Encyclopedia of Buddhism

The Routledge *Encyclopedia of Buddhism* is a complete, careful, accurate and up-to-date one-volume desk reference, documenting the history, doctrines, schools, rituals, sacred places, basic ideas and concepts, and globalization of the entire Buddhist tradition. In addition, it provides bibliographic references to the leading scholarship by scholars from around the world. As such, it is an indispensable tool for students, teachers, and researchers from a wide range of disciplinary backgrounds, as well as to the general reader.

The *Encyclopedia* is characterized by its wide range of contents, primary sources, and both the depth and quality of its entries. It allows its readers to quickly access information on all topics included in the volume.

It covers the study of Buddhism, Buddhist canons and literature, Buddha, Dharma, Sangha, Nikaya Buddhism, Mahayana Buddhism, Vajrayana Buddhism, Buddhist meditational systems, sacred places in Buddhism, practices and rituals, biographies of famous Buddhists (including ideal types), Buddhist ethics, Buddhist art(s), engaged Buddhism, Buddhism and technology, women in Buddhism, Buddhism in India, South and Southeast Asia, Tibet, China, Korea, Japan, and Buddhism in the Western World.

All readers of the *Encyclopedia* will benefit from a scholarly but readable work that lends itself to being approached from almost any starting point, and guides the reader to an increased knowledge of Buddhism through very easy access to all relevant materials.

Damien Keown is Professor of Buddhist Ethics at Goldsmiths College, University of London. **Charles S. Prebish** holds the Charles Redd Endowed Chair in Religious Studies at Utah State University. They are the editors of two Routledge series: World Religions and Critical Studies in Buddhism and are the authors of *Introducing Buddhism*.

Encyclopedia of Buddhism

Edited by

Damien Keown

Charles S. Prebish

Routledge
Taylor & Francis Group
LONDON AND NEW YORK

First published 2007
Reprinted 2008, 2009

This edition published in paperback 2010
by Routledge
2 Park Square, Milton Park, Abingdon, Oxon OX14 4RN

Simultaneously published in the USA and Canada
by Routledge
270 Madison Ave, New York, NY 10016

Routledge is an imprint of the Taylor & Francis Group, an informa business

Typeset in Times New Roman and Optima
by Taylor & Francis Books
Printed and bound in Great Britain
by MPG Books Ltd, Bodmin

British Library Cataloguing in Publication Data
A catalogue record for this book is available from the British Library

Library of Congress Cataloging-in-Publication Data
A catalog record for this book has been requested

ISBN13: 978-0-415-31414-5 (hbk)
ISBN13: 978-0-415-55624-8 (pbk)
ISBN13: 978-0-203-49875-0 (ebk)

Contents

Illustrations

Figures

Tables

Contributing editors and editorial advisory board

Introduction

Many scholars consider the Frenchman Eugène Burnouf to be the founding father of Buddhist Studies as a discipline. In the century and a half since Burnouf's seminal work *Introduction to the History of Indian Buddhism* (1845), the academic study of Buddhism has grown enormously. The International Association of Buddhist Studies boasts a membership of approximately 500 members, and there are thousands of university courses on Buddhism in North and South America, the United Kingdom, Europe, Asia, and Australia. Moreover, as Buddhism has globalized in the past half-century, millions of individuals beyond Asia have begun the serious practice and study of all aspects of the Buddhist teachings.

In spite of this great interest in Buddhism, there has been to date no accessible single volume that adequately covers all aspects of the Buddhist tradition. Such books have been limited by size and price, thus minimizing their overall effectiveness as a complete reference tool for scholars and students. Buddhist dictionaries suffer the same dilemma, making many compromises in their determination of what materials are included and excluded. And both are hindered by the fact that the entire Buddhist tradition is simply too vast a topic to be properly handled by one individual.

This encyclopedia seeks to remedy the above problems and fill the present lacuna in Buddhist Studies with a single-volume desk reference that is complete, accurate, and up to date. It documents the history, doctrines, schools, rituals, sacred places, basic ideas and concepts, and globalization of Buddhism. The *Encyclopedia of Buddhism* is a scholarly but readable work that lends itself to being approached from almost any starting point, and guides readers to an increased knowledge of Buddhism through easy access to relevant materials. The volume is characterized by its careful selection of relevant subject matter and the depth and quality of its entries. In addition, it facilitates further research by providing bibliographical references to the leading scholarship As such, the editors hope it will become an indispensable tool for students, teachers, and researchers from a wide range of disciplinary backgrounds, as well as to the general reader.

Rationale

Before embarking on this project the editors gave careful thought to the format that would best meet the needs of readers. The standard method in composing a work of this kind is for the editor to compile a list of topics beginning with A and ending with Z and then marshal an army of contributors to write the entries. The problem with this method is that it can lead to an idiosyncratic selection of subjects, and a highly subjective assessment of the relative importance of individual topics. The coverage can also be superficial, and nothing is more frustrating to the reader than to find only a sentence or two on the topic that interests him, and pages and pages on the editor's pet subject. Further, as the work of many hands, often produced with little or no contact between contributors, this methodology inevitably results in a fragmented and often uneven final product.

To overcome as many of these problems as possible, the editors of this volume determined beforehand that the following eight general categories would be of most interest to readers and should provide the basis for the volume.

1. Buddhist history (in Asian cultures).
2. Major Buddhist traditions and schools.
3. Significant persons.
4. Canons, texts, and other literature.
5. Concepts and ideas.
6. Rituals and customs.
7. Sacred places.
8. The Buddhist diaspora.

We then assembled a dedicated team of twenty-three leading specialists in different fields of Buddhist Studies, and asked *them* to take responsibility for both determining the key subjects of interest within their individual fields and writing the corresponding entries on those topics. The contributing editors (who simultaneously constituted the editorial advisory board to the project) then determined how best to meet the requirement for coverage of these topics in relation to their own areas of expertise. This was followed by negotiation among the group as to the best division of labor to ensure that no important subject was overlooked and duplication was kept to a minimum.

No encyclopedia is ever complete, and at every stage a trade-off has to be made between breadth and depth. In the present work, the division of subject matter is as follows:

25 per cent – major topics: twenty-four entries of 5,000 words. (These are listed as the **main survey entries** in the **List of entries by major topic**.)
30 per cent – significant persons, canons, texts, and literature: entries of 1,500 words.
30 per cent – important concepts, ideas, rituals, customs, sacred places, diaspora: entries of 1,000 words.
15 per cent – miscellaneous entries of 500 words.

An important objective of this volume was to provide substantive in-depth coverage of key areas, as opposed to wide but superficial coverage after the fashion of a dictionary. For this reason there are no entries in the present work of fewer than 500 words, and each key subject area (for example, those involving major Buddhist schools and traditions) is covered by a 5,000-word overview entry which gives a comprehensive and detailed introduction to the topic. These longer entries form the backbone of the encyclopedia. Further information is then available in the form of shorter entries of 1,500 and 1,000 words on specific aspects of the topic (for example, significant individuals, concepts, and places). Perhaps some readers will feel that this methodology is too restrictive, but we feel it strikes the right balance and manages to avoid the dictionary-style superficiality to which some encyclopedias are prone in their anxiety to have a separate entry on every topic and term.

How to use this encyclopedia

In this work there are 340 alphabetically ordered **entries** which, in almost half a million words, cover the entire Buddhist tradition. In addition to a **list of entries A–Z**, the reader will find a **list of entries by major topic** to guide them through the work thematically. The **main survey entry** for each topic is indicated in this list. This work covers several thousand years of history stretching across a number of different cultures and languages, therefore we have also included a **chronology of Buddhist history** and a **pronunciation guide** preceding the main text. A selection of over forty black-and-white **illustrations** is spread throughout this volume to provide a visual sense of Buddhist art, culture, and life.

Finding information in a traditional encyclopedia can be something of a lottery. For example, a reader seeking information on the Buddha might well have to search under several separate entries such as "Buddha," "Śākyamuni," "Siddhārtha Gautama," and "Tathāgata," which could be widely distributed at the beginning, middle and end of the text. A novice unaware of the relation between these terms might well miss important information by failing to check under all four headings. To some extent this problem can be overcome through the use of cross-referencing, and in this work full use is made of this method in the form of **see also** lists at the end of entries to ensure that every entry connects to other related ones. In this way, more or less regardless of whatever starting point the reader chooses, he or she will be led to specific information on the required topic. Nevertheless, to avoid this potentially time-consuming journey, as also the problem of a distorted or incomplete perspective, the editors feel that the best starting point for research is the appropriate **major topic entry**. By browsing through this the reader will receive a comprehensive orientation and be introduced to all the most important aspects of a topic. Specific shorter entries can then be consulted as required on particular areas of interest. A thorough, analytical **index** at the end of the work will also help the reader find topics of interest as they are discussed throughout the work.

Although this encyclopedia will provide information in sufficient depth to satisfy most readers, as an aid to further research a complete list of **references and further reading** and a **guide to the Buddhist scriptures** are provided at the end, indicating the main sources drawn upon for the articles and including the most important publications in each main subject area.

Acknowledgements

A work such as this depends on the cooperation of many individuals. Given its innovative and focused approach, the number of contributors is much smaller than for a conventional volume of this kind: instead of the usual list of several hundred names our team of collaborators amounts to fewer than thirty highly dedicated scholars who have worked as a close-knit team in the production of the work. No doubt this arrangement played an important part in helping us complete the project ahead of schedule. The editors are accordingly deeply grateful to all our contributors and advisory board members for lending their time and expertise to this undertaking. Particular thanks go to Professors Alan Sponberg, Jim Deitrick, and John Powers for stepping in at a late stage to take over responsibility for the areas of Mahāyāna Buddhism, Engaged Buddhism, and Vajrayāna Buddhism, respectively.

On the editorial side we wish to thank Dominic Shryane of Routledge's London office who helped in the initial administration of the project, and Susan Cronin who took over responsibility after the project was transferred to New York.

The editors have worked hard to make this volume distinctive. Our aim was not just to produce another reference work on Buddhism, but to be innovative in adopting a new format and methodology that would make this work stand out amongst its rivals. We wanted to put in the hands of readers a volume that would respond to the needs of those seeking authoritative orientation on the key areas of Buddhist doctrine and practice, both historically and in the modern world, without a bewildering abundance of superficial information on minor points of detail. We hope we have succeeded, and have contributed to raising awareness of a religious tradition that is fast becoming part of everyday life in the modern world both East and West.

Pronunciation guide

In the course of its long history Buddhism has spread to every part of Asia. One result of this is that Buddhist concepts have come to be expressed in languages as diverse as Sanskrit, Pāli, Tibetan, Chinese, Mongolian, Japanese, Korean, Thai, Sinhala, Vietnamese and many more. As this book is intended to reflect the cultural diversity of Buddhism, it contains terms drawn from all the major Buddhist languages. Following the scholarly convention, however, the primary language used is Sanskrit. Sanskrit served as the *lingua franca* of ancient India, just as Latin did in medieval Europe, and most of the translations made into other Asian languages were based on Sanskrit originals. The most important scriptures of Mahāyāna Buddhism were composed in a variant of Sanskrit known as Buddhist Hybrid Sanskrit, while the earliest Buddhist scriptures are preserved in Pāli, a literary language derived from Sanskrit.

Sanskrit and Pāli

One feature of Asian languages like Sanskrit is that their alphabets are larger than those of Western languages. In order to represent the additional characters diacritical marks have to be added to the Roman letters. These typically take the form of symbols such as dots and dashes placed above or below certain characters. These symbols do not affect the alphabetical order of entries in the present work, but do affect pronunciation in various ways. As far as Sanskrit is concerned, the most important of these is that a macron above a vowel serves to lengthen it, roughly doubling the length of the sound. Thus the character "ā" is pronounced as in "far" rather than "fat." With respect to consonants, an underdot (ṭ, ḍ, etc.) indicates that the tongue touches the roof of the mouth when pronouncing these letters, giving the characteristic sound of English when spoken with an Indian accent. For the most part the other marks do not affect pronunciation enough to be of any special concern. A summary of the most important points in connection with the pronunciation of Sanskrit and Pāli terms is shown below:

ā	pronounced as in far
ī	pronounced as in seek
ū	pronounced as in brute
ṛ	pronounced as in risk
ñ	pronounced as in Spanish *mañana*
ś or ṣ	pronounced as in shoe
ṅ/ṃ	pronounced with a nasal sound as in ring
c	pronounced ch, as in church

More detailed guidance on the pronunciation of Sanskrit can be found in Chapter 1 of Michael Coulson, *Sanskrit: An*

Introduction to the Classical Language (London: Teach Yourself Books, 1992).

Chinese

The transcription and pronunciation of Chinese poses special problems because there are two systems in use for transcribing it, namely Wade-Giles and Pinyin. The latter was introduced in 1979 by the People's Republic of China as its official system, and is the form used in the present work. Pinyin has gained acceptance among specialists, but students will also encounter Wade-Giles in introductory and popular literature. A helpful guide on converting from Wade-Giles to Pinyin can be found in A.C. Graham, *Disputers of the Tao* (La Salle, Illinois: Open Court, 1989), pp. 441–4. Neither Pinyin nor Wade-Giles, however, provides a way of representing the sounds of spoken Chinese with any accuracy as the same characters in Chinese may be pronounced in one of four different tones.

Japanese

The transcription of Japanese is relatively unproblematic, and this book uses the widely adopted Hepburn system. The characters used correspond closely to their Roman equivalents, with the exception of the long vowels ō and ū. As in the transliteration of Sanskrit, the macron over the letter indicates that the sound of the vowel is emphasized and lengthened, thus *kōan* is pronounced "koh-an," with the emphasis on the first syllable.

Tibetan

In contrast to Japanese, Tibetan orthography and pronunciation poses many complex problems. This is despite the fact that a standard system of transliteration exists that does not rely on diacritics, namely the system devised by Turrell Wylie and explained in his article "A Standard System of Tibetan Transcription" (*Harvard Journal of Asiatic Studies*, vol. 22 (1959): 261–7). The present work adopts this method of transliteration, but difficulties still remain. Not least among these is the fact that Tibetan words frequently contain letters that are not pronounced (this is also a feature of English, as in words such as "through," "ought," and so forth). Even more problematic from the point of view of alphabetization is that in Tibetan these redundant letters are often found at the start of a word: thus the term for a senior monk – lama – is in fact spelled "blama." As this book is intended primarily for a general readership, the policy of using a simplified phonetic form for the spelling of Tibetan words has been adopted while putting the correct transliteration from the Tibetan in brackets, thus: lama (*blama*).

Korean

The Korean system of writing is known as Hangŭl, and the present work uses the standard conventions for transcription into English. This method uses the standard Roman alphabet pronounced for the most part as in English, with the exception of the two vowels ŏ (pronounced as in cot) and ŭ (pronounced as in burn).

Chronology of Buddhist history

Prior to sixth century BCE

Vedic period in India (*c.* 1500–1000)
Composition of the *Brāhmaṇas* (*c.* 1000–800)
Composition of early *Upaniṣads* (*c.* 800–500)

Sixth century BCE

Life of Laozi
Life of Confucius (552–479)

Fifth century BCE

Life of the Buddha Śākyamuni (*c.* 485–405)
Reign of Bimbisāra (*c.* 465–413)
Council of Rājagṛha (*c.* 405)

Fourth century BCE

Alexander the Great in India (*c.* 327–325)
Reign of Chandragupta Maurya (322–298)
Megasthenese at court of Chandragupta (303)
Second Buddhist council at Vaiśālī (*c.* 305)
Non-canonical Buddhist council at Pāṭaliputra (*c.* 284)
Beginning of Buddhist sectarianism

Third century BCE

Reign of Indian king Aśoka (272–231)
Third Buddhist council at Pāṭaliputra (250)
Aśoka's missionary Mahinda introduces Buddhism to Sri Lanka (247)

Second century BCE

Beginning of Mahāyāna Buddhism (*c.* 200)
Beginning of composition of *Prajñāpāramitā* literature
Stūpa construction at Sañcī (*c.* 200–000)
An Shigao arrives in China and establishes first translation bureau (148)

First century BCE

Reign of Duṭṭhagāmaṇi Abhaya in Sri Lanka (101–77)
Abhayagiri monastery founded in Sri Lanka (*c.* 100–000)
Pāli Canon written down in Sri Lanka (29–17)

First century CE

Reign of King Kaniṣka in India
Fourth Buddhist council at Kaśmīr (*c.* 100)
Composition of *Lotus Sūtra* and other Buddhist texts
Buddhism enters Central Asia and China

Second century CE

Life of Indian Buddhist philosopher Nāgārjuna

Third century CE

Expansion of Buddhism to Burma, Cambodia, Laos, Vietnam, and Indonesia

Fourth century CE

Life of Indian Buddhist philosophers Asaṅga and Vasubandhu
Development of Vajrayāna Buddhism in India
Translation of Buddhist texts into Chinese by Kumārajīva (344–413), Huiyuan (334–416), and others
Gupta dynasty in India, Buddhist philosophy and art flourish (350–650)
Buddhism enters Korea in 372

Fifth century CE

Nālandā University founded in India
Life of Buddhist philosopher Buddhaghosa in Sri Lanka (*c.* 400–500)
Chinese pilgrim Faxian visits India (399–414)

Sixth century CE

Life of Paramārtha (499–599)
Bodhidharma arrives in China from India (*c.* 520)
Sui Dynasty in Chinese history (589–617); beginning of golden age of Chinese Buddhism
Development of Tiantai, Huayan, Pure Land, and Chan of Chinese Buddhism
Life of Zhiyi (538–97)
Buddhism enters Japan from Korea (552)
Prince Shotoku sponsors Buddhism in Japan (572–621)
Buddhism flourishing in Indonesia

Seventh century CE

First diffusion of Buddhism in Tibet (*c.* 600)
Life of Dharmakīrti; flourishing of logic and epistemology (*c.* 600)
Tang Dynasty in Chinese history (618–907)
Life of Wŏnhyo (617–86); foundation of "unitive Buddhism" in Korea
Life of Songtsen Gampo (618–50); establishment of Buddhism in Tibet
Life of Ŭisang; introduction of Hwaŏm (hua-yen) into Korea (625–702)
Chinese pilgrim Xuanzang visits India (629–45)
Life of Huineng (638–713); Northern–Southern schools controversy
Pala Dynasty in India (650–950)
Unified Silla period in Korea (668–918); Buddhism flourishes
Chinese pilgrim Yijing travels to India (671–95)

Eighth century CE

Life of Padmasambhava (*c.* 700)
Northern–Southern schools controversy in Japan (*c.* 700)
Esoteric school (Zhenyan Zong) develops in China (*c.* 700)
Construction of Borobudur (*c.* 700–800)
Mahāyāna and Tantric Buddhism flourish in India (700–1100); consolidation of school of logic and epistemology
Nara period in Japanese history (710–84)
Academic schools (Jōjitsu, Kusha, Sanron, Hossō, Ritsu, and Kegon) proliferate in Japan
Great debate between Tibetan and Chinese Buddhist schools
Council of Lhasa in Tibet (742)
Nying-ma-pa school of Tibetan Buddhism begins
First Tibetan monastery at Samye
Life of Saichō (767–822); founding of Tendai school
Life of Kūkai (774–835); founding of Shongon school
Heian period in Japanese history (794–1185)

Ninth century CE

Founding of Vikramaśīla monastery in Tibet (*c.* 800)
Reign of Lang Darma (836–42) and suppression of Buddhism in Tibet
Great Buddhist persecution in China (845)

Tenth century CE

Sung dynasty in China (960–1279)
Koryŏ period in Korea (978–1392)
First complete printing of Chinese Buddhist canon (Szechuan edition) in 983
Atīśa (982–1054) arrives in Tibet from India (1042)

Eleventh century CE

Life of Mar-pa (1012–97) and origins of Kagyü school of Tibetan Buddhism
Life of Naropa (1016–1100)
King Anawrahtā unifies Burma and gives allegiance to Theravāda Buddhism (1040–77)
Life of Milarepa (1040–1123); becomes greatest poet and most popular saint in Tibetan Buddhism
Life of Ŭich'ŏn (1055–1101)
Sakya Order of Tibetan Buddhism begins (1073)
Life of Gampopa (1079–1153)
Revival of Theravāda Buddhism in Sri Lanka and Burma
Decline of Buddhism in India

Twelfth century CE

Construction of Angkor Wat (*c.* 1100)
Theravāda Buddhism established in Burma
Life of Hōnen (1133–1212); founds Jōdo-shū in Japan
Life of Eisai (1141–1215); founds Rinzai Zen school of Japanese Buddhism
Life of Chinul (1158–1210); Chogye Order founded; development of Sŏn in Korea
Life of Shinran (1173–1262); founds Jōdo Shinshū in Japan
Kamakura period in Japan (1185–1392)
Nālandā University sacked by Mahmud Ghorī (1197)

Thirteenth century CE

Buddhism disappears from north India. Traces linger in south (*c.* 1200)
Printing of *Tripiṭaka Koreana* (*c.* 1200)
Life of Dōgen (1200–53), founds Sōtō Zen school in Japan
Life of Nichiren (1222–82), founds school of Japanese Buddhism named after him
Life of Ippen (1239–89); foundation of Jishū school
Sakya Paṇḍita converts Mongols to Buddhism (1244)
Theravāda declared state religion of kingdom of Sukhothai (Thailand) (*c.* 1260)
Life of Butön (1290–1364); collects and edits Tibetan Buddhist Canon

Fourteenth century CE

Life of Tsongkhapa (1357–1419); Gelukpa Order founded in Tibet
Theravāda Buddhism declared state religion of Thailand (1360)
Ming dynasty in China (1368–1644)
Ch'osŏn period in Korea; Buddhism suppressed
Laos and Cambodia become Theravāda

Fifteenth century CE

Tibetan Kanjur printed in China

Sixteenth century CE

Office of Dalai Lama instituted by Mongols

Seventeenth century CE

Life of Dalai Lama V and beginning of rule of Tibet by Dalai Lamas

Control of Japanese Buddhism by Tokugawa Shōgunate (1603–1867)
Life of Bashō; Buddhist influence on haiku and the arts in Japan

Eighteenth century CE

Colonial occupation of Sri Lanka, Burma, Laos, Cambodia, and Vietnam; Western domination of South and Southeast Asia
Mongolian Buddhist canon translated from Tibetan (1749)

Nineteenth century CE

Beginning of the academic study of Buddhism by Western scholars (*c.* 1800)
Royal Asiatic Society founded (1823)
Reign of Rama IV in Thailand; reform of Thai *sangha* (1851–68)
First Buddhist temple founded in the United States, in San Francisco (1853)
Meiji Restoration in Japanese history (1868), marking end of military rule
Life of Nishida Kitarō, founder of Kyoto school (1870–1945)
New religions begin to emerge in Japanese Buddhism
Fifth great Buddhist council in Mandalay
Theosophical Society founded (1875)
Publication of Sir Edwin Arnold's *The Light of Asia* (1879)
Pāli Text Society founded in England by T.W. Rhys Davids (1881)
Mahabodhi Society founded by Anagārika Dharmapāla (1891)
Life of B. Ambedkar, conversion of Untouchables in India (1891–1956)
Buddhist Churches of America founded (1899)

Twentieth century CE

Taishō Shinshū Daizōkyō edition of Chinese Buddhist Canon printed in Tokyo (1924–9)
The Buddhist Society founded in London (1924)
Wŏn Buddhism founded in Korea (1924)
Nichiren Shōshū Sokagakkai formally established (1937)
Risshō Kōseikai founded (1938)
People's Liberation Army enters Tibet (1950)
World Fellowship of Buddhists founded (1950)
Sixth great Buddhist council at Rangoon (1954–6)
Dalai Lama flees Tibet to India (1959)
Friends of the Western Buddhist Order founded (1967)
Development of Engaged Buddhism (1970)
Vajradhatu Foundation founded (1973)
International Association of Buddhist Studies founded (1976)
International Network of Engaged Buddhists founded (1989)
United Kingdom Association of Buddhist Studies founded (1995)

Twenty-first century CE

Destruction of standing Buddha statues at Bāmiyān by Taliban regime (2001)

List of entries A–Z

List of entries by major topic

Academic study of Buddhism (Prebish)

Academic study of Buddhism **(main survey entry)**
Anglo-German school of Buddhist Studies
Bareau, André
Conze, Edward
Current issues in Buddhist Studies
de Jong, Jan Willem
Franco-Belgian school of Buddhist Studies
Hirakawa, Akira
Lamotte, Étienne
Leningrad school of Buddhist Studies
Major professional societies
North American school of Buddhist Studies
Poussin, Louis de La Vallée
Prominent Buddhist Studies journals
Rhys Davids, Thomas W.
Robinson, Richard Hugh
Scholar-practitioners in Buddhist Studies

Biographies of famous Buddhists and ideal types (Schober)

Acharn Mun
Aśoka
Aung San Suu Kyi
Buddha, bodies of
Buddhadasa
Disciples of Buddha
Famous Buddhists and ideal types **(main survey entry)**
Sayadaw, Mahāsī
Siddhārtha Gautama, life of
U Nu

Buddha (Harvey)

Bodhisattva career in the Theravāda
Buddha **(main survey entry)**
Buddha, dates of
Buddha, early symbols
Buddha, family of
Buddha, historical context
Buddha, relics of
Buddha, story of
Buddha, style of teaching
Buddha and *cakravartin*s
Buddhas, past and future
Ennobling Truths/Realities
Ennobling Truth/Reality, the First
Ennobling Truth/Reality, the Second
Ennobling Truth/Reality, the Third: *nirvāṇa*
Ennobling Truth/Reality, the Fourth: The Ennobling Eightfold Path
Not-Self (*anātman*)
Pratyeka-buddhas

Buddhism and technology (Lancaster)

Computers and the Buddhist cultural heritage
Cyber-Buddhism
Digital input of Buddhist texts
Digital research resources

Electronic publications
Technology and Buddhism **(main survey entry)**

Buddhism and the modern world (Baumann)

Australia, Buddhism in
Buddhism, psychology, and therapy
Buddhism and Western lifestyle
Buddhism in the Western world **(main survey entry)**
Buddhist adaptations in the West
Diasporic Buddhism: traditionalist and modernist Buddhism
Ecumenicism and intra-Buddhist activities
Europe, Buddhism in
Global Buddhist networks: selected examples
New Buddhist roles
North America, Buddhism in
Southern hemisphere, Buddhism in the
Western Buddhism: Diamond Sangha
Western Buddhism: Friends of the Western Buddhist Order
Western Buddhism: Insight Meditation Society
Western Buddhism: Shambhala International

Buddhism in China (Jones)

Bodhidharma
Chan
China, Buddhism in **(main survey entry)**
China, early schools
Faxiang
Huayan
Huineng
Kumārajīva
Lushan Huiyuan
Lüzong
Pure Land school, China
Tiantai
Zhenyan Zong
Zhiyi

Buddhism in India (Hayes)

Abhidharma schools
Anātmavāda
Asaṅga
Candrakīrti
Dharmakīrti
India, Buddhism in **(main survey entry)**
Madhyamaka school
Nāgārjuna
Nirvāṇa
Pramāṇika movement
Ratnakīrti
Śāntideva
Śantirakṣita
Tathāgatagarbha in Indian Buddhism
Vasubandhu
Yogācāra school

Buddhism in Japan (Swanson)

Dōgen and Sōtōshū
Genze riyaku – worldly benefits
Hōnen and Jōdoshū
Hongaku shisō – original enlightenment
Honji-suijaka/shinbutsu shūgo – Buddhist syncretism in Japan
Japan, Buddhism in **(main survey entry)**
Kenmitsu (exoteric–esoteric) Buddhism
Kūkai and Shingon Buddhism
Mikkyō and ritual in Japanese Buddhism
New Buddhist lay movements in Japan
Nichiren and Nichirenshū
Pilgrimage in Japan
Pure Land movements in Japan
Rinzai tradition
Saichō and Tendai
Shinran and Jōdo Shinshū
Shōtoku Taishi and Buddhism in ancient Japan
Shugendō
Sōshiki Bukkyō (funeral Buddhism)
Zen

Buddhism in Korea (Park)

Chinul
Hwaŏm Buddhism
Hyujŏng

Buddhism in South and Southeast Asia (Bond, Wickremeratne)

Buddhism in Tibet (Powers)

Buddhist arts (Kinnard)

Buddhist canons and literature (Lang)

Buddhist ethics (Keown)

Abortion
Ahiṃsā
Animals and the environment
Cloning
Ethics **(main survey entry)**
Ethics, theories of
Euthanasia
Human rights
Sexual ethics
Skillful Means (*upāya-kauśalya*)
Stem cell research
Suicide
Vegetarianism
War and peace

Buddhist meditational systems (McMahan)

Dhyānas
Dzogchen
Kōan
Meditation (Chan/Zen)
Meditation, modern movements
Meditation, visualization
Meditation in the Pāli Canon and the Theravāda tradition
Meditation in the *Visuddhimagga*
Meditation traditions, Vajrayāna
Meditational systems **(main survey entry)**
Sādhana
Śamatha
Vipaśyanā
Zazen

Dharma (Keown)

Cosmology and rebirth
Decline of the *Dharma*
Dependent Origination (*Pratītya-samutpāda*)
Dharma **(main survey entry)**
Dharmacakra
Karma

Mahāyāna Buddhism (Sponberg)

Archetypal Buddhas and *Bodhisattvas*
Bodhisattva path
Buddha-fields and pure lands
Buddha nature and *tathāgatagarbha*
Lotus Sūtra of the True Dharma (*Saddharmapuṇḍarīka Sūtra*)
Mahāyāna Buddhism **(main survey entry)**
Perfection of Wisdom literature
Vimalakīrti Sūtra

Nikāya Buddhism (Hallisey, Keown)

Abhidharma
Abhidharmakośa
Aśvaghoṣa
Councils
Dharmaguptakas
Harivarman
Kaniṣka
Katyāyanīputra
Mahāsāṃghika
Nikāya Buddhism **(main survey entry)**
Sammatīyas/pudgalavādins
Sarvāstivāda
Sautrāntika
Vātsīputrīyas
Vinayas

Practices and rituals (Walters)

Chanting practices
Charity (*dāna*)
Deity cults
Full moon day and other calendrical observances
Funerals and other life-cycle rituals
Healing and protective practices
Medical practices
Monastic rituals
Moral discipline
New Year and national festivals
Pilgrimage
Politics
Preaching and *Dharma* transmission
Rituals and practices **(main survey entry)**
Worship

Sacred places in Buddhism (Trainor)

Sangha (Prebish)

Socially engaged Buddhism (Deitrick)

Vajrayāna Buddhism (Powers)

Women in Buddhism (Fenn)

A

ABHIDHARMA

Abhidharma denotes a style of systematic and philosophical interpretation of the Buddha's teachings that was developed by Buddhist scholastics in *Nikāya* Buddhism. The formation of distinct traditions of *Abhidharma* thought and literature was gradual, becoming clearly visible about the third century BCE and reaching an apex around the fourth century CE, but the practice of *Abhidharma* was coincident with the formation of the separate schools that are characteristic of *Nikāya* Buddhism. The philosophical systems subsequently created in these different schools, however, exerted an influence that went beyond the communities of their creation. Their contents were the subject of mutual exchange and debate among different schools and they left an enduring imprint on the philosophical systems that developed in Mahāyāna communities, notably the Yogācāra.

The meaning of the term "*Abhidharma*" is not easily specified, in large part because the term quickly became overdetermined as a category in the communities that valued *Abhidharma* as an intellectual and religious practice. A straightforward analysis of the word suggests that *Abhidharma* practice is a more advanced or "higher" (*abhi*) study of the Buddha's teachings (*dharma*), and this interpretation was frequently endorsed by Buddhist scholastics. The complexity of meaning that the term quickly acquired in use, however, can be seen in the enumeration of twenty-four different meanings for the word in some texts of the later Sarvāstivāda.

Whatever the complexities of the term might be, it is clear that *Abhidharma* is a method of scholastic analysis and interpretation. As an intellectual practice, *Abhidharma* was philosophical in its concerns for first principles, coherence and consistency, as well as in its rigorous self-consciousness about its methods of interpretation and epistemology. As a religious practice, *Abhidharma* was commonly given three goals. It was meant to be an aid to understanding the world and especially a person through the identification of the metaphysical elements and constitutive processes that make the world and a person what they are. It was also meant to provide assistance in the defense of authentic Buddhist metaphysical positions against the challenges of non-Buddhist rivals and Buddhist heretics. In having this purpose, we can see that *Abhidharma* was a reaction to the conditions of doctrinal difference that characterized *Nikāya* Buddhism as much as it helped to create those differences. Finally, *Abhidharma* was seen as having a soteriological purpose as the discriminatory knowledge that *Abhidharma* inculcated contributed to the personal and salvific transformation that was the reason for the existence of Buddhist monastic life. Indeed, the metaphysics discerned through *Abhidharma* analysis came to be identified with the insight gained in the course of higher spiritual attainments.

Three intellectual practices are at the core of *Abhidharma* thinking, each furthering the three religious goals just mentioned. First is standardization. *Abhidharma* standardized the teachings of the Buddha largely through the making of lists of key doctrines which in turn were interpreted as the essential core of Buddhist thought and practice. Second is elaboration. *Abhidharma* literature developed and critically elaborated the basic ideas found in the Buddha's teachings by explaining them in detail and by applying them to new contexts. The third practice of *Abhidharma* thinking is systematization. *Abhidharma* thinkers connected the basic categories of their lists to each other with an eye to removing apparent inconsistencies and also to display their mutual interdependence and coherence.

It is possible to speculate that the origins of *Abhidharma* thinking lie in the practice of list-making as a means of stabilizing and standardizing the Buddha's teachings. A text in the canon of the Theravāda school (*Dīgha Nikāya* 33) explicitly connects the practice of list-making with the rationale of protecting the teaching of the Buddha against loose interpretations and distortions. This text explains how the Buddha heard that after the death of one of his contemporaries, disputes arose among that teacher's students about what he had actually taught and how his teachings were to be interpreted. To prevent something similar occurring at his death, the Buddha asked for a list of his key teachings to be prepared. Śāriputra did so and recited his list in front of the Buddha, who accepted it as an accurate summary of his teachings. It is worth adding here that this account has the appearance of being a charter for *Abhidharma* practice, especially as Śāriputra is frequently identified as a founding figure for *Abhidharma* itself.

It is not necessary to accept the historical accuracy of this account to see its general truth. Lists, or *mātṛkā*, are centrally visible in the earliest examples of *Abhidharma* literature, but, equally significant, they are also prominent in other canonical texts that seem to prefigure actual *Abhidharma* literature. The creation of *mātṛkā* was not unique to *Abhidharma*. Lists of rules are also seen in *Vinaya* literature, where they are followed by explanations and elaborations of these rules, a pattern that looks very similar in its structure to what can be noted in the *Abhidharma*'s own combination of lists and explanations.

The need for the coherence and standardization afforded by *mātṛkā*, whether in the *Vinaya*, in the Buddha's sermons (*sūtra*) or later in the *Abhidharma*, is obvious. As is well known, the Buddha had a long teaching career, one which lasted more than forty-five years, and over this long career he taught people with different capabilities and in a variety of contexts. He directed his teaching accordingly, sacrificing a systematic presentation of his thought for the effectiveness of his teaching particular people. According to Buddhist accounts, the record of his teaching that was left at his death thus required a standardization and systematization that the Buddha himself did not provide.

The *Abhidharma* was never, however, only a practice of list-making for the purposes of standardization and the reliable transmission of the Buddha's teachings. The *Abhidharma* was also directed to explanation and elaboration, making explicit what was left unsaid in the Buddha's own sermons. It is possible to see a model for this aspect of *Abhidharma* practice in the Buddha's career as well, especially in his practice of engaging in dialogues which took the format of questions and answers that allowed for new elaborations and clarifications to be introduced. Questions and answers are a distinctive feature of many *Abhidharma* texts.

With respect to their *Vinaya* and *Sūtra* literature, the different schools of *Nikāya* Buddhism showed considerable overlap and commonality, suggesting that these parts of their canons crystallized to a large degree before the process of school formation got well underway. This is not the case with respect to their collections of *Abhidharma* literature. Indeed, the *Abhidharma* collections of the various schools of *Nikāya* Buddhism are so different that we must conclude that *Abhidharma* was integral to the processes by which they became differentiated. This means that *Abhidharma* practices and goals were also put in the service of school formation and the defense of *Abhidharma* positions became as much an apologetic method as a soteriological practice. Inevitably, the apologetic purposes to which *Abhidharma* practice was directed tended to be at the expense of its other intellectual and religious goals, with a defense of mere dogmatism often the result.

See also: ***Abhidharmakośa*; Dharmaguptakas; Katyayanīputra; *Nikāya* Buddhism; Sarvāstivāda; Sautrāntika.**

CHARLES HALLISEY

ABHIDHARMA SCHOOLS

The precise beginnings of *abhidharma* are obscure to us now, but in general it can be said that what eventually came to be called *Abhidharma* grew out of attempts to clarify and systematize the teachings attributed to the Buddha and in so doing to provide a theoretical framework for the variety of practices recommended for those who aspired to realize the goals of those teachings. The word *Abhidharma* itself is open to several interpretations, but generally the prefix *abhi* is taken to mean either "above" or "toward," so that the entire compound can be understood to refer to the highest reality or that which leads one toward the highest reality. The great *Abhidharma* scholar Vasubandhu explains that the word primarily refers to *nirvāṇa*, the greatest good; a secondary meaning is wisdom, as that leads one to *nirvāṇa*; and a tertiary meaning is a text that contains wisdom. Whatever the derivation of the word, the genre of literature known as *Abhidharma* was seen as a set of texts that spoke of the principles of Buddhism in the most literal and straightforward way, without rhetorical flourish, without poetic tropes or ornamentation and without the ambiguities and vagueness of colloquial speech. While the *sūtras* contain the Buddha's discourse in colloquial speech, and often in poetry and satirical narratives, the *Abhidharma* literature claims to contain what the Buddha really meant when he spoke in various roundabout ways.

It took no more than a few generations for followers of the Buddha to divide into schools of interpretation, each with its own set of emphases. As the community divided on various issues, a variety of canons came into being. Four versions of the code of monastic discipline evolved, along with different versions of the discourses of the Buddha. Several of the canonical schools had their own *Abhidharma* division as well. While differences in the monastic codes and the discourses are relatively minor, the differences in the *Abhidharma* divisions of the different canons are more stark. Of the earliest schools of Buddhism, the *Abhidharma* systems of only two of them, the Theravādins and the Sarvāstivādins, survived down through the millennia. The Theravādin *Abhidharma* is still studied in Sri Lanka, Myanmar, Thailand, Laos and Cambodia, while derivatives of the Sarvāstivādin *Abhidharma* were influential in East Asian and Central Asian Buddhism and are still studied in Tibet and Mongolia.

The Theravādin *Abhidharma* (*Abhidhamma* in Pāli) is based on seven books in the *Abhidhamma-piṭaka*. The *Dhammasaṅgaṇī* (*Enumeration of Dharmas*) contains enumerations and definitions of all factors of experience that are held to be ultimately real. These include all the mental factors that can accompany acts of awareness, the different types of awareness, the primary physical elements and the classes of matter made up of those elements, and *nirvāṇa* (Pāli *nibbāna*). The *Vibhaṅga* (*Analysis*) classifies the ultimate factors of experience into categories and distinguishes between how those factors are defined in the discourses of the Buddha and in the books of *Abhidharma*. The *Dhātukathā* deals with the same material as the first two books but presents it in the form of questions and answers, rather like a catechism. The *Puggalapaññatti* defines and characterizes the types of human beings, and especially those who have made progress along the path to *nirvāṇa*. The *Kathāvatthu* (*Issues for Discussion*) was composed around the time of the Emperor Aśoka and chronicles all the points of dispute among eighteen schools of Buddhism that had evolved during the first two centuries of the community's existence. The *Yamaka* comprises ten chapters dealing with such things as the classification of all mental factors into the categories of wholesome, unwholesome, and neutral; the five aggregates of *dharmas* that form the basis of our idea of a person or self; the four noble truths; and the three types of *karma* (mental, verbal and corporal). The largest book of the Theravādin *Abhidharma* is the *Paṭṭhāna* (*Relations*), which gives an exhaustive account of the Buddhist theory of causality as contained in the doctrine of Dependent Origination (*pratītya-samutpāda*). The study of these books of *Abhidharma* is designed to help the practitioner replace the habit of seeing life in personal terms with the habit of seeing life as the arising and falling of impersonal events that are unworthy of being invested with either attachment or aversion. Studying the canonical books of *Abhidharma* directly is a daunting task, so many Theravādin practitioners have entered the terrain of *Abhidharma* by studying the Wisdom section of Buddhaghosa's comprehensive work on Buddhist theory and practice entitled *Visuddhimagga* (*Path of Purification*).

The Sarvāstivāda school is also known as the Vaibhāṣika school, because most of its doctrines are found in the great commentary (*vibhāṣa*) to a text summarizing the seven *Abhidharma* texts of that school's canon. According to Yaśomitra, who wrote an extensive commentary to Vasubandhu's *Abhidharmakośa*, each of these seven texts was written by a different author. These texts are the *Jñānaprasthāna* by Kātyāyanīputra, the *Prakaraṇapāda* by Vasumitra, the *Vijñānakāya* by Devaśarman, the *Dharmaskandha* by Śāriputra, the *Prajñaptiśāstra* by Maudgalyāyana, the *Dhātukāya* by Pūrṇa, and the *Saṃgītiparyāya* by Mahākauṣṭhila. Other authorities, however, name other books than these. These seven books were all translated into Chinese and are still extant in translation but not in the original Sanskrit. What is still extant in Sanskrit is the work that eventually surpassed those texts in popularity, namely Vasubandhu's *Abhidharmakośa*, which became the principal work studied by many Sanskrit-using Buddhists in

India and the translation of which was studied by most Tibetan monastics.

The *Abhidharmakośa* consists of eight main chapters and a ninth chapter that may have circulated originally as a separate work. The eight main chapters are all written in verse and accompanied by a prose commentary also written by Vasubandhu. The text opens with a chapter entitled *Dhātunirdeśa*, which lays out the constituents of the material world and of the world of consciousness and provides the basic categories into which these constituents can be classified. The next chapter focuses on the twenty-two faculties (*indriyas*) discussed in Buddhist texts; these include the sense faculties, the reproductive faculties, the life force, and the faculties or powers that motivate the life of Buddhist practice, such as faith, mindfulness, and wisdom. The third chapter, called *Lokanirdeśā* (description of the world) offers an extensive cosmology in which all the six realms of living beings are contained, namely the two superhuman celestial realms, the human realm, the animal realm, the realm of ghosts and disembodied spirits, and the eight great hell realms. Each of these six realms is divided into subrealms, and each is described in detail. The fourth chapter begins with the observation that all the realms in the world are produced by the ripening of *karma*, so this next chapter lays out an elaborate theory of *karma* and its ripening. This chapter discusses actions of the body, speech and mind and distinguishes between the actions of ordinary people and of people acting under the protection of vows, such as those of monastic discipline. Each individual *karma*, or action, that is performed has the immediate effect of establishing a habit, which then predisposes one to act in similar ways in the future. All action is conditioned by underlying proclivities known as *anuśayas*, and these make up the subject matter of the fifth chapter. The proclivities that produce afflictions (*kleśas*) are discussed, along with the methods by which each specific affliction can be uprooted through intellectual understanding in combination with contemplative exercises. The sixth chapter deals with the stages of development as a practitioner leaves behind the habits of undisciplined people and gradually eliminates the obstacles to *nirvāṇa*. The seventh chapter, called *Jñānanirdeśa* (*Explanation of Knowledge*), offers a detailed account of the knowledge of each of the four truths, namely the knowledge of distress (*duḥkha*), knowledge of its cause, knowledge of its cessation, and knowledge of the path leading to the cessation of distress. This chapter also discusses the various forms of extraordinary abilities, or what many people would now call psychic powers, recognized throughout Buddhist literature. The last of the eight principal chapters treats the various levels of meditative achievement (*samāpatti*). The chapter ends with a claim that the Buddha's *Saddharma* (truth) is twofold, for it comprises both the word and the accomplishment of the word. The word itself is the *Vinaya*, the *Sūtras* and the *Abhidharma* divisions of the Buddhist canon. The accomplishment is the realization of what those words convey, and it resides in the exemplary behavior of accomplished practitioners. The word, says Vasubandhu, will last for a very long time, but the accomplishment will fade much more quickly. In fact, he says, it has already all but disappeared in his time and will steadily decline even more in the future. The independent treatise that has come to be regarded as a ninth chapter to the *Abhidharmakośa* is a critique of the views of the so-called Pudgalavādins (personalists), who held the view that there is a person that is neither identical with nor different from the five aggregates of traditional Buddhism.

Building upon the basic framework of the Sarvāstivādin *Abhidharma* was a system of *Abhidharma* of the Yogācāra school, which presents *Abhidharma* from a Mahāyāna perspective and lays out the many stages of the career of a *bodhisattva*. This system had a lasting impact on East Asian Buddhism. Like the two systems of *Abhidharma* discussed earlier, the Yogācāra system presents a complete view of the world and of human consciousness and offers a roadmap to perfection for the practitioner to follow.

See also: **Abhidharma; Canons and literature; India, Buddhism in; Pāli canon.**

RICHARD P. HAYES

ABHIDHARMAKOŚA

The *Abhidharmakośa* or *Treasury of Higher Teachings* is a key *Abhidharma* text in verse written by Vasubandhu and summarizing Sarvāstivādin tenets in eight chapters with a total of about 600 verses. Vasubandhu, the half-brother of Asaṅga, was probably born during the late fourth century CE in northwest India, where he initially studied Sarvāstivādin *Abhidharma* as presented in the *Mahāvibhāṣā*. Dissatisfied with those teachings, he wrote the *Abhidharmakośa* as a summary and critique of the *Mahāvibhāṣā* incorporating many Sautrāntrika arguments. Later in his life he is said to have converted to Mahāyāna and become one of the most influential founders of the Yogācāra school.

The subjects covered in the *Abhidharmakośa* include all the main aspects of Buddhist psychology and metaphysics. The verses of the main text are commented on in the accompanying *bhāṣya* or "exposition", an auto-commentary in which Vasubandhu criticizes the views of the Sarvāstivādins in the *Mahāvibhāṣā*. The *Mahāvibhāṣā* formed the basis of debate between the schools of the Small Vehicle for many centuries, and many shorter treatises such as the *Abhidharmakośa* were composed to criticize and supplement it. Other scholars reacted in turn to the views expressed in the *Abhidharmakośa*, for example Sanghabhadra, a mid fifth-century CE scholar of the Sarvāstivāda school, based in Kashmir. He is thought to have been a younger contemporary of Vasubandhu and wrote the *Abhidharma-nyāya-anusāriṇī* as a refutation of Vasubandhu's critiques of Sarvāstivāda contained in the *Abhidharmakośa*.

The nine chapters in the *Abhidharmakośa* deal with what is perceived (*dhātu*), the sense-faculties (*indriya*), the world (*loka*), *karma*, the proclivities (*anuśayas*), the Noble Ones (*āryapudgala*), knowledge (*jñāna*), meditation (*samādhi*), and refutation of the concept of a self (*anātman*). The commentary (*bhāṣya*) includes an additional chapter in prose refuting the idea of the "person" (*pudgala*) as held by some Buddhists.

As well as the original Sanskrit, translations exist in Tibetan, Chinese and Mongolian, and also in English and French, the latter in six volumes being completed by Louis de La Vallée Poussin during the First World War shortly before his death (English translation by Leo Pruden, 1988). A large number of subcommentaries on the *bhāṣya* have been preserved in Tibetan translations.

The *Abhidharmakośa* later became the basic text of the Kośa school, a minor school of Buddhism during its early period in China. The Abhidharmakośa-*bhāṣya* was translated into Chinese by Paramārtha between 563 and 567 and by Xuanzang between 651 and 654. The school always had a tenuous existence, and by 703 the imperial court registered specialists in this text as belonging to the Faxiang school. However, it did flourish during a time when Japan actively sought Buddhist teachings and texts, and it was transmitted to that country as the "Kusha school", one of the "Six Schools" of Nara Buddhism.

See also: ***Abhidharma*; *Abhidharma* schools; Poussin, Louis de La Vallée; Sarvāstivāda; Sautrāntika; Vasubandhu.**

DAMIEN KEOWN

ABORTION

The Buddhist belief in rebirth clearly introduces a new dimension to the abortion debate. For one thing, it puts the question "When does life begin?" – a key question in the context of abortion – in an entirely new light. For Buddhism, life is a continuum with no discernible starting point, and birth and death are like a revolving door through which an individual passes again and again.

In keeping with traditional Indian medical thought, the Buddha explained conception as a natural process that occurs when three specific conditions are fulfilled (*Majjhima Nikāya* 1.256). On this understanding, (1) intercourse must take place (2) during the woman's fertile period, and (3) there must be available the spirit (*gandharva*) of a deceased person seeking rebirth. When these conditions are present the *gandharva* (this is simply a figurative way of referring to the *vijñāna* or consciousness of a recently deceased person) "descends" into the womb and a new life comes into being. Thus from the earliest times Buddhist sources have been quite clear that individual human life begins at conception. The ancient authorities, of course, had an imperfect knowledge of embryology, particularly concerning ovulation and conception, but their understanding of foetal development as a gradual process with a definite starting point was not very different from that of modern science.

Once consciousness has "descended" into the womb and conception has occurred, the embryo develops through a set number of stages. In *The Path of Purification* (236), Buddhaghosa lists four stages of the early embryo during the first month after conception. The first stage is the *kalala*, in which the tiny embryo is described as "clear and translucent", and is likened to "a drop of purest oil on the end of a hair." The following three stages are the *abudda*, the *pesi* and the *ghana*, terms which connote increasing density and solidity. Sometimes a fifth stage, *pasākhā* ("five branched"), is mentioned, which is when the protuberances of the limbs and head become visible. After the first month, the phases of pregnancy were enumerated by reference to the number of months from conception.

Interpreting the traditional teachings in the light of modern scientific discoveries such as ovulation, the most common view among Buddhists today, particularly those from traditional countries, is that fertilization is the point at which individual human life commences. As a consequence, abortion is widely seen as contrary to the First Precept. Abortion is explicitly mentioned in the monastic precept against taking human life (the Third *Pārājika*) which states "A monk who deliberately deprives a human being of life, even to the extent of causing an abortion, is no longer a follower of the Buddha" (*Vinaya* 1.97).

Despite the condemnation of abortion, the case histories recorded in the *Vinaya* disclose that monks, particularly in their capacity as medical practitioners, occasionally became illegally involved in procuring and performing abortions. Monks frequently acted as counsellors to families, and often were drawn into the kinds of problems which arise in family life, such as an unwanted pregnancy. The motives reported in the sources for seeking an abortion include: concealing extramarital affairs, as when a married woman becomes pregnant by her lover; seeking to prevent an inheritance by killing the rightful heir prior to birth; and domestic rivalry between co-wives because of the pregnancy of one affecting the position and status of another. Sometimes monks brought their medical knowledge to bear in an attempt to cause a miscarriage. The methods used included ointments, potions and charms, pressing or crushing the womb, and scorching or heating it. Monks who were involved in performing or procuring abortions were expelled from the *sangha* for life, the severest sanction available.

Other more popular literature describes the evil karmic consequences of abortion, sometimes in lurid detail. Stories in the *Dhammapada* commentary, the *Petavatthu* (Stories of the Departed), and the *Jātakas* (such as the *Saṃkicca Jātaka*), narrate the evil consequences which follow an abortion, such as the loss of offspring in future lives, acts of revenge, and rebirth in hell. At both a popular and scholarly level, therefore, the early teachings are consistent in depicting abortion as an immoral act that brings karmic suffering in its wake.

Turning now to the contemporary situation, things are less tidy and consistent than in the classical sources. There is considerable variety across the Buddhist world, much divergence between theory and practice, and a fair amount of what might be called "moral dissonance" whereby individuals experience themselves as pulled in opposing directions. In the more traditional Buddhist countries such as Sri Lanka and Thailand, abortion is illegal with certain limited exceptions, such as when necessary to save the mother's life or in the case of rape. The relevant Thai law is the Penal Code of 1956, which imposes strict penalties: a woman who causes an abortion for herself or procures one from someone else can expect to face a penalty of three years in prison or a fine of 3,000 baht, or both. Official statistics report only a tiny number of abortions per year, but this massively underestimates the number performed. Illegal abortions are very common, with perhaps 300,000 each year in Thailand in the hundreds of illegal abortion clinics. According to a 1987 study the majority of abortions (around 80–90 per cent) were performed for married women who were mostly agricultural workers. The study also confirmed that abortion was the accepted method of birth control among these women, suggesting that if better contraception was available the number of abortions would drop considerably.

An interesting aspect of the Thai situation is the low profile maintained by Buddhist monks, who rarely comment or become involved on either side of the argument. With rare exceptions, monks do not picket abortion clinics, go on protest marches or counsel women who are considering having an abortion, as clergy or activists in the West might do. This is not because they have no position on the matter, and if pressed almost all would agree that abortion is immoral. For the most part, however, they regard it as a secular or "village" matter in which they have no direct involvement, and seem content to leave the decision to the conscience of the individuals involved. To a large extent this apparent aloofness has to do with matters of decorum and the high status in which the monkhood is held. Most Buddhist layfolk, and particularly women, would feel embarrassment at discussing such intimate matters with monks, and prefer to discuss the problem with a doctor or other secular professional. Many monks, too, feel that these questions are not proper for one who has renounced the world and is pursuing the spiritual life. This attitude is changing, although slowly.

Turning to the example of a Mahāyāna country, in the face of a high rate of abortion of perhaps one million per annum or more, Japanese society has searched its ancient cultural heritage and evolved a unique response. This takes the form of the *mizuko kuyō* memorial service for aborted children. *Mizuko* literally means "water-child," a concept which has its origins in Japanese mythology, and *kuyō* means a ritual or ceremony. The *mizuko kuyō* ceremony can take many forms, but would typically involve the parents, and sometimes other members of the family, erecting an image of the *bodhisattva* Jizō (the patron *bodhisattva* of small children) and paying their respects to it by bowing, lighting a candle, striking gongs, chanting verses or a hymn, and perhaps reciting a short Buddhist *sūtra* like the *Heart Sūtra*. It is also customary to provide a memorial tablet and a posthumous Buddhist name, which allows the deceased child to be recognized within the family structure. The rite may be repeated at intervals, such as on the anniversary of the abortion.

The ritual, however, is not without its critics. The majority of Buddhist organizations in Japan do not endorse *mizuko kuyō*, regarding it as a modern innovation based on questionable theology and lacking any basis in the *sūtras*. One of the largest Buddhist organizations in Japan, the Jōdo Shinshū, actively opposes the rite for this reason, pointing out that according to orthodox Buddhist teachings a ritual cannot wipe away the bad *karma* caused by an abortion. The more unscrupulous temples in Japan have also sometimes exploited the ritual commercially, promoting the idea of *tatari*, or retribution from departed spirits. The idea has been suggested, often accompanied by lurid pictures, that an aborted foetus becomes a vengeful spirit that causes problems for the mother unless placated by the ritual. Undoubtedly, many temples saw the ritual simply as a money-making scheme and ruthlessly exploited vulnerable women.

In Western countries some Buddhists feel that there may be circumstances in which abortion is justified. They point out that early Buddhist attitudes were formulated in a society which took a very different view of the status of women from that of the modern West. It has also been argued that abortion rights are integral to the emancipation of women and are necessary to redress injustice. Buddhists who are sympathetic to this view and who support the notion of the woman's "right to choose" may recommend meditation and discussion with a Buddhist teacher as ways in which the woman can get in touch with her feelings and come to a decision in harmony with her conscience. As the encounter between Buddhism and Western values proceeds, discussions over the abortion question are certain to continue, hopefully producing more light than heat, in contrast to the dominant pattern in the West in recent decades.

See also: **Ethics; Euthanasia; Japan, Buddhism in; Moral discipline; *Vinaya Piṭaka*.**

DAMIEN KEOWN

ACADEMIC STUDY OF BUDDHISM

Introductory studies

Although there was very little reliable information in the West pertaining to Buddhism prior to the nineteenth century, one can find such landmark works as Simon de la Loubère's *Du Royaume de Siam*, published in 1691, which began to offer an initial glimpse of the Buddhist world. It was not until the appearance of Michel François Ozeray's *Recherches sur Buddhou* (1817), however, that the picture began to brighten. Additionally, as early as 1821, the Danish scholar R.K. Rast ventured to Ceylon to study Pāli and Sinhalese, and to collect palm-leaf manuscripts. Four years later, in 1825, the first publication of the Buddha's biography appeared in *Asiatic Journal*, written by the Russian scholar Issak Jacob Schmidt, who hailed from St. Petersburg. Soon, the pioneering efforts of Henry Thomas Colebrooke, Brian Houghton Hodgson, Alexander Csoma de Körös, and Eugène Burnouf, followed by their intellectual heirs, brought the reliable study of Buddhism to Europe, and eventually, to the rest of the world.

To a large extent, the early interest in Buddhism was philological, converging on the increasing availability of Sanskrit and Pāli manuscripts that were appearing on the European continent. Perhaps the most thorough examination of this development was Russell Webb's "Pali Buddhist Studies in the West," serialized in the now defunct journal *Pali Buddhist Review*, and which systematically reviewed the developments of Pāli and Buddhist Studies in virtually all European countries, as well as Canada and the United States. Also worthy of note is William Peiris' *The Western Contribution to Buddhism*, which contains much historical detail and interesting character sketches of the early scholars of Buddhism. Jan W. de Jong's *A Brief History of Buddhist Studies in Europe and America* also offers valuable information, although America is virtually absent from the volume despite its title. There is also much useful information in Edward Conze's article, "Recent Progress in Buddhist Studies," published in his anthology *Thirty Years of Buddhist Studies* (1968/2000), and in Guy Richard Welbon's *The Buddhist Nirvāṇa and Its Western Interpreters* (1968). There are also some useful case-specific studies, such as Charles Prebish's chapter "The Silent Sangha: Buddhism in the Academy" in his volume *Luminous Passage: The Practice and Study of Buddhism in America (1999)*.

Perhaps the only conclusion that might be drawn from the above, insofar as conclusions are even possible, is that several distinctions appear obvious from an examination of the above sources. First, following the pioneering work on this topic by Constantin Régamey, it can be said that geographic associations seem to identify at least three classical "schools" of Buddhology: the Anglo-German, Leningrad, and Franco-Belgian. The Anglo-German (and oldest) school was led by Thomas W. Rhys Davids and Hermann Oldenberg, while the Leningrad school included Fedor Stcherbatsky, Otto Rosenberg, and E. Obermiller. The Franco-Belgian school included primarily Louis de La Vallée Poussin, Jean Przyluski, Sylvain Lévi, Paul Demiéville, and Étienne Lamotte. The Anglo-German school almost exclusively emphasized the Pāli literary tradition, and according to Conze it dominated the scholarly scene in Europe until around 1914. The Leningrad school, which developed after 1916, worked diligently on Buddhism's scholastic literature, attempting to define, largely through etymological studies, the meaning of Buddhism's extensive technical terminology. It is clearly closer to the Franco-Belgian school that followed than to the Anglo-German. It had largely died out by 1940, with the deaths of Stcherbatsky and Obermiller. The Franco-Belgian school utilized the Sanskritic materials, along with their corresponding translations and commentaries in Chinese and Tibetan. It added other disciplinary approaches, such as that of sociology, to the philological and philosophical inquiries of its predecessors.

The development of Buddhist Studies in Europe

Many scholars consider Eugène Burnouf to be the father of modern Buddhist Studies, and it was his work (co-authored with Christian Lassen) that led to the publication of the first Pāli grammar in the West, in Paris in 1826. As early as 1837, George Turnour published a text and translation of the first thirty-eight chapters of the *Mahāvaṃsa*, but the first full Pāli text was not published until 1855: Viggo Fausboll's edition of the *Dhammapada* (along with an Italian translation). The first Pāli Dictionary, by Robert Caesar Childers, did not appear until 1875. By then, bits and fragments of many Pāli Buddhist texts had been published in various sources such as the *Journal of the Royal Asiatic Society*, *Journal Asiatique*, and others.

Burnouf had been especially interested in Buddhist texts composed in Sanskrit, but after his death in 1852 thirty years passed before Émile Senart published an edition of the *Mahāvastu*. Pāli studies, however, championed by the Anglo-German school, thrived. In 1881 Thomas W. Rhys Davids founded the Pāli Text Society in London, and the first issue of the *Journal of the Pāli Text Society* appeared the following year. When Rhys Davids died in 1922, his wife (Caroline Augusta Foley) succeeded him. By then, virtually all of the Pāli Canon had been edited and published, as well as a series of non-canonical texts such as the *Milindapañha* and others. Pāli studies also proceeded in Germany, largely through the work of Friedrich Spiegel, Hermann Oldenberg, Karl Neumann, and Karl Seidenstucker. In addition, many manuscripts were discovered in the cave temples of Turfan by German expeditions.

In the 1860s a number of individuals were born who fueled both the Franco-Belgian and Leningrad schools. One of the first of these was Sylvain Lévi, an early leader of Sanskrit Buddhist studies. In 1892 he published the first chapter of the *Buddhacarita*, and eventually discovered a text of the *Mahāyānasūtrālaṅkāra*, which he published in 1907. Louis de La Vallée Poussin (a Belgian) was born shortly after Lévi, and began his studies under him at the Sorbonne in 1891. Perhaps his greatest works are his French translation of Vasubandhu's *Abhidharmakośa*, and of the *Vijñaptimātratāsiddhi*. La Vallée Poussin's most famous student was the Belgian Étienne Lamotte. Before his fortieth birthday, he had already published translations of the *Saṃdhinirmocana*, Vasubandhu's *Karmasiddhiprakaraṇa*, and Asaṅga's *Mahāyānasaṃgraha*. His *Histoire de bouddhisme Indien* has become a classic text in Buddhist Studies. Fedor Stcherbatsky studied under I.P. Minaev, among others, and in 1903 published a Russian translation of Dharmakīrti's *Nyāyabindu*, along with Dharmottara's *ṭīkā*, which was eventually translated into English in two volumes as *Buddhist Logic*. He is best known for two shorter works: *The Central Conception of Buddhism and the Meaning of the Word "Dharma"* (1923) and *The Conception of Buddhist Nirvāṇa* (1927).

England, Germany, France, Belgium, and Russia were not the only places where the study of Buddhism prospered in Europe. Denmark, Holland, Italy, and Scandinavia also produced significant scholars and publications. In Denmark, Dines Andersen, along with the Swedish scholar Helmer Smith, edited the first volume of the *Critical Pāli Dictionary*. This work was continued by V. Trenckner at the Royal Danish Academy of Sciences and Letters. In 1865, a Chair in Sanskrit was created at the University of Leiden in Holland, and was first held by the eminent scholar Hendrik Kern. Kern's legacy was continued through the long work of Jan W. de Jong, who trained many of today's leading scholars of Buddhism from his post at the Australian National University. Italy's great contribution to Buddhist Studies comes in the form of its foremost scholar, Giuseppe Tucci, and the publication series of its society of orientalists: Instituto per il Medio ed Estremo Oriente, in Rome.

The legacy of the above pioneers of Buddhist Studies is far too extensive to document in this short presentation. The best condensation of the current state of affairs in the various European countries can be found in Russell Webb's article "Contemporary European Scholarship on Buddhism," published as Series Continua I of *Buddhica Brittanica: The Buddhist Heritage*, edited by Tadeusz Skorupski in 1989. It outlines all the major scholars, publications, and professional societies in Europe. Moreover, Webb is currently working on a complete monograph devoted to Buddhist Studies in Europe.

Japan

In the last half-century the study of Buddhism by Japanese scholars has flourished, and it is necessary to add a Japanese school of Buddhology to the previously cited Anglo-German, Leningrad, and Franco-Belgian schools. Although likely split into Tokyo and Kyoto subschools, the Japanese school of Buddhology seems to emphasize sound philology, as well as a keen interest in textual studies and a generally doctrinal orientation. It strives for objectivity in its scholarship, as opposed to specifically sectarian approaches to its work. It has benefited from the pioneering leadership of scholars such as Junjirō Takakusu, Gadjin Nagao, Akira Hirakawa, Jukido Takasaki, Hajime Nakamura, and others, whose interests have spanned the horizon of topics on the Buddhist Studies landscape.

Buddhist Studies in North America

Thomas Tweed's *The American Encounter with Buddhism 1844–1912: Victorian Culture and the Limits of Dissent* (2006) is a wonderful and complete introduction to the early pioneers of the American Buddhist movement. For those unwilling to wade through more than 200 pages of Tweed's meticulous prose, a pleasant narrative can be found in Rick Fields' chapter on "The Restless Pioneers" in *How the Swans Came to the Lake* (1992). Unfortunately, there are no such books or chapters documenting the development of the academic study of Buddhist Studies in America – the largest venue of the discipline – and the existence of such work remains a *desideratum*. As a result, we can only sketch a very short overview of Buddhist Studies in America.

As note, although some might consider Eugène Burnouf the founding father of Buddhist Studies as a discipline, in the United States, the beginning of Buddhist Studies seems inextricably bound to three primary individuals: Paul Carus, Henry Clarke Warren, and Charles Rockwell Lanman. Carus arrived in America in the 1880s with a Ph.D. from Tübingen, eventually becoming the editor of *Open Court* journal and later of the Open Court Publishing Company. Although he wrote more than a dozen books of his own, including the still widely read *The Gospel of Buddhism* (1894), Carus is probably best known for bringing D.T. Suzuki to America and employing him at Open Court for many years.

Henry Clarke Warren and Charles Rockwell Lanman were more scholarly in their approach than Carus, and worked diligently to establish the Buddhist literary tradition in America. Lanman had studied Sanskrit under William Dwight Whitney, earning his doctorate in 1875 before moving on to Johns Hopkins University, and eventually becoming Professor of Sanskrit at Harvard University in 1880. Warren, though horribly deformed as a result of a childhood accident, had studied Sanskrit with Lanman at Johns Hopkins, and followed his learned master back to Harvard, where the two struck up an alliance that culminated in the creation of a new publication series known as the Harvard Oriental Series. Hendrik Kern's edition of the *Jātakamālā*, or collection of Buddhist birth stories, was the first edition, with Warren's famous *Buddhism in Translations* becoming the third volume in 1896.

Following Warren's death in 1899, and with Lanman moving on to other studies in the Indic tradition, the development of Buddhist Studies was left to others. One of these early trailblazers was Eugene Watson Burlingame, who had studied with Lanman at Harvard before shifting to Yale, where he worked industriously on a variety of Pāli texts. By 1921 he had published a three-volume translation of the *Dhammapada* commentary in the Harvard Oriental Series. Burlingame was followed by W.Y. Evans-Wentz, a 1907 Stanford graduate, who studied extensively in Europe, and is best known for his collaborative compiling of the translations of his teacher, Kazi Dawa-Sandup. Their translation of the *Tibetan Book of the Dead*, although unreliable and now entirely superseded, became extremely popular. By the time of Evans-Wentz's death in 1965, a new group of Buddhological scholars had developed on the American scene, including such committed scholars as Winston King, Richard Gard, and Kenneth K.S. Ch'en.

Despite the work of these early educators, it was not until after 1960 that Buddhist Studies began to emerge as a significant discipline in the American university system and publishing industry. During the Vietnam War years and immediately thereafter, Buddhist Studies was to enjoy a so-called "boom," largely through the efforts of such leading professors as Richard Hugh Robinson of the University of Wisconsin, Masatoshi Nagatomi of Harvard University, and Alex Wayman of Columbia University. No doubt there were many reasons for the increased development of Buddhist Studies, not the least of which were the increase in Area Studies programs in American universities; growing government interest in things Asian; the immense social anomie that permeated American culture in the 1960s; and the growing dissatisfaction with (and perhaps rejection of) traditional religion. During the 1960s, a formal graduate program was instituted at the University of Wisconsin, offering both an M.A. and a Ph.D. in Buddhist Studies. Interdisciplinary programs emphasizing the study of Buddhism were soon available at Berkeley and Columbia as well. As other programs arose, such as the program at the Center for the Study of World Religions at Harvard University, and the History of Religions program at the University of Chicago, it became possible to gain sophisticated training in all aspects of the Buddhist tradition, and in all Buddhist canonical languages as well. As a result, a new generation of young Buddhologists was born, appearing rapidly on the campuses of many American universities, and rivaling their overseas peers in both training and insight.

This picture of expanding American Buddhology is perhaps not so rosy as one might think, rapid growth notwithstanding. As interest grew, funding for graduate education did not keep pace, and would-be Buddhologists no longer had the luxury of being able to spend six or eight or even ten *fully funded years* in preparation for the Ph.D. As a result, the breadth and scope of their training was compromised, resulting in an accelerated urgency for specialization. The consequence was that very few new Buddhologists were appearing with the complete philological training and geographical comprehensiveness of their teachers. Thus, it became usual to find individuals focusing on *one tradition*, such as Indian or Tibetan or Chinese or Japanese Buddhism, but rarely *all* of the traditions. And if the distinctions that characterize the Anglo-German, Franco-Belgian, and Leningrad schools, mentioned above, are accurate, the "American" school is equally divided within itself.

Current Buddhist Studies

More than twenty years ago, an article on recent Buddhist literature titled "Buddhist Studies American Style: A Shot in the Dark," was published, explaining at the outset that the conjured image of Inspector Clouseau "falling through banisters, walking into walls, crashing out of windows, and somehow miraculously getting the job done with the assistance of his loyal Oriental servant," was not an accidental choice on the author's part; that Buddhist Studies was just as erratic as poor Clouseau. At that time, a similar argument could have easily been made for Buddhist Studies throughout the world.

Lately, though, Buddhist Studies has begun to engage in the useful process of self-reflection, and the results of that inquiry are fruitful and inspiring. In winter 1995, the *Journal of the International Association of Buddhist Studies* devoted an entire issue to the topic of Buddhist Studies as an academic discipline, providing the occasion for scholars to reflect on various aspects of the field. José Cabezón, a Buddhist scholar and former Tibetan lama, summarized the critical question:

> Although the academic study of Buddhism is much older than the International Association of Buddhist Studies and the journal to which it gave rise, the founding of the latter, which represents a significant – perhaps pivotal – step in the institutionalization of the field, is something that occurred less than twenty years ago. Nonetheless, whether a true discipline or not – whether or not Buddhist Studies has already achieved disciplinary status, whether it is proto-disciplinary or superdisciplinary – there is an apparent integrity to Buddhist Studies that at the very least calls for an analysis of the field in holistic terms.

In another interesting article entitled "The Ghost at the Table: On the Study of Buddhism and the Study of Religion," Malcolm David Eckel wrote in his conclusion:

> It is not just students who are attracted to religious studies because they "want to know what it is to be human and humane, and intuit that religion deals with such things." There are at least a few scholars of Buddhism who feel the same way. For me the biggest unsettled question in the study of Buddhism is not whether Buddhism is religious or even whether the study of Buddhism is religious; it is whether scholars in this field can find a voice that does justice to their own religious concerns and can demonstrate to the academy why their kind of knowledge is worth having.

In a recent (2002) issue of *Tricycle: The Buddhist Review*, Duncan Ryuken Williams, an ordained Sōtō Zen priest and university professor, compiled a short list of institutions which offer graduate study in Buddhism. Although Williams' listing included the expected sorts of categories ("Most comprehensive programs," "Institutions with strength in Indo-Tibetan Buddhist Studies," and so forth), he also included a category called "Practitioner-friendly institutions," indicating yet another aspect to the current study of the Buddhist tradition: the "scholar-practitioner."

Publication venues and professional societies in Buddhist Studies

The international community of Buddhist Studies scholars is extremely active in publication. Preliminary survey data collected in the United States suggests that this group significantly outperforms scholars identified generally in the Religious Studies community. To accommodate this need, a number of journals are devoted exclusively to the publication of Buddhist materials. They include the *Journal of International Association of Buddhist Studies*, *Buddhist Studies Review*, *The Eastern Buddhist*, *Pacific World*, and the *Journal of the Pāli Text Society*. A number of other journals, although not exclusively devoted to Buddhism, also are popular resources among Buddhologists. These include: *Buddhist–Christian Studies*, *Journal of Asian Studies*, *Journal of the American Oriental Society*, *Journal of the American Academy of Religion*, *History of Religions*, *Japanese Journal of Religious Studies*, *Philosophy East and West*, *Monumenta Nipponica*, and the *Journal of Chinese Philosophy*. Books are regularly published by both university and trade/commercial presses. Among the former, the University of Hawai'i Press, University of California Press, Oxford University Press, Princeton University Press, State University of New

York Press, University of Chicago Press, Columbia University Press, and Cambridge University Press appear to be the most favorite. Among the latter, Routledge, Snow Lion, Wisdom Publications, and Shambhala lead the way.

Although the number of professional societies devoted exclusively to the study of Buddhism is very small, they represent an extremely active group. Dating back to the founding of the Pāli Text Society in 1881, there has been a steady stream of interest in Buddhism. Forty years later, D.T. Suzuki founded the Eastern Buddhist Society in Japan. In more modern times, the two most prominent professional societies are the International Association of Buddhist Studies, founded in the United States in 1976 by A.K. Narain, and the United Kingdom Association of Buddhist Studies, currently under the direction of Peter Harvey. Also highly significant is the "Buddhism Section" of the American Academy of Religion, founded in 1981 by George Bond and Charles Prebish, and currently co-chaired by Janet Gyatso and Charles Hallisey.

Scholar-practitioners in Buddhist Studies

Virtually everyone who begins an academic career in Buddhist Studies eventually pores over Étienne Lamotte's exciting volume *Histoire de Bouddhisme Indien des origines à l'ère Śaka*, either in the original French or in Sara Webb-Boin's admirable English translation. That Lamotte was a Catholic priest seems not to have influenced either his understanding of or his respect for the Buddhist tradition, although he did worry a bit from time to time about the reaction of the Vatican to his work. Edward Conze, arguably one of the most colorful Buddhist scholars of the twentieth century, once remarked:

> When I last saw him, he had risen to the rank of Monseigneur and worried about how his "Histoire" had been received at the Vatican. "*Mon professeur*, do you think they will regard the book as *hérétique*?" They obviously did not. His religious views showed the delightful mixture of absurdity and rationality which is one of the hallmarks of a true believer.

Why does there seem to be such a bifurcation of study and practice in Buddhism? José Cabezón, in an article in the *Journal of the International Association of Buddhist Studies*, candidly says:

> Critical distance from the object of intellectual analysis is necessary. Buddhists, by virtue of their religious commitment, lack such critical distance from Buddhism. Hence, Buddhists are *never* good buddhologists. Or, alternatively, those who take any aspect of Buddhist doctrine seriously (whether pro or con) are scientifically suspect by virtue of allowing their individual beliefs to affect their scholarship. Good scholarship is neutral as regards questions of truth. Hence, evaluative/normative scholarship falls outside the purview of Buddhist Studies.

What has been the response to the educational leadership gap on the part of Buddhist communities? Again, the explanation is twofold. On the one hand, there is a movement in some Buddhist communities to identify those individuals *within the community itself* who are best suited, and best trained, to serve the educational needs of the community, and confer appropriate authority in these individuals in a formal way. Recently, Sakyong Mipham Rinpoche, son of Chögyam Trungpa and now head of the Shambhala International community, declared nine community members "Acharyas," an Indian Buddhist designation for a respected teacher. These individuals, one of whom holds the Ph.D. degree from the University of Chicago with specialization in Buddhism, were authorized to take on enhanced teaching and leadership roles in their community and beyond. On the other hand, virtually everyone who writes on Western applications of Buddhism sees it almost exclusively as a lay movement, devoid of any significant monastic component. Emma Layman, one of the earliest researchers in the field, said as much in 1976: "In general, American Buddhists are expected to lead their lives within the lay community rather than in a monastic setting." Later, Rick Fields echoed the same sentiment when he proclaimed: "Generalization of any kind seems to dissolve in the face of such cultural and religious diversity." As such, it does seem safe to suggest that lay practice is the real heart of scholar-practitioners of Buddhism. As a result, Western Buddhist communities have looked to the growing number of scholar-practitioners to provide an expanding role and reliable fund of knowledge to their community members.

The role of technology in Buddhist Studies

Until quite recently, introductory texts on Buddhism did not include a single word about the role of computer technology in the development of Buddhist Studies. The earliest formal interest in the application of computer technology to Buddhism seems to have occurred when the International Association of Buddhist Studies formed a Committee on Buddhist Studies and Computers at its 1983 meeting in Tokyo. Jamie Hubbard, in an amusing and highly significant article called "Upping the Ante: Budstud@millenium.end.edu," pointed out: "The three major aspects of computer technology that most visibly have taken over older technologies are word processing, electronic communication, and the development of large scale archives of both text and visual materials." Hubbard went on to relate his first experiences with IndraNet, an online discussion forum sponsored by the International Association of Buddhist Studies in the mid-1980s and co-managed by Hubbard and Bruce Burrill with equipment donated by Burrill. Apart from a small bevy of faithful participants, there was little interest in the forum and it died a largely unnoticed death within two years. Nonetheless, of the three impact-items cited by Hubbard, it was clearly electronic communication that was to have the most important and continuing consequences for the discipline of Buddhist Studies.

Early in the 1990s, a profusion of online discussion forums (or "e-mail discussion lists"), similar in nature to the one described, began to proliferate and thrive on the Internet. Although these forums were global in scope, the vast majority of subscribers and participants were from North America. One of the very first of these was "Buddhist." Although the traffic on the list was often frenetic, with messages that were sometimes delivered as late as six months after they were composed, it was an exciting beginning. Because the list was unmoderated, and most often concerned with various aspects of Buddhist practice and popular issues within modern Buddhism, the number of postings eventually became sufficiently unwieldy that the owner decided to bequeath the list to a new owner-manager, and the list was moved to McGill University in Canada.

During one of the periods in which the "Buddhist" list had broken down, Richard Hayes, a professor on the Faculty of Religious Studies at McGill University, surveyed a number of subscribers to the list and discovered that many of these individuals favored beginning a separate list that was not only restricted to academic discussions of Buddhism but moderated as well. In collaboration with James Cocks, who worked in the computer center at the University of Louisville, a new discussion forum called "Buddha-L" was created, initially monitored by Cocks under guidelines composed by Hayes. The forum considered scholarly discussions of virtually all aspects of Buddhism, as well as issues related to teaching Buddhism at the university level, and occasional postings of employment opportunities in academe. Hayes confessed that, because of the narrow, academic nature of the forum, his expectation was for a small but dedicated number of subscribers. Within a year, however, the group had over 1,000 subscribers. In addition to the above groups, a number of other discussion groups built an early but substantial following among Buddhists on the Internet. Perhaps the best known of these additional groups is "ZenBuddhism-L," founded in August 1993 at the Australian National University by Dr. T. Matthew Ciolek, Head of the Internet Publications Bureau of the Research School of Pacific and Asian Studies at the Australian National University.

In February 1992, an "Electronic Buddhist Archive" was established by the Coombs Computing Unit of the Australian National University. Under the direction of T. Matthew Ciolek, it was positioned as a subsection of the Coombspapers FTP Social Sciences/Asian Studies research archive which had been initiated several months earlier. It contained over 320 original documents in ASCII (plain text) format, including bibliographies, biographies, directories, Buddhist electronic-texts, poetry, and the like. It also offered a unique collection of previously unpublished transcripts of teachings and sermons by many famous twentieth-century Zen masters such as Robert Aitken Rōshi, Taizan Maezumi Rōshi, Hakuun Yasutani Rōshi, and others.

E-mail discussion forums and Buddhist databases were not the only form of early Buddhist activity on the Internet. As early as 1993, the first electronic Buddhist journal made its appearance. Called *Gassho*, it was edited by its founder, Barry Kapke, who operated it and other enterprises under a broad, umbrella-like organization known as DharmaNet International, founded in 1991. According to Kapke, it was published "as a service to the international Buddhist community, inclusive of all Buddhist traditions." Kapke used the past tense in the above description because *Gassho* went on hiatus following the May–June 1994 issue. Quite simply, its rapid growth exceeded the capability of its entirely volunteer staff to keep up. Just as a new issue was nearly completed for December 1996, both Kapke's home computer and its Internet server crashed, resulting in a loss of all materials for that issue. While no new issues have followed this devastating loss, it was clear from the first issue (available in both online and hard-copy versions), in November–December 1993, that *Gassho* presented a vision of a new kind of Buddhist community. Its masthead referred to it as an "Electronic Journal of DharmaNet International and the Global Online *Sangha*." *Gassho* notwithstanding, another online electronic journal would eventually provide the occasion for an immensely rapid, and continued, growth in electronic Buddhist Studies by exploiting yet another electronic medium for the dissemination of information: the World Wide Web.

The *Journal of Buddhist Ethics* was born in July 1994. It was originally planned as a traditional, hard-copy scholarly journal by its editors, who quickly learned that potential publishers had little interest in a highly specialized, purely academic journal that was not likely to turn a profit. One of the co-editors, Damien Keown, suggested publishing the journal online, where there would be no expenses, and where the journal could provide a useful service to its constituent community, however tiny it might be. Once a technical editor was added to the staff, plans rapidly moved ahead, making the journal available via the World Wide Web, as well as through FTP and Gopher retrieval. The journal went online on 1 July

1994 with no articles, but with a WWW page outlining the aims of the journal and listing its editorial board members. It advertised its presence on a small number of electronic newsgroups, and within a week had 100 subscribers. The journal's first "Call for Papers" was made after Labor Day, and by the end of 1994 it had over 400 subscribers in twenty-six countries. It currently has over 6,000 subscribers in more than fifty countries.

Along with other new features, added to the journal's basic emphasis on scholarly articles devoted to Buddhist ethics, the journal began a new section called "Global Resources for Buddhist Studies." Rather quickly, the editors discovered that many communities of Buddhist practitioners began requesting that links to their own developing World Wide Web pages be listed with the *Journal of Buddhist Ethics*. In other words, it became clear that the World Wide Web in general was indeed growing immensely and quickly, furnishing a unique opportunity for communication that Buddhist communities had never known before. Although it was by no means unique in its establishment of a jumping-off point for the exploration of additional Buddhist resources of all kinds on the Web, along with DharmaNet International and the WWW Virtual Libraries at the Australian National University, and a newer Buddhist Gateway known as the Buddhist Resource File, the *Journal of Buddhist Ethics* provided a new way of thinking about Buddhist communities, one that augmented Gary Ray's cybersangha and Barry Kapke's global online sangha.

More recently, and with an exceedingly more sophisticated technology, major Buddhist Studies sites have been created throughout the world, many prompted by the groundbreaking work of Charles Muller in Japan. These sites provide such items as Buddhist texts in their original languages, constantly updated Buddhist dictionaries, and a wide variety of electronic tools – such as Unicode fonts – for worldwide information exchange in Buddhist Studies. Coupled with the global reach of Buddhist Studies professional societies such as the International Association of Buddhist Studies and the United Kingdom Association of Buddhist Studies, and international forums for virtually instant communication (like the H-Buddhism online community of scholars created by Charles Muller), the discipline of Buddhist Studies begins the twenty-first century with a vision unimagined even a quarter-century earlier.

See also: **Anglo-German school of Buddhist Studies; Current issues in Buddhist Studies; Franco-Belgian school of Buddhist Studies; Leningrad school of Buddhist Studies; Major professional societies; North American school of Buddhist Studies; Prominent Buddhist Studies journals; Scholar-practitioners in Buddhist Studies.**

CHARLES S. PREBISH

ACHARN MUN

Acharn Mun (1870–1949) is widely considered an *arhat* in the Thai forest tradition. Born in northeastern Thailand, he was known for his commitment to life as a wandering forest ascetic and for being an accomplished meditation master. Throughout his life, Acharn Mun preserved some distance from the Thai center of power and the monastic establishment in Bangkok. After his death, his image was the object a modern cult of amulets believed to embody his magical protection (*iddhi*).

According to the hagiography composed by his disciple, Acharn Maha Boowa, Acharn Mun's quest for enlightenment began with a prophetic dream that revealed to him the possibility of *nirvāṇa* in this life. To quiet and control his agile mind, Mun spent the early years of his monastic career in strict ascetic practice (*dhūtaṅga*) and *vipassanā* meditation. His perseverance was challenged by the lack of a teacher and by a brief hiatus from monastic life, after which he became fully ordained in the *Vinaya*-oriented and royally sponsored *Thammayut* lineage.

When Mun commenced his wandering peripatetic practice in the late nineteenth century, neither the forest tradition nor *vipassanā* meditation was widely practiced in Thailand. Mun observed strict ascetic practices (*dhūtaṅga*) that included wearing rag robes, eating only food that was put into his alms bowl, dwelling in the forest, under trees and in caves, and so forth. The forest was seen as the untamed and dangerous domain of wild beasts, especially tigers and elephants. Mun used meditation, especially walking meditation, to conquer the fears of the mind and invoke the protection of the *Dhamma*. Acharn Mun was ethnically Laotian with a dedicated lay following in the northeast regions of Thailand. His charisma and solitary forest practice posed a challenge to the modern Thai state. A series of *sangha* reforms in 1902, 1941, and 1962 aimed to integrate the independent forest tradition by encouraging Mun and his disciples to take up permanent residence at established monasteries.

Mun spent many years in solitary forest practice. His peripatetic wandering took him into the forests of the Thai northeastern frontier and into Laos, where he remained in solitary forest practice for many months. His solitary endeavors usually entailed supernatural feats. He would emerge from the forest with spiritual renewal and compassionate motivation to teach his disciples. For instance, during his stay in the Srikara Cave in the mountains of Nakhon Nakoy, his unfaltering meditation enabled him to overcome the physical challenges by the resident demon and to convert him to the *Dhamma*. Like a *bodhisattva*, he would postpone his immediate enlightenment to teach his disciples. He repeated this pattern throughout the decades of his life. His culminating retreat to the mountains of Chiengmai lasted for eleven years (1929–40) and led him to the attainment of an *arhat*. When he passed away in 1949, his body was cremated and his remains are said to have turned into clear crystal-like relics.

His legacy included a number of close disciples, foremost among them his biographer, Acharn Mahaa Boowa. After Mun's hagiography was serialized in a popular Buddhist magazine in the early 1970s, his charisma continued to grow and gave rise to a cult of amulets. His small, encased image was particularly sought after by the Bangkok elites who believed the amulet would grant protective powers to the person wearing it. Despite the focus on Acharn Mun's powers at the nation's center, the forest tradition eventually fell victim to rapid modernization, deforestation and political forces seeking to integrate the independent charisma of forest monks in Thailand.

See also: **Famous Buddhists and ideal types.**

JULIANE SCHOBER

ACTIVIST WOMEN IN CONTEMPORARY BUDDHISM

The activist women discussed here are those women working around the world to enact and establish egalitarian relationships among the sexes, both within the Buddhist *sangha* and throughout society. As Judith Simmer-Brown notes in her study of "women's *Dharma*" in the West, however, it is impossible to write comprehensively about the diverse activities of these women as so few of them have yet been the subjects of research or documentation. For this reason, our treatment of the topic will necessarily be selective, concentrating heavily on the activities of Western women, especially in the United States, which have been more thoroughly studied and written about than the activities of others in other parts of the world.

Much of the activity of these Western women is theoretical in nature, undertaken with the intention of grounding their more overt attempts to realize egalitarian relationships intellectually in the Buddhist tradition. This theoretical activity receives its impetus from the fact of the historical dominance of Buddhism by men and the many arguments and rationalizations which have been generated over the centuries for relegating women to second-class status within the tradition. Contemporary activist women counter these traditions by insisting that not only are there contrary resources in the Buddhist tradition for constructing more egalitarian relationships among the sexes, but, even more fundamentally, Buddhism is itself inherently egalitarian. According to this line of reasoning, the patriarchy of traditional Asian Buddhist traditions represents a corruption of the original intention and internal logic of the Buddhist tradition, and egalitarianism is, therefore, advocated as normative for the tradition.

In support of such claims, advocates of Buddhist egalitarianism often cite the admission of women into the monastic *sangha* by the Buddha and the many accounts of spiritual achievement by women in various contexts throughout the centuries. Even more fundamentally, they ground their arguments in the most basic teachings of Buddhism about the interrelatedness of all phenomena (*pratītya-samutpāda*; *śūnyatā*) and no-self (*anātman*). These teachings are interpreted as undercutting categorical distinctions between "male" and "female" and as thus implying a fundamental egalitarianism at the heart of Buddhism. Relying on the Mahāyāna teaching of "emptiness" (*śūnyatā*), for instance, influential American scholar-practitioner Rita M. Gross argues that "'male' and 'female,' like all other labels and designations, are empty and lack substantial reality. Therefore, they cannot be used in a rigid and fixed way to delimit people." She concludes, moreover, that:

> no major Buddhist teaching provides any basis for gender privilege or gender hierarchy and that these doctrines, in fact, mandate gender equality at the same time as they undercut the relevance of gender . . . To be true to its own vision, Buddhism needs to transcend its androcentrism and patriarchy.

Gross and others commonly insist, therefore, that Buddhism's recent historical encounter with the West represents an "auspicious coincidence" or "magical meeting," in which Buddhism may finally and fully realize its inherent but socially suppressed sexual equality. Unfortunately, the egalitarian implications of Buddhist teachings have generally been ignored and actively side-stepped by male elites throughout the centuries. These, it is charged, have operated according to the patriarchal values of traditional Asian cultures rather than according to the inherent logic of the Buddhist tradition. Buddhism's arrival on the shores of America, where the values of democracy and equality are already firmly established, now provides an unprecedented opportunity for the tradition to realize its own inherent equality. American Buddhist women may thus even "model and theorize sane gender arrangements" for the rest of the world.

Critics, of course, hear in such statements a neo-colonial or "Orientalist" bias, which erects its own kind of hierarchy among the cultures of "East" and "West," a hierarchy of equality and "sanity" on the one hand, and patriarchy and, presumably, "insanity" on the other hand. Western women are thus pictured as being uniquely (and superiorly) in the position "to manifest, in everyday reality, what the Buddhist *Dharma* has said explicitly and implicitly for so long" (Gross), but has been prevented from doing by its involvement in "the patriarchal hierarchical societies" of Asia (Boucher). Critics suggest that with such arguments, Western feminist Buddhists are hoist by their own petard. In other words, like the misogynists they criticize, they reify the "empty" distinction between "Asia" and "the West" and mistake this distinction for being relevant to questions about who may and who may not realize the ultimate and "true" meaning of Buddhism.

Fortunately for those working to establish egalitarian relationships within Buddhism, this criticism takes aim at the claims of Western women to be in a superior position to recognize and realize the inherent egalitarianism of Buddhism, and, not, directly at least, at their more basic claims about Buddhism's inherent egalitarianism. Western women are free, therefore, to admit their own hubris in declaring the superiority of their position, without necessarily being forced to concede their fundamental insights about the egalitarian implications of Buddhist teachings. It may be true, in other words, that Buddhism is inherently egalitarian, as they argue, without it simultaneously being true that this egalitarianism may only, or even only best, be realized among American Buddhist practitioners who may then, like big sisters, export their more enlightened insights to the rest of the world.

At the practical level, contemporary activist women are working to institutionalize egalitarianism in various ways throughout the world. In Theravāda countries, for example, efforts have focused, to a large degree, on the roles and statuses of dedicated female practitioners, who have been denied the opportunity of full ordination for centuries. Interestingly, many of these women have resisted full ordination, arguing that full ordination would bring with it institutionalized subordination to the men's *sangha* and governmental supervision. In Sri Lanka, for instance, *dasa sil matavo* or "ten-precept women," who take the ten precepts, shave their heads, don saffron and white robes, chant scriptures, meditate, and serve societal needs, have received both the respect and donations of laypeople without having to succumb to the institutional authority of Theravāda's male elite. At the same time, however, they have been denied status and resources by not being fully ordained. Moreover, the traditional hierarchy of the men's and women's *sanghas* remains unchallenged by their actions. For this reason, debate continues among Sri Lankan and other Theravādan women about whether or not they should work toward the re-establishment of the women's *sangha* or maintain their status as dedicated laypersons.

In other parts of the world, especially in the West, this problem is being largely side-stepped with arguments that distinctions between monastics and laity are as spurious as distinctions between males and females, and thus that practical distinctions between monastics and householders should be leveled as well. Some carry the argument even further to include distinctions between human and non-human beings, and thus many contemporary activist women support and form alliances with various ecological movements and advocate for the full inclusion of all beings in what American activist Joanna Macy calls the "eco-*sangha*." The efforts of contemporary activist women in Buddhism thus have implications for issues far beyond those surrounding the roles and statuses of women and men in Buddhism.

See also: **Buddhist women, anthropological approaches to; Feminist approaches in Buddhism; Women in Buddhism: an historical**

and textual overview; Women in Korean Buddhism; Women in modern Buddhism; Women in Tibetan Buddhism.

JIM DEITRICK

AHIṂSĀ

One of the most basic principles of Buddhist ethics, and one for which it is universally admired, is *ahiṃsā*. It finds expression in Buddhist ethics in many moral codes, but particularly as the first of the Five Precepts (*pañca-śīla*) which prohibits "onslaught on living creatures" (*pāṇātipāta*). Although *ahiṃsā* literally means "non-harming" or "non-violence", it embodies much more than these negative-sounding translations suggest. *Ahiṃsā* is not merely the absence of violence, but involves a deeply positive feeling of respect for living beings, a moral position associated in the West with the terms "respect for life" or "the sanctity of life."

In India, *ahiṃsā* seems to have been emphasized most among the unorthodox renouncer (*śramaṇa*) movements such as Buddhism and Jainism which emphasized concern (*dayā*) and sympathy (*anukampā*) for living creatures, and an increasing empathy with them based on the awareness that others dislike pain and death just as much as oneself. As the *Dhammapada* notes, "All tremble at violence, all fear death. Comparing oneself with others one should neither kill nor cause to kill" (v. 129).

Under the influence of *ahiṃsā*, animal sacrifice, which had played an important part in Brahmanical religious rites in India from ancient times, was rejected by both Buddhism and Jainism as cruel and barbaric. Due in part to their influence, blood sacrifices in the orthodox Brahmanical tradition came increasingly to be replaced by symbolic offerings such as vegetables, fruit and milk. Many Buddhists – especially followers of the Mahāyāna in East Asia – have embraced vegetarianism, as this diet does not involve the slaughter of animals. Many Hindus have also emphasized the importance of *ahiṃsā*, and the concept was promoted especially by Gandhi, who made it the cornerstone of his religious and political teachings in the twentieth century.

Among the ancient renouncer movement (*śramaṇas*), *ahiṃsā* was sometimes taken to extremes. Jain monks, for example, took the greatest precautions against destroying tiny forms of life such as insects, even unintentionally. Their practices had some influence on Buddhism, and Buddhist monks often used a strainer to make sure they did not destroy small creatures in their drinking-water. They also avoided travel during the monsoon to avoid treading on insects and other small creatures which become abundant after the rains. Concern is even apparent in early sources about the practice of agriculture because of the inevitable destruction of life caused by ploughing the earth. In general, however, Buddhism regards the destruction of life as morally wrong only when it is caused intentionally (in other words, when the death of creatures is the outcome sought).

As a result of its association with *ahiṃsā*, Buddhism is generally perceived as non-violent and peace-loving, an impression which is to a large extent correct. While Buddhist countries have not been free from war and conflict, Buddhist teachings constantly praise non-violence and express disapproval of killing or causing injury to living things. In the words of the *Dhammapada*, "He who has renounced violence towards all living beings, weak or strong, who neither kills nor causes others to kill – him do I call a holy man" (v. 405).

See also: **Ethics; Moral discipline; Vegetarianism; War and peace.**

DAMIEN KEOWN

AJAṆṬĀ AND ELLORĀ

Two of the most famous sites in the Indian Buddhist world are the cave temple complexes of Ajaṇṭā and Ellorā. Ajaṇṭā is the earlier of the two, having been begun probably in the middle of the sixth century CE, during the Gupta period (although the caves may have been occupied by monks much earlier). The caves at both sites consist of dozens of large *caitya* halls, *vihāras*, and which are elaborately adorned with *stūpas*, decorative carvings, stone images of Buddhas, *bodhisattvas*, and female deities (See Figure 7). At Ajaṇṭā there are some thirty caves, built during two major phases of construction, which are often thought to correspond to a Theravāda and a Mahāyāna monastic presence at the site. Although there is evidence that such an understanding of the site is warranted, it is also important to note that the caves contain a mixture of styles and motifs, reflecting a complex layering of artistic influences – often drawn from other important sites, such as Sārnath, Bodhgayā, Amarāvatī, Sāñcī, and Bhārhut.

Although there are many impressive stone images in the caves, what is perhaps most remarkable about the art at Ajaṇṭā is the intricate paintings that decorate their walls: paintings of various scenes from the Buddha's life, with a particular emphasis on ones taken from the *Jātakas*. In Cave 1, for instance, there are paintings of Padmapāṇi, Vajrapāṇi, and Avalokiteśvara – indicating that it belongs to the Mahāyāna phase of the site – along with images of the Śākyamuni setting out from the palace, being tempted by Māra, etc. Although these painted images were no doubt intended as decorations, they also would have served as ritual aids in the monks' meditation activities.

The caves at Ellorā, which date to a period between 600 and 730 CE, are most striking for their numerous *bodhisattva* images, many of which appear to be placed, within the caves, in *maṇḍalas*. Indeed, there is strong evidence at Ellorā – the particular *bodhisattvas* represented, as well as their very precise arrangement – that this was a very early tantric center in India. Certainly Śākyamuni figures prominently in Ellorā's art, as he does throughout all periods of Indian Buddhism, but he is jointed by a whole range of other figures, many of which coincide with important early Buddhist tantric texts, such as the *Mañjuśrīmūlakalpa*.

Thus, for instance, in Cave 11, which dates to the latter part of Ellorā's excavations, an elaborate series of *maṇḍalas* is cut into the caves walls. In one part of the cave, in the first shrine, Śākyamuni (or perhaps the *dhyāna* Buddha Akṣobhya, who figures prominently in early tantric *maṇḍālas*) presides over a collection of *bodhisattvas*: Avalokiteśvara, Mañjuśrī, Vajrapāṇi, Kṣitigarbha, and others. Although the presence of these figures, and even their arrangement in a *maṇḍala*, could possibly part of mainstream Mahāyāna practice, it seems likely that this cave, and others (such as Cave 12) at Ellorā, were made by and for Buddhists who included tantric practitioners. As such, then, the caves at Ellorā provide compelling evidence of a doctrinal shift taking place in India, one that began, perhaps, in the south, and gradually migrated north into the Pāla monastic

Figure 1 Row of seated Buddhas, Ellorā, India

realms, and eventually into Nepal and Tibet.

See also: **Art, Buddhist; Sacred places.**

JACOB N. KINNARD

AMBEDKAR, B.R.

Dr. Bhimrao Ramji (B.R.) Ambedkar (1891–1956) is venerated by his *dalit* ("oppressed," often derogatorily called "untouchable") Buddhist followers side by side with Siddhartha Gautama. To these Indian Buddhist converts, he is the "*Bodhisattva*," "Maitreya Ambedkar," turning the wheel of *Dharma* anew for a new and modern age. His exposition of Siddhartha's teachings, *The Buddha and His Dhamma* (posthumously published in 1957), is often referred to as their "bible" and its novel interpretation of the Buddhist path commonly constitutes their only source of knowledge on the subject. To them, Ambedkar is their liberator – and, indeed, a liberator of the world – leading all people, regardless of their social status, from oppression and injustice to freedom and humanity, just as Gautama Buddha did 2,500 years ago. Even among those who do not revere him, Ambedkar is still widely recognized as one of India's most significant persons of the twentieth century, most remembered for agitating against Gandhi in favor of secularization and the dismantling of the Hindu caste system, supervising the writing of India's democratic Constitution, and, through the sheer force of his personality, initiating the revival of Buddhism in India that culminated in his veneration as a modern-day Buddhist saint.

Ambedkar was born on 14 April 1891, in Maharashtra in western India. Born into the Mahar caste of mostly landless "village servants" or day-laborers, he was considered despicably "untouchable" by the Hindu society in which he grew up. Though ostracized throughout his life, in the liberalizing India of the early twentieth century he was able to earn high school and college degrees – unprecedented accomplishments for an "untouchable" – before also earning graduate degrees in the United States and England, including a Ph.D. in economics from Columbia University in New York (where he studied with John Dewey, among others) and a D.Sc. from the University of London for his thesis, *The Problem of the Rupee.* He was also admitted to the Bar in England before pursuing post-graduate studies in economics at the University of Bonn, and eventually returning to India, where, in the late 1920s, he entered politics and established himself as a leader of the Mahar civil rights movement in Maharashtra. It was in this capacity that he eventually led approximately 500,000 *dalits,* mostly Mahars, to convert to Buddhism in a mass conversion ceremony in Nagpur on 14 and 15 October 1956 – with millions following in the years since – just months before his death on 6 December of the same year.

As a politician, Ambedkar championed the rights of the so-called "scheduled castes," incorporating provisions for the protection of their rights in the Constitution, which he is given credit for writing almost single-handedly. Like some of his contemporaries, he saw the roots of Indian oppression in the religiously sanctioned social discrimination of the caste system. Unlike many of these contemporaries, however, who worked simply to reform Hinduism, Ambedkar became increasingly convinced that members of the scheduled castes could only be liberated, socially and spiritually, by extricating themselves from the Hindu religion and converting to some other, more empowering, faith. In 1935 he publicly declared that, though he had unfortunately been born a Hindu, he had no intention of dying one, and began to advocate for the mass exodus of *dalits* from Hinduism. The question was to which religion to convert.

Ambedkar approached this question systematically and pragmatically, weighing religions for their potential to contribute to the social and spiritual liberation of India's outcastes. In the end, he settled on Buddhism, though Christianity is said to have been a serious contender and may have even won out if not for his observation that Indian Christian converts, especially from among the lower castes, commonly failed to live out their own, potentially liberating, praxis. While he eventually decided in favor of Buddhism, the Buddhism upon which he settled and about which he wrote in *The Buddha and His Dhamma* was, in many respects, unlike any form of Buddhism that had hitherto arisen within the tradition. Gone, for instance, were the doctrines of *karma* and rebirth, the traditional emphasis on renunciation of the world, the practice of meditation, and the experience of enlightenment. Gone, too, were any teachings that implied the existence of a trans-empirical realm or the efficacy of magic in this one. Most jarring, perhaps, especially among more traditional Buddhists, was the absence of the Four Noble Truths, which Ambedkar regarded as the invention of wrong-headed monks.

Against the testimony of tradition, Ambedkar instead portrayed the Buddha as a rationalist social reformer, concerned with the well-being of persons in this world and their liberation from oppressive social conditions. As he put it, "The center of his [that is, the Buddha's] *Dhamma* is man and the relation of man to man in his life on earth." The *nirvāṇa* toward which the Buddha's teachings lead is not some other-worldly *nirvāṇa*, but a "kingdom of righteousness on earth" in which people are freed from poverty and social discrimination and empowered to create for themselves happy lives.

This novel interpretation of Buddhism was no doubt born of Ambedkar's experiences as an outcaste Hindu and the need for a religion relevant to the lives of his fellow *dalits*. He recognized, for instance, that many of Buddhism's traditional teachings would not only offend *dalits*, but, more importantly, would not be conducive to their social and spiritual emancipation. They needed a religion that would empower them to change their situation, not one riddled with "superstitions," like *karma* and rebirth, which blame oppressed people for their own misery. Accordring the Ambedkar, the historical Buddha's teachings provided such empowerment, but only when stripped of the misguided interpolations of escapist monks.

For his novel interpretation of Buddhism, Ambedkar is sometimes pejoratively accused of having created a "neo-" or "new Buddhism" that might more properly be called "Ambedkarism." He and his *dalit* followers, of course, reject this characterization, preferring to think of their Buddhism as a "*navayāna*," a new vehicle for the transmission of the authentic Buddhist *Dharma*. While, in true reformist fashion, Ambedkar rejected centuries of interpretation of that *Dharma*, he nevertheless regarded himself not as an inventor of a new Buddhism, but as a reviver of an original Buddhism that had been smothered under centuries of misguided interpretation. For this he is venerated as one virtually on par with Siddhartha Gautama himself.

In discussing Ambedkar's veneration among his followers, however, it is important to acknowledge their adamant refusal to endow him – or Siddhārtha – with the aura of a supernatural being or to worship him as such. Ambedkar's iconography clearly depicts a human being, even if he is occupying space traditionally reserved for the gods. He invariably stands tall (in the ancient iconographic posture of *samabhaṅga*, or no bends), wearing eyeglasses, a blue suit, white shirt, and red tie. He holds a book in his hand – often labeled "*Bharat*" ("India") and identified with the Constitution – and in his pocket is a fountain pen. His right hand is sometimes raised in a posture signifying oration or teaching. The iconography speaks of a modern man, a man of learning, a self-made and upright man who inspires others to the same. Though, like Siddhārtha Gautama, he taught the path to liberation, also like Gautama he is still a man and the instillation of his down-to-earth image at shrines like those dedicated to the gods of Hinduism publicly proclaims and reinforces the *dalits*' rejection of those gods in favor of what they perceive as the liberating *praxis* of Ambedkar's this-worldly, modern, rational, and socially engaged Buddhism.

While critics often point out that Ambedkar failed to lead the majority of *dalits* in India to reject Hinduism and embrace Buddhism, it must still be acknowledged that he sparked a revival of Buddhism in India that has attracted millions of followers who claim to find in his exposition of the Buddha's teachings the remedy for their social and spiritual ills. Ambedkar no doubt himself hoped to lead more to Buddhism, but even so, the revival he initiated is perhaps the most significant Buddhist movement to arise in India since Siddhartha Gautama instituted the religion 2,500 years ago. For this, he deserves recognition as one of Buddhism's most significant modernist reformers and will certainly be remembered as such in all subsequent histories of the tradition.

See also: **Buddhist peace groups (in Asia and the West); Engaged Buddhism; Global Buddhist networks: selected examples; Human rights; India, Buddhism in.**

JIM DEITRICK

ANAGARIKA DHARMAPALA

Anagarika Dharmapala was one of the key figures in the movement for the revival of Buddhism in Ceylon (now Sri Lanka) during the British colonial period. Born in 1864 as Don David Hēvāvitarana, he was the son of a prominent family that had both profited from the colonial expansion of the economy and supported the Buddhist renaissance and its protest of the colonial repression of Buddhism. Through his family he became well acquainted with the two outstanding *bhikkhus* (monks) who led the early revival of Buddhism, Hikkaduve Sumangala and M. Gunananda.

In 1880 he met the leaders of the Theosophical Society, Madame Helena Blavatsky and Colonel Henry Olcott, who came to Ceylon to aid the Buddhists. Becoming a member of the Theosophical Society, he went to India in 1884 to work with Blavatsky and Olcott. They advised him to devote himself to "the good of humanity" and to study Pāli and Buddhist philosophy. He returned to Colombo and served as the General Secretary of the Buddhist Section of the Buddhist Theosophical Society and also edited its newspaper. During this period he vowed to live as a *brahmacārin* and took the name Anagarika Dharmapala. By doing this he created a new role for himself as a spiritual seeker who was neither a monastic nor a lay person. This role allowed Dharmapala to traverse the Buddhist path while also working actively in the world.

Dharmapala worked with Olcott to establish Buddhist schools in Ceylon in order to offset the colonial dominance of the Sinhala people and the associated suppression of Buddhism. By traversing the rural backcountry of Ceylon with Olcott, Dharmapala came to realize the desperate need for the Sinhala people to assert their heritage to resist the British colonial oppression. Dharmapala had another life-changing discovery during this period when he traveled to India and visited the site of the Buddha's enlightenment at the *Bodhi* tree in Bodhgayā. He was shocked to find the temple there crumbling and the shrine in the control of a Hindu. He vowed beneath the *Bodhi* tree to work to rescue Buddhism from neglect, both in India and back home in Ceylon. These became his causes for the rest of his life. He worked to revive the Buddhist tradition and the Sinhala Buddhist identity from the subjugation and neglect of centuries of colonialism. Dharmapala became a champion of the cause of Sinhala Buddhist nationalism and argued that the recovery of their true Buddhist identity represented the best response that the Sinhalas could make to the problems of the modern context. Re-establishing Buddhism and Buddhist values would enable them to restore the "glorious civilization" of ancient antiquity that Buddhism had inspired and anchored.

In 1893 Dharmapala traveled to the West, first visiting London, where he was the guest of Sir Edwin Arnold, author of *The Light of Asia*, and Ms Annie Besant. Then he went to Chicago to represent Buddhism at the Parliament of the World's Religions. The Parliament represented the first great council held in the West in which Christian delegates shared the stage with representatives from the Asian and other religious traditions. Although only twenty-nine years of age, Dharmapala was clearly the most celebrated interpreter of Buddhism at the Parliament. He made several speeches during the conference and received glowing reviews in the local newspapers for his articulate explanations of Buddhism. Three themes about which he spoke at the conference represented central pillars of his campaign to restore Buddhist identity and pride. First, he argued that Buddhism is a religion that is perfectly compatible with modern science. Although Christians were embroiled during that period in a great debate about evolution, Dharmapala said that the Buddha's teachings were entirely consistent with the doctrine of evolution. The Buddha taught, he argued, that the cosmos was a continuous process unfolding in obedience to natural laws.

Second, Dharmapala also declared that not only was Buddhism more compatible with science than was Christianity, but also its ethical teachings were filled with more compassion and love than he had witnessed being practiced by the Christian missionaries in Ceylon.

The third point that Dharmapala stressed in his addresses was that Buddhism was a religion of optimism and activism, not a religion of negativism and pessimism. That had been one of the chief criticisms of Buddhism developed by the colonial missionaries, who charged that Buddhism taught people to withdraw from life in order to seek their own welfare rather than participating in life for the benefit of all. For Dharmapala the idea that Buddhism requires one to be engaged with the world, not disengaged, was central. In his life and work he symbolized this ideal of Buddhist activism and engagement.

Following the Parliament, Dharmapala traveled around the world, eventually returning to Ceylon where he promoted Sinhala Buddhist nationalism and identity. Breaking with Olcott and the Theosophists, he founded the Mahā *Bodhi* Society to work for the restoration of the Bodhgayā shrine in India. He published a newspaper and began to motivate Buddhists to defend their heritage in both Lanka and India. In 1915 the British exiled him to Calcutta on grounds of sedition because of his attempts to rouse the Sinhala Buddhist nationalists. Although he was later allowed to return to Ceylon, Dharmapala chose to spend much of the rest of his life in India working for the protection and revival of Buddhism there. Through his work at home and abroad, Dharmapala raised the consciousness of the Buddhists by proclaiming that Buddhism was superior to any imported religion from the West. He encouraged his fellow Buddhists to live simple and moral lives following the Buddha's *Dharma*, and he drafted a set of guidelines for lay life which he called the *Gihi Vinaya* or Daily Code for the Laity. Toward the end of his life and until his death in 1933, Dharmapala took ordination as a *bhikkhu* in Theravāda Buddhism and accepted the name Sri Devamitta Dharmapala.

See also: **Buddhism and Western lifestyle; Buddhism in the Western world; South and Southeast Asia, Buddhism in; Sri Lanka, Buddhism in.**

GEORGE D. BOND

ANĀTMAVĀDA

According to the history of the propagation of the Buddha-dharma offered in the *Vinaya Piṭaka*, the first two discourses that the Buddha delivered were to a band of ascetics with whom he had formerly trained. The topic of one of these discourses was why none of the constituents of a person qualifies as a self. Beginning with the physical body, the Buddha observes that no one can simply will the body to be as one wishes it to be. One cannot by a simple act of will make an unhealthy body healthy, an injured body healed, an old body young, or an unattractive body comely. This suggests that the body is not fully within one's control, and whatever is not within one's control cannot be considered to be either one's property or one's self. Exactly the same kinds of observations are then applied to each of the non-material aspects of a person. One is not in control of what feelings (*vedanā*) arise, for if one were then one would not have unpleasant feelings. Similarly, one is not in full control of which concepts (*saṃjñā*) arise, nor of one's habits of character (*saṃskāra*), nor of what types of awareness (*vijñāna*) arise. Therefore, none of the five collections (*skandha*) of characteristics (*dharma*) that make up a person can be called either a self or a property belonging to the self. Moreover, there is nothing outside these five collections that can be called "I" or "mine." Everything that can be experienced or thought about, then, is not the self (*anātman*). This claim that nothing is the self came to be seen as the one doctrine of Buddhism that distinguished it from all other teachings in India. Vasubandhu, for example, argues that no path but the Buddhist path can lead to a liberation from suffering, because no other path is founded on the principle of non-self.

Closely associated with the doctrine of non-self are the doctrines that all experiences are impermanent (*anitya*) and unsatisfactory (*duḥkha*). Some canonical discourses begin with the observation that all complex things, being composite, are liable to decomposition. Whatever is impermanent cannot bring lasting satisfaction and so is ultimately unsatisfactory, and whatever is unsatisfactory is not what one wishes to think of as one's self. Although impermanence, unsatisfactoriness and lack of self always occur together, they may be seen as distinct features. Understanding that these three features are found in all things is an important step in losing one's attachment to what one experiences. By letting go of attachment to experiences, one simply witnesses the flow of events without clinging, without resistance and without giving in to the temptation to identify oneself with them.

Moreover, seeing that no possible experience can lead to lasting satisfaction is what makes it possible to stop striving for new experiences and for further existence. The absence of any desire for further existence is called *bhavanirodha* or *nirvāṇa*, which is the ultimate goal of all Buddhist practice.

As the doctrine of non-self was eventually worked out in greater detail, it was said that the idea of a self has a basis, namely the five collections of characteristics. If there were no body or awareness or habits of character, there would be no idea of a self or of a personal identity. The idea of a self is therefore a derivative idea, not a datum of experience. Moreover, it is a complex idea, as it would not arise without a combination of data of experience arising together. This observation eventually gave rise to the doctrine, expressed by Vasubandhu and others, that simple data are substantially real while complex things have only a conceptual existence. A concept is nothing but the grouping of experienced data for some purpose. A concept therefore does not correspond to a thing in the world but rather is a purposeful way of arranging sensations of things that are things in the world. This insight gave rise to a claim, common in many forms of Buddhism, that conceptual thinking, being based always in some kind of purpose or desire, is an obstacle to the purpose-free acceptance of things as they are and that the most sure path to *nirvāṇā* is therefore through direct experience rather than through discursive thinking and other kinds of intellectual activity.

The doctrine of non-self took an important new direction in the writings of Nāgārjuna. Buddhists before him had argued that a notion of personal identity is something that the mind superimposes upon *dharmas*, which are the phenomena such as color, shape, sound, smells and so forth that are given in sensory experience. In the view of these earlier Buddhists, then, *dharmas* have a substantial existence while personal identity has only a conceptual existence. Nāgārjuna's insight was that even these *dharmas* lack substantial existence. No personal self can be found in *dharmas*, because *dharmas* themselves have no self. The way that Nāgārjuna expressed this notion is that all *dharmas* are devoid or empty (*śūnya*) of their own natures (*svabhāva*) because their natures are given to them by their causes and conditions, each of which is also lacking its own nature.

Nāgārjuna's commentators would later point out that an "own-nature" (*svabhāva*) is to a *dharma* as a self (*ātman*) is to a person. This amounts to saying that the doctrine of non-self is true because it turns out that nothing at any level of analysis has a nature it can call its own. What began, then, as the Buddha's simple observation that there is nothing over which one is in control evolved into a thoroughgoing metaphysical doctrine that nothing at all has an independent essence. Whether one thinks of the doctrine in its simpler or its more evolved form, the doctrine of non-self became the distinctive hallmark of Buddhism in India.

See also: **India, Buddhism in; Not-self (*anātman*).**

RICHARD P. HAYES

ANGKOR

The sprawling temple complex at Angkor, in Cambodia, is best known as a Hindu site. It was created under the patronage of the king Suryavarman II (ruled 1113–50). Dedicated to the Hindu god Viṣṇu, it was planned as a model of the cosmos, with Mount Meru at its center. Angkor Wat's rising series of towers and courtyards are vertically dominated by a 213-foot lotus-blossom-shaped central tower. Angkor is probably the largest religious structure in the world.

One of the most impressive complexes at Angkor is Angkor Thom, literally "the great city," the last capital of the Khmer empire and, during its peak, a sprawling city of nearly a million inhabitants. Within the city are the remains of dozens of structures, including Suryavarman's palace and the Phimeanakas, the state temple. At the center of Angkor Thom rises the Golden Tower of the Bayon, a soaring Buddhist temple which is surrounded by more than thirty lesser towers and several hundred stone shrines which originally would have housed (based on inscriptional evidence) a vast array of Buddha and *bodhisattva* images, as well as images of Prajñāpāramitā, Tārā, and lesser Buddhist deities (most of these images were long ago removed from the temple). A particularly common image type seems to have been a seated Buddha sheltered by the *nāga* (serpent) Mucalinda. One of most well-known features of the site is the dozens of smiling faces that adorn the smaller towers surrounding the main structure. It is unclear who or what these images represent, although it is generally agreed that they are the compassionate *bodhisattva* Avalokiteśvara, perhaps modeled on the face of Jayavarman VII himself. These massive faces, which are placed on each side of each of the smaller towers, look out to the four cardinal points and seem to signify the omnipresence of the *bodhisattva* Avalokiteśvara, the one who sees all.

In part because it is laid out as a massive *maṇḍala*, the Bayon at Angkor Thom seems to be intended to represent a microcosm of the universe, divided into four parts by the main axes that run through the center of the complex. The temple is situated at the exact center of the axes and stands as the symbolical link between heaven and earth.

The temple itself, as it now stands, consists of three levels. The lower two are lined with bas-reliefs and the third includes a central sanctuary. It is a massive structure, with various courtyards, image niches (or galleries), towers, and terraces. The massive central tower rises to 130 feet. In addition to the images drawn from the Mahāyāna and Hindu pantheons – reflecting, perhaps, a religious syncretism on the part of the Khmer rulers – many of the bas-reliefs at the Bayon depict mundane scenes – fishing, festivals, the marketplace, and cockfights – as well as scenes of royal processions and large-scale military battles.

See also: **Art, Buddhist; Sacred places; *Stūpa*.**

JACOB N. KINNARD

ANGLO-GERMAN SCHOOL OF BUDDHIST STUDIES

In the nomenclature utilized by Constantin Régamey in his 1951 volume *Der Buddhismus Indiens*, the Anglo-German school of Buddhist Studies was the earliest of the three buddhological schools he identified – the other two being the Franco-Belgian and Leningrad schools – and it dominated the scene in Europe until around 1915. The two leading exponents of the Anglo-German school were Thomas W. Rhys Davids (1843–1922) in England and Hermann Oldenberg (1854–1920) in Germany. This school focused exclusively on the Buddhism revealed in the Pāli Canon, which it believed represented the oldest, original, and purest Buddhism. Virtually all of this presumption, however, was eventually stripped away in the debate on "precanonical" Buddhism prompted by Stanislaw Schayer in the 1930s. Edward Conze believes that this school has few, if any, advocates left in the scholarly buddhological world because of the untenability of the school's presumptions. Later, we shall see that, while the underlying basis for the school (that is, that the Theravāda tradition preserved in the Pāli literature is the earliest, original form of Buddhism) is no longer imagined to be accurate, exclusive study of this tradition remains strong, and especially so in England.

While study of the Pāli texts existed in Europe long before the founding of the Pāli Text Society by Thomas W. Rhys Davids in 1881, it was the formation of that society that provided a crystallization of Pāli Buddhist Studies. Additionally, it was in London that Rhys Davids first met Hermann Oldenberg, and it was their collaboration as colleagues and text editors that fueled the study of the Theravāda tradition, which included an enormously lively and constructive debate that raged throughout Europe over the proper understanding of the term *nirvāṇa*. Together, Rhys Davids and Oldenberg are best known for their three-volume set titled *Vinaya Texts*, which was published between 1881 and 1885. Singly, however, each scholar distinguished himself with an impressive set of editions and translations. In 1880 Rhys Davids translated the *Jātaka Nidānakathā*, and the following year published *Buddhist Suttas* in the Sacred Books of the Buddhists series, edited by Max Müller. In 1890 and 1894 he published the two volumes of the *Questions of King Milinda*. In 1884 he edited the *Abhidhammattha-saṅgaha*. Along with his friend J.E. Carpenter, he edited volumes I and II of the *Dīgha Nikāya* in 1890 and 1911. Rhys Davids went on to translate all three volumes of the *Dīgha Nikāya*, in collaboration with his wife (Caroline Augusta Foley Rhys Davids), as *Dialogues of the Buddha*, completed in 1910 and 1921. Oldenberg published an edited text of the *Dīpavaṃsa* in 1879, and followed with his monumental edition of the five volumes of *The Vinaya Piṭakaṃ*. He also introduced Western scholars to the famous texts known as the *Theragāthā* and *Therīgāthā*. His volume *The Buddha, His Life, His Doctrine, His Community* remains a classic today, more than a century and a quarter after its initial publication, as do Rhys Davids' *Manual of Buddhism* (1877) and *Buddhist India* (1903).

Thomas W. Rhys Davids and Hermann Oldenberg were not the only stalwarts of the Anglo-German school of Buddhist Studies. Caroline Augusta Foley Rhys Davids was born in 1858, and married T.W. Rhys Davids in 1894. Her editions of Pāli texts and English translations were as numerous and valued as those of her husband, and she was blessed with no less energy than he. Her secondary works, such as *Gotama the Man* and *Sakya or Buddhist Origins* made enormous impact in emphasizing the Theravāda tradition. Following her husband's death in 1922, she carried on as president of the Pāli Text Society.

Other important British Pāli scholars and writers who worked diligently in the Anglo-German school included Lord Chalmers, F.L. Woodward, George Turnour, Robert Childers, and William Stede. Lord Chalmers, born in 1858, was a major patron of the Pāli Text Society who edited and translated texts for the society; he went to Ceylon in 1913 to serve as governor. F.L. Woodward was born in 1871. Although he was an excellent editor and translator of Pāli texts, he was best known in Ceylon for his work in the education of Buddhist boys, a role he managed well as head of Mahinda College. George Turnour was best known for an English translation of the *Mahāvaṃsa*, which Thomas W. Rhys Davids called "the foundation of all Pāli scholarship." Robert Childers, who served in the Ceylon Civil Service from 1856 until 1864, was best known for a two-volume set (published in 1872 and 1875) of his *Dictionary of the Pāli Language*. William Stede was a longtime collaborator with Thomas W. Rhys Davids. Together, in 1921, they published *The Pāli Text Society's Pāli–English Dictionary*, which remains the standard reference today. He had a long association with the London School of Oriental and African Studies, from which he retired in 1949. He was also a president of the Pāli Text Society.

No two British Pāli scholars made a greater impact through the early and middle portion of the previous century than Isaline Blew Horner and Edward J. Thomas. A librarian by formal training, Horner first visited Ceylon in 1923. Miss Horner was one of the most proficient editors and translators in the long history of the Pāli Text Society, whose presidency she took in 1959 and maintained for many years. Her six-volume English translation of the *Vinaya Piṭaka*, published as *The Book of the Discipline* (between 1938 and 1966), remains the standard today. Her important volume,

Women Under Primitive Buddhism (published in 1930) was one of the first gender-related volumes published in Buddhist Studies; and her following volume, *The Early Buddhist Theory of Man Perfected* (published in 1934), was one of the first considerations of the theory of the *arahant*. For her important service to the study of Pāli Buddhism, she was awarded an honorary D.Litt. degree by the University of Ceylon in Peredeniya. No less important in England was Edward J. Thomas. Unlike his predecessors, Thomas left school at fourteen and for the next twelve years worked as a gardener. Eventually, he returned to school, learning Sanskrit and Pāli at Cambridge. His *The History of Buddhist Thought* was one of the first volumes devoted solely to Buddhist philosophy, and along with *The Life of the Buddha as Legend and History*, helped to further define the Anglo-German school of Buddhist Studies.

While Oldenberg is perhaps the best known of the German members of the Anglo-German school, he is by no means the only important member: George Grimm, Karl Neumann, Wilhelm Geiger, and perhaps one or two others are noteworthy in the formative period. Although he was the author of eight books, his volume *The Doctrine of the Buddha: The Religion of Reason and Meditation*, first published in German in 1915, was his most famous. He was most interested in the *anattā* doctrine, and found himself at odds with Buddhaghosa's understanding of rebirth. Karl Neumann was one of the very earliest scholars of Buddhism in Germany. He earned his doctorate in 1891, having been inspired by the works of Schopenhauer. He worked on translations of the *Sutta Nipāta* and *Dīgha Nikāya*, but his work was cut short by his premature death on his fiftieth birthday. Wilhelm Geiger was born in 1856, and gained fame as the first German scholar to study Pāli, and to edit Pāli texts. He visited Ceylon in 1895, eventually publishing a translation of the *Mahāvaṃsa* between 1908 and 1930. Geiger's Pāli grammar has also been a valuable asset to Pāli scholars for nearly a century.

Although Conze maintains that the tripartite division of schools of Buddhist Studies breaks down after 1935, there remains a strong group of scholars in both England and Germany who still retain the basic focus of the Anglo-German school, although their scholarship has been greatly enhanced by a wider and broader understanding of the Buddhist tradition than that maintained by their predecessors. In England, the foremost Pāli and Theravāda scholar today is Richard Gombrich, recently retired Boden Professor of Sanskrit at Oxford. His work in training a new generation of buddhological scholars remains a consummate achievement, as is his work with the Pāli Text Society and United Kingdom Association of Buddhist Studies. Also noteworthy is Peter Harvey of the University of Sunderland, whose introductory volumes on Buddhism and Buddhist ethics have become standards in the field. K.R. Norman's work in editing Pāli texts has also been a staple product of the Pāli Text Society. Rupert Gethin, the current president of the Pāli Text Society, has equally enhanced the study of Theravāda Buddhism in general and throughout Europe, as has retired scholar Lance Cousins, a brilliant and resourceful Pāli scholar. In Germany, the legacy of Pāli scholarship was maintained by Heinz Bechert at Göttingen, who trained a new generation of German scholars and was a rigorous critic in the spirit of Jan W. de Jong. Oskar von Hinüber, too, has done admirable work on the Pāli tradition, especially focusing on *Vinaya* materials. Despite the fact that Buddhist Studies today involves far more than simply the Pāli tradition, the Anglo-German school of Buddhist Studies has bequeathed a great legacy to modern Buddhist Studies.

See also: **Academic study of Buddhism; Horner, Isaline Blew; Rhys Davids, Caroline Augusta Foley; Rhys Davids, Thomas W.**

CHARLES S. PREBISH

ANIMALS AND THE ENVIRONMENT

Buddhism is often seen as an "eco-friendly" religion with an expanded moral horizon encompassing not just human beings but also animals and the environment. It is generally thought to have a more "enlightened" attitude to nature than Christianity, which has traditionally taught that humankind is the divinely appointed steward of creation, holding authority over the natural order. As, according to Buddhist teachings, human beings can be reborn as animals, and vice versa, the Buddhist worldview suggests a much closer kinship between species whereby different forms of life are interrelated in a profound way. On a more theoretical level, the doctrine of Dependent Origination is interpreted by some East Asian schools (notably Kegon) as teaching that the entire cosmos has an underlying metaphysical unity in terms of which all phenomena are linked in a delicate and complex web of relationships. The image of "Brahma's net" is often used to illustrate this concept, the net being a web of jewels which glisten and reflect one another in their many different facets.

At the same time, the idea that Buddhism is deeply in tune with "green" values and a natural ally of the "animal rights" and other activist movements requires qualification. There is no doubt that Buddhist literature contains many references to animals and the environment, but when the context of these references is examined they often turn out to have little in common with the modern conservationist agenda or concern to reduce animal suffering. Human beings remain the primary focus of Buddhist teachings, many of which presuppose an anthropomorphic perspective (the view that value belongs to humans alone and nature is to be protected for their sake and no other). For example, a hierarchy can be seen within the scheme of the six realms of rebirth (*gati*). Animals occupy one realm and humans another, and it is clearly preferable to be born in the latter than the former. A "precious human rebirth" is given special prestige as the most auspicious form of rebirth from which to attain liberation.

Animals

A visitor to any Buddhist country will see many examples of spontaneous kindness towards animals. A custom common in many Buddhist countries is that of "releasing life," a practice whereby animals kept in captivity are released upon payment of a small fee. Typically small birds are set free from their cages, and it is believed that merit is gained by the donor for this act of kindness. The First Precept has a direct bearing on the treatment of animals as it prescribes non-violence not just towards human beings but to "*pāṇa*" or "creatures". The *Sutta Nipāta* states: "Let him neither kill, nor cause to be killed, any living being, or let him approve of others killing, after having refrained from hurting all creatures, both those that are strong and those that tremble in the world" (v. 393). It is often stated that enlightened beings "show kindness and live with compassion for the welfare of all living beings" (*Aṅguttara Nikāya* 1.211). Abstaining from violence is a requirement of the Eightfold Path under the headings of Right Action and Right Livelihood. Right Action is said to include abandoning the taking life of life (*Dīgha Nikāya* 2.312) and Right Livelihood forbids certain professions such as trade in flesh and weapons (*Aṅguttara Nikāya* 3.208). A categorical ban is imposed on hunting, butchering and other similar professions (*Majjhima Nikāya* 1.343). All the above directives are clearly directed towards the protection of animals. Animal sacrifices, moreover, are severely criticized, and alternative sacrifices using oil, butter and molasses are praised (*Dīgha Nikāya* 1.141).

The environment

It is difficult to state definitively whether early Buddhism believed plants and vegetation to be on a par with other beings that suffer or whether they were considered to be non-sentient. One detailed list of precepts includes a rule that forbids causing injury to seeds and crops (*Dīgha Nikāya* 1.5), and there are *Pātimokkha* injunctions that prohibit damage to vegetation, classifying it as a form of life with a single sense-faculty (*eka-indriya jīva*) (*Vinaya* 3.155). It is not clear, however, whether these rules have to do with ecology or with Buddhist monks living up to the expectations of the laity, who would certainly have expected them to keep up with their scrupulous rivals such as the Jains. Elsewhere bad *karma* is said to follow the cutting of a branch or tree that once gave fruit and shade (*Aṅguttara Nikāya* 3.369), and merit is promised to those who plant groves and parks (*Saṃyutta Nikāya* 1.33). The great Buddhist emperor Aśoka (third century BCE) planted trees and also medicinal herbs. Further, in popular belief trees and plants merited respect as the abode of deities.

As for the wilderness that forms an important part of the ecological agenda today, Buddhism gives no specific injunctions for its conservation, although aesthetic references to wild nature are found. One of the most effective arguments for preserving the wilderness lies in what has come to be known as the "hermit strand" in Buddhism. This has to do with the advice given to hermits to live in natural surroundings in order to pursue the path of liberation without distraction (for example, *Majjhima Nikāya* 1.274). The Buddha himself chose to dwell in forests in order to pursue spiritual ideals (*Dīgha Nikāya* 3.54), and the fact that the main events in his life – such as his birth, enlightenment, first sermon and death – all took place under trees or in parks seems to associate him with natural environments. The Buddha left a palace to live in the forest, and if there were no wilderness the religious seeker like himself would be unable to seek refuge from active life.

Also influential in defining ethical attitudes toward the natural world are the four *Brahma-vihāras*. Referred to as the "sublime attitudes," universal love (*metta*), compassion (*karuṇā*), sympathetic joy (*muditā*) and equanimity (*upekkha*) foster feelings that lead to the protection of the natural world and ensure its well-being. A truly compassionate and loving human being would find it hard to reconcile these sentiments with callous environmental damage and cruel blood sports pursued merely for the sake of enjoyment. The Mahāyāna emphasis on the "great compassion" (*mahā-karuṇā*) of *bodhisattvas*, and the Yogācāra notion of the "embryonic Buddha" (*tathāgata-garbha*) which holds that the universal seed of Buddhahood is present in all living beings – including animals – further strengthen the ethical identification between self and others which is important to ecological concern.

Various perspectives on animals and the environment are currently being developed by writers and activists working within the field of socially engaged Buddhism in an effort to apply the traditional teachings to contemporary ecological concerns.

See also: **Ahiṃsā; Aśoka; Cosmology and rebirth; Ethics.**

DAMIEN KEOWN

ANURĀDHAPURA

Located approximately 200 kilometers north of the present capital of Sri Lanka, Colombo, Anurādhapura was the center of government and religion in the island from *c.* 400 BCE until the end of the tenth century CE. The kings of the Anurādhapura period ensured the prosperity of the city and the country by constructing a massive system of irrigation tanks and canals that supported the agricultural economy. Anurādhapura has been regarded by Buddhists as a sacred city, because of its history and because the great kings of the Anurādhapura period, who sought to emulate Aśoka by dedicating themselves to protecting the Buddha, the *Dharma* and the *Sangha*, graced Anurādhapura with many Buddhist shrines and sacred places.

The *Mahāvaṃsa* proclaims that the Buddha visited Anurādhapura, and that later Aśoka's son, Mahinda Thera, came there to establish the *Dharma* with the help of King Devānaṃpiya Tissa (r. 250–210 BCE). Devānaṃpiya Tissa and later kings such as Duṭṭhagāmaṇi (161–137 BCE) venerated the Buddha by presiding over the enshrinement of relics including a branch of the *Bodhi* tree under which the Buddha attained enlightenment, the Buddha's right collar-bone and the tooth relic. Enormous *stūpas* such as the Mahāthūpa and the Thūpārāma focused the devotion of the Buddhists on these relics. Three large monasteries, Mahāvihāra, Abhayagiri, and Jetavana, representing three major monastic *nikāyas*, reflected the power of the *sangha* in Anurādhapura. They influenced the court and shaped the practice of Buddhism. A rivalry existed between the monasteries, but over time the Mahāvihāra became the center of Sinhala Theravāda orthodoxy in the country and extended its influence to the wider South and Southeast Asian region.

The Mahāvihāra's interpretation of the *Dharma* was established by the great commentator Buddhaghosa who went from India to Sri Lanka during the reign of King Mahānama (409–31 CE). Buddhaghosa lived and worked at the Mahāvihāra in Anurādhapura where he wrote his systematic treatise on the Theravāda path, the *Visuddhimagga*. After writing this work, Buddhaghosa went on to compose commentaries on some of the major books of the *Tripiṭaka*. In his introductions to these commentaries, Buddhaghosa explained that he was not setting out his own ideas but relying on the "pre-eminent teachers of yore ... who are like unto the banners of the Mahāvihāra." That is, Buddhaghosa based his work on the ancient Sinhala commentaries that served as the basis for the Mahāvihāra's interpretation of the *Dharma*. Although Buddhaghosa was relying on the earlier, authoritative sources, the works he produced, especially the *Visuddhimagga*, provided new and authoritative presentations of the meaning and the practice of the *Dharma*. The *Visuddhimagga* set out in elaborate detail the nature of the path to liberation which consisted of *sīla*, *samādhi* and *paññā*. Because Buddhaghosa wrote his *Visuddhimagga* and commentaries in the Pāli language, they came to be studied by Buddhists in South and Southeast Asia, thereby extending the influence of the Sinhala Theravāda orthodoxy of the Mahāvihāra. The *Mahāvaṃsa*, the "Great Chronicle," was compiled in the fifth century CE and represented earlier Sinhala accounts of the history of Lanka preserved by the Mahāvihāra.

The capital of the country was moved to Polonnaruwa at the end of the tenth century CE to gain more protection from invaders from south India. However, Anurādhapura remained the spiritual center of Sri Lanka from that time to the present.

See also: **Commentarial works; Pāli canon; South and Southeast Asia, Buddhism in; Sri Lanka, Buddhism in.**

GEORGE D. BOND

ARAHANT

When the great Theravāda commentator, Buddhaghosa, wrote the *Visuddhimagga* delineating the nature of the gradual path to enlightenment, he placed the *arahant* at the completion of that path. The *arahant* stands as a transcendent figure in Theravāda, one who has followed to its end the way of *Dharma* set out by the Buddha. Having mastered the gradual path of development, the *arahant* has spanned the distance between the ordinary person or *puthujjana* and the enlightened state. In this way, the *arahant* represents a figure that incorporates two somewhat paradoxical qualities, shared humanity and otherness. For this reason, the *arahant* serves as both an exemplar for other Buddhists and a being venerated by other Buddhists.

The qualities that set the *arahant* apart from the ordinary person are explicated in the *Visuddhimagga* and in some key *sūtras* in the Pāli *Tipiṭaka*. The *arahants* are said to perfect the "three trainings": the training in higher morality, *adhisīla-sikkhā*; the training in higher concentration, *adhicitta-sikkhā*; and the training in higher wisdom, *adhipaññā-sikkhā*. The training in higher morality involves, first, the *sīla* of *Pātimokkha* restraint. Fulfilling this form of morality, the *arahant* perfects the key virtues that constitute the foundation of Buddhist ethics. The *arahant* develops compassion, generosity, and non-violence. All of the virtues that are represented in the ten precepts of Buddhism come into play as the *arahant* lives dependent on the gifts of others, practices right sexual conduct, and clings to the truth. The texts place great emphasis on truthfulness and the importance of avoiding all forms of negative speech, gossip or frivolous speech. At the next levels of the training in higher morality, the *arahant* perfects "livelihood purification" and then the "*sīla* concerning requisites." Perfecting the *sīla* on these levels, the *arahant* learns to live with only a simple begging bowl and a robe and foregoes immoral and destructive ways of living in the world.

In the training in higher concentration, the *arahant* attains the perfection of *samādhi*. This training includes the restraint of the sense faculties. Controlling the senses rather than letting the senses control the mind, the *arahant* develops a pure mind. This purity is strengthened by perfecting mindfulness, *sati*, and clear comprehension. To complete the perfection of *samādhi*, the *arahant* must eliminate the five hindrances or *nīvaraṇas*: sensuality, ill-will, sloth and torpor, excitement and flurry, and doubt. The texts describe these as the characteristics of ordinary people, *puthujjanas*, and by eliminating them the *arahant* transcends the ordinary plane of existence. Conquering the *nīvaraṇas* is also associated with the attainment of the series of trance states or *jhānas* that mark the perfection of *samādhi*. Commenting explicitly on the distance between those reaching this stage and the ordinary person, the texts say that these adepts are as happy as prisoners set free or as people who find their way out of the wilderness.

The final stage of the path, the training in higher wisdom, *adhipaññā-sikkhā*, involves the *arahant*'s attaining the "six higher knowledges," *abhiññās*. The first three of these *abhiññās* represent the attainment of powers similar to those of the yogis and holy men in Indian tradition. The *arahant* acquires the ability to do miraculous deeds such as flying through the air, walking on water, and passing through solid rock. In addition, the *arahant* gains the ability to hear all things, to penetrate the minds of other beings, to see into the past and the future, to recall previous births, and finally to extinguish the cankers, *āsavas*. The texts indicate that final attainment, the destruction of the *āsavas*, is the most important because it signifies the conquest of all negative mental states that bind beings to *saṃsāra*.

To further distinguish the *arahant* from the ordinary person and to emphasize the length of the gradual path, the Theravāda divided the path into four stages that extend over many lifetimes of an individual. These four stages are called the four paths or the four noble persons, *ariya puggalā*. They include: the path of the stream-enterer (*sotāpatti magga*), the path of the once-returner (*sakadāgāmi-magga*), the path of the non-returner, (*anāgāmi-magga*), and the path of the *arahant*.

Clearly, the description of the path to *arahant*ship represents a catalogue of the ideal Buddhist life, and the *arahants* who completed the path have been venerated by many Buddhists. Theravāda Buddhism has a rich hagiographical literature that extols the virtues of the great *arahants* and portrays them as models for other Buddhists on the path. For example, the legends of Sāriputta and Moggallāna relate the story of two Brahmin youths who renounced their wealth and privilege in order to seek liberation. Similarly, Mahā Kassapa, although born into a wealthy family, gave it all up to become a forest-dwelling renunciant. As a result of his perfection of the *dharmic* virtues, Mahā Kassapa became a master of *iddhi* or the miraculous powers that accompany wisdom. The conquest of desire for and attachment to worldly things represents one of the most frequent themes in the legends of the *arahants*. The female *arahant*, Subhā, for example, is immortalized in the *Therīgāthā* for her complete non-attachment to the material world. While living the monastic life in the forest, Subhā was accosted by a man who praised her beautiful eyes and tried to induce her to go with him. Subhā rebuffed the man by plucking out her own eye and offering it to the man.

The *arahants* play a prominent role in Buddhism down through history. The Mahāyāna sources relate the story of the sixteen *arahants* or *arhats* whom the Buddha requested to remain in the world for the sake of the *Dharma* until Maitreya appears. The relics of the great *arahants* have been venerated with *stūpas* and shrines in various Buddhist countries. The Emperor Aśoka dedicated shrines to the *arahants* as did the later kings of Sri Lanka, Myanmar, and Thailand.

Although, during most of Buddhist history, Buddhists seem to have regarded *arahant*ship as a remote goal attainable only in one's future lives, in recent times with the emergence of the *vipassanā* meditation movement in Theravāda some Buddhists have begun to view the ideal of *arahant*ship as attainable here and now. These same Buddhists have identified some contemporary figures as *arahants* living among us today, thus giving new life to the *arahant* ideal.

See also: **Meditation, modern movements; Meditation in the *Visuddhimagga*; Moral discipline; *Stūpa*; South and Southeast Asia, Buddhism in; *Vinaya Piṭaka*.**

GEORGE D. BOND

ARCHETYPAL BUDDHAS AND *BODHISATTVAS*

Throughout its history South Asian religiosity has expressed itself through a diverse plurality of divine beings, most notably the various *devas* or "shining ones." Buddhism is no exception to this rule, although in the development of its own distinctive celestial pantheon it does offer a fascinating variation on the prevailing notion of divinity common to Vedism, Brahmanism, and popular Hinduism. Ancient India experienced a decisive turning point during the "Age of the Wanderers" (*c.* 600–400 BCE) when the prevailing Brahmānic religious hegemony was increasingly challenged by a varied and inchoate range of new ideas and practices introduced by the *śrāmaṇas* ("strivers"), a highly heterogeneous movement of spiritual seekers, visionaries, and ascetics, having little more in common than their persistence in exploring spiritual alternatives to the status quo. While falling generally within that *Śrāmaṇic* movement, the teachings of Siddhārtha Gautama, the "historical Buddha," represent a distinctive relationship to the more traditional notions of gods and goddesses current at his time. While the Buddha clearly rejected the spiritual authority of the *Vedas*, he saw no reason to reject out of hand the popular pantheon of divine and other mythological beings. Indeed, *devas* turn up frequently in the earliest Buddhist scriptures, along with various other non-human beings – *yakṣas, rakṣasas, gāruḍas, kiṃnāras, gandharvas, māras,* etc. With the possible exception of the *māras*, none of these were Buddhist innovations: they were all familiar features of the commonly accepted cosmology of the day. However, the Buddha did qualify his acceptance of this popular pantheon in one decisive way: all these beings were seen to be subject to the vicissitudes of *saṃsāric* existence along with humans, animals and all other sentient beings. This represented a significant "demotion" for the *devas*, who were considered in the popular cosmology to be immortal beings enjoying great power and wealth, dwelling in their heavenly realms much as did their cousins in Persia, Greece, and Rome. The Buddha saw no reason to question the existence of these *devas*, but more significantly he asserted that their "immortality" was a delusion, one held by humans as well the gods themselves. The gods and demi-gods might lead a relatively pleasant existence for many eons, but the only true escape from the suffering of the *saṃsāric* cycle of repeated death and rebirth was, the Buddha asserted, the path to awakening and *nirvāṇa* he had rediscovered, following in the footsteps of the previous buddhas ("awakened ones"). This the gods too must learn, and thus the Buddha was deemed to be "the teacher of both men and gods" (*satthā devamanussānaṃ*).

Soon, however, and quite naturally, the buddhas themselves became the objects of the devotional sensibility that extended the traditional Indian rituals of hospitality to the practice of venerating all exalted beings, human and divine alike. And the buddhas were, for Buddhists, quite a special class of beings. True, they were human-born; and indeed, the liberation from suffering they had realized was accessible to all beings – not just to the (not so) immortal gods. But in becoming awakened they had left behind all the bonds of *saṃsāric* existence. They were no longer subject to the suffering of rebirth, and this made them quite special – more than human, more even than divine. The Buddha presented his *Dharma* as universal and eternal, and very quickly his followers began to imagine and venerate the buddhas of the past and the future in similar terms. One of the earliest forms of meditation was *buddhānusmṛti* or "recollection of the Buddha(s)," a practice common to all schools of Buddhism in which the practitioner would call the Buddha to mind, recollecting all his special qualities, physical and spiritual. The Theravāda commentator Buddhaghosa tells us that the practitioner: "attains the fullness of faith, mindfulness, understanding and merit ... He conquers fear and dread ... He comes to feel as if he were living in the Master's presence ... His mind tends towards the plane of the Buddhas" (in Ñāṇamoli's translation).

What this text and other non-Mahāyāna sources indicate is that from the earliest days of the tradition, Buddhists have understood meditation to include the possibility of encountering the Buddha(s), and even transporting oneself to the plane on which they live now, in some realm quite distinct from that of their former (or future) earthly existence. Following that precedent, the Mahāyāna scriptures boldly envisioned a cosmos replete with myriads of Buddha-lands, each with its own buddhas and *bodhisattvas.*

And then, going a step further, they developed a more universalized "buddhology" to support that view, one that eventually recognized the enlightened mind of the Buddha(s) as working on three different planes.

We see this most clearly in later Mahāyāna sources, especially those associated with the Yogācāra school, which developed a comprehensive system comprising three distinct "bodies" (*kāya*) of the Buddha(s), three cosmological levels of their activity in the world: their *Dharma* Body (*Dharmakāya*), their Body of Communal Enjoyment (*sambhogakāya*) and their Body of Magical Transformation (*nirmāṇakāya*). The first of these evolved slowly from a less cosmologically framed notion holding that Śākyamuni's true or "real" body was the "body" of his *Dharma*, his *Dharmakāya*. At first referring perhaps only to the "corpus" of his teachings or doctrine, the term *dharmakāya* eventually came to refer to all those qualities that constitute buddhahood – and eventually, and even more broadly, to the enlightened mind shared by all buddhas. In its full-blown Mahāyāna expression, the *Dharma* Body of the Buddha thus takes on the cosmological and even ontological dimensions of ultimate reality – the thusness (*tathatā*) of all things (*dharmas*), which is also to say the intrinsically pure and radiant consciousness of all the buddhas. The Body of Communal Enjoyment and the Body of Magical Transformation are, by contrast, bodies of manifest form (*rūpa*) appearing as if they are physical, material bodies. The first of the two, the *sambhogakāya* or Body of Communal Enjoyment, encompasses the manifestation of enlightenment/thusness in its archetypal form. Here we enter into the cosmology of the various pure lands or Buddha-fields inhabited by the "archetypal" or "ideal" buddhas and *bodhisattvas*, who are, in fact, simply the spontaneous manifestation of the compassion of the *Dharmakāya*. But to encounter one of these archetypal manifestations of enlightenment, one must reach quite a high level of meditative skill, including developing the ability to "visit" other, more ideal planes of existence, whether through meditative practice or through rebirth. For those lacking that ability, the *Dharmakāya*'s emanation of compassion extends down even further, manifesting in its third aspect, the Magical Body (*nirmāṇakāya*), the apparently human physical body of earthly buddhas like Śākyamuni. It is a significant feature of the Mahāyāna that some of its earliest scriptures reflect an elaborate cult practice focused on one or another of the archetypal *sambhogakāya* emanations. The expanded cosmology of the Mahāyāna *sūtras* offered rich opportunities for innovative forms of practice. Through new and increasingly elaborate forms of visualization meditation, devotees could encounter, venerate and eventually identify with their chosen archetypal figure, exploring and cultivating the particular qualities of enlightenment expressed by that particular figure. The Mahāyāna was thus soon equipped with its own rich and diverse pantheon of *sambhogakāya* Buddhas and *bodhisattvas*, each manifesting and making more accessible a particular aspect of the *Dharmakāya*, much as the pure light of the sun can be prismatically refracted into the infinitely differentiated spectrum of the rainbow.

Five buddha families

Just as world-systems in the Mahāyāna cosmology are as numerous as the sands of the Ganges, so too are the Buddhas and *bodhisattvas* that inhabit them. Some were recognized as especially important quite early, and others emerged over time, especially as the later Mahāyāna in the India began to absorb Tantric iconographic elements. This proliferating pantheon of archetypal figures was soon organized into various arrays and eventually into the more complex cosmograms (*maṇḍalas*) of the Vajrayāna. The goal was not only to work out a system based on the distinctive qualities and attributes of the individual figures, but also to explore their interrelationships as a composite manifestation of the whole of the enlightened mind. The initial step was to group the Buddhas and *bodhisattvas* into "families." The earliest Vajrayāna literature, for example, recognized three such families: the Buddha or Tathāgata family, the Lotus family, and the Vajra family. This configuration eventually evolved further into the more geometrically balanced configuration found in the *Maṇḍala* of the Five *Jinas* ("conquerors"), so called because they have utterly conquered greed, hatred, and delusion. While the earlier three-family scheme sought to establish a hierarchical relation between the families, the five-family *maṇḍala* depicts a synchronic map or cosmogram to be used by the practitioner to explore the Enlightened Mind in all its aspects. Over time the interlocking symbolism of this *maṇḍala* became very rich indeed, providing a useful structure for introducing some of the most important *sambhogakāya* Buddhas and *bodhisattvas.* The cosmogram is in this case divided into five domains, four in the cardinal directions and one in the center, each comprising a "family" of related *bodhisattvas* and other archetypal beings under the aegis of the specific Buddha presiding in that domain. While this fully developed *maṇḍala* or cosmogram is clearly influenced by the later Tantric period of Indian Buddhism, the principal figures were well known and venerated much earlier.

Akṣobhya and Vajrapāṇi

The *maṇḍala* is visualized as a grand three-dimensional palace, and entering from the east one encounters first the domain of Akṣobhya ("Imperturbable") Buddha, who presides over the Vajra (Diamond or Thunderbolt) family. Akṣobhya was very likely the first archetypal Buddha to become the focus of a dedicated cult-practice, although texts related to the cult of Amitābha appear early in the Mahāyāna period as well. The main source describing Akṣobhya's attributes and encouraging his veneration is the *Akṣobhyavyūha Sūtra*, a "Pure Land *sūtra*" describing Abhirati ("Intense Delight"), Akṣobhya's Buddha-field located "far, far away to the east." He also plays a role in another Mahāyāna *sūtra*, the *Aṣṭasāhasrikā-prajñāpāramitā*, and there he is associated especially with the quality of wisdom, and in particular with the unshakable (*akṣobhya*) confidence arising from insight into the emptiness (*sūnyatā*), which is to say the thusness (*tathatā*) of all things. Usually blue in color, Akṣobhya is depicted manifesting the earth-touching gesture (*mudrā*), and has the elephant as his accompanying animal. He is associated with *ālaya-vijñāna*, the highest of the eight modes of cognition of Yogācāra Buddhism, and demonstrates the mirror-like wisdom (*adarśana-jñāna*) that sees and reflects everything just as it is. Like Sukhāvatī, Amitābha's Pure Land, Akṣobhya's Abhirati Buddha-field is a veritable paradise, and one well suited to *Dharma* practice. The fruit of Akṣobhya's *bodhisattva* vows and his impeccable moral conduct over multiple lifetimes, Abhirati has no obstructing mountains, gullies, brambles or gravel. Its very earth is golden in hue and as soft as cotton. There is no lying, no illness, nor anything ugly or smelly. No jails even: for one of Akṣobhya's vows was that he would always save criminals about to be punished, even at the expense of his own life. But unlike Sukhāvatī, Abhirati has women as well as men, and children too, all living in perpetual harmony. The Vajra family's *bodhisattva* protector, Vajrapāṇi, began his career as an early, if rather obscure figure accompanying Padmapāṇi as one of Śākyamuni's two principal attendants. The Buddhist strategy for dealing with potentially threatening autochthonous spirits has been one of assimilation and conversion, and it is Vajrapāṇi, bearer of the all-powerful thunderbolt, who becomes best known for subduing all hostile forces and mental states.

Ratnasambhava and Jambhala

Presiding over the Jewel (*ratna*) family is the Buddha Ratnasambhava ("jewel-born" or "jewel producing"), whose position in the southern quadrant of the *maṇḍala* is associated with fecundity and productivity, including all the highest attainments of human culture. Whereas Akṣobhya is associated with the dawn sky in the east, Ratnasambhava's realm basks in the warmth of the noon-day sun at its highest, nurturing all of life. He is thus depicted as yellow in color, and a golden light radiates from his body, abundantly infusing everything with its life-giving radiance. Manifesting the gift-bestowing gesture with his right hand, he holds his emblem, the "wish-fulfilling" jewel (*cintāmaṇi*), in his left, and his animal is the horse. He transforms the affliction of pride into the Wisdom of Sameness (*samatā-jñāna*) which, seeing the commonality of all life-forms, allows him to care for them equally, each according to its needs. While neither Ratnasambhava nor his *bodhisattva* protector Ratnapāni ("bearer of jewels") developed their own dedicated cult following, Jambhala, another of the *bodhisattvas* in the family, has become rather popular because of his association with the generation of wealth. He is the Buddhist assimilation of Kubera, originally king of the *yakṣas* and later the Hindu god of wealth. In his Buddhist guise he is most typically depicted in his benign aspect as a portly and prosperous merchant, holding in one hand a citron (*jambhala*), and in the other a mongoose, which, when squeezed, disgorges a stream of jewels. Expressing well the qualities of richness and abundance – both spiritual and material – associated with the Ratnasambhava Jewel family, he has become a patron saint of business enterprises.

Amitābha and Avalokiteśvara

To the west resides Amitābha ("infinite light"), glowing red in the rays of the setting sun. Also know as Amitāyus ("infinite life") he is associated especially with meditation – and hence depicted with his hands cupped in the meditation *mudrā*. His palace is made of brilliantly red rubies, and there he presides over the Lotus family, which includes a number of important cult figures including Śākyamuni, Padmasambhava, and two of the earliest documented archetypal *bodhisattvas*: Mañjuśrī and Avalokiteśvara. Amitābha became, in East Asia at least, the most important Buddha of all, because of the attractions of his Pure Land, where all who have faith and confidence in the efficacy of his vows will be reborn in extraordinarily pleasant surroundings, there eventually to complete the journey to full enlightenment. This Land of Happiness and Well-being (*Sukhāvati*) is frequently depicted in East Asian art, with beautiful rivers and groves. So perfect are the conditions that women are born there as men, no longer having to bear the physiological burden of procreation. Amitābha's lotus emblem symbolizes receptivity, and his animal is the peacock, known in Asia for its ability to digest the poison of snakes and transform it into the brilliant hues of its plumage. Amitābha is thus said to transmute the poison of greed into the Wisdom of Discrimination (*pratyavekṣaṇa-jñāna*). The *bodhisattva* protector of the Lotus family is Avalokiteśvara, who, along with his Buddha family counterpart Mañjuśrī, is one of the two earliest and devotionally most important of the *bodhisattvas*. As a pair they express the two aspects of the Buddha's enlightenment, Mañjuśrī his wisdom and Avalokiteśvara his compassion. As enlightened compassion incarnate and active in the world Avalokiteśvara ("the lord looking down from above") has in Indo-Tibetan Buddhism a feminine aspect, the hugely popular feminine cult-figure Tārā ("savioress"), and in China he changes gender completely to become Guanyin. Because of a famous chapter in the *Lotus Sūtra* in which he is depicted as capable of saving beings from all sorts of dangers and misfortunes, and because of his association with Amitābha's Sukhāvatī Pure Land, he (or she) became probably the most popular object of petitionary prayer, especially where there is a concern to advert danger.

Amoghasiddhi, Viśvapāṇi, and Green Tāra

Appearing dark green in the mysterious light of the midnight sky, Amoghasiddhi presides over the Action (*karma*) family in the northern quadrant of this cosmogram. He is accompanied by two *garuḍas*, winged half-men, half-horse beings, while his emblem is the double-thunderbolt (*viśva-vajra*), both pairs indicating his association with strong and powerful "all-accomplishing attainment" (*amogha-siddhi*). His gesture is that of fearlessness, with his green color and northern domain bringing associations of nature at its most undomesticated. Envy is the affliction transformed by his All-accomplishing Wisdom (*kṛtyānuṣṭhāna-jñāna*). Perhaps the latest of this group of five to emerge, he is relatively undifferentiated, but remains all the more awesome for that. The protector of his family is Viśvapaṇi ("bearer of all"), but there are few other *bodhisattvas* associated with the Action family, perhaps because Amoghasiddhi, like his southern counterpart Ratnasambhava, seems never to have been the focus of a special cult. One other figure warrants mentioning, however, because of her popularity in Tibet. There Avalokiteśvara's feminine form Tārā came to have both a white and a green form, deriving from her manifestation as the two wives, one Nepali and one Chinese, of the Tibetan King Songtsen Gampo (seventh century CE). Indeed, the king is said to have converted to Buddhism under the benign influence of these two Tārās. In her green form, Tārā is depicted with one leg extended, indicating her willingness to step into the world out of compassion for all beings – hence her association with Amoghasiddhi and his Action family.

Vairocana and Mañjuśrī

Finally, having fully circumambulated the outer palaces of the *maṇḍala*, the practitioner turns inwards to enter the domain of the Buddha family, presided over by Vairocana, the "Illuminator." A universalization of the more human Śākyamuni, Vairocana is the Buddha of the highly mythological *Avataṃsaka Sūtra*, a Mahāyāna scripture dating from the second (or perhaps third) century CE. In this text he is said to preside over the *dharmadhātu*, the idealized universe as experienced in all its "unfixed" luminosity and accessible only to the most skilled meditator. His Buddha body is pure and tranquil, emitting great beams of light that extend throughout the cosmos. He:

> has the miraculous power of manifesting all the images of the *Dharmadhātu* within one single particle of dust . . . revealing in a single pore of his skin the whole history of all the worlds in the ten quarters from their first appearance until their final destruction.
>
> (translated by Suzuki)

This theme of the interconnectedness or interpenetration of all things became especially central to the Huayan (Jap. Kegon) school in East Asia, where

Vairocana is especially venerated. He comes to be associated with the color white – or perhaps more accurately with the unrefracted pure light of the sun that appears colorless by virtue of comprising all colors. His animal is the lion and his *mudrā* is that of "Turning the Wheel of the *Dharma*," the gesture of teaching, and thus his emblem is the golden *Dharma*-Wheel (*dharmacakra*). He is said to transform the affliction of ignorance (*avidyā*) into the highest of the five Buddha wisdoms, the *dharmadhātu-prakṛti-jñāna*, the Primordial Wisdom of the *Dharmadhātu*. Mañjuśrī is the *bodhisattva* protector of the Buddha family. Recognized by his flaming sword and his "sweet voice" (*mañjughoṣa*), he is the *bodhisattva* of wisdom, and especially the *prajñā* wisdom that discerns emptiness and dispels all delusions.

Over the centuries leading up to the demise of Buddhism in India, the Mahāyāna pantheon of archetypal buddhas and *bodhisattvas* continued to evolve and expand, especially under the influence of the Tantric symbolism and ritual central to the Vajrayāna extension of the Mahāyāna. One of the many innovations added to the basic cosmogram sketched above is the addition of female counterparts for each of the buddhas, each with her own iconography, and all understood to be fully enlightened female buddhas.

See also: ***Bodhisattva*** **path; Buddha; Buddha, bodies of; Buddha-fields and pure lands; Buddhas, past and future; Mahāyāna Buddhism.**

Alan Sponberg

ARIYARATNE, A.T., AND THE *SARVŌDAYA ŚRAMADĀNA* MOVEMENT

Buddhist layperson Ahangamage Tudor (A.T.) Ariyaratne is the founding director of Asia's largest non-governmental organization, the *Sarvōdaya Śramadāna* Movement, a network of grass-roots, self-help community development agencies dedicated to fostering economic, cultural, and spiritual "awakening" among Sri Lanka's rural poor. In more recent years, Sarvōdaya has also worked to foster peace among the country's warring ethnic factions, to advocate for a more participatory democracy responsive to the needs of local communities, and to provide relief to the victims of the devastating tsunami of 2004. *Sarvōdaya Śramadāna*, which acknowledges its roots in Gandhian-style social activism, is, at the same time, promoted by Ariyaratne as fostering a distinctively Buddhist and Sri Lankan form of *sarvōdaya* (literally "the welfare of all"), which he renders as "the awakening of all" to stress its Buddhist character.

Sarvōdaya traces its origins to 1958, when Ariyaratne – then a teacher at Colombo's prestigious high school, Nalanda College – and several of his colleagues arranged for their students to spend time living and working among the country's rural poor. This "holiday work camp in a backward village," as it was called, was meant to broaden the horizons of the affluent students by exposing them to the realities of life among Sri Lanka's outcaste poor, as well as to the rewards of manual labor. The initial camp – which involved forty students, twelve boy scouts, over a dozen teachers, and a number of government workers in digging latrines, planting gardens, repairing a school, and constructing a temple – was deemed a success by the educators, and additional work camps were initiated. Though not primarily intended, it soon became obvious that the *śramadāna* (literally "giving of one's energy") camps, as they came to be called, not only enhanced the students' education, but also benefited the villagers, who were reportedly "inspired and uplifted" by their associations with the "gentlemen from Colombo" who worked and ate with them and otherwise treated them as equals. The educational mission of the *śramadāna* camps thus shifted, in time, to include the villagers themselves as its primary beneficiaries.

The typical *Sarvōdaya* program begins with an invitation from a village to conduct a program for its benefit. *Sarvōdaya* leaders meet with the village's religious and secular leaders to organize a village council, or "family gathering," at which villagers discuss their most urgent needs (such as a road or better sanitation system). Everyone, including children, is encouraged to participate and the village is aided in organizing a *śramadāna* camp wherein villagers work together to solve the problems they deem most significant. After the work camp, groups of children, mothers, farmers, elders, etc., are formed to organize additional projects relative to their particular needs – for example, a parents' group may organize childcare or farmers a cooperative marketing venture. These efforts are meant to contribute to the self-sufficiency of the village, promote the development of local leadership, and distribute the power of decision-making to those most affected.

For Ariyaratne and the *Sarvōdaya* Movement, the concept of *śramadāna* captures the essence of the movement, and, indeed, of the Buddhist path itself. It is a reinterpretation of the Buddhist virtue of *dāna* (giving or generosity), which has traditionally been understood in Theravāda Buddhism as the giving of alms to Buddhist monastics, a form of merit-making directed primarily at gaining a better rebirth for the giver. *Sarvōdaya* broadens the scope of *dāna* to include giving to one's entire community, and lays emphasis on the possibility of giving, not just material goods, but also one's efforts to benefit others. Such giving is taken, in turn, as a means of advancing toward the interrelated "dual awakening" of self and society, perhaps even in this life.

At the heart of this understanding of *dāna* is a critique of traditional Theravāda conceptions of the Buddhist path, which characteristically regard the path as something best pursued by spiritual elites living aloof from but dependent upon society. While Ariyaratne is sometimes criticized by traditionalists for the mundane character of the "awakening" he promotes, he does not so much reconceive the Buddhist notion of awakening as he does the path according to which it is achieved. He accepts traditional, transmundane interpretations of *nirvāṇa*, in other words, but promotes an alternative, "socially engaged," means for its attainment, and thus conceives of the *Sarvōdaya* Movement as empowering villagers, not only to improve their present existence, but to work toward ultimate spiritual liberation, as well.

It is this emphasis on the spiritual potential of the laity that has prompted some to characterize Ariyaratne's Buddhism as a form of "Protestant Buddhism," a term coined by anthropologist Gananath Obeyesekere to describe the Protestant-influenced Buddhism of turn-of-the-twentieth-century Sri Lankan revivalist Anagarika Dhammapala and his Western Theosophical patrons, Henry Steel Olcott and Madame Helena Blavatsky. The suggestion in so characterizing Ariyaratne's Buddhism, of course, is that its emphasis on the spiritual potential of the laity may derive more from Protestant Christian (that is, colonial) influences than from Buddhism. It might also, therefore, represent a kind of "heresy," too much at odds with the more traditional interpretations of the Buddhist path to be considered truly Buddhist. Of course, Ariyaratne rejects this characterization, promoting his "engaged Buddhism" as not only consistent with the original teachings of the Buddha, but as truer to them than so-called "traditional" interpretations. The latter, avers Ariyaratne, arose only recently during the colonial period as clerics and scholars conspired with colonial rulers to undercut the social force of indigenous, Buddhist ways of life by interpreting Buddhism in thoroughly other-worldly terms. According to Ariyaratne, vestiges of the older, more humane and socially relevant Buddhist culture live on in Sri Lanka's villages, and it is from these vestiges that he claims to draw his vision for personal and social awakening. While some also see in this a romanticizing of life in Sri Lanka's pre-colonial villages, it is not surprising that this nationalist rhetoric finds an audience among those whose traditional ways of life, whatever their character, have been disrupted by centuries of colonial rule and neo-colonial consumer capitalism. Neither is it surprising that Ariyaratne's confidence in the spiritual potential of common villagers is welcomed among those who are accustomed to being told that their poverty is deserved recompense for some crime committed in a previous life and that they are, therefore, unworthy of awakening in this one. For them, Ariyaratne and the *Sarvōdaya* Movement offer not only hope, but guidance and resources for progressing toward awakening, even in the midst of their present poverty and oppression.

Whatever the source of its ideology, from its inception the *Sarvōdaya* Movement attracted widespread attention and quickly drew thousands of volunteers from all over the country. It is estimated that by 1966, hundreds of camps were organized with over 300,000 volunteers. In 1967, the movement began to receive funding from European development agencies which propelled the rate of its growth even further and prompted Ariyaratne, in 1972, to resign his position at Nalanda College in order to dedicate himself full-time to directing the movement's efforts. Over the years, Ariyaratne has been a charismatic and outspoken promoter of the movement, remaining committed to its fundamental ideology of human-centered development, even when threatened with the loss of foreign and government aid. Today, despite various setbacks, the movement boasts having revitalized village life in over half the villages in Sri Lanka. It has, in the process, also become a potent political force, as noted previously, offering Sri Lanka a purportedly indigenous and Buddhist alternative to Western models of development and governance.

In response to the ethnic conflict that began to ravage Sri Lanka in the late 1970s, Ariyaratne and the *Sarvōdaya* Movement have worked more recently to establish peace and reconciliation on the island nation. In 1983, *Sarvōdaya* began to organize inter-ethnic and inter-religious peace conferences, Gandhian-style peace walks, and peace meditations, all aimed at "creating peace within the 'psychosphere' through meditational practices." These events have, in many cases, attracted tens and even hundreds of thousands of participants. It is estimated that 650,000 people from 15,000 villages participated in the largest of these peace meditations, held in Anuradhapura in 2002. For his peace efforts, Ariyaratne was awarded Japan's Niwano Peace Prize in 1992 and India's Mahatma Gandhi Peace Prize in 1996.

See also: **Buddhist economics and ecology; Buddhist peace groups (in Asia and the West); Engaged Buddhism; Global Buddhist networks: selected examples; Macy, Joanna; Maha Ghosananda; Nhat Hanh, Thich.**

JIM DEITRICK

ART, BUDDHIST

Overview

The very nature of sculptural images in Buddhism is complex and often embedded in significant controversy, both within the tradition itself and within the scholarly world that interprets such images. Further, the conception and function of images varies considerably within the Buddhist world, not only over the course of history, but also according to the particular ritual, devotional, and decorative context in which any particular image is situated, and, necessarily, according to the image's very particular cultural context. It is thus important from the outset to recognize that although it is possible to make general statements about the nature and function of sculptural and pictorial images in Buddhism, it is also nearly always possible to find examples that seem to contradict such generalizations.

The Buddha's followers began to depict the Buddha very early on in sculpture, perhaps even before he had died, although because no such images survive this point is ultimately only speculation. The Buddha himself is recorded in some commentaries on the Pāli *suttas* to have said that objects associated with him – corporeal relics, primarily, but also objects he came into contact with, such as his robe and begging bowl, as well representational images – would be permissible only if they were not actually worshipped, as such worship would necessarily be involved in attachment; rather, such images could, he said, provide an opportunity for reflection on the *Dharma* and for meditation.

In other places, however, the tradition records that the Buddha actually sanctioned his sculptural representation. For instance, there is an oft-repeated story about a king named Prasenajit – in many versions of the story his name is Udayana – which provides one of the clearest expressions of a reason for making images of the Buddha. The story, as recorded by the Chinese pilgrim Faxian in the fifth century, goes as follows:

> When [the] Buddha went up to heaven for ninety days to preach the faith to his mother, King Prasenajit, longing to see him, caused to be carved in sandal-wood from the Bull's Head mountain an image of [the] Buddha and placed it where [the] Buddha usually sat. Later on, when [the] Buddha returned to the shrine, the image straightaway quitted the seat and came forth to receive him. [The] Buddha cried out, "Return to your seat: after my disappearance you shall be the model for the four classes in search of spiritual truth." At this, the image went back to the seat. It was the very first of all such images, and is that which later ages have copied.[1]

Whether this is in fact a very early story that was still popular in Faxian's time, or whether it is a much later "explanation" for the existence of Buddha images, the image clearly is intended to "fill in" for the Buddha in his absence, to make him present in some sense. The nature of this presence, however, is extremely complex, and has been a matter of considerable debate, as will be explored later.

Although the Pāli texts and commentaries make mention of images that are contemporary with the Buddha himself, in fact the earliest surviving Buddhist sculpture dates to considerably later. The earliest Buddhist art coincides with the Mauryan dynasty (fourth to second centuries BCE), and is typically associated with the great figure of Aśoka and his active promulgation of Buddhism through the use of inscriptions on stone pillars, many of which were adorned with various potent Buddhist symbols. Aśoka is also credited with providing rock-cut dwellings for Buddhist monks, caves that were adorned with various artistic motifs, as well as with building thousands of *stūpas* (funereal monuments), many of which were quite elaborately decorated, thus establishing the use of visual images in the communication of certain basic Buddhist ideas.

Buddhist art really began to flourish in the second and first centuries BCE, under the patronage of the Śuṇga dynasty. It was during this period that large monastic complexes were established at Bodhgayā in northern India, at Bhārhut and Sāñcī in central India, at Amarāvatī and Nāgārjunakoṇḍa in southern India, and at Bhājā, Nāsik, Kārlī, and other cites in western India. Significantly, however, the Buddha himself is absent from these very early images. Instead of representing his physical form, early Buddhist artisans employed a range of visual symbols to communicate aspects of the Buddha's teachings and life story: the wheel of *Dharma* (*dharmacakra*), denoting his preaching ("turning") his first sermon, and also, with its eight spokes, the eight-fold Buddhist path; the *Bodhi* tree, which represents the place of his enlightenment (under a pipal ficus tree at Bodhgayā) and also serves to signify the enlightenment experience itself (as well as the very powerful moment of enlightenment, the beginning of Buddhism); the throne, symbolizing the Buddha's status as "ruler" of the religious realm, and also, through its emptiness, his passage into final *nirvāṇa*; the deer, evoking both the place of his first sermon, the deer park at Sārnāth, and also the protective qualities of the *Dharma*; the footprint (or footprints), which denote both his former physical presence on earth and the reality of his temporal absence; the lotus, symbolic of the individual's journey up through the "mud" of existence, to bloom, with the aid of the *Dharma*, into pure enlightenment; and the *stūpa*, the reliquary in which are contained the Buddha's physical remains, a powerful symbol of both his physical death and his continued presence in the world. Later Buddhism added countless other symbols to this iconographic repertoire: in the Mahāyāna, for instance, the sword becomes a common symbol of the incisive nature of the Buddha's teachings; in the Vajrayāna, the *vajra*, or diamond (or thunderbolt), is a ubiquitous symbol of the pure and unchanging nature of the *Dharma*.

Much of the very early Buddhist art produced in India is narrative in both form and function, presenting episodes from the Buddha's life and scenes from his prior lives. At Bhārhut and Sāñcī, Bodhgayā, and Amarāvatī, huge *stūpas* were erected as part of the large monastic complexes that began to be built at these sites as early as the third century BCE, and on and around these *stūpas*, particularly on the railings that encircled the monuments themselves, elaborate carvings were made. Many of these were scenes from the Buddha's prior lives, which were also verbally recorded in the *Jātaka* and *Avadāna* literature; there were representations of prior Buddhas; and there were also depictions of key events in the Buddha's life, such as his miraculous conception, his birth, and his departure from the palace in search of enlightenment (again with the Buddha himself absent).

It has typically been assumed that because the earliest Buddhist artistic images did not depict the Buddha, there must have been a doctrinally based prohibition against such depictions. First articulated by the French art historian Alfred Foucher in 1917, this idea – generally referred to as the "aniconic thesis" – has deeply influenced our understanding of early Buddhist art. The basic assumption by those who adhere to this thesis has been that there must have been a prohibition against representing the Buddha in the early centuries after his death, perhaps because the Buddha had, at the time of his *parinirvāṇa*, passed for ever out of existence, and therefore could only be represented by his absence.[2]

Recently, however, scholars have begun to rethink this basic assumption, and to re-evaluate early sculptural images in Buddhism. They have argued that perhaps these early sculptures are not reflective of a theological position which prohibits the physical representation of the Buddha (much like the Jewish or Islamic or Protestant prohibition against representations of the divine), but instead frequently represent events that took place after the Buddha's death, and scenes of worship at prominent places of pilgrimage linked to key events in his life – such as Bodhgayā, Lumbinī, Rajgirī – and are thus intended to serve as ritual records and blueprints, visual prompters for correct veneration.

Regardless of where one stands on this debate, it is fairly certain that early Buddhist artisans and their patrons did not have a single purpose in making artistic images. There is, in fact, a wide variety of forms in early Buddhist art: in some cases, they seem to represent scenes from the Buddha's life simply without the Buddha present; in others, Buddhist artisans seem to have represented the Buddha's absence with an empty throne, and often depicted the throne itself as an object of veneration; and in still other images, they represented the Buddha's physical relics or a *stūpa* containing his relics being worshipped in place of the Buddha. Given this variety of forms in early Buddhist art, it seems clear, at any rate, that early Buddhists had a complex understanding of both the form and function of representations of the Buddha, and that any attempt to articulate a univocal theory of early Buddhist art – such as that put forth in the aniconic thesis – is probably misguided, precisely because of the complex interactions of original intent, ritual and aesthetic context, and individual disposition. Fundamentally, Buddhist images project a polyvalent potential.

Actual images of the historical Buddha began to appear some time around the turn of the first millennium, prominently in two regions: in Mathurā, near modern Agra, and in Gandhāra, in what is now modern Afghanistan. In Mathurā, large standing images of the Buddha were made in the red sandstone that was indigenous to the region. The Buddha in these images is typically standing, depicted as broad-shouldered, wearing a robe, and marked by various *lakṣaṇas*, the thirty-two auspicious marks with which he was born and which are described in several early texts – these included the *uṣṇīṣa*, or protuberance atop the head, elongated earlobes, webbed fingers, *dharmacakra* on the palms, etc. In the Gandhāra region, in contrast to Mathurā, the Buddha was typically depicted in what appears to be a Greek style of representation, wearing a robe that resembles a toga, and with distinctly Western facial features, details that may be evidence that an iconographic exchange took place with the Greeks who inhabited the region at the time of Alexander the Great. Many of the Gandhāran Buddha images depict him seated, forming the *dharmacakra mudrā* – literally the "turning of the wheel of *Dharma* gesture" – with his hands. In other images he is presented in a meditational posture, his body withered by the years of extreme asceticism that preceded his enlightenment. These different iconic forms were employed by Buddhist artisans (and their royal, monastic, and lay patrons) to emphasize both different moments in the Buddha's life story as well as to convey visually different aspects of the *Dharma*.

By the fifth century CE, the Buddha was represented in a large array of forms and sizes. Some of these representations were truly colossal, such as the recently destroyed images at Bāmiyān, in modern Afghanistan, cut out of cliffs, reaching upwards of 30 meters (100 feet), a practice that would continue throughout the Buddhist world for the next millennium. The sheer size of these images seems to have been intended to convey an understanding of the superhuman qualities of the Buddha, many of which were also expressed in contemporary biographical stories contained in various *nikāyas*, the *Lalitavistara*, *Buddhacarita*, and several other well-known texts. Further, such massive images would have served as a potent means to attract new followers.

As the various Mahāyāna schools emerged and developed in India, Tibet, and later in East Asia, the Buddhist pantheon expanded tremendously, and this expansion was reflected in art and iconography. In India, particularly in the northeast, there was a virtual iconographic explosion after the eighth century. Although images of various *bodhisattvas* had been produced in the early art of Gandhāra and Mathurā, they became particularly prominent in the Mahāyāna as it developed in India.

As Buddhism spread beyond India, an elaborate iconographic lexicon related to arhats, monks, and saints emerged. In China, the veneration and representation of important patriarchs became prominent; *arhats* were frequently represented, occasionally individually but more commonly in groups. In the Chan schools in particular, where monastic lineage was central, portraits of important patriarchs were common. Most prominent was Bodhidharma, who is typically depicted as an aged monk deep in meditation; sometimes he is depicted floating in the ocean atop a reed, representing his voyage from India to China. He is also represented in a kind of aniconic form, as an abstract face painted on papier mache or wooden balls, and occasionally as a lascivious old man, often in the company of courtesans, conveying Chan's understanding that enlightenment can be found in the most mundane, and even the most conventionally polluting, of activities. In Tibet, images of Padmasambhāva, who is said to have introduced Buddhism and tamed the demons who inhabited the region, are common; he is frequently depicted as a robed monk, with a crown, often holding an alms bowl and *vajra*. Prominent monks such as *Atīśa* and Xuanzang are common in both the sculpture and painting of China and Japan. In Japan in particular, individual monks, often specific to a particular monastery, are presented in remarkably realistic images, sometimes life-size three-dimensional sculptures. As with images of Śākyamuni, such sculptures function as meditational aids to be emulated, pedagogical prompters, and outright objects of devotion (See Figure 2).

It is important to note, however, that although a wide variety of figures began to be represented in Buddhist sculpture by the first few centuries of the first millennium of the common era – *bodhisattvas*, monks, *arhats*, as well as an array of female figures – there is throughout Buddhist history a continued and consistent emphasis on the image of Śākyamuni, the "historical Buddha." Thus despite the great variety of Buddhist schools, and their particular iconographic developments, among the most common artistic images in the Buddhist world are those associated directly with Śākyamuni's life story – his birth, his attainment of enlightenment, his preaching of the first sermon, and his death.

Figure 2 Buddha images, Gakyonsa Monastery, North Kyongsang, Korea

Indeed, perhaps the most common artistic image in all of Buddhism is of the seated Buddha displaying the *bhūmisparśa mudrā*. What makes this iconographic form so important, and thus so ubiquitous, is that it marks the very beginning of Buddhism, as well as the *Dharma*'s tremendous power. Just at the point at which he is about to attain *bodhi*, Śākyamuni is confronted by Māra, who realizes that he is about to be defeated by this man who has discovered the means with which to cut through all artifice and to conquer death (Māra is the very embodiment of death). Māra, however, who is also the embodiment of illusion and subterfuge, creates all manner of illusion and temptation to distract and defeat the Buddha-to-be. He unleashes his various armies – appropriately named desire, discontent, hunger and thirst, craving – but Śākyamuni is unmoved. Māra then uses his own daughters to tempt Śākyamuni, to stir in him lust and desire, but again to no avail. So finally Māra assaults him verbally, and challenges his very right to be beneath the *Bodhi* tree, his right to achieve enlightenment. Śākyamuni responds that all of the millions of offerings that he has made in the past have given him the right to enlightenment. Māra, however, persists; he says there is no witness to support Śākyamuni's claims. Śākyamuni's response is the exact moment depicted in *bhūmisparśa mudrā* images: he reaches out his right hand and touches the earth. The *bhūdevī*, the goddess of the earth (who is also sometimes depicted in the images), is impartial and free from malice, and thus serves as the ideal character witness, creating a terrific earthquake to confirm the Buddha's enlightenment. Māra, death (and hence rebirth) is thereby defeated.

Finally, although from the moment they appear in the Buddhist world visual images were intended to narrate aspects of the Buddha's life and teachings and therefore function on the ground as visual texts to be read, they were also very much intended to be objects of ritual worship. A wide range of texts are available for making and consecrating Buddhist images, from locally produced manuals in the vernacular to pan-Buddhist iconographic manuals. Perhaps the most common form of worship in the Buddhist world is *Buddha pūja*, literally "honoring the Buddha." This is a ritual that typically involves making some sort of offering to a Buddha image (or to a relic or a *stūpa*) – a flower, a small lamp, food, or even money. Many images, particularly the stelae that were abundantly produced in the medieval Indian milieu – although this is also an iconographic theme on some of the very earliest Buddhist images – actually depict such worship as part of the sculpture, usually along the base of the image, at what would, in a ritual context, be eye-level for the worshipper. The iconography in such cases, then, serves as a kind of visual guide to proper ritual action.

Buddhist iconography is also frequently intended to focus the mind of the worshipper on the Buddha and his teachings, to serve as a visual aid, and to help the practitioner engage in *Buddha anusmṛti*, or "recollection of the Buddha." This important form of meditation involves contemplating the Buddha's magnificent qualities and internalizing them, very often with the use of an image, either a sculpture or a painting. The iconography of such images, then, serves a mimetic function, in that the meditator is to emulate the iconographically presented Buddha, and in the process to create a mental image by internalizing the external iconographic form; in short, the practitioner is to become like the image, and in the process like the Buddha himself.

Architecture

As with Buddhist artistic images, the variety of architectural forms in the Buddhist world is staggering. The most basic architectural form in Buddhism is the *stūpa*, the ubiquitous burial mounds that are found, sometimes in great abundance, throughout the Buddhist world – in monastic complexes, in villages and cities, and sometimes in extremely remote locations where Buddhists attempted to establish their religion. Originally intended to house the physical relics of the Buddha (*dhātu*, or *śarīra*), in its most rudimentary form the *stūpa* is a hemispherical dome or mound of varying height and diameter; some *stūpas* are only a few inches high, others rise to over 30 meters (100 feet). Although the earliest *stūpas* were quite simple, very early on in the history of Buddhism the *stūpa* became one of the physical foci of monastic and lay life, and developed into an elaborate symbolic structure, as evinced by the great Indian *stūpas* constructed at Sāñcī and Bhārhut and Amarāvatī in the early centuries of the first millennium, or, several centuries later, the magnificently complex structures at Borabadur in Indonesia, or Angkor Wat in Cambodia. Likewise, in Sri Lanka, several huge monastic complexes were constructed beginning as early as the fourth century BCE, such as the Thūpārāma at Anurādhapura, the Mahāthūpa, and the Abhayagiri *dāgaba*, structures that reached nearly 120 meters (400 feet) in height.

Typically, larger *stūpas* were (and continue to be) situated at the center of a temple complex, surrounded by railings, with gates at the four points of the compass where there were gateways (*toraṇa*) on which were frequently carved images of the Buddha, scenes from his life, *Jātaka* and *Avadāna* stories, etc. As Buddhism expanded across South and East Asia, temple structures took on decidedly local characteristics – the intricate pagodas of Japan, for instance, or the thousands of distinctly Burmese temples that stretch nearly as far as the eye can see at Pagan – although the basic model has always been the *stūpa*.

In the traditional Buddhist temple, clustered around the main *stūpa* are several monastic structures. The *caitya* hall, for instance, is the place where a range of rituals would take place, and where the monks in residence at the monastery, as well as laypersons in some contexts, would gather to hear *Dharma* talks. The first such halls may have been wooden, although the most famous examples of *caityas* are the elaborately carved cave structures located at Ajaṇṭā and Ellorā. In India free-standing *caitya* halls appeared as early as the third century CE. Traditionally the *caitya* was a rectangular hall with columns running down the walls, allowing for an open space in the center that was used for collective rituals; there was usually only one entrance (and thus only one source of light), at the opposite end of which was located a *stūpa*. Some *caityas* are elaborately decorated with images, while others are quite spare. As is the case with the development of *stūpa* architecture, *caityas* took on the specific stylistic character of their locales.

Vihāras, monastic dwellings, have taken many forms throughout the history of Buddhism. The earliest *vihāras* seem to have been simple cave dwellings. By the medieval period in India, however, *vihāras* had developed into complex temple structures. The sprawling medieval *Mahāvihāra* at Nālandā in northeastern India, for example, was in fact a huge complex of several different monasteries (constituted by different sectarian identities), with elaborate *caitya* halls, large *stūpas*, and multiple shrines. At Nālandā there were several *stūpas* that were surrounded by brick towers that were then decorated with a variety of stucco images set in individual niches. Likewise, at Pāhārpur, in modern Bangladesh, under the patronage of the Pāla kings a huge, three-leveled *stūpa* was erected, with terraces on which devotees could circumambulate the main structure, around which were built several smaller temples.

Perhaps the most famous of all Buddhist architectural structures is the Mahābodhi Temple at Bodhgayā. Dating probably to the Gupta period, although a structure may have been built at the site as early as the Mauryan period, under the patronage of Aśoka himself, the temple – which has been repaired and essentially rebuilt several times – remains the most venerated structure in all of Buddhism. The present-day temple at Bodhgayā consists of a large central structure that rises to some 50 meters (160 feet), above four smaller temples, around which is a high wall; image niches cover virtually the entire surface of the temple and the surrounding walls, along with several elaborately decorated gates. Inside the temple itself are several stories that house Buddha images. Around the central courtyard, within the confines of the outer walls, are dozens of images and smaller *stūpas*, many containing the remains of prominent monks. Because of its significance, marking as it does the place where Buddhism began, the Mahābodhi Temple has been replicated throughout the Buddhist world, both in large-scale monuments and in smaller, portable shrines.

Notes

1 H.A. Giles, trans., *The Travels of Fa hsien* (Cambridge: Cambridge University Press, 1923), pp. 30–1.

2 See Alfred Foucher, "L'Origine grecque de l'image du Bouddha," *Annales du Musée Guimet* (Chalon-sur-Saone: Bibliothèque de vulgarisation, 1913), pp. 231–72. In this highly influential article, Foucher first articulates the view that the origins of the earliest Buddha images were Greek; see also Foucher's "The Beginnings of Buddhist Art," in his *The Beginnings of Buddhist Art and Other Essays in Indian and Central Asian Archaeology* (Paris: Paul Geuthner, 1917), pp. 1–29. Perhaps the most vocal opponent of this theory was Ananda Coomaraswamy; see his "The Origin of the Buddha Image," *The Art Bulletin*, vol. 9 (1927): 1–43; and also see his "The Indian Origin of the Buddha Image," *Journal of the American Oriental Society*, vol. 46 (1926): 165–70. For a more recent discussion of the issue, see Susan Huntington, "Early Buddhist Art and the Theory of Aniconism," *Art Journal*, vol. 49 (1990): 401–7, a useful survey of the relevant points here. See also Vidya Dehejia, "Aniconism and the Multivalence of Emblems," *Ars Orientalis*, vol. 21 (1992): 45–66; and S. Huntington's response, "Aniconism and the Multivalence of Emblems: Another Look," *Ars Orientalis*, vol. 22 (1993): 111–56 (and Dehejia's brief response, on p. 157). Also see A.K. Narain, "First Images of the Buddha and *Bodhisattvas*: Ideology and Chronology," in A.K. Narain (ed.) *Studies in Buddhist Art of South Asia* (New Delhi: Kanak Publications, 1985), pp. 1–21; see also John Huntington's article, in the same volume, "The Origin of the Buddha Image: Early Image Traditions and the Concept of Buddhadarūpanapunyā," pp. 24–58. One of the most fruitful discussions on this subject, and one that has been far too often ignored, is found in Paul Mus' article, "The Iconography of an Aniconic Art," *RES*, vol. 14 (1987): 5–28.

See also: **Art, Gupta; Art, Mauryan; Art, Pāla; Art and ritual; Art and Zen; Art as ritual; Art in Sri Lanka; Art in Thailand; Sacred places; *Stūpa*; Tibet: an expanded pantheon; Tibet: *maṇḍalas*.**

JACOB N. KINNARD

ART, BUDDHIST PRESENCE IN

Once Buddhists did begin to represent the Buddha himself in sculptural images, it appears that they did so, on the most basic level, because they wished to see him, but of course the Buddha was not in the world to be seen. Images, then, were intended, in part, to bridge this gap, to allow the followers of the Buddha to continue to see him, and to be in his presence, despite the fact that he was, after his *parinirvāṇa*, absent from the world. On one level, this may seem to contradict the emphasis in the Pāli Canon on the primary importance of the *Dharma*, and certainly this issue is occasionally raised in the early texts, such as the famous incident in the *Mahāparinibbāna Sutta* when the Buddha upbraids his chief disciple, Ānanda, for being too attached to the physical Buddha. In this instance, the Buddha assures Ānanda that he can, and indeed must, proceed on his own. First, he must be diligent and earnest in his own efforts – he must be "a lamp unto himself" and not rely on anything other his own self-effort to understand and apply the teachings. Second, Ānanda and the other disciples must realize that after he is physically gone, it is the Buddha's teaching that will endure, not his physical form. As the Buddha puts it: "O Ānanda, that *Dhamma* and *Vināya* (monastic rules) have been made known and taught to you by me; after I'm gone that is your teacher" (*Dīgha Nikāya* 2.145 and 154).

The tension is not so easily resolved, however, and there is also a consistent emphasis in the Pāli Canon and its commentaries on the power of the Buddha's physical presence and the importance of seeing his physical form. Frequently, this desire to see the living Buddha is used as an opportunity to emphasize certain key doctrinal points, such as the fundamental truth of impermanence and the need to cultivate detachment, and also to emphasize the importance of learning and applying the *Dharma* – and not devotion to the person of the Buddha – as that which leads to enlightenment. In the *Saṃyutta Nikāya* of the Pāli Canon, for instance, there is a story about a young monk named Vakkali. This rather frail monk has fallen ill and is visited by the Buddha, who is concerned about his health. When the Buddha asks him how he is faring, however, Vakkali replies that he has long desired to see the Blessed One but because of his illness he has been unable to satisfy this desire. The Buddha sharply rebukes him: "Enough, Vakkali! What is the sight of this putrid body to you? He who sees the *Dhamma*, Vakkali, he sees me; he who sees me, he sees the *Dhamma*" (*Saṃyutta Nikāya*). The point of this passage is quite clear: attachment to the physical body of the Buddha is pointless – if not actually a hindrance – as the vision of the Buddha and the "vision" of the *Dharma* are equal. However, it is important also to note that the very fact that the desire to see the Buddha is raised in the texts at all indicates that on some level the desire for vision and visualization of the Buddha, long after he had physically passed out of this world, were marked as significant within the Buddhist community.

In another version of the Vakkali story, which occurs in the commentary on the *Dhammapada*, Vakkali is a young Brahmin who one day sees the Buddha and is so struck with his appearance that he joins the *sangha* in order to see the Blessed One constantly. As a monk, he is so attached to the physical form of the Buddha that he follows him everywhere, to the point that he neglects his *Dharma* study and meditational exercises. The Buddha upbraids him in the same way, reminding him that seeing the *Dharma* is seeing the Buddha, but Vakkali is unable to leave the Buddha's side. The Buddha finally attempts to cure him by forbidding the young monk to accompany him on the rains retreat; Vakkali, however, responds by vowing to hurl himself off a cliff. In order to save him, the Buddha in this version actually creates an image of himself for Vakkali, who is overjoyed at the sight of this image. The Buddha then delivers a short sermon and Vakkali attains the status of an *arahant*.

Thus as much as early Buddhist texts emphasized the danger of becoming too attached to the physical form of the Buddha, there is also frequently a kind of celebration of the joy one receives from a vision of the Buddha. Part of this certainly is grounded in the basic equation in Indian thought of vision and knowledge. However, there is also a tension that is maintained in these examples, a tension between seeing that is salvifically efficacious and seeing that is a salvific hindrance. Thus it is not enough just to see the Buddha, but to see him in the correct way. Images, likewise, fundamentally effect a kind of presence, bring the Buddha into view and provide a kind of access to his *Dharma*. However, images can also be a hindrance to progress on the path if they are seen in the wrong way, if they become objects to which the viewer is overly attached.

See also: **Art, Buddhist**

JACOB N. KINNARD

ART, GUPTA

The Gupta period, which began in the beginning of the fourth century CE and lasted for approximately 200 years, has often been held up as the pinnacle of Indian art – indeed, as the pinnacle of classical Indian civilization, although this, too, is largely an Orientalist projection, in part because it was in this period that many of the essential aspects of Indian iconography – Buddhist, Hindu, and Jain – were first developed. Certainly this is a particularly fecund period in Buddhist art. However, many of the basic themes that art articulated in the Buddhist art of this period are ones that have already appeared previously, in the Bactro-Gandhāran images and in those produced early at Mathurā.

Images of Śākyamuni predominate in this period. Standing images, in particular, are very common. These images present a distinctly Indian Buddha – in acontrast to those produced in Gandhāra, for instance – and an iconographic style that would persist in India for centuries. Large standing images of the Buddha found at Mathurā – a center of Buddhist activity – present the Buddha in the guise of a monk, with an elaborately and delicately carved robe and a particularly calm visage, as if to emphasize his enlightenment; similar images have been found at Sarnāth and Bodhgayā as well.

During this period what appears to be a standardized set of Buddha images is first articulated: birth, enlightenment, first sermon, death. Two oft-reproduced images from Sarnāth present the Buddha preaching his first sermon – an event that took place at Sarnāth – his hands forming the *dharmacakra mudrā*, a large halo behind him, and with an image of the wheel of *Dharma* at the bottom of the image, along with his first disciples and two small deer. From this point on, this becomes the standard way to depict this event in the Buddha's life.

Perhaps the most significant development in Buddhist art during the Gupta period were a series of cave temples and monasteries. Beginning in the fifth century, Buddhists began carving out elaborate caves at Ajaṇṭā in the Deccan, caves which have survived remarkably intact. At Ajaṇṭā there are twenty-eight caves that were excavated in a remarkably brief period. Together they made up an elaborate monastic complex, home to hundreds of monks, with lecture halls, dining areas, and sleeping quarters, all of which were adorned with sculptures and paintings – Buddha and *bodhisattva* images, *Jātaka* stories, etc. – which functioned both as decorations, visual narratives of the Buddha's biography, objects of devotion, opportunities for the making of merit (on the part of the donors), and as aids to meditational practices. Similar, although significantly less elaborate, caves were carved in the fifth century at nearby Aurangabad, as well as at Ellorā (although these are predominantly Hindu); at these sites, significantly, the sculptures seem to reflect a more distinctly Mahāyāna character, with a preponderance of *bodhisattvas* and the early articulation of elaborate *maṇḍala* schemes.

See also: **Art, Buddhist.**

JACOB N. KINNARD

ART, MAURYAN

The fourth century BCE marks an important point for the development of Buddhism and Buddhist art, as it was during this period that Buddhism received its first substantial state patronage, from the Mauryan dynasty, particularly from Aśoka (r. 273–232 BCE). Aśoka, of course, stands as the model Buddhist king, the embodiment of *Dharma*, and he is credited with, among other things, establishing the standard of royal support for *sangha* by building monastic shelters, planting trees and digging wells to aid travelers, erecting pillars and tablets inscribed with basic Buddhist doctrine, and spreading the physical remains of the Buddha throughout India. These latter were particularly important in the spread and growth of Buddhism; enshrined in *caityas* and *stūpas*, they became objects of devotion and important gathering places, often associated with significant events in the Buddha's life. The very earliest Buddhist art appeared on the Aśokan pillars, and on and around the *stūpas*. For instance, Aśoka is credited with having established the monastic complex at Bodhgayā, where the Buddha attained enlightenment, and to have marked the actual place with the *Vajrāsana*, the "diamond seat" upon which the Buddha attained enlightenment. Whether or not the *Vajrāsana* that is presently *in situ* at Bodhgayā is the one erected by Aśoka, it carries a tremendous symbolic significance as the very spot where Buddhism began, and it has served as the basic template for other representations of the Buddha's throne.

The pillars themselves have frequently been understood by scholars to have been symbolically connected to the ancient Indic image of the *axis mundi* (the image of such a pillar, connecting heaven and earth, appears in the *Ṛg Veda*, in the story of Indra, the cosmic king, slaying the demon Vṛtra); it has thus been posited that Aśoka, in erecting these pillars, wished to evoke this ancient image of the cosmic king. Be that as it may, the pillars were frequently topped with animals – notably the bull, lion, elephant, and horse – and, more significantly in the context of the rise of Buddhist art, the image of the *dharmacakra*, the wheel of *Dharma* that evokes the Buddha's first sermon as well as the status of the king as the worldly *cakravartin*, the great wheel-turner who appears in several early Buddhist texts. Thus Aśoka's pillars served to visually connect the earthly king to the dharmic realm, thereby establishing a consistent theme in the history of Buddhist art.

Aśoka is also credited with having spread Buddhism by first dividing the Buddha's relics – according to standard accounts, into an astonishing 84,000 portions – and enshrining them in *stūpas* throughout India. Artistically, the *stūpa* is a rather basic physical structure, essentially a dome or mound. However, the *stūpa* was visually connected to both the Buddha's life (and, therefore, his teachings) and to his *parinirvāṇa*. As an image of his death, the *stūpa* was able to convey the important message of the impermanence of all phenomenon. But clearly the *stūpa*'s symbolic valence extended beyond the image of the Buddha's death. The Buddha himself is credited as pronouncing, shortly before his death, that the places where his physical remains were enshrined would provide opportunities to contemplate his teachings. What is more, the relics themselves were considered to be saturated with the Buddha's physical presence, and thus the *stūpa* could also be understood not just to symbolize or represent the Buddha's pastness, but also to evoke his continued presence in the world. Early Buddhist artisans also began to embellish *stūpas* with narrative motifs, with what, in some sense, can be seen as "visual texts" that were intended to be "read" by laypersons and monks.

See also: **Art, Buddhist; Aśoka.**

JACOB N. KINNARD

ART, PĀLA

The last significant lineage of Buddhist kings in India, the Pālas, spanned from about 750 to 1200 CE, and held sway over a substantial portion of the Indian subcontinent. Their political capital, Pāṭaliputra (modern Patna) was located in the heart of the strongly Buddhist northeast, and they were, at various times, patrons of monasteries at Bodhgayā, Nālandā, Vikramaśīḷa, and elsewhere. This was a period of tremendous change in Buddhism, and although it is the *bodhisattva* that is the hallmark of the Mahāyāna, and although significant *bodhisattva* iconographic forms emerged during the Pāla period, Śākyamuni is undoubtedly the single most commonly represented being during this period, particularly in the *Māravijaya* form, which presents the Buddha at the moment of defeating the evil Māra, the embodiment of temptation, illusion, and death in Buddhism. In these images, the Buddha is seated in what is sometimes called the *bhūmisparśa mudrā*, or "earth-touching gesture," visually evoking the moment when the Buddha calls the earth goddess as witness to his enlightenment, marking the final defeat of Māra. This iconographic form, sometimes presenting the Buddha as a crowned figure and including the seven jewels (*saptaratna*) of the ideal king, became extremely popular in medieval north India, where it seems to have been complexly involved in royal support of Buddhism by the Pālas, evoking as it does the image of the *dharmarāja*, the righteous ruler.

By the eighth century, a fairly common means of representing the Buddha in the monastic stronghold of northeastern India was a standardized set of eight scenes, known as the *aṣṭamāhapratihārya*, that presented a kind of condensed version of the Buddha's life – birth, enlightenment, first sermon, various miraculous events in his biography, and death – which enabled the viewer of the image to participate ritually and imaginatively in the entire life of the Buddha by looking at and venerating a single image. In this sense, then, such images were more than visual texts or narratives; they served as means to visual pilgrimages, and as such not only recorded past events in the Buddha's life and ongoing ritual activity, but also allowed the viewer to participate in the Buddha's life. In short, they evoke a sense of the Buddha's continued presence in the world despite his physical absence.

The various Mahāyāna schools articulated complex understandings of the continued presence and power of the Buddha in the world, understood broadly as *buddhatā*, or "buddha-ness," and this was borne out in Pāla-period sculpture. One particularly common manifestation of *buddhatā* was the set of five celestial Buddhas, sometimes called *Jina* or *Dhyāni* Buddhas, more properly deemed the *pañcatathāgatas*, a set that represents the manifestation of different aspects of the Buddha's teaching and salvific power and which is depicted in both sculpture and painting. The five are Vairocana, Akśobhya, Ratnasaṃbhāva, Amitābha, and Amoghasiddhi.

A wide range of divine and semi-divine female figures were also depicted in Pāla-period Mahāyāna iconography, many of which are elaborately described in medieval texts such as the *Sādhanamālā* and *Niṣpannayogāvalī*. The female divinity Tārā, who in many respects is the female equivalent of Avalokiteśvara, emerges in the Mahāyāna as a divine savior who protects and nurtures her devotees; with her name literally meaning "star," she was perhaps originally associated, in particular, with guiding sailors, and is sometimes referred to as *jagat tāriṇī*, the "deliverer of the world." She is depicted in numerous forms, sometimes seated with a book, sometimes standing displaying variations of the *abhayamudrā* (the gesture of no fear) or making a hand gesture of giving (*varada mudrā*), and is intimately associated with the lotus, denoting her characteristic purity.

Some time around the eighth century, the extremely important Perfection of Wisdom texts (*Prajñāpāramitā Sūtras*) became personified in the figure of Prajñāpāramitā, wisdom incarnate, a goddess-like figure who is often textually described as the divine "mother" of all enlightened beings. In one striking image that seems to date to about the eighth century and which was made in what is now modern Bihar, Prajñāpāramitā is seated with her legs folded across her lap in what is known as the *vajraparyakāsana* position. She is two-armed, her hands forming the *dharmacakra mudrā*; to either side of her are two lotuses, and on top of each is a book, no doubt the Perfection of Wisdom text she embodies. She is flanked by two female attendants, and at the base of the stele, between two lions, are two kneeling worshippers and a deer. What is particularly interesting about this image is the way in which the female deity is depicted in precisely the way Śākyamuni is depicted preaching his first sermon at the deer park in Sārnath, forming the *dharmacakra mudrā*, including the details of the worshippers at the bottom of the image, the wheel of *Dharma*, and the deer. It may well be that the artisans who made this image, or the monks or laypersons who sponsored it, intended to make a visual point here, one that is made in the Perfection of Wisdom *sūtras*: namely, that in the mainstream Mahāyāna schools it is the *Prajñāpāramitā* texts that are the supreme form of the *Dharma*, the true source of *buddhavācana*.

See also: **Art, Buddhist.**

JACOB N. KINNARD

ART AND RITUAL

Although from the moment they appear in the Buddhist world visual images were intended to narrate aspects of the Buddha's life and teachings, and therefore function on the ground as visual texts to be in some way read, they were also very much intended to be objects of ritual worship. A wide range of texts are available for making and consecrating Buddhist images, from locally produced manuals in the vernacular to pan-Buddhist iconographic manuals. For instance, the *Sādhanamālā* and *Niṣpannayogāvalī* are two well-known and widely circulated medieval Indian iconographic manuals, written in Sanskrit and still in use today, that discuss and describe three-dimensional icons – as well as paintings and *maṇḍalas* – in sometimes minute detail. Further, they lay out the proper way to construct an image – the purifying rituals to be performed prior to the start of work, the materials to be used, the iconographic details, the specific proportion – as well as detailed instructions for the ritual practices that are associated with the image.

Perhaps the most common form of worship in the Buddhist world is *buddha pūja*, literally "honoring the Buddha." This is a ritual that typically involves making some sort of offering to a Buddha image (or to a relic or a *stūpa*) – a flower, a small lamp, food, or even money – in return for which positive *karma*, or merit (*puṇya*) is generated. Many images, particularly the stelae that were abundantly produced in the medieval Indian milieu, actually depict such worship as part of the sculpture, usually along the base of the image, at what would, in a ritual context, be eye-level for the worshipper. The iconography in such cases, then, serves as a kind of visual guide to proper ritual action.

Perhaps the most commonly repeated textual discussion of images in Buddhism involves the construction of an small statue of the Buddha to fill in for Śākyamuni when he is absent, and images of the Buddha continued to be made in order to create a sense of the teacher's presence in light of his physical absence from the world. Another important strategy to negotiate this absence of the Buddha as a teacher and guide is the practice of *buddha anusmṛti*, "recollection of the Buddha." Although in texts this is typically portrayed as a meditational practice, *buddha anusmṛti* is also a mediating practice, in that it can *make present* the absent Buddha, and it is a ritual that explicitly involves the use of artistic images.

In Buddhaghosa's important meditational text, the *Vimuttimagga*, the author says this about *buddha anusmṛti*: "If a man wishes to meditate on the Buddha, he should worship Buddha images and such other objects." In the Mahāyāna text entitled the *Pratyutpanna-buddha-saṃmukhāvasthita-samādhi Sūtra*, literally the "*Sūtra* on the Direct Encounter with the Buddhas of the Present," the authors lay out the ritual means by which practitioners can mentally transmit themselves into the presence of this or that particular manifestation of the Buddha. There are several very relevant discussions in this text on the use of images in this text. The Buddhist who wishes to be in the presence of the living Buddha must imagine the Buddha's physical body as resembling a sculptural (or painted) image, and images are to be used to aid in the visual – and visionary – encounter with the Buddha. By gazing at the artistically created *physical* image, the practitioner is thus able to conjure up a detailed mental image of the Buddha; in turn, it is via this mental visualization that one is fully able to recollect the Buddha, a process that, if perfected, effectively brings the Buddha into the present.

See also: **Art, Buddhist.**

Jacob N. Kinnard

ART AND ZEN

At the heart of Zen Buddhism is the attempt to actualize emptiness, *śūnyatā*. This is most typically realized through intense meditation, exemplified by Dogen's *zazen*, "just sitting," technique, whereby the practitioner develops a mode of being without thinking, a way of being in the world as the world is happening, in flux – this is, in essence, experiencing the world as the Śākyamuni said, *yathābhūtam*, as it is, impermanent. The art of Zen is fundamentally an extension of the basic goal of Zen. Zen artists, particularly painters, attempt to visually articulate the immediacy of experience, to capture not a single moment, a representation, but rather to embody a flowing, ongoing experience. They wish, in short, to capture the flux of emptiness, and to do so in such a way that both the producer of the artistic image and the participant in it experiences this dynamism and flow.

Zen art began in China, but it is in the monasteries of Japan that it really matured and flourished. From the Kamakura period in the fifteenth century on, landscape painting, especially ink-drawing (*suibokuga*), became particularly prominent in the Zen tradition. The point of this art is not to create a representation of nature; on the contrary, the artist – or more properly the monk – trains him or herself not to attempt to accurately render the landscape, but rather to harmoniously connect with the natural world, and to spontaneously create a painting that dynamically captures this connection. Zen painting, therefore, is devoid of emotions and exaggeration. It is an art form that is fundamentally not intended to narrate a story – although some Zen paintings are "illustrations" of Zen stories – or to convey any sort of symbolic content. Rather, like a *kōan*, a Zen painting is intended to provide a means for the artist and the viewer to enter into the reality of emptiness.

Portrait painting has also been an important tradition in Zen, reflecting the emphasis on monastic lineage in the Zen tradition. In part intended to preserve the image and memory of important monks, Zen portraiture also serves a meditational function, in much the same way that Buddha images do, allowing the practitioner to meditate, using the visual image, on the various qualities that were embodied in the Zen master. Zen artists also painted objects, including animals – the heron and ox were particularly common – and fruits. One of the most famous of all Zen paintings is actually by the Chinese by Mu Qi (d. 1270), and depicts six persimmons. This very influential painting captures the essential inscrutability of Zen paintings: the six persimmons may symbolize the stages of enlightenment, or the creative process or mental states of Mu Qi when he worked on the painting, or they may be intended to symbolize nothing at all but instead to capture the simplicity of the particular moment apprehended by the painter.

One of the best-known and most influential of all Zen painters, Sesshu Toyo (1420–1506), presents a good example of the sort of intense preparation necessary to master Zen painting. At twelve he entered a Zen monastery to train as a monk. He then went to China to study painting and, upon his return to Japan, eventually settled in a small monastery near Yamaguchi. Sesshu created both portrait paintings and landscapes, developing a sharp, immediate technique of painting that demanded utter concentration, with each brush stroke beginning subtly, moving boldly across the paper, and then fading out or abruptly ending. No corrections were possible – the painter spontaneously responds to what he or she sees, such that there is no mediation, no distinction between the object and the subject. One is to not so much see such a painting, but rather enter into it, into the changing seasons, the dynamism of a waterfall, the flux of the natural world.

Zen ink paintings are also often abstract in composition, such as paintings of a simple circle, or *enso*, the outside form of which conveys the material world and the endlessness of *saṃsāra*, the inner space utter emptiness. Zen artist monks also painted simple calligraphic images of letters and words. A common form of calligraphy is *ichigyo sho*, or "one-line calligraphies," which are very short – five to seven characters – sayings or bits of poetry painted vertically on a scroll. Even simpler are the *ichiji-kan*, "one-word barriers," which consist of a single character – such as MU, the verbal expression of nothingness, or KU, emptiness – usually in bold brush strokes, that serves as, essentially, a visual *kōan*. Again, the point of such paintings is to focus the mind, as in meditation, to eliminate all distractions, all distinctions between painter, brush, paper, object. One of the most famous Zen calligraphers is the monk Hakuin (1685–1768), one of the most important Zen patriarchs who, among other things, was instrumental in reviving *kōan* practices and establishing the Rinzai school. Although he did not take up painting until very late in life, his mode of calligraphy became extremely influential; it emphasized a kind of bold, almost raw immediacy. Significantly, Hakuin and his followers viewed this mode of painting as a way of spreading Zen to the illiterate – although it should be noted that an illiterate farmer in eighteenth-century Japan would never have only looked at such a painting, but would also have received verbal instructions about how to look properly.

In Zen, the art of the garden was profoundly important as a ritual act. On the most basic level, the Zen garden reflects the monks' deep connection with the natural world – also reflected in Zen landscape painting – and the sense of the interconnected whole that is the cosmos. To construct a garden, and to tend it, was analogous to ordering and focusing the mind. To view the garden, likewise, was an act of purification, in that the viewer ideally would become one with the clean, ordered world of the garden. But the Zen garden also functions in a similar matter to the *kōan*, a visual and physical world posing an answerless question: what does the garden mean, or symbolize? From one perspective, such gardens are constructed with a high degree of symbolic resonance: sand can symbolize water; rocks can signify mountains or islands; moss can signify a forest. But on another level, the participant in the Zen garden is to transcend such symbolic interpretations. The garden is precisely what it is. In Kyoto, as part of the famous Ryoan-ji temple, there is a simple rectangular garden enclosed by a wall. The garden itself consists only of sand and fifteen stones and a small amount of moss: there are no animals, essentially no plants. The garden is like the emptied mind in meditation, and at the same time a means to attain that mind.

Finally, an essential part of Zen art is the tea ceremony, which was rooted in the contact between Zen monks and the nobility in medieval Kyoto. Fundamentally, the tea ceremony was (and still is) a mode of combining a deep sense of aesthetic simplicity, highly structured ritual, and meditation. Indeed, the tea ceremony is traditionally said to embody four essential Zen principles: harmony (*wa*), reverence (*kei*), purity (*sei*), and tranquility (*jaku*). Initially, the tea ceremony was steeped in luxury, no doubt because of its roots in the Japanese nobility, but it was significantly reformed beginning in the early sixteenth century. Sen no Rikyo, the son of a fish merchant, and hence himself a man of humble origin, essentially domesticated the tea ritual, moving it from a formal pavilion to an ordinary residence – ideally a simple hut – thereby removing the earlier class exclusivity from the ceremony. There is very little decoration in a Rikyo-style tea room: a hanging scroll or a vase of flowers; the intent of this simplicity is to cultivate an awareness of all of the individual details, the harmony in simplicity. Indeed, at the heart of this form of tea ceremony is the concept of *wabi*, "desolation." The point of this highly formal, artistic ritual is essentially the same as that of Zen meditation: to focus and still the mind by concentration, and to surrender the individual self to the flow of experience. But the tea ceremony also reflects the Zen emphasis on harmony, on the importance of being engaged, truly, with the things of the world. Thus every element in the tea ceremony – the tea bowl, the canister, the water pot, the cups, etc. – is individually produced, so as not to be a "mere cup," but rather to be a unique, individual object, yet one that only functions as part of the entire group and, indeed, as part of the entire ritual.

See also: **Art, Buddhist; Japan, Buddhism in; Zen.**

JACOB N. KINNARD

ART AS RITUAL

Three-dimensional images are essential to a wide range of rituals in Buddhism, from the simplest form of veneration of the Buddha (*buddha pūja*) to very elaborate mediations on the magnificent qualities of the Buddha (*buddha anusmṛti*). Such images are not only the object of ritual action, however; their imagining, construction, and consecration are also important ritual actions in themselves.

Before an image can be constructed it must first be imagined through meditation on the Buddha, on his physical form, his mental perfections, his compassion, etc. Although the specific rituals involved in this imaging vary considerably across the Buddhist world, the maker of the image typically must purify him or herself, sometimes through the recitation of specific texts or verbal formulas (*mantras*), and then enter into meditations in which the physical body (*rūpakāya*) of the Buddha is imagined in great detail, often to the point that he appears to the meditator as a living being. In the *Mañjuśrīmūlakalpa*, a medieval Indian text that deals with meditational rituals and image painting, elaborate preparatory rituals (*sādhana*) are laid out, rituals that involve a range of visualizations that are intended to make the *bodhisattva* an active presence and to create a mental image of an entire world that is then to be reproduced in the painting (*paṭa*).

The actual construction of the image, by a monk or a highly trained artisan, can involve a long series of complex rituals, many of which are laid out in pan-Buddhist iconographic manuals such as the *Sādhanamālā* and *Niṣpannayogāvalī*, the *Mañjuśrīmūlakalpa*, and numerous local texts. In some instances, such as in contemporary Thailand, each action on the part of the artisan is accompanied by the recitation of a particular auspicious verse or *mantra* as specified in a ritual manual.

Once an image has been properly constructed, it must then be ritually consecrated, through a ritual known as the *buddha abhiṣeka*. In contemporary Thailand, for instance, this ritual takes place in a monastic setting, and involves the chanting of special protective verbal formulas (*parittas*) and the offering of particular auspicious material objects. Through the course of the consecration ritual, the image is, essentially, imbued with all of the qualities of the Buddha himself; indeed, it is instructed in Buddhist doctrine, told the life story of Śākyamuni, and actually ordained, after which point it is treated, essentially, like the living Buddha.

In the Zen context, two-dimensional images are often objects upon which to meditate, but the painting of an image, much like the writing of a *kōan*, is also itself an act of meditation, intended to cultivate mindfulness. Although landscapes are common in Zen painting, one of the common images is the simple open circle (*enso*), the image of *śūnyatā* itself, evoking also the loss of self that is at the core of Zen practice. The single, spontaneous stroke captures the moment, and when done properly embodies mindfulness. The actual painting, be it a landscape, portrait, or circle, is not intended to be simply a representation of something, but also a dynamic capturing of the ongoing ritual moment of the act of painting.

See also: **Art, Buddhist.**

JACOB N. KINNARD

ART IN CHINA

Buddhism first appeared in China probably in the first century CE, but it took several centuries to really establish itself. Early Chinese Buddhism was a decidedly syncretic tradition, a mixture of the Theravāda and Mahāyāna, along with elements of the indigenous traditions of Taoism and Confucianism. Of particular importance in this early Chinese milieu was the *Saddharmapuṇḍarīka*, the *Lotus Sūtra*, and the *Amitāyus Sūtra*, one of the first Indian Buddhist texts to be translated from Sanskrit into Chinese.

Indian monks came from India to China beginning in the fourth century CE, bringing with them not only Indian Buddhist texts but also images and iconographic manuals. The earliest Buddhist art in China was decidedly Indian in style and form, bearing a marked resemblance to images from the Central Asian region of Gandhāra, the Gupta milieu, and the cave temples of the Deccan, in particular.

During the fifth and sixth centuries, Buddhist art flourished particularly in the Northern Dynasties. One of the most distinctive features of the Chinese Buddhist art produced under the patronage of the Northern Dynasties are the many monastic cave complexes spread throughout the country. As at the Indian sites of Ellorā and Ajaṇṭā – which may have served as the models for these caves – the Chinese caves contain a wealth of Buddhist sculpture and painting.

Dunhuang, in northwestern China, situated along the Silk Route in a remote region near the Gobi Desert, was begun in the fifth century and continued to be actively excavated for another 600 years. It was a massive complex of nearly 500 caves, decorated with elaborate paintings and sculptures spanning across the doctrinal divisions of Buddhism. Among the caves at Dunhuang, there are: mural paintings of the Buddha's life and stories from the *Jātakas*; paintings which illustrate a whole range of Mahāyāna *sūtras*; there are images of Śākyamuni in various poses; and there are countless images of *bodhisattvas*, other Buddhas, and the extended Buddhist pantheon; paintings and sculptures depicting important donors who sponsored the excavation and embellishment of the caves; and there are caves on whose walls are painted thousands of *sūtras*. The monks and artisans at Dunhuang clearly had a vast array of texts available to them; indeed, a cache of some 40,000 *sūtras* was discovered hidden in the caves at the end of the nineteenth century, many of them texts which had long been considered lost.

The Longmen cave temple complex was, like Dunhuang, constructed beginning in the late fifth century. It too is a huge complex, with over 2,000 caves and upwards of 100,000 images. One of the most impressive images at Longmen is the huge Vairocana that dominates the Fengxian Temple. Carved directly out of the rock cliffs, Vairocana sits in meditation, surrounded by several standing *bodhisattvas*. Similar caves are also found at Yungang. Here, in particular, there seems to be an incorporation of the image of the emperors of the Northern Wei dynasty, who sponsored Longmen and Dunhuang as well, into the Buddhist iconography. In Cave 20 of the complex, there is a 15-meter (45-foot) seated Buddha accompanied by a smaller standing *bodhisattva*; the face of the seated Buddha is thought to be that of Wei emperor Wencheng, who was the chief royal sponsor of the caves' excavation. Likewise, in other caves various members of the royal family are depicted as Buddhas and *bodhisattvas*. This reflects not only the importance of royal patronage in the establishment of Buddhism in China, but also the concept, first articulated by the monk Fu Guo, that the emperor was considered the living embodiment of the Buddha.

Chinese temples, pagodas, seem to have been modeled on Indian *stūpas*, although the actual shape and form of the typical Chinese pagoda is markedly different from anything found in India. The basic pagoda has a square base, and rises up in layers of overlapping rectilinear layers, with each successive layer overlapping the one directly beneath it. As in the case of Indian temples and *stūpas*, pagodas typically contain both relics and sculptural images.

In addition to the Buddhist art that was produced as part of the various cave complexes, Chinese Buddhists also constructed and ritually venerated a variety of specifically Chinese sculptural forms. One particularly interesting aspect of the depiction of *bodhisattvas* is the typically genderless nature of the *bodhisattva* images. This may have been a result of Chinese interpretations of the Pure Land texts, which stress that in a Buddhakṣetra there is no gender distinction, or it may have been caused by the popularity of the *Lotus Sūtra* and its emphasis on Avalokiteśvara's skillful means and selfless compassion, through which he could transform himself into any form in order to protect his devotees. In China Guanyin became the supreme mother goddess, the protector of mothers and children, depicted sculpturally as a beautiful white-robed young woman.

In addition to Guanyin, other *bodhisattvas* were depicted in Chinese sculpture as well; of particular note are Samantabhadra and Maitreya, because they are transformed into uniquely Chinese forms. Samantabhadra, who figures prominently in the *Saddharmapuṇḍarīka* and *Avataṃsaka Sūtras*, is the embodiment of universal knowledge who spontaneously emanates teachings throughout all of space in ways that are appropriate to their particular, is Puxian in Chinese Buddhist art. He is often depicted with Śākyamuni, accompanied by Mañjuśrī. As Puxian, however, he is typically depicted with feminine characteristics, riding an elephant with six pairs of tusks, carrying a lotus-leaf parasol, with similar dress and features to some feminine depictions of Kuan Yin. Maitreya, the *bodhisattva* of the future, is transformed in later Chinese sculpture – after the Tang period (618–907 CE) – into Budai, a laughing, pot-bellied figure who seems to be the integration of a variety of local cult figures into the Buddhist pantheon. Budai goes about the countryside spreading good cheer and befriending children.

In addition to images of Buddhas and *bodhisattvas*, images of the *luohan*, patriarchs or *arhats*, were extremely important in Chinese Buddhist art, particularly in the Ch'an milieu. Although representations of *luohan* can be traced to the fourth century, it was after the eight century that a group of eighteen patriarchs became an iconographic set, and this number was eventually expanded, to the point that groups of 500 or 1,000 *luohan* were not uncommon. These figures are sometimes depicted as serious monks, often in meditation, sometimes rendered with striking realism, and included not only local Chinese patriarchs, but also Nāgārjuna and Bodhidharma. However, another, more esoteric, tradition emerged in which the *luohan* were often presented as caricatures of human emotions and urges.

See also: **Art, Buddhist.**

JACOB N. KINNARD

ART IN SRI LANKA

Buddhism arrived very early in Sri Lanka, probably in the third century BCE. It has always been intimately intertwined with the country's history, and especially linked to kingship: one of the hallmarks of the great Buddhist kings of Sri Lanka is the magnificent temple structures they constructed. Two, in particular, stand out: Anurādhapura, which flourished from the third century BCE until the tenth century CE; and Polonnaruwa, built in the eleventh and twelfth centuries under the patronage of Parakramabahu I. As with the early Indian monastic temples – Sāñcī, Bārhut, Amarāvatī – Anurādhapura and Polannaruwa are dominated by massive *stūpas*, but also feature a vast range of Buddha images, architectural detail, and so-called aniconic images (footprints, empty thrones, etc.). At Polonnaruwa, at Gal Vihāra, huge images of the Buddha – standing, meditating, and reclining – were carved directly out of a rocky hillside. These are massive images, affecting a sense of the majesty and power of the Buddha.

On a more modest but no less significant scale is the art, particularly painting, to be found inside the many temples spread throughout the island, art which has both an essential doctrinal function and also a ritual dimension – what might, in some contexts, be called a "visual liturgy." In the Dambulla cave temples, for instance – first excavated as early as 100 BCE – there are elaborate paintings depicting various heavens and hell, some of which are quite graphic, as well as various *Jātaka* scenes. Painted in the middle of the nineteenth century, under the patronage of King Kīrti Śrī, these paintings present a fascinating example of Buddhist artistic practice.

These temple images serve several important visual, ritual, and doctrinal functions: they link the sacred places of Sri Lanka to the Buddha himself, who mythically visited the island after his enlightenment, and in the process tell the stories of these visits, as textually recorded in the Sri Lanka Buddhist chronicles; in the process, they thus help establish a specifically Buddhist pilgrimage circuit on the island, and lay out a kind of map of these specific sacred places. These paintings also present images of the twenty-four prior Buddhas; they illustrate the life of the Buddha; they depict a variety of *Jātaka* stories. In short, these painted images tell the ongoing story of Buddhism.

In contemporary Buddhist temples, images can range from very traditional stone and metal Theravāda images to distinctly modern (or post-modern) images made of plastic. At the Dikkawella Wevurukannala temple, south of Matara, on the far southern tip of the island, for example, there is one of the most gaudy, garish displays of Buddhist art anywhere in the world. The Buddha's life story is portrayed using hundreds of life-sized images. Particularly impressive are the many depictions of Buddhist hell. Scenes of the various tortures that await those who engage in karmically inefficacious acts are graphically portrayed: red demons hack a man in half using a huge saw; a woman is boiled in a cauldron of oil; Yāma and Māra are depicted as almost comically ghoulish demons; transgressors are poked and prodded and burned, and so on. Although they may not be classified as high art, these images, too, serve a specifically Buddhist function, reminding their viewers of the very real cause-and-effect workings of *karma*.

See also: **Art, Buddhist.**

JACOB N. KINNARD

ART IN THAILAND

Buddhism was first introduced into what is now Thailand some time between the third and sixth–seventh centuries, by Indian traders and missionizing monks. The earliest Thai Buddha images, which date to the eighth century, were produced Dvarati region of central Thailand, a region originally inhabited by the Mon, who were the first indigenous Thais to adopt Buddhism (although they also adopted aspects of Hinduism as well). These early images are strongly influenced by the Buddhist art of India, particularly that produced in the Gupta milieu, and there is, as in the Indian context, an emphasis on the key moments in the Buddha's biography – *Jātaka* stories, the Enlightenment, defeat of Māra, the first sermon, etc.

From the ninth century Thai artisans drew heavily on Khmer motifs, as well as the art of Sri Vijaya to the south, incorporating, in particular, Mahāyāna themes and motifs into the Buddhist art they produced. From the thirteenth century, once the Theravāda had been introduced from Sri Lanka, there emerged a distinctly Thai tradition of Buddhist art, centered in the kingdom of Sukothai, the first Thai capital. Clustered around Wat Mahathat, the "Great Relic" temple, are hundreds of elaborately decorated stone *stūpas*, along with numerous Buddha images. Especially common during this period were walking Buddha images and images of the Buddha in the *bhūmisparśa mūdra*. Buddha images from Sukothai are particularly stylized. The artisans who produced them seemed to have literally drawn on various descriptions of the Buddha in the Pāli Canon – especially those that discuss the *lakṣaṇas*, the Buddha's distinct physical characteristics – and not on the human form, and the images often appear distorted and almost abstract. Images produced during the Ayutthaya period (mid-fourteenth to eighteenth centuries) extended this basic thematic and stylistic trend, and tended to emphasize various standing forms of the Buddha, as well as the *Māravijaya* episode.

The ritual treatment of Buddha images in Thailand is particularly important. In temples throughout contemporary Thailand, an elaborate series of rituals is performed to properly consecrate and "enliven" a Buddha image. The *buddha abhiṣeka* ritual includes the chanting of special protective verbal formulas (*parittas*) and the offering of particular auspicious material objects. Through the course of the consecration ritual, the image is, essentially, imbued with all of the qualities of the Buddha himself; indeed, it is instructed in Buddhist doctrine, told the life story of Śākyamuni, and actually ordained, after which point it is treated, essentially, like the living Buddha.

Perhaps the most famous image in Thailand is the Emerald Buddha, an image that is intimately connected to kingship and considered to possess a range of magical powers (See Figure 3). According to various legendary accounts, the Emerald Buddha was created in India in 43 BCE by Nāgasena in Pāṭaliputra, from where it was transported to Cambodia and ensconced in Angkor Wat; the image then, according to the legends, was moved about constantly, from Ayutthaya, Laos, and then eventually Chiang Rai, and finally to Bangkok, where it became the palladium of the Thai kingdom. Although various mytho-historical accounts of the image are extremely important, particularly the *Chronicle of the Emerald Buddha*, it seems more likely that the image was actually created in the fifteenth century. The Emerald Buddha itself is a relatively small image, about 26 inches high, with the Buddha seated cross-legged, in the *virāsana* pose; it is of jade, not emerald. The image has, historically, been paraded in royal processions as part of a wide range of political and religious rituals, and in times of crisis: during a major cholera epidemic in the 1820s, for instance, the Emerald Buddha was processed through the streets of Bangkok to spread its protective powers. The image has also typically been brought out in procession during periods of drought. As with images of the Buddha throughout South and Southeast Asia, the significance of the Emerald Buddha, then,

Figure 3 Buddha image, Ayutthaya, Thailand.

lies less in its status as an artistic object and more in its function as the mark of legitimacy of the Buddhist kings of Thailand, and the belief that it protects the country.

See also: **Art, Buddhist.**

JACOB N. KINNARD

ASAṄGA

Reliable biographical details for any Indian personality before the end of the first millennium CE are difficult to find, but few figures are as shrouded in mystery and legend as the Mahāyāna teacher Asaṅga, who probably lived from some time around 290 until some time around 380 CE. During his long life he made numerous contributions to the literature of what came to be known as the Yogācāra (also known as Vijñānavāda and Cittamātra or mind-only) school. He is traditionally said to be the older brother of Vasubandhu, although traditional biographies disagree on whether these two great figures were full brothers or half-brothers with a common father and different mothers. Both men are supposed to be from Gandhāra, which is now in Pakistan, and to have been born into a Brahman family of a father who was a priest in the royal court. The older brother entered into monastic life and took the religious name Asaṅga, by which name we know him today.

The traditional biographies report that Asaṅga was taken to Tuṣita heaven by Maitreya and was there given five texts by the future Buddha. Modern scholars tend to be skeptical of the traditional account; some have attributed these five texts to an unattested persona called Maitreyanātha, while others have attributed them to Asaṅga himself. Whatever the case may be, these texts are regarded as foundational to Mahāyāna scholasticism and are in one way or another associated with Asaṅga. These five texts are *Abhisamayālaṃkāra* (*Ornament of doctrine*), *Madhyāntavibhāga* (*Distinguishing the Middle from the Extremes*), *Dharmadharmatāvibhāga* (*Distinguishing Dharmas and Dharmahood*), *Mahāyānasūtrālaṃkāra* (*Ornament of the Mahāyāna Sūtras*), and *Ratnagotravibhāga* (*Distinguishing the Families of the [Three] Jewels*), also known as *Uttaratantra*. The first of those five texts is connected with ideas set forth in the perfection of wisdom (*prajñāpāramitā*) cycle of *sūtras*, and the fifth is an apology of the *tathāgatagarbha* doctrine; many modern scholars have expressed doubts about these two texts being by the same author as the other three. The remaining of these three texts offer theories that are foundational to the theories and practices of the Yogācāra school. The doctrines expounded in these five texts are discussed in the entries on Yogācāra school and *Tathāgatagarbha*.

Aside from those five texts that were either composed by or revealed to Asaṅga, there are other important Yogācāra texts attributed to Asaṅga. The most extensive of these is known as *Yogācārabhūmi* (*Stages in the Practice of Yoga*), which presents *Abhidharma* theory from the *Vijñānavāda* (awareness only) perspective. Another text offering a Mahāyāna, and especially *Vijñānavāda Abhidharma* is the *Abhidharmasamuccaya* (*Collection of Writings on Abhidharma*). A third treatise is the *Mahāyānasaṃgraha* (*Compendium on Mahāyāna*).

Modern study of Asaṅga's influence has been somewhat fragmented, and we still lack a complete account of this man and his thought. Even before a definitive study is done, however, we are in a position to count him among the most creative and influential thinkers in the history of Indian Buddhism and indeed in the entire history of Indian philosophy.

See also: **India, Buddhism in; Mahāyāna Buddhism; Vasubandhu; Yogācāra school.**

RICHARD P. HAYES

AŚOKA

The Mauryan emperor Aśoka (r. *c.* 265–238 BCE) ruled for nearly four decades over most of South Asia. After his military defeat of the Kaliṅgas in 260 BCE, he is said to have converted to Buddhism. He sponsored the Third Buddhist Council at Pāṭaliputra where, under his royal patronage, monastic precursors of the Theravāda lineages prevailed, establishing an institutional complementarity between Buddhist kingship, the laity, and the *sangha* that came to define in large measure what is now called traditional Theravāda orthodoxy. What is known about this important Buddhist king derives from two types of sources. There are rock edicts and pillars erected during his reign that indicate the extent of his empire and Buddhist literature composed centuries after his time.

When the Brāhmī language in which his edicts had been composed fell into oblivion, Aśoka's public pronouncements remained shrouded in myth until James

Prinsep deciphered them in 1837. Constructed as part of the consolidation of his empire, they speak to his political philosophy, non-violent conquest by the power of the *Dhamma*. Aśoka advocated *Dhammic* rule as the basis for social justice, liberality towards one's subjects and religious tolerance. However, scholars debate the extent to which his understanding of *Dhamma* was specifically Buddhist. The edicts mention *Dhamma* missionaries he sent throughout his empire and beyond to preach to the population. Aśoka is also credited with the construction of 84,000 *stūpas* said to contain relics of the Buddha. While this is likely a mythical number, Aśoka's *stūpas* nonetheless underscore the cultic veneration of the Buddha in the rituals of his empire over which he ruled by the power of the *Dhamma*. Aśoka's son Mahinda and his daughter Sanghamittā both joined the *sangha* and are credited with establishing Buddhism in Sri Lanka after they converted King Tissa (*c*. 306 BCE).

Aśoka's emissaries are said to have reached the Mon regions of southern Burma and central Thailand. Nonetheless, it is important to separate Aśokan history from the mythical and cultural dimensions his kingship assumed in later Theravāda Buddhist political theory. Other works like the Sanskrit Aśokāvadāna, Pāli texts such as Buddhaghosa's commentary on the *Visuddhimagga*, chronicles like the Sinhala *Mahāvaṃsa* and *Dīpavaṃsa*, as well as later, vernacular accounts dating to the classical and traditional Buddhist kingdoms in Southeast Asia similarly exalted his rule. He embodied the Ten Royal Virtues (*dasarājadhamma*) that inform good governance, namely generosity, moral virtue, self-sacrifice, kindness, self-control, non-anger, non-violence, patience and righteousness. His reign came to be seen as the conceptual model for a Universal Monarch, the *cakkavatti*, who conquers and rules by the peaceful force of the *Dhamma*. The Aśokan model was particularly influential in the classical kingdoms of Buddhist Southeast Asia. Aśoka's patronage of the Buddha's dispensation (*sāsana*), his support for monastic orthodoxy and his sponsorship of *stūpa* veneration were themes central to the reigns of Theravāda kings who sought to emulate his imperial use of Buddhism to consolidate their kingdoms and legitimate their power.

See also: **Famous Buddhists and ideal types; India, Buddhism in.**

JULIANE SCHOBER

AŚVAGHOṢA

Aśvaghoṣa was an Indian poet who wrote in Sanskrit in perhaps the first or second centuries CE. Aśvaghoṣa is best known for his biography of the Buddha, the *Buddhacarita*, which may be the earliest complete account of the Buddha's life from his conception until his death. Moreover, the *Buddhacarita* is composed in an accomplished literary Sanskrit and the career and works of Aśvaghoṣa point to the broad involvement of mainstream communities in the creation of a composite Buddhist civilization in South Asia throughout the first millennium of the Common Era. Aśvaghoṣa is often considered to be the greatest Sanskrit poet before Kalidāsa in the fifth century CE.

As Aśvaghoṣa is primarily a literary figure, not a scholastic thinker, it is impossible to identify him with any distinctive school of Buddhist thought current at his time. His importance is as a figure of mainstream Buddhism, rather than as a member of any particular movement of thought. His works do reveal a solid competence in Buddhist thought, however, as well as a close awareness of some traditions of Hindu thought, notably the Sāṃkhya school. Later Buddhist schools in China claimed him as a Mahāyāna thinker: the *Awakening of Faith in the Mahāyāna* (Chinese: *Da sheng qi xin lun*) was attributed to him, although the scholarly consensus now is that this text is an original text composed in China by someone else.

Chinese biographies say that Aśvaghoṣa was born as a Brahmin and was a critic of Buddhist thought until his conversion. In this, Aśvaghoṣa is portrayed in a manner similar to other Buddhist thinkers who were his contemporaries. Whether or not the specifics of these accounts are accurate, the general sociology is consistent and revealing. Buddhism seems to have existed as an elite and prestigious learned community at this time, one that was nourished by conversions that coincided with social advancement rather than as a full-scale community that was sustained across the stratifications of society. Thus we see little reference from this time to Buddhist thinkers having had parents who themselves were Buddhists. Less common, however, is the prestige attributed to Aśvaghoṣa. One Chinese biography says that when the great Kuṣāṇa king, Kaniṣka, conquered northern India, he demanded the relics of the Buddha's begging bowl and Aśvaghoṣa as tribute. Chinese sources also say that Aśvaghoṣa participated in the fourth Buddhist council, convened by Kaniṣka, and was an advocate of Mahāyāna positions. These Chinese sources are interested in Aśvaghoṣa as a religious figure, and they portray him as one of the successors of the Buddha as a teacher.

It is as a literary figure that Aśvaghoṣa claims the attention of the modern historian. He is an excellent and representative example of the centrally visible role of Buddhists in the creation of the pan-Asian cosmopolitan culture that was transmitted in and associated with Sanskrit. Sanskrit fragments of the *Buddhacarita* have been found far beyond South Asia, in Central Asia, and translations of Aśvaghoṣa's work were made into Chinese and Tibetan. The *Buddhacarita* was also widely admired by non-Buddhist writers in Sanskrit across South Asia. In addition to the *Buddhacarita*, Aśvaghoṣa also wrote another narrative poem in a highly literary style of Sanskrit, the *Saundarananda*, which tells the story of the Buddha's conversion of his cousin, Nanda, as part of which Nanda ended his marriage to become a monk.

The religious sociology assumed in Aśvaghoṣa's works is noteworthy. His works acknowledge respectfully the existence of religious communities other than Buddhist ones, and they portray patterns of tolerant and respectful interaction between different religious communities as well as successful persuasion of others to adopt Buddhist positions. Frequently showing connections between different religious communities while affirming the superiority of the Buddhist traditions, Aśvaghoṣa's works seem representative of mainstream Buddhism's ability in the early centuries of the Common Era to provide resources that enabled movement across the boundaries of religious, regional, and social communities that existed at the time.

See also: **Buddha, story of; Famous Buddhists and ideal types; Hagiographies; Siddhārtha Gautama, life of.**

CHARLES HALLISEY

AUNG SAN SUU KYI

The 1991 Nobel Peace Prize Laureate Aung San Suu Kyi (b. 19 June 1945) is known as a pro-democracy activist in Burma and as an eloquent advocate of socially engaged Buddhism. She was born as the youngest of three children to Aung San (1915–47), the national hero, and later martyr, of Burma's independence, and Daw Khin Kyi, who served as her country's ambassador to India in the early 1960s. Suu Kyi spent her youth in India and England, where she earned her B.A. degree in politics, philosophy, and economics from St Hugh's College,

Oxford University, in 1967. During the 1970s, she worked at the United Nations in New York as special assistant to Secretary General U Thant. Returning to England, she married Michael Aris, a Tibetanist and subsequently professor at Oxford University, and traveled with him to Bhutan. They raised two sons, Alexander and Kim, in England, where Aung San Suu Kyi focused on graduate studies and academic writing about her father's political life and Burma's colonial and intellectual histories at Oxford and Kyoto. When her mother fell ill in 1987, Suu Kyi returned to Burma where she quickly emerged as the symbol for a national struggle for democracy amidst popular unrest in 1988. These events constituted a watershed in Burma's national history with political repercussions that continue to shape the lives of fifty million people.

Already under house arrest by 1989 and barred from campaigning, Suu Kyi became Secretary General of her party, the National League for Democracy (NLD), which won 82 percent of the popular vote in 1990. With the military regimes unwilling to relinquish power despite legitimate elections, she dedicated her life to the Burmese struggle for democracy, endured extended house arrest (1989–95; 2000–2; and 2003–present) and campaigned relentlessly for her party's platform of good governance and grass-roots engagement with the country's pressing needs in health care, education, and human rights.

Her intellectual biography includes numerous humanitarian awards and honorary degrees. She published a collected volume, *Freedom from Fear*, which focuses on her father's political life and colonial and intellectual history in Burma and India. Her *Letters from Burma* are reminiscent of Martin Luther King Jr.'s civil rights campaign from the Birmingham jail. In this finely calibrated collection of weekly letters to Burmese and foreign audiences, Suu Kyi presents cultural narratives and moral parables advocating Buddhist inspiration and social change. In her political speeches, such as "Empowerment for a Culture of Peace and Development," she makes powerful appeals for the universal needs of freedom from want and freedom from fear, human rights, and particularly the rights of women.

Her commitment to modern Buddhist ethics and a socially engaged Buddhist worldview characterizes her religious biography. She frequently remarked that the spiritual strength she draws from meditation helped her persevere in her work despite many years of house arrest and tremendous personal sacrifice. Her public presence is highly charismatic and popular with Burmese and Western audiences. The national struggle for democracy she symbolizes in Burma is guided by nonviolence and the ideals of Mahātma Gandhi and other modern saints, such as Nelson Mandela and Martin Luther King. Like many public figures of her time, her model bridges both a colonial and postcolonial world in Burma. Against a traditional Buddhist and cultural background in which men gain spiritual power by renouncing the world, Aung San Suu Kyi models a modern alternative to Buddhist saintliness by choosing, as a woman, to withdraw from the world in order to find religious inspiration to change the political, social and humanitarian conditions in her country. As of this writing, she remains under restrictive house arrest, following a violent attack on her and her supporters by agents of the regime in May 2003.

See also: **Famous Buddhist and ideal types.**

JULIANE SCHOBER

AUSTRALIA, BUDDHISM IN

After two centuries oriented towards Europe, Australia in 2005 increasingly describes itself as part of Asia. This changed self-description reflects the growing trade relations with Asian countries but also the fact that Asian immigrants make up 6 percent of the population of twenty million (2005). Thanks to immigration, Buddhism has become the second-largest religion in the country. In both Australia and New Zealand, Buddhism is becoming more and more mainstream.

History

Buddhism's arrival in Australia and New Zealand most likely goes back to Chinese immigrations in the middle of the nineteenth century. Chinese coolie laborers and gold-miners arrived in 1848 and 1863, respectively. The Chinese were birds of passage and usually stayed only five years. Their ubiquitous joss houses were scattered throughout the eastern states of Australia and formed a syncretic blend of Taoist, Confucianist, and Buddhist rites and beliefs. A lasting religious influence did not occur and was also hindered by the Christianization of those who remained. The nineteenth century also saw the arrival of Sinhalese and Japanese workers. The roughly 500 Sinhalese and about 3,600 Japanese celebrated Buddhist festival days and withdrew to their small temples to be isolated from the hostile and racist environment. In 1901, the Immigration Restriction Act stopped any further immigration from South and East Asia and implemented the White Australia Policy, declared as Christian-led.

Theosophist and spiritualist ideas had been around as Henry Steel Olcott, the prominent Theosophist Buddhist, toured Australia and New Zealand for several months in 1891, and again 1897. Olcott lectured on the wisdom of the East, but despite interest in the small upper educated classes, Buddhist groups were not formed. It took until 1925 for three Australian converts to form the Little Circle of *Dharma* in Melbourne, followed by the Buddhist Study Group in 1938. Both discussion groups were small and short-lived, the latter promoting Buddhism as a "workable psychology adaptable for modern problems." In contrast to other Western countries, women, both articulate and demanding, became important for organizing Buddhism in the early 1950s in Australia. Marie Byles promoted Buddhism through articles and books and led "Silent Retreats"; in 1952 American-born nun Sister Dhammadinna (1881–1967) came with thirty years' experience in Sri Lanka to promote meditation and Theravāda Buddhist teachings to Euro-Australians; Natasha Jackson (1902–90) became the leading voice of the 1953 formally constituted Buddhist Society of New South Wales, in Sydney. She and her companion Charles F. Knight (1890–1975) robustly favored an intellectualized approach to Buddhism and confined the society's work to literary studies and publications based on Pāli Buddhism. Also in 1953, Buddhists in Melbourne founded the Buddhist Society of Victoria, being more eclectic and Mahāyānist in its approach. Though eminent Buddhist visitors like U Thittila and Nārada Thera lectured to packed auditoriums, many adopted Buddhism as a kind of hobby.

This rationalist, not practice-oriented, approach to Buddhism was increasingly questioned from the early 1960s onward, as artists and others discovered Zen ideas and practices, and as Japanese teachers came to Australia and New Zealand. Zen groups started to emerge, likewise Sōka Gakkai circles and groups. The arrival of Asian teachers was possible because politically the Asian immigration ban of 1901 was lifted. Australian "white-only policy" officially ended in 1973 and enabled an increase of Asian teachers and immigrants. The mid-1970s saw the arrival of Tibetan Buddhist teachers and the founding of local groups and centers. A Buddhist plurality emerged during the 1980s with Buddhists, many from the counterculture, founding more groups, centers, and first monasteries. Similar developments came about five to ten years later in New Zealand than in Australia. Also, from the late 1970s on, refugees from Cambodia, Laos, and Vietnam in particular came to Australia and New Zealand. During the 1980s they established their temples and pagodas. Chinese, Korean, Japanese, and Sinhalese further added to the Buddhist plurality and each gave their stamp to now existent multiculturalism. As an official policy, this became more prominent in the late 1970s. Processes of institutionalization continued and from 1990 to 1996 the Taiwanese Fo Kuang Shan Order built the huge Nan Tien Ssu Temple located in Wollongong, New South Wales. It is the biggest Buddhist complex in the southern hemisphere. During the 1990s, the number of Buddhist organizations (groups, centers, temples) rapidly grew from 167 in 1995 to 315 in 2000, and to 378 in 2002 according to the online listing provided by BuddhaNet. For New Zealand, 101 organizations had been listed in 2005; the national census in 2001 specified 41,000 Buddhists among 3.8 million people (1.1 per cent). The number of Buddhists in Australia grew explosively: within twenty years, the figure multiplied from a comparatively few 35,000 in 1981 to 200,000 in 1996 and again to 356,000 people in 2001 according to the census (1.9 per cent of Australia's population). The sharp increase was primarily caused by processes of immigration, in particular of Vietnamese people. Ethnic Buddhists far outweigh convert Buddhists. Estimates speak of about 85 percent ethnic Buddhists to 15 percent convert Buddhists in Australia and New Zealand.

As in other Western countries, Buddhism in Australia and New Zealand is markedly characterized by its plurality. Theravāda and Tibetan Buddhism make up a fourth, Mahāyāna rather more than a third and non-sectarian Buddhism 15 per cent according to their numbers of groups. Ecumenical or intra-Buddhist organizations exist in the bigger cities and arrange, for example, joint Vesakh celebrations. These ecumenical societies bring together the different traditions to achieve common goals and to have a visible and active presence in the community, particularly in regard to representation to the various levels of government. Despite these efforts, as in other Western countries, a gap continues between immigrant Buddhism and Euro-Australian Buddhism, both internally diverse and heterogeneous.

See also: **Buddhism in the Western world.**

MARTIN BAUMANN

AYUTTHAYA

Ayutthaya (Ayudhyā) is the name of an extensive kingdom that was centered in the city of Ayutthaya, located in the Chao Phraya river basin about fifty-five miles north of present-day Bangkok, Thailand. Founded in the middle of the fourteenth century, the Ayutthaya kingdom dominated the region for over four centuries. In the sixteenth century, a Myanmar (Burmese) invasion gained control for thirty years, followed by a return to Thai control and a period of great prosperity. In the seventeenth century, Ayutthaya was one of the greatest cities in the world, a cosmopolitan trading center with a population estimated at one million. Several European powers, including the Portuguese, Dutch, English, and French, maintained trading enclaves there, beginning with the Portuguese who first established relations in the early sixteenth century. The Ayutthaya kingdom came to an end in 1767 when a Myanmar invasion left the city in ruins. At the height of its influence in the sixteenth century, the empire extended over central Thailand, including the kingdom of Sukhothai which had dominated the region during the thirteenth and fourteenth centuries, as well as southeastern Myanmar, parts of the

Khmer empire in present-day Cambodia, and the Malay peninsula.

The Ayutthaya empire drew extensively upon Khmer cultural ideals and artistic traditions, including a Buddhist *devarāja* tradition that identified the king as both god (*deva*) and future Buddha (*bodhisattva*). In keeping with this identification, the royal palace was regarded as equivalent to Indra's (Śakra's) abode situated atop Mount Meru at the very center of the cosmos (See Figure 4). Extensive building activities under King Ramathibodi I (1351–69), including the construction of many monumental Buddhist monastic complexes, gave material form to this ideal cosmology. Although the city plan as a whole did not conform to this symbolic ideal as rigidly as some other Southeast Asian capitals, the basic orientation of the city around the king's palace with a central Buddhist monastery, Wat Mahathat, reflected the *devarāja* and *cakravartin* ideals according to which the king's omnipotent rule radiated outwards from the capital over his domain. At its height the city had 550 major buildings, more than 400 of them related to Bud-

Figure 4 Royal Palace, Ayutthaya, Thailand.

dhist monastic complexes. The massive construction, and reconstruction, activity undertaken by a succession of Ayutthaya kings bears witness to the great wealth that flowed into the kingdom through agricultural production and its prominence as a center of trade. These royal expressions of *dāna*, pious generosity, also reflect Theravāda Buddhist ideals of kingship according to which the king's meritorious support of the *sangha*, exemplified by his construction of Buddhist temples, bears witness to his karmic fitness for rule and his destiny as a future Buddha. The Ayutthaya court, which employed both brahman priests and Buddhist monastics in its religious rituals, integrated Hindu and Buddhist religious ideals in the service of maintaining royal authority. The extensive ruins of the ancient city, marked by Khmer-influenced central towers (*prang*) and Sri Lankan-style relic monuments (*chedi*), testify to the confluence of diverse cultural forms that characterized Ayutthaya's long history. The Ayutthaya historical park was added to the list of World Heritage Sites in 1991..

See also: **Ajaṇṭā and Ellorā; Aśoka; Bodhgayā; Borobudur; Buddha, relics of; Cave temples; *Mantras*, *mudrās*, and *maṇḍalas*; Pagan; Sacred mountains; Sacred places; Sāñcī; Sārnāth; South and Southeast Asia, Buddhism in; *Stūpa*.**

KEVIN TRAINOR

B

BAREAU, ANDRÉ

French Buddhologist André Bareau (1921–93) was regarded as perhaps the world's leading authority on Indian Buddhist sectarianism. Born in Saint-Mandé (Val-de-Marne), he engaged in Oriental studies under Paul Demiéville and Jean Filliozat at the Sorbonne. He received his doctorate in 1951 for his translation of the Abhidhamma text known as the *Dhammasaṅgaṇī*. In 1956 a position as Director of Studies in Buddhist Philology was created for him at the Sorbonne, and he remained in that position until his retirement in 1973. Two years prior to his official retirement, he assumed the Chair of Buddhist Studies at the Collège de France, where he remained until 1992. He also served on the initial editorial advisory board of the *Journal of the International Association of Buddhist Studies*. During his career, he traveled extensively in India, Nepal, Sri Lanka, Thailand, and Cambodia.

His classic books *Les Premiers Conciles bouddhiques* and *Les Sectes bouddhiques du petit Véhicule*, both published in 1955, are still considered the outstanding research volumes in that area. These two volumes conclusively demonstrated that the earliest schism in Buddhism *did not* occur at the second Buddhist council of Vaiśālī, as previously thought, but occurred, according to Bareau, at a later date (possibly thirty-seven years later during the reign of Mahāpadma Nanda). Bareau believed the cause of Buddhism's first schism focused on supposed disciplinary laxity of the future Mahāsāṃghika sect, as well as on five theses concerning the nature of liberated individuals known as *arhants*, set forth by the notorious monk Mahādeva. Bareau's thesis has since been criticized, and perhaps proved incorrect, by the published research of Charles Prebish, Janice Nattier, Lance Cousins, and others. Bareau's volume on Buddhist sectarianism remains the only research publication to exhaustively list and catalogue the specific doctrinal theses of each of the earliest so-called Hīnayāna sects. Bareau also published a number of other landmark volumes, including *L'Absolu en philosophie Bouddhique: Evolution de la notion d'Asaṃskṛta* (1951) and *Recherches sur la biographie du Bouddha dans les Sūtrapiṭaka et les Vinayapiṭaka anciens* (1963, 1971). He was also known for his prolific list of instructive professional articles, which included such works as "La construction et le culte des Stūpa d'après les Vinayapiṭaka," published in *Bulletin de l'École Française D'Extrême-Orient* in 1962.

Bareau's academic and intellectual approach focused on working with the earliest original texts available in each of the pertinent canonical languages of Sanskrit, Pāli, and Chinese, an approach he shared with his Belgian colleague and contemporary, Étienne Lamotte. In a career that spanned more than forty years, he also found time to publish books for a popular audience, such as his anthology of texts on Buddha's life and teaching known as *En suivant Bouddha* (published in 1985).

Despite his immense reputation and work which influenced a generation of Buddhological scholars throughout the world, André Bareau lived quietly in the Paris suburbs amidst his large family. His obituary notice in the journal *Buddhist Studies Review*, published in London, also notes his profound love of cats.

See also: **Academic study of Buddhism; Franco-Belgian school of Buddhist Studies.**

CHARLES S. PREBISH

BATCHELOR, MARTINE

Martine Batchelor is one of the first women in Europe to become ordained. She was an ordained Korean Zen nun from 1975 to 1985 at Songgwang Sa monastery. She was a member of the Sharpham North Community and a founding teacher at Sharpham Buddhist College and Contemporary Enquiry. She is a co-founder of Gaia House. She has taught worldwide, published several books and articles and now resides in France, where she was born.

In an interview, "Very Good *Dharma* Friends," she states that she was politically active as a teenager but upon reading a copy of the *Dharmapada* she realized that if she was going to change the world she first needed to change herself. She shelved her desire to become a journalist and set out traveling. While in Thailand she met some Korean monks and went to Korea to study Zen meditation. She remained, was ordained, and studied with the late Master Kusan. She translated his talks and teachings and went with him on tour in America. In 1985 she returned to Europe, and she and her new husband were able to ease their way out of monastic life and into lay life through participation in the Sharpham North lay community.

Her published works include *The Way of Korean Zen* (1985), a translation of Master Kusan's writing, *Walking on Lotus Flowers* (1996), *Principles of Zen* (1999), *Meditation for Life* (2001) and *The Path of Compassion* (2004). She is co-author with Kerry Brown of *Buddhism and Ecology* (1992) and has contributed many articles in anthologies and on the Web. She and her husband lead numerous workshops on ecology and meditation in Europe and the United States.

Regarding the Buddhist influence on society, Batchelor notes that Buddhism has always been conditioned by its social setting and will be influenced by contemporary society as well. One must be careful however, with adaptation. For example, although Buddhism and psychotherapy can work well together, one must be clear that Buddhism is not psychotherapy. Carefully used by a skilled teacher they can complement each other, balancing the danger of using meditation as an escape from problems and the psychotherapeutic danger of becoming self-absorbed with one's problems.

Batchelor focuses on providing Buddhist teachings that are adapted to contemporary issues. She stresses that it is insufficient simply to study Buddhist ethics or meditate. It is necessary to work on ethics, concentration and wisdom at the same time. Her writings on meditation, particularly her *Meditation for Life*, have been praised for their accessibility. Each chapter of the book begins with background, moves on to instruction and finishes with a guided meditation. It is enhanced by pictures taken by her husband, Stephen. In *Walking on Lotus Flowers* she has collected the experiences of a wide variety of Buddhist women, including Tenzin Palmo who spent twelve years in cave meditation. Her versatility is further demonstrated in her most recent book, *The Bodhisattva Precepts*, which combines both her linguistic abilities (it is a translation of the Chinese *Brahmajāla Sūtra*) and her social concern (the publisher's description states that it "demonstrates an ancient ground for socially engaged Buddhism").

Martine Batchelor is one of a growing number of Western teachers and practitioners who are consciously adapting Buddhism to a modern context and bringing their insights to bear on contemporary problems.

See also: **Women in Buddhism: an historical and textual overview.**

MAVIS L. FENN

BODHGAYĀ

Bodhgayā (also known as Buddhagayā), the traditional site of Gautama Buddha's enlightenment, is by far the most well known and commonly visited of the historical places associated with his life. One Buddhist tradition maintains that this spot is the center of the earth, the only place capable of bearing the weight of a Buddha's extraordinary attainment, and it is thus the place where all Buddhas gain enlightenment (though the species of tree under which they sit varies from Buddha to Buddha). Located in the north Indian state of Bihar about eight miles south of the town of Gayā (itself an important Hindu pilgrimage site), the temple complex is oriented around a great *pīpal* tree, more commonly known as the *Bodhi* tree, which is believed to be a direct descendent of the tree under which the *bodhisattva* Siddhārtha gained perfect enlightenment. This tree, the polished sandstone platform (*vajrāsana* or "diamond throne") that lies sheltered beneath it just to the east, and the adjoining temple, which ascends 170 feet over the temple complex, provide the primary religious focus for the great numbers of Buddhist pilgrims who travel there from around the world.

A third-century BCE Aśokan inscription records that the Emperor Aśoka made a pilgrimage to the place of the Buddha's enlightenment, and some archeological remains at Bodhgayā, including the sandstone *vajrāsana* beneath the *Bodhi* tree, have been dated to that period. A carving of an open-air two-storied tree shrine (*bodhighara*) discovered on a first-century BCE railing pillar at Bhārhut bears an inscription identifying it as a depiction of Śākyamuni's (Gautama's) enlightenment; this carving has given rise to considerable speculation about earlier structures surrounding the *Bodhi* tree. Based on textual descriptions and frequent depictions of similar tree shrines at Sāñcī, Bhārhut, and Amarāvatī, it appears likely that *bodhigharas* were a feature of many early Indian Buddhist monasteries, and *bodhigharas* have been a characteristic element of Sri Lankan monastic architecture from the introduction of Buddhism in the third century BCE to the present day. The dating of the temple that presently dominates the Bodhgayā complex remains uncertain, though scholars have suggested a date around the fifth century for the construction of a structure very similar in appearance to the present-day temple. The temple was subject to several renovations over the course of the centuries, and there is evidence that the location of the *Bodhi* tree may have shifted with the construction of the temple that dominates the site today.

The Gupta period (fourth to sixth centuries CE) was a time of expansion at Bodhgayā. A large monastery called the Mahābodhi Saṅghārāma, built under the patronage of a Sri Lankan king for the benefit of Sri Lankan pilgrims to Bodhgayā, was constructed in the fourth century. This reflects long-standing connections between Bodhgayā and Sri Lanka which, according to widely accepted tradition, began in the third century BCE when the nun Sanghamittā brought a branch of the *Bodhi* tree from Bodhgayā to Anurādhapura, the ancient Sri Lankan capital, where it has been nurtured and venerated continuously to the present day.

In addition to the *Bodhi* tree and *vajrāsana* which are associated with the moment of the Buddha's enlightenment and the events that immediately preceded it, several other cultically significant places were distinguished at Bodhgayā, including those linked with the seven-week period following his attainment of Buddhahood. During the first week he is said to have remained seated in meditation beneath the *Bodhi* tree while he experienced the joy of liberation; during the second week he stood to the side gazing upon the tree with unblinking eye as a gesture of gratitude; in the third he walked back and forth along a jeweled promenade; in the fourth he sat contemplating the *Abhidharma* in a jeweled chamber while his body gave forth multicolored rays of light; and in the fifth he meditated beneath the Ajapāla banyan tree; at this time, according to one tradition, he overcame the temptation presented by Māra's three daughters. During the sixth week, as he sat in meditation under the Mucalinda tree, a great storm arose and Mucalinda, a mighty serpent deity (*nāga*) who dwelt at the bottom of the nearby lake, coiled himself around the Buddha's body and raised his cobra hood to protect him from the elements. During the seventh week, the Buddha sat in meditation beneath the Rājāyatana tree and at that end of the week he was approached by two merchants, Trapuṣa and Bhallika, to whom the Buddha gave some strands of hair for veneration. These incidents and their locations are mentioned in Faxian's and Xuanzang's accounts and they are distinguished at Bodhgayā today. The tradition of the seven weeks became an important iconographic theme in Sri Lanka and Southeast Asia, and in some images from Myanmar the seven weeks are depicted in parallel with the "eight great marvels." The story of the Buddha's hair relics became important in Myanmar, where there is a Mon tradition that the two merchants came from that region and were responsible for bringing the relics back to Myanmar; they were eventually enshrined in the Shwedagon *stūpa* in Yangon (Rangoon). Two copies of the Bodhgayā complex including the shrines connected with the seven weeks were also constructed in Myanmar and Thailand in the fifteenth century, providing Buddhists with the opportunity to venerate the shrines locally without traveling to India.

Buddhist communities in northeastern India flourished under the patronage of Pāla rulers (eighth–twelfth centuries CE), and Pāla-era sculptural remains from Bodhgayā testify to a vibrant and diverse artistic tradition, strongly influenced by Tantric Buddhist iconography. With the end of the Pāla dynasty and the rise of Turkish Muslim attacks on Buddhist monastic centers, Buddhism virtually disappeared from north India. From the thirteenth to the early nineteenth centuries, Bodhgayā appears to have been largely neglected, though later pilgrimage accounts indicate that a trickle of Buddhist devotees continued to visit the site. When Francis Buchanan, a British colonial officer, visited Bodhgayā in 1811, he found it in ruins, noting that it had then become part of a Hindu pilgrimage circuit centered at the nearby town of Gayā, reflecting in part the Vaiṣṇava tradition that the Buddha was an *avatāra* of Viṣṇu. At that time the site was under the supervision of a group of Hindu Vaiṣṇava ascetics who had established a small monastery there in the seventeenth century. Two royal missions from Burma came to Bodhgayā in the first half of the nineteenth century, and in 1875 the Burmese government gained permission to undertake renovations. As the renovation proceeded, the British colonial administration disapproved of some of the repairs and in 1880 a British archeological officer was appointed to work with the Burmese. The temple as it appears today is largely the result of this major renovation, which attempted to restore the structure to its Pāla-era appearance based on two small stone models found in India. Several other large-scale reproductions of the Bodhgayā temple were constructed throughout Asia, and copies survive in Myanmar, Thailand, Nepal, Tibet, and China. In addition, the Bodhgayā temple, along with the Buddha seated in the earth-touching posture (*bhumisparśa mudrā*), is represented on large numbers of small pressed-clay votive tablets found in Southeast Asia.

By the end of the nineteenth century, a major conflict had emerged over who should have legal custody of the site. Spearheading the movement to give Buddhists exclusive control over Bodhgayā was the Buddhist reformer Anagārika Dharmapāla. Dharmapāla, inspired in part by some newspaper articles written by Sir Edwin Arnold that decried Hindu worship at Bodhgayā, founded the Mahabodhi Society in 1891 with the aim of establishing Buddhist control. Physical conflict resulted from an attempt by Dharmapāla and his supporters to place a Buddha image inside the temple, and the question finally ended up in the courts. It was not resolved until 1949, when the Bodh Gaya Temple Act gave custody of the site to a joint Hindu–Buddhist committee, and inter-religious tensions continue over the administration of the site. The history of the conflict points to some of the powerful forces that have contributed to communal conflict in Asia in the twentieth century, including nineteenth-century Orientalist categories that aligned particular ethnic communities with exclusively defined religious traditions, often without regard to the complexities and ambiguities of actual religious practice, and the emergence of religious revival movements linked with nationalism and anti-colonialist impulses.

Despite this behind-the-scenes conflict over who has the right to control Bodhgayā, the complex today continues to draw many Hindus as well as Buddhists from all over the world. Buddhists from several countries have erected temples and other facilities to support the large numbers of pilgrims and tourists who flock there. A considerable diversity of Buddhist traditions are represented, including new Buddhist communities founded in the twentieth century, such as members of the Dalit Buddhist community and Buddhists from Europe and North America. Most Buddhists who visit Bodhgayā perform some form of clockwise circumambulation around the temple; in the case of some Tibetan Buddhists, this takes the form of measuring out the circuit with full-body prostrations. Many people take a fallen leaf from the *Bodhi* tree as a pilgrim's memento. In 2002 Bodhgayā was named a World Heritage Site, and efforts are currently underway to control development in the surrounding area and to reduce the increasing pollution from auto emissions, which threaten the health of the *Bodhi* tree.

See also: **Ajaṇṭā and Ellorā; Anagarika Dharmapala; *Arahant*; Aśoka; Buddha, relics of; Faxiang; Kuśinagara; Lumbinī; Pāṭaliputra; Sacred places; Sārnāth; Vaiśālī.**

KEVIN TRAINOR

BODHI TREE

Bodhi tree or Bo tree is the name commonly given to the tree under which Gautama Buddha gained perfect awakening (*bodhi*) at Bodhgayā. What is believed to be a descendant of the original tree presently stands there, along with an Aśokan-era (third century BCE) sandstone platform (*vajrāsana* or "diamond throne") marking the place of the Buddha's enlightenment, and these presently receive the veneration of great numbers of Buddhists from around the world who come to Bodhgayā on pilgrimage. The current *Bodhi* tree belongs to the *Moraceae* family and is one of several species of fig trees; its Latin name is *Ficus religiosa*, and Sanskrit texts refer to it as the *pippala* or *aśvattha*. Its distinctive heart-shaped leaves are widely associated with the Buddha's enlightenment, though Buddhist canonical sources record the tradition that several other species of tree have served as *Bodhi* trees for previous Buddhas. The Pāli *Mahāpadāna Sutta* (*Dīgha Nikāya* no. 14), for example, identifies six different *Bodhi* trees for the six Buddhas who immediately preceded Gautama, and the introduction to the Pāli *Jātaka* commentary (*Nidāna-kathā*) identifies the names of the trees associated with eighteen other earlier Buddhas. The *Bodhi* tree is numbered among the seven things that come into existence at the moment that a *bodhisattva* gains his final rebirth (Skt. *sahajāta*s).

There is a long history of tree veneration in ancient India. Ancient seals from the Indus Valley civilization (c. 2300–1750 BCE) depict *pippala* trees in contexts that appear to have cultic significance, and several species of trees, including the *pippala*, figure prominently in Vedic and Brahmanic literature. Indian Buddhist tradition absorbed this widespread reverence for certain kinds of trees that were commonly thought to be the dwelling places of spirits and demons. There are numerous Buddhist textual references to shrines (*caityas*) associated with trees, and trees and the superhuman beings with which they were linked figure prominently in Buddhist iconography. Particular trees are also important in biographical traditions about Gautama Buddha. For example, his mother was said to have given birth to him standing, supported by the branch of a nearby *śāla* tree that had miraculously bent itself down for her to grasp. Another tradition maintains that while he was still a young boy, he fell spontaneously into a high level of meditative absorption while seated beneath a rose-apple tree (Skt. *jambu*). Trees also figure significantly in the episodes surrounding his enlightenment, including Sujātā's gift of food, given to him while seated beneath a banyan tree (Skt. *nyagrodha*) under the misapprehension that he was a tree spirit who had ensured her fertility. Biographical traditions centered on the seven weeks that followed the Buddha's enlightenment also identify three specific trees under which he meditated during that time. Finally, the Buddha's final passing away is said to have taken place between two *śāla* trees.

A justification for venerating the *Bodhi* tree and, by extension, other trees that the Buddha used for meditation, appears in one of the *Jātakas* called the *Kāliṅgabodhi Jātaka* (no. 479). In response to the request of a group of Śrāvastī residents for a place where they could leave their offerings for the Buddha while he was away from his Jetavana residence, the Buddha explained to his disciple Ānanda that three types of shrines (Pāli *cetiyas*, Skt. *caityas*) are permitted for a Buddha: a bodily relic (*sārīrika*) shrine, a relic-of-use (*pāribhogika*) shrine and a commemorative (*uddesika*) shrine. He then clarified that the great *Bodhi* tree, a shrine by virtue of the Buddha's use of it, is the only one of the three that was permitted while a Buddha is still alive. The narrative shifts to the account of a past life in which Ānanda was a king traveling on the back of an elephant. Suddenly the elephant was unable to go any further, despite the king's violent goadings. The Buddha, who in that life was the king's chief priest, explained that they could not proceed because they had approached the precincts of the great *Bodhi* tree where all Buddhas gain their perfect awakening. The king then held a week-long festival of veneration for the tree, and at the end of his life was reborn as a *deva* in the Heaven of the Thirty-Three.

Outside of India, the *Bodhi* tree has had the greatest ongoing religious and historical significance in Sri Lanka. The history of the great *Bodhi* tree is the subject of an extensive literature composed in Pāli and Sinhala. As recounted in the Pāli *vaṃsa* literature, the transmission of Buddhism from India to Sri Lanka in the third century BCE was closely connected with the arrival of a branch of the *Bodhi* tree, brought by the Emperor Aśoka's daughter, Sanghamittā, a Buddhist nun who was also linked with the transmission of the women's monastic ordination lineage. Chapters 18 and 19 of the *Mahāvaṃsa* recount how the branch from the southern side of the *Bodhi* tree miraculously detached itself and planted itself in a golden pot, which Sanghamittā and a group of Buddhist nuns brought by ship to Sri Lanka; this was the fulfillment of the Buddha's prediction given just before his final passing away as recorded in an earlier chapter of the text.

The *Mahāvaṃsa* also preserves a tradition that the *Bodhi* tree planted in the ancient Sri Lankan capital of Anurādhapura bore a miraculous fruit that put forth eight shoots; these were planted at various locations around the island. Four other branches bore similar fruit, producing a total of thirty-two shoots that were then planted in other locations in Sri Lanka. The importance of this tradition can be seen, for example, in the case of Bellanwila Rājamahā Vihāra, a prominent temple located in the outskirts of Colombo. This temple was founded in the mid-nineteenth century and consequently lacks the antiquity and prestige associated with Sri Lankan temples founded under royal patronage; nevertheless, it claims a special status for having one of the thirty-two shoots that sprang from the original *Bodhi* tree in Anurādhapura. The Bellanwila *Bodhi* tree is widely known for its special powers to ensure the health of infants and children.

Nearly every temple in Sri Lanka possesses a *Bodhi* tree, though only a small minority claim direct descent from the tree at Bodhgayā. The *Bodhi* tree, along with the *stūpa* and image hall, represent the Buddha for the purposes of making offerings. The *Bodhi* tree is typically surrounded on four sides with a wall upon which flower offerings can be placed, and some have a special place where water scented with sandalwood can be poured upon the tree's roots. Usually the pot in which the water has been placed is first circumambulated clockwise around the tree (*pradakṣinā*). It is also common for people to offer lighted oil lamps and flags and banners which are suspended from tree branches. Beginning in the 1970s, a new *Bodhi* tree-centered ritual called *Bōdhi-pūjā* ceremony was popularized by a charismatic monk named Pānadurē Ariyadhamma Thera. The ceremony, which typically includes an offering of water or milk to the *Bodhi* tree, is notable for its strong congregational and affective character and its use of melodic Sinhala chanting.

See also: **Anurādhapura; *Arahant*; Aśoka; Bodhgayā; Buddha, early symbols; Buddha, relics of; Kuśinagara; Lumbinī; *Mantras, mudrās,* and *maṇḍalas*; Pāṭaliputra; Sacred places; Sārnāth; *Stūpa*; Worship.**

KEVIN TRAINOR

BODHIDHARMA

In traditional Chan histories, Bodhidharma is the Indian monk-missionary who brought Chan to China. Legend depicts him as a south Indian prince who left the household life and, after attaining enlightenment, became the twenty-eighth "patriarch" through whom the Buddha's original enlightenment experience had been transmitted from mind to mind without the use of "words and letters." Upon bringing Chan to China, he became the first Chinese patriarch, and occupies the first position in all master–disciple lineages in East Asia.

According to the legend, Bodhidharma arrived in Canton via the sea route in 526 CE, and was invited to the court of Emperor Wu of the Liang dynasty in the south. Expecting the master's praise for the temples he built and his lavish support of the *sangha*, the emperor received instead enigmatic responses and a brusque dismissal of his activities. Bodhidharma then left for the north, reportedly crossing the Yangtze River on a reed, and arrived at the Shaolin Temple. Finding the resident clergy weak and vulnerable to the depredations of local bandits, he taught them self-defense, from which evolved the famous Shaolin style of martial arts. He then sequestered himself in a cave for nine years and sat gazing at the wall. Once, enraged at his drowsiness, he ripped off his eyelids and threw them down to the ground, where they sprouted as tea plants. In addition, his legs are said to have withered away because of his constant sitting. (This is the origin of the *Daruma* doll, a Japanese toy shaped like an egg with large, lidless eyes and a weighted bottom that springs upright again when knocked over.) Huike, the man who would become his disciple and the second Chinese patriarch, came to him for study during this period, but was unable to get Bodhidharma's attention. The latter looked up and received him only after the former cut off his arm as an offering. When Bodhidharma died at the age of 160, he was buried at the Shaolin Temple, but the same day one of the monks who was traveling met him heading west holding up a single sandal. When the monk returned, he recounted the story, whereupon the other clergy opened the tomb and found only a single sandal inside.

While most of the above story is clearly legendary, there is no reason to doubt the historicity of the man himself. Numerous early records speak approvingly of him (or someone by that name) as a wise and compassionate monk, and there exists a work attributed to him called *The Two Entrances and Four Practices,* which speaks of a practice called "wall-contemplation." Other records confirm that he came from the west, that he was well practiced in meditation, and that among his disciples was one named Huike. *The Two Entrances and Four Practices* gives his teaching on meditation and wisdom in terms that anticipate later Chan practice. However, far from being an iconoclastic and mysterious figure who rejects "words and letters," these early sources present him as a master of a particular scripture, the *Laṅkāvatāra Sūtra*, and remark on his willingness to speak quite plainly and openly about his understanding of the teachings. All earlier sources report that he himself claimed to be over 150 years old. The "historical" and "legendary" Bodhidharmas are both worth study, and reveal different facets of Chinese Chan history and self-image.

See also: **Chan; China, Buddhism in; Japan, Buddhism in; Zen.**

CHARLES B. JONES

BODHISATTVAS

Perhaps the single most striking development in the art of the Mahāyāna in India is the preponderance of *bodhisattva* images, especially the *bodhisattvas* Mañjuśrī, Avalokiteśvara, and Maitreya. Images of Manjuśrī first began to be made in India sometime around the fifth or sixth century, and may have first been made at Ellorā. Relatively soon thereafter he was sculpturally depicted in several different forms. He is perhaps most frequently depicted as a young man or boy (*mañjuśrī kumāra*), or as a crowned royal figure. In some Indian images, Mañjuśrī sits cross-legged atop a lotus, displaying the *dharmacakra mudrā*, echoing a common textual-image of Mañjuśrī as the source of the Buddha's wisdom. In others, he stands and forms the *varada mudrā*, or "gift-giving" gesture, conveying the sense in which he offers his followers the gift of the *Dharma*. In numerous Mahāyana texts, particularly in the *Prajñāparāmitā sūtras*, Manjuśrī – "pleasing splendor" – is intimately involved with the central Buddhist concept of *prajñā*, the penetrating wisdom that leads to enlightenment; he is frequently the interlocutor in Mahāyāna texts, and is sometimes the Buddha's teacher.

Two iconographic elements that typically are frequently included in sculptural depictions of Mañjuśrī are especially important in this regard: (1) the book – the *Prajñāparāmitā* (Perfection of Wisdom) text of which he is the embodiment – sometimes held aloft, sometimes clutched close to the chest, and, more frequently, perched atop one or more of the lotuses that he typically holds; and (2) the sword, which conveys the sense of *prajñā* as slashing through ignorance and delusion. There are, for instance, numerous bronze images that were found at the important site of Kurkihār, dating to the ninth or tenth centuries, that depict a seated Mañjuśrī holding a book aloft in his left hand, and a small ball, perhaps a piece of fruit, in his right; visually, an image such as this seems to convey a kind of dual emphasis on *prajñā*, in that in addition to the book, the piece of fruit in the right hand can be seen as a representation of Mañjuśrī's offering of the fruit (*phala*) of enlightenment to his followers. Several Mahāyāna texts espouse the benefits of seeing an image of Maṇjuśrī (and also reciting his various names): in keeping with a pervasive connection between seeing and knowing, to see such an image is to partake in the *prajñā* which the *bodhisattva* embodies, and, such texts state, can in itself lead to enlightenment.

Although textually Mañjuśrī is afforded the highest status in the Mahāyāna Buddhist pantheon, it is Avalokiteśvara who is the single most popular figure in the Buddhist world after the Buddha himself. Images of Avalokiteśvara seem to have been first made sometime around the third century CE in northwestern India, in Gandhāra and Mathūra. As perhaps the most paradigmatic of all *bodhisattvas*, he is the embodiment of compassion, the *bodhisattva* who sees all suffering and comes to the aid of his devotees. Sculpturally he is depicted in a vast range of forms, and there is a tremendous variety of iconographic elements associated with him. Frequently he has several eyes, denoting his compassionate omniscience, and sometimes multiple heads, as in the *daśamukha* (ten-faced) iconographic form (prevalent particularly in Nepal); he also nearly always has multiple hands, in which he holds various implements that aid him in his salvific endeavors. In the *Saddharmapuṇḍarīka Sūtra* and several other mainstream Mahāyāna texts he is described as a great protector whom one invokes against a standardized set of perils (snakes, beasts, robbers, poisons, storms, and so forth), which are also sometimes iconographically depicted with him (See Figure 5). This apotropaic conception of Avalokiteśvara is emphasized in several early sculptures of the *bodhisattva*, which depict him as the guardian of the faithful, saving them from the same perils described in the texts. At Kanheri, for instance, in Cave 90, there is a sixth-century image of Avalokiteśvara, accompanied by the female figures Tārā and Bhṛkuṭī, along with ten perils from which he protects his devotees. It is, however, in

Figure 5 Carved sandalwood mural of Buddhas, Munsusa Monastery, South Kyongsang, Korea.

the Buddhist stronghold of the northeast that Avalokiteśvara is most prominent in sculpture.

Although he become very important in the Buddhist art of East Asia, Maitreya, the Buddha of the future, appears less frequently than either Mañjuśrī or Avalokiteśvara in Indian sculpture. Like Avalokiteśvara, Maitreya images first appear in the Gandhāra and Mathurā regions, probably dating to about the third century CE. In Indian Buddhist sculpture he typically is depicted as a crowned, royal figure (often with a Buddha image or *stūpa* in his forehead) seated on a throne. Unlike other *bodhisattvas*, he does not sit in the lotus position, but rather in what appears to be a "Western" posture, with his feet on the ground, an iconographic detail that may have been intended to convey the notion that he is ready to "step" into the world when the time has come for him to descend from the Tuṣita heaven in which he resides. He sometimes forms the "no fear" gesture (*abhayamudrā*), or the *dharmacakra mūdra*, as it is he who will deliver the final version of the *Dharma* that will release all beings from *saṃsāra*.

See also: **Art, Buddhist; *Bodhisattva* career in the Theravāda; *Bodhisattva* path; Mahāyāna Buddhism.**

JACOB N. KINNARD

BODHISATTVA CAREER IN THE THERAVĀDA

Arhats, Buddhas, and *bodhisattvas*

In the early schools, such as the Sarvāstivāda and Theravāda, Buddhas were seen as very rare in human history, and to differ from (other) *arhats* (Pāli *arahats*) mainly in that they rediscovered the liberating truth when it had been lost to human society, and had a more extensive knowledge than (other) *arhats*. Dedicated followers of the early schools generally aimed to use the Buddha's teachings to help liberate themselves from *saṃsāra*, the round of rebirths, as quickly as possible, by becoming *arhats*.

Mahāyānists, however, saw the *arhat* ideal as having insufficient compassion, for it involved leaving other beings to their fate within *saṃsāra*. As the status of a Buddha was elevated, and the gap between the state of an *arhat* and a Buddha increased, Buddhahood came to be seen as the goal that all should strive for in the Mahāyāna. The Mahāyāna or "great (spiritual) vehicle" came to be seen as superior to the Hīnayāna, or "lesser vehicle," which was a term often applied to followers of the pre-Mahāyāna schools, though in Tibet the two terms are still sometimes used simply as terms for people of different levels of motivation. The Mahāyāna saw itself as the *bodhisattva-yāna*, or "vehicle of the *bodhisattvas*," namely the way to be followed by those aiming at full Buddhahood. The *Hīnayāna* was seen to comprise: (1) the *śrāvaka-yāna*, or "vehicle of the disciples," which concerned those whose aim was to become an *arhat*, and (2) the *pratyekabuddha-yāna*, or "vehicle of the individual Buddhas," for those aiming to be non-teaching Buddhas.

That *arhats* came to be seen as somewhat selfish by the Mahāyāna may be partly a product of certain people claiming to be *arhats* who were not yet perfect. For a Theravādin, the notion that an *arhat* is selfish is absurd. Such a person is, by definition, one who has destroyed the "I am" conceit, the very root of selfishness; they are also characterized as being compassionate (*Aṅguttara Nikāya* 1.211). The best type of person is one who both works for his or her own spiritual welfare and is a good teacher of others (*Aṅguttara Nikāya* 2.95).

That said, the Mahāyāna does put compassionate concern for others in a more central place on the path than does the Theravāda and other early schools. Moreover, Theravādins acknowledge that Buddhahood is a higher goal than *arhat*ship. The Theravādin commentator Buddhaghosa says, of moral virtue: "that motivated by craving, the purpose of which is to enjoy continued existence, is inferior; that practiced for one's own deliverance is medium; the virtue of the perfections practiced for the deliverance of all beings is superior" (*Visuddhimagga* 13).

Theravādins agree that the path to Buddhahood is a longer one than that to *arhat*ship. As this world still has the Buddha's teachings to guide it, though, it is seen as appropriate for most to use these and take *arhat*ship as their highest goal, whether this be attained in the present or a later life. Thus most Theravādins can be seen to be *śrāvaka-yāna* in their level of motivation. Nevertheless the tradition also holds out the possibility, for a heroic few, of taking the long path of the *bodhisattva* so as to become a perfect Buddha. Thus while the *bodhisattva-yāna* is the normative path in the Mahāyāna, it is an optional path in the Theravāda. Theravādins may select which of three kinds of Buddhas, or awakened ones, they aspire to become: a disciple (*sāvaka*)-*buddha* or *arhat*, an individual Buddha (*pratyekabuddha*) or a *sammā-sambuddha*, a perfect Buddha who rediscovers the *Dharma* and teaches it to others. In the *Cariyāpiṭaka* commentary, one dedicated to the first of these goals is referred to as a *sāvaka-bodhisatta*, and one dedicated to the last as a great (*mahā*)-*bodhisatta*. In most contexts, though, the term *bodhisatta* refers to the latter. This term, note, was originally equivalent to Sanskrit *bodhisakta*, meaning "one bound for awakening" or "one seeking awakening," though in time it came to be Sanskritized as *bodhisattva*, a "being (for) awakening."

Gautama Buddha's *bodhisattva* career: a model for other *bodhisattvas*

In the Pāli Canon, the Buddha refers to himself as a *bodhisattva* in his life as Gautama prior to his becoming a Buddha (e.g. *Majjhima Nikāya* 1.17) and in his immediately prior life (*Majjhima Nikāya* 3.119–20, *Dīgha Nikāya* 2.108). Yet his role as a *bodhisattva* is seen to have started long before this. It is held that a "hundred thousand eons and four incalculable periods ago," in one of his past lives, Gautama was an ascetic named Sumedha (Megha in the Sanskrit *Mahāvastu* 1.193–248, Sumati in the *Divyavādāna*) who met and was inspired by a previous Buddha, Dīpaṃkara (Pāli Dīpaṅkara: "Light-maker"). As Rupert Gethin puts it, "What impressed Sumedha was Dīpaṃkara's very presence and his infinite wisdom and compassion, such that he resolved that he would do whatever was necessary to cultivate and perfect these qualities in himself". He is said to have thrown himself down in the mud so that Dīpaṃkara would not need to walk in it and resolved to strive for Buddhahood. He knew that, while he could become an *arhat* disciple of Dīpaṃkara, the path he had chosen instead would take many many lives to complete:

> 54. While I was lying on the earth it was thus in my mind: If I so wished, I could burn up my defilements [become an *arhat*] today.

55. What is the use, while I (remain) unknown, of realizing *Dharma* here? Having reached omniscience (*sabbaññuta*), I will become a Buddha in the world with its gods.

56. What is the use of my crossing over alone, being a man aware of my strength? Having reached omniscience, I will cause the world together with the gods to cross over.

57. By this my act of service (*adhikāra*) towards the supreme among men, I will reach omniscience, I will cause many people to cross over.

(*Buddhavaṃsa* IIA.54–7).

In the *Buddhavaṃsa*, to be a *bodhisattva*, one must once make a mental resolve (*mano-paṇidhāna*), then make aspirations (*abhinīhāras*) in the presence of a succession of Buddhas, perform an act of service (*adhikāra*) for each Buddha as a guarantee of one's deep seriousness of purpose, and each Buddha must make a declaration (*vyākaraṇa*) that one's aspiration will succeed. For it to do so, a person must (IIA.59): be human, a male, with a root motivation, see a Buddha, be a renunciant, have special qualities, do an act of service (*adhikāra*), and have willpower (*chandatā*). On the matter of gender, it is notable that in the Mahāyāna, where the *bodhisattva* role is not just for a heroic few, it is not restricted to males, though it is still generally said that a perfect Buddha will be male. In the Theravāda, the goal for most, *arhat*ship, can be attained by a man or woman.

Jātaka stories and developing the perfections

The ascetic Sumedha is seen to have gone on to develop his moral and spiritual qualities in many lives, in which he meets various past Buddhas. From the *Buddhavaṃsa* and other such works, at these meetings he is variously: a brahmin (six times), a warrior-noble (five times), a matted-hair ascetic (three times, including as Sumedha), a *cakravartin* emperor (twice), a serpent-deity (*nāga*) king (twice), and once each a seer, a brahmin who becomes an ascetic, a warrior-noble who becomes a seer, a district governor, a god, a nature-spirit-general, and a lion. In his last human life, he was Prince Vessantara, who is banished for giving away the state's auspicious white elephant, and then even gives away his children and wife, all to bring his generosity to perfection. His life between this and his life as Gautama was in the Tusita (Skt. Tuṣita) heaven, the realm of the "delighted" gods, said to be the realm where the *bodhisattva* Metteyya (Skt. Maitreya and Maitrī) now lives, ready for a far-distant period in human history after Buddhism has become extinct, and he can become the next Buddha (*Dīgha Nikāya* 3.76).

A rich kind of literature dealing with the lives of the *bodhisattva* who became Gautama Buddha consists of the *Jātaka* stories. The Pāli Canon *Jātaka* section contains 547 of these in verse form, and the commentarial prose expands these into a range of morality tales, which no doubt partly drew on and adapted Indian folk tales. There are also a number of post-canonical *Jātaka* tales. In such stories, the *bodhisattva* is seen as a moral hero (and sometimes a more fallible being), whether as a human, animal or god. The fact that there are 547 *Jātaka* stories is not seen to imply that the Buddha had only 547 past lives – these are seen as without number – or even 547 lives since resolving to become a Buddha.

The *Cariyāpiṭaka*, or "Basket of Conduct," is a short text (thirty-seven pages) of the Pāli Canon, one of the last to be included. This focuses on certain *Jātaka* stories (and some not traceable there) to exemplify the *bodhisattva*'s ten "perfections" (Pāli *pāramīs*, Skt. *pāramitās*) inasmuch as they were developed in the current world eon: generosity (*dāna*), moral discipline (*sīla*, Skt. *śīla*), desirelessness (*nekkhamma*, Skt. *naiṣkāmya* or *naiśkramya*, "renunciation"), wisdom (*paññā*, Skt. *prajñā*), energy (*viriya*, Skt. *vīrya*) patience (*khanti*, Skt. *kṣānti*), truthfulness (*sacca*, Skt. *satya*), resolute determination (*adhiṭṭhāna*, Skt. *adhiṣṭhāna*), lovingkindness (*mettā*, Skt. *maitrī*) and equanimity (*upekkhā*, Skt. *upekṣā*). In the Pāli Canon, this list is only found in this text and the *Buddhavaṃsa* (IIA.117–66), though its individual items are valued elsewhere in it. Each quality is said to exist as a perfection, then as a "higher perfection" (*upapāramī*), then as an "ultimate perfection" (*paramattha-pāramī*; *Buddhavaṃsa* I.77). According to the *Apadāna*, one of the latest texts of the Pāli Canon, for the first perfection, ordinary giving of things is the first of these levels; the gift of body parts, such as an eye (as in the Sivi *Jātaka*, no. 499) is the second, and the highest kind is the giving of wife and children (as in the Vessantara *Jātaka*, no. 547). The *Dīgha Nikāya* commentary (p. 427), though, sees the giving of one's life as the highest level.

Shanta Ratnayake reports that the *Cariyāpiṭaka* commentary holds that, for the *bodhisattva*, "Due to his wisdom, he becomes disentangled from *saṃsāra*, but due to his compassion he remains in it," that wisdom acts as the purifier of all the perfections, compassion is the cause, root and ground of them, and that skillful means (Pāli *upāya-kosalla*) is needed in developing them. This all, of course, parallels ideas in Mahāyāna texts.

Bodhisattvas other than Sumedha/Gautama

In the Theravāda tradition, the only well-known *bodhisattva* apart from Gautama prior to his Buddhahood is Metteyya/Maitreya. In time, however, texts developed that referred to other *bodhisattvas*. The late fourteen-century *Dasabodhisattuppattikathā*, or "Account of the Arising of Ten *Bodhisattvas*," talks in glowing terms of Metteyya and nine following *bodhisattvas*. H. Saddhatissa, who edited and translated this, sees it as very devotional in spirit and influenced by "popular Hindu and Mahāyāna practices". Much of its content is on past lives of the ten *bodhisattvas*, which are mainly on their training under Buddhas before Gautama. The names of the Buddhas that they will in future become are given as: Metteyya ("The Kindly One"), Rāma, Dhammarāja ("King of *Dharma*"), Dhammasāmi ("Lord of *Dharma*"), Nārada, Raṃsimuni ("Ray-sage"), Devadeva ("God of Gods"), Narasīha ("Lion Among Men"), Tissa, Sumaṅgala ("Good Blessing"). Of these, seven are identified as having been characters mentioned in the Pāli Canon as meeting Gautama Buddha: King Pasenadi, three brahmins (Caṅkī, Subha, Todeyya), the *asura* (jealous god) Rāhu, and two elephants, Nālāgiri, whom the Buddha tamed, and Pārileyya, whom the Buddha spent some time alone with in a forest. Metteyya is said to have been a monk named Ajita at the time of Gautama, though the *Anāgatavaṃsa*, or "Chronicle of the Future", says this will be the lay name of Metteyya in the life when he becomes a Buddha. In the Pāli Canon and its commentaries, there is actually no mention of Gautama making a "declaration" of the future Buddhahood of the person who will be the next Buddha. Such a declaration, though, is referred to in the Lokottaravādin *Mahāvastu* (3.240, 245), though without naming the person.

Other than Maitreya, of the *bodhisattvas* named in Mahāyāna texts, Avalokiteśvara or Lokanātha, "Lord of the World," was also known in Sri Lanka, though he has now evolved into the minor *deva* Nātha, whose consort is Tārā. In Thailand, which has a Chinese minority, statues of Guanyin, the Chinese form of Avalokiteśvara, are sometimes found within the precincts of Theravādin temples. The deity Viṣṇu, who in Hinduism is seen as sustainer of the universe, and as including the Buddha as one of his incarnations (*avatāras*), is seen by Buddhists in Sri Lanka as a *bodhisattva*.

As regards humans seen as *bodhisattvas*, in the late fourth century in Sri Lanka, King Buddhadāsa, who was very active in providing medical services for his people, "lived openly before the people the life that *bodhisattvas* lead and had pity for (all) beings as a father (has pity for) his children" (*Cūḷavaṃsa* XXXVII.108–9), and later King Upatissa is said to have fulfilled the ten perfections (*Cūḷavaṃsa* XXXVII.180). A tenth-century inscription of King Mahinda IV says that only *bodhisattvas* could be kings of the island. Various Burmese kings, such as Kyanzittha (1040–1113), declared themselves *bodhisattvas*, and in Thailand, King Lu T'ai (fourteenth century), author of the *Traibhūmikathā*, on Buddhist cosmology, aspired to be a Buddha. In twentieth-century Sri Lanka, the prime ministers S.W.R.D. Bandaranayake and Dudley Senanayake in the 1950s were seen by some followers as having been *bodhisattvas*. The association between kings and *bodhisattvas* relates to their role in pursuing public welfare, the link between Buddhas and *cakravartin* emperors, both being seen to be born with the "thirty-two marks of a great person," and the fact that the last human life of Gautama prior to his Buddhahood was seen to have been as Prince Vessantara.

Some Theravādin monks have also been seen or seen themselves as *bodhisattvas*. The monks of the Anurādhapura monastery at least likened the great fifth-century commentator Buddhaghosa to the *bodhisattva* Metteyya (*Cūḷavaṃsa* XXXVII.242–3), and the author of the commentary on the *Jātakas* ended his work with a vow to develop the ten perfections so as to become a Buddha. In twentieth-century Sri Lanka, venerable Doratiyāwe (*c*. 1900) refused to use certain esoteric meditation methods as they would make him a stream-enterer or an *arhat*, whereas he had vowed to become a Buddha in the future. Also the lay revivalist and reformer Anagārika Dharmapāla saw himself as a *bodhisattva*.

See also: ***Bodhisattva* path; Buddha; Buddha and *cakravartins*; Buddhas, past and future; Hagiographies; *Jātakas* and other narrative collections; *Pratyeka-buddhas*.**

PETER HARVEY

BODHISATTVA PATH

Of the various streams of doctrine and practice that eventually converged to become Mahāyāna Buddhism, perhaps the most fundamental is the notion that supreme, perfect awakening (*anuttara-saṃyaksambodhi*) is to be achieved by means of the *bodhisattva* path, and achieved not just by buddhas but by all followers of the *Dharma*. Over the course of the first four or five centuries of the Common Era, Mahāyāna Buddhists generated an increasingly rich and complex map of the *bodhisattva*'s career, incorporating and revalorizing many elements from the earlier tradition while simultaneously adding a number of crucial and distinctive innovations unique to the Mahāyāna.

Any survey of these developments must begin with the notion of the *bodhisattva* and how it was transformed and expanded by the earliest Mahāyānists. In the scriptures of early conservative Buddhism a *bodhisattva* (lit.: "an awakening-[bound] being") was a buddha-to-be: that is, a being destined to become a buddha in the present life-time or in some future one. A buddha was distinguished not just by his awakening, but especially by the fact that he was able to complete his *bodhisattva* career at a time when the *Dharma* of previous buddhas was no longer current in the world. He was able, in other words, to reassert the universal truth afresh for the benefit of all beings. This was seen as an unusual and exceedingly rare occurrence; buddhas were few and far between. At the same time, awakening was available to all. Hence the need for another category of liberated being, the *arhat*. An *arhat* was, like a buddha, fully liberated from ignorance and craving; the crucial difference was that whereas a buddha had to reinvent the wheel of the *Dharma* (in the last of his life-times as a *bodhisattva*, at least), the *arhat* achieved his or her liberation by following a buddha's teaching. By following the path of the auditor or "hearer" (*śrāvaka*), anyone could become an *arhat*, whereas only a very few could be *bodhisattvas* destined to become buddhas, for the simple reason that, by definition, there could be only one buddha in the world at any given time. The mode of practice pursued by those few who were *bodhisattvas* bound for buddhahood came to be known as the *bodhisattva-yāna* (vehicle or "conveyance") or the *bodhisattvācaryā* (career or course of practice), while parallel to that was the path or vehicle by which "auditors" (*śrāvakas*) progressed through hearing the teaching of a buddha.

This *śrāvaka-yāna* leading to *arhat*ship was the normal aspiration of all the Buddha's followers. Indeed, aspiring to become a buddha would no doubt have seemed foolish and unnecessary, if not actually presumptuous. But however much this was the conventional view, it was to be seriously challenged by the Mahāyānists, who retained the distinction between *bodhisattva* and *arhat*, but radically reoriented it with their assertion that all true disciples of the Buddha were in fact *bodhisattvas*, whether they realized it or not, as full and complete buddhahood, with its concern for the eventual liberation of all beings, was surely the only true goal of the Buddha's teaching. Failing to realize this fact, they asserted, some people would humbly pursue the lesser goal of arhatship, only to come eventually to see that they were in fact *bodhisattvas* destined for the same compassionate enlightenment as all buddhas. Others would, whether from ignorance or arrogance, think that they had achieved all there was to achieve having become *arhats*, thus stubbornly restricting themselves to achieving less than their full potential and perhaps even generating extremely negative *karma*-formations through their denigration of the Mahāyāna view and the texts expressing it. Early Mahāyāna texts like the *Aṣṭasāhasrikāprajñāpāramitā* and the earliest strata of the *Lotus* or *Saddharmapuṇḍarīka Sūtra* tended to depict *śrāvakas* and *arhats* sympathetically and optimistically as simply having not *yet* seen that they were destined to become *bodhisattvas* and buddhas, whereas later Mahāyāna works typically take a more polemical stance, the exclusive superiority of the *bodhisattva* path over all other paths being seen now as the product of the most spiritually insidious and debilitating delusion. As the *bodhisattva* ideal evolved, the notion of the *arhat* not only became redundant, but came to represent the very problem that was to be avoided.

But what was it that distinguished the *bodhisattva* from the *śrāvaka*, and ultimately the buddha from the *arhat*? The difference lay, more than anywhere else, in the altruistic orientation of the *bodhisattva*. Only in the fulfillment of this aspiration or vow (*praṇidhāna*) was it possible, the Mahāyāna scriptures asserted, for the Great Compassion (*mahākaruṇā*) of the buddhas to be realized. This was the critical turning point on the spiritual path, the point where the *bodhisattva* path departed decisively from that of the *śrāvakas*. So crucial was that turn, that the early Mahāyānists flagged it clearly with their notion of the arising of the *bodhicitta*, the "awakening-mind," by which they meant specifically the arising of the aspiration to seek awakening not just for oneself but for the benefit of all sentient beings. It was this that launched one on the *bodhisattva* path, and the inspiration came from the qualities and virtues manifested by the Buddha himself.

These spiritual qualities of the Buddha, which inspired the early Mahāyānists even more than the doctrinal content of his teaching, were identified in the early literature as the "perfections" (*pāramī* or *pāramitā*) he had cultivated over many previous lifetimes, and it was they that became, along with the notion of the *bodhicitta*, the foundation for the *bodhisattva* path. While present in all the early scriptures, they were especially the focus of the *Jātaka* tales, which told stories of the Buddha's earlier lives, including the positive qualities he cultivated on the path to his eventual buddhahood. So central are these "perfections" or virtues in the *Jātaka* stories, and so popular were they among lay Buddhists, that their popularity has become one of the key arguments for seeing the Mahāyāna as a lay-oriented or lay-inspired form of early Buddhists. But the full-time practitioners, or at least some of them, whether forest-dwelling meditators or monastery-bound textual redactors, would have had just as much reason to be inspired by these qualities, and it is much more likely they who formulated this innovative *bodhisattva* ideal and they who wrote the texts to support it.

From the various early lists of the Buddha's qualities and virtues, they fashioned a progressive list of six that eventually became the core of the *bodhisattva*'s practice. Beginning with generosity (*dāna*) and morality (*śīla*), the *bodhisattva* lays the foundation for forbearing patience (*kṣānti*) and vigor (*vīrya*), which in turn makes possible the meditative absorption (*dhyāna*) that culminates in *prajñā*, a nonconceptual, direct insight into the nature of existence. Whereas the conservative tradition most typically characterized the goal of liberation in negative terms, seeing it as the elimination of the psychological and spiritual defilements driving continual rebirth in *saṃsāra*, the Mahāyāna was inclined to emphasize what they took as the positive counterpart to that same soteriological process. And of all the positive virtues, it was the *prajñā* insight into the nonsubstantiality of all "things" that they saw as the most important. The latter was, in their view, inseparable from a life of skillfully compassionate activity undertaken for the benefit of all beings. Eventually four additional *bodhisattva* perfections or virtues were added to the path of practice so that the sequence corresponded to the ten *bodhisattva* stages or "grounds." As the earliest *Prajñāpāramitā Sūtras* repeatedly stress, however, it is *prajñā* that is both the source and the ultimate culmination of all the other virtues. Indeed, *Prajñāpāramitā*, personified as the goddess of transformative wisdom or insight, became for the Mahāyānist the "mother of all buddhas."

Along with the notion of the *bodhisattva* virtues, the Mahāyāna also retained other elements of the early conservative soteriology, in particular the catalog of basic *Dharma* practices summarized by the Buddha shortly before his death and subsequently known as the thirty-seven *bodhipakṣya dharmas* or "factors conducive to awakening." These comprised the four stations of mindfulness (*smṛtyupasthāna*), the four abandonments (*prahāṇa*), the four types of supernatural power (*ṛddhipāda*), the five moral faculties (*indriya*), the five spiritual strengths (*bala*), the seven components of awakening (*bodhyaṅga*), and the Noble Eightfold Path (*āryamārga*). But even while retaining many of the earliest practices, the Mahāyānists did not hesitate to expand their own, more positively framed formulations. With the *Daśabhūmika Sūtra* we come to a more distinctly Mahāyāna depiction of the path, divided now into the ten stages or "grounds" (*bhūmi*) from which the *sūtra* takes its name. Developed most likely from an earlier list of seven stages and occurring with later variations, this Mahāyāna teaching seeks to outline the path of the *bodhisattva* in its entirety. The *Daśabhūmika* formulation enumerates the *bhūmis* as:

1 The *Pramuditā* or Joyful Stage, where the *bodhisattva* perfects the virtue of generosity (*dāna*), while rejoicing in *bodhi* and in his aspiration to be of benefit to all sentient beings.
2 The *Vimalā* or Immaculate Stage, where the *bodhisattva* perfects the virtue of morality (*śīla*), becoming free of all afflictions and impurities.
3 The *Prabhākarī* or Luminous Stage, where the *bodhisattva* perfects the virtue of patience (*kṣānti*) while bringing the light of his insight to all the world.
4 The *Arciṣmatī* or Radiant Stage, where the *bodhisattva* perfects vigor (*vīrya*) and the thirty-seven *bodhipakṣya dharmas*, while burning away ignorance and craving.
5 The *Sudurjayā* or Difficult-to-Conquer Stage, where the *bodhisattva* perfects his or her meditative absorption (*dhyāna*) and understanding of the Four Noble Truths, becoming increasingly impervious to the attacks of Māra, the tempter.
6 The *Abhimukī* or Face-to-Face Stage, where the *bodhisattva* perfects direct insight (*prajñā*) into the principle of conditionality (*pratītyasamutpāda*), standing now "face-to-face" with enlightenment.
7 The *Dūraṅgamā* or Far-going Stage, where the *bodhisattva* perfects the virtue of skillful means (*upāya*), established now at the pinnacle of existence (*bhūtakoṭi*) and able to help all beings effectively; with the culmination of this stage the *bodhisattva* becomes "irreversible," assured of reaching the ultimate goal.
8 The *Acalā* or Immovable Stage, where the *bodhisattva* perfects the virtue of aspiration (*praṇidhāna*), choosing to manifest at will wherever need is the greatest, and unmoved by thoughts of phenomena or of their emptiness.
9 The *Sādhumatī* or Stage of Good Intelligence, where the *bodhisattva* perfects the virtue of strength (*bāla*), while acquiring the four modes of analytical knowledge (*pratisaṃvid*).
10 The *Dharmameghā* or Cloud-of-the-*Dharma* Stage, where the *bodhisattva* perfects the virtue of wisdom (*jñāna*), acquiring a radiant body replete with jewels, able now to manifest multiple bodies and other magical powers in service of benefiting sentient beings.

There are other arrangements of the stages of the *bodhisattva* path, some identifying as many as fifty-two steps, but the last important addition to the Mahāyāna effort to map the *bodhisattva* path comes with the incorporation into the Mahāyāna of the Sarvāstivādin doctrine of the fivefold path. In its Mahāyāna formulation this schema begins with the Path of Accumulation (*saṃbhāramārga*), initiated by the arising of the *bodhicitta* and involving one's initial practice of all the perfections. Next comes the Path of Preparation (*prayogamārga*), which consists in cultivating a deeper understanding of emptiness (*śūnyatā*). This culminates in the Path of Vision (*darśanamārga*), the third step, which is characterized by a direct experience of *prajñā* insight and marks the beginning of the *bodhisattva*'s practice of the first of the ten stages outlined above. Fourth is the Path of Cultivation or Development (*bhāvanamārga*), which consists in fully traversing the ten stages. And finally comes the Stage of No-more-Learning (*aśaikṣamārga*), which constitutes full and complete Buddhahood.

See also: **Bodhisattvas; India, Buddhism in; Mahāyāna Buddhism.**

ALAN SPONBERG

BÖN

In traditional Buddhist histories, the Bönpo (practitioners of Bön) commonly appear as the enemies of the *Dharma*, who are said to have been primarily responsible for the initial obstacles it encountered in Tibet. In early dynastic histories, the Bönpo are priests of the royal cult, whose main responsibilities were performance of rituals for the health and well-being of the kings and overseeing their funeral rites. Prior to the introduction of Buddhism to Tibet, there does not seem to have been an organized religion of "Bön" aside from this royal cult, and it was only after Tibet's loosely organized indigenous religious practitioners were confronted with a rival system that the religion of Bön began to develop.

Lacking a canon, the Bönpos appropriated literature from Tibetan Buddhism, and changed some of the terminology and doctrines. The Bönpos, however, assert that their religion was established before Buddhism and that Buddhists borrowed their scriptures. They claim that their founder was a sage named Dönpa Shenrap (sTon pa gshen rab, "Supreme Holy Man"), who brought Bön to Tibet from Takzik (rTag gzigs, which appears to roughly correspond to Persia) by way of Shangshung (Zhang zhung, probably an area of western Tibet with Mount Kailash at its center). He is said by Bönpos to be superior to Śākyamuni Buddha, whose doctrine was borrowed from Shenrap's.

The focus of traditional Bön ritual and practice was the indigenous gods and spirits of Tibet. Many Bön practices are concerned with propitiating and subduing malevolent forces and with protecting people from their destructive power. In recent decades, however, the Bön tradition in exile has been undergoing an image makeover, and many of the old shamanistic Bön priests have been replaced by younger monastics whose outward appearance and religious practices closely parallel those of mainstream Tibetan Buddhism. Contemporary Bönpos generally deny that this is actually a change in the tradition, however; rather, they claim that they are returning to the original teachings and practices of Shenrap, which became corrupted (largely as a result of the malevolent influence of Tibetan Buddhism). Bönpos commonly distinguish three types of Bön: (1) the old Bön, which emphasized shamanistic and animistic practices; (2) the new or reformed Bön, which focuses on study and oral debate, along with meditation; and (3) "swastika Bön" (*gyung drung bon*), the "eternal Bön" taught by Shenrap.

The term *bön* has roughly the same range of meanings for Bönpos that *chos* (Skt. *dharma*) has for Tibetan Buddhists. It refers to the teachings and practices of the tradition, and is associated with truth and reality. In Bön scholastic philosophy, it also refers to the basic constituents of the universe, which in combinations constitute the phenomena of experience. Like Tibetan Buddhists, the Bönpos divide their canon into two sections, Translations of Teachings (*bKa' 'gyur*) and Translations of Treatises (*bsTan 'gyur*). The former contains the teachings of Shenrap, and the latter comprises commentarial treatises and philosophical and cosmological texts. Many of these are nearly identical to works in the Tibetan Buddhist canon, with Bön terms substituted for Buddhist ones (e.g. *bön* for *chos*).

See also: **Tibet, Buddhism in.**

JOHN POWERS

BOROBUDUR

Borobudur is a massive pyramid-shaped *stūpa* located in a volcanic region on the Indonesian island of Java. It was built in the late eighth and early ninth centuries by the Sailendra kings of central Java, and was rather mysteriously abandoned only a century or so after its completion.

The temple is built in the shape of a huge lotus, and is composed of six rectangular stories, with three circular terraces around a central *stūpa*. This is truly one of the most impressive monuments not only in Buddhism but in the world, presenting, essentially, a physical model of the entire cosmos, one that allows the worshipper to traverse the Mahāyāna path in a condensed manner.

The *stūpa* is nearly 100 feet tall, and the square base has sides which are nearly 400 feet long. The sheer number of artistic images at Borobudur is staggering: there are nearly 1,500 narrative panels, from the *Jātakas*, *Avadānas*, and other sources; there are over 1,200 decorative panels; the monument has some 500 Buddha images and nearly 1,500 *stūpas*.

Borobodur seems to present a microcosm, albeit a massive one, of the world, allowing the worshipper to go on physical pilgrimage that mimics the religious journey laid out by Buddhism. The lower part of the monument has five levels, diminishing in size as they go up. The sides of each of the first four levels have sculpture galleries around the sides, with stairs on all four sides, linking all levels of the monument. The worshipper begins by going through four galleries adorned with various images and *Jātaka* and *Avadāna* scenes, and then entering a terrace with seventy-two *stūpas*, each of which houses an image of the Buddha, arranged in three concentric circles surrounding the much larger central *stūpa*.

In much the same way that a *maṇḍala* offers a kind of visual pilgrimage, Borobudur – which is itself laid out as a kind of three-dimensional *maṇḍala* – can be seen as a physical monument that allows the pilgrim to follow the course of enlightenment. Thus as one slowly circumambulates the monument, moving around and up, the narrative panels allow one to visually move from the world of base desires and impulses, where humans are bound by their greed and lust; the pilgrim would then ascend to the next level, where there are images of the form realm where these desires are controlled but one is still bound to the material world; finally, in the next level of the monument, there are images of the formless realm, the realm of freedom from such hindrances. Indeed, of the nearly 500 panels on the upper three levels of the monument, about a third present scenes from the *Gaṇḍavyūha*. This important text, part of the larger *Avataṃsaka* (Flower Ornament) *Sūtra*, narrates the pilgrimage of a young man named Sudhana as he travels from teacher to teacher in search of enlightenment. Sudhana's journey illustrates the importance of gaining wisdom and compassion before one is able to reach enlightenment. What one clearly sees at Borobudur, then, is the degree to which Buddhist art has not only a decorative function, but an instructive one – the panels, essentially, visually guide one on his or her physical and religious pilgrimage.

See also: **Art, Buddhist; Sacred places.**

JACOB N. KINNARD

BUDDHA

This entry focuses on how the nature of a Buddha was understood in the early texts of Buddhism, typified by the Pāli Canon, rather than on the story of the historical Buddha, which is the subject of another entry, or on developed ideas on the nature of Buddhas in the Mahāyāna, on which see Buddha, bodies of, and Mahāyāna Buddhism (main survey article).

The term "Buddha" is not a proper name, but a descriptive title meaning "Awakened One" or "Enlightened One." This implies that most people are seen, in a spiritual sense, as being asleep – unaware of how things really are. As "Buddha" is a title, it should not be used as a name, as in, for example, "Buddha taught that ... " In many contexts, "the

Buddha" is specific enough, meaning the Buddha known to history, Gautama (Pāli Gotama). From its earliest times, though, the Buddhist tradition has postulated other Buddhas who have lived on earth in distant past ages, or who will do so in the future. The Mahāyāna tradition also postulated the existence of many Buddhas currently existing in other parts of the universe. All such Buddhas, known as *samyak-sambuddhas* (Pāli *sammā-sambuddhas*), or "perfect fully Awakened Ones," are nevertheless seen as occurring only rarely within the vast and ancient cosmos. More common are those who are "buddhas" in a lesser sense, who have awakened to the truth by practicing in accordance with the guidance of a perfect Buddha such as Gautama: *arhat*s (Pāli *arahats*). There are also said to be *pratyekabuddhas* (Pāli *paccekabuddhas*), "individual Buddhas" who attain enlightenment without the benefit of a perfect Buddha's teaching, and who give no systematic teachings themselves.

As "Buddha" does not refer to a unique individual, Buddhism is less focused on the person of its founder than is, for example, Christianity. The emphasis in Buddhism is on the *teachings* of the Buddha(s), and the "awakening" of human personality that these are seen to lead to. Nevertheless, Buddhists do show great reverence to Gautama as a supreme teacher and an exemplar of the ultimate goal that all strive for, so that probably more images of him exist than of any other historical figure.

The key role of a perfect Buddha is, by his own efforts, to rediscover the timeless truths and practices of *Dharma* (Pāli *Dhamma*) at a time when they have been lost to society (*Aṅguttara Nikāya* 1.286–7). Having discovered it for himself, he skillfully makes it known to others so that they can fully practice it for themselves and so become *arhats* (*Majjhima Nikāya* 3.8). Teaching *Dharma*, he initiates a spiritual community of those committed to *Dharma*: the four assemblies (Skt. *pariṣats*, Pāli *parisās*) consisting of the monastic community (*sangha*) of monks and nuns, and laymen and laywomen followers. Any of these who gains true insight into *Dharma* becomes a member of the Noble *Sangha* (stream-enterers, once-returners, non-returners and *arhats*). As founder of a monastic *sangha* and propounder of the rules of conduct binding on its members, a Buddha also fulfils a role akin to that of "law-giver."

As to gender, the early texts say that while a woman can be an *arhat*, it is impossible for her to be an *arhat* who is also a perfect Buddha (*Majjhima Nikāya* 3.65–6, *Aṅguttara Nikāya* 1.28), just as a female cannot be a *cakravartin* ruler, a Śakra (Pāli Sakka) – chief of the thirty-three gods of the Vedic pantheon – a great Brahmā deity, or a Māra, an evil tempter-deity. Gender is something that can change between rebirths, however. The Theravādin tradition also saw it as necessary for a person to be male to be a *bodhisattva*, one heroically aiming at perfect Buddhahood. The Mahāyāna thought otherwise, though it had different views on the level of advanced bodhisattva-hood that could be attained while in a female body, and sometimes held that a woman could be a perfect Buddha.

The process of becoming a Buddha is seen to take many lives of dedicated practice. It is held that "a hundred thousand eons and four incalculable periods ago," in one of his past lives, Gautama was an ascetic named Sumedha (in some Sanskrit texts, Megha or Sumati) who met and was inspired by a previous Buddha, Dīpaṃkara (Pāli Dīpaṅkara). He therefore resolved to strive for Buddhahood, by becoming a *bodhisattva* (Pāli bodhisatta), a being (*sattva*) who is dedicated to attaining perfect enlightenment (*bodhi*) (*Buddhavaṃsa* ch. 2). He knew that, while he could soon become an enlightened disciple of Dīpaṃkara, an *arhat*, the path he had chosen instead would take many lives to complete. It would, however, culminate in his becoming a perfect Buddha, one who would bring benefit to countless beings by rediscovering and teaching the timeless truths of *Dharma* in a period when they had been forgotten by the human race. He then spent many lives, as a human, animal and god, building up the moral and spiritual perfections necessary for Buddhahood. Some of these lives are described in what are known as *Jātaka* stories, of which there are 537 in the Theravādin collection (canonical verses plus commentarial prose expansion). Over the ages, he also met other past Buddhas. In his penultimate life he was born in the Tuṣita (Pāli Tusita) heaven, the realm of the "delighted" gods. This is said to be the realm where the *bodhisattva* Maitreya/Maitrī (Pāli Metteyya) now lives, ready for a future period in human history long after Buddhism has become extinct, when he will become the next Buddha (*Dīgha Nikāya* 2.76).

Epithets of the Buddha

In the *suttas* (Skt. *sūtras*) of the Pāli Canon, the most common way of referring to the Buddha is as *Bhagavat* (stem form) or *Bhagavā* (nominative form); the *suttas* frequently say, near their start, "At one time the *Bhagavā* was staying at . . . " The term *Bhagavā* is variously translated as: "Blessed One," "Exalted One," "Fortunate One," "Lord." It implies one who is full of good qualities. A common refrain on the qualities of the Buddha (for example *Dīgha Nikāya* 2.93), now often chanted in a devotional context, is:

> Thus he is the *Bhagavā*, because he is an *arhat*, perfectly and completely awakened (*sammā-sambuddho*), endowed with knowledge and (good) conduct, well-gone (*sugato*), knower of worlds, an incomparable charioteer for the training of persons, teacher of gods and humans, Buddha, *Bhagavā*.

The term *Tathāgata* is used by the Buddha to refer to himself in his nature as an enlightened being, for example "A *Tathāgata* knows . . . " It is not used when he is giving details of his life as the individual Gautama. *Tathāgata* literally means either "Thus-gone" or "Thus-come." The "thus" alludes to the true nature of reality, truth. *Dīgha Nikāya* 3.135 explains a *Tathāgata* as: he speaks factually and at a suitable time; he is fully awakened to all that any being experiences; from the time of his awakening, all he says is "exactly so" (*tath'eva* – "just thus"); "as he speaks, so he does (*tathā-kārī*), as he does, so he speaks (*tathā-vādī*)."

Buddha: human, god, or . . . ?

While modern Theravādins sometimes say that the Buddha was "just a human," such remarks have to be taken in context. They are usually intended to contrast the Buddha with Jesus, seen as the "Son of God," and to counter the Mahāyāna view of the Buddha's nature, which sees it as far above the human. These remarks may also be the result of a somewhat demythologized view of the Buddha. In the Pāli Canon, Gautama was seen as *born* a human, though one with extraordinary abilities because of the perfections built up in his long *bodhisattva* career. Although once he had attained enlightenment, he could no longer be called a "human," as he had perfected and transcended his humanness. This idea is reflected in a *sutta* passage where the Buddha was asked whether he was a god (*deva*) or a human (*Aṅguttara Nikāya* 2.37–9). In reply, he said that he had gone beyond the deep-rooted unconscious taints (Skt. *aśravas*, Pāli *āsavas*) that would make him a god or human – a god being merely a being in one of the higher realms of rebirth – and was therefore to be seen as a buddha, one who had grown up in the world but who had now gone beyond it, as a lotus grows from the water but blossoms above it unsoiled.

The *suttas* do contain some very "human" information on the Buddha, though. It is said that he was once teaching a group of laypeople "till far into the night." After they retire, he asks Śāripūtra (Pāli Sāriputta) to teach the monks, as "My back aches, I want to stretch it," and then retires to sleep (*Dīgha Nikāya* 3.209). In the *Mahāparinibbāna Sutta* (*Dīgha Nikāya Sutta* 16), we find the eighty-year-old Buddha expressing "weariness" at the prospect of being asked about the rebirth-destiny of each and every person who has died in a locality (*Dīgha Nikāya* 2.93), saying,

> I am old, worn out . . . Just as an old cart is made to go by being held together with straps, so the *Tathāgata*'s body is kept going by being strapped up. It is only when the *Tathāgata* . . . enters into the signless meditative concentration that his body knows comfort.
>
> (2.100)

In his final illness, he is extremely thirsty, insisting that there be no delay in his being given water to drink (2.128–9) the stream he asks for it from is found to be clear even though recently churned up by many passing carts).

Elsewhere in the same text miraculous details about him are reported, as when he crosses the Ganges by his psychic power (2.89). He states that if he had been asked, he would have had the power to live on "for a *kalpa* (Pāli *kappa*), or the remainder of one" (2.103), with *kalpa* generally meaning "eon," but possibly here meaning the maximum human life-span at that time, of around 100 years. The causes of earthquakes are said to include key events in the Buddha's life: his conception; birth; enlightenment; first sermon; giving up any remaining will to live, in his final illness; and his passing into final *nirvāṇa* at death (2.108–9). Again, on the nights of his enlightenment and final *nirvāṇa*, he has very clear and bright skin, whose shining nature made golden robes look dull in comparison (2.133–4), and when he lies down between two *sāl*-trees, where he will die, these burst into unseasonal blossom in homage to him, and divine music is heard in the sky (2.137–8). Finally, after his death, the text reports that the gods prevent his funeral pyre from igniting until the senior disciple Mahā-kāśyapa (Pāli Mahā-kassapa) arrives at the site (2.163).

The above material suggests a transcendence which emerges *from* and yet goes *beyond* the human condition. This is perhaps another case of a Buddhist "middle way" avoiding two extremes: neither simply a human nor solely transcendent. That said, one of the early schools, the Lokottaravādins, or "Transcendentalists," had a different view. One of their surviving texts is the *Mahāvastu*, which grew over a number of centuries, perhaps beginning in the late second century BCE. While its outlook has often been seen as foreshadowing certain Mahāyāna ideas, it has itself been shown to incorporate whole passages from early Mahāyāna scriptures, and may have been influenced by Mahāyāna concepts up to as late as the fifth century CE. It sees Gautama as "transcendental" even before his Buddhahood. He leaves the Tuṣita heaven in a mind-made body to bestow his blessings on the world, and though highly spiritually developed he pretends to start from the beginning, making "mistakes" such as asceticism (*Mahāvastu* 1.169–70). As a Buddha, he is an omniscient being who is ever in meditation. No dust sticks to his feet, and he is never tired. He eats out of mere conformity with the world, and so as to give others a chance to make much good *karma* by giving him alms food. For such a world-transcending being, it was felt that all incidents in his life must have occurred for a special reason. The *Mahāvastu* thus gives much attention to the Buddha's biography, and also includes many *Jātaka* tales on his past lives. In examining his development to Buddhahood, a series of ten stages of the *bodhisattva* career were outlined. This idea was also important in the Mahāyāna, though the details are different. Unlike the Mahāyāna, the Transcendentalists still saw the goal for most people as *arhat*ship, the way of the *bodhisattva* being only for extraordinary individuals.

The Buddha's psychic powers and extra-sensory perception

While Jesus is more often associated with so-called "miraculous" wonders than the Buddha, these are also attributed to him. In gaining hearers for his message, the Buddha did not always rely on his charisma, reputation and powers of persuasion. Psychic powers are not seen as supernatural miracles, but as the supernormal products of the great inner power of certain meditations. A late canonical passage (*Paṭisambhidāmagga* 1.125) describes his "marvel of the pairs," which later legendary material ascribes to the Buddha while staying at Śrāvastī (Pāli Sāvatthī; *Dhammapada commentary* 3.204–16). This describes a public challenge in which the Buddha was asked to display his psychic powers in the hope that he would abstain and thus appear to lack such abilities. He therefore agreed to meet the challenge at a later date, when he rose into the air and produced both fire and water from different parts of his body. Occasionally, the Buddha is said to have used his powers for physically healing a devout supporter, such as bringing a long and very painful childbirth to an end (*Udāna* 15–16), or curing a wound without leaving even a scar (*Vinaya* 1.216–18). However, he made it an offence for monks to display psychic powers to laypeople (*Vinaya* 2.112), and saw teaching as a much better way to influence others than such a means (*Dīgha Nikāya* 1.211–14). He generally regarded psychic powers as dangerous, as they could encourage attachment and self-glorification. In a strange parallel to the temptation of Jesus in the desert, it is said that he rebuffed Māra's temptation to turn the Himālayas into gold (*Saṃyutta Nikāya* 1.116).

The *suttas* not infrequently refer to a set list of psychic powers (Skt. *ṛddhis*, Pāli *iddhi*s), including walking on water, flying, and multiplication of one's bodily form (for example *Dīgha Nikāya* 1.77–8), which may be developed on the basis of attainment of meditative *dhyāna* (Pāli *jhāna*). Maudgalyāyana (Pāli Moggallāna), one of the Buddha's two chief disciples, was famed for such powers. *Dīgha Nikāya* 1.77 describes a related power of generating a mind-made body (*manomaya-kāya*). Not surprisingly, the Buddha is attributed with all these powers, and in one passage he says that he could carry out all the forms of psychic power either with his mind-made body or with his normal body composed of the physical elements (*Saṃyutta Nikāya* 5.282–3).

Dīgha Nikāya 1.79–80 also describes two forms of extra-sensory perception: hearing sounds at great distances – whether human or divine – and reading the minds of others. Such powers are often described as being used by the Buddha, as when reporting what a god says, or reporting what "someone might think" when a person in his audience had just thought this, before going on to carefully respond to such a line of thinking. It is said that mind-reading is carried out by one of four ways: by noting visible signs; by noting sounds, human or divine; by noting something implied by sound; or by probing someone's mind, to see what he or she thought (Skt. *vitarka*, Pāli *vitakka*) they will have next, while one is oneself in second *dhyāna* (a state free of *vitarka*) (*Dīgha Nikāya* 3.103–4)

Overall, the attitude to such wonders in the Pāli Canon is: they are real possibilities for human beings to develop; they may be spiritually useful in aiding others; but they should not be sought for their own sake, and a person may become attached to them if they are not careful.

Did the Buddha claim to be omniscient? (Skt. *sarva-jña*, Pāli *sabba-ññū*)?

In one passage, the Buddha *denies* that he teaches, "There is no renunciant or brahmin who is omniscient (*sabba-ññū*) and all-seeing (*sabba-dassāvī*), who can have complete knowledge and vision; that is not possible" (*Majjhima Nikāya* 2.126–7). Rather, he teaches, "There is no renunciant or brahmin who knows all, who sees all, *simultaneously*; that is not possible." Accordingly, in another *sutta*, the Buddha does *not* accept that "The renunciant Gautama claims to be omniscient and all-seeing, to have complete knowledge and vision thus: 'Whether I am walking or standing or sleeping or awake, knowledge and vision are continuously and uninterruptedly present to me.'" Rather, what he *does* claim is the "threefold knowledge" (Skt. *traividyā*, Pāli *tevijjā*) – as experienced on the night of his enlightenment – that he could: "in so far as I wish," remember his past lives; "in so far as I wish," see beings being reborn according to their *karma*, and directly know his state of liberation (*Majjhima Nikāya* 1.482).

The *suttas* attribute the claim to *continuous* omniscience (as expressed above) to Mahāvira, the Jain leader, though they also say that he prevaricated when actually asked a question (*Majjhima Nikāya* 2.31). Ānanda also jokes that some teachers make this claim yet have to ask people's names, fail to get alms food, and get bitten by dogs – so that they then cover themselves by saying that they knew these events were destined, so did not avoid them (*Majjhima Nikāya* 1.519).

At *Aṅguttara Nikāya* 2.25, the Buddha says:

> Monks, in the world with its gods, *māras*, and *brahmās*, in this generation with its renunciants and brahmins, gods and humans, whatever is seen, heard, sensed, and cognized, attained, searched into, pondered over by the mind – all that do I know . . . I fully understand.

Admittedly, the terms "omniscient" or "all-seeing" are not included in the list of 100 or so epithets of the Buddha uttered ecstatically by the householder Upāli (*Majjhima Nikāya* 1.386–7). Nevertheless, within certain late texts of the Pāli Canon, the Buddha is referred to as omniscient and/or all-seeing (*Paṭisambhidāmagga* 1.131, 133, 174, *Buddhavaṃsa* IIA.57, *Kathāvatthu* III.1), and in line with such passages, the postcanonical Theravādin *Milindapañha* (p. 102) (which the Burmese include in the Pāli Canon) says:

> The Lord was omniscient, but knowledge-and-vision was not constantly and continuously present to the Lord. The Lord's omniscient knowledge was dependent on the adverting (of his mind); when he adverted to it he knew whatever it pleased (him) to know, being able to do this quicker than someone opening or closing their eyes.
>
> (p. 106)

The Sarvāstivādin *Abhidharmakośabhāṣya* (ch. 9) says much the same, though it refers to the Mahāsaṃghikas as holding that a Buddha *can* know all *dharma*s in one instant.

That said, the above claims relate to the Buddha once he was actually a Buddha, not before this, during his spiritual quest. Moreover, the "threefold knowledge," as the key example of the Buddha's knowledge, says little about the future other than knowledge of how particular beings will be reborn. At *Dīgha Nikāya* 3.134, when the issue of whether the Buddha's great knowledge extends to the future is raised, he claims that it does; but the example of such knowledge that is given is that he knows that he will have no further rebirths. In other contexts, though, the Buddha claims to know things in the distant future, such as that the next Buddha, in a golden age in the distant future, will be Metteyya (Sanskrit Maitreya; *Dīgha Nikāya* 3.76). This, though, could be construed as based on knowledge of the current spiritual maturity of Maitreya, and of the long time between any two Buddhas in the past. The Buddha being seen as having a kind of omniscience is of course a ground for Buddhists trusting his teaching.

Buddha-fields

Early Buddhism contained the idea that there are countless worlds spread out through space (e.g. *Aṅguttara Nikāya* 1.227). The Theravādin commentator Buddhaghosa refers (*Visuddhimagga* 414) to these in its idea of different kinds of "Buddha-fields" (Skt. *Buddha-kṣetras*, Pāli *Buddha-khettas*): the field of birth, consisting of the 10,000 worlds that quaked at the Buddha's birth; the field of his authority, consisting of many hundreds of thousands of worlds where various *parittas*, or protective chants of his, have power, and the field of his range of knowledge, which is immeasurable. In the Mahāyāna, there developed the idea that heavenly Buddhas create their own Buddha-fields as ideal realms in which to attain awakening.

The Buddha and other *arhats*

In the early Buddhist texts, the Buddha is himself said to be an *arhat* (Pāli *arahat*) and to be in most respects like any other *arhat* ("worthy one"): one who has destroyed attachment, hatred and delusion and the rebirth they lead to, and fully experienced *nirvāṇa* in life. Any *arhat*'s experience of *nirvāṇa* is the same; however, a perfect Buddha is seen as having more extensive knowledge than other *arhats*. For example, he can remember as far back into previous lives as he wants, while other *arhats* have limitations on such a power, or may not even have developed it. What he teaches is just a small portion of his huge knowledge (*Saṃyutta Nikāya* 5.438), for he only teaches what is both true and spiritually useful (*Majjhima Nikāya* 1.395). Moreover, a perfect Buddha is someone who, by his own efforts, rediscovers the *Dharma* and teaches it anew when it has previously been lost to society. Other *arhats* can then teach based on their own experiential understanding, but this is gained from practicing under the guidance of a perfect Buddha.

The Buddha and *Dharma*

Of the three refuges, Buddha, *Dharma* and *Sangha*, the first two are particularly closely related. The Buddha chides a monk who had too much uncritical faith in him, so as to be always following him round: "Hush, Vakkali! What is there for you in seeking this vile visible body? Vakkali, whoever sees *Dharma*, sees me; whoever sees me, sees *Dharma*" (*Saṃyutta Nikāya* 3.120). This close link between the Buddha and *Dharma* is reinforced by another *sutta* passage, which says that a *Tathāgata* can be designated as "one who has *Dharma* as body" (*Dhamma-kāya*) and as "*Dharma*-become" (*Dhamma-bhūta*) (*Dīgha Nikāya* 3.84). These terms indicate that a Buddha has fully exemplified the *Dharma*, in the sense of the Path, in his personality or "body": he embodies it. Moreover, he has fully realized *Dharma* in the supreme sense by his experience of *nirvāṇa*, the equivalent of the supreme *Dharma*: *Aṅguttara Nikāya* 1.156 and 158 have parallel passages on the *Dharma* refuge and *nirvāṇa*, as "visible here and now, timeless, inviting investigation, leading onward, to be experienced individually by the wise." The *arhat* is no different in these respects, for he is described as "become the supreme" (*brahma-bhūta*) (*Saṃyutta Nikāya* 3.83), a term which is used as an equivalent to "*Dharma*-become" in the above passage. Any enlightened person, Buddha or *arhat*, is one who is "deep, immeasurable, hard-to-fathom as is the great ocean" (*Majjhima Nikāya* 1.487). Having "become *Dharma*," their enlightened nature can only really be fathomed by one who has "seen" *Dharma* with the "*Dharma*-eye" of stream-entry. While Christians see Jesus as God-become-human, then, Buddhists see the Buddha (and *arhats*) as human-become-*Dharma.*

The commentary (2.314) on the above *Saṃyutta Nikāya* 3.120 says:

> Here the Blessed One shows *Dharma*-body-ness, as stated in the passage, "The *Tathāgata*, great king, has *Dharma* as body. For the ninefold supramundane *Dharma* is called the *Tathāgata*'s body." Here, the supramundane *Dharma* refers to *nirvāṇa* along with the four "path" and four "fruit" experiences that know it in the eight kinds of Noble persons.

In the *Milindapañha*, it is explained (p. 73), that while it is not possible to point out where the Buddha is after his death, "it is possible ... to point to the Lord by means of the *Dharma*-body; for *Dharma* ... was taught by the Lord." Buddhaghosa also says of the Buddha, "whose *Dharma*-body brought to perfection the treasured qualities of the aggregates of virtue etc. [concentration, wisdom, freedom and knowledge and understanding]" (*Visuddhimagga* 234). Thus the Buddha is seen as very closely related to the *Dharma* that he taught and practiced, and which in the highest sense is *nirvāṇa*, the unconditioned.

The thirty-two marks of a great man

The *Lakkhaṇa Sutta* (*Dīgha Nikāya, Sutta* 30; 3.142–79) describes "thirty-two marks or characteristics (Skt. *lakṣaṇas*, Pāli *lakkhaṇas*) of a great man (Skt. *mahā-puruṣa*, Pāli *mahā-purisa*)" that the Gautama was seen as born with. These were held to foretell a future as either a Buddha or a *cakravartin* (Pāli *cakkavatti*), a compassionate emperor, ruling the world according to the ethical values of the *Dharma*. The concept of such marks is said to have been referred to in the Brahmanic tradition (*Dīgha Nikāya* 1.88, 2.16, *Majjhima Nikāya* 2.134, *Suttanipāta* vv. 999–1003 and p. 106), and Jain texts (see Mahāvīra, the founder/reformer of Jainism, as having had them). One might see the "marks" as intended as either as physical in the normal sense, or as aspects of a "spiritual" body which only sensitive people could sense. Each mark is said to be caused by a particular excellence in a past life, and to be indicative of a particular quality of the life of a Buddha or *cakravartin*. The essentials of the *sutta* are in Table 1.

The *Lakkhaṇa Sutta* then elaborates on the parallels between a Buddha and a *cakravartin*; gives a detailed expression of a notion of a Buddha's spiritual body, and links this to past *karma* in a very detailed way. In this respect, it accords with the general idea that "This body ... is not yours, it is not another's: it is to be seen as old *karma* which is constructed, thought out, felt" (*Saṃyutta Nikāya* 2.64–5).

The above marks were later used as a basis for visualizing the Buddha and the qualities he embodied, and then for the form of Buddha-images when these developed (no. 32 coming to be shown as a protuberance on the head, called the *uṣṇīṣa*, Pāli *uṇhīsa*, or turban). Meditators may have also mindfully thought of the marks in relation to their own bodies so as to help arouse the related qualities.

Bodies of the Buddha

From the above, we thus see various concepts of Buddha-bodies. A Buddha:

Table 1 The thirty-two marks of a great man according to the *Lakkhaṇa Sutta*

Mark/characteristic (quote).	Past karmic cause of the mark and what it portends for the present life (précis).
1. Well planted are his feet, evenly he lowers his foot to the ground, evenly he lifts it, evenly he touches the ground with the sole of his foot.	*Past deeds*: unwavering good conduct in body, speech and mind, in generosity, self-discipline, observance of holy days, in honoring parents. *In the present*: he cannot be impeded by any enemy, whether external or from within the mind.
2. On the soles of his feet and on the palms of his hands wheels arise – with a thousand spokes, with rim and hub, adorned in every way and well-defined within.	*Past deeds*: protected and helped others. *In the present:* he has a great retinue of followers.
3. He possesses extended heels.	*Past deeds*: non-violence and compassion. *In the present*: he is long-lived.
4. Long are his fingers and long are his toes.	As for 3.
5. Soft and tender are his hands and feet.	*Past deeds*: became loved through the four bases of sympathy: generosity, pleasing speech, beneficial conduct and impartiality. *In the present:* followers are well disposed to him.
6. Net-like are his hands and feet.	As for 5.
7. His feet have raised ankles like conch shells.	*Past deeds:* an explainer of true welfare and of *Dharma. In the present:* becomes the foremost person among laypeople (as a *cakravartin*) or renouncers (as a Buddha).
8. His lower leg is like the antelope's, well shaped and pleasing.	*Past deeds:* quickly became skilled in crafts and sciences. *In the present:* quickly learns those things beneficial to a *cakravartin* or a Buddha.
9. While standing and without bending, he touches and rubs all over his knees with both palms.	*Past deeds:* knew the nature of individuals and what they needed. *In the present:* rich in material or spiritual possessions.
10. Covered in a bag is that which garments must conceal.	*Past deeds:* reunited long-lost friends and relatives. *In the present:* many physical, or spiritual, sons.
11. Golden is his color and his skin shines as gold—like the most splendid lord of the gods.	*Past deeds:* never angered, however provoked, and gave away soft fabrics. *In the present:* will receive fine fabrics.
12. Subtle is his skin; due to the subtlety of his skin, neither dust nor stain sticks to his body.	*Past deeds:* keen to enquire of the wise about good and bad actions. *In the present*: great wisdom.
13. He has separate hairs on his body; the hairs arise singly, one to each pore.	*Past deeds:* did not lie, a truth-speaker, reliable, non-deceiving. *In the present:* citizens, or monks and nuns, will do what he requests.
14. He has hairs on his body which turn upwards. Dark up-turned hairs, black in color curling in rings and turning auspiciously to the right.	As for 7.
15. His frame is straight like a *brahmā's.*	As for 3 and 4.

Table 1 (*continued*)

Mark/characteristic (quote).	Past karmic cause of the mark and what it portends for the present life (précis).
16. Seven outflowing places has he: on both hands there are outflows, on both feet there are outflows, on both shoulder-tips there are outflows, at the top of the back there is an outflow.	*Past deeds*: gave good food to others. *In the present:* he receives good food.
17. Lion-like is the upper part of his body.	*Past deeds:* worked to benefit others in faith, morality, learning, renunciation, *Dharma*, wisdom, and material possessions. *In the present:* cannot lose anything, material or spiritual.
18. Filled is the hollow between his shoulders.	As for 17.
19. He is proportioned like the sphere of the Banyan tree. As is his body, so is the span of his arms. As is the span of his arms, so is his body.	As for 9.
20. Smoothly rounded are his shoulders.	As for 17 and 18.
21. He releases the highest of tastes. Taste-bearing flows that arise in the neck when in happiness he turns upwards are carried all round.	*Past deeds:* avoided physically harming others. *In the present:* little illness, good digestion, also equable and tolerant of exertion.
22. Lion-like is his jaw.	*Past deeds:* avoided idle chatter, but spoke on *Dharma* and discipline. *In the present:* cannot be overcome by any opponent, external or internal.
23. Forty are his teeth.	*Past deeds:* avoided slander, but delighted in harmony. *In the present:* his citizens or monks and nuns will not be divided.
24. Level are his teeth.	*Past deeds:* avoided wrong livelihood, i.e. by means of cheating, bribery, deception, killing, theft. *In the present:* citizens or monks and nuns will be pure.
25. Undivided are his teeth.	As for 23.
26. Utterly white are his teeth.	As for 24.
27. Mighty is his tongue.	*Past deeds:* avoided harsh speech, but spoke in an agreeable way. *In the present:* will have a persuasive voice.
28. He has the voice of a *brahmā, soft as the Indian songbird.*	As for 27.
29. Very blue are his eyes.	*Past deeds:* looked at others in a straightforward, open, direct and kindly way, not furtively. *In the present:* will be popular and loved by all types of people.
30. His eye-lashes are like those of a young calf.	As for 29.
31. The filament that arises between his eyes is white like soft cotton.	As for 13.

embodies *Dharma*, or perhaps has "a *Dharma*-body" consisting of Path qualities; can meditatively generate a mind-made body; has a body, perhaps in the sense of a spiritual body, endowed with the thirty-two marks; as well as a normal physical body.

After his death, Buddhists have particularly looked to his two-fold heritage: the *Dharma*-body of his teachings and his physical remains. While the Theravāda tradition emphasizes that the Buddha, since his death, is beyond contact with the world and cannot respond to prayer or worship (cf. *Milindapañha* 95–101), something of his *power* is still seen to remain in the world, to be drawn on through the practice of his teachings, the chanting of portions of them in protective blessing chants (Pāli *parittas*) and the bodily relics which remained after his cremation (see entry on Buddha, relics of).

As seen from the entry on Ennobling Truth/Reality, the Third, in its discussion of *nirvāṇa* beyond death, the Buddha did not accept any of four views on an enlightened person after death: that he "is," "is not," "both is and is not" and "neither is nor is not." In practice, this is taken to mean that he is not non-existent, but that his state cannot be expressed in words. What seems fairly clear from the early texts is that, as one can only be individualized by the conditioned aggregates of body and mind, that state cannot be one in which he exists as an individual being.

See also: ***Bodhisattva* career in the Theravāda; Buddha, dates of; Buddha, early symbols; Buddha, family of; Buddha, historical context; Buddha, style of teaching; Buddhas, past and future; Ennobling Truths/Realities; Ennobling Truth/Reality, the First; Ennobling Truth/Reality, the Second; Ennobling Truth/Reality, the Third: *nirvāṇa*; Ennobling Truth/Reality, the Fourth: the Ennobling Eightfold Path; *Pratyeka-buddhas*.**

PETER HARVEY

BUDDHA, BODIES OF

Conceptions about the body, or bodies, of the Buddha articulate the ways in which Buddhist communities envision an enlightened presence among sentient beings. In all branches of the tradition, conceptions about the Buddha's spiritual and physical body have profoundly influenced doctrines about the person of the Buddha and about the nature of Buddhahood, ideas about his presence or absence from the world of impermanence, and ritual practices validating such ideals. These notions differ across the Buddhist tradition in ways that are specific to each community. Ideas about the bodies of the Buddha are expressed in the doctrines, histories, and cosmologies of Theravāda, Mahāyāna, and Vajrayāna communities, profoundly shaping their social character and development.

Theravāda

The Theravādins view the Buddha as having lived and transcended the life of conditioned human existence. While his physical body turned into relics, his spiritual body became synonymous with the scriptural tradition, the higher stages of the path, and with enlightenment itself, according to Buddhaghosa's *Path of Purification* (1960 edition: 443–5). One finds many references to the Buddha's bodies in canonical texts, commentaries, and chronicles composed in the Theravāda tradition. Similar ideas referring to his physical remains, i.e. his relics (*rūpakāya*) and the body of his spiritual teachings, *dhammakāya*, are expressed in the *Saṃyutta Nikāya* and *Dīgha Nikāya*. Together, they constitute the Buddha's legacy he entrusted to the laity and to the *sangha* respectively. The conception of the Buddha's two bodies was foundational to the identity and cultural organization of many Theravāda Buddhist communities. In 1977 Frank Reynolds observed that "*dhammkāya* and *rūpakāya* embody two basic Buddhological realities on which

Theravāda religion has historically grounded itself," profoundly shaping the social formation of Theravāda Buddhist communities. Popular veneration of his relics engendered *stūpa* cults and image veneration, whereas support for his teachings motivated monastic learning and scholarship. This understanding of the Buddha developed early in the history of the tradition. By the time the Pāli Canon assumed its classic form in Sri Lanka during the fifth century CE, the conception of the two bodies was firmly established in the Theravāda tradition. In light of its profound impact on the organization of Theravāda societies, it stands to reason that the doctrine of the two bodies should also structure the end of the Buddha's dispensation (*sāsana*). Various myths claim that his relics reconstituting his body to deliver a final sermon will mark the end of this Buddha's era. On that occasion, multitudes throughout the cosmic realms will be enlightened.

Rūpakāya

The *Mahāparinibbāna Sutta* tells the story of his final departure from the world of rebirth (*saṃsāra*) and the funerary rites of a universal monarch (*cakkavatti*) he received from the early Buddhist community. The doctrinal development of the Buddha's bodies is linked closely to this account. Accordingly, the Buddha's body was ritually washed, venerated and finally cremated. Among the physical remains found in his funeral pyre were bone fragments and teeth that were subsequently distributed and enshrined in *stūpas* (reliquary mounts or *cetiya, Pāli*) at sites throughout all cardinal directions. *Stūpas* containing the Buddha's relics have been constructed at sites associated with his life, including his birthplace at Lumbinī, the place of his enlightenment at Bodhgayā – the most important Buddhist pilgrimage site in India – the site of his first sermon at Banares, the modern city of Mumbai, and the site of his death at Kuśinagara. The cultic veneration of the Buddha's *rūpakāya* became central to Aśoka's (*c.* 265–238 BCE) state cult of 84,000 *stūpas*. He ordered the original sites of the Buddha's relics to be opened and their contents to be relocated and enshrined in *stūpas* he commissioned throughout his empire. *Stūpas* became pilgrimage sites under lay sponsorship that functioned initially independently from monasteries, receiving both alms and veneration from the general population.

The Theravāda tradition recognizes three classes of objects that make up the Buddha's *rūpakāya*: namely, his physical relics (*sarīradhātu*), objects he used (*paribhogadhātu*) and reminders of him (*uddesikadhātu*), such as footprints of the Buddha atop Sri Lanka's Adam's Peak. Consecrated Buddha images were eventually included among the class of items designated as *rūpakāya*. The sponsorship of images and the construction of *stūpas* also developed into important ways to celebrate the Buddha's *rūpakāya*. While such sacred objects were considered inherently powerful, their containment at certain sites was seen as an indication of a layperson's righteous power to grant protection to them. Such cultic practice not only created a ritual presence for a Buddha who is absent from the world, they also defined and organized hierarchically the Buddhist communities that engaged in this popular practice. Donald Swearer describes the Buddha's physical remains as structuring Buddhist cosmography and defining Buddhist communities. The Buddha's physical presence, in the form of relics or consecrated images, therefore defines a Buddhist landscape and identifies a cosmic center, or *axis mundi*, within it. It is around such defining cosmic centers that Buddhist kings mobilize and organize merit-making communities. Lay sponsors derive great merit and rewards in future lives from their support of the Buddha's *rūpakāya*.

Dhammakāya

The Buddha's *dhammakāya* (born of the *Dhamma*) constitutes his mind-made or spiritual body that comprises all his good qualities. The Buddha's *Dhamma* also comprises his teachings, his message, his scriptural legacy and the universal law. The Buddha uses this body when he accomplishes miraculous acts like visiting his mother in Tāvatiṃsa heaven to teach to her the *Abhidhamma*. His teachings were initially compiled, systematized, and memorized at the first Buddhist council, which his disciples convened shortly after his death (*pārinirvāṇa*). The Theravāda tradition believes that its canonical texts preserve the original and complete teachings of the Buddha and defines its mission as safeguarding its orthodoxy. Subsequent Buddhist councils compiled new renditions of the *tipiṭaka* that were stripped of perceived accretions.

In the Theravāda cultures of Sri Lanka, Burma, Laos, and Cambodia, it is the primary responsibility of the *sangha* to teach, practice, and preserve the *dhammakāya*. Hence, memorization of all three canonical baskets (*tipiṭaka*) constitutes an achievement few monks are able to attain through study and monastic examinations over the course of a lifetime. Those monks who achieve this distinction are considered enlightened *arhats*, as knowing the Buddha's *Dhamma* completely is tantamount to that Spiritual attainment. Efforts to missionize the *dhamma*, donations of books containing the *Dhamma*, and supporting its preservation in other ways are acts that bestow great merit and future rewards upon individuals who support monks in these activities.

Mahāyāna and the Buddha's three bodies

The doctrine of the three bodies of the Buddha (*trikāya*) reflects this broader range of Mahāyāna innovations that included cosmological worldviews, doctrinal developments, and devotional practices. While there is already some evidence of a third, supra-natural body mentioned in the Pāli scriptures, it was the development of the Mahāyāna literatures that brought about extensive rethinking of the Buddha's bodies. These new conceptions were more diverse than their Theravādin counterparts and allowed for the Buddhist imagination to envision other times, other places and other Buddhas.

The classic Mahāyāna conception of the Buddha's bodies developed during the first century CE and envisioned him to possess three bodies (*trikāya*). His *dharmakāya* was the collection of the Buddha's *dharmas* and perfected qualities such as his compassion, wisdom, etc. The Buddha's *dharmakāya* was understood as the eternal principle of Ultimate Truth, the Universal Law, the supreme state of absolute knowledge, his unchanging essence, and the source of his emanations in the human realm. *Nirmāṇakāya* was the emanation body, a magical body the Buddha created to teach the *Dharma* among sentient beings at select moments in time. The notion of the Buddha as possessing a magical and temporary body discounted any earlier understanding of Siddhartha Gautama Śākyamuni, or of earlier Buddhas, as historical human beings. By contrast, the appearance of a Buddha in time and place was merely a magical transformation of his unchanging and eternal *dharmakāya*. This innovation opened the Mahāyāna imagination to the notion of the simultaneous existence of multiple Buddhas, each within his or her own universe or Buddha-field. His third body was the glorified or enjoyment body (*sambogha-kāya*). It is the Buddha in his heavenly contemplation and he appears in this form to *bodhisattvas* in pure lands. The reward the *bodhisattva* receives for his devotional practice is his own transfiguration into the *samboghakāya*.

The new Mahāyāna *sūtras* professed to be the authentic, revealed word of the Buddha that contained teachings appropriate to a dispensation in decline. Beginning with the *Lotus Sūtra*, they presented the founding figure of the Theravāda tradition as conditional truth the Buddha created intentionally through skillful means (*upāya*) for the benefit and eventual enlightenment of lesser minds. While stressing the eternal and all-pervading presence of the Buddha in countless cosmic worlds, this vision of the Buddha's bodies authorized devotional developments within the Mahāyāna tradition as well as the notion of teachings appropriate to the times of a dispensation in decline.

However, the new devotionalism was not the only development engendered by these innovations. The Yogācāra school in the fourth century in India proposed that enlightenment constitutes the realization of emptiness (*śūnyatā*), i.e. that all existence is ultimately empty. Mahāyāna thinkers engaged in doctrines concerning the Discernment of Wisdom (*prajñāpāramitā*) added to this idea of emptiness that the attainment of enlightenment rests on developing *bodhicitta*, the mind of enlightenment, through discernment of wisdom and the non-arising of *dharmas*.

Vajrayāna and the incarnate Buddha

Other developments envisioned the nature of Buddhahood and enlightenment altogether differently. Esoteric Vajrayāna, known as the Diamond Vehicle, considers the human body the site for divine and enlightened beings to become manifest. It sees the human body as the womb of potential Buddhahood in the future. *Tathāgatagarbha*, the embryonic qualities of "one who has thus come," are believed to be eternally present in all sentient beings. It constitutes the kernel of pure Buddha nature, a hidden treasure of enlightenment yet to be realized. Among Tibetan Buddhist, lamas like the Dalai Lama are considered Buddhas who, free from karmic constraints, choose the emanation body (*nirmāṇakāya*) of their next incarnation. Enlightened beings choose to become manifest in different human beings. Donald Lopez notes that "The institution of the incarnate lama has been central to the organization of Tibetan society and ... [the primary] means by which authority and charisma, in all of their symbolic and material forms, are passed from one generation to another."

See also: **Famous Buddhists and ideal types; India, Buddhism in; Mahāyāna Buddhism.**

JULIANE SCHOBER

BUDDHA, DATES OF

Indian culture has not been as concerned with recording precise dates as have Chinese or Graeco-Roman culture, so datings cannot always be arrived at with accuracy. A key reference point for dating the Buddha is the inauguration of the reign of the Buddhist emperor Aśoka (Pāli Asoka). There are references in Aśokan edicts to the sending of ambassadors to certain Hellenistic kings, an event generally dated by scholars at *c.* 268 BCE. The Pāli sources of Theravāda Buddhism say that the Buddha died 218 years before this: the "long chronology." As all sources agree that Gautama was eighty when he died (e.g. *Dīgha Nikāya* 2.100), this would make his dates *c.* 566–486 BCE. An alternative "short chronology" is recorded in Sanskrit sources of north Indian Buddhism preserved in East Asia, according to which he died 100 years (or something more) before Aśoka's inauguration, which would make his dates 448–368 BCE – though in East Asia, the traditional date of the Buddha's death was actually 949 or 878, and in Tibet, 881 BCE. In the past, modern scholars have generally accepted

486 or 483 BCE for this, but the consensus is now that they rest on evidence which is too flimsy.

Carbon dating indicates that certain sites associated with the Buddha in the Pāli Canon were not settled prior to 500 BCE (plus or minus 100 years), which makes the Buddha's death unlikely to have been as early as 486 BCE (Härtel 1991–2). Moreover, a consideration of Jain historical data suggests that both the Buddha and Mahāvira, the Jain leader, who died a little before the Buddha, died between 410 and 390 BCE.

Richard Gombrich has argued that, as a result of recent research of Hellenistic historians, Aśoka's consecration may be dated anywhere between 267 and 280 BCE. Moreover, 100 and 218 (like our "two centuries and a score years") are best seen as ideal round numbers. Gombrich has calculated a number *between* 218 and 100–136 from figures associated with a lineage of teachers in the *Dīpavaṃsa*, a chronicle of Sri Lanka. This ends with the death of a king that occurred in 303 CE, though earlier parts of the text and certainly its sources could be rather earlier. The figure of 218 years itself comes from the *Dīpavaṃsa* (6.1), though Gombrich holds that it is based on a misunderstanding of figures in an earlier part of the text. The focus of the early chapters of the *Dīpavaṃsa* is on monastic matters, and especially the authentic transmission of the *vinaya* or monastic code of discipline. By collating various figures in the text, supplemented by some from the later *Mahāvaṃsa* chronicle, and reinterpreting what some of them refer to, thus removing internal inconsistencies, he derives the following information:

16 AB (after the death of the Buddha), the *Vinaya* expert Upāli (aged sixty) ordains Dāsaka, who is likely to have been twenty, minimum age for ordination as a monk.

33 AB, Dāsaka (aged thirty-seven) admits Soṇaka (aged fifteen) as a novice.

41 AB, Dāsaka (aged forty-five) ordains Soṇaka (aged twenty-three) as a monk.

52 AB, Soṇaka (aged forty) ordains Siggava (probably aged twenty).

102 AB, Siggava (aged sixty-four) ordains Tissa (probably aged twenty).

136 AB, Tissa is aged fifty-four at the inauguration of Aśoka; Mahinda is fourteen.

142 AB, Tissa (aged sixty) ordains Mahinda, aged twenty.

Gombrich explains that, as a result of the numbers being given in round years, thus discounting part years, there is a margin of error for the figure of 136, so that the correct figure could be between 132 and 142. Given the additional uncertainty of the date of Aśoka's inauguration, this gives the date of the Buddha's death as between 422 and 399 BCE, with a greater likelihood for a date in the middle of this range.

Why the discrepancy with the *Dīpavaṃsa*'s own assertion that Aśoka was inaugurated as emperor 218 years AB? Gombrich argues that: (1) the text is more approximate on dates relating to kings than to monks; (2) 218 is the sum of conventional numbers 100 + 100 + 18, noting that while the second council is said to have been 100 AB, evidence indicates it was 60 AB; (3) in a damaged part of the text (*Dīpavaṃsa* 5.95), a list of ages at death for a lineage of monks adds to 219 if taken as years lived after ordination (giving an implausible average age of ninety-two), and it was mistakenly read this way by the monk who continued the text from Chapter 6; (4) a list of years for a line of monks (*Dīpavaṃsa* 5.96) is not the age at which they became "patriarchs" (there was no such role then), but is the length of time they knew the *Vinaya* by heart, between learning it as novices and dying; such a reading removes discrepancies in the *Dīpavaṃsa* figures that arise from other interpretations.

There exists no final scholarly consensus as yet for the Buddha's dates – Cousins finishes his review of the evidence by talking of a "reasonable probability" of a date around 400 BCE for the Buddha's death – though if one sets aside the margins of error that Gombrich acknowledges, his research indicates 484–404 BCE. Bringing the date of the Buddha forward, note, does not necessarily place him in a later phase of the development of Indian religion. This is because the Hindu *Upaniṣads* are themselves generally dated relative to the Buddha's dates.

In Theravāda countries, the traditional dating – of uncertain antiquity – places the Buddha's death in 544/3 BCE, based on the "long chronology" and a misdating of Aśoka's inauguration. On this basis, Theravādins celebrated 1956 as "Buddha *Jayantī*" year, the 2,500th anniversary of the Buddha's final *nirvāṇa*. This was regarded as a time of resurgence in Buddhism. The new dating of the Buddha's death as *c.* 404 BCE would make 1997 the 2,400th anniversary of the Buddha's final *nirvāṇa*, 2097 as the 2,500th anniversary of this, and 2017 the 2,500th anniversary of his birth. As Buddhism is seen to decline over the ages (*Saṃyutta Nikāya* 2.24) a later date for the Buddha is, from a Buddhist perspective, good news!

See also: **Buddha; Buddha, historical context; Buddha, story of.**

PETER HARVEY

BUDDHA, EARLY SYMBOLS

A notable feature of early Buddhist art is that it did not depict Gautama, or any previous Buddha, in a human form; even before his enlightenment, Gautama is only shown by symbols. This must have been because of the feeling that the profound nature of one nearing or attained to Buddhahood could not be adequately represented by a human form. Even contemporary Brahmanism only portrayed minor deities such as *yakṣas* (Pāli *yakkhas*) in non-symbolic ways; the major gods were represented only by symbols. Early Buddhism used a range of symbols to represent the Buddha and his nature, and these have continued in use even after portrayals of him in human form developed from the second century CE.

Bodhi trees

The most important focus of devotion in early Buddhism would have been the Buddha's bodily relics within the ten original *stūpas*. More numerous than these, and second in importance, were trees grown from the cuttings or seeds of the three under which Gautama attained Buddhahood, and the original tree itself: *bodhi* ("awakening" or "enlightenment") trees. These were greatly revered as tangible links with the Buddha's great spiritual powers, like bodily relics. They were accordingly seen as having wondrous powers, as seen in the *Mahāvaṃsa* chronicle (XVIII.38–44), which says that when Emperor Aśoka (Pāli Asoka, *c.* 268–239 BCE) wished to take a cutting of the original tree to send to Sri Lanka, a branch severed itself from the tree, floating in the air while it grew roots, and later emitted rays of light in six colors. Bodhi trees were also reminders and symbols of Gautama's attainment of awakening and the awakened state itself, which role could also be fulfilled by any species of the same tree (*aśvattha* (Pāli *assattha*), *pīpal* or *ficus religiosa*) or depictions of such a tree.

In pre-Buddhist India, there was already a cult of sacred trees such as the *aśvattha*. They were often surrounded by a railing and had a mud platform at the base as a place to put offerings to the tree or to the minor deity seen as inhabiting it. When worshipped, they were seen as fulfilling wishes and granting fertility. The

Buddha frequently recommended the roots of trees as places for his monks to meditate, and he meditated beneath one on the night of his enlightenment. According to *Vinaya* 1.1–4, the Buddha stayed near the bodhi tree for four weeks after his enlightenment. The *Nidānakathā* (p. 77) says that, for the second of these, the Buddha continually contemplated the tree with feelings of deep gratitude for its having sheltered him at his most important time.

As in pre-Buddhist worship of trees, devotion to bodhi trees was expressed by watering them, attaching flags to their branches, and placing offerings such as flowers on the platform at their base. Devotees would also perform the act of clockwise circumambulation or *pradakṣiṇā* (Pāli *padakkhiṇā*), literally "keeping to the right." This action is a common one in the Buddhist tradition; it is also performed round a *stūpa* and, especially in Tibet, round any sacred object, building, or person. Keeping one's right side towards someone is a way of showing respect to them: in the *suttas*, people are often said to have departed from the Buddha keeping their right side towards him. The precedent for actual circumambulation may have been the Brahmanic practice of the priest walking around the fire-sacrifice offerings or of a bride walking around the domestic hearth at her marriage. All such practices demonstrate that what one walks around is, or should be, the "centre" of one's life.

Originally Buddhist tree-shrines were, like their predecessors, simply surrounded by a wooden railing (*vedikā*). During Aśoka's time the increasing popularity of the religion led to the development of more elaborate enclosures known as "*bodhi*-houses" (*bodhi-gharas*). From their gallery devotees could circumambulate and water the trees without churning up a sea of mud.

On stone reliefs that embellished *stūpas*, the Buddha could also be symbolized by a bodhi tree, or his life could be symbolically depicted by a bodhi tree (awakening), *Dharma*-wheel (first sermon) and *stūpa* (*parinirvāṇa* at death). In a wider sense, these three symbols represent the Buddha's nature as an Awakened One, as the teacher of a universal message and as passed into *nirvāṇa*. Past Buddhas could also be symbolized by their bodhi trees, said to be of a range of species (*Dīgha Nikāya* 2.2–8). Buddhists also prize the heart-shaped leaves of bodhi trees, especially of descendents of the original tree, an aged revered specimen of which grows on the putative spot where this grew, in Bodhgayā.

The lotus

One of the most common and important early Buddhist symbols is the lotus. In India this has always been looked upon as the most beautiful of flowers. Its bursting into blossom above the water made it a symbol for the birth of gods and the birth of the world. In the Brahmanical *Rig Veda*, the fire god Agni is said to have been born from a lotus; in the *Brāhmaṇas* and *Āraṇyakas*, the lotus was the seat of the creator Prajāpati or the base on which he placed the earth after he had dredged it up from the cosmic ocean. The lotus was particularly associated with the goddess Śrī or Śrī-Lakśmī, described in a late portion of the *Rig Veda* as "lotus-born" and holding a lotus in her hand. According to Coomaraswamy, she and the lotus represented the earth, the waters (of life) and all the potential and creative energy latent in the waters: "that wherein/whereon there is or can be manifestation."

In early art, medallions depicting a circle of open lotus petals were particularly common (Figure 6(b)), but motifs involving lotuses and Śrī-Lakṣmī were also used to depict the birth of Gautama. Yet the lotus did not just symbolize physical birth:

> Just as, monks, a lotus, blue, red or white, though born in the water, grown up in the water, when it reaches the surface stands there unsoiled by the water; just so, monks, though born in the world, grown up in the world, having overcome the world, a *Tathāgata* abides unsoiled by the world.
> (*Saṃyutta Nikāya* 3.140; cf. *Majjhima Nikāya* 1.169)

Just as the lotus blossom grows up from the mud and water, so one with an enlightened mind develops out of the ranks of ordinary beings, by maturing the spiritual potential latent in all. Like the *Bodhi* tree, the lotus is a symbol drawn from the vegetable kingdom. While both suggest spiritual *growth*, the lotus emphasizes the *potential* for growth, whereas the *Bodhi* tree indicates the *culmination* of this growth: awakening.

The fact that drops of water roll off a lotus (cf. "like water off a duck's back") gives this unsoiled flower an added symbolic meaning in Buddhism, as a simile for non-attachment. As Maudgalyāyana (Pāli Moggallāna) says of himself, "he is not soiled by conditioned phenomena as a lotus is not soiled by water" (*Theragāthā* 1180). *Nirvāṇa* is also likened to a lotus in being "unsoiled by defilements" (*Milindapañha* 318), as it is beyond attachment, hatred and delusion that worldly beings are involved in. *Milindapañha* 375 also shows other aspects of lotus symbolism: the "earnest student of yoga" must be like the lotus above water, for "having overcome and risen above the world, he must stand firm in the supramundane state"; like a lotus trembling in the slightest breeze, he or she must also "exercise restraint among even the slightest defilements; he should abide seeing the peril (in them)."

The *Dharma*-wheel

The *Dharma*-wheel (*dharma-cakra*, Pāli *dhamma-cakka*) has been one of the major Buddhist symbols since early times. A crucial key to the understanding of its meaning are the canonical stories of just and compassionate emperors of the past known as *cakravartin*s or "wheel-turners," for whom a glowing thousand-spoked "divine wheel" appears on a full moon night. The king anoints the wheel with water, setting it spinning. He then urges it to roll forth and accompany him in the peaceful conquest of the four directions of the whole world. The wheel is the first of the *cakravartin*'s seven "treasures," and such a list, also beginning with the wheel, occurs in the Brahmanical *Rig Veda* as pertaining to Agni or Soma-Rudra; the *Mahābhārata* 1.18 also lists seven "treasures" which appear at the churning of the cosmic ocean, starting with the "mild moon of 1,000 rays"; five of the seven "treasures" are the same in all three lists if the moon disc is seen as a kind of wheel.

In Buddhist stories on the *cakravartin*, the wheel's continuing presence is a sign that a compassionate ruler is still on his throne. The key aspect of its meaning is that it symbolizes the emperor's just rule radiating outwards to all the lands of the earth. The commentator Buddhaghosa explains that on the exterior of the wheel's rim are 100 parasols, each accompanied by two spear-heads. The latter symbolize the emperor's power of peaceful conquest, while the parasols as emblems of royalty represent all the kings of the earth who come willingly to accept the righteous rule of the emperor (*Dīgha Nikāya* commentary 2.617–19).

The "treasure-wheel" and the *Dharma*-wheel are said, not surprisingly, to look exactly alike. For practical purposes each is depicted with fewer than 1,000 spokes and 100 parasols (Figure 6(a)). In time the spear-heads disappeared and the parasols degenerated into residual bumps. While the parasols on the *cakravartin*'s wheel stand for kings who come to accept his rule, on the *Dharma*-wheel they can be seen to represent the great beings who come to follow the teachings of the *Dharma*. These

Figure 6(a) Wheel design from Sāñcī, first century CE.

Figure 6(b) Lotus medallion design from the railing on the Bhārhut *stūpa* (second century BCE).

include kings, spiritually advanced teachers of other sects and also gods. The Buddha taught for the benefit of "gods and humans" and Śakra (Pāli Sakka), that is, Indra, the ruler of the Vedic gods, is said to have become a stream-enterer (*Dīgha Nikāya* 2.288), while a Great Brahmā deity, seen by brahmins as the overlord or "creator" of the world, is said to have requested the Buddha to teach the world (*Vinaya* 1.5–7). The protective parasols and sharp spears also suggest, respectively, the Buddha's compassion and wisdom.

It is in the Buddha's first sermon, "The Setting in Motion of the *Dharma*-wheel," that the notion of the "*Dharma*-wheel" is rooted. In this, the wheel does not roll until the first member of the Buddha's audience gains insight into his teachings, so attaining the "*Dharma*-eye" (Skt. *dharma-cakṣu*, Pāli *dhamma-cakkhu*), thus becoming a stream-enterer. At this the gods are said to have cried out, "The supreme *Dharma*-wheel rolled thus by the Lord in the deer park at Sārnāth cannot be rolled back by . . . anyone in the world." By his act of teaching, so that there was the first experiential realization based on it, the Buddha inaugurated the "rule" or influence of *Dharma* in the world, paralleling how a *cakravartin* inaugurates his rule. This link is explicitly made when the Buddha says to Śāriputra (Pāli Sāriputta), "Just as the eldest son of a *cakravartin* ruler rolls on aright the wheel set rolling by his father, even so do you, Śāriputra, roll on aright the supreme *Dharma*-wheel set rolling by me" (*Saṃyutta Nikāya* 1.191).

In its simplest sense, then, the *Dharma*-wheel represents the transmission of *Dharma* in the first sermon. From this it naturally came to symbolize the Buddha as teacher, the *Dharma* as teaching, and the power of both to transform people's lives. The two are, of course, intimately related, with the Buddha embodying the *Dharma*. As with most symbols, the meaning of the *Dharma*-wheel is multivalent. In *Rig Veda* 1.164, the sun is likened to a revolving wheel, "the immortal wheel which nothing stops, on which all existence depends." Buddhaghosa likens the spokes of the *Dharma*-wheel to the sun's rays and the hub to a full moon. It seems appropriate, then, to see the radiating spokes of the *Dharma*-wheel as suggesting that, like the sun, the Buddha shed the "warmth" of his compassion and the light of his wisdom on all who came to him.

In the *Rig Veda*, the solar deity Mitra is said to be the "eye of the world": that is, the sun both illuminates and watches over the world. Certain *Dharma*-wheels (Figure 7) are reminiscent of an eye in their appearance, and can thus be seen as symbolizing the spiritual vision of the Buddha at whose death certain followers said, "The eye has disappeared in the world!" (*Dīgha Nikāya* 2.158). The eye-like nature

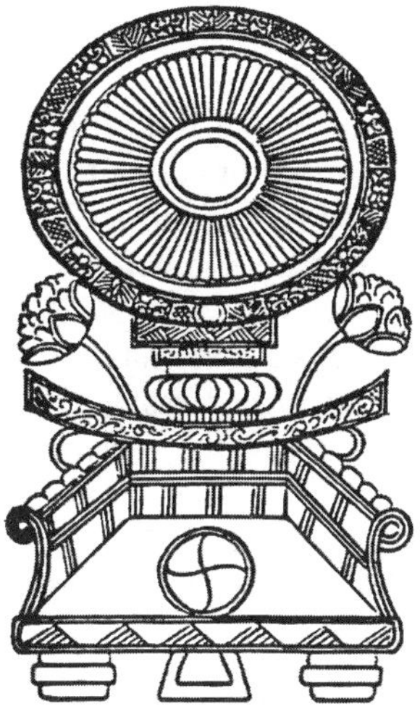

Figure 7 Symbolic portrayal of the Buddha giving his first sermon. The design is from a relief from a *stūpa* at Nāgārjunakoṇḍa (third century CE).

of the *Dharma*-wheel also links to its first "turning" when a disciple of the Buddha first gained the "*Dharma*-eye." In all this there may well be a pun on *cakra*, wheel, and *cakṣu*, eye (Pāli *cakka* and *cakkhu*).

In the *Rig Veda*, the wheel is a possession of the god Varuṇa, the "universal monarch" (*sam-rāj*) and lord of *ṛta*, cosmic order. The wheel is also a symbol of the regular course of things, and thus of cosmic order, in that the one wheel of the sun's chariot is said to have twelve, five or 360 spokes, corresponding to the number of months, seasons or days in the year. In Buddhism, the *cakravartin*'s rule according to *Dharma* leads to peace and order in his realm. It thus seems appropriate to take the regularly spaced spokes of the *Dharma*-wheel as symbolizing the spiritual harmony and mental integration produced in one who practices the *Dharma*.

In the *Bṛhadāraṇyaka Upaniṣad* (2.5.15), all gods, worlds, and beings are said to be held together in the *ātman* (Self) like spokes in the hub and felly of a wheel; in *Chāndogya Upaniṣad* (7.15.1) all is said to be fastened on *prāṇa*, the vital breath, like spokes in a hub. In the Buddhist "wheel-turner" legend, the state of the empire depends on the emperor. The *Dharma*-wheel, then, with its spokes firmly planted in the hub, can be seen to symbolize that the Buddha, by discovering and teaching *Dharma*, firmly established its practice in the world. The radiating spokes can be seen as representing the many aspects of the path taught by the Buddha, though it should be noted that they do not just have eight spokes representing the factors of the Eightfold Path, the overall path consisting of many interrelated skilful qualities.

The spokes of the *Dharma*-wheel are not only fixed in but also converge on the hub. This can be taken to symbolize that the factors of the *Dharma* in the sense of path lead to *Dharma* in the sense of *nirvāṇa*. In this respect it is worth noting that the Buddha said that his "setting in motion of the *Dharma*-wheel" was the "opening of the doors" to the "deathless" (*amata*), i.e. *nirvāṇa* (*Vinaya* 1.6). When *Dharma*-wheels were placed above the gateways to *stūpas*, it may have been to symbolize that the *Dharma* offers an entrance to deathlessness.

As the centre of a spinning wheel is still, so the Buddha's mind was seen as ever still, even when he was busy teaching. In line with this, the hubs of some *Dharma*-wheels are in the form of open lotuses, suggesting the non-attachment of the Buddha's mind. As the centre of a wheel is an empty hole, so the Buddha's mind was empty of any idea of an unchanging "I," the root of all suffering.

In early Buddhist art, *Dharma*-wheels often appear on top of pillars, the most famous example being that at Sārnāth erected by Aśoka. It probably symbolized the power of both the Buddha and Aśoka, who may well have been inspired by the *cakravartin* ideal. As the legendary wheel remains aloft near the ruler's palace while he rules but starts to sink down when he is near death (*Dīgha Nikāya* 3.59), it appears most appropriate to place it high up on a pillar, to symbolize the health of imperial rule or of the sovereignty of the *Dharma*.

The "vase of plenty"

An early Buddhist symbol of some importance which became one of the eight auspicious symbols in the Sinhalese and Tibetan traditions is the *pūrṇa-ghaṭa* (Pāli *puṇṇa-ghaṭa*) or *pūrṇa-kumbha*, the "vase of plenty." It is also an auspicious symbol in Hinduism, probably equivalent to the golden *kumbha* containing *amṛta*, the gods' nectar of immortality, which emerged at the churning of the cosmic ocean by the gods.

In Buddhism, water pouring out from an upturned *kumbha* is likened to a noble disciple getting rid of unskillful states (*Saṃyutta Nikāya* 5.48 and *Aṅguttara-Nikāya* 5.337), and a *kumbha* being gradually filled by drops of water is likened to a person gradually filling himself with evil or karmically fruitful qualities (*Dhammapada* 121–2). In this way the *kumbha* is generally likened to the personality as a container of bad or good states. Quite often, though, a full *kumbha* is used as a simile for a specifically *positive* state of being: a person who truly understands the four Ennobling Truths is like a full *kumbha* (*Aṅguttara Nikāya* 2.104); a person of wide wisdom (*puthu-pañño*), who bears in mind the *Dharma* he has heard, is like an upright *kumbha* which accumulates the water poured into it (*Aṅguttara Nikāya* 1.131).

The implication of these passages is that the full *kumbha* would be a natural symbol for the personality of someone who is "full" of *Dharma*: a Buddha or *arhat*. While the Hindu *pūrṇa-ghaṭa* contains *amṛta*, the Buddhist one contains *Dharma*, that which makes life fruitful and brings a person to the Buddhist *amṛta* (Pāli *amata*), the "deathless": *nirvāṇa*.

In early Buddhist art, the "vase of plenty" was often shown with a lotus or *Bodhi* tree sprouting from it, so suggesting spiritual growth from the reservoir of *Dharma* which it symbolized. Figure 8 shows two vases as part of a composite symbol. The upper vase has the disc of an open lotus shown at its lip. Above the lotus is a *triśūla* (Pāli *tisūla*) or trident which represents the three Buddhist "treasures" (*tri-ratnas*, Pāli *ti-ratanas*): the Buddha, *Dharma* and *Sangha*.

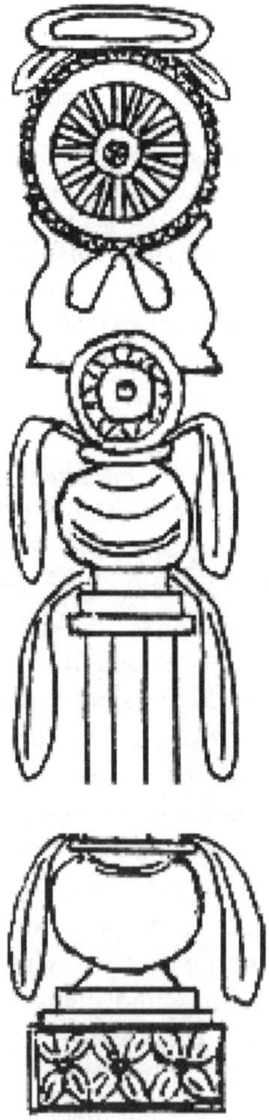

Figure 8 Composite symbol design from the railing of the *stūpa* at Sārnāth, early centuries CE.

Buddha footprints and feet

Like relics and *bodhi* trees, footprints of the Buddha (*Buddha-padas*), in the form of depressions in rocks, are seen as tangible links with him that also act as reminders that the he actually walked on earth and left a spiritual "path" for others to follow. Whether they were part of the earliest Buddhist cult is unclear, but they were used in symbolic representations of his presence in scenes from his life.

One of the most famous "footprints" is the depression measuring 1.7 by 0.85 meters in the rock on top of Mount Siripāda (Adam's Peak) in Sri Lanka. The Chinese Buddhist pilgrim Faxian records having seen it in 412 CE. The sixth-century *Mahāvaṃsa* (1.77–8), based on earlier chronicles, refers to the "footprint" as having been made by the Buddha when he once flew to Sri Lanka by means of his meditation-based psychic power.

Other than putative "real" Buddha footprints, large depictions of the Buddha's feet also became important. By at least the second century CE, these were used as cult objects in the art of Amarāvatī and Gandhāra. On them were various symbols such as wheels, a type of mark of a great man said to have been on the body of Gautama from his birth, lotuses and *svastikas*, an ancient Indian auspicious sign, also used in Jainism and Hinduism, whose name derives from *su* + *asti*, well + be; its form was originally to suggest the rotation of the sun in the sky. Later art embellished such feet or footprints with up to 108 (= 2^2 x 3^3) auspicious signs such as the sun, moon and Mount Meru – a huge mountain said to be the centre of the world (seen as a flat disc): all marvelous things of importance, though shown as "lower" than the Buddha. Such symbols also sometimes adorn the feet of images of the Buddha reclining, while *svastikas* sometimes appear on the chests of Buddhas in East Asia.

Aniconic "bodies" of the Buddha

In early Buddhist art, symbols were often combined to form aniconic "bodies" of the Buddha, so paving the way for the development of images of him in human form, as in Figure 9, where a *Dharma*-wheel stands for the Buddha's head, a short pillar or column for his body and a throne, again suggestive of the Buddha's sovereignty, for his legs. Sometimes, a column fringed by flames represents the body of the Buddha. Such flaming columns were no doubt intended to recall the story of the Buddha's conversion of three fire-worshipping ascetics by overcoming, with his meditative psychic power, two venomous snakes by returning their heat and flames with his own (*Vinaya* 1.24–5). Flaming columns may also recall the "wonder of the pairs" at Śrāvastī (Pāli Sāvatthī) where the Buddha is said to have risen into the air with a mass of fire coming from the upper part of his body and a mass of water from the lower part (*Dhammapada* commentary 3.204–5 and *Paṭisambhidāmagga* 1.125). Again, flaming columns may symbolize the spiritual energy of the Buddha, later symbolized by flames arising from the crown of the head

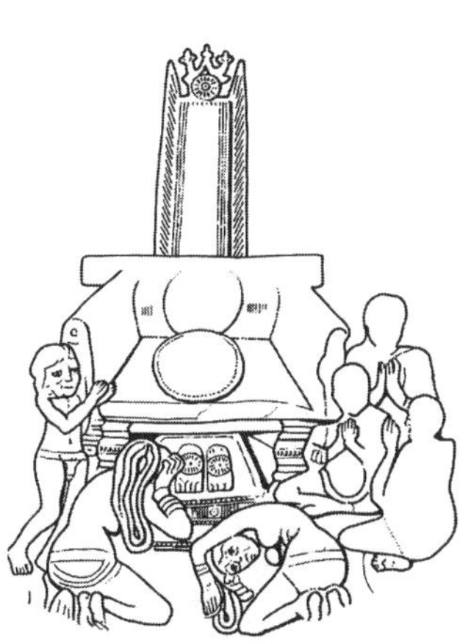

Figure 9 Rāhula being presented to his father, the Buddha (second century CE *stūpa* railing at Amarāvatī).

of Thai and some Sri Lankan Buddha images. As expressed at *Dhammapada* v. 387, "all day and night the Buddha shines in glory."

Stūpas

The final and perhaps most important symbol of early Buddhism is the *stūpa* (Pāli *thūpa*) or "(relic) mound." These are known in Sri Lanka as a *dhātu-gabbha* (Pāli), "womb/container for (relic)-elements," which in Sinhala is *dāgoba* (Figure 10). The mispronunciation of this by Portuguese colonialists may be the origin of the word "pagoda," now mainly used for the multi-roofed East Asian form of the *stūpa*. In Thai, the term used for a *stūpa* is *cedi* (from Pāli *cetiya*, Skt. *caitya*: a shrine) (Figure 11), and in Tibetan *mchod rten* (pronounced *chorten*).

Figure 11 A *stūpa* in Chiang Mai, Thailand.

Stūpas became important in Buddhism because of the holy relics they contained, their symbolizing the Buddha and his *parinirvāṇa* (entry into *nirvāṇa* at death), and in some cases their location at significant sites. Relics placed in *stūpas* are said to have been those of Gautama, *arhats* and even of past Buddhas. Where funerary relics could not be found, hair or possessions of holy beings, copies of bodily relics or possessions, or Buddhist texts came to be used in their place. The *stūpa* is more than a symbol of the *parinirvāṇa*. It is a complete symbol-system incorporating many of the other symbols discussed above, representing the Buddha and the *Dharma* he embodied.

Figure 10 A *stūpa* in Sri Lanka.

Though the development of the Buddha image provided another focus for devotion to the Buddha, *stūpas* remain popular to this day, especially in Theravāda countries. They have gone through a long development in form and symbolism, but this entry concentrates on their early significance.

The best-preserved ancient Buddhist *stūpa*, dating from the first century CE in its present form, is at Sāñcī in central India. It was built over one dating from the third century BCE, which may have been built or embellished by Aśoka. Its diagrammatic representation in Figure 12 gives a clear indication of the various parts of an early *stūpa*.

The four gateways (*toraṇas*) of this *stūpa* put it, symbolically, at the place where four roads meet, as specified in the *Mahāparinibbāna Sutta* (*Dīgha Nikāya*

2.142). This is probably to indicate the openness and universality of the Buddhist teaching, which invites all to come and try its path, and also to radiate loving-kindness to beings in all four directions. In a later development of the *stūpa* in north India, the orientation to the four directions was often expressed by means of a square, terraced base, sometimes with staircases on each side in place of the early gateways. At Sāñcī, these gateways are covered with carved reliefs of *Jātaka* stories on the career of Gautama as *bodhisattva* and also, using symbols, of his final life as a Buddha. Symbols also represent previous Buddhas.

Encircling the Sāñcī *stūpa*, connecting its gateways, is a stone railing (*vedikā*), originally made of wood. This marks off the site dedicated to the *stūpa*, and encloses the first of two paths for circumambulation (*pradakṣiṇā-pathas*). The *stūpa* dome, referred to in Sri Lanka and certain early texts as the *kumbha* or "vase," is the outermost container of the relics, which are housed in an inaccessible chamber near the dome centre in a series of containers, the innermost one often of gold. The dome is thus associated with the "vase of plenty," and symbolically acts as a reminder of an enlightened being as "full" of uplifting *Dharma*. In the third century CE Divyāvadāna, the dome is also called the *aṇḍa* or "egg." As the relics within are sometimes called *bījas*, "seeds," this is all suggestive of *stūpa*-devotion as leading to a fruitful

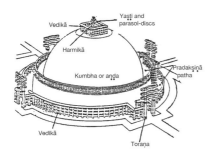

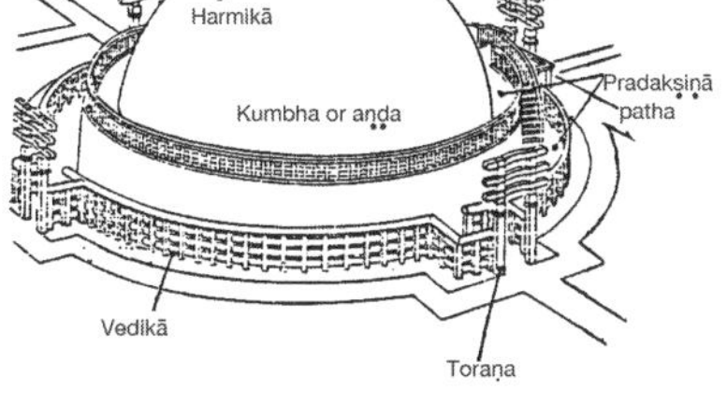

Figure 12 The Great *Stūpa* at Sāñcī.

spiritual life, and to the production of new enlightened ones in the future. From above, the circle of the *stūpa* dome is also suggestive of a *Dharma*-wheel or an open lotus medallion, and inner radial walls in some *stūpas* enhance this imagery. In Burma, the tapering shape of their *stūpas* is also likened to that of a lotus bud.

On top of the Sāñcī *stūpa* is a pole (skt. *yaṣṭi*, Pāli *yaṭṭhi*) and discs, which represent ceremonial parasols. As parasols were used as insignia of royalty in India, their inclusion on *stūpas* can be seen as a way of symbolizing the spiritual sovereignty of the Buddha. The kingly connection probably derives from the ancient custom of rulers sitting under a sacred tree at the centre of a community to administer justice, with mobile parasols later replacing such shading trees. The parasol-structure on *stūpas* also seems to have symbolized the Buddhist sacred tree, which in turn symbolized enlightenment. This is suggested by a second-century BCE stone relief of a *stūpa* which shows it surmounted by a tree with parasol-shaped leaves. The structure at the base of the pole and discs (the *harmikā*, "top enclosure") has also been found, on a number of *stūpas*, to have resembled the design of *bodhi*-tree enclosures.

The parasol pole was often mounted on top of an eight-sided axial pole inside the *stūpa*, sometimes called a *yūpa*. This was originally the term for a Vedic post where animals were tethered prior to being sacrificed. Some early Buddhist *stūpas* had a wooden axis, and these may have originally been Brahmanical sacrificial posts on a sacred site taken over by Buddhists. For Buddhism, the idea of "sacrifice" suggested the self-sacrifices of the path: in the *Kūṭadanta Sutta* (*Dīgha Nikāya* 1.144–7), the best "sacrifice" is explained in terms of the path, and at *Dīgha Nikāya* 3.76, a *yūpa* is where a future *cakravartin* ruler distributes goods to all and then becomes a monk. In the *Milindapañha* (21–2), the monk Nāgasena is described as:

> bearing aloft the *yūpa* of *Dharma* . . . thundering out the thunder of Indra (the Vedic rain god) and thoroughly satisfying the whole world by thundering out sweet utterances and wrapping them round with the lightning flashes of superb knowledge, filling them with the waters of compassion and the great cloud of the deathlessness of *Dharma*.

That is, Vedic symbolism is effectively put to Buddhist use.

Another term for the *stūpa* axial pillar is *indra-kīla* (Pāli *inda-khīla*), or "Indra's stake." This was a term for the huge stone pillars used to secure open the gates of cities in India and Sri Lanka. The term derived from Vedic mythology, in which the god Indra was seen to stabilize the earth by staking it down. In early Buddhist texts, the term is used as an image for the unshakeability of the mind of an *arhat* or stream-enterer (*Saṃyutta Nikāya* 5.444, *Suttanipāta* 229, *Dhammapada* 95, *Theragāthā* 663). The *stūpa* axis representing their unshakeable mind fits in well with the idea of the dome, as a *kumbha*, symbolizing the enlightened person as full of *Dharma*-related qualities.

The axial pillar is also linked to Mount Meru, home of many of the gods, with the base of the circular dome as like the circle of the earth, home to humans. Here, the *stūpa* superstructure, linked to the *Bodhi* tree, is suggestive of the Buddha, who stands above both humans and gods as their teacher.

In later *stūpas* the top part was fused into a spire, and several platforms were often added under the dome to elevate it in an honorific way. It then became possible to see each layer of the structure as symbolizing a particular set of spiritual qualities. In the *Caityavibhāgavinayabhāva Sūtra* and the *Stūpalakṣaṇakārikāvivecana*, respectively from the first and second centuries CE, a *stūpa*'s seven layers from the bottom up to the *harmikā* are seen to symbolize the seven sets of qualities making up the "thirty-seven factors conducive to awakening": the four applications of mindfulness, the four right efforts, the four bases of success, the five faculties, the five powers, the seven factors of awakening (the dome), and the factors of the Eightfold Path (*harmikā*). The spire of the *stūpa* symbolizes the thirteen powers and ten knowledges of a Buddha. At *Dīgha Nikāya* 2.120, the Buddha, not long before his death, taught the seven sets as to be practiced to prolong the holy life. They can be seen to summarize the *Dharma* that he embodied.

Overall, the *stūpa* can be seen to symbolize the Buddha and *Dharma*. Indeed, in some early *Vinaya*s where a *stūpa* is seen as having its own property (land and offerings), it is sometimes seen as "the property of the *stūpa*" and sometimes as the "property of the Buddha." That the *stūpa*'s basic configuration symbolizes the Buddha's enlightened person is suggested by a simile at *Saṃyutta Nikāya* 4.194–5. This likens the body (*kāya*) to a city with six gates (the senses, including the mind), at the centre of which sits the "lord of the city" (consciousness), who receives a message (*nirvāṇa*), from messengers (calm and insight) from the four directions. He sits in the middle of the city, where four roads meet, representing the four great elements (*mahā-bhūtas*) that are the basis of the body. As a *stūpa* is also ideally at a crossroads, and the relics at its centre are also termed *dhātus*, another term for elements, it is akin to the "city" of the Buddha's personality, centered on a consciousness that has experienced *nirvāṇa*.

See also: **Art, Buddhist; *Bodhi* tree; Bodhgayā; Buddha; Sacred places; Sāñcī; *Stūpa*; *Stūpas* of Sāñcī, Bhārhut, and Amarāvatī.**

PETER HARVEY

BUDDHA, FAMILY OF

The historical person known as "the Buddha" was born into the Gautama (Pāli Gotama) clan and was given the name Siddhārtha (Pāli Siddhattha). He was born in the republic of Śākya (Pāli Sakka, Sakyā, Sākiyā), for which reason he is generally known in the Mahāyāna tradition as Śākyamuni (Pāli Sakyamuni) Buddha, "Śākyan Sage" Buddha, though in Theravāda Buddhism, he is usually referred to as Gotama Buddha. The Śākyan capital was Kapilavastu (Pāli Kapilavatthu).

His father was Śuddhodana (Pāli Suddhodana) and his mother (Mahā)-Māyā (*Dīgha Nikāya* 2.52), though as she died seven days after his birth, he was brought up by her sister, Mahā-Prajāpatī (Pāli Mahā-Pajāpatī), who was also married to his father. He had no brothers or sisters but had a half-brother in Sundara-Nanda, son of Mahā-Prajāpatī. The Theravāda tradition says he also had a half-sister, Sundarī-Nandā (*Therīgāthā* commentary 83 and *Aṅguttara Nikāya* commentary 1.363). Both later ordained and became *arhats.*

It is said (*Mahāvastu* 1.355) that the Buddha's father had three brothers: Dhautodana (Pāli Dhotodana), Śuklodana and Amṛtodana (Pāli Amitodana), as well as a sister Amṛtikā (Pāli Amitā). The Theravāda tradition gives him *four* brothers, including both a Sukkodana, and Sukkhodana, and adds another sister, Pamitā (*Suttanipāta* commentary 1.357, *Mahāvaṃsa* II.18–22). The *Mūlasarvastivāda Vinaya* names the sisters as Amṛtikā Śuddhā, Droṇā and Śuklā, thus paralleling their brothers' names.

The *Mahāvastu* (1.355–7) names his mother and Mahā-Prajāpatī's siblings, all sisters, as Mahāmāyā, Atimāya, Anantamāya, Cūlīyā, and Kolīsovā, and says that these were married to Śuddhodana's five (above, three!) brothers. The Theravāda tradition just refers to their siblings as two brothers, Suppabuddha and Daṇḍapāṇi.

The Buddha had cousins in: (1) Ānanda, seen in the Theravāda tradition as son of Amitodana; seen in the Lokottaravādin *Mahāvastu* (3.176–7) as son of Śuklodana and a Mṛigī; (2) Devadatta, seen in the Theravāda tradition as son of his maternal uncle Suppabuddha and paternal aunt Amitā (though at *Vinaya* 2.189, Devadatta is called Godhiputta, Godhi's son); (3) *Mahāvastu* (3.176–7) sees him as son of Śuklodana, and brother of Ānanda and Upadhāna. Both Ānanda and Devadatta ordain as monks. *Mahāvastu* 3.176–7 adds Aniruddha (Pāli Anuruddha), Mahānāma and Bhaṭṭika as sons of Amṛtodana, and Nandana and Nandika as sons of Śukrodana, with the first and last two of these becoming monks. Aniruddha becomes a notable *arhat*, and remains calm when the Buddha dies (*Dīgha Nikāya* 2.156–7). He emphasized the four applications of mindfulness (*Saṃyutta Nikāya* 5.294) and was described as the monk who was foremost in the "divine eye" (*Aṅguttara Nikāya* 1.23).

The identity of Gautama's wife is somewhat unclear. In the Theravāda tradition, the *Buddhavaṃsa* (XXVI.13) calls his wife and mother of Rāhula (Rāhulamātā) Bhaddakaccā; the *Mahāvaṃsa* (II.21–4) and the commentary to the *Aṅguttara Nikāya* (1.204–5) calls her Bhaddakaccānā, and the former sees her as his cousin, sister of Devadatta. The *Mahāvastu* (2.69), however, implies that Gautama's wife, whom it calls Yaśodharā, was not Devadatta's sister, as he woos her. The *Buddhavaṃsa* commentary (p. 245) also calls Gautama's wife Yasodharā (Skt. Yaśodharā), which is the more common name used in north Indian Sanskrit texts such as the *Divyāvadāna* (p. 253). The Mahāyānized Sarvāstivādin *Lalitavistara* calls her Gopā, daughter of maternal uncle Daṇḍapāṇi, and some texts give him three wives: Yaśodharā, Gopikā and Mṛgajā. The *Mahāvastu* (2.73) sees Yaśodharā as daughter of

Śāykan Mahānāma. It also refers (3.177) to a Mahānāma as son of Gautama's maternal uncle Amṛtodana, as does the Theravāda tradition, but if Gautama married Amṛtodana's granddaughter, there would have been a notable age difference.

Śuddhodana

While later tradition portrays him as a *rājā* in the sense of a king, the Śākyan land was an oligarchic republic, and Śuddhodana was probably chosen by fellow nobles. When it was predicted that his son would be either a great ruler or a Buddha, it is said that he sought to protect him from the unpleasant side of life that might prompt him to renounce worldly life and seek enlightenment.

Most traditions agree that the Buddha returns to Kapilavastu in response to a request from his father. During this time, the Buddha gradually brings his father round to accepting his teachings and, though he never became a monk, he attains the different levels of sanctity, becoming a stream-enterer, once-returner, and then non-returner and is an *arhat* at the time of his death (*Therīgāthā* commentary 141). While in Kapilavastu, many relatives of the Buddha become monks. Śuddhodana gets the Buddha to agree that no one could be ordained without the permission of their parents (*Vinaya* 1.82–3). The *Mahāvastu* (3.176) also says that he got the Buddha to agree that no more than one son from each family could ordain, and none if he were an only son.

(Mahā)-Māyā

The Theravādin *Nidānakathā* relates that at the time of Gautama's conception, Mahā-Māyā dreamt that she was transported to the Himālayas where a being in the form of an auspicious white elephant entered her right side. Near the end of her pregnancy, she journeyed from Kapilavastu to the home of her relatives to give birth, as was the custom. On the way, she and her party passed the pleasant Lumbinī grove, where she stopped to enjoy the flowers and birdsong. Here she went into labor, holding onto a tree. The *sutta* account (*Majjhima Nikāya* 3.122–3) says that Māyā had a pregnancy of ten lunar months, then gave birth standing up, with the baby, unsmeared by blood or fluids, set down on the ground by four *deva*s, and a warm and cool stream of water appearing from the sky as a water-libation for mother and child.

The *sutta* says that Māyā died seven days after giving birth, with a later text saying that she was then in her forties (*Vibhaṅga* commentary 278). The *sutta* says she was reborn in the Tuṣita (Pāli Tusita) heaven (in some traditions, the Trāyastriṃśa, Pāli Tāvatiṃsa, heaven). Later texts say that the Buddha spent one rainy season visiting the Trāyastriṃśa heaven to teach her the *Abhidharma*, which led to her becoming a stream-enterer (*Dhammapada* commentary 3.216–17).

Mahā-Prajāpatī

Five years after his enlightenment, Mahā-Prajāpatī Gotamī is said to have gone to the Buddha with 500 other Śākyan women, whose husbands had recently ordained, to seek ordination, even though a nuns' order did not yet exist (*Vinaya* 2.253–5). The *Therīgāthā* commentary (141) says that her husband had recently died. At first the Buddha refuses to accede to her request, though he accepts after Ānanda asks on her behalf and has the Buddha agree that women are capable of the various grades of enlightenment, up to *arhat*ship. The *Dhammapada* commentary (1.115) says that Mahā-Prajāpatī was herself already a stream-enterer, and she soon becomes an *arhat* after her ordination as the first nun. However, in the *Dakkhiṇāvibhaṅga Sutta* (*Majjhima Nikāya* 3.253–7), she is portrayed as still a layperson at a time when the nuns' order already exists.

Verses 157–62 of the *Therīgāthā* are attributed to her, and her death at the age of 120 is described in 189 verses in the *Therīapadāna*. Here, as Gotamī, she is portrayed as paralleling the Buddha, Gotama, both having a "final great *nirvāṇa*" (*mahā-parinirvāṇa*; v. 75). She says that she has the six "higher knowledges," as had the Buddha and certain other *arhats* (v. 78), and then showed the first of these by rising into the air and multiplying her form, and so forth (vv. 80–90). She then goes through the same series of meditative states that the Buddha was to go through at his death, before passing into final *nirvāṇa*, at which there is an earthquake and flowers fall from the sky, as at the Buddha's death (vv. 145–9). The Buddha then praises her as "with wisdom vast and wide" (v. 183). It is interesting that in this text, Mahāprajāpatī addresses Ānanda as her "son" (vv. 63–5), and that Ānanda collects her bones after her cremation (v. 178).

Ānanda

For the last twenty-five years of the Buddha's life, Ānanda was his faithful personal attendant and, in effect, secretary. He accepted this position on the conditions that he did not get any special food or robes but that he could ask the Buddha whatever he wished, and that the Buddha would repeat to him any teachings he had given when he was absent. He was very helpful to enquirers, by answering questions himself or arranging for them to discuss matters with the Buddha – unless the Buddha was ill or very tired. When the Buddha was old and approaching death, he said to Ānanda, "For a long time, Ānanda, you have been in the *Tathāgata*'s presence, showing lovingkindness in acts of body, speech and mind, beneficially, blessedly, wholeheartedly, and unstintingly" (*Dīgha Nikāya* 2.144). Ānanda had a very enquiring mind and if the Buddha just smiled, he would ask the reason.

Even prior to his enlightenment (though he was then a stream-enterer), the Buddha said of him, "Monks, Ānanda is a learner. Yet it would not be easy to find his equal in wisdom" (*Aṅguttara Nikāya* 1.225). The Buddha described him as his foremost monk of those "who have learned much . . . are of good memory (*satimant*) . . . of good behavior . . . resolute . . . personal attendants" (*Aṅguttara Nikāya* 1.24–5).

Ānanda was the most popular teacher of the nuns; he often taught them and was also in charge of arrangements for regularly sending teachers to them. He was also a popular teacher among laywomen. His services were often sought for consoling the sick, advising, for example, practice of the four applications of mindfulness (*Saṃyutta Nikāya* 5.176–8).

At the first council, Ānanda was asked to be present to recount what he had heard of the Buddha's teachings. So as to ensure he was enlightened, like all the others at the first council, he put in a special effort on the night before and so became an *arhat* (*Vinaya* 2.284–6). The initial words of most discourses, "Thus have I heard," are said to have been Ānanda's words at the first council.

Nanda

Nanda is said to have been reluctantly persuaded by his half-brother, the Buddha, to ordain, even though he had just married. He pined for his wife and wished to disrobe, but the Buddha persuaded him to stay by showing him the more beautiful goddesses that his meditations might give him access to. Later he realized the base level of this motivation for staying a monk, and went on to become an *arhat* (*Udāna* 22–3). He is later praised as chief of monks who guard the sense-doors (*Aṅguttara Nikāya* 1.25).

Devadatta

Devadatta is portrayed as someone oriented to gain and fame (*Aṅguttara Nikāya* 4.160). In his youth he is seen as a jealous rival of his cousin the Buddha, and in many *Jātaka* stories, on past lives of the Buddha, he also appears as a problematic character, though one who also did good deeds. He is said to have ordained in the Buddha's *sangha*, attained worldly psychic powers (*Vinaya* 2.183) and was originally well thought of as a monk (*Vinaya* 2.189). When the Buddha was in his seventies, though, his jealousy led him to attempt to take over as head of the *sangha* (*Vinaya* 2.188), and he conspired with Prince Ajātaśatru (Pāli Ajātasattu) in this (*Vinaya* 2.184–203). While the latter succeeded in his plot to kill his father, Bimbisāra, Devadatta tried three times to kill the Buddha without success. In two of these, his attempt is via soldiers of Ajātaśatru and a drunken elephant; in the other, he himself rolled a large rock down a hill at the Buddha; while the rock broke into pieces, a fragment cut the Buddha's foot.

Devadatta then sought to improve his reputation by trying to persuade the Buddha to make vegetarianism and certain voluntary ascetic practices – such as living only at the root of a tree – compulsory; the Buddha refused (*Vinaya* 3.171–2). Criticizing the Buddha, Devadatta then tried to cause a schism in the *sangha* (*Vinaya* 3.174–5, *Udāna* 60–1), but those who initially supported him were persuaded otherwise by the Buddha's two chief disciples, Śāriputra (Pāli Sāriputta) and Maudgalyāyana (Pāli Moggallāna). Devadatta then became ill and is said to have died when the earth swallowed him up. It is said he would be reborn in hell for many ages (*Vinaya* 2.200, *Aṅguttara Nikāya* 3.402), but the *Milindapañha* (pp. 108–13) says that he would eventually become a *pratyeka-buddha*.

Rāhula

In the Theravāda tradition, Gautama's renunciation is a week after his son Rāhula's birth, and he takes a last fond look at him and his wife, but does not wake them, lest his renunciation becomes impossible (*Nidānakatha* 62). In the Mūlasarvāstivādin *Vinaya*, however, his son is conceived on the night of his renunciation, so that Gautama fulfills his duty as a husband, and Rāhula is not born until not long before Gautama's enlightenment.

When the Buddha went back to Kapilavastu, the boy Rāhula was sent by his mother Rāhulamātā (Mother-of-Rāhula) to ask for his (royal) inheritance; so the Buddha had Śāriputra ordain him as a novice (*Vinaya* 1.82). The Buddha taught him constantly for some time after his ordination, later describing him as "Chief among my monk disciples who desire training" (*Aṅguttara Nikāya* 1.24). In time, he becomes an *arhat* (*Majjhima-Nikāya* 3.280). In verses attributed to him in the *Theragāthā* (v. 295), he says "They know me as 'lucky' Rāhula, fortunate for two reasons; one that I am the Buddha's son, and the other that I am one with vision into the truths."

Gautama's wife

The *Mahāpadāna Sutta*, while giving the names of the mothers and fathers of various Buddhas, mentions no wives, though it mentions many female musicians that surrounded the past Buddha Vipassī in his youth (*Dīgha Nikāya* 2.21). The *Ariyapariyesanā Sutta* makes no mention of Gotama having had a wife and son, but says "while still young, a black-haired young man endowed with the blessing of youth, in the prime of life, though mother and father wished otherwise and wept with tearful faces, I . . . went forth" (*Majjhima Nikāya* 1.163). This perhaps suggests the "going forth" might have been in the late teens and prior to marriage – though it is said in the *Mahāparinibbāna Sutta* that Gotama was twenty-nine at his renunciation (*Dīgha Nikāya* 2.151). In the *Ariyapariyesanā Sutta*, the Buddha refers in general terms to "wife and son" as amongst various things which are subject to birth, ageing, sickness and death (*Majjhima Nikāya* 1.162), with a wise person "having understood the danger in what is subject to birth . . . to ageing."

All traditions agree, though, that the Buddha had a son called Rāhula. As seen above, the Theravādin *Buddahavaṃsa* calls Rāhula's mother Bhaddakaccā or Bhaddakaccānā. The latter is described at *Aṅguttara Nikāya* 1.25 as chief of the Buddha's nuns who have great "higher knowledges" (such as memory of past lives); the commentary affirms that she was an *arhat*. In the *Jātaka* commentary, it is said that Rāhulamātā ordained so as to be near her son and the Buddha, her ex-husband, being known as the nun Bimbā-devī (*Jātaka* 2.392–3). In the Thai tradition is a late text known as "Bimbā's Lament" (Strong 2001: 96–7) in which Gautama's wife laments having been left and that Gautama did not immediately come to see her when he returned to Kapilavastu.

The Buddha's wife is identified as having previously been a key character in many *Jātaka* stories, on past lives of the Buddha. The best-known example is as Maddī, wife of Prince Vessantara (Skt. Viśvantara), whose perfect generosity even entails him giving her away when asked (*Jātaka* VI.479–593). The tradition indicates, though, that she and many of the Buddha's relatives had the great benefit of becoming *arhats* through his teachings.

See also: **Buddha; Buddha, story of; *Jātakas* and other narrative collections.**

PETER HARVEY

BUDDHA, HISTORICAL CONTEXT

Social and material conditions of the day

The Buddha taught in the region of the Ganges basin in northeast India, at a time of changing social conditions, where the traditions of small kin-based communities were being undermined as these were swallowed up by expanding kingdoms, such as those of Magadha and Kośala (Pāli Kosala). A number of cities had developed which were the centers of administration and of developing organized trade, based on a money economy. These included Śrāvastī, Rājagṛha and Vaiśālī (Pāli Sāvatthī, Rājagaha and Vesālī), in all of which the Buddha was to spend much time, though he came from one of the smaller kin-based republics: Śākya (Pāli Sakka, Sakyā, Sākiyā).

The religious context

While the Buddha was innovative, he needed to express himself using categories and concepts that were comprehensible to his culture and addressing their concerns. How did this color the Buddha's message, and does it mean, as some claim, that Buddhism carries "unnecessary cultural baggage" from its early period? To address such questions, it is necessary to understand that period, how the Buddha related to its ideas and practices, and the similarities and differences between his teachings and those of his contemporaries. It should be noted that the period had its own diversity, and some "modern" ideas (such as materialism and skepticism) are not new ideas that Buddhism now has to relate to for the first time: it has already responded to ancient versions of these in India.

In the Buddhist *suttas*, the religious teachers/practitioners of the day are usually summed up as "*brāhmaṇas* and *śramaṇas*." The first were the priests of the still dominant sacrificial Vedic religion, also known as Brahmanism; scholars generally use the modernized form "brahmins" (occasionally "brahmans") to refer to them. The second were various renunciants who rejected the authority of the Vedic texts and, while sharing certain concerns of later Vedic religion, sought their own solutions to the problems of life. Buddhism itself originated as a *śramaṇa* (Pāli *samaṇa*) tradition.

Vedic culture and Brahmanism

Brahmanism, which around 200 BCE began to develop into the religion now known as Hinduism, had entered the northwest of the Indian sub-continent by around 1500 BCE, brought by a nomadic people who seem to have come from an area now in eastern Turkey, southern Russia and northern Iran. In this area, people spoke a postulated Aryan (Skt. *Ārya*) language, the basis of a number of "Indo-European" languages spread by migration from there to India, Iran, Greece, Italy and other parts of Western Europe. The form of the language spoken in India was Sanskrit (from which Pāli is derived). The influx of the Aryans brought to an end the declining Indus Valley Civilization, a sophisticated city-based culture which had existed in the region of Pakistan since around 2500 BCE. The religion of the Aryans was based on the *Veda*, orally transmitted teachings and hymns seen as revealed by the gods: the *Rig Veda Saṃhitā* (*c.* 1500–1200 BCE), three other *Veda Saṃhitās*, and later compositions known as *Brāhmaṇas* and *Upaniṣads*. The Aryans worshipped thirty-three gods known as *devas*, anthropomorphized principles seen as active in nature, the cosmos, and human life. The central rite of the religion was one in which the priests sang the praises of a particular *deva* and offered him sacrifices by placing them in a sacrificial fire. In return, they hoped for such boons as health, increase in cattle, and immortality in the afterlife with the *devas*. In the *Brāhmaṇas* (*c.* 1000–1800 BCE), animal sacrifices came to be added to the earlier offerings, such as grain and milk. The enunciation of the sacred sacrificial verses, known as *mantras*, was also seen as manipulating a sacred power called *Brahman*, so that the ritual was regarded as actually coercing the *devas* into sustaining the order of the cosmos and giving what was wanted.

Brahman and Brahmā

In the early *Upaniṣads*, *Brahman* came to be seen as the substance underlying the whole cosmos, and as identical with the *ātman*, the universal Self which the yogic element of the Indian tradition had sought deep within the mind. By true knowledge of this identity, it was held that a person could attain liberation from reincarnation after death, and merge back into *Brahman*.

Richard Gombrich argues that Buddhist commentators who wrote centuries after the Buddha no longer recognized allusions to Brahmanical ideas in the *suttas* and that, in particular, "The central teachings of the Buddha came as a response to the central teachings of the old *Upaniṣads*, notably the *Bṛhadāraṇyaka*", this being the only clearly pre-Buddhist *Upaniṣad* other than the *Chāndogya*.

In the Buddhist *suttas*, there is no unambiguous reference to the neuter *Brahman*, in the sense of an impersonal ground-of-being or divine force, but many references to the male deity Brahmā – indeed, more than one of these – the personal embodiment of *Brahman* in Brahmanism. Nevertheless, in the *Upaniṣads*, Brahmā is only referred to a few times. In the *Chāndogya Upaniṣad*, he is referred to at 3.11.4 as he who teaches a sacred formulation of truth (*brahman*) to

Prajāpati – the main creator god referred to in the *Upaniṣads*, with whom Brahmā is sometimes identified, who then teaches it to Manu, a key human ancestor. Again at 8.15.1, he teaches Prajāpati, who teaches Manu, about a certain way of living leading to the world of *Brahman*, beyond rebirth. The post-Buddhist *Muṇḍaka Upaniṣad* begins "Brahmā arose as the first among gods, as the creator of all ... he disclosed the knowledge of *Brahman*." In later Hinduism, Brahmā comes to be seen as creating the world on behalf of the highest deity, seen as either Viṣṇu or Śiva.

Within Buddhism, several terms contain the term *brahma-*, which could mean either Brahmā or *Brahman*, but in either case reflect the influence of Brahmanical terminology: the term *brahmacariya*, literally "*brahma*-conduct," is used to refer to celibacy and the religious "holy life" that it is a key ingredient of; the qualities of lovingkindness, compassion, empathetic joy and equanimity, which are said to lead to rebirth in the world of a *brahmā* (*Dīgha Nikāya* 1.235–2), are described as *brahma-vihāras*, usually translated as "divine abidings;" the Buddha is said to be *brahma-bhūta*: to have "become brahmā/*brahman*" (*Dīgha Nikāya* 3.84;), perhaps simply meaning "become the supreme," for *brahmā* could also mean "the best," as at *Saṃyutta Nikāya* 5.4–6, where people refer to a fine chariot as "the *brahmā* of chariots;" the *arhat*, or Buddhist saint, is also sometimes seen as the true brahmin, as in *Dhammapada* verses 383–423.

In the *Tevijja Sutta* (*Dīgha Nikāya* 1.237–9), the Buddha ridicules brahmins for claiming to know the way to union with Brahmā/*Brahman* when none of them has actually experienced this. In the *Kūṭadanta Sutta*, it is claimed that the Buddha was asked by a brahmin on the best way to conduct the (Brahmanical) sacrifice. He replies with a story about a past king who was asked the same, and was advised first to prevent poverty in his land, then to conduct a completely nonviolent sacrifice (*Dīgha Nikāya* 1.134–41). This is a good example of Buddhism replacing ritual sacrifice with ethical action.

Moreover, while fire had a positive valence in Brahmanism as the medium of communication with the gods, in Buddhism it was used as a symbol of the "burning" quality of such things as greed, hatred, and delusion, and the whole process of grasping at life. Again, while thinking of the problems of human nature as being casued by desire and spiritual ignorance is found in both the *Upaniṣads* and Buddhism, the understanding of these is different. Seeing the spiritual quest as relating to ideas of Self is found in both, though in different ways.

Varṇa

The great responsibility of the brahmin priests in their ritual support for cosmic order was reflected in them placing themselves at the head of what was regarded as a divinely ordained hierarchy of four social classes, the others being those of the *kṣatriyas* or warrior-leaders of society in peace or war, the *vaiśyas*, or cattle-rearers and cultivators, and the *śūdras*, or servants. A person's membership of one of these four *varṇas*, or "complexions" of humanity, was seen as determined by birth; in later Hinduism the system incorporated thousands of lesser social groupings and became known as the caste, or *jāti*, system.

At the time of the Buddha, most brahmins practiced priestly duties of either sacrifice or austerities, plus things such as truthfulness and study of the Vedic teachings. Some were saintly, but others seem to have been haughty and wealthy, supporting themselves by putting on large, expensive, and bloody sacrifices, often paid for by kings. At its popular level, Brahmanism incorporated practices based on protective magic spells, and pre-Brahmanical spirit-worship no doubt continued.

The Buddhist critique of Brahmanical thinking on the four *varṇas* can be seen at *Dīgha Nikāya* 3.81–4. Here brahmins claim to belong to the only pure class, being "the true children of Brahmā/an, born from his/its mouth, Brahma-born, Brahma-created, Brahma-heirs"; while this might be seen as a reference to the neuter *Brahman*, there is here a clear allusion to the *Puruṣa-Sūkta*, a *Rig Veda* hymn on the sacrifice of the primal man, with brahmins being said to come from the mouth of the primal man, namely the part which utters sacred speech. The Buddha's response to this claim, though, is to point out that brahmins are actually born of brahmin *women*. Moreover, people of any of the classes can act well or badly: behavior, not birth, is what is important, as also emphasized by *Suttanipāta* verse 136:

> Not by birth does one become an outcaste,
> not by birth does one become a brahmin.
> By (one's) action does one become an outcaste,
> by (one's) action does one become a brahmin.

Elsewhere, the Buddha gets a brahmin to examine the traditional qualities of a brahmin, which refer to family lineage, knowledge of the Vedic *mantras*, good appearance, virtue and wisdom, and strip away the first three, leaving virtue and wisdom as the only things that really matter (*Dīgha Nikāya* 1.9–24). It is, though, not appropriate to see the Buddha as arguing like a modern egalitarian against any notion of social class. He simply argues against ideas of superiority based on birth. Elsewhere, he argues that the particular social stratification of his day in India is not a universal sacred norm, as different stratifications are found elsewhere.

As regards the social background of the Buddha's disciples, we have some information. The commentary to the *Theragāthā* and *Therīgāthā* describes the background of 328 monks and nuns and indicates that over two-thirds came from urban areas. It also indicates that: 41 percent were brahmin, 23 percent *kṣatriya*, 30 percent *vaiśya*, 3 percent *śūdra* (servants), and 3 percent "outcaste" (below the *śūdras* in the Brahmanical hierarchy). Of these, the brahmins do not generally appear to have been traditional village priests, but urban dwellers perhaps employed as state officials. State officials and merchants were the dominant groups in urban society, but neither had an established niche in the *varṇa* system (though merchants later came to be seen as *vaiśyas*). These groups seem to have been particularly attracted to the Buddha's message, which addressed people as individuals in charge of their own moral and spiritual destiny, rather than as members of the *varṇa* system. Respect should be based on moral and spiritual worth, not birth: it had to be earned. Indeed, in urban society, people's worldly attainments increasingly depended on personal effort, rather than on traditionally ascribed social position. The Buddhist emphasis on karmic results as depending on adhering to universal, rather than *varṇa*-bound, moral norms was thus congenial. The Buddha taught all who came to him without distinction, and urged his disciples to teach in the local languages or dialects of their hearers (*Vinaya* 2.139). In contrast, the brahmins taught in Sanskrit, which had by now become unintelligible to those who had not studied it, and only made the Vedic teachings available to males of the top three *varṇas*.

Karma and rebirth

The idea of reincarnation is first clearly stated in the *Upaniṣads*, seeming to have developed as an extension of the idea, found in the *Brāhmaṇas*, that the power of a person's sacrificial action might be insufficient to lead to an afterlife that did not end in another death. The *Upaniṣads*, perhaps because of some non-Aryan influence, saw such a death as being followed by reincarnation as a human or animal. Non-Aryan influence was probably more certain in developing the idea that it was the quality of a person's *karma*, or "action," that determines the nature of their reincarnation in an insecure earthly form; previously, "*karma*" had only referred to sacrificial action. Nevertheless, Brahmanism continued to see *karma* in largely ritual terms, and actions were judged relative to a person's *varṇa*.

While the *Upaniṣads* were starting to move away from the sacrificial ways of thinking which permeated early Brahmanism, they were still affected by it. In Buddhism we see a decoupling of *karma* from its link to ritual by identifying it with the mental impulse behind an act; the ethical quality of this was the key to an action's being good or bad, not its conformity with ritual norms. Even in Buddhist ritual, which is mild by comparison with brahmin ritual, this still holds good.

Dharma

A key term of Brahmanical thought was *Dharma*, seen as the divinely ordained order of the universe, an order which also includes the order of human society, as seen in the *varṇa* system and in the four stages of life that a male of the top three classes should go through: student, married householder, semi-retired forest-dweller, and ascetic renunciant (*saṃnyāsin*). All of these classes and stages entailed particular duties, also known as *dharmas*. The concept of *Dharma* thus includes both how things are and how they should be. An analogy to this in Western thought is the concept of "law," which as a "law of nature" is how things are, and as a legal "law" is how things should be. Likewise, a standard such as the meter rule in Paris is both something that exists and something that determines what things of that type *should be*.

In Buddhism, *Dharma* (Pāli *Dhamma*) is also a central term. Here, the emphasis is not on fixed social duties, but primarily on the nature of reality, practices aiding understanding of this and practices informed by an understanding of this, all aiding a person to live a happier life and to move closer to liberation.

Concerns for connection and enumeration

On the meaning of *Upaniṣad*, Patrick Olivelle states:

> The earliest usage of the important term *upaniṣad* indicates that it [means] ... "connection" or "equivalence." In addition, the term implies hierarchy; the Upaniṣadic connections are hierarchically arranged, and the quest is to discover the reality that stands at the summit of this hierarchically interconnected universe.

While this relates to the *Upaniṣads*' probing of secret inner relationships between the microcosm and macrocosm, ultimately between *ātman* and *Brahman*, Buddhism too contains much on the connections between things, though here expressed in terms of causal connections rather than mystical correspondences (though a concern with these returns in tantric Buddhism). Buddhism likewise contains the idea of a hierarchy of worlds which can be experienced in meditation or entered on being reborn after death.

Just as Buddhism has a concern for (causal) connections, so it has a concern for analysis, often into lists of items, for example the four Ennobling Truths/

Realities, the five components of personality, the six elements (*dhātus*): earth, water, fire, wind, space and consciousness. This accords with a concern, in brahmin as well as in various *śramaṇa* teachings, to enumerate the various elements of a person and the cosmos. This is all part of seeing the *Dharma* of things: their basic order or pattern.

In Hinduism, this approach in time crystallized into the Sāṃkhya, or "Enumeration," school. While this was not founded as a separate school until around 400 CE, early forms of the ideas which it systematizes are found in texts such as the *Kaṭha* and *Śvetāśvatara Upaniṣads* (*c.* 300–100 BCE?). In the story of the Buddha's life, one of the teachers he goes to is Ārāḍa Kālāma (Pāli Āḷāra Kālāma). In the *Buddhacārita* of Aśvaghoṣa (second century CE), Ārāḍa is attributed with teachings that are in certain respects similar to those of early Sāṃkhya (XII.17–42), concerning how components of personality evolve and in which the *ātman* is the inner knower (XII.20) who is not the agent of action (XII.26).

Yoga

Brahmins learnt of yogic techniques of meditation, physical isolation, fasting, celibacy, and asceticism from ascetics whose traditions may have gone back to the Indus Valley Civilization. Such techniques were found to be useful as spiritual preparations for performing the sacrifice. Some brahmins then retired to the forest and used them as a way of actually carrying out the sacrifice in an internalized, visualized form. Out of the teachings of the more orthodox of these forest-dwellers were composed the *Upaniṣads.*

The Buddha can clearly be seen as part of the broad yogic tradition of India. Gavin Flood describes yoga as a practice shared by many of the brahmin and *śramaṇa* renouncers from the period which includes the origin of Buddhism:

> The term *yoga*, derived from the Sanskrit root *yuj*, "to control," "to yoke" or "to unite," refers to those technologies or disciplines of asceticism and meditation which are thought to lead to spiritual experiences of profound understanding or insight into the nature of existence ... The concept of yoga as a spiritual discipline not confined to any particular sectarian affiliation or social form, contains the following important features:
>
> - consciousness can be transformed through focusing attention on a single point;
> - the transformation of consciousness eradicates limiting mental constraints or impurities such as greed and hate;
> - yoga is a discipline, or range of disciplines, constructed to facilitate the transformation of consciousness.

"Yoga," as a term, is more used in Hinduism than in Buddhism, and indeed Hinduism contains a school based on a particular systematization of yoga practices and ideas known as the Yoga school, which shares many theoretical ideas with the Sāṃkhya school. *Kaṭha Upaniṣad* (6.10–11) talks of yoga as the steady control of the senses which, along with the cessation of thinking, leads to the highest state. *Śvetāśvatara Upaniṣad* (2.8–14) says that the yogin should hold the body erect, calm the breathing till it stops, and restrain the mind, so as to know the true *ātman*.

Forms of Buddhist meditation which emphasize concentration – generally known as *śamatha* (Pāli *samatha*) – are akin to yogic meditative discipline. They certainly aim at single-pointed concentration in which the mind seems to unite with its object, which has a transformative effect on consciousness, and which undermine qualities such as greed and hatred (though insight is needed to completely eradicate these). In the higher states attained by *śamatha*, normal thought is transcended, and in the highest, all mental activity is transcended. For the Buddhist goal, though, *śamatha*, or calm, has to be complemented by *vipaśyanā* (Pāli *vipassanā*), or insight, and the very *deepest* levels of *śamatha* are not prerequisites for enlightenment.

The *śramaṇas*

By the time of the Buddha, the ideas expressed in the *Upaniṣads* were starting to filter out into the wider intellectual community and were being hotly debated, both by brahmins and by *śramaṇas*, who were somewhat akin to the early Greek philosophers and mystics. The *śramaṇas* rejected the Vedic tradition and wandered free of family ties, living by alms, in order to think, debate, and investigate altered states of consciousness through meditative practices and austerities.

While *śramaṇa* literally means "one who strives," it is variously translated. Common translations are: (1) "recluse," but while some *śramaṇas* were loners, and most may have spent periods of solitary meditation, they also depended on contact with the laity for alms, and many also taught the laypeople; (2) "ascetic," but while practices such as fasting and going naked in all weathers were common among *śramaṇas*, Buddhist *śramaṇas* avoided all but mild asceticism. More satisfactory translations are "renunciant" or "renunciate." A term which also included those from the Brahmanical tradition that abandoned normal worldly life was *parivrājaka* (Pāli *paribbājaka*), or "wanderer," though the term later used specifically in Brahmanism was *saṃnyāsin*. Another common term, and that preferred in Buddhism, was *bhikṣu* (Pāli *bhikkhu*), "almsman."

Many *śramaṇas* came from the new urban centers, where old certainties were being questioned, and increasing disease from population concentration may have posed the universal problem of human suffering in a relatively stark form. They therefore sought to find a basis of true and lasting happiness in a changing and insecure world.

Jainism

One of the major *śramaṇa* groups was that of the Jains. Jainism was founded, or at least led in the Buddha's day, by Vardhamāna the Mahāvīra, or "Great Hero." Buddhists *suttas* referred to them as Nigraṇthas ("without bonds"), and to Vardhamāna as Nigraṇtha Jñātaputra (Pāli Nigaṇṭha Nātaputta). The latter appears in the *suttas* as a contemporary of the Buddha who died before him.

Buddhism and Jainism emerged from a similar strand of Indian culture, and have many similarities. Both Gautama Buddha and Vardhamāna are seen as coming from the *kṣatriya* class, and both were born in the northeast of the Indian sub-continent (Vardhamāna in Patna). Both lived a renunciant life from a similar age (Gautama, twenty-nine; Vardhamāna, thirty) and spent a number of years of strict ascetic practice – up to six in the case of Gautama, at the end of which he rejected extreme asceticism, twelve in the case of Vardhamāna, who continued to advocate such practices. Both then attained some form of enlightenment and went on to teach others and led monastic and lay followers. Unlike Gautama, Vardhamāna died aged seventy-two, after a period of voluntary starvation.

Doctrinally, Buddhism and Jainism have much in common. Both postulate countless past rebirths, with no creator of either the world or the round of rebirths. The human world goes through vast cycles of improvement and decline (the details differ), and is currently in a period of decline. Rebirths exist at many levels (again, details differ) and a being's *karma* (action) determines how it is reborn. Liberation is by the self-effort of the individual, under the guidance of their tradition. Beings have freedom of action, and are not puppets of fate. Both traditions rejected the efficacy of the Vedic fire sacrifice and emphasize, in their different ways, non-violence to all forms of life. Both seek liberation from the round of rebirths, which is seen as entailing repeated suffering.

It is clear that Buddhists and Jains were taking part in a similar quest, and language used by each may have been alluded to, commented on, critiqued and re-interpreted by the other. Ex-Jain Buddhists would also have brought some Jain modes of expression with them.

The terms *Tathāgata* and *arhat* (Pāli *arahat*) are used in both religions, applied to their founders, and both use the term *nirvāṇa* for their highest goal, though they understand it differently. Both founders were seen to have been endowed with the "thirty-two characteristics of a great man." The concept also existed in Brahmanism, and this is reflected in the fact that when each tradition started to portray their founders, they look very similar: a meditating Buddha and Mahāvīra are hard to tell apart (though the Jain images lack a dot on the forehead, may be totally naked, and have a diamond-shaped symbol on the chest). Both traditions see their founders as one in a line of similar figures: Buddhism has its past Buddhas and Jainism sees Vardhamāna as twenty-fourth of a line of *Jinas*, "Conquerors" (of bondage) or *Tīrthaṃkaras*, "Fordmakers" (those who show a way beyond for others). The one before him is called Pārśva, who lived perhaps only 250 years earlier, suggesting that *śramaṇa* traditions were well established by the time of the Buddha.

That said, Jainism has a number of key teachings of which Buddhism is critical. A key focus is on the *jīva* – life-principle, sentient essence or soul – an unchanging, eternal substance, but with changing attributes. Buddhism emphasizes that no permanent Self/soul can be found to exist. The *jīva* is seen as an individual self, unlike the universal Upaniṣadic *ātman*, which Jainism rejects. There are an infinite number of *jīvas*, just as the Sāṃkhya and Yoga schools of Hinduism accept an infinite number of *puruṣas*, inner "persons." Each *jīva* is directly knowable, the "I" of "I did," "I do," "I shall do": the agent of action, as well as the subject of knowledge, consciousness, the enjoyer/eater of experiences including karmic fruits. In this, it is much more like the Western concept of self or soul than either the universal *ātman* or the *puruṣa*, with the latter being beyond both body and mind; a passive observer, rather than an agent. The *jīva* is seen to expand or contract to fill the body it dwells in (it has a size and weight), and to have a very close relationship to its body: it is neither identical with nor different from it. It is by nature different from what is *ajīva*, non-sentient: matter, space, and time. *Jīvas* exist in all living things, including plants and even stones, earth, rivers, raindrops, flames, fires, gases, and winds. Life is prolific but is imprisoned in many forms, subject to suffering: the pains of an animal, of a tree being cut down, or even iron being beaten. This range of sentient things is much greater than is acknowledged in Buddhism, which certainly does not include things such as iron, and is ambivalent on plant life: one cannot be reborn as a plant, but plants *may* have a kind of rudimentary sentience.

The *jīva* is seen as by nature bright, omniscient, immortal and blissful, but is obscured by karmic "matter": here, there are some similarities with early Buddhist ideas on the basic nature mind (*citta*) as being radiant (*Aṅguttara Nikāya* 1.10), and related later ideas on the Buddha-nature as present in all beings.

The aim of Jainism is to liberate the *jīva* from the round of rebirths, so that it will float to the "top" of the universe, to exist in blissful, omniscient isolation from the world and its problems. This notion of liberation is again reminiscent of those in the Sāṃkhya and Yoga schools of Hinduism. The notion of the universe as definitely spatially limited is not shared with Buddhism.

Liberation is seen to come by freeing the *jīva* from bondage by removing its encrustation of *karma*, seen as a kind of subtle matter. The methods of doing so are two-fold:

1. wearing out the results of previous *karma* by austerities (*tapas*) such as fasting, pulling out the hair (at ordination) and going unwashed (washing also harms vermin and even water); penances are done for bad actions, and some monks and even very pious laity practice *sallekhanā*: fasting to death when old;
2. to avoid the generation of new karmic matter, self-restraint, total non-violence to any form of life, and vegetarianism. Such good conduct generates some karmic results, but unlike bad *karma*, these spontaneously destroy themselves.

The Buddha saw the Jain theory of *karma* as somewhat mechanical and inflexible. Buddhist texts attribute to Jainism a kind of karmic fatalism: "Whatever this individual experiences, whether pleasant, unpleasant or neutral, all this is because of previous action. Thus, by burning up, making an end to ancient actions, by non-doing of new actions, there is no overflowing into the future" (*Majjhima Nikāya* 2.214). Buddhism, in contrast, sees past *karma* as only one of several causes of present pleasure or pain (*Saṃyutta Nikāya* 4.230–1). The austerities Jainism advocates are seen in Buddhism as ineffective and extreme.

Buddhist and Jain ethics share an emphasis on avoiding the killing of any living being, though in Jainism, while intentional harm is worse, even unintentional harm is to be constantly guarded against, so as to avoid accumulating the *karma* of killing. Just as Buddhism recruited well amongst merchants, so did Jainism, particularly because trading had a lower likelihood of causing death to any kind of *jīva* than many other modes of livelihood.

Jain monks, like Buddhist ones, live by alms, but the Jain ones have preserved a basically wandering life, also found in early Buddhism, except during the Indian rainy season. In developing a more settled renunciant lifestyle, ordered by rules of community, the Buddhists can be seen to have invented monastic life. Buddhism and Jainism both emphasize constant awareness and equanimity. They share meditations on the impurity of the body and the impermanence and unsatisfactoriness of the world, though Jainism emphasizes these more. A common Jain meditation is "abandoning the body," a form of standing meditation.

Both Buddhism and Jainism are critical of dogmatic or one-sided views, both comparing these to the views of blind men quarrelling over the nature of an elephant after only ever having felt a small part of it, then over-generalizing from this. The Buddhist use of this simile is at *Udāna* 67–9; the Jain use is discussed on the Jain World website: http://www.jainworld.com/phil/anekant.htm. In time, the Jains developed a theory of knowledge including *anekānta-vāda*, the doctrine of many-sidedness, and *syād-vāda*, the doctrine that all knowledge is relative. Knowledge is relative, partial and limited for the unliberated *jīva*, whose natural omniscience is still obscured. This limits the perceptions and perspectives of the unliberated, so that what they say will only ever be partially true: any statement about an object will always be relative to a particular context. Jainism thus advocates meditation on the different aspects of things. For example, free will and determinism both have aspects of truth to them, and the *jīva* is both unchanging (in its inner nature) and changing (in its qualities). Here, there are *some* similarities with the Buddhist idea that the truth is often a "middle way" between extreme opposing views. The Jain idea that existence is a complex organic whole with many interrelated, interdependent factors can also be related to Buddhist ideas.

The Ājīvikas

The Ājīvikas (Pāli and Sanskrit, though the spelling Ājīvaka is also found in Pāli), were an ascetic *śramaṇa* group that were important rivals to the Buddhists and Jains in their early days. They survived in India to around the fourteenth century CE, but then died out. Consequently, all we know of them now is through depictions of them in the literature of competing religions. The best study of them is by A.L. Basham.

The Ājīvikas (literally, "Those who make a living") originated when certain ascetics were united under the leadership of the determinist Maskarin Gośāla (Pāli Makkhali Gosāla). Gośāla spent six years in shared asceticism with the Jain leader Vardhamāna before the two quarreled and went their own ways. Their followers, however, were often in contact, and had a mutual respect for each other. In Jain texts Gośāla claimed to be the twenty-fourth *Tīrthaṃkara*, as did Vardhamāna.

The Ājīvikas, like the Buddhists and Jains, saw the world as working according to natural law rather than the will of a divine being, but differed from both in denying the efficacy of *karma*; rather, the destiny of beings was rigidly determined by *niyati*: "destiny" itself. Ājīvika belief focused on the *jīva*, though this seems to have been understood as material in nature. "Destiny" was seen to drive it through a fixed progression of types of rebirths, over vast cycles of time, from a low form of animal to an advanced human who becomes an Ājīvika ascetic. Near the end of this process, it would pass seven times from one human body to another without dying, by a process of reanimation, before leaving the round of rebirths. Here, the notion of past ages is similar to Jain and Buddhist beliefs, and the figure of seven is reminiscent of the Buddhist belief that a "stream-enterer," one who had glimpsed *nirvāṇa*, would have at most seven more rebirths before fully attaining it.

Both Vardhamāna and the Buddha criticized Ājīvika fatalism as a pernicious denial of human potential and responsibility: Gośāla's teachings are described as being more harmful than those of any other teacher (*Aṅguttara Nikāya* 1.33).

The Ājīvikas, like the Jains, seem to have practiced non-injury and vegetarianism, and had female as well as male ascetics. Their practices also included not accepting food specially prepared for them, from a pregnant woman, or from where there was a dog which might also want to eat; and rigorous asceticism, such as fasting, nakedness, and perhaps disfiguring initiations. They aimed to die by self-starvation (as Vardhamāna in fact did), as a fitting way to end their last rebirth. Amongst the various ascetics referred to in the *suttas*, it is possible that some otherwise unassigned ones were Ājīvikas, because of their nakedness and extreme asceticism. In the *Pāṭika Sutta*, for example, there is reference to a naked ascetic whose practice was to move and eat like a dog (*Dīgha Nikāya* 3.6–7).

The *Sāmaññaphala Sutta* includes teachings attributed to a number of *śramaṇa* groups (*Dīgha Nikāya* 1.52–9). In many of these is a concern for enumeration of types of things, as referred to above. The *sutta* includes teachings not only of Gośala but also of Pūraṇa Kassapa (Skt. Purṇa Kāśyapa) and Pakuddha Kaccāyana (Skt. Kakuda Kātyāyana). Their teachings seem also to have had an influence on the Ājīvikas, and other Pāli texts attribute some of

Purṇa's and Gośāla's views to each other (*Aṅguttara Nikāya* 3.383–4, *Saṃyutta Nikāya* 3.69).

The *Sāmaññaphala Sutta* says that Purṇa taught that by one who kills, robs, commits adultery and lies, no evil (*pāpa*) is done, and by one who gives, no good *karma* accrues (*Dīgha Nikāya* 1.52). That is, he seemed to deny the reality of good and evil. The *sutta*'s characterization may be more a *reductio ad absurdum* than a straight description, though. It may be that Purṇa taught that the *jīva* was a passive, non-involved observer of the actions of the body, which were then seen as determined by *niyati*, as Gośāla taught. Such a notion of a passive on-looking Self beyond morality is found elsewhere in early Indian thought. In *Bṛhadāraṇyaka Upaniṣad* 4.4.22, it is said of the *ātman* that, "He does not become more good by good actions or in any way less by bad actions". In the Sāṃkhya and Yoga schools, the *Puruṣa* is an uninvolved spectator of the actions carried out by body and mind.

Kakuda's views are characterized as concerning seven unchanging, eternal elemental bodies (*kāyas*): earth, water, fire, air, pleasure, pain and the *jīva*. These do not affect each other, such that "there is neither slain nor slayer ... whoever cuts off a man's head with a sharp sword does not deprive anyone of life, he just inserts the blade in the intervening space between these seven bodies" (*Dīgha Nikāya* 1.56). The first four of these elementals are found in Buddhism, though not as eternal, as the four primary elements of the material world. Again, the *Sāmaññaphala Sutta* may be trying to reduce the view to absurdity by seeing it as denying that any life is destroyed when someone is decapitated. Yet there is an echo, here, of a passage in the post-Buddhist *Kaṭha Upaniṣad* (2.19; cf. *Bhagavad Gītā* 2.19) when, speaking of the eternal, indestructible *ātman*, it says: "If the killer thinks that he kills; if the killed thinks that he is killed; both of them fail to understand. He neither kills, nor is he killed".

The materialists

A small group of *śramaṇas* referred to in Buddhist texts are said to hold to "annihilationism" (*ucchedavāda*), on account of them saying that a person is completely destroyed at death, thus denying rebirth. The Buddha saw most other views of the day as some form of the opposite extreme, "eternalism" (Skt. *śāśvata-vāda*, Pāli *sassata-vāda*), which says that what survives death is some eternal Self, soul or life-principle. Buddhism taught that a person continues as an ongoing flow of changing conditions (according to the doctrine of Dependent Origination), this being a "middle" teaching that avoids both annihilationism and eternalism (*Saṃyutta Nikāya* 2.20–1).

The annihilationists denied any kind of self other than one which could be directly perceived, and held that this was annihilated at death. Characterization of them in Buddhist texts varies between seeing them as accepting an unchanging Self which is then destroyed at death (which is seen as odd: if an unchanging Self exists, it would not be destroyed by death), and denying any Self or surviving Self (*Saṃyutta Nikāya* 4.400–1). The *Brahmajāla Sutta* says they believed in up to seven kinds of Self (*attā*), the first of which consists of gross matter, two consist of subtle matter, and four are completely formless, mental; but they are all seen to be entirely destroyed at death (*Dīgha Nikāya* 1.34–6). Here, the first kind were materialists, and these seem to have been the most typical of the "annihilationists," akin to the Cārvāka or Lokāyata, a mainly materialist school of later Indian thought.

The aim of these renunciants was to lead an abstemious, balanced life which enjoyed simple pleasures and the satisfaction of human relationships. They denied the idea of rebirth, and also those of *karma* and *niyati*. Each act was seen as a spontaneous event without karmic effects, and spiritual progression was not seen as possible. According to the Pāli tradition, in the Buddha's day their main spokesman was Ajita Kesakambalī (also referred to as Ajita Kesakambala; Skt. Ajita Keśakambalin). In the *Pāyāsi Sutta* (*Dīgha Nikāya, Sutta* 23), we also find the materialist Prince Pāyāsi, who denies rebirth on what he takes as empirical grounds. Once he had conducted a gruesome experiment on a condemned criminal, sealing him in a jar so that he suffocated, he failed to see any *jīva* escaping when the seal was broken (*Dīgha Nikāya* 2.332–3).

As described in the *Sāmaññaphala Sutta*, Ajita's views are that a human being is composed of earth, water, fire and wind, which disperse at death, with the sense-faculties dispersing to space, and both fools and the wise are equally destroyed at death. Moreover,

> there is no [worth in] what is given ... there is no fruit or result of good or bad deeds, there is no this world or other world, there is no mother or father (as beings to be respected) ... no renunciants or brahmins ... who proclaim this world and the next, having realized them by their own higher knowledge.
>
> (*Dīgha Nikāya* 1.55)

This latter passage is found elsewhere in the *sutta*s (e.g. *Majjhima Nikāya* 3.71–2) as the content of "wrong view," with Buddhist "right view" as the precise opposite, so as to assert the value of giving, self-sacrifice, respect for parents, the efficacy of *karma*, the reality of various types of rebirth worlds and of spiritual progress. Philosophical materialism is of course more common in the modern world than in ancient India, but it was not absent there. The Buddha was aware of this kind of position and clearly rejected it.

The skeptics

The final group of *śramaṇas* were the skeptics, seen in the Pāli tradition as led by Sañjaya Belaṭṭhaputta (Skt. Sañjayī Vairaṭiputra or Sañjayi Vairaṭṭīputra). They responded to the welter of conflicting theories on religious and philosophical issues, and the consequent arguments, by avoiding commitment to *any* point of view, so as to preserve peace of mind (*Dīgha Nikāya* 1.58–9). They avoided any commitment on the matters of rebirth, *karma*, and the destiny of an enlightened person after death. On the first two issues, the Buddha gave definite, positive teachings, while on the third he also preserved a silence, though probably for different reasons. The skeptics held that knowledge was impossible, and would not even commit themselves to saying that other people's views were wrong. In the *Brahmajāla Sutta*, the (wrong) views of four kinds of prevaricating "eel-wrigglers" are given (*Dīgha Nikāya* 1.25–8). The first three views result from the wish to avoid speaking falsely on what is wholesome or unwholesome, getting attached to one's view, or being cross-examined by others. Sañjayī's view is given last, and attributed to his dullness. Yet given that the Buddha's two chief disciples, Śāriputra and Maudgalyāyana (Pāli Sāriputta and Moggallāna), started as disciples of Sañjayī (*Vinaya* 1.39), it is unlikely that he was simply a dullard. The Buddha shared his wish to step aside from the "jungle" of conflicting views, and avoid dogmatic assertions built in flimsy grounds.

Overview

With the materialists, the Buddha shared an emphasis on experience as the source of knowledge, and with the skeptics he shared a critical evaluation of current beliefs on rebirth, *karma* and self. He saw the materialists and skeptics as going too far, however, in denying or doubting the

Table 2 Early Indian Views on philosophical issues

	Rebirth exists	A person's own karma determines how he or she is reborn	A permanent Self exists	Spiritual salvation is possible
Brahmins	Yes	Yes (ritual karma being most important)	Yes	Yes
Jains	Yes	Yes	Yes	Yes
Buddhists	Yes	Yes	No evidence for this	Yes
Ājīvikas	Yes	No	Yes	Yes, but not by personal effort
materialists	No	No	Self exists, but it is destroyed at death.	No
skeptics	?	?	?	?

principles of *karma* and rebirth, which he held were shown to be true by (meditative) experience (*Majjhima Nikāya* 1.402). Buddhism, then, did not uncritically absorb belief in *karma* and rebirth from existing Indian culture, as is sometimes held. These ideas were very much up for debate at the time.

Table 2 lists some of the views of the various groups in ancient India on certain philosophical issues of the day.

See also: **Buddha; Buddha, dates of; Buddhas, past and future; Dependent Origination (*pratītya-samutpāda*); *Karma*.**

PETER HARVEY

BUDDHA, RELICS OF

In the *Mahāparinibbāna Sutta*, not long before the Buddha's death, Ānanda asked him what was to be done with his *śarīra* (Pāli *sarīra*), his mortal body. He responded that the funeral arrangements were not for monks such as him to concern themselves with, but for wise laypeople. When Ānanda nevertheless asked how the body should be treated, the Buddha said that it should be treated like that of a *cakravartin* monarch: wrapped in 500 alternating layers of new linen cloth and carded cotton wool, placed in an oiled iron coffin, and then cremated. A *stūpa* (Pāli *thūpa*) or funerary mound should then be erected, by implication for the remains, at a place where four roads meet, "And whoever lays wreaths or puts sweet perfumes and colors there with a devout heart, will reap benefit and happiness for a long time" (*Dīgha Nikāya* 2.141–2). That is, the veneration of a *stūpa* and its content is seen to arouse positive mental states, which have a karmically beneficial effect. It is also said that a *stūpa* is appropriate for a *cakravartin* ruler, a *pratyekabuddha*, and a (Noble) disciple of the Buddha.

The cremation was done by local Malla leaders, and "what had been skin, under-skin, flesh, sinew, or joint-fluid, all that vanished and not even ashes or dust remained, only the *śarīras* remained." The Mallas then honored the *śarīras* for a week. However, as seven other peoples were keen to ask for a share of them, to avoid conflict the brahmin Droṇa (Pāli Doṇa) divided them into eight, to be placed in eight *stūpas*. Droṇa was granted the urn that they were gathered in, and another people got the funeral pyre embers, and these two items were also placed in *stūpas*, making a total of ten original *stūpas* (2.164–7).

The nature of relics

As suggested before, the main term translated as "relics" is the plural of *śarīra*. In the singular, the term is used for a corpse in a cemetery (e.g. *Majjhima Nikāya* 3.91, *Aṅguttara Nikāya* 3.58), though it is also used of a living body as that which wears out with old age (*Dhammapada* 151), or which becomes lean and pale with grief (*Suttanipāta* 584), and a repeated passage is "Willingly, let only my skin, sinews and bones remain, and let the flesh and blood dry up in/on my *śarīra*, but my energy shall not be relaxed so long as I have not attained what can be attained by manly strength" (e.g. *Majjhima Nikāya* 1.481). Overall, the *śarīra* is best seen as the "mortal body"; indeed it is the term for the body used in questions on whether the *jīva*, the life-principle, is identical with the body or not, questions that the Buddha set aside, unanswered (e.g. *Majjhima Nikāya* 1.157).

In the *suttas*, the term only seems to be used in the plural in relation to a single corpse in the case of the Buddha or an *arhat*: at *Saṃyutta Nikāya* 2.83, the *arhat* knows that when he dies, "here itself, all that is experienced, with no delight for him, will become cool, and *śarīras* will be left over." Here the term can be seen to mean something like "remains," though rather special remains. Bones and teeth are included, indeed the Sanskrit *Mahāparinirvāṇa Sūtra* refers to *asthis* (bones) rather than *śarīras*, as being left after the Buddha's cremation, and bones and teeth are amongst famous Buddha-relics. Nevertheless, in the *Dīgha Nikāya* commentary (2.603–4), Buddhaghosa reports that the *śarīras* of the Buddha were of three types, "like jasmine buds, like washed pearls, and like (nuggets) of gold" and in three sizes: as big as mustard seeds, broken grains of rice, or split green peas. John Strong refers to these as "transmogrified somatic substances ... the result of a process of metamorphosis brought on not only by the fire of cremation but also by the perfections of the saint ... whose body they re-present" and that "There is nothing surprising in this, Buddhist relics the world over appear more as jewel-like beads than as burnt bones" (See Figure 13).

In Korea, when monks are cremated, only such items are treated as relics, not bones, and also in Thailand, except that there the bones are preserved in case they *become* relics. In the Tibetan tradition, the website of the Gelugpa Kopan monastery in Nepal (http:// kopan-monastery.com.tour/lamakonchogrelic.html) says that these kind of relics "like pearls, jewels or crystalline deposits ... may manifest within the ashes of the great master's body when it is cremated. They appear as a result of the purity of the spiritual master's mind and may spontaneously multiply over a period of time."

Of the relics of Geshe Lama Konchog, it says that six weeks after his cremation, "One set of two relics had multiplied to become thirty-seven relics, and another had multiplied into twenty-eight. The bones are constantly producing pearl-like and golden-type relics; and from the ashes

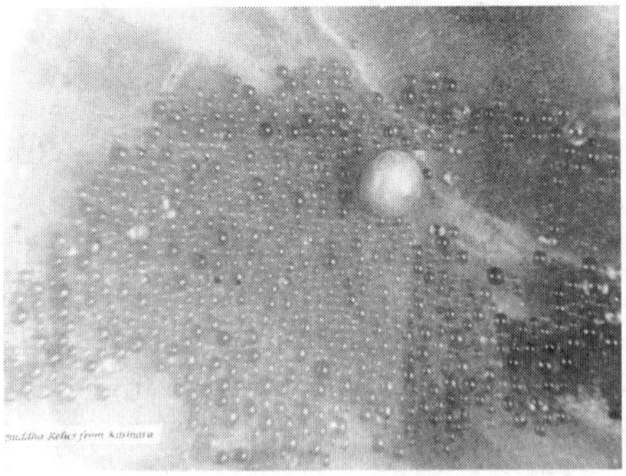

Figure 13 Relics from Kuśināra, where the Buddha passed away, given by India to Thailand and then divided up. These are one of the portions given to two British Buddhist centers.

relics are manifesting as well." Lama Zopa Rinpoche says on the website:

> One has to make very strong and extensive prayers and preserve pure morality for many lifetimes in order to create the causes that produce relics . . . Relics are manifested and remains are left behind as a result of the kindness of holy beings in order for us sentient beings to collect merit and purify obscurations.

As well as the above, nail-cuttings and hair of enlightened persons came to be treated as relics, and sometimes copies of relics were enshrined as if they were relics. The *Nidānakathā* (p. 81) refers to the newly awakened Buddha as giving a few of his hairs to his first (lay) disciples, for them to revere. The hairs are here referred to as *dhātus*, "elements," and any kind of relic is sometimes referred to in Pāli as a *sarīra-dhātu*, "element of the mortal body" (*Vimānavatthu* commentary 165), with a shrine (*cetiya*) for it being a *dhātu-cetiya* (*Dhammapada* commentary 3.29).

The cult of relics

In the past in the West, perhaps because of Protestant aversion to Catholic relic veneration, it was thought that Buddhist relic veneration was only a concern of the laity, but the textual, archaeological and contemporary evidence does not support this.

Richard Gombrich holds that the cult of relics was probably invented by Buddhists, as in Brahmanism a corpse was seen as very impure, and should be deposited outside of a settlement, not at a crossroads in it. However, as in other parts of the world, there may well have been a warrior-noble tradition of revering the relics of dead kings and heroes, interred in burial mounds (tumuli), out of both respect for and fear of the dead. The Buddha said that his corpse should be treated like that of a *cakravartin* monarch, and in the *Aṅguttara Nikāya*, when the wife of a *rājā* Muṇḍa dies, he tells his treasurer to place the body (*sarīra*) in an oiled iron coffin (3.58 – as with the Buddha), and after the cremation of the *sarīra*, he has a *stūpa* built for it (3.62). Moreover, in the *Mahāparinibbāna Sutta*, the demand for the Buddha's relics by various leaders and peoples arises without any prompting. In any case, even in Brahmanism/Hinduism, the tombs of *renunciants* receive some devotion.

Physical relics are seen as the most powerful focus for Buddhist devotion, and hence they are usually contained in the key Buddhist symbol, the *stūpa*. The Sri Lankan chronicle the *Mahāvaṃsa* (XXX.100) says that there is equal karmic fruitfulness in devotion to the Buddha's relics as there was in devotion to him when he was alive. It is likewise said that "when the relics are seen, the Buddha is seen" (XVII.3) and the *Vibhaṅga* commentary (431) says "while the relics endure, the enlightened ones endure." At *Milindapañha* 341, it is said that through Buddhist practice one can "buy" various things – e.g. a long life, heavenly rebirth, *nirvāṇa* – from the Buddha's "bazaar," which consists of his teachings, shrines (Pāli *cetiyas*) for his *sarīras* and things used (*pāribhogikas*), and the *Sangha*-jewel. Here, these seem to stand respectively for the *Dharma*, Buddha and *Sangha*. *Jātaka* (4.228) sees these two shrines as the first two of three kinds, clearly in descending order of importance: *sarīrika-cetiya, pāribhogika-cetiya* and *uddesika-cetiya*. The last of these refers to a shrine "indicating" the nature of a Buddha, which at first were symbols of the Buddha, and then images. The second kind of shrine is for things used by a Buddha, including his alms bowl and robe, and sites of key events in his life, which became important places of pilgrimage. The most important "used" item, though, is the tree under which the Buddha attained enlightenment, its saplings and in later tradition even any member of the species *aśvattha* (*ficus religiosa*) which became known to Buddhists as the *bodhi* or Enlightenment tree.

The *Buddhavaṃsa* (ch. XXVIII) refers to a range of relics: those in the original ten *stūpas*, a tooth in the heaven of the thirty-three gods headed by Śakra (Pāli Sakka), one in the realm of the *nāgas* (serpent-deities), one each in the Gandhāra and Kaliṅga regions, teeth and hair taken by gods of other world-systems, and a range of possessions such as bowl, staff and robe in various parts of India or heavens, hence (v. 13) "The ancients say that the dispersal of the relics of Gautama, the great seer, was out of compassion for living beings."

The heritage of the Buddha included not only his bodily relics and things used by him, but also his teachings, the *Dharma*. Consequently, the idea of *Dharma*-relics developed, to be installed in *stūpas* or images as physical relics were. *Dharma*-relics could be whole *sūtras*, short formulae known as *dhāraṇīs*, or key verses written on gold plates, such as those from *Vinaya* 1.40 that mean: "Those *dharmas* which proceed from a cause, of these the *Tathāgata* has told the cause, and that which is their stopping: the great renunciant has such a teaching" (Strong 2004: 8).

In their role as reminders of a Buddha or *arhat*, they point to their spiritual qualities, their teachings and the fact that they have actually lived on earth. This in turn shows that it is possible for a human being to become a Buddha or *arhat*. Yet relics are also tangible links with awakened ones and their spiritual powers, and are thought to contain something of the spiritual force and purity of the person they once formed part of. In the *Aṣṭsāhasrikā Prajñāpāranitā Sūtra*, while a copy of the *sūtra* is seen as more venerable than a world full of physical relics, these are still to be revered as "they have come forth from this perfection of wisdom, and are pervaded by it" (p. 95). As an awakened person was free of spiritual faults and possessed great energy for good, it is believed that his or her relics were somehow affected by this. They are therefore seen as radiating a kind of beneficial power.

Miraculous powers are hence attributed to relics, as seen in a story related in the *Mahāvaṃsa* (XXXI.97–100). When King Duṭṭhagāmaṇi (161–137 BCE) was enshrining some relics of Gautama in the great *stūpa* at Anurādhapura, Sri Lanka, they rose into the air in their casket and then emerged to form the shape of the Buddha. In a similar vein, the *Vibhaṅga* commentary (p. 433) and the *Anāgatavaṃsa* says that at the end of the 5,000-year period of the Buddhist era, when all practice and understanding of Buddhism has disappeared from the world, all the relics in Sri Lanka will assemble, travel through the air to the foot of the *Bodhi* tree in India where the Buddha attained awakening, there to be joined by all other relics, and will form the shape of the Buddha, emit rays of light and then burn up in a flash of light. This is referred to as the *parinirvāṇa* (complete extinction) of the *dhātus*.

Buddha-relics can be seen to remind devotees both of the impermanence of the Buddha and of his entry to the deathless (*nirvāṇa*); they are a presence that reminds them of the absent Buddha; while from a body that generally putrefies, they are from a person purified of defilements and long outlast the putrefying aspects of the body. In these respects, they have a liminal nature, conditioned traces of one awakened to the unconditioned, to which they are a tantalizing doorway. John Strong also sees them as expressions of the Buddha's biography, "they sum up a biographical narrative; they embody the whole of the Buddha's coming and going, his life-and-death story; they reiterate both his provenance and his impermanence"; they are also extensions of the biography, as they have travels and adventures of their own, after his death.

It is said that in the third century BCE, the devout Buddhist emperor Aśoka (Pāli Asoka) opened most of the original ten *stūpas* and redistributed their relics around his empire to be installed in "84,000" *stūpas* as focuses of devotion. When Buddhism spread to other countries, relics were sought. Thus, in the reign of Aśoka, after Mahinda, the emperor's son, took the religion to Sri Lanka, relics were obtained from India and, it is said, the Buddha's right collarbone and right eye-tooth were obtained from the heaven of Śakra (*Mahāvaṃsa* XVII.11–15), to be enshrined in a *stūpa* in the capital Anurādhapura. A tooth-relic was later enshrined in the Temple of the Tooth, Kandy, where there is an annual festival in honor of it, and possession of it came to be seen as a requirement of the king of Sri Lanka; in Southeast Asia, too, the possession of relics was seen to confer legitimacy on a king. In Burma, in the ancient capital Pagan, the Shwe zigon *stūpa* is said to contain a collarbone, frontlet bone and tooth of Gautama. In the present capital Yangon (Rangoon), the 112-meter-high gold-covered Shwe dāgon *stūpa* is said to contain some hairs of Gautama Buddha and belongings of three previous Buddhas. In seventh-century China, a finger-bone of the Buddha was presented to an emperor, and in the Tang dynasty (618–907) capital, there were festivals honoring this and several tooth-relics. In the Unified Silla period in Korea (668–918), temples were built for Buddha-relics such as small skull fragments, teeth and clothing. In China, the complete body of Huineng, the sixth Chan patriarch (638–713), is honored: having not decayed after death, its lacquered form, sitting in the meditation posture, has been revered in a grotto. Moreover, in both Theravāda and Mahāyāna lands, temple images to be used for devotion are consecrated in a ceremony which may include the placing of some kind of relics in them.

One way in which diplomatic links have been made between countries is for them either to share a portion of the relics that they have, or to loan them. Even Communist China has done this to build links with Buddhist countries. A modern manifestation of Buddhist cooperation is the pooling of relics from various countries to place in a 152-meter bronze statue of Maitreya Buddha that is scheduled to be completed in 2008 in the place where the Buddha passed away in India (http://www.maitreyaproject.org/en/index.html).

See also: **Buddha; Buddha, bodies of; Buddha, early symbols; Buddha and *cakravartins*; Sacred places.**

PETER HARVEY

BUDDHA, STORY OF

As the first of the "three refuges," the Buddha is a source of inspiration to Buddhists, and the events of his life are seen to illustrate points of teachings. This entry covers the figure of the historical Siddhārtha Gautama (Pāli Siddhattha Gotama) and the account of him as a "Buddha" as preserved in the Buddhist tradition. To understand the role of the Buddha within Buddhism, one needs to see how events in his life are seen to connect with central Buddhist concerns. The events have a connection to history, and scholars have a duty to understand history; but history is not just the critical quest of what "actually happened," it is also the study of how traditions have understood such events and set them within a broader mythic framework.

This entry looks both at the "story" of the Buddha and at characterizations of his qualities and character. A full discussion of early concepts of his nature is dealt with in the main survey entry on the Buddha.

Historical outline of the Buddha's life

Gautama was born in the small republic of the Śākya (Pāli Sakka, Sakyā, Sākiyā) people, which straddles the present Indian–Nepalese border and had Kapilavastu (Pāli Kapilavatthu) as its capital. From his birth among these people, Gautama is known in Mahāyāna tradition as Śākya-muni, "the Śākyan sage." The republic was not Brahmanized, and rule was probably by a council of household-heads, perhaps qualified by age or social standing. Gautama was born to one of these rulers, so that he described himself as a *kṣatriya* (member of the warrior-noble class) when talking to brahmins, and later tradition saw him as the son of a king. Gautama was thus no "prince," but a person of aristocratic background who took to the life of a renunciant (Skt. *śramaṇa*, Pāli *samaṇa*) in response to reflection on the common problems of human frailty and suffering. After a period of religious searching, he had a key religious experience at the age of thirty-five, after which he was known as a Buddha, or "awakened one." He attracted a range of disciples in northeast India, some of whom he ordained as monks or nuns, and lived to the age of eighty.

Sacred biographies

In the early Buddhist texts, there is no continuous life of the Buddha, as these concentrated on his teachings. Only later did a growing interest in the Buddha's person lead to various schools producing continuous "biographies," which drew on scattered accounts in the existing *Sutta* and *Vinaya* textual collections, and floating oral traditions. These "biographies" include the Mahāyānized Sarvāstivādin *Lalitavistara* (first century CE); the Lokottaravādin *Mahāvastu* (first century CE), which also includes a range of other material; Aśvaghoṣa's poem, the *Buddhacarita* (second century CE); and the Theravādins' *Nidānakathā* (second or third century CE). There are also sculptural reliefs that pre-date such developed biographies of the Buddha. The details in all these are in general agreement, but while they must clearly be based around historical facts, they also contain legendary and mythological embellishments, and it is often not possible to sort out one from the other. While the bare historical basis of the traditional biography will never be known, as it stands it gives a great insight into Buddhism by enabling us to see what the meaning of the Buddha's life is to Buddhists: what archetypal lessons it is held to contain.

In the Tibetan tradition, the story is structured around twelve deeds said to be done by all Buddhas: descending from the Tuṣita heavenly rebirth realm; conception; birth; education as a youth; marriage and birth of a son (for Gautama this was Rāhula); renunciation; period of asceticism, which is then abandoned; sitting down to meditate to attain Buddhahood; conquest of the evil tempter-deity Māra; attainment of Buddhahood; teaching the *Dharma*; death. The Theravādin tradition talks of thirty features that are the rule (*dhammatā*) in the life of any Buddha.

The developed "biographies" are best seen as hagiographies, belonging to a genre of literature which is mythic in format and aiming to exemplify certain key truths in an archetypal saintly life. In modern usage, to say something is "mythic" is sometimes seen as equivalent to saying that it is "false." Yet in its original meaning "myth" means a (meaningful) "story." If one thinks that the meanings conveyed by mythic material are false, then one might say that the myth conveys a falsehood; but it is not false simply in being mythic. One pervasive modern "myth" is the idea of "progress": an account of human history which highlights certain features as significant as part of an overall direction in history.

The Buddha's early career

The Buddha's life-story is set as the culmination of a broader story relating to Gautama's past lives. Like all other beings, he is seen to have had countless past lives, but at a certain point he met a past Buddha and resolved to work over many lives to build up the perfections needed to become a Buddha himself.

In his penultimate life, it is said that Gautama was born in the Tuṣita (Pāli Tusita) heaven, the realm of the "delighted" gods. This is said to be the realm where the *bodhisattva* Maitreya (Pāli Metteyya) now lives, ready for a future period in human history when Buddhism will have become extinct, and he can become the next Buddha (*Dīgha Nikāya* 2.76). The *Lalitavistara* tells that Gautama chose the time in human history in which to be reborn for the last time.

The early texts clearly see the conception and the other key events of Gautama's life, such as his birth, enlightenment, first sermon, and death, as events of cosmic importance; for at all of them they say that light spread throughout the world and the earth shook. The *Nidānakathā* relates that at the time of the conception, Mahāmāyā, his mother, dreamed that she was transported to the Himālayas where a being with the appearance of an auspicious white elephant entered her right side. When she recounted this dream to her husband, Śuddhodana (Pāli Suddhodana), he had it interpreted by sixty-four brahmins. They explained that it indicated that his wife had conceived a son with a great destiny ahead of him. Either he would stay at home with his father and go on to become a *cakravartin* (Pāli *cakkavatti*) ruler, a universal emperor – which the *suttas* say that he had been many times in previous lives (*Aṅguttara Nikāya* 4.89) – or he would become a wandering renunciant and become a great religious teacher, a Buddha.

The *Accariyabbhūtadhamma Sutta* (*Majjhima Nikāya* 3.11–28) is a short discourse which starts with monks remarking on the Buddha's ability to remember past Buddhas, and then has Ānanda recite a number of "wonderful and marvelous qualities" of the Buddha that he has heard from him, the first of which are:

- the *bodhisattva* was "mindful and fully aware" when he appeared in the Tuṣita heaven, remained there, and left there to enter his mother's womb;
- when he appeared in his mother's womb, a great light spread out, even to spaces between worlds where there was no sunlight, and "this ten-thousand-fold world system shook" (as also at his birth);
- moreover, four gods (*devas*) came to guard him and his mother;
- once he was in the womb, his mother was virtuous, celibate, happy and healthy.

While the above *Sutta* simply talks of birth from the womb, the *Mahāvastu* (2.20) and the *Lalitavistara* and *Buddhacarita* (I.9–11) say that the birth was from the uninjured right side. John Strong says that the idea that he was born without passing through the birth canal may be connected with the Indian idea that the trauma of this blots out memory of past lives. However, Buddhist texts refer to many *arhats* as having this ability, though not as born in an out-of-the-ordinary way. More relevant is the idea that while spiritually advanced beings can have clear awareness at conception, and some during gestation, only a perfect Buddha can retain this at birth (*Dīgha Nikāya* 3.103, 231, and its commentary

885–6, and *Abhidharmakośabhāṣya* 3.16–17). It may have been thought by some that this required a non-vaginal birth.

The *Nidānakathā* account relates that Gautama was born in the pleasant Lumbinī grove, where his mother had stopped off on a trip to give birth in her parents' home. It is said that she gave birth standing, holding onto a tree. The *sutta* accounts say that the baby was set down on the ground by four gods (*devas*), and that a warm and a cool stream of water appeared from the sky as a water-libation for mother and child. He immediately stood, walked seven paces, scanned in all directions, and said in a noble voice that he was the foremost being in the world, and that this would be his last rebirth (*Majjhima Nikāya* 3.123).

Gautama's birth under a tree fits the pattern of the other key events in his life: attaining enlightenment under another tree, giving his first sermon in an animal park, and dying between two trees. This suggests his liking for simple natural environments where he could be in harmony with all forms of life.

As his mother had died a week after giving birth (*Majjhima Nikāya* 3.122), Gautama was brought up by his father's second wife, his mother's sister, Mahāprajāpatī (Pāli Mahā-Pajāpatī). The early texts say little on his early life, except that it was one of lily pools, fine clothes and fragrances, with female musicians as attendants in his three palaces (or, at least, buildings on high platforms: Pāli *pāsādas*; *Aṅguttara Nikāya* 1.145). The later biographies portray him as having been an eager, intelligent, and compassionate youth. They relate that his father was keen that he should stay at home to become a great king, and so surrounded him with luxuries to ensure that he remained attached to the worldly life. At sixteen, he was married to Yaśodharā (Pāli Yasodharā), and at twenty-nine they had a son named Rāhula.

Renunciation

In the Pāli Canon, a text covering the period from the Buddha's renunciation to his first disciples becoming *arhats* is the *Ariyapariyesanā Sutta* (*Majjhima Nikāya* 1.160–75). It was from a wealthy background that Gautama renounced the worldly life of pleasure and set out on his religious quest. The lead-up to this crucial transition is described in different ways in the early and later texts. The *suttas* portray it as the result of a long consideration. Even from his sheltered existence, he became aware of the facts of ageing, sickness and death. Realizing that even he was not immune from these, the "vanities" of youth, health, and life left him (*Aṅguttara Nikāya* 1.145–6). He therefore set out to find the "unborn, unageing, undecaying, deathless, sorrowless, undefiled, uttermost security from bondage – *nirvāṇa*" (*Majjhima Nikāya* 1.163). He realized, though, that:

> House life is crowded and dusty; going forth [into the life of a wandering renunciant] is wide open. It is not easy, living life in a household, to lead a holy-life as utterly perfect as a polished shell. Suppose I were to shave off my hair and beard, put on saffron garments, and go forth from home into homelessness?
>
> (*Majjhima Nikāya* 1.240)

The *Dīgha Nikāya* (2.151) says that the transition occurred at the age of twenty-nine, the *Nidānakathā* (pp. 60–2) seeing this as just after the birth of his son. Such later texts portray the renunciation as arising from a sudden realization rather than from a gradual reflection. In this, they follow the model of a *sutta* story of a previous Buddha, Vipassī (*Dīgha Nikāya* 2.22–9), which sees the lives of all Buddhas as following a recurring pattern. The *Nidānakathā* relates that, on three consecutive days, Gautama visited one of his parks in his chariot. His father had the streets cleared of unpleasant sights, but the gods ensured that he saw a worn-out, grey-haired old man, a sick man and a corpse. He was amazed at these new sights, and his charioteer explained to him that ageing, sickness and death came to all people, thus putting him in a state of agitation at the nature of life. In this way, the texts portray an example of the human confrontation with frailty and mortality, for while these facts are "known" to us all, a clear realization and acceptance of them often does come as a novel and disturbing insight. On a fourth trip to his park, Gautama saw a saffron-robed renunciant with a shaven head and a calm demeanor, the sight of whom inspired him to adopt such a lifestyle. This account of seeing four signs is a good example of a mythic form of truth-telling. That night, he left his palace, taking a long last look at his son, who lay in his sleeping wife's arms, knowing it would be difficult for him to leave if she awoke. The Buddhist tradition sees his leaving of his family as done for the benefit of all beings; moreover, after he became a Buddha, he is said to have returned to his home town and taught his family, with his son ordaining under him as a monk. His renunciation of family life stands as a symbolic precedent for the monastic life of Buddhist monks and nuns. Indeed, the term for the Buddha's renunciation is the "great going forth" (Skt. *mahā-pravrajya*, Pāli *mahā-pabbajjā*), *pravajya* being the term for ordaining as a novice monk.

Spiritual quest

After Gautama's renunciation, the tradition allots a six-year span to his spiritual quest. The *suttas* tell that he first sought out teachers from whom he could learn spiritual techniques, going first to Ārāḍa Kālama (Pāli Āḷāra Kālāma; *Majjhima Nikāya* 1.163–7). He soon mastered his teachings and then enquired after the meditational state on which they were based. This was the "sphere of nothingness," a mystical trance attained by yogic concentration, in which the mind goes beyond any apparent object and dwells on the thought of nothingness. After Gautama quickly learned to enter this state, Ārāḍa offered him joint leadership of his group of disciples, but he turned down the offer as he felt that, while he had attained a refined inner calmness, he had not yet attained enlightenment and the end of suffering. He then went to another yoga teacher, Udraka Rāmaputra (Pāli Uddaka Rāmaputta), and again quickly grasped his doctrine and entered the meditational state on which it was based, the "sphere of neither-perception-nor-non-perception." This went beyond the previous state to a level of mental stilling where consciousness is so attenuated as to hardly exist. In response, Udraka acknowledged him as even his own teacher, for only his dead father (Rāma) had previously attained this state. Again Gautama passed up a chance of leadership and influence on the grounds that he had not yet reached his goal. Nevertheless, he later incorporated both the mystical states that he had attained into his own meditation system, as possible ways to calm and purify the mind in preparation for developing liberating insight. He in fact taught a great variety of meditational methods, adapting some from the existing yogic tradition, and can be seen as having been one of India's greatest practitioners of meditation.

Having experimented with one of the methods of religious practice current in his day, he next tried ascetic self-mortification as a possible route to his goal. The *suttas* tell that he settled in a woodland grove at Uruvilvā (Pāli Uruvelā) and resolved to strive earnestly to overcome attachment to sensual pleasures by intense effort, trying to dominate such tendencies by force of will (*Majjhima Nikāya* 1.77–81; 1.240–6). He practiced non-breathing meditations, though they produced fierce headaches, stomach pains,

Figure 14 Carved wooden image of the fasting Buddha, Korea.

and burning heat all over his body. He reduced his food intake to a few drops of bean soup a day, till he became so emaciated that he could hardly stand and his body hair fell out. At this point, he felt that it was not possible for anyone to go further on the path of asceticism and still live (See Figure 14). Nevertheless, though he had developed clarity of mind and energy, his body and mind were pained and intranquil, so that he could not carry on with his quest. He therefore abandoned his practice of harsh asceticism.

At this point, he might have abandoned his quest as hopeless, but he thought "might there be another path to awakening?" (*Majjhima Nikāya* 1.246). He then remembered a meditative state that he had once spontaneously entered while concentrating on the earth being cut by a plough. He recollected that this state, technically known as the "first *dhyāna*" (Pāli *jhāna*), was beyond involvement in sense-pleasures, which he had been attempting to conquer by painful asceticism, but was accompanied by deep calm, blissful joy, and tranquil happiness. He wondered whether it was a path to awakening, and, seeing that it was, he resolved to use it. On his taking sustaining food to prepare himself for this meditation, his five companions in asceticism shunned him in disgust, seeing him as having abandoned their shared quest and taken to luxurious living.

One of the points implicit in the account of the Buddha under the two yoga teachers is that, though he attained refined and subtle states, these were not acceptable as the end-point of his quest, as he had not yet attained its true goal. He was also clearly not interested in leading disciples unless he had something truly worthwhile to teach. In the spiritual quest of the Buddha, it is also interesting to note that:

- with the two yoga teachers, he attains two mystical states which are among four "formless" (Skt. *ārūpya*, Pāli *arūpa*) states: ones which *leave behind* perception of anything whatsoever material – but this does not lead to his goal;
- in his ascetic phase, he tries to go for *mastery over* the body and its desires by force of will, but this exhausts him and drives him to a painful dead end;
- he then turns to a path which requires him to build up a healthy body and attain inner states of happiness, not pain. This path of *dhyāna* is, in effect, one of *mindful awareness of* the body, rather than ignoring it (in formless states) or trying to forcefully repress it. This approach of awareness rather than ignoring or forcefulness is found in many other aspects of Buddhist practice.

Temptation by Māra

One *sutta* (*Suttanipāta* vv. 425–49) outlines a temptation sequence which the later texts put at this juncture. It refers to a Satan-like figure known as Māra, "Death-bringer," also commonly called "the Bad One" (Skt. *pāpīyāṃs*, Pāli *pāpimant*): a deity who has won his place by previous good works, but who uses his power to entrap people in sensual desire and attachment, so as to stay within his realm of influence. This is the round of rebirth and repeated death, so that Māra is seen as the embodiment of both sensual desire and death. Māra came to the emaciated ascetic with honeyed words. He urged him to abandon his quest and take up a more conventional religious life of sacrifice and good works, so as to generate good *karma* (karmic fruitfulness or "merit"). In response, Gautama replied that he had no need of more good *karma*, and scorned the "squadrons" of Māra: sense-desire, jealousy, hunger and thirst, craving, dullness and drowsiness, cowardice, fear of commitment, belittling others, obstinate insensitivity, and self-praise. Māra then retreated in defeat.

This account, clearly portraying the final inner struggle of Gautama, gains dramatic color in the later texts, where Māra's "army" of spiritual faults bore witness to the fact that he had done many charitable acts in previous lives. Taunting Gautama that he had no one to bear witness to *his* good deeds, Māra tried to use the power of his own good *karma* to throw Gautama off the spot where he was sitting. Gautama did not move, however, but meditated on the spiritual perfections that he had developed over many previous lives, knowing that he had a right to the spot where he sat. He then touched the earth for it to bear witness to his store of karmic fruitfulness. The earth quaked, and the earth goddess (known variously as Sthāvarā, Dharaṇī, Bhūmidevī, Bhū Devī, Pṛthivī, Kṣiti, Vasundharā) appeared, wringing from her hair a flood of water, accumulated in the past when Gautama had formalized good deeds by a simple ritual of water-pouring. At the quaking and flood, Māra and his army fled. This is commemorated by countless images and paintings as a victory over evil. These show Gautama seated cross-legged in meditation with his right hand touching the earth: the "earth-witness" (Skt. *bhūmi-sparśa*) or "conquest of Māra" (Pāli *māra-vijaya*) gesture.

Māra's location in the scheme of worlds is not specified in the *suttas*. It is certainly not hell, which is presided over by the god Yama. The Theravāda commentary to the *Majjhima Nikāya* (1.28) says that Māra dwells in the heaven of the "Masters of the Creations of Others," the highest of the six heavens of the realm of sense-desire, a realm which also includes all beings except the higher gods. As with the Christian Satan, a "fallen angel," Māra is seen as having had a good past, but as using his power to a perverted end. He goes for power over beings of the sense-desire realm rather than seeking to attain a higher rebirth or an end to rebirth. The next higher heaven is the beginning of the realm of pure or elemental form, where the brahmā gods dwell: beings who perceive the world in a purer, more direct way, untainted by sense-desire (though still with other limitations). Māra is thus seen to exist at a transition point in the process of spiritual development. The brahmā levels correspond to the *dhyānas*, meditative trances free of sense-desire, ill-will, and certain other spiritual hindrances. Māra is seen as being unwilling to make the step to this state. Instead of developing the power to *transcend* the realm of sense desire, he goes for *power over* it. This is always a possibility. In human terms, it parallels the situation of a spiritual teacher who uses his or her influence over others to manipulate them for his own ends.

However, a Māra is not stuck for ever in this state. Maudgalyāyana (Pāli Moggallāna), one of the Buddha's two chief disciples – an enlightened *arhat* – says that long ago, at the time of the previous Buddha Kakusandha (Pāli), he had been a Māra named Dūsin (*Majjhima Nikāya* 1.333).

The scope of Māra's influence is sometimes seen as the realm of both the five senses (*Saṃyutta Nikāya* 5.148–9) and the (unenlightened) mind (*Saṃyutta Nikāya* 1.115). At a philosophical level, Māra is a term for all that is *duḥkha*, all the limited, conditioned processes that make up the world and living beings. Here it is equivalent to "subject to death."

*The enlightenment or awakening (***Bodhi***)*

Free of the spiritual hindrances represented by Māra, Gautama then developed deep meditations as a prelude to his awakening, seated under a species of tree which later became known as the *Bodhi*, or "Awakening" tree. The *sutta* account (*Majjhima Nikāya* 1.247–9) describes how he entered the first *dhyāna*, and then gradually deepened his state of concentrated calm till he reached the fourth *dhyāna*, a state of great equanimity, mental brightness and purity. Based on this state, he went on to develop, in the course of the three watches of the moonlit night, the "threefold knowledge" (Skt. *trai-vidyā*, Pāli *te-vijjā*):

- memory of up to 100,000 previous lives (and of past universes);
- seeing the rebirth of others according to their *karma*;
- insight into the Four Ennobling Truths on life's pains (Skt. *duḥkha*, Pāli *dukkha*), their origin, cessation, and path to this, and of the same fourfold scheme applied to the "taints" (Skt. *āśravas*, Pāli *āsavas*): sense-desire, (attachment to) becoming, ignorance and views – seen as spiritual faults which fester in the mind and keep it unenlightened.

On the phrase "threefold knowledge" Richard Gombrich comments, "There is no reason why this particular set of attainments – of which the last one is indeed composite – should be called 'three knowledges' if they were not intended to parallel and trump the 'three knowledges' of brahmins", namely knowledge of the contents of their three *Veda-saṃhitā* texts.

The third knowledge, completed at dawn, brought the perfect awakening Gautama had been seeking, so that he was now, at the age of thirty-five, a Buddha. *Dhammapada* verses 153–4 are said to record his words of joyful exultation at this achievement of the end of craving and spiritual ignorance, and attaining the unconditioned *nirvāṇa*, beyond ageing, sickness and death.

The Canonical account (*Vinaya* 1.1–7, *Majjhima Nikāya* 1.167–70) then says that the new Buddha stayed under or near the *bodhi* tree for four weeks, at the place now called Bodhgayā. After meditatively reflecting on his awakening, he pondered the possibility of teaching others, but thought that the *Dharma* he had experienced was so profound, subtle, and "beyond the sphere of reason" that others would be too subject to attachment to be able to understand it. At this, the compassionate Great *Brahmā* deity Sahampati became alarmed at the thought that a fully awakened person had arisen in the world, but that he might not share his rare and precious wisdom with others. He therefore appeared before the Buddha and respectfully asked him to teach, for "there are beings with little dust in their eyes who, not hearing the *Dharma*, are decaying." The Buddha then used his mind-reading powers to survey the world and determine that some people were spiritually mature enough to understand his message. On deciding to teach, he declared, "Opened for those who wish to hear are the doors of the Deathless." The entreaty of the compassionate Brahmā is seen by Buddhists as the stimulus for the unfolding of the Buddha's compassion, the necessary complement to his enlightened wisdom for his role as a perfect Buddha, a "teacher of gods and humans."

Gautama wished to teach his two yoga teachers first of all, but gods informed him that they were now dead, a fact which he then confirmed by his meditative knowledge. He therefore decided to teach his former companions in asceticism. Intuiting that they were currently in the animal park at Ṛṣivadana (Pāli Isipatana; now called Sārnāth) near Benares, he set out to walk there, a journey of about 100 miles.

The first sermon

The Canonical account (*Vinaya* 1.10–12; *Saṃyutta Nikāya* 5.420–4) relates that, on his arriving at the animal park, Gautama's five former companions saw him in the distance and resolved to snub him as a spiritual failure. As he approached, however, they saw that a great change had come over him and, in spite of themselves, respectfully greeted him and washed his feet. At first they addressed him as an equal, but the Buddha insisted that he was a *Tathāgata*, a "Thus-gone" or "Truth-attained One," who had found the Deathless and could therefore be their teacher. After he twice repeated his affirmation, to overcome their hesitation, the ascetics acknowledged that he had a newfound assurance and were willing to be taught by him.

Gautama then gave his first sermon. This commences with the idea that there is a "middle way" (Skt. *madhyama-pratipad*, Pāli *majjhima-paṭipadā*) for those who have gone forth from the home life, a way which avoids both the extremes of devotion to mere sense-pleasures and devotion to ascetic self-torment. Gautama had himself previously experienced both of these spiritual dead-ends. The middle way which he had found to lead to enlightenment was the *ārya* (Pāli *ariya*), or Ennobling, Eightfold Path (Skt. *mārga*, Pāli *magga*). The idea of a middle way runs through much of Buddhism. The term is applied both to a middle way of practice, for which the first sermon is the *locus classicus*, but also, even in the early texts, to a middle way of understanding, avoiding extreme views.

Gautama then continued with the kernel of his message, the Four Ennobling Truths/Realities. He then emphasized the liberating effect on him of his full insight into these truths, such that he was now a Buddha. As a result of this instruction, one member of Gautama's audience, Kauṇḍinya (Pāli Koṇḍañña), gained transformative experiential insight into the truths taught, so that Gautama joyfully affirmed his understanding. This insight is described as the gaining of the stainless "*Dharma*-eye," by which Kauṇḍinya "sees," "attains," and "plunges into" the *Dharma*, free from all doubt in the Buddha's teachings. This experience is technically known as "stream-entry," a crucial spiritual transition brought about by the first glimpse of *nirvāṇa* (though it may also refer to a person's going straight to a higher level of insight). Kauṇḍinya's gaining of the *Dharma*-eye is clearly seen as the climax of the first sermon, for as soon as it occurs the exultant message is rapidly transmitted up through various levels of gods that "the supreme *Dharma*-wheel" had been set in motion by the "Lord," and could not be stopped by any power. The "Setting in motion of the *Dharma*-wheel" (Skt. *Dharma-cakra-pavartana*, Pāli *Dhamma-cakka-ppavattana*) thus became the title of the *sutta* of the first sermon (*Saṃyutta Nikāya* 5.420–4). The image of setting a wheel in motion is intended to symbolize the first transmission of experiential *Dharma*-understanding from the Buddha to a disciple, inaugurating an era of the spiritual influence of the *Dharma*.

After Kauṇḍinya was ordained, thus becoming the first member of the monastic *sangha*, the Buddha gave more extensive explanations of his teachings to the other four ascetics, so that, one by one, they attained the *Dharma*-eye and were then ordained. Later the Buddha gave his "second" sermon, on the factors of personality being "not-Self," at which his disciples all attained the full experience of *nirvāṇa* – as he himself had done at his awakening – so as to become *arhats* (Pāli *arahats*).

Other disciples, monastic and lay, followed, so that soon there were sixty-one *arhats*, including the Buddha. Having such a body of enlightened monk-disciples, the Buddha sent them out on a mission to spread the *Dharma:* "Walk, monks, on tour for the blessing of the manyfolk, for the happiness of the manyfolk, out of compassion for the world, for the welfare, the blessing, the happiness of gods and humans" (*Vinaya* 1.21). As the teaching spread, Gautama in time gained his two chief disciples, Śāriputra (Pāli Sāriputta), famed for his wisdom and ability to teach, and Maugalyāyana (Pāli Moggallāna), famed for his psychic powers developed by meditation. Five years after first ordaining monks, Gautama initiated an order of nuns, in response to the repeated requests of his foster-mother Mahāprajāpatī (Pāli Mahāpajāpatī), and the suggestion of his faithful attendant monk Ānanda.

The middle years

The Canon gives only incidental reference to events between the sending out of the sixty *arhats* and the last year of the Buddha's life. The general picture conveyed is that he spent his long teaching career wandering on foot, with few possessions, around the Ganges basin region. Though he was of a contemplative nature, loving the solitude of natural surroundings, he was generally accompanied by many disciples and spent much of his time in or near the new towns and cities, especially Śrāvastī, Rājagṛha, and Vaiśālī (Pāli Sāvatthī, Rājagaha, and Vesālī).

The Buddha's contribution to a disciple's spiritual development

In the Pāli Canon, much emphasis is placed on a disciple's own effort: "By oneself is evil done; by oneself is one defiled. By oneself is evil left undone; by oneself is one made pure. Purity and impurity depend on oneself; no one can purify another" (*Dhammapada* verse 165). Also: "You yourself must make the effort; Buddhas only point the way" (*Dhammapada* verse 276).

Nevertheless, the role of the Buddha in "pointing the way" is by no means neglected: the individual must tread the path him/herself, but the Buddha is seen, so to speak, as a wise map-maker to guide the journey. This is also acknowledged in a passage at *Dīgha Nikāya* 2.100, where the Buddha is old and ill and explains that he has made his teachings explicit, so that a disciple should "live with himself as an island, with himself as a refuge . . . with *Dharma* as an island, with *Dharma* as refuge" by developing careful mindfulness of body and mind. This not only counsels self-reliance, but also reliance on *Dharma* – which other passages emphasize as being discovered, taught and embodied by the Buddha.

His role as a way-discoverer is seen in a passage (*Saṃyutta Nikāya* 2.105–7) where he gives a simile of a man who, while wandering in a forest, discovers an ancient path to a once populated city. Likewise he himself discovered the Ennobling Eightfold Path to *nirvāṇa*, the end of suffering, the "ancient" path traveled by past Buddhas, and made it known (see also Buddha, style of teaching).

The Buddha's appearance, voice, mode of conduct and presence

At one point, an admiring brahmin says of the Buddha:

> Sirs, the renunciant Gautama is handsome, comely, and graceful, possessing supreme beauty of complexion, with sublime beauty and sublime presence, remarkable to behold. [He] ... is a good speaker with a good delivery; he speaks words that are courteous, distinct, flawless, and communicate the meaning.
>
> (*Majjhima Nikāya* 2.166–7)

Amongst the "thirty-two marks" of a Buddha are that he had "the voice of a brahmā" (*Dīgha Nikāya* 3.173), which is explained thus of a brahmā deity:

> his voice had eight qualities: it was distinct, intelligible, pleasant, attractive, compact, concise, deep and resonant. And when he spoke in that voice to the assembly, its sound did not carry outside. Whoever has such a voice as that is said to have the voice of a brahmā.
>
> (*Dīgha Nikāya* 2.212)

One *sutta* describes a young brahmin visiting the Buddha to see if his reputation as a Buddha and *arhat* is deserved. After seeing that he is endowed with the thirty-two marks, he stays with him for seven months, closely observing his every move (*Majjhima Nikāya* 2.135). His consequent description of him includes:

> He walks neither too quickly nor too slowly ... He does not walk looking about ... When seated indoors, he does not fidget with his hands. He does not fidget with his feet. He does not sit with his knees crossed. He does not sit with his ankles crossed. He does not sit with his hands holding his chin. When seated indoors, he is not afraid, he does not shiver and tremble, he is not nervous ... and he is intent on seclusion ... He washes his bowl without making a splashing noise ... (When eating) he turns the mouthful over two or three times in his mouth and then swallows it ... He takes his food experiencing the taste, though not experiencing greed for the taste ... (After he has washed his bowl) he is neither careless of his bowl nor over-solicitous about it ... When he has eaten, he sits in silence for a while, but he does not let the time for blessing go by ... (After taking leave from a donor's house) he walks neither too fast nor too slow, and he does not go on as one who wants to get away.
>
> (pp. 137–9)

This portrays the Buddha as one whose movements and actions are measured and balanced, expressing absolutely no hint of greed, restlessness, fear, indifference, over-concern, or aversion. Were his manner to have expressed any hint of these, the implication is that this would have shown that he was not enlightened.

The early texts portray the Buddha as a charismatic, humanitarian teacher who inspired many people. He even elicited a response from animals; for it is said that an elephant once looked after him by bringing water when he was spending a period alone in the forest (*Vinaya* 1.352). A person who bore enmity towards him, however, was his cousin Devadatta, one of his monks. Jealous of his influence, Devadatta once suggested that the ageing Buddha should let him lead the monastic *sangha*, and then plotted to kill him when the request was turned down (*Vinaya* 2.191–5). In one attempt on his life, Devadatta asked his friend, Prince Ajātaśatru (Pāli Ajātasattu), to send soldiers to waylay and assassinate the Buddha. Sixteen soldiers in turn went to do this, but all were too afraid to do so and became the Buddha's disciples instead. In another attempt, the fierce man-killing elephant Nālāgiri was let loose on the road on which the Buddha was traveling. As the elephant charged, the Buddha calmly stood his ground and suffused the elephant with the power of his loving-kindness, so that it stopped and bowed its head, letting the Buddha stroke and tame it.

The Buddha's compassion

The Buddha's friendly disposition is shown in how he greeted people. It is stated,

> Now it is the custom for Buddhas, for lords to exchange friendly greetings with incoming monks. So the Lord spoke thus to the monk Kassapagotta: "I hope, monk, that things went well with you, I hope you had enough to support life, I hope you have come on the journey with but little fatigue . . . ?"
>
> (*Vinaya* 1.313)

Once, the Buddha is said to have found a monk with dysentery, smeared with his own excrement, whom the other monks were not tending. He therefore washed him himself and laid him on a comfortable couch. After this, he tells the other monks: "Monks, you have not a mother, you have not a father who might tend you. If you, monks, do not tend to one another, then who is there who will tend you? Whosoever, monks, would tend me, he should tend the sick" (*Vinaya* 1.302).

After the Buddha eats a meal offered by Cunda which helps to trigger his final illness, he is concerned lest Cunda might feel remorse and blame himself; thus the Buddha says that his offering is to be seen as karmically very uplifting (*Dīgha Nikāya* 2.135–6).

In general, the Buddha's most dominant expression of compassion is his careful teaching of others so as to aid their movement to enlightenment. This is particularly seen when the Buddha agrees to the request of Brahmā Sahampati for him to teach after his enlightenment, when it is said that he, "out of compassion for beings," surveyed the world, saw that there were some who were ready to understand his profound teaching, and decided to teach (*Vinaya* 1.6–7).

The passing away of the Buddha

The *Mahāparinibbāna Sutta* (*Dīgha Nikāya* 2.72–167) deals with the last year of the Buddha's life. During this period, Ānanda asked about the fate of the *sangha* after his death, clearly wondering who would lead it. In reply, the Buddha said that he had taught the *Dharma* without holding anything back, and that the *sangha* depended on the *Dharma*, not on any leader, even himself. Members of the *sangha* should look to their own self-reliant practice, with the clearly taught *Dharma* as guide: with themselves and the *Dharma* as "island" and "refuge" (*Dīgha Nikāya* 2.100). Later the Buddha specified that, after his death, the *sangha* should take both the *Dharma* and monastic discipline (*vinaya*) as their "teacher" (2.154).

Though unwell for the last three months of his life, the Buddha continued to wander on foot. Finally, he could only continue by overcoming his pain through the power of meditation. His journey ended at the small village of Kuśinagarī (Pāli Kusinārā), where he lay down on a couch between two trees, in bloom out of season. The text says that gods from ten regions of the universe assembled to witness the great event of a Buddha's death: his "great passing into *nirvāṇa*" (Skt. *mahā-parinirvāṇa*, Pāli *mahā-parinibbāna*; 2.138–9).

When asked what should be done about his funeral arrangements, the Buddha remarked that this was the concern of the laity, not the *sangha*, but that his body should be treated like that of a *cakravartin* (Pāli *cakkavatti*) ruler. After his cremation, the Buddha's relics were placed in eight *stūpas*, with the bowl used to collect the relics and the ashes of the funeral fire in two more.

Even on his death-bed, the Buddha continued to teach. A wanderer asked whether other *śramaṇa* leaders had attained true knowledge. Rather than say that their religious systems were wrong and his right, the Buddha simply indicated that the crucial ingredient of any such system was the Ennobling

Eightfold Path: only then could it lead to full *arhat*ship. He saw such a Path as absent from other teachings that he knew of.

Not long after this, the Buddha asked his monks if any had final questions that they wanted answering before he died. When they were silent, he sensitively said that, if they were silent simply out of reverence for him, they should have a friend ask their question. They remained silent. Seeing that they all had a good understanding of his teachings, he therefore gave his final words. According to the Pāli tradition, these were: "Conditioned things (Pāli *saṅkhāras*) are subject to decay. Attain perfection through heedful attentiveness (*appamādena*)!" (2.156). In a Sanskrit version of the *Mahāparinirvāṇa Sūtra*, though, his last words were:

> Monks, gaze upon the body of the Tathāgata! Examine the body of the Tathāgata! For the sight of a completely enlightened Buddha is as rare an event as the blossoming of the *udumbara* tree. And, monks, do not break into lamentation after I am gone, for all karmically constituted things [better: conditioned things] are subject to passing away.

He then made his exit from the world, in the fearless, calm and self-controlled state of meditation. He passed into the first *dhyāna*, and then by degrees through the three other *dhyānas*, four "formless" mystical states, and then the "cessation of perception and feeling." He then gradually descended back to the first *dhyāna*, moved back up to the fourth *dhyāna*, and died from here (2.156). Buddhists see this event not so much as a "death" as a passing into the deathless (Skt. *amṛta* Pāli *amata*), *nirvāṇa*.

See also: **Buddha; Buddha, family of; Buddha, relics of; Buddha and *cakravartins*.**

PETER HARVEY

BUDDHA, STYLE OF TEACHING

The Buddha's style of teaching is generally portrayed as one of skillful adaptation to the language, mood and concerns of his hearers, responding to the questions and even the non-verbalized thoughts of his audience and taking cues from events. By means of a dialogue with his questioners, he gradually moved them towards sharing his own vision of truth. When brahmins asked him about how to attain union with the deity Great Brahmā after death, he did not say that this was impossible, but that it could be attained by meditative development of deep lovingkindness and compassion, rather than by bloody Vedic sacrifices (*Dīgha Nikāya* 1.235–52). He often gave old terms new meanings, for example calling the *arhat* the "true brahmin," and using the term *ārya* (Pāli *ariya*), the Sanskrit term for the "noble" Āryan people who brought the Vedic religion to India, in the sense of spiritually noble.

A key Mahāyāna doctrine is that the Buddha taught with "skillful means" (*upāya-kauśalya*), not only in the sense of appropriately selecting for a particular audience from what he knew to be true, but also in the sense of teaching things which were not fully true but which would help motivate certain people's level of practice. In earlier text collections such as the Pāli Canon, only the first kind of skillful means is found. An example is at *Udāna* 22–3. Here, the monk Nanda, the Buddha's half-brother, says that he wishes to disrobe to return to a beautiful girl he had married soon before ordaining. To dissuade him, the Buddha enabled him to see the goddesses of the heaven of the Thirty-three, which Nanda admitted were far more beautiful. While this motivated him to remain a monk, as practice would enable rebirth in such a realm, other monks were critical of the basis of this motivation. Ashamed, he thus meditated intently until he became an *arhat*.

The Buddha's skill in teaching is suggested by his saying:

> I recall teaching *Dharma* to an assembly of many hundreds. Perhaps each person thinks: "The renunciant Gautama is teaching *Dharma* especially for me." But it should not be so regarded; the *Tathāgata* teaches *Dharma* to others only to give them knowledge.
>
> (*Majjhima Nikāya* 1.249)

The Buddha also says that he has attended many hundreds of each of the eight kinds of assemblies: of warrior-nobles, brahmins, householders, renunciants, gods of the realm of Four Great Kings, the Thirty-three gods, and Brahmā gods. In each case: "before I sat down with them, spoke to them or joined in their conversation, I adopted their appearance and speech, whatever it might be," such that after he had taught them, they did not know whether he was a god (*deva*) or a human (*Dīgha Nikāya* 2.109).

The Buddha showed even-mindedness when gaining disciples. A General Siṃha (Pāli Sīha), who was a great supporter of Jain monks, once decided to become a lay disciple, but the Buddha advised him that such a prominent person as himself should carefully consider before changing his religious allegiances (*Vinaya* 1.236). Already impressed by the Buddha's teaching, Siṃha was even more impressed by the fact that he did not jump at the chance of gaining an influential disciple. On affirming that he still wished to be a disciple, the Buddha advised him that he should not deprive Jain monks by withdrawing his generous support, but continue this while also supporting Buddhist monks, as he now wished to do.

The Buddha treated questions in a careful, analytic way, and divided these into four types (*Aṅguttara Nikāya* 2.46):

- those that can be answered categorically, straightforwardly;
- those that can be answered in a qualified way in accordance with a careful analysis of the question;
- those to be answered by a counter-question, to clarify what is being asked, reveal presuppositions, or draw attention to a parallel situation so as to draw conclusions from it;
- those not to be answered, but set aside, as question-begging and fraught with misconceptions.

The roles of investigation and faith

The Buddha did not mind if others disagreed with him, but censured misinterpretations of what he taught. He emphasized self-reliance and the experiential testing-out of all teachings, including his own. He was well aware of the many conflicting doctrines of his day, a time of intellectual ferment. Rejecting teachings based on authoritative tradition, or mere rational speculation, he emphasized the careful examination and analysis of experience, as seen in the famous *Kālāma Sutta*. Here he spoke to the Kālāma people, who had had a string of teachers visiting them, speaking in praise of their own teachings and disparaging those of others (*Aṅguttara Nikāya* 1.189). In response to their perplexity over which teacher to believe, the Buddha said that they were right to feel uncertain:

> Do not accept anything on the grounds of report, or a handed-down tradition or hearsay, or because it is in conformity with a collection (of teachings) (*piṭaka-sampadānena*), or because it is the product of (mere) reasoning (*takka-hetu*), or because of inference (*naya-hetu*), or because of reflection on appearances (*ākāra-parivitakkena*), or because of reflection on and approval of a view (*diṭṭhi-nijjhāna-kkhantiyā*), or because it has the appearance of what

> ought to be (*bhavya-rūpatāya*), or because (you think) "this renunciant is our revered teacher." When you, O Kālāmas, know for yourselves: "these *dharmas* are unwholesome and blameworthy, they are condemned by the wise (*viññu-garahitā*); these *dharmas*, when accomplished and undertaken, conduce to harm and suffering," then indeed you should reject them.

Accordingly, he gets them to reject the *dharmas* (which must here mean mental states as much as teachings conducive to these) of greed, hatred and delusion, as leading to behavior which breaks the moral precepts, and to take up non-greed, non-hatred and non-delusion, as seen in someone who mindfully radiates loving-kindness, compassion, empathetic joy and equanimity in all directions.

Given what the above criticizes as sole sources of knowledge, what is left is one's own direct experience, checked in relation to the views of "the wise" presumably to get one to critically assess one's experience and ensure that one is not jumping to unwarranted conclusions from it. The "wise" are the *viññū*, or the "discerning," as referred to in a common chant on the *Dharma* refuge (e.g. S.IV.41), which says that the *Dharma* is "to be personally experienced by the wise (*paccataṃ veditabboviññūhi*)." In the later Sanskrit works the *Tattvasaṃgraha* and *Jñānasamuccayasāra*, a verse attributed to the Buddha says, "Just as the experts test gold by burning it, cutting it and applying it on a touchstone, my statements should be accepted only after critical examination and not out of respect for me."

Only occasionally, for example before his first sermon, did the Buddha use his authority, but this was not to force people to agree with him, but to get them to listen so that they could then gain understanding. He also advised his disciples not to react emotionally when they heard people speaking in blame or praise of him, but to assess calmly the degree to which what was said was true or false (*Dīgha Nikāya* 1.3).

The Buddha emphasized that his teachings had a practical purpose, and should not be blindly clung to. He likened the *Dharma* to a raft made by a man seeking to cross from the dangerous near shore of a river, representing the conditioned world, to the peaceful other shore, representing *nirvāṇa* (*Majjhima Nikāya* 1.134–5). He then rhetorically asked whether such a man, on reaching the other shore, should lift up the raft and carry it around with him there. He therefore said, "*Dharma* is for crossing over, not for holding on to." That is, a follower should not grasp at Buddhist teachings and practices (*dharmas*), but *use* them for their intended purpose, and be free of any attachment to them when they had fully accomplished their goal. The *Dharma* is seen to point out truths about reality that, when fully understood, are liberating. But one of the truths about reality is that attachment brings suffering, so one should not be attached even to *Dharma*. Indeed, to do so entails that one has probably misunderstood it in some way. Note, though, that the man in the parable does not separate himself from the raft before he has reached the "other shore." This would be rather unwise! Moreover, many ordinary Buddhists do have a strong attachment to Buddhism.

While the Buddha was critical of blind faith, he did not deny a role for soundly based faith or "trustful confidence" (Skt. *śraddhā*, Pāli *saddhā*) for, to test out his teachings, a person had to have at least some initial trust in them. Indeed, an important set of path qualities is the five faculties: *śraddhā*, energy, mindfulness, meditative concentration, and wisdom. Even in Theravāda Buddhism, which often has a rather rational, unemotional image, a very deep faith in the Buddha, *Dharma* and *Sangha* is common. Ideally, this is based on the fact that some part of the Buddha's path has been found to be uplifting, thus inspiring confidence in the rest. Many people, though, simply have a calm and joyful faith (Skt. *prasāda*, Pāli *pasāda*) inspired by the example of those who are well established on the path.

The *Caṅkī Sutta* (*Majjhima Nikāya* 2.171–6) discusses how there can be a reliable "awakening to truth (*saccānubodhaṃ*)." It describes how a layperson assesses a monk as to the presence of states of greed, hatred or delusion, such that these might cause the monk to lie or give bad spiritual advice. If he sees that the monk's mind is purified of these, he reposes *śraddhā* in him. Consequent to this, a series of activities follows, each being "of service" to the next: "approaching," "drawing close," "lending ear," "hearing *Dharma*," "remembering *Dharma*," "testing the meaning," "reflection on and approval of *Dharma*," "desire-to-do," "making an effort," "weighing up," "striving," and finally, "he realizes with his person (*kāyena*) the highest truth itself; and penetrating it by wisdom, he sees." Here, "reflection on and approval of *Dharma* (*dhamma-nijjhānakkhantiyā*)" is similar to "reflection on and approval of a view," as mentioned in the *Kālāma Sutta* as an unreliable source of certainty. Here something very close to it (though it concerns *Dharma*, not a "view") plays *a* part in a sequence of events culminating in knowledge. It can be seen as helping to prepare the right conditions for the arising of knowledge, as does *śraddhā*, but it is not itself *the same* as knowledge, nor is it directly productive of it. The quality of *śraddhā*, though, can still exist once true knowledge arises, in the form of joyful appreciation for what has become directly known.

The Buddha's selection of what to teach

The Buddha is seen as saying, "I have taught *Dharma*, Ānanda, making no 'inner' and 'outer': the *Tathāgata* has no (closed) 'teacher's fist' in respect of teachings" (*Dīgha Nikāya* 2.101). That is, he has no secret inner teaching, but has been explicit with all that pertains to enlightenment. In the *Abhayarājākumāra Sutta*, he says that he teaches from what he knows to be true, what is connected to goal of the spiritual life, whether or not others find it agreeable to hear, and at the appropriate time (*Majjhima Nikāya* 1.395). What he taught, compared to what he directly knew, was like a few *siṃsāpa* leaves in his hand compared to the numerous leaves in a grove of *siṃsāpa* trees. He had not taught that which did not aid progress to *nirvāṇa*, but taught that which did: the Four Ennobling Truths (*Saṃyutta Nikāya* 5.438–9).

When Mahāyāna texts came to be composed, they claimed that the Ennobling Truths were only the Buddha's preliminary teachings, with higher ones held back for those who could understand them. How, then, might a Mahāyānist take the above statements? There seem to be different possibilities, including:

1 The *Dīgha Nikāya* 2.101 statement might itself be seen as a provisional teaching.
2 One might accept the Mahāyāna claim that the Mahāyāna teachings *were* taught by the historical Buddha, but that some refused to listen to them, or pass them on.
3 One might say that the *Saṃyutta Nikāya* 5.438–9 passage might allow that teachings that did not "aid progress" early in Buddhist history could have come to do so by the time of the Mahāyāna, and perhaps that the Buddha foresaw this.

See also: **Buddha; Buddha, story of; Disciples of the Buddha; Skillful Means.**

PETER HARVEY

BUDDHA AND *CAKRAVARTINS*

While Gautama renounced the option of political power in becoming a Buddha, he did give teachings on how best to govern a realm. Moreover, Buddhism became a force for shaping civilization in this world, not just a means for transcending it. The Buddha is seen as linked to, though surpassing, one who is able to compassionately rule the human world, the *cakravartin* (Pāli *cakkavatti*), a "wheel-turning" king (*rājā*), or "universal monarch." The term may have originally meant an all-powerful monarch "whose chariot wheels turn freely," that is, "whose travels are unobstructed," expressing the aspiration for worldwide rule, though India had known no large empires by the time of the Buddha. The term also occurs in pre-Buddhist Brahmanical and Jain texts.

The paralleling of a *cakravartin* and a Buddha is seen in the following ideas:

1 Both a Buddha and a *cakravartin* are born with a body endowed with the "thirty-two characteristics of a great man" (*Dīgha Nikāya* 2.142–79).
2 Both a Buddha and a *cakravartin* are *Dharma-rājās*, as they each honor, revere and are dependent on *Dharma*. The one rolls the wheel of sovereignty, the other the *Dharma*-wheel (*Aṅguttara Nikāya* 1.109–10).
3 The seven treasures of a *cakravartin* (*Dīgha Nikāya* 2.172–7) are paralleled by the seven awakening factors of a Buddha (*Saṃyutta Nikāya* 5.99): mindfulness (paralleling a divine wheel that appears in the sky); *dharma*-investigation (a flying noble white elephant); energy (a flying noble white horse); joy (a radiant eight-faced jewel); tranquility (a beautiful and gentle woman as wife); meditative concentration (a wise treasurer-steward); and equanimity (a wise counselor).
4 A Buddha and a *cakravartin* are the two persons who bring happiness to the world (*Aṅguttara Nikāya* 1.76).
5 There cannot be two of either of them in the same world-system at the same time (*Majjhima Nikāya* 3.65).
6 The small town where the Buddha died, Kuśinagarī (Pāli Kusinārā), was once the wondrous capital, with a dazzling *Dharma*-palace, of a *cakravartin*, Mahāsudarśana (Pāli Mahāsudassana) whom the Buddha had been in a past life (*Dīgha Nikāya* 2.169–99).
7 The Buddha says that, due to his past cultivation of lovingkindness, he had many good rebirths, including many times seven as a *cakravartin* (*Aṅguttara-Nikāya* 4.89).
8 The Buddha instructed that after his death, his body should be dealt with as should that of a *cakravartin* (*Dīgha Nikāya* 2.142).

These parallels indicate the idea of a Buddha having universal spiritual "sovereignty" – in the sense of influence – over humans and gods. The title of the Buddha's first sermon, the *Dharmacakra-pravartana Sūtra* (Pāli *Dhammacakkappavattana Sutta*), the "Setting in Motion of the Wheel of *Dharma*," suggests the idea that this sermon inaugurated the period of the Buddha's spiritual influence in the world. Such an influence is of course seen as superior to that of a *cakravartin*.

The nature of a *cakravartin*

It is said that a person who is to be a *cakravartin* is a moral and compassionate ruler (*Majjhima Nikāya* 3.172–7). On a full moon day dedicated to religious observance, he goes to an upper room of his palace and a beautiful thousand-spoked divine wheel appears in the sky to him. A fourteenth-century Thai text sees it as like a second full moon, and it is clear from the canonical texts that others can see it. It is anointed by the *cakravartin* and it goes to each of the four directions, to the ends of the earth, followed by the *cakravartin* and his army. Other kings welcome him, and he teaches them to keep the five moral precepts. He thus conquers the earth, but without violence. Of the *cakravartin* Mahāsudarśana, that the Buddha had once been, it is said that he practiced the four meditative *dhyānas* (Pāli *jhānas*) and radiated to the four directions lovingkindness, compassion, empathetic joy and equanimity (*Dīgha Nikāya* 2.186). The *Cakkavattisīhanāda Sutta* (*Dīgha Nikāya* 3.58–79) refers to a *cakravartin* as ruling the four continents and living for many hundreds of thousands of years, but as renouncing the world when the divine wheel slips from its place, indicating that he did not have long to live, with the wheel then disappearing after his renunciation (pp. 59–60). The wheel reappears for his son when he fulfils the duties of a *cakravartin*: honoring and depending on *Dharma*, protecting all the people of his realm as well as animals and birds, preventing both crime and poverty, and periodically going to brahmins and renunciants to ask for advice on what is wholesome and unwholesome (pp. 60–1). There is then a line of seven more *cakravartins*, but the eighth one did not prevent poverty (p. 65), which sets in train a long moral decline in society, starting with theft, then violence. As morality declines, human life-span declines from its prior 80,000 years till it lasts only ten years, in a "sword-period" of mutual violence (p. 73). Those who survive this, by having hidden in the forest, are then so pleased to see others alive that they pledge to live morally again, and as they do so, human life-span starts to increase, till it gradually climbs back to 80,000 years, in a prosperous period when greed, fasting, and old age are the only diseases (pp. 74–5). Then, the text narrates, a new *cakravartin*, called Saṅkha, will arise, and also the next Buddha, Maitreya (Pāli Metteyya), under whom the *cakravartin* will become a monk and then an *arhat* (pp. 75–6). But of course this golden age will not last for ever, and it is pointed out that even those who live for 80,000 years still die (*Aṅguttara Nikāya* 4.136–9). Moreover, it is said that the happiness of a heaven is greater than that of a *cakravartin* (*Majjhima Nikāya* 3.173–8).

Steven Collins both re-translates and discusses the *Cakkavattisīhanāda Sutta* at length. For him, it is:

> a story of decline and revival ... an elaborate way of giving narrative form to a ... sense of the futility of temporal goods ... [It] depicts life in time, however good or bad, as slightly absurd; and thereby its opposite, timeless *nirvāṇa*, as the only serious thing in the long run.

According to Collins it is a "parable" whose aim is to "induce in its audiences ... a sense of detachment from or at least a (briefly) non-involved perspective on, the passage of time".

It is said that *cakravartins* rule over one to four continents, and only exist when human life-span is not less than 80,000 years (*Abhidharmakośabhāṣya* III.95–6). While perfect Buddhas have clear awareness in the womb from conception to birth, and *pratyekabuddhas* have this at conception and some time after, *cakravartins* have clear awareness simply at conception, unlike other beings who lack this quality at any time in the womb (*Abhidharmakośabhāṣya* III.17). This places *cakravartins* at a high grade of spiritual development, but below that of a *pratyekabuddha*. However, while they are reborn in a heaven, they are not free of the possibility of future bad rebirths (*Saṃyutta Nikāya* 5.342).

The *cakravartin* is in many ways the ideal layperson, and the ideal's emphasis on compassionately bringing benefit to the whole world in some way foreshadows ideas later attached to the *bodhisattva* ideal in the Mahāyāna. It is also notable that in Mahāyāna art, advanced *bodhisattvas* are often portrayed wearing the decorations of royalty in a way that is reminiscent of the early idea that a *cakravartin* monarch is one role fulfilled by a *bodhisattva* on his way to perfect Buddhahood.

In Buddhist history, Emperor Aśoka (Pāli Asoka; r. 268–239 BCE) is seen to have in effect embodied the *cakravartin* ideal, though he did not explicitly claim to have been a *cakravartin*. Later kings have made this claim, such as the founder of the Chinese Sui dynasty (585–618) and, in Burma, kings Kyanzittha (1040–1113) and Alaungpaya (1752–60), who saw themselves as both *bodhisattvas* and *cakravartins*.

See also: **Buddha; Buddha, story of; *Pratyeka-buddhas*.**

PETER HARVEY

BUDDHA-FIELDS AND PURE LANDS

The theme of paradises, both earthly and otherworldly, is common to most cultural traditions, and Buddhist cosmology and soteriology both offer especially fertile ground for the elaboration of various types of paradisiacal realms. Most prominent among these are the buddha-fields (*buddhakṣetra*) of Mahāyāna literature, along with their East Asian equivalents, the "pure lands" or *jingtu*, which are at the center of the primary mode of devotional practice in Chinese, Korean, and Japanese Buddhism. Buddhists have always worked within more than a single cosmology; even in the scriptures of the conservative early schools one finds, alongside the dominant single-world system, a "cosmology of thousands" (*sāhasra*). The former is seemingly limited to, or at least focused on, this world conceived as a flat disk with heavens above and hells below. But beyond that immediate frame of reference, the earliest Buddhists recognized a system of 10,000 worlds, systematized in terms of periods of cosmic time. These worlds are classified temporally, in terms of the frequency with which buddhas arise in different types of world system, just as the over-arching structure for the cosmos as a whole is explained in terms of thousands of worlds arising and falling according to the various divisions of cosmic time. Later, in the Mahāyāna, we find the development of an even more elaborate cosmology, framed in terms of an even more vast and incalculable (*asaṃkhyeya*) number of parallel world systems. In this Mahāyāna system it is the spatial dimension that becomes the organizing focus, with the concept of time becoming virtually meaningless in a cosmic drama spread over so vast a stage. The occurrence of buddhas repeatedly turning the wheel of the *Dharma* anew was thus the basis for both temporal and spatial imagination and speculation. How often might a buddha appear in any given world? In which of the parallel world systems making up the cosmos, and in how many, are buddhas proclaiming the eternal *Dharma* even now?

It is within this cosmological context that the notion of the *buddhakṣetra* (Buddha-field) arose. The realm of a buddha's activity is his buddha-field, and the nature and quality of that field varied, some being "pure" (*viśuddha*), some "impure" (*aviśuddha*), and some "mixed" (*miśraka*). The Sahā-realm, in which we humans live, is the *buddhakṣetra* of Śākyamuni Buddha, and it is considered to be an impure *buddhakṣetra*, one still in the midst of a long process of purification arising from the effects of Śākyamuni's ministry. But beings are not limited to any single world system or *buddhakṣetra*. Especially in the Mahāyāna cosmology, they can seek to be reborn in a *buddhakṣetra* less afflicted by suffering and thus more conducive to enlightenment. These are the "pure lands" constructed through the power of the salvific vows (*praṇidhāna*) of various *bodhisattvas* and buddhas, both "historical" and archetypal. While these purified *buddhakṣetras* offer a more attractive existence than this Sahā-world, one free of gross suffering, the point of seeking rebirth in a buddha-field is not simply to enjoy its paradisiacal pleasures but, much more importantly, to take advantage of the supportive conditions it offers to gain the ultimate release from all rebirth more quickly and easily than would be the case if one were to be reborn repeatedly in this impure Sahā-world. Particularly powerful among these supportive conditions is the salvific efficacy or grace (*adhiṣṭhāna*) generated by the vow of the presiding buddha or *bodhisattva*. These vows are deemed to have such a powerful karmic effect that one is assured an end of unfavorable rebirths, even if the work of personal liberation is still to be completed.

In the Pāli scriptures of Theravāda Buddhism the term "buddha-field" (Pāli *buddhakhetta*, Skt. *buddhakṣetra*) refers to the realm in which a buddha lives and teaches, and to the domain of Śākyamuni Buddha in particular. Tradition held that immediately prior to the final lifetime when he was to become enlightened, Śākyamuni Buddha dwelt in Tuṣita heaven, one of the lower celestial heavens within this world system. This was taken as the pattern for all buddhas, past and future, of this Sahā-world, and indeed the *bodhisattva* Metteyya (Skt. *Maitreya*), is said to be living presently in Tuṣita, awaiting his rebirth as the next Buddha. It is easy to see how this belief soon led aspirants to pray for eventual rebirth with Metteyya as participants in a Buddhist millennium when it would be far easier to complete the Buddhist path. That aspiration developed, in turn, into a specialized cult in early Mahāyāna circles, one that became very popular in China before it was eventually eclipsed by the cult of Amitābha. There are thus significant parallels between the Theravāda goal of rebirth in Tuṣita and the Mahāyana pure land cults, but still the Tuṣita heaven is not, as part of the Sahā-world system, a "pure land" in the Mahāyāna sense. Nor is Maitreya considered to be building or embellishing Tuṣita to make it more conducive to the enlightenment of his devotees. Indeed, their ultimate goal is to be reborn back in the human realm with him when his time as the next Buddha arrives, there to enjoy the fruits of his lifetimes of practice.

There are other early sources for pure land devotionalism. Those aspiring to rebirth in the later Mahāyāna pure lands are encouraged to meditate on the virtues of their chosen Buddha, a practice of *buddhānusmṛti* ("recollection or contemplation of the Buddha") which probably stems from such early stories as Piṅgiya's verses in the *Sutta Nipāta* (vv. 1140 and 1142), in which Pingiya reports how in his old age he no longer needs to visit the Buddha in person because he constantly keeps the master in his mind's eye. Still, however far back we can trace their roots, the later pure lands have many features which represent a substantial and distinct Mahāyāna development. They are intentionally created through the power of the *bodhisattva*'s vow to perfect the virtue of compassion through constructing for devotees an ideally purified world, a Buddhist "New Jerusalem." The earliest surviving reference to a *bodhisattva* vowing to accomplish the purification of such a buddha-realm (*buddhakeṣtra-pariśuddhi*) is likely to be a passage in the *Aṣṭasāhasrikāprajñāpāramitā Sūtra* which asserts that one sign that a *bodhisattva* has reached the stage of irreversibility on the path to buddhahood is that he or she has the aspiration: "Thus will I act that in my Buddha-field, after I have won full enlightenment, there shall be no states of woe at all!" (XX.382; according to Conze's 1973 translation).

The utopian aspects of the pure land have ample precedent in the visionary depiction of highly idealized cities or mansions located within this world system. We see this in the wonders of Vimalakīrti's palace in Vaiśālī and also in the various realms Sudhana encounters in his quest for Vairocana's tower in the *Gaṇḍavyūha Sūtra*. Another, probably earlier, example is found in the thirtieth chapter of the *Aṣṭasāhasrikā*, where we are told of the *bodhisattva* Sadāprarudita's journey to the east to find the town of Gandhavati (literally, "possessing fragrance"), which is said to be 500 leagues away and built of the seven precious things. It has 500 rows of shops arranged beautifully on the terraced banks of the golden river, Jambu, which supplies the city's moats with water pleasantly "neither too cold nor too hot" and covered with fragrant flowers. All the inhabitants are prosperous and they are continuously entertained by many bells strung round the city, which when stirred by the breeze produce music as harmonious as that of the Gandharvas. There Sadāprarudita is to seek out the mansion of the *bodhisattva* Dharmodgata, where all the inhabitants of the city, "both women and men, divert, enjoy and amuse themselves, they have constant joy in the parks and on the ponds and they feel and taste the five kinds of sense-pleasure" (according to Conze's 1973 translation). But the *bodhisattva* Dharmodgata enjoys these pleasures only for a certain time, we are told, before turning to the higher pursuit of proclaiming the Perfection of Wisdom from a magnificent pulpit especially built for his teachings by the good citizens of the town. Note that, for all their mythic extravagance, these more worldly *Dharma* paradises are still located within the geography of South Asia, within this Sahā-realm. But even in the same scriptures we begin to find still more highly idealized pure lands located in fantastic realms spread across all the reaches of the cosmos.

The *Vimalakīrti Nirdeśa Sūtra* depicts such an ethereal and highly spiritualized pure land – the Sarvagandhasugandhā Universe (lit. "most excellently fragrant of all fragrances"). While this land is somewhat reminiscent of Dharmodgata's city of Gandhavati, what we have now is not an earthly city but a whole celestial universe located "in the direction of the zenith, beyond as many buddha-fields as there are sands in the forty-two Ganges rivers," where "all the houses, the avenues, the parks, and the palaces are made of various perfumes" (according to Thurman's 1976 translation). There the Buddha Sugandhakūṭa ("pinnacle of excellent fragrances") presides, teaching the *Dharma* by means of alluring perfumes rather than through words and concepts. Vimalakīrti does insist that time and space, however vast, are ultimately unreal for the spiritually adept, and elsewhere in the same scripture we are told that when *bodhisattvas* purify their minds sufficiently even this Sahā-realm is revealed to be a pure land. Nonetheless, it was the "cosmically distant" pure lands that ultimately became the most popular focus of Mahāyāna devotionalism, and the tradition has generated a rich variety of choices. Best known today is Amitābha's Sukhavatī ("[land] of happiness"), which is said to lie to the west of our world system, but there are also other, possibly earlier, examples as well: to the east, for example, is Akṣobhya's Abhirati ("surpassing delight"), and there are also the Padma ("Lotus") Pure Land of Buddha Padmottara, Bhaiṣajyaguru Vaiḍūryaprabha's Vaiḍūrynirbhāsā, and Queen Śrīmālādevī's unnamed pure land, which is yet to be realized in the future. Extravagant in the (dharmically conducive) sensual delights they offer, each of these purified realms has its own special features. Sukhavatī is replete with fragrant flowers, jeweled trees, and melodious rivers, while all the mountains and ravines have been leveled for the convenience of its inhabitants, among whom no women are to be found. But in Abhirati, by contrast, we find not only lovely forests and rivers but also happy families with many women and children, and the women are said to be forever free of the pains of menstruation. Different though they are, all these ideal realms have two things in common. They come into existence as the salvific fruition of a *bodhisattva*'s vow to perfect the virtue of great compassion (*mahākaruṇa*), each manifesting in every aspect the perfection of Buddhist morality. And once the devotee secures rebirth there, he or she is assured a pleasurable existence, even while ever more diligently and effectively pursuing the ultimate goal of awakening.

See also: **Cosmology and rebirth; Mahāyāna Buddhism; Pure Land movements in Japan; Pure Land school, China.**

ALAN SPONBERG

BUDDHA NATURE AND *TATHĀGATAGARBHA*

The Buddha proclaimed his teaching to be a "middle path" between the extremes of eternalism and annihilationism, the one extreme including all views that posit a permanent, immutable essence or soul, and the other, all claims that the self is totally annihilated at death, thus leaving no basis for karmic continuity from one lifetime to the next. But despite his clear statement of this middle way, over the centuries the Buddha's interrelated teachings of no-self (*anātman*), impermanence (*anitya*), and suffering (*duḥkha*) have given rise to persistent charges of pessimism if not outright nihilism. Nāgārjuna's radical extension of the *anātman* doctrine to assert that all "things" (*dharmas*) are empty of any intrinsic existence served only to exacerbate the fear of nihilism, even among many within the Buddhist tradition. The Mahāyāna teaching that all beings possess the *tathāgatagarbha* sought to address these fears, real or imagined, even if at the price of raising the specter of the other extreme, eternalism. While philosophically problematic, the concept served a vital psychological role in reassuring followers of the path that they were indeed in possession of all that is needed to realize the goal. It is no accident, one is inclined to think, that this teaching became increasingly popular from the mid-third century CE, a time when some within the Yogācāra school were raising the possibility that certain beings, the so-called *icchantikas*, were so ensnared in their desire (*icchā*) that they would never be capable of overcoming their negative karmic conditioning. Moreover, this was during the Gupta period, a high point in Hindu philosophical resurgence, which may also have contributed to the increasing popularity of *tathāgatagarbha* speculation. Originally presented in terms of simple but suggestive analogies rather than philosophical argument, the basic idea was that all beings possess, innately, the essence of the Buddha's enlightenment, something that can, in other words, serve as a basis for the development of the positive qualities that eventually lead to Buddhahood. But the question of how the apparently essentialist implications of that notion are to be squared with the doctrines of *anātman* and *śūnyatā* (emptiness [of intrinsic existence]) gave rise to a tension that runs through Mahāyāna thought right down to the present.

The term *tathāgatagarbha* is variously translated as the matrix (or womb, or germ, or embryo = *garbha*) of the Buddha (*tathāgata* = the "thus-gone"/"thus-come" [one]) – or, less literally, as the Buddha nature or Buddha essence possessed by all sentient beings. The doctrine is found in several key Mahāyāna scriptures, including the *Tathāgatagarbha Sūtra*, the later recensions of the (Mahāyāna) *Mahāparinirvāṇa Sūtra*, the *Śrīmālādevīsiṃhanāda Sūtra* ("Sūtra of the Lion's Roar of Queen Śrīmālādevī") and, less centrally, in the *Laṅkāvatāra Sūtra*. There is little evidence that it was an important teaching in Indian Buddhism, but it eventually became very influential indeed in the Buddhism of Tibet and East Asia. The Tibetan assimilation of the doctrine is based on the *Ratnagotravibhāga* (or *Uttaratantra*), a treatise (*śāstra*) ascribed in the earliest Chinese translations to Sāramati, but considered by a later Tibetan tradition to be the work of Maitreya. In East Asia the *Ratnagotravibhāga* was eclipsed by the popular and influential *Dasheng Qixin Lun* ("The Awakening of Faith in the Mahāyāna"), a treatise ascribed to Aśhvaghoṣa (first to second century CE), but much more likely to be an original Chinese work. Both these key works are largely based on the *Śrīmālā Sūtra*, which thus became the primary scriptural source for the doctrine, though there are significant differences of interpretation within the various schools of Tibetan and East Asian Buddhism. In neither case do we have a school based primarily on the *tathāgatagarba* teachings, yet it would not be an exaggeration to say that they came to have a formative influence on every aspect of Buddhism in both regions.

In the *Tathāgatagarbha Sūtra*, perhaps the earliest and certainly the simplest formulation of the doctrine, we find it briefly presented in terms of nine suggestive, if not very precise, similes. The *tathāgarbha* is, this *sūtra* asserts, like the calyx of an unopened lotus blossom, like honey still in the comb, like unthreshed grain still in the husk, like gold in ore, like a treasure buried beneath a poor man's house, like a seed still in its hull, like a buddha image wrapped in a dirty cloth, like one destined to become a world ruler while still enclosed in the impurities of the womb, and like a golden statue still lodged within its clay mold. Note that some of these analogies suggest a potentiality yet to be fulfilled, while others seem to refer to an actuality as yet unrecognized. Therein lies the fundamental ambiguity that was left to the later tradition to resolve – in significantly different ways. The *Mahāparinirvāṇa Sutra* added to the controversy with its view that the *tathāgatagarbha* is a real, permanently existing element which is to be understood precisely as the Self (*ātman*) – present in all sentient beings, yet difficult to perceive accurately as it is obscured by adventitious defilements. It is what makes it possible for beings to become enlightened. But then a later section (or interpolation?) of the same *sūtra* paradoxically has the Buddha suggesting that this depiction of the *tathāgatagarbha* as *ātman* is a strategy for converting non-Buddhists who fear the apparent nihilism of his teaching. Thus he teaches Self where there is no-Self, and "no-Self" where is Self.

The *Śrīmālā Sūtra* and the *Ratnagotravibhāga* (with its *Vyākhyā* commentary) associate the *tathāgatagarbha* possessed by all beings with the *dharmakāya* of buddhas, understanding the former to be the latter when still obscured by defilements. But both texts continue, seemingly, to argue that this purified *tathāgatagarbha*-qua-*dharmakāya* is intrinsically pure and never truly defiled, concluding that the *dharmakāya* as untainted thusness (*tathatā*) is not only permanent but unchanging as well. Both texts conclude that the mystery of how this can be the case is inconceivable to the deluded mind, and therefore remains a matter of faith to be resolved only by the arising of full enlightenment. From that common point the Chinese understanding diverges from the Tibetan interpretations, with the influential *Tasheng Qixin Lun* framing the relationship of *tathāgatagarbha* to *dharmakāya* more in terms of the cosmological evolution of the *tathāgatagarbha* as One Mind (= *dharmākāya*), evolving from its primordial state, to manifest differentiation and defilement, and eventually with awakening, reverting back to its pure, primordial state. The links between these ideas and later developments – the "pure awareness" of *rDzogs chen* and the "primordial enlightenment" (*hongaku*) of Japanese Tendai and Shingon, for example – are evident, but warrant further research.

See also: **India, Buddhism in; Mahāyāna Buddhism; *Tathāgatagarbha* in Indian Buddhism; Yogācāra school.**

ALAN SPONBERG

BUDDHADASA

Likely the most innovative thinker in the modern Theravāda tradition, Buddhadasa Bhikkhu (1926–93) has reinterpreted core principles of Theravāda doctrine to renew their moral relevance in the modern world. He has been recognized as the intellectual architect laying the foundation for socially engaged Buddhism. Although he spent most his career in the forest meditation retreat he built, his influence through his philosophical scholarship, teaching and lectures had far-reaching impact well beyond Bangkok and Theravāda Buddhism.

He received his basic education as a temple boy in his home village in southern Thailand. Following his full ordination at age twenty as Phra (Ngeuam) Indapanno, he resolved to sit for monastic examinations in Bangkok. However, he soon became disenchanted with the ecclesiastical hierarchy and educational conventionalities of the Thai *sangha* and returned to rural southern Thailand where he founded a forest meditation retreat, Suan Mokkhabalarama, the Garden of the Power of Liberation in 1932. This forest retreat became the center of his activity where he studied, practiced and taught the *dhamma*.

He argued that suffering is rooted in attachment to notions of "I" and "mine." One's efforts to overcome the First Noble Truth and eradicate suffering bring spiritual rewards that eventually lead to abandoning selfishness, realizing unsurpassable voidness, *nibbāna*. His reflections on *dhamma* which he glossed as Nature, the One Reality, Truth, and the Law of Nature led him to assert the spiritual interdependence of all material, physical and social realities and have guided him in the formulation of a modern Buddhism moral imperative, dhammic socialism. Ending suffering was therefore not an other-worldly activity withdrawn from social and personal concerns. Rather, *nibbāna* was to be attained by direct engagement with the world (*saṃsāra*).

For Buddhadasa, democracy had primarily moral, rather than political, relevance. Throughout his career, he gave public speeches in which he explained Buddhist philosophical foundations for political ideologies, often adopting perspectives that were not consonant with the mainstream of Thai public opinion. In the 1940s, he lectured on "Buddha-*Dhamma* and Peace" and on "Buddha-*Dhamma* and the Spirit of Democracy." During the 1970s, when Southeast Asia, and Thailand in particular, feared the threat of communism, he chose to speak on "Socialism According to Religious Principles." For Buddhadasa, the type of socialism that could help the world was dhammic socialism, governed by the practice of morality and wisdom. The social imperative motivating concern for others and the greater social good was informed by dhammic morality and correctness and recognized the fundamental interdependence of nature. Socialism was therefore intrinsic to Buddhist history as the practice of politics was indeed the practice of morality (*sīla*). "For the authority of *dhamma* to function in society, it must act through institutions and rulers" (viz. the Ten Virtues of Rulers, *rājadhamma*).

Among those who sought out his counsel through the decades are Thai lawyers, educators, medical doctors and social progressives like Sulak Sivaraksa, founder of many civil organizations including the International Network of Engaged Buddhists. Buddhadasa's legacy continues to be realized at his forest hermitage, now called Suan Mokkh International, that serves a meditation center, think-tank for social activists and inter-religious dialogue, as well as educational facilities for *dhamma* missionaries.

See also: **Famous Buddhists and ideal types.**

JULIANE SCHOBER

BUDDHAS, PAST AND FUTURE

While Gautama (Pāli Gotama) Buddha was not seen as the continuer of an historical tradition, his authenticity was backed up through the idea that he was one of a long line of Buddhas spread through cosmic time. This paralleled the established Jain tradition that Mahāvīra, a contemporary of the Buddha, was the twenty-fourth Tīrthaṃkara or "Ford-maker" (guide to liberation). The *Mahāpadāna Sutta* (*Dīgha Nikāya* 2.1–54) has the Buddha referring to himself and a number of past Buddhas, with basic details of their lives (See Table 3).

Additionally, for each of the above Buddhas, there is given: his clan, the type of tree under which he attained enlightenment, names of two chief disciples, name of attendant monk, and names of parents. It is elsewhere said that Gotama, as the brahmin Jotipāla, became a monk under Kassapa Buddha (*Majjhima Nikāya* 2.45–54).

The *Mahāpadāna Sutta* goes on to describe key events of the life of Vipassī

Table 3 Table showing details of previous Buddhas

Name	*Lived*	*Social class*	*Life-span*	*Number of assemblies of* Arhat *monk disciples*	*Number in each*
Vipassī (Skt. Vipaśyin) (Insightful)	91 eons ago	warrior-noble	80,000 years	3	6,800,000 100,000 80,000
Sikkhī (Skt. Śikhin) (Crested)	31 eons ago	warrior-noble	70,000 years	3	100,000 80,000 70,000
Vesssabhū (Skt. Viśvabhū) (Bull-like (?))	31 eons ago	warrior-noble	60,000 years	3	80,000 70,000 60,000
Kakusandha (Skt. Krakucchanda or Krakutsanda)	present eon	brahmin	40,000 years	1	40,000
Konāgamana (Skt. Konakamuni) (Shower of Gold)	present eon	brahmin	30,000 years	1	30,000
Kassapa (Skt. Kāśyapa)	present eon	brahmin	20,000 years	1	20,000
Gotama (Skt. Gautama)	present eon	warrior-noble	100 years	1	1,250

Buddha. Of all these, it is said, "This, monks, is the rule (*dhammatā*; literally *dharma*-ness)." That is, the lives of all Buddhas follow the same basic pattern; they are not accidental, except in minor details. Accordingly, Vipassī's story gives the basis for later retellings of Gotama Buddha's life, and can be seen as the earliest Buddha-legend (the story of seeing an ill person, an aged person, a corpse, and a calm renunciant come from the account of Vipassī's life). The Buddha ends the *sutta* by saying, "And so it is, monks, that by his penetration of the principle of *Dharma* (*dhamma-dhātu*), the *Tathāgata* remembers the past Buddhas" (*Dīgha Nikāya* 2.53).

The above shows that the early Buddhist tradition did not see the *Dharma* as discovered and taught by a unique individual, but rather by a unique *type* of individual, who emerges in widely separated periods of human history, yet according to a given pattern that itself relates to *Dharma*, the basic pattern of things, in which the basic parameters are set and only the particular details are left to fill in. In the *Dīgha Nikāya* (3.114), the Buddha affirms that both in the past and in the future, there will be Buddhas equal to him.

Cosmic cycles of eons

The *Mahāpadāna Sutta* sees the present eon (Skt. *kalpa*, Pāli *kappa*) as "fortunate" in containing several Buddhas. Its length is suggested by saying that at the time of its Buddha Kakusandha, there was a mountain that took four days to climb or descend; now it takes only an hour to do so (*Saṃyutta Nikāya* 2.191–2).

Regarding the nature of an "eon," there are said to be:

> these four incalculables (*asaṅkeyyas*) of an eon. What four? When the eon rolls up (*saṃvaṭṭati*), it is no easy thing to reckon: so many years ... so many hundreds of thousands of years. When the eon being rolled up stands still, it is no easy thing to reckon ... When the eon rolls out (*vivaṭṭati*) ... When the eon being rolled out stands still ...
>
> (*Aṅguttara Nikāya* 2.142)

These four phases, in which a world-system comes to be destroyed, remains destroyed, develops, and remains before being destroyed again, came to be known as a "great eon" (*mahā-kalpa*), the usual referent when "an eon" is referred to. Once, the Buddha is asked the length of an eon (the commentary glosses: "a great eon"). He says that if there were a solid stone mountain a league (*yojana* – perhaps seven miles) high, and it was stroked once a century with a piece of fine cloth, it would wear away before an eon came to an end – though the cycle of rebirth goes back many hundreds of thousands of eons, without discernible beginning (*Saṃyutta Nikāya* 2.181–2).

During the time that a world remains, the maximum life-span of humans is seen to vary from 80,000 years to ten years (*Dīgha Nikāya* 3.68–75), being lower when morality is poorer. Nevertheless, however long it is, people still die: at *Aṅguttara Nikāya* 4.136–9 is the story of a teacher (Gautama in a past life) at a time when people lived for 80,000 years, who taught that life was short. In the Sarvāstivādin tradition, the *Abhidharmakośabhāṣya* (III.90–92) holds that in the period when a world remains "rolled out," there are twenty intermediary (*antara*) eons: in the first, life-span descends from an unlimited period to ten years, then eighteen in which it goes from ten to 80,000 years and back, and in the last it goes from ten to 80,000. Then there are twenty intermediary eons for the world to be destroyed, twenty in which it is quiescent, and twenty in which it develops again: thus eighty in all to a great eon. The Theravāda tradition talks of sixty-four intermediary eons to a great eon

(*Dīgha Nikāya* commentary, p. 162), presumably sixteen per world-phase.

Somewhat confusingly, the term *asaṃkheyya* (Pāli *asaṅkeyya*), "an incalculable," is also used for a unit which is a huge number of "great eons." This is seen when the *Visuddhimagga* (p. 411) says that the great disciples can recollect 100,000 past eons, the two chief disciples an incalculable and 100,000 eons, a *pratyeka-buddha* two incalculables and 100,000 eons, and a perfect Buddha has no limits. The *Abhidharmakośabhāṣya* (III.93d–94a) explains that it takes a *bodhisattva* three *asaṃkheyyas* to become a perfect Buddha, and that each of these consists of 1,000 million million great eons.

The twenty-eight Buddhas of the *Buddhavaṃsa*

In the *Buddhavaṃsa*, a relatively late text of the fifth *Nikāya* of the Pāli Canon (perhaps third to second century BCE), accounts are given of twenty-four Buddhas prior to Gotama, adding Dīpaṅkara (Skt. Dīpaṃkara: "Light-maker") then seventeen others before Vipassī. In the *Buddhavaṃsa*, Dīpaṅkara is said to have lived "a hundred thousand eons and four 'incalculables' ago" (IIA.1), when the present Buddha, as the ascetic Sumedha, first made his aspiration for Buddhahood. The text also names three Buddhas prior to Dīpaṅkara, such that the Theravāda school has a list of twenty-eight Buddhas of the past and present. In the later Theravāda tradition, there are around twenty-five works on such past Buddhas. As assigned to eons by the *Dīgha Nikāya* commentary (pp. 410–11):

- in one eon: Taṇhaṅkara, Medhaṅkara, Saraṇaṅkara, Dīpaṅkara (these names seem to echo the Jain "Tīrthaṃkara" as a general term for past Jain enlightened ones);
- an incalculable eon (*asaṅkheyya-kappa*) without Buddhas, except that in its final (great) eon: Koṇḍañña;
- an incalculable without Buddhas, except that in its final eon: Maṅgala (Blessing), Sumana (Uplifted Mind), Revata, Sobhita (Radiant One);
- an incalculable without Buddhas, except that in its final eon: Anumodassin (Unexcelled Insight), Paduma (Lotus), Nārada;
- an incalculable without Buddhas, except that in its final eon (100,000 eons ago): Padumuttara (Supreme Lotus);
- 70,000 eons later (= 30,000 eons ago): Sumedha (Very Wise), Sujāta (Well Born);
- 18,000 eons ago: Piyadassin (Pleasing to See), Atthadassin (Seer of the Goal), Dhammadassin (Seer of *Dharma*);
- ninety-four eons ago: Siddhattha (Attained to his Goal);
- ninety-two eons ago: Tissa, Phussa (Excellent);
- ninety-one eons ago: Vipassī;
- thirty-one eons ago: Sikhī, Vessabhū;
- in this fortunate eon: Kakusandha, Koṇāgamana, Kassapa, Gotama, and the next Buddha, Metteyya.

In the above, "an incalculable eon" must be that which is many great eons; if it meant the "incalculable of an eon," of which there are four in a great eon, there would be Buddhas appearing in each of these, though *one* is when the physical world is non-existent.

The intervening eons empty of Buddhas are also said to contain no *cakravartin* emperors or solitary Buddhas (Skt. *pratyeka-buddhas*, Pāli *pacceka-buddhas*). All these Buddhas are seen to attain enlightenment at the same firm spot on earth (*Dīgha Nikāya* commentary 424), as only it can support the weight of such an attainment (*Jātaka* 4.229). The above list includes only twenty-seven past Buddhas, but the *Buddhavaṃsa* says that there have been countless others (XXVII.20). Indeed, this is implied by the idea that *each* past Buddha must, as a *bodhisattva*, have met *earlier* Buddhas. In the Lokottaravādin *Mahāvastu*, the Buddha says that he knew, in the past, 800 Buddhas called Dīpaṃkara, and, for example, 90,000 named Kāśyapa (1.57–8). There is also a list of the names of past Buddhas that runs to four pages in translation (1.136–41).

Past Buddhas were venerated in Emperor Aśoka's time (mid-third century BCE), as one of his pillar inscription says he enlarged the *stūpa* of Konākamana (as he called him). In stone reliefs at Bhārhut, in the second century BCE, the seven Buddhas of the *Mahāpadāna Sutta* are represented by their seven *bodhi* trees. In Sri Lanka, a periodic fundraising event for temples that runs for three to six nights uses dancing, drumming and lay chanting on the lives of the twenty-four Buddhas before Gotama, and past Buddhas are sometimes represented by a row of Buddha images at temples.

Future Buddhas

In the *Cakkavattisīhanāda Sutta*, it is said that the next Buddha will be Metteyya (Sanskrit Maitreya and Maitrī), "The Kindly One," who will come later in the present eon after human life-span has dipped to ten years then again climbed back to 80,000 years, and at a time of a future *cakravartin* emperor (*Dīgha Nikāya* 3.75).

All Buddhist traditions agree that Maitreya is currently in the Tuṣita (Pāli Tusita) heaven, awaiting his future time as the next Buddha on earth. He was the focus of a considerable cult in Central Asia, China, Korea and Japan, and messianic cults focused on him have existed in both Burma and Korea. In China, as his popularity came to be eclipsed by that of Amitābha Buddha, as in Japan, he often came to be represented by the fat and jolly Budai, a tenth-century Chan monk who had come to be seen as an incarnation of him. His cult has remained strong in Korea, though.

In Sri Lanka, many people aspire to be reborn as a human at the time Maitreya is a Buddha, and attain enlightenment as one of his disciples. At the end of blessings (*anumodanā*) on receiving a donation, Sri Lankan monks may say, "With the aid of these acts of karmic fruitfulness, may you see Maitreya and attain *nirvāṇa*." Even the great Theravādin commentator Buddhaghosa aspires, at the end of his *Visuddhimagga* (pp. 837–8), that by the power of his good *karma*, he can be reborn in the Tāvatiṃsa heaven of the stream-enterer god Sakra (Pāli Sakka), there to become a stream-enterer himself, and then to be a human at the time of Metteyya and become an *arhat*. Most temples in Sri Lanka have an image of Metteyya, who is always shown as a *bodhisattva* decorated with divine ornaments, never as a Buddha. In low-country temples, his iconography seems to have been influenced by portrayals of the Mahāyāna *bodhisattva* Avalokiteśvara, as he has a Buddha in his crown and sometimes holds a lotus.

While the Mahāyāna tradition is rich in the idea of many *bodhisattvas* who will be Buddhas in the future, this idea is not absent in the Theravāda. There is, for example, the *Dasabodhisattuppattikathā* or "Account of the Arising of Ten *Bodhisattvas*," which talks of Metteyya and nine following *bodhisattvas*. In the Theravādin tradition, *Anāgatavaṃsa*, or "Chronicle of the Future" also has much to say on Metteyya, as does the *Māleyyadevatheravatthu*. In the Sanskrit tradition, the *Maitreyavyākaraṇa* describes his coming as a Buddha.

In the contemporary world, an important Buddhist project is the building of a 152-meter (500-foot) bronze statue of Maitreya Buddha at Kuśinagarī, where the Buddha passed away. This project is headed by Lama Zopa Rinpoche, who is collecting relics from various Buddhist countries to place in the image (http://www.maitreyaproject.org/en/index.html).

The issue of multiple Buddhas

While the Mahāyāna came to postulate many Buddhas in the universe at the same time, the position of the Pāli Canon and similar early text collections is that "It is impossible, it cannot come to pass that two perfectly enlightened Buddhas should arise simultaneously in a single world-system. This is not possible" (*Majjhima Nikāya* 3.114; *Dīgha Nikāya* 2.225). (This would, of course, imply that Mahāvīra, the Jain leader, though sometimes called a Buddha, was not really one.) In the *Milindapañha*, the reason for this is said to be that this "ten-thousand world-system" (or galaxy) can only sustain the special qualities of one Buddha at once, otherwise it will tremble and come to an end, like a one-person boat sinking if two people embark on it: dispute might arise among some of their followers, and neither would be supreme, unrivaled in the world (pp. 236–9). This still left open the question of whether Buddhas might simultaneously exist in *different* "world-systems": a possibility that the Mahāyāna later made use of, postulating countless Buddhas spread throughout the vastness of the universe.

See also: ***Bodhisattva*** **career in the Theravāda; Buddha; Buddha, story of; Cosmology and rebirth; Mahāyāna Buddhism;** ***Pratyeka-buddhas*****.**

PETER HARVEY

BUDDHISM, PSYCHOLOGY, AND THERAPY

Western psychology has influenced Buddhism just as Buddhist ideas and methods are in the process of affecting Western psychology and therapeutic forms. In specific schools and aspects Buddhism is getting psychologized, whereas on the reverse side psychologists are becoming Buddhists. The encounter and mutual exchange have become strong and prominent since the 1960s, though contacts and adoptions date back a few decades earlier.

Western psychology as a new and independent discipline emerged in the late nineteenth and early twentieth centuries with psychologists and psychoanalysts such as William James (1842–1910), Sigmund Freud (1856–1936), and Carl Gustav Jung (1875–1961). Psychological approaches analyzed and systematized the influence of the unconscious on the conscious and on psycho-somatic problems of a person. In particular, Jung, among others, had been fascinated by Tibetan Buddhism as an entrance into the collective unconscious, and Tibetan symbols as expressions of so-called archetypes. Jung stimulated an interest in Buddhist images and in the idea of making use of Buddhist concepts to learn more about the conscious and unconscious mind.

The credit of instigating the encounter of Buddhism and psychology on a much broader level undoubtedly goes to Daisetz T. Suzuki (1870–1966). Suzuki's *Essay in Zen Buddhism* (1927) interpreted Zen Buddhist concepts in psychological terms devoid of realignments to the Japanese Buddhist context. Zen practice was rationalized through minimizing the importance of pietistic, ritualistic, and sacramental dimensions of practice in favor of an instrumental or goal-directed approach. Zen, according to Suzuki, forms the basic and universal experience of all religions. *Satori* (Jap.) or the breakthrough to enlightenment is renamed in psychological terms as an "insight into the unconscious." Suzuki portrayed Zen as a technique and psychological experience consisting of the alleged ahistorical essence of spirituality. Suzuki's emphasis on direct experience met with and strongly stimulated the rising interest of the American Beat generation and its praise of anti-rational and non-conventional ways of thinking and experimenting during the 1950s. The meeting of Freudian psychologist Erich Fromm, Richard de Martino, and Zen teacher Suzuki in 1959 at a conference and the subsequent publication *Zen Buddhism and Psychoanalysis* (1960) can be seen as the first major encounter between Western psychology and (Eastern Mahāyāna) Buddhism. Fromm had been fascinated by the idea that Zen practice and Buddhist ideas may strongly contribute to processes of healing and a better understanding of the way the conscious and unconscious interrelate. Suzuki underscored that Zen and its practice are means to set creative impulses inherent in humanity's capacity free and to enable freedom.

The fascination with Zen, poetry, and literacy as well as the use of drugs and psychedelics made a peculiar mix during the 1950s and 1960s in North America. Spokespersons such as Timothy Leary, famous for his experiments with psychedelic drugs, and professor of psychology Richard Alpert, who returned from India as Baba Ram Das, fostered interest in both Buddhism and psychology. Humanistic psychology spoke in terms of development and setting free one's energy and potentials; transpersonal psychology started to employ so-called disciplines of consciousness such as yoga and meditation in order to enable an entrance to the varied areas of consciousness. A mutual and ongoing process has been carried on since then: the psychologizing of Buddhism respectively of specific forms of meditation, and a Buddhization of psychology.

The psychologization of Buddhism is restricted to those Westerners who have taken up Buddhism as their new orientation in life (converts). Strong emphasis is placed on inner, individual experience and on the transformative force of Buddhist insight. Quite a number of practitioners value Buddhism primarily as another, somewhat exotic form of psychological training. Though approaches towards a psychologization and next secularization of Buddhist meditation forms can be found in Tibetan Buddhism, for example Shambhala training, and specific Zen centers, for example Toni Parker and Joko Beck Sensei, the *vipassanā* movement has become most prominent in this line. *Vipassanā* (insight meditation) with its flagships the Insight Meditation Society (IMS), in Massachusetts, and Spirit Rock Meditation Center, in California, reduced the use of Buddhist vocabulary, employing instead Western psychological notions. As a substitute for speaking explicitly of Buddhism, the practice of meditation is renamed as gaining insight into the practitioner's moment-to-moment experience and of lifestyles that reflect these insights. The approach is explicitly non-sectarian and does not speak of being religious. Rather, *vipassanā* meditation is called an awareness technique fostering awakening, freedom, and psychological healing. A step further in this direction of *vipassanā*-derived mindfulness practices are approaches that teach meditation in hospitals, clinics, prisons, and schools without any hint of its previous Buddhist context. Jon Kabat-Zinn and many others following in his steps use meditation and body awareness methods to reduce stress and bring about an inner calmness.

The avoidance of Buddhist terms and the explicit use of Western psychological notions mirror, at least with regard to the IMS, the strong efforts to indigenize and Westernize Buddhist meditation and ideas. If Western psychology can be labeled an "indigenous belief," as suggested by Gil Fronsdale, this process of adopting psychological vocabulary follows the common line of Buddhism to adapt to a new culture and its worldview. Subsequently, a Western Buddhist form in this terminology can be expected to strongly stress individualism which focuses on personal experience, inner transformation and a very American-styled freedom. It remains to be seen whether Buddhism's aim and intention to understand the nature of suffering (Skt. *duḥkha*), and by this process to enable man and woman to reach spiritual enlightenment, will be buried under the Western obsession with the personal self and the "I," or whether the transformative spiritual appeal remains despite such adaptation processes.

The Buddhization of psychology can be followed up in the way that many psychologists and therapists have also become Buddhists. Emphasis is placed on the fact that both psychology and Buddhism attain to the mind and deal with the forces and formation of the mind, the conscious, and unconscious. Buddhists, however, underscore that Buddhist meditation and Buddhist teachings go beyond and further than Western psychology, in that they aim to enable non-attachment and a freedom of the very idea of an I or personal self. Spiritually oriented psychotherapists strive to enrich approaches of Western psychology with the insights of Buddhist teachings. Mark Epstein's *Thoughts without a Thinker: Psychotherapy from a Buddhist Perspective* (1995) as well as *The Couch and the Tree: Dialogues between Psychoanalysis and Buddhism*, edited by Anthony Molino (1998), may serve as prime examples of such Buddhist endeavors to transform Western psychology (which itself is very heterogeneous).

The psychologization of Buddhism and the Buddhization of psychology are prominent at work in North America, but also to a growing extent in Europe and other Western countries. The strong emphasis of focusing on the mind, on psychological healing and on the practice of meditation leaves out, to a varying extent, the collective as well as the ritual and devotional dimensions of Buddhism. Debates among Buddhists will continue whether a shortened, a focused, or a new and in this way specifically Western form and emphasis of Buddhism is emerging.

See also: **Buddhism and Western lifestyle; Buddhism in the Western world; Buddhist adaptations in the West.**

MARTIN BAUMANN

BUDDHISM AND WESTERN LIFESTYLE

Since the 1990s, the media has styled Buddhism as trendy, cool and a "lifestyle religion." This is observable in reports in newspapers, magazines, and television in Europe, North America, and also Brazil. The message told is that Buddhism is championed as a fashionable accessory, an item acquired to be "in." Indeed, a rapidly increasing number of people put up a Buddha figure in their living room for purposes of decoration, have a recent book of the teachings of the fourteenth Dalai Lama on their nightstand desk, and put up Tibetan prayer flags in their garden. The commercialization of Buddhism is well on its way in parts of the Western world; it has created a specialized industry which today sells goods styled as Buddhist, and tomorrow distributes articles related to Feng Shui or Celtic esotericism. Accessorizing with "things Buddhist" provides a touch of intellectuality, exoticism, and cosmopolitanism. Socially, it distances itself from less well-off classes which still, according to their understanding, follow long-established lines of beliefs such as "outdated" Christianity. Certainly this trend exists in sections of the urban, educated and well-off strata of society. However, media reports in such lifestyle magazines usually fail to mention that earnest and committed Buddhists – both convert and immigrant

Buddhists and their descendants – have been a part of the Western societies for more than a century.

Despite its enormous heterogeneity, Buddhism in the West is characterized by laicization, feminization, integration, and egalitarianism. These marks have a direct influence on the lifestyle of Buddhists in the West, in particular of convert Buddhists. The vast majority are lay Buddhists, both male and female, who live with their partner or family, have a job, enjoy their hobbies, and are part of ordinary social networks. Being Buddhist is not discernible from the outside (except for monks and nuns) and Buddhists do not walk around with a bright smile all the time, or with glowing eyes and sophisticated ideas. The integration of Buddhism into ordinary life is a big issue and topic in the West – the integration of Buddhist ideas and practices into the practice of householders, family people (including children), and professionals. In contrast to Asia (generally speaking), Western lay converts are not content to be merely devotional supporters of monastic personnel, as are increasingly the descendants of immigrant Buddhists. Rather, they study Buddhist texts and practice meditation at home and in the Buddhist center. Much of the ritual, ceremony and Asian customs have been abandoned and left behind. Ideally, Western Buddhists continuously strive to act according to the ethical precepts and the Noble Eightfold Path. In this way they engage to combine Buddhist values and their ordinary Western lifestyle.

The feminization of Buddhism in the West and the emphasis on egalitarianism have given female Buddhists a much greater voice than in almost all schools and traditions in Asia. Women are Buddhist teachers, authors, directors of centers, and much more. Also, as Jack Kornfield, prominent *vipassanā* teacher at Spirit Rock Center, California, styled it, the feminization has brought about a softening and an opening of the Buddhist spirit and practice. It balances the long-established primacy of the mind and the gaining of enlightenment through conquering oneself, with an awareness of the body and community. Western Buddhist lifestyle therefore is no longer characterized by an emphasis on individuality, cold rationality, cognition, and restriction, as had been typical for parts of the early periods of adoption. Rather, community experience, embracement of the joys and hardships of life, and connectedness to one's body have become apparent.

This amalgamation of Buddhist ideas and practices with ordinary life also relates to non-traditional lifestyles or alternative sexual preferences of gay, lesbian, bisexual, and transgendered people. Undoubtedly a taboo topic in most Asian countries, this "queer community," as author Roger Corless labeled it, has come out and forth within Buddhist groups and circles, more prominently so in North America. A number of Buddhist gay, lesbian, and bisexual groups have emerged and it is not uncommon for some centers to run courses or retreats exclusively for gays or lesbians. Integration of these Buddhists involves not a distancing, but the provision of means and locations to meet, exchange, and support.

Despite the prominence of lay Buddhism in the West, becoming a monk or nun, wearing the robe, and keeping the *Vinaya* rules is an option followed by a slowly growing number of Western converts. Within immigrant Buddhist communities, the option is also taken, though much less than necessary, to staff the temples; therefore, lay people often administer ceremonies, as do personnel imported from Asia. It is still perplexing for many non-Buddhist people to see a Theravāda monk, a Zen nun, or a Tibetan Buddhist *lama* in the streets of Western cities. However, some of the puzzlement has dispersed, giving way to interest and respect. Though the ordained strive to keep the monastic rules and vows, changes to Western context and life were inevitable: the robe might be augmented by warmer clothing; in specific Theravāda schools, more than the usual one daily meal is allowed; in some monasteries both monks and nuns live in the same location though in different parts of the premises; hierarchical structures and the subordination of nuns have been replaced by egalitarian and democratic forms. However, much has been kept and not adapted to the Western lifestyle: the head is shaven, robes worn, money is not taken or possessed, and celibacy is practiced. Although a monastic life has gained more sympathy among convert Buddhists, quite a number of previously ordained have disrobed. The rules have proved to be too demanding, in particular with regard to the precepts requiring celibacy; support of a lay community was too weak; encouraging fellow monastics were lacking, as well as relevant monastic training. A few Western schools such as the Diamond Sangha and the Friends of the Western Buddhist Order have created new roles for ordained personnel, where the lifestyle is neither monastic nor structured by the *Vinaya* rules; nevertheless, specific precepts are taken, commitment is high and dedication strong.

Buddhists again and again discuss whether Western lifestyle, with its obsession on the "I" and its praise of consumerism, will water down a committed Buddhist life and Buddhist teachings and practices. Buddhists in the West, both converts and immigrants, debate this question and are eager to create new Western Buddhist ways of life.

See also: **Buddhism, psychology, and therapy; Buddhism in the Western world.**

MARTIN BAUMANN

BUDDHISM IN THE WESTERN WORLD

During the twentieth century, Buddhism spread globally. Buddhists founded groups, centers, and temples in Australia and New Zealand, in Africa, in most countries of Europe, and in South and North America. Buddhism outside of Asia is marked by a heterogeneity and diversity that is observable in all thus-denoted "Western" countries. The entire range of Buddhism's main traditions and subtraditions can be found outside of Asia, often in one country. Further, often a major city is home to some forty, fifty or more different Buddhist groups, centers, and temples. Buddhists of divergent traditions and schools have become neighbors – a rarity in Asia itself. Additionally, Western Buddhists founded new orders and organizations, signaling ambitious moves to create indigenized forms of Buddhist practices, teachings, and institutions. The Western institutionalization of Buddhism accelerated rapidly in the closing three decades of the twentieth century. Likewise, academic research matured and has become a recognized subject with a wealth of scholarly studies since the 1990s.

The designation "the West" or "Western world" is primarily defined as a term of difference. It takes up common understandings in the study of Buddhism to loosely denote those geographic regions which are not a part of Asia. Not too long ago, the study of Buddhism was exclusively restricted to the various regions in Asia, their texts, and historical developments in antiquity and medieval times. Language skills and philology provided the key approach and Buddhologists rarely, if at all, engaged in the study of modern or even contemporary times. Times have changed dramatically and many scholars with an original focus on texts and histories of long ago have developed an interest in contemporary Buddhism as well. In addition, other scholars trained in social scientific methods started to research contemporary Buddhism, both in Asia and beyond. It is from this perspective of a label of difference and the establishing of a new field of research within the study of Buddhism that this and other articles use the notion "West" and "Western world." It goes without saying that a homogeneity is definitely not implied and that the notion is used primarily in a pragmatic way.

Buddhism in the West is deeply marked by its heterogeneity and, in one categorical typology, the division of Buddhism into the two strands of immigrant, ethnic or traditionalist Buddhism on the one hand, and, on the other, convert, "white," or modernist, diasporic Buddhism. For both strands the issues of gender equality, prominence of lay Buddhists, employment of egalitarian and democratic principles, the meeting of Buddhist schools and traditions, and social engagement are challenges and ideals. These are, however, discussed and transposed along different lines and emphases in the two strands. This article offers a descriptive overview of the history, or rather histories, of Buddhism outside of Asia, and points to main themes and current issues.

Early encounters

Very early information about Buddhist concepts can be traced to the records of the Greek philosopher Plutarch (first century CE). Plutarch writes about the Indo-Greek king Menander (Menandros, *c.* 155–130 BCE) and his conversation with the Buddhist monk Nāgasena, documented in the Pāli text *Milindapañha* (*The Questions of King Milinda*). The rise of Christianity, and later of Islam, blocked further exchange until Franciscan friars traveled to Mongolia in the thirteenth century. From the sixteenth century onwards, travelers and Jesuit missionaries to Tibet, China, and Japan left fragmentary accounts of Buddhist rituals and concepts. First records of the so-called "false god" Bod or Fo arrived in Europe accompanied by drawings of exotic and stereotyped Asian figures and postures.

The late seventeenth century witnessed the first attempt to send Buddhist monks to Europe. In 1686, the Siamese king Narai sent some ten ambassadorial emissaries, including three Thai *bhikkhus*, to inform Don Pedro, Catholic king of Portugal, about Siam's customs and religious beliefs. The embassy included ritually carried religious texts, most likely a collection of Thai *suttas* (texts). Unfortunately, the Portuguese vessel was shipwrecked off the west coast of southern Africa. The Siamese noblemen and monks were rescued and later shipped home to Siam from the Cape Colony. The messengers never reached Europe and it was more than two centuries later that a fully ordained Theravāda monk arrived in Europe.

In the course of European colonial expansion, administrators and officials gathered information about the customs and history of the peoples and regions that were subjected to British, Portuguese, and Dutch domination. Texts and descriptions were collected and translated in the late eighteenth century. A distinction had not yet been clearly made between Hindu and Buddhist treatises, however. Simultaneously, in Europe the Romantic movement gave rise to a glorifying enthusiasm for the East, and for India in particular. The Asian world and its religious and philosophical traditions were discovered along with efforts aimed at tracing a genuine and pure spirituality that was supposedly lost in Europe through the victory of rationalism.

Discovery of Buddhism through texts

The credit for first systematizing the increasing amount of information on Buddhist texts and concepts goes to the Paris-based philologist Eugène Burnouf (1801–52). His *L'Introduction à l'histoire du buddhisme indien* (1844) presented a scientific survey of Buddhist history and doctrines. Burnouf imposed a rational order on ideas hitherto perceived as unrelated, in this way creating the prototype of the European concept of Buddhism. In the mid-nineteenth century, Europe witnessed a boom of studies and translations, paving the way for an enhanced knowledge of and interest in the teachings. At this time Asian religion was essentially treated as a textual object located in books, Oriental libraries, and institutes of the West.

The writings of the German philosopher Arthur Schopenhauer (1788–1860) inspired wide interest in Buddhist philosophy and ethics among intellectuals, academics, and artists. In the United States, the nineteenth-century transcendentalists Ralph Waldo Emerson, Henry David Thoreau, and Walt Whitman praised Indian philosophy and introduced translations, produced in Europe, to members of the American middle and upper classes. Circles of aesthetic conversation and textual sources were the mediators that initiated the spread of and provided for the public presence of Buddhist ideas in Europe and the United States. The appeal of Indian spirituality was strengthened by the intervention of the Theosophical Society, founded by Helena P. Blavatsky (1831–91) and Henry Steel Olcott (1832–1907) in 1875 in New York. In addition, Sir Edwin Arnold (1832–1904) published his famous poem *The Light of Asia* in 1879, followed by Olcott's *Buddhist Catechism* in 1881. Both works praised the Buddha and his teaching. Echoing this overt glorification of the Asian religion, a few Europeans became the first self-converted followers of the teaching in the early 1880s.

Though more Westerners took up Buddhist teachings as their new orientation in life, another twenty years passed before the first Buddhist organizations outside of Asia were formed. In Germany, the Indologist Karl Seidenstücker (1876–1936) established the Society for the Buddhist Mission in 1903 in Leipzig. Likewise, the first British monk, Ananda Metteyya (Allen Bennett McGregor, 1872–1923), formed the Buddhist Society of Great Britain and Ireland in 1907 in London. By means of lectures, pamphlets, and books, the first professed Western Buddhists tried to win members from the educated middle and upper social strata. These and related activities were polemically commented on by Christian clergy, who criticized the "nihilism" of Buddhism and the "foreignness" of the Asian religion to European society. This debate was strengthened when a few committed men, including Anton F. Güth (1878–1957), ordained as Nyānatiloka, became monks in the Theravāda tradition in the early twentieth century and temporarily remained in Europe. Nyānatiloka's attempt to establish a *vihāra* (monastery) in Switzerland in 1910 failed, and he founded his later famous Island Hermitage in south Ceylon (Sri Lanka) in 1911.

Internationalization: toward a global Buddhism

To a certain extent the incipient Buddhist activities in Western countries relied on reformist approaches and modernist reinterpretations of Asian Buddhist concepts. In Ceylon (Sri Lanka), the center of South Asian Buddhist revival, educated urban Buddhists who had been influenced by Orientalist concepts emphasized the rational and scientific aspects of Buddhist teachings. These modernist Buddhists portrayed Buddhism as text-based, pragmatic, rational, universal, and socially active. Both European scholarship and the Western glorification of Buddhist ideas strengthened national and religious self-confidence in South Asia, further generating ideas of a missionary outreach. In addition, in 1880 Olcott and Blavatsky visited Colombo, Ceylon, and publicly took refuge in the Buddha, *Dharma*, and *Sangha*, becoming the first Westerners to do so in an Asian country.

In the two decades that followed, Olcott and the Ceylonese Anagārika Dharmapāla (1864–1933) worked together to renew the importance of Buddhism. In 1891, Dharmapāla set up the Mahā *Bodhi* Society, its aim being to restore the neglected site of Bodhgayā in north India and to resuscitate Buddhism in India. These activities led to Dharmapāla's invitation to the World Parliament of Religions in Chicago in 1893. His well-received speech at this paramount event for the formal debut of Asian religions in the United States established Dharmapāla as the main spokesman of Buddhist revival in South Asia. It was in Chicago in 1893 as well that Carl Theodor Strauss (1852–1937) became the first American to formally convert to Buddhism on American soil. In the years to come Strauss and Dharmapāla worked jointly and traveled extensively around the world to spread Buddhist teachings. Overseas branches of the Mahā Bodhi Society were formed in the United States (1897), Germany (1911), and Great Britain (1926), in this way establishing the Society as the first international Buddhist organization and its founder as the first global Buddhist missionary or propagandist.

Buddhism brought by immigrants

A different, nonmodernist, and religiously more tradition-oriented line of Buddhism reached Western countries with the arrival of Chinese and Japanese migrants to the United States West Coast and later to South America. Gold had been discovered in California in 1848, and miners from China came in hopes of unearthing a fortune. By the 1880s the number of Chinese in California, Montana, and Idaho had grown to over 100,000 people. Upon their arrival, the immigrants built Chinese temples, the first two in San Francisco in 1853. During the next fifty years hundreds of so-called joss-houses, where Buddhist, Taoist, and Chinese folk traditions mingled, appeared throughout the western United States.

In striking contrast to the high esteem that Buddhist texts and ideas had gained among East Coast intellectuals, Americans on the West Coast devalued East Asian culture as exotic, strange, and incomprehensible. The Chinese laundrymen, cooks, and miners were regarded as unwelcome immigrants. In 1882, the Chinese Exclusion Act restricted further immigration of Chinese nationals. In a similar way, Japanese who had come to the United States in search of work beginning in the 1870s faced racism and social exclusion. Buddhism was regarded as a foreign religion, causing a threat to the relationship between Japanese and American people. Nevertheless, two Jōdo Shinshū priests were sent in 1899 to support the spiritual needs of Japanese laborers, and the Buddhist Mission to North America became formally established in 1914.

More migrants from Japan arrived in Latin and South America around the turn of the century. Japanese workers traveled to Mexico and Peru in 1897, and to São Paulo in Brazil in 1908. The laborers intended to work for only a few years on the plantations and then return to Japan. Most often, however, their stay turned into long-term residence. During the 1920s and 1930s, the Japanese workers built provisional installations that functioned as temples and Buddhist monks from various Buddhist traditions stayed to serve the religious and cultural needs. The only lasting temple was the Kōmyōji temple of the Jōdo Shinshū in Cafelândia in São Paulo, founded in 1932. Japanese workers were expected to assimilate as quickly as possible to Brazilian culture, which also meant conversion to Roman Catholicism. A fair number did, as the Japanese saw conversion as necessary to the process of Brazilianization. However, the decision to change their status from sojourner to immigrant resulted in efforts to ensure the preservation of Japanese culture and identity. Japan's defeat in the Second World War brought an end to the migrants' hopes for return. Staying for long and with the aim of preserving their religious identity, Buddhist Japanese and their descendants established more temples. The Mission of Sōtō Zenshū in Brazil founded Busshinji Temple in 1956, followed by the influx of other Buddhist traditions since the 1970s.

As with Brazil, the Second World War was a watershed for Japanese people in the United States. Acculturative processes had begun during the 1920s and 1930s to meet the needs of the American-born generation; these processes included education programs and such adaptations as referring to Buddhist temples as churches and to priestly personnel as minister or reverend. Paradoxically, adaptation accelerated tremendously during the time of the internment camps. From 1942 to 1945, some 111,000 people of Japanese ancestry were interned, almost 62,000 of them being Buddhists, the majority Jōdo Shinshū. Religious services in the camps were conducted in English, a demand that was later established as the norm. Of similar importance, formerly tight bonds with the mother temples in Japan dissolved. This emancipation from the normative Japanese model was expressed in the organization's new name: no longer a "Mission [from Japan] to North America," it became reincorporated as the Buddhist Churches of America in 1944.

Chinese in the United States remained mostly concentrated in Chinatowns along the West coast. As the numbers of Chinese dropped as a result of the Chinese Exclusion Act, so too did the number of temples. The other strand of Buddhism in the United States – made up of those who had converted to Buddhism – was no more successful at initiating Buddhist activities during the first half of the twentieth century. The appearance of the Japanese Rinzai Zen monk Shaku Sōen (1859–1919) at the World Parliament of Religions gave momentum to the practice of Zen meditation, which was strengthened by two disciples sent by Shaku Sōen to the United States: Zen masters Nyōgen Senzaki (1876–1958) and Sokei-an Sasaki (1882–1945). Although they stayed in the United States for years, the meditation groups they set up were met with little interest. It was not until D.T. Suzuki (1870–1966) returned to North America for a long stay in the 1950s that a psychologically reshaped Zen became popular.

Buddhism in Europe during the first half of the twentieth century

The First World War brought an end to the incipient Buddhist movements in Europe. But Buddhism was taken up again immediately after the war, especially in Britain and Germany. In contrast to the early period, Buddhism was now beginning to be practiced, at least by its leading proponents. The teachings were not only to be conceived by the mind, but also applied to the whole person. Religious practices such as spiritual exercises and devotional acts became part of German and British Buddhist life during the 1920s and 1930s.

In 1921, Georg Grimm (1868–1945) and Seidenstücker started the Buddhist Parish for Germany. The committed group saw itself expressly as a religious community of Buddhist lay followers. Lectures by Grimm were attended by 500 to 1,000 listeners. In Berlin, Paul Dahlke (1865–1928) built the famous Buddhist House in 1924. In this house, which served as both residence and monastery, Dahlke led the same kind of ascetic and religious life as South Asian Buddhist monks. The divergent interpretations of the teachings of the Pāli Canon by Grimm and Dahlke led to the formation of two independent schools, which polemically disputed the central teaching of *anattā* (Pāli "no-self"). Both schools continued their work during the Nazi period, albeit restricted to small, private circles, at times under political control. Buddhists were regarded by the Nazis as pacifists and eccentrics. With the exception of those who had abandoned their Jewish faith and become Buddhists – about a third of all Buddhists in German-speaking areas during the 1920s – no official or public persecution of Buddhism took place.

In London, Christmas Humphreys (1901–83) formed the Buddhist Lodge of the Theosophical Society in 1924. The society opened a Buddhist shrine room in 1925 and regularly celebrated Buddhist festival days. As a result of Anagārika Dharmapāla's missionary efforts in Britain during the mid-1920s, British Buddhists founded a branch of the Mahā Bodhi Society (1926) and established a Buddhist monastery with three resident *bhikkhus* (monks) in London (1928–40, reopened in 1954). It was the first time that several Theravāda monks stayed for a long period outside of Asia and lived according to the *Vinaya* (monastic rules) in that unfamiliar place.

In Europe, it was undoubtedly those who had adopted Buddhism as their new orientation in life who dominated the small Buddhist scene. Except for a few Buddhist activists like Anagārika Dharmapāla or a few Japanese Zen Buddhists (Zenkai Omori, D.T. Suzuki) on academic visiting tours, so far no Asian Buddhist migrants had come to Europe. There is an important exception to this pattern, however: in the early twentieth century, Mongolian Tibetan Buddhists from Kalmykia and Buryatia in Russia had established sizeable communities in St. Petersburg, the tzarist Russian capital until 1917. In St. Petersburg, Kalmyk and Buryat people built a Gelugpa temple and monastery in 1909–15. The first Buddhist monastery on European soil thus was established not by Western convert Buddhists, but by so-called ethnic or migrant Buddhists led by the Buryat-Mongol *lama* Agvan Dorzhev. During the Communist Revolution in 1917, however, the temple was desecrated. Following the comparative calm of the 1920s, Buddhists and scholars were persecuted and murdered under Stalin's dictatorship (1930s to 1953). Not until the 1980s did Buddhists see conditions improved in Russia.

The 1950s and 1960s: spread and pluralization

In contrast to the first half of the twentieth century, the second half witnessed a boom of Buddhism outside of Asia. Western countries experienced a heavy influx of Asian immigrants and a tremendously expanded interest in Buddhist meditation, liturgy, and teachings among Westerners. World War II had brought an end to public Buddhist activities in Europe, except for London. However, after 1945 Buddhists re-established former Theravāda groups or founded new ones. Buddhist lectures were well attended and Buddhist books and journals well received. From the 1950s onwards, new Buddhist traditions were brought to Europe. Japanese Jōdo Shinshū was established in Britain (1952) and Germany (1956). The writings of Suzuki and Eugen Herrigel (1884–1955) popularized Zen meditation and art. Tibetan Buddhism won its first Western converts in Berlin in 1952 through the establishment of the Western branch of the order Arya Maitreya Mandala, founded by the German-born Lama Govinda in 1933 in India. In addition, the activities of Buddhist missionary organizations from South Asia gained momentum, an example being the Lanka Dharmaduta Society, founded in 1952, which sent Theravāda *bhikkhus* to the Berlin Buddhist House with the aim of spreading the *dharma*.

Buddhism spread more and more widely in various European countries as attractive books and translations became more readily available. Simultaneously, Asian teachers began visiting new Buddhist groups to lecture and conduct courses on a regular basis. During the 1960s a considerable change occurred in the way that members and interested people wanted to experience Buddhism both spiritually and physically. Meditation became popular, and Buddhists and sympathizers filled courses in Theravāda *vipassanā* meditation and Japanese Zen meditation. Zen seminars (Jap. *sesshin*) took place in increasing numbers, with teachers coming from Japan to guide newly formed groups.

In the United States, lecture tours by Suzuki instigated an upsurge of interest in Zen concepts and meditation. At the same time, "Beat Zen" and "Square Zen" created by Allan Watts, Allen Ginsberg, Gary Snyder and Jack Kerouac, popularized Zen and attracted members of the emerging counterculture. Japanese teachers such as Sōtō Zen master Shunryu Suzuki settled in the United States as immigration regulations were relaxed during the mid-1950s and 1960s. In addition, various meditation centers were founded as young Americans returned from Japan having received a traditional religious education. Notable among these was Philip Kapleau (b. 1912), author of the instrumental *The Three Pillars of Zen* (1965) and founder of the Rochester Zen Center in New York (1966), and Robert Aitken (b. 1917), founder of the Diamond Sangha in the 1960s. Both were disciples of Zen master Hakuun Yasutani (1885–1974), founder of the Zen school Sanbo Kyodan in 1954. In addition to the explosive interest in Zen meditational practice, further Buddhist traditions arrived from Asia with Sri Lankan, Thai, Chinese, Taiwanese, Korean, and Japanese teachers. Among these traditions and schools, one of the most vigorous turned out to be the Sōka Gakkai from Japan. It claimed a membership of 500,000 people – both Japanese immigrants and Caucasian converts – in the mid-1970s.

The first lasting Australian Buddhist organization was founded in 1953, with a membership of mainly well-educated citizens. Leading Australian Buddhists, such as Charles F. Knight (1890–1975) and Natasha Jackson (1902–90), regarded Buddhism as a triumph of rationalism and used it as a foil in their attacks on Christianity. Their specific approach was strongly intellectualized, and they went to great lengths to prove that Buddhism was fully consonant with scientific thinking. As in Europe and the United States, Zen, Pure Land, and Sōka Gakkai were also imported into Australia during the 1960s.

In general, during this time two characteristics stand out in contrast to the previous phases: Buddhism was no longer dominated by a single main tradition, as had been the case in Europe with Theravāda and in the United States with Mahāyāna Buddhism. Rather, since the 1950s, Buddhist teachers of various traditions arrived from Asia to win converts and to found centers. A plurality of Buddhist traditions emerged, substantially supplemented by the various Buddhist strands formed by immigrant Buddhists. Second, the shift from intellectual interest to practical application deepened and spread through increased interest in meditation.

From the 1970s onward: rapid increase and ongoing pluralization

The Zen boom of the 1960s was followed by an upsurge of interest in Tibetan Buddhism. Tibetan teachers such as Tarthang Tulku (b. 1935) and Chögyam Trungpa (1939–87) arrived in the United States in 1969 and 1970 and formed organizations that established European branches during the 1980s. Beginning in the mid-1970s, high-ranking *lamas* conducted preaching tours in Europe, North America, and Australia, extending to South Africa and South America in later years. Many Westerners who were involved in the protest movements and counterculture of the late 1960s became fascinated by Tibetan Buddhist rituals and symbols and the lives of the *lamas*. Within two decades, converts to Tibetan Buddhism were able to found a multitude of centers and groups, which at times outnumbered those of all other Buddhist traditions in a given country.

This rapid increase, accompanied by an expansion of existing institutions, led to a considerable rise in the number of Buddhist groups and centers associated with convert Buddhists. In Great Britain, for example, the number of Buddhist organizations nearly quintupled from seventy-four to 400 between 1979 and 2000. In Germany, interest in Buddhism resulted in an increase from approximately forty to more than 600 groups, meditation circles, centers, and societies between 1975 and 2005. In North America, Don Morreale's *Complete Guide to Buddhist America* (1998) listed 1,062 meditation centers in 1997, the majority having been founded since the mid-1980s. Similar patterns are observable in Australia, where the number of Buddhist groups rose from 167 to 378 between 1991 and 2002. As a result of large-scale immigration, especially of Vietnamese people, the number of Buddhists in Australia multiplied by ten in two decades from 35,000 to 356,000 (1981 to 2001). Similar to Europe and North America, numerous schools, branches, and traditions of Theravāda, Mahāyāna, Tibetan, and non-sectarian Buddhism have gained a firm standing in Australia, and in New Zealand as well.

In a parallel development, considerable numbers of Buddhists from Asian countries have come to Western Europe, North America, and Australia since the 1960s. In Europe, and France in particular, large communities of refugees from Vietnam, Laos, and Cambodia have emerged. Paris has become the center for Southeast Asian Buddhist migrants, though the largest Vietnamese pagoda in Europe was inaugurated in Hanover, Germany, in 1991. Further, many refugees, migrants, and business people from Asian countries have found asylum or a place to work in Western Europe. Similarly, in Canada and the United States hundreds of thousands of migrants arrived after immigration regulations were relaxed in the mid-1960s.

Whether in North America, Western Europe, or Australia, in the process of settling down migrants established their own religious and cultural institutions to preserve their identity and heritage. By visiting pagodas and temples, performing customary acts of devotional worship, and jointly celebrating Buddhist festivals, immigrant Asian Buddhists gained a home away from home. Most Asian migrant communities have turned out to be markedly conservative, presenting a primarily stable and familiar environment for their members in the socio-culturally foreign and often discriminatory environment. With the rise of second and third generations, established role models and hierarchies are changing. Immigrant Buddhists in the West point to language issues and they call for briefer, acculturated rituals, forms, and contents. Estimates of the total numbers of Buddhists in Europe amount to around one to two million, two-thirds of them Asian immigrants, at the beginning of the twenty-first century. In North America the number may be three to four times higher than in Europe, with Buddhists of Asian ancestry making up the vast majority.

Buddhism also grew in both South America and South Africa, beginning in the 1970s. Zen has captured the interest of non-Japanese Brazilians since the late 1970s, resulting in the establishment of numerous local meditation groups and centers. Likewise, Japanese traditions of Nichiren, Shingon, and Pure Land have gained followings. Tibetan Buddhism, arriving in Brazil the late 1980s, also experienced a boom during the 1990s. As in other non-Asian countries to which

Buddhism spread, a plurality of schools and traditions has become established.

In South Africa, after an attempt to convert Indian migrant Hindus to Buddhism beginning in 1917, small Buddhist groups were formed during the 1970s in metropolitan centers. Followers of Tibetan, Zen, Nichiren, and Theravāda came together for joint meetings and a non-denominational rather than tradition-wise orientation was characteristic. One of South Africa's main Buddhist reference points became the Buddhist Retreat Center near Ixopo, formally inaugurated in 1980. In contrast to a prevalent ecumenical spirit, since the mid-1980s the various groups have begun sharpening their doctrinal identity and lineage adherence. In many cases hitherto loose bonds with the Asian parent tradition or headquarters were strengthened. During the 1990s, Tibetan Buddhism gained a strong following as teachers started to stay longer in South Africa. Likewise, Zen teachers and Theravāda *bhikkhus* settled in the country and firmly established their traditions.

Main themes and current issues

Buddhism's plurality in the West

Buddhism outside of Asia is deeply marked by its plurality and heterogeneity. A multitude of schools and traditions have successfully settled in urbanized, industrialized settings. The general traditions of Theravāda, Mahāyāna, and Tibetan Buddhism are internally heavily subdivided according to country of origin (e.g. Theravāda from Sri Lanka, Thailand, Myanmar, or Laos); lineage (e.g. Tibetan Buddhism following Dge lugs [Gelug], *Karma* Bka' brgyud [Kagyu], Sa skya [Sakya], or Rnying ma [Nyingma]); teacher (Asian and Western, manifold); and emphasis on specific Buddhist concepts and practices. Flourishing in the West, these various Asian-derived schools and traditions did not remain unchanged, and various subschools have evolved. In addition, a second generation of Western teachers, disciples to Western, not Asian, masters, is maturing. These manifold developments have given birth to both traditionally-oriented schools and to independent schools and centers favoring innovation and the creation of a "Western Buddhism." Noteworthy examples of the latter include the Insight Meditation Society in the United States, the Friends of the Western Buddhist Order, founded by the British Sangharakshita in 1967, Shambhala International, successor to Chögyam Trungpa's Vajradhātu, the Diamond Sangha founded by Robert Aitken, and the Order of Buddhist Contemplatives created by the late Rev. Master Jiyu Kennett Rōshi in 1975.

The marked plurality of Buddhism outside of Asia has been intensified by the globalization of once-local organizations. The British-based Friends of the Western Buddhist Order has spread worldwide. Organizations formerly restricted to the United States, such as the Insight Meditation Society or Aitken's Diamond Sangha, have established branch centers in Europe, Australia, and elsewhere. This global outreach also came to apply to American Zen teachers, including Richard Baker Rōshi, Bernard Glassman Rōshi, and the late Prabhasadharma Rōshi, as well as to prominent Vietnamese and Korean meditation masters, including Thich Nhat Hanh and the late Seung Sahn. Tibetan Buddhist organizations have created similar global organizations. *Lamas* and teachers tour the globe untiringly on visits to the multitude of local groups and centers. New global Buddhist organizations were founded, including, among others, the Sōka Gakkai, the Fo Kuang Shan Order, the Kwan Um Zen school, the Association Zen International, Shambhala International, and Ole Nydahl's Diamond Way Buddhism under the spiritual guidance of the seventeenth Karmapa Trinlay Thaye Dorje (one of the current two Karmapas, the other being Urgyen Trinley Dorje). Sogyal Rinpoche founded Rigpa and Geshe Kelsang Gyatso the New Kadampa Tradition.

This global outreach and dispersion of a formerly local or nationally based Buddhist group was greatly intensified by the World Wide Web. Buddhist centers maintain their own websites, linked to sister centers and parent organizations, and facilitating the exchange and spread of information. Numerous so-called cyber-*sanghas* are available online, thus establishing a new form of Buddhist community. In these ways Buddhism adapts, as it has done continuously during its 2,600 years of history, to new cultural, political, and technological environments.

Current issues

The past three decades have also shaped in more clarity the contours of possible new forms of adapted, i.e. Westernized Buddhism. Apart from those orders and schools mentioned above as forerunners in creating variations of "Western Buddhisms," scholars and (mainly) Western convert Buddhists pointed to some marked features which will shape emerging forms of "Western Buddhisms" (in the plural). Buddhism in the West to a large degree is characterized by the engagement and involvement of lay people and practitioners. Lay teachers instruct meditation and lay people – not monks and nuns as commonly in many countries in Asia – practice meditation and study texts. The lay involvement also affects the fields of responsibility and activity of monastics who in the West have no monopoly on teaching, spreading the *Dharma* and much more. Another prominent issue is the critical evaluation of women's roles, called by Jack Kornfield and others the "feminization of Buddhism." This feminization includes issues such as gender equity associated with the role of both women and men; the emergence of a feminist Buddhism; the question of ordination and practicing as a nun; and scandals of misuse of authority leading to sexual exploitation.

Further, in many convert groups democratic and egalitarian principles rank high. Buddhists emphasize consensual decision-making and, for example, vote on who may be the head of a center or school. Such an anti-hierarchical structure is less prominent in many Buddhist traditions in Asia. Next, in many convert groups and publications, a close linkage to Western psychological concepts is notorious. Also, social engagement has appeared as a prominent topic, lectured about and practiced by many. Some engaged Buddhists and groups work for the transformation of society in terms of Buddhist social activism, environmentalism, and ecology. The list of issues grows, with questions related to the integration of Buddhist practice and household family life; to the rarely raised issue of racism and exclusion of blacks and people of color; to the unavoidable shifts and changes of immigrant Buddhist communities with the growing up to the next generation, rising intermarriage rates and active Christian missionary interference; to the banalization and commercialization of Buddhism; and, last but not least, to the area of intra-religious dialogue with Jews and Christians, and, in particular, intra-Buddhist encounter and meeting. Conspicuously, quite a number of Buddhist teachers have studied in more than one Buddhist tradition and utilize multiple meditation techniques and refer to more than just one Buddhist school. Also, elements of non-Buddhist traditions are being integrated into the teachings and specific meditation practice. This eclectic incorporation is held as being meaningful to the new context and as a bridge to provide a better understanding of Buddhist concepts.

Buddhism in the West in the early twenty-first century is in the making and shaping. Contextualized, i.e., Western forms of Buddhism will emerge – certainly no uniform or homogenous tradition. Indigenized forms of immigrant, or traditionalist, Buddhism will come about in the run of four to five generations. This will only occur when the now close bonds to the Asian home country tradition loosen and the country of residence's own teachers, interpretations, and practices emerge. On the side of convert, or modernist, Buddhisms, future developments will demonstrate which of the adaptations and innovations will survive in the long run. It is not unlikely that processes of recoupment and a closer re-orientation to the Asian (former) mother tradition will occur – often both at home in Asia and in the Western country.

See also: **Buddhism, psychology, and therapy; Buddhism and Western lifestyle; Diasporic Buddhism: traditional and modernist Buddhism; Ecumenicism and intra-Buddhist activities; Global Buddhist networks: selected examples; New Buddhist roles; Western Buddhism: Diamond Sangha; Western Buddhism: Friends of the Western Buddhist Order; Western Buddhism: Insight Meditation Society; Western Buddhism: Shambhala International.**

MARTIN BAUMANN

BUDDHISM IN TIBET TODAY

Since the invasion and annexation of Tibet by China in the 1950s, the country has seen periods of extreme repression followed by relative relaxation of restrictions on religious practice. The government of the People's Republic of China is officially committed to the Marxist notion that "religion is the opiate of the masses," and its constitution indicates that as the society develops, religion will naturally wither and die. Despite this, the constitution also guarantees that "every citizen of the PRC shall have freedom of religious belief."

The contradictions inherent in these two views have strongly affected recent events in Tibet. During the early period of invasion and the Cultural Revolution of the 1960s and 1970s, Chinese troops and Tibetan cadres destroyed thousands of monasteries and subjected most religious leaders to "struggle sessions" (*thamzing*), in which they were accused of being "class enemies" and often brutally beaten or killed. For decades religious practice was severely curtailed by Chinese authorities, who saw it as a vestige of Tibet's "feudal" society and an impediment to progress. Buddhism has also been strongly linked to Tibetan nationalism and resistance to Chinese rule, with monks and nuns often leading protests and putting up anti-Chinese posters.

The central symbol of Tibetan resistance is the Dalai Lama, who heads a government-in-exile in India, which China views as the center of international agitation against its rule in Tibet. In Tibet itself, Buddhists have largely resisted government attempts to eradicate their religion, and by all accounts religious practice is flourishing in Tibet today. Pilgrimages and ceremonies that were banned by the government in the past have been revived, and many of the monasteries that were destroyed or closed down have been rebuilt. The Barkhor – the most popular pilgrimage circuit in Tibet, located in the heart of old Lhasa – teems with pilgrims from all over the Tibetan plateau, who circumambulate the Jokhang shrine and make prostrations. The pilgrimage route around Mount Kailash draws thousands of pilgrims every year, but government surveillance of religious activities and suspicion of monks and nuns remains pervasive. Several of the largest monasteries have Chinese military encampments next to them, and during a visit to Tashihlünpo Monastery in 2001, I was told that the seventy-three monks there were constantly watched by twenty-four Chinese security personnel. Monks and nuns who escape into exile commonly report that they were allowed only an hour or two per day for study of Buddhist philosophy and practice, while most of their time was spent in political indoctrination classes run by Communist cadres.

Some pro-China academics in the West have painted a relatively rosy picture of religious freedom in Tibet today, but Buddhists there often tell a different story to Western visitors, and human rights groups who have studied the situation have concurred that there is little if any religious freedom in Tibet today. Official government policy is that only "patriotic" religious groups will be allowed to practice, and those deemed unpatriotic should be suppressed vigorously. As more and more Tibetans flee into exile and as the Chinese occupation of the country continues, it seems likely that religion will come under increasing pressure and that its vitality will wane.

See also: **Tibet, Buddhism in.**

JOHN POWERS

BUDDHIST ADAPTATIONS IN THE WEST

Buddhism's history in the West is also a history of adaptation and innovation. Buddhists who came as refugees or skilled immigrant workers and people who had converted to Buddhism both had to adapt Buddhist forms, teachings, and practices in order to preserve Buddhism in the new Western settings. The maintenance of a Buddhist tradition was needed to strike a balance between conservation and innovation, between continuity and adaptation. Following the explosive growth of Buddhism from the 1970s onward, Buddhism on the convert side is on the brink of creating structures, concepts, and lifestyles of Western Buddhisms (in the plural). Immigrant Buddhists and their descendants are still too few in their new Western home country to favor a new, Western-adapted form of their Buddhist tradition (an exception are the Japanese Jōdo Shinshū Buddhists in the Americas). Thus far, many in a conservative manner emphasize modes of preservation and eschew transformation. Nevertheless, numerous modifications and changes were unavoidable and issues such as language use; leadership; the religious education of the next generation, i.e. the transmission of tradition; the role and status of women; and the complexes of ritual, teaching, and organizational form are emphatically debated. Adaptations such as the shortening of rituals and festivals, improvised religious places, and expanded responsibilities of the monks and nuns had come about as a result of constraints and the shortcoming of the diaspora situation. Westernized "ethnic" forms have not yet developed, with the notable exception of the Buddhist Churches of America (Jōdo Shinshū of American-Japanese), masterfully described and analyzed by Kenneth K. Tanaka.

In marked contrast, the strand of convert, or modernist, Buddhists did not wait long to adapt and change Buddhist practices, teachings, and ways of life. Selection and adaptive combination with Western concepts and forms had been guiding principles. Western Buddhists selected practices of meditation and the study of texts as central features of Buddhism. In Asia, in many traditions commonly only monastics engage in these practices. In the West, ritual and cosmological views (such as different worlds of rebirth) have very often been abandoned and looked down upon as "Asian customs." Western Buddhists translated texts written in Asian languages and unavoidably gave Western-biased interpretations. Often, terms from psychology and therapy were employed. They founded registered societies with membership status, fees and fixed regular times for gatherings. Most often these groups and societies strongly advocate consensual decision-making and equality of the sexes. Further, they underscore that Buddhist ideas and ideals as learnt in study groups and weekend retreats should be integrated in the family and the local community. Most often, laypeople, not monks or nuns, function as teachers and advisors. Some training programs for forthcoming teachers are much shorter than established programs of the tradition in Asia. In some cases, initiation and ordination is given fairly soon. Overall, in many instances Buddhism has been squeezed into the existing shapes and structures of Western societies. Employing linguistic terms, the grammar of Western society remained unchanged while a different lexicon, the one of Buddhist terms and concepts, was superimposed. Rarely, the grammar of Western society was questioned and changed. However, engaged orders and groups such as the Buddhist Peace Fellowship and other committed endeavors strive to build a less violent, less greedy, and more socially responsible world.

Western Buddhists have already molded incipient forms that can be labeled "Western Buddhism." Among these are the Friends of the Western Buddhist Order, Shambhala International, Insight Meditation Society, and Diamond Sangha. New Buddhist roles and a blend of Buddhism and Western lifestyle were created. Importantly, these and other features of adaptation translate differently according to the regional context, i.e. socio-cultural contexts as different as North America, Brazil, South Africa, and New Zealand.

See also: **Buddhism, psychology, and therapy; Buddhism and Western lifestyle; Buddhism in the Western world; Diasporic Buddhism: modernist and traditionalist Buddhism; New Buddhist roles.**

MARTIN BAUMANN

BUDDHIST ECONOMICS AND ECOLOGY

Over the course of the past several decades, a number of people, working mainly within Theravāda Buddhism, have labored to construct a "Buddhist economics" as a challenge and alternative to the capitalist- and Marxist-influenced economies which have come to dominate Asia during the post-colonial period. A few are likewise working in the West to envision and enact economic relationships that are consistent with, and that even promote, Buddhism's quest to liberate all beings. Indeed, the first such attempt was undertaken by Western economist E.F. Schumacher in his article aptly entitled "Buddhist Economics," first published in 1966 but not widely read until 1973 when it was republished in his influential book, *Small is Beautiful: Economics as if People Mattered*. Schumacher here notes the damage done to rural economies and traditional ways of life by the "heedless" modernization of Burma's economy. He suggests that rather than rushing to modernize its economy, Burma should recognize that the country's traditional Buddhist way of life calls for a distinctively Buddhist economics rooted in equally distinctive Buddhist values and concerns. Schumacher conceives of this economics as a "Middle Way between materialist heedlessness and traditional immobility," an economics characterized by the "keynote" of "simplicity and nonviolence," but, nevertheless, capable of producing "extraordinarily satisfactory results."

More recent attempts to construct a Buddhist economics continue to play on Schumacher's theme of "simplicity and nonviolence," often introducing "compassion" and "justice" into the mix, as well. As noted above, these attempts come mainly from South and Southeast Asia, among such notable persons as Buddhadāsa Bhikkhu, P.A. Payutto (a.k.a.

Dhammapitaka Bhikkhu), Sulak Sivaraksa, A.T. Ariyaratne, H.N.S. Karunatilake, and Padmisiri De Silva. Thich Nhat Hanh and the Dalai Lama often also lend their support to these efforts. British activists Ken Jones and Christopher Titmuss are widely recognized for their attempts to construct a "green Buddhism" along similar lines, in opposition to the growth economies of contemporary Europe.

Most proponents of Buddhist economics identify themselves as "engaged Buddhists," and thus ground their socially transformative economic visions in the same ideas about interrelatedness that govern engaged Buddhist discourse in general. Their attempts to construct a distinctively Buddhist economics are not typically driven by theoretical concerns, however, but, as seen in the case of Schumacher above, arise directly in response to the violence and suffering they see generated by capitalist and Marxist economic systems taking hold around the globe. Buddhist economics thus starts, in most cases, with a critique of Western-style economies and their deleterious effects upon humans and their world.

Western economies are criticized fundamentally for their "materialist" assumptions, which are characterized as inevitably leading to dehumanizing, oppressive, and ecologically destructive consequences. These assumptions, it is argued, create a vision of the role of economics as working fundamentally to maximize the satisfaction of human desires through the maximal production and consumption of material goods in society. Moreover, the common view of Western economics as a "value-free science" leads it to measure the strength of any given economy strictly in relation to its ability to satisfy a relatively great number of desires through the production and consumption of a relatively great number of material goods, with no attention given to the nature of the goods produced or of the desires satisfied. Western economics is charged, therefore, with being committed solely to the value of material consumption, even at the expense of human happiness, justice, and ecological integrity.

By exposing the "materialist" nature of the "goods" which Western economic systems pursue, their Buddhist critics mean first to reveal the pretensions of their claims to value-neutrality, showing them, indeed, to be committed to the value of maximizing the satisfaction of human desires through the production and consumption of material goods. Critics mean, also, of course, to hold this value up for critique, a critique which follows along relatively predictable lines. When viewed from a Buddhist perspective, in other words, it is instantly recognized that such an economics is inherently unstable and leads inevitably to suffering (*dukkha*). Indeed, this "materialist" economics flies directly in the face of the central insights of the First and Second Noble Truths. What is called for, therefore, is a different sort of economics, an economics founded upon Buddhist assumptions and geared toward the production of Buddhist "goods." What is called for, in other words, is an economics directed toward the realization of enlightenment and liberation.

Buddhist economics works, therefore, not to maximize the satisfaction of human desires, but to produce the material conditions wherein liberation from suffering may productively be sought and achieved by all. As such, only those forms of production that contribute to the "purification of human character" factor positively into its calculations. In this vein, Buddhist economics strives foremost after economic simplicity and the meeting of basic human needs (for Ariyaratne, aspiring to create a society in which there is neither poverty nor affluence; for Payutto, striving to satisfy people's desire for well-being (*chanda*), but not their selfish and sensuous desires for pleasure and power (*taṇhā*); providing opportunities for work for everyone, so that everyone may benefit from the character-shaping benefits of work, especially of work done in service of others in community; limiting society to the use of "intermediate" or labor-intensive technologies as tools rather than replacements for human labor, again, so that everyone may participate in the character-building practices of labor; ideally using only locally available and renewable resources in an ecologically responsible manner; aspiring toward national self-sufficiency; and avoiding production that causes harm to others, either through its processes or through its products.

Buddhist economists take inspiration for their economic vision from a variety of traditional sources, including the traditional monastic *sangha* – which is held up by Sulak Sivaraksa, for example, as a "prototype" of the ideal Buddhist community geared toward the liberation of all its members; the Buddha's teachings contained, especially, in the Pāli Canon – which are interpreted by Buddhadāsa as exemplifying a kind of religious or "Dhammic socialism" wherein everyone works generously for the well-being of the community; the examples of numerous legendary kings, including, of course, the legendary King Aśoka, who is remembered for his compassionate and "Dhammic" rule; and, finally, traditional South and Southeast Asian (rural) cultures, which are seen by Ariyaratne and others as containing the remnants of harmonious pre-colonial social structures founded upon Buddhist principles of social organization.

Critics of Buddhist economics, like buddhologist Richard Gombrich and anthropologist Gananath Obeyesekere, perhaps not unexpectedly view Buddhist economic theories as naïvely founded on a sentimentalized and romanticized vision of pre-colonial Asian village life. They point out also that most proponents of Buddhist economics hail from the urban middle classes, and charge them, therefore, with "projecting" from these locations their own bourgeois values upon a "fantasy" of pre-colonial village life that never really existed.

Regardless of the sources of their vision, Buddhist economists have had some measure of success in seeing their theories realized in practice, especially through the Sri Lankan *Sarvōdaya Śramadāna* movement, which represents one of the world's few real-life experiments with an alternative to the capitalist and Marxist economies of the West. For this reason, the movement has attracted the attention not only of Buddhists, but of economists and other social theorists throughout the world, who are likewise critical of traditional Western economics and wish to discover less destructive and dehumanizing forms of social organization. Only time, of course, will determine how influential such movements might become in the future or what power they might possess for effecting a positive transformation of economies, not only in Asia, but of other societies throughout the world.

See also: **Ariyaratne, A.T.; Buddhist peace groups (in Asia and the West); Engaged Buddhism; Global Buddhist networks: selected examples; Nhat Hanh, Thich; Sivaraksa, Sulak.**

JIM DEITRICK

BUDDHIST PEACE GROUPS (IN ASIA AND THE WEST)

The term "peace" has various meanings. On the one hand, it is commonly used to refer to an inner state of calm, equilibrium, contentment, or serenity. On the other hand, "peace" is conceived as an external, social condition, one free of hostilities, especially warfare, but also in its ideal form free of other, more subtle forms of civil and interpersonal strife. The former is commonly thought of as the more "spiritual" of the two meanings, while the latter is regarded as "worldly" or "mundane." As a "religion" concerned with "spiritual" matters, Buddhism is typically defined in relation to the first, more "spiritual," meaning of peace, as a *praxis* for producing inner, "spiritual" or "otherworldly" states of tranquility within practitioners. To the extent that this accurately describes Buddhism, the entire religion might be thought of as one big "peace group."

In recent years, some, who call themselves "engaged Buddhists," have offered interpretations of Buddhism which conceive of "inner" and "outer," "otherworldly" and "mundane," as inseparable and interrelated aspects of a single reality. Seen from this perspective, "inner peace" is utterly inconceivable without and ultimately indistinguishable from "outer, worldly peace," and vice versa. Buddhism, for engaged Buddhists, is not merely a *praxis* for the attainment of inner or other-worldly states of peace, therefore, but simultaneously a *praxis* for the realization of outer, this-worldly peace, as well.

Engaged Buddhist peace activists thus work theoretically to demonstrate Buddhism's relevance for the pursuit of worldly peace through the elucidation of Buddhist principles of social action grounded in this fundamental principle of interrelatedness. They also work practically in the world to realize outer peace through the implementation of these principles in their individual and corporate acts. The Buddhist peace groups discussed here are organizations that work practically to establish "outer" peace through Buddhist practice. It should be stressed, however, that the goal of these Buddhist peace groups is not "merely" to create worldly peace. Just as they disparage more entrenched understandings of Buddhism that conceive of the religion as working solely to produce inner peace within individuals, so do engaged Buddhists typically eschew interpretations that focus exclusively on outer peace. In other words, they see their peace activism as complementing, rather than displacing, more "traditional" forms of Buddhism, which they perceive as concentrating unduly on the realization of inner peace alone. While many such engaged Buddhist peace groups have arisen in recent decades, only a few of the more prominent and influential will be discussed here.

Tiep Hien Order and Community of Mindful Living

The *Tiep Hien* Order or Order of Interbeing was founded by Vietnamese monk Thich Nhat Hanh in 1966. The Order consists of monks, nuns, and laypersons who are ordained by Nhat Nanh to live according to the Order's fourteen engaged Buddhist precepts. These precepts are grounded theoretically in the interrelatedness of all phenomena and so bind followers not to turn away from the suffering of others brought on by war and injustice, but to realize their own complicity in this suffering and do something to help its victims. In this vein, Nhat Hanh and his Order advocate a radical and principled non-violence which regards all forms of coercion as inherently unskillful means of realizing peace both within and without. As Nhat Hanh says, "There is no way to peace; peace is the way." Thus, Nhat Hanh and his followers work for peace in the world, first and foremost through the establishment of peace within themselves through Buddhist mindfulness practice. They tend also to concentrate on the realization of peaceful interpersonal relationships at work and at home, in the belief that this peace will radiate outward to the rest of society. The Community of Mindful Living is a California-based offshoot of the *Tiep Hien* Order which provides support for individuals and meditation groups throughout the world who are not ordained members of the Order but, nevertheless, wish to "be peace" and live according to the Order's precepts.

Buddhist Peace Fellowship

The Buddhist Peace Fellowship (BPF) was founded in the United States in 1978 by Robert Aitken – a peace activist, American Zen "lay-*rōshi*," and director of the Diamond Sangha on the island of Maui – along with his wife, Anne, and student, Nelson Foster. BPF "strives to offer a public witness ... for peace and protection of all beings; raise humanitarian, environmental, and social justice concerns among Buddhist communities; [and] bring a Buddhist perspective to contemporary peace, environmental, and social justice movements." The forty-five chapters of this loosely organized association of Buddhists and Buddhist sympathizers set their own agendas, in some cases serving simply as discussion, meditation, or support groups, while, in others, participating in and organizing more overt forms of social work and political activism, including anti-war and anti-nuclear protests and various social service projects. At the national and international levels, BPF works mainly to foster communication among its chapters and individual members, while also occasionally facilitating large-scale projects, including raising financial support for Tibetan Buddhist refugees; conducting workshops on conflict resolution; sponsoring speaking tours by Thich Nhat Hanh and other engaged Buddhist leaders; and conducting intensive retreats and workshops dedicated to the establishment of peace through engaged Buddhist practice.

Nipponzan Myōhōji

One of engaged Buddhism's oldest peace groups is Japan's Nipponzan Myōhōji, a relatively small group of approximately 1,500 members, which nevertheless attracts widescale attention with its Gandhian-style "peace walks" and prolific building of "peace pagodas" throughout the world. This movement of Nichiren Buddhist monastic and lay practitioners was founded in 1918 by Fujii Nichidatsu, although its anti-war and anti-nuclear activities did not begin until after the dropping of the bombs on Hiroshima and Nagasaki at the end of the Second World War. These holocausts convinced Fujii of the "madness, folly, and barbarousness of modern war" and likewise compelled him to espouse a radical non-violence, inspired by Gandhi's notion of *ahiṃsā* and his own, some might say novel, interpretation of the *Lotus Sūtra*. This radical non-violent activism renounces violence even in defense of oneself and strives instead to attain world peace through the chanting of *daimoku* and participation in non-violent peace activism.

Dhammayietra

The *Dhammayietra* is an annual "peace walk" led by Cambodia's Supreme Patriarch Maha Ghosananda. It typically proceeds through politically unstable regions of the country in order to advocate for peace and draw attention to other important issues facing Cambodia, such as the dangers of deforestation and land-mines. These well-organized events attract thousands of participants each year who are provided with extensive training in non-violent conflict resolution. Ghosananda, who has repeatedly been nominated for the Nobel Peace Prize, also travels widely throughout the world, encouraging peace and reconciliation through the implementation of engaged Buddhist principles of non-violent social activism.

Sarvōdaya Śramadāna

The Sri Lankan *Sarvōdaya Śramadāna* Movement is a network of grass-roots, self-help community development agencies dedicated to fostering economic, cultural, and spiritual "awakening" among the country's rural poor. In response to the ethnic conflict that began to ravage the country in the late 1970s, the movement has also worked more recently to establish peace and reconciliation on the island nation. Toward this end, *Sarvōdaya* regularly organizes inter-ethnic and inter-religious peace conferences, Gandhian-style "peace walks," and "peace meditations," all aimed at "creating peace within the 'psychosphere' through meditational practices." These events have, in many cases, attracted tens and even hundreds of thousands of participants. It is estimated that 650,000 people from 15,000 villages participated in the largest of the peace meditations, held in Anuradhapura in 2002.

Zen Peacemaker Order

The Zen Peacemaker Order (ZPO) was founded in 1996 by Bernard Tetsugen Glassman Rōshi and his late wife, Sandra Jishu Holmes Rōshi. ZPO is dedicated to the three tenets of "not knowing, thereby giving up fixed ideas about ourselves and the universe; bearing witness to the joy and suffering of the world; and healing ourselves and others." Among the better known of its various activities, ZPO periodically organizes "street retreats" or "homeless *sesshins*" and Nipponzan Myōhōji-style "peace walks" at the Auschwitz-Birkenau Nazi death camp. These and other ZPO activities "bear witness" to the world's suffering and act for ZPO practitioners as a kind of *kōan* practice in which they meditatively become one with the social problems they are trying to solve.

Although these and other engaged Buddhist groups and individuals often disagree about the best or appropriate means for achieving peace in the world, they all agree that such peace is inseparable from the peace which Buddhism has traditionally sought to realize within individuals. As seen from these examples, each, in its own way, works to combine more traditional Buddhist practices with overt forms of social action, based upon the basic conviction that inner and outer peace are interrelated aspects of a single, overriding peace.

See also: **Ariyaratne, A.T.; Buddhist peace groups (in Asia and the West); Dalai Lama (and the Tibetan struggle); Engaged Buddhism; Glassman, Bernard Rōshi; Global Buddhist networks: selected examples; Macy, Joanna; Maha Ghosananda; Nhat Hanh, Thich.**

JIM DEITRICK

BUDDHIST WOMEN, ANTHROPOLOGICAL APPROACHES TO

Buddhist Studies has been dominated from the outset by textual studies. The privileging of texts over practice arises for a variety of reasons. Questions of class and gender also influenced early studies. Western and Asian scholars often frowned upon popular practice as superstitious, not "true" religion, and because women were secondary their practice was overlooked, ignored, or discounted.

The study of what people do, what they say they do, and what it means individually and culturally was left to anthropologists. There was little convergence between Buddhist Studies and Anthropology until relatively recently. A study by Fenn in 2000 indicated that about 50 percent of departments where Buddhist Studies are offered have now moved towards an integration of social scientific method with their traditional historical and philological offerings. With the influence of feminist studies in religion, scholars began to turn their attention to the presence, or absence, of materials dealing with women.

Anna Grimshaw spent a year in the remote Himalayan nunnery of Julichang attached to the Rizong monastery in Ladakh. There she shared the hardship of the nuns, whose primary function was the production of goods for the monastery to which they were attached and by which they were supervised. While allowed in the temple on some ritual occasions, they were marginal to the spiritual life of the monastery. Rituals they did perform tended to be those that would be polluting to the monks but were necessary for the laity. Both Grimshaw's study and that of Faith Adiele, who spent time at Wat Phra Singh, a forest monastery in Thailand, affirmed both the internalization of negative views of laity towards women's spiritual capabilities and the women's own belief that they must be reborn as men before they could attain enlightenment.

Paula Arai's study of nuns in the Sōtō Buddhist tradition in Japan indicates that this internalization is not universal. These nuns tend to live more disciplined lives than the monks and strive for enlightenment. Arai's study embeds their story in the history of the order and how they have come to virtual parity with male monastics in a relatively short period of time.

Kim Gutschow, who spent three years with the nuns of Zangskar, puts their lives in a wider sociological and economic context and shows how the relationship between the nuns and monastery and village are beginning to change as a result of politics, globalization and feminist ideas.

Studies such as those noted above are valuable, particularly when combined with historical and sociological materials, because they allow us to balance textual materials, producing a complex rather than a reductionist view of women in religion. Further, they provide a wealth of ideas and experience for those who look to improve the conditions under which Buddhist women practice.

See also: **Women in Buddhism: an historical and textual overview.**

Mavis L. Fenn

BURMA (MYANMAR), BUDDHISM IN

Although the origins of Buddhism in Burma (now officially known as Myanmar) are difficult to document, Buddhist tradition holds that the *Dharma* arrived in the region very early as a result of visits from the Buddha himself and missions from the Third Buddhist Council held during the reign of the Emperor Aśoka. If these accounts are difficult to prove historically, they nevertheless serve as crucial guides to the important and formative role that Buddhism has held in the culture. Relating that the Buddha made numerous trips to the area during his lifetime, the *Sāsanavaṃsa* says that he first flew with 500 *arahants* to visit Sudhammapura (Thaton) in the Rāmañña country. On this visit he is said to have established the people in the three refuges and the five precepts and to have donated hair relics.

Another legend says that two merchants, Tapussa and Bhallika, met the Buddha and offered him food. In return, the Buddha gave them the hair relics that came to be enshrined in the Shwedagon Pagoda in Yangon. Later the Buddha is said to have visited Aparānta to spread the *Dharma* and left his footprint at Shwesettaw near Saccabandha mountain. He also visited Arakan where he created the Mahāmuni image of himself, which stands today in the Arakan pagoda in Mandalay. In this way, the legends of the Buddha's various visits provided a basis for the tradition and for practices such as relic worship and pilgrimage that continue to the present.

The chronicles' accounts of the emissaries sent out by Moggaliputta Tissa Thera at the conclusion of the Third

Council say that two of the missionaries, the *arahants* Soṇa and Uttara, came to Suvaṇṇabhūmi or Thaton. Arriving there, the *theras* (elders) established the *Dharma*, defeated the demons, and preached the *Brahmajāla Sutta*. Although the mission of Soṇa and Uttara to Suvaṇṇabhūmi is not mentioned in the two Rock Edicts of Aśoka (Edicts V and XIII) that list the countries to which Aśoka sent missionaries, it is mentioned in the Kalyānī inscriptions of Pegu (*c*. 1476). The Buddhists of Myanmar also believe that the great commentator Buddhaghosa was a native son who returned to Myanmar after writing or editing his commentaries and the *Visuddhimagga* in Sri Lanka. These legends and the preceding accounts of the Buddha's visits serve to establish for the Buddhists the authority and authenticity of the Buddhist tradition in Myanmar. One of the chief purposes of these accounts was undoubtedly to support the Buddhism of Myanmar in its rivalry with the Sinhala Buddhism of Lanka.

The classical period of Buddhism in Myanmar began with King Aniruddha (Anawratha) who came to power in Pagan in 1044 CE. Aniruddha was converted to a Sinhala form of Theravāda Buddhism by a Mon monastic, Shin Arahan, who came to assume the role of primate of the religion and adviser to the king. It seems probable that before the time of Aniruddha, and even afterwards in many parts of the country, various forms of Hinduism and Buddhism were practiced, including Mahāyāna and Tantric forms. But Aniruddha instituted a measure of Theravāda orthodoxy and negotiated exchanges of Buddhist texts and monastics with Sri Lanka. In response to a request from King Vijayabāhu I of Sri Lanka, Aniruddha sent monks and scriptures to Sri Lanka. In return, Vijayabāhu sent Pāli texts and a replica of the tooth-relic of the Buddha. Aniruddha also conquered Thaton and transplanted its monks and their volumes of scriptures and commentaries to Pagan.

The successors to King Aniruddha continued this tradition of support for Buddhism and established a strong pattern of mutual support between the monarchy and the *sangha*. Buddhism not only gave authority to the king, viewing him as a world-ruler or *cakkavattin* (Skt. *cakravartin*), but it also came to define the national identity and later, in the modern period, shaped Burmese nationalism.

Soon after the time of Aniruddha, King Kyanzittha (1084–1113), continued this patronage of Buddhism, completing the Schwezigon pagoda containing three relics of the Buddha and restoring the Mahābodhi temple at Bodhgayā. King Narapatisithu (1173–1210) strengthened the ties with the Mahāvihāra in Sri Lanka. During this time some prominent monks visited Sri Lanka and returned to spread the Mahāvihāra tradition in Myanmar. Two Mon monks, Uttarajīva Mahāthera and a novice named Chapaṭa, journeyed to Anuradhapura in 1180. Chapaṭa and four other monks remained there for a decade or "ten rains retreats" and underwent re-ordination as elders in the Mahāvihāra lineage. When these monks returned to Myanmar, they refused to associate with the Myanmar *bhikkhus* (monks) and established a branch of the *sangha* that came to be called the *Sīhaḷa Sangha*. Swearer notes that this event "marked the permanent establishment of Sinhala Buddhism in mainland Southeast Asia and brought about a schism in the Burmese Buddhist *sangha*". The Mahāvihāra form of Buddhism influenced the politics and the practice of Buddhism in Myanmar during the following centuries. In the chronicles, Chapaṭa and his *Sīhaḷa Sangha* are called the "later school" and the Myanmar monks are called "the earlier school." Even after the fall of Pagān in the thirteenth century, King Wareru sent monks to Sri Lanka to bring back the Mahāvihāra ordination and reform the *sangha*.

Among the many later kings who both supported Buddhism and benefited from the support of the *sangha* were Dhammaceti (Dhammazedi) (1472–92) and Mindon-Min (1852–77). Dhammaceti was a former Mon *bhikkhu* who became king through the favor of a queen who had been his student. On assuming the throne, Dhammaceti began a reform of the *sangha* to correct the sectarianism and lack of discipline that prevailed. He dispatched two delegations of *bhikkhus* to Sri Lanka to receive the Mahāvihāra ordination, and on their return he sponsored a great ordination or re-ordination ceremony that is said by the Kalyānī inscription to have included 15,666 *bhikkhus*. This massive reform had the effect of confirming the dominance of the Sīhaḷa school and ending much of the dissension and corruption in the *sangha* in Lower Myanmar for many years. Mindon-Min ruled in Upper Myanmar in the period just before British annexed the entire country. After moving the capital to Mandalay, he presided over a peaceful period and actively supported Buddhism. He initiated yet another purification of the *sangha* that was made necessary in part by the chaos created in the hierarchy and discipline of the *sangha* by the British rule in Lower Myanmar. He required the monks to take vows to adhere to the *Vinaya* code of discipline. Mindon-Min also convened the Fifth Buddhist Council which met for three years (1868–71) and produced a new edition of the *Tripiṭaka*. Carved on marble slabs, this edition of the *Tripiṭaka* was enshrined in Mandalay.

Although Theravāda Buddhism attained dominance through the reforms carried out by these kings and the influence of the *Sīhaḷa Sangha*, other varieties of Buddhism continued to be practiced in Myanmar at various times and on various levels. Evidence of Mahāyāna Buddhism and belief in *bodhisattvas* such as Avalokiteśvara can be found in temple art from the eleventh century CE. Tantric influences are believed to be evident in some of the temples and literature of the Pagān period. Discussions of the Buddhism of Myanmar should also take note of the popular worship of *nats* or spirits. The Buddhist tradition in Burma has always comprised a dual system similar to the systems of other Theravāda countries, with the dominant Buddhist cosmology incorporating and accommodating the popular worship of spirits or *nats*.

The British colonial rule of Myanmar represented a serious disruption in the patterns and continuities that had shaped the country's history, and in the period after independence in 1948 the powers that emerged tried in various ways to restore those patterns while also addressing contemporary problems. The British undermined both the monarchy and the *sangha*, the two institutions that had shaped the culture for the ethnic Myanmar majority. At the same time, the British strengthened the role of the minority ethnic groups and encouraged immigration. After independence, U Nu, the first prime minister of the Union of Burma, advocated a form of Buddhist socialism that re-established the links between the ruler and Buddhist values. He sought to restore the *sangha* to their traditional place by establishing a Buddhist *Sāsana* Council and convening a new *Sangha* Council. But U Nu's idealistic attempt to establish a Buddhist socialism was not to last. Mounting a coup, General Ne Win overthrew U Nu's government in 1962 and set up a military government. That government and its successor, which still holds power at the present time, continued to both patronize the *sangha* and seek legitimation from Buddhism even though one could question their commitment to the principles of the *Dharma*.

See also: **Aśoka; Aung San Suu Kyi; Buddha and *cakravartins*; Commentarial works; Pilgrimage; Sacred places; South and Southeast Asia, Buddhism in.**

GEORGE D. BOND

BUTÖN

Butön (Bu ston rin chen grub, 1290–1364) was a great scholar, artist, and abbot of Zhalu monastery in Tsang in west central Tibet. He became a monk at seventeen, was ordained at twenty-three, and studied monastic disciple (*Vinaya*), *sūtras*, *tantras*, and treatises on logic and epistemology (*pramāṇa*) with the eminent scholars of his day. He became abbot of Zhalu in 1320, and after he retired in 1356, he continued to teach and write. Butön collected and classified Buddhist manuscripts into the two divisions of the Tibetan Buddhist canon: the Kanjur (*bka' gyur*), works attributed to the Buddha, and the Tenjur (*bstan 'gyur*), works and commentaries written by Indian yogins and scholars. He built the temple at Zhalu that housed this vast manuscript collection and painted the murals on its walls. His elaborate depictions of *maṇḍalas* became the iconographic templates for artists working on other temples and his editorial work influenced subsequent blockprint editions of the Tibetan canon. When he died in 1364, the Zhalu monks recited the entire Kanjur three times in commemoration of his life's work.

Butön took from Narthang (*sNar thang*) monastery a vast collection of manuscripts, gathered from surrounding central Tibetan monasteries and hermitages, and brought them to Zhalu. Butön culled the duplicates and added 1,000 more texts to complete his edition of the Kanjur and Tenjur. Some of these texts had been translated centuries earlier from Sanskrit manuscripts. The translations from Pāli of thirteen Theravāda discourses by his teacher, Nyi ma Gyaltsen (Nyi ma rgyal mtshan dPal bzang po), and Ānandaśrī were recent. He compared the Tibetan translations against Sanskrit originals, revised some of these translations and corrected others. The lack of Sanskrit originals led him to exclude some Tantras accepted as genuine by the Nyingma (*rNying ma*) school from his edited canon. Butön's edition of the Tenjur was completed in 1334, and his catalogue to it in 1335. In the catalogue, he indicated that the ruler of the Zhalu region funded the project and invited scribes from central and western Tibet to assist Butön in preparing the manuscript version of the Tenjur.

The Zhalu school's importance declined after Butön's death, but his works remain influential to the present day. Tibetan historians from the fourteenth century onward cite his *Doctrinal History* (*chos 'byung*) of Buddhism, and E. Obermiller's English translation makes it the best-known Tibetan historical work in the West. Butön's *Doctrinal History* provides information on Buddhism in India and Nepal, including detailed accounts of the lives of the Buddha and prominent Indian scholars, the development of Buddhism in Tibet, on his editorial methods for classifying Buddhist texts, and an index to the translations of the Kanjur and Tenjur. Butön's collected works (*gsung 'bum*) number more than 200 texts. He composed commentaries on numerous fundamental texts of Tibetan Buddhism, including the *Perfection of Insight (Prajñāparamitā) Sūtras* and the *Wheel of Time (Kālacakra) Tantra*.

See also: **Pāli canon; Tibet, Buddhism in; *Tripiṭaka*, Sanskrit and Prakrit; *Tripiṭaka*, Tibetan; *Tripiṭaka* and word of the Buddha.**

KAREN C. LANG

C

CAMBODIA AND LAOS, BUDDHISM IN

The logic of territorial contiguity, Buddhism, and politics both secular and related to Buddhism, defined the history of Cambodia. Hemmed in by Thailand, Laos, and Vietnam, the south of Cambodia alone confronted the Gulf of Siam, making her open to Indic Hindu cultural and religious influences primarily via trade. The Khmers made up almost 90 percent of Cambodia's ethnic population.

Before Theravāda Buddhism became predominant in the fourteenth century, Mahāyāna Buddhism and, as elsewhere in the peninsula, animism had taken strong root. Theravāda Buddhism made its presence felt in the reign of King Jayavarman VII, who reigned 1181–1201. The original Cambodian empire at the height of its power extended over parts of northern Thailand, Laos and Vietnam, providing an aura of a golden age to later rulers. Later, however, Cambodia closer to modern times lost considerable territory to Vietnam, a neighbor she traditionally feared, and to Thailand. The French who became the paramount power in the region established a protectorate in Cambodia in 1863, and later in 1889 made all of Cambodia a French colony, increasing its size by successfully compelling Thailand in 1907 to return three Cambodian provinces Thailand had appropriated in the eighteenth century.

However, Cambodia's relations with Thailand were closer on account of a strong common Theravāda tradition, in contrast to those with Vietnam. Thailand, with an older Buddhist tradition and unfettered by colonialism, extended a benign fraternal tutelage over Cambodia. An independent Theravāda Buddhist tradition was fostered by Cambodia's rulers of the nineteenth century beginning with Duang (1848–60), and continued more forcefully by his successor Norodhom (1860–1914), whose reign broadly coincided with that of Mongkut in Thailand. A notable feature was the importation of the Dhammayuttika *Nikāya* (monastic group) that Mongkut had created in Thailand as a countervailing reformed sect to the older Mahānikāya sect. As rulers both Duang and Norodom espoused the Dhammayuttika sect, which received added legitimacy when, as a result of the efforts of Mongkut, five Cambodian monks went to Sri Lanka to return with Buddhist relics and saplings from the Bo tree in Anurādhapura.

With the death of Mongkut, Thai influences on Cambodia became perceptibly less. Chulalongkorn, though concerned with the condition of Buddhism in Cambodia, was by inclination cosmopolitan and secular. In any event, the differences between the newly established Dhammayuttika sect and the older Mahānikāya Order were more to do with style than substance.

Meanwhile the French colonial government adopted multiple strategies towards Buddhism. Unlike in Vietnam, there was no Mandarin class influencing court policies, a class the French used in ruling Vietnam. The French were faced with a problem in Cambodia. The Buddhist monks in spite of the absence of an organizational structure comparable with Thailand were potentially an *imperium in imperio*, given their ubiquity, universal presence and the reverence traditionally shown to Buddhist monks. At the end of the nineteenth century an official survey revealed the existence of well over 2,000 monasteries. The fluid political situation in countries across the borders of Cambodia, the politicization of the Cambodian monkhood or their manipulation, was a veritable sword of Damocles.

As if to give substance to official misgivings, the monks in Cambodia in the modern period from 1820 to 1916 led rebellions that, however, were suppressed without difficulty in spite of a conniving backdrop of peasant unrest fused with millennial ideologies. The latter had potential to latch on to the age-old visions of the glories of the Khmer empire dominated by powerful rulers. The French in a sense legitimized the phobias by forbidding Buddhist monks from learning martial arts or practicing indigenous medicines, which reputedly had talismanic powers making their users invincible. The king under French colonial rule was at best a ceremonial figurehead, the head of a spiritual Buddhist state, with its rituals and ceremonies of largely symbolic significance and as an entity running the affairs of Buddhism, but constrained to show deference to the policies of the colonial authority. The government contained the potential political danger of the monks by keeping in place existing regulations prohibiting monks from voting or holding office. The restrictive policies found favor with conservative Buddhist elements in Cambodia as in other Buddhist countries confronting modernization. Monks functioned best immured in monasteries and attending to the spiritual needs of the laity, avoiding both social and political involvement. Moreover the French placed restrictions on the construction of new monasteries, and insisted that monasteries be certified by the state following ordination.

More effective were French policies of restructuring the educational system with a view to undermining the traditional Cambodian penchant for looking to Thailand for higher monastic learning and thereby coming within the ambience of Thai cultural and covert political ideologies. Comparable importance was attached to changing the dependence on monasteries as the sole source of primary and secondary education, in a strategy to undermine the traditional Buddhist influence on education. At secondary and higher levels, two new institutions, while seeming to focus on scholarly Buddhist studies, encouraged the creation of secular intellectual elite. A mix of educational reform, modernization, and economic opportunities created the classic bifurcation characteristic of countries under the fiat of sustained Western colonization.

With the phasing out of French rule in 1953, there was a critical power vacuum in Cambodia. In 1946 when belatedly the right to form political parties was conceded, to the right of the political spectrum there was the Nagara Vatta, which enjoyed a measure of royal support and stood for liberal democracy basing its support on the middle class, but clearly lacked a rural base. Its rival UIF had the support of Buddhist monks and was strongly pro-communist. Popular support with no viable focal point to turn to rallied round Prince Sihanouk who had ascended the throne in 1941. His popularity with radical left forces was strong following his uncompromising stand against the American presence in Vietnam, and the forced use of Cambodian territory in the war against the Vietming. Above all he had led Cambodia to formal political independence in 1953. Sihanouk was aware of the rising tide of communist popularity in the rural areas, where communism appealed to an emasculated Buddhist monkhood with no point of legitimate political focus as well as to an impoverished rural mass. The king tried to popularize Buddhist Socialism, visualizing a society ethicized by Buddhist values that would avoid the greed of capitalism and the negative egalitarianism of communist redistribution of economic wealth and productive potential. The utopianism appealed neither to the wealth-producing bourgeoisie nor to the mass of the rural disadvantaged. Sihanouk conceded that he had failed, reflecting philosophically on the mismatch of idealism and limitations of human nature driven by self-interest. He was ousted in a coup that brought in Lon Nol as head of a new Khmer Republic

Lon Nol, who had the backing of the Americans, was pro-Buddhist and anti-communist. His notably brief tenure of office, marred by illness, failed to prevent the Khmer Rouge from taking complete control of Cambodia in April 1975 under the leadership of Pol Pot, who until he was deposed by Vietnamese forces in 1979, unleashed a reign of terror directed at Buddhism and the *sangha*, bringing both to the point of near extinction. Viscerally committed to Marxist ideologies in their most elemental forms, Pol Pot understood that the real obstacle to the establishment of a communist state was Buddhism, which in effect meant the traditional order of monks. Tactically, however, he made a distinction between Buddhism and its ethical positions, and the order of monks representing the latter as a parasitic class who used *karma* to legitimize their privileged position enabling them to live otiose lives of little utility to society at large. The nuance's distinction appealed to rural youth and to younger monks at the lower end of the monastic hierarchy. Above all it legitimized the take-over of monasteries, putting them to secular uses, the expulsion of older monks, forcing them to work in the fields, the destruction of monasteries and *stūpas*, the decapitation of Buddha images and the cynical use of palm leaf manuscripts to roll cigarettes: acts which reverberated in the Buddhist world and may have overall had the ironical effect of undermining the communist appeal in South and Southeast Asia.

His successors in the post-Vietnamese era of healing were wiser and quick to learn from his mistakes, notably the People's Republic of Kampuchea and the Buddhist Liberal Democratic Party. They understood the dialectic that those who aspired to usher in a new order of society would serve their interest best by recognizing the legacies of the past to make the new order a viable synthesis. The new dispensation made a commitment to Buddhism, gave the *sangha* recognition, and made provision for a king. It was clearly an emblematic gesture but counted in a society that attached great value to symbols, leaving the reality to be achieved at some future point.

Meanwhile the land-based kingdom of Laos in its pre-European phase was dominated by Thailand and Vietnam, especially the latter. Some of the territories appropriated by Thailand to the west of Laos became part of French Indo-China. Laos traditionally was a Buddhist country with strong links between Buddhism and the state. Successive rulers fostered Buddhism and the monastic order to legitimize their authority. In the rural areas, where the bulk of the population lived, the links between the monastic order and the laity were strong constantly reinforced by legitimizing rituals. Laos attracted foreign scholars and enjoyed a reputation as a center for Buddhist studies. The picture of stability and tranquility was shattered with the advent of France and the gradual expansion of French power in the nineteenth century. Although Laos was an appendage in the larger context of French interests in Vietnam and Cambodia, French power had far-reaching implications for Laos. It put an end to the idea of Laos being a Buddhist state, and sundered the links between the monastic order and the ruler and his claims to legitimacy, with the king becoming the titular head of a virtually non-existing Buddhist state, beholden to the French for the modicum of influence he exercised.

Less than a century of French colonial rule led to an irreversible bifurcation in Laotian society. French rule created a Europeanized elite susceptible to Western cultural mores and, more importantly, to ideologies of capitalism and liberalism. However, French rule also opened pathways to the mesmerizing influence of Marxist-Leninist ideologies that swept through Asia in the throes of decolonization. French rule, which formally ended in 1954, ushered in a prolonged period of acrimonious conflict between the RIG, the Royal Pathet Lao who stood for democratic forms of government and economic liberalism, and the PL, the communist Pathet Lao, inspired by literalist exegetical interpretations of Marxist-Leninism. In an expedient coalition which brought the two parties to work together, the ministry of religious affairs came within the control of a staunchly ideological communist who immediately and effectively followed policies of demolishing the traditional institutional infrastructures of Buddhism, eroding the power of the *sangha* in the rural areas. In any event the communist Pathet Lao which had long been active in the rural areas, was easily able to seize power in 1975 to establish the Lao People's Republic. The Pathet Lao ideologues, sensing the importance of Buddhism and the tactical need to legitimize their authority, worked out an extraordinarily detailed and complex synthesis of Marxist-Leninist ideologies and Buddhism, committed in the process to one consistent principle that in situations where the two ideologies could not be harmonized, it was Buddhism that had to yield the point. In this way Laos earned the distinction of becoming the first Marxist state in the region.

See also: **Buddha and *cakravartins*; Politics; South and Southeast Asia, Buddhism in.**

ANANDA WICKREMERATNE

CANDRAKĪRTI

One of the most important commentators and authors of the Madhyamaka school, Candrakīrti probably lived in the middle of the seventh century CE. The two works for which he is best remembered are an independent treatise known as *Madhyamakāvatāra* and a commentary to Nāgārjuna's *Mūlamadhyamakakārikā*, entitled *Prasannapadā Madhyamakavṛtti*.

As a commentator to Nāgārjuna's work, Candrakīrti begins with an extended criticism of previous commentators to the same work who had attempted to defend Nāgārjuna's doctrine of the emptiness of all beings by employing the formal structures of Dignāga's inferential schemata. Dignāga's style of inference made use of inferential signs in the form of properties that were known to occur only in the presence of other properties so that observation of the sign could be used as evidence for the presence of some other property. So if emptiness is a property, said these previous commentators, it should be possible to find other properties that could be used as signs of its presence in things. This inferential strategy was severely criticized by Candrakīrti as ill-conceived, for it makes the mistake of seeing emptiness as a property like any other observable property, such as color or texture or weight. This is a mistake because emptiness is not a property of things as much as it is a name for the fact that things are dependent upon conditions, and this fact can be directly observed and therefore does not require inference to be known.

In his criticism of his predecessors, Candrakīrti's principal worry seems to have been that they were coming close to regarding emptiness as a doctrinal commitment about the nature of things that needed to be defended against other claims about the ultimate nature of things. Candrakīrti's understanding of Nāgārjuna's work was that Nāgārjuna had been trying to provide an antidote to the disease of having dogmatic views (*dṛṣṭi*) that required defense. The urge to defend one's views disturbs one's own peace of mind and potentially disrupts one's harmonious relations with others, and thus stands as an obstacle to both wisdom and compassion. The power of Nāgārjuna's work, according to Candrakīrti, was that it provides a means of eliminating the compulsion to defend one's views by showing that all views are provisional and contingent rather than absolutely true. The logicians who followed Dignāga were seeking certainty, whereas the whole point of the Madhyamaka method was to learn to live without certainty. According to Candrakīrti, therefore, the method of analysis used by Nāgārjuna was intended to show the ultimate inadequacy of all claims to truth. This inadequacy could only be shown by examining one view at a time and finding it inadequate. What follows from Candrakīrti's understanding of Nāgārjuna's method is that conventional ways of viewing the world need not be abandoned, but need only be held with an understanding that they are not ultimately grounded in reality. Wisdom, therefore, is not a matter of giving up conventional truth in favor of a higher truth but a matter of using conventional truth without clinging to it.

See also: **India, Buddhism in; Madhymaka school; Mahāyāna Buddhism.**

RICHARD P. HAYES

CANONS AND LITERATURE

All the world's major religious traditions have scriptures that their followers regard as sacred or authoritative. This claim of sanctity or authority distinguishes these religious scriptures from all other writings. The Abrahamic traditions of Judaism, Christianity, and Islam share a common identity as "People of the Book." While the Qu'ran is a single unified work, the Hebrew Bible and the Christian Bible are compilations drawn from multiple sources, but all these books derive their authority from divine revelation. The word "canon," which is used most often in the Christian context, refers to religious writings that believers regard as authentic and definitive. In the broadest sense, a canon includes all writings considered authentic, without excluding the possibility that other writings may be added to the canon later. In a more restricted use, a canon is a body of scriptures, closed at some specific point, often by the convening of an ecclesiastical council, such as the fourth-century CE Council of Nicea that decided the twenty-seven works that belong in the New Testament. After a restricted canon has been established and accepted by the faithful, it becomes closed to the possibility of new revelations. A less restrictive concept of canon allows for new writings to develop and to gain acceptance as canonical among the believers who faithfully transmit these texts from one generation to the next.

Buddhist canons

As Buddhists have no single authoritative book, it is inappropriate to speak of a Buddhist canon. There are multiple Buddhist canons with varying criteria for inclusion. Complete sets of authoritative scriptures exist in Pāli, Chinese, and Tibetan languages and there are partial canons of scriptures preserved in Sanskrit and various Prakrit languages. The difficulties of interpreting texts across cultures also contributed to an evolving canonization process. A vibrant oral commentarial tradition influenced the composition of many works included in these canons. Each of these canons is a unique compilation, shaped by different hands over centuries. The monastic scholars who compiled the different editions and redactions of the Pāli, Chinese, and Tibetan canons differed among themselves over which works were authentic and worthy of canonical inclusion and which works were spurious and ought to be excluded. The Theravāda tradition of Burma/Myanmar accepted as canonical four works excluded by other Theravāda Buddhists. Particular editions of the Chinese and Tibetan canons also differ both in the arrangement of the texts included and in their number.

These Buddhist canons are compilations of heterogeneous works composed at different times. The compilers of the Pāli, Chinese, and Tibetan canons determined a scripture's authenticity by using criteria that were modified as the Buddhist community itself changed. The Pāli canon's criteria for inclusion were the most conservative. Scriptures spoken by Gautama Buddha or his enlightened disciples and passed down in secure line of transmission were regarded as authentic. While Theravāda tradition considered the canon closed at the Council of Rājagṛha in the year of the Buddha's death, in fact the Pāli canon remained open to additions at least until the time of Buddhaghosa (*c.* fifth century CE). The Chinese and Tibetan canons remained open to additions of new scriptures well into the fourteenth century. These canons include scriptures originally composed in the literary languages of Pāli and Sanskrit but also in several vernacular languages that were all translated into Chinese or Tibetan. The scriptures included in Chinese and Tibetan canons were attributed not only to Gautama Buddha's inspiration, but also to the inspiration of multiple Buddhas and *bodhisattvas* throughout the entire cosmos. Their compilers judged a scripture's authenticity based upon transmission in a faithful lineage of Indian teachers. The task of discriminating Indic originals from indigenous authors' forgeries was made even more difficult by the proliferation of Mahāyāna *sūtras* and *tantras* that claimed to be products of dreams, revelations, and visions.

The formation of the *Tripiṭaka*

The Buddhist word most often translated as "canon" is *Tripiṭaka*, the three baskets (*piṭaka*) of the Buddha's teachings containing his discourses (*Sūtra*), the monastic code (*Vinaya*), and scholastic teachings (*Abhidharma*). As the Buddha lay dying he advised his grieving disciples that they must look to his teaching for inspiration and guidance after he had gone. He did not choose to appoint any one of his numerous disciples to succeed him but instead gave each of them the responsibility for guiding their lives according to the precepts he had set down for them during his lifetime. His parting advice encouraged his disciples to gather together and come to an agreement on the teachings that he had handed down to them. Traditional accounts of early Buddhist history record that 500 of these disciples who had attained the enlightened status of saints (*arhat*) met together at Rājagṛha during the first three-month rainy-season retreat after their teacher's death. They gathered together to collect what they had remembered of the teachings they had heard the Buddha give during the forty-five years of his lengthy teaching career. This select group agreed upon an authoritative body of teachings to serve as their guide and to provide both continuing inspiration and a means for settling future disputes.

Buddhist tradition holds that at the Council of Rājagṛha, Kāśyapa – Gautama Buddha's oldest disciple – requested that Ānanda recite the Buddha's discourses and Upāli recite the rules that govern monastic life (*Vinaya*). The assembled disciples' communal recitation of these teachings signified agreement on their authenticity. After the Buddha's death, his disciples passed down orally these two fundamental collections of teachings. The *Sūtra Piṭaka* included all of the remembered discourses spoken by the Buddha, along with those discourses spoken by his disciples with his authorization. The *Vinaya Piṭaka* comprised rules and regulations binding on monks and nuns, along with explanations of the circumstances that led their adoption. The Theravāda school, the sole surviving school of at least eighteen schools that flourished in the centuries after the Buddha's death, believed that a third collection of summaries (Skt. *mātṛkā*, Pāli *mātikā*) and scholastic interpretations of Buddhist teachings was added later. This last of the Buddhist canon's three baskets, the *Abhidharma Piṭaka*, contained the "higher teachings." The *Abhidharma Piṭaka* included texts in which monastic scholars arranged, classified, and made into a coherent system all of the unsystematic teachings found throughout the *sūtras*. These three collections of scriptures were passed down orally for several centuries. Within the Indian Buddhist community, separate groups of Buddhist monastics transmitted different parts of the canon, as there were only a rare few with exceptional memories who knew the entire *Tripiṭaka*.

Inscriptions on Buddhist monuments at Bhārhut and Sāñcī refer to two of the traditional three baskets of the Buddhist canon. These inscriptions, some dating back to the first century BCE, record that certain monastics specialized in the recitation of the disciplinary code while others specialized in the recitation of particular discourses. Inscriptions at the Buddhist sites of Nāgārjunakoṇḍa and Amarāvatī in southern India distinguish between monastics who recited the collection of lengthy discourses and those who recited the collection of medium-length discourses. Many extant canonical texts show evidence of the formulaic phrases linked together in repeated patterns that is characteristic of oral literature. Experienced Buddhist reciters (*bhāṇaka*) could easily string together these formulaic phrases into a well-structured composition for the education and enjoyment of their audiences. As a consequence of different reciters specializing in memorizing discourses of differing lengths, identical or similar text or segments of text occur in two or more places in the canon. Comparison of different recensions of a particular scripture suggests that these reciters had no fixed text. The minor differences that exist are those common to oral literature: the titles, locations, characters may change; some material may be abridged or eliminated while other material, often explanatory in nature, may be added. The changes that occur over time in oral literature render problematic any attempts to separate the supposed original teachings of Gautama Buddha from those of his later and often sectarian followers.

As Buddhism spread into different regions of the Indian sub-continent and to the island of Sri Lanka, Buddhist scriptures must have been transmitted and preserved in number of different languages or dialects. Linguistic and sectarian differences motivated particular monasteries to compile their own canonical collections. At some point the eighteen or more schools that developed in these regions may have chosen to translate their *sūtra* holdings, which had been preserved up to that point in different regional dialects, into a standardized language capable of being understood by monastics from monasteries in other areas. This standardized "church" language used for the recitation and preservation of scriptures was probably not identical with any particular spoken language. The Theravāda school preserves its canonical scriptures in Pāli; one of these standardized "church" languages that bear the traces of other regional languages. According to Theravāda tradition, King Aśoka's son, the monk Mahinda, brought Buddhist teachings to Sri Lanka in the third century BCE. During the reign of King Vaṭṭagāmaṇi (*c.* 29–17 BCE), the Theravāda school's collection of the Buddha's teachings and scholarly commentaries on them were written down because monks feared that the teachings could be lost in times of war, famine, or monastic strife. The monks of the Mahāvihara, the first monastery built in Sri Lanka, produced a canon of Pāli scriptures that legitimated and defined their conservative teachings against controversial teachings favored by monks of the newer Abhayagiri monastery, built and patronized by King Vaṭṭagāmaṇi. It is impossible now to determine the extent to which this canon written down many centuries ago resembles the present Pāli canon.

Other schools preserved their own holdings of the Buddha's teachings in their own preferred languages. When the various Buddhist schools in India began to commit their scriptures to written form, their development of a standardized "church" language continued in a different direction than that of the Theravāda monks who compiled the canon in the Pāli language. Perhaps because of the increasing influence of Sanskrit grammatical works, such as Patañjali's *Mahābhāṣya* (*c.* second century BCE), the language in which Buddhist scriptures were written down became progressively more "Sanskritized." Evidence from inscriptions found at northern Indian sites like Mathurā, Śrāvastī, and Sārnāth, indicate that this "Sanskritization" process was already underway by the first century CE. This growing influence and prestige of Sanskrit led monks to insert Sanskrit vocabulary items and grammatical forms into the composition of Buddhist texts, perhaps as early as the second century BCE. The language of these Buddhist Sanskrit texts, in which Sanskrit and middle Indo-Aryan forms were juxtaposed, is sometime referred to as "Buddhist Hybrid Sanskrit."

All schools transmitted their own set of *Sūtra* and *Vinaya* texts; many also passed down *Abhidharma* texts. All the *Sūtras* began with the line, "Thus have I heard," indicating the importance of the oral transmission, even after writing came into use. There are four or five *Sūtra* collections (*Āgamas*, *Nikāyas*) considered canonical by the eighteen mainstream (*śrāvakayāna*) schools. The *Long Discourses* (*Dīrgha*) and the *Middle Length Discourses (Madhyama)* are arranged by length. The *Connected Discourses* (*Saṃyukta*) are arranged topically, and the *Increasing-by-One Discourses* (*Ekottara*) are arranged in increasing order of their topics from one to eleven. A fifth collection, the *Collection of Minor Texts* (*Kṣudraka*), was rejected by some and considered as a separate division (*piṭaka*) by others. The reciters of the *Long Discourses* (*Dīrgha bhāṇaka*) grouped the *Collection of Minor Texts* under their *Abhidhamma Piṭaka*. The schools' *Vinaya Piṭaka*, which focuses on monastic discipline and the history of the monastic order, were less varied than either the *Sūtra Piṭaka* or the *Abhidharma Piṭaka*. Different schools' *Vinayas* rules and regulations for monks and nuns ranged from 218 to 263 for the monks and from 279 to 380 for the nuns. The narrative accounts of how these rules developed were also subject to local variation. The *Mūlasarvāstivādin Vinaya*, preserved in Tibetan translation, contains a rich narrative tradition that explained how particular rules were formulated. The earliest *Abhidharma* texts were elaborate lists or summaries of technical terms. In later *Abhidharma* texts, Buddhist scholars debated divergent interpretations of doctrine. Only the *Abhidharma Piṭakas* of the Theravāda and Sarvāstivāda have survived and each contained seven quite distinct books. The fifth book of the Theravāda school, the *Book of Disputed Points* (*Kathāvatthu*) was believed to have been compiled as a record of debates at the third monastic council held at Pāṭaliputra during the reign of King Aśoka (r. 272–231 BCE). Interscholastic debate over the interpretation of the Buddha's teachings contributed to the writing and rewriting of *Abhidharma* textbooks, These texts' authors, though they debated different teachers' interpretations of doctrine, shared certain fundamental assumptions: the world consisted of a finite number of phenomena (*dharma*); these phenomena exist ultimately, and *arhat*s realize *nirvāṇa* through an analysis of these phenomena. The *Abhidharma* texts contained in the last of the three baskets of the Buddhist canon were regarded as the word of the Buddha on the grounds that these texts were written on the basis of an outline or summary (*mātṛkā*) that the Buddha himself formulated. The questions answered in these texts are answered in the same way the Buddha would have answered had he been asked the questions.

The fallibility of human memory, contested interpretations of scripture, and the composition of new texts, prompted questions over which teachings could be relied upon as the Buddha's word. Buddhists began to develop criteria to determine which texts could be considered the word of the Buddha (*buddhavacana*) and which could not. The texts did not need to be spoken by the Buddha as he could authorize other monastics to speak in his place. The criteria set forth in the *Scripture on the Great Indications* (*Mahāpradeśa Sūtra*) judge a text's authenticity based on its provenance from the Buddha or a learned member of the *sangha* and on its harmony with the received body of his teachings (*Sūtra*, *Vinaya*, *Abhidharma*). A *sangha* of elders indicated a teaching as reliable if someone heard it spoken by the Buddha, by a group of monastics who were specialists in the *Sūtra*, *Vinaya*, or in the *Abhidharma*, even by a single monastic who is a specialist in any of the areas. Other criteria were developed in the Theravāda text, the *Guide (Nettipakaraṇa)* and in the *Mūlasarvāstivāda Vinaya*: a teaching is authoritative if it agrees with recognized *sūtras*, if it is reflected in the *Vinaya*, and if it does not contradict reality (*dharmatā*). The *Scripture on the Four Reliances* (*Catuḥpratisaraṇa Sūtra*) prescribed four criteria for determining which texts should be recognized as the Buddha's word. One should rely on: (1) the teaching (*Dharma*) rather than the person (*pudgala*); (2) the meaning (*artha*) rather than the letter (*vyañjana*); (3) the definitive meaning (*nītārtha*) rather than the interpretable meaning (*neyārtha*); and (4) direct intuitive knowledge (*jñāna*) rather than conceptual, discursive knowledge (*vijñāna*).

Closed and open canons

The development of different criteria for determining authentic Buddhist teaching presumes the existence of some recognized corpus of works against which new scriptures could be judged. When and to what extent this corpus of works became closed remains unknown. Of all the canonical collections, the Theravāda collection of scriptures preserved in Pāli is the most restricted. The repeated copying of these manuscripts, first written down in the first century BCE, enabled this canon to survive intact. Even the Theravāda school is not united over which texts belong in the *Collection of Minor Texts.* The Burmese edition of Pāli canon includes in its *Collection of Minor Texts* four texts: the *Compendium of Discourses* (*Suttasaṃgaha*), the *Guide*, the *Piṭaka Instructions* (*Peṭakopadesa*), and the *Questions of King Milinda* (*Milindapañha*). The *Compendium of Discourses* contains commentary on the discourses and the *Guide* and the *Piṭaka Instruction* are both handbooks useful for explaining the discourses' meaning. The *Questions of King Milinda* comprises the monk Nagasena's explanations and illustrations of Buddhist teachings to a first-century BCE Indo-Greek king, Meander.

Buddhist settlements flourished in the Indo-Greek region of Gandhāra (northern Pakistan and eastern Afghanistan) under the first century CE patronage of the Kuṣāṇa dynasty king, Kaniṣka. The fifty-five Gāndhārī manuscripts in the *Senior Collection* and the twenty-nine Gandhārī scrolls of the British Library collection suggest that Gandhāran monastery libraries had a canon in Gāndhārī, a middle Indo-Aryan vernacular language. Many of the *sūtras* in the *Senior* and British Library collections correspond to Pāli canonical *suttas.* Parallels to known canonical literature include the *Words of Dharma* (*Dharmapada*) and the *Rhinoceros Horn Sūtra* (*Khaḍgaviṣaṇa Sūtra*) of the *Collection of Minor Texts.* The British Library collection also includes *Abhidharma* texts and many stories of eminent monastics (*Avadāna*). While the sectarian affiliation of these monasteries is uncertain, all the Gāndhārī scriptures belong to some mainstream tradition. As some of these texts have no known parallels and may be locally composed materials, the Gāndhārī canon appears to be open to the addition of local compositions.

Monastics belonging to mainstream schools also wrote commentarial works explaining *Sūtra*, *Vinaya* and *Abhidharma* texts that later achieved canonical status. The *Great Commentary* (*Mahāvibhāṣā*) on the Sarvāstivāda *Abhidharma* text, *Foundation of Knowledge* (*Jñānaprasthāna*), explains and criticizes Sarvāstivāda teachers' competing views. Many of these teachers' commentaries, now lost in their original language of composition, have been translated into Chinese and incorporated into the Chinese canon. The most influential *Abhidharma* commentary in both the Chinese and Tibetan canons is *The Treasury of Abhidharma* (*Abhidharmakośa*) written as a response to the *Great Commentary*, by Vasubandhu (fourth century CE).

During the first few centuries CE both the authors of *Abhidharma* exegetical works (*śāstra*) and the unknown authors of new *sūtras* were engaged in a reinterpretation of Buddhist literature. No definite date for the composition of these new *sūtras* is known but their translation into Chinese during the latter part of the second century CE suggests that that they were composed in India a century or two earlier. Like the older scriptures, these new compositions were considered the Buddha's word, as whatever is well spoken by a disciple of the Buddha does not contradict his word. The dialogue between the Buddha and his disciples in these new scriptures reflected the concern among this later generation of Buddhists that some of the mainstream theories and practices were no longer effective. These new discourses criticized the traditional path of the *arhat* for displaying a self-centered concern with his or her own attainment of *nirvāṇa*. Some of these new discourses may have first arisen within mainstream Mahāsaṅghika monastic circles in south India but the compilers of the Chinese and Tibetan canons considered them to belong to the Mahāyāna tradition.

Although the origins of the Mahāyāna movement remain obscure, most scholars agree that it developed in monastic circles, perhaps as early as the second century BCE. Chinese pilgrims who traveled to India as late as the seventh century reported that the minority of monks who supported the Mahāyāna lived in the same monastic institutions as other monks whom they criticized for following an inferior path (Hīnayāna). The new *sūtras* they created, though often expanded in length (*vaipulya*), were modeled on older paradigms. The creators of these new Mahāyāna *sūtras* disputed the mainstream canons' claims to represent a complete collection of the Buddha's teachings. These *sūtras* were presented in the form of dialogs between Śakyamuni Buddha and his disciples that took place in various regions in central India, often on Vulture Peak. The anonymous creators of these Mahāyāna *sūtras* and the *Dharma* preachers (*dharmabhāṇakas*) who memorized and recited them in public regarded these works as the Buddha's word on the grounds that "Whatever is well spoken is the word of the Buddha." The Buddha to these anonymous authors and *Dharma*-preachers revealed some of these *sūtras* in meditations, visions, and dreams. Other *sūtras*, the *Perfection of Insight* scriptures (*Prajñāpāramitā Sūtra*), claimed to be teachings entrusted by the Buddha to semi-divine beings, the serpent-like *nāgas*, until the time came when there were people receptive to their profound, deep teachings. Each *sūtra* proclaimed its own unique authoritative status and the vast quantities of merit that the devout could acquire from hearing, preaching, copying, and preserving these texts.

The Mahāyāna movement created large quantities of new *sūtras* that the faithful regarded as being the authentic word of the Buddha. The earliest extant manuscript copy of a Mahāyāna *sūtra*, *The Perfection of Insight Sūtra in Eight Thousand Lines* (*Aṣṭasāhasrikāprajñāpāramitā*), was recently discovered among a cache of Buddhist Sanskrit manuscripts, which may have come from a monastic library in Bāmiyān, Afghanistan. This incomplete manuscript was produced around the second century CE. The Schøyen collection of manuscripts from the second to eighth centuries includes both Mahāyāna *sūtras* and mainstream works, which supports the idea that monastic libraries preserved both mainstream and Mahāyāna works. Some early Mahāyāna *sūtras* – the *Immovable One's Pure Land* (*Akṣobhya-vyūha*), the *Pure Land of Bliss* (*Sukhāvatīvyūha*), and the *Bhaiṣajya Guru Sūtra*, found at in Bāmiyān and at Gilgit (located in Pakistan and northern India) – depict the pure lands of Mahāyāna Buddhas. These pure lands resulted from the fulfillment of vows taken by Akṣobhya (the Immovable) Buddha, Amitābha (Infinite Light) Buddha, and Bhaiṣajya (Medicine) Buddha when they began the *bodhisattva* path. The stages of *bodhisattva* path and the *bodhisattva*'s journey are also the focus of two influential scriptures included within the vast *Flower Garland* (*Avataṃsaka*) collection, the *Ten Stages* (*Daśabhūmika*) *Sūtra* and the *Array of Flowers* (*Gaṇḍavyūha*) *Sūtra*. Because of this focus on the acts of *bodhisattvas*, collections of Mahāyāna *sūtras* were described as a "*bodhisattva* canon" (*bodhisattvapiṭaka*). This canon remained open to new Mahāyāna works. It is uncertain whether these compositions in

Buddhist Sanskrit and various Prakrits ever formed an independent canon comparable to the Theravāda school's exclusive canon of works in Pāli.

As Mahāyāna Buddhism continued to develop, *tantras*, a new genre of Buddhist literature, were added to the vast collection of Mahāyāna texts. These *tantras*, like some early Mahāyāna *sūtras*, claimed to be revelations acquired from Buddhas through meditation, visions, and dreams. Some of these scriptures may date back as early as the fifth century CE but most were composed between the eighth and eleventh centuries, when the Vajrayāna path was followed in both lay and monastic circles. The *tantras* were written in a non-standard Sanskrit that often used coded language (*sandhya bhāṣā*) that required a teacher (*guru*) to initiate and instruct disciples about these scriptures' hidden meanings. Teachers' explanations also aided students in the practice of specific rituals and visualization techniques incorporated in the *tantra*s. The scriptures from the Highest Yoga (*anuttarayoga*) class of *tantra*s such as the *Secret Assembly (Guhyasamāja) Tantra*, and the *Wheel of Time (Kālacakra) Tantra* use sexual imagery to depict the stages of the Vajrayāna path to liberation. *Tantras* also generated an extensive commentarial literature, composed by monastic exegetes, to explain the context of these sexual images and the meanings of coded language. These *tantras* were accepted into the open canon of Mahāyāna Buddhism as exegesis revealed that their teachings were in accord with the authentic word of the Buddha.

Multiple Chinese and Tibetan canons

The Chinese and Tibetan canons remained open to the enormous quantities of both mainstream and Mahāyāna literature that Buddhists brought first into China and later into Tibet. The compilers of the Chinese and Tibetan canons adopted different strategies for the incorporation of all this material. The Chinese preserved multiple translations of the same text, while the Tibetans preferred to exclude earlier and less accurate translations. Chinese and Tibetan translations of Mahāyāna literature not only provide access to material long lost in India but they also show how this literature underwent considerable change over several centuries of translation.

Buddhism spread across the Silk Road through Central Asia to China with monks and pious laity bringing along hand-copied Buddhist manuscripts. The *Scripture in Forty-two Sections* (*Sishi'er zhang jing*), a short collection of passages from mainstream Buddhist scriptures (*Āgamas*), is traditionally regarded as first text translated into Chinese at the request of Emperor Ming (r. 58–75 CE). An Shigao (fl. 148–170 CE), the Chinese name of a Parthian Buddhist, translated more than twenty works, mostly mainstream *Sūtra* and *Abhidharma* texts, in the capital city of Luoyang. The Indo-Scythian monk Lokakṣema (fl. 170–90), also working in Luoyang, is credited with the introduction of Mahāyāna Buddhist works. He translated many Mahāyāna *sūtras*, including a partial translation of *The Perfection of Insight Sūtra in Eight Thousand Lines* (*Aṣṭasahaśrikāprajñāpāramitā*), the *Sūtra of Concentration of Direct Encounter with the Buddhas of the Present* (*Pratyutpanna-buddhasammukhāvasthitasamādhi Sūtra*) and the *Land of Bliss Sūtra* (*Sukhāvatī-vyūha*) which introduced the meditative practice of visualizing Amitābha Buddha and his Western Buddha Land. Kumārajīva (343–413), a Central Asian monk, and his team of assistants at Chang An produced elegant and accurate Chinese translations of nearly 100 texts. His translations of the *Lotus Sūtra* and the *Teaching of Vimalakīrti Sūtra* improved on earlier efforts. He also translated Sarvāstivāda *Vinaya* works, the three treatises (*san lun*) on which the Chinese branch of the Madhyamaka school was based and the *Great Perfection of Insight Treatise* (*Dazhidulun*), which incorporates some of his oral commentary on these Madhyamaka treatises. Chinese readers preferred Kumārajīva's stylish translations to those of Xuanzang (596–664), whose meticulous translations retained traces of the Sanskrit syntax and grammar he had studied during his years in India.

The Tang dynasty (618–907) catalogs of monastic library holdings were compiled after the translation of most scriptures into Chinese was completed. Catalogs distinguished between new or old translations, authentic Indian texts and spurious scriptures, complete and abridged translations, mainstream and Mahāyāna works, and those texts with known and unknown translators. Zhisheng's *Catalog of the Kaiyuan era on Buddhism* (*Kaiyuan shijao*) completed in 730 was the most thorough in its chronological arrangement of translations and descriptions of different translators and translations. This catalog influenced organization of all subsequent East Asian editions of the canon, including the modern Taishō. Not all efforts to exclude inauthentic texts succeeded. Some spurious texts credited to well-known foreign translators were accepted as genuine, such as Kumārajīva's translation of the *Brahma's Net Sūtra* (*Fanwang Jing*), an apocryphal text on Mahāyāna precepts.

A complete canon of scriptures was not produced until 927, when the Song court authorized the carving of the canon onto wooden printing blocks. The massive work of carving 13,000 blocks with the contents of over 1,000 works was completed in 984 (See Figure 15). This edition, which was widely disseminated, effectively closed the canon. The Chinese canon's translations of texts spread to Korea, Vietnam, Japan and literary Chinese became the "church" language of East Asian Buddhism. The Mongol rulers of the Liao dynasty printed another set of blocks in 1055 based on the Shu edition. On these two editions, the eleventh-century Korean Koryŏ dynasty editions were made. The first complete Japanese editions of Chinese canon were completed in the seventeenth century, and the nineteenth and early twentieth centuries saw the completion of three more Japanese editions. The 1924–34 Taishō Shinshū Daizōkyō edition, in eighty-five volumes containing 2,920 texts, has become the standard reference for the Chinese canon. The Taishō edition of the canon contains more of the traditional *tripiṭaka* of *Sūtra*, *Vinaya*, and *Abhidharma* texts. Historical works, biographies of eminent monks and nuns, meditation and ritual manuals, and even reproduction of iconographies are included. The first fifty-five volumes of the Taishō edition contain the scriptures of the Chinese canon; Japanese texts are included in Volumes 56 to 84. Volume 85 contains Dunhuang texts and apocryphal texts composed in China; Volumes 86 to 97 reproduce iconographies, and Volumes 98 to 100 provide bibliographical information.

Beginning in the seventh century, Tibet received large numbers of Buddhist scriptures from India and China that Tibetans, working with foreign Buddhist teachers, translated into Tibetan. At Samye and other smaller monasteries, teams of Tibetan translators working with Indian

Figure 15 Library of traditional Tibetan books (*dpe cha*) printed from woodblocks, Leh Palace, Ladakh.

and Chinese collaborators had produced a large body of translated texts, kept in monastery and palace libraries. The ninth-century catalog of translations held in the Denkar palace listed *sūtras*, followed by *tantras* and *dhāraṇīs*, hymns of praise, texts on monastic discipline (*Vinaya*), and *sūtra* commentaries and other treatises. Nearly 500 of its 736 titles are *sūtras*, beginning with the *Perfection of Insight* (*Prajñāpāramitā*) *Sūtras*, *Flower Garland* (*Avataṃsaka*) *Sūtras*, *Jewel Peak* (*Ratnakūṭa*) *Sūtras*, miscellaneous Mahāyāna *sūtras*, and ending with Hīnayāna *sūtras*. A small number of *sūtras* and *sūtra* commentaries were listed as translations from Chinese.

Early in the fourteenth century, at Narthang monastery, Tibetan scholars compiled translations made over a 500-year period and determined which of these to include in an authoritative collection of Buddhist scripture. The Tibetan edition of the Buddhist *tripiṭaka* is divided into two parts: translations of the Buddha, the Kanjur (*bka 'gyur*), and translations of the treatises attributed to Indian masters, the Tenjur (*bstan 'gyur*). Monks learned in the canon began work in 1311 on the first Kanjur and Tenjur collections, each totaling over 100 volumes. Butön Rinchendrup (Bu ston Rin chen 'grub, 1290–1364) played a major role in selecting, editing, and classifying these texts. He compared the massive collection of manuscripts at Narthang with those listed in Denkar catalog and in the catalogs of several monastic libraries. His arrangement of texts was based on the catalogs' lists, but he went beyond their simple inventories of manuscripts to establish criteria for limiting the number and type of texts included in the Kanjur and Tenjur. The most important criterion was that the text was an accurate translation of a genuine Indic manuscript. Numerous esoteric ritual texts and manuals were not incorporated into the Tibetan canon because Butön doubted the Indian provenance of many *tantras*. The Kanjur has three main sections: *Vinaya*, *Sūtra*, and *Tantra*. The *Vinaya* section's texts on monastic discipline are from the Mūlasarvāstivādin schools. The *Sūtra* section includes *Perfection of Insight Sūtras*, *Flower Garland Sūtras*, *Jewel Peak Sūtras*, and miscellaneous *sūtras*, primarily Mahāyāna. The Tantra section's more than 300 texts follow Butön's arrangement into four main classes: *Action Tantra* (*Kriyā Tantra*), *Performance Tantra* (*Caryā Tantra*), *Yoga Tantra*, and *Highest Yoga* (*Ānuttarayoga*) *Tantra*. The arrangement of the Tenjur's collection of more than 3,000 texts begins with *Hymns of Praise to the Buddhas*, followed by *Commentaries on the Tantras* and *Commentaries on the-Perfection of Insight Sūtras*, Mādhyamika treatises, Yogācāra treatises, *Abhidharma* treatises, *Vinaya* commentaries, *Avadāna* and *Jātaka* stories, letters, and technical treatises on logic and epistemology (*pramāṇa*), linguistics (*śabdavidyā*), medicine, iconography, poetic meters, and political treatises (*nītiśāstra*), and Atiśa's minor treatises. Kanjurs and Tenjurs come from different regions of Tibet and have a complex history of transmission. The sections and the number and order of the individual texts within sections are not the same in all Tibetan *Tripiṭakas*. Differences occur in classifying the sequence of the Buddha's teachings and reflect sectarian preferences in the inclusion and order of specific *tantras*.

Practical canons

Modern scholars distinguish between the formal canon of the Pāli, Chinese and Tibetan *Tripiṭakas*, the definitive sources of interpretative authority, and the ritual or practical canon that contemporary monastics draw upon when conducting rituals and preaching sermons. This second type of canon may include selected portions of the *Tripiṭaka*, as well as texts on the *Dharma* that are consistent with the canonical content. Many small monasteries and nunneries have no complete collection of the canon. Their collections may consist of non-canonical commentaries, story collections (*Jātaka*, *Avadāna*), often in local languages, and popular ritual texts.

Theravāda monks study the Pāli canon with the aid of vernacular commentaries. Sinhala commentaries (*sannayas*) often include the Pāli text, a Sinhala gloss, and an explanation of its contents. Burmese and Thai commentaries (*nissaya*) explain the text, and justify its importance in the tradition and absorbing and replacing the text. *Nissayas* often rewrite and expand the Pāli text by adding new sections and using the text as the foundation for studying grammar and vocabulary. These vernacular commentaries introduce selected texts to monastic students and form their understanding of Theravāda Buddhist doctrine. Tibetan monastic students similarly reply on textbook commentaries (*yig cha*) that summarize a canonical text's general meaning. Tibetan doxographies (*grub mtha'*), which are also concise summaries of teachings, are also frequently studied and memorized by monastic students.

Monastic libraries contain large numbers of ritual texts and ritual manuals, as performance of rituals is an important part of life of a Buddhist temple. Ritual manuals guide monks and nuns in the performance of consecration rituals, which bring together the lay and monastic communities in consecration of a temple, a *stūpa*, or an image. Laypeople also invite monastics to chant ritual texts for protection against illness and misfortune, but also as blessings for new houses, new businesses, and new marriages. The most important ritual activities that Buddhist monastics perform for the laity concern the dead and the dying, and all Buddhist monastic institutions instruct their members in the proper recitation of ritual texts at funeral and memorial services.

See also: ***Abhidharma*; Butön; Textual authority: the *Catuḥpratisaraṇa Sūtra*; Hagiographies; *Jātakas* and other narrative collections; Kumārajīva; Pāli canon; *Tripiṭaka*, Chinese; *Tripiṭaka*, Sanskrit and Prakrit; *Tripiṭaka*, Tibetan; *Tripiṭaka* and word of the Buddha; *Vinaya Piṭaka*; *Vinayas*.**

KAREN C. LANG

CAVE TEMPLES

The Buddhist tradition has a long history of cave temple construction, ranging from caves little altered from their natural condition that served as residences for individual Buddhist renunciants, to massive, multi-storied structures carved deep into rock that provided for the residential and ritual needs of large communities of Buddhist monastics, as well as the diverse interests of the laity who supported their construction and maintenance. Even before the time of the Buddha, caves in India were associated with ascetic retreat, and the *Sakkapañha Sutta* of the *Dīgha Nikāya* recounts that the Buddha was staying in a cave near Rājagṛha, the capital of the state of Magadha, when the great god Sakka (Skt. Śakra) descended from his celestial residence to ask him a series of questions about the *Dharma*; this tradition was known to the Chinese pilgrims Faxian and Xuanzang who mention the site in their accounts. A series of rock-cut caves in Bihar, India, excavated during the Mauryan period (third century BCE) are the earliest intact architectural structures in India, and three of these bear inscriptions proclaiming that they were donated by the great emperor Aśoka to shelter Ājīvika renunciants (one of several early renunciant movements that vied with early Buddhists for patronage). These caves may have provided the model for an extensive series of cave temples, including both *caitya* halls and *vihāras*, constructed at more than two dozen sites in the Ghāts of western India between 100 BCE and 200 CE.

Ajaṇṭā, one of the most famous of the western India cave complexes, saw two major phases of construction, one during the first centuries BCE–CE that produced two *caitya* halls and three monastic residences (*vihāras*), and a second period of much more extensive construction in which twenty-five additional caves were fashioned within a period of less than twenty years (*c.* 462–80 CE). It is this latter set of fifth-century cave temples that is famous for its remarkably well-preserved sculptures and paintings (See Figure 16). Ajaṇṭā's history, known in part through the large collection of donatory inscriptions found there, illuminates the close connection between dynastic politics and *sangha* patronage in central India during the fifth century. The spatial and ritual organization of Ajaṇṭā's cave temples also illustrates the means through which transcendent Buddhas and *bodhisattvas* were physically localized and integrated into local systems of religious practice that addressed a wide range of mundane and supramundane interests.

Caves also played an important role in the early history of Buddhism in Sri Lanka where more than a thousand cave dwellings with inscriptions dating from the third century BCE to the first century CE have been identified. In contrast to the numerous *stūpas* and *vihāras* built under royal patronage in the ancient capital of Anurādhapura, only a very small percentage of the early Buddhist cave dwellings were donated by members of the royal family; the largest group of donors comprised local or regional leaders and their families. In addition, few of these cave dwellings were situated near *stūpas*; instead, many were located near pathways for meditation, suggesting that they were intended to shelter forest-dwelling monastics committed to meditational discipline. Most of these dwellings were little more than natural caves with only minor modifications to render them more habitable, including enclosure of the cave's mouth and the construction of drip ledges to divert rainwater.

Figure 16 Wall painting of the Buddha preaching, Ajaṇṭā, India, Cave 16.

Dambulla in central Sri Lanka is the site of the largest cave complex on the island, with five caves housing more than 150 sculpted Buddha images as well as many images of gods, *arhats* and royal patrons. Inscriptional evidence indicates that several caves in the area were donated as monastic dwellings as early as the second century BCE, though since at least the eleventh–twelfth centuries, the cave complex has functioned as a set of image halls. Major renovations and expansions of the complex took place under royal patronage during the twelfth and eighteenth centuries. The thousands of wall paintings that now cover the caves' interior surfaces include depictions of important episodes in Gautama Buddha's life, as well as important events in the history of Sri Lankan Buddhism; most of these paintings date from the eighteenth century.

Indian Buddhist traditions were carried along the great trade network known as the Silk Road from northwest India, through central Asia, and into China, which has the largest collection of Buddhist cave temples in Asia. Several of the most well known of the Chinese cave complexes are found near the ancient city of Dunhuang in Gansu Province, then an important desert outpost situated near the confluence of the northern and southern branches of the Silk Road. In the fourth century CE, a wandering Buddhist monk named Yuezun built a meditation cave at Mogao, which is situated about fifteen miles from Dunhuang. A succession of nearly 500 highly decorated cave constructions followed over the next millennium, built with the patronage of local governors, prominent *sangha* members, and local groups of traders.

Over the course of the 1,000-year period that Mogao was an important Buddhist center, the region came under the domination of several different regional powers, and the interior decorations reflect diverse cultural traditions, including pictorial and sculptural influences from Gandhāra, central Asia, and China. The iconography of the caves also reflects the diversity of Mahāyāna traditions, with images of Maitreya, Amitābha (Pure Land Buddhism), and Tibetan Tantric Buddhas, *bodhisattvas*, and deities abounding. Analysis of the spatial and compositional organization of these cave temples opens a window on to the religious world of medieval China, providing a sense of the numerous levels of religious and secular authority and their relationship to the aspirations of a diverse groups of people, ranging from religious elites engaged in meditation and textual study to itinerant traders seeking the protection of powerful Buddhas and *bodhisattvas* as they faced the perils of the Silk Road. Buddhist tradition, with its doctrines of rebirth and *karma*, brought to China a new understanding of temporality and a new set of powerful religious agents with the power to affect one's future course of life. Within the idealized iconography of the cave temple, the relationship of these agents to one another was visibly displayed, and the ritual means for interacting with them for one's benefit made available.

The cave temples at Mogao gradually lost their patronage and prestige from the fourteenth century onward. The site was largely deserted in the 1890s when a Daoist priest named Wang Yuanlu settled there and began to restore some of the caves. In 1900 he discovered a vast library of Buddhist manuscripts, numbering in the tens of thousands, that had been sealed in a secret chamber to protect them from Arab armies that were sweeping into the region at the beginning of the eleventh century. Word of his discovery gradually made its way to Europeans exploring the region, and much of the contents of the vast library was purchased and taken into European collections; these included Buddhist texts, silk and paper paintings, textiles, and other sorts of documents that have provided considerable insight into the daily life of the time. In 1961 the Chinese government designated Mogao a nationally protected site, and in 1987 it joined the list of World Heritage Sites, which now includes other Chinese Buddhist cave complexes such as Yungang in Shanxi Province, Longmen in Henan Province, and Dazu in Sichuan Province.

See also: **Ajaṇṭā and Ellorā; Angkor; Anurādhapura; Aśoka; Sacred mountains; Sacred places; *Stūpa*.**

KEVIN TRAINOR

CHAN

The history of this school in China is long and complex. The word *chan* is the Chinese rendering of an Indic word for meditation (*dhyāna*), and according to traditional accounts, a lineage of legendary meditation masters existed in India from the time of the Buddha himself. This lineage was established one day when, in the middle of an assembly, the Buddha held up a flower without saying a word. All in the audience were puzzled by this gesture, except for Mahākāśyapa, who understood the meaning and smiled. The

Buddha then confirmed Mahākāśyapa's understanding and publicly "transmitted his *Dharma*" to him. This direct, "mind-to-mind transmission" then passed through twenty-eight generations of "patriarchs" in India, the last of whom, Bodhidharma, traveled to China in 526 CE and became the first of the Chinese patriarchs.

Bodhidharma passed the *Dharma* on to his disciple, Huike (487–593), who is renowned for his dedication and perseverance: when he first approached Bodhidharma for teaching, the latter ignored him and continued his meditation. After standing patiently in the snow for several days, Huike finally cut off his arm and offered it to Bodhidharma as a token of his earnestness. After this, Bodhidharma agreed to teach him. (Other sources say Huike's arm was cut off by bandits.)

In time, Huike, the second Chinese patriarch, transmitted his *Dharma* through three other "patriarchs" to the sixth, Huineng (638–713). Historically, not much is known about Huineng. His name appears on lists of the "ten great disciples" of the fifth Chan patriarch Hongren (601–674). Other than this, sources vary widely as to the details of his life and teaching, rendering an objective biography difficult to construct. However, while he may be historically obscure, the Chan school honors him as the sixth patriarch, the fountainhead of the so-called "Southern school" of Chan, and the main character in the classic, *The Platform Sūtra of the Sixth Patriarch* (Ch. *Liu zu tan jing*).

Huineng is most important within the tradition as the figure who carried on the true teaching and practice of "sudden enlightenment." In the *Platform Sūtra*, there is a famous episode in which Huineng, represented as an illiterate, unordained worker hulling rice in the monastery kitchen, bests Hongren's senior disciple Shenxiu (605?–706) in a poetry contest. Hongren had arranged this contest in order to see who among his disciples was most enlightened and would thus merit designation as his successor and become the sixth patriarch. Shenxiu submitted a verse which speaks of the need to wipe away the dust (representing defilements) that accumulates on the mirror (the mind). Later generations took this as a statement of the "gradual enlightenment" position. Huineng's verse, dictated to a monk and written on a wall, speaks of the ultimate non-existence of both mind and defilements, a view more compatible with the position of "sudden enlightenment." Huineng himself is said to have returned to south China after his training with Hongren at his East Mountain Monastery, was finally ordained a monk, and eventually settled in the Caoxi Temple in Xinzhou.

It is worth examining the positions of "sudden" and "gradual" enlightenment, as they constituted the polarities in a controversy that shook the nascent Chan school during the eighth century. At issue was the question: does one have to work towards enlightenment, gaining it step by step over a period of time, or does it manifest fully developed in an instant? The former position required a long period of study and practice, undergirded by careful observance of moral precepts. The latter rested on the Mahāyāna idea that all dualities are ultimately unreal, including such dyads as ignorance–enlightenment, practice–attainment, and *saṃsāra-nirvāṇa*. Using this critique, proponents of sudden enlightenment asserted that, as there was nowhere to go and nothing to change, enlightenment could occur instantaneously, taking literally no time at all.

In the end, largely resulting from the efforts of Huineng's disciple Shenhui (670–762), the "sudden enlightenment" position came to dominate Chan, and the stories of Huineng transmitted through the *Platform Sūtra* and other sources attained quasi-scriptural status. The result was that subsequent Chan *rhetoric* stressed the immediacy of enlightenment, while in actual *practice* seekers continued to meditate, study, and observe the precepts. In time, every Chan monk and nun came to trace his or her "*Dharma*-lineage" back to Huineng, giving him the status of common ancestor within all subsequent Chan lineages, even for schools founded outside of the "Northern" and "Southern" schools of Shenxiu and Huineng, such as the Oxhead school founded by Farong (594–657).

Other lineages of masters and students emerged between the eighth and tenth centuries. The designation "Five Houses" was given in the tenth century to five early lineages, of which only two, the Caodong and Linji, survived more than a few generations. The term "Five Houses" was first coined by Fayan Wenyi (885–958), founder of the latest of the "houses" to appear.

The five were as follows:

1 Guiyang, named after Mounts Gui and Yang, where its headquarter temples were located. The founder was Guishan Lingyou (771–853).
2 Linji, founded by Linji Yixuan (d. 866).
3 Caodong, named after Mount Dong, home of the founder Dongshan Liangjie (807–69), and Mount Cao, home of his disciple Caoshan Benji (840–901).
4 Yunmen, founded by Yunmen Wenyan (864–949).
5 Fayan, founded by Fayan Wenyi.

The period beginning with Bodhidharma and culminating with the emergence the "Five Houses" is one of transition: while the earlier masters were known as students and teachers of the *Laṅkāvatāra Sūtra*, after the conclusion of the controversy and the acceptance of "sudden enlightenment," the school came to define itself as one that eschewed scriptural study and conventional practices, and attempted to point directly to the mind as the fount of enlightenment.

This iconoclastic self-definition created a problem: If all words and all the usual Buddhist practices are potential objects of clinging, then how should the teachers teach, how should they certify genuine achievement, and how could they distinguish the truly enlightened from the charlatans? This perplexity led to a period of intense experimentation and creativity as teachers sought ways to impart the content of their experience directly to students. Thus, during the late Tang and the Song dynasties (roughly 750–1260), the school entered into a period sometimes described as "the golden age of Chan," where masters employed "shock Chan" techniques to evoke a direct, experiential understanding. These techniques, pioneered by such figures as Mazu Daoyi (709–88), Huangbo (d. 850), and Linji Yixuan (d. 866), included beating with sticks, shouting directly into students' ears, bizarre behavior, and seemingly nonsensical answers to students' questions. Many stories of such masters were recorded in a new genre of literature called "Recorded Sayings" (Ch. *yulu*).

The atmosphere of free experimentation spilled over into the arts. In poetry, Hanshan (seventh or eighth century) represented the free spirit, living apart from normal monastic routines and leaving his poems on trees and rock faces in the mountains. Painters played with more spontaneous, less mannered styles of painting, seeking to manifest the uncalculating, naturally enlightened mind by capturing the essence of their subject with only a few quick, decisive strokes.

In teaching, such creativity and spontaneity was difficult to maintain over the long term, and eventually a way was found to appropriate and institutionalize the methods of "shock Chan." By the late Song, masters began directing students to study and contemplate the stories of masters contained in the "recorded sayings" literature, with a view to placing themselves into the stories and attempting to see directly the mind of the characters depicted therein. As students had success with this technique, the stories that were found most effective were used again and again, and came to be regarded as *gongan* (Jap: *kōan*), or "public cases," and became standardized. These were subsequently anthologized into *gongan* collections such as the *Gateless Barrier* (*Wumen guan*) and the *Blue Cliff Record* (*Biyan lu*). With a *gongan* as the basis of practice, a student might begin by contemplating the entire story, but as he or she delved more deeply into it, concentrate on a so-called "capping phrase" (Ch. *hua tou*), a practice called "contemplating the word" (Ch. *kanhua chan*). This style of Chan was propagated most avidly by the Linji monk Dahui Zonggao (1089–1163).

Other schools, such as the Caodong school, rejected this method, claiming that its emphasis on a formal, goal-oriented practice violated the basic principle of sudden enlightenment, which held that all beings were already perfectly enlightened and liberated just as they were. This school stressed the practice of "silent illumination" (Ch. *mozhao*), in which students simply sat with no goal in mind save to realize their already perfect buddhahood. The Linji school, in turn, criticized this practice for its inertness and quietism.

By the Yuan and Ming dynasties, *gongan* practice had become overly formalized, and critics of the Chan school argued that it mistook witty banter for genuine enlightenment. Practitioners of "silent illumination" came in for criticism on the charge that their practice led to mere laziness and torpor. While a few reformers emerged in the mid-Ming, such as Zipo Zhenke (1543–1603) and Hanshan Deqing (1546–1623), several influential Chan followers, such as the literatus Yuan Hongdao (1568–1610) ultimately rejected it in favor of more serious moral practice or Pure Land Buddhism.

In the modern period, reformers and accomplished masters such as Xuyun (1840–1959) and Laiguo (1881–1953) helped to instill respect for Chan once again, and social trends such as modernization, urbanization, and the general rise in educational levels has given the laity increased time and inclination to take up the practice. In the West, the scene has been dominated by Japanese Zen, but some Chinese Chan masters, such as Shengyan (1930–) and Xingyun (1927–) have developed followings in East Asia, Europe and America.

See also: **Bodhidharma; China, Buddhism in; Dōgen and Sōtōshū; Meditation (Chan/Zen).**

CHARLES B. JONES

CHANTING PRACTICES

Chanting is central to most Buddhist practices and rituals. In addition to conveying religious sentiments and ideas, Buddhist chants are believed able to establish and renew moral discipline, produce enlightenment, ward off obstacles and exorcise demons, bring rain, make deities and *bodhisattvas* appear and/or transfer merit to other beings.

Namaskāra and *stotra*

Buddhist rituals almost invariably begin with some form of chanted salutation (*namaskāra*) to the Buddha or comparable devotional object. The most common Theravāda salutation is "praise to him, the Blessed One, the Worthy One, the Great Enlightened Buddha" (*namo tassa bhagavato arahato sammāsambuddhassa*). More elaborate Pāli and/or Sanskrit eulogistic verses (*stotra*), or their vernacular equivalents, are also commonly encountered in the chanting which accompanies a given Buddhist ceremony. These salutatory chants set a reverential tone, and may be considered meritorious deeds (*puṇyakarma*) and sources of power in their own right. *Namaskāra* is often followed by additional liturgical chants including the Triple Refuge (*triśaraṇa*) and disciplinary formulas (such as the *pañca śīla* and/or *bodhisattva* vows).

Especially in Mahāyāna traditions, *namaskāra* may be directed to a Buddha or *bodhisattva* other than Śākyamuni. *Namaskāra* to Amitābha Buddha (Ch. *Nianfo*, Jap. *Nembutsu*) is the basis for numerous practices and rituals among East Asian Pure Land Buddhists (see separate entry). Praise to the *Lotus Sūtra* (Jap. *namu myōhō renge kyō*) is similarly central to Nichiren practice. In such cases *namaskāra* serves as the very basis of ritual and practice, whether as the source of power to heal, protect and bless, as an object of meditation, or as the key to higher religious attainments such as birth in the Pure Land.

Mantras and *kōans*

Like some forms of *namaskāra*, Buddhist *mantras* can invoke powerful forces (usually identified deities and *bodhisattvas*) in times of need or for general protection and blessing, and can also serve as the focus for meditative practices.

Though *mantras* originated in pre-Buddhist (Vedic) Indian tradition, and some of the *mantras* found in Buddhist texts are clearly Hindu in content, uniquely Buddhist *mantras* also figure significantly, especially in esoteric traditions in Japan and the Tibetan world; Shingon, for example, isolates and elaborates five types of *mantra* recitation. Typically semi-intelligible, secret, and non-grammatical but suggestively guttural and alliterative, *mantras* might be chanted for assistance in crisis, such as the *mantra* "*Oṃ tāre tuttāre ture svāha*" to invoke Tārā; as part of regular daily rituals, such as the *Heart Sūtra mantra* "*gate gate paragate parasaṃgate bodhi svaha*" chanted during morning and evening rituals in Chinese and Taiwanese temples; or perpetually, such as Avalokiteśvara's *mantra* "*Oṃ mani padme hūm*," which is chanted six times daily in some Tibetan monasteries and kept perpetually spinning throughout the universe by means of "prayer wheels" and, more recently, hard disk drives.

Used as meditative devices, *mantras* (or their "seed syllables") are powerful not only in combating worldly problems but also in effecting states of attainment including ultimate liberation. This is one of several ways in which they can fruitfully be compared with the practice of chanting *kōans* in Japanese Zen. Though the *kōan* is literally intelligible its meaning is likewise extra-linguistic, it is typically short and pithy like a *mantra*, and is sometimes recited in meditation, especially on the individualized recommendation of a meditation master.

Sūtra recitation

Because *sūtra* recitation can play a prominent role in healing and protective rites, preaching, *Dharma* study and teaching, devotional practices, and monastic training regimens and daily routines, Buddhists have developed diverse *sūtra* chanting styles and associated practices, including constructing ritual enclosures for *sūtra* chanting, holding massive (traditionally royally funded) recitations of the entire *Tripiṭaka* or corresponding "canonical" collections, having *sūtras* inscribed on stone or canonical manuscripts recopied, and the provision of musical accompaniment (Korean *Pomp'ae* is a fully musical Buddhist chanting tradition). In addition to their intrinsic beauty, Buddhism's unique and varied chanting styles help emphasize particularly significant passages and messages in the *sūtras* being chanted, enhance the devotional atmosphere, and aid memorization.

See also: ***Mantras*, *mudrās*, and *maṇḍalas*; Ritual texts; Rituals and practices; *Sangha*; *Vinaya Piṭaka*.**

JONATHAN S. WALTERS

CHARITY (*DĀNA*)

Charity (*dāna*, cognate with "donate") is first in all the lists of "perfections" which *bodhisattvas* cultivate, and in the Theravāda version of Gautama Buddha's paradigmatic *bodhisattva* path, charity is also the last of the perfections fulfilled. According to the *Jātaka* this achievement occurred during the *bodhisattva*'s penultimate birth when as King Viśvāntara he relinquished his children and wife at a decrepit beggar's request. Among Theravāda Buddhists the wrenching but enormously popular story (Pāli *Vessantara-jātaka*) has served as a central motif for temple arts, dramatic performances, embellished literary and oral traditions, and vernacular idioms and pop songs. Though other Buddhists have privileged different *Jātakas* more in line with the suffering *bodhisattva* ideal, in which his perfection of *dāna* entails giving away his own life – as in the famous story (not found in the Pāli *Jātaka*) of feeding himself to a starving tigress so she can feed her cubs (*Vyāghra-Jātaka*) – the same importance is placed upon charity as the foundation and expression of religious perfection. In addition to the vast wealth he gave away during his previous lives, the Buddha himself is portrayed in all the traditions as the giver of the best charity, the gift of his teachings (*Dharma-dāna*). *Dāna* is first of the four means by which a Buddha or *bodhisattva* is said to attract masses of people to himself (*saṃgraha-vastu*).

Charity was central to Buddhist practice from the very beginning. The earliest texts are replete with stories of laypeople – sometimes beggars but more often kings – providing gifts (*dāna*) to the *sangha*, daily in the form of almsfood and other refreshment, and periodically in the form of robes and other monastic requisites, land and other properties, and service; Buddhist histories narrate royal charity to the religion at length, making *dāna* the very substance of Buddhist kingship. Our earliest hard evidence of Buddhist practice is of charity, namely the *stūpas* and associated ornaments constructed by donors beginning with Emperor Aśoka Maurya but soon coming to include elite ministers, merchants, and kings as well as guilds, families, neighborhoods, and whole towns in various regions, who left stone inscriptions documenting their gifts (an imperial practice which traveled with Buddhism to Sri Lanka, Southeast Asia, and East Asia). Around the time of Aśoka, Buddhists also deepened the early Buddhist justification of charity as a sure way to gain heaven by making heaven just a stop along the way to *nirvāṇa*, the achievement of which, beginning with texts like *Apadāna*, is explicitly linked to charity (or other meritorious deeds) performed during previous lives.

Though in the *Jātakas* the category *dāna* includes any kind of charitable contribution, in the early post-Aśokan inscriptions and parallel texts like *Apadāna* the term comes to denote specifically *Buddhist* charity, and both make clear that as this happened the opportunities for performing it grew increasingly ritualized. The range of Buddhist charitable actions can be explored in three groups: almsgiving practices and rituals, other material charity, and nonmaterial charity.

Almsgiving

Providing basic sustenance for monks and nuns has been the primary form of Buddhist charity from the religion's beginnings, and almsgiving so clearly dominates the category that in many Buddhist languages the term *dāna* always implies almsfood unless some other sort of *dāna* is stipulated. In the descriptions of the Buddha's own almsgathering practices found in the early texts we can see the origins of the rituals of invitation, begging customs, and ceremonial (such as ornamental enclosures, chanting scriptures, preaching, use of images and other ritual objects, processions and drumming) which have characterized almsgiving rituals in the various traditions. The Buddha himself usually went outside the monastery to collect alms (or others having gone brought alms to him), and the practice of wandering alms-begging (Pāli *piṇḍapāta*) survives in pockets around the world, especially in Southeast Asia. *Vinaya* stipulations and local custom dictate the sorts of interactions which occur during *piṇḍapāta*, including rules for greeting, serving, receiving thanks, and hearing sermons. Typically, the recipients of *dāna* remain passive, neither requesting nor refusing what is offered (or not), and in countries such as Thailand where wandering alms-begging (Thai *biṇṭhabat*) is still widely practiced (though monks and nuns tend to have established routes and to know their donors) the transaction is conducted silently and impersonally.

More commonly in other parts of the Buddhist world monks and nuns keep stores of food for preparation in monastic kitchens and/or donors bring alms to their temples or invite them to their homes. From ancient times kings provided favored monks with stores of food, or they or other laity set up charitable funds (Thai *munithi*), precisely so that they would not have to spend time begging, a practice which continues in the Thai king's grants of a monthly allowance (Thai *nittayaphat*) to senior monks. Even in countries where such in-temple almsgiving is the rule, on certain occasions monks may still practice *piṇḍapāta* or ritualized forms thereof, as with some Zen monks who, in groups of three, wander about chanting "*Ho* ... *u*" ("Rain of *Dharma*") for donations of uncooked rice and money (typically, not looking donors in the eye), eight times monthly. By contrast, in Burma only ten-precept-holding women (Burmese *thila-shin*, "nuns") are provided uncooked rice, as opposed to the cooked food provided for monks, as a symbol of their greater self-reliance. In all these instances the underlying principle remains the same, that providing *dāna* to monks and nuns is an especially fruitful opportunity for merit-making and other religious goals; donors must sometimes make "reservations" months in advance in order to gain the opportunity to provide a particular monk or nun alms, perhaps in order to ritually transfer the merit of the *dāna* to deceased relatives on their proper death anniversaries.

Other material charity

Classical texts (for example *Aṅguttara Nikāya* 4.239) provide lists of the eight (sometimes ten) items suitable for *dāna* to monks and nuns, beginning with food but including other sorts of things which are typically provided as *dāna*: water, clothes, vehicles, garlands, scented ointment, conveniences for lying down or dwelling, and lighting. These have been interpreted liberally to embrace a vast range of gifts typically made to the *sangha*: betel leaves and nuts, cigars, cigarettes, sweets, staples, alms-bowls (food); tea, soda, butter, wells and ponds (drinks); robes, sandals, umbrellas (clothes); oxen, bicycles, cars, planes (vehicles); rosaries, flowers, gold ornaments (garlands); medicines, lotions and oils, incense (scented ointment); buildings, couches and chairs, mats, beds, sheets, pillows and pillowcases, kitchen utensils, curtains, gardens, forest groves and agricultural fields, soap and toothpaste (conveniences for sitting and dwelling); ornate lamps, candles, kerosene, electrification (lighting).

Beyond such gifts to individual monks and nuns, *dāna* also includes large-scale, usually corporate (and sometimes state-sponsored) efforts to create and improve institutions belonging to the religion as a whole, such as *stūpas* and other Buddhist monuments, or temples. Fundraising, inauguration and completion, as well as many aspects of the construction itself involve rituals of blessing, worship, protection and/or geomancy, and may be subject to determination of auspicious times, the presence of particular participants such as senior monks or political leaders, and the preferences of donors; these rituals are often celebrated with large festivals that may include speeches, dramas, sporting events, auctions, sermons, meditation practice, and so forth. Beginning with Aśoka Maurya, Buddhists have also variously conceived of public works (roads and bridges, hospitals, forests and parks, charity kitchens, animal preserves, rest-houses for pilgrims, irrigation works, and so on) as falling within the scope of *dāna*; as mentioned, as *bodhisattva* the Buddha performed many sorts of *dāna* which were not specifically Buddhist, from feeding beggars (and tigers!) to creating such public works when born as a king. It should be noted that although monks and nuns do not typically provide *dāna* to other monks and nuns, they have, from an early date, engaged in these sorts of additional material *dāna* practices, as in the Chinese view of the *sangha* as *bei tian* or a "field of compassion" which provides hospitals, soup kitchens and other forms of charity to the poor.

Non-material charity

Though *dāna* generally implies material offerings, in practice the tradition has recognized a variety of non-material forms of *dāna* as well, especially the contribution of human labor (called *śrama-dāna*) for the construction, restoration and improvement of Buddhist monuments (for example, baking or laying bricks for a new *stūpa* or temple or whitewashing or otherwise ornamenting an existing one) or other public works (such as helping to build roads, tanks, and parks, or volunteering one's services to the sick, poor, needy, animals, and so forth). Another especially important non-material type of *dāna* is the *Dharma-dāna* or "gift of truth" mentioned previously; the Buddha's paradigmatic generosity with his teachings is widely praised in Buddhist texts as the most salubrious form of charity, and it has been emulated by preachers across the tradition as a primary way for monks and nuns to further cultivate the perfection of charity (*dāna-pāramitā*).

See also: **Aśoka; *Bodhisattva*; Ethics; *Jātakas* and other narrative collections; Politics; Preaching and *Dharma* transmission; *Stūpa*.**

JONATHAN S. WALTERS

CHINA, BUDDHISM IN

Buddhism has been part of the Chinese religious scene for approximately 2,000 years, and while it has adapted itself well to Chinese culture, it still remains a "foreign religion" in the minds of many Chinese.

The transmission of Buddhism into China: the Han period (1–221)

Buddhism first entered China some time during the first century CE, probably with foreign traders who came into north-western China via the Silk Road or from the maritime route along the southeastern coast. For the first two centuries or so, the Han Chinese people took very little notice of this religion, as it existed within immigrant and trading communities outside the ambit of Chinese culture. It was a foreign religion, which immediately marked it as "barbarian," a derogatory designation that would haunt it for many centuries. In addition, the Eastern Han dynasty (25–221 CE) was, by and large, a period of stability and prosperity, and the Chinese were not seeking new religious ideas; the old Confucian system appeared to be working quite well. For all these reasons, Chinese historians never wrote about Buddhism for its own sake during this time, but only brought it up in passing if it figured in the affairs that interested them. Consequently, historical references to Buddhism are scant.

Nevertheless, the intellectual elites did begin, slowly and reluctantly, to take notice of Buddhism late in this period. As interest grew during the second century, a few monks began to settle in China permanently and, in response to inquiries from Chinese associates, started translating scriptures into Chinese. One of the earliest scriptures in Chinese was the *Sūtra in Forty-two Sections*, a compilation of extracts from various *sūtras*, forming a kind of "reader" or primer. Notable among the earliest known translators were An Shigao (date unknown) and Lokakṣema (second century).

We first find a member of the Chinese elite taking an interest in Buddhism in the year 65 CE, when an imperial edict written with regard to Liu Ying, the king of Chu, mentions that he "recites the subtle words of Huang-Lao (i.e. Daoist scriptures), and respectfully performs the gentle sacrifices to the Buddha." The edict goes on to say that the thirty bolts of silk that Liu Ying had sent to the court should "be sent back in order to contribute to the lavish entertainment of the *upāsakas* (Buddhist laymen) and *śramaṇas* (Buddhist clergy)." While this edict mentions explicitly the king's practice of Buddhism, and recognizes the presence of Buddhist clergy and laity, it is equally clear that Liu Ying's practice of Buddhism consisted mainly of the offering of sacrifices, and was conjoined with Daoist practice. This last point is significant, as we shall shortly see. Otherwise, this remains an isolated narrative; no other reliable historical document of the first two centuries CE even mentions Buddhism.

The period of national disunity (221–581)

With the fall of the Han dynasty in 221 CE and the ensuing fragmentation of the realm into the Three Kingdoms, interest in Buddhism among the Chinese increased. The unstable situation inspired many prominent members of society to withdraw from worldly affairs and seek for new spiritual paths. At the same time, the division of China into kingdoms north and south of the Yangtze River gave Buddhism in these two regions different characters. In the North, greater proximity to India and Central Asia via the Silk Road meant that Buddhism in this region received a greater number of monks and meditation teachers from India, Kashmir, Scythia, Parthia, and the oasis kingdoms lining the Silk Road where it skirted the Taklamakan Desert, and so it tended to emphasize religious practice over textual study. In addition, from the early fourth century to the late sixth, the North was often under non-Chinese rule. These "barbarian" rulers favored Buddhism and many monks served as court advisors, ritual specialists, and thaumaturges, giving Buddhism in the North a more overtly ritual, practical, and political character.

Many of the literati had fled the troubles of the North and migrated to the Southern Kingdoms, bringing with them their emphasis on literary skill. In addition to this, the Northern Kingdoms blocked their access to the living traditions of India and Central Asia, and so the South developed a more literary approach to Buddhist study. During this time, Daoan (312–85) produced the first catalogue of Buddhist scripture, and he and his disciples worked to produce critical editions of scriptures and treatises, identify as "spurious" those that had no available Indic original, and develop principles for translating texts into Chinese. The Kuchean monk-translator Kumārajīva arrived in 402 and, with official support, opened a translation bureau in the North, producing seventy-two translations of Buddhist texts of such quality that many are still considered the standard even after later re-translation. His rendering of Indian *Madhyamaka* texts led to the foundation of the Sanlun (or "Three Treatise") school that specialized in Madhyamaka philosophy. Also, the dissemination of Buddhist texts and teachings among the educated elite, along with the fact that different members of literati families or circles of associates might be involved in different religious paths, led to a prolonged exchange of ideas between Buddhism and Daoism, and Buddhism absorbed and modified many Daoist ideas and terms.

The arrival of Kumārajīva also marked the beginning of a new era in the appropriation of Buddhist thought in China, and to understand this, we must first look at the mixing of Buddhism with Daoism that took place prior to his arrival.

Interactions with Daoism

It must be emphasized that Buddhism came to China from India, a land with a culture and set of languages vastly different from Chinese culture and language. As an essential first step in grasping Buddhist concepts and translating them into the Chinese language, translators looked for points of contact, similarities in thought and expression that could be used as a bridge. The most obvious place to find such equivalences was Daoism, which, like Buddhism, had meditation practices and engaged in metaphysical speculations. As already noted above, the first Chinese figure known to have embraced Buddhism, King Liu Ying, practiced it in conjunction with "Huang-Lao," or Daoist sacrifices and thought inspired by the mythical Yellow Emperor (Huang di) and Laozi, the purported author of the *Daode Jing*, the most basic of Daoist texts.

Translators attempting to render Buddhist thought into Chinese sometimes resorted to a process called "matching meanings" (*geyi*), using pre-existing Chinese religious terms to translate Buddhist ideas. (The other option was not to translate at all, but simply to represent the sounds of the Sanskrit terms by using Chinese characters for their phonetic value rather than their semantic meaning, a process that often made texts nearly unintelligible if too many terms were rendered in this way.) Using this method, translators used the Daoist terms *wu* ("non-being") or *benwu* ("original non-being") as a translation equivalent for the Buddhist term "emptiness." These were misleading, as the Daoist concepts refer to an original state of chaos, or to phenomena in an unmanifest state, and indicate a matrix of potentiality out of which particular phenomena arise. Emptiness, on the other hand, refers to the lack of an abiding essence in living beings and in non-living phenomena. In the case of living beings, it denies the existence of a "soul" or of any constant element at all that always carried over from one life to the next unchanged.

This mistake allowed the Chinese to suppose that a "soul" or a "self" transmigrated as a way of understanding the mechanics of reincarnation, even though Buddhism had from its inception explicitly denied the existence of any such thing. The use of a Daoist term to translated "emptiness" allowed for this error. It was not until Kumārajīva came and explained the matter that the Chinese finally understood the true meaning of the doctrine of emptiness, and how rebirth could take place without the literal transmigration of an abiding self from body to body. Nevertheless, during these four centuries of Buddhist–Daoist interaction, a good deal of Daoist thinking entered into Buddhism, and affected its subsequent development: for example, the idea that all phenomena form a unified, living cosmic entity greatly affected the growth of Tiantai thought. In addition, "root-branch" (*ben-mo*) thinking, which indicated that all apparently unrelated phenomena can be traced down to a single source and therefore can be dealt with in a unified manner, helped shape Chan's teaching of a single practice that would address all problems, however apparently unrelated they may be.

Other significant figures of the Northern and Southern Kingdoms period include Daosheng (360–434) a great textual scholar; Lushan Huiyuan (344–416) and Tanluan (476–542), who helped establish the Pure Land teachings; the Sanlun master Sengzhao (374–414); and the great translator Paramārtha (499–569), whose translations of Indian "mind-only" literature paved the way for the future establishment of the Faxiang school.

The Sui-Tang period (581–907)

General overview

China was reunified by the Sui dynasty in 581 CE, which was quickly toppled by the Tang dynasty in 618. The Tang dynasty held power for almost 300 years, and this period became one of China's golden ages. Buddhism flourished during this period, although it also suffered severe setbacks. Increased affluence and patronage enabled many original thinkers and practitioners to establish schools of Buddhism more in keeping with Chinese cultural and intellectual patterns and less dependent upon pre-existing Indian schools of thought. At the same time, Buddhism made more inroads among the common people, particularly in the form of the Pure Land movement and, to a lesser extent, in Chan.

Prosperity brought its own difficulties. As the numbers of ordained clergy increased, the government became concerned about the revenue and labor pool that would be lost because of the clergy's tax- and labor-exempt status. In addition, even at Buddhism's inception in China some traditional Confucian scholars had decried it as a foreign religion that violated basic Chinese values, especially the loyalty that all citizens owed to the state and the filial piety that sons and daughters owed their parents. Daoists sometimes saw Buddhism as a competitor rather than as an ally. In the past, the government instituted ordination examinations and issued certificates to control the size of the *sangha*, and twice during the Northern and Southern Kingdoms period the state had suppressed Buddhism (in 446 and 574). In the year 845, the Tang court was incited to suppress Buddhism once again, and for three years it pursued a policy of razing monasteries, forcing clergy back into lay life or even killing them, and burning books, images, and properties. Unlike the previous two persecutions, this suppression happened in a unified China and affected all areas to some extent. Scholars formerly thought that this event marked the end of Buddhism's intellectual and cultural dominance, as the *sangha* never recovered its former glory. However, others have pointed out that, according to other indicators such as numbers of monastics and extent of property holdings, Buddhism remained a vital force in Chinese society even after this persecution.

Another significant development during the Sui-Tang period was the adoption of vegetarianism as the norm for both clergy and laity. Even though Buddhism has always regarded all living beings as equal and discouraged the eating of meat, in most Buddhist countries, and during Buddhism's early period in China, most Buddhists still ate meat and ate vegetarian meals only as a special practice at certain times. During the Sui-Tang period, however, vegetarianism became the norm for all clergy, and, to a lesser extent, for laity. Following the teachings of the *Laṅkāvatāra Sūtra*, the prescribed diet eschewed not only meat and wine, but also the "five pungent vegetables." The lists of these five vegetables vary, but always include garlic and onions, which were thought to be too *yang* or "hot" and thus to lead to increased sexual arousal. They were also thought to foul the breath, thus making it difficult to gain an audience for teaching.

Tiantai

The Tiantai school founded during this period represents one of the first truly original schools of Buddhism to emerge in China. This was a school that took its name from the site of its head temple, Mount Tiantai in Zhejiang Province on China's eastern seaboard. The *de facto* founder was the monk Zhiyi (538–97), but tradition regards him as the third patriarch of the school after Huiwen (fl. *c.* 550), and Zhiyi's teacher, the meditation master Huisi (515–77). Tiantai is known for a number of innovative features: its system of doctrinal classification (Ch. *panjiao*), its highly articulated system of meditation, and its doctrine of the Three Truths. As indicated above, this latter development showed an influence of Daoist thought insofar as it represented ultimate truth as a living, organic, dynamic force that operated in the world rather than as a simple statement of the lack of essence in things, as the Sanlun school had taught. Tiantai was also unique in Chinese Buddhism for positing an ultimate reality that contained both pure and impure aspects; ignorance and evil were as much a part of it as purity and truth. According to Zhiyi, even the impure and evil aspects of truth served a function.

Faxiang

The Faxiang school traces its origin to the Indian monk-translator Paramārtha (499–569), who arrived in China in 546. Although he brought and translated many texts with him, he was best known for his teaching of Asaṅga's *Mahāyāna-saṃgraha* (*Compendium of the Mahāyāna*). This text, known in China by its short title *Shelun*, became the focal text for the Shelun school. This text points out that all of the reality that any living being perceives arises from "seeds" implanted in consciousness by the *karma* of past deeds. The world we know, therefore, is an evolution of consciousness.

Later, the great Chinese pilgrim and translator Xuanzang (602?–64) traveled to India and brought back many more Indian *Cittamātra* ("mind-only") texts, and a new school consolidated around him and his new translations, superseding the older Shelun school. However, the school taught the existence of *icchantikas*, those who could never achieve Buddhahood because they lacked the capacity (literally, "seeds") for it. This did not suit the atmosphere of Chinese Buddhism, which believed implicitly in universal salvation, and so the school did not survive past the first generation of Xuanzang's disciples, the best-known of whom was Kuiji (632–82). Even though the school did not survive as an institution, however, its teachings remained a viable subject of study, and it came to prominence again in the twentieth century during the Buddhist "revival" in China because proponents saw its subtle psychology as most compatible with modern scientific thought.

Huayan

The Huayan school derives its name from the scripture that forms its primary object of study, the *Avataṃsaka Sūtra* (Ch. *Huayan jing*), a text that attempts to describe in words the way the world appears to an enlightened mind. The scripture had been known and studied in China at least since the year 420, when Buddhabhadra completed the first translation. Later, a group of scholars gathered around Dushun (557–640) to study the "Chapter on the *Bodhisattva* Grounds" in this translation. Consequently, they were called the *Dilun* ("treatise on the grounds") school, and this is commonly regarded as the forerunner of the Huayan school itself. Dushun's disciple Zhiyan (602–68) also specialized in studying and preaching this *sūtra*. However, the real founder of the Huayan school was Zhiyan's disciple Fazang (643–712), although he is traditionally listed as the school's third patriarch.

Fazang, perhaps because of his Central Asian ancestry, had some facility with Indian languages, and so was called to the capital Chang'an to assist with Xuanzang's translation work. He broke with the latter, and later was asked by Empress Wu Zetian to assist the Indian monk Śikṣānanda with a new translation of the *Avataṃsaka*, which came out in 704. However, it was not Fazang's skill as a translator but his facility in expounding the abstruse philosophy of the *sūtra* in accessible language and appealing metaphors that helped attract imperial patronage and consolidated the school's position and status.

After Fazang, the next patriarch is Chengguan (738–820 or 838). Also versed in Indian languages, Chengguan assisted the monk Prajñā to produce a 40-fascicle version of the last section of the *sūtra*, the *Gaṇḍavyūha*, and his teaching activities and prolific commentaries on the *sūtra* further established the school on a secure basis.

The fifth and last patriarch was Guifeng Zongmi (780–841), also acknowledged as a patriarch in the Chan school. Like his predecessors, he achieved great eminence for his learning and teaching, and served in the imperial court, assuring continued patronage. However, the great persecution of 845 took place four years after his death, and this school, dependent as it was on royal patronage for maintenance of its academic facilities and the upkeep of its masters, perished at that time.

Huayan is widely regarded as the most advanced of all Chinese Buddhist philosophies, because of its doctrine of the interpenetration of all phenomena with each other through a causal nexus in which everything in the cosmos is regarded as the total cause of everything else. Huayan's handling of the questions of the part and the whole, and the many and the one, give it the most unitive vision of reality to be found in any Chinese Buddhist school.

Chan

By this school's own account, a lineage of meditation masters who passed the enlightened mind directly from master to student without verbal teaching existed in India from the time of the Buddha himself. The last of these Indian masters, Bodhidharma, traveled to China in 526 and became the first of the Chinese patriarchs, passing the *Dharma* on to his disciple, Huike (487–593). In time, the *Dharma* was transmitted from Huike, the second Chinese patriarch, to the sixth, Huineng (638–713). Historically, this was a period of transition: while Bodhidharma and his followers were known as scholars of the *Laṅkāvatāra Sūtra*, the school came to define itself in later years as one that eschewed scriptural study and attempted to point directly to the human mind itself as the fount of enlightenment.

In addition to this shift away from literary study, a controversy broke out in the early eighth century over the relationship between practice and enlightenment. In Chan lore, this was epitomized as the struggle between proponents of "gradual enlightenment," represented by Huineng's fellow disciple Shenxiu (605?–706), and "sudden enlightenment," propounded by Huineng himself. "Sudden enlightenment" really meant "instantaneous enlightenment," enlightenment that took literally no time to achieve because to have Buddha-nature, the capacity to achieve Buddhahood, meant that one was already a Buddha just as one was. With nowhere to go and nothing to achieve, the only task for the practitioner was to realize what he or she had been all along;

this could be achieved in a moment. After this view became normative in Chan circles, all conventional practices – scripture chanting, ritual, even meditation itself – came under suspicion of gradualism. When done in quest of enlightenment, they appeared to violate the principle of universal Buddha-nature.

The rejection of written and oral teachings and the acceptance of sudden enlightenment as the orthodox position led to a period of experimentation and creativity as teachers sought for ways to impart the content of their experience directly to students. Thus, during the late Tang and early Song dynasties, the school entered into a period described as "the golden age of Chan," where masters employed "shock" techniques to evoke in their students a direct experience of their innate enlightenment. These techniques, pioneered by such figures as Mazu Daoyi (709–88), Huangbo (d. 850), and Linji Yixuan (d. 866), included beating with sticks, shouting directly into students' ears, bizarre behavior, and nonsensical answers to students' questions. Many stories of such masters were recorded either in a new genre of literature called "Recorded Sayings" of individual masters, or in collections of *gongan* (meaning a legal precedent or case) that recorded individual encounters and dialogues with masters, often recounting an individual's moment of enlightenment.

While the above represents Chan's self-image, it remains the case that in most monasteries designated as "Chan" or "meditation" centers, monks and nuns followed conventional practices and routines, performing devotional services in the morning and evening, chanting scriptures, studying doctrines, and cultivating proper monastic decorum. It is likely that many of the stranger stories of Chan masters remained in memory precisely because they contrasted starkly with ordinary behavior, and served to show that even the most proper clerical conduct and perfect practice of meditation could become objects of clinging to be resisted with occasional skillful violations.

Pure Land

Pure Land Buddhism is also a complex and highly variegated set of schools of thought that are bound by a common belief that devotees must undertake some practice directed at Amitābha, the Buddha of the western direction, either to gain a vision of him or to attain rebirth in his Land of Utmost Bliss (*Sukhāvatī*) after death. The first appearance of Amitābha-centered thought and practice in China came in 179, when Lokakṣema produced a translation of the *Pratyutpanna-samādhi Sūtra*, a work that extolled a type of meditation which would cause all the Buddhas to appear before the practitioner. Based on this text, in the year 402 the monk Lushan Huiyuan (334–416) gathered together a group of 123 clergy and local literati in his Donglin Temple (in modern Jiangxi Province), where they all practiced this visualization of Amitābha together with the intention of gaining rebirth in Sukhāvatī. The group that Huiyuan formed later came to be known as the White Lotus Society (Ch. *Bailian she*), and Huiyuan's name headed the list of Chinese Pure Land patriarchs compiled later.

The appearance of translations of the "Three Pure Land *sūtras*" (The *Longer* and *Shorter Sukhāvatīvyūha Sūtras* and the *Meditation Sūtra*) provided a fuller recounting of the Pure Land mythologem of Amitābha Buddha, his Pure Land, and his vows, providing the basis for new understandings of Pure Land theology and practice. The master Tanluan (476–542) devoted himself to the oral invocation of Amitābha's name as a means of gaining rebirth, based upon the forty-eight vows of the Buddha as recorded in the *Longer Sukhāvatīvyūha Sūtra*, one of which was that, if devotees could not achieve rebirth in his Pure Land by reciting his name ten times, he would not accept Buddhahood. Tanluan also taught others to follow this practice, and so became one of the first popularizers of the method of *nianfo* (Buddha-recitation). Another master, Daochuo (562–645) counseled people to recite the Buddha's name as much as possible as a way of purifying the mind, using beans as counters. He wrote a commentary on the *Meditation Sūtra* called the *Anle ji* (*Collection of Ease and Bliss*) that included a compilation of scriptural passages supporting the efficacy of the practice and defending it against detractors. His disciple Shandao (613–81) also wrote in support of the oral recitation of the Buddha's name and composed a number of liturgical works for societies formed for laypeople to practice together, but he devoted his intellectual energy to composing a commentary on the *Meditation Sūtra*, a work which teaches a complex set of difficult visualizations as a means of attaining a vision of Amitābha in this life, and advocated "auxiliary practices" to be done in combination with the "true practice" of chanting the name. These three masters and their successors formed the leadership for a Pure Land movement concentrated in north China.

During the Song dynasty, monks associated with the Tiantai school began recruiting laypeople into large-scale societies for organized liturgies of reciting the Buddha's name, and the practice of gathering people together for Buddha-recitation retreats remains common to this day. The practice of Pure Land became widespread during later times with the encouragement and writings of later "patriarchs" such as Yunqi Zhuhong (1535–1615), Ouyi Zhixu (1599–1655), Chewu (1741–1810), and Yinguang (1861–1940). Under their hands, the emphasis of the practice changed from a means of gaining a vision of the Buddhas to a way of invoking the "other-power" of Amitābha so that he would meet one at the time of death and conduct one to the Pure Land. This rationale for practice was reinforced by compilations of "rebirth stories" that recounted the death scenes of devotees and gave evidence that they had indeed reached the Pure Land. It is no longer a "school," but simply a practice available to any Chinese Buddhist, and most resort to it as a sort of "safety net" regardless of any other practice or branch of learning they may pursue.

School of the Three Stages

The school of the Three Stages was established during the Sui dynasty by the monk Xinxing (540–94), and took as its basic theory that Buddhist practitioners were divided into three levels or stages: those who could grasp the ultimate teaching of the One Vehicle, those who could grasp the lower teaching of the Three Vehicles, and those who in ignorance could not grasp any teaching with accuracy. Believing all people to be in the third category, they declared all teaching and practice futile. However, they also believed in the presence of Buddha-nature in all things, giving the world a pervasive sanctity along with its pervasive degeneracy. As a sign of this universality of Buddha-nature, they would prostrate before all people and other beings to honor them as Buddhas.

Esoteric Buddhism

"Esoteric Buddhism" is a general term for certain Buddhist schools and practices originally derived from or influenced by Hindu tantric practices. Rendered into Chinese as either *Mizong* ("secret school") or *Zhenyan zong* ("*mantra* school"), it imported Tantric Buddhism from India and adapted it for the temperament and mores of Chinese culture. A nascent school can be detected as far back as the third century, but the main transmission of the school into China began with the arrival of the India monks Śubākarasiṃha (637–735), Vajrabodhi (671?–741), and Amoghavajra (705–74) at the capital in the eighth century.

Entrance into this school required a ritual initiation at the hands of a master in a recognized lineage of masters and disciples and empowerment by a divine guardian. Once empowered, the practitioner then took part in rituals that involved ritual gestures (*mūdrās*), verbal formulas (*mantras*) frequently rendered in a modified Sanskrit and unintelligible to the listener, and mental visualizations of Buddhas and *bodhisattvas*. The effects of these rituals included not only the attainment of Buddhahood, but also this-worldly effects such as rainmaking and healing. However, because of the expense of building the elaborate ritual spaces and obtaining ritual texts, vestments, and implements, the school was never large, and was confined mostly to the capital. Simplified elements of its practices persist to the present in Chinese Buddhist rituals and devotional services.

The Song and Yuan periods (960–1344)

After the Tang, the intellectual vigor of Buddhism was eclipsed by the rise of Neo-Confucianism in the Song dynasty. Nevertheless, there were significant figures and movements during this time. Many figures worked to reconcile the very different outlooks and methods of the Chan and Pure Land schools, notably Yongming Yanshou (904–75). As noted above, this was also the period during which many Tiantai monks such as Siming Zhili (960–1028) established lay societies for the propagation of Pure Land practices.

The Ming and Qing periods (1344–1911)

Buddhism saw something of a revival during the latter half of the Ming dynasty, a development that has sometimes been attributed to the rapid expansion of the civil service examination system. During this time, millions of young Chinese men worked relentlessly to prepare for an examination that only 1 or 2 per cent could pass, which left an oversupply of disaffected but highly literate men in society who turned their intellectual energies to Buddhism as an alternative to the Confucian system that had let them down. Many of them turned to Chan thought and practice, attracted by its radical relativizing of the present world and society. Monastic leaders who came forward to fuel this revival included Zhuhong (1532–1612), Zhenke (1543–1603), Hanshan Deqing (1546–1623), and Ouyi Zhixu (1599–1655). The layman Li Zhi (1527–1602) and other literati focused on artistic pursuits such as poetry and painting while discussing Chan philosophy over wine; some of the more extreme were identified as propounding "crazy Chan" (*kuang chan*).

Pure Land experienced a revival at this time as well. As noted above, Yunqi Zhuhong and Ouyi Zhixu led the revival, and the layman and literatus Yuan Hongdao (1568–1610) synthesized Pure Land and Huayan thought in his *Xifang helun* (*Comprehensive Treatise on the West*). Many at this time also attempted to reconcile Chan practice with its reliance on individual accomplishments, and Pure Land with its stress on Amitābha's "other-power." These attempts were not always successful, and some level of tension between the two persists to this day.

From the Ming to the Qing dynasty, Buddhism stagnated (although it remained strong in the central eastern seaboard) until the end of the nineteenth century, when there was another revival of interest in it as a potential part of the Chinese heritage that could be brought out to counter Western culture's claims of superiority. During the early years of the twentieth century, figures such as Ouyang

Jingwu (1871–1943) and the monk Taixu (1889–1947) sponsored new editions of the scripture and advocated a modernized educational system that would bring Buddhism into alignment with modern currents of thought.

The modern period (1911–present)

During the early Republican period (1912–49), many secular modernizers pushed measures through the government to confiscate the properties of "backward" Buddhism for use as schools or government buildings, and Buddhists organized to resist. While they had some success on this front, the constant war caused the government to reverse its long-standing exemption of Buddhist monks from military service, and many were taken from the monasteries and put into uniform. The Communist victory in 1949 cut short the revival of Buddhism, as the new regime tried to undercut all societal support for religion in general. The Cultural Revolution proved a catastrophe for Buddhism during the 1960s and 1970s, as Red Guards destroyed many temples and treasures, and clergy were forced to return to lay status and submit to re-education. However, after the death of Communist leader Mao Zedong in 1976 and the passing of many of his allies, the government has grown more tolerant, and many monasteries are back in operation. Currently, the Chinese Buddhist Association (Zhongguo Fojiao Xiehui) is a thriving organization, and Chinese universities sponsor the academic study of Buddhism. To what extent Buddhism will recover from the setbacks of the Mao era still remains to be seen.

Chinese Buddhism has also grown in places outside of mainland China such as Taiwan, Singapore, Hong Kong, and Malaysia, and has increasingly been exported to Western countries, although it still lags far behind Tibetan, Southeast Asian, and Japanese Buddhism in popularity in those places. Meanwhile, modernizing movements have begun placing less emphasis on escape from the world and more on this-worldly activities. Going under the name "Humanistic Buddhism" or "Engaged Buddhism" (Ch. *renjian fojiao*), these movements advocate for women's issues, environmental protection, and social justice on Buddhist grounds, even as more traditional practices and goals endure side-by-side with them.

See also: **Chan; China, early schools; Faxiang; Huayan; Huineng; Kumārajīva; Lushan Huiyuan; Lüzong; Pure Land school, China; Tiantai; Zhenyan Zong; Zhiyi.**

CHARLES B. JONES

CHINA, EARLY SCHOOLS

Buddhism entered China some time around the turn of the first millennium CE. However, the Chinese at first had only a rudimentary idea of its teachings. The time between Buddhism's inception in China during the Han dynasty and its full flowering during the Tang (618–907) was a time of exploration and learning, during which Chinese and immigrant thinkers translated texts and debated their meaning. Several schools appeared at this time, which we must understand as relatively small groups of masters and students who concentrated their efforts either on a single text or set of texts, or on the teachings of a particular school of Indian Buddhism.

Satyasiddhi (Ch. *Chengshi zong*)

This school took as its focus the text *Satyasiddhi Śāstra* (Ch.: *Chengshi lun*) written by the third-century Indian sage Harivarman and translated by Kumārajīva (343–413). Harivarman had sought to establish the emptiness of both persons and phenomena by analyzing both into smaller and smaller building blocks, until at the end only eighty-four elements remained. Such analysis would show the constructed nature of all objects thus devaluing them and reducing grasping; this would lead to *nirvāṇa*. This school was very small, and was soon superseded by the Sanlun school, whose reasoning was more theoretically rigorous and less dependent on such analytical thought experiments.

Sanlun

This school's name means "Three Treatises," and indicates its focus on three works devoted to *Madhyamaka* philosophy that had recently been translated by Kumārajīva: the *Zhong lun* (*Treatise on the Middle [Way]*) and the *Bailun* (*Treatise in One Hundred [Verses]*), both by Nāgārjuna (second century CE), and the *Shi'er men lun* (*Treatise on the Twelve Gates*) by his disciple Āryadeva. The primary teaching of these works had to do with the doctrine of Two Truths: the Conventional or Worldly Truth, and the Absolute Truth. The first represented the way in which unenlightened beings perceived the world from their own particular subjective angles in a way that, while true, was limited and partial. The second was the truth as seen by an enlightened mind, which could see the self and the world as they were in themselves, apart from all subjective viewpoints and conditions.

After Kumārajīva's death, the main proponent of the school was his disciple Sengzhao (374–414). Sengzhao digested the complex and foreign thought of the three Indian treatises into a more native idiom in his brief works *The Immutability of Things*, *The Emptiness of the Unreal*, and *Prajñā is not Knowledge*. In these works he criticized commonly held ideas about the way in which things exist, the sequence of events in time (particularly causes and effects), and conventional knowledge as lacking in profound wisdom.

After Sengzhao, the main transmission of the Sanlun teachings passed through a line of disciples that included Senglang, Sengquan, and Falang (507–81). The school, never large, found it difficult to gain acceptance for its critique of reality, which appeared overly negative to the Chinese. Toward the end of Falang's life, Zhiyi (538–97) was having success in propagating his new Tiantai teachings which, among other things, analyzed the final nature of reality not as a static "emptiness," but as living mind that he designated "Middle-way Buddha-nature." Under this name, Zhiyi could speak of truth as a dynamic power in the world revealing the marvelous nature of things.

Responding to this competition, the last great Sanlun master, Jizang (549–643), brought innovative new ideas into the school's teaching. He analyzed the traditional Two Truths of Sanlun into three levels. Where there was originally (1) the Worldly Truth of Being countered by the Absolute Truth of non-being or emptiness, Jizang took two further steps. (2) Where a Worldly version of the Two Truths could affirm either being or non-being, the next level of Absolute Truth critiqued both being and non-being as artificial constructs. (3) Finally, where a Worldly Truth might affirm or criticize both being and non-being, Absolute Truth would neither affirm nor deny either being or non-being. Thus, the Two Truths constantly led the believer into ever-greater depths of realization in a dynamic process that might have rivaled that of the Tiantai system. However, in the end, Tiantai won out, and the Sanlun school slipped into oblivion.

Nirvāṇa school

This school focused its attention and study on the *Mahāparinirvāṇa Sūtra*, first translated into Chinese in the early fifth century. This scripture had particular interest as it presented teachings given by the Buddha on his deathbed, and was thus thought to represent his final word. Three translations of this *sūtra* exist in the Chinese canon, and controversies surrounding the first and second of these played a role in the establishment of this school. The first, translated in 418 by Faxian (fourth to fifth centuries) and Buddhabhadra (359–429), included material that appeared to support the view that beings called *icchantikas* lacked Buddha-nature, the potential for Buddhahood, and thus were doomed to *saṃsāra* for ever. Daosheng (360–434), a prominent monk who worked with Kumārajīva in the capital, felt strongly that such a teaching violated the spirit of Mahāyāna Buddhism and publicly stated that this translation must be incomplete. For daring to contradict scripture, he was denounced and left the capital, convinced that he would eventually be vindicated. In 422, another, longer translation by Dharmarakṣa (385–433) appeared which showed that the earlier translation had indeed been incomplete, and contained a clear statement that *all* beings possessed Buddha-nature. Daosheng returned to his teaching post with renewed prestige.

The *Nirvāṇa* school emphasized what it understood to be the scripture's central teachings: (1) *Nirvāṇa* is not annihilation but an eternal and joyous state. (2) All beings have Buddha-nature and are capable of attaining *nirvāṇa*. (3) This Buddha-nature is not only the potential for Buddhahood, but identical with emptiness. This removed this term's negative connotations and provided a more positive vision of the true nature of things. (4) As the ultimate nature of things is undivided and without characteristics that one could grasp, then the wisdom that realizes this must arise and comprehend it, not in a piecemeal fashion, but all at once. (5) Although living beings have no self that travels through *saṃsāra* and is the subject of suffering, this does not mean that there is no self that realizes wisdom and *nirvāṇa*; rather, wisdom reveals Buddha-nature as the true self beyond ignorance and suffering.

These teachings and this text gained popularity because of the controversy surrounding Daosheng, and because of Dharmarakṣa's efforts in promoting his translation. His student Daolang (date unknown) composed a commentary explaining further the identity between Buddha-nature and emptiness, thus helping spread the notion that truth is an active force working in the world, and not just a static idea about the nature of reality. Another group of monks and laymen, acting under orders of King Wen of the Liu-Song dynasty (r. 424–53) took the previous two translations and collated their contents, adding polish to the text and rationalizing its section headings to produce the "Southern Text."

The *Nirvāṇa* school, however, never had an institutional structure or identity. Rather, it existed as a lineage of masters and students devoted to the study and propagation of one text. These lineages came to an end with the founding of the Tiantai school, which subsumed study of the *Mahāparinirvāṇa Sūtra* by placing this text alongside the *Lotus Sūtra* as the highest expressions of Buddhist truth.

School of the Three Stages (Ch. *Sanjie jiao*)

This school was established by the monk Xinxing (540–94). Based on his interpretation of the *Lotus Sūtra*, he taught that living beings were divided into three categories according to their capacities. The first and highest group could grasp the unified teaching of the One Vehicle, the second the teaching of the Three Vehicles (separate teachings for *śrāvakas*, *pratyekabuddhas*, and *bodhisattvas*), while the third, comprising the majority of beings, had no ability to distinguish truth from delusion. Xinxing believed that all people belonged to this third group, and so his followers did not live in monasteries or perform the usual practices, as they felt such efforts would be futile. Instead, they lived in courtyards and outbuildings and circulated among the people, maintaining a strict discipline to purify themselves. They also believed that Buddha-nature was present in all things, giving the world a pervasive sanctity along with its pervasive degeneracy. In recognition of this universal Buddha-nature, they prostrated before all people and other beings to honor them as Buddhas.

During the seventh century, their advocacy of almsgiving led to the establishment of the Inexhaustible Treasury at the Huadu Temple in Chang'an, which functioned as a lending institution. As alms came in, its wealth grew until it alarmed the imperial court. This, plus its claims regarding the depravity of the age and the illegitimacy of the ruling authorities, finally induced the court to ban the school and seize its assets in 713.

Dilun school

This school took its name from the conventional short title of the Buddhist text upon which it concentrated. The full title is *Shi di jing lun* (*Treatise on the Scripture of the Ten Grounds*), a work by the Indian scholar Vasubandhu (fourth century). This text aroused considerable interest among Chinese Buddhists, and also directed their attention to Buddhabhadra's translation of the *Avataṃsaka Sūtra* (Ch. *Huayan jing*), as the *Dilun* provided commentary on the eighth fascicle of this work, which contained a discussion of the ten stages through which a *bodhisattva* passes on the way to Buddhahood. Thus, *Dilun* scholars generally were familiar with the *Huayan Sūtra* as well. During the Tang dynasty, when the Huayan school was established on the basis of the *Huayan Sūtra*, it quickly absorbed *Dilun* scholars into its fold.

Shelun school

This school was closely connected with the Indian monk and translator Paramārtha (499–569), who arrived in China in 546 bearing many scriptures. He resided in China during a particularly turbulent time in its history, which forced him to move frequently. Nevertheless, he managed to produce sixty-four works in 278 fascicles. In particular, he emphasized the translation and study of Consciousness-only texts, of which the most important was his translation of the *Mahāyānasaṃgraha* by Asaṅga. Known in China by its abbreviated title *Shelun*, it had already been translated by Buddhabhanta, but Paramārtha's translation was easier to read and more complete. The Shelun school gathered around Paramārtha to study this text, but by the next century the Chinese monk-pilgrim Xuanzang (*c.* 596–664) produced translations of other Consciousness-only texts, and his Faxiang school absorbed the students of the Shelun school.

See also: **China, Buddhism in; Kumārajīva; Madhyamaka school.**

CHARLES B. JONES

CHINUL

Pojo Chinul (1158–1210), with the epithet Moguja, played a significant role in revitalizing Sŏn Buddhism in the twelfth century and was one of most important figures in Korean Sŏn Buddhism. According to Chinul's stele, the major source of information on his life, he joined a monastery at the age of eight (1165). Chinul mainly trained himself without noticeably influential mentors until the age of twenty-five (1182), at which time he passed the government examination for monks. Instead of taking a governmental post, Chinul continued his own practice. He moved between several different monasteries and finally settled down at the Songgwang monastery in 1200 where he trained disciples, gave *Dharma* talks, and wrote on Buddhism until his death.

Chinul's Buddhism developed around the core Chan doctrine that the mind is the Buddha. The doctrinal foundation of Chan Buddhism claims that everyone already has an innate Buddha nature. To Chinul, this original mind is pure and clear. The mind recaptures self-nature through introspection, which Chinul described as "observing the radiance" (Kor. *kwanjo*). This task of looking within one's mind to locate the source of one's own awakening constitutes the core of Chinul's Buddhist thought. In his *Kwŏnsu chŏnghye kyŏlsa mun* (*Encouragement to Practice: the Compact of Samādhi and Prajñā Community*), written for the establishment of the Compact of Samādhi and Prajñā Community in 1190, Chinul attempted to correct his contemporaries' idea that Buddhahood can no longer be attained at the age of the end of *Dharma*. Chinul argued that none of the Buddhist *sūtras* confirmed such an idea. He asserted that one's own mind is the source of awakening. Chinul further emphasized that awakening is possible by upholding the conviction that one's own nature is originally clear, thus enabling the removal of defiled thoughts through the equal practice of *samādhi* and *prajñā*.

In *Susim kyŏl* (*Secrets of Cultivating the Mind*, *c*. 1203–5), Chinul repeated his view that the mind is the Buddha. Here he contends that observing precepts or memorizing entire Buddhist *sūtras* will not help attain Buddhahood if done without the acknowledgement that the body of a sentient being is equipped with the Buddha nature. In this text, Chinul reveals his stance in Sŏn soteriology through his explanation of "sudden awakening followed by gradual cultivation." The fact that no Buddhahood exists outside the mind makes possible sudden enlightenment, whereas the habit of sentient beings distinguishing themselves from the Buddha necessitates gradual cultivation. Following the sudden awakening in which the identity between sentient being and Buddha becomes clear, gradual cultivation continues until one completely embodies the fact that the quiet and empty mind is the nature of both sentient beings and the Buddha.

Chinul's exploration of the mind continues in his *Chinsim chiksŏl* (*Straight Talk on the True Mind*, *c*. 1205) where he argued that there is no other *Dharma* or teaching than seeing through one's own mind. In the section "Right Faith in the True Mind," Chinul explains the distinction between the scholastic school and the meditational school with regard to their respective views on faith. Faith in the former lies in causation, whereas faith in the latter lies in the belief that one is originally the Buddha. The nature of the true mind, however, transcends causation; its essence is the Buddha nature in each sentient being, and all the activities of daily life reveal its function.

Chinul found the philosophical foundation of his ideas about enlightenment and the true mind in every sentient being in the Hwaŏm Buddhist theory of "Nature Origination." In his posthumous work, *Wŏndon sŏngbul ron* (*Treatise on the Complete and Sudden Attainment of Buddhahood*), Chinul interpreted "Nature Origination" as it was presented in the "Appearance of the *Tathāgatas*" chapter of the *Huayan jing*. Here he sided with the lay Buddhist scholar in Tang China, Li Tongxuan (635–730), and disagreed with Fazang (643–712), the designated third Patriarch of Huayan Buddhism. Chinul argued that Fazang's approach to the teachings in the *Huayan jing* according to ten different levels suggests that Fazang lacked faith in the intrinsic identity between sentient beings and the Buddha. Unlike Fazang, Li understood "Nature Origination" as the revelation of the "Buddha of the Unmoving Wisdom" (Kor. *pudongji pul*), with which every sentient being is equipped. The "Buddha of the Unmoving Wisdom" is also described as the original wisdom of universal bright light (Kor. *kŭnbon po'gwangmyŏngji*), which Chinul identified with the true nature of sentient beings. As every sentient being already has this wisdom, characterized by its simultaneously empty, calm, and alert nature, enlightenment is sudden.

In *Kanhwa kyŏrŭi ron* (*Treatise on Resolving Doubts about Hwadu Meditation*), another posthumous work, Chinul proffered Kanhwa Sŏn as the best way to realize this "Original Wisdom of Universal Light." Quoting Dahui Zonggao's (1089–1163) teaching on Kanhua Chan, Chinul clarifies the difference between Hwaŏm's and Sŏn's actualization of the Buddha nature. From the perspective of those who have attained awakening, both the Buddha and sentient beings are the "Buddha of the Unmoving Wisdom"; from the position of sentient beings, however, the difference between the Buddha and sentient beings needs to be emphasized. Hence, in *Wŏndon sŏngbul ron*, the radical sameness between the Buddha and the sentient being is confirmed, whereas in *Kanhwa kyŏrŭi ron*, the reality of sentient beings, who still failed to look within themselves to realize the relationship between themselves and the Buddha, is foregrounded. Here Chinul urged Sŏn practitioners of his time to grasp these differences through the practice of *hwadu* (critical phrase) meditation. Following Dahui, Chinul distinguishes between the practice of "live words" (Kor. *hwalgu*; Ch. *huoju*), which is a nondualistic embodiment of reality, and that of "dead words" (Kor. *sa'gu*; Ch. *siju*), which is a dualistic speculative approach to Buddhist teaching. Chinul endorsed the practice of live words as the fastest way to attain awakening, but reserved it for those who demonstrated a high maturity level in their practice.

In bringing together Hwaŏm philosophy and Sŏn meditation, Chinul was much influenced by Guifeng Zongmi (780–841), who was himself both a patriarch of the Heze Chan tradition and the fifth patriarch of Huayan Buddhism. Composed less than a year before his death, the *Pŏpchip pŏrhaeng rok chŏryo pyŏngip saki* (*Excerpts from the Dharma Collection and Special Practice Record with Personal Notes*, 1209) is Chinul's most scholarly work. It comments on the excerpts of Zongmi's *Dharma Collection* and expounds Chinul's views on the different Chan schools in China, including his idea on the relation between Hawŏm and Sŏn Buddhism, and his theory of sudden awakening followed by gradual cultivation.

Chinul's Buddhism has been frequently characterized with the three phrases found on his stele: the gate of equal practice of *samādhi* and *prajñā*; the gate of complete and sudden awakening based on faith and understanding; and the gate of the short-cut approach of *hwadu* meditation. These three aspects of Chinul's Buddhism are also explained in line with the three awakening experiences Chinul experienced between 1182 and 1198. The first took place in 1182 at the Chŏngwŏn monastery as he read a passage in Huineng's *Platform Sūtra of the Sixth Patriarch*. This passage stated that, as the self-nature of suchness gave rise to thoughts, even though our six sense organs encountered various forms of outside worlds, the nature of the true suchness was always self-reliant. This passage provided the foundation for Chinul's constant emphasis on the true mind, and for his encouragement of being awakened to the nature of one's mind. The occasion for the second awakening occurred when Chinul was exposed to Li Tongxuan's *Huayan lun* (*Expositions on the Flower Garland Sūtra*) in 1185 at the Pomun monastery. In the "Appearance of the *Tathāgatas*" chapter, a passage states that a particle of dust contains 1,000 volumes of *sūtras*. In the *Expositions*, Li explains that the body of sentient beings is originally the Buddha of Unmoving Wisdom, which provided Chinul with the intrinsic connection between scriptural Buddhism and Sŏn practice. The third awakening took place in 1198 while he was in retreat at the Sangmuju hermitage. A passage from the *Dahui yulu* (*Records of Dahui*) touched Chinul's mind. The passage states that Sŏn does not exist separately from our daily existence: one cannot find Sŏn in a quiet place, in a bustle, nor in speculations; however, one cannot find Sŏn separate from them either.

During the 1990s, T'oe'ong Sŏngch'ŏl (1912–93) asserted the sudden awakening followed by sudden cultivation as an authentic form of Sŏn practice, criticizing Chinul's position of sudden awakening followed by gradual practice. Sŏngch'ŏl's claim kindled a debate on the nature of Sŏn enlightenment in Chinul's and Sŏngch'ŏl's Buddhism known as the subitist–gradualist debate.

By demonstrating Hwaŏm Buddhism as a theoretical ground of Sŏn Buddhist thought, Chinul provided a philosophical foundation for Sŏn Buddhism, which since then has become a major host to the development of the rapport between scholastic and meditational schools in Korean Buddhism. Through the compact community movement, the first religious society in the history of Korean Buddhism, Chinul also provided mental and physical space for collective Sŏn practice. By introducing and endorsing Kanhwa Sŏn, Chinul had managed to set the foundation of the Korean form of Sŏn practice that continues until today.

See also: **Korea, Buddhism in.**

JIN Y. PARK

CHÖDRÖN, PEMA

Pema Chödrön is a teacher in the Karma Kagyu school of Vajrayāna (Tantric) Buddhism. She was a student of the late Chögyam Trungpa Rinpoche until his death in 1987. Her current teachers are the head of the Shambhala organization, Sakyong Miphram Rinpoche (Trungpa's son and lineage holder) and Dzigar Kangtrul Rinpoche. Pema Chödrön is the former director and current resident teacher at Gampo Abbey, a monastery on Cape Breton Island, Nova Scotia, Canada, that focuses on reinterpreting Buddhist teachings and monastic practice for Western needs. She travels extensively and her teachings appear widely in books and popular Buddhist magazines such as *Tricycle* and *Shambhala Sun*.

Born Deidre Blomfield-Brown in 1936 in New York City, Pema Chödrön was one of the first American-born women to become a fully ordained nun (*bhikṣuṇī*). In her thirties, after the failure of her second marriage, she began a spiritual quest to help her deal with the anger and disappointment in her life. She came across an article by Trungpa Rinpoche on dealing with negative emotions, and while on a trip to Europe she met Lama Chime Rinpoche with whom she studied for several years. Lama Chime encouraged her to work with Trungpa, whom she met in 1972. After taking the novice initiation from the Sixteenth Gyalwa Karmapa in 1974, she became Trungpa's student. The Vajrayāna tradition does not confer full ordination on women and so, encouraged by her teachers, she took full ordination in Hong Kong in 1981.

When the decision was made to move Shambhala headquarters to Nova Scotia and build a monastery there, Pema Chödrön was named by Trungpa as its first director. Prior to this, she had been the co-director of the Karma Dzong meditation center in Boulder, Colorado. Organizational chaos and scandal erupted within the community in the late 1980s and early 1990s until Miphram Rinpoche was appointed as the new head/protector (Sakyong) by senior lineage holders in both the Nyingma and Kagyu schools.

Throughout this period of intense turmoil, Chödrön was perceived both within and outside the organization as a calm, grounded and respected monastic presence.

While Chödrön is undoubtedly an able administrator and disciplined monastic, it is her role as a teacher that accounts for her public prominence. To date, she is the author of seven books: *The Wisdom of No Escape* (1991), *Start Where You Are* (1994), *Awakening Loving-Kindness* (1996), *When Things Fall Apart* (1997), *The Places That Scare You* (2001), *Comfortable with Uncertainty* (2003) and *Shantideva's The Way of the Bodhisattva* (2005); as well as several audio collections: *Pure Meditation* (2000), *Good Medicine* (2001), *Compassion Box and the Pema Chödrön Collection* (2004).

Chödön's focus is on the daily struggles of modern life experienced by her Western lay audience. She follows the traditional pattern of Buddhist teaching, beginning with an analysis of suffering. This analysis is centered on the individual suffering wrought by the frustrations of modern life: alienation, disorientation, fear, depression, etc.; and their social consequences: alcoholism, violence, dysfunctional relationships with others, and mental and physical illnesses. In *The Places That Scare You* she refers to our bondage to the "three lords of materialism" that cause us to misuse substances to run away from insecurity and pain and seek "special" states of mind through drugs, sports, and spiritual practices as well. Our certainty that we know reality, an illusion, causes further pain. We cling to our "selves," ideas and opinions, practices, and thus become isolated from others. Our root bondage and addiction however, is ego-clinging and it is from this that suffering emerges. Hope lies in the recognition that our true nature is one of openness and compassion and that we are connected to others. We discover this nature through connecting with our underlying energy, the source of our wisdom.

The specific means to connect with our true nature, to become enlightened, is through training the mind (*lojong*) and developing compassion through taking upon ourselves the pain of others and emitting positive energy into the world in its stead (*tonglen*). There are seven steps to the mind training, synthesized in a series of "slogans." They are designed to clear the mind of illusion, connect with the underlying energy that sustains all things, and produce an awareness of emptiness. *Tonglen* practice develops one's compassion. These practices work in concert to produce an individual who is open to the world, able to sustain themselves and others.

While Chödrön follows the traditional teaching pattern in Buddhism (stating the problem, the origin of it, the fact that it can be solved and the program to solve it) and technical terms such as *lojong* and *tonglen* do arise in her teaching, the fact that the focus audience is Western requires a style of teaching that fits her audience. Her style is relaxed and peppered with personal anecdotes. She laughs often in interviews. She frequently uses the term "we" indicating a connection with her audience. She is often "in conversation" with others, bell hooks and Alice Walker, for example, which also conveys a sense of intimacy with her audience. Like most Western teachers, she draws in material from other traditions and uses insights drawn from outside the Buddhist tradition as well. Her authority to teach is conveyed in a variety of ways, from the formal (robes and shaved head, references to her teacher, her position as resident teacher at Gampo Abbey) to the informal (her life experience and personal demeanor).

The message itself is presented primarily in Western, humanistic prose and focuses on practical matters. How do we apply teaching and practice to everyday life? Ironically, one begins with the self. Our original nature is enlightenment.

Thus, as Chödrön notes in *Start Where You Are*, we already have the wisdom and compassion necessary to heal ourselves. The practices are designed to develop in us a level of trust that this is so and transform us into a person of *bodhicitta* – that is, an individual who is compassionate, has clarity of sight, and is open. And we start where we are.

Three techniques guide us in confronting the daily joys and sorrows of life ("Don't Give Up"): Examine whatever happens in life in a non-judgmental manner; see the "poisons" of life (lust, hatred, and so on) as "medicine" (wisdom in disguise) and tap into their energy through "relaxing in the moment." Discussed in "Good Medicine for This World," this appears to mean fully experiencing joy and sorrow, taking in the painful and transforming it into the positive. Finally, one should see whatever arises as enlightened wisdom. This is the Buddhist insight of seeing and accepting that both joy and sorrow are a natural part of life. Heaven and hell are in the perception of them.

Chödrön's importance within Shambhala and the popularity of her teachings ensure that she will continue to make an important contribution to the Westernization of Buddhism.

See also: **Women in Buddhism: an historical and textual overview.**

MAVIS L. FENN

CHRONICLES AND PILGRIMAGE RECORDS

Sri Lanka

The Sri Lankan chronicles (*vaṃsa*) and pilgrims' accounts of their travels provide historical information about the development of Buddhism in India and neighboring regions. The *Island Chronicle (Dīpavaṃsa)* was compiled around the fourth century CE; the *Great Chronicle (Mahāvaṃsa)* begins with the fourth century and ends with fall of Śri Vikramarājasiṃha, last king to rule Kandy (1798–1815). Chinese and Tibetan pilgrims followed the trade routes to India, visited its sacred sites, and collected texts, which they brought back to their homelands. Faxian (334–420) wrote the first account of a pilgrimage to India, *Foguo ji* (*An Account of Buddhist Kingdoms*) and a Tibetan monk, known by his Sanskrit name Dharmaśvamin (1197–1264), the last, *Itinerary to India* (*Rrgya gar lam yig*).

Theravāda chronicles record the merit Buddhist kings acquire through their support of Buddhism. The *Island Chronicle* narrates Sri Lankan history from the legendary visits of Gautama Buddha to the reign of Mahānāma (334–61). The text also depicts Mahinda's (*c.* 280–222 BCE) conversion of Devānampiya Tissa (r. 247–207 BCE), who built Mahāvihāra, the first monastery at Anurādhapura. Both the *Island Chronicle and* the *Great Chronicle*, attributed to Mahānāma (*c.* sixth century), indicate that threats posed by famine, war, and conflict between Mahāvihāra monks and monks at Abhayagiri, built by Vaṭṭagāmaṇi (r. 29–17 BCE) motivated the writing down of Buddhist texts in the first century BCE. The *Great Chronicle* includes new material from Sinhala commentaries and devotes eleven chapters to King Duṭṭhagāmaṇi's (r. 101–77 BCE) conquest over the Tamils. The continuation of the *Great Chronicle*, also known as the *Short Chronicle* (*Cūlavaṃsa*), a title introduced by nineteenth-century Europeans, covers medieval and early modern Sri Lankan history. Tibboṭuvave Buddharakkhita wrote Chapters 97–100 at the request of Kīrti Śri Rājasiṃha (r. 1747–80) and Hikkaḍuve Sumaṅgala (1826–1911) wrote the appendix in 1877. Other Pāli chronicles include translations from earlier Sinhala works: the tenth-century *Chronicle of the Great* Bodhi *Tree* (*Mahābodhivaṃsa*) of Upatissa on Saṅghamittā's (*c.* 280–221 BCE) bringing a cutting of the *Bodhi* tree to Anurādhapura and the twelfth-century *Chronicle of the Stūpa* (*Thūpavaṃsa*) on King Duṭṭhagāmaṇi's building of the Mahāthūpa in Anurādhapura. The fourteenth-century *Saddhammasaṅgaha* (*Compendium of the True Teaching*), composed by Dhammakitti Mahāsāmi chronicles the first three councils in India, Buddhism's entry into Sri Lanka, Duṭṭhagāmaṇi's reign, and the compilation of subcommentaries (*ṭīkās*) by Mahākassapa during the reign of Parakkamabāhu (1153–86). The final chapters describe the merit acquired through copying the *Tipiṭaka* and listening to the Buddha's teachings.

China

Acquiring copies of Buddhist texts and studying Buddhist teachings motivated Chinese pilgrims' travel to India. Faxian, Xuanzang (596–664) and Yijing (635–713) all recorded their travels. Faxian left China in 399 to acquire a complete set of *Vinaya* texts in India. His journal described Buddhist practices and pilgrimage sites he visited in Central Asia, India and Sri Lanka. He returned to China in 414 with Mahīśāsaka school *Vinaya* texts and *sūtras* from the *Long and Connected Collections* (*Dīrgha*, *Samyukta*). The famous translator Xuanzang (596–664) left Chang An in 629, and between 635 and 641 traveled throughout India, visiting all the major Buddhist sites. His *Record of the Western Regions of the Great Tang* (*Da tang xi yu ji*), written in 646, provided detailed information about Bodhgayā and the Mahābodhi Temple. He described his studies at Nālandā and Valabhī monasteries, which housed several thousand monks, studying Buddhist and Hindu scriptures and secular subjects. He observed that monks with Mahāyāna interests lived together with their Hīnayāna brethren and notes the decline of Buddhist monasteries in the Deccan. After returning to Chang'an in 645 with 600 Sanskrit manuscripts, relics, and statues, Xuanzang devoted the rest of his life to textual translation. Yijing (635–713), in his *Account of Buddhism, Sent from the South Seas* (*Nanhai jigui neifa zhuan*), narrates his journey from Guangzhou by boat to acquire Mūlasarvāstivādin school *Vinaya* texts. He arrived at Sumatra, a center of Buddhist learning in the seventh century, where he studied Sanskrit, before traveling on to study at Nālandā and Valabhī, where he observed the increasing importance of esoteric rituals. After ten years in India, he returned to China in 689 and began translating the texts he had acquired.

Tibet

Dromtön (Tib. 'Brom ston, 1005–64) wrote an account of his teacher, Atiśa (*c.* 980–1055). Dromtön's *Itinerary* (*'Brom ston lam yig*) describes how Atīśa and his disciple transform themselves into wrathful Vajrayāna deities to calm the storm that threatens their journey to Sumatra. Dromtön's *Itinerary* also recorded the journey of Nagtso Losawa (Nag tso lo tsa ba) to Vikramalaśīla monastery, where he stayed until Atiśa returned from twelve years of studying in Sumatra with Guru Suvarṇadvīpa. Vikramalaśīla's abbot was reluctant to allow Atīśa to leave India with Nagtso for Tibet because he feared losing a good scholar to the hazards of travel in areas plagued by Muslim raiders. The Tibetan pilgrim, Dharmaśvamin, confirmed both the lack of scholarly monks in India and the dangers of Muslim invaders. Dharmaśvamin, who arrived in Nepal in 1226 and spent eight years near Katmandu, observed the growing popularity of Vajrayāna beliefs and the decline of monasticism. When he arrived at Bodhgayā in 1234, he found it almost deserted because the monks feared Muslim invaders. He spent a brief three months in Bodhgayā, Rājagṛha and Nālandā before his return to Tibet. These accounts of pilgrimages (*lam yig*) to Buddhist sacred sites in India, Nepal, and Tibet, described a route that other intrepid pilgrims could follow, but other pilgrimage accounts that depicted travels to the mythical kingdom of Shambhala described paths only advanced Vajrayāna practitioners could travel.

Japan

Most pious pilgrims described travels to India, but Ennin, a Japanese Tendai monk (794–864), traveled to China to study Buddhism. He spent nine years in China (838–84) at monasteries on Mount Wutai and in Chang'an, studying Sanskrit, and the diverse traditions of Pure Land, Esoteric Buddhism, Chan and Tiantai. His travel diary, *The Record of a Pilgrimage to China in Search of the Law* (*Nitto Guho Junrei Koki*) recorded detailed information about Chinese Buddhism, including the growing persecution of Buddhists under the reign of the Tang emperor. In 847 Ennin returned to Japan and became the chief priest of the Tendai sect at Enryakuji, where he erected buildings to store the *sūtras* and religious instruments he brought back from China.

See also: **Canons and literature; Pilgrimage; Pilgrimage in Japan; Pilgrimage in Tibetan Buddhism.**

KAREN C. LANG

CLONING

The birth of Dolly the sheep caused a furor when it was announced to the world on 24 February 1997. What made this birthday so special was that Dolly was unlike any other sheep, not solely because she was created by scientists in the laboratories of the Roslin Institute in Edinburgh, but because she had been produced by means of a new technology that threatens to revolutionize the way we think about the basis of life itself. Since the 1950s scientists had been experimenting with cloning tadpoles and frogs, but Dolly was the first mammalian clone, and her genetic proximity to the human species gave cause for deep reflection and concern as the implications for human beings were assessed. Dolly has since been followed by mice, goats, pigs, cats and horses, and it seems only a matter of time until the technique is perfected for use on human beings. It is in connection with this prospect – chilling to some and exciting to others – that profound moral issues arise.

The Raelian religious cult claimed that a first cloned child – significantly named Eve – was delivered by caesarean section on 26 December 2002. Similar claims followed, but none has been verified, and the scientific community remains highly sceptical. Conventional research teams have claimed more modest success. In 2001 US-based Advanced Cell Technology claimed to have produced the world's first cloned embryos, but none grew beyond six cells, and in February 2004 a team in South Korea announced that it had grown thirty cloned embryos to the blastocyst stage, a claim later shown to be false.

The science of cloning

A clone is a genetic duplicate – a kind of photocopy – of another individual. The word "clone" is from the Greek *klon*, meaning a twig, and the idea of cloning resembles the way horticulturalists take cuttings from a mature plant and grow them into identical copies of their parent. Cloning in human beings replaces the normal process of sexual intercourse. Instead of an ovum being fertilized by a sperm, the nucleus of an unfertilized ovum is removed and replaced with a nucleus of a somatic cell from a donor (a skin cell is typically used for this purpose). The ovum is then stimulated and its cells begin to divide and reduplicate as in the case of a normal embryo. The developing embryo is placed in the womb and develops into an individual with the same genetic makeup as the donor of the cell nucleus. As the technique involves the transfer of the nucleus of a somatic (bodily) cell to an embryo, the cloning technique goes by the scientific name of Somatic Cell Nuclear Transfer, or SCNT.

In traditional reproduction each parent contributes twenty-three of the forty-six chromosomes that will define the child's genetic identity. A cloned child, however, inherits all forty-six of its chromosomes from a single DNA source.

The type of cloning just described is known as "reproductive cloning." This is where the aim of the procedure is to produce a baby, either a baby sheep as in the case of Dolly, or a human baby. An alternative type of cloning procedure is known as "therapeutic cloning." Here the aim is not to produce a living copy of an individual, but to carry out experimentation on early embryos as part of a program of scientific research. The broad aim of this research is to understand better the process of genetic development in order to prevent abnormalities and to develop treatments using gene therapy to alleviate chronic hereditary diseases such as Huntingdon's disease and cystic fibrosis. Treatments of this kind, which are known as somatic therapies, work by targeting and repairing genetically abnormal cells, for example by introducing missing genes.

Objections to cloning

In the furore which followed the birth of Dolly, cloning met with widespread condemnation by churchmen and politicians around the globe. Religious opposition was led by the theistic traditions, notably Christianity, Judaism and Islam. These religions teach that life is a gift from God, and for them the creation of life in the laboratory seems to usurp the divine authority of the creator. The Bible teaches that God created human beings in his image by breathing life into the bodies he formed from clay, and to seek to duplicate this miracle in a laboratory seems to some an act of great hubris. Reproductive cloning is also in conflict with the biblical model of sexual generation: We are told in the book of Genesis that God created human beings "male and female" and enjoined them to multiply through sexual union, a practice which subsequent Christian authorities regard as appropriate only within the constraints of marriage. Cloning respects none of these religious precedents and in the eyes of many believers threatens to undermine divinely sanctioned norms governing family and social life.

Many of these theological objections disappear when cloning is viewed from a Buddhist perspective. As Buddhism does not believe in a supreme being, there is no divine creator who might be offended by human attempts to duplicate his work. Nor does Buddhism believe in a personal soul, or teach that human beings are made in God's image. Its view of creation and cosmology is very different from that of the Bible, and does not seem to carry with it any normative principles or obligations relating to reproduction. There is no theological reason, then, why cloning could not be seen as just another way of creating life, neither intrinsically better nor worse than any other.

Supporters of cloning regard the objections to it as overstated, and point out that clones have been with us throughout history in the form of identical twins. The fact that two individuals share the same genetic code, they say, has never threatened the fabric of society. Further, just as identical twins differ (for example, in the curvature of the skull and the shape of internal organs), an individual produced by cloning would be only a fuzzy copy of the DNA donor. There are several reasons for this. Even with identical DNA there are underlying differences at the molecular level which will become greater as the clone develops. The DNA supplied by the mother (mitochondrial DNA) can also subtly alter the overall genetic "mix." Another important reason is that the development of an individual brain is always a unique process, and while DNA may determine the rough layout of the wiring it cannot control the operation of trillions of neurons and synapses. Environmental factors also play an important part in individual development, and have a profoundly formative influence on personality, perhaps even greater than that of DNA. Each individual undergoes a different set of experiences over the course of a lifetime, and these experiences shape character and personality, making every individual unique. No two individuals are ever the same, regardless of their DNA, and the fear of armies of identical mindless clones being directed by evil dictators is therefore more a product of science fiction than scientific fact.

Conclusion

What conclusions can be drawn about the ethics of cloning from a Buddhist perspective? The first point to reiterate is that the technique itself need not be seen as theologically improper or immoral: cloning is just another way of creating human life. IVF programs have created "test-tube babies" since 1968, and the fact that fertilization takes place in the laboratory rather than in the bedroom does not appear to have resulted in any serious harm to the children born through the technique.

As regards therapeutic (as opposed to reproductive) cloning, however, Buddhism is likely to have strong reservations. Creating human life only to destroy it in the course of experimentation, for example by harvesting stem cells, seems directly contrary to the principle of *ahiṃsā*. Regardless of the benevolent motivation for such experimentation (which also typically involves scientific curiosity, fame, and financial rewards) Buddhism would not sanction engaging in death-dealing experiments or accept the utilitarian moral logic of destroying one life to save another (or even many more). Quite apart from the problems surrounding the technique itself, cloning must also be subject to the same general moral standards that apply to any other human activity. This means that the motivation of those involved must be wholesome (free from greed, hatred and delusion), and the reasonably foreseeable consequences for individuals and society at large must be taken into account. Many reservations have been expressed in the latter regard, from the erosion of human dignity to a return to the eugenics programs of the 1930s and 1940s, and these fears cannot be dismissed lightly. In contrast, few clear benefits to cloning human beings have been identified, and though experiments on embryos have been going on for years the medical breakthroughs promised have failed to materialize. Scientific curiosity seems to be the main factor motivating cloning experiments at present, and overall Buddhists are likely to be sceptical about the need for this curiosity to be satisfied at the price of destroying human life in its early stages on a large scale.

See also: **Abortion; *Ahiṃsā*; Ethics; Stem cell research.**

DAMIEN KEOWN

COMMENTARIAL WORKS

Gautama Buddha provided his disciples with an oral commentary on his teachings. Generations of disciples added their own oral comments, some of which were included after these scriptures were written down. The concise and easily memorized prose or verse of the root texts required oral and written commentaries to clarify and elaborate their meaning and to impose a structural unity. The written commentaries, a genre of literature modeled on oral explanations, often paraphrased individual words, analyze the components of compound words and the grammatical relations between them, in addition to explanations of the religious and philosophical issues raised by the text.

The Pāli canon's *Collection of Minor Texts* (*Khuddaka Nikāya*) includes the *Exposition* (*Niddesa*), a commentary in two parts, the *Major and Minor Expositions* (*Mahāniddesa, Cullaniddesa*), that used synonyms to explain the words in three early canonical texts, the *Section on the Eights* (*Aṭṭhakavagga*), the *Section on the Ultimate Path* (*Pārāyanavagga*), and the *Rhinoceros Horn Scripture* (*Khaggavisāṇasuttanta*) and briefly commented on the texts' meaning. According to Buddhaghosa (*c.* fifth century CE), by the first century BCE only one monk's memory preserved the *Exposition*. Buddhaghosa translated the Sinhala commentaries he studied at Mahāvihāra monastery into Pāli. He is credited with writing Pāli commentaries on the entire canon. These commentaries and his *Path of Purification* (*Visuddhimagga*), a lengthy exposition of the Buddha's teachings, remain the most influential explanations of the Theravāda tradition.

Theravāda monks also study the Pāli canon with the aid of vernacular commentaries. Sinhala commentaries (*sannayas*) often include the Pāli text, a Sinhala gloss, and an explanation of its contents. Burmese and Thai commentaries (*nissaya*) explain the text, and justify its importance in the tradition and absorbing and replacing the text. *Nissayas* often rewrite and expand the Pāli text by adding new sections and using the text as the foundation for studying grammar and vocabulary. These vernacular commentaries introduce selected texts to monastic students and form their understanding of Theravāda doctrine.

Commentaries defended a text's viewpoint but many also advocated new views or criticize other teachers' positions. Debate over the interpretation of the Buddha's teachings contributed to the writing and rewriting of *Abhidharma* commentaries between the first and fourth centuries CE, the same period that saw the rise of new Mahāyāna *sūtras* and commentaries on *sūtras*. The *Great Commentary* (*Mahāvibhāṣā*) on the Sarvastivāda *Abhidharma* text, *Foundation of Knowledge* (*Jñānaprasthāna*), recorded Vaibhāṣika teachers' views. In response to the *Great Commentary*, Vasubandhu (fourth century CE) wrote *The Treasury of Abhidharma* (*Abhidharmakośa*) and his own commentary on it. According to Vasubandhu's *Logic of Explanation* (*Vyākhyāyukti*), commentaries should explain the text's purpose, subject matter, word order, and its logical consistency. Nāgārjuna (*c.* 150–250) in his major work, *Verses on the Middle* Way (*Mūlamadhyamakakārikā*) explained the purpose and logical consistency of the *Perfection of Insight Scriptures'* (*Prajñāpāramitā Sūtra*) teachings on emptiness (*śūnyatā*). Nāgārjuna's subject matter and use of logic became the debated subject of eight Indian commentaries, including the *Light of Insight* (*Prajñāpradīpa*) of Bhāvaviveka (*c.* 500–70) and the *Clear Words* (*Prasannapadā*) of Candrakīrti (*c.* 550–650).

The translation of Indian commentaries into Chinese and Tibetan inspired Chinese and Tibetan scholars to compose commentaries. The translation and interpretation of Indian texts became fused when the translators' explanations of the scripture were incorporated into the text itself. The *Treatise on the Great Perfection of Insight* (Ch. *Dazhidulun*), attributed to Nāgārjuna, contains explanatory material contributed by its translator, Kumārajīva (343–413). Many *Abhidharma* commentaries, including the *Great Commentary* and the *Treasury of Abhidharma*, were translated into Chinese, often more than once. Vasubandhu's *Treasury of Abhidharma* was first translated by Paramārtha

(499–569) and later by Xuanzang (596–664). Most Chinese commentaries were written on *sūtras*, particularly on the *Lotus Sūtra* (*Saddharmapuṇḍarīka*), the *Diamond Sūtra* (*Vajracchedika*), the *Heart Sūtra* (*Hṛdaya*), the *Vimalakīrti Sūtra*, the *Nirvāṇa Sūtra*, and the *Descent to Laṅka* (*Laṅkāvatara*) *Sūtra*. Commentarial style changed over time. The *zhu* commentary, influenced by oral commentary necessary in communicating the meaning of an Indian text to a Chinese audience, incorporated these explanatory glosses into the text. The *shu* commentary, prevalent in the sixth to ninth centuries, was composed in monastic circles for a sophisticated scholarly audience. This type of commentary began with an introduction that explains the history of the text's translation and transmission, along with an explanation of its purpose, basic thought, and its relations to other teachings. The commentary's core clarified the text's central teachings and its conclusion praises the text's appeal. The popularity of Chan and Pure Land teachings from the tenth century onward contributed to the demise of scholarly commentaries.

Most Tibetan commentaries focus, not on *sūtras*, but on treatises (*śāstras*), such as Vasubandhu's *Treasury of Abhidharma*, Dharmakīrti's (*c.* seventh century CE) *Commentary on Valid Cognition* (*Pramāṇavārttika*), Candrakīrti's *Entrance to the Middle Way* (*Madhyamakāvatāra*) and Maitreyanātha's (*c.* 270–350) *Ornament for Realization* (*Abhisamayālaṅkāra*), itself a commentary on the *Perfection of Insight in 25,000 Lines* (*Pañcaviṃśatiprajñāpāramitā Sūtra*). Butön (Tib. Bu ston, 1290–1364) lists five types of commentaries in his *Doctrinal History* (*'chos 'byung*): (1) extensive explanations of the words and the concise meaning; (2) explanations of the words; (3) explanations of the most difficult points in the text; (4) explanations of the general meaning; and (5) condensed explanations. Extensive explanations provide a detailed textual analysis and often a critique of other scholars' views. The textbooks (*yig cha*) used in monastic colleges are commentaries that summarize a text's general meaning. In word commentaries, the words of the root text are highlighted with small circles underneath them or printed larger than the surrounding commentarial text. Tibetan doxographies (*grub mtha'*) are also concise summaries of teachings, frequently studied and memorized by monastic students. Bhāvaviveka's *Blaze of Reasoning* (*Tarkajvālā*), a commentary on his own *Verses on the Heart of the Middle Way* (*Madhyamakahṛdayakārikāḥ*) that defends the Madhyamaka position and criticizes the Vaibhāsika and Yogācāra schools and the non-Buddhist Vaiśeṣika, Sāṅkhya, Mīmāṃsā, and Vedānta schools, influenced the development of the Tibetan doxographies. These doxographies present the main tenets of the six non-Buddhist Indian schools: Vaiśeṣika, Sāṅkhya, Mīmāṃsā, Vedānta, Jaina, Lokāyata; and the four Buddhist schools: Vaibhāṣika, Sautrāntika, Yogācāra, and Madhyamaka, in a hierarchical order that puts the author's own school at the top.

See also: ***Abhidharma*; *Abhidharma* schools; *Abhidharmakośa*; Canons and literature.**

KAREN C. LANG

COMMUNITY IN VAJRAYĀNA BUDDHISM

Vajrayāna and society in medieval India

Community has played a central role in Vajrayāna Buddhism since its inception. Early Buddhist *tantric* texts describe small groups of practitioners living outside the Indian mainstream, often residing in such marginal areas as cremation grounds, wilderness areas, or cemeteries. Some of their practices were perceived by the rest of society as abhorrent, and there are numerous references to their being shunned and despised. In this context, it is not surprising that the fellowship of other *tantrists* would assume a central importance, and this is still true today, even in the Tibetan cultural area, in which Vajrayāna is firmly entrenched in the mainstream and where it is regarded as the supreme Buddhist practice.

In the seventh and eighth centuries, particularly in modern-day Bengal and Bihar, India witnessed the development of new religious communities, whose members referred to themselves as "adepts" (*siddha*, Tib. *grub thob*). Among them were various groupings of widely revered figures, referred to as "great adepts" (*mahāsiddha*, Tib. *grub thob chen po*). The most influential grouping of Buddhist *siddhas* is found in Abhayadatta's (*c.* twelfth-century) hagiography *Lives of the Eighty-Four Adepts* (*Caturaśīti-siddha-pravṛtti*), which includes such luminaries as Virūpa, Kāṇha, Tilopa, and his student Nāropa. Many of the *siddhas* are also known through compositions of prose and poetry, particularly for inspired verse compositions (*dohā*).

The *siddhas* constitute a strange collection of tribal people, outcastes, beggars, criminals, and some upper-caste members. They are often described as wearing ornaments of human bone and carrying skullcaps, having long, matted hair and covered with animal skins, and they reportedly defeat demons, fly through the air, pass through solid objects, and travel to the land of the *ḍākinīs* (female buddhas who are guardians of tantric lore), where they receive esoteric instruction. The goal of *siddha* practice is the acquisition of supernatural powers (*siddhi*, Tib. *dngos grub*), which are said to be aids on the path to buddhahood.

The *siddhas* considered themselves to have transcended ordinary religious and social norms, and their texts report orgiastic gatherings called *gaṇacakra* in which they copulated in cemeteries and consumed substances that were considered polluting by Hindu and Buddhist orthodoxy, such as alcohol, beef, and even human flesh. Their pantheon incorporated various fearsome tribal and local deities that were associated with low-caste groups, as well as demons and other unsavory characters. Their antinomian practices are described as skillful means to help adepts transcend ordinary conceptuality and are connected with the doctrine of emptiness (*śūnyatā*), according to which all phenomena are devoid of any inherent nature, and so by extension anything can be appropriated in the path to liberation.

One of the most important *siddhas* was Nāropa (1016–1100), who according to tradition was a well-established scholar at the monastic university of Nālandā. One day in his study he saw a shadow fall across his texts, and when he turned he saw a hideously ugly old woman, who challenged him to explain the true meaning of what he was studying. He confessed that while he understood the surface meaning, he lacked insight into the deeper truths of the scriptures, and the woman (who was a *ḍākinī*) urged him to seek out the great master Tilopa. Nāropa subsequently left Nālandā and eventually found Tilopa, who subjected him to a series of difficult and often painful tests before finally agreeing to give him tantric teachings and initiations.

Nāropa's story has a number of typical elements found in *siddha* biographies: a statement regarding the future *siddha*'s caste and occupation, a description of an existential crisis, the search for a guru who can teach a path to resolution of the crisis, a period of training (often involving tasks that are anathema to one's previous caste status or are dispiriting or humiliating), and a final resolution in which the *siddha* attains full awakening and manifests spectacular magical feats. The specificity of descriptions of the *siddhas*' early lives, their social situations, and the large corpus of works attributed to them in Tibetan canons leave little doubt that some of them were historical figures, but their biographies are also intermingled with mythological and magical elements and so are problematic as historical sources. The *siddhas* are both individuals and archetypes, and their stories are remembered for their personal distinctiveness and because they represent core ideals of Vajrayāna doctrine and practice.

Today in the Tibetan cultural areas, the *siddhas* are culture heroes, and their modern successors, *tantric lamas* (who often trace their practices and initiations back to Indian masters), are believed to have inherited their teachings, practices, and also their charisma, which are now integrated into the mainstream social system. In Tibetan Buddhist communities, the *lama* plays a central role, and most *lamas* are expected to possess magical powers that can aid the community. People come to *lamas* with a range of pragmatic concerns, including advice regarding life choices, marriage, interpersonal relations, family matters, the weather, health of their animals, and concerns about the future. Many *lamas* are experts in astrology and use it to provide advice to their constituents, and *lamas* who gain reputations for being particularly gifted or powerful will attract customers from near and far.

Identity and practice

Beginning with the early *siddha* cults, tantric initiation involves gaining membership in a community. One's identity as a tantric practitioner is closely connected to the initiations one has received and the liturgies of visualization (*sādhana*) one performs. Those who take the fourteen root vows of *tantra* become part of the Vajrayāna tradition, but one's immediate community includes those who belong to a particular lineage, who have received empowerments (*abhiṣeka*) from the same guru, and who regularly perform the same *sādhanas*. Within a particular lineage, feelings of belonging may vary considerably, however, and some people take initiations as a form of blessing but do not intend to engage in regular subsequent practice of *sādhanas*. More committed practitioners are urged to perceive members of the lineage as their "*vajra* brothers and sisters" and to rely on them as a support group.

While Vajrayāna in India may have originated with antisocial cults that lived at the margins of society and openly rejected its norms, within a short time it had been incorporated into the curriculum of north Indian monastic universities like Nālandā and Vikramaśīla. From at least the eighth century, *tantric* initiations and rituals were part of the routine of these institutions, and scholar monks engaged in study and commentary on tantric texts. As *tantra* became part of the monastic mainstream, there was a growing tendency to interpret the more extreme passages in *tantras* metaphorically, and this has continued in Tibet, where Vajrayāna is regarded by all four Buddhist orders as the supreme path and where it is an integral part of the society.

Vajrayāna and society

Tibetan Buddhists often engage in activities that were once confined to select groups of initiates. *Tantric* initiations are commonly given to large groups of people who have no intention of taking on any practice commitments, but who view the initiation as a blessing that brings merit. The annual Kālacakra initiation given by the Dalai Lama draws thousands of people from all over the Tibetan cultural area and from around the world, and most will not take the higher initiations that require regular performance of *sādhanas*.

Tantric rituals are also performed by lamas for a variety of practical uses, such as health, long life, etc. Today once-secret *tantric* ceremonies are enacted annually in festivals in Ladakh and other areas of the Himalayan region for the entertainment of the general populace, including Western tourists who flock to these events with cameras and video recorders. The monks who perform dances (*'cham*) that often depict *tantric* themes and Buddhas justify their activities by stating that the audience only perceives the outward form but has no notion of the underlying meaning of the rituals, and so there is no violation of the vow of secrecy, which enjoins *tantrists* not to openly display Vajrayāna mysteries. In recent years, troupes of *tantric* monks touring Western countries have become a common sight. They often construct sand *maṇḍalas* that were originally designed for Vajrayāna initiation, but are now created in public venues such as art galleries, universities, or halls for the entertainment of non-Buddhists.

Pilgrimage

Religiously inspired travel is hugely popular among Tibetan Buddhists, who believe that one acquires merit by making pilgrimages to sacred places or people. One of the most popular pilgrimage destinations is Mount Kailash, which is visited by thousands of Buddhists every year. Many travel for months to get there, and some make the journey in a series of prostrations, in which they lay the front of their bodies flat on the ground with hands extended, then get up and place their feet at the point where the tips of the fingers reached, after which they perform another prostration. When they arrive at Mount Kailash, they may continue the process, and many make multiple circuits around the mountain by this method. The pilgrimage itself is meritorious, but if one adds additional religious details or voluntarily takes on supraordinate difficulties, the merit is increased greatly.

The Tibetan cultural area has innumerable places that are associated with a great human master or the activity of a Buddha, and these are popular destinations for pilgrims. Many *tantric* practitioners travel to caves in which great *siddhas* like Padmasambhava or Milarepa are reputed to have practiced meditation. It is believed that such places are imbued with the charisma of the masters who practiced there, and one may tap into the residual power created by their meditation. Many of these places are in remote areas, and the difficulty of accessing them, the time and effort required, and the distances involved all contribute to their appeal and to the merit one gains by making the journey.

However, pilgrimage is not generally viewed as difficult by Tibetans. Pilgrims often travel in groups and regard their journey as a holiday, one that is often made with family and friends, which brings health benefits, and also generates merit that will contribute to well-being in the present life and to better rebirths.

The most popular pilgrimage destination for Tibetan Buddhists is Lhasa, the holiest city of Tibetan Vajrayāna. Until the Chinese invasion and annexation of Tibet in the 1950s, it was the residence of the Dalai Lamas, the most influential reincarnate *lamas* in Tibetan Buddhism, and it was also the site of some of Tibet's largest monasteries and popular annual festivals. During the widespread destruction of Tibetan cultural institutions and the massacre of its population during the invasion and the Cultural Revolution of the 1960s and 1970s, thousands of monasteries and temples were destroyed and countless *lamas* and other Buddhist practitioners died, but with the lifting of some of the harshest aspects of religious persecution in the late 1980s Tibetans began rebuilding monasteries and other religiously significant sites, and pilgrimage to these places is increasing in popularity. Some festivals that were once banned by the Chinese have been revived, and pilgrims can travel to areas that were previously restricted.

The most widely visited pilgrimage destination is the Barkhor in Lhasa, a circuit around the Jokhang, the holiest shrine of Tibetan Buddhism, which houses the image of Jowo Rinpoche (reputedly of Śākyamuni Buddha as a young prince, brought to Tibet by the Chinese princess Wen Cheng). Every day large crowds of pilgrims from all over the Tibetan cultural area come to the Barkhor and make the circuit, many making prostrations, intoning *mantras*, and often combining their visit with some form of Vajrayāna practice, because the holy precincts are believed to be a particularly auspicious place for religious activities. The large numbers indicate that faith in Buddhism remains strong for many Tibetans, despite the persecution they have endured, but many *lamas* lament what they see as a tendency to preserve the outward forms of Buddhism while gradually destroying its inner vitality and the culture that once sustained it.

See also: **Tibet, Buddhism in; Vajrayāna Buddhism.**

JOHN POWERS

COMPUTERS AND THE BUDDHIST CULTURAL HERITAGE

The cultural heritage of Buddhism is preserved at thousands of sites throughout Asia. Some sites are the remains of the ancient past, while others are contemporary centers for practice. Images are among the most important means of preserving and presenting records of these sites. For decades scholars of Buddhist art, architecture, and religious practices photographed important works of art in caves, monasteries, and archaeological sites. The earliest method of presenting these photographs to audiences was to project lantern slides (glass-enclosed films, sometimes hand-painted) onto a screen. The first major advance over this older technology was 35mm color film. By 1939 the clumsy and fragile glass slides were replaced with transparent plastic slides inserted into cardboard frames. These could be arranged in trays and projected automatically to accompany lectures. This became the most common technology for depicting Buddhist cultural heritage, whether art objects or architectural structures. Buddhist scholars fully exploited it for nearly fifty years, until the arrival of the computer.

Computer image display requires the analog data of color and form to be translated into digital data. This was first made possible by the development of the digital scanner, which allowed images on film and paper to be copied into digital memory and displayed on a computer screen. Once images could be captured and stored, digital projection technology was developed to imitate the function of slide projectors. Early computerized images were not immediately accepted by art historians because they did not have sufficient resolution to compete with 35mm slides. Scholars working with Buddhist art and artifacts needed the ability to display very fine detail. Image resolution, measured in "dots" (or pixels) per inch, determines the amount of detail available in an image, and high-resolution scans require large amounts of computer memory. As computer memory measured in megabytes and gigabytes became increasingly affordable, digital scanners began to be able to create images whose resolution equaled or exceeded that of 35mm color slides, and computer projection became the most common method of image display in scholarly circles. In 2004 Kodak announced that it would no longer produce slide projectors, and classroom presentations on Buddhist heritage sites shifted from film to digital projection.

The shift to computer projection was driven by developments within the field of computer technology. But while it allowed images on paper, film, and blueprints to be converted into digital files, the strategies for using these files did not depart from the older film technologies. Even the development of digital cameras that could record images directly as electronic data did not change the essential methodology of scholarship.

A new method of capturing images did eventually revolutionize the scholarship of heritage sites: 3-D laser scanning allowed scholars to collect millions of points of color and shading with a quick pass of the sensor and to create finely detailed three-dimensional images of structures, down to the level of a hairline crack in a pillar. Preservation of laser-scanned "points" gave researchers accurate and detailed records of artifacts, structures, and fragments from heritage sites.

Photographs and laser-scanned details of the textures and forms of extant objects made it possible to create virtual reality (VR) reconstructions of a structure's former appearance. More than just a picture or a graphic display, VR reconstructions could be linked to a wealth of information, photographs, texts, and analytic software. Laser scanning began to revolutionize the field of archaeology by enabling researchers to keep detailed on-site field records. Northwestern University's Professor Sarah Fraser, supported by a grant from the Andrew W. Mellon Foundation, led the way with a project at the Dunhuang caves in northwest China. Using imaging technology at the site, the team was able to create digital reconstructions of some of the most important caves. The project started with Cave 196 and by 2002 had been expanded to twenty caves in all. VR technology made it possible to reconstruct images of the caves' past glory without doing any damage to the fragile surfaces of the physical ones.

Collateral technologies have provided additional tools for the scholar of heritage sites. Geographic Information Systems, or GIS, has been one of the most important of these. GIS uses global positioning systems (GPS) to determine the exact location of any site on earth, as well as the precise location of any point within a site. One of the most fully developed projects making use of these technologies is the work being done at Angkor Wat, Cambodia, under Professor Roland Fletcher of the University of Sydney. There, an international group of researchers using radar, laser scans, space photographs, and GIS technology, is developing a complete description of the site, including the size and nature of the urban center that once surrounded these impressive Buddhist ruins. Ground-penetrating radar has been able to reveal the structure of ancient rice fields that are invisible even to an archaeologist walking over the terrain. This new data has made it possible to revise earlier speculations about Angkor Wat and opened up the possibility of interdisciplinary cooperation.

The Electronic Cultural Atlas Initiative (ECAI), an international project organized in 1997 by Professor Lewis Lancaster of the University of California, Berkeley, brought together a large number of cultural heritage project leaders to work on technology issues. ECAI's mission is to develop methodologies designed for the changing technology. Departing from standard library and archive procedures, ECAI adopted a method of cataloguing data according to "place" and "time," using GIS data for latitude and longitude, and Common Era (CE) dates for historical dates. This makes it possible to create maps and animations to indicate change over time. By mid-2005 more than 100 projects involving Buddhist materials had been registered in the ECAI clearinghouse. These include two Silk Road atlases, one headed by Professor Ruth Mostern of the University of California, Merced, and the other by Mr. Aming Tu at Chung-Hwa Institute of Buddhist Studies in Taiwan; a database of Korean

Buddhist monasteries, led by Professor Heungkyu Kim of Korea University, Seoul; and the reconstruction of the Aizu monastery in Japan, directed by Professors Janet R. Goodwin of the University of Aizu and James M. Goodwin of UCLA.

In order to make GIS work for Buddhist scholars, it was necessary to develop historical gazetteers that establish the location of ancient names of important sites. Modern gazetteers record contemporary inhabited places but omit the older names, which may be found only in ancient texts. Further recommendations on how to mark up heritage data has been explored by Professors Michael Buckland and Ray Larson of the University of California, Berkeley, who expanded the idea of the gazetteer by combining the place-names and feature types (monasteries, mountains, shrines, etc.) of the traditional gazetteer with biographical data for personal names and a record of events associated the location. Professors Paul S. Ell and Ian Gregory at Queen's University, Belfast, and Dr. Linda L. Hill of the University of California, Santa Barbara, reviewed the use of GIS for such an expanded gazetteer. The China Historical GIS (CHGIS), an international collaborative project of Harvard and Fudan universities, was one of the first attempts to use GIS for mapping the locations of thousands of Buddhist monasteries in East Asia. Under the leadership of Professors Jianxiong Ge at Fudan and Peter Bol at Harvard, with technical support from Merrick Berman of MIT, CHGIS promises to add a new dimension to the study of Chinese and Buddhist cultural patterns. Professor David F. Germano of the University of Virginia added Tibetan place names and biographical data. This work was supported by grants from the Henry Luce Foundation and the National Endowment for the Humanities.

Software development for heritage data in GIS was essential. The TimeMap software project under the direction of Professor Ian Johnson of the University of Sydney's Archaeological Computing Laboratory provided a method of authoring maps using heritage data from a clearinghouse that marks up by latitude and longitude as well as by time. Through such software, polygons representing the extent of a cultural pattern can be quickly constructed. They can also be changed as the timeline designation is shifted from one century, year, or day to another. A number of Buddhist projects registered with the TimeMap software represent major applications of GIS to cultural data.

In addition to offering new methods for capturing images of cultural sites, the Internet opened the way for worldwide dissemination of the information. The Rubin Museum of Art in New York City was one of the pioneering groups in making high-resolution scans of Buddhist art and heritage objects freely available on the Internet. Thousands of Tibetan Buddhist paintings were scanned and posted on the museum's website, where they were made available to users. Thus, the Internet made it possible, for the first time, to study in great detail the complex art of Tibet. The museum opened in 2004, but the digital images were available earlier.

Whether used on its own, or in combination with technologies such as VR and holography, digitized data has been an invaluable tool for Buddhist scholarship. Cultural heritage sites are in constant danger of damage and destruction. Fortunately, photographs, digital data sets, and written material posted at many Internet websites provide valuable information for scholars and others with an interest in these important sites. VR has a place in reconstructing ancient sites as a scholar believes them to have been. It can also be used with holographic technology to display three-dimensional images of the reconstructions, on a computer screen or projected onto the site itself. One example of the role the computer can play in the event of destruction is the response of the

Huntington Photographic Archive at Ohio State University immediately following the destruction of the Bamiyan Valley Buddha statues in March 2001. Professor John Huntington posted scores of photographs from his collection on the archive's website for use by researchers, reporters, and students.

Buddhist studies have tended to focus on textual sources. The turn toward investigating the cultural aspects of the tradition marked a distinct shift both in focus and in presentation of source materials. While textual study exploits the search and retrieval capabilities of computer technology, cultural study requires more sophisticated image technologies and analytical tools such as 3-D scanners, GIS, VR and holography. Coordinating textual and cultural technologies remains a major challenge for the field. In the early decades of these new approaches, cultural studies will often be determined by advances in computer software use.

LEWIS R. LANCASTER

CONZE, EDWARD

Edward Conze was a world-famous Buddhologist primarily known for his landmark work on the *Prajñāpāramitā* or Perfection of Wisdom literature. If a single individual had to be identified who had advanced the general understanding of Mahāyāna Buddhism in the scholarly community during the middle portion of the previous century, it would be Edward Conze. With more than twenty books, over 100 articles, and well over 100 reviews to his credit, he must be counted among the world's most erudite and prolific scholars of Buddhism. Born in London in 1904, he was later educated in the Gymnasium in Germany, where he described himself as always being the first, and the naughtiest, in his class. He had a special gift for languages, and by age twenty-four knew fourteen. Within Buddhist Studies, he was well versed in Pāli, Sanskrit, Chinese, Tibetan, and Japanese. He received his Ph.D. in Philosophy (in Germany) in 1928. Conze rediscovered Buddhism in the 1930s, primarily through the writings of D.T. Suzuki and Har Dayal, and he suggests that between 1933 and 1948 he was transformed from an "ardent young communist" to a "dedicated Buddhist scholar." Unlike other scholars of Buddhism, Conze published two volumes of his "memoirs" as *The Memoirs of a Modern Gnostic* in 1979. About the parts of this work, Conze states:

> The first surveys my intellectual development, including those factors which helped or hindered it. The second fills in some of the details and gives me ample opportunity to comment on many things. The third part contains everything which has been deemed libelous, brutally frank, or politically impermissible. By common consent Part III cannot be published in my lifetime, and must wait for the 21st Century, if ever there should be such a thing.

Nobody, though, seems to have ever seen this dubious Part III.

Conze's *Perfection of Wisdom* publications are obviously far too numerous to list, but included editions and translations of the *Vajracchedika*, *Aṣṭasāhasrikā*, *Pañcaviṃśatisāhasrikā*, *Abhisamayālaṃkāra*, *Aṣṭadaśasāhasrikā*, and a dictionary of *Prajñāpāramitā* literature. In addition, his other major books on Buddhism include *Buddhism: Its Essence and Development* (1951), *Buddhist Thought in India* (1962), and *Thirty Years of Buddhist Studies* (1967). One of Conze's collaborators, Arthur Waley, said of him that, "To Dr. Conze, the questions that Buddhism asks and answers are actual, living questions, and he constantly brings them into relation both with history and with current actuality." For his contribution to Buddhist Studies, Conze was honored with a festschrift volume in 1979 titled *Prajñāpāramitā and Related Systems: Studies in Honor of Edward Conze.*

Conze traveled extensively, teaching often in the United States. He believed that Buddhist Studies could only be put on a firm foundation when one standardized the translation of Buddhism's basic textual terminology, and it was on this project that he worked diligently in North America, first at the University of Wisconsin in 1963, and later in Seattle with Leon Hurvitz. He was an early forerunner of what we have today called the "scholar-practitioner," noting "Although one may originally be attracted by its remoteness, one can appreciate the real value of Buddhism only when one judges it by the results it produces in one's own life from day to day." Conze died in 1979.

See also: **Academic study of Buddhism; Anglo-German school of Buddhist Studies.**

CHARLES S. PREBISH

COSMOLOGY AND REBIRTH

To a considerable extent, Buddhism drew upon pre-existing Indian notions and did not invent an entirely original cosmology of its own. As Buddhism spread to other parts of Asia, this scheme remained dominant although it was adapted in various ways to accommodate local beliefs. This article describes early Buddhist cosmology as set out in Indian sources composed during the first millennium or so of Buddhism's existence.

There is a good deal of fluidity in the earliest cosmological notions, but as they became more settled in the centuries following the Buddha's death, Buddhism came to envisage the world as divided into two broad categories: animate and inanimate. It pictures the inanimate part as a kind of receptacle or container (*bhājana*) in which various kinds of living beings (*sattva*) make their homes. The physical universe is formed out of the interaction of the five primary elements, namely earth, water, fire, air and space (*ākāśa*). In Indian thought, space is considered as an element in its own right rather than just a void or the absence of other elements. From the interaction of these elements worlds are formed, such as the one we now inhabit. This world is not unique, however, and there are thought to be other worlds "as numerous as the sands of the Ganges" inhabited by beings like ourselves. Groups of these worlds cluster together to form "world-systems" known as *cakravālas*, which are roughly equivalent to the modern concept of a solar system. These are said to be found everywhere throughout the six directions of space (to the north, south, east, west, above, and below). The world we live in is therefore not the centre of the universe, as contemporary Western authorities believed, and Buddhist cosmological notions are much more in line with those of modern astronomy in the way the latter envisages the scale and extent of the cosmos.

The world-systems conceived of by Buddhism were believed to evolve and be destroyed over vast periods of time known as *kalpas*, which are measured in millions of years. Worlds come into being through the interaction of impersonal material forces, flourish for a while, and then embark on a downward spiral at the end of which they are destroyed in a great cataclysm caused by natural elements such as fire, water or wind. In due course the process starts up again and the worlds once again evolve to complete a full cycle of time known as a "great eon" (*mahākalpa*).

The operation of these natural forces has an impact on the living creatures who inhabit the worlds which are created and destroyed. Interestingly, some sources see the effect as two-way, and suggest that it is the actions of the inhabitants of the various worlds that to a large extent determine their fate. For instance, when people are greedy and selfish the rate of decline is accelerated, and when they are virtuous it slows down. This view at first seems at variance with the contemporary scientific viewpoint, but on reflection seems in harmony with modern ecology and the belief that selfish exploitation of natural resources, such as by burning fossil fuels, plays a part in the decline of the natural environment, for example by causing global warming. According to Buddhist belief, a world in which people are wise and virtuous would last considerably longer and be a more pleasant place to live than one inhabited by an ignorant and selfish population. Buddhist cosmology, therefore, seems to have important implications for contemporary ecology.

There is no one Buddhist "creation myth" as such, but one well-known early text known as the *Aggañña Sutta* tells an interesting story about how the world began. It takes us back to the time when a previous world-system had been destroyed, and a new one was once just beginning to evolve. Just before a world is destroyed, the living beings which inhabit it are reborn into a spiritual realm where they await the eventual evolution of a new world. When the new world begins to appear, they are reborn into it as ethereal beings who have translucent bodies which show no distinction between the male and female genders. Slowly, the fabric of the new world becomes denser, and the spirit-like beings reborn there feel an attraction to its material form and begin to consume it like food. As they do this, their bodies become correspondingly grosser and take on a material form similar to the one we have now. As this matter is consumed, however, food becomes scarcer, and competition for it leads to violent conflict. In order to keep the peace, the story continues, the people elect a king, who then enforces laws and punishes those who break them. This event marks the beginning of social life.

Some scholars interpret this text not so much as a creation myth as a satire on the beliefs of the Buddha's Brahmin rivals who insisted that the structure of society set out in the caste system was eternal and divinely ordained. Whichever way we read it, however, a primary point of interest is that the myth presents a view of the origins of the world which is quite unlike the one taught in Christianity. In the Buddhist account the world is not the work of a divine creator, and creation is not a once-and-for-all event. Nevertheless, both faiths seem to agree on one thing at least: that humankind is in its present predicament because of a "fall" which was caused by some serious moral failing. In the Judeo-Christian tradition the fall is attributed to pride and disobedience, while Buddhism sees our present dilemma as being caused by the existence of primordial desire.

The six realms of rebirth

Once a world-system has evolved, it assumes an archetypal structure within which are found qualitatively different modes of existence, some more pleasant than others. The sources commonly speak of six domains or "'realms" of rebirth, although the earliest sources mention only five. Some of these realms are visible to us here and now, while others are not. The ones we can see are the human and animal realms, and the ones we cannot see are those of the gods, the Titans or *asuras*, and hell. On the borderline is the realm of the ghosts, beings who hover on the fringes of the human world and who are occasionally caught sight of as they flit between the shadows.

As the wheel of *saṃsāra* moves around, beings migrate through the various domains in accordance with their *karma*, or the good and evil deeds committed in each rebirth. The scheme of the six realms is commonly depicted in the form of a wheel known as the "wheel of life" (*bhavacakra*), which sets out the relative position of each of the six domains (Figure 17).

If we look at the circular diagram of the *bhavacakra*, we see that there are three realms below the line and three above. This simple division reflects a qualitative difference in that the three realms below the middle line (hell, the ghosts, and animals) are particularly unfortunate places to be reborn, while those above the line (heaven, the *asuras*, and the human world) are more pleasant. The wheel of life is often depicted in Tibetan *thangkas* or wall hangings and is used as an illustration for didactic and meditational purposes. In this format the wheel is a symbolic representation of the process of cyclic rebirth or *saṃsāra*, and shows the six realms (the whole of *saṃsāra*) in the grasp of the demon Yama, the Lord of Death. On some accounts the wheel represents a mirror held up by Yama to a dying person and revealing the various possibilities for the next rebirth open to them. At the very centre of the wheel are shown three animals: a cock, a pig and a snake, which represent the "three poisons" of greed (*rāga*), hatred (*dveṣa*) and delusion (*moha*). It is these forces that create bad *karma* and fuel the endless cycle of rebirth. Placing these mental forces at the centre of the diagram reveals the important point that for Buddhism the cosmos is in a very real sense psychologically driven and arises and ceases in conjunction with the state of mind of the individual. The close connection between psychology and cosmology is also seen in meditational theory, where the various levels of trance (*dhyāna*) are conceived of as pseudo-physical planes in the manner explained below.

Figure 17 Wheel of life (*bhavacakra*) wall mural in the entrance to Rumtek Monastery, Sikkim.

In one sense the notion of the cosmos having a hierarchical structure is not unfamiliar in the West. Traditional Christian teachings depict God dwelling at the summit of his creation surrounded by angels and saints, while Satan inhabits an infernal region beneath our feet. Human beings are somewhere in between, poised between these two eternal destinations. Traditional teachings also speak of a fourth domain – purgatory – existing as a temporary abode for departed souls undergoing purification in order to be worthy to enter heaven. This gives us a total of four possible states or modes of existence.

To these four the Buddhist scheme adds one more by separating the animal realm from that of human beings. The final remaining domain is that of the *asuras* mentioned above. These are figures from Indian legend and mythology who did battle with the gods in a cosmic struggle between good and evil. In Buddhist teachings they are depicted as warlike demons, consumed by hatred and a lust for power, who cannot refrain from expressing their violent impulses in a futile struggle for a victory they never achieve. Instead, hatred breeds more hatred, and one battle leads simply to the next. However, the *asuras* are not of great importance in this scheme, and as noted, are absent from the earliest conceptions of the hierarchy, which speak only of five realms. It is not impossible that they were added simply to balance the circle.

Despite the similarities, there are also some important differences to the Christian conception of the destinations that await us in the next life. The most notable is that in the Buddhist scheme no one is condemned to abide permanently in any given realm. Hell is not a place of permanent damnation, nor is heaven a place of eternal happiness. The wheel revolves continuously, and individuals may move repeatedly in and out of any of the six destinations or *gatis*, as they are known. In this respect the Buddhist hell is more like the Christian purgatory. The second difference is that the Buddhist hell is more varied, and is thought to have cold as well as hot areas in which the departed spirits suffer by freezing until their evil *karma* is purged.

Above hell is the world of the ghosts, who suffer in a particular way. The denizens of this realm are pictured as people who were selfish and greedy in their previous life and who are now suffering the consequences by being denied the ability to enjoy the pleasures they crave. In popular art they are depicted as having swollen stomachs and tiny mouths through which they can never pass enough food to satisfy their constant hunger. Generosity is a highly regarded virtue in Buddhism, and the selfish merit a special punishment all of their own. These wraiths live in the shadows of the human realm, coming out in the twilight to consume the offerings left out for them by pious layfolk (See Figure 18).

The last of the three unfortunate realms is that of the animals. Rebirth in animal form involves physical suffering through being hunted both by humans and by other predators, and also has the disadvantage that animals are unable to reason and understand the cause of their predicament. Driven mainly by instincts they cannot control, and being without a language capable of conveying the subtleties of Buddhist teachings, animals can only hope for an existence relatively free from pain and to be born in a better condition in the next life. Buddhist folktales depict animals as being capable of virtuous behaviour to some degree, in keeping with modern studies which seem to suggest the higher mammals are capable of altruistic behaviour. For the most part, however, animals are greatly restricted in their capacity for autonomous moral choices. Although there is no dogma on this point Buddhism seems to envisage the realm of animal rebirth as limited to mammals, which means that contrary to popular belief you are unlikely to "come back as an ant." However, there are also some early sources which speak of human beings being reborn as worms, so it is not possible to be categorical on this point.

Figure 18 Wall mural depicting the sufferings of the hungry ghost (*preta*) realm, Haedongsa Monastery, Andong, Korea.

The human world is found in the fourth segment of the *bhavacakra*. Because it is so auspicious, and forms a kind of anteroom for *nirvāṇa*, rebirth as a human being is thought of as of great value, and a rare and difficult thing to attain. The great benefit of human existence is that it reminds us constantly of the facts of suffering and impermanence, and so our minds are constantly focused on the factors which spurred the Buddha to attain enlightenment. Had he remained cosseted within the palace walls (a situation perhaps analogous to that of the gods) he would never have found a permanent solution to life's problems. In addition to this, human beings are endowed with reason and free will, and are in position to use these faculties to understand Buddhist teachings and choose – if they wish – to follow the Noble Eightfold Path. While suffering certainly exists in human life, it is not unremittingly painful. There are many pleasant experiences too, such that on balance the human realm is thought to offer an appropriate "middle way" between the less attractive alternatives. Suffering is thus like the grit in the oyster, which in time producing the priceless pearl of *nirvāṇa*.

The most pleasant of the six realms of rebirth is undoubtedly heaven, which appears at the top of the diagram. Heaven is the residence of the gods (*deva*), who are beings who have accumulated sufficient good *karma* to justify a rebirth in paradise. The top five heavens are known as the "Pure Abodes", and are reserved for those known as "non-returners" (*anāgāmin*). These are individuals in the human world who are on the point of gaining enlightenment and will not be reborn again as human beings. There are no special theological overtones associated with a heavenly rebirth: the gods do not create the cosmos, control human destiny, forgive sins, pass judgment, demand worship, or perform any of the other functions we associate with God in the theistic traditions. Nor is heaven a place of permanent salvation: the gods are subject to the law of *karma* just like anyone else, and in due course they will be reborn in a lower realm.

Mythology locates the heavens above the great mountain known as Meru which was believed to lie at the centre of the world. Just as there are multiple hells, so there is a proliferation of heavens arranged in hierarchical order. Later sources (from the fifth century CE onwards) subdivide the heavenly realm into twenty-six different levels or "mansions" which are increasingly sublime. If we add to these the five other realms of rebirth shown in the *bhavacakra* we reach a total of thirty-one possible rebirth-destinations. The lower heavens were thought to be located on the slopes of Mount Meru, the higher terrestrial ones on its summit, with the more sublime heavens floating on top of it in space.

The gods at the different levels live for different periods of time. At the lower levels their life-spans are hundreds of times those of humans, and at the top their lives are measured in billions of years. Time is believed to be relative, however, and the gods perceive it differently according to their station: thus a million years of human time might seem like a week to the gods on the lower levels, and a day to the gods at the summit.

It might seem strange to say that rebirth in heaven is not the ultimate goal, and this statement needs some qualification. In practice, many if not most Buddhists would be only too happy to find themselves in heaven in their next rebirth, and many (both monks and laymen) make efforts to bring this about by the performance of good deeds and the like. However, all Buddhists accept that heaven is at best only a proximate goal, and the final aim is to attain *nirvāṇa* and put an end to rebirth altogether. There is even a *danger* to being reborn in heaven, namely that of becoming complacent and losing sight of the omnipresence of suffering. Being insulated from the more painful aspects of life causes the gods to lose sight of the painful realities the Buddha drew attention to in the First Noble Truth, and to slacken in their efforts to reach *nirvāṇa*. For this reason the human world is generally regarded as preferable and as the best place of rebirth.

The three spheres

Buddhist cosmology often seems untidy and contradictory, and this is because it is made up of competing schemes which do not always integrate perfectly with one another. For example, alongside the scheme of the six realms of rebirth just described is found an ancient Indo-European conception of the world as divided into three layers, probably based originally on the model of earth, atmosphere, and sky. In this tripartite model the surface of the earth is the domain of human beings. Above it are various atmospheric phenomena which as clouds, lightning and thunder, which became personified and regarded as divinities (for example like the Norse god Thor, who was thought to produce thunder by striking his hammer). Above the zone of the lower atmosphere where these intermediate phenomena take place is a higher realm, perhaps identified with the location of the sun, moon and stars. Buddhists imagined that matter became increasingly rarefied and refined in the higher levels, and eventually tapered away into realms which seem to consist of pure thought.

In the tripartite model, the lowest and most earthly of the three spheres is known as the "sphere of sense-desires" (*kāmāvacara*), and includes all of the realms up to the sixth heaven above the human world. Next is the "sphere of pure form" (*rūpāvacara*), a rarefied spiritual space in which the gods perceive and communicate by a kind of telepathy. This extends up to level twenty-seven. Highest of all is the "sphere of formlessness" (*arūpāvacara*), a state without material shape or form (*rūpa*) in which beings exist as pure mental energy.

The gods in the four highest levels, collectively known as the sphere of formlessness, are thought to apprehend phenomena in four increasingly subtle ways: in the lowest (level twenty-eight) it seems that all that exists is infinite space; in the second (level twenty-nine) as if there is nothing but infinite consciousness; in the third (level thirty) there is a pervasive impression of "nothingness," or the idea that even consciousness itself has been transcended. After leaving behind even the thought of "nothingness," there arises an ineffable state of mind known as "neither perception nor non-perception" (level thirty-one). This is the summit of existence and the highest state in which anyone can be reborn. As already noted, Buddhist ideas about cosmology dovetail with its meditational theory, and the names of the two highest levels of rebirth (levels thirty and thirty-one) bear the same names as the two highest stages of meditation. Access to these places or states can thus be gained either by being reborn in them or by tuning into their "frequency" through meditation.

See also: ***Dhyānas*; *Karma*.**

Damien Keown

COUNCILS

Councils were the mechanism by which the Buddhist monastic order attempted to limit the social and intellectual fragmentation that was endemic to its organization. The Buddhist monastic order (*sangha*) is organized in a segmentary fashion. Within any segmentary social organization, social identity and location are defined in terms of lineages rather than in terms of identifying characteristics or marked boundaries. In the Buddhist monastic order, one was ordained by someone, one was always the student of someone, and one belonged to his lineage; consequently, one's social location came from one's relations to the monks that one's teacher had also ordained and taught, monks who were fellow members of one's particular lineage. As is easily seen, fragmentation is inherent in segmentary social organizations wherever they occur. In the case of the Buddhist monastic order, students of a teacher go on to have their own students who, in turn, are more related to each other than to the monks who are in lineages of the other students of their teacher's teacher. With this inherent fragmentation of segmentary social organizations, in which an individual is related in varying degrees and in different ways and located within overlapping groups, competition and conflict are not uncommon. It should be no surprise, perhaps, that the earliest divisions in *Nikāya* Buddhism were around issues of monastic practice, and thus consequently about social locations within the larger monastic order.

One way that can be used to settle conflict between segmentary lineages is to claim a deeper genealogical connection between them by saying that the members of groups in competition and conflict are all students of a common teacher – teacher's teacher and so forth – and we can safely assume that such arguments were continually made in the Buddhist monastic order even if these arguments and the monks who made them did not make it into the historical record available to us. We might also speculate that the common tendency found across *Nikāya* Buddhism to identify a particular monk as the founder of a certain school, such as Katyāyanīputra with the Sarvāstivādins, was intended to maintain connections among groups that otherwise would be exclusively differentiated by positions of doctrine or practice.

The Buddhist councils can be seen as similar attempts to maintain relations of harmony among segmentary lineages by claiming the deepest genealogical connection possible: the Buddha and his teachings. When councils failed to establish such a deep connection, however, schism replaced fragmentation, and lineages that had merely been differentiated were subsequently separated by new divisions and perceived as unrelated groups.

Historical sources produced in the different schools of *Nikāya* Buddhism describe five different Buddhist councils. For modern historians, there is considerable doubt about even the broadest accuracy of these accounts, and perhaps they are best taken as descriptions of ideals that could motivate and guide subsequent action in unrecorded councils rather than as accounts of actual events. The different accounts are also frequently sectarian in their historical claims, generally attributing the deep genealogical connection to the Buddha and his teachings to the group or school which produced the account and portraying rival groups as beyond the pale. Such accounts obviously played a centrally visible role in the self-understanding of particular schools of *Nikāya* Buddhism and in defining their place in the history of the Buddha's legacy.

The first council described in Buddhist sources is said to have been held at the time of the Buddha's death in Rājagṛha under the sponsorship of the king of Magadha. Modern scholarship is generally skeptical about the accuracy of these accounts, even to the point of questioning whether it occurred at all. As portrayed, however, the first council was paradigmatic for subsequent councils in *Nikāya* Buddhism, particularly in its affirmation of the role of the king in re-establishing monastic unity. The purpose of the first council was to establish what it was that the Buddha had taught in order that his teachings might serve as the guiding rule for Buddhist practice.

A second council is said to have been held approximately 100 years after the death of the Buddha in Vaiśālī, and modern historical scholarship generally accepts that this council did occur in some fashion. The apparent cause of this council was concern over emerging differences in practice among different communities of Buddhist monks. Monks in Vaiśālī had accepted a set of practices which a visiting monk found objectionable when he observed them. These practices were about a variety of things, including the consumption of food, collective ritual practice, and the handling of money by monks. In general, it seems that the practices either assumed or created conditions that loosened the requirements of monastic life. A judgment was made by an appointed set of senior monks (*sthavira*) against the new practices, but many monks refused to abandon them and as a result of this refusal the monastic order began to be accepted as internally divided, rather than just fragmented.

Buddhist sources number these first two councils as the first and second, respectively. Modern scholarship identifies another council that is described in

Buddhist sources and which occurred approximately half a century after the second council at Vaiśālī. This council was held at Pāṭaliputra and attempted to resolve the monastic divisions that had festered after the second council. It failed, and the monastic community divided into two groups, the Sthaviras and the Mahāsāṃghikas, with each *nikāya* developing its own canon and especially its own *Vinaya*, as a way of claiming a genealogical connection to the Buddha.

Another council, numbered the third in Theravādin sources, was also held in Pāṭaliputra and was convened by the great Indian emperor, Aśoka, in the third century before the Common Era. It was concerned with doctrinal issues that had emerged within the monastic order and it is portrayed as affirming an orthodoxy as it was preserved by the Theravāda school itself. It may be the case that this council was a strictly Theravādin event, as it is mentioned in only Theravādin sources.

A fifth council was held in the first century of the Common Era in northwest India and was convened by the Kuṣāṇa emperor, Kaniṣka and presided over, according to some sources, by Aśvaghoṣa. It was exclusively a Sarvāstivādin council and it was primarily concerned with issues of *Abhidharma* doctrine based on the texts of the Sarvāstivādins. The *Vibhāṣā*, the great commentary on the foundational text of Sarvāstivādin *Abhidharma*, Katyāyanīputra's *Foundation of Knowledge* (*Jñānaprasthāna*), is said to have been composed at this council.

See also: **Kaniṣka; Katyāyanīputra; *Nikāya* Buddhism; Pāṭaliputra; *Sanghas*, sectarian; Sarvāstivāda.**

CHARLES HALLISEY

CURRENT ISSUES IN BUDDHIST STUDIES

Scholarly studies chronicling the academic investigation of Buddhism by Western researchers, and the issues driving those investigations, are extremely sparse in the literature. Since 1950, only a handful of reliable publications have emerged to inform the understanding of the discipline of Buddhist Studies. The most useful of these include: (1) U.N. Ghosal's "Progress in Buddhist Studies in Europe and America," in P.V. Bapat's *2500 Years of Buddhism* (1956); (2) Edward Conze's "Recent Progress in Buddhist Studies," originally published in *The Middle Way*, 34 (1959), and later included in his edited volume *Thirty Years of Buddhist Studies* (1968); Williams Peiris' *The Western Contribution to Buddhism* (1973); (4) Jan W. de Jong's "A Brief History of Buddhist Studies in Europe and America," in *The Eastern Buddhist*, NS 7 (1974); (5) de Jong's follow-up "Recent Buddhist Studies in Europe and America 1973–83," in *The Eastern Buddhist*, NS 17 (1984); (6) de Jong's eventual book *A Brief History of Buddhist Studies in Europe and America* (second, revised edition, 1987); (7) Charles Prebish's "Buddhist Studies American Style: A Shot in the Dark," in *Religious Studies Review* 9 (1983); (8) his follow-up chapter "The Silent Sangha: Buddhism in the Academy," in *Luminous Passage: The Practice and Study of Buddhism in America* (1999); (9) Russell Webb's "Pāli Buddhist Studies in the West," serialized in the now defunct *Pāli Buddhist Review*; and (10) Webb's "Contemporary European Scholarship on Buddhism," in Tadeusz Skorupski's edited volume *The Buddhist Heritage* (1989).

Perhaps the only conclusions that might be drawn from the above literature, insofar as conclusions are even possible, is that several distinctions appear obvious from an examination of these sources. First, geographic associations abound, which seem to identify at least four well-developed "schools" of Buddhology: the Anglo-German, led by Thomas W. Rhys Davids and Hermann Oldenberg;

the Franco-Belgian, led by Louis de La Vallée Poussin, Jean Pryzluski, Sylvain Lévi, Paul Demiéville, and Étienne Lamotte; the Leningrad, led by Fedor Stcherbatsky, Otto Rosenberg, and Eric Obermiller; and the American, led by Richard H. Robinson, Masatoshi Nagatomi, Alex Wayman, and Leon Hurvitz. To these, we might now also add a Japanese school, led by Junjirō Takakusu, Gadjin Nagao, Akira Hirakawa, Jukido Takasaki, Hajime Nakamura, and others. Second, and perhaps more importantly, the above categorizations describe reflect the "style" and emphasis of the scholarship involved. The Anglo-German school almost exclusively emphasized the Pāli literary tradition, and focused almost entirely on philological issues. The Franco-Belgian school utilized the Sanskritic materials, along with their translations and commentaries in Chinese and Tibetan, as well as moving beyond merely philological studies. The Leningrad school, emphasizing doctrinal issues, placed itself closer to the Franco-Belgian than the Anglo-German school, and the American school seemed to cover the entire roadmap of the above-mentioned schools.

What all of the above schools lacked was an element of self-reflection in their collective work. Lately, however, the discipline has become keenly aware of this desideratum, and has begun to engage in a useful process of self-reflection, broadly conceived, and the results of that inquiry are fruitful and inspiring. For example, the entire winter 1995 issue of the *Journal of the International Association of Buddhist Studies* (*JIABS*) was devoted to the topic "On method," providing the occasion for scholars to reflect on various aspects of the discipline. In that issue, seminal articles by IABS president D. Seyfort Ruegg, Luis O. Gómez, and José Cabezón raised important new concerns.

Near the outset of his article in the above issue of the *JIABS*, Gómez notes that:

> A scholarly discipline is not only a matter of disinterested intellectual effort, for it is evidently also a matter of the abstract application of intellectual curiosity through the medium of a discourse accessible, intelligible, and valuable to the intellectual elite, yet supported by a community that is interested in the veneer of learning.

He goes on to suggest that the difference between Buddhist Studies and Christian Studies is:

> that Buddhist Studies continues to be a Western enterprise about a non-Western product, a discourse about Buddhism taking place in a non-Buddhist context for a non-Buddhist audience of super-specialists, whose intellectual work persists in isolation from the mainstream of Western literature, art, and philosophy, and occasionally even from the mainstream of contemporary Buddhist doctrinal reflection.

This suggests that buddhological scholars find themselves in a very complicated and difficult arena in which to carry out their work.

For Gómez, it is the rich tradition of critical methods within Buddhism that provides the opportunity for successful intellectual exploration. He suggests including but moving beyond purely philological works to an examination of matters of lexicon, systems of thought, examination of the doctrinal traditions, textual histories, and the development of a profound critical awareness. He also recognizes that "we cannot forget the communities of new believers in the West, for whom a secular non-sectarian Buddhist scholarship will probably become a necessity."

Cabezón approaches the dilemma of modern buddhological study from a somewhat different perspective, beginning with institutional concerns. He says,

> It is often the case that a common pattern of institutional support provides a discipline

> with homogeneity. This is lacking in Buddhist Studies . . . Unlike other disciplines – even ones that are structurally homologous to our own, like Judaic Studies – Buddhist Studies has few secular institutional homes that it can call its own.

Nonetheless, Cabezón prognosticates that "what will guarantee the stability and longevity of the discipline is not the *insistence on homogeneity*, which in any case can now only be achieved through force, but instead by *embracing heterogeneity.*" Further, he champions methodological and theoretical heterogeneity, suggesting that buddhological scholars dismiss the series of all too prevalent stereotypes about their scholarship, not the least of which is that Buddhists never make good buddhologists. He argues aggressively for scholar-practitioners. Additionally, he suggests that buddhologists move beyond written texts: "There is today a call for the increased investigation of alternative semiotic forms – oral and vernacular traditions, epigraphy, ritual, patterns of social and institutional evolution, gender, lay and folk traditions, art, archaeology and architecture." There is little doubt that as Buddhist Studies continues the process of self-reflection, important new insights will emerge that will shape the discipline in the current century.

See also: **Academic study of Buddhism.**

CHARLES S. PREBISH

CYBER-BUDDHISM

There have been many predictions about how the future will be structured and determined by technology. One of the first was made by Marshall McLuhan ("the medium is the message"), who predicted that the changes created by modern technology would bring modern culture more in line with ancient oral traditions than with those of print culture. While print culture requires a high level of organization for the production of publications, cyber-culture tends to be decentralized and diffuse.

McLuhan's prescient appraisal can, to some degree, be seen in the emergence of cyber-Buddhism. With web pages that can be created easily and made available through the World Wide Web, cyber-Buddhism began to develop its own cultural patterns. For example, just as oral traditions used imagery to reinforce the spoken word, so too color and pictures accompany website textual data in the world of cyber-technology. A large number of images, from museum collections to graphics associated with ritual performances, populate web pages containing Buddhist material. In 2005 Google could report 231,000 images associated with the word search "Buddhist" and more than half a million for the word "Buddha." In addition, just as oral performances were constructed on the spot by the "singer," so too the Web allows for spontaneity and immediacy. Erik Davis, in *TechGnosis: Myth, Magic, and Mysticism in the Age of Information* (1998), explores this aspect of the interface between technology and religious practices.

Given these old/new patterns, Buddhist users of the Internet face an issue that was common to all in the first years of the new technology: how to define the "ethics of the virtual," or, in Gary Snyder's expressive words, the "Etiquette of Freedom." C.C. Hsieh of Academia Sinica in Taiwan, one of the earliest pioneers in computer science, has stated that the issue of the ethics of dealing with the virtual is one of the most pressing matters in terms of virus, hacking, identity theft, incorrect information, slander, and so forth. In his classes at the University of California, Davis, Snyder asks questions about the values that guide a life in which one can express oneself without interference or control. The answer, for this Buddhist poet, is found in the "wild." Nature and respect for survival, he suggests, can provide the guidance, or the "etiquette." Over time, cyber-communities have worked to create the mores that guide the behavior and decisions made within the realm of computer technology.

The World Wide Web was welcomed by many as a way to establish a cyber-community of Buddhists. Some even predicted the emergence of a single global Buddhist community, or *sangha*, through the connections made possible by the new technology. This approach can be seen in the work of Charles Prebish in publications such as *Luminous Passage: The Practice and Study of Buddhism in America* (1999). The group that wished to develop this new cyber-community proposed to use the core message of the Buddha's teaching as the basic content. Gary L. Ray published *CyberSangha: The Buddhist Alternative Journal* as a vehicle for new ideas and positions not held by the traditional Buddhist groups. The role of Buddhist women also found expression on the Internet. Sakyadhītā, an international association of Buddhist women formed in 1987 in Bodhgayā, India, began to use the Internet as a primary tool for realizing their stated mission of "compassionate social action through networking, education, publications, and practical training."

Ven. Pannyavaro, an Australian monk, edits an extensive website, BuddhaNet, in an effort to aid the development of what he termed an "online cyber *sangha*." As one of the vice-presidents of the World Fellowship of Buddhists, Ven. Pannyavaro provides a continuing and thoughtful appraisal of the role of new technology from within the inner circle of Buddhist leaders. As he uses the Internet for one aspect of his teaching, the difference he reports between the number of people coming to his live lectures and those who visit the website indicates how powerful the new medium of communication is. While sixty people might come to his center during one week, the website might be accessed by over 50,000 each day. Many of these visitors also send emails to the site. This is an unprecedented response to a Buddhist publisher and indicates the importance of the cyber-community.

Even with such a large involvement in a single site, the idea of a large unified global community of Buddhists communicating on the Web has not yet been realized. In place of a single cyber-community of Buddhists the Internet gives voice to the diverse ethnic forms of Buddhism and to traditional teachers. Ven. Pannyavaro, for example, is an ordained Theravāda monk and a member of the official organizational structure of Buddhism, so his site could hardly be described as an alternative to the existing Buddhist community. Also, while massive amounts of Buddhist data have been placed on the Internet by Buddhist communities, there is no sign of an emerging single focus. Once the technology was found to be well suited to spreading information about particular forms of religious belief and practice, websites produced by ethnic communities representing traditional teachers began to proliferate. Thousands of web pages began to appear as Buddhist groups around the world announced their programs and activities online. Thus, rather than fostering a unified *sangha*, the Web allows a greater diversity of opinions to reach audiences around the world. No single voice could dominate the new medium. It was, said one scholar, not just a "postmodern experiment," it was perhaps best described as "transmodern" a decentralized mass movement that is pluralistic and philosophically diffuse.

It is increasingly difficult to keep abreast of the extent and precise characteristics of Buddhism on the Internet. Not only it is impossible to encompass the data at the present, it is also beyond our resources to preserve all of the past data that has appeared And, as many of the early cyber-Buddhist sites are no longer maintained, it is unlikely that we can ever reconstruct a complete history of how the *Dharma* made its appearance in the new technology. Lacking a full understanding of the present and the past, we must await future analyses that can view the ways in which the millions of pages of Internet data persisted and stimulated new ways of thinking and communicating.

Professor Jim Taylor of the University of Adelaide, Australia has approached the issue from the point of view of modernity studies. He explores the idea of a major shift in the concept of space. Using the Thai environment, he discusses the transformation of religious space that occurs when the physical monastery, with its campus of buildings, is replaced by a virtual electronic space. As a result, he suggests that religion in modern urban settings may give privilege to the new technology, or simulated place, over physical space.

As mentioned, the hope for a unified Buddhist presentation on the Web was to some degree an attempt to escape from the dominance of culture-based traditions. The culturally contextualized Buddhism of Thailand, Sri Lanka, Tibet, Japan, Taiwan, or Korea requires interested persons to be immersed in more than just the basic teachings. For many, this cultural context constitutes a major barrier to the spread of the Buddhist tradition. The attempt to construct a Buddhist community apart from the older forms of the tradition is reminiscent of the Buddhist explorers from Victorian-era groups in England and their later counterparts in North America. When Colonel Henry Steel Olcott announced his conversion to Buddhism, he urged the modern Buddhist community to turn away from "superstitious" practices and find in their ancient texts a logical and comfortable teaching for the modern world. Quite naturally, Olcott carried into Buddhism many of the collective cultural practices of his own time. Later scholars would define the filtered Buddhism of this type to be "Protestant Buddhism." Those who sought to free the tradition from its ethnic roots could not help but describe the religion through the lenses of their own heritages. While the publications and influence of these nineteenth- and twentieth-century European and North American converts were significant, no large community of Buddhists has emerged entirely separate from ethic forms of the religion. The cyber-Buddhist community faced many of the same issues. Websites dedicated to new ways of viewing the religion and its teaching have appeared. Without the financial backing of the traditional religious communities, however, many appear for a short time and are then closed or no longer maintained or updated.

Another hope for cyber-Buddhism was the creation of an environment where individuals could speak freely and without the restrictions imposed by traditional structures and beliefs. This hope was partially realized as opinions began to be expressed about gender, sexuality, and political issues in Buddhism. These ideas were presented in asynchronous discourses that appeared in web journals (weblogs, or blogs) and wikis ("What I Know Is"), creating situations where the user was not only the receiver of information but could also be a provider. As more information was placed on the Internet through these innovative forms, serious questions were raised about how to judge their content. Blogs were conversations among individuals, and the greatest value of these conversations was in the moment of the encounter. Recording or preserving past conversations was not given high priority. But, even while ephemeral materials are difficult to preserve and study, there are numerous examples of the value of being able to look back and review the information contained in these less prized formats. Cyber-Buddhism clearly found an important avenue of expression in these media. Without some appraisal of the nature of these interchanges, it may be impossible to reconstruct the shifting perceptions of the first and second decades of Internet communication about Buddhism.

The academic domains where data are reviewed, edited, and curated, resisted the wiki model. Online encyclopedias such as Wikipedia allowed large set of Buddhist data to be accessible on the Web; however, the nature and value of the material could vary widely. Nonetheless, the persistence of the approach indicates the importance of this type of web-linked communication. A public forum came into existence through the medium of the wiki that allowed Buddhist scholars and interested individuals to circulate their material and receive responses from others. As communities of scholars form the users as well as the providers of the wiki content, the networking fosters contacts that would never occur with printed research material. Educators were also faced with the challenge of evaluating student work that had been written based on Internet data rather than traditional library research. Some mourned that students had lost the ability to write and read in the traditional fashion. In reality it is clear that their students were using websites for reading and blogs and text-message strategies for writing. This shift away from printed sources to digital resources for the study of Buddhism created a new type of cyber-scholarship. The understanding of the Buddhist tradition was being directly influenced by these changes.

A more formal presentation of Buddhist material appeared on a number of Internet sites that were both academic and sectarian. *Pacific World*, for example, is an annual journal in English devoted to the dissemination of historical, textual, critical, and interpretative articles on Buddhism generally and Shinshū Buddhism particularly. It is intended to serve both academic and lay readers. Another example of this type of cyber-Buddhism is the publication of *The Buddhist Himalaya*, one of the several projects of Nāgārjuna Institute of Exact Methods in Kathmandu. It promotes the study of Buddhist philosophy, art, iconography, history, biography, monuments and manuscripts in the Himalayan countries of Nepal, (northern) India, Tibet, and Bhutan. From BuddhaNet came a non-sectarian Buddhist magazine, *Buddha-Zine*. *Shenpen Osel*, published by Kagyu Shenpen Osel Choling (KSOC) in Seattle, Washington, is a more sectarian online journal that seeks to present teachings of the Kagyu lineages. These online resources constitute a response of the religious communities making use of the older ways of presenting ideas.

The ever-growing amount of online data creates an obvious need to help users locate digital material on Buddhism. In the early days of the Internet, Barry Kapke set up DharmaNet International as a central site for Buddhist information. Other efforts were also made to construct single portals to access available web-based data. Dr. T. Matthew Ciolek at Australia National University was another pioneer in this effort, and his site Buddhist Studies WWW Virtual Library became perhaps the best-known and most widely used portal for online Buddhist content. The Center for Buddhist Studies at National Taiwan University created a large database of online Buddhist texts and resources available in both English and Chinese. The Ohio State University maintained a mirror site of the material in order to make it more available. A number of sites provided more specialized portals. For example, the Halifax Zen Center opened the site Zen Cyber-Bones, which provides a listing of online resources on Zen Buddhism.

The task of creating portals for Buddhist studies was formidable. In the first few years of the Internet, it was possible to have a good idea of what the major websites were. But as the number of sites increased, the task of mastering them called for new approaches, and portals were replaced by powerful search engines. One of the early examples of this expanded capability was the commercial engine maintained by Lycos. In 1996 Lycos reported that their software had an index of 60 million documents. Other competitors appeared, such as Google and Yahoo! By 2005 Yahoo! would claim that their index covered 20 billion documents. Using these engines, Google hits for the word "Buddhism" resulted in a report of 5,490,000 documents; "Buddhist" resulted in 7,730,000. Yahoo reported 3,430,000 results for "Buddhist Studies," 21,900,000 for "Buddhist," and 16,000,000 for "Buddhism." It has become impossible for any single group to explore, classify, and evaluate these millions of pages, and tens of thousands of new ones are added every month. The need for search engines to develop more semantic elements and the ability to search within the content of the documents as well as the titles and key words became an ever more important task.

Alongside the sites that maintain extensive links to important web pages, others provide content directly. The most impressive Buddhist-operated sites for full text data, extensive references to online sites, and well-designed search aids are in Taiwan. One of these, known as CHIBS (Chung-Hwa Institute of Buddhist Studies), contained the first online version of the Chinese Buddhist canon. This site, offering a host of language classes, important journal articles dating back to the nineteenth century, and special projects relating to the Silk Road, was different from those whose primary offerings are portal services for links to other sites. CHIBS is a content-rich site where users can find hard-to-locate materials as well as advanced data sets. A less well-known site, the Library of Luminary Buddhist Institute, was an outstanding example of how a website can combine links with internal data. Both CHIBS and the Library of Luminary Buddhist Institute were set up and directed by monastics and trained lay persons as the major content providers. Another project is exemplified by the CyberSangha Buddhist Library, a collection of online Buddhist texts set up by the Santavihara Foundation. These groups conceive of their roles as a type of practice devoted to cyber-activities.

Another example of how the Internet helps to promote new forms of communication is Internet radio. The Internet Multicasting Service, launched in 1993 through the efforts of Carl Malamud, allows radio programs to go out over the Internet. One of the important stations that helped to initiate this type of activity for the Buddhist community was Lamrim.com, Tibetan Buddhist Internet Radio. As the title suggests, this 24-hour station offers on-demand programming about Tibetan practices, with lectures and chanting. Another example is the Savanata Sisilasa, Dhamma Talks Internet Radio, which became the first Internet station to broadcast in the Sinhala language. Through these radio stations, sound was given a place in the technology alongside the more prevalent text and image data.

The cyber-Buddhist tradition is firmly established and is becoming a part of the religious tradition. A poem Gelek Rinpoche wrote in 1993 to thank Michael Roach for his role in helping to create Buddhist databases for the canonic literature indicates the acceptance of the new technology by a senior lama. He wrote:

> Your deeds are pure,
> And white,
> A moon in the sky
> That lights
> Our great books . . .

LEWIS R. LANCASTER

D

DALAI LAMA (AND THE TIBETAN STRUGGLE)

Tenzin Gyatso, the Fourteenth Dalai Lama of the Tibetan *Gelugpa* (lit. "Model of Virtue," a.k.a. Yellow Hat) sect, is undeniably the most widely recognized Buddhist leader in the world today. As the head of the Tibetan community-in-exile, which generally regards him as the legitimate secular and spiritual leader of Tibet, he has consistently advocated for Tibetan autonomy while also calling upon Tibetans to love their Chinese overlords, even as their enemies, and to employ non-violent means as they resist foreign rule. He has received numerous awards and honors, including the Nobel Peace Prize in 1989 for his non-violent teachings.

The Dalai Lama was born Lhamo Thondup on 6 July 1935, in the north-eastern Tibetan province of Amdo. The title he bears means roughly "The Teacher Whose Wisdom is as Great as the Ocean." It was officially bestowed upon him on 22 February 1940, when he was enthroned as the *tulku* (lit. "apparent body") or reincarnation of the previous Dalai Lama, Thubten Gyatso, who died on 17 December 1933. He was also renamed Jetsun Jamphel Ngawang Lobsang Yeshe Tenzin Gyatso ("Holy Lord, Gentle Glory, Compassionate, Defender of the Faith, Ocean of Wisdom") at this time. During his childhood, he pursued traditional monastic studies, while his regent ruled in his name, but was forced to assume full responsibility as head of state at the age of fifteen on 17 November 1950, in response to the invasion of the country by the Chinese and the political instability that ensued. He nevertheless continued his monastic training, and in 1959 was awarded the *geshe lharampa* degree (roughly equivalent to a doctorate in Buddhist philosophy), just weeks prior to fleeing Tibet in March for a life of exile in India.

For centuries, the Dalai Lamas – who are considered incarnations of Chenrezig or Avalokiteśvara, the so-called "*Bodhisattva* of Compassion" – and their regents have exercised political control over large areas of the Tibetan Plateau by involving themselves in a series of "priest–patron" relationships, first with the Mongolian, and later the Manchurian, rulers of Central Asia and China. In exchange for their spiritual guidance – and, no doubt, legitimation of their rule – these overlords backed the Dalai Lama's rule of Tibet as their vassals. With the collapse of Manchurian rule of China in the early twentieth century, Tibet's relationship with China underwent radical change.

For a brief period, from the collapse of the Manchurian Qing dynasty in 1912 to the rise of Mao Zedong and the Communists to power in 1949, Tibet enjoyed virtual independence. This independence ended as the Communists consolidated power in China and began to extend their control over the region of Tibet in 1950. The Tibetans mounted a predictably ineffective resistance against the Chinese People's Liberation Army, and the Dalai Lama's attempts both to win the support of Western nations and to negotiate a Chinese withdrawal ultimately met with failure. In 1959 the Dalai Lama fled Tibet for India, where he has since lived in exile with tens of thousands of other refugees in the city of Dharamsala, called "Little Lhasa," the seat of Tibet's unrecognized government-in-exile.

The consequences of direct Chinese rule of Tibet have been, by most reports, catastrophic for the Tibetan people, their culture, and the ecology of the region. It is reported, for instance, that as many as one million Tibetans have died either by torture and execution at the hands of Chinese, or from malnutrition and starvation brought on by two periods of famine resulting from Communist mismanagement of agricultural resources. In addition, the Buddhist traditions of Tibet have been subject to extreme attack, especially during the Cultural Revolution, when monks and nuns were forced to reenter lay life against their will and more than 6,000 religious sites were destroyed. The Chinese government has also implemented a massive population transfer program with the apparent goal of making Tibetans a minority in their own land and eroding the traditional culture of the region. With regard to the natural environment, China has reportedly used Tibet as a nuclear-waste dumping ground, while also clear-cutting her eastern forests, destroying ecosystems, and threatening numerous species of wildlife with extinction.

In response to these catastrophes, the Dalai Lama and the Tibetan community-in-exile have engaged in the two-fold task of preserving Tibetan culture while also working to re-establish Tibetan independence. In regard to the latter, there has been disagreement between the Dalai Lama and the elected government-in-exile, with the latter agitating for total independence from China and preparing for direct rule, and the former working to reach a "Middle Way" compromise that would recognize Chinese rule while also allowing for the self-governance of Tibet. The Dalai Lama's Five Point Peace Plan, which he first proposed before members of the United States Congressional Human Rights Caucus on 21 September 1987, calls for the transformation of Tibet into a demilitarized "zone of peace," the abandonment of China's population-transfer policy, respect for the Tibetan people's fundamental human rights and democratic freedoms, restoration and protection of Tibet's natural environment, and the commencement of "earnest negotiations" on the future status of Tibet vis-à-vis China. Even more recently, he has proposed that Tibet be administered as a self-governing democracy "in association with the People's Republic of China." Though China would control her defense and most of her dealings with foreign nations, Tibet would still, under this proposal, be ruled internally by a democratically elected government. To date, no such compromise has been reached.

Much of the strategy of the Dalai Lama and other Tibetans living in exile who are working to free Tibet from Chinese rule has been to raise consciousness of their plight around the world and enlist foreign governments to support their cause. They have generally been more successful at the first than the second of these goals. Much of this success owes to the public relations genius of the Dalai Lama and his ability to use his office and various media to publicize the plight of the Tibetan people globally. He travels routinely, giving speeches to crowds of tens of thousands and meeting with heads of state and religious leaders, as well as Hollywood celebrities and producers who have helped to broadcast his message to millions through movies such as *Kundun* and *Seven Years in Tibet*. The Dalai Lama has also published numerous very popular essays and books, including *The Art of Happiness* (with Howard C. Cutler), *The Compassionate Life*, *Ethics for a New Millennium*, and *Freedom in Exile: The Autobiography of the Dalai Lama*.

While the Dalai Lama's teachings undoubtedly grow out of his training and experience as a Tibetan Buddhist *lama* and in response to the specific needs of his people, they have also been promulgated as universal teachings relevant to everyone, regardless of their religion or context. These "engaged Buddhist" teachings focus on the equality and interdependence of all persons as seekers of "happiness" and their equal right to pursue their happiness freely, in concert with others. While some observers see this notion of equality as grounded in Buddhist doctrines, such as the universal Buddha-nature, the Dalai Lama only sometimes makes this connection explicit, preferring instead to develop his teachings along non-sectarian lines. Unlike some contemporary Buddhist theorists, who see a conflict between basic Buddhist teachings and notions of human rights, the Dalai Lama embraces human rights as consistent with Buddhism. As noted above, he is an ardent advocate of non-violence and the power of truth, though he also recognizes that violence is, in many cases, inevitable, and in some, even necessary. The key for him, even when resorting to violence, is to do so only out of a sense of compassion, even for those upon whom violence must be perpetrated. Notably, he was roundly criticized by pacifists for his failure to condemn the United States' invasion of Iraq in 2003, although he did exhort the US to "think seriously [about] whether a violent action is the right thing to do" prior to the war.

The future of Tibet and the Tibetan people in exile is, of course, difficult to predict. The refugees, though still considering Dharamsala (lit. "House of Rest") their temporary home, have lived in exile for over forty years and it is sadly coming to look more and more like their permanent residence. While some in the Chinese government undoubtedly fear uprisings in Tibet should the Dalai Lama die in exile, some also speculate that the government may use his death as an opportunity to select and train the next Dalai Lama in China. For his part, the Dalai Lama has claimed that he will never be reborn in a Tibet ruled by the Chinese, and may even forego rebirth altogether. Still, as long as his homeland is threatened by foreign domination, he thinks it likely he will return to help further lead his people toward liberation. At any rate, the search for and naming of the next Dalai Lama is certain to be one of the most politically contentious and significant episodes in the history of the office.

See also: **Buddhist peace groups (in Asia and the West); Dalai Lamas; Engaged Buddhism; Global Buddhist networks: selected examples; Human rights; Maha Ghosananda; Nhat Hanh, Thich; Tibet, Buddhism in; Tibetan Buddhism in exile.**

JIM DEITRICK

DALAI LAMAS

One of the most significant innovations of Tibetan Buddhism is the institution of reincarnating lamas (*sprul sku*). This is based on the Mahāyāna beliefs that Buddhas and *bodhisattvas* take repeated rebirths for the benefit of sentient beings and that they are able consciously to choose their rebirth situations. The Dalai Lama lineage began in the sixteenth century, when the Mongol chieftain Altan Khan gave Sönam Gyatso (bSod nams rgya mtsho, 1543–88) the Mongol title "*ta le*" ("ocean"), which implied that he was an "ocean of wisdom." The members of this lineage are believed by Tibetan Buddhists to be physical emanations of the buddha Avalokiteśvara (Tib. sPyan ras gzigs).

The title was retrospectively accorded to Sönam Gyatso's two predecessors, and was passed on to his successor, Yönden Gyatso (Yon tan rgya mtsho, 1589–1617), who was a great-grandson of the Mongol chieftain Altan Khan. The birth of a Dalai Lama in the Mongol royal family created a close bond between the Gelukpa Order (with which the Dalai Lamas are most closely associated) and the Mongol khans, and this connection led to the fifth Dalai Lama, Ngawang Losang Gyatso (Ngag dbang blo bzang rgya mtsho, 1617–82), taking control of the country with the help of Mongol forces in the seventeenth century.

From this time onward, the Dalai Lamas were the rulers of most of the Tibetan plateau. During the fifth Dalai Lama's lifetime, construction began on the Potala, a huge palace that sits on a hill in Lhasa, the capital of Tibet. Until the Chinese invasion of the 1950s, it was the seat of the Tibetan government.

The sixth Dalai Lama, Tsangyang Gyatso (Tshangs dbyangs rgya mtsho, 1683–1706), deviated significantly from the paradigms of his predecessors. Preferring a life devoted to romance and poetry rather than religion, he moved out of the Potala and into an apartment in the village below. He is best known for his romantic poetry, but Tibetans do not question his authenticity. The seventh Dalai Lama, Kelsang Gyatso (1708–57), was by all accounts an exemplary monk and scholar, but his next few successors died young and failed to exert significant influence.

The thirteenth Dalai Lama, Tupden Gyatso (1876–1933), was one of the most powerful members of the lineage. He consolidated power over most of the Tibetan plateau, and worked to establish Tibet's independence and to develop its ability to defend itself against foreign aggression. His efforts to modernize the army and education systems were mostly scuttled after his death by conservative monastic leaders, however, and his successor, Tenzin Gyatso (bsTan 'dzin rgya mtsho, 1935–), inherited a militarily weak and divided country. Following early Chinese attacks on eastern Tibet, he was invested with full authority at the age of sixteen, and after Chinese troops conquered his country he tried to work with the interim administration. Following a popular uprising in Lhasa in 1959, he fled into exile in India, where he subsequently established a government-in-exile in Dharamsala, Himachal Pradesh. Since that time, he has become the most potent symbol of Tibetan resistance and an international spokesman for Tibetan Buddhism, drawing huge crowds all over the world. In 1989 he was awarded the Nobel Peace Prize in recognition of his efforts to find a peaceful resolution to the crisis in his homeland.

See also: **Tibet, Buddhism in; Vajrayāna Buddhism.**

JOHN POWERS

DE JONG, JAN WILLEM

Born in Leiden on 15 February 1921, Jan de Jong was initially educated at the University of Leiden between 1942 and 1945. His primary interest was Chinese, but he also trained in Sanskrit and Japanese.

Hindered in the Netherlands by the difficulty of studying during the German occupation, following the war he went to Harvard in 1946. There he studied under W.E. Clark and established life-long friendships with the well-known Sanskritists Daniel H.H. Ingalls and Franklin Edgerton. Between 1947 and 1950, he studied under Paul Demiéville at the Sorbonne and the Collège de France in Paris. During this period, he also learned Tibetan and Mongolian. He eventually completed his Ph.D. at Leiden, with a dissertation titled *Cinq Chapîtres de la Prasannapadā*, which was eventually published in Paris. Between 1950 and 1953, he served as Research Assistant at Leiden, then Lecturer (1953–6), and in 1956 became the first Professor of Tibetan and Buddhist Studies in the Netherlands. Along with his colleague F.B.J. Kuiper, he launched the well-known *Indo-Iranian Journal*, which he co-edited until 1998. They also established a monograph series of the same name. In 1965, de Jong became Head of the Department of South Asian and Buddhist Studies at the Australian National University in Canberra, and later he became Dean of the Faculty of Asian Studies. By that time, he had visited Japan, first in 1963, and again every ten years thereafter. In 1996, during his last visit, he served as a visiting professor at the International College of Advanced Buddhist Studies. In 1998, de Jong developed cancer, and died on 22 January 2000.

Along with his fluency in Buddhist languages, Jan de Jong also knew English, French, German, Italian, Danish, and Russian. From this solid linguistic base, he read voraciously and began to develop a huge personal library that totaled more than 10,000 volumes by the time of his death. Because of his unique capacity for reading copious numbers of books and monographs, and his personal interest in text-critical scholarship, de Jong's venue of choice for his personal writing was reviewing books. One scholar noted that of his 870 total writings, 700 were book reviews. These were no simple writings either. Some extended to twenty pages, and all were typified by what another scholar referred to as his "hypercritical" approach. They offered philological observations, criticisms of textual and grammatical points, bibliographic omissions, social and doctrinal misunderstandings, and the like. He remains no doubt the most brutal reviewer of books in the history of Buddhist Studies.

To celebrate his sixtieth birthday, his colleagues L.A. Hercus, F.B.J. Kuiper, T. Rajapatirana, and E.R. Skrzypczak honored him with a festschrift entitled *Indological and Buddhist Studies.* Some of de Jong's writings have appeared in two separate collections, one edited by Gregory Schopen as *Buddhist Studies by J.D. de Jong* in 1977, and the other by de Jong himself as *Tibetan Studies* in 1994. A bibliography of his work between 1949 and 1973 was also published by the Faculty of Asian Studies of the Australian National University. His book *A Brief History of Buddhist Studies in Europe and America* provides much information on the discipline of Buddhist Studies, although it barely mentions American scholars.

See also: **Academic study of Buddhism.**

CHARLES S. PREBISH

DE SILVA, RANJANI

Ranjani de Silva has been *the* prime mover in the re-establishment of the *bhikkhunī sangha* in Sri Lanka although she has remained a laywoman herself. She was president of Sakyadhītā International from 1995 to 2000 and is currently president of Sakyadhītā Sri Lanka. In 2004 she received a United Nations Outstanding Buddhist Women award. She also founded a Sakyadhītā training center for *dasasilmātās* (ten-precept women) in 1993.

An article in the *Sunday Observer* Online (4 April 2004) provides some personal background. She was born in Mirissa, Mathara, Sri Lanka and completed high school at the women's high school, Sujata Vidyalaya. She was interested in Buddhism from childhood. She worked as the manager of the Personnel and Administration Department of the State Engineering Corporation for twenty-three years. While there, she was very involved in welfare work for the employees, experience that would be valuable to her in training *dasasilmātā*s for work in the community after their ordination.

In 1984 after an early retirement she took a ten-day meditation course. The course was given by Ayya Khema, a German-born Theravāda nun who lived in Sri Lanka for several years. Through Ayya Khema, one of the conference organizers, she attended the first Sakyadhītā conference in Bodhgayā in 1987. There she was able to compare the state of the *dasasilmātās* with the nuns she met from other countries. She was determined to improve the living conditions and training of Sri Lankan nuns. Immediately after her return, she trained ten *dasasilmātās* for hospital service and formed a chapter of Sakyadhītā from a group of fifty women of the All Ceylon Women's Buddhist Congress. Their first president was scholar Kusuma Devendra (who went on to become fully ordained in 1996). Inspired by the second conference in Thailand, she invited Sakyadhītā to hold the third in Colombo. In "Reclaiming the Robe" she notes that the Supreme Advisory Council of the Ministry of Buddhist Affairs opposed the conference and tried to demand that the ordination issue not be mentioned so as not to give women "false hopes" that ordination might be reinstated. The women refused, and with the help of two senior, respected monks the conference was convened.

The two monks, Ven. Mapalagama Vipulasar Thera and Ven. Inamaluwe Sumangala Thera, supervised the training of additional nuns who received ordination at Sārnāth in 1996 and Bodhgayā in 1998. There are about 400 fully ordained nuns who appear to be generally well respected by the broader community, yet still the Advisory Council refuses to acknowledge them. Thus, nuns receive no government funding but manage on donations from the laity. In addition, there are about 3,000–4,000 *dasasilmātās* throughout the country, mostly in rural areas. De Silva has been able to get some funding from the Heinrich Böll Foundation for the nuns at the main center.

Ranjani de Silva believes that monastic resistance to the re-establishment of the *bhikkhunī sangha* is simply based upon reluctance on the part of the male hierarchy to share wealth, power and prestige with a strong and active community of women. The monastic issues of *Vinaya* lineage are settled. The public complaints by conservative monks have been answered by Pāli and Buddhist scholars who are supportive of the efforts for full ordination.

Ranjani de Silva continues to work tirelessly on behalf of the nuns of Sri Lanka. When five *dasasilmātās* were ordained at His Lai temple in the United States in 1988 they returned to Sri Lanka to silence and marginalization, and reverted to lives as *dasasilmātās.* Now their ordination is greeted with celebration. They go on alms rounds and are becoming respected leaders within their communities. This change is caused, in large part, by Ranjani de Silva.

See also: **Women in Buddhism: an historical and textual overview.**

MAVIS L. FENN

DEATH AND DYING IN TIBETAN BUDDHISM

All traditions of Tibetan Buddhism emphasize the importance of awareness of the immanence of death and the impermanent nature of cyclic existence. There is an extensive literature on death and dying in Tibetan, and in recent years Tibetan teachings on these topics have hit a responsive chord in the West. Two of the key focal points of this literature are the uncertainty of the time of death and the preciousness of a human rebirth. Death can occur at any moment, and when it does only religious practice will be of any use. Moreover, rebirth as a human being is very rare, and humans are uniquely positioned to take advantage of Buddhist teachings and practices and thus attain liberation, so wise people should decide to devote their energies to following the Buddhist path.

Of particular importance in Tibetan Buddhism are teachings on the "intermediate state" (*bardo*, Skt. *antarābhava*), the period between lives during which one's consciousness makes the transition from one body to another. The classic work on this is entitled *Liberation through Hearing in the Intermediate State* (*Bar do thos grol*), a manual used to guide the dead through the *bardo*. According to this text, during the death process the coarser levels of consciousness drop away as the physical body degenerates. At the moment of death, the "mind of clear light" (*'od gsal sems*, Skt. *prabhāsvara-citta*) manifests, and all conscious knowledge of one's past life is left behind.

During the *bardo* process, one encounters various intense sights and sounds, including bright lights of different colors. If one has previously engaged in death meditation, one may be able to recognize that these are merely manifestations of one's own mind that present opportunities for meditative practice, and even liberation. Successful meditators may emerge from the *bardo* as fully awakened Buddhas, but this only happens in exceptional cases.

If one dies violently, the *bardo* process may last for a short time, but with natural death one may remain in the *bardo* for up to seven days. If one is an advanced meditator who is able to control the death process, it can be extended for up to forty-nine days, after which one will take rebirth unless one has managed to use the opportunity to escape from cyclic existence.

Tibetan *bardo* literature assumes *tantric* physiology, which conceives the human body as having 72,000 channels through which subtle energies called "winds" (*rlung*, Skt. *prāṇa*) and "drops" (*thig le*, Skt. *bindu*) move. The most important are the central channel and the two channels on its right and left. During the process of death, the winds that are the bases of consciousness dissolve into the right and left channels, and then in turn they all coalesce in the wind of the central channel. At the same time, the energies that had held the drops in place weaken, and they move to the heart *cakra*. When all the winds dissolve into the "indestructible drop" the mind of clear light manifests. This is the moment of actual death according to tantric medical theory, and the beginning of the *bardo* process.

See also: **Tibet, Buddhism in.**

JOHN POWERS

DECLINE OF THE *DHARMA*

From the earliest times it was felt that the *Dharma*, in the sense of the body of Buddhist teachings or Buddhism as a religion, would not endure long in the present age. The general context for such an outlook is provided by Buddhist cosmological notions which depict the universe as undergoing vast cycles of progress and decline and locate the present age as in the latter category. While the *Dharma* as ultimate truth will endure for ever, the *Dharma* as an earthly institution is like everything else caught up in a downward spiral which is slowly but surely accelerating.

Predictions about the decline and disappearance of the True *Dharma* (*saddharmavipralopa*) were made from the earliest times and repeated down the centuries, particularly when calamities of one kind or another seemed to threaten the survival of the religion. The Buddha himself stated that because of the admission of women into the *sangha* the True *Dharma* would last only 500 years instead of 1,000 (*Saṃyutta Nikāya* 2.224). This calculation is used by later sources which evolve a three-stage theory of decline: first, that of the True *Dharma* (*saddharma*); second, that of the Counterfeit *Dharma* (*pratirūpakadharma*); and third, that of the End of the *Dharma* (*paścimadharma*). During the first, which would last 500 years, the teachings of the Buddha would be transmitted with minimal distortion, and beings had a good chance of understanding and practicing them, and of achieving enlightenment (*bodhi*). During the second period, also 500 years, the substance would be gone and only the outer forms of practice would remain. Fewer beings would attain the goal at this time. During the third period, even the semblance of genuine practice would disappear, and beings would be left to their own devices. There is considerable variation among the sources over the length of each phase of decline, with some claiming that the first phase lasts for 1,000 years and the second for 500.

The notion of the decline of the *Dharma* was particularly emphasized in East Asian Buddhism. In China, *The Scripture Preached by the Buddha on the Total Extinction of the Dharma* (fourth–fifth century CE) is one of the earliest of a large body of Chinese Buddhist texts describing the degeneration of the Buddha's teaching caused by moral laxity and depravity within the religious community. In Japan the concept of decline was known as *mappō*, and according to most calculations of the time of the Buddha's death, the world was already in the period of *mappō*. While this may appear to be cause for despair, many in East Asia actually responded to this analysis not by giving up, but by advocating new and creative doctrines. In response to *mappō*, new schools arose, such as the Pure Land and Nichiren schools, asserting that the Buddha had foreseen and provided for the advent of this final age by preparing texts and teachings suited for beings born in this time. These teachings had been discovered and propagated to counter the adverse conditions of *mappō* and give beings hope for liberation. This assertion validated texts, teachings, and practices that obviously conflicted with what was known of early Buddhism by arguing that the difference between the first period of the True *Dharma* and the present period made it necessary that the teachings be significantly different. It was felt that the degenerate conditions of the present age demanded such measures.

See also: ***Dharma*; Japan, Buddhism in.**

DAMIEN KEOWN

DEITY CULTS

Everywhere Buddhism eventually took root, people had been propitiating and petitioning deities and similar non-human beings for centuries or even millennia prior to becoming Buddhist. India's Vedic as well as pre-Vedic gods (*deva*), snake-gods (*nāga*), and protector-beings (*yakṣas*) were paralleled by the *deviyo* and *yaku* of Sri Lanka, Thai *phī*, Burmese *nats*, Japanese *kami* or the *Bon-po* deities of Tibet, beings believed real and capable of rendering both assistance and harm to humans, especially in connection with nature and farming or hunting, childbirth, physical and mental health and disease, and group honor.

Buddhism's relationship with these different deity cults has ranged from condemnation to assimilation, but especially among more traditional segments of the population deity cults have constituted an important aspect of ritual and practice throughout Buddhist history. Scholars differ on whether these cults should be viewed as separate religions that coexist with Buddhism (especially in Tibet and Japan, where Bon-po and Shintō, respectively, are institutionalized as such), as syncretic additions to Buddhism, or as fully integrated dimensions of Buddhism. Others still would treat both Buddhism and the pre-Buddhist cults as part of a single, larger Tibetan, Sinhala or Khmer religion.

The Buddha and the gods

The Buddha himself was raised in a theistic world, and his own ambiguous relationship with non-human beings has played out in the history of the religion. On the one hand, he at least questioned (and in some instances seems flatly to have denied) the relevance, morality, and even the existence of deities and similar beings. But on the other hand even the earliest traditions have him interacting with gods (especially Brahmā and Śakra), *nāgas* (such as Muccalinda), and malevolent beings (including Māra and various *yakṣas* and *rākṣasas*), which means the early Buddhists at least entertained their discursive (and perhaps their ontological) reality. These beings are portrayed universally – though not always enthusiastically – submitting to the greater authority of the Buddha; many *dhāraṇīs* and *parittas* invoke that authority to assemble supernatural forces of sometimes formidable dimension, and huge statues of *yakṣas* armed with clubs stood at ancient Buddhist sites demonstrating Buddhist command of the resultant power. Similar ambiguity is seen in the Buddha's response to deity-related practices, some of which (notably animal sacrifice) were condemned while others, as in the Buddha's famous advice to Sigāla (*Dīgha Nikāya* 3.180–93), were reinterpreted in Buddhist guise.

Contention and assimilation

Though countless myths record the initial antagonism of indigenous deities to the Buddha, *sangha*, and relics, they invariably end in harmonization; at the very least, the *deva*s or *kami* in question respond to the compassion shown them by the Buddha or his followers with a promise to stop harassing them. But in many cases these indigenous deities end up becoming Buddhists themselves, in varying degrees, promising that they will actively serve the religion (often in return for periodic worship and recognition) even as they retain their original character. Thus, like the *yakṣas* of ancient India, the Chinese deity Wei To was believed to protect monasteries and *Dharma*, and shrines were provided for him in traditional Chinese monastic complexes; whole classes of protective deities (*Qie lan*) were invoked daily as part of afternoon devotions. Similarly, each Tibetan sect honors a high patron deity to whom its rituals are dedicated. In Sri Lanka, Buddhist temples are the primary venues for Buddhist worship of the originally Hindu deities starting with Viṣṇu whose statues are ubiquitously found in them; the gods are conceived of as fellow Buddhists (sometimes even as *bodhisattvas*, Sinh. *budu wena deviyo*) whose good works in the world are attempts at progressing along the Buddhist path.

Indeed, the line between deities and *bodhisattvas* (and in Mahāyāna and Vajrayāna contexts existing Buddhas and their various fierce and benevolent emanations) is often blurred: all Buddhas have lived lives as gods while cultivating the *bodhisattva* path; intercessionary *bodhisattvas* and Buddhas like Avalokiteśvara and Vairocana have been conflated with indigenous deities such as the Chinese goddess of mercy Guanyin and the Japanese supreme solar *kami* Amaterasu Ōmikami, respectively; like deities, whom their statues often resemble, *bodhisattvas* are installed in temples, petitioned for worldly help, celebrated with festivals and provided with additional forms of worship generally reserved for deities proper (for example, the celebration of Guanyin's birthday in China) or, in the case of fierce emanations, propitiation as might be offered a malevolent being. In other cases still – as happened often with the *kami* in Japan – indigenous deities have been so Buddhicized as to lose their original character altogether. At the furthest end of the scale, some deities – such as the variously conceived guardian deities of the four directions (*Vidyārājas*, Jap. *Myō-ō*), or various classes of supernatural beings not encountered outside Buddhist contexts – appear to have been Buddhist from the start.

Purposes and methods of worship

Scholars have identified numerous, overlapping reasons that deity cults have been so thoroughly integrated into Buddhism. Clearly, centuries-old traditions are not easily eradicated, and it appears that Buddhists have never even tried to effect it. In addition to the Buddha's own tolerance of others' religious beliefs and practices, in some cases the accommodating attitude which characterized the historical spread of Buddhism has been portrayed as conscious strategy to help localize and muster support for the religion. Other scholars have stressed the ways that interceding deities and/or *bodhisattvas* can soften the harsh edge of personal soteriological responsibility and *karmic* absoluteness at the core of the early Buddhist tradition; by intervening in worldly affairs these figures fulfill what would appear from their ubiquity in human religious history to be a basic religious need. Finally, the integration of these cults can be seen as compassionate outreach to the beings themselves, who like all beings are subject to suffering.

Worship of deities and related classes of beings varies as much as do the deities themselves. Offerings (*pūjā*) to images and other surrogates, processions, salutation (*namaskāra*) and eulogy (*stotra*), annual festivals and associated rites like the empowerment of *yantras*, *maṇḍalas* and amulets appear very similar to their strictly Buddhist counterparts, though the differences are consistently marked by different types of offering or different content in eulogies. Deity-related rites may be performed independently, but more often they integrate Buddhist elements and/or are themselves integrated into Buddhist full moon day rites, processions and festivals.

Especially in esoteric traditions, deity rituals may also involve more intimate relationships with these beings including visualization and initiation or even self-transformation into them; intentional or unintentional possession by deities and related beings is commonly encountered throughout the Buddhist world, and traditions of healing, exorcism, rain-making and prognostication have developed in relation to it.

See also: **Buddha, bodies of; Buddha, relics of; Cosmology and rebirth; Famous Buddhists and ideal types; Holidays and observances; *Mantras*, *mudrās*, and *maṇḍalas*; South and Southeast Asia, Buddhism in; Vajrayāna Buddhism.**

JONATHAN S. WALTERS

DEPENDENT ORIGINATION (*PRATĪTYA-SAMUTPĀDA*)

The doctrine of Dependent Origination (Skt. *pratītya-samutpāda*, Pāli *paṭicca-samuppāda*) is a fundamental Buddhist teaching on causation and the ontological status of phenomena. The term *pratītya-samutpāda* is variously translated as

"Dependent Origination," "Dependent Arising," and "Origination-in-Dependence," but these alternative translations all express the same central concept, namely that nothing arises independently or from itself alone. The doctrine teaches, instead, that all phenomena arise in dependence on causes and conditions.

The doctrine of Dependent Origination is expressed in its simplest form in the Sanskrit phrase "*idaṃ sati ayaṃ bhavati,*" or "when this exists, that arises." This postulate can be expressed in the logical form A→B (when condition A exists, effect B arises), or as its negation −A→−B (where condition A does not exist effect B does not arise). An important implication of this teaching is that there is nothing that comes into being through its own power or volition, and there are therefore no entities or metaphysical realities (such as God or a soul) that transcend the everyday nexus of causes and effects. In this respect the doctrine dovetails with the teaching of no-self (*anātman*). Early sources indicate that the Buddha became enlightened under the *Bodhi* tree when he fully realized the profound truth of Dependent Origination, and saw that all phenomena are conditioned (*saṃskṛta*) and arise and cease in a determinate series.

There are various formulations of the doctrine in early sources, but the most common one illustrates the soteriological implications of causality in a series of twelve stages or links (*nidāna*) showing how the problem of suffering (*duḥkha*) and entrapment in *saṃsāra* arises because of craving and ignorance. Some early texts mention fewer than twelve stages, while others vary the order slightly, but the settled formulation of twelve links becomes established at quite an early date and remains the standard formulation from then on.

The twelve links in the process (often shown around the rim of the "wheel of life" or *bhavacakra*) are:

1 ignorance (*avidyā*);
2 formations (*saṃskāra*);
3 consciousness (*vijñāna*);
4 name and form (*nāma-rūpa*);
5 six sense spheres (*ṣad-āyatana*);
6 contact (*sparśa*);
7 feelings (*vedanā*);
8 craving (*tṛṣṇā*);
9 grasping (*upādāna*);
10 becoming (*bhava*);
11 birth (*jāti*);
12 old age and death (*jarā-maraṇa*).

The significance of the links is open to interpretation, but one popular understanding followed by both Buddhaghosa and Vasubandhu is that the series extends over three lives. Thus (1)–(2) relate to the previous life, (3)–(7) to the conditioning of the present existence, (8)–(10) to the fruits of the present existence, and (11)–(12) to the life to come.

In narrative form the sequence describes a pattern of events which explains how we come to find ourselves afflicted by suffering in the manner described in the First Noble Truth. The first link, ignorance, signifies that in our previous lives we failed to heed the Buddha's teachings and accumulated *saṃskāras* or karmic formations (the second link) which in turn caused our consciousness to arise in the present life (the third link). As human beings we exist in two dimensions with a mind and body (the fourth link) and experience the world through certain sense-modalities (the fifth link). Relating to the world in this way we make contact (the sixth link) with external reality. The sensory stimulus we receive from the outside world causes us to respond emotionally to it (the seventh link): for example, either we like it, don't like it, or are neutral towards it. A preference develops for certain kinds of feelings over others, and we seek more of those we like and less of those we do not like (the eighth link). These preferences become stronger and we begin to grasp (the ninth link) at particular options and opportunities which promise further experiences of the kind desired. We become habituated to patterns of behaviour which then become our mode of being (the tenth link, and the last in the second life). At death, the impetus to experience the same pleasures anew leads us to be reborn again (the eleventh link), and inevitably to old age and death (the twelfth and final link).

Above we have described the sequence in a forward-moving direction illustrating how suffering arises, but it can also be used to show how suffering is ended when the process is unwound. Indeed, a description of how the same structure becomes the way of achieving enlightenment follows most summaries of the twelve links in Pāli sources. This alternative formulation describes how when ignorance is removed, the karmic formations (*saṃskāras*) also cease, as do consciousness, mind and body and the six senses. Sense contact likewise ceases, as do feeling, craving, grasping, becoming, and birth, old age, and death. The formulation of the twelve links of Dependent Origination thus shows how causal factors operate in generating both the problem of suffering and its solution.

Various later schools came to their own, sometimes radical, understanding of the doctrine. Chief among these is that of the Madhyamaka, for whom Dependent Origination came to be synonymous with emptiness (*śūnyatā*). According to Nāgārjuna, the doctrine of Dependent Origination could only be coherent if phenomena were devoid of self-essence (*svabhāva*). The term *svabhāva* means intrinsic nature, self-being or own-being, in the sense of a permanent and unchanging identity or substratum of the kind denied in the "no-self" (*anātman*) teachings. According to the *Abhidharma*, the *svabhāva* was the unique and inalienable "mark" or characteristic (*lakṣaṇa* or *sva-lakṣaṇa*) by means of which entities could be differentiated and classified. For example, the *svabhāva* of fire was identified as heat, and the *svabhāva* of water was defined as fluidity. By identifying the *svabhāva* of an entity a taxonomy of real existents could be produced. Thus the schools of the Hīnayāna, while denying a self of persons (*pudgala-nairātmya*) nevertheless accepted the substantial reality of those elements (*dharmas*) which composed the world at large, including five *skandhas* or "aggregates" of the individual subject. Beginning with Nāgārjuna, the Madhyamaka undercut this teaching by denying the substantial reality not just of the self (*ātman*) but of all phenomena, a view known as *dharma-nairātmya*. All entities were therefore seen as alike in lacking a discrete mode of being or self-essence (*svabhāva*), and in sharing instead the common attribute or "mark" of emptiness (*śūnyatā*). Such a conclusion, Nāgārjuna reasoned, was required by the doctrine of Dependent Origination and indeed was its true meaning, for if things enjoyed a more permanent mode of being, it would be impossible for them to be originated and cease to be in the way the doctrine describes. The world would instead be a static place full of frozen unchanging entities in which nothing was ever produced or destroyed, which is clearly not what we perceive. However, Nāgārjuna also maintained that from the perspective of the higher level of truth (*paramārtha-satya*), that is, from the viewpoint of the enlightened, the claim that anything at all is ever produced or originated is incoherent. He begins his *Verses on the Middle Way* (*Mūla-madhyamaka-kārikā*) with the magisterial statement: "Nowhere are there any entities which have originated (i) from themselves, (ii) from another, (iii) from both together, or (iv) from no cause at all." As later commentators explained the four possibilities, the first means that it would be pointless for entities to originate from themselves, for what would be the point if they already exist? If they originated from something else, alternatively, how can an infinite regress be avoided, for if X causes Y, then presumably something in turn causes X, and so on? Option (iii) merely combines the faults of (i) and (ii), while the final option (iv) means that the production of things in the world would be totally random because entities could come into being at any time for no reason at all. In this way Nāgārjuna and his followers felt it had been demonstrated that any kind of cause–effect relationship between really existent entities (those of the kind which possessed *svabhāva*) was impossible, leading to the conclusion that the doctrine of Dependent Origination entailed the emptiness (*śūnyatā*) of all phenomena.

See also: ***Abhidharma*; Cosmology and rebirth; Ennobling Truths/Realities; Madhyamaka school; Nāgārjuna.**

DAMIEN KEOWN

DHARMA

Etymology

Etymologically, the world *Dharma* derives from the Sanskrit root *dhṛ*, which has the general sense of "to bear, sustain, hold or support." In the different Buddhist languages it is translated in a variety of ways. The Pāli form of *Dharma* is *Dhamma*, and the Prākrit form *Dhama* is also found. In the Chinese Buddhist canon the standard translation for *Dharma* is *fa*, a term with the sense of a law or orderly way or method. In Japanese the term *hō* is used, and in Korean, *pŏp*.

Dharma is a rich and complex term with many nuances and shades of meaning, and it is not possible to find a single word in English which will accurately represent all its meaning. Many translations for *Dharma* have been proposed including "religion," "truth" and "natural law," but none really captures the scope of this comprehensive term, and it is preferable to leave *Dharma* untranslated rather than use a translation that may have restricted or misleading connotations. The range of meaning of the term is illustrated by the fact that in different contexts *Dharma* can mean a universal moral order, a norm, religion, righteousness, a doctrine, truth, duty and proper conduct, as well as referring in a more technical sense to the entities and phenomena we perceive in the world around us. This use of *dharma* as a technical term referring to sense-data and the objects of perception (indicated in this article by the use of lower case) is particularly associated with the *Abhidharma* tradition, and constitutes a development which can be discussed separately. Accordingly, this article is divided into two main parts: the former explores *Dharma* as "religious teachings" under the heading of "Buddhist *Dharma*," while the latter treats *dharma* as a technical term in *Abhidharma*.

Early Indian conceptions

As far back as Vedic times (approximately 1,500 BCE) there existed the concept of a cosmic order governing all natural phenomena. The term most commonly used to describe this regulatory principle was *ṛta*, but this term became less important after the Vedic period and was eventually replaced by *Dharma*, a term also found in Vedic literature, for instance in the *Ṛg-veda*, the most important corpus of Vedic scripture. Down the centuries the term has been employed by all the Indian religions traditions and is one of the main terms adherents use to denote their faith. For example, Hindus commonly refer to their religion as the *sanatana-dharma* ("eternal doctrine") while Buddhists describe themselves as followers of the *Buddha Dharma* ("teachings of the Buddha").

Buddhist *Dharma*

In Buddhism, *Dharma* is classified as one of the Three Jewels (*triratna*) or "triple gem" revered by all Buddhists and constituting the nucleus of the faith, namely the Buddha, the *Dharma* (the teachings) and the *Sangha* (the monastic community). The Three Jewels are also referred to as the "three refuges" (*triśaraṇa*), particularly when used as a profession of faith. The formal procedure by which a layman becomes a Buddhist is by "taking refuge," which involves repeating three times the formula "I take refuge in the Buddha, I take refuge in the *Dharma*, I take refuge in the *Sangha*."

The Buddha is the one who discovered (as opposed to invented) the *Dharma* in our era, and the *Sangha* is the custodian and transmitter of its content through subsequent generations. The *Dharma* itself, however, is transhistorical and exists whether or not it has been perceived by anyone or preserved and disseminated as a body of teachings over time by the *Sangha*. In this respect it is akin to a universal law, something like the law of gravity. Gravity existed before the apple fell on Newton's head, and the ignorance of its nature made no difference to its effects on our lives. The Buddha, like Newton, has drawn our attention to an important truth about the world we live in, although neither created anything that was not there before. In this respect some sources compare the *Dharma* to a lost city in the jungle which existed continuously despite no one being aware of it, until one day a traveller stumbled upon it.

Turning the wheel of Dharma

The Buddha's first sermon was entitled "The Discourse on Setting in Motion the Wheel of the *Dhamma*" and was preached in the Deer Park at Sārnāth, near Vārāṇasī (Benares) to five ascetics who were previously his companions. In this discourse (*Saṃyutta Nikāya* 56.11) the Buddha speaks first of all of the "Middle Way" and the avoidance of two extremes: one is the pursuit of sensual pleasures and the other is self-mortification. He identifies the Middle Way with the Noble Eightfold Path, and describes it as leading to knowledge, peace, and enlightenment. He then proceeds to elucidate *Dharma* in the form of the Four Noble Truths as follows:

> Now this, monks, is the Noble Truth of suffering (*duḥkha*). Birth is suffering, aging is suffering, illness is suffering, death is suffering. Contact with what is unpleasant is suffering, and separation from what is pleasant is suffering; not to get what one wants is suffering. In short, the five aggregates of clinging (*upādāna-skandha*) are suffering.
>
> Now this, monks, is the Noble Truth of the arising of suffering. It is this craving (*tṛṣṇā*) which leads to renewed existence, accompanied by delight and lust, seeking delight now here and now there in the form of craving for sensual pleasures, craving for existence, and craving for non-existence.
>
> Now this, monks, is the Noble Truth of the cessation of suffering. It is the cessation and complete fading away of that craving, the renunciation and relinquishing of it, freedom from it, non-reliance on it.
>
> Now this, monks, is the Noble Truth of the way leading to the cessation of suffering. It is this Noble Eightfold Path, that is, right view, right resolve, right speech, right action, right livelihood, right effort, right mindfulness, right meditation.

The Buddha stated that it was through thoroughly understanding these four truths that he himself had awakened, and while he was in the course of preaching the sermon one of the five ascetics present, a man by the name of Kondañña, also gained "the dust-free stainless vision of the *Dhamma*," the essence of which was defined as "Whatever is subject to origination is subject to cessation," a reference to the doctrine of Dependent Origination (*pratītya-samutpāda*). By giving this first sermon the Buddha had set in motion "the Wheel of the *Dhamma*

(*dhamma-cakka*)" which henceforth could not be stopped by anyone in the world. At this wondrous event, the text records, the gods began to rejoice all the way from the lowest heavens up to the highest and "the ten-thousandfold world system shook, quaked, and trembled, and a glorious radiance of immeasurable extent manifested itself in the world."

A number of interesting points about *Dharma* are revealed in this discourse. First we see that *Dharma* is identified with a set of core teachings: the Middle Way, the Four Noble Truths, and the doctrine of Dependent Origination (*pratītya-samutpāda*). The practice of the Middle Way involves following the Eightfold Path, which is divided into three components of Morality (*śīla*), Meditation (*samādhi*) and Wisdom (*prajñā*). Morality is the foundation of Buddhist practice, and is often spoken of in terms similar to those used of *Dharma* as that which bears or supports. Morality is often compared to the earth, which provides the foundation for any kind of building project. *Milinda's Questions* (34) compares the practice of morality to the work of a town planner who first clears the site for a new city, removing all the stumps and thorns, before laying out the streets. Morality facilitates the practice of meditation, which in turn is conducive to the development of wisdom and the arising of knowledge and a vision of things as they really are. Thus the *Dharma* as a set of religious teachings leads to a correct vision of *Dharma* understood as the way things are in reality. However, this is not simply a theoretical vision, for one must also act rightly and fulfil the requirements of *Dharma* as a moral agent in the world. In this sense the path and the goal embrace both moral conduct and understanding, and Buddhist ethico-religious teachings and the underlying nature of things converge in a seamless unity. That religion is not thought merely to be a collection of concepts divorced from reality is illustrated by the way the natural world itself quaked and shook when the wheel of *Dharma* was set in motion.

The vision of *Dharma* the Buddha achieved is not easy to attain, and the Buddha was well aware of how delusion and the passions can obscure the mind's apprehension of the truth. He stated:

> This *Dhamma* I have attained is deep, difficult to see or comprehend, calm and sublime, beyond the realm of mere logic, to be apprehended by the wise (alone). Yet beings delight in sensuality, take pleasure in sensuality, rejoice in sensuality. It is hard for such beings to see this truth, namely conditionality or Dependent Origination. And it is hard to see this truth, namely the calming of all formations, the rejection of all attachments, the destruction of craving, dispassion, cessation, *nirvāṇa*. If I were to teach the *Dharma* others would not understand me, and that would be wearisome and troublesome for me.
>
> (*Majjhima Nikāya* I.167f)

Once again in this passage we see *Dharma* expressly identified with the key doctrine of Dependent Origination and note that the practice of *Dharma* culminates in *nirvāṇa*. Thus we might say that *Dharma* in an ontological sense means the true nature of things in the world, and *Dharma* in a soteriological sense denotes the path and the goal that lies at its end, namely *nirvāṇa*.

The political dimension of Dharma

There is an important political dimension to the word *Dharma* which is evident in many early discourses and which takes on concrete form in the later history of Buddhism. The *Aggañña Sutta* provides an account of the origins of social life which intended to undermine the Brahmin claim that the caste system is an aspect of *Dharma* and therefore a legitimate social institution. Instead, basing itself on the theory of Dependent Origination, the *sutta* narrates how a new world-system comes into being and explains the sequence of events by which society evolves the institution of kingship. On this account citizens elect a king in order to enforce social order and restrain evil-doers who, motivated by craving (*tṛṣṇā*) seek to deprive others of what is rightfully theirs. The first king, known as Mahā-sammata (literally, "having the approval of the majority"), was chosen because of his own moral purity and charged with the enforcement of *Dharma*. He was expected to rule impartially, in accordance with the provisions of *Dharma*, for the well-being of all. The explanation of the meaning of the word "king" (*rāja*) was supposedly "he pleases others by *Dhamma*, hence he is a king" (*dhammena pare rañjetīti kho … rājā*).

The greatest of all kings are those known as *cakravartins*, a word meaning "wheel turner". The wheel that these great rulers turn is the wheel of *Dharma*. Whereas the Buddha turned the wheel of the *Dharma* in the religious sphere, the cakravartin turns it in the political sphere. Both a Buddha and a *cakravartin* are said to bear the thirty-two marks (*dvātriṃśādvara-lakṣaṇa*) of the superman (*mahāpuruṣa*) on their bodies. The *cakravartin* unites all regions under his benign leadership. Wherever he travels he is welcomed and people voluntarily submit to his rule out of respect for his adherence to the principles of *Dharma*. The *cakravartin* represents the Buddhist political ideal of the just ruler or universal monarch who brings peace and prosperity to his subjects, and various kings in history have been seen as embodying this ideal, notably Aśoka.

The grandson of Candragupta Maurya, son of Bindusāra, and third encumbent of the Mauryan throne from *c.* 272 to 231 BCE, Aśoka was perhaps the greatest exponent of the principles of *Dharma* in the political sphere that Buddhism has ever known. Aśoka is famous for the edicts he ordered to be carved on rocks and pillars throughout his kingdom. A total of thirty-three inscriptions have been found which provide invaluable historical and chronological information on early Indian Buddhist history. A great patron of Buddhism, it can be seen from the edicts that the content of Aśoka's *Dharma* is essentially that of a lay Buddhist. *Dharma* consists, he tells us, of "Few sins and many good deeds of kindness, liberality, truthfulness and purity" (Pillar Edict 2). In his edicts Aśoka offers fatherlike advice to his subjects, commending moral virtues such as peacefulness, piety, religious tolerance, zeal, respect for parents and teachers, courtesy, charity, sense-control and equanimity. No reference is made to the technical aspects of Buddhist doctrine as expounded in the Four Noble Truths. He relates in Rock Edict XIII that after his bloody conquest of the Kaliṅga region of northeast India, he repented of his warlike ways and became a lay Buddhist. From then on he attempted to rule according to *Dharma* as a "*Dharma-rāja*" or righteous king. He appointed officers known as "superintendents of *Dharma*" (*dharma-mahāmātra*), to propagate the religion. However, in the best tradition of Indian kingship, Aśoka supported all religions. One of the edicts towards the end of his reign, known as the "schism edict," condemns schism in the *Sangha* and speaks of monks being expelled. This seems to confirm accounts in Buddhist chronicles of his involvement in a council at Pāṭaliputra around 250 BCE, reckoned as the "Third Council" by the Theravāda tradition. This involvement seems to suggest the ruler has authority over the *Sangha* in the political sphere and a duty to enforce orthodoxy. His duties also seem to extend to the promotion of religion. The edicts also record that Aśoka sent ambassadors to five named kings reigning in the Hellenistic world, which again seems to support the Buddhist tradition that he did much to promote the spread of the *Dharma*. He is credited with sending his son Mahinda, himself a monk, to Sri Lanka to establish Buddhism there, as well as sending missionaries to other parts of Southeast Asia.

In the modern world kingship is no longer regarded as an appropriate form of political organization and has been replaced by modern alternatives such as democracy and communism. Buddhists today are wrestling with the question of what form of political organization best expresses the requirements of *Dharma*. In the latter half of the twentieth century Southeast Asia was torn by ideological wars between capitalism and communism. Buddhists could be found on both sides of this divide, and some activists saw in communism a "selfless" social system that seemed to express the Buddhist teaching of no-self in a concrete political form. Some Chinese communists tried to argue that life in a commune where all property was held in common and all individuals worked jointly for the advancement of the community was the ideal form of life for a *bodhisattva*. Others disagreed, and saw the values of capitalism and liberal democracy as more in keeping with Buddhist teachings on free will and personal responsibility. Since the widespread collapse of communism at the end of the last century many Buddhists seem to favour a centre-left democratic style of government as most in keeping with Buddhist ideals. However, whether democracy expresses the requirements of *Dharma* better than any other political system, and whether and how it is in harmony with the classical ideal of the righteous king, are questions which have been little explored so far.

Dharma as *Abhidharma* term

Abhidharma (Pāli, *Abhidhamma*) is a term meaning "higher doctrine" and denotes the scholastic analysis of religious teachings. The earliest *Abhidharma* material was composed over several centuries beginning around 300 BCE and formed the substance of the various collections of canonical scholastic treatises (*Abhidharma Piṭaka*) of the different early schools. Influential later non-canonical compendia of *Abhidharma* teachings include the *Abhidharma-kośa* of Vasubandhu and the *Abhidharma-samuccaya* of Asaṅga (both probably late fourth century CE). The *Abhidharma* represents an attempt to classify and analyse material contained in the Buddha's discourses (*sūtras*) using a special analytical framework and technical terminology. The fundamental doctrines discussed are those already presented in other parts of the canon, which are therefore taken for granted.

This was a kind of tidying-up exercise designed to bring the unsystematic data contained in the Buddha's discourses under some kind of general rubric. In the early teachings a multitude of phenomena are mentioned, many of a psychological kind but others relating to the natural world. A key early classification was that of the individual subject into five aggregates or components (*skandhas*), namely matter or form (*rūpa*), feelings and sensations (*vedanā*), ideation (*saṃjñā*), mental formations (*saṃskāras*) and consciousness (*vijñāna*). The nature of the external world was classified under the perceptual categories of the *āyatanas* and *dhātus*. The twelve *āyatanas* are the six sense-organs (eye, ear, nose, tongue, body and mind), and their corresponding objects (forms, sounds, smells, tastes, tangible objects and ideas). The eighteen *dhātus* are the six senses, their six objects and the resultant six sense-consciousnesses generated as a result of the contact between the senses and their objects. These are as eye-consciousness (*cakṣur-vijñāna*), ear consciousness (*śrota-vijñāna*), smell-consciousness (*ghrāṇa-vijñāna*), tongue-consciousness (*jihvā-vijñāna*), body-consciousness (*kāya-vijñāna*) and mind-consciousness (*mano-vijñāna*).

The sources exhibit a scholastic fondness for producing further lists of items and then seeking to classify them in different ways. One example which relates to virtuous qualities is the thirty-seven "constituents of enlightenment" (*bodhi-pākṣika dharma*). The thirty-seven items comprise the four foundations of mindfulness (*smṛti-upasthāna*), the four efforts or restraints (*prahāṇa*), the four bases of supernatural power (*ṛddhipāda*), the five spiritual faculties (*indriya*), the five powers (*bala*), the seven limbs of enlightenment (*bodhyaṅga*) and the Eightfold Path (*aṣṭāṅga-mārga*). With respect to negative qualities various kinds of defilements (*kleśa*) are mentioned and categorized under different headings, such as unwholesome roots (*akuśala-mūla*), hindrances (*nīvaraṇa*), fetters (*saṃyojana*), latent tendencies (*anuśaya*), and so on. These groupings are scattered throughout the texts, and in some early *suttas* the attempt is made to arrange them in a systematic manner. Examples include the *Dasuttara Sutta*, which lists 550 *dharmas*, the *Saṅgīti Sutta*, which extends this further, and the *Anupada Sutta*. However, this attempt was of a limited nature and it fell to the *Abhidharma* tradition to make a more comprehensive effort at systematic classification.

Going far beyond anything found in the *Sutta Piṭaka*, the *Abhidharma* sought to develop a comprehensive taxonomy or system of classification into which all phenomena, whether mental or physical, could be located.

The first attempt at a comprehensive Abhidharmic classification is found in the *Dhammasaṅganī*, the first book of the *Abhidhamma Piṭaka* of the Theravāda school. The *Dhammasaṅganī* takes the untidy lists of items from the *Sutta Piṭaka* and classifies them in various ways, but primarily according to whether they are morally good (*kusala*), bad (*akusala*) or neutral (*avyākata*). The meaning of the first two is clear, and the last category contains four items which relate to either non-moral or trans-moral phenomena. These are: (1) resultant consciousness (*vipākacitta*) or mental states which are the result of earlier ones; (2) functional consciousness (*kriyācitta*), or neutral states of mind; (3) matter (*rūpa*); and (4) the unconditioned (*nirvāṇa*). The *Dhammasaṅganī* does not speculate much about the ontological status of the various *dharmas* it classified, but with the passage of time there was a tendency for the *Abhidharma* to conceive of the items appearing in the lists as enjoying a privileged mode of being: one could be sure they, at least, really existed, as they had been identified as key components of reality by the scholastic tradition. Thus over time the *Abhidharma* began to move towards a realist view of the *dharmas* it had identified, and to treat *dharmas* as basic components of the natural world roughly in the way a scientist might conceive of the world as made up of different combinations of the hundred or so elements known to modern chemistry. *Dharmas* thus came to be understood as the basic building-blocks which in their various permutations constitute the world as we know it. By some time around the fifth century CE views of this kind are found in the writings of Theravāda scholars such as Buddhadatta and his junior contemporary Buddhaghosa. Buddhadatta's work the *Abhidhammāvatāra* ("Introduction to Abhidhamma") adopts a new fourfold system of classification of the 170 *dhammas* it recognized into matter (*rūpa*), mind (*citta*), mental factors (*cetasikas*) and *nirvāṇa*, apparently derived from models which had become influential in India by this time such as that of the Sarvāstivāda, which will be examined in detail below. This was the system subsequently followed by later writers in the later medieval period, such as Anuruddha, author of the *Abhidhammathasaṅgaha*. However, the main intellectual developments in the *Dharma* theory took place not in Sri Lanka but on the Indian mainland, and the school that was most innovative in this respect was the Sarvāstivāda.

The Sarvāstivāda

The Sarvāstivāda was an important school of Indian Buddhism that separated from the main body of the Elders (Sthaviras) around the middle of the third century BCE. Its name means "the school that holds that everything exists" and this derives from its philosophical views concerning the nature of phenomena. Like other early schools such as the Theravāda, its ontology was pluralist and realist, and the Sarvāstivādins believed (not unlike the ancient Greek atomists) that reality could be analysed into a collection of discrete entities, or *dharmas*. While agreeing with other schools that conditioned *dharmas* are momentary (*kṣanika*), they nevertheless maintained that they also enjoy real existence both in the past and future. Four theories were proposed to explain this, which we cannot go into here, except to note that according to the first, *dharmas* exist from beginningless time and simply undergo a change of mode from latent to manifest. Time itself, it was suggested, was simply the change of mode undergone by *dharmas*. Theories of this kind were developed as a solution to difficulties arising out of the Buddhist denial of enduring substances in the no-self (*anātman*) doctrine, which gave rise to problems concerning causation, temporality, and personal identity. The conventional scholastic solution was to posit a theory of instantaneous serial continuity according to which phenomena (*dharmas*) constantly replicate themselves in a momentary sequence of change (*dharma-kṣanikatvā*). Thus reality was conceived of as cinematic, like a filmstrip in which one frame constantly gives way to the next: each moment is substantially existent in its own right, and collectively they produce the illusion of stability and continuity. The distinctive Sarvāstivādin solution was to claim that time was relational, and that *dharmas* existed in all three times, just as a woman could be a mother and a daughter simultaneously. Although the Sarvāstivādins were apparently expelled at the council of Pāṭaliputra, they went on to become extremely influential, particularly in the northwest of India in Kashmir and Gandhāra, where they survived until Buddhism disappeared from the sub-continent. The school possessed its own canon, much of which survives today, and is renowned for its *Abhidharma* texts, especially the *Mahāvibhāṣā* composed under the supervision of Vasumitra at the Council of Kaniṣka (second century CE). The school is alternatively known as the Vaibhāṣika, from the name of this text, and gave rise to a dissident tradition known as the Sautrāntika.

The Sarvāstivādin classification of dharmas

Sarvāstivādin sources distinguish seventy-five *dharmas* in total, of which seventy-two are "conditioned" (*saṃskṛta*) and three are "unconditioned" (*asaṃskṛta*). The three unconditioned *dharmas* are: (1) space (*ākāśa*), and two states of emancipation; (2) through discerning knowledge (*pratisankhyānirodha*) and; (3) through non-discerning knowledge (*apratisankhyānirodha*). These three are unconditioned in the sense that they are not subject to the law of causality and so do not pass through the phases of production (*jāti*), duration (*sthiti*), decay (*jarā*) and destruction (*anityatā*) which affects all conditioned phenomena. The remaining seventy-two *dharmas* were grouped into four main categories: matter (*rūpa*), mind (*citta*), mental concomitants (*caitta*) and formations not connected to thought (*cittaviprayukta*).

*Matter (***rūpa***)*

Matter or form consists of the first five of the six sense faculties (*indriya*) and their respective objects (*viṣaya*). Thus the senses of seeing (*cakṣur-indriya*), hearing (*śrotra-indriya*), smell (*ghrāṇa-indriya*), taste (*jihvā-indriya*), and touch (*kāya-indriya*) have material form (*rūpa*), sound (*śabda*), smell (*gandha*), taste (*rasa*), and touch (*spraṣṭavya*) as their objects. The eleventh *dharma* in the group was "unmanifest action" (*avijñapti*), a problematic concept not accepted by all branches of the Sarvāstivāda which relates to inward dispositions as yet not manifest in physical action. The intention, choice or resolution to do something was thought of as a kind of internal shadow of the outward act which left a subtle material trace in the body of the agent at some level.

*Mind (*citta*)*

The second category contains only one element, that of pure thought or consciousness.

*Mental concomitants (*caittas*)*

The third category contains forty-six elements or factors associated with mental activity. The first ten of these are general factors thought to be of broad scope (*mahābhūmika*) that accompany all mental activity. These are:

feeling (*vedanā*);
conception (*saṃjñā*);
volition (*cetanā*);
contact (*sparśa*);
attention (*manaskāra*);
motivation (*chanda*);
inclination (*adhimokṣa*);
mindfulness (*smṛti*);
meditation (*samādhi*);
understanding (*prajñā*).

Ten further basic factors accompany every good (*kuśala*) moment of consciousness. These are:

faith or confidence (*śraddhā*);
energy (*vīrya*);
equanimity (*upekśā*);
modesty (*hrī*);
embarrassment at wrongdoing by others (*apatrāpya*);
non-craving (*alobha*);
non-hatred (*adveṣa*);
non-injury (*ahiṃsā*);
serenity (*praśrabdhi*);
non-heedlessness (*apramāda*).

Six "general defiled factors" (*kleśa-mahābhūmika-dharmas*) accompany negative thoughts:

delusion (*moha*);
heedlessness (*pramāda*);
torpor (*kausīdya*);
lack of faith (*aśraddhā*);
sloth (*styāna*);
restlessness (*auddhatya*).

Ten minor defiled factors (*upakleśa*) which may be present at specific times are:

anger (*krodha*);
hypocrisy (*mrakṣsa*);
stinginess (*mātsarya*);
jealousy (*īrṣyā*);
envious rivalry (*pradāsa*);
causing harm (*vihiṃsā*);
enmity (*upanāha*);
deceit (*māyā*);
trickery (*śāṭhya*);
conceit (*mada*).

Two factors are present alongside all negative states of mind. These are known as "universally unwholesome elements" (*akuśala-mahābhūmika-dharma*) and are:

shamelessness (*āhrīkya*);
immodesty (*anapatrāpya*).

Eight indeterminate (*aniyata*) factors can be associated with good, bad or indeterminate states of mind. These are:

attention (*vitarka*);
discursive thought (*vicāra*);

drowsiness (*middhā*);
remorse (*kaukṛtya*);
greed (*rāga*);
hatred (*pratigha*);
pride (*māna*);
doubt (*vicikitsā*).

Factors disassociated from thought (*cittaviprayukta*).

The following fourteen factors do not fall into the category of either mind or matter and for the most part are natural forces which control the way *dharmas* interact.

acquisition (*prāpti*), a force which binds *dharmas* together into groups;
rejection (*aprāpti*), a force which disengages *dharmas* from one another;
homogeneity (*sabhāgatā*), a force which unites similar *dharmas*;
non-perception (*āsaṃjñika*), a force which brings out the attainment of the meditative state of non-perception;
attainment of non-perception (*asaṃjñisamāpatti*) produced by the effort to attain a trance state;
the "attainment of cessation" (*nirodhasamāpatti*), a trance in which all thought and feeling are suspended;
the life force (*jīvitendriya*), the faculty which determines lifespan;
origination (*jāti*);
duration (*sthiti*);
decay (*jarā*);
impermanence (*anityatā*);
force imparting meaning to letters (*vyañjana-kāya*);
force imparting meaning to sentences (*nāmakāya*);
force imparting meaning to phrases (*pādakāya*).

The Yogācāra

Yogācāra means "the practice of yoga" and is the name of a Buddhist school which taught the doctrine of *citta-mātra* ("mind only"); it was also known as the Vijñānavāda ("the way of consciousness"). The school developed in the fourth century CE and its leading exponents were Maitreyanātha, Asaṅga, and his brother Vasubandhu.

The basic postulate of the school is that consciousness (*vijñāna*) itself is the fundamental and only reality and that the apparent diversity of the empirical world is the product of instability and obscuration in the individual field of consciousness. The standard form of the doctrine distinguishes eight functions or aspects of consciousness, the most fundamental being the *ālaya-vijñāna* or "storehouse consciousness," which is the foundation of personal identity. Beginning with this list of eight consciousnesses this school compiled a list of 100 *dharmas* in five categories. These are:

1–8 Mind (*citta*), which consists of the eight consciousnesses, being the six listed by the Sarvāstivāda plus the coordinating mental organ (*manas*) and the storehouse consciousness (*ālaya*).
9–59 Mental concomitants (*caitta*).
60–70 Form (*rūpa*).
71–94 Factors separate from the mind (*citta-viprayukta-saṃskāras*).
95–100 Unconditioned (*asaṃskṛta*) *dharmas*.

(See Table 4)

The Madhyamaka

Not all schools were as keen on compiling tables of *dharmas* as those mentioned above. A notable exception is the Madhyamaka, the "Middle School", founded by Nāgārjuna in the second century CE. The school claims to be faithful to the spirit of the Buddha's original teachings, which advocate a middle course between extreme practices and theories of all kinds. The adoption of any one position, it was argued, could immediately be challenged by taking up its opposite. The

Table 4 The classification of *dharmas* by three major schools

	Theravāda	Sarvāstivāda	Yogācāra
Rūpa (form)	28	11	11
Citta (mind)	89	1	8
Caitta (mental concomitants)	52	46	51
Viprayukta (dissociated)	0	14	24
Asaṃskṛta (unconditioned)	1	3	6
TOTAL	170	75	100

truth, accordingly, was thought to lie somewhere in between and to be arrived at through a process of dialectic in the course of which opposing positions are revealed as self-negating. The Madhyamaka applied this principle to philosophical theories concerning the nature of reality and was sceptical of the *Abhidharma* project of constructing a taxonomy of phenomena. For them the very assertion that "things exist" or that "things do not exist" was an extreme view and to be rejected. The Madhyamaka therefore challenged the notion of the substantial reality of *dharmas*, arguing that if things truly existed in this way, and were possessed of a real nature or "self-essence" (*svabhāva*), it would contradict the Buddha's teaching on selflessness (*anātman*) and, moreover, render change impossible. What already substantially exists, they argued, would not need to be produced; and what does not substantially exist already could never come into being from a state of non-existence. Thus real existence cannot be predicated of *dharmas*, but neither can non-existence as they clearly enjoy a mode of being of some kind. The conclusion of the Madhyamaka was that the true nature of phenomena can only be described as "emptiness" or "voidness" (*dharma-śūnyatā*), and that this emptiness of self-nature is synonymous with the doctrine of Dependent Origination (*pratītya-samutpāda*) taught by the Buddha. This reasoning is set out in Nāgārjuna's terse "Middle Verses" (*Mūla-madhyamaka-kārikā*), the root text of the system.

See also: ***Abhidharma*; Cosmology and rebirth; Madhyamaka school; Nāgārjuna; Sarvāstivāda; Yogācāra school.**

DAMIEN KEOWN

DHARMACAKRA

The *dharmacakra* (Pāli *dhammacakka*) or "wheel of the *Dharma*" is a symbol of the Buddhist teachings in the form of a wheel. The symbolism of the wheel derives from the name of the First Sermon given by the Buddha in the Deer Park at Sārnāth, known as the "Discourse on Setting in Motion the Wheel of the Law" (*Dharmacakra-pravartana Sūtra*), found in the *Saṃyutta Nikāya* and elsewhere in the Pāli Canon. Representations of the *dharmacakra* often show a deer on either side of the wheel, making explicit reference to this event. In this important early text the Buddha sets out the Four Noble Truths and their three aspects, often spoken of as three "turnings" of the wheel. The three turnings denote the content of the particular Truth, what is to be done in respect of it, and its culmination. For example, the First Noble Truth concerns suffering; this Truth is to be "fully understood," and its culmination is understanding the nature of suffering.

In later Buddhism the second and third "turnings of the wheel" are understood differently, as referring to the promulgation of new teachings. Not uncommonly the Mahāyāna is said to be a second turning, and the Vajrayāna the third. This idea of a progression in the teachings is also used for sectarian purposes to legitimate the superiority of certain schools. The *Sandhinirmocana Sūtra* (second century CE), for example, equates the Buddha's teachings in his First Sermon concerning the Four Noble Truths with the first turning of the wheel. The doctrine of emptiness (*śūnyatā*) as taught in the *Prajñāpāramitā* literature is said to constitute the second, and the teachings of the Yogācāra school as set out in the *Sandhinirmocana Sūtra* itself are then presented as the third and highest "turning" or phase of doctrinal teachings.

The *Dharma* resembles a wheel in that it is thought to be eternal in having neither a beginning nor an end. It is also "turned" at different times by different Buddhas who renew its impetus by spreading the *Dharma* in different eras. Like a wheel the *Dharma* is also pictured as "rolling forward," progressively gaining momentum as it spreads throughout the world carried by monks and nuns as part of their missionary activity.

Different representations of the wheel symbolize different aspects of doctrine. A wheel with eight spokes connotes the Eightfold Path, and one with twelve spokes the three turnings of the wheel described above. Alternatively, representations with twelve spokes can recall the twelve links of the doctrine of Dependent Origination (*pratītya-samutpāda*). Sometimes there are

Figure 19 Dharma wheel, Thai Dvāratī style (seventh–ninth century).

many spokes, as shown in the accompanying illustration (Figure 19).

The *dharmacakra* is also represented in a stylized hand gesture known as the *dharmacakra mudrā*. In this *mudrā* the thumb and index fingers of both hands touch at their tips to form a circle. Statues of the Buddha making this particular gesture call to mind the First Sermon in the Deer Park at Sārnāth. The symbol of the wheel is not unique to Buddhism and is also found in Jainism, as well as being used today on the flag of India.

See also: **Art, Buddhist; Buddha, early symbols; *Dharma*.**

DAMIEN KEOWN

DHARMAGUPTAKAS

The Dharmaguptakas were a school of *Nikāya* Buddhism that was particularly prominent in northwest India and which played a key role in the transmission of Buddhism across Central Asia and to China. Its *Vinaya* literature was particularly important in China. The Dharmaguptakas draw our attention to a number of key processes in the history of *Nikāya* Buddhism, but especially the role of regionalism in the formation of separate schools, and especially the role of language in school definition. It seems that the Dharmaguptakas used Gāndhārī as their language of religious authority and their canon was transmitted in this language: it is also the case that in some circumstances Sanskrit was also used by the Dharmaguptakas, as fragments of Dharmaguptaka texts have been found in Sanskrit in Central Asia.

The name of the Dharmaguptakas is unproblematic in its meaning: they are "the protectors of the *Dharma*." This was a common ordination name for monks, however, and it is possible that their name follows the common pattern of other *Nikāya* Buddhist schools. That is, it is a derivative from the name of a monk called Dharmagupta and some Buddhist sources do explain the name of the school in this fashion. Dharmagupta was said to be in the ordination lineage of the *arhat* Maudgalyayāna.

It is likely that the Dharmaguptakas appeared as a distinct group in the second century BCE, although it is unclear from exactly which school it was that they separated. Buddhist sources commonly associate their separation with the Mahīśāsakas, one of the schools within the Sthaviravādin lineages of *Nikāya* Buddhism, but some affinities with the Sarvāstivādins are also sometimes suggested. The division between the Mahīśāsakas and the Dharmaguptakas seems to have been over a disagreement about the efficacy of worship and donative rituals. The Mahīśāsakas said that there was more merit from worshipping and making offerings to the monastic order, while the Dharmaguptakas argued that there is more merit from worshipping and making offerings to a *stūpa*, a monument sacralized by its physical connections with the Buddha himself. This disagreement, which ultimately concerns doctrinal positions about the nature of the Buddha after his death, also suggests that the ritual practices of mainstream Buddhism, which frequently served as a social grammar transcending the doctrinal divisions that kept the various schools separate, could themselves become the object of disagreements leading to new school formation.

Like other major schools in *Nikāya* Buddhism, the Dharmaguptakas had their own canon. The Dharmaguptaka canon was not only distinct in being transmitted in Gāndhārī, but in its structure it was quite different from the canons of the Theravāda school and the Sarvāstivādin schools, although with respect to the sermons of the Buddha, the *Sūtra Piṭaka*, there seems to be common elements in the different canons. It is the arrangement of the parts that is significantly different. The Dharmaguptaka version of the *Sūtra Piṭaka* was apparently the source for the first Chinese translations of the *Āgamas*.

Notably, the Dharmaguptakas seem to have had a special section of their *Sūtra Piṭaka* devoted to *Jātakas*, narratives about the former lives of the Buddha, a feature that is suggestive of the degree to which the Dharmaguptakas were centrally visible in the social grammar of mainstream Buddhism. It may be that the Dharmaguptaka position in their disagreement with the Mahīśāsakas is also indicative of their embeddedness in mainstream Buddhism because the Dharmaguptakas were known for a position that the Buddha was not to be considered as belonging to the *sangha* or Buddhist monastic order. The intrinsic superiority of the Buddha to the monastic order as an object of worship and merit-making would have been foundational to any understanding of Buddhist cultic activity.

The Dharmaguptakas also had their own *Abhidharma*, and this portion of their canon appears in structure to be very different from what is found with the Theravādins and the Sarvāstivādins. There is a possibility that a text surviving in Chinese, the *Śāriputrabhidharma Śāstra* (the treatise on the *Abhidharma* of Śariputra) is in fact from the Dharmaguptaka *Abhidharma*, but this text is also sometimes associated with the Vātsīputrīyas.

Inscriptional evidence locates the Dharmaguptakas in areas closely associated with the Oaka and Kuṣāṇa empires. These would include the Gandhara regions of northwest India, Bactria, and Mathurā. The association of the Dharmaguptakas with the Gandhara region helps us to understand their use of Gāndhārī as an authoritative language for their religious texts. It seems to have been the case that the Dharmaguptakas used Gāndhārī as a trans-local language, and texts in that language circulated in non-Gāndhārī-speaking areas in Central Asia, such as Khotan.

It seems that the Dharmaguptakas flourished with patronage from various Indo-Scythian kingdoms from the first century BCE until the second centuries CE, although other schools, such as the Mahīśāsakas and the Sarvāstivādins, were clearly also present in the Gandhāra region. The recent appearance of a cache of Buddhist manuscripts transmitted in Gāndhārī makes it clear that this region was a center of Buddhist intellectual life during this time, a center as significant as anything found in northern or central India. These materials make it very clear too that Buddhist life was already highly localized by this point, because we find examples of texts, notably narrative literature, that have no counterparts in the literatures of other schools associated with other regions.

See also: **Canons and literature; *Nikāya* Buddhism; Sarvāstivāda; Sautrāntika; *Stūpa*.**

CHARLES HALLISEY

DHARMAKĪRTI

One of the most influential thinkers in the history of Indian Buddhism, Dharmakīrti was probably active in the first half of the seventh century CE. He was a critic of Īśvarasena, who is said to be a disciple of Dignāga (fl. *c.* 480), who is now seen as the founder of what came to be known as the epistemological movement (*pramāṇavāda*) within Indian Buddhist scholasticism. Dharmakīrti was the author of a philosophical corpus that almost completely overshadowed Dignāga's work and became the cornerstone for most Buddhist scholasticism for the next six centuries in India.

Dharmakīrti's largest work is entitled *Pramāṇavārttika*, which takes as its point of departure Dignāga's collection of writings on logic and epistemology entitled *Pramāṇasammucaya*. *Pramāṇavārttika* contains four chapters in verse, to one of which the author supplied his own prose commentary. One chapter, entitled *Pramāṇasiddhi*, is a polemical defense of the claim that the Buddha is a source of knowledge about liberation from the root causes of discontent (*duḥkha*). What justifies the claim that he is the source of this particular knowledge is that no one knew it before he proclaimed the four noble truths, and what justifies the claim that what he said qualifies as knowledge is that one who acts on what the Buddha taught will not be disappointed. The Buddha taught these truths, says Dharmakīrti, because of his extraordinary compassion for sentient beings in distress, a compassion cultivated over the course of innumerable lifetimes. Defense of this claim leads to a lengthy discussion of the plausibility of the doctrine of rebirth, a doctrine that Dharmakīrti defends against the criticisms of various materialists who had argued that consciousness depends on processes in the physical body and therefore necessarily ends when the physical body dies and decomposes.

In other chapters of *Pramāṇavārttika*, Dharmakīrti has detailed discussions of sensory knowledge (*pratyakṣa*), inferential reasoning as a means of acquiring new knowledge for oneself, and the presentation of arguments in dialogue whereby one may impart to others what one has learned through the senses and through reasoning. In this work Dharmakīrti links sensory experience to ultimate truth (*paramārthasatya*) and relegates all conceptual knowledge and verbally communicated knowledge to the level of conventional truth. Having a correct conceptual grasp of the Buddha's insights is necessary but not sufficient for attaining *nirvāṇa*. In addition to correct understanding, one must also have a direct experience of the truths taught by the Buddha. This experience, argues Dharmakīrti, is essentially an experience of one's own mind, for the mind is the ultimate source of what is experienced as external objects. Thus Dharmakīrti's philosophy has much in common with trends in the Yogācāra school, especially with the focus on the mind and the emphasis on the importance of experiencing the flow of phenomena without imposing a duality of comprehending subject and comprehended object upon what is experienced. Unlike other Yogācāra treatises, the conclusions in Dharmakīrti's works are based entirely on reason and do not in any way depend on the authority of tradition (*āgama*).

See also: **India, Buddhism in; Mahāyāna Buddhism; *Pramāṇika* movement.**

RICHARD P. HAYES

DHYĀNAS

Dhyānas (Pāli *jhānas*) are highly refined states of concentration in which attention is completely absorbed in its object. They are considered to be fruits of meditation practices emphasizing tranquility and calm (*śamatha*) and are preliminary to the attainment of insight (*vipaśyanā*) into the true nature of phenomena. In Pāli explications, meditators embark on the *dhyānas* after overcoming the "five hindrances" to the development of meditative concentration: sensual desire, ill will, sloth and torpor, restlessness and remorse, and doubt. The *dhyānas* are usually presented as a succession of states, each more elevated than the last: (1) a state consisting of applied thought, discursive examination, happiness, joy, and one-pointed concentration; (2) the stilling of applied thought, while retaining discursive examination, happiness, joy, and one-pointed concentration; (3) the stilling of discursive examination while retaining happiness and joy, and the arising of equanimity and mindfulness; and (4) a state of mindfulness and equanimity transcending pleasure and pain, joy and grief (*Majjhima Nikāya* 3.92). Beyond these are even more refined states of concentration that transcend all physical elements, the four formless *dhyānas* (*arūpadhyāna*): awareness of (1) endless space, (2) unlimited consciousness, (3) nothingness, and (4) neither perception nor non-perception. Some accounts of these stages of meditation include a state beyond the *dhyānas* – the "cessation of perception and feeling," a condition of deepest calm in which all cognitive processes are temporarily suspended.

There exists some ambivalence about the *dhyānas* in Pāli literature. While they are described and recommended in a number of *sūtras*, biographies of the Buddha present Gautama, during his pre-enlightenment asceticism with the *śramaṇas*, perfecting the practice of the *dhyānas* and recognizing that they did not bring him to the ultimate understanding he sought. Thus, as elevated as they may appear, the *dhyānas* are generally not considered ends in themselves and can even be sources of subtle attachment (*Majjhima Nikāya* 1.294ff., *Visuddhimagga* 18.16ff.). They are not themselves sufficient to the attainment of awakening and in some *sūtras* are not considered requisite. They are, instead, forms of "pleasant abiding here and now," as well as a solid basis of concentration upon which practices more directly conducive to awakening can be undertaken.

In some forms of Buddhism, the term *dhyāna* took on a life of its own, particularly in its adoption by the Chan school – Chan is the Chinese adaptation of the term *dhyāna*, which then became "Zen" in Japan. Thus Chan/Zen became the "meditation school," in which the term *dhyāna* was applied more broadly to meditation practices in general rather than to the specific states of concentration outlined in Pāli literature.

See also: **Chan; Mahāyāna Buddhism; Meditation (Chan/Zen); Meditation,**

modern movements; Meditation, visualization; Meditation in the Pāli Canon and the Theravāda tradition; Meditation in the *Visuddhimagga*; Meditation traditions, Vajrayāna; Meditational systems; *Nikāya* Buddhism; South and Southeast Asia, Buddhism in; *Śamatha*; *Vipaśyanā*; *Zazen*.

DAVID L. MCMAHAN

DIASPORIC BUDDHISM: TRADITIONALIST AND MODERNIST BUDDHISM

Buddhism in the West is a Buddhism which succeeds in maintaining its Buddhist identity in diasporic contexts. The term "diaspora" received a widespread popularity within the social sciences and cultural studies during the last decade of the twentieth century. For the purpose here, "diaspora," as an analytical category de-contextualized from its Jewish origin and usage, will denote a religious-cultural group and tradition which survives and endures in a territory which is geographically and culturally different from the region where the group and/or religious tradition has had its origin. In this way, Buddhism sustains its specific contents, rituals, and practices in the diasporic West. Although the notion "diaspora" commonly is employed for migrant groups and emphasizes an identificational difference of this group from the host society's dominant cultural and religious orientations, the analytical heuristics can be used for the side of Western convert Buddhism as well.

The two main, internally heterogeneous strands or lines of Buddhism – that of migrant or immigrant and that of convert Buddhism – face similar difficulties in order to maintain the religious identity: processes of institutionalization and community building; processes of identity formation, retention, and possible loss; changes of Buddhist tradition in the diasporic context such as traditionalization, adaptation, and innovation. Further, questions of the use of language arise. The immigrant group is faced by the need to keep, or not to keep, the former home and ritual language, whereas the convert side has to decide to what extent Asian vocabulary has to be taken up or a language has even to be learned. Of contested importance are likewise the means of transmitting the religious tradition to the next generations; the question of leadership and power; the role and status of women, and that of lay teachers. In particular, in the doctrinal sphere processes of universalization, standardization, and loss by assimilation occur. Effects of compartmentalization come to the fore in the way that Buddhism is relegated to specific places and times. Buddhism is less "caught" in daily life (as in many Asian countries), but increasingly taught, be it in Sunday classes and summer camps and, predominantly on the convert side, explained in books and weekend retreats.

The binary differentiation of Buddhism's Western past and presence along the categories of immigrant and convert Buddhism is attractive because of its wide applicability. It easily systematizes the apparently diffuse and disparate field. The dichotomy goes back to the heuristic typology of "two Buddhisms," proposed by Charles S. Prebish (1979, 1993) and later adopted by others. As the terms indicate, the line of immigrant Buddhism is constituted by migrants from Asian Buddhist countries while the other is made up of Western people having converted to Buddhism. However, the labels are restricted to the first generation of each strand only: that is, to those who actually immigrated and those who took up Buddhism as their new orientation in life. Applied to consecutive generations and a longer span of time those categories become increasingly blurred and without explanatory value. Indeed, Buddhists of Chinese and Japanese origin live in the fifth or sixth generation in the Americas and a second generation of "convert" Buddhists is coming up.

In order to overcome the shortcomings, an analytical perspective is suggested, which does not relate to people's actions and ethnic ancestry, but to religious concepts held and practices followed. Set up as Weberian ideal types, a main difference with regard to Buddhist worldviews and religious acts is suggested along the terms traditionalist and modernist Buddhism. The strands themselves are not monolithic, but rather are heterogeneous, and consist of different traditions and schools. Though this differentiation has been established along religious and organizational changes which took place in the nineteenth and early twentieth century in Theravāda South Asia, the categorization seems transferable to Mahāyāna and Tibetan Buddhism as present in the West. The designations relate back to the threefold systematization of Buddhism in South Asia as established by leading buddhologists. The cumulative Buddhist tradition is differentiated along the periods of canonical or early Buddhism, traditional or historical Buddhism, and reformist, Protestant or modern Buddhism. During the period of Theravāda traditionalist Buddhism, ranging roughly from the third century BCE to the nineteenth century, the soteriological goal of attaining *arhant*ship (becoming an *arahant*, an enlightened person) in this life was increasingly perceived to be attainable only after an immensely long, gradual path of purifying oneself from imperfections. Monks and laity came to perceive *nibbāna* many future existences away. Devotional acts such as merit-making rituals, *deva* and spirit cults as well as protective and healing ceremonies became integral to Buddhism. Modernist Buddhism emerged as a response of Buddhist monks and leaders to the challenges posed by the impact of colonialism, missionary Christianity, and economic transformations in the late nineteenth century. In close interchange with the glorified image of Buddhism in Europe and North America, Buddhist reformers laid an emphasis on rationalist elements in Buddhist teachings; a heightened recognition and use of texts; a tacit elimination of traditionalist cosmology and ritual practices; a renewed emphasis on meditational practice; a stress on social reform and universalism; and the importance of the possibility of reaching awakening or *nibbāna/nirvāṇa* in this life. Both forms coexisted in suspense, modernist Buddhism forming a clear minority confined mainly to the educated middle strata of society.

Western spiritual seekers and enthusiasts, having become Buddhists and some monks (very few nuns), from the late nineteenth century onwards, received their teaching predominantly from modernist Buddhists. In their reformist ambitions these Asian modernizers emphasized meditational practices; a text-based rational approach; a purge of folk-religious practices; lay involvement; and the possibility of reaching enlightenment in this life. This modernist Buddhism was imported on a larger scale by Western Buddhist teachers, who had been taught in Asia during the 1960s and thereafter. It had also been exported from Asia by traveling monks and lay instructors. Since then the emphasis on modernist Buddhist elements has become characteristic for the very vast majority of Western Buddhists. In a typically reformist attitude Western Buddhists stress skipping traditionalist Buddhism and seeking guidance from the thus perceived "original" words of the Buddha.

In contrast, traditionalist Buddhism in the West has a very different focus and form. In Western countries, this strand can be found in many temples founded by Asian migrants, immigrants, and their descendants. Clear emphasis is placed on the monk lay hierarchy, in which the monk (less the nun) embodies the ideal of a pious Buddhist life and aspiration.

Traditionalist Buddhists engage in various forms of acquiring merit (Pāli *puñña*) in order to gather good "deeds" or "actions" to achieve better circumstances in both this and subsequent existences. They donate to the *sangha* by giving *dāna*, take part in ritualized chanting and *pūjas* (worship), and at times participate in meditation. Also, the laity might request a variety of so-called folk-religious practices from the monks, including palm-reading, fortune-telling, countering evil spells, and preparing protective amulets. The practices and the belief in their right-working, usefulness and benefit have their basis in cosmological and ontological views that are taken for granted, also in diasporic Western contexts.

Religiously, in quite a number of diaspora temples, pagodas, and centers visited by both Buddhists of Asian ancestry and of Euro-American origin, these major lines of Buddhism come together. However, there is an intersection without interaction, forming parallel worlds and distant congregations, as Paul Numrich noticed (1996). Modernist Buddhists, predominantly Western converts but also a slowly growing number of Asian immigrant descendants, focus on meditation and studying texts. Traditionalist Buddhists perform devotional acts and rituals. The terms "modernist" and "traditionalist" Buddhism analytically direct attention on the religious differences instead of focusing on ethnic ancestry, skin-color difference, and citizenship. Further, attention can be paid to tensions between the strands and their religious focus. In this respect, a typical difficulty of a religion in diaspora comes to the fore: it is the dilemma of both, so to say, staying true to the thus-perceived "original" – either to the transplanted tradition or the "word of the Buddha" – and at the same time adapting to the constraints of the new socio-cultural context. Such processes of adaptation affect both strands in the way that traditionalist Buddhists willingly or reluctantly see a need to modernize their tradition in Western contexts, especially so as the next generation remains not unaffected by rationalized, de-mythologized, and egalitarian worldviews. However, a linear development from traditionalist to modernist interpretations certainly does not exist. Though some ritual activities might be disregarded and considered inappropriate in a diasporic temple, there exists also the strength and traditionalist potential to withstand and oppose thus-labeled assimilative trends of demythologization and modernization. Likewise, modernist Buddhism is affected in the way that spokespersons already questioned the emphasis on individualism, cognitive, and rational elements. Some suggested an orientation favored within traditionalist Buddhism towards collective forms, devotional and ritual acts, and faith in order to live a Buddhism which also takes the body and community and not only the mind and individual person into account. Second, some modernist Buddhists in their efforts to indigenize the *Dharma* have been strongly affected by Western psychology, its vocabulary and worldviews. In this way psychologized and secularized interpretations of Buddhist meditation have gained widespread popularity in Western countries. This understanding does not relate to Buddhist terms and concepts any more but accentuates meditation as an awareness technique to reduce stress and to foster psychological healing. One may speak of post-modernist forms of Buddhism, though at times the Buddhist origin is neither acknowledged nor taken into account any longer. For this reason, former Buddhist meditational practices have become assimilated to the diasporic context to such an extent that cardinal Buddhist ideas – the concepts of impermanence (Skt. *anitya*), suffering (*duḥkha*), and no-self (*anātman*) – have lost their intentional impulse and goal-oriented direction towards enlightenment (Skt. *nirvāṇa*).

See also: **Buddhism, psychology, and therapy; Buddhism and Western lifestyle; Buddhism in the Western world; Buddhist adaptations in the West; Ecumenicism and intra-Buddhist activities; New Buddhist roles.**

MARTIN BAUMANN

DIGITAL INPUT OF BUDDHIST TEXTS

The material that follows cannot be documented from print publications. It is of two types. A great deal of the information is available through browser searches, while other sections are in the nature of a personal memoir. I have been fortunate to have lived through the era that is described and to have come into contact with all of the researchers mentioned. For the Internet information, the ease of search through a browser makes it less important to mention every existing website for each project. Future readers will have access to expanding information, and current websites will disappear over time. Because a good deal of this information appears in print for the first time in this article, I hope this publication will serve as an introduction to the history of the input of Buddhist material.

The first Buddhist materials to be digitized were the canonic texts. Because of the size and variety of these canons the computer was a promising storage and retrieval tool for scholars and researchers. At the same time this literature was held in high esteem by the religious communities, which were willing to raise the sizeable sums of money needed to digitize and make it available. Scholars were also supportive, although slow to acknowledge digital sources when annotating articles and books. While a passage might be located by searching the CD-ROM and online versions of the canons, it was generally more acceptable to reference the print versions in footnotes. Standard rules for citation had to be developed, and scholars needed to be reminded that using a digital source without referencing that fact constituted a new form of plagiarism. As with all new technologies, early uses imitated the former ones. When Buddhist texts became available in digital form they were viewed in the same way as print versions had been. Later users began to exploit the full potential of the electronic versions for analyzing structure and pattern as well as for searching and retrieving data.

Pāli

On 30 May 1988, *Vaiśākha Pūjā* Day, the Digital *Tipiṭaka* Development Team at the Mahidol University Computing Center, Thailand, announced the completion of the first major project to digitize Buddhist texts. The Siam edition of the Pāli *Tipiṭaka* in forty-five volumes had been successfully digitized and released with an application program called BUDSIR (Buddhist Scriptures Information Retrieval). The work had been directed by Professor Supachai Tangwongsan. Released first on a WORM (Write Once Read Many) drive, it later became available on a CD-ROM (Compact Disk-Read Only Memory), and several hundred copies were distributed by the American Academy of Religion and Mahidol University. With the entire *Tipiṭaka* available in digital format, researchers no longer had to seek out those few libraries in the world whose collections contained the whole Pāli canon.

BUDSIR made it possible for the first time to digitally search for and retrieve every example of any word, sentence, or phrase in the *Tipiṭaka*. Then, in 1991, His Majesty King Bhumibol Adulyadej issued a directive to include the seventy volumes of the *Aṭṭhakathā* (Commentary) along with the *Tipiṭaka* texts. Completed in 1994, all 115 volumes were released on CD-ROM with a BUDSIR IV upgrade that incorporated new international standards and other user requirements. Two years later BUDSIR IV for Windows was released, redesigned with a graphical user interface (GUI) to facilitate text comparison and a new audio feature that allowed the computer to reproduce the sound of the words of the Pāli texts. In 1997 a Thai transcription was added, with a new search engine that was able to display multi-script retrieval. In addition, translation tables from Roman and Thai scripts made it possible to view the texts in Devanagari, Sinhalese, Burmese, or Khmer. At this point, a dictionary of Pāli–Thai equivalents was linked to the database, allowing quick reference for Thai language readers. Finally, in 2002, BUDSIR was upgraded again to allow users to access and search the data online. New features continued to be added until 2004, when the Devanagari and Sinhalese scripts could be used for retrieval.

Within a decade of the release of the Siam edition, a number of groups began to digitize other editions of the canon. The Vipassana Research Institute (VRI) in India chose to digitize the *Chaṭṭha Sangayana* edition produced in 1956 at the culmination of the Sixth Buddhist Council. The Indian government had commissioned the Nalanda Institute to prepare a print version in Devanagari, and VRI prepared a reprint of 135 volumes. By 1997 a CD-ROM of the Devanagari edition was available, along with software to convert the Devanagari into Roman and Burmese script. Software upgrades included five additional script options, the ability to install the data on Chinese Windows, and the expansion of the number of volumes to 216.

In 1991 the Sri Vajiragnana Dharmayatanaya, a *bhikkhu* training center in Maharagama, Sri Lanka, began to digitize the Sri Lankan version of the Pāli *Tipiṭaka*. The edition used as the basis for the input was the fifty-eight-volume *Buddha Jayantī Tipiṭaka* that had been compiled and published during the 1960s and 1970s with government support. The digital input was under the auspices of the Amarapura branch of the *sangha* headed by Ven. Madihe Pagnnaseha Mahanayake Thera. The work of creating machine-readable versions was completed in 1994, though a number of errors remained. At that point, the Colombo branch of the Sasana Sevaka Society undertook further proofreading and annotation. Known as the Sri Lanka *Tripiṭaka* Project (SLTP), it was mirror sited with the *Journal of Buddhist Ethics* in 1999.

The Pāli Text Society and Dhammakaya Foundation

The most commonly used version of the Pāli canon for scholarship has been the edition prepared by the Pāli Text Society of Oxford (PTS). PTS was formed in 1881 by Professor Thomas William Rhys Davids to translate and publish Buddhist literature. Scholars recognized the importance of digitizing the PTS version of the canon, and in 1988 Professors Jamie Hubbard of Smith College and Robert Thurman of Columbia University prepared a funding proposal to the National Endowment for the Humanities (NEH). When the NEH did not select the project for support, Professor Hubbard turned to the Buddhist community. In December 1988 Professor Hubbard joined Professor Lewis Lancaster of the University of California, Berkeley, at a meeting of the World Buddhist Federation at the Hsi Lai Temple in Los Angeles, where they demonstrated the potential of computers for reading and working with text material. Hearing of this presentation, the Dhammakaya Foundation indicated an interest in the digital project. By 1990 volunteers began inputting and proofreading the texts. As the team was unable to locate all of the PTS texts in Thailand, the library of the University of California, Berkeley, supplied the missing works.

Difficult copyright issues delayed the signing of a memorandum of understanding until April 1996, when Professor K.R. Norman of PTS went to Thailand and signed the agreement for a joint venture between PTS and the Dhammakaya Foundation. The CD-ROM was released in June. Called EPaliText version 1.0, it contained the digital version of PTS's Pāli language volumes and a search engine. The publication coincided with the celebration of the Golden Jubilee of His Majesty King Bhumibol Adulyadej, and the first copies of a revised version, known as Palitext version 1.0, were presented to the monarch in November 1996. Five hundred copies of the CD-ROM were distributed worldwide. While the Pāli language version was being input, the Dhammakaya Foundation also started work on the English translations of the PTS texts. As of May 2005, this English material had not appeared in digital format.

Fragile Palm Leaves manuscript preservation project

Palm-leaf manuscripts continued to be made, even after printing had become the technology of choice for recording Buddhist texts. Those palm-leaf documents still available in collections often date to the nineteenth century when copying Pāli texts was still a major form of merit-making. By the latter part of the twentieth century, however, the preservation of these manuscripts was no longer assured. In 1994 the Fragile Palm Leaves manuscript preservation project was formed to rescue them from neglect and destruction. One of the leaders of this movement was Peter Skilling. By 2000 the group had collected more than 5,000 manuscripts with 10,000 titles; in early 2001 the Fragile Palm Leaves Foundation was registered under Thai law. A catalogue of the manuscripts in Pāli and Burmese was compiled in cooperation with the PTS. As new computer technology became available, images of the manuscripts were scanned into digital databases. This project was established in cooperation with the Lumbinī International Research Institute in Nepal.

Tibetan canon editions and commentaries

The major work of digitizing the canonic texts of Tibet was initiated by Geshe Michael Roach, an American monk who was influenced by his teacher Khen Rinpoche Geshe Lobsang Tharchin, the longtime head lama of the Rashi Gempil Ling Temple in Howell, New Jersey. The endeavor was given the title Asian Classics Input Project (ACIP), and is coordinated from the USA with monastic university computing centers in South Asia, including Sera Mey, Sera Jey, Ganden Jangtse, Drepung Loseling, and Sakya (Rajpur). Refugee camps, especially the southern Indian settlements of Rabling and Dekey Larsoe, are also involved. Working with the refugee council of His Holiness the Dalai Lama, local groups in India made space available, while ACIP provided the hardware, training, and workers' salaries. In addition to preserving Tibetan canonic texts, the project provides Tibetan youth with training in computer technology.

ACIP is also compiling a digital catalogue of Tibetan woodblock prints from two large Russian collections. The St. Petersburg Branch of the Institute of Oriental Studies of the Russian Academy of Sciences has 25,000 volumes containing nearly 200,000 titles. The Oriental Library of the University of St. Petersburg has an additional 3,300 xylographic copies. By 2005 the number of titles cataloged from these two collections reached 50,000, far exceeding the 1,000 entries in the next-largest print catalogue of similar titles. This is a good example of how the amount of data available online and in distributed digital formats exceeds the amount available in print.

With the St. Petersburg projects under way, ACIP turned its attention to the Tibetan materials in Mongolian archives in Ulan Bator, an estimated 1.4 million titles. These include many duplicates, as well as a large number of texts preserved at Mongolia's main Buddhist monastery, Gangdan Tekchen Ling, that were scattered or ill-housed during the troubled times after 1937. ACIP has estimated that it may take several decades to complete the work on these materials and that, when it is done, the titles will far outnumber those included in the St. Petersburg catalogue.

There are a number of other efforts in Nepal and India to digitize the literary classics of Tibetan Buddhism's major schools. Many of these projects, which focus on the writings of important figures in Tibetan history, combine print output with digital publication of rare texts. For example, the Nitartha International Document Input Center in Kathmandu used a computer-generated script to print the collections of the *Karma Kagyu* masters. The ability to create and use new fonts and to produce clear copies for print output has enhanced many of the organization's publications. Ironically, the computer has stimulated much of the growth in print publications.

The Drukpa Kagyu Heritage Project (DKHP), also based in Kathmandu, has been closely associated with these attempts to collect and publish the writings of particular masters. Under the direction of Ven. Tsoknyi Rinpoche and Tony Duff, the DKHP has led the way in developing word-processing software for Tibetan materials, which they have shared with other projects. There are a host of projects in this field. Software engineers Leigh Brassington and Marvin Moser were involved in the early development of Tibetan software. Some of the DKHP's most advanced input projects are: the complete works of Dilgo Khyentse Rinpoche, under the direction of Matthieu Ricard; the anthology of Jigma Lingpa at the Namdroling Monastery; the Gomang Pharkhang Project of Peter Gilks; the materials originally found at Mindroling; the collection of Taklun Kagyu texts being input by Sonam Tobgyal in Toronto.

Sanskrit editions

The digitizing of Sanskrit materials has been delayed because there is no religious community to provide the support for such work. The most significant Sanskrit text preservation project used microfilm and was undertaken by the Nepal–German Manuscript Preservation Project (NGMPP), founded by Dr. Wolfgang Voigt and Professor Dr. Klaus Ludwig Janert. An agreement between the government of Nepal and the German Research Council launched the project in 1970, and Professor Dr. Albrecht Wezler served as director general from 1982 until the work was completed in 2002. The project has microfilmed more than 180,000 Sanskrit and Tibetan manuscripts consisting of nearly five million folios. A number of Buddhist texts were included in this international project, which is an excellent candidate for future digitization.

While there has never been a coordinated effort to digitize the complete body of Sanskrit texts that exist either in manuscript or in published critical editions, early efforts were made by individual scholars. These projects usually involved a single text or a group of texts relating to the particular interest of the researchers involved. This has been particularly true in Japan, where private data sets have been created for a variety of texts. Few of these have ever been made available to a large audience.

One project to digitize some of the most important Sanskrit texts was initiated by Professor Jong-cheol Lee of the Academy of Korean Studies, Seoul, when he was a graduate student at the University of Tokyo. Jong-cheol Lee set up a small input center in India, financed mainly with his own money, with some additional support from the Center for Buddhist Studies at the University of California, Berkeley. The goal of this long-term web-based project is to create a Sanskrit database for a polyglot Buddhist dictionary that will include mappings among Sanskrit, Tibetan, Chinese, and Korean.

As a follow-up to the Pāli project at Mahidol University, Professor Supachai also digitized several thousand pages of Sanskrit texts, which he plans to make available in the future.

Professor Lewis Lancaster, working with a grant from the Fo Guang Shan Educational and Cultural Foundation, mounted a new project in 2000 with the Nagarjuna Institute of Exact Methods in Kathmandu, Professor Min Bahadur Shakya, Director. An input center was set up in Kathmandu to digitize a set of published editions of Mahāyāna Sanskrit texts as well as Tantric texts from manuscripts. The digitized texts were put online by the University of the West in Los Angeles for free public use.

Central Asian languages

Professor Dr. Jost Gippert of the University of Frankfurt established the Thesaurus Indogermanischer Text-und-Sprachmaterialien (TITUS) to create a database of Buddhist texts written in Central Asian Indo-European languages. During the first phase of the project, slides of the manuscripts were prepared, scanned, and stored as graphic images. During the second phase, the texts were input using Unicode for the various scripts to allow display as a screen font.

The Chinese Buddhist canon

It is difficult to establish exactly when Chinese Buddhist texts began to be digitized. In 1986 a group at the Institute of World Religions of the Chinese Academy of Social Sciences in Beijing formed a "Bureau of the Chinese Buddhist Canon." One of the first and most difficult issues the group dealt with was the lack of a digital font containing all of the ancient characters of the canon. Several attempts were made to create software that could reproduce the glyph form for any possible combination of the elements of Chinese characters. While thousands of these combinations were constructed, the effort did not result in the creation of a usable font. In the 1990s Professor Fan Guang Chang reported at an international meeting of the Electronic Buddhist Text Initiative (EBTI), that 106 volumes of the canon had been digitized, along with various art, artifacts and other cultural data. He also indicated that a project was under way to digitize one of the Ming dynasty editions of the Chinese canon. The distribution of this data has not yet been documented.

The Zen texts project of Hanazono University

One of the earliest and most influential centers for research on digitizing Buddhist texts was the International Research Institute for Zen Buddhism (IRIZ) at Hanazono University in Kyoto. Under the leadership of Dr. Urs App, IRIZ explored the problems of computer input, including characters that did not exist in any of the available fonts. Working with Dr. Christian Wittern, Dr. App played another important role as well, making the scholarly community aware of the potential usefulness of digital technology. His 1991 publication of the first volume of *The Electronic Bodhidharma* in many ways announced the arrival of the new technology for Buddhist studies. Print publications were followed in 1995 by the release of ZenBase CD1, a digital resource for the study of texts from this important school of Buddhism. It is hard for later generations to understand the range of problems faced by those who explored digital technology before the commercial development of software, large capacity memory, and personal computers. Pioneering scholars such as App and Wittern made contributions that were essential to the process that unfolded over the following two decades. Together with other scholars, they helped define the issues of computing for the humanities and influenced the way computer engineers approached the development of tools and standards.

Professor C.C. Hsieh of Academia Sinica in Taiwan played a crucial role in the various digital input projects. In the 1980s he led the first major project to digitize a Chinese archive, the twenty-five dynastic histories of China, inspiring other Buddhist scholars to proceed with the canonic input. The dynastic history database of forty million characters proved that a large amount of information in Chinese characters could be digitized for search and retrieval.

The *Koryŏ* edition

The oldest complete set of printing blocks for the Chinese Buddhist canon is found at the Jogye Order's Haein Monastery in South Korea. Known as the *Koryŏ* edition, it consists of more than 83,000 blocks carved in the thirteenth century from the Northern Song's *Kaipao* edition. Prints from Haein Monastery's blocks were used to produce the nineteenth-century Tokyo edition of the canon, as well as the twentieth-century *Taisho Issaikyo* metal-type edition. In 1993 Professor Lewis Lancaster received support from Korea's lay Buddhist community to digitize Haein's *Koryŏ* edition.

Professor Lancaster, working with Drs Urs App, Christian Wittern, and Sungtaek Cho, located an input facility at the Shanghai Chemical Research Institute, whose computer center had installed the newest technology in the late 1980s. In order to accommodate this project, the institute received permission to load the font set of traditional characters into their system. A staff was assembled, and nearly two million characters (of the more than fifty-two million total for the whole canon) were digitized. At the same time, Vens Cheongnim and Hyemuk of Haein Monastery had also begun to experiment with digitizing the *Koryŏ* edition and held a summit conference to discuss how the work could be accomplished. The two projects were joined in 1994, and the data input was turned over to Seoul. Fundraising efforts resulted in Samsung Corporation adopting the project. Samsung set up a dedicated laboratory and employed over thirty full-time typists and six engineers for one year to input the content of all 83,000 printing blocks. The work was completed in January 1996, and the first CD-ROM was made available. At about the same time, the Haein Monastery was designated a UNESCO World Heritage Site, partially in recognition of the importance and aesthetic quality of the *Koryŏ* printing blocks. Proofreading began in April 1997, after a fundraising project supported by a month-long advertisement in Korea's *JoongAng Ilbo* newspaper solicited donations from the general public. In order to make the digital version look like the block prints, a new font was developed that followed the glyph patterns of the thirteenth-century scribes. This required creating more than 30,000 user-defined characters. Known as the *Tripiṭaka Koreana*, the project is still ongoing under the leadership of Ven. Cheongnim.

Chinese Buddhist Electronic Text Association

While the *Taishō Issaikyō* has been the most widely used edition of the Chinese Buddhist canon produced under the

Northern Song, copyright issues delayed its digitization. The publisher of the print version, Daizo Shuppansha, Inc., undertook the initial input as a commercial project. Working with the late Professor Ejima Yasunori of Tokyo University, four CDs were produced for separate volumes of the print edition. To recover their production costs, the publisher charged a very high price for each disk, and income proved insufficient to justify the project financially. As a result, the work came to a halt while alternate approaches were explored. An agreement was eventually reached which allowed Daizo Shuppansha to retain the copyright for the content while giving the Chinese Buddhist Electronic Text Association (CBETA) of Taiwan permission to distribute it without charge online and on CD-ROM. This agreement was a milestone in the development of intellectual property rights as they apply to information available on the Internet. The leaders of the CBETA team were Ven. Hui-min and Mr. Aming Tu.

Once the copyright license had been granted, CBETA set to work in 1998 on an electronic version. As with similar projects, donations from the religious community made the work possible. Support came from the Chung-Hwa Institute of Buddhist Studies, the Yin-Shun Foundation of North America and the Buddhist *Bodhi* Foundation. In 1999 Volumes 5–10 of the *Taishō Issaikyō* were the first to be released. This was followed by an updated release for Volumes 1–55 and 85 of the print edition. At this point CBETA provided the entire content of the Northern Song edition as found in the Haein Monastery printing blocks, with a few additions. Volume 85, for example, contained texts from Dunhuang manuscripts. CBETA was able to move rapidly toward digital publication in part because of the efforts of Mr. Hsiao Chen-kuo, a Buddhist layman who had been digitizing the data for some years. As he had done the work out of religious commitment, Mr. Hsiao released his data for use with CBETA. In addition, Dr. Christian Wittern converted the digital *Tripiṭaka Koreana* to Big Five extension for use in the digital publication. As the *Taishō* text is a copy of the *Koryŏ* block prints, the data were easily adopted for CBETA. CBETA credits a number of individuals for the data input, including Tseng Kuo-Feng and Leo Flamenco. In 2004 the project was enlarged to include materials from the *Zokuzokyo*, texts that do not occur in the core of the Chinese canon contained in *Taishō* volumes 1–55. With the CD-ROM and Internet versions of the Chinese canon from CBETA, Buddhist scholars finally had a useful digital resource. While the *Tripiṭaka Koreana* had been completed earlier, it was CBETA that finally introduced the digital canon to a wide audience.

SAT

Work on digitizing the Chinese canon has also been done in Japan. The group most responsible is *Samganikikritam Taishō Tripitakam* (SAT), also known as the Association for Computerization of Buddhist Texts (ACBUT). As the copyright for the print edition of the *Taishō* is held in Japan, an early attempt was made to digitize the edition in Tokyo. However, the nature of the project shifted after the untimely death of Professor Ejima Yasunori and the effort was later led by Professors Moro Shigeki of Hanazono University, Kyoto, and Ishii Kosei of Komazawa Junior College, Tokyo. SAT was able to negotiate the license for CBETA in Taiwan and thus make the *Taishō* available to the world. Rather than limiting their activity to digitizing, SAT began exploring ways of dealing with the many variant readings in the multiple translations of the Buddhist texts and researching the best practices for using the digital version of the canon.

Hong Kong

In 1999 a separate project in Hong Kong produced a CD-ROM with Volumes 1–85 of the *Taishō*. Because it can be read only with one reader that runs only on a version of Microsoft Windows for traditional Chinese characters, it did not find a ready audience. Given the easy availability of CBETA on the Web at this time, it was not possible to make an impact using complex and restrictive methods.

Chinese Buddhist manuscripts

In addition to the canonic projects already discussed, another major digital project was underway at the British Library in London. The International Dunhuang Project (IDP), under the leadership of Dr. Susan Whitfield, has scanned thousands of manuscript pages collected by British archaeologist Sir Aurel Stein in the early twentieth century. Colin Chinnery was a major figure in the development of this resource. The digital versions of the Chinese Buddhist manuscripts that constitute the majority of documents from Dunhuang's Cave 17, in particular, constitute a major step forward for research. Scholars now have Internet access to documents that were previously available for limited use only at the British Library. This resource is invaluable for future textual criticism of Chinese canonic readings. A digital map with photographs from the Stein archive provides context for the locations of the archeological sites that contained the Buddhist materials.

Persistence of digital data

The long-term preservation of data presents challenges that major libraries have not yet solved. CD-ROMs and DVDs will last only as long as their layers remain sealed, currently estimated at thirty to forty years. Even when material is stored at supercomputer centers, it is questionable whether the functional formats of the data will be usable after several decades. As platforms and software become obsolete, the data will have to be transferred to keep it current. The cost of high-level data security and continual software and hardware upgrades will put long-term funding pressure on libraries and archives. ACIP is addressing this challenge by backing up their digital material with microfilm, which is thought to have a life-span of a century or more. Acid-free paper also remains an essential storage option. Scanned images printed onto acid-free paper have centuries of potential usefulness. There is probably no one issue as critical as the possibility of loss, as scholars and institutions opt to make use of digital information.

The transfer of digital data creates a broad range of new problems that will require well-coordinated solutions to avoid a quagmire of incompatible platforms, codes, categorization systems, and unnecessarily repeated work. To address these concerns, Electronic Buddhist Text Initiative convened its first informal meeting at the University of California, Berkeley, in 1992, with sixteen persons present. This has been followed by more or less annual meetings, each marking a clear development in the scope and sophistication of the digital projects discussed. EBTI's administration moved to Dongguk University in Seoul in 2001, where it continues to serve the scholarly community.

Buddhist response to digital canonic developments

During the time Mahidol University was digitizing the Siam edition of the Pāli canon, Ven. Chao Khun Phra Dhammapitaka (Bikkhu Prayudh Payutto), a senior Thai monk, served as adviser to the project and worked closely with

Professor Supachai on proofreading the texts. Later, Bikkhu Payutto began speaking and writing about the impact the new technology might have on Buddhism. He began by noting that the amount of data available electronically has so surpassed the storage capacity of the human mind that we are becoming increasingly dependent on the computer. As a consequence, he suggests that Buddhists might have to choose between remaining "a natural humanity living in a natural world, or . . . attempt[ing] to make a 'scientific human' for the scientific world." Also, whereas our traditional understanding of Buddhist doctrine is based on sensory data, as described in great detail throughout the Pāli texts, Bikkhu Payutto asks whether the vast amount of new data available to us might one day challenge our previously held opinions. He suggests that his fellow Buddhists think how this might affect their understanding of the basic doctrines of the tradition.

Using the concept of creating benefit to frame another issue, Bikkhu Payutto also recommends that Buddhists evaluate whether technology is "creating benefit" or merely "seeking benefit." Weighing benefit for "self" against benefit for "others," this Buddhist monk implies that seeking benefit at any cost is quite different from creating lasting benefit.

On 7 December 2000 a solemn procession of Jogye Order monks carried a crystal *stūpa* into the Olympic Pavilion in Seoul, South Korea. Sealed inside the *stūpa* was a CD-ROM containing the recently completed digital *Tripiṭaka Koreana*. In this ritual moment, the digital world became part of Buddhist religious tradition, and the Jogye Order's celebration provided telling evidence of the acceptance of the digital canon as a sacred object.

See also: **Cyber-Buddhism; Digital research resources.**

LEWIS R. LANCASTER

DIGITAL RESEARCH RESOURCES

During the 1980s and 1990s the production of digital tools for Buddhist Studies was directed mainly toward digitizing the textual record and exploring methods for making the texts available and searchable. Thus, it is not surprising that digital dictionaries and encyclopedias for use with these texts were the focus of the following round of activity. In the beginning these tended to be digital versions of works published originally in print. The multi-volume *Fo Guang Buddhist Dictionary* (Hsing Yun 1988–99) added a new level of sophistication to Chinese publications on the Buddhist tradition when it was published in print in 1989. It was eventually digitized and issued on CD-ROM. Likewise, after expanding their 1983 *Dictionary of Buddhist Terms and Concepts*, Sōka Gakkai released print and digital versions in 2002. This major revision, *The Dictionary of Buddhism*, included over 2,700 terms and cross-references for doctrinal terms, as well as events in Buddhist history, commentaries, and a focus on the tradition of Nichiren Buddhism and the *Saddharmapuṇḍarīka Sūtra*.

The development of digital research and reference works in Buddhist studies faced some formidable challenges. The lack of standardization added complexity to the building of new reference tools. As groups such as Fo Guang Shan and Sōka Gakkai attempted to create digital tools based on paper publications, they faced the increasing likelihood that rapid development of new software would soon render their products obsolete. Innovators such as these were faced with the time-consuming task of learning how to use the newest software. Platform and character coding choices had to be made within a context in which there was no compatibility among alternatives. While the digital dictionaries were first released on CD-ROM, newer technology brought the DVD into use at about the same time as the World Wide Web was becoming a powerful research environment. It also became obvious that there were great differences between the print and digital editions. The print edition could be reissued many times without the need for major revisions. But while sweeping changes in the digital world made the data easier to disseminate and use, each new development required reworking the material.

Another type of resource that followed the digitizing of texts was the dictionary of multilingual equivalents. In Buddhist studies, Professor Charles Muller of Toyo Gakuen University, Tokyo, was a major figure in developing this type of resource. In 1986 Professor Muller began compiling the digital *Dictionary of East Asian Buddhist Terms* (DEABT), along with the companion *Dictionary of East Asian Literary CJK Terms* (DEALT), with the thought of producing a new print dictionary. In the end, however, Muller put the material into HTML format and distributed it on the Web in 1995. At that time users were able to access 3,000 Buddhist terms in Chinese, Japanese, and Korean. As with all digital projects, the material required continuous updating – a daunting task involving XML markup. Three years after he posted the first HTML version on the Internet, Professor Muller had converted the entire text from S-JIS to Unicode and re-released it. Within another six months the dictionaries functioned with Document Type Definition (DTD) markup that allowed for eXtensible Style Language (XSL) files. The project is now known as the *CJKV–English Dictionary* (*Chinese, Japanese, Korean, Vietnamese–English Dictionary*), with the subtitle of *A Dictionary-Database of CJK Characters and Compounds Related to East Asian Cultural, Political, and Intellectual History.* It contains more than 50,000 word entries. As an additional user resource, Professor Muller prepared a digital version of *The Korean Buddhist Canon: A Descriptive Catalog*, compiled by Professor Lewis Lancaster of the University of California, Berkeley, in collaboration with Sung-bae Park.

As a result of sharing the news of his efforts on the Internet, Professor Muller came in contact with Professor Michael Beddow, a scholar of German Studies from the University of Leeds who had trained in computer programming. It was Professor Beddow who had conceived of ways to use programming code to produce some of the functions Professor Muller sought for his dictionary. While Professor Beddow had no background in East Asian languages, his long-term interest in using XML markup for the storage and retrieval of lexicographical documents made him an invaluable collaborator. Within six weeks of the first email contact between the two scholars, Professor Muller's markup structure was upgraded to use XPointers, which made it possible to retrieve a single dictionary entry from files that contained hundreds of words. This allowed the dictionary to be used immediately as it existed at that moment.

Another important development in producing Buddhist dictionaries came with the online version of *The Pāli Text Society's Pāli–English Dictionary.* A grant from the US Department of Education provided funds for the University of Chicago and the Triangle South Asia Consortium (TSAC) in North Carolina to construct an electronic version of this and other South Asian dictionaries. *The Pāli Text Society's Pāli–English Dictionary* contains 160,000 citations, as well as etymologies for the main entries. This is part of the Digital South Asia Library at the University of Chicago and is included in the web page of *Digital Dictionaries of South Asia (DDSA)*. A number of dictionaries that include Buddhist terms are under construction at this site. The initial versions of these dictionaries are simulations of the paper editions and have yet to employ more sophisticated coding to facilitate cross-referencing. The eventual size and importance of the *DDSA* site will eventually require that it settle some of the most pressing problems for online Buddhist and other reference works. Not the least of these challenges is long-term preservation. This problem has occupied the library community since 1996, when the Commission on Preservation and Access (CPA) and the Research Libraries Group (RLG) created the Task Force on Archiving of Digital Information and published a report outlining the challenges the new technology poses within the traditional library system.

Other facsimile dictionaries began to appear on the Internet. One type was represented by the *Buddhist Dictionary: Manual of Buddhist Terms and Doctrines*, compiled in print by Nyānatiloka Mahāthera and revised several times. The coverage of terms was to some extent defined by the listings found in the Pāli canon *Abhidhamma* and the content focused on doctrinal descriptions rather than linguistic or lexical strategies.

Another dictionary project was mounted at the University of Cologne under the title *The Cologne Digital Sanskrit Lexicon (CDSL)*. This project started with the goal of producing digital editions of the bilingual Sanskrit dictionaries that were produced in the nineteenth century. The project is important for Buddhist studies because it will provide the largest Sanskrit lexicon available. Further, the team at Cologne promises to create digital tools designed for the analysis of Sanskrit texts. Professor Jong-Cheol Lee of the Academy of Korean Studies set in motion a project called *The Construction of a Sanskrit Database for a Polyglot Buddhist Dictionary.* This is a digital project that will attempt to provide the Buddhist vocabulary that is missing from the nineteenth-century Sanskrit dictionaries.

Online Tibetan Buddhist dictionaries were developed early and their range has been impressive. The first of these were mainly the work of individual scholars which was later incorporated into the digital versions. One of the first online compilations of Tibetan words with English equivalents was started by Dr. James Valby while he was a student at the University of Saskatchewan in the 1970s and 1980s. Over time, he assembled most of the listings in Sarat Chandra Das' 1902 dictionary, part of H. Jaeschke's (1881), as well as glossaries from English translations of Tibetan works. By the time it appeared online under the name *James Valby's Tibetan–English Dictionary for MS-DOS* it contained some 53,000 entries. Professor Eric Schmidt and his staff expanded Dr. Valby's work, producing the *Rangjung Yeshe Tibetan–English Dharma Dictionary (RYD)* – also called the *Rangjung Yeshe Tibetan–English Dictionary of Buddhist Culture* – from other projects and some of their own information. In addition to Dr. Valby's 64,477 entries, the *RYD* staff included Richard Barron's Glossary of 4,869 entries; 83,000 words and equivalents from the *rdzogs chen*, *Mahāmudrā*, and other literature; Ives Waldo's Glossary of 122,000 terms; and 18,440 entries from Jeffrey Hopkins' *Tibetan–Sanskrit–English Dictionary.* After some 300,000 entries were collected, compared, and duplicates removed, the *RYD* online dictionary contained nearly 180,000 individual terms and phrases. This was an advance over print dictionaries such as that of Sarat Chandra Das with fewer than 30,000 entries, though many tasks remain to make the dictionary fully usable. It did not provide source references for each entry, and it combined words from different parts of speech without differentiation. Also, it did not follow the lexical strategy of listing definitions in order of their frequency of usage. Professor David F. Germano and his team at the University of Virginia have provided a continuing source of encyclopedia and lexical information with their *Tibetan Himalayan Digital Library* (*THDL*) project. The team has compiled a thematic vocabulary of Lhasa, a gazetteer with information on Tibetan place names, and terminology of Tibetan Tantric practice.

Another important type of resource was a Tibetan word-processing program called TibetDoc that was developed by Tony Duff and a team of scholars in Kathmandu. TibetDoc was designed for online dictionary production and is an example of a product created by a group of scholars willing to explore the programming requirements of their research projects. While most scholarly research relies on the computer, few researchers pay attention to the programming code upon which their research increasingly depends. Mr. Duff recognized that digital research in Tibetan materials requires writing code that makes it possible for scholars to produce and transmit documents easily.

Mr. Duff and the Padma Karpo Translation Committee (PKTC) produced *The Illuminator Tibetan–English Dictionary* (*ITED*) containing 25,000 entries organized by semantic fields and parts of speech. It is a major accomplishment for a single editor to compile such a large digital resource. While the *ITED* has fewer entries than the *RYD*, it provides more comprehensive information for each term. The PKTC and Duff have also prepared facsimile digital versions of other important dictionaries. These include the Das dictionary, Geshe Chodrak's *Tibetan–Tibetan Dictionary* published in the 1940s, and the ninth-century *Mahāvyutpatti Sanskrit–Tibetan–English Glossary.* PKTC's digital version of Das' dictionary allows users to access a number of terms found under a variety of entries which are not available for search in the print version. Geshe Chodrak produced his important lexical reference work in 1940, and it remains the last Tibetan-language dictionary ever published. It provided help for Tibetan readers, but was also an invaluable tool for scholarly research. While the *Bod rgya tshig mdzod chen mo* (*The Great Chinese–Tibetan Dictionary*), published in the 1980s, has tended to supersede Chodrak's work, the digital version of the original work revived interest in its content. The *Mahāvyutpatti* remains important because it is one of the earliest glossaries for Sanskrit–Tibetan equivalents.

A growing number of online resources has made the Internet the first choice of many students and scholars of Buddhist studies. Despite problems regarding procedures for annotating and referencing information, the shift from paper to digital resources is an established reality because of the many advantages offered by the new technologies.

See also: **Cyber-Buddhism; Digital input of Buddhist texts.**

LEWIS R. LANCASTER

DISCIPLES OF THE BUDDHA

The early Buddhist tradition defines the Buddha's disciples broadly as listeners (Skt. *śrāvaka*, Pāli *sāvaka*) who have professed their faith in the Triple Gem. Despite this general definition, *śrāvakas* constitute a critical category in the formation of the early Buddhist community, in the compilation of the Buddha's teachings and in the transmission of the *Dharma*. Disciples played important roles in the growth of the community and in the initial popularization of the teachings.

The concept of discipleship acquired specific meanings in the hagiographies of the Buddha's most celebrated followers. The texts offer multiple accounts of the lives of his closest disciples. In many of *Jātaka* tales, their association with the Buddha is even extended into past lives. While scholars glean some biographical information about the disciples from texts, the significance of these narratives lies primarily in the fact that they illustrate the perfection of virtues (*pāramitā*) and give didactic examples of the disciples' life stories. In particular, accounts of the Great Disciples illustrate the practice of virtues and of Higher Path Stages leading to the ideal of *arhat*hood itself. There is evidence of cults venerating the Sixteen *arhats* who were known for their longevity and forest practice prior to the seventh century in India (as noted by Reginald Ray in 1994). Some great disciples like Śāriputra, Upāli and Mahāpiṇḍola were also the focus of cults in Southeast Asia. Ānanda's dedicated service and personal attention to the Buddha continues to be emulated as an important mode of practice in Burma today.

The early Buddhist community encompassed different types of disciples, ordained monks (*bhikkhu*) and nuns (*bhikkhunī*) as well as lay supporters, including both men (*upāsaka*) and women (*upāsīka*) who took refuge in the Triple Gem, the Buddhist Confession of Faith. Among the earliest converts were five of the Buddha's previous fellow ascetics who formed the initial core of the ordained community (See Figure 20). His most generous lay supporter was a wealthy merchant, Anāthapiṇḍika, who donated the land required to transform the *sangha*

Figure 20 The Buddha preaching the first sermon to five disciples, Sārnāth, India.

from a mendicant to a sedentary community. Recruiting from all social strata of Indian society, the Buddha's disciples also comprised kings like Bimbisāra, and Prasenadi who commissioned the first image. Finally, the Buddha's early disciples included a considerable number of relatives. Among them were his son, Rāhula, and at least two cousins, his devoted personal assistant Ānanda and his challenger, Devadatta. Through Ānanda's intervention with the Buddha, his aunt and foster mother Mahāprajāpatī received permission to form the ordained order of nuns.

During the Buddha's ministry, disciples are believed to have excelled in attaining the Final Path Stages and enlightenment because they benefited from direct and unmediated access to his sermons. The texts describe in several ways the extraordinary experiences of the disciples in the early Buddhist community. Accounts of their spiritual accomplishments have been compiled in the *Psalms of the Brethren*, *Theragāthā*, and in the *Psalms of the Sisters*, *Therīgāthā*. The semi-canonical Birth Stories of the Buddha, the *Jātakas*, project into past lives his association of several of his closest disciples to underscore their karmic affinity with the Buddha. While countless passage of the Theravāda canon make mention of the Buddha's great disciples (*aggasāvaka*), several of them, and especially Śāriputra, Ānanda, and Upāli were important redactors of the Buddha's teachings. Although Śāriputra passed away prior to the Buddha's *pārinirvāṇa* and the compilation of his teachings at the First Buddhist Council, he is credited with compiling several of the *Nikāyas* of the *Sutta Piṭaka*.

With the exception of Ānanda, who attained enlightenment only after the Buddha's *pārinirvāṇa*, all of the Great Disciples became *arhats* by following the Buddha's model. In Theravāda Buddhism, and to lesser extent in other branches of the tradition, the sacred biographies of the great disciples therefore constitute significant didactic narratives. Although not entirely systematized, their hagiographic traditions emphasize the practice of select virtues (*pāramitā*) each of the great disciples perfected in their mastery of the Path. The hagiographies of each of the great disciples are not preserved as continuous narratives, but are dispersed throughout the texts. Several publications attempt to fashion continuous narratives from these accounts and a highly useful treatment is found in Nyānaponika Thera's *Great Disciples of the Buddha* (2003). The following sections summarize some of the mythic accounts of the Buddha's most important disciples.

Ānanda

Among all of the great disciples, Ānanda is described as the Buddha's most devoted personal attendant. He functioned not only as secretary to his master, but appears to have been also an effective intermediary for those seeking access to the Buddha. He is said to have been a cousin and childhood friend of the Buddha. Upon joining the *sangha*, Ānanda requested that the Buddha grant him unlimited access at all times. Tradition also asserts that Ānanda's focus on the Buddha's personal well-being kept him from attaining enlightenment during the Buddha's life. His fellow disciples required him to meditate prior to ascertaining his enlightenment, a stipulation they imposed on his participation at the First Council where he is said to have recited sections of the *Sutta Piṭaka*.

In the Burmese tradition, Ānanda's watchful attentiveness to the Buddha's needs inspired ritual and meditation practices among devotees who seek to emulate his service to the Buddha and his physical needs. In the course of these often elaborate rituals, devotees may offer food, candles, and fragrances the way they imagine Ānanda to have done to Buddha images "as if the Buddha was present." In solitary practice and also as part of communal rituals, Burmese devotees make offering to the Buddha "as though he was alive" and in the manner attributed to Ānanda. During the eleventh century, King Kyanzittha built one of Pagan's most renowned temples, the monumental and ornate Ānanda Temple. Its terraces display scenes from the *Jātakas* and the Defeat of Māra's Army, one of the Buddha's visions during his enlightenment.

Sāriputta

The tradition attributes to Sāriputta the most discerning insights into the *Dharma*. Together with Moggallāna, he was the Buddha's chief disciple (*mahāsāvaka*) who quickly attained the *Dhamma* eye and became an *arhat*. Sāriputta is usually depicted to the right of the Buddha, while Moggallāna stands to his left. The two disciples are said to have shared the responsibility of oversight over the *sangha*. Sāriputta predeceased the Buddha and did not participate in the First Buddhist Council or in the subsequent formation of the community.

Sāriputta's distinguishing virtue was wisdom. He is credited with the systematization of the *dhamma* and was especially accomplished in the *Abhidhamma*, the philosophical basket of the *Tipiṭaka* that concerns causality and mastery of the Final Path Stages. Tradition claims that Sāriputta followed the Buddha as he ascended the Jeweled Staircase on his way to preach the *Abdhidhamma* to his mother in *Tāvatiṃsa* Heaven. Sāriputta recorded there and then this basket of the canonical texts. Like Ānanda and Moggallāna, Sāriputta is frequently identified in the concluding remarks of *Jātaka* stories as having encountered and traveled with the Buddha-to-be through previous lifetimes.

Moggallāna

Moggallāna is recognized as a master of psychic powers (*iddhi*) that endowed him with clairvoyance and clairaudience. He had the ability to read minds, to travel with his mind-made body and to transform himself into other beings. He was known to use magical powers in battles with supernatural beings, such as in his fight with the giant serpent that darkened the world and wrapped itself around Mount Meru (*Visuddhimagga* XII.106–16). Moggallāna was a close friend of Sāriputta and passed away shortly after his friend's death. The *Jātakas* identify these two chief disciples in many of the concluding sections of the stories as having shared many previous lives with the Buddha-to-be.

Mahākassapa

Mahākassapa's strength was in the practice of austerities (*dhūtaṅga*), an ability the Buddha is said to have recognized in him when he gave Mahākassapa robes made of rags and invited him to join the *sangha*. Mahākassapa is an accomplished practitioner of meditation, capable of reaching the highest stages of trance (*dhyāna*). When the Buddha had passed away, he oversaw the distribution of the Buddha's relics and presided over the First Council to preserve the integrity of the *Dharma*. Having assumed the leadership of the *sangha* in this way, he designated Ānanda as his successor by giving him the Buddha's alms bowl and imparting in him the *Dharma*. Mahākassapa entered *pārinirvāṇa* while meditating in a cave at Mount Kukkatapāda, which Chinese sources locate in southwest China and where his body is said to remain intact until the coming of Meitrya. The Chan tradition recognizes Mahākassapa as the only disciple to whom the Buddha transmitted the *Dharma* in silence, while holding up a lotus flower. This episode furnishes the textual precedent for the later Chan practice of the silent transmission of the *Dharma* from a teacher to his selected disciple. Receiving the silent *Dharma* transmission commissions the disciple to propagate these teachings after his teacher departs from this world.

These brief descriptions do not exhaust the disciples' long lists of accomplishments. For instance, Upāli was a low-caste barber who joined the *sangha* and eventually excelled in the monastic discipline of the *Vinaya*. Inasmuch as stories concerning the lives of the Buddha's disciples may have inspired or legitimated particular practices, they also illustrate the perfection of specific virtues (*pāramitā*). Lastly, in concluding these remarks on the Buddha's disciples, it is worth noting that the Mahāyāna and Vajrayāna traditions generally disregard *sāvakas* and *arhats* because they consider them inferior to the path of a *bodhisattva*. However, some Mahāyāna texts describe the Buddha's disciples as having been charged to remain in the world until the coming of the next Buddha, Maitreya.

See also: ***Arahant*; *Bodhisattvas*; Famous Buddhists and ideal types.**

JULIANE SCHOBER

DŌGEN AND SŌTŌSHŪ

Dōgen (1200–53) was the transmitter and founder of the Japanese Sōtō tradition of Zen Buddhism, and one of the most profound thinkers in the history of Buddhism in Japan.

Dōgen was born on the outskirts of Kyoto, the son of aristocratic lineage. His parents died when he was young, however, and he became determined to be a Buddhist renunciant. He was ordained at Enryakuji and studied at the Tendai headquarters on Mount Hiei, but soon became disillusioned with what he saw as a corrupt institution, dominated by political intrigue and warrior monks involved in armed battles against other temples such as Kōfukuji and Miidera. He struggled with and was unable to resolve his doubts concerning the Tendai teaching that all sentient beings have Buddha-nature. After leaving Mount Hiei he studied the Rinzai tradition under Myōzen (1184–1225), a disciple of Eisai (1141–1215), with whom he left for China in 1223. While in China he met an elderly monk, the chief cook of a monastery, who taught Dōgen the importance of discipline and practice in daily life. After visiting numerous Linji (Rinzai) monasteries, he discovered his "authentic teacher" in Ru-jing (1163–1268), a priest in the Caodong (Jap. Sōtō) Chan tradition. After three years of intense practice, he was recognized as having attained enlightenment. Dōgen's enlightenment experience occurred when he overheard Ru-jing scolding another monk for drowsing off, saying, "You must drop off body and mind" (Jap. *shinjin datsuraku*), a phrase that came to have profound implications for Dōgen's philosophy and practice.

Dōgen returned to Japan in 1227 with his *dharma* transmission and was enthusiastic in propagating his understanding of the teachings of the Buddha. Running into opposition from Tendai priests, he eventually settled at Eiheiji, a temple in the mountains of Echizen far removed from bustle and center of secular power, which eventually became the headquarters of the Sōtō school. He spent much of his time maintaining an austere practice and writing essays on Zen practice, explanations, compilations of monastic rules, and Japanese verse. His philosophical essays, written over a period of many years, were compiled into the *Shōbōgenzō* (Treasury of the Eye for the True Dharma), a monumental collection of discourses on Buddhist thought and practice. A well-known collection of Dōgen's talks, the *Shōbōgenzō-zuimonki*, was compiled by his disciple Ejō (1198–1280).

Dōgen's approach to practice is summarized in the phrase "just sitting" (*shikantaza*), reflecting the idea that sitting in meditation (*zazen*) is the only true way of enlightenment. He also taught that practice itself is the attainment of enlightenment (*shūshō-ichinyo*). His reinterpretation and re-reading of the famous Buddhist phrase that "all things have the Buddha-nature" to mean that "all existence is Buddha-nature" is particularly well known.

Dōgen is recognized as one of the most profound Buddhist philosophers in Japanese history, and his stark and uncompromising approach to life and Buddhist practice has been influential even in the West. His Sōtō school is still one of the two largest Zen schools in Japan.

In contrast to the starkness of Dōgen, the Sōtō school became a major network of Buddhist temples in Japan through incorporating a wide variety of popular practices and beliefs. Keizan Jōkei (1264–1325), the founder of Yōkōji and Sōjiji (eventually the head temple of the largest and dominant Sōtō branch), is considered by some to be the true founder of the Sōtō school, as it was through his (and his successors') activities that Sōtō expanded into one of the largest Buddhist networks in Japan. Disputes between the Eiheiji and Sōjiji lineages over matters such as the legacy of Dōgen and Keizan, performance of rites, institutional authority, and so forth have continued into the modern period.

Keizan promoted the traditional magico-religious beliefs of the Japanese along with Zen meditation, thus allowing Sōtō temples to proliferate and prosper among the common people. Local beliefs and practices, such as the deities and practices associated with the mountains of Hakusan and Kumano, and the networks focused on such cults, were incorporated into the activities of Sōtō temples. In the Tokugawa period (1600–1868) Sōtō temples, as with other Buddhist schools, gained much support from the government policy requiring all families to register at and support a local temple, and eventually led to the dominance of funerary rituals and family memorial services (see article on *Sōshiki Bukkyō* [funeral Buddhism]), a situation which continues to this day with the predominance in Japan of "zazenless Zen" – that is, a vast network of "Zen" temples where *zazen* (sitting in meditation) is rarely practiced.

A popular figure from the Sōtō tradition is Ryōkan (1758–1831), a renowned poet and calligrapher. Ryōkan was born the eldest son of a village elder and Shinto priest; he was expected to succeed his father but unexpectedly entered a Zen temple at the age of seventeen. He took his vows under Kokusen, at whose temple, Entsūji, Ryōkan underwent severe practices for over ten years. After his master's death Ryōkan wandered around the country for a number of years and finally settled in a simple retreat near his home village. He lived a simple and frugal existence, writing poetry on the joys of a simple life and stressing the unity of all Buddhist teachings. In his later years Ryōkan developed a strong relationship with the nun Teishin, a widow forty years his junior. They exchanged a series of poems, which were collected by Teishin, along with other poems by Ryōkan, into *Hachisu no tsuyu* (Dew on the Lotus). Ryōkan left no immediate disciples, but his poetry in a variety of styles is still widely read and admired.

See also: **Japan, Buddhism in; Meditation (Chan/Zen); Zen.**

PAUL L. SWANSON

DZOGCHEN

Dzogchen (*rdzogs chen*), or "great perfection" comprises a set of teachings emphasizing distinctive meditation practices associated with the Nyingma (*rnying ma*) school of Tibetan Buddhism, as well as the non-Buddhist Bön tradition of Tibet. They are considered the highest meditation teachings (*atiyoga*) among the three inner tantras (*mahāyoga*, *anuyoga*, and *atiyoga*). In contrast to the other two yogas, *dzogchen* involves no visualization of deities or the body's subtle energies, but instead works directly with the mind to reveal its own primordially pure nature.

Dzogchen teachings distinguish between the ordinary (and ultimately illusory) mind (*sems*, Skt. *citta*) and the "mind in-itself" (*sems nyid*). Ordinary mind consists of appearances, dualistic apprehension, and discursive thought. It is not a container of thoughts but rather a veil of concepts that obscures the true nature of reality. Mind in-itself is the true nature of mind characterized by pure awareness (*rigpa*), which is Buddha-nature. The Nyingma tradition asserts that this Buddha-nature is not merely potential – as asserted by the Gelugpa school – but actual in every person. The goal of the practice, then, is not to *develop* one's Buddha-nature but to *reveal* it. This primordial nature of mind, while considered to be self-arisen and beyond causes and conditions, is the source and basis of all mental phenomena – indeed, of all phenomena – and is not a "thing" that can be made into an object of conceptual representation. It transcends all ideation, linguistic reference, and comparison, and is described as luminous and akin to space – omnipresent, transparent, unobstructed, limitless, and eternal. Jigme Lingpa (1730–98), an important scholar of *dzogchen*, described it as the all-embracing background against which phenomena arise and into which they disappear.

Dzogchen is considered an advanced and rapid path to enlightenment that cuts directly to this primordial level of mind, often in a sudden enlightenment experience. The primary technique cultivates the ability to observe the coming and going of thoughts and phenomena without preference or rejection against the background of pure awareness. The nineteenth-century *dzogchen* master Patrul Rinpoche directs practitioners "neither to suppress nor indulge, neither accept not reject, in any way, the thoughts or emotions which are the energy of *rigpa*. 'Rest in the aspect of awareness, beyond all description'". Still other *dzogchen* techniques direct the meditator to cut off the flow of adventitious thoughts, temporarily dispelling all aspects of ordinary consciousness in order to directly apprehend the pure mind, which manifests spontaneously. Once *rigpa* is clearly recognized, the meditator rests in that primordial state, and there is no difference between meditation and non-meditation. All actions, including ordinary, everyday activities, are said to become spontaneous manifestations of the *dharmakāya*. Thus liberation and the natural flow of activity are co-extensive – thoughts arise but do not bind and are liberated instantly "like a snake uncoiling its own knots" (Patrul).

See also: **Meditation, visualization; Meditation traditions, Vajrayāna; Meditational systems; *Sādhana*; *Śamatha*; *Vipaśyanā*.**

David L. McMahan

E

ECUMENICISM AND INTRA-BUDDHIST ACTIVITIES

The founding of regional associations and national umbrella unions with the aim of bringing together different Buddhist schools and traditions has been strongly supported by Western Buddhists from the mid-1970s onwards. Undoubtedly, since the first divisions occurred, Buddhist history has seen similar endeavors to bring together divergent traditions. In modern times, prominent previous intra-Buddhist examples have been Henry Steel Olcott's "Fundamental Buddhist Beliefs" in his famous *Buddhist Catechism* (1881) and the founding of the World Fellowship of Buddhists by its first president, G.P. Malalasekera, in 1950. Like the latter, ecumenical unions in Western countries have strongly fostered a communal spirit and feeling of solidarity among the different Buddhist groups, schools and traditions. Apart from these organizational activities, there have also been other intra-Buddhist ideas, such as specific approaches to reunite Buddhism and practices by founding a new school or tradition. Examples of such eclectic efforts are the Arya Maitreya Mandala (founded by Lama Govinda in 1933) and the Friends of the Western Buddhist Order. Voices to create a "Navayāna," or new vehicle merging different Buddhist ideas and practices, have primarily remained written drafts.

The joining together of different Buddhist groups and schools under an organizational umbrella followed both pragmatic reasons and the stimulating of solidarity feeling. Buddhists in a country wanted to speak with one voice and have a representative body towards the public and administration. At the same time, it was apparent that Buddhists both in the East and in the West often stress their differences rather than their common ground. In particular, Western Buddhists experienced a territorial proximity of different schools and traditions. The establishment of umbrella associations attempted to manage this new neighborhood plurality and to cope with Buddhism's minority status by joining forces.

Buddhists have founded national unions in Germany (1955), Australia (1958), Austria (1976), Switzerland (1976), the Netherlands and Norway (both 1979), Italy (1985), France (1986), Denmark (1992), Great Britain (1994), Belgium and Portugal (both 1997). Various local associations and regional councils came into being in North America from the 1980s onwards.

In Europe, a main aim of such umbrella associations was to achieve the recognition of Buddhism as a public body by the state. The status would entitle to special rights such as to teach Buddhism in schools and access to broadcast time on television and radio. Also, official acknowledgement of Buddhism would help to secure a place and standing in the country and, importantly, would ensure that Buddhist groups were not considered "sects" or "cults." The process to set up the legally required organization as representative of all Buddhists and headed by a democratically elected committee strongly promoted an "ecumenical" spirit (a self-designation). Further, the adoption of a commonly accepted "Buddhist Confession" (again, a self-designation, coined by German Buddhists) served as a catalyst for the flourishing of Buddhist cooperation, strengthened an intra-Buddhist dialogue, and standardized doctrinal contents. State recognition of Buddhism was achieved in Austria (1983), Portugal (1998), and Italy (2000), though not in Germany. Intra-Buddhist activities encompass, among others, joint celebrations of Buddhist festivals, providing non-sectarian information about Buddhism by publications, Internet sites, and congresses, and participating in interreligious dialogue and alliances. Buddhists are eager to praise their "unity in diversity." Nevertheless, it is important to perceive that quite a number of Buddhist groups and centers deliberately do not join a national umbrella organization. Also it is important to recognize that organizations and temples of immigrant Buddhists have rarely become members. Consequently, questions of representation and who speaks for Buddhism in a country remain. Buddhist plurality often remains dominated by the plurality of convert Buddhists.

See also: **Buddhism in the Western world; Buddhist adaptations in the West.**

MARTIN BAUMANN

ELECTRONIC PUBLICATIONS

Electronic publications have been distributed in two ways: on CD-ROMs and DVDs on the one hand, and over the Internet on the other. CD-ROMs and DVDs appeared first and dominated until the Internet became the main means of disseminating electronic materials. By 1980 the impact of digital materials in the humanities was sufficiently advanced to warrant the attention of Susan Hockney, who published *A Guide to Computer Applications in the Humanities*, announcing that machine-readable text was a viable scholarly resource and was destined to become central to textual scholarship.

Some digital publications reproduce material that already exists in print. The most important early computer-based projects in the humanities, including Buddhist studies, involved digitizing existing paper, film, or microfiche documents. Recognizing the problem of preserving these early digital documents, Lou Burnard established the Oxford Text Archive (OTA) in 1976 to collect electronic texts from multiple sources. This was followed two years later by the formation of the Association for Computers and the Humanities (ACH), attracting primarily textual scholars. Professor Robert Kraft and members of the American Academy of Religion (AAR) and the Society of Biblical Literature (SBL) established the Computer Assisted Research Group (CARG). Within two years, CARG's newsletter had become the most sophisticated publication geared toward scholars working in textual analysis, especially those in the field of the Hebrew Bible. A few Buddhist scholars attended the AAR's annual meetings, but they lacked the canonic databases that had become central to Greek and Hebrew scholarship. The best resource for studying the discussions at CARG meetings is Professor John Abercrombie's *Computer Programs for Literary Analysis.* Many of the software advances in biblical studies made by CARG members as early as the 1980s have not yet been equaled in Buddhist textual studies.

The 1990s saw a proliferation of electronic and print publications dealing with the issues presented by digital material. *Research and Educational Applications of Computers in the Humanities* (REACH), launched in 1989 and edited by Eric Dahlin, was an important electronic publication. The only similar venture in Buddhist studies was the *Electronic Bodhidharma*, edited by Urs App and published by the International Research Institute for Zen Buddhism in Kyoto. *Humanities and the Computer: New Directions*, edited by David S. Mial, described the influence of the digital world on the various fields of the humanities. New methods of tracking the rapid and continuous growth of material on the Internet also appeared in the 1990s. One of the most complete of these aids was the work of Dr. T. Matthew Ciolek of the Australia National University, Canberra ACT. His "virtual library" site included an annotated bibliography of digital resources as well as a catalog and portal for accessing the large lists of available Internet materials. The Buddhist portion of the site housed on the Coombs server in Canberra opened in 1994 and was known as *Buddhist Studies WWW Virtual Library.* The Association for Asian Studies (AAS) in Ann Arbor, Michigan, made a digital version of its *Bibliography of Asian Studies* available in 1998; its more than 500,000 entries included many Buddhist titles.

As the number of Internet sites grew, and students increasingly relied on this type of information, many in the scholarly community raised concerns about how to judge the quality of such material. One response was a joint effort by the universities of Wisconsin, Ohio State, and Minnesota to create a catalogue of resources for Asian studies that had been reviewed by their academic staffs. This was given the name *The Digital Asia Library/Portal to Asian Internet Resources* and was housed at the Madison campus of the University of Wisconsin.

While many of these digital publications appeared first on paper or film, a growing number were published originally on the Internet. In the beginning, most of these sites attempted, as nearly as possible, to reproduce the formats of similar paper or film publications, as seen in the bibliographical references cited above. This was especially true of digital periodicals, which aimed to give scholars the same credit they would have received for printed ones, and it was an indication that online information publishing was coming of age. Some of the most important digital journals for Buddhist studies are the *Journal of Buddhist Ethics*, edited by Damien Keown and Charles S. Prebish, the *Journal of Global Buddhism*, and the *International Journal of Tantric Studies.*

Findings published in digital journals that are peer-reviewed, carefully edited, and produced in accordance with established standards of scholarly print publications, are not significantly different from those that appear in printed journals, and have some very significant advantages. They can be prepared and posted quickly, and they can be made available to researchers and scholars worldwide. Search and retrieval functions are available through browsers and other Internet software, eliminating the need for indexes. With over 6,000 subscribers, the *Journal of Buddhist Ethics* probably has the largest readership of any peer-reviewed periodical in the field of Buddhist studies. While the readership of print journals can be gauged only by citations and bibliographical references over years, the number of visitors to a website can be counted and even analyzed immediately. A graphic example of what digital publication can mean for scholarly material was provided when David Rumsey and Cartography Associates scanned the Japanese Historical Map Collection of the East Asian Library of the University of California, Berkeley, and made it available to online users. This collection of historical maps had been preserved in a locked facility with carefully controlled access for fifty years. During this period some twenty-five scholars had registered and spent time with the collection. The day the website opened nearly 25,000 people visited the site and hundreds of thousands visited during the ensuing months.

Similar results were achieved when the *Taishō Issaikyō* version of the Chinese Buddhist canon was published on CD-ROM and, later, on DVD. Hundreds of scholars secured and began using these disks, transforming the way the canon was read and studied. However, these hundreds of users were dwarfed by the thousands who visited the online version made available without cost by the Chinese Buddhist Electronic Text Association (CBETA). Although the print edition had been a standard for many decades, scholars throughout the world quickly shifted their allegiance to the searchable digital version. Similar results have been achieved with other Buddhist and canonic materials that have been made available for free on the Internet.

Another source of information of interest to Buddhist scholars was the many online course websites created by faculty who started to communicate with their students in this medium. Because web browsers can locate these data, the readership for a syllabus is often far larger than the number of students registered for the course. Excellent bibliographies, outlines, and readings became accessible in this way. While these are not publications in the ordinary sense, they represent an important presentation of research and information for the field of Buddhist studies. Some of these sites, such as the one maintained by Professor John R. McRae of Indiana University, provide links to other recommended sites, as well as to mirror-sited material that can be used directly. "Courseware" allowing students to post questions and comments was another innovation in teaching and research. Many of these online discussions can also be located through browser searches, so they have joined the list of digital publications.

Digital libraries are also beginning to be available online. For Buddhist studies, the Himalayan and Tibetan Digital Library at the University of Virginia, under the guidance of Professor David F. Germano, marks a major development of specific data. The advantage of a digital library is that metadata can be much more complex than that of the traditional library, which is limited by the call numbers of classification schemes such as that of the Library of Congress. Call numbers can be quite useful for shelving and retrieving volumes listed by author and title, or even by basic subject categories. However, they are extremely limited compared to the thousands of markup fields available for data in XML which make it possible to conduct very detailed and focused searches. One of the first attempts to determine a standard markup scheme for the humanities and social sciences is the Text Encoding Initiative (TEI) developed under the leadership of C. Michael Sperberg-McQueen and Lou Burnard. After years of discussion and preparation, a comprehensive manual of more than 1,000 pages has been placed on the Internet. Dr. Christian Wittern has led the way in using TEI for Buddhist text markup. While TEI offers an appealing array of classifications dealing with multiple content subcategories, such as event, place, author, and type, complex software is required to insert the metadata into texts. Recognizing the difficulties of such a detailed markup scheme, a new version called TEI Lite provides a simpler method. Future research will depend on automated markup for many of the TEI categories; for example, using digital gazetteers to detect place-names and feature types within large sets of data.

The digital library presents many challenges for Buddhist Studies, as well as for other disciplines. The library must house data, provide metadata tags, and develop technology for display and analysis. There is no clear model yet for how this will be done. Researchers will have to decide whether these online resources are to be repositories that hold data and allow it to be searched by commercial software, or whether they will provide their own system of access and retrieval. The University of Virginia's Himalayan and Tibetan Digital Library provides users with access software and instructions for using it. However, this is a collection of specific data focused on Buddhist studies. It is not a model that can be easily followed by libraries whose collections include data from a wide range of disciplines.

The most perplexing problem for digital publications will be the development of a sustainable and accessible model. Much of the data that was digitized early in the development of online resources for the humanities will not be available in the future. No arrangements were made to transfer the information from one platform to another. The end of support for the software in a university server often marks the end of all access to the data dependent upon the system. Digital libraries cannot guarantee to keep their current functional software working and available in perpetuity. The Electronic Cultural Atlas Initiative (ECAI) and the California Digital Library (CDL) are experimenting with the publication of multimedia materials. As a way of preserving material for the future, content is placed in primitive formats such as ASCHII text files and JPEG image files, apart from the software the author used to display and navigate through the material. The data is then stored at the San Diego Supercomputer Center. At some time in the future, when the software used by the authors is no longer available or being supported, users will be given access to the stored data and screen shots to use with whatever software they are using. One of the first digital data sets of Buddhist materials to be entered into this system will be the Koryŏ Chinese Buddhist canon.

Digital resources have grown rapidly since Buddhist and other scholars in the humanities began using the technology in their work. Appraisals of the role of the computer in scholarship are helpful, but each decade brings new approaches and challenges that transcend anything previously conceived. This will remain true as long as the technology continues to develop rapidly.

One of the great weaknesses of periodical publication in the humanities has been the length of time between the completion of articles and the availability of the material in a library reading room. This problem is not limited to Buddhist studies. Digital publication offers more timely dissemination. As more students turn to the Internet as the main, or even sole, source of information for research and reading, the need for adequate Buddhist resources in the medium becomes a critical issue.

See also: **Cyber-Buddhism; Digital research resources.**

Lewis R. Lancaster

ENGAGED BUDDHISM

Engaged Buddhism (also called "socially engaged Buddhism") is commonly recognized as one of the most significant movements in contemporary Buddhism. It is a diverse phenomenon, or, perhaps more accurately, a network of diverse phenomena – an international network of groups and individuals who share a common interest in finding Buddhist solutions for contemporary social problems. Like the Christian social gospel and more recent liberationist movements, engaged Buddhist movements typically focus on overcoming suffering and oppression in this world, and, therefore, mine the traditions of Buddhism for resources that will allow them effectively to address such widespread social problems as economic and social oppression, war, hunger, disease, social and geographic dislocation, environmental degradation, and spiritual malaise. While engaged Buddhist movements often develop in isolation from one another in response to the particular needs of particular communities, they are all, in various ways, Buddhist responses to the same set of modernizing influences (see below) and thus share many traits and concerns in common. Moreover, these movements and individuals often recognize their similarities and have joined together through such institutions as the International Network of Engaged Buddhists (INEB) to organize a relatively cohesive global network. The term "engaged Buddhism," therefore, refers simultaneously to diverse groups and individuals who seek to transform society according to Buddhist principles, as well as to a loosely organized religious movement of global significance.

Prominent examples of socially engaged Buddhist figures and movements originating in Asia include the following.

- Vietnamese Zen (*Thien*) monk and founder of the *Tiep Hien* Order or Order of Interbeing, Thich Nhat Hanh. Nhat Hanh is credited with coining the term "engaged Buddhism" in 1963 to describe the socially relevant Buddhism he has sought to create throughout his career, a Buddhism which has grown primarily in response to the twentieth-century clashes of Vietnam with Western powers and the wars that tore the country apart for decades. He has consistently worked to bring peace, not only to the Vietnamese, but also to Americans and others throughout the world. Living in exile in France since 1966, he encourages followers to achieve peace within through mindful practices – to "be peace," as he puts it – as the most effective way for achieving peace and reconciliation in the world. He was nominated for the Nobel Peace Prize by Martin Luther King, Jr. in 1967.
- The fourteenth Dalai Lama of the Tibetan Gelugpa sect, Tenzin Gyatso, who, for decades, has led the Tibetans' non-violent struggle to save their culture and liberate themselves from foreign domination. While the Dalai Lama is commonly considered both the spiritual and temporal leader of Tibet, he and tens of thousands of Tibetans have lived in exile since 1959, when they were forced to flee their homes in response to Chinese invasions and subsequent attempts to eradicate their indigenous religious and cultural traditions. Like Thich Nhat Hanh, the Dalai Lama has also spread his non-violent Buddhism throughout the world, especially in the West, where he tours and publishes widely. He was awarded the Nobel Peace Prize in 1989 for his non-violent resistance to Chinese rule.
- The Burmese National League for Democracy led by Buddhist scholar and statesperson Aung San Suu Kyi. Suu Kyi was awarded the Nobel Peace Prize in 1991 for her non-violent efforts to liberate Burma (Myanmar) from its military dictatorship and establish democracy and human rights in the country. She was elected

Burma's Prime Minister in 1990, but the military *junta* refused to transfer power to her and her party, and she has since lived much of her life under house arrest.

- The *Dalit* Buddhism of Dr. B.R. Ambedkar and his former "untouchable" followers in India, millions of whom have converted to Buddhism in protest against the social discrimination of the Hindu caste system and thereby initiated the most significant revival of Buddhism in India since its virtual disappearance from the region centuries ago. For Ambedkar and his followers, Buddhism is not merely a means for rejecting caste, but also a self-empowering and liberating *praxis* that enables practitioners to achieve happy and fulfilling lives in this world.
- The Sri Lankan *Sarvōdaya Śramadāna* community development movement engineered by educator A.T. Ariyaratne. *Sarvōdaya* is a network of grassroots, self-help community development agencies dedicated to fostering economic, cultural, and spiritual "awakening" among Sri Lanka's rural poor. In recent years, *Sarvōdaya* has also worked to foster peace among the country's warring ethnic factions, to advocate for a more participatory democracy responsive to the needs of local communities, and to provide relief to the victims of the devastating tsunami of 2004.
- The social reformism of the Siamese (Thai) Buddhist layperson Sulak Sivaraksa, founder of the INEB and a host of other non-governmental organizations. At the heart of Sulak's engaged Buddhism is an unremitting criticism of the structural causes of suffering which he sees at work in Western-style capitalism and militaristic societies throughout the world, and an unflinching commitment to building "a spiritual, green and just society" founded upon Buddhist-inspired principles of social and economic development. In typical engaged Buddhist fashion, he insists that "the transformation of society must first begin with the self," though he also encourages followers to work actively in the world for peace and justice. He was nominated in 1994 for the Nobel Peace Prize and in 1995 was given the so-called "Alternative Nobel Prize" or Right Livelihood Award "for his vision and commitment to a future rooted in democracy, justice and cultural integrity."
- Sōka Gakkai International (SGI), which originated in Japan but has since become a global religious movement. Sōka Gakkai is rooted in the teachings and practices of Nichiren Shōshū Buddhism, and takes as its fundamental aim the goal of "contributing to peace, culture, and education based on the philosophy and ideals of the Buddhism of Nichiren Daishōnin." For SGI, Nichiren's is fundamentally a humanistic philosophy which "enables individuals to cultivate and bring forth their inherent wisdom … and realize a society of peaceful and prosperous coexistence." Its current president, Daisaku Ikeda, has been awarded the United Nations Peace Award, the Simon Wiesenthal Center's International Tolerance Award, and the Rosa Parks Humanitarian Award.
- Cambodian monk Maha Ghosananda, who is often called the Gandhi of Cambodia for his efforts to bring peace and reconciliation to his war-ravaged country. Insisting that "national peace can only begin with personal peace," he is perhaps best known for leading the annual series of *Dhammayietra* peace walks, which one commentator describes as acting to "sanctify the land" and transform the practice of walking meditation into a form of social commentary. Ghosananda has received numerous nominations for

the Nobel Peace Prize, and was awarded Japan's Niwano Peace Prize in 1998.

- The Taiwanese Buddhist nun Cheng Yen, who founded the Tzu Chi Foundation in 1966. Tzu Chi is a network of Buddhist relief organizations dedicated to providing charity, medical care, education, and "culture" to persons in need. It has over four million members and branches in twenty-eight countries. Cheng Yen has received numerous international awards for her compassionate relief efforts.

Engaged Buddhist movements originating in the West include the following.

- The Buddhist Peace Fellowship, founded by Robert and Anne Aitken and Nelson Foster in the United States in 1978. Its initial aim was "to bring a Buddhist perspective to the peace movement, and to bring the peace movement to the Buddhist community." It has since expanded its range of concerns to include environmental, feminist, and social justice issues, and has also worked to foster dialogue among the disparate cultures of American "white" and "ethnic" Buddhisms. In 1995, it initiated the Buddhist Alliance for Social Engagement (BASE), which provides instruction and support for engaged Buddhist social service and activist volunteers, primarily in the San Francisco Bay area.
- Bernard Tetsugen Glassman Rōshi and the Zen Peacemaker Order (ZPO), which Glassman and his wife, Sandra Jishu Holmes Rōshi, founded in 1996. Among the better known of its various activities are "street retreats" or "homeless *sesshins*" and pilgrimages that ZPO periodically organizes to the Nazi death camp at Auschwitz-Birkenau. These and other activities "bear witness" to the world's suffering and act, for Glassman, as a kind of *kōan* practice in which activist practitioners meditatively become one with the social problems they are trying to solve.
- The "Despair and Empowerment Workshops" of American Buddhist activist and scholar Joanna Macy. These workshops, which employ techniques adapted from Buddhist *vipassanā* meditation, offer participants the opportunity to "transform despair and apathy, in the face of overwhelming social and ecological crises, into constructive, collaborative action." Macy's workshops have been attended by thousands around the world, and her insights disseminated even more widely through such popular books as *Despair and Personal Power in the Nuclear Age* and *World as Lover, World as Self.*
- The social and political activism of the United Kingdom's Ken Jones and Christopher Titmuss, who critique Western society and politics and offer, instead, a "green" Buddhist vision for social change. Titmuss is author of numerous books, including *Mindfulness in Daily Living*, and has twice stood for Parliament for the Green Party (1986 and 1992). Jones is author of *Beyond Optimism: A Buddhist Political Ecology*, *The Social Face of Buddhism: An Approach to Political and Social Activism*, and *The New Social Face of Buddhism: A Call to Action* (with American engaged Buddhist scholar, Kenneth Kraft), and is one of the most prominent members of the UK Network of Engaged Buddhists.

Given the diversity of these and countless other engaged Buddhist groups and individuals throughout the world, it is impossible to define with precision the contours of the movement as a whole. Nevertheless, its outlines are roughly traceable. Many observers agree that engaged Buddhism is most fundamentally a product of the profound interpenetration of Asian and Western cultures that has occurred over the past several centuries. Although it is possible to point to examples of Buddhist social concern throughout Buddhism's many histories, Christopher Queen's characterization of the "shape and style" of contemporary engaged Buddhism as a recent phenomenon has received a widespread support. On this view, the movement represents one of the most significant ways in which Buddhism is adapting in response to its recent colonial and post-colonial encounters with the West. It is perhaps best characterized, therefore, as a kind of "Protestant Buddhism," growing in response to, and to a large degree in reaction against, the modernizing forces of industrialization, diversification and commodification of labor, urbanization, militarization, secularization, and homogenization of cultures, while simultaneously adapting elements of Western cultures for its own use, including new technologies and the drive to realize, as B.R. Ambedkar puts it, "a kingdom of righteousness on earth." Even in Europe and America, the emergence of engaged Buddhism is only made possible, and perhaps even necessitated, by the recent intermingling of Asian and Western cultural forms and the desire to render Buddhism relevant to the problems of modern life.

The origins of engaged Buddhism are commonly traced to the late nineteenth-century revival of Buddhism in Sri Lanka under the leadership of Anagarika Dharmapala and his Western, Theosophical patrons, Col. Henry Steel Olcott and Madame Helena Blavatsky. As historian Stephen Prothero and others have demonstrated, the Buddhism these figures fashioned with their *Buddhist Catechism* and Buddhist flag was influenced as much by Olcott's and Blavatsky's native Western culture as it was by Dharmapala's need to protest against the forced dominance of this culture over his own and the suffering it had caused for the Sinhalese people. The impetus for the rise of this and most other engaged Buddhist movements, especially in Asia, is thus not merely the intermingling of Asian and Western religious and social forms, but the imposed dominance of the one over the other and the unprecedented suffering brought on by the continuing influence of modernity throughout the world.

Both Robert N. Bellah and Donald K. Swearer have worked to understand Buddhism's various responses to modernity, and their insights are useful for understanding engaged Buddhism. Buddhism, they observe, has tended to respond to modernity in one of two ways. On the one hand, "neo-traditionalist" (Bellah) or "fundamentalist" (Swearer) movements have arisen, which strive to keep change to a minimum while also using modern ideas and methods in their defense of traditional values. At the opposite extreme, "reformist" movements strive to engage the "tensions, dislocations and 'evils' of the contemporary age" head-on by "applying creative interpretations of traditional beliefs and practices as part of their solution" (Swearer). Moreover, they tend to promote these "creative interpretations" as "a return to the early teachers and text, a rejection of most of the intervening tradition, [and] an interpretation of the pristine teaching ... as advocating social reform and national regeneration" (Bellah). According to this typology, engaged Buddhism is clearly reformist in character, creatively reinterpreting Buddhist traditions for modern circumstances.

The distinctiveness of engaged Buddhism among other reformist movements is manifested in the particular shape of its "creative interpretations," which typically center on the pairing of "inner peace and world peace" and the conjoining of personal and social practices to which this pairing leads. Even more fundamental is the notion that all phenomena are "interrelated" or "interdependent," which is how engaged Buddhists typically gloss the traditional Buddhist teachings of *pratītya-samutpāda* and *śūnyatā* (emptiness).

Interdependence implies for engaged Buddhists that where there is no separate, individual self (*anātman*), there is a larger "ecological" self that comprises the total web of "interbeing." The title of Joanna Macy's book, *World as Lover, World as Self*, conveys this idea succinctly. For Macy and others within the movement, self and others are so intimately connected that work toward the betterment of the self *ipso facto* benefits others, and vice versa. More poignantly, the interrelatedness of self and others implies that individuals cannot be liberated from suffering so long as others continue to suffer in the world. Engaged Buddhists, therefore, typically stress the social and this-worldly aspects of liberation and work toward the achievement of "mundane awakening" for all.

In keeping with this goal of mundane awakening – which comprises social, economic, political, as well as spiritual dimensions – engaged Buddhists have construed several styles of social activism that are often regarded as distinguishing the movement from other Asian and Western religious and secular social activist movements, and thus as offering distinctively Buddhist solutions to contemporary social problems. This distinctiveness is rooted in the conviction, noted above, that social change and inner change are inseparable. Not all engaged Buddhists agree about the practical implications of this inseparability, however, and this, then, represents one of the most common areas of disagreement among them.

For a few, the notion that "inner peace leads to world peace" implies that personal, "spiritual" work is enough to bring about desired social changes. Robert Aitken suggests, for instance, that because the body is "all creation without restriction," by improving oneself, one is simultaneously improving all creation. Scholar Kenneth Kraft notes, too, that some Buddhist teachings give precedence to the mind in constructing reality and thus lend credence to the view that the spiritual practice of the individual is the most convenient and effective means for effecting and maintaining social, and even cosmic, harmony. For others – undoubtedly a majority – however, the interrelatedness of self and world suggests that personal, "spiritual" work that is focused exclusively on self-betterment is spiritually and socially insufficient and belies a false understanding of the Buddha's teachings on the interrelatedness of all phenomena. Rather, it is argued, personal transformation naturally drives one to work overtly and compassionately in the world for the betterment of others. The claim is often made that unless one is working "outwardly" for peace, one cannot hope to experience real "inner" peace, either.

Even among those who agree that the doctrine of interrelatedness properly leads to overt activity directed at the achievement of world peace, there are still disagreements about what this entails. Most agree that they must begin with the self, to cultivate peace and understanding within through the practice of mindfulness. Even here, though, the social implications of mindfulness practice are commonly stressed. The intention of mindfulness is not merely to advance its practitioners toward the experience of personal liberation. Indeed, this goal is often not mentioned at all. Rather, it has the purposes of bettering the world through the activities of self-betterment; helping practitioners experience a more vital relationship to other beings and the entire cosmos; making practitioners more mindful in the carrying out of their daily affairs, and, thereby, improving their interpersonal relationships; and/or making practitioners more mindful in their efforts toward social and political reform. As this analysis of engaged Buddhist mindfulness practice implies, however, engaged Buddhists tend to disagree about the other means by which they ought to work for social change.

While some advocate simple meditation and self-betterment as the best, if not only, means for bringing about social change, a second position contends that, as individuals transform themselves, they should also engage with others in a more compassionate and loving manner, and thereby contribute through the conduct of their everyday lives to a better society. Advocates of this position point out that these positive social effects, though small, are hardly insignificant, and, indeed, some would argue that even the smallest actions can produce great effects that ripple outward throughout society. Breathing and smiling, for instance, are stressed by Thich Nhat Hanh and his followers as effective means for achieving positive social change. "If we are peaceful, if we are happy, we can smile and blossom like a flower, and everyone in our family, our entire society, will benefit from our peace."

Yet a third approach contends that reliance on personal betterment and improved personal relations as means for positive social change remains unsatisfactory. It is also necessary, they contend, to work more actively and systematically in the world for peace and justice. American activist Patricia Marx Ellsberg, for instance, responding to her experiences at a retreat with Thich Nhat Hanh, complains of having felt uncomfortable with the underlying assumption of the retreat, "that if enough individuals change, society will change." She proposes, instead, in a manner reminiscent of the Christian social gospel and other liberationist movements, that society is more than an aggregate of individuals; it is shaped also by social structures and concentrations of power. For Ellsberg, "these forces need to be challenged and transformed" before there can be real peace.

In this vein, engaged Buddhists also commonly advocate viewing people as "co-responsible" for the goods, as well as the evils of social life. Stressing the corporate dynamics of social ills, they encourage everyone, not only to admit their own complicity in the structures of social and environmental oppression, but also to take responsibility for correcting those structures. At the same time, they insist that the goal of social and political activism is not "victory" over some other, "evil" group of oppressors, but harmony among all humans and nature. The "outer" work of Buddhism is not to fight or defeat an enemy, but, as with its inner, meditative practices, the healing and transformation of the social and ecological self.

Among the more common ways in which engaged Buddhists seek overtly to transform society are education, the mass dissemination of their ideas, civil disobedience, and participation in the institutions of political power. Some have started vocational schools, for instance, which train adults in a particular skill, and pre-schools, which allow parents to engage in full-time work or attend school themselves. Others have founded primary and secondary schools, and still others, universities. With regard to the use of mass media and marketing, many of these leaders and movements have cultivated relationships with politicians, other religious leaders of renown, publishers, and even celebrities and film producers to bring international attention to their causes and activities. Consider, for instance, the public relationships of the Dalai Lama with actor Richard Gere and Thich Nhat Hanh with the late Trappist monk Thomas Merton. Also note the spate of popular Hollywood movies produced in recent years that sympathetically depict the oppression of Tibetans by the

Chinese, as well as the inordinate number of books that have been published by engaged Buddhist leaders – Thich Nhat Hanh alone having produced over eighty titles. With regard to politics, some lobby and otherwise attempt to pressure governments, while others, like the Sōka Gakkai in Japan, have founded their own political parties and run candidates for office.

Whether working toward personal betterment alone as a means of transforming society or in conjunction with social service and/or social and political activism, there is almost unanimous agreement among engaged Buddhists that social transformation must be pursued non-violently. The grounds for non-violent social activism is again the belief that all things are interrelated, that means and ends are inseparable, or, as Joanna Macy puts it, that means are "ends-in-the-making." If the goal is peace, engaged Buddhists insist, peaceful means must be employed to achieve it. Some, like Thich Nhat Hanh, push the ideal of non-violence to the extreme, eschewing even non-violent forms of coercion, while others, like the Dalai Lama and the Tibetan Struggle movement, see a need to coerce, but never in ways that cause harm.

In their "inner" and "outer" efforts to transform oppressive social structures, engaged Buddhists are also frequently critical of the "hierarchical" and "dualistic" Buddhist structures they have inherited from established Buddhist forms. These structures, they contend, unduly concentrate power in the hands of a few, usually men, while also valorizing monastic withdrawal from, rather than engagement with, the world. Engaged Buddhists thus commonly work to construct more egalitarian Buddhist institutions that value life in the world as much as, if not more than, monastic withdrawal and provide as much opportunity for female as male leadership to emerge. Much attention has also been paid, not only to defining how practitioners might engage in full-fledged Buddhist practice while simultaneously engaging the social world, but also to articulating why the practice of Buddhism in family and social life is superior to monastic withdrawal.

Finally, some engaged Buddhists, especially in the United States and Europe, have gone beyond attempts to level distinctions between monastics and the laity, and have insisted also on a leveling of the distinctions between human and non-human life, and even non-living matter. Americans Joan Halifax and Bill Devall, for example, have each argued that the notion of the *sangha* ought to be expanded to include, among other things, "other species, plant and animal, as well as environmental features and unseen ancestors and spirits." This "ecocentric *sangha*," or what engaged Buddhist poet Gary Snyder calls the "Great Earth Sangha," must take into account the rights of other species and even inanimate objects. The *sangha*, for these engaged Buddhists, is not limited solely to monastics or even humans, or further, even to sentient beings; all of reality is the *sangha* and every identifiable aspect of that reality – be it animal, plant, ecosystem, planet, or solar system – has an equal place within "the Buddhist ecological community."

In sum, engaged Buddhists typically direct their activities toward the cessation of suffering in all its forms, personal, social, and environmental, which are characteristically regarded as interrelated aspects of a single, inseparable suffering. Awakening, too, is inseparably personal, social, and ecological, and so engaged Buddhists work to transform not only themselves, but the world, as well. Indeed, most concentrate on the transformation of the world as an effective means for realizing change within, and, therefore, advocate outward work for peace in conjunction with inner meditative practices. Importantly, the institutional expression of engaged Buddhism is in many respects openly hostile toward more traditional forms of Buddhist organization, typically opting for "democratic" and "non-hierarchical" forms of establishment, over the more "patriarchal" and "dualistic" structures of tradition Buddhist forms. Thus, distinctions between the laity and the monastic *sangha* are intentionally blurred, if not altogether erased, throughout the movement, as are, sometimes, distinctions between human and non-human beings.

A question that persists among engaged Buddhist practitioners and scholars alike that deserves attention in closing is how new (in what sense and to what degree) is engaged Buddhism? On the one hand are those who interpret Buddhism as traditionally silent on and disengaged from this-worldly social concerns, inherently lacking a social ethics, and leading its followers to escape the world, certainly not to transform it. On this interpretation, engaged Buddhism is thoroughly unprecedented in its attempt to develop and apply a distinctively Buddhist social ethics where previously there was none. On the other hand are those who say that "all Buddhism is socially engaged," that contemporary engaged Buddhist groups are new only in the sense that they express in contemporary forms an ongoing tradition of Buddhist social engagement, a tradition, moreover, that has been generally ignored by scholars and recent Buddhist practitioners, succumbing in both cases to the pressures and interests of colonial rule. Engaged Buddhism is thus a revival of an "original" Buddhism, nearly lost under centuries of misguided (mis-)interpretation. Thomas Freeman Yarnell further argues that portraying the movement as new in the first, unprecedented, sense, as is commonly done especially among Westerners, continues the legacy of colonialism by presuming to "appropriate, own, and reinvent Buddhism from the ground up."

While Yarnell's critique deserves serious consideration, it is still not easy to ignore the novelty of engaged Buddhism with respect to more traditional Buddhist forms and the various ways in which it has grown both by adapting to and reacting against modernity. It is true, perhaps, that Buddhists have historically worked to realize the social implications of their faith and have thus consistently developed and applied distinctively Buddhist social ethics relevant to their own particular contexts. At the same time, it is also true that modernity presents novel challenges for Buddhism, which the tradition is meeting in new, and even unprecedented ways. It seems reasonable to conclude where we began, therefore, by observing that the "shape and style" of engaged Buddhist social ethics are unprecedented, even if there is nothing new about Buddhist social engagement, *per se*. Whatever else one notices about engaged Buddhism, it is impossible to overlook the indelible impression left by its various encounters with the West, an impression which arguably constitutes its single most defining characteristic.

See also: **Ariyaratne, A.T.; Buddhist economics and ecology; Buddhist peace groups (in Asia and the West); Dalai Lama (and the Tibetan struggle); Glassman, Bernard Rōshi; Global Buddhist networks: selected examples; Macy, Joanna; Maha Ghosananda; Nhat Hanh, Thich.**

JIM DEITRICK

ENNOBLING TRUTHS/ REALITIES

What are generally known as the four "Noble Truths" (Skt. *ārya-satyas*, Pāli *ariya-saccas*) are the focus of what is seen as the first sermon of the Buddha (Skt. *Dharmacakrapravartana Sūtra*, Pāli *Dhammacakkappavatana Sutta*; *Vinaya* 1.10–12; *Saṃyutta Nikāya* 5.420–4), and form the framework for many key teachings of the Buddha. As found in the early *sutta/sūtra* collections known as the *Nikāyas* or *Āgamas*, they are an advanced teaching intended for those who have been spiritually prepared to hear them. When teaching laypersons, the Buddha frequently began with a "step-by-step discourse" (Skt. *anupūrvikā kathā*, Pāli *anupubbi-kathā*), on giving and moral observance as leading to a heavenly rebirth, and then on the advantages of renouncing sense-pleasures (by meditative calming of the mind). Such teachings were used to inspire his hearers and help them gain a state of mind which was calm, joyful and open. In this state of readiness, they would then be taught the Four Ennobling Truths (for example *Vinaya* 1.15–16), being a *Dharma*-teaching "particular" or "special" (Skt. *sāmutkarṣikī*, Pāli *sāmukkaṃsikā*) to Buddhas, or their "elevated" teaching. If the mind is not calm and receptive, talk of *duḥkha* (Pāli *dukkha*) – suffering/pain/unsatisfactoriness/stress/anxiety/angst – may be too disturbing, leading to states such as depression, denial, and self-distracting tactics. The Buddha's own discovery of the four Truths was from the fourth *dhyāna* (Pāli *jhāna*), a state of profound meditative calm, "When the mind was thus concentrated, purified, bright, unblemished, rid of defilement, pliant, malleable, steady, and attained to imperturbability" (*Majjhima Nikāya* I.249). The Mahāyāna later came to see the teaching on the four Truths as themselves preliminary to higher teachings, but there is none of this in the *Nikāyas* or *Āgamas*. In these, they are not teachings to go beyond or unproblematic simple teachings, but deep realities to explore.

The Ennobling Truths concern (1) *duḥkha*; (2) the origination (*samudaya*, or cause) of *duḥkha*, namely craving (Skt. *tṛṣṇā*, Pāli *taṇhā*); (3) the cessation (*nirodha*) of *duḥkha* by the cessation of craving (this cessation being equivalent to *nirvāṇa*); and (4) the path (Skt. *mārga*, Pāli *magga*) that leads to this cessation. The same fourfold structure of ideas (*x*, origination of *x*, its cessation, path to its cessation) is also applied to a range of other phenomena, such as the experienced world (*loka*; *Saṃyutta Nikāya* 1.62) and to each of the twelve links of Dependent Origination (e.g. *Saṃyutta Nikāya* 2.43). The reality described by the twelve links is actually seen to lie behind the Four Ennobling Truths. The links go into detail on the origination (second Truth) of *duḥkha* (first Truth). The cessation/stopping of all the links is equivalent to the third Truth, and the fourth Truth; the path is what leads to this, itself being a series of positive conditions.

If *duḥkha* is perceived in the right way, it is said to lead to "faith" or "trustful confidence" (Skt. *śraddhā, Pāli saddhā*) in the Buddha's teachings. From faith, other states successively arise: gladness, joy, happiness, meditative concentration, and deepening states of insight and detachment, culminating in destroying the causes of *duḥkha* (*Saṃyutta Nikāya* 2.30). This suggests that some initial understanding of *duḥkha* supports spiritual practice which leads to greater insight into it and ultimately liberation from it.

In Brahmāṇism, the term *ārya* (Pāli *ariya*) referred to the "noble" people who migrated into India, while in Buddhism it is used in a spiritual sense. In the first sermon, each of the Truths is called an *ārya-satya*, a noble-truth. The standard translation "noble truth" is a possible meaning, though the least likely one. The commentators interpret it as: "truth of the noble one(s)," "truth for a noble one," in the sense of "truth that will make one a noble," or, sometimes, "noble truth." Here, "noble ones" are those who are partially or fully enlightened: stream-enterers, once-returners, non-returners and *arhats*, along with Buddhas. It actually sounds a little odd to call a truth "noble," and the reason the "noble ones" are as they are is precisely because they have had insight into the Truths. While Norman prefers "truth of the noble one (the Buddha)," he acknowledges that the term may be deliberately multivalent. In line with "truth for a noble," an apposite rendering is "Ennobling Truth."

Note also that, "The word *satya* (Pāli *sacca*) can certainly mean truth, but it might equally be rendered as 'real' or 'actual thing,' hence we have 'four "true things," or "realities"'". The first sermon says of these: the first is "to be understood"; the second is to be "to be abandoned"; the third is "to be realized," literally, "to be seen with one's own eyes"; the fourth is "to be developed/cultivated." This makes most sense if the *satyas* are four "Ennobling Realities": the second of these is a reality to abandon, not a truth to abandon! It is also apparent that these Ennobling Realities are not something that Buddhists should respond to with "belief." To "believe" them is to mishandle them, rather than to treat them appropriately by respectively understanding, abandoning, realizing, and developing them.

See also: **Ennobling Truth/Reality, the First; Ennobling Truth/Reality, the Second; Ennobling Truth/Reality, the Third: *nirvāṇa*; Ennobling Truth/Reality, the Fourth: the Ennobling Eightfold Path.**

PETER HARVEY

ENNOBLING TRUTH/ REALITY, THE FIRST

On the first Reality (Skt. *satya*, Pāli *sacca*), the first sermon states (*Vinaya* 1.10, *Saṃyutta Nikāya* 5.421):

> This, monks, is the Ennobling Reality that is *duḥkha* (Pāli *dukkha*):

1 birth is *duḥkha*, ageing is *duḥkha*, sickness is *duḥkha*, death is *duḥkha*;
2 sorrow, grief, pain, unhappiness and unease are *duḥkha* [omitted at *Vinaya* 1.10];
3 association with what one dislikes is *duḥkha*, separation from what one likes is *duḥkha*, not to get what one wants is *duḥkha*;
4 in short, the five groups (as objects) of grasping are *duḥkha*.

(Numbers added)

The word *duḥkha* refers to all those things which are unpleasant, imperfect, and which we would like to be otherwise, "Rich in meaning and nuance . . . Literally 'pain' or 'anguish,' in its religious and philosophical contexts, *duḥkha* is, however, suggestive of an underlying 'unsatisfactoriness' or 'unease' that must ultimately mar even our experience of happiness". *Duḥkha* has been translated in many ways: for example, "suffering," "pain," "unsatisfactoriness," "anguish," "unease," "stress," "ill." Of these, the first is the most common, though it is only appropriate in a general, inexact sense. The English word "suffering" is either a present participle (as, for example, in "he is suffering from malaria") or a noun (for example, "his suffering is intense"). In the common translation "birth is suffering," it does not make sense to take "suffering" as a present participle – it is not something that birth *is doing*. If "suffering" is intended as a noun, though, it is not the case that birth or ageing are themselves *forms of* suffering – they can only be occasions for or causes of suffering, which is an experience, a mental state.

In actual fact, in the first Ennobling Reality, *duḥkha* in "birth is *duḥkha*" is an adjective, not a noun. The Pāli for the first Ennobling Reality moves from *duḥkha* as a neuter noun, in "This . . . is the Ennobling Reality which is *duḥkha*," to *duḥkha* as an adjective. This is seen by the fact that its gender (shown by the word ending) changes in accord with that of the word it qualifies, for example, the feminine noun "birth." This should be reflected in the translation, which it is not in "This is the Noble Truth of suffering: birth is suffering." Indeed, in English there is no adjective from "suffering." Ṭhānissaro Bhikkhu translates the first sermon: "Now this, monks, is the noble truth of stress: Birth is stressful, aging is stressful." This has a shift from noun to adjective and captures many of the connotations of *duḥkha*. Nevertheless "stress/stressful" is somewhat distant from the basic everyday meaning of the word *duḥkha*, which is "pain" as opposed to "pleasure" (*sukha*). These, with neither-*duḥkha*-nor-*sukha*, are the three kinds of feeling (*vedanā*) (e.g. *Saṃyutta Nikāya* 4.232). *Saṃyutta Nikāya* 5.209–10 explains the first of these as the "faculties" of pain (*duḥkha*) and of sadness/unhappiness (*domanassa*): that is, bodily and mental *duḥkha*. This shows that the primary sense of *duḥkha* is physical "pain," but that it also refers to mental pain, unhappiness (and then, in Buddhism, beyond this). The same spread of meaning is seen in the English word "pain," for example in the phrase, "the pleasures and pains of life."

Yet while one could translate "ageing is painful," "painful" is probably too associated with physical pain to English speakers to suggest the depth and spread of the meaning of *duḥkha*. There is, though, the slightly colloquial expression in which it is said that something or other "is a pain," such as a traffic jam, getting old, a hard task. This usage is what amounts to an adjectival phrase, saying that whatever it is applied to – whether a bodily sensation, a state of mind, an external thing or a situation – is unpleasant, unwanted, troublesome, stressful. That this captures the tone of the *Nikāyas*' talk of *duḥkha* can be seen from a passage saying that the five aggregates are to be seen "as a pain (*dukkha*), as a disease, as a boil, as a dart, as a misfortune, as a sickness" (*Saṃyutta Nikāya* 3.167). Indeed, the *Paṭisambhidāmagga* (2.241–2), a canonical Theravādin interpretative text, says that in contemplating something as *duḥkha*, one should see it:

> as *duḥkha*, as a disease, as a boil, as a dart, as a misfortune, as a sickness, as a plague, as a distress, as a danger, as a menace, as not a protection, as not a cave of shelter, as not a refuge, as devoid, as a disadvantage, as the root of misfortune, as murderous, as with-taints, as prey to Māra (meaning the evil, tempter deity, or simply death), as of the nature of birth, ageing, grief, lamentation, despair and defilement.

One can thus translate the first Ennobling Reality: "This is the Ennobling Reality that is pain: birth is a pain, ageing is a pain . . . "

Phenomena listed as *duḥkha*

Of the kinds of *duḥkha* outlined in the first sermon, it can be seen that:

- types (1) and (2) (see numbering above) occur occasionally;
- type (3) are frequent, daily occurrences; and
- type (4) "in short, the five groups (as objects) of grasping (*upādāna-skandhas*) are a pain" is pervasive in its extent.

In the term *upādāna-skandha*, *skandha* (Pāli *khandha*) means "mass," "group," "aggregate," or perhaps "bundle." The *skandhas* are the five kinds of processes making up a person, body and mind: material form (*rūpa*), feeling (*vedanā*), labeling/cognition/perception (Skt. *saṃjñā*, Pāli *saññā*), constructing activities (Skt. *saṃskāras*, Pāli *saṅkhāras*) and consciousness/discernment (Skt. *vijñāna*, Pāli *viññāṇa*).

Now it is very common to see the *upādāna-skandhas* translated as "groups of grasping" or "aggregates of grasping," but this can be misleading. Grasping (*upādāna*) is a specific mental state which would best be classified as an aspect of the fourth *skandha*, "constructing activities"; so there cannot be five groups that are *types of* grasping. Thus "groups (as objects) of grasping" or "grasped at groups" is better.

Nevertheless, there are hidden nuances in the word *upādāna*. Its root meaning is "taking up," so while its abstract meaning is "grasping" or "clinging," its concrete meaning is "fuel," the "taking up" of which sustains a process such as fire. Richard Gombrich comments that the *Nikāyas* are rich in fire-related metaphors because of the importance of fire in Brahmanism, and then argues that the term *upādāna-skandha* is also part of this fire imagery: they can each be seen as a "bundle of fuel" (p. 67) which "burn" with the "fires" of *duḥkha* and its causes. They may not each be forms of grasping or clinging, but are each sustaining objects of, or fuel for, these. Thus the first Ennobling Reality can also be seen to end: "In short, the five bundles of grasping-fuel are a pain."

In the Fire Sermon (*Saṃyutta Nikāya* 4.19–20), the six senses and their objects, along with the sensory stimulation and feeling that these lead to, are seen as metaphorically "on fire" with attachment, hatred and delusion – key causes of *duḥkha* (pain) – and the ageing and death and so forth that are themselves *duḥkha* ("a pain"). The pervasiveness of *duḥkha* in its most subtle sense can be seen in a parallel passage where a very similar range of phenomena are together said to be tantamount to *duḥkha*, and also to "a being" (*Saṃyutta Nikāya* 4.39). However, *nirvāṇa* is the "extinction" of these "fires."

Aspects of *duḥkha*

The pervasive nature of *duḥkha*, of all that is "a pain," can be seen at *Saṃyutta Nikāya* 4.259, where Śāriputra (Pāli Sāriputta) is asked, "What, now, is *duḥkha*?" He replies: "There are, friend, three kinds of painfulness (Pāli *dukkhatā*): the painfulness of pain (*dukkha-dukkhatā*); the painfulness of conditioned things (*saṅkhāra-dukkhatā*); and the painfulness of change (*vipariṇāma-dukkhatā*)." The first of these is physical and mental pain. The second is "a pain," painful, as a result of being a limited, conditioned state, imperfect. The third is pleasant while it lasts but is associated with the pain of loss.

Duḥkha is indeed one of the three characteristics (Skt. *lakṣaṇas*, Pāli *lakkhaṇas*) of conditioned existence: "all conditioned things (Skt. *saṃskāras*, Pāli *saṅkhāras*) are impermanent (Skt. *anitya*, Pāli *anicca*); all conditioned things are *duḥkha*; all states (Skt. *dharmas*, Pāli *dhammas*, which includes *nirvāṇa*, the unconditioned *dharma*) are not-Self (Skt. *anātman*, Pāli *anattā*)" (e.g. *Aṅguttara Nikāya* 1.286–7). It is frequently said that what is impermanent is *duḥkha*, and what is *duḥkha* cannot be rightly taken as "this is mine, I am this, this is my Self" – in other words it is not-Self (e.g. *Majjhima Nikāya* 1.138–9). This clearly sees impermanence as a key reason for something being *duḥkha*, and something's being "a pain" as reason not to take it as a permanent Self. Moreover, taking an impermanent thing as such a Self is a cause of more *duḥkha* (*Saṃyutta Nikāya* 3.19).

What is *duḥkha* is not only *duḥkha*

The quality of *duḥkha* pervades all conditioned states, yet does not exhaust them. It is said of each *skandha* that is steeped in both *duḥkha* and pleasure (*sukha*). It is by being enamored with or attached to the pleasant aspects that people become "captivated" and "defiled." Wise attention to their *duḥkha* aspects leads to them turning away or letting go (Pāli *nibbindanti*) and experiencing non-attachment (*virāga*), purification (*Saṃyutta Nikāya* 3.68–70). Thus the Buddha says in respect of each of the *skandhas*:

> The pleasure and gladness that arise in dependence on it: this is its attraction [Pāli *assādo*]. That it is impermanent, a pain, and subject to change; this is its danger [*ādīnavo*]. The removal and abandonment of desire and attachment [*chanda-rāga*] for it: this is the escape [*nissaraṇaṃ*] from it.
> (*Saṃyutta Nikāya* 3.27–8)

Buddhism, then, does not say that "life is suffering," as the first Ennobling Reality is sometimes glossed, but that pain and suffering are an endemic part of life that must be calmly and fully acknowledged in one's response to the nature of conditioned existence. It is also worth bearing in mind that the Buddhist path itself can generate considerable joy (Skt. *prīti*, Pāli *pīti*) and happiness, even if this is imperfect and conditioned.

What kind of statement is "This is *duḥkha*"?

To what extent is it a description, and to what extent is it a judgment? Many words have aspects of both; for example, "liar" is a description which also contains an implicit judgment. When something is said to be "*duḥkha*" in the sense of physical or mental pain, the descriptive aspect is predominant, though there is an implied "this is unfortunate." When something is said to be "*duḥkha*" in the sense of being "a pain" as a result of being conditioned, limited, and imperfect, the judgmental aspect is to the fore, for that which is *duḥkha* is here clearly being unfavorably compared with what is unconditioned and unlimited, namely *nirvāṇa*. The clear message is: if something is *duḥkha*, do not be attached to it. At this level, *duḥkha* is whatever is not *nirvāṇa*, and *nirvāṇa* is that which is not *duḥkha*. This does not lead to a useless circular definition of the two terms, though, for *duḥkha* is that which is conditioned, arising from other changing factors in the flow of time, and *nirvāṇa* is that which is unconditioned.

Does saying that something is *duḥkha* mean that it: (1) is "a pain" *only when grasped at* or (2) is *by its very nature* "a pain"? Both seem to be implied in the Theravādin *Nikāya* collection:

1 grasping at anything leads to psychological pain (because all conditioned things are subject to impermanence) – even physical pain is worse when one craves for its ending,
2 but also conditioned things are to be seen, in themselves, as *duḥkha* in the sense of being limited and imperfect, and thus incapable of offering lasting satisfaction. Indeed, it is said that the death of a liberated person (*arhat*) only brings the *duḥkha skandhas* to an end (*Saṃyutta Nikāya* 3.109–12), so a living *arhat*'s *skandhas* are still *duḥkha* in *some* sense. Conditioned things may also, in a straightforward sense, be forms of physical or mental pain.

Yet to see the many things described as "*duḥkha*" as being so in an adjectival sense – "painful," "a pain," "stressful" – rather than as a noun – "suffering," "unsatisfactoriness" – suggests that they are not entities whose very nature is a thing which is *duḥkha*. Their being *duḥkha* is a *quality* that they have. Is such a quality to be seen as (a) like being "red," which depends on a perceiving observer, or "heavy," which depends on being on a massive planet, or (b) is it like the quality of reflecting light waves of a certain wavelength, or having a certain mass (which, unlike "weight" is seen as constant wherever a body is placed in space)? Is *duḥkha* (a) a *relational* quality or (b) an *absolute* quality of conditioned process-events?

On the "absolute" view, process-events need to completely stop, be transcended, for *duḥkha* to be *fully* absent: as in *nirvāṇa* beyond death or as a timeless experience during life. Theravādins tend to this view. On the "relational" view, all that is needed for a complete absence of *duḥkha* is for craving to stop; there is no "*duḥkha*" or "being a pain" apart from those who crave for or against what is experienced as "a pain." This kind of perspective is taken up in the Mahāyāna, in which the conditioned, *duḥkha* factors which make up *saṃsāra*, the world of rebirth, when seen with the eye of wisdom, are no different from *nirvāṇa*, in which there is nothing of *duḥkha*. That is, when what is experienced as painful is fully understood, there is an experience beyond any pain, as wisdom transforms how this is perceived.

See also: **Buddha; Cosmology and rebirth; *Dharma*; Ennobling Truth/Reality, the Second; Ennobling Truth/Reality, the Third: *nirvāṇa*; Ennobling Truth/Reality, the Fourth: the Ennobling Eightfold Path.**

PETER HARVEY

ENNOBLING TRUTH/ REALITY, THE SECOND

If the Buddha focused on *duḥkha* (Pāli *dukkha*) in the first Ennobling Truth/Reality, the second picks out a key cause for its arising: "It is this craving (Skt. *tṛṣṇā*, Pāli *taṇhā*), giving rise to rebirth, accompanied by delight and attachment, finding delight now here, now there" (*Vinaya* 1. 10, *Saṃyutta Nikāya* 5.421).

Tṛṣṇā is not just "desire" – for desire can be for good things. Indeed *chanda*, desire-to-act, can be very positive, even though it can *also* be directed in unwholesome ways. Amongst the sets of positive spiritual qualities in the *Nikāyas* are the four "bases of success" (in meditative development), and one of these is "the basis of success that is furnished both with concentration gained by means of desire-to-act [*chanda*] and with the activities of endeavor" (*Dīgha Nikāya* 2.213). So, Buddhism does not see all "desire" as problematic. This can be seen in some of the early *arhats*' non-attached appreciation of natural beauty: "With clear water and wide crags, haunted by monkeys and deer, covered with oozing moss, those rocks delight me" (*Theragāthā* v. 1070).

Tṛṣṇā contains an element of psychological compulsion. It can be seen as a driven, restless will, ever on the look-out for new objects to focus on. It is clinging desires, mental thirst, and drives directed at aspects of the changing, unreliable world, demanding that things be like this and not like that. This propels people into situation after situation involving pain, disquiet, and upset. The more strongly a person craves, the greater the frustration if what is craved for is not attained. Also, the more things a person craves for, the more opportunities there are for painful frustration, *duḥkha*.

The first and second Ennobling Realities are intimately connected: the more that a person ignores the *duḥkha* aspects of what he/she craves, the more likely craving will continue, and thus more *duḥkha*. The more the *duḥkha* aspects are contemplated, the weaker craving will be, and thus the less *duḥkha* will arise.

Craving is analyzed in various ways. One way is to describe it as craving for visual objects, for sounds, tastes, smells, touchables and mind objects (*Majjhima Nikāya* 1.51). That is, it is a reaching out towards these, construing them as able to offer lasting satisfaction. It can be experienced in the mind's unwillingness to settle into calm stillness: in its need to turn towards things to think and "chew" on. It can also be experienced in attachment to such stillness, once it is experienced.

The first sermon identifies three types of craving: "craving for sensual pleasures, craving for existence, craving for non-existence," that is, sensual-craving, craving for continuance, craving for ending, or the urges "want pleasure," "want more," "don't want/want different."

Sensual craving is the most obvious form, focused on sex, sexual fantasies or on other sensual pleasures such as those from food or what one wears. It is the mind's erratic energy moving towards these in the spirit of "must have." Craving for continuance is the urge to keep pleasant sensations and situations going, and the related view that they can carry on unchanged. It is also the drive for self-protection, for ego-enhancement, and for eternal life after death as "me." Craving for ending is the urge to get rid of unpleasant sensations, situations or people. In intense form, it can be an impulse to suicide.

All of these reactions lead to pain when they are frustrated. When fulfilled, they offer fleeting satisfaction only – to be followed by a search for more. That is, they cannot really be fulfilled, any more than a colander can be filled with water. Just as it is filled with holes, so craving has a "hole" in it that can never actually be "filled" by the things it chases. However much such wanting is fed, it is never satisfied. A sigh of relief is sooner or later followed by the restless hunt for something else to chase after or latch hold of. Buddhism suggests that peace lies in stepping aside from this driven-state, in calmly working with how things are, not reacting for or against. Even, in time, for or against craving: let it be, and it will go. Latch onto it and it will flare up.

Note that, as regards rebirth, while some form of craving is seen to determine *that* a being is reborn, *how* they are reborn is seen as the result of their *karma*. An enlightened person is not reborn, as they lack craving, though they may have generated good and bad *karma* in their final life, prior to their enlightenment. This is the position in early and Theravāda Buddhism, at least. In Mahāyāna Buddhism is the idea that an advanced *bodhisattva* can *choose* to remain in the round of rebirths for longer than would otherwise be necessary, so as to build up further perfections towards perfect Buddhahood. However, this remaining is sometimes seen to need a small remnant of attachment.

Craving for an end to craving

While craving is to be abandoned for *duḥkha* to be transcended, craving for an end to craving may play a part in the path to the end of *duḥkha*, as well as *chanda* directed to this goal. In one passage, it is said that a monk, hearing of another monk who has attained enlightenment, may aspire that he too may one day attain this, hence, "This body comes into being through craving (that is, craving causes rebirth); and yet it is by relying on craving that craving is to be abandoned" (*Aṅguttara Nikāya* 2.146). Here, spiritual craving spurs on someone's spiritual practice which then brings all craving to an end. Can such spiritual craving be skillful, like *chanda*? A post-Canonical Theravādin text, the *Nettipakaraṇa* (p. 87), says, "There are two types of craving, skillful and unskillful. Unskillful craving leads to *saṃsāra*, skillful craving is abandonment, it leads to diminution."

Yet spiritual craving can, like any other craving, bring some *duḥkha*, and indeed it is said that "grief based on renunciation" occurs when someone has "longing" for the goal of the path (*Majjhima Nikāya* 3.218; 1.303–4). Indeed it is said that one may desire to go beyond all that is *duḥkha*, but this "is not to be got by wishing" (*Dīgha Nikāya* 2.307). Moreover, near the end of the path, spiritual desire may be what holds a person back from the highest attainment. Thus it is said that a monk becomes an *arhat* (Pāli *arahat*) when he realizes the impermanent, conditioned nature of a certain meditative state that he is in; though if he has attachment to *Dharma* and delight in it, he becomes a non-returner, the spiritual attainment just *short* of *arhat*ship (*Majjhima Nikāya* 1.350).

Other causes of *duḥkha*

While the first sermon picks out craving as the key condition for the arising of *duḥkha*, other passages set this in a context of a range of contributory conditions. In the twelve links of Dependent Origination, the first is spiritual ignorance (Skt. *avidyā*, Pāli *avijjā*), ingrained misperception of the nature of reality, so that the four Ennobling Truths/Realities are not directly seen. Such ignorance – and ignore-ance – feeds into and sustains other conditions, that lead on to pleasant and unpleasant feelings, that often elicit craving in response, and this in turn is seen to feed grasping (*upādāna*): for sensual pleasures, for fixed ways of doing things, for fixed and limiting views, and to the idea of Self. Behind the latter lies the deep-seated "'I am' conceit," the gut feeling of an "I" who is seen as either superior to, inferior to, or as good as other people. The causes of *duḥkha* are sometimes also summarized as attachment (*rāga*), hatred (Skt. *dveṣa*, Pāli *dosa*) and delusion (*moha*). Such causes include both cognitive faults – ignorance, mis-seeing, delusion – and affective ones – craving, attachment, hatred – and mixed ones, such as conceit and grasping at views. These feed into and support each other: negative emotion clouds the mind and distorts perception, and misperception sustains negative emotion.

See also: **Buddha; Cosmology and rebirth; Dependent Origination (*pratītya-samutpāda*); *Dharma*; Ennobling Truth/Reality, the First; Ennobling Truth/Reality, the Third: *nirvāṇa*; Ennobling Truth/Reality, the Fourth: the Ennobling Eightfold Path.**

PETER HARVEY

ENNOBLING TRUTH/ REALITY, THE THIRD: *NIRVĀṆA*

As expressed in the Buddha's first sermon, this says:

> This is the Ennobling Reality that is the cessation (*nirodha*) of pain (Skt. *duḥkha*, Pāli *dukkha*): it is the remainderless fading away and cessation of that very craving, the giving up and relinquishing of it, freedom from it, non-reliance on it.
>
> (*Vinaya* 1.10; *Saṃyutta Nikāya* 5.421)

That is, when craving is ended, the true end of *duḥkha* is experienced: *nirvāṇa* (Pāli *nibbāna*). *Nirvāṇa* literally means "extinction," here meaning the going out of the "fires" of attachment (*rāga*), hatred (Skt. *dveṣa*, Pāli *dosa*) and delusion (*moha*) and the *duḥkha* they bring. The first full experience of *nirvāṇa* is had when a person becomes an *arhat* (Pāli *arahat*), one who has reached the goal of the Ennobling Eightfold Path and thus brought rebirth, even in the subtlest of heavens, to an end. The "destruction of attachment, hatred and delusion" is how both *nirvāṇa* and *arhat*ship are explained at *Saṃyutta Nikāya* 4.252. The path is not seen to cause *nirvāṇa*, but is just the path to it, just as a mountain is not caused by the path to it (*Milindapañha* 269). The path simply causes the destruction of the craving and so forth that stops *nirvāṇa* being experienced.

The two domains of *nirvāṇa*

Nirvāṇa is first attained during life by an *arhat* and then finally at death. The *Itivuttaka* (38–9) explains that there are two "domains (*dhātus*) of *nirvāṇa*": (1) that "with remainder of the grasped-at" (Skt. *sopadhi-śeṣa*, Pāli *sa-upādi-sesa*), that is, with the five aggregates (Skt. *skandhas*, Pāli *khandhas*) of the living *arhat* still remaining; and (2) that "without remainder of the grasped-at" (Skt. *nir-upadhi-śeṣa*, Pāli *an-upādi-sesa*). The first is described as the destruction of attachment, hatred and delusion in a living *arhat* who still has the five senses through which pleasure and pain are experienced. The second is what happens at the end of an *arhat*'s life, when all such experiences "become cool," like a fire gone out. The Theravādin commentaries explain the first as *kilesa-parinibbāna*, or "extinguishing of the defilements," and the second as *khandha-parinibbāna*, or "extinguishing of the aggregates."

Characterizations of *nirvāṇa*

Whether in life or beyond death, *nirvāṇa* is seen as very hard to describe. The Buddha says:

> This *Dharma* won by me is deep, difficult to see, difficult to understand, peaceful, sublime, not within the scope of reason, subtle, to be experienced by the learned ... that is to say Dependent Origination. This too were a matter difficult to see, that is to say the tranquilizing of all constructing activities (Pāli *saṅkhāra-samatha*) the renunciation of all clinging (*upadhi*), the destruction of craving, non-attachment (*virāga*), cessation (*nirodha*), *nirvāṇa*.
>
> (*Majjhima Nikāya* 1.167)

The term "*nirvāṇa*" is only one of many used for the goal of the Ennobling Eightfold Path. A section in the *Saṃyutta Nikāya* (4.360–73) first expresses this goal as the "unconditioned" or "unconstructed" (Pāli *asaṅkhata*, Skt. *asaṃskṛta*) that which has not been subject to the *saṅkhāras* (Skt. *saṃskāras*), the "constructing activities" (fourth aggregate), or any other conditioning factors: *Dīgha Nikāya* 3.275 explains the goal as a cessation that is the leaving behind of the "constructed, dependently arisen (*paṭicca-samuppanna*)." The "unconstructed" is then replaced successively with a list of terms in this Pāli text: the uninclined, the taintless (*anāsava*), truth/reality (*sacca*), the beyond (*pāra*), the subtle, the very-hard-to-see, the undecaying, the constant (*dhuva*), the undisintegrating, the non-manifestive (*anidassana*), the unelaborated (*nippapañca*, Skt. *niṣ-prapañca*), peace (*santa*), the deathless (*amata*), the sublime (*panīta*), the auspicious (*siva*), the secure (*khema*), the destruction of craving, the marvelous, the amazing, the unailing, the unailing state, *nirvāṇa*, the unafflicted, non-attachment, purity (*suddhi*), freedom (*mutti*), the unclinging (*anālaya*), the island (amidst the flood), the shelter, the place of safety, the refuge (*saraṇa*), the destination (*parāyana*). This list mixes negative terms (such as the unconditioned, the deathless, non-attachment), positive images (such as the sublime, the peaceful), and poetic imagery (such as the island). Elsewhere, the goal of the path is the "cessation of the world" (*loka-nirodha*, e.g. *Saṃyutta Nikāya* 1.62), that is, an experience in which the normal world of lived experience stops, drops away. In some passages (e.g. *Paṭisambhidāmagga* 1.91–2), it is seen as: the "signless" (*animitta*), beyond all perceptual cues; the "undirected" (*appaṇihita*, Skt. *apraṇihita*), beyond all goal-directedness; and "emptiness" (*suññatā*, Skt. *śūnyatā*), empty of attachment, hatred and delusion, and realized through recognizing everything, including itself, as empty of Self.

Perhaps the most famous passages on *nirvāṇa* are in the *Udāna*. *Udāna* pp. 80–1 says:

> Monks, there exists (*atthi*) the unborn (*ajāta*), unbecome, unmade, unconstructed (*asaṅkhata*). Monks, if that unborn ... were not, there would not be apparent the leaving behind (*nissaraṇa*), here, of the born, made, constructed.

Itivuttaka pp. 37–8 in turn explains this "leaving behind" as "peace ... unarisen (*asamuppana*) ... the cessation of *duḥkha*-states, the tranquilizing of constructing activities, bliss (*sukho*)."

Udāna p. 80 says on such a state:

> There exists (*atthi*), monks, that sphere (*āyatanaṃ*) where there is: (i) neither solidity, cohesion, heat, nor motion; (ii) nor the spheres of infinite space, infinite consciousness, nothingness, or neither-perception-nor-non-perception; (iii) neither this world, nor a world beyond, nor both,

> nor sun-and-moon; (iv) there, monks, I say there is no coming, nor going, nor maintenance, nor falling away, nor arising; (v) that, surely, is without support (*appatiṭṭha*), non-functioning (*appavatta*), objectless (*anārammaṇa*) – (vi) just this is the end of *duḥkha*.

Here:

1 are the four physical elements, literally "earth," "water," "fire," and "wind," which are the primary components of material form (*rūpa*) and common objects of meditation to attain the *dhyānas* (Pāli *jhānas*), meditative states, of the level of elemental form (*rūpa*);
2 are the four formless states which are both further levels of meditative experience and corresponding levels of rebirth;
3 is a way of referring to any rebirth and the realm of space;
4 uses terms normally employed when talking of the process of moving from one rebirth to another;
5 will be discussed below, and
6 shows that the passage is on *nirvāṇa*.

Nirvāṇa's relation to the elements of the conditioned world

Nirvāṇa exists, then, yet is beyond even subtle meditative states and levels of rebirth and is hard to discern and pin down. The above enigmatic passage, while the most well known of its type, is complemented by others, especially at *Aṅguttara Nikāya* (5.318–26), which help to illuminate it. At 5.318–19, Ānanda asks the Buddha whether there is a meditative state in which a person does not perceive solidity in solidity (the same for cohesion, heat and motion), does not perceive the sphere of infinite space in this sphere (the same for the other three formless spheres), does not perceive this world in this world (or the world beyond in it), yet he still perceives something: *nirvāṇa*.

Here, *nirvāṇa* is perceived not by looking away from the items of the world, such as solidity, but by looking "through" them, so to speak. Even when applying the mind to various items, they are not perceived, as such: in solidity, no solidity is recognized. Solidity is perceived, as it were, as empty of "solidity": *saṃjñā* (Pāli *saññā*) – "perception" or "interpretation," that which classifies or labels experience – does not latch onto a perceptual "sign" (*nimitta*) as a basis for seeing solidity as solidity. Rather, the mind perceives *nirvāṇa*. In a parallel passage at 5.324–6, the Buddha describes a monk who meditates in such a way that that "in solidity, the perception of solidity is *vibhūta*." "*Vibhūta*" can mean "made clear" or "destroyed," again suggesting that an insight arises which renders solidity "transparent," so to speak, enabling the vision of *nirvāṇa*.

Such passages raise interesting questions about the nature of the relationship between *nirvāṇa*, the unconditioned, and the conditioned factors which make up normal experience, the world of *saṃsāra*. The Mahāyāna later comes to say that *nirvāṇa* and *saṃsāra* are not ultimately different, cannot be differentiated, both being "empty" of inherent existence. The above passages hint in this direction, but no more than this. In any case, the above passages are probably on the knowing of *nirvāṇa* as an object of insight, but not the full experience of it.

Is *nirvāṇa* experienced all the time by the *arhat*?

Another issue on the nature of *nirvāṇa* is whether the form of it during life is something that the *arhat* experiences all the time. The Theravāda tradition sees *nirvāṇa* as the experience which destroys a person's defilements and hence makes them an *arhat*, but also says that the *arhat* can enter a special state, the "fruit" (*phala*) of arhatship, which takes the timeless realm of *nirvāṇa* as its object.

The *suttas* preserved by the Theravādins not only suggest that *nirvāṇa* in life is an episodic experience, but that it is actually a state in which all conditioned states of body and mind stop. This is indicated by a number of passages which see the goal of the path as the stopping/cessation (*nirodha*) of all the links of Dependent Origination, a state known during life (e.g. *Saṃyutta Nikāya* 3.58–61; *Suttanipāta* 726–39). If all the links stop, then all a person's normal functioning, including the sentient body (*nāma-rūpa*), the six senses, and feeling must be suspended. This suggests that the full experience of *nirvāṇa* in life is a timeless, transcendent experience. This cannot be the same as an *arhat*'s normal state of consciousness, in which he or she is not free from the *duḥkha* of physical pain, though they are not mentally perturbed by this (*Milindapañha* 44–5).

Nirvāṇa as a radically transformed consciousness?

Suttas in the Theravādin collection suggest something even more radical. This is that, when fully experienced, *nirvāṇa* is a timeless state of objectless consciousness. Certain passages indicate that the state in which all the links of Dependent Origination stop is one in which consciousness (Skt. *vijñāna*, Pāli *viññāṇa*) remains in a certain "stopped" form. Normally, consciousness is "supported" (Pāli *patiṭṭhita*) on some or other "object" (*ārammaṇa*) and hence conditions the arising and continuance of the sentient body (*Saṃyutta Nikāya* 2.66). However, in a passage on the cessation/stopping (*nirodha*) of the links of Dependent Origination (*Saṃyutta Nikāya* 3.54–5), it is said that when attachment (*rāga*) for any of the five aggregates is abandoned, consciousness is without either object or support (*patiṭṭhā*), so as to be "unsupported" (*apatiṭṭhita*), "without constructing activities" (*anabhisaṅkhāra*), "released" (*vimutta*), so that there is attainment of *nirvāṇa*. This description of an "unsupported" consciousness that lacks an object very closely matches part (v) of the above *Udāna* 80 description of *nirvāṇa*: "that, surely, is without support (*appatiṭṭha*), non-functioning (*appavatta*), and objectless (*anārammaṇa*)." Such a consciousness is the only thing that matches this description of *nirvāṇa*.

There are also two parallel passages which seem to equate *nirvāṇa* with a form of consciousness. At *Dīgha Nikāya* 1.221–3, the question is raised:

> Where do solidity, cohesion, heat and motion have no footing? Where do long and short, course and fine, foul and lovely (have no footing)? Where are sentiency (*nāma*) and body (*rūpa*) stopped without remainder?

The Buddha replies:

> Consciousness: non-manifestive (*anidassana*), infinite, accessible from all round (*sabbato paha*). Here it is that solidity . . . (as above). With the stopping of consciousness, here, this is stopped.

The Theravādin commentary sees this as on *nirvāṇa* (note that, above, *anidassana* is one of the synonyms for *nirvāṇa*), but tries to make the word *viññāṇa* mean "is to be known by consciousness" rather than "consciousness," which is implausible. It also sees the last line as about the complete cessation of consciousness at an *arhat*'s death, yet the last line seems to be about the same situation as is the first line, on a consciousness which has not simply ended. At *Majjhima Nikāya* 1.329–30, the Buddha also speaks of a "Consciousness: non-manifestive, infinite, shining in every respect (*sabbato-pabha*) that is not reached by the solidness of solidity . . . by the allness of the all." Elsewhere the "all" (*sabba*) is equated with the six senses and their objects

(*Saṃyutta Nikāya* 4.16–17), that are in turn equated with *duḥkha* (*Saṃyutta Nikāya* 4.38–9). This suggests that a nirvanic form of consciousness untouched by *duḥkha* is meant at *Majjhima Nikāya* 1.329–30.

Nirvāṇa beyond death

What can one say on *nirvāṇa* beyond death? The Buddha was repeatedly asked what happened to an enlightened person after death. Could it be said that he (i) "is" (*hoti*), (ii) "is not," (iii) "both is and is not" or (iv) "neither is nor is not"? He did not agree with any of these statements, and the second, equivalent to complete annihilation at death, is particularly criticized (*Saṃyutta Nikāya* 3.109–12). While his reasons for leaving these questions undetermined was partly because they were a time-wasting distraction from the path to enlightenment (*Majjhima Nikāya* 1.426–31), he also saw them as based on a misconception, being asked by people who viewed the five aggregates as somehow related to a permanent Self (*Saṃyutta Nikāya* 4.395). That is, they were asking about what happens to an enlightened *Self* after death. As the Buddha saw "Self" as a baseless idea, he therefore answered no questions that presumed its existence.

It is interesting that the above questions are framed using the Pāli word *hoti*, usually used for saying that something *is something else*, e.g. "the brahmin is a minister," and not *atthi* (Skt. *asti*), "exists." Beyond death, one cannot say *what* an *arhat* is:

> There exists no measuring of one who has gone out (like a flame). That by which he could be referred to no longer exists for him. When all phenomena (*dharmas*) are removed, then all ways of describing have also be removed.
>
> (*Suttanipāta* v. 1076)

At *Majjhima Nikāya* 1.486–7, *hoti* is replaced by *upapajjati*, "arises" in rebirth, and the death of an enlightened person is again likened to a fire going out – though in Indian thought of the day, an extinct fire was simply seen as going into another, undifferentiated state, as the potential for fire was seen as in all material things. The indescribable state of an enlightened person after death is in fact linked in some passages to a transformed form of consciousness. At *Saṃyutta Nikāya* 1.121–2, a monk attains *nirvāṇa* at the very time of death: his consciousness is not "supported" in any rebirth, and "with an unsupported (*appatiṭṭhitena*) consciousness, the clansman Godhika attained *nirvāṇa*."

There are thus suggestions that *nirvāṇa*, whether in life or beyond death, is an "unsupported," "objectless," "stopped" form of consciousness, which is radically different from the form of conditioned consciousness that normally occurs within the five aggregates, including all the subtle transformations of this in meditative states. Such suggestions are not taken up in the Theravāda school, though, which rests content with silence on the state of an enlightened person after death, and sees *nirvāṇa* as a timeless, transcendental realm that can be fully known as an object by the *arhat*, the first experience of which makes him or her an *arhat*. However *nirvāṇa* is seen, it is also clear that it is also something that a stream-enterer, one who gains the first level of experiential knowledge of the four Ennobling Truths, also gains a distant glimpse of.

Nirvāṇa in the *Mahāyāna*

In the Mahāyāna, the goal of becoming an *arhat* was seen as insufficiently compassionate, as it entailed leaving the round of rebirths at death, not staying in it to develop additional qualities needed to become a full Buddha, who could bring countless benefits to the world.

Hence the true path, trodden by the *bodhisattva*, is that which goes to full Buddhahood. At stage six of the ten-stage *bodhisattva*-path, wisdom equivalent to that of an *arhat* is attained, but the advanced *bodhisattvas* do not pass into "*nirvāṇa* without remainder of the grasped-at" at death, but voluntarily remain in the round of rebirths to work further towards Buddhahood, and continue to aid beings. They are no longer attached to *saṃsāra*, aimlessly wandering on in rebirths, but nor are they attached to post-mortem *nirvāṇa* beyond rebirths. Moreover, in their wisdom they know that *saṃsāra* is not ultimately different from *nirvāṇa*, for both are empty of a separate essence. They are thus seen to experience a *nirvāṇa* that is *apratiṣṭhita*: "unsupported" or "non-abiding" in either *saṃsāra* or *nirvāṇa*. It is intriguing that the term *apratiṣṭhita* is used, for this is the equivalent of Pāli *appatiṭṭhita*, used in the early texts of nirvanic consciousness. For the Mahāyāna, a being can still operate in the world in such an "unsupported" state, this being one of *non-attachment* to *saṃsāra* or *nirvāṇa*; in the Pāli *sutta*s, it seems to indicate a state where the conditioned world has dropped away, and consciousness is without *any object*, even "*nirvāṇa*."

See also: **Buddha; Buddha, bodies of; Cosmology and rebirth; *Dharma*; Ennobling Truth/Reality, the First; Ennobling Truth/Reality, the Second; Ennobling Truth/Reality, the Fourth: the Ennobling Eightfold Path.**

PETER HARVEY

ENNOBLING TRUTH/REALITY, THE FOURTH: THE ENNOBLING EIGHTFOLD PATH

The fourth of the Four Ennobling Truths/Realities is the Ennobling Eightfold Path (Skt. *āriya aṣṭaṅgika-mārga*, Pāli *ariya aṭṭhaṅgika-magga*). This is seen in the first sermon as the "middle way" of practice (Skt. *madhyama-pratipad*, Pāli *majjhima-paṭipadā*): "That middle way awakened to by the *Tathāgata* (Thus-gone/Truth-attained One), which gives rise to vision, which gives rise to knowledge, which leads to peace, to direct knowledge, to awakening, to *nirvāṇa*," and the "way leading the cessation of pain (Skt. *duḥkha*, Pāli *dukkha*)." The first sermon says that the Ennobling Eightfold Path is "to be developed/cultivated (*bhāvetabban*)" (*Vinaya* 1.11; *Saṃyutta Nikāya* 5.422) and it is elsewhere said to be "the best of conditioned states" (*Aṅguttara Nikāya* 2.34). The Path has eight factors (*aṅga*s) each described as right or perfect (Skt. *samyak*, Pāli *sammā*): (1) right view, seeing or understanding, (2) right resolve, (3) right speech, (4) right action, (5) right livelihood, (6) right effort, (7) right mindfulness, and (8) right concentration. The Path-factors are not "steps" on the Path but more like qualities that are needed to effectively travel to *nirvāṇa*, the end of *duḥkha*.

The Path-factors are grouped into three sections (*Majjhima Nikāya* 1.301). Factors 3–5 pertain to *śīla* (Pāli *sīla*), moral discipline; factors 6–8 pertain to *samādhi*, meditative unification of the heart/mind (*citta*); factors 1–2 pertain to *prajñā* (Pāli *paññā*), or wisdom; *śīla, samādhi*, and *prajñā* are always given in this order. Accordingly, the Path essentially comprises cultivation of three aspects of a person's character:

- *Moral discipline* addresses bodily and verbal conduct, so as to act in a more morally wholesome, virtuous way, restraining overt expressions of greed, hatred and delusion.
- *Meditative unification* addresses the inner expressions of greed, hatred and delusion in the emotions, calming these by refining the quality of attention.

- *Wisdom* addresses aspirations and understanding of the nature of reality, which is seen to improve as progress in meditation develops, and insights based on this can arise. Wisdom challenges misperceptions of reality, in order ultimately to remove even latent, underlying forms of greed, hatred and delusion that are not always apparent in conscious thought.

Moral discipline is seen as a good foundation of the other two, though it is also strengthened and deepened by them. This is because unwholesome actions – counteracted by moral discipline – strengthen the hindrances to meditative success. Meditation helps weaken these, and so aids virtuous behavior, as does wisdom: moral discipline and wisdom are said to be like two hands that wash each other (*Dīgha Nikāya* 1.124).

The Ennobling Eightfold Path and the ordinary eightfold path

The eight factors (*aṅgas*) of the Path exist at two basic levels, the ordinary (Skt. *laukika*, Pāli *lokiya*), and the transcendent (Skt. *lokottara*, Pāli *lokuttara*) or Noble (Skt. *ārya*, Pāli *ariya*), so that there is both an ordinary and an Ennobling Eightfold Path (*Mahācattārīsaka Sutta*: *Majjhima Nikāya* 3.71–8). Most Buddhists seek to practice the ordinary Path, which is perfected only in those who are approaching the lead-up to stream-entry. At stream-entry, a person gains a first glimpse of *nirvāṇa* and the "stream" which leads there, and enters this, the *Ennobling* Eightfold Path. This form of the Path, then, has first to be found before it can be practiced. One might perhaps think of attaining the Ennobling Path as like reaching a key base camp for the ascent of a mountain.

Each Path-factor is a state which is skillful or wholesome (Skt. *kuśala*, Pāli *kusala*), and progressively wears away its opposite "wrong" factor, until all unskillful states are destroyed. The form of the Path which immediately leads up to becoming an *arhat* (Pāli *arahat*) has two extra factors, right knowledge (Skt. *samyag-jñāṇa*, Pāli *sammā-ñāṇa*,) and right freedom (Skt. *samyag-vimukti*, Pāli *sammā-vimutti*), making it tenfold. The *Mahācattārīsaka Sutta* gives a clear analysis of the Path. The details are as follows, with some information added from other texts.

Right view (Skt. *samyag-dṛṣṭi*, Pāli *sammā-diṭṭhi*)

At the "ordinary" level, right view is in the form of correct belief:

> there is gift, there is offering, there is (self-) sacrifice [these are worthwhile]; there is fruit and ripening of deeds well done or ill done [what one does *matters* and has an effect on one's future]; there is this world, there is a world beyond [this world is not unreal, and the unenlightened are reborn in another world after death]; there is mother and father [it is good to respect parents, who establish one in this world]; there are spontaneously arising beings [some of the worlds one can be reborn in, for example some heavens, are populated by beings that come into being without parents]; there are in this world renunciants and brahmins who are faring rightly, and who proclaim this world and the world beyond having realized them by their own super-knowledge [spiritual development is a real possibility, actualized by some people, and it can lead, in the profound calm of deep meditation, to memory of past rebirths in a variety of worlds, and awareness of how others are reborn in such worlds according to their *karma*].

This helps make a person take full responsibility for their actions. It can also implicitly be seen to cover intellectual, and partial experiential, understanding of the four Ennobling Truths/Realities. The concerns of ordinary right view are also the focus of the three "bases for effecting karmic fruitfulness" (Skt. *puṇya-kriyā-vastus*, Pāli *puñña-kiriya-vatthus*): giving (*dāna*), moral discipline (Skt. *śīla*, Pāli *sīla*), and meditative cultivation (*bhāvanā*) (*Dīgha Nikāya* 3.218).

At the Noble or "transcendent" level, right view is in the form of right seeing: flashes of transformative direct insight into the Ennobling Realities in the form of the faculty of wisdom: knowledge which penetrates into the nature of reality. It is not based on the concepts of ultimate "existence" or ultimate "non-existence," as are speculative viewpoints, but on insight into the middle way of Dependent Origination. It sees: (1) how the world arises according to conditions, so that "non-existence" does not apply to it – it is not a pure illusion; and (2), how the world ceases from the cessation of conditions, so that it does not have substantial, eternal "existence" either (*Saṃyutta Nikāya* 2.16–17). Noble right view, then, directly knows the world as an ongoing flux of conditioned phenomena.

Right resolve (Skt. *samyak-saṃkalpa*, Pāli *sammā-saṅkappa*)

A "*saṃkalpa*" is seen as springing from what one focuses perception on, and to potentially lead on to desire-to-do, yearning and seeking something out (*Saṃyutta Nikāya* 2.143), reminiscent of the *saṃkalpa*/resolve that the brahmins made before carrying out a sacrificial ritual. At the "ordinary" level, it is resolve for: (a) peaceful "desirelessness" or "renunciation" (Skt. *naiṣkāmya* or *naiśkramya*, Pāli *nekkhamma*), and away from sense-pleasures (*kāmas*); (b) non-ill-will (Skt. *avyābādha*, Pāli *avyāpāda*), equivalent to lovingkindness, and away from ill-will; (c) non-injury (Skt. *ahiṃsā*, Pāli *avihiṃsā*), equivalent to compassion, and away from any desire to injure. At the Noble level, it is focused mental application (Skt. *vitarka*, Pāli *vitakka*) in accord with right seeing. One of great wisdom is said to be able to apply himself or herself to whatever *vitarka* or *saṃkalpa* he or she pleases: "Thus he is master of the mind in the ways of *vitarka*, also he is one who attains at will, without difficulty and without trouble, the four *dhyānas*" (*Aṅguttara Nikāya* 2.36). It is seen to both spring from and aid right view, both being part of wisdom. It aids right view as it is a repeated application of the mind to an object of contemplation, so that this can be rightly seen and understood to be impermanent, *duḥkha*, not-Self – just as a money changer assesses a coin as genuine or false by eye, but in doing so needs the help of his hands in turning the coin over and tapping it (*Visuddhimagga* 515). That is, carefully applying the mind to something helps one understand it in a deep and discerning way.

Right speech, action and livelihood

For each of the three Path-factors that come under moral discipline, these are well established at the ordinary level of the Path, and become natural at the Noble level.

Right speech

Right speech (Skt. *samyag-vācā*, Pāli *sammā-vācā*) is: (a) "abstaining from false speech:" truthful speech (equivalent to the fourth of the five lay ethical precepts); (b) "abstaining from divisive speech": speech focused on absent people's good points rather than on real or imagined bad points; (c) "abstaining from harsh speech": speech which is kindly and not angry or abrasive; (d) "abstaining from frivolous speech": speech which does not involve wasted words, or speaking just for the sake of speaking.

Right action

Right action (Skt. *samyak-karmanta*, Pāli *sammā-kammanta*) is equivalent to the first three of the five lay precepts: (a) "abstaining from onslaught on living beings": avoiding intentional killing of, or injury to, any living being; (b) "abstaining from taking what is not given": avoiding theft and cheating; (c) "abstaining from wrong conduct in regard to sense-pleasure": avoiding causing suffering to others or oneself by inconsiderate or greedy sensual activity.

Right livelihood

Right livelihood (Skt. *samyag-ājīva*, Pāli *sammā-ājīva*) is making one's living, lay or monastic, in such a way as to avoid causing suffering to others (human or animal) through cheating them (*Majjhima Nikāya* 3.75) or physically harming or killing them by: "trade in weapons, living beings, meat, alcoholic drink, or poison" (*Aṅguttara Nikāya* 3.208).

Right effort, mindfulness and concentration/unification

For the Path-factors that come under meditative unification, they are at the Noble level once Noble right view guides them.

Right effort

Right effort (Skt. *samyag-vyāyāma*, Pāli *sammā-vāyāma*) is endeavor directed at developing the mind in a wholesome way: (a) avoiding the arising of unwholesome states (such as greed, hatred or delusion); (b) undermining unwholesome states which have arisen; (c) developing wholesome states, as in meditation practice; (d) maintaining wholesome states which have arisen.

Right mindfulness

Right mindfulness (Skt. *samyak-smṛti*, Pāli *sammā-sati*) is a crucial aspect of any Buddhist meditation, and is a state of keen awareness of mental and physical phenomena as they arise within and around one. It is explained as practicing the four applications or presencings of mindfulness (Skt. *smṛty-upasthānas*, Pāli *sati-paṭṭhānas*) – mindful observation, within oneself and others, of the qualities and changing nature of: (a) body (*kāya*) (including breathing, bodily postures, movements, parts, elements and stages of decomposition after death); (b) feeling (*vedanā*) whether pleasant unpleasant or neutral; (c) states of mind (*citta*); (d) *dharmas* (Pāli *dhammas*): basic patterns in the flow of experience, such as the five *skandhas* (Pāli *khandhas*) comprising body and mind, the five hindrances (desire for sense-pleasures, ill-will, dullness and drowsiness, restlessness and worry, and vacillation), the four Ennobling Realities, and the seven factors of awakening (mindfulness, discrimination of *dharmas*, energy, joy, tranquility, meditative unification, and equanimity).

Right concentration / unification

Right concentration/unification (Skt. *samyak-samādhi*, Pāli *sammā-samādhi*) refers to states of inner collectedness, peace and mental clarity arising from attention closely focused on a meditation object. Attained by unification of the mind's energies, these are the four *dhyānas* (Pāli *jhānas*), meditative (lucid) trances. As described at *Dīgha Nikāya* 1.73–6: (a) the first *dhyāna*, which is "endowed with mental application (Skt. *vitarka*, Pāli *vitakka*) and examination (*vicāra*), born of detachment (from sense-desires and unwholesome states), filled with (uplifting) joy (Skt. *prīti*, Pāli *pīti*) and (contented) happiness (*sukha*)," with the joy and happiness suffusing the entire body; (b) the second *dhyāna*, in which there is no longer mental application and examination, and whose joy and happiness are "born of concentration"; (c) the third *dhyāna*, endowed with equanimity and (strong) mindfulness, but without joy; (d) the fourth *dhyāna*, also endowed with equanimity and strong mindfulness, but without happiness, a state in which the mind is "serene, purified, cleansed, without blemish, with defilements gone, become pliable, workable, firm and imperturbable," ready for deep insight. *Aṅguttara Nikāya* 1.235 describes the *dhyānas* as what "training in higher mind (*adhi-citta-*)" involves. The Theravādin *Abhidharma* (*Vibhaṅga* 263–4) specifies the key *dhyāna* factors as: mental application, examination, joy, happiness, and one-pointedness of mind (Skt. *cittaikagratā*, Pāli *cittass'ekaggatā*) in the first; joy, happiness and one-pointedness of mind in the second; happiness and one-pointedness of mind in the third; and equanimity and one-pointedness of mind in the fourth. Details of these factors are given in the *Visuddhimagga* (142–7).

The unfolding of the Path-factors

The order of the eight Path-factors is seen as that of a natural progression, with one factor following on from the one before it. Right view comes first because it knows the right and wrong form of each of the eight factors; it also counteracts spiritual ignorance, the first factor in Dependent Origination. From the cool believing or knowing of right view blossoms a right resolve, which has a balancing warmth. From this, a person's speech becomes improved, and thus his or her action. Once he is working on right action, it becomes natural to incline towards a virtuous livelihood. With this as basis, there can be progress in right effort. This facilitates the development of right mindfulness, whose clarity then allows the development of the calm of meditative concentration. Neither the ordinary nor the Ennobling Path is to be understood as a single progression from the first to eighth factor, however. Right effort and mindfulness work with right view to support the development of all the Path-factors: the Path-factors mutually support each other to allow a gradual deepening of the way in which the Path is trodden. In terms of the division of the Path into moral discipline, meditation and wisdom, the Path can be seen to develop as follows. Influenced by good examples, a person's first commitment will be to develop moral discipline, a generous and self-controlled way of life for the benefit of self and others. To motivate this, he or she will have some degree of preliminary wisdom, in the form of appropriate belief, outlook and an aspiration, expressed as *śraddhā* (Pāli *saddhā*), trustful confidence or faith in the wholesome qualities of the Path and those rich in these. With moral discipline as the indispensable basis for further progress, some meditation may be attempted, perhaps starting with chanting Buddhist formulas and short texts. With appropriate application, meditation will lead to the mind becoming calmer, stronger, and clearer. This will allow experiential understanding of the *Dharma* to develop, so that deeper wisdom arises. From this, moral discipline is strengthened, becoming a basis for further progress in meditation and wisdom. With each more refined development of the moral discipline–meditation–wisdom sequence, the Path spirals up to a higher level, until the crucial transition of stream-entry is reached. The Ennobling Path then spirals up to *arhat*ship.

The Noble persons

Any person not yet on the Ennobling Path is known as a *pṛthagjana* (Pāli *puthujjana*), an "ordinary person." Such people are seen as, so to speak, "deranged" (*Vibhaṅga* commentary 186), as they lack the mental balance of those on the Ennobling Path, the eight kinds of "Noble (Skt. *ārya*, Pāli *ariya*) persons." These comprise the Noble *Sangha*, which with the Buddha and *Dharma* are "three refuges" of a Buddhist.

The first Noble person is someone who, by strong insight into the "three marks" of conditioned phenomena (as impermanent, *duḥkha* and not-Self), is one "practicing for the realization of the fruit which is stream-entry" (*Aṅguttara Nikāya* 4.293). He or she goes on to become a stream-enterer (Skt. *srotāpanna*, Pāli *sotāpanna*), the second kind of Noble person, who is sure to become an *arhat* within seven lives (*Aṅguttara Nikāya* 1.235). He or she is free from rebirths as a hell-being, animal, ghost or jealous god (*asura*), as he has completely destroyed the first three of ten spiritual "fetters" (*saṃyojanas*; *Saṃyutta Nikāya* 5.357). The first fetter is "views on the existing group" (Skt. *satkāya-dṛṣṭi*, Pāli *sakkāya-diṭṭhi*), that is, taking any of the five aggregates as "Self" or somehow related to a "Self." This is destroyed by deep insight into the four Ennobling Realities and Dependent Origination. The second fetter is vacillation in commitment to the three refuges and the worth of morality. The stream-enterer thus has unwavering confidence in the refuges and unblemished morality (*Saṃyutta Nikāya* 2. 9–70). This is because he has "seen" and "plunged into" the *Dharma* (*Majjhima Nikāya* 1.380), giving him trust in *Dharma* and in the "*Dharma*-become" Buddha, and is himself now a member of the Noble *Sangha*, whether or not he or she is a monastic. The third fetter destroyed is "clinging to disciplines and observances," for although his morality is naturally pure, he or she knows that this alone is insufficient to attain *nirvāṇa*. The common "rites and rituals" instead of "disciplines and observances" (Skt. *śīla-vrata*, Pāli *sīla-bbata*) is a mistranslation, though no doubt the fetter does refer to attachment to various fixed ways of doing things.

The Theravādin *Abhidharma* denies that one practicing for stream-entry has yet got rid of any fetters: he may no longer overtly express "views on the existing group" or experience vacillation, but he or she still possesses the underlying tendencies for these. On these grounds, those who disagreed with the Theravādins on this issue (identified by the commentary as those of the Andhaka and Sammitiya schools) held them to have already overcome these two fetters, though still having that of clinging to disciplines and observances (*Kathāvatthu* III.5). The person practicing for stream-entry is explained by the *Puggala-paññatti*, a text of the Theravādin canonical *Abhidharma*, as equivalent to the faith-follower (*saddhānusārī*) and *Dharma*-follower (*dhammānusārī*). These are referred to at *Majjhima Nikāya* 1.477–9 as part of a list of seven types of Noble persons, differentiated by the spiritual qualities prevalent in them. Neither person has yet destroyed any spiritual taints (Skt. *āśravas*, Pāli *āsavas*), but both have the faculties of faith, mental strength, mindfulness, concentration and wisdom, though to different degrees. The former "has sufficient faith in and love for the *Tathāgata*" and the latter "with wisdom he has gained a reflective acceptance of those teachings proclaimed by the *Tathāgata*." One can see them as representing spiritually developed Buddhist followers who emphasize, respectively, faith and wisdom. In one passage (*Aṅguttara Nikāya* 4.75–6), the faith-follower is replaced by the "dweller in signlessness (*animitta*-)," which *Visuddhimagga* 659–60 explains in relation to deep understanding of impermanence.

By deepening his insight, a stream-enterer may become one practicing for the realization of once-returning, and then a once-returner (Skt. *sakṛdāgāmin*, Pāli *sakadāgāmin*). A once-returner can only be reborn once in the sense-desire world, as a human or lower god. Any other rebirths will be in the higher heavens. This is because he or she has destroyed the gross forms of the next two fetters, sensual desire and ill-will. The next Noble persons are the one practicing for the realization of non-returning, and the non-returner (*anāgāmin*). The non-returner has destroyed even subtle sensuous desire and ill-will, so that great equanimity is the tone of his or her experience, and he cannot be reborn in the sense-desire world. His insight is not quite sufficient for him to become an *arhat*, and if he does not manage to become one later in life, he is reborn in one or more of the five "pure abodes" (Skt. *śuddhāvāsas*, Pāli *suddhāvāsas*) the most refined heavens in the pure form world, where only non-returners can be reborn. In these he matures his insight till he becomes a long-lived *arhat*-god. The highest pure abode is the "supreme" (Skt. *akaniṣṭha*, Pāli *akaniṭṭha*) heaven, which the Mahāyāna *Laṅkāvatāra Sūtra* (p. 361) sees as where *bodhisattvas* finally attain perfect Buddhahood. There is, though, the suggestion that the quickest kind of non-returner experiences *nirvāṇa* in a between-lives state (later called the *antarā-bhava*), and is not reborn in any state (*Saṃyutta Nikāya* 5.69–70).

The final two Noble persons are the one practicing for the realization of *arhat*ness, and the *arhat* himself. The *arhat* destroys all the five remaining fetters: attachment to the pure form or formless worlds, the "'I am' conceit" (perhaps now in the form of lingering spiritual pride), restlessness, and spiritual ignorance. These are destroyed by the Tenfold Path, which brings *duḥkha* and all rebirths to an end in the blissful experience of *nirvāṇa*.

In one explanation of Path-progress, *Aṅguttara Nikāya* 1.233–4 explains that stream-enterers and once-returners have fully developed moral discipline and have a modicum of meditation and wisdom; non-returners have also fully developed their meditation, and *arhats* have fully developed all three qualities.

See also: **Buddha; Cosmology and rebirth; *Dharma*; Ennobling Truths/Realities; Ennobling Truth/Reality, the First; Ennobling Truth/Reality, the Second; Ennobling Truth/Reality, the Third: *nirvāṇa*; Ethics; Meditational systems.**

PETER HARVEY

ETHICS

Morality is woven into the fabric of Buddhist teachings and there is no major branch or school of Buddhism which fails to emphasize the importance of the moral life. The scriptures of Buddhism speak eloquently of virtues such as non-violence and compassion, and the "Golden Rule" is held up as the principle which should inform our relationships with others. Although newcomers to Buddhism are often struck by the variety of the different Asian traditions, as divergent in form as Zen and Tibetan Buddhism, at the level of moral teachings there is much common ground. Although some would disagree, it does not seem unreasonable to speak of a common moral core underlying the divergent customs, practices and philosophical teachings of the different schools. This core is composed of the principles and precepts, the values and virtues which were expounded by the Buddha in the fifth century BCE and which continue to guide the conduct of some 350 million Buddhists around the world today. This essay will review the main features of these moral teachings making reference to more specific entries on individual topics which will be found elsewhere in this encyclopedia.

Dharma

The ultimate foundation for Buddhist ethics is *Dharma*. *Dharma* has many meanings, but the underlying notion is of a universal law which governs both the physical and moral order of the universe. *Dharma* can best be translated as "natural law," a term which captures both its main senses, namely as the principle of order and regularity seen in the behaviour of natural phenomena, and also the idea of a universal moral law whose requirements have been discovered by enlightened beings such as the Buddha (note that Buddha discovered *Dharma*, he did not invent it). Every aspect of life is regulated by *Dharma*; the physical laws which regulate the rising of the sun, the succession of the seasons, and the movement of the constellations. *Dharma* is neither caused by nor under the control of a supreme being, and the gods themselves are subject to its laws, as was the Buddha. In the moral order, *Dharma* is manifest in the law of *karma*, which, as we shall see below, governs the way moral deeds affect individuals in present and future lives. Living in accordance with *Dharma* and implementing its requirements is thought to lead to happiness, fulfillment and salvation; neglecting or transgressing it is said to lead to endless suffering in the cycle of rebirth (*saṃsāra*).

In his First Sermon, the Buddha was said to have "turned the wheel of the *Dharma*" and given doctrinal expression to the truth about how things are in reality. It was in this discourse that the Buddha set out the Four Noble Truths, the last of which is the Noble Eightfold Path which leads to *nirvāṇa*. The Path has three divisions – morality (*śīla*), meditation (*samādhi*), and insight (*prajñā*) – from which it can be seen that morality is an integral component of the path to *nirvāṇa*.

The Eightfold Path and its three divisions

1 Right view
2 Right resolve
3 Right speech
4 Right action
5 Right livelihood
6 Right effort
7 Right mindfulness
8 Right meditation.

Karma

The doctrine of *karma* is concerned with the ethical implications of *Dharma*, in particular those relating to the consequences of moral behaviour. *Karma* may be defined as a principle of moral retribution in terms of which good and bad deeds bring about pleasant and unpleasant consequences in the future as well as a transformation in the agent's present moral status. The remote effects of karmic choices are referred to as the "maturation" (*vipāka*) or "fruit" (*phala*) of the karmic act. Performing good and bad deeds is compared to planting seeds that will fruit at a later date. Good *karma* is often referred to as "merit" (Skt. *puṇya*, Pāli *puñña*), and its opposite, bad *karma*, is known as *pāpa*. Some Buddhists go to extreme lengths to accumulate merit, for example by making large donations to the *sangha* or funding lavish construction projects for the building of temples and the like.

Belief in *karma* is common to many Indian religions and did not originate with the Buddha. As it is one of the "givens" of Indian thought, rarely does the Buddha seek to justify or defend the idea of *karma* explicitly. However, the notion permeates his teachings and frequent reference is made to it in the early discourses. There, the Buddha reserves a particular censure for those of his contemporaries who denied the belief that moral acts entailed future consequences (this was known as *akiryavāda* or "the doctrine of non-retribution"). Six teachers were criticized by him, and the fullest exposition of their views is to be found in an early discourse entitled *The Fruits of the Religious Life* (*Sāmaññaphala Sutta*), the second discourse of the *Dīgha Nikāya* of the Pāli Canon. The text relates how the king of Magadha, Ajātaśatru, went to visit the six teachers and questioned them concerning the fruit of the religious life. After receiving unsatisfactory responses, he eventually visited the Buddha and was "pleased and delighted" at the Buddha's account of the religious life and its culmination in *nirvāṇa*. The views of the six briefly were as follows: Pūraṇa Kassapa denied that the religious life had any purpose whatsoever, good and evil deeds being equally devoid of religious significance. Makkhali Gosāla was a determinist who taught that a person's destiny was preordained by fate, while Ajīta Kesakambala held a materialist view according to which a man or woman is utterly annihilated at death. Pakudha Kaccāyana espoused a doctrine of fatalistic pluralism, according to which human beings are a compound of elemental substances which are dispersed at death. All of the above four were ethical nihilists (*natthikavādin*) and denied the existence of moral causation. The fifth, Sañjāya Belaṭṭhaputta, was described as an "eel wriggler" because he refused to take a stand on any position, and the Jain leader Nigaṇṭha Nātaputta, while accepting the doctrine of moral retribution (*kiriyavāda*) reduced the religious life to physical discipline and self-mortification. In view of their failure to appreciate the true purpose of the religious life and the place of morality within it, all six teachers were roundly condemned by the Buddha.

In Buddhism *karma* involves a complex of interrelated ideas which embraces both ethics and belief in reincarnation. Not all the consequences of what a person does are experienced in the lifetime in which the deeds are performed. *Karma* that has been accumulated but not yet experienced is carried forward to the next life, or even many lifetimes ahead. Early sources refer to five possible rebirth destinations known as *gatis*. These are as a god, a human being, a hungry ghost, an animal, or in hell. To these later sources add a sixth, the realm of the titans (*asura*), powerful and aggressive warlike beings. Rebirth in the human world is regarded as the most fortunate location, because it involves the best mix of pleasure and pain appropriate to the quest for *nirvāṇa*. When reborn in the human world, certain key aspects of a person's rebirth are thought of as karmically determined. These include the family into which one is born, one's social status, physical appearance, and of course, one's character and personality, because these are simply carried over from the previous life.

Karma is not the same as determinism, and the doctrine of *karma* does not claim that everything that happens to a person is determined in advance. Such was the erroneous belief held by Makkhali Gosāla, one of the sectarian teachers mentioned above. Instead, many of the good and bad things that happen in life can simply be accidents. *Karma* does not determine precisely what will happen or how anyone will react to what happens.

Precepts

In common with Indian tradition as a whole, Buddhism expresses its ethical requirements in the form of duties rather than rights. These duties are thought of as implicit requirements of *Dharma*. The most general moral duties are those found in the Five Precepts, such as the duty to refrain from evil acts such as killing and stealing. On becoming a Buddhist one formally "takes" (or accepts) the precepts in a ritual context known as "going for refuge," and the form of words used acknowledges the free and voluntary nature of the duty assumed.

The most widely known precepts in Buddhism are the Five Precepts, comparable in standing to the Ten Commandments of Christianity. The Five Precepts are undertaken as voluntary commitments in the ceremony of "taking refuge" when a person becomes a Buddhist. They are as follows:

1 I undertake the precept to refrain from harming living creatures.
2 I undertake the precept to refrain from taking what has not been given.

3 I undertake the precept to refrain from sexual immorality.
4 I undertake the precept to refrain from speaking falsely.
5 I undertake the precept to refrain from taking intoxicants.

Apart from the Five Precepts various other lists of precepts are found, such as the Eight Precepts (*aṣṭāṅga-śīla*) and the Ten Precepts (*daśa-śīla*). These are commonly adopted as additional commitments on the twice-monthly holy days (Skt. *poṣadha*, Pāli *uposatha*), and supplement the first four of the Five Precepts with additional restrictions such as the time when meals may be taken. Another set of precepts similar to the Ten Precepts is the Ten Good Paths of Action (*daśa-kuśala-karmapatha*). Precepts like these which apply to the laity are comparatively few in number compared to those observed by monks and nuns, as explained below.

Vinaya

A term often found paired with *Dharma* is *Vinaya*. Particularly in early sources, the compound "*Dharma-Vinaya*" ("doctrine and discipline") is used to denote the whole body of Buddhist teachings and practice. Originally, the Buddhist monastic Order (*sangha*) existed as just another sect within a broad community of wandering teachers and students known as *parivrājakas* or *śramaṇas.* From these simple beginnings evolved a complex code for the regulation of monastic life which eventually became formulated in the portion of the canon known as the *Vinaya Piṭaka*, referred to above. The *Vinaya Piṭaka* also contains a large number of stories and biographical material relating to the Buddha, as well as a certain amount of historical matter regarding the Order (*sangha*).

The Prātimokṣa

The purpose of the *Vinaya* is to regulate in detail life within the community of monks and nuns and also their relationship with the laity. In its final form the text is divided into three sections, the first of which contains the set of rules for monks and nuns known as the *Prātimokṣa* (Pāli *Pāṭimokkha*), also referred to as the *Prātimokṣa Sūtra* (Pāli *Pāṭimokkha Sutta*). The derivation of the term *prātimokṣa* is uncertain, perhaps "that which should be made binding" or "that which causes one to be released (from suffering)." Different schools had their own versions of the *Vinaya* and the number of the rules slightly varies in each. Those which have survived belong to the schools of the Theravāda, Mahāsāṃghika, Mahīśāsaka, Dharmaguptaka, Sarvāstivāda and Mūlasarvāstivāda, although only the Theravāda *Vinaya* survives complete in its original language. In the Theravāda *Vinaya* the rules for monks number 227. Across all schools the rules for monks vary from 218 to 263, and for nuns from 279 to 380. The rules are not all ethical and deal mainly with the behavior of the members of the Order in respects of food, clothes, dwellings, furniture, etc. The rules are arranged in eight sections, in decreasing degree of punishment and therefore roughly corresponding to the degree of importance attached to their observance. The rules are recited once a fortnight on the days of the full moon and the new moon, and anyone who has infringed any of the rules is called upon to declare the transgression.

Virtues

Although the precepts, whether lay and monastic, are of great importance there is more to the Buddhist moral life than following rules. Rules must not only be followed, but followed for the right reasons and with the correct motivation. It is here that the role of the virtues becomes important, and Buddhist morality as a whole may be likened to a coin with two faces: on one side are the precepts and on the other the virtues. The precepts, in fact, may be thought of simply as a list of things which a virtuous person will never do.

Early sources emphasize the importance of cultivating correct dispositions and habits so that moral conduct becomes the natural and spontaneous manifestation of internalized and properly integrated beliefs and values, rather than simple conformity to external rules. Many formulations of the precepts make this clear. Of someone who follows the first precept it is said, "Laying aside the club and the sword he dwells compassionate and kind to all living creatures" (*Digha Nikāya* 1.4). Abstention from taking life is therefore ideally the result of a compassionate identification with living things, rather than a constraint which is imposed contrary to natural inclination. To observe the first precept perfectly requires a profound understanding of the relationship between living beings (according to Buddhism, in the long cycle of reincarnation we have all been each other's fathers, mothers, sons, and so forth) coupled with an unswerving disposition of universal benevolence and compassion. Although few have perfected these capacities, in respecting the precepts they habituate themselves to the conduct of one who has, and in so doing come a step closer to enlightenment.

The task of the virtues is to counteract negative dispositions called *kleśas* (what are known in the West as "vices"). The lengthy lists of virtues and vices which appear in Buddhist commentarial literature are extrapolated from a key cluster of three virtues, the three "cardinal virtues" of non-attachment (*arāga*), benevolence (*adveṣa*) and understanding (*amoha*). These are the opposites of the three "roots of evil" (or "three poisons"), namely greed (*rāga*), hatred (*dveṣa*) and delusion (*moha*). Non-attachment means the absence of that selfish desire which taints behavior by allocating a privileged status to one's own needs. Benevolence means an attitude of goodwill to all living creatures, and understanding means knowledge of Buddhist teachings such as the Four Noble Truths. While these are the three most basic Buddhist virtues, there are many others, some of the most important of which are discussed below.

Dāna

A key virtue for lay Buddhists in particular is *dāna*, which means "giving" or "generosity." The primary recipient of lay Buddhist generosity is the *sangha* – because monks and nuns possess nothing they are entirely dependent on the laity for support. The laity provides all the material needs of the monastic community, everything from food, robes and medicine to the land and buildings which constitute the monastic residence. In the *kaṭhina* ceremony, which takes place following the annual rainy season retreat in countries where Theravāda Buddhism is practised, cotton cloth is supplied to the monks by the laity for the purpose of making robes. The relationship is not just one-way, for in return monks provide *Dharma* teachings to the laity, and the gift of the *Dharma* is said to be the highest of all gifts. At all levels of society – between family members, friends and even strangers – generosity is widely practiced in Buddhist countries and seen as an indication of spiritual development. This is because the generous person, as well as being free from egocentric thoughts and sensitive to the needs of other, finds it easier to practice renunciation and cultivate an attitude of detachment. The story of Prince Vessantara, the popular hero of the *Vessantara Jātaka*, is well known in South Asia. Vessantara gave away everything he owned, even down to his wife and children. Many Theravāda sources praise *dāna*, and Mahāyāna sources emphasize the extreme generosity of *bodhisattvas* who are disposed to give away even parts of their bodies, or their lives, in order to aid others. As we shall see below, *dāna* is also the first of the "Six Perfections" (*pāramitā*) of a *bodhisattva*.

Ahiṃsā

Ahiṃsā is a fundamental Buddhist virtue. Literally meaning "non-harming" or "non-violence", it includes in addition more positive overtones including compassion (*karuṇā*) and sympathy (*anukampā*) for all living creatures. *Ahiṃsā* is a pre-Buddhist concept which came to prominence among the unorthodox renouncer (*śramaṇa*) movements such as Buddhism and Jainism. These groups rejected the Brahmanical practice of animal sacrifice and sometimes went to extreme lengths to avoid harming even tiny forms of life such as insects. The Jains are particularly famous for the scrupulous care they take to avoid causing harm even unintentionally Their practices had some influence on Buddhism, and Buddhist monks often used a strainer to make sure they did not destroy small creatures in their drinking-water, as well as avoiding travel during the monsoon to avoid treading on insects and other small creatures which become abundant after the rains.

Compassion

Compassion (*karuṇā*) is a virtue which is of importance in all schools of Buddhism but which is particularly emphasized by the Mahāyāna (see below). In early Buddhism, *karuṇā* figures as the second of the four *Brahmavihāras* or "Divine Abidings." These are states of mind cultivated especially through the practice of meditation. The four are lovingkindness (*maitrī*), compassion (*karuṇā*), sympathetic joy (*muditā*) and equanimity (*upekṣā*). The practice of the four *Brahmavihāras* involves radiating outwards the positive qualities associated with each, directing them first towards oneself, then to one's family, the local community, and eventually to all beings in the universe. In Mahāyāna iconography and art the symbolic embodiment of compassion is the great *bodhisattva* Avalokiteśvara, "the one who looks down from on high." He is portrayed as having a thousand arms extended in all directions to minister to those in need and is constantly appealed to by those in difficult circumstances. In the course of time in Buddhism there appeared a doctrine of salvation by faith according to which the mere invocation of the name of a Buddha was sufficient, given the extent of the Buddha's compassion, to ensure rebirth in a "Pure Land" or heaven.

Mahāyāna morality

In the Mahāyāna, the *bodhisattva* who devotes himself or herself to the service of others becomes the new paradigm for religious practice, as opposed to the *arahant*, or saint in the early tradition, who is criticized for leading a cloistered life devoted to the self-interested pursuit of liberation. Schools which embraced the earlier ideal are henceforth referred to disparagingly as the Hīnayāna ("Small Vehicle"), or the Śrāvakayāna ("Vehicle of the Hearers"). In the Mahāyāna great emphasis is placed on the twin values of compassion (*karuṇā*) and insight (*prajñā*), and the *bodhisattva* practices six special virtues known as the "Six Perfections" (*pāramitā*). These are generosity (*dāna*), morality (*śīla*), patience (*kṣānti*), perseverance (*vīrya*), meditation (*samādhi*) and insight (*prajñā*). It can be seen that three of these (*śīla, samādhi* and *prajñā*) coincide with the three divisions of the Eightfold Path of early Buddhism, demonstrating both continuity and change in the evolving moral tradition.

The Mahāyāna did not reject the ethical teachings of early Buddhism but subsumed them under an expanded framework of its own within which three levels were identified. The first level was known as "Moral Discipline" (*saṃvara-śīla*) and consisted of the scrupulous observance of the moral precepts. The second level was known as the "Cultivation of Virtue" (*kuśala-dharma-saṃgrāhaka-śīla*) and was concerned with the accumulation of the good qualities necessary for the attainment of *nirvāṇa*. The third category was known as "Altruistic Conduct" (*sattva-artha-kriyā-śīla*) and consisted of moral action directed to the needs of others. The Mahāyāna claimed that the early followers had access only to the first level and that their moral practices were deficient in lacking concern for the well-being of others. The Mahāyāna is not a monolithic system and there is no one "official" code of ethics for either laymen or monks. The *Vinayas* of the early schools were not rejected and continued to be observed by monks and nuns alongside the new teachings recommended for *bodhisattvas* in Mahāyāna literature.

*Skillful means (*upāya-kauśalya*)*

An important innovation in Mahāyāna ethics was the doctrine of skillful means (*upāya-kauśalya*). This teaching was taken by some to mean that the clear and strict rules encountered in the early sources which prohibit certain sorts of acts could be interpreted more in the way of guidelines rather than as ultimately binding. In particular, *bodhisattvas*, the new moral heroes of the Mahāyāna, could claim increased latitude and flexibility based on their recognition of the importance of compassion. The pressure to bend or suspend the rules in the interests of compassion results in certain texts establishing new codes of conduct for *bodhisattvas* which sometimes allow the precepts to be broken. In some of these, such as the *Upāya-kauśalya Sūtra* (*c.* first century BCE), even killing is said to be justified to prevent someone committing a heinous crime and suffering karmic retribution in hell. The result is a form of Buddhist "situation ethics" similar to the utilitarian-influenced ethical teachings of Joseph Fletcher in a Christian context.

Tantra

In *tantric* teachings, too, the precepts are sometimes set aside. *Tantra*, alternatively known as the Vajrayāna (Diamond Vehicle) or Mantrayāna (Vehicle of Mantras), is a form of Buddhism that developed in India in the sixth century CE and is characterized by antinomianism and the use of magical techniques which aim to speed the practitioner to enlightenment in a single lifetime. One of the basic techniques of *tantra* is to transmute negative mental energies into positive ones using a form of mystical alchemy which is believed to transform the whole personality. By liberating energy trapped at an instinctual level in emotions such as fear and lust, it was thought that practitioners could do the psychological equivalent of splitting the atom and use the energy produced to propel themselves rapidly to enlightenment. In certain forms of *tantra* such practices involved the deliberate and controlled reversal of moral norms and the breaking of taboos in order to help jolt the mind out of its conventional patterns of thought into a supposedly higher state of consciousness. Examples of such activities include drinking alcohol and sexual intercourse, both serious breaches of the monastic rules. While some practitioners understood such teachings literally, however, others saw them as merely symbolic and simply useful subjects for meditation.

Buddhist ethics in the West

Despite an abundance of moral teachings of the kind described above, Buddhism down the centuries has shown little interest in ethics as a philosophical discipline.

There are few treatises on the subject and it appears that both ethics and politics were not subjects that Buddhist scholars felt drawn to pronounce on. Perhaps this is caused by the different cultural histories of East and West. As everyone knows, the Greeks invented democracy, and the discipline of political science (which included ethics as a subsidiary) arose to develop constitutions founded on ethical principles such as justice. Buddhism, by contrast, grew under a system which the Greeks would have regarded as despotism. The sciences of politics and ethics are largely redundant where kings or tyrants rule: what one finds in their place is statecraft. As throughout its long history Buddhism has lived predominantly under non-democratic political systems, perhaps it is not surprising that we do not find ethics and politics in its curriculum.

There are further reasons which might explain this discrepancy, such as that Buddhism is fundamentally a renouncer tradition which rejected social life and the systems of religious law that govern it (as exemplified in the Hindu *Dharmaśāstra* tradition, for example). Another possibility is that Buddhism simply developed expertise in other areas, notably psychology. Buddhist thinkers instinctively seek to explain ethical problems in terms of psychology, as if ethical concepts such as right and wrong could be equated with states of mind such as greed and hatred. While psychology can shed light on individual motivation, however, it can give no account of more abstract notions such as justice, a concept central to Greek ethical thought but rarely, if ever, discussed in Buddhist literature.

It is only since Buddhism arrived in the West that a nascent discipline of Buddhist ethics has developed. The beginning of the discipline can conveniently be dated to 1964 when Winston King, referring to "the almost total lack of contemporary material on Buddhist ethics in English," published his book *In the Hope of Nibbana*. King specified an interest in six aspects of Theravāda ethics and raised general questions about the role of ethics in Buddhism. In the 1970s a number of Sri Lankan scholars, notably Jayatilleke and Premasiri, began to pose more explicit theoretical questions. Adopting Western terminology, Jayatilleke asked of Buddhist ethics: "Is it egotistic or altruistic? Is it relativistic or absolutistic? Is it objective or subjective? Is it deontological or teleological? Is it naturalistic or non-naturalistic?"

Some writers feel that before raising questions of the above kind we must pause to reflect on the methodological problems which such comparisons raise. (Questions of this kind are discussed further in the entry on *Ethics, theories of*.)

The focus on Theravāda ethics continued with the publication in 1970 of the Ven. Hammalawa Saddhatissa's descriptive work *Buddhist Ethics*, which has remained in print for over thirty years. During this time only a small number of other books have appeared, despite an explosion of Western interest in Buddhism and a flood of publications on other aspects of Buddhist thought. There was no scholarly journal devoted to Buddhist ethics until the author of the present article and Charles S. Prebish founded the online *Journal of Buddhist Ethics* in 1994.

Socially engaged Buddhism

More or less coinciding with the birth of Buddhist ethics was the appearance of a related movement known as "socially engaged Buddhism." While Buddhist ethics is concerned with the specifics of individual conduct, engaged Buddhism focuses on larger questions of public policy such as social justice, poverty, politics and the environment. Clearly there is a connection, and it can be no coincidence that both these disciplines have arisen at roughly the same time as

Buddhism encounters the West. Perhaps we can see Buddhist ethics and engaged Buddhism as corresponding to two of the major branches of Western thought – ethics and politics – which for one reason or another never attained an autonomous status in the canon of Buddhist learning.

Four styles of Buddhist ethics

One modern Buddhist writer on engaged Buddhism – Christopher Queen – has suggested that there are four different "styles" of Buddhist ethics. The first is called "The Ethics of Discipline," in which the conduct caused by mental impurities fuelled by the "three poisons" of greed, hatred and delusion are combated by observing the five vows of the laity. Here the focus is on the individual Buddhist practitioner. Then there is "The Ethics of Virtue" in which the individual's relationship comes more clearly into focus by engaging in such practices as the *Brahmavihāra*s mentioned earlier, namely lovingkindness, compassion, sympathetic joy, and equanimity. This marks a shift from observing strict rules to following a more internally enforced ethical framework. Third, there is "The Ethics of Altruism" in which service to others predominates. Finally, there is the comprehensive "Ethics of Engagement" in which the three previous prescriptions for daily living are applied to the overall concern for a better society, and this means creating new social institutions and relationships. Such an approach involves, as Queen maintains, awareness, identification of the self and the world, and a profound call to action. (It will be seen that this fourfold model builds on the threefold classification of Mahāyāna ethics described above.) With such an expanded concept of morality in mind, a number of engaged Buddhist activists have worked to extend the traditional principles of morality into a carefully developed plan of Buddhist social ethics.

Summary

We might summarize the key points of this survey by saying that Buddhist moral teachings are thought to be grounded in the cosmic law of *Dharma* rather than commandments handed down by God. Buddhism holds that the requirements of this law have been revealed by enlightened teachers and can be understood by anyone who develops the necessary insight (*prajñā*). In leading a moral life a person becomes the embodiment of *Dharma*, and anyone who lives in this way and keeps the precepts can expect good *karmic* consequences such as happiness in this life and a good rebirth in the next. Buddhist moral teachings emphasize self-discipline (especially for those who have chosen the life of a monk or nun), generosity (*dāna*), non-violence (*ahiṃsā*) and compassion (*karuṇā*). Mahāyāna Buddhism places a special emphasis on service to others, which at times has led to a conflict between compassion and keeping the precepts. While the notion of skilful means and *tantric* teachings have both had some influence on Buddhist ethics, however, the mainstream view has remained that the precepts express requirements of *Dharma* and should not be contravened. Questions of a more theoretical nature still outstanding include whether we can legitimately make use of Western concepts to understand the nature of Buddhist ethics, and if so how it is to be classified.

See also: **Abortion; *Ahiṃsā*; Cloning; *Dharma*; Ennobling Truths/Realities; Moral discipline; Skillful Means; War and peace.**

DAMIEN KEOWN

ETHICS, THEORIES OF

In the course of Buddhist history there never arose a branch of learning concerned with the philosophical analysis of moral norms. On the whole there seems to be a remarkable lack of interest or curiosity about the concepts and principles which underlie Buddhist moral teachings. On very few occasions, for instance, do we see the Buddha moving to a discussion of theoretical questions about ethics, or responding to ethical and political conundrums of the kind put to Jesus by the Pharisees, such as whether it was right to pay taxes to the Romans (Matthew 22:17). The great Buddhist thinkers of the past left no legacy in the form of treatises on ethics. There is not even a word for "ethics" in the early Indian texts – the closest approximation to it is *śīla*, often translated as "morality," but closer in meaning to disciplined behavior or self-restraint. Speculation on Buddhist ethical theory is thus a recent development and so far has proceeded mainly by drawing comparisons with Western models.

Three of the most influential theories of ethics in the West have been deontology, utilitarianism and virtue ethics. Deontological ethics had as one of its leading exponents Immanuel Kant (1724–1804). This approach to ethics emphasizes notions of duty and obligation and is characterized by looking backwards for justification. For example, a deontologist might suggest that the reason I am morally obliged to give $5 to Tom is because I promised to do so when I borrowed the money from him yesterday. My promise thus gave rise to a moral obligation which I now have a duty to discharge. Deontological systems of ethics typically emphasize rules, commandments and precepts, which impose obligations we have a duty to fulfil. Utilitarianism, by contrast, associated with Jeremy Bentham (1748–1832) and John Stuart Mill (1806–73), seeks justification in the future through the good consequences that are expected to flow from the performance of an act. Utilitarians would justify the repayment of my debt by pointing to the happiness it will give Tom to have his money returned, the benefit of the maintenance of our friendship, the advantage of being able to ask Tom for another loan if the need arises, and the general good to society as a whole which flows from people keeping promises. They will weigh this up these consequences against the disadvantages of not repaying the loan – such as the loss of friendship, confidence and trust – and conclude that the former of these alternatives is better and hence the morally correct choice.

Virtue ethics offers something of a middle way between the other two and tends to look both to the past and to the future for justification. According to virtue ethics, of which Aristotle (384–322 BCE) was a chief exponent, what is of primary importance in ethics are neither pre-existing obligations nor pleasant outcomes, but the development of an individual's character so that he or she becomes habitually and spontaneously good. Virtue ethics seeks a transformation of the personality through the development of correct habits over the course of time so that negative patterns of behavior are gradually replaced with positive and beneficial ones. The way to act rightly, according to virtue ethics, is not simply to follow certain kinds of rules, nor seek pleasant consequences, but first and foremost to *be* or *become* a certain kind of person. As this transformation proceeds, the virtuous person may well find that his or her behavior spontaneously comes increasingly into line with conventional moral norms. In virtue ethics, however, in contrast to deontology, these norms are internalized rather than externally imposed. With respect to the consequences of moral conduct, it will not infrequently turn out that a person who adopts a consistent plan of life and lives according to a consciously chosen and integrated set of values will be the happier for it. There is here a similarity with utilitarianism which sees the moral life as geared to the production of happiness. Aristotle called the state of well-being which results from living rightly *eudaimonia*, a term often translated as "happiness" but which really means something like "thriving" or "flourishing." Virtue ethics thus proposes a path of self-transformation in which a person comes gradually to emulate certain ideal standards of behavior disclosed in the conduct of teachers or sages who have already progressed further than us towards the goal of human fulfillment. The behavior of these role-models provides a template on which to shape our own conduct: their positive qualities reveal the virtues we should emulate, and the actions they systematically avoid become codified in the form of precepts which serve to guide their followers.

Comparative ethics

Can any of the three theories just outlined help us understand the nature of Buddhist ethics? Before making comparisons we must pause to reflect on the methodological problems which such comparisons raise. Is it legitimate simply to compare Western ethics with Eastern ethics in a straightforward way, or are there cultural, historical and conceptual differences which might distort or invalidate such a comparison? It may be that the assumptions and presuppositions of Western thought are not compatible with those of Buddhism, and an insufficiently sensitive or nuanced comparison may simply force Buddhism into a Procrustean bed resulting in the neglect of important aspects of its teachings simply because they have no Western analogue. One might wonder, for example, whether Buddhism even fits the Western category of a "religion", and, if not, how it should be classified. Problems of this kind have exercised the minds of scholars working in the nascent field of comparative ethics in the last few decades, but as yet there is no agreed methodology for undertaking a comparative study.

Despite the possible pitfalls in drawing comparisons between East and West it seems important to make the attempt in order to gain some theoretical understanding of the structure of Buddhist ethics. It can be noted that scholars working in other branches of Buddhist philosophy have not hesitated to draw comparisons between Buddhist and Western thinkers and concepts. One difference is that in studying these branches of Buddhist thought, Western scholars were joining in a conversation among Buddhists themselves which had begun centuries ago. Where ethics is concerned, however, there is no ongoing discussion in which to participate and the conversation is only just beginning.

Virtue ethics

With the above caveats entered, I think it fair to say that the growing consensus among scholars is that Buddhist ethics bears a greater resemblance to virtue ethics than any other Western theory. There are sufficient points in common to speak at least of a "family resemblance" between the two systems. This is because Buddhism is first and foremost a path of self-transformation which seeks the elimination of negative states (vices) and their replacement by positive or wholesome ones (virtues). This is the way one becomes a Buddha. The transformation of the "man in the street" (*pṛthagjana*) into a Buddha comes about through the cultivation of particular virtues (paradigmatically wisdom and compassion) leading step by step to the goal of complete self-realization known as *nirvāṇa*. There are differences too: virtue ethics as developed in the West does not involve a belief in reincarnation or rebirth. It may, however, be thought to teach a "naturalized" theory of *karma* in which the good consequences of moral action become manifest in the present as opposed to future lives. Virtue, as Aristotle said, is its own reward, and the virtuous person (in the virtue ethics tradition this means a morally authentic and psychologically integrated agent, not someone who is merely sanctimonious or pious) can expect to lead a more fulfilled and rewarding life, thus reaping the good consequences of their virtue, so to speak, in real time.

Not all scholars would agree with the identification just made between Buddhism and virtue ethics. An alternative view, also worthy of serious consideration, is that Buddhist ethics cannot be accommodated entirely within any of the available Western theoretical models. We have already noticed that Buddhism has features in common with all the theories outlined so far. In common with deontology Buddhism has rules and precepts which approach the status of moral absolutes. Early sources tirelessly repeat that certain acts, such as taking life, are not to be done under any circumstances, and rules of this kind are typical of deontological ethics.

Perhaps an even closer similarity exists between Buddhism and utilitarianism. After the fashion of utilitarianism, many scriptural sources advise Buddhists to reflect deeply on the consequences of their moral choices. According to utilitarianism, right acts are those which bear good consequences, and in Buddhism the doctrine of *karma* teaches that there is a close relationship between good deeds and future happiness.

The Mahāyāna doctrine of Skilful Means also has a utilitarian aspect because it seems to prioritize successful outcomes over respect for the precepts. When coupled with an emphasis on compassion it may be thought to resemble the Christian utilitarian hybrid known as "situation ethics" promoted by Joseph Fletcher, in which the maximization of love in the world is the only standard of right and wrong. But again there are differences. While utilitarianism relies solely on consequences for moral justification, Buddhism also places great weight on intention (*cetanā*). Another way of stating the difference between the two systems is to say that whereas Buddhism teaches that acts have good consequences because they are good acts, utilitarianism holds that acts are good because they have good consequences.

See also: **Ethics; Precepts, lay; *Vinaya Piṭaka*.**

DAMIEN KEOWN

EUROPE, BUDDHISM IN

Around the turn of the twenty-first century, Buddhism in many European countries has become "in" as a fashionable, "cool," and trendy religion. Public interest in Buddhist meditation and top representatives like the Dalai Lama and Thich Nhat Hanh have made it well known that Buddhism has become established in the Occident. Many long-time practicing Buddhists strongly welcome this development though at the same time they are aware that Buddhist practices, concepts, and symbols have become commercialized and trivialized. Popularity and media interest have their price and some fear a sell-out of Buddhism's spirituality and liberating potential.

History

Intellectual and ethical interests of Westerners clearly dominated the first encounters between Buddhism and Europe. Asian immigrants with a Buddhist background did not arrive until the second half of the twentieth century. Fragmentary and distorted information about Buddhist customs, rites and concepts had trickled into Europe since the sixteenth century, brought by Jesuit missionaries and travelers to the Far East. Around 1800, as texts and descriptions about Indian religions became known in literate and academic circles in Europe, a glorifying enthusiasm for the East took hold. Following the studies of the French philologist Eugène Burnouf, who in 1844 presented a scientific survey of Buddhist history and doctrines for the first time, a boom of translations, studies and portrayals came about. The writings of Arthur Schopenhauer (1788–1860) stirred up a particular interest in Buddhist philosophy and ethics among artists, academics and intellectuals. The discovery of Buddhism was primarily treated as a textual object, being located in books, oriental libraries and academic institutes.

England, Germany, and France had been the countries foremost in studying and textualizing Buddhism. The same applies for the ensuing developments of adopting Buddhism and establishing societies. In 1903, Indologist Karl Seidenstücker (1876–1936) formed the Society for the Buddhist Mission in Germany in Leipzig. This and other, often only short-lived, societies praised Buddhism as the "religion of reason," the religion that rested on insight and knowledge alone. Lay followers, very rarely ordained clergy, had been instrumental in efforts to spread and establish Buddhism in Europe. After the disaster of World War I, Buddhists began to practice and not only to discuss the teachings. In the societies or "parishes" religious practices (such as worship, spiritual exercises, and devotional acts) took on. In Germany, Georg Grimm (1868–1945) and Paul Dahlke (1865–1928) founded their own parishes and circles, respectively. During the Nazi regime, thanks to their marginalized status, Buddhist activities were able to continue, albeit restricted to small, private circles, at times under political control. In London, Christmas Humphreys (1901–83) formed an eclectic Buddhist Theosophical Society in 1924, followed by the establishment of a branch of the Mahā Bodhi Society in 1926. It should not go unmentioned that in St. Petersburg, the tsarist Russian capital until 1917, migrant Buddhists from Kalmykia and Buryatia had built a Gelugpa temple and monastery in 1909–15. Following the Communist Revolution in 1917 and Stalin's dictatorship (1930s to 1953), Buddhist activities were banned in both western and eastern parts of Russia.

For the most part, lay followers, texts of the Pāli Canon, and small numbers characterized the first century of encounter between Europe and Buddhism (1850 to 1950). Philosophical, ethical and cognitive interests stood out clearly. From the 1950s onwards, this pattern had to give way successively to a plurality of Buddhist traditions. New Buddhist traditions were brought to Europe. Japanese Jōdo Shinshū (True Pure Land Teachings) came to Britain and Germany. Zen Buddhism became known through the writings of Daisetz T. Suzuki and Eugen Herrigel. Sōka Gakkai (Nichiren Buddhism) traveled with Japanese businessmen and students and they founded groups in Britain, France, Italy, Germany, and elsewhere. From the 1960s on, a multitude of new groups, societies and institutions were founded in most countries of Western Europe. Buddhism spread widely as attractive books and translations became readily available. Simultaneously, Asian teachers started visiting the incipient groups, lecturing and conducting courses on a regular basis. During the 1960s, a considerable change occurred in the way that members and interested people wanted to experience Buddhism both spiritually and physically. Meditation became very popular. Zen seminars took place in increasing numbers, with teachers coming from Japan to guide the newly formed Zen groups. Also, increasing number of young Europeans started to travel to India or Burma in search of "Indian spirituality" and religious guidance.

The Zen boom of the 1960s and 1970s was followed by a sharp rise of interest in

Tibetan Buddhism. Tibetan teachers (the *lamas*) had first come to England, France, and Switzerland in the late 1960s, and had established small centers. From the mid-1970s on, however, as further high-ranking *lamas* conducted preaching tours in Europe, Tibetan Buddhism took off. Many members of the protest movements and the counterculture of the late 1960s became fascinated by Tibetan Buddhist rituals, symbols, and the lives of the monks. In addition to the personal charisma of the numerous Tibetan teachers, the outstanding appearances of the fourteenth Dalai Lama inspired the Western followers. Since his first journey to Europe in 1973, the Dalai Lama has repeatedly visited centers all over Europe. For many, the Gelukpa monk is a living symbol and embodiment of deep spirituality, social engagement, and altruism. Within only two decades, converts to Tibetan Buddhism were able to found a multitude of centers and groups, at times outnumbering all other traditions in a country.

Tibetan Buddhism, Japanese, Korean and Vietnamese Zen, Nichiren and Pure Land Buddhism, and Theravāda Buddhism raised a steadily increasing interest in Western Europe. Also, organizations with no alignment to a specific tradition had their share; prominent among these are the Friends of the Western Buddhist Order. Within only three decades, the number of groups and centers multiplied. In many cities a plurality of some twenty to fifty Buddhist schools and traditions has come about. Also, Eastern European countries have witnessed a growing interest in Buddhism following the political changes since 1989. Numerous Buddhist groups, Tibetan and Zen groups in particular, have been founded in Poland, the Czech Republic, Hungary, and western parts of the Russian Federation. Visits by European and North American Buddhist teachers, as well as a longing for spiritual alternatives to the established Roman Catholic and Orthodox Churches, brought about a steady growth of Buddhism in Eastern Europe.

In addition to the strand of Western convert Buddhists, since the 1960s many Buddhists from Asian countries have come to Western Europe. In France, large communities of refugees from Vietnam, Laos, and Cambodia have emerged, especially in Paris. In Great Britain, the Netherlands, Germany and Switzerland, and other Western European nation-states, refugees, migrants and businessmen from Asian countries have found asylum or a working place. In the process of settling down, they founded religious and cultural institutions to preserve their identity and heritage. Such temples and pagodas have become enlarged as more financial resources and organizational skills were available. At times, these migrant institutions form representative and clearly visible places of Buddhism's presence in Europe, such as the Vietnamese pagodas in Hanover (Germany) and Lørenskog (Norway), the Thai Wat Srinagarindravaram in the canton Solothurn (Switzerland), and the Thai Buddhapadipa Temple in London.

The most recent establishment of Buddhism outside of Asia has come about in Israel, since the 1990s. Israel is the most accepting Near Eastern nation to consent to an establishment of Buddhist groups and centers, comparatively speaking. Vipassanā centers can be found in Bahrain and Oman, and a Zen center now functions in Oman. Though the encounter between Buddhism and Judaism is widely discussed in North America through the fact that quite a number of Jews have turned to Buddhism and became influential teachers – a line of conversion very prominent in Germany and Austria until 1933 – the settlement of Buddhism in Jewish Israel is little known. Buddhism came into Israel not via Asian migrants (who are allowed as temporary workers only), but rather through traveling teachers and ordained personnel of Western and Asian origin, respectively. Since the 1990s, various Buddhist traditions have been able to establish centers, numbering approximately twenty-five in 2005. The Dalai Lama visited Israel in 1994 and 2000, yet a Gelukpa group did not come into existence. The Tibetan Karma Kagyu tradition has been more successful in establishing a foothold through the visits of the dynamic (though contested) Ole Nydahl in the late 1990s. Zen Buddhism is represented by different traditions, also through traveling masters, such as Thich Nhat Hanh. There are also *Vipassanā* meditation groups. Thus far, Buddhist developments are recent and the overall number of practitioners and groups is small.

Current situation

As a result of the rapid developments from the 1970s on, a plurality of Buddhist schools and traditions has evolved in many European countries. The monolithic resonating notion of Buddhism in Europe conceals the internal diversity and far-ranging heterogeneity. Theravāda, Mahāyāna and Tibetan Buddhist traditions, along with non-aligned groups or centers, can be found in a single country, often even in one major city. Convert Buddhists have been eager to found numerous groups, centers, and retreat houses. In contrast, Asian or immigrant Buddhists established only a few institutions compared to their absolute numbers. A main reason is that the pattern and structure of religious life and practice differ considerably from those of convert Buddhists. Though numbers are difficult to state, in many European countries Buddhists of Asian origin – altogether totaling about 700,000 people – outnumber convert Buddhists by two and at times three to one. Informed guesses for the total Buddhist population of Europe range from one to two million. While the figures of immigrants and refugees from Asian countries can be stated more or less exactly for each country, the opposite applies for convert Buddhists and sympathizers. Despite the statistical difficulties, so far in no European country do Buddhists form more than 1 percent of the population.

Compared to North America, intra-Buddhist activities and platforms are strong and prominent in Europe. National umbrella organizations of Buddhist societies and centers exist in most countries. The awareness of Buddhists from different schools and traditions in becoming neighbors fostered such joint activities. Also, endeavors to secure state recognition of Buddhism as a public body have accelerated what has become called an "ecumenical" Buddhism (a self-designation). Official state recognition has been granted in Austria, Portugal and Italy thus far.

Overall, Buddhists in Europe look toward a promising future. They praise their unity in diversity and point to increasing intra-Buddhist activities. Buddhist organizations have become professional, Buddhist publishers have come into existence, and a second generation of well-trained Western teachers is maturing – those who have been students of Western, not Asian, teachers. The number of ordained personnel is growing, as is the number of full-time lay teachers. The media has discovered Buddhism and some spokespersons as worthwhile for cover stories. Typically, interest is directed towards the side of convert Buddhists and it is they who speak out and represent Buddhism in public. The gap between migrant and convert Buddhists is apparent in most countries and in their national umbrella organizations. Both strands face their own challenges though issues of leadership, language, gender, and the next generation are common. Notwithstanding the increased interest in things Buddhist, Buddhism will certainly remain a minority tradition in Europe during the twenty-first century. Buddhists hope, however, that being a Buddhist in Europe will be regarded less as a trendy affair or as a clinging to Asian roots, and rather as being an accepted dialogue partner with competence, among others, in spirituality, devotion, compassion and religious liberation.

See also: **Buddhism and Western lifestyle; Buddhism in the Western world; Ecumenicism and intra-Buddhist activities.**

MARTIN BAUMANN

EUTHANASIA

Attitudes towards euthanasia will be influenced to a large degree by the perspective one adopts on suicide. As suggested in the entry on suicide, one interpretation of the evidence in early Buddhist sources is that the Buddha regarded suicide as wrong, but did not to judge too harshly those who took their own lives in circumstances of great pain or distress.

By "euthanasia" here is meant intentionally causing the death of a patient by act or omission in the context of medical care, and we have in mind mainly cases of *voluntary* euthanasia, that is, when a mentally competent patient freely requests medical help in ending his or her life. Two principal modes of euthanasia are commonly distinguished, namely active and passive. Active euthanasia is the deliberate killing of a patient by an act, for example, by lethal injection. Passive euthanasia is the intentional causing of death by omission, for example, by not providing food, medicine, or some other requisite for life. Some commentators see this distinction as morally significant, whereas others do not. Given the importance Buddhism places on intention in moral evaluation, it would seem to matter little whether the fatal outcome is achieved by active or passive means. Note that on the definition in use here the borderline case of administering painkillers which may simultaneously hasten death does not count as euthanasia of either kind, because the doctor's intention in such circumstances is normally to kill the pain, not the patient.

There is no term synonymous with "euthanasia" in early Buddhist sources, nor is the morality of the practice discussed in a systematic way. Given that monks were active as medical practitioners, however, circumstances occasionally arose where the value of life was called into question. These circumstances are outlined in certain of the case histories preserved in the *Vinaya*. In the sixty or so cases reported under this rubric, about one third are concerned with deaths that occurred following medical intervention of one kind or another by monks. In some of these cases the death of a patient was thought desirable for "quality of life" reasons such as the avoidance of protracted terminal care (*Vinaya* 2.79) or to minimize the suffering of patients with serious disabilities. In those cases where there was an intention to bring about the death of the patient, the judgment was that the monks involved should be expelled from the *sangha*.

The rule which applies in such cases occurs in the *Vinaya* under the rubric of the third *pārājika*, the rule prohibiting the taking of human life. The circumstances in which the rule was introduced have a bearing on both suicide and euthanasia. The commentary to the third *pārājika* relates how as a result of practicing a specific form of meditation known as "contemplation of the impure," certain monks developed disgust and loathing for their bodies. So intense did this become that many proceeded to kill themselves, and lent assistance to one another in doing so. When the Buddha learned what had taken place he proclaimed the third *pārājika*, the monastic rule against taking human life, in the following words:

> Should any monk intentionally deprive a human being of life or look about so as to

> be his knife-bringer, or eulogise death, or incite [anyone] to death saying "My good man, what need have you of this evil, difficult life? Death would be better for you than life" – or who should deliberately and purposefully in various ways eulogise death or incite anyone to death: he is also one who is defeated, he is not in communion.
>
> (*Vinaya* 3.72)

The precept is directed specifically at those who lend assistance to others in ending their lives, what the precept calls acting as "knife-bringer." The above episode shows the Buddha directly intervening to prevent monks committing suicide with the assistance of others. Such a prohibition, as well as applying to euthanasia, would also seem to include "physician-assisted suicide," which is where the physician assists the patient who wishes to die by prescribing lethal drugs but crucially not administering them himself. The rule established by the Buddha in the case cited above is an ecclesiastical one which technically is binding only on monks and nuns. However, it may also be thought to express an underlying moral perspective in terms of which any intentional taking of life – even one's own – is seen as wrong.

Despite its opposition to both suicide and euthanasia Buddhism does not appear to hold that there is a moral obligation to preserve life at all costs. Recognizing the inevitability of death is a central tenet of Buddhist teachings. Death cannot be postponed for ever, and Buddhists are encouraged to be mindful and prepared for the evil hour when it comes. To seek to prolong life beyond its natural span by recourse to ever more elaborate technology when no cure or recovery is in sight is a denial of the reality of human mortality and would be seen as arising from delusion (*moha*) and excessive attachment (*tṛṣṇā*).

Following this line of reasoning, in terminal care situations there would be no need to go to extreme lengths to provide treatment where there is little or no prospect of recovery. Any course of treatment that is contemplated must be assessed against the background of the overall prognosis for recovery. Rather than embarking on a series of piecemeal treatments, none of which would produce a net improvement in the patient's overall condition, it would often be appropriate to reach the conclusion that the patient was beyond medical help and let events take their course. In such cases it is also justifiable to refuse to administer, or to withdraw, treatment that is either futile or too burdensome in the light of the overall prognosis.

See also: ***Ahiṃsā*; Ethics; Moral discipline; Suicide.**

DAMIEN KEOWN

F

FAMILY LIFE

Although the primary models for the most effective religious lifestyle in Buddhism are the celibate monastic or the committed *bodhisattva*, members of the laity have always constituted the great majority of Buddhist practitioners. As such, the interpersonal familial social relationships of the laity are especially important, and were occasionally the focus of Buddha's most pointed and specific instructions. Hammalawa Saddhatissa, in his classic volume *Buddhist Ethics*, notes that "The duties of children to their parents were stressed in India from a very early date." He goes on to point out that the "*Rukkhadhamma Jātaka* expressed the value of the solidarity of a family, using the simile of the trees of a forest; these are able to withstand the force of the wind whereas a solitary tree, however large, is not." Perhaps the most famous and important of Buddha's family-oriented sermons is the *Sigālovāda Sutta* of the *Dīgha Nikāya*, in which Buddha provides explicit instructions to the layman Sigāla, who is trying to honor his father's dying wish that he honor the six directions. Buddha likens worshiping the six directions to proper actions towards six different categories of persons. The six directions: east, south, west, north, nadir, and zenith, respectively correspond to parents, teachers, wife and children, friends and companions, servants and workpeople, and religious teachers and Brahmins. Before expounding on the specific requirements of proper social and familial relating, Buddha encourages Sigāla, generally, to keep the precepts, avoid acting from impulse, hatred, fear, or delusion.

The first relationship addressed by Buddha is that of parents and children. On the relationship between parents and children, Buddha's instructions are straightforward and explicit. As the *Sigālovāda Sutta* proclaims:

> In five ways a child should minister to his parents as the eastern quarter: once supported by them, I will now be their support; I will perform duties incumbent on them; I will keep up the lineage and

> tradition of my family; I will make myself worthy of my heritage; I will make alms offerings on their behalf after they are dead.
>
> In five ways parents thus ministered to, as the eastern quarter by their child, show their love for him: they restrain him from vice; they exhort him to virtue; they train him to a profession; they contract a suitable marriage for him; and in due time they hand over his inheritance.

These relational expectations are maintained throughout the Buddhist tradition, and especially so in East Asia, where filial piety plays an outstanding role as the foundational basis of ethical life. Kenneth Ch'en even notes that one Chinese rendering of the above text translates one of the child's duties as "not to disobey the commandments of the parents."

The *Sigālovāda Sutta* also offers a similar dyadic pattern of husband–wife relational expectations:

> In five ways should a wife as western quarter be ministered to by her husband: by respect, by courtesy, by faithfulness, by handing over authority to her; by providing her with adornment. In these five ways does the wife, ministered to by her husband as the western quarter, love him: her duties are well performed, by hospitality to the kin of both, by faithfulness, by watching over the goods he brings, and by skill and industry in discharging all her business.

Because, as noted above, most marriages in early Buddhism were arranged, Buddha occasionally offered advice to a man's daughters on how to conduct themselves in marriage. Peter Harvey summarizes one of these passages, from the *Aṅguttara Nikāya*, this way:

> (1) Regarding her husband, she gets up before him, retires after him, willingly does what he asks, is lovely in her ways and gentle in speech, not being one to anger him; (2) she honours all whom her husband respects, whether relative, monk or brahmin; (3) she is deft and nimble in her husband's home-crafts, such as weaving; (4) she watches over servants and workpeople with care and kindness; and (5) she looks after the wealth her husband brings home.

It should also be noted that divorce, although generally infrequent in early Buddhism, was permitted.

As we move into the modern world, and especially considering Buddhism's recent and continued globalization, the problem becomes significantly more complicated. For example, to my knowledge, only one popular Buddhist publication addresses the issue of Buddhist family life with regularity: *Turning Wheel: Journal of the Buddhist Peace Fellowship.* For many years the journal has run a regular "Family Practice Column." Between 1995 and 1997 it was written by Patrick McMahon from the Spirit Rock community, and since 1997 it has been (mostly) supervised by Mushim Ikeda-Nash. The column regularly discusses marriage, intimacy, death, and even cooking in Buddhist perspective. In addition, the journal occasionally devotes an entire issue to family-related matters. The Winter 1996 issue, for example, focused on "Family – What is It?" This compelling issue discussed the full range of Buddhist lifestyle issues in America, from Buddhist marriage to children returning home to care for ageing and dying parents. One article, "On Retreat for Twenty Years," even identified parenting as essential Buddhist practice. A number of years later – in Fall 1998 – the journal identified an entire issue as the "Back-to-School Issue," discussing the Buddhist transformation of education ... in the public schools, monastery, family, university, reform school, and the garden.

A careful search of the Internet also yields precious little in the way of family-oriented Buddhist sites. Ron Epstein has compiled a useful little reference file titled "Buddhism and Respect for Parents" with links to some classic Buddhist sources. Another offered a tidy list of materials under the rubric "Family *Dharma* Connections," and included "*Dharma* Lessons and Daily Practice," "Buddhist Holidays," "Children's Books," "Book Reviews," "Children's Videos," and "Mindful Divorce."

Nonetheless, as we can see from the above, all familial relationships, like interpersonal relationships throughout Buddhism, are steeped in the ethical values and standards typified by the four "divine abodes" (*brahmavihāras*) of lovingkindness (*maitrī*), compassion (*karuṇā*), joy (*muditā*), and equanimity (*upekṣā*). These qualities remain a powerful benchmark against which Buddhist family life throughout the world, including modern America, is invariably measured.

See also: **Holidays and observances; *Sangha*.**

CHARLES S. PREBISH

FAMOUS BUDDHISTS AND IDEAL TYPES

This essay presents an overview of extraordinary religious accomplishment by ideal individuals as they are interpreted within the schools and branches of the Buddhist tradition. The varieties of ideal practice, types of paths pursued, and stages of spiritual attainments range widely within these traditions. Similarly, the categories and classes of beings to whom extraordinary accomplishments are ascribed are complex and their distinguishing traits range widely. For more detailed discussions of particular ideal types, readers are referred to specific entries in this encyclopedia.

This essay explicates how Buddhist communities come to believe that ideal religious attributes are manifest in certain individuals. It begins with a consideration of the ways in which Buddhist communities provide the social and ethical contexts that foster and support the religious achievement of individuals. The discussion focuses next on ideal types and how their achievements are understood in Theravāda, Mahāyāna, and Vajrayāna Buddhism. Where appropriate, the discussion points to salient individuals and their sacred biographies to illustrate how ideal traits are embodied in the lives of these ideal individuals. Any discussion of famous Buddhist individuals and their religious achievements is necessarily selective at the cost of more, and perhaps better, examples and some of these constitute separate entries in the encyclopedia. It is also important to underscore that the religious truths about particular individual accomplishments are always subject to validation by teachers and to acceptance by communities. The selective focus on individual lives thus serves primarily to illustrate broader themes characteristic of ideal types and their practice of the path.

Throughout the Buddhist tradition, designations given to ideal types, such as Buddhas, *bodhisattvas* and *arhats*, refer to classes of religious achievement that reflect beliefs about ideal path action in pursuit of enlightenment. While there are a considerable number of such ideal types, interpretations of their relative ranking and worth vary from one tradition to another. For instance, Theravādins view the attainment of an *arhat* as the highest possible achievement during this dispensation, whereas *bodhisattvas* figure far less prominently in their beliefs and practices. By contrast, Mahāyāna and Vajrayāna tend to discount the status of *arhats* and *śrāvakas* as temporary and less desirable than the path of a *bodhisattva*. Divergent interpretations about ideal types are therefore common across the Buddhist traditions. Classificatory designations may also refer to a specific individual. For instance, the term "Buddha" is at once an honorific, a title that designates someone who achieved moral perfection without the aid of a teacher. It is a common designation for the Buddha of the current era, Siddhārtha Gautama Śākyamuni. The life of the Buddha is understood as modeling and illustrating the culmination of moral perfection. The dual uses of the term "Buddha," however, are not the only ways in which categories of ideal accomplishment and the biography of individuals are linked.

Another way to map ideal types onto individual lives is through the extensive use of sacred biography in the Buddhist tradition. The didactic illustration of ideal types in hagiographies is a hallmark of the Buddhist tradition. Stories about the life of the Buddha and *Jātaka* stories about his previous lives and individuals close to him are widely told throughout the Buddhist world. Much of the popularity of such stories about the lives of the Buddha, his disciples and his community appear to lie in the didactic exemplification of moral virtues. Their salience may also be attributed to the ways in which they allow Buddhists to relate to – and by extension participate in, the hagiographies of Buddhas, *bodhisattvas* and *arhats*. Sacred biographies of individual Buddhist saints thus offer models for the attainment of Buddhist virtues and create a mythic interpretative framework through which Buddhists participate in extraordinary religious accomplishments ascribed to ideal types.

Ideal communities

Enlightenment is generally an experience that characterizes the spiritual achievement of an individual rather than groups. Nevertheless, Buddhist communities are important contexts for the production of ideal types as they provide the moral, ethical, and material grounding for ideal types and their cultivation of the path of enlightenment. Buddhist communities play a significant role in the validation of moral achievements by Buddhist saints. Enlightenment is usually recognized by the individual's teachers or attributed by close disciples in the community. In the absence of a centralized ecclesiastical hierarchy, Buddhist communities are vital in the social process of validating the exemplars of ideal types living among them.

In most world religions, the validation of sacred biographies is a complex process. For instance, the Catholic Church relies on a lengthy process of compiling saintly biographies to determine whether individuals meet the criteria of sainthood. Upon the death of a potential candidate, biographical information is gathered from devotees in the inner circle, from the community, and from ecclesiastic superiors to determine what evidence can be adduced to make the case for sainthood. Did miracles occur in the life of the saint? Can other signs of divine intervention be identified? How does the life story of a particular individual resonate with the biographical patterns of previous saints? And, in the last analysis, does the ecclesiastical hierarchy of the papacy concur with the findings in the official biography compiled to ascertain an individual's saintly status?

By contrast, Buddhist communities tend to rely on the confirmation of teachers and on communal validation of individual path attainments. Although teachers may question disciples on matters of doctrine, textual knowledge, visionary experiences, and meditative attainments, becoming a Buddhist saint is not a process subject to the authority of a centralized institution that determines the standards by which such attainments are recognized. Frequently, it is the inner circle of disciples who attribute extraordinary attainments to their spiritual teacher. In most Buddhist communities, monastic rules of conduct prohibit monks from proclaiming their own enlightenment.

Buddhist communities are generally constituted by vows like taking refuge in the Triple Gem or the vow to seek *bodhisattva*hood. Communities are also affirmed by the fields of merit they generate through the practice of ritual and by the presence of some form or embodiment of enlightenment such as a Buddha relic or image. In other cases, vows to ascetic practice or vows to become a *bodhisattva* may constitute the basis of a community. In many ways, the early Buddhist community that existed during the Buddha's lifetime represents the ideal community in the eyes of the later tradition. Many in the community are said to have attained enlightenment, because ordained and lay followers had direct access to the Buddha's teaching. Great merit is gained from being in the presence of a Buddha. Many of the disciples were said to have attained moral perfection as well and merit was also generated by their proximity. Since that time, the dispensation and the *Dharma* are thought to have declined and the ideal conditions of the early community have deteriorated.

The *sangha*, the ordained monastic community, constitutes another kind of ideal community that offers its members the moral context and ethical conditions conducive to the attainment of enlightenment. Reginald Ray's exhaustive study of Buddhist saints examines diverse models of enlightenment among the domesticated, resident *sangha* and among forest monks, showing that multiple ideal types of enlightenment have been central to the development of the tradition in India from its earliest times. Monastic modes of practice are safeguarded by the rules of the *Vinaya*, the code of discipline that guides monastic practice. The *sangha* recognized a number of ways in which individual monks may follow the path to moral perfection. The ideal community of the *sangha* of the four quarters, the *catudissa sangha*, is constituted in the performance of monastic rituals. When a local chapter of monks carries out ritual acts within the consecrated boundaries of a *sīmā*, an ordination hall, it enacts rituals the ideal community of the *catudissa sangha* as each chapter acts in ritual contexts as part of an undivided monastic community.

Traditional Theravāda Buddhism also envisions an ideal, utopian community created through the performance of *paṭivedha sāsana*. This vision of social harmony emerges from the fields of merit created by large numbers of enlightened *arhats* within a polity. Their presence will also enhance the material circumstances of their lay supporters who will in turn be able to support more enlightened monks. The just rule of a *dhammarāja*, a king who rules in accordance with the *Dhamma*, is central to realizing the goals of *paṭivedha sāsana*.

Another example of an ideal Buddhist community may be found among the inner circle of disciples and close followers of a charismatic individual at the center of his cult community. Such communities often have millennial aspirations. Their social organization and the mobilization of resources tend to focus on celebrating the life of its central charismatic figure. In many ways, these communities see themselves as having already achieved the conditions of perfect social harmony derived from the field of merit this charismatic leader generates. Expectations of an imminent realization, such as the appearance of a future Buddha like Maitreya – or the limited time of an already enlightened being like the presence of Acharn Mun in Thailand – are typical features of such social groups. In the absence of such central charismatic sources, the communities tend to dissipate as hastily as they emerged.

The future Buddha Maitreya currently awaits his descent to the human realm in Tūṣita heaven. The cult of Maitreya became a model for later celestial *bodhisattvas* and celestial Buddhas. Each of these celestial beings was imagined to preside over distinct Buddha-fields in which they create ideal conditions for practicing the *Dharma*. Indian Mahāyāna traditions and later traditions envisioned Buddhas presiding over Buddha-fields that exist simultaneously in countless universes. The ideal communities that characterize the presence of celestial beings are represented most clearly in devotional Pure Land traditions like the Western paradise of the Buddha Amitābha, Sukhāvatī. *Bodhisattvas* are rewarded with rebirth into this realm for their devotion and chanting of Amitābha's name, the Buddha of infinite light.

Ideal communities in the Vajrayāna tradition are invoked in visions of divine beings that inhabit *maṇḍalas*, the macrocosmic abodes of Buddhas and *bodhisattvas*. In traditional Vajrayāna, the cosmic Buddha Mahāvairocana is seated at the center of the *maṇḍala*, while the Buddhas Akṣobhya, Ratnasambhava, Amitābha and Amoghasiddhi surround him in each cardinal direction. Another *maṇḍala* transformation is found in the tantric master Dārikapa's commentary on the *Heart Sūtra*. An important aspect of Tantric practice is the adept's realization that his or her body constitutes a microcosm of this divine space, encompassing a divine presence. Through rituals and visualization practices (*sādhana*), teachers (*gurus*) guide their initiated disciples in the creation of Buddha-worlds, embodying divine beings and enacting divine realms, while striving for the ultimate knowledge that emptiness (*śūnyatā*) is the ultimate reality and the seed (*tathāgatagarbha*) of enlightenment.

Buddhist communities generally create specific identities that define and locate them within the tradition. They also seek to create and emulate within their boundaries the presence of ideal types to demonstrate and illustrate their adherence to particular visions of enlightenment. Thus, particular visions of ideal communities tend to correspond with specific visions of individual ideal types.

Perfected individuals

Categories of ideal types abound in the Buddhist tradition. Much of the diversity in doctrine and practice among Buddhist schools can be described as divergent conceptions about the nature of enlightenment and about the ways to master the path to moral perfection. Beliefs about path action envision ideal types of individuals who either embarked upon the path to achieve Buddhist spiritual goals or who have already attained moral perfection. In the Theravāda tradition, that path is open only to human beings, while other branches of Buddhism, particularly those in East Asia, also entertain the option of *nirvāṇa* for other sentient beings. Regardless, mythical and historical individuals embody in their practice normative accomplishments and ideals. Recognizing an enlightened being proceeds almost always on the basis of one's teacher's pronouncement and communal validation. Self-proclamation is uncommon and falsely claiming enlightenment is considered a transgression in the monastic community. Notwithstanding such restrictions, ideal types may have, from time to time, used the power of suggestion to reveal their spiritual accomplishment to their communities. One of the ways in which this is accomplished and which is nearly universal to Buddhist cultures, is by emulating in one's own life significant and multivalent episodes reminiscent of the hagiography of ideal types. Experiences that are reminiscent of normative models are often seen as evidence for enlightenment that elicit communal validation. For instance, when the monk Acharn Mun left his community in northeastern Thailand and retreated to solitary meditation in the forest, his followers expected that he would seek extraordinary spiritual experiences. His hagiographies recount his forest retreat as the culmination of his spiritual path and credit him with enlightenment when he re-emerged to join society.

Western literature labels *arhats* as "saints." The Theravāda tradition and its precursors considered them to be permanently and fully enlightened as the path of an *arhat* follows, by definition, the model a preaching Buddha (*sammāsambuddha*) has set out for his community. Becoming an *arhat* is the culmination of this type of path action and constitutes the ultimate normative ideal in the early Buddhist community and later Theravādin communities.

In the Indian mainstream Buddhism, there was a general recognition that achieving moral perfection required countless lives, even for a Buddha. This expectation lessened the certainty of most ordinary sentient beings to attain *nirvāṇa* in the foreseeable future. However, those who transcend in their practice of meditation into the final stages of the path, each with its specific meditative stage (*dhyāna*), are considered the streamwinners (*srotāpanna*). Their karmic trajectory assures the attainment of enlightenment within just a few life-spans. Some traverse this "distance" within just one lifetime, while others toil longer along the way. The next stage is that of the once-returner (*sakadāgāmin*) who requires only one further rebirth before attaining moral perfection. Non-returners (*anāgāmin*) attain enlightenment after their departure from this life without rebirth in this world. Finally, those who are no longer tainted by the evils of lust, delusion, ignorance and becoming and have achieved insight, clairvoyance and magical powers (*iddhi*) transcend into the enlightenment of an *arhat*, the final stage of this path.

Outstanding among the *arhats* are the Buddha's great disciples who, with the exception of Ānanda, all achieved enlightenment during the Buddha's lifetime. Among this inner circle, each of the great disciples is known for having perfected a specific virtue in the mastery of his path. The Buddha's chief disciples, Sāriputta and Moggallāna, are frequently depicted in Buddhist iconography as standing to his left and right respectively. While Sāriputta was known for perfecting the virtue of insight, Moggallāna excelled in the use of magical powers (*iddhi*) derived from the higher stages of meditation. Upāli's virtue was memorizing the *Vinaya* and Ānada's distinction rested in his personal devotion to the Buddha. The Theravādin list of six virtues (*pāramī*) perfected in the mastery of the path was later extended to comprise ten virtues in the Mahāyāna tradition.

Theravāda

Becoming an *arhat* is the ideal goal in the Theravāda tradition and its precursors. It is also primarily a path most appropriately pursued by monks whose final spiritual attainment is sheltered by a community of ordained renouncers who uphold the *Vinaya*. The Theravādin tradition upholds that the monastic context is a necessary condition for *arhats* to maintain their existence. Laypeople, by contrast, may potentially attain enlightenment although their path may be more difficult than the practice of the path within the *sangha*. While the tradition maintains that the enlightenment of lay *arhats* is equal to the enlightenment of monks, it also maintains that lay *arhats* are unable to sustain their lives within society and must either join the *sangha* upon reaching enlightenment or become completely extinct.

In the Theravāda tradition, becoming an *arhat* is predominantly a monastic path. While most monks are not expected to become *arhats* and transcend the cycle of rebirth, there are at least two primary venues for the monastic pursuit of higher path stages. *Pariyatti* focuses on the preservation and study of Buddhist canonical texts and the commentarial literature that developed in the course of two millennia. This type of monastic practice requires a great deal of memorization as well as written transmission of textual practices. Contemporary Burma celebrates monks who have passed the requisite examinations that qualify them as having memorized the Pāli *Tipiṭaka* in its entirety. Their achievement of complete knowledge of the Buddha's word is understood to be one of the venues by which a monk becomes an *arhat*.

The other path is that of meditation. This practice (*paṭipatti*) centers on cultivating the higher states of meditation. In modern contexts, this practice is found at meditation monasteries, in forest hermitages or even in solitary forest practice. Examples of the former include the well-known Mahāsī meditation center in Rangoon and its affiliated monasteries throughout Burma and abroad. Traditionally, the practice of meditation was closely associated with the forest (*āraññavāsī*) tradition and with solitary practice of the path apart from the distractions that necessarily accompany monastic life in towns and cities. Ascetic practices (*dhūtaṅga*) like sleeping under the open sky, sleeping seated in meditation, observing a restricted diet, or wearing rags taken from charnel grounds, are the hallmark of the forest tradition. Debates have ensued from time to time between town-dwelling monasteries and forest hermitages concerning their respective faithfulness to the monastic rules of conduct (*Vinaya*). The charisma that resulted from the solitary practice of austerities (*dhūtaṅga*) in the forest often enhanced the reputation of forest monks. Some of these monks were eventually recognized as having attained moral perfection as a result of their practice of the path of meditation. Tambiah's 1984 study of the Thai forest tradition and the cult of amulets surrounding Acharn Mun explicates the production of charisma by forest saints and its appropriation by a modern, contemporary nation-state. In 1983 Carrithers presented biographies of monks in the Sinhalese forest tradition, while in 1997 Kamala chronicled the demise of the forest tradition in modern Thailand, where it was outlawed in the late twentieth century to counteract and contain ecological critiques to rampant deforestation in the service of modernization.

In contrast to Mahāyāna and Vajrayāna Buddhism, the concept of a future Buddha (*bodhisattva*) was not a predominant ideal type in Theravāda Buddhism. It carried rather specific and restricted meanings ascribed to certain individuals. In the classical kingdoms of Buddhist Southeast Asia, aspirations of laypeople to attain eventual enlightenment were made most evident in the royal titles kings assumed. While most kings shaped their political roles as *dhammarājas* who ruled in accordance with the Buddhist universal law, some added the title of a wheel-turner (*cakkavatti*), a designation that is attributed to the Buddha in his sacred biography. In traditional Theravāda cultures, there was a common expectation that righteous kings would attain enlightenment in some distant future. For instance, traditional Burmese culture employs a separate nomenclature when referring to kings, monks, the Buddha and his icons. The exalted beings at the apex of the social status hierarchy were addressed with the term *Hpaya*, and a royal prince may be referred to as a future buddha (*Hpayalaun*). However, when the Burmese king Bodawpaya (1782–1819) proclaimed himself to be the future Maitreya, his royal court turned against him. Even in dynastic contexts, validation by the community remains an essential aspect.

The traditional distinction between the abilities of laypeople and monks to become enlightened has been challenged by not only by the Mahāsāṃghika, but also by later traditional esoteric cults within Theravāda and by the profound transformations in Buddhist roles that characterizes Buddhist modernities. As Buddhist monastic authority weakened during colonial rule, Buddhist lay organizations, and especially lay meditation movements, assumed leadership within this vacuum of religious authority. More laypeople claimed to have reached the higher path stages. Alternatively, their meditation teachers and close community recognized them for attaining the higher meditative stages of the path (*jhāna*). For instance, the Burmese meditation teacher U Ba Khin was recognized as having reached enlightenment upon passing from this world. While lay *arhats* in the Theravāda tradition do not constitute a conventional ideal of lay practice, various lay voices among mediation movements have sought to lay claim to aspirations of *nibbāna* with growing frequency and perhaps even urgency in recent times.

Mahāyāna scholars locate the doctrinal schisms concerning the validity of ideal types during the second century after the Buddha's death, when at least two opposing viewpoints emerged from the debates among monastic communities. Precursors of the Theravāda, the Sthaviravāda, maintained that the spiritual attainments of *arhats* and *śrāvakas* were valid and permanent, while the great assembly, the Mahāsaṃghika, argued that the path of a *bodhisattva*, a Buddha-to-be, held greater rewards than either of the other two. Textual sources available to us were composed after the schism occurred and present sectarian retrospectives couched in a partisan rhetoric about divergent views on ideal path action and attainment. Some of the later Vajrayāna texts similarly claim that the path they advocate offers still greater rewards than can be realized within either the Theravāda or Mahāyāna traditions. Some of today's literature continues to employ pejorative terminology that identifies Theravāda lineages and their precursors with the Lesser Vehicle (Hīnayāna), while describing Mahāyāna schools and their precursors as belonging to the Greater Vehicle. Such discussions appropriate, rather than contextualize, textual sources and the partisan views of Buddhist history they portend. Quite apart from these rhetorical concerns, however, there is no doubt that Buddhist doctrinal thought underwent far-reaching innovations and transformations with the rise of Mahāyāna schools, practices and ideals. These entailed major changes in soteriology, doctrine and cosmology that came to define Mahāyāna Buddhism from the first century onward. While some Mahāyāna schools refer to a group of sixteen *arhats*, the *bodhisattva* path became the normative ideal of the tradition.

Eventual enlightenment as a Buddha, rather than enlightenment as an *arhat* who emulates the model of a Buddha, constitutes the culmination of the *bodhisattva* path. The *bodhisattva* path was conceived not only as a monastic ideal, but also as a path open to laypeople. A *bodhisattva* has taken a vow to practice the path leading Buddhahood and postpone its culminating achievement for the benefit of his community. Wisdom, compassion and service to the community are the distinguishing marks of the *bodhisattva* path. With time, *bodhisattvas* came to be seen as savior figures that choose active involvement in their communities, while Buddhas became increasingly removed from the temporal concerns of the community. In contrast to notions of successive Buddhas who formed part of a lineage of initially seven and later twenty-four Buddhas and linked successive dispensations, new Mahāyāna conceptions posited the existence of multiple Buddhas, Buddha worlds and *bodhisattvas* at any one time. Most significantly, the new Mahāyāna schools regarded Siddhārtha Gautama, the historical Buddha of the Theravāda tradition, as one of many manifestations of an eternal and unchanging

Dharma body. New Mahāyāna doctrinal developments inspired a reconceptualization of the three bodies of the Buddha, *trikāya*.

By the second century CE, a new and influential Mahāyāna *sūtra*, the *Lotus Sūtra*, charted the *bodhisattva*'s path as perfecting devotion and leading to enlightenment in the pure lands. The *Lotus Sūtra* depicted the divinity of celestial Buddhahood and glorified the celestial Buddha Amitābha who presided over the Western Pure Land of Bliss (Sukhāvatī). Although central to the narrative of the *Lotus Sūtra*, the Buddha Amitābha was one in a set of five celestial Buddhas, with one in the center and the others presiding over a Pure Land in each of the four cardinal directions. The central figure in the narrative is the celestial *bodhisattva* Avalokiteśvara, the *bodhisattva* of compassion. Avalokiteśvara eventually was recognized as the patron saint of Tibet. He is also known in Chinese as Guanyin and in Japanese as Kannon. Hōnen, the famous Japanese founder of Pure Land (*Jōdo*) Buddhism, is said to have attained enlightenment in 1175 and thereafter dedicated his remaining lifetime to chanting Amitābha's name. His disciple Shinran (1173–1263) claimed that this practice alone was sufficient for salvation in the Pure Land. The Pure Land paradigm advocated the *bodhisattva*'s path of devotion in order to gain access to a blissful eternal existence and the promise to fall back into unhappy states. The *bodhisattva*'s path in impure lands like the realm of ordinary human existence emphasizes wisdom and compassion to ameliorate suffering among ordinary human beings.

Vajrayāna

While it is difficult to locate the origins of tantric Buddhism or Vajrayāna, the Thunderbolt or Diamond Vehicle, there is textual evidence of its presence in South Asia by the fourth century CE. Indian tantric literature extols the supernatural powers achieved by the *mahāsiddhas*, the ideal type of attainment in the Vajrayāna tradition. *Mahāsiddhas* are yogic adepts whose *siddhi* signified their transcendent powers of Buddhahood. Tantric Buddhism in India comprises the famous Eighty-Four *Mahāsiddhas* that include adepts like Nāropa, the famous abbot of the ancient monastery at Nālandā in Bihār, northeast India. Nāropa's six yogas are among well-known Vajrayāna teachings in Bengal during the eleventh century, by which time *tantric* Buddhism had also been well established in Tibet. The tradition, however, credits Marpa (1012–96) and his disciple Milarepa with its transmission into Tibet.

In contrast to other tantric traditions, Buddhist *tantras* are ritual manuals and instructions the Buddha is said to have taught to select disciples. These secret teachings emphasize the yogic path of contemplation in which the *bodhisattva* transcends both emptiness (*śūnyatā*) and compassion (*karuṇā*) to experience nonduality. The *tantric* initiate is guided in the mastery of this path by a guru or teacher who gradually shares his esoteric knowledge through a complex series of guided experiences, visualizations and ritual practices. Central to *tantric* practice is the identification with and invocation of a divinity or Buddha whom the *guru* embodies.

In the Tibetan tradition, celestial *bodhisattvas* chose to manifest themselves in individuals who are recognized, by means of oracles and divination, as living embodiments of enlightened beings. Most famous among many lineages of divine incarnation that are recognized in the Tibetan Vajrayāna tradition is the incarnation of the *bodhisattva* Avalokiteśvara in the person of the Dalai Lama, Tibet's spiritual and temporal leader. The current Dalai Lama, His Holiness Tenzin Gyatso (b. 1935) is the fourteenth Dalai Lama in this lineage and was recognized as the incarnate *bodhisattva* of compassion at the age of two. He grew up and studied within the monastic setting of the Gelukpa lineage. He was enthroned as Tibet's spiritual and political leader in 1940 and completed his doctorate in Buddhist philosophy at the age of twenty-five after passing monastic examinations and public debates on doctrinal matters. Following the Chinese invasion in 1959, he left Tibet and dedicated himself to re-establishing Tibetan Buddhism in exile. Since 1960, he leads the Tibetan government in exile from Dharamsala, India. He received the Nobel Peace Prize in 1989 in recognition of his non-violent struggle to free Tibet from Chinese domination. His monastic lineage, the Gelukpa Order, is one of several prominent monastic traditions in this branch of Buddhism.

Other famous *lamas* include the Panchen Lama who ranks second in the Gelukpa Order; the Nyingma Lama, Tarthang Tulku (b. 1935) who established the Tibetan Nyingma Meditation Center in Berkeley, California; and Trungpa Rinpoche Vidyadhara Chögyam (1939–87) who initially followed a distinguished monastic career. He left the *sangha* and Tibet in 1963 to relocate to the United Kingdom and the United States where he founded multiple meditation centers.

One Buddha, many Buddhas

The conceptions of Buddhahood vary widely across the tradition. Buddhists imagined, personified, and also abstracted visions of complete enlightenment in forms they considered to be present and absent, human and divine, immersed in humanity and removed from it. The imaginarium of the Buddhist world is articulated in the kinds of Buddhas it entertains.

Silent Buddhas (*pratyekabuddha*) constitute a highly ambiguous category among ideal Buddhist types. They are known across the tradition and distinguish themselves from other Buddhas through the absence of a community. They achieved enlightenment without a teacher and do not teach to a community, and yet Ray (1994) notes the presence of *stūpas* dedicated to silent Buddhas in India.

By contrast, the preaching Buddha (*sammāsambuddha*) of the Theravādin community is seen as a historical figure, an exceptional human being who mastered the path to enlightenment without a teacher through countless rebirths. He exemplified the path to enlightenment and resolved to teach his community. In this manner, he set into motion the Wheel of the Universal Law. The legacy he left to his community comprised the body of his relics (*rūpakāya*) and of his teachings (*dhammakāya*).

In the Mahāyāna traditions, we find a conception of the Buddha that is increasingly removed from this world. The historic Siddhārtha Gautama Śākyamuni comes to be seen as a temporal manifestation of a *Dharma* that is eternal and unchanging. The idea of a single Buddha makes way to an infinite number of Buddhas. Some, like the Pure Land Buddha Amitābha, are divine, and eternal. They preside over Buddha-fields, far removed from the world of human beings whose path becomes one of devotion and meditation.

In the Vajrayāna tradition, enlightened beings like Buddhas and *bodhisattvas* chose to become incarnate in exalted human beings. At the same time, the tantric master (*guru*) has realized his or her potential for Buddhahood (*tathāgatagarbha*) and the initiate in their own manifestations of divine realities. The presence of Buddhahood is no longer limited in time or space, but is entirely a function of the individual's realization of enlightenment.

As Buddhism finds new articulations in modern contexts, new ideals of enlightenment have begun to emerge. For instance, the eminent Thai monk Buddhadasa, who many believe to have attained *arhat*hood himself, advocated a new type of path that simultaneously encompassed enlightenment and involvement with the world. Others developed his philosophical innovations within the framework of socially engaged Buddhism. In doing so, they invited new conceptions of ideal types that compass the modern Buddhist saint who is an ascetic removed from the world only to alleviate suffering through his or her exemplary involvement with the world. Other conceptions of ideal types are likely to develop as Buddhist communities become established across the globe. In this sense, Buddhism does not entertain a finite number of saints, neither the classifications of ideal types nor the individuals believed to have attained such distinctions. Regardless of their characteristics or the times and places of their appearance, their accomplishments will always be subject to the validation of Buddhist communities.

See also: **Acharn Mun; *Arahant*; *Bodhisattvas*; *Bodhisattva* career in the Theravāda; Buddha, bodies of; Disciples of the Buddha; Siddhārtha Gautama, life of.**

JULIANE SCHOBER

FAXIANG

Faxiang ("*Dharma*-characteristic") was a school of Chinese Buddhism that taught that all of reality is an evolution of a fundamental level of consciousness; because of this, it is often referred to as the *Weishi*, or "consciousness-only" school.

This school derives from pre-existing streams of Indian Mahāyāna thought based on the writings of Asaṅga and Vasubandhu which crystallized into the Indian Yogācāra (or Cittamātra or Vijñānavāda) school. This school held that there are within each individual's mind eight levels of consciousness: the five senses, the mind that gathers and processes their sensory data, a seventh mind that is the center of thought and will be called *manas*, and finally, an eighth level called the *ālayavijñāna* or storehouse-consciousness. This last contains "seeds," potentialities implanted by karmic acts which would give rise in the future to all perceptions and actions when conditions become right for their fruition. In unenlightened beings, these seeds came to maturity as mistaken perceptions of reality. A mistaken perception of an ongoing "self" arose because the seventh mind, perceiving the *ālayavijñāna*, mistook it for a stable, permanent entity, which it was not, as its set of "seeds" was always changing as new seeds were added and old ones exhausted their potential. This error gave rise to a further misapprehension as the mind artificially divided phenomena into "self" and "other," not realizing that all things were equally projections of the *ālayavijñāna*. Enlightenment came about when beings realized that all things were merely evolutions of the *ālayavijñāna*, that is, were "consciousness-only," thus eradicating any remaining notion of a separation of self and other, or that phenomena enjoyed any kind of independent existence.

Another feature of Faxiang thought was the analysis of the world into three levels of perception and existence, called the "three natures" (Ch. *san xing*). The first, representing objects of perception, was called the "other-powered nature" (Skt. *paratantra-svabhāva*, Ch. *da qi xing*) as they arose only in dependence upon causes and conditions external to themselves. The second was the "imaginary nature" (Skt. *parikalpita-svabhāva*, Ch. *suo zhi xing*), and represented things as mistakenly perceived by the unenlightened, that is, as independently existing things that are separate and distinct from the consciousness that perceives them. The third was called the "consummate nature" (Skt. *pariniṣpanna-svabhāva*, Ch. *cheng shi xing*), and represented things perceived correctly by an enlightened consciousness, that is, as evolutions of that consciousness with no distinction between subject and object.

A third feature of this school's teaching that was to have decisive consequence for its fortunes in China was the idea that there were certain beings, called *icchantikas*, who lacked any seeds of Buddhahood in their makeup. Having no potentiality for Buddhahood, they would never achieve it, and thus would be forced to suffer in *saṃsāra* for ever.

This school in China traces its origin to the Indian monk-translator Paramārtha (499–569), who arrived in China in 546 during a particularly turbulent period of history. He suffered much during his stay in China, having to move frequently to flee from political unrest and incurring the jealousy of rival monks. It is amazing that, despite these constant interruptions, he managed to translate sixty-four works in 278 fascicles before his death. Among the many texts that he brought and translated, he was best known for his translation and promotion of Asaṅga's *Mahāyānasaṃgraha* (*Compendium of the Mahāyāna*), a fundamental Indian Yogācāra text. Known in China by its short title *Shelun*, it became the basis for the Shelun school that studied it intensively.

Later, Yogācāra thought developed further under the great Chinese pilgrim and translator Xuanzang (602?–64), who traveled in India for seventeen years collecting scriptures and studying languages, and became the second of the great translators of Buddhist texts after Kumārajīva. Xuanzang left for India without government leave in 629, primarily to pursue an interest in Vijñānavāda or consciousness-only philosophy. He returned in 645, bringing many texts and gifts from famous Indian monasteries and kings. The emperor questioned him for many days about his travels, and offered him an official post, which Xuanzang refused. He dedicated the remainder of his life to translating the texts he brought back. Because his output was so extensive (seventy-three items in all) and of such high quality, and because he retranslated many texts that already existed in Chinese using new vocabulary of his own devising as translation equivalents, his activity is held to mark the transition from the "old translation" period (dominated by Kumārajīva's work) to the "new translation period." In addition to his translations, Xuanzang also published a travelogue called *The Record of Western Lands of the Great Tang [Dynasty]* (*Da Tang xi you ji*), which has proved an invaluable source for Indian history. This work also became the basis for the Chinese literary classic, *The Journey to the West*. As a result of his work, a new school consolidated around him, superseding the older Shelun school. However, the teaching of *icchantikas* did not suit the atmosphere of Chinese Buddhism, which took universal salvation as an object of faith, and so the school did not survive past the first generation of Xuanzang's disciples, the best-known of whom was Kuiji (632–82). The lack of compassion perceived in the doctrine of *icchantikas* was so unpopular that the system of doctrinal classification put forward by the Huayan school shortly after Xuanzang's passing placed Faxiang at the level of "elementary Mahāyāna," just one step above Hīnayāna.

While it may have lost pride of place, Faxiang thought never suffered complete rejection. Its seminal idea, that all reality is a projection of the mind, became a fundamental belief of all Chinese Buddhists, and "the triple world is mind-only" was a stock phrase repeated endlessly in classic texts. Interestingly, when Buddhism experienced a revival of interest among intellectual circles in the late nineteenth and early twentieth centuries, Faxiang studies came to the forefront once again. The revivers saw in Faxiang's subtle psychological analysis the best chance for harmonizing traditional Buddhist philosophy with the modern scientific viewpoint.

See also: **China, Buddhism in; Kumārajīva.**

CHARLES B. JONES

FEMINIST APPROACHES IN BUDDHISM

Early scholars of women in Buddhism such as Isaline Blew Horner tended to take an apologetic approach in regard to Buddhist attitudes towards women. Placed against a somewhat distorted presentation of women in Brāhmaṇical religion, Buddhism was presented as radically egalitarian at its inception. Evidence to the contrary was routinely attributed to later "monkish" redactors.

Recent scholarship is grounded in gender studies and feminist theory and tends to follow the pattern established by Western feminist scholarship: revelation of sexism and misogyny; the attempt to recover positive figures (male and female) for a "usable history" (one which can be used to reconstruct the tradition in more egalitarian or androgynous ways) and visions of a reconstructed tradition.

Karen Lang examines stock phrases in the *Therīgāthā* and *Therāgāthā*. She reveals that while the enlightened shared common values, there were distinctions between the manner in which men and women utilized stock phrases and images. Liz Wilson examines female images in post-Aśokan hagiographic literature with a focus on meditation. Particularly important are meditations on death and impermanence. These texts engender *saṃsāra* as female and nuns tended to take their own bodies as meditation subjects. In short, they internalized the view of women as symbolic of death and desire. Serinity Young also found an enduring association with women and death as well as anxiety about the stability of male sexuality. She argues that the integration of the symbolic female marked the physical exclusion of real women.

Miranda Shaw attempts an historical recovery of the central role of women in Indian Tantra. Studying a variety of texts, forty of them written by women, she argues that women were central figures in the development of Tantric ritual rather than being exploited as ritual implements or altars. It was the gradual appropriation of *Tantra* by celibate monks in Tibet that pushed egalitarian Tantra to the margins.

Ann Klein and Rita Gross are two scholars who have thoroughly examined feminism, its value to Buddhism and Buddhism's potential value for feminism. Klein approaches the matter from a philosophical perspective. She is careful to note that this is a "conversation" between the two, as the Tibetan context cannot simply be moved to a Western, twentieth-century context, nor is the psychological "journey" the same as the Buddhist path to enlightenment. Gross attempts a reconstruction of Buddhism along feminist lines. Given the scope of her material, an historical survey, analysis and reconstruction, it is not surprising that the work generated considerable discussion.

Dialogue among scholars regarding history, practice, theory and interpretation marks maturity in a field of study. Bernard Faure's recent study, *The Power of Denial*, engages several of the works mentioned previously and others in his study of the changes in Buddhist history and doctrine in Japan caused by gender and politics. This provides evidence that in the same way as contemporary practice and the use of social scientific method have become acceptable so too has the study of women in Buddhism and feminist method(s).

See also: **Women in Buddhism: an historical and textual overview.**

MAVIS L. FENN

FRANCO-BELGIAN SCHOOL OF BUDDHIST STUDIES

In the nomenclature utilized by Constantin Régamey in his 1951 volume *Der Buddhismus Indien*, the "Franco-Belgian" school of Buddhist Studies was the latest of the three schools of Buddhist Studies that developed prior to 1935 (the other two being the "Anglo-German" and "Leningrad" schools). The school was predominantly shaped by Louis de La Vallée Poussin, Jean Pryzluski, Sylvain Lévi, Paul Demiéville, Étienne Lamotte, and their literary heirs. About this school Régamey says,

> These scholars continue on the lines of the Russian school. They do not, however, slavishly follow Buddhist scholasticism, but use all the sources which are today available, supplementing their philological and philosophical analysis with the data of ethnology, sociology, etc. They have abandoned as fruitless the attempt to reconstruct a pure Buddhism, are convinced that Buddhism is as much the work of the Buddhists as of the Buddha himself, and find the entire wealth and the true face of this religion in the manifoldness of its aspects, and the multiplicity of its sects or schools.

In light of the above, it would be fair to say that the Franco-Belgian school is closer to the Buddhist Studies done today than either of the other above-mentioned schools. Its principles and multi-lingual approach clearly dominate contemporary European scholarship on Buddhism, as Russell Webb's research on the topic indicates, and guide the development of the North American school, as well as current research in Japan.

At the heart of this school is Louis de La Vallée Poussin. Belgian by birth, this seminal scholar was able to study Indology in Paris with such luminaries as Sylvain Lévi and Emile Senart, as well as with Hendrik Kern in Leyden. Although he is best remembered for his French translation of Vasubandhu's *Abhidharmakośa*, published between 1923 and 1931, as well as his 1930 translation of Xuanzang's *Vijñaptimātratāsiddhi*, the lifelong issue that fueled La Vallée Poussin's work was his struggle to understand the concept of *nirvāṇa*. About his passion to understand *nirvāṇa*, Guy Welbon notes, "From his publication of *Bouddhisme: Études et matériaux* in 1898 until his last article, 'Buddhica,' published posthumously in 1938, he devoted more time manuscripts to the meaning of the Buddhist *nirvāṇa* than had any European previously." To this quest, La Vallée Poussin brought his use of all the Buddhist canonical languages and his recognition that Pāli Buddhism represented only one aspect of the overall Buddhist tradition. Unfortunately, like his predecessor Senart, he also believed Buddhism to be one of the forms of Hinduism. As early as 1898, he stated this directly: "Buddhism is one of the forms of Hinduism, at every point comparable to the popular or learned religions organized under the aegis of the Brahmins and the patronage of the Vedas." Forty years later, he said the same thing: "In short, Buddhism is only the 'buddhized' aspect of contemporaneous Hinduism." He even saw the *Vinaya* tradition as having emerged from Hinduism: "From an incoherent jumble of practices collected all together in the tradition of the yoga have emerged the *Vinayas* and the customs of the different schools." Despite the above, his monumental genius shaped the Buddhist Studies of his time.

Although only six years older than La Vallée Poussin, Sylvain Lévi (1863–1935), as noted above, was one of his teachers in Paris. He was a brilliant Sanskritist, who also knew Chinese, Tibetan, and Kuchean. Some scholars suggest his greatest accomplishment was the discovery of the Sanskrit text of the *Mahāyānāsūtrālaṅkāra*, which he edited and translated into French in 1907. Almost twenty years later, he published the *Viṃśatikā* and *Triṃśikā* along with their commentaries. He also worked on the *Buddhacarita*, Chinese translations of the *Milindapañha*, and the *Divyāvadāna*. He was a frequent collaborator of other scholars, having done important work with Stcherbatsky on Yaśomitra's *Sphuṭārtha*; with S. Yamaguchi, on the *Mādhyantavibhāga-ṭīkā*; and with Junjirō Takakusu, which resulted in the publication (between 1929 and 1931) of three fascicles of the encyclopedic dictionary of Chinese Buddhist terms known as *Hōbōgirin*. Lévi traveled throughout his career, having visited Nepal as early as 1905, India, Japan, Korea, Siberia, and Russia. Like La Vallée Poussin, his work helped spawn much interest in the Yogācāra-Vijñānavāda tradition.

Perhaps less well known than Lévi and La Vallée Poussin was Paul Demiéville (1894–1979). His biography by Gisèle de Jong, which was checked by Demiéville himself, appears in *Choix d'Études bouddhiques* and in *Choix d'Études sinologiques*. Although born in Switzerland, he became a French citizen in 1931. Between 1931 and 1945, he was a professor at the École des Langues Orientales, and between 1946 and 1964, at the Collège de France. He served as redactor-in-chief of *Hōbōgirin*, and as either director or co-director of the esteemed journal *T'oung Pao*, where he published many of his buddhological articles. His complete bibliography appears in the latter-named journal, but he is best known for his 1952 volume *Le Concile de Lhasa* and his 1951 article in *T'oung Pao*, "A propos du Concile de Vaiśālī." His obituary in the 1979 *Journal of the International Association of Buddhist Studies* refers to him not only as a sinologist and a buddhologist, but also as a "Tun-huang-ologist."

Sharing in Demiéville's interest in early Buddhist history, and especially its various councils was Jean Przyluski (1885–1944). Also a student of Sylvain Lévi, he translated many texts from Chinese that concerned northwest India. Interested particularly in geographical matters, particularly in how they related to the development of the various early Buddhist schools, he also studied Buddha's *parinirvāṇa* and the first Buddhist council of Rājagṛha. His classic book, *Le Concile de Rājagṛha*, was published in Paris between 1926 and 1928. Along with Marcel Lalou, he created the well-known *Bibliographie Bouddhique*, cataloging Buddhist publication between 1928 and 1958.

The best-known, and perhaps greatest, of this school's generation of buddhological scholars is Étienne Lamotte. In his long life (1903–83), Lamotte not only served as a professor at the Catholic University of Louvain, but also attained the rank of monseigneur in the Roman Catholic Church. He was an Honorary Fellow of the International Association of Buddhist Studies and the Royal Asiatic Society of Great Britain, and an Honorary Member of the École Française d'Extrême-Orient and the Société Asiatique. Simply put, it was Lamotte's erudition and brilliance that typified, and brought to fruition, the work of his teacher Louis de La Vallée Poussin. All scholars of Buddhist Studies read the entirety of his panoramic *Histoire du bouddhisme Indian, des origins à l'ère Śaka*, either in French or Sara Boin-Webb's English translation. He is sometimes referred to as "the greatest authority on Buddhism in the Western world."

The legacy of the above buddhological figures for the current, and future, generation of Buddhist Studies scholars cannot be minimized. Nor can the legacy of the Franco-Belgian school of Buddhist Studies be considered as anything less than formative for the entire discipline. For this school of Buddhist Studies, the view of the Buddhist tradition throughout Asia was utterly expansive. Their approach to Buddhist Studies training involved, in the first place, a comprehensive study of all the Buddhist canonical languages. Unfortunately, it suggests a tradition of philological erudition that is rarely seen today, and especially so in North America. Because graduate education has been so very expensive, students are no longer able to spend sufficient time in the university to master Sanskrit, Pāli, Chinese, Tibetan, and Japanese. As a result, it has become quite normal for students to take the "Sanskrit and ... " approach, learning Sanskrit as the *lingua franca* of their training, and then learning the one additional language that reflects their area of interest. Additionally, as the number of scholars with Ph.D. degrees in Buddhist Studies proliferates in North America and throughout the world, the competition for a declining number of jobs becomes so keen that individuals entering the academic world eschew the kind of additional training advocated in the Franco-Belgian school in favor of joining the job market as quickly as possible in order to pursue the academic goal of tenure.

Despite the above, the advocates of the Franco-Belgian school can still be seen throughout Europe. In France, the recently deceased André Bareau epitomized the school's approach in his brilliant, encyclopedic work on early Indian Buddhist history and sectarianism. In Belgium, the tradition continued to be maintained by Charles Willemen. In Italy, the school's approach continues through the Instituto Italiano per il Medio ed Estremo Oriente, begun in 1933 by Giuseppe Tucci. In Switzerland, the University of Lausanne, under Tom Tillemans, has a thriving program. Scandinavian countries, including the University of Oslo and the University of Stockholm, have also preserved the tradition of this school's Buddhology. In the Netherlands, before her recent death, Ria Kloppenborg maintained Buddhist Studies at Utrecht. These are only a few of the many remnants of the Franco-Belgian school of Buddhology's lineages in Europe. As Edward Conze said, "The principles of the Franco-Belgian school have now been universally adopted by all scholars working in the field, whatever country they may live in." Although published many years ago, this statement remains true today.

See also: **Academic study of Buddhism; Bareau, André; Lamotte, Étienne; Poussin, Louis de La Vallée.**

CHARLES S. PREBISH

FULL MOON DAY AND OTHER CALENDRICAL OBSERVANCES

Long before the Buddha, South Asians already considered the "sabbaths" (*upoṣadha*) which commence the forty-eight lunar weeks (consisting of six to nine days each) – namely the days of new moon (typically the first day of the lunar month), waxing moon, full moon (typically the fifteenth day) and waning moon – to be especially auspicious for religious activity. Early in the Buddha's career he allowed his monks to participate in silent attendance amidst the crowds that would converge on such days for Vedic sacrifices and chanting, or debates about the various *śrāmaṇic* teachings. This rule was later amended to permit them to chant the *Prātimokṣa* together there, an important ritual that has continued into the present. *Upoṣadha* also emerged as a key focus of lay Buddhist practice during the Buddha's own lifetime; these sabbaths remain the principle Theravāda occasions for adoption of the quasi-monastic eight precepts (*aṣṭāṅgaśīla*) and commitment of the entire day to *Dharma* practice.

Already transformed into special occasions for large Buddhist gatherings by *Prātimokṣa* and *aṣṭāṅgaśīla*, the significance of *upoṣadha* days was enhanced by famous events in the Buddha's life and in the history of the *sangha* which from an early date came to cluster about them, especially the twelve full moon days. Most important among these was certainly the full moon day of the month called *Vaiśākha*, corresponding to April–May, under which the Buddha was believed to have been born, enlightened, and to have passed into *nirvāṇa*. Theravāda Buddhists continue to celebrate the day (Sinh. *Wesak*) with great pageantry in Sri Lanka and Southeast Asia. Chinese celebrations of the Buddha's birthday with joyous processions on the eighth day of the second lunar month perhaps echo the ancient Indian schematization. In Japan the three events of *Vaiśākha* are celebrated separately as *Nehan-e* (day of final passing) on the fifteenth day of February or March, when some Buddhists venerate a painting of the event and chant the Buddha's last sermon; *Kanbutsu-e, Kōtan-e*, or *Busshō-e* (Buddha's birthday), celebrated on the eighth day of April and also known as the festival of flowers (*Hanamatsuri*); and the day of enlightenment (*Jōdo-e*), 8 December, which is remembered in solemn religious services and, among Zen Buddhists, a week-long retreat called *rōhatsu daisesshin* entailing intensive simulation of the Buddha's path to *nirvāṇa*.

But all the full moon days boast such layers of association with famous events from Buddhist history believed to have occurred on them, and serve as landmarks of monthly and annual ritual cycles such as the beginning and end of the *varṣa* retreat or the Great Prayer Festival at Lhasa, the fortnightly *Prātimokṣa* recitation, the beginning of pilgrimage or ordination "seasons," and annual obligations to deities. Their special status also made them logical venues for the dedication of newly constructed or restored Buddhist monuments, special *pūjās, parittas* and processions, and temple fund-raising festivals. In the former British colonies of Ceylon and Burma the status of the full moon day became a contentious political issue, and eventually resulted in their protection with blue laws and government holidays paralleling Sundays.

Yet the sorts of monthly and annual Buddhist festivals and other religious practices thus described, whether held on *upoṣadha* days or not, have constituted only part of any individual Buddhist's annual ritual cycle. In addition to annual festivals of the national sort, lived ritual calendars also generally include periodic rites for the dead, anniversaries of the birth or death of revered monks and nuns, and any individual's periodic religious practice such as daily *pūjā* or recitation of the five precepts, monthly adoption of the *aṣṭāṅgaśīla* (or in the case of monks and nuns, *Prātimokṣa*), periodic almsgiving, and pilgrimage practices.

See also: **Holidays and observances; Monastic rituals; *Sangha*; South and Southeast Asia, Buddhism in; *Vinaya Piṭaka*; Worship.**

JONATHAN S. WALTERS

FUNERALS AND OTHER LIFE-CYCLE RITUALS

Life-cycle rituals celebrate and often sacralize the processes of birth and becoming in most world religions but are conspicuously underdeveloped in Buddhism, which has stressed instead aversion to these processes. Celebration of birth, the beginnings of education, puberty, marriage and other major life transitions certainly occur in Buddhist cultures, but they tend to draw heavily on other (especially indigenous/pre-Buddhist) religious traditions and/or to lack the participation of Buddhist clergy; in some instances, such as the Sinhala Buddhist marriage ritual and the American Buddhist conversion ceremony, they are distinctly modern. Two important exceptions to this generalization are the monastic life, which is marked with a series of rites of passage, and funerals, which Buddhists everywhere have seized on as an opportunity for proclaiming the *Dharma* and helping the departed in the next life. After discussing Buddhist funerals this article explores how Buddhism has been partially incorporated into pre-funerary life-cycle rituals, too.

Buddhist funerals

Funerals are so famously Buddhist that especially in East Asia even non-Buddhists turn to the religion for them; some Japanese monks are considered impure because of their proximity to funerals, cremations, and cemeteries. Monastic roles as funerary experts may originate in the cemetery meditations and shroud-wcaring practiccs of thc carly Buddhist community, symbolically continued today in the practice of presenting Theravāda monks with robes that have been kept on coffins, which in turn reflect basic Buddhist understandings of death's inevitability.

Monks and nuns may play a role before, during and after cremation (the dominant method) or burial of the dead. While a body lies in state they may chant blessings or preach sermons, typically large community events with various associated rites (such as water-pouring, corpse anointing, corpse viewing, charity and merit-transference) included according to local custom, financial ability, and so forth. Similar chanting and/or preaching may accompany cremation itself, although the level of participation of monks and nuns in this part of funereal culture varies considerably by region (Japanese monks may take part in the actual cremation; Sinhalese monks typically avoid the pyre altogether). All traditions celebrate post-funereal rites at specified intervals during which chanting, preaching and/or charity provided in the deceased's name is believed to provide him or her assistance in the afterlife, symbolized in the provision of food for the dead (e.g., the Thai *Bun Khaw Saak*). Post-cremation rites are especially pronounced in the case of important personages such as emperors and temple patrons, but all the dead can be assisted as is evident in the Japanese "All Souls' Day" (*Obon*) and related festivals of the dead such as the Hungry Ghost Festival (Ch. *Da Jui*) celebrated in China, Malaysia, Singapore and Vietnam. Tibetans have developed the most elaborate Buddhist ritual techniques for assisting a being through dying and death.

Not surprisingly, Buddhists have been especially concerned to properly conduct the funerals of monks, nuns and parallel *religieux*. Monastic funerals typically include especially large gatherings of laypeople and clergy, ornate pyres shaped like *stūpas* or temples, and special practices for naming, viewing, cremating, and later enshrining and even worshiping remains, especially of those deemed particularly advanced. Like their lay counterparts, the monastic deceased are likewise remembered and served in post-cremation rites on death anniversaries. In addition to local incumbents the death anniversaries of founders and saints are observed with rites and sometimes festivals in various sectarian temples, and Chinese monasteries traditionally contained ancestor halls (*zu tang*) designed for the worship of past abbots on the first and fifteenth days of the lunar month.

Other life-cycle rites

Despite doctrinal aversion to other life-cycle rituals, in practice they have often been accommodated, and Buddhism has *de facto* become part of them. Thus protective rituals and/or worship at particular

Figure 21 Villagers in Zanskar celebrating the birth of a child.

Buddhist temples or sacred sites are widely part of pre-natal and post-natal custom throughout the Buddhist world (See Figure 21). Buddhist blessings and/or the presence of Buddhist monks might likewise lend a Buddhist overlay to traditional and modern life-cycle rites from first reading of the alphabet to high school or university graduation. In Thailand, temporary ordinations function as a male puberty rite, and monastic blessings regularly precede weddings. Elsewhere, especially in recent times, monks and Buddhist symbols have come to play an even greater role in marriage rituals, sometimes even performing them. Retirement from active life might also become a focus of Buddhist ritual if, as is often the case, it coincides with ordination or adoption of the eight or ten precepts.

See also: **Ethics; Rituals and practices; Tibet, Buddhism in; *Stūpa*.**

JONATHAN S. WALTERS

G

GANDHĀRA

Actual images of the Buddha seem to first appear sometime around the turn of the first millennium – thus a century or two after the great *stūpas* were first constructed – during the reign of the Kuṣāṇa dynasty, specifically during the rule of Kaniṣka. Although it is not certain where the first images were actually made – and it is possible that earlier images were made, but made of perishable material such as wood that has not survived – some of the earliest images of the Buddha come from what is now western India, Pakistan, and Afghanistan (a broad region known as Gandhāra). This area had close political and cultural ties to the Bactrian region to the west (modern Tadzhikistan), an area that was, since the time of Alexander, made up of a rich cultural mix – Persians, Greeks, Parthians, Chinese, Indians, and Scythians all lived there. The Buddhist art from this region is sometimes referred to as Graeco-Roman, or Hellenistic, because many of the images are strikingly similar to those produced in Greece and Rome during the same period, and it seems likely that Buddhist artisans working in these areas were influenced by these images. However, the idea that the actual representation of the Buddha derived from the Graeco-Roman world, put forth by several prominent early Orientalists, in no small part because this thesis emphasized the dominance of Western culture – is an interpretative stretch that has been largely discredited. Indeed, Buddha images also began to appear at about the same time in the Swat valley in what is now Pakistan and to the south in Mathurā.

Typical Buddha images from the Bactro-Gandhāran region produced during the Kuṣāṇa period depict him standing or seated, sometimes preaching, sometimes meditating, displaying what would become standard hand gestures (*mudrās*): the *abhaya mudrā* (no fear), *dharmacakra mudrā* (teaching), and *dhyāna mudrā* (meditation). He is typically dressed as a monk – wearing a simple robe with no other adornments – with an *uṣṇīṣa* on the top of his head and with markedly elongated earlobes (a sign of his former royal status). In some of these images the Buddha is depicted along with his followers, particularly in scenes portraying him teaching. In one of the most famous of the images from this period, now in the Lahore Museum, Śākyamuni is depicted as a strikingly gaunt meditating figure, with sunken stomach and cheeks and dramatically protruding ribs, an image that conveys the extreme austerities he experienced prior to his enlightenment. Also common in both the Bactro-Gandhāra tradition are images of the first sermon delivered at Sārnāth – often including his first disciples – and images of his *parinirvāṇa*; the defeat of Māra is also a common motif.

Another important development during this period is the emergence of images of *bodhisattvas*, particularly Maitreya and Avalokiteśvara, reflecting the emergence of various early Mahāyāna schools in the region during the first centuries of the Common Era. Stylistically these images are often quite different than the Buddha images produced in this period. The *bodhisattvas* are often depicted as royal figures, wearing only partial robes – similar to a dhoti, with a bare torso – and adorned with armbands, necklaces, earrings, and elaborate headdresses, as well as various *lakṣaṇas* (bodily marks). Significant in this regard is the relative paucity of images presenting scenes from the *Jātaka* tales; consistent with basic Mahāyāna doctrine – and reflected in such texts biographical texts as the *Lalitavistara* and *Divyāvadāna* – the emphasis in Bacto-Gandhāran art is predominantly on Śākyamuni himself or on the various *bodhisattvas*, not on the prior lives of the Buddha.

A further development in the art of this period that warrants mention here is the representation of various figures most typically associated with the Pure Land schools, reflective of certain doctrinal innovations particular to the Kuṣāṇa milieu. In one such image, now in the Lahore Museum, Amitābha (or Amitāyus) is depicted displaying the *dharmacakra mudrā*, teaching his disciples in Sukhāvatī (the western celestial pure land over which he presides).

See also: **Art, Buddhist; Sacred places.**

Jacob N. Kinnard

GELUK

Tsong Khapa (Tsong kha pa bLo bzang grags pa, 1357–1419), the founder of the Gelukpa (dGe lugs pa) Order, was one of the great scholars and religious reformers of Tibetan Buddhism. His writings indicate a profound concern with what he perceived as tendencies toward laxness in monastic discipline among his contemporaries, and the Gelukpa ("System of Virtue") Order emphasizes intensive study, meditative practice, and strict adherence to the rules of the *Vinaya*. Tsong Khapa considered himself to be reviving the Kadampa (bKa' gdams pa) tradition, founded by Atīśa (982–1054) and his Tibetan disciple Dromdön. Like Atīśa, Tsong Khapa considered cenobitic monasticism to be the most effective path for the vast majority of Buddhist practitioners, but he also believed that the sexual yogas of highest yoga *tantra* (*rnal 'byor bla na med rgyud, anuttara-yoga-tantra*) are essential for the final attainment of Buddhahood.

In 1410, Tsong Khapa founded Ganden (dGa' ldan) Monastery, which remains one of the major institutions of the order. Partially destroyed by the Chinese invasion of the 1950s, it has been rebuilt in south India. The "Throne Holder of Ganden" (*dGa' ldan khri rin po che*) is the head of the Geluk Order. Following Tsong Khapa's paradigm, modern Gelukpa monasteries have a program of study that can take over thirty years to complete, which culminates in the *geshe* (*dge bshes*, literally "spiritual guide") degree for successful candidates. The core of this training program is oral philosophical debate based on standard textbooks (*yig cha*), Indian Buddhist scriptures, and the writings of Tsong Khapa and his main disciples.

Initially a small reformist sect, the Gelukpas became the dominant Order of Tibetan Buddhism during the lifetime of the fifth Dalai Lama, Ngawang Losang Gyatso (Ngag dbang blo bzang rgya mtsho, 1617–82), who gained political control over most of the Tibetan plateau with the help of Mongol backers. From that time until the Chinese invasion in the 1950s, the Dalai Lamas were rulers of large areas of the Tibetan plateau, but in 1959 the fourteenth Dalai Lama, Tenzin Gyatso (1935–) fled into exile and established a headquarters in Dharamsala, India.

Tsong Khapa's main works on Buddhist philosophy and practice are the *Great Exposition of the Stages of the Path* (*Lam rim chen mo*) and the *Great Exposition of Secret Mantra* (*sNgags rim chen mo*), which respectively discuss the standard Mahāyāna path of the *bodhisattva* and the esoteric practices of *tantra*. Tsong Khapa follows the traditional Indian Mahāyāna gradualist paradigm, which begins with the notion that ordinary beings are afflicted by adventitious defilements, which are progressively eliminated through the practice of virtue and cultivation of good qualities. This process involves a combination of intensive study and long-term meditative practice, which requires many lifetimes for most practitioners. Tsong Khapa also emphasizes, however, the notion that the practices of highest yoga *tantra* can greatly shorten the time required for the attainment of awakening and that advanced practitioners may reach the final stage of the path in as little as one human lifetime. One of Tsong Khapa's most important notions is the "three principal aspects of the path" (*lam gtso bo rnam gsum*): (1) the intention definitely to leave cyclic existence; (2) generating the intention to attain awakening in order to benefit other sentient beings; and (3) the correct view of emptiness. These constitute the necessary basis for practice according to the Geluk system.

See also: **Tibet, Buddhism in; Vajrayāna Buddhism.**

JOHN POWERS

GENZE RIYAKU – WORLDLY BENEFITS

Genze riyaku, lit. "benefits in the present world," is a pervasive aspect of religious (including Buddhist) activity in Japan. It refers to the acquisition of "practical benefits" in this present life (not the next life, after death), both traditional and modern – relief from disease, entrance to the university of one's choice, safe childbirth, success in business, protection from evil spirits, safe travels and avoidance of traffic accidents, maintaining a harmonious family life, peace of mind, and so forth – through religious activities such as prayer, the purchase of amulets, chanting or copying the Buddhist scriptures, performance of rituals, and so forth. A modern Japanese dictionary defines it as "the belief or faith that blessings from the gods and buddhas will be provided in this life, based on a worldview that is focused on the present world."

Throughout Japanese history, Buddhist figures and institutions have been called upon to provide practical benefits through the performance of Buddhist ceremonies: for rain against drought, for "protection of the country" (*gokoku*), for repelling foreign invasions (e.g., the Mongol invasions in the thirteenth century), for blessing the enthronement of a new emperor, and so forth. Historically the term has been used to refer to spiritual as well as material benefits to be gained through faith in Buddhist figures, such as Kannon

(Avalokiteśvara, the *bodhisattva* of compassion) or Yakushi (Bhaiṣajyaguru, the healing Buddha), or through adherence to certain texts (such as the *Lotus Sūtra*) or Buddhist images (such as the Amida icon at Zenkōji) or traditions (such as legends of efficacy associated with certain sacred sites). Even the Jōdo Shin tradition, which officially discourages reliance on "magical" means, is heir to a collection of "poems on worldly benefits" (*genze riyaku wasan*) written by their founder, Shinran.

The term is especially prominent in reference to new religious movements, which often promise their followers concrete benefits for their daily lives, and offer many followers who witness to the experience of such benefits. There have also been various scandals in modern Japan over exorbitantly priced "spiritual" goods and extravagant promises of efficacy, relying on the market for *genze riyaku*. The promise of "worldly benefits," however, is no less pervasive at traditional Buddhist temples in modern Japan, where a vast array of means for practical benefits are made available to the willing religious consumer.

See also: **Japan, Buddhism in.**

PAUL L. SWANSON

GLASSMAN, BERNARD RŌSHI

Bernard Tetsugen Glassman Rōshi is the first of pioneering Zen missionary Taizan Maezumi Rōshi's twelve *Dharma* heirs and the first American-born Buddhist to receive *Dharma* transmission in Japan's Sōtō tradition. He is accurately described as one of American Zen's best-known innovators and, with his founding of an international network of community development organizations and the activist Zen Peacemaker Order, Glassman has more recently earned a reputation as a leader of America's engaged Buddhist movement.

Bernard Glassman was born on 18 January 1939, in Brooklyn, New York, to Eastern European Jewish immigrants. He was educated in applied mathematics at the Polytechnic Institute of Brooklyn and the University of California at Los Angeles, where he received his Ph.D. while also working in the aerospace industry. In 1970, he was ordained as a Sōtō priest and began *kōan* practice with Maezumi Rōshi at the Zen Center of Los Angeles. In 1976, he completed *kōan* practice and received *Dharma* transmission (he later also received *inka* from Maezumi in 1995), at which time he quit the aerospace industry and devoted himself full time to teaching Zen. In 1979, with the support of Maezumi, Glassman founded the Zen Community of New York (ZCNY).

It was as abbot of ZCNY that Glassman began to experiment with novel methods for teaching Zen to Americans. The first of his innovations, criticized by some as a sell-out to capitalism and by others as a distraction from his more legitimate duties as teacher of *zazen* and *kōan* practice, was Greyston Bakery, founded in 1982. First conceived as a means of supporting ZCNY and a venue for engaging students in "work-practice," the multi-million-dollar enterprise has since evolved into a network of "welfare to work" community-development companies and not-for-profit agencies, united under the umbrella of the Greyston Mandala Foundation. These various enterprises, which include Greyston Bakery, Greyston Family Inn, and Maitri House, provide housing and job development, social services, child care, and HIV-related healthcare for "the economically disenfranchised" of New York, and through its international affiliates, other locations throughout the world.

In 1996, Glassman and his late wife, Sandra Jishu Holmes Rōshi, founded the Zen Peacemaker Order (ZPO). ZPO is dedicated to the three tenets of "not knowing, thereby giving up fixed ideas about ourselves and the universe; bearing witness to the joy and suffering of the world; and healing ourselves and others." Among the better known of its various activities, ZPO periodically organizes "street retreats" or "homeless *sesshins*" and pilgrimages to the Nazi death camp at Auschwitz-Birkenau, inspired by similar events sponsored by Japan's Nipponzan Myōhōji. These and other activities "bear witness" to the world's suffering and act, for Glassman, as a kind of *kōan* practice in which activist practitioners meditatively become one with the social problems they are trying to solve.

Although Glassman Rōshi has been criticized for his innovations and, more poignantly, for his willingness to work within what many engaged Buddhists perceive as the inherently oppressive structures of capitalism, he defends his various innovations as so many necessary and "expedient means" for adapting the *Dharma* to the West.

Glassman is author of a number of popular books, including *Instructions to the Cook: A Zen Master's Lessons in Living a Life That Matters* (with Rick Fields) and *Bearing Witness: A Zen Master's Lessons in Making Peace.*

See also: **Ariyaratne, A.T.; Buddhist peace groups (in Asia and the West); Engaged Buddhism; Global Buddhist networks: selected examples; Maha Ghosananda; Nhat Hanh, Thich; Sivaraksa, Sulak.**

JIM DEITRICK

GLOBAL BUDDHIST NETWORKS: SELECTED EXAMPLES

During the late twentieth century numerous Buddhist organizations have become globally spread. The process started in the 1970s with the worldwide expansion and institutionalization of Zen, Tibetan Buddhist, Theravāda, *vipassanā*, Nichiren, and non-sectarian orders, schools, and traditions. While most of the global Buddhist organizations operate along the model of central headquarters and affiliated satellites, a few organize themselves as networks with nodal points in a global net. Each model carries advantages and disadvantages for the organization. The centrally organized institution is strong in distributing teachers, financial resources, authorization for a newly founded group, know-how, education schemes and much more. This form with power and resources concentrated proves to be useful for an accelerated dispersion, especially so to regions less developed in Buddhist terms like South and Latin America, and Africa. On the other hand, the centrality hinders processes of adaptation to and indigenization in the very local context. The other model, the non-hierarchical network with independent though affiliated centers, facilitates such processes of adaptation and the provision of answers to questions of the local context. On the other hand, the insistence on independence requires it to generate its own resources; the less tight structure enables an easier break away.

The first Buddhist organization with a worldwide diffusion was the 1891-founded Mahā Bodhi Society. Its founder Anagārika Dharmapāla toured the world for three decades and founded oversea branches in the United States and Europe. A century later and thanks to rapidly improved means of transportation and communication, the logistical maintenance of a global organization has improved. Current examples of globally spread organizations with local groups, centers, and temples in all parts of the Western world are the Sōka Gakkai International with its president Daisaku Ikeda (Nichiren Buddhism); the Fo Kuang Shan Order established by Master Xingyun in Taiwan; the Korean Kwan Um Zen school founded by late Zen master Seung Sahn; the Association Zen International following the teachings and practices of late Deshimaru Rōshi; the

Diamond Sangha founded by Robert Aitken (all Mahāyāna); Shambhala International, formerly Vajradhatu, established by the late Chögyam Trungpa; Diamond Way Buddhism led by the Danish-born Ole Nydahl; the Foundation for the Preservation of Mahāyāna Tradition (FPMT) founded by the late Lama Thubten Yeshe; the New Kadampa Tradition of Geshe Kelsang Gyatso; Sogyal Rinpoche's Rigpa organization; (all Tibetan Buddhism); the Thai Forest Tradition, inspired by late Ajahn Chah; *vipassanā* lineages following U Ba Khin, S.N. Goenka (a disciple of U Ba Khin), and Mahāsi Sayādaw (all Theravāda); the tradition-wise non-affiliated Friends of the Western Buddhist Order founded by Sangharakshita (Dennis Lingwood). A few organizations might have gone unmentioned; other teachers with a global outreach must be mentioned, including, among others, foremost the Fourteenth Dalai Lama; Thich Nhat Hanh and his Order of Interbeing; Richard Baker Rōshi, Bernard Glassman Rōshi, the late Prabhasadharma Rōshi and more *vipassanā*, Theravāda, Zen and Tibetan teachers, monks, nuns and priests.

At times, an organization is split off from its former mother tradition: Geshe Kelsang Gyatso and his followers opted out of the FPMT in 1982 and declared the founding of the New Kadampa Tradition (NKT) in 1991. The NKT claims more than 800 groups and centers worldwide in 2005, leaving the FPMT numerically far behind. Ole Nydahl's similar dynamic Diamond Way Buddhism is a Western, lay-based form of the Tibetan Karma Kagyu tradition. As such it is not a split-off as the Seventeenth Karmapa Trinlay Thaye Dorje (one of the current two Karmapas, the other being Urgyen Trinley Dorje) is its spiritual head. The Diamond Way website listed 481 groups and centers in forty-nine countries in 2005. The exclusive standpoints, the claim to represent "the" Buddhism, and the Westernized form have made the teachings and practices of both organizations attractive to followers in all Western worlds. Both teachers are disputed and are controversial, however.

With the exception of the Sōka Gakkai and the Fo Kuang Shan Order, most globally spread Buddhist organizations primarily approach converts, not immigrant Buddhists and their offspring. A global organization of nationally defined Buddhist diasporas such as Vietnamese, Chinese, Japanese, Korean, Thai, and Tibetan has not yet emerged.

See also: **Buddhism in the Western world.**

MARTIN BAUMANN

GORAMPA

Gorampa (Go rams pa bSod nams seng ge, 1428–89) was the greatest scholar of the Ngorpa tradition of the Sakya Order of Tibetan Buddhism, one of the two main branches of Sakya (the other being Tsarpa). Both are named after the monasteries that are the seats of the traditions. Ordained as a novice monk at age ten, when he was nineteen Gorampa traveled to central Tibet, and subsequently joined Nalendra Monastery. Later he traveled to Ngor Ewam Chöden (Ngor E wam chos ldan) Monastery and studied with the renowned teacher Ngorpa Günga Sangpo (Ngor pa Kun dga' bzang po, 1382–1456). Gorampa was given the full monastic ordination by his successor, Muchen Gönchok Gyeltsen (Mu chen dKon mchog rgyal mtshan, 1388–1456), at age twenty-six. During his stay at the monastery, he devoted himself to the study of *tantra*, along with epistemology (Tib. *tshad ma*, Skt. *pramāṇa*).

He distinguished himself in debate and scholarship, and was appointed assistant instructor at a small training center named Dreyül ('Bras yul). During this time he composed a number of works on Buddhist philosophy, including a commentary on Sakya Pandita's (Sa skya På'ita Kun dga' drgyal mtshan, 1182–1251) *Clear Differentiation of the Three Vows* (*sDom gsum rab dbye*).

In 1474 he moved to a small study center at Danak (rTa nag) Valley in the Tsang province of central Tibet, which he named Tupden Namgyel (Thub bstan rnam rgyal). There he lectured on a range of topics, including tantra, epistemology, and *Vinaya*, and composed a number of influential texts, including a commentary on Sakya Pandita's *Treasure on the Science of Valid Cognition* (*Tshad ma rigs gter*) and an exposition of Madhyamaka philosophy entitled *Definitive Meaning of the Middle Way* (*dBu ma spyi don*). He became abbot of Ngor Monastery in 1483 at age fifty-three, and died while *en route* to Tupden Namgyel. He was cremated at Tupden Namgyel, and his remains are enshrined there.

His collected works comprise more than 100 texts in thirteen volumes and cover a range of subjects. He composed five works on the three vows according to Sakya Pandita's system, and he is regarded within the Sakya tradition as being the authoritative interpreter of these topics. His discussions of Mādhyamaka philosophy generated heated controversy with the Gelukpa Order because of their trenchant criticisms of Tsong Khapa's philosophy. In his *Differentiation of Views* (*lTa ba'i shan 'byed*), he identified three perspectives regarding the understanding of emptiness (Tib. *stong pa nyid*, Skt. *śūnyatā*): (1) viewing the extreme of permanence as the middle way; (2) viewing the extreme of annihilation as the middle way; and (3) Madhyamaka who are free from extremes. Gorampa characterized Tsong Khapa's position as belonging to the second group, and particularly took issue with his notion that emptiness should be understood as denial of inherent existence (Tib. *rang bzhin*, Skt. *svabhāva*). Gorampa's position is that ultimate reality transcends all verbal formulations and all dichotomies and that it must be directly perceived through introspective meditation. It cannot be described in words, nor can it be accurately understood through inference, as Tsong Khapa believed.

See also: **Tibet, Buddhism in.**

John Powers

GUHYASAMĀJA-TANTRA AND *GUHYAGARBHA-TANTRA*

The *Secret Assembly Tantra*

The *Guhyasamāja-tantra* (*Secret Assembly Tantra*, Tib. *gSang ba 'dus pa'i rgyud*) and the *Guhyagarbha-tantra* (*Secret Womb/ Embryo Tantra*, Tib. *gSang ba snying po'i rgyud*) are assigned to the highest yoga *tantra* class by Tibetan doxographers. The *Guhyasamāja* is particularly important for the Gelukpa Order, and is the basis of its system of *tantric* theory and practice, while the *Guhyagarbha* is the main *tantra* of the "great yoga" (Skt. *mahāyoga*, Tib. *rnal 'byor chen po*) class for the Nyingma Order. The *Secret Assembly* is further classified as a "father *tantra*," meaning that its primary teaching concerns the development of the "illusory body" (Skt. *māyā-deha*, Tib. *sgyu lus*). Its primary deity is Guhyasamāja, who is visualized as being dark blue in color and as having three faces and six arms, surrounded by a retinue of four female Buddhas: Māmakī, Locanā, Pāṇḍarvāsinī, and Tārā.

The *Secret Assembly* was originally composed in Sanskrit, and later translated into Tibetan and Chinese. The earliest Tibetan translation dates from the eighth century. Alex Wayman considers it to be one of the earliest *tantras* and dates it to the fourth century, but its developed systems of doctrine and practice make this unlikely, and it is doubtful that it existed in its present form before the eighth century. The *Secret Assembly* is divided into two sections: a "root *tantra*" (Skt. *mūla-tantra*, Tib. *rtsa ba'i rgyud*) of seventeen parts; and a section referred to as "higher *tantra*" (Skt. *uttara-tantra*, Tib. *bla ma'i rgyud*). When first introduced to Tibet, both of these *tantras* generated significant controversy because of their apparently unorthodox teachings. The *Secret Assembly* opens with the standard phrase for *sūtras* and *tantras*, "Thus have I heard at one time: The Bhagavan [Buddha] was residing in . . . ," but instead of a location in India, the Buddha is said to be "residing in the vaginas of the women who are the body, speech, mind, and heart of all the *tathāgatas* [buddhas]." The *bodhisattvas* in the assembly are so scandalized to see the Buddha *in flagrante delicto* and exhorting them to such practices as offering feces and semen to buddhas and killing sentient beings that they collectively faint. After being revived by the Buddha's power, they are informed that even the *tathāgatas* entertain doubts regarding the esoteric teachings of the *Secret Assembly*.

In Section 16, for example, the Buddha is said to instruct his audience: "You should kill living beings, speak lying words, take things that are not given, and have sex with many women." When performed in the context of *tantric* practice, actions that are proscribed in Buddhist moral codes become means conducive to liberation. *Tantric* practitioners must transcend attachment even to conventional morality and overcome disgust with substances that are considered polluting by traditional Hindus and Buddhists, such as semen, blood, and feces. Only when one has reached a state of complete indifference toward the things of the world is it possible to attain the total equanimity of a Buddha. The main mental afflictions of desire, aversion, and obscuration are presented as "wish-fulfilling gems" (Skt. *cintā-maṇi*, Tib. *yid bshin nor bu*) for *tantric* adepts who are able to transmute them by means of esoteric practice.

The Buddha further advises the assembly to "have sex with women in various modes of existence in the three worlds" as part of their vows relating to desire. Skillful use of the emotion of anger involves slaying "all of those conceived as sentient beings" with the "*vajra* of meditation." Further, the Buddha asserts that skillful use of delusion involves performance of "fearful and terrible actions," all of which are "conducive to the awakening of a buddha."

In stark contrast with other Buddhist teachings that praise yogins who overcome anger, desire, and obscuration, the *Secret Assembly* asserts that those who have especially strong negative emotions are best suited for the supreme practices: "Those who belong to the families of desire, anger, and obscuration are well versed in non-discrimination, and so they attain the best success (Skt. *siddhi*, Tib. *dngos grub*) in the supreme and highest manner." Equally scandalous from the point of view of Indian social hierarchies, the Buddha Vajradhara states that people of mixed caste, basket-weavers and others practicing lowly occupations, murderers, and greedy people "succeed in this excellent path, the supreme Great Vehicle." Those who revile their teachers, who covet others' property, who are promiscuous, who eat feces and urine, and who indulge in incest "attain great success in the supreme truth of the Great Vehicle." Even one who has sexual intercourse with the mother of the Buddha will attain Buddhahood through the extraordinary practices of the *Secret Assembly*.

The text then goes on to outline a complex meditative visualization in which the central Buddha Guhyasamāja is surrounded by a retinue of other Buddhas in a vast cosmic *maṇḍala*, suggesting, as Tibetan exegetes commonly claim, that the overtly scurrilous practices taught previously are part of an internal yoga designed to wean the mind from any sort of attachment – even positive attachment to moral practice and conventional behavior – in order to attain the perspective of a Buddha, who views all aspects of cyclic existence as being equal.

The *Secret Womb Tantra*

The *Guhyagarbha-tantra* is an important source for the Nyingma great perfection (*rdzogs chen*) system. Longchen Rapjampa (kLong chen rabs 'jam pa, 1308–64) describes this text as "the highest summit of all vehicles, the source of all verbal transmissions, the great shortcut of the vehicle of all Buddhas of the three times, the most secret [teaching of all]" (*Illumination of Darkness in the Ten Directions, Tib. Phyogs bcu mun sel*). Tibetan doxographers regard it as a highest yoga *tantra*, and Nyingma scholars view it as the most important work of the "great yoga" class. The *tantra* opens with the statement that the Buddha was dwelling in Akaniṣṭha heaven, "endowed with great bliss that is the identity of the indestructible body, speech, and mind of all the *tathāgatas* of the ten directions and four times."

The *Secret Womb* comprises a collection of nineteen texts in the Tibetan Buddhist canon. The main ones are a short version in twenty-two chapters, an intermediate length version in forty-six chapters, and a long version in eighty-two chapters. The first describes a *maṇḍala* populated by forty-two peaceful deities and fifty-eight wrathful ones, and its central teaching holds that all things manifest spontaneously (*thams cad rang snang*), and mind and primordial wisdom also manifest spontaneously (*sems dang ye shes rang snang*).

A supplementary text describes the Buddha-body as the basis of meditative attainments, the creation of *maṇḍalas*, control of winds and drops within subtle energy channels, along with the process of purification of the aggregates (Skt. *skandha*, Tib. *phung po*) that comprise the psycho-physical continuum of a living being. The long version of the *tantra* focuses on the qualities (Skt. *guṇa*, Tib. *yon tan*) of Buddhas, and the intermediate version on their awakened activities (Skt. *karma*, Tib. *phrin las*). Other texts in the *Secret Womb* cycle deal with a wide range of topics relating to tantric theory and practice.

After it was introduced to Tibet, it became the subject of controversy. Like the *Secret Assembly*, it contains a number of passages that appear to be at odds with conventional Buddhist morality and practice. The kings of Burang ('Pu rangs), who were supporters of Buddhism, reportedly rejected the *Secret Womb* as heretical on the basis of its teachings regarding sexual union (*sbyor ba*) and "liberation" (*sgrol ba*, which involves liberating beings from their negative *karma* by killing them). According to some sources, this involved the slaying of animals – and possibly humans – but Tibetan exegetes interpret such passages allegorically. According to Longchen Rapjampa, these two practices are internal yogas involving merging one's vital energies with the primal source of all existence, which leads to liberation of these energies from their ordinary constraints.

In the *Official Edict* (*bKa' shog*) catalog of Yeshe Ö (Ye shes 'od, fl. mid-eleventh century), the eleventh chapter focuses on a detailed denunciation of the practices of sexual union and deliverance, and the famed translator Rinchen Sangpo (Rin chen bzang po, 958–1055) echoed these sentiments in his *Refutation of Errors Regarding Secret Mantra* (*sNgags log sun 'byin*). Some Tibetan critics asserted that the *Secret Womb* was actually a composition of the tantric adept Vairocana and not a genuine *tantra* of Indian origin, but after an old Sanskrit version was discovered by Śākyaśrī (1127–1225) at Samye (bSam yas) Monastery it was generally accepted as authentic.

According to Nyingma doxographers, *tantras* of the great yoga class like the *Secret Womb* are mainly concerned with the basis of realization of Buddhahood, which is the fundamental nature of reality (*gnas lugs*). Great yoga practices mainly involve the generation stage, in which one mentally creates a vivid image of a Buddha in front of oneself, endowed with all the physical and mental qualities of a fully awakened being. The emphasis is on practice, which is deepened in the completion stage. This involves imagining that the visualized Buddha merges with oneself and that one is transformed into a buddha, possessing the body, speech, and mind of an awakened being and performing the activities of Buddhahood. The completion stage is the main focus of the "subsequent yoga" (Skt. *anuyoga*, Tib. *rjes su rnal 'byor*) class of *tantras*, while "supreme yoga" (Skt. *atiyoga*, Tib. *rdzogs chen*) teaches that from the point of view of Buddhahood appearances and emptiness interpenetrate and are inseparable.

The view of great yoga emphasizes the ground of practice – the generation stage – and the conduct it describes is connected with ritual actions. Great yoga texts are concerned with activities such as empowerment (*dbang bskur*), engagement in practice (*'jug pa*), meditation (*bsgom pa*), conduct (*spyod pa*), and result (*'bras bu*). The techniques of great yoga are said to be a gradual path to Buddhahood, while those of subsequent yoga are aimed at spontaneous realization of one's innate buddha-nature. Supreme yoga combines both in a comprehensive unitive vision of the path. Subsequent yoga focuses on the path to Buddhahood, in this case the completion stage and meditative techniques designed to actualize meditative stability. Supreme yoga is concerned with the result of practice, i.e. the full actualization of Buddhahood.

Some Tibetan commentators view the *Secret Womb* as a condensed form of the teachings of the *Secret Assembly*, despite the fact that the two share little in common in terms of either doctrine or practice. Drigung Beldzin ('Bri gung dpal 'dzin, *c.* fifteenth century), for example, credits Padmasambhava with composing the *Secret Womb* as a "condensed version" of the *Secret Assembly* that summarizes its main points (*Chapter Differentiating Dharma and Non-Dharma, Chos dang chos ma yin pa rnam par dbye ba'i rab tu byed pa*, p. 265).

See also: **Tibet, Buddhism in; Vajrayāna Buddhism.**

JOHN POWERS

H

HAGIOGRAPHIES

Among the most popular genres of Buddhist literature are works that relate the lives of Buddhas and exemplary Buddhist practitioners. Unlike modern biographies that provide detached, factual accounts of their subject's lives, hagiographies and Buddhist life stories (Pāli *apadāna*, Skt. *avadāna*) combine facts and historical details with myths and legends. While these lives have their roots in oral tradition and in the art of the storyteller, most are not wholesale fabrications of invented lives. Their authors recreate the personal history of extraordinary people in a compelling story to educate and inspire an audience. These stories, often used by Buddhist preachers, illustrate the moral and intellectual values that govern the lives of Buddhas and their disciples and make them worthy of admiration, if not veneration.

The Buddha's life has generated numerous hagiographies compiled by pious Buddhists over the millennia. Narratives about Gautama Buddha's quest for enlightenment, his teaching, and his death occur in the *Sūtra* and *Vinaya* sections of the Buddhist canon. Stories that depicted his entire extraordinary life history, beginning with the descent from Tuṣita heaven, must have been in circulation by the first century BCE, when artists began to carve them onto the *stūpas* at Bhārhut and Sāñcī. Sanskrit hagiographies, the *Great Story* (*Mahāvastu*), the *Graceful Description* (*Lalitavistara*), and Aśvaghoṣa's *Acts of the Buddha (Buddhacarita)* appeared around the first to second centuries CE. These Sanskrit hagiographies all referred to the Buddha's past lives (*Jātaka*). The *Story of Connections* (*Nidānakathā*), the introduction to the Pāli *Jātaka* tales (*c.* third to fourth century CE), provided the connections between all the Buddha's past lives and his present life.

The Pāli canon's *Collection of Minor Texts* (*Khuddaka Nikāya*) included the *Lineage of the Buddha* (*Buddhavaṃsa*) and the *Stories* (*Apadāna*). In the *Lineage of the Buddha*, when the Buddha granted Śāriputra's request to speak about his aspiration for Buddhahood, he wove his own past births and meritorious actions into an account of the life histories of the twenty-four Buddhas who preceded him. The *Stories*' accounts of Buddha's disciples, 547 elder monks (*thera*) and forty elder nuns (*therī*) indicate that all in previous lives had honored a Buddha, who predicted that as a result of their merit they would become enlightened under Gautama Buddha. The stories explaining how they became *arahants* reflected the disciples' celebration of their enlightenment in the *Monks' Verses* and *Nuns' Verses* (*Theragāthā, Therīgāthā*).

Avadānas, one of twelve genres of Buddhist Sanskrit literature, were likely composed between the first and the fourth century CE in Sarvāstivāda communities in northwest India from where they spread along the Silk Road to China. The stories, some that the Buddha told about his own past lives, illustrated the workings of *karma* and emphasized the importance of generosity, morality, and devotion. Like the *Jātaka* stories, these stories of prominent monastics and laypeople depicted their spiritual progress through the cultivation of moral virtues over many lifetimes. Among the many of the fragmentary Gāndhārī manuscripts recovered from sites in modern Pakistan and Afghanistan are *Avadānas* that utilized local characters to make these moral tales even more vivid.

The *Hundred Stories* (*Avadānaśataka*), translated into Chinese in the third century CE, related how past meritorious acts led the Buddha, monks and nuns to enlightenment and how generous or ungenerous acts resulted in respective rebirths in heaven or in the realm of hungry ghosts (*preta*). Among the thirty-eight stories included in the *Divine Stories* (*Divyāvadāna*) are tales that explained Śāriputra's and Maudgalyāyana's early entrance into *nirvāṇa* and how merchants' moral virtues and devotion led them to become wealthy. The *Story of Aśoka* (*Aśokāvadāna*) combined fact and legend about King Aśoka (*c*. 272–231 BCE) in its focus on his acts of merit. The acts began with a childhood offering of a handful of earth to a Buddha in past life that resulted in his rebirth as a universal monarch (*cakravartin*). The text emphasized the cruel Aśoka's conversion to Buddhism through a monk's miraculous intervention, his subsequent benevolent deeds, his pilgrimage to Buddhist sites, his redistribution of the Buddha's relics and his erection of 84,000 *stūpas.*

Fact and legend were also combined in the Sanskrit hagiographies of eminent Indian monks translated into Chinese by the Central Asian monk Kumārajīva (343–413 CE). These hagiographies depicted the impressive intellectual abilities of Nāgārjuna and Āryadeva and their willingness to use any means (even magical) to convert others to the truth. These hagiographies' sources portrayed their subjects as *bodhisattvas*, the spiritual exemplars of the Mahāyāna movement whose virtues begin with generosity and culminate in wisdom.

Chinese hagiographies of eminent monks, like Confucian biographies, emphasized their subjects' scholarship, and moral rectitude, but also credited their subjects with miraculous deeds. These hagiographies included particular details and anecdotes drawn from individuals' lives, while simultaneously depicting them as examples of generalized religious values. The *Biographies of Eminent Monks* (*Gaosheng zhuan*) by Huijao (497–554) distinguished ten categories of eminent monks, including translators, scholars, wonder-workers, meditators, ascetics, ritual specialists, reciters, merit-makers, and preachers. The *Biographies of Nuns* (*Biqiuni zhuan*), compiled by the monk Baochang in 516, praised the intellectual accomplishments of nuns at a time when few women were educated. This popular genre included *Further Biographies of Eminent Monks* (*Xu gaosheng zhuan*) by Doaxuan (596–667), *Song Biographies of*

Eminent Monks (*Song gaoseng zhuan*) by Zanning (919–1001), *Biographies of Eminent Monks Compiled during the Ming Dynasty* (*Ming gaoseng zhuan*) by Ruxing and the *Further Biographies of Nuns* (*Xubiqiuni zhuan*) completed in 1939 by Zhenhua (1909–47). Pure Land hagiographies, such as the thirteenth-century *Comprehensive Record of the Buddhas and Patriarchs* (*Fozu tongyi*) and *Selections on the Land of Bliss* (*Lebang wenlei*) used the compelling deathbed testimonials of monks and laity to spread the faith. These Chinese hagiographies were written to guide and inspire faithful Buddhists but also to seek new converts and royal patrons.

Hagiographies, most on the lives of adepts (*siddha*), formed an important part of the Vajrayāna tradition. Most stories in Abhayadatta's twelfth-century *Lives of the Eighty-four Siddhas* (*Caturaśitisiddhapravṛtti*) focused on the crucial encounter of a lay practitioner with a charismatic teacher whose guidance leads to liberation in one lifetime. The stories depicted the adepts' extraordinary powers, acquired from meditation and esoteric yogic practices, and their miraculous deeds that inspired others to follow the Vajrayāna path. Tibetan hagiographies often adopted a sectarian viewpoint. The doctrinal history (*'chos 'byung*) of Longchenpa (Tib. Klong Chen pa, 1308–64) concentrated on the exemplary lives of Padmasambhava and the Nyingma (Tib. Rnying ma) tradition's treasure discoverers (*gter ston*). Tsangnyon Heruka (Gtsang smyon he ru ka, 1452–1507) and Pema Karpo (Pad ma dkar po, 1527–97) similarly concentrated on the Kagyu (Tib. *bka' rgyud*) hagiographies. Tsangyon's *Life of Milarepa* remains the most popular retelling of Milarepa's transformation under the strict guidance of the Indian adept Marpa from sorcerer to enlightened *yogin*. Unlike this version of Milarepa's liberation story (*rnam thar*), esoteric Tibetan hagiographies were written for specialized audiences with the superior abilities and expert training that would enable them to understand Vajrayāna practices.

See also: **Buddha; Buddha, early symbols; Canons and literature; Chronicles and pilgrimage records; *Jātakas* and other narrative collections.**

KAREN C. LANG

HALIFAX, JOAN

Joan Halifax's teaching provides a good example of engaged Buddhism. It combines Zen meditation and practice, and social concern and action. She has practiced Buddhism since the 1960s, receiving Zen training with Master Seung Sahn, the Lamp Transmission from Thich Nhat Hanh and *inka* from Rōshi Bernie Glassman. In terms of social concern and action she is the founder, abbot, and head teacher of the Upaya Zen Center in New Mexico, a Zen monastery that funds a wide variety of projects including the Upaya Prison Project of which she is the founder and director. She founded the Ojai Foundation, a spiritual "think tank." She is a founding teacher of the Zen Peacemaker Order which engages in a wide variety of social initiatives. Academically she is an anthropologist and has been on staff at the University of Miami Medical School, an Honorary Research Fellow at Harvard, and has taught worldwide. Since the 1970s she has worked extensively with the dying and is director of Being With Dying.

Joan Halifax is an individual whose academic training, Buddhist practice, and personal life have come together in an amazing confluence. Her work with shamans and the Huichol Indians, and studying rites of passage that "restored order in the heart" went some way toward healing mental suffering she had endured for several years but she felt a need to deepen her meditation practice and so took refuge with Seung Sahn in 1976.

While Halifax has been involved in a wide variety of projects including teaching shamanic perspectives on the environment, it is for her work with the dying that she is best known. As a shamanic anthropologist she acted as a link between traditional healers and modern medicine, providing her with an understanding of a wide variety of world views. As a clinician she knows the physiological aspects of death and dying. As a Buddhist practitioner and teacher she brings compassion and a wealth of thought and practice on impermanence and death. All of this comes together as she works with the dying, their friends and family to transform suffering.

As well as working with caregivers, both professional and family, to deal with the dying in compassionate ways, she also deals with the dying themselves. As was the case in medieval times, people today also wish for "a good death." The Middle Ages had a wealth of literature and art specifically to deal with dying. Since the 1970s people like Halifax and Elisabeth Kübler-Ross have tried to address these lacunae in modern Western culture. Halifax is able to use Buddhist concepts and practices to help those who wish to make their death meaningful for themselves in psychological or spiritual terms.

One can also see how the Prison Project is an extension of this work. People in prison are cut off from family and friends, networks of support. They are, in a sense, socially dead. Stress, anxiety and isolation can be countered through meditation and trained staff and post-release workers.

Joan Halifax is a good example of Buddhist women who are engaged in the attempt to restructure society in compassionate ways.

See also: **Women in Buddhism: an historical and textual overview.**

MAVIS L. FENN

HARIVARMAN

Harivarman was an Indian monk of the late third or early fourth century who wrote an important scholastic work, *The Treatise on the Establishment of Truth* (Chinese *Chengshi Lun*, Sanskrit title reconstructed as *Tattvasiddhi Śāstra* or *Satyasiddhi Śāstra*). Harivarman's treatise was a central text in Chinese Buddhist discussions in the fifth and sixth centuries, but lost its prominence when it was condemned as a "Hīnayāna" work by Jizang (549–623), the systematizer of the Sanlun ("Three Treatises") school, and by Daoxuan (596–667), the founder of the Lu school ("school of monastic disciplines"). Indeed, it seems that Harivarman was more important as a thinker in China than he was in India, a useful reminder that the works of Indian *Nikāya* Buddhism often assumed a different trajectory when they were received in new institutional settings in Tibet and East Asia.

Chinese sources say that Harivarman's family of birth was brahmin, and that he originally studied the doctrines of the Sāṃkhya school of Hindu philosophy. He is also said to be a student of the great Buddhist thinker Kumāralāta, who perhaps was an early Sarvāstivādin, but he is also claimed in the intellectual lineage of the Sautrāntikas; Kumāralāta was said to have been the teacher to the teacher of Vasubandhu (fourth–fifth century CE), a prominent figure in Buddhist intellectual history across Asia.

The Treatise on the Establishment of Truth was translated by Kumārajīva (344–413). It does not survive in Sanskrit and there do not seem to be any references to it in other Indian sources. It can be compared to the systematic treatises of *Abhidharma* found in the Sarvāstivādin school, and to Vasubandhu's *Abhidharmakośa* (*The Treasury of Systematic Thoughts*). Its basic format of questions and answers follows some of the distinctive contours of *Abhidharma* literature in all schools of Buddhism. As was typical of such works, *The Treatise on the Establishment of Truth* covers in an integrated fashion a variety of foundational topics ranging across the Three Jewels (the Buddha, his teaching, and the Buddhist monastic order), the Four Noble Truths, and the theory of two truths, Buddhist meditative practice, and the nature of reality and of wisdom. The scholastic affiliation of Harivarman is not clear from *The Treatise on the Establishment of Truth*, and some have suggested that it should be placed within the Sautrāntika lineage; others have suggested that its orientation seems similar to the Bahuśrutīyas, one of the Mahāsaṃghika lineages. It does include considerable criticism of the doctrinal positions of the Sarvāstivādins.

The translation of *The Treatise on the Establishment of Truth* by Kumārajīva gave it a different profile when it first was received in China. Kumārajīva was associated with the introduction of Madhyamaka thinking in China and Harivarman was read within this framework. *The Treatise on the Establishment of Truth* does have a strong theme on emptiness, one of the distinctive concerns of the Mādhyamaka, and Harivarman was initially read as an authoritative interpreter of Mādhyamaka positions. *The Treatise on the Establishment of Truth* became the focus of a separate school, a textual community, and more than twenty-five commentaries were produced on it by the end of the sixth century. Subsequently, its heritage was absorbed into the resources of "Three Treatises" school, a Mādhyamaka school across throughout East Asia.

See also: ***Abhidharmakośa*; Nāgārjuna; *Nikāya* Buddhism; Sarvāstivāda; Sautrāntika.**

CHARLES HALLISEY

HEALING AND PROTECTIVE PRACTICES

Buddhists, especially monks and nuns, have been famed for their skills as healers since the time of the Buddha; the *Vinaya* and later hagiographical traditions variously attribute healing powers and medical practices to the Buddha himself. These practices spread with the religion and may have played an important role in its initial successes outside India; they were developed into unique regional traditions of medical and extra-medical healing over time and through interaction with indigenous symbols and rites. This article surveys extra-medical traditions of Buddhist healing, protection and exorcism, while specifically medical practices are treated separately.

Power words

Generating the power to heal, ward off malevolent human and non-human forces, or bring rain and general blessings on society and the earth has been the specific focus of a genre of chanted Buddhist texts called *dhāraṇī* in Sanskrit, and *paritta* in Pāli, under which labels practitioners in particular Buddhist schools have anthologized, and perform, certain Buddhist *sūtras*, verses and various apocryphal material believed especially powerful in these ways. These collections share much material in common across sectarian lines, especially early *sūtras* (or portions thereof), such as the Pāli *Ratana Sutta and Āṭānāṭiya Sutta*, which were believed to have been chanted originally (by the Buddha) for a particular curative or protective purpose, but they also diverge widely, especially in the apocryphal texts adjoined to the early *sūtras* in each collection. These apocryphal materials address changing local circumstances and exhibit local distinctiveness as well as considerable trans-local (inter-sectarian) contestation. Debates over pronunciation of the *suttas* in the dominant *paritta* collection, *Catubhāṇavarapāli*, and over the contents of its apocryphal appendix (*upagrantha*), for example, caused a serious rift between the Theravāda kingdoms of

Kandy and Ayutthaya in the mid-eighteenth century. Originally non-Buddhist, related practices which Buddhists later adopted and developed, such as *mantra* recitation in South Asia, are sometimes incorporated into *dhāraṇī* texts and performances.

Dhāraṇī or *paritta* (and likewise *mantra*) recitation is sometimes an elaborate affair involving a quorum of monks, nuns and/or lay chanters, platforms and other decorations, and accoutrements such as offerings of flowers, food, incense, and/or valuables; images; scrolls or palm leaf manuscripts; thread and water to be purified then distributed; specific ritual acts of boundary-creation, consecration, and so forth. In such circumstances it may last for many hours or even days and weeks at a time. In different circumstances, especially emergencies, it might be a much abbreviated affair, for which shorter liturgies and/or selections of particularly powerful recitations have been preserved in the different Buddhist traditions.

Power objects

Buddhists from all traditions have maintained that the power (*bala*) produced by these practices – which is variously conceived as a force (*ānubhāva*) associated with the Triple Gem or the words themselves, or as the participation of deities and *bodhisattvas* in Buddhist projects – permeates the area within which the recitation occurs, serving whatever curative or protective need may exist. But Buddhists have also maintained that this power can be contained and transported for later/perpetual use, whether in objects that have been chanted upon (such as amulets, thread, images, water, boundary stones, and door frames) or in physical embodiments of the chanted words themselves, which might be diagrammed as *yantra*s in Sri Lanka, tattooed on the body in Southeast Asia, worn as amulets in China or written on slips of paper or distilled into pills and ingested in Tibet.

Other healing and protective practices

While *dhāraṇī* or *paritta* and *mantra* recitation have been the most prominent Buddhist healing and protective practices, in different regions monks and nuns have established themselves as experts in local, originally non-Buddhist arts such as exorcism (which is especially prominent in Tibet and Sri Lanka), divination (especially in East Asia) and astrology (especially in South and Southeast Asia). In some circumstances particularly revered monks or nuns, sacred objects (such as *Śrī Mahā Bodhi* in Sri Lanka) or particular *bodhisattvas* or deities may also be approached for healing and protection. Especially notable in this regard are the Tibetan cult of Bhaiṣajyaguru "the *bodhisattva* of healing" and the Japanese cult of Binzuru, whose images are often found outside temples and worshipped for their believed healing powers.

Finally, it is important to note that according to many, especially advanced Buddhist practitioners through the ages, the most powerful forms of healing and protection come from the self-cultivation of morality, wisdom and mindfulness, which naturally deters and potentially transforms wild animals and snakes, violent or otherwise ill-spirited people and supernatural beings, and even natural calamity. This force is sometimes even conceived as a literal shield effected by deities, *bodhisattvas* and/or Buddhas in the practitioner's service, or as a spontaneous result of his or her own perfected being.

See also: **Mantras, mudrās, and *maṇḍalas*; Medical practices; Rituals and practices; *Vinaya Piṭaka*.**

JONATHAN S. WALTERS

HEVAJRA-TANTRA

The *Hevajra-tantra* (Tib. *Kye rDo rje rgyud*) is classified by Tibetan doxographers as belonging to the highest yoga *tantra* corpus and as a mother *tantra*, meaning that it is primarily concerned with the wisdom aspect of practice. Mother *tantras* focus on techniques relating to the mind of clear light realizing emptiness. The original treatise was written in Sanskrit, and it was later translated into Tibetan and Chinese. According to Tibetan tradition, the text that exists today under the title *Hevajra-tantra* is a condensed version of the original *tantra*, which comprised 500,000 verses, but there is no evidence that such a text ever existed.

The main Buddhas discussed in the *tantra* are Hevajra and his consort Nairātmyā. Hevajra is described as having eight faces, four legs, sixteen arms, and he tramples four demons (Skt. *māra*, Tib. *bdud*) with his feet. He appears in a wrathful aspect and wears a garland of severed heads. His body is smeared with ashes, and his skin is dark black, but his inner nature is tranquil and blissful. His retinue includes eight female Buddhas: Ghasmarī, Pukkasī, Ḍombiṇī, Vetālī, Gaurī, Caṇḍālī, Śavarī, and Caurī.

The text opens with the words: "Thus have I heard at one time: The Bhagavan [Buddha] dwelt in the vagina (*bhaga*) of the Vajrayoginī who is the body, speech, and mind of all Buddhas," apparently indicating that the two were in sexual embrace. In answer to a question from Vajragarbha, the *tantra*'s main interlocutor, the Buddha describes the wondrous attainments of Hevajra. "*He*" is said to imply his perfection of the quality of compassion, and "*Vajra*" indicates that he has similarly perfected wisdom. Hevajra is further declared to be the essence of Vajrasattva and other Buddhas.

Vajragarbha is informed that through the secret teachings he is about to receive he can attain the perfection of Buddhahood, along with an extensive list of magical powers. These include spells for producing rain, destroying enemy armies, gaining mastery over a young woman, and altering the course of the sun and moon.

The ideal of the text is a fully realized being (Skt. *siddha*, Tib. *grub thob*) who wanders freely, uninhibited by social conventions, who has "passed beyond oblations, renunciation, and austerities, and who is liberated from *mantra* and meditation."

> There is nothing that one may not do, and nothing that one may not eat.
>
> There is nothing that one may not think or say, nothing that is either pleasant or unpleasant.
>
> (I.7,24)

Tantric rituals are described in which groups of yogins gather at cemeteries or mountain caves, wrapped in animal skins or burial shrouds, and feast on forbidden substances such as dishes made from the flesh of humans, cows, horses, elephants, and dogs, or from the flesh of a hanged criminal or a slain warrior. In addition to magical spells and violent acts, the *tantra* describes sexual yogas and rites of initiation in which the guru places drops of sexual fluids on the tongues of students. At one point Vajragarbha and other *bodhisattvas* are so shocked by the apparently scurrilous words of the Buddha that they faint, after which he revives them and reassures them that the new teachings are merely a more advanced version of what they had previously been taught.

Some of the actions described in the *Hevajra* are clearly meant to be treated symbolically, and the *tantra* itself makes it clear in several places that certain practices are only to be visualized as means to help trainees transcend attachment to ordinary reality and moral codes, and are not exhortations for literal observances. In other cases, such as the descriptions of orgiastic rites and sexual practices, the detail and explicitness of the descriptions indicate that they are probably meant to be taken literally. The question of which apparently questionable *tantric* teachings are to be treated as allegorical is one of the main concerns of Indian and Tibetan commentators on this and other *tantric* texts, who commonly assert that these pronouncements are codes for various aspects of well-established Buddhist doctrines and practices or that they are to be enacted in the mind and not physically. Thus when Vajragarbha asks the Buddha to outline the proper code of conduct for tantric practitioners, he is told:

> You should kill living beings.
> You should speak lying words.
> You should take what is not given.
> You should frequent others' wives.
> (II.3, 29)

In the following verses, the Buddha explains that "killing living beings" involves cultivating "singleness of thought" (Skt. *eka-citta*, Tib. *sems gcig*); "speaking lying words" refers to the vow to save all sentient beings; "what is not given" is a woman's bliss (presumably in sexual yoga); and "frequenting others' wives" is meditation focused on Nairātmyā, Hevajra's consort. Despite the Buddha's reassurances, the fact that tantras which taught yogas of sexual union (*sbyor*) and "deliverance" (*sgrol*, involving slaying living beings) were condemned in Tibet indicates that some *tantric* practitioners probably took them literally. However, the *Commentary on the Condensed Meaning of the Hevajra-tantra* (Skt. *Hevajra-piṇḍārtha-ṭīkā*, Tib. *Kye'i rdo rje bsdus pa'i don gyi rgya cher 'grel pa*) cautions that "the rites of ritual slaying and so forth that have been described [in the *tantra*] are intended to frighten living beings in order to subdue them, and thus establish them [on the correct path]. If one were really to kill them, one would be violating a vow of the great seal (*phyag chen po'i dam tshig*) and would fall into the Avīcī hell" (15.86b, 5–6).

In common with other highest yoga *tantras*, the *Hevajra* stresses the importance of the guru and of unfailing devotion as a prerequisite for trainees. The teachings are potentially dangerous if misunderstood or misapplied, and the coded language used in the *Hevajra* must be explained by the oral instructions of a qualified teacher, who is the present embodiment of a lineage hearkening back to the original propagation of the text. Initiation into the Hevajra *maṇḍala* is also a precondition for practice of this *tantra*, following which students are required to regularly construct the complex visualizations described in the text during sessions of meditation. With repeated practice, trainees develop the ability to mentally visualize the *maṇḍala* of Hevajra and his retinue, and to populate the symbolic universe of the liturgical practice (Skt. *sādhana*, Tib. *grub thabs*) with Buddhas and *bodhisattvas*, envisioned in ever-increasing detail and complexity. The ultimate aim is to transform the mind of the practitioner, reconstructing perceptions, motivations, and thoughts in accordance with the symbolic nuances of the figures of the *sādhana* and their Buddhist connotations.

The central teaching of the *tantra* is the "inseparability of cyclic existence and *nirvāṇa*" (Skt. *saṃsāra-nirvāṇa-abheda*, Tib. *'khor 'das dbyer med*). In chapter five, Vajragarbha is told:

> In reality there is neither form nor perceiver,
> Neither sound nor hearer,
> Neither smell nor one who smells,
> Neither taste nor taster,
> Neither touch nor one who touches,
> Neither thought nor thinker.
> (I.5, 1)

The *tantra* further declares that from the point of view of ultimate reality there is no meditator nor anything on which one meditates, no deities nor *mantras*. Rather, reality is characterized by undifferentiated unity. The soteriological purpose of these teachings is revealed in chapter nine, where Vajragarbha is told:

> That by which the world is bound,
> By the same things it is released from bondage.
> But the world is deluded and does not understand this truth,
> And one who does not possess this truth cannot attain perfection.
> (I.9, 19)

Those who perceive reality in accordance with ordinary appearances and conventions remain trapped by them, while adepts employ the very things that bind beings consumed by passion and other negative mental states as the means of escape from cyclic existence. Ultimately cyclic existence and *nirvāṇa* are perspectives, and so there is no real difference between them: "all beings are Buddhas, but this is hidden by obscurations; but when they are removed, they are then actually Buddhas" (II.4, 69). One who understands this insight remains unpolluted by negative emotions and can indulge in any behavior.

The *Hevajra* conceives of humans in terms of a mystical physiology. Within the bodies of humans there are thirty-two principal energy channels (Skt. *nāḍī*, Tib. *rtsa*), through which the winds and drops circulate. The three main channels are: *lalanā* (Tib. *brkyang ma*), located on the left side of the spinal column and associated with wisdom; *rasanā* (Tib. *ro ma*), located on the right side and associated with method; and *avadhūti* (Tib. *kun 'dar ma*), which is roughly contiguous with the spine and integrates the two primary aspects of practice. A primal energy called *caṇḍālī* (Tib. *gtum mo*) resides at the base of the central channel, and the *tantra* contains instructions for causing it to rise through a series of stages (Skt. *cakra*, Tib. *rtsa 'khor*) located at the navel, heart, throat, and head. This process results in increasing bliss and mastery of supernatural powers.

> Caṇḍālī ignites in the navel.
> She burns the five *tathāgatas* [Buddhas].
> She scorches Locanā and the other female Buddhas.

The *tantra* explains that this means that when *caṇḍālī* (who is both a Buddha and the personification of the primal energy that one causes to rise through the *cakra*s) blazes, she burns the Buddhas that represent conventional Buddhist teachings and practices, which enables the adept to move on to the more advanced instructions of the *Hevajra*. The text also turns the tables on those who cling to old orthodoxies, claiming that they are the real heretics, while only those who embrace *tantric* teachings are able to attain the supreme state of buddhahood.

According to Tibetan tradition, the text was first revealed to humans by Saroruha, who also composed a commentary on it, along with rituals related to its teachings. The *Hevajra-tantra* is one of the most influential *tantras* for Tibetan Buddhists, particularly for the Sakya Order. It is the basis of the Sakya system of "path and result" (*lam 'bras*), a graduated system of meditation in which each stage requires mastery of the one preceding it. The path and result system teaches that the path of practice and its result are inseparable, like cyclic existence and *nirvāṇa*. The result subsumes the path because it is produced by it, and the path similarly subsumes the result because it is the means by which it is attained. Traditional histories state that it was originally brought to Tibet by the translator Drokmi ('Brog mi, 993–1077), who inherited it through a lineage of masters beginning with Vīrūpa. The lamas of the Khön ('Khon) family are the hierarchs of the Sakya tradition, and the first member to adopt the path and result teachings was Sachen Günga Nyingpo (Sa chen Kun dga' snying po, 1034–1102), who founded Sakya Monastery, the main seat of the Order, in 1073.

See also: **Tibet, Buddhism in; Vajrayāna Buddhism.**

John Powers

HIRAKAWA, AKIRA

In a long career that spanned more than six decades, Akira Hirakawa was acknowledged to be one of the leading scholars of Buddhism worldwide, having made contributions to the field on a wide and far-reaching series of topics, ranging from the *Vinaya Piṭaka* to the beginnings of Mahāyāna. Born in 1915 in Toyohashi City, he did both undergraduate and graduate study at the Tokyo Imperial University in the Department of Indian Philosophy and Sanskrit Philology. He eventually joined that department as a Research Assistant in 1946, and four years later was appointed Associate Professor in the new Department of Indian Philosophy at Hokkaido University. In 1954 he returned to Tokyo to become an Associate Professor, and was granted Full Professorship in 1962. Following his retirement from the University of Tokyo in 1975, he taught Buddhist Studies at Waseda University for a decade. When the International College for Advanced Buddhist Studies was founded in 1996, Professor Hirakawa joined the faculty as Chairman and Professor, and he remained there until his death in 2002.

In a memorial tribute in the 2003 edition of the *Journal of the International Association of Buddhist Studies*, Kotabo Fujija states that, "It would not be an overstatement to say that Hirakawa's professional career began and ended with a study of the *Vinaya-piṭaka*." Hirakawa's doctoral dissertation focused on the *Vinaya*, and its publication in 1960 as *Ritsuzō no Kenkyū* (*A Study of the Vinayapiṭaka*) remains perhaps the most complete secondary volume on the *Vinaya* in print, utilizing all the Buddhist languages and literatures. In 1970, he also published *Shan-Chien P'i-P'o-Sha: A Chinese Version by Saṅghabhadra of Samantapāsādikā* (in collaboration with P.V. Bapat), and in 1982, *Monastic Discipline for the Buddhist Nuns: An English Translation of the Chinese Text of the Mahāsāṃghika-Bhikṣuṇī-Vinaya* (in collaboration with Z. Ikuno and Paul Groner). In fact, half of the *Collected Works of Akira Hirakawa*, published in seventeen volumes in Tokyo between 1988 and 2000, are devoted to his work on the Buddhist *sangha*. The last five of these volumes represent entirely new work.

In the West, Professor Hirakawa is perhaps best known for his book *A History of Indian Buddhism: From Śākyamuni to Early Mahāyāna*, which was edited and translated into English by Paul Groner, and published in 1990. This volume represents only a portion of Hirakawa's surveys of the Buddhist tradition. Throughout his long career, he remained profoundly interested in the development of the Mahāyāna tradition. His 1963 article "The Rise of Mahāyāna Buddhism and Its Relationship to the Worship of Stūpas" was considered groundbreaking, and has influenced the thinking of numerous other scholars of the Buddhist tradition, then and now. Most recently, it has been questioned and criticized, yet it remains one of the landmark articles that is considered classic reading for all Buddhological scholars.

Throughout his eighty-seven years, Professor Akira Hirakawa remained an avid researcher and publisher, who was respected throughout the entire discipline of Buddhist Studies. He was one of the discipline's most prolific scholars, and his career accomplishments were recently summarized in a booklet published in 2003 by the Library of the International College for Advanced Buddhist Studies.

See also: **Academic study of Buddhism.**

CHARLES S. PREBISH

HOLIDAYS AND OBSERVANCES

Introduction

As in all religious traditions, Buddhism has many holidays and observances that are designed primarily to commemorate auspicious persons and events, to provide an occasion for merit-making, or both. Although not initially concerned with ritual endeavors, early in its history festivals began to appear, thus providing the occasion for Buddhists to reaffirm their commitment to the tradition, acknowledge community solidarity, and in the process, to develop a seasonal calendar of religious events. Although all Buddhist traditions seem to recognize the birth, death, and enlightenment of Buddha as occasions worthy of recognition and celebration, other festivals tend to be case specific to the *Nikāya*, Mahāyāna, and Vajrayāna schools. In countries populated by the one surviving *Nikāya* Buddhist sect, Theravāda, generally but not exclusively in South Asia, traditional New Year celebrations are popular. Additionally, the rain retreat period is celebrated, as is the ceremony ending the rain retreat. The robe-giving ceremony, known at *kaṭhina*, is also popular. Religious ceremonies tend to emphasize the monastic tradition rather than the secular. In the Mahāyāna countries of East Asia, Confucian, Taoist, and Shintō traditions are often woven into Buddhist events. There is a highly popular "hungry ghost" festival in China, corresponding to a "feast for the dead" ceremony in Japan. In Vajrayāna northern Asia, the death of Tsong Khapa is celebrated in the Fall, as well as a New Year festival, somewhat symbolic of Buddhism's victory over the indigenous Bön tradition. Within the specific schools of Buddhism in the various countries, festivals particular to that group are also celebrated (See Figure 22).

Figure 22 Votive lanterns for deceased family members, Pulguksa Monastery, South Kyongsang, Korea.

Theravāda festivals

In Theravāda countries, beginning with the first full moon day in mid-April, Buddhists celebrate the start of the Buddhist New Year. The New Year festival generally lasts for three days. It is a time for cleansing and reflection, and often involves humanitarian acts such as releasing caged birds, or rescuing fish from ponds and streams which are drying out. On the occasion of the New Year festival, Buddhists often make a renewed effort to rededicate themselves to appropriate Buddhist principles in the coming year. The following month provides the occasion for the *Vesākha Pūja* – sometimes called "Buddha Day" – which celebrates Buddha's birthday, enlightenment, and death. Houses are often decorated, paintings with stories of Buddha's life displayed, and other, similar acts of reverence for Buddha are entertained. Shortly thereafter, on the next full moon, Buddhists celebrate the *Āsāḷha Pūja*, which commemorates Buddha's renunciation and first sermon. This time also marks the beginning of the rainy season retreat, providing the occasion for monastics and laity alike to deepen their religious endeavor. On the full moon marking the end of the three-month rain retreat period, the monks hold the "Invitation Ceremony" or *Pavāraṇā*, during which time the laity is collectively blessed, and offerings to the monastic community are made. Coincident with this ceremony is that of the *kaṭhina* rite, when the monks receive new robes, and offerings of goods and money are made to the monasteries.

Other, less formal festivals can be noted in the Theravāda tradition. The end of the rainy season is often marked by the observance of Ānāpānasati Day, marking the occasion when Buddha gave his important instructions on the mindfulness of breathing (as recorded in the *Ānāpānasati Sutta* of the *Majjhima Nikāya*). Some Theravāda countries also observe *Abhidhamma* Day, in April, which presumably commemorates the occasion on which Buddha ascended to the Tuṣita heaven to teach *Abhidhamma* to his mother. Other famous festivals include the Plowing Festival in May, celebrating Buddha's first pre-enlightenment experience at age seven; the Elephant Festival in May, and the Tooth Festival in August in Sri Lanka, worshipping one of Buddha's relics housed on the island.

Mahāyāna festivals

Many of the Mahāyāna observances, such as Buddha's birth, enlightenment, and death, coincide with those of the Theravāda tradition. In Japan, for example, Buddha's birth is celebrated in April as Hanamatsuri, while his enlightenment is celebrated in February as Nehan, and his death is marked in December with the Rōhatsu holiday. In China the Ullambana Festival, or the Festival of the Hungry Ghosts, celebrated during the first fifteen days of the eighth lunar month, is especially important. It is a time for worshipping and making offerings to ancestors, hoping to help them achieve a better rebirth. This time for engaging in the classic Buddhist transfer of merit practice became known as the O-bon Festival in Japan. At that time, graves are washed, *sūtras* are chanted, and other offerings made in recognition of dead ancestors. Another well-known Mahāyāna festival is that marking the birthday of Avalokiteśvara (Guanyin in Chinese). It marks an occasion, in March, to celebrate the compassion of this important celestial *bodhisattva*. The dates of these holidays vary from country to country, but continue to emphasize the spirit of the underlying theme of the celebration. Many Chinese celebrations have been secularized by the communist regime on the mainland, but continue as powerful religious observances in Taiwan, and Western Chinese expatriates.

Vajrayāna festivals

Vajrayāna lands, like the traditions above, note the traditional Buddhist festivals. The various schools of Tibetan Buddhism, though, also have festivals to honor their founders, with the death of Tsong-kha-pa being particularly noteworthy. In addition the Tibetan New Year festival is especially important. Held in February, it is preceded by monastic celebrations that include ritual dancing, chanting, and music. The entire event is said to drive away evil spirits and help beings progress on the Buddhist path. There is also an impressive five-day celebration known as Monlam (Tib. *sMon lam*) or "Great Vow," which marks the occasion in which rival teachers and evil forces were overcome.

Other celebrations

As noted above, individual sectarian traditions have added festivals which are case specific to their particular affiliation. Some of these have been generated as a result of Buddhism's rapid globalization in the modern world, highlighting various Western holidays recast in Buddhist context in Western Buddhist communities. Others represent Westernized versions of the traditional Buddhist holidays noted in the *Nikāya*, Mahāyāna, and Vajrayāna traditions notes above.

See also: **Family life; *Sangha*.**

CHARLES S. PREBISH

HŌNEN AND JŌDOSHŪ

Hōnen (Genkū; 1133–1212) was a Tendai Buddhist priest who, by advocating the sole practice of verbal recitation of the Buddha Amida's name (*nenbutsu*), became the founder of the Jōdoshū (Pure Land school) and a central figure in the development of the new Buddhism of the Kamakura era.

Hōnen was born in a village in Mimasaka province (Okayama) in the midst of a period of struggle following the Genpei wars. He entered a Tendai monastery in 1141 at the young age of eight years, after his father was killed in a local skirmish. At the age of fourteen he moved to the Tendai headquarters on Mount Hiei, where he was ordained.

Hōnen soon became known for his dedication to practice and his mastery of the Buddhist scriptures. He was well versed in the multifarious Tendai traditions, but was drawn to Pure Land teachings. In 1150 he entered the Kurodani area of Mount Hiei, where he stayed for twenty years and focused on Pure Land practices (including visualization as well as invocational *nenbutsu*) under the Tendai monk Eikū (d. 1179). Through Genshin's *Ōjōyōshū* he discovered the writings of the Chinese Pure Land master Shandao (613–81), whom he would later declare to be his only master. Upon reading Shandao's admonition, "Do not cease thinking upon Amida's name for even a moment. This is an act that ensures rebirth in the Pure Land, for it is in accordance with the vow of that Buddha," he was awakened to the saving grace of Amida through the verbal invocation of his name. He later wrote that this moved him to "immediately throw away all other practices for the sole practice of nenbutsu."

Soon after this experience, in 1175 at the age of forty-two, Hōnen left Mount Hiei to go and live in Ōtani in the outskirts of Kyoto, where he started preaching the "exclusive *nenbutsu*" (*senju nenbutsu*), the practice of the verbal *nenbutsu* as the only way to assure birth in the Pure Land. This is taken as the founding of the Jōdoshū, the first independent Pure Land school of Buddhism.

Hōnen's teaching, and especially his successful lectures and discussions at Ōhara in 1886 (or 1889) and at Tōdaiji in 1190, attracted a large number of followers (including Shinran). He formulated his teachings in *Senchaku hongan nenbutsu shū* (*Collection of Passages on the Nenbutsu Selected by the Primal Vow*) in 1198.

Opposition to Hōnen's teachings grew in proportion to his success. In 1204 the Tendai school tried to ban *nenbutsu*, and Hōnen responded by composing a *Seven-Article Injunction* in an attempt to curb the excesses of some of his followers. In 1207 the priests of Kōfukuji presented the *Kōfukuji Petition*, a list of nine "errors" committed by *nenbutsu* followers, to the emperor in another attempt to ban the movement. A scandal involving some of Hōnen's followers with ladies of the court finally led to Hōnen being forced into exile to the island of Shikoku in 1207. Although he was allowed to return to Kyoto in 1211, he died the next year. On his deathbed he composed his *One-Page Testament*, a concise summary of his *nenbutsu* beliefs.

Hōnen and his followers were subject to severe criticism by members of the traditional Buddhist schools, who were loath to admit their teachings or to recognize their movement as a legitimate Buddhist school. Eventually Chion-in (in Kyoto, the location of Hōnen's tomb, and whose famous bell often is shown on TV to ring in the New Year in Japan) emerged as the headquarters of the belatedly recognized Jōdo school.

In the Tokugawa period (1600–1868), the Jōdo school was known for its academies (*danrin*) for the training of priests, and for the activities of its popular Buddhist preachers in teaching the general public. The Jōdo school has been overshadowed in modern Japan both in numbers and influence by the Jōdo Shin school of Shinran, Hōnen's disciple and devoted follower, yet still maintains an active presence in the Buddhist world.

See also: **Japan, Buddhism in; Pure Land movements in Japan.**

PAUL L. SWANSON

HONGAKU SHISŌ – ORIGINAL ENLIGHTENMENT

Hongaku shisō refers to the idea that all sentient beings (and even all things) originally or inherently (*hon*) have the potential to become enlightened or awakened (*kaku*), or are already endowed with enlightenment – that they are Buddhas just as they are. The term can be translated in a number of ways, none of them entirely satisfactory. "Original enlightenment" is the most common, but this has too strong a temporal connotation. "Innate awakening" or "inherent enlightenment" has a substantialist ring that seemingly contradicts the basic Buddhist teaching of *anātman* (no substantial self) and *pratītya-samutpāda* (dependent origination), and "originary enlightenment" is too awkward. In any case it shares a similar meaning with other problematic Buddhist terms such as Buddha-nature and *tathāgatagarbha* (storehouse or womb of Buddhahood) that imply an endowed potential or even presence of Buddhahood in all beings.

The earliest appearance of the compound *hongaku* is found in the *Awakening of Faith* – a text almost certainly compiled in China – and contemporaneous apocryphal Chinese texts such as *The Sūtra of the Benevolent Kings* and *Vajrasamādhi Sūtra*, indicating that the term is a Chinese formulation rather than a translation of any single Sanskrit (or Central Asian language) term. In the *Awakening of Faith*, *hongaku* is used in contrast to *shigaku* – the "inception" or "actualization" of enlightenment, that is, the process by which one realizes enlightenment – hence the English rendering "original" enlightenment. The key passage in the *Awakening of Faith* states, "'original enlightenment' indicates a contradistinction to the process of the actualization of enlightenment; the process of actualization of enlightenment is none other than [realizing] identity with original enlightenment."

This idea of original enlightenment had an immense influence on the development of East Asian Buddhism, including the Huayan, Chan, and Tiantai traditions, leading even to debates over "the Buddha-nature of non-sentient beings." In Japan, *hongaku* thought took on a life of its own. Its influence was strong in the Shingon school, particularly through Kūkai's extensive use of the *Shakumakaen-ron*, an apocryphal commentary on the *Awakening of Faith* attributed to Nāgārjuna. The development of *hongaku shisō* was especially prominent in the Tendai school, where an identifiably independent movement called *hongakumon* (the "gate" of original enlightenment), or *Tendai hongaku shisō* (Tendai thought of original enlightenment) developed in the medieval period. Texts devoted to *hongaku shisō* made their appearance in the late Heian and Kamakura periods (tenth to thirteenth centuries CE), some of them attributed to prominent Tendai figures like Saichō, Genshin, and Ryōgen. These texts include the *Honri taikō shū*, attributed to Saichō, which interprets the most important Tendai teachings in terms of *hongaku*; "Hymns on Original Enlightenment" (*Hongaku-san*), with commentary attributed to Ryōgen and Genshin; and texts such as the *Shuzen-ji ketsu*, attributed to Saichō, which contains details on the oral transmissions (*kuden*) of *hongaku* ideas, practices, and lineages. In these texts emphasis was placed on oral transmissions, with their accompanying lineages, and a subjective hermeneutics of understanding through the "mind of contemplation" (*kanjin*).

It is no accident that these developments took place contemporaneously with the syncretistic *honji-suijaku/shinbutsu shūgo* movement, that is, the tendency to emphasize the unity or interrelationship between Buddhist and "Shintō" deities and practices. The influence of *hongaku* can also be seen in the growth of Shugendō, as well as in all the Buddhist movements that developed in and after this period, such as the Pure Land schools, the Zen schools, and the Nichiren schools. Building on the Mahāyāna idea of the "identity of *saṃsāra* and *nirvāṇa*," *hongaku* thought evolved into an ethos of "absolute non-duality" and total affirmation of the conventional, mundane world. This ideal is perhaps best expressed in the phrases claiming that "the grasses, trees, mountains, and rivers all attain Buddhahood" (*sōmoku kokudo shikkai jōbutsu*; *sansen sōmoku shikkai jōbutsu*), phrases that turn up almost incessantly in Japanese literature, art, theatre, and so forth. This religious ethos constituted the status quo for most of Japanese history, and continues to dominate today.

There are a few exceptions to the dominance of *hongaku* thought in Japan. Hōchibō Shōshin, a Tendai scholar of the twelfth century, was critical of *hongaku* thought, pointing out that it should not be understood to mean that sentient beings are "already" enlightened, and that such an interpretation denies causality and is the Buddhist heresy of "naturalism" (*jinen gedō*). In the seventeenth century, Myōraku Jisan and Reikū Kōken and the Tendai Anraku school urged a revival of a more strict adherence to the Buddhist precepts, in response to what they perceived as a decadence encouraged by the *hongaku* ethos. These were exceptions, however, and the *hongaku* ethos has survived as an unquestioned assumption in much of Japanese Buddhism.

The importance of *hongaku* in Japanese Buddhism has been brought to the fore in contemporary Japan through the work of scholars such as Shimaji Daitō, Hazama Jikō, and Tamura Yoshirō, who considered *hongaku* in a positive way and even claimed it to be the climactic development of Mahāyāna Buddhism. In contrast, *hongaku* thought has been rejected as "not Buddhism" in the stimulating and controversial writings of Hakamaya Noriaki and Matsumoto Shirō, who have promoted a "Critical Buddhism" that rejects substantialist ideas such as Buddha-nature and *hongaku* in favor of reaffirming "causality" or "conditioned co-arising" as the basic teaching of Buddhism. They reject *hongaku* as a non-Buddhist substantialism (introducing the neologism *dhātu-vāda*), and claim that the *hongaku* ethos promotes social discrimination, ethnocentrism, and an uncritical acceptance of the status quo through an emphasis on *wa* ("harmony", or forced conformity). The *hongaku* ethos has also been criticized by Kuroda Toshio, a historian whose theories on "exoteric–esoteric" (*kenmitsu*) Buddhism claim that *hongaku* thought was the dominant orthodoxy of medieval Japan, and that these structures continue to be influential in modern Japan.

See also: ***Honji-suijaka/shinbutsu shūgo*** **– Buddhist syncretism in Japan; Japan, Buddhism in; *Kenmitsu* (exoteric–esoteric) Buddhism.**

PAUL L. SWANSON

HONJI-SUIJAKU/SHINBUTSU SHŪGO – BUDDHIST SYNCRETISM IN JAPAN

Honji-suijaku (lit. "original ground and hanging traces") and the more general *shinbutsu shūgo* ("amalgamation of Buddhas and *kami* [local Japanese deities]") refers to various forms of interaction and combinatory associations between Buddhist and local Japanese deities and practices in Japan. The terms *honji* and *suijaku* derive from Tiantai/Tendai interpretations of the *Lotus Sūtra*, in which the second half of the *sūtra* reveals the "original" and eternal aspect of the Buddha, while the first half concerns the temporary "traces" of the Buddha or Buddhas in this conventional, historical world. Building on this paradigm, the Buddhas are seen as basic and "original," while the local Japanese deities (*kami*) are seen as historical manifestations of this "original ground."

In a wider and more general sense, *shinbutsu shūgo* refers to the long and complicated interrelationship between Buddhism (at first an imported, "foreign" religion) and the various local deities and their cults indigenous to Japan. This relationship, or amalgamation, has been seen as a historical process in which at first the Buddhist figures are considered as foreign deities to be accepted or rejected, undergoing a period of initial conflict and eventual acceptance. As Buddhism became the accepted paradigm, *kami* were perceived by some as sentient beings in need of salvation – as deluded beings reborn as *kami* due to their bad *karma*, and thus in need of and seeking Buddhist liberation. In some contexts *kami* were accepted as guardians or protectors of Buddhism, as Indian and Chinese deities and figures had done so in previous times and other places. Finally, as in the Tendai context, *kami* were defined and accepted as "traces" of Buddhas or *bodhisattvas*, as manifestations of the compassion of these Buddhist figures. A term often seen in this context is *wakō dōjin*, lit. "softening one's light and mixing with the dust," a phrase originally from Laozi but used in this context to manifest the activity of a Buddha or *bodhisattva* as appearing in this world to help and save other beings.

These different kinds of relationships, however, did not necessarily occur independently in a clear historical progression, and each of these relationships or associations can still be found in Japan today. Although there are many examples of a direct link claimed between a certain Buddha and a certain *kami* (such as that between Dainichi [Mahāvairocana], the "Great Sun" Buddha, and Amaterasu Ōmikami, the Sun Goddess), more often there is a complicated web of interconnections and combinatory associations that differ over time and place. The Kumano cult, for example, earlier claimed Amida and Kannon as the "original ground" of the Kumano deities at Hongū, Shingū, and Nachi, yet at a later time defined the connections between Buddhist figures and local *kami* into a much more complicated scheme, such as the *Kumano jūni gongen* (the twelve avatars of Kumano), which incorporated not only Amida and Kannon but other figures such as Yakushi (Bhaiṣajyaguru), Jizō (Kṣitigarbha), Śākyamuni, and Nagārjuna. Neither was there always a one-to-one correspondence between Buddha and *kami* – sometimes a Buddhist figure served as the "ground" for many *kami*, and sometimes a *kami* had many Buddhist "grounds."

Neither was this "amalgamation" a total fusion of the elements into a blob of indistinguishable parts; identifiably Buddhist and *kami* figures and practices existed side by side, at times in interrelated harmony, and at times in competition. The relationship between the Tendai temple complex on Mount Hiei and the Sannō cult of the Hie Taisha shrines at the foot of the mountain in Sakamoto, for example, was usually one of mutual support without merging all elements into a unit of indistinguishable parts. Most religious complexes in Japan, up to the modern period, included both "Buddhist" temples and shrines of local cults or deities.

These combinatory associations, however, were not always smooth, noncontradictory, or without conflict. Ise Shrine, for example, has a long history of not allowing "Buddhist" elements within its precincts. In the Tokugawa period (1600–1868) some argued that the *kami* were the "original ground" and the Buddhas and *bodhisattvas* the "traces." The whole combinatory paradigm of the amalgamation of Buddhas and *kami* was radically challenged and institutionally destroyed by the Meiji government at the end of the nineteenth century through a series of laws demanding the "separation of *kami* and Buddhas" (*shinbutsu bunri*). Temples and shrines, formerly sharing common grounds, were forced to physically separate into "Buddhist" and "Shintō" compounds, and to conduct their affairs independently. Religious figures were forced to choose between being a "Buddhist" or "Shintō" priest. Uncounted Buddhist temples and objects were destroyed. Shugendō, seen to be hopelessly amalgamated, was proscribed, and Shugendō institutions and centers were turned into Shintō shrines.

This forced separation was brought to an end at the close of World War II, but institutionally the damage has been done. Nevertheless, a sense of combinatory practices and associations is still a strong part of the Japanese religious ethos, wherein many Japanese take their newborn to be blessed at a Shintō shrine, get married in a Christian church, and participate in Buddhist funeral and memorial services. Also, many of the new religious movements in contemporary Japan combine elements from a variety of traditions.

See also: **Japan, Buddhism in.**

PAUL L. SWANSON

HORNER, ISALINE BLEW

I.B. Horner (1896–1981) was a female pioneer in scholarship on Buddhism. Carmen Blacker, in her obituary of Horner noted that she began translating and publishing Pāli texts when, as librarian of Newnham College at Cambridge, she received the library of Lord Chalmers (1931). This was not, however, her first introduction to Buddhism. According to R.E. and C.W. Igleden at age twelve, while visiting relatives in Kent, she met T.W. Rhys Davids and Caroline Augusta Foley Rhys Davids at lunch. This was her only encounter with T.W. Rhys Davids. She had correspondence with C.A.F. Rhys Davids, who encouraged her in her studies. This led to the publication of *Women Under Primitive Buddhism* (1930), the first book dedicated to a study of women in the early tradition. The first section of the book deals with materials drawn from the Commentaries, *Jātaka* and the *Milindapañha*, and deals with their presentation of women in the roles of mother, daughter, wife, widow and worker. The material for study of *bhikṣuṇī* comes from the *Vinaya*, particularly *Cullavagga X* and the *Bhikṣuṇī Vibhaṅga*. While she gives these texts more historical weight than scholars of today likely would deem prudent, she was not unaware of the problems of bias, lacunae and redaction of these texts over a considerable period of time. She pieced together a picture of the first *bhikṣuṇīs*, their reasons for joining the *sangha*, their aspirations and successes. Despite the passage of seventy years since its publication, *Women Under Primitive Buddhism* remains a mainstay on syllabi on women and Buddhism and her translations of the *Vinaya* remain in use. Her production was impressive: *The Early Buddhist Theory of Man Perfected* (1934), *Living Thoughts of Gotama the Buddha* (with A.K. Coomaraswamy, 1948), *Ten Jātaka Stories* (1954–9), contributions to Edward Conze (ed.) *Buddhist Texts Through the Ages* (1954), numerous journal articles and several volumes of the Pāli *Vinaya*.

She was also an organizer and patron. In 1950 she founded the World Federation of Buddhists, from 1939 to 1949 she was elected to the governing body of Newnham College, she was honorary secretary for the Pāli Text Society from 1942 to 1959 and president and honorary treasurer from 1959 to her death in 1981. For a period of time she *was* the Pāli Text Society and in 1969 she established a trust fund for the Society to ensure that it would be able to continue its publishing.

As well as her financial assistance to the Pāli Text Society, she donated funds for a library extension to the University of Ceylon (now Sri Lanka), and personally helped students with their work. Her work and dedication was marked by an Honorary Doctorate of Literature from the University of Ceylon in 1964 and an Order of the British Empire in 1980.

There appears to be little written on her personal life. She never married, and was known for her sharp wit and her love of flowers and animals, especially her cat.

See also: **Anglo-German school of Buddhist Studies; Women in Buddhism: an historical and textual overview.**

MAVIS L. FENN

HUAYAN

The Huayan school's highly abstract philosophy was traditionally considered the highest expression of Chinese Buddhist thought. Its unitive vision of all things forming a single, integrated reality, in which every part affected both the whole and all other parts, formed the foundation for the practices of other schools of Buddhism in China, even those as disparate as Chan and Pure Land.

History

The school derives its name from the scripture that forms its primary object of study, the *Avataṃsaka Sūtra*, or *Huayan jing* in Chinese. The scripture had been known and studied in China at least since the year 420, when Buddhabhadra completed the first translation. The *sūtra*'s primary goal is to show the reader how the world appears to a completely enlightened Buddha or advanced *bodhisattva*. It presents a universe conceived as empty of inherent existence and as arising and annihilating each moment in response to the activities of mind. The Buddha, realizing that all reality arises in this way, and having perfect control of his mind through his meditation, is able to produce effects at any distance which may appear to unenlightened beings as magic, but which to him simply manifest reality-as-it-is: mind-made. His transformations are not different in quality from those worked by ordinary beings as they pass from life to life; the crucial difference is that the Buddha is aware of the process and can control it. The Buddha sees that the universe lacks disparate objects with solid boundaries between them, but is instead a constant flow and flux in the basic transformations of mind.

As a result of this fluidity and lack of solid boundaries, all of reality is seen as perfectly interpenetrating. This interpenetration occurs at two levels. First, the ultimate nature of reality, the noumenon, is perfectly expressed in all individual phenomena. More concretely, the single primal Buddha Vairocana is the ground of all reality. As he emanates all individual phenomena, he perfectly pervades all things. Second, because of this complete pervasion of noumenon (Vairocana) into all phenomena, all phenomena perfectly interpenetrate each other. Each individual thing arises out of the same matrix of transformations, and so each implies and influences all of the others. Everything is within everything else, and yet there is no confusion of one phenomenon with another.

The final chapter, the *Gaṇḍavyūha*, depicts the journey of a youth named Sudhana as he visits one teacher after another, eventually seeing a total of fifty-three. Each teacher deepens his awareness, and the group represents every level of being, from the prostitute Vasumitrā to the greatest *bodhisattva* Samantabhadra. By the end of his journey, Sudhana experiences the falling of the boundaries that separated his own body and mind from the rest of reality and he sees the ocean of flux that is the *dharmadhātu*, or field of *dharmas*. His realization renders all former obstacles transparent to him and he wanders unimpeded through the cosmos as he wills.

A group of scholars around Dushun (557–640) were attracted to the "Chapter on the *Bodhisattva* Grounds" in the eighth fascicle of this translation. Consequently, they were called the *Dilun* ("discourse on the grounds") school, and this is commonly taken as a forerunner of the Huayan school itself. Dushun's disciple Zhiyan (602–68) also specialized in study and preaching the *sūtra*. However, credit for the foundation of the Huayan school proper goes to Zhiyan's disciple Fazang (643–712; also called Xianshou), although, in deference to his illustrious predecessors, he is listed as the school's third patriarch.

Fazang, perhaps because of his Central Asian ancestry, had some facility with Indian languages, and so was called to the capital Chang'an to work in Xuanzang's translation bureau. He broke with the latter, and later was asked by Empress Wu Zetian to assist the Indian monk Śikṣānanda (date unknown) with a new translation of the *Avataṃsaka*. However, it was not Fazang's skill as a translator, but his facility in expounding the abstruse philosophy of the *sūtra* in accessible language and appealing metaphors that helped attract imperial patronage and consolidated the school's position.

After Fazang, the line of patriarchs continued with Chengguan (738–820 or 838). Also versed in Indian languages, Chengguan assisted the monk Prajñā to produce a 40-fascicle version of the last section of the *sūtra*, the *Gaṇḍavyūha*, which added new material to the end and brought the *sūtra* to a more satisfying conclusion. In addition, Chengguan's teaching activities and his prolific commentaries on the *sūtra* further established the school on a secure basis.

The fifth and last patriarch was Zongmi (780–841), who was also acknowledged as a patriarch in the Chan school. Like his two predecessors, he achieved great eminence for his learning and teaching, and served in the imperial court, assuring continued patronage. However, four years after his death, the next emperor instigated the most wide-ranging persecution of Chinese Buddhism in premodern history, and this school, dependent as it was on royal patronage for maintenance of its academic facilities and the upkeep of its masters, perished at that time.

Doctrinal classification

Before the foundation of the Huayan school, Zhiyi (538–97), founder of the Tiantai school, had already established criteria for taking the highly varied corpus of Buddhist texts and teachings and placing them into an overall structure that brought order and explained discrepancies. However, his system had developed some deficiencies after his death. Fazang therefore constructed a Huayan scheme of doctrinal classification, or *panjiao*, in order to correct these problems. He established a single hierarchy of teachings:

1 The doctrine of the Hīnayāna was lowest because it recognized only the lack of selfhood in living beings, but not in other phenomena, and also because it lacked compassion for others and set as its goal only the liberation of the individual.
2 The elementary Mahāyāna recognized the lack of selfhood in both beings and phenomena, but it still lacked compassion because it failed to discern

Buddha-nature in all beings, and thus taught that some beings could never attain Buddhahood. This was the level in which Fazang placed the Faxiang school.

3 The advanced Mahāyāna covered the doctrines of the Tiantai school, which recognized the emptiness of both beings and phenomena, acknowledged the universality of Buddha-nature and thus the potential of all beings to become Buddhas, and its teachings of the Three Truths reaffirmed the provisional existence of things even as it taught their ultimate emptiness.

4 The Sudden Teaching covered texts and schools that inculcated the experience of sudden enlightenment, which appeared at once without prior doctrinal or scriptural study. This included the *Vimalakīrti Nirdeśa Sūtra* and the Chan school.

5 The Perfect Teaching, as found in the *Avataṃsaka Sūtra* affirmed the perfect interfusion of all phenomena within the One Mind and within each other, and the simultaneity of past, present, and future. This doctrine revealed completely the content of the enlightened mind. This was the position of the Huayan school itself.

The doctrine of interpenetration

The Huayan school considered its greatest advance to be its teaching of perfect interpenetration. This school had already shown that all particular phenomena subsist completely in the body of Vairocana, and that Vairocana was not to be found apart from or transcendent over them. Thus it taught the perfect interpenetration of the absolute, called "principle," and phenomena.

Fazang went further, and asserted the perfect interpenetration of all phenomena with each other. To illustrate this, he resorted to many images and metaphors to make his meaning clear. One was the parable of Indra's net, which described the world in terms of the fishing net of the Hindu god Indra. At each node of the net was a jewel, and each jewel reflected the light of every other jewel perfectly, thus causing its own light to be part of their light and accepting their light as part of its own.

He also used the example of a house and one of its rafters as metaphors for the relationship of principle and phenomena. The rafter is part of the house, and because a house is nothing other than its parts, and the parts cannot be parts unless they are integrated into the whole house, the house and the rafter create each other: a house with no rafters is hardly a house, and a rafter not integrated into a house is merely a piece of lumber. This conveys the view of the interpenetration of principle and phenomena. However, because the house does not exist apart from its parts, the rafter then depends upon all the other parts of the house being in place for the house to exist and give it its meaning as a rafter. Furthermore, based on the axiom that any change in a thing makes it an unrelatedly different thing, Fazang asserted that if the rafter were removed and another one put in its place, the house would then be a different house, and all its other parts would then undergo a complete change of state from being part of one house to being part of another. Thus, the rafter (or any individual part) totally determines the being of all other parts. In this way, Fazang demonstrated that every particular phenomenon in the cosmos exercises a complete and determinative role in the being of all other particular phenomena, and in turn has its own being completely determined by all other particular phenomena. Consequently, all phenomena interfuse without obstruction.

See also: **China, Buddhism in; China, early schools; Japan, Buddhism in.**

CHARLES B. JONES

HUINENG

Huineng (638–713) was an early Chan monk who, while historically obscure, is honored as the sixth "patriarch" (Ch. *zu*) of Chinese Chan, the fountainhead of the so-called "Southern school" of Chan, and the main character in the classic *The Platform Sūtra of the Sixth Patriarch* (Ch. *Liu zu tan jing*).

From a historical perspective, not much is known about Huineng. His name appears on lists of the "ten great disciples" of the fifth Chinese Chan patriarch Hongren (601–74). Other than this, sources vary widely on the details of his life and teaching, rendering a true biography difficult to reconstruct.

Whatever the actual facts of his life, he is more important within the traditional accounts as the figure who carried on the teaching and practice of "sudden enlightenment" against the opposing position of "gradual enlightenment." In the biographical section of the *Platform Sūtra*, Huineng is depicted as an illiterate woodcutter. One day, while returning home, he passed by a temple and heard a voice from within chanting the *Diamond Sūtra*. Instantly, he understood the *sūtra*'s teaching and was enlightened. Thereupon, he went to Hongren's East Mountain Monastery. Hongren at first refused to accept him, saying that Huineng's rude southern accent revealed him to be unfit for study. To this, Huineng retorted that in the *Dharma* there is neither north nor south, whereupon Hongren admitted him, but did not ordain him. Instead, he put Huineng to work hulling rice.

There follows a famous episode in which Huineng bests Hongren's senior disciple Shenxiu (605?–706) in a poetry contest that Hongren had arranged in order to see whose enlightenment was most profound and would thus merit designation as his successor. Shenxiu's verse, which speaks of the need to wipe away the dust (representing defilements) that accumulates on the mirror (the mind), is taken as a statement of the "gradual enlightenment" position, while Huineng's, dictated to a monk and written on a wall, speaks of the ultimate non-existence of both mind and defilements, a view more compatible with the position of "sudden enlightenment." After seeing Huineng's poem, Hongren realized that he thoroughly understood the true *Dharma*, and, calling Huineng into his quarters at night, privately transmitted his *Dharma* to him, along with first patriarch Bodhidharma's robe and bowl. He then advised Huineng to flee the monastery, fearing that the other monks would harm him out of jealousy. Huineng is said to have returned to south China after his training with Hongren, was finally ordained a monk, and eventually settled in the Caoxi Temple in his hometown of Xinzhou.

Historians have pointed out many problems with this story. Records show that Shenxiu and Huineng never resided at Hongren's monastery at the same time, and the copious doctrinal teachings that fill the remainder of the *Platform Sūtra* hardly support the image of the Sixth Patriarch as illiterate. However, there is evidence for Huineng having occupied the Caoxi Temple: to this day a body coated in red lacquer is kept there that is said to be Huineng's.

See also: **Bodhidharma; China, Buddhism in; China, early schools; Chan; Zen.**

CHARLES B. JONES

HUMAN RIGHTS

Political events in the course of the twentieth century have placed the issue of human rights squarely on the agenda of many Buddhists. The Chinese invasion of Tibet, the bitter ethnic conflict in Sri Lanka, the wars which have ravaged large parts of Southeast Asia and Indo-China, and the experience of military dictatorship in Burma, have all provided contemporary Buddhism with first-hand experience of the abuse of human rights on a large scale. In protesting such abuses, leading Western and Asian Buddhists routinely express their concerns about social justice using the vocabulary of human rights. Followers of the movement known as "socially engaged Buddhism" commonly appeal to the concept of human rights as a basis for their calls for social justice and an end to such practices as the use of child labor in the developing world.

Rights

Worthy though such causes are, however, it is not clear whether the concept of rights has any basis in Buddhist teachings. There appears to be no term in Buddhist sources corresponding to the notion of "rights" in the way understood in the West. The concept of a right emerged in the West as the result of a particular combination of social, political, and intellectual developments which have not been repeated elsewhere. From the Enlightenment in the eighteenth century, it has occupied centre-stage in legal and political discourse, and provides a supple and flexible language in terms of which individuals may express their claims to justice. In the simplest terms a right may be defined as an exercisable power vested in an individual. This power may be thought of as a benefit or entitlement, which allows the rightholder to impose a claim upon others or to remain immune from demands which others seek to impose.

If Buddhism has no concept of rights, how appropriate is it for Buddhists to use the language of rights when discussing moral issues? A Buddhist may argue that the discourse of rights is not inappropriate for Buddhism because rights and duties are related. A right can be regarded as the converse of a duty. If *A* has a duty to *B*, then *B* stands in the position of beneficiary and has a *right* to whatever benefit flows from the performance of his duty on the part of *A*. Although rights are not explicitly mentioned in Buddhist sources, it may be thought that they are implicit in the notion of *Dharmic* duties. If a king has a duty to rule justly, then it can be said that citizens have a "right" to fair treatment. At a more general level, if everyone has a duty not to take life, then living creatures have a right to life; if everyone has a duty not to steal, then everyone has a right not to be unjustly deprived of their property. Thus it might be argued that the concept of rights is implicit in *Dharma*, and that rights and duties are like separate windows onto the common good of justice.

Human rights

Contemporary human rights charters, such as the United Nations Universal Declaration on Human Rights of 1948, set out a list of basic rights which are held to be possessed by all human beings without distinction as to race or creed. Many Buddhists subscribe to such charters, and Buddhist leaders such as the Dalai Lama can often be heard endorsing the principles these charters embody. Certain of these rights seem to be foreshadowed in Buddhist sources: a right not to be held in slavery can be found in the canonical prohibition on trade in living beings (*Aṅguttara Nikāya* 3.208). It is also arguable that other human rights are implicit in the Buddhist precepts. The right not to be killed or tortured, for example, may be thought of as implicit in the First Precept.

On the whole, however, traditional sources have little to say about the kinds of questions which are now regarded as human rights issues. In the absence of an explicit concept of rights, of course, this is not unexpected, but if it is to endorse the concept of human rights and lay claim to these rights for its followers, Buddhism must provide some account of how the idea of human rights can be grounded in Buddhist doctrine. How might it do this? It might begin by pointing out that human rights are closely tied to the notion of human dignity. Many human rights charters, in fact, explicitly derive the former from the latter. In many religions human dignity is said to derive from the fact that human beings are created in the image of God. Buddhism, of course, makes no such claim. This makes it difficult to see what the source of human dignity might be, but if it is not to be sought at a theological level, it must be sought at the human level. In Buddhism, it seems that human dignity flows from the capacity of human beings to gain enlightenment, as demonstrated by the historical figure of the Buddha and the saints of the Buddhist tradition. A Buddha is a paradigm of human perfection, and it is in the profound knowledge and compassion which he exemplifies – qualities which all human beings can emulate – that human dignity seems to be grounded. Buddhism teaches that we are all potential Buddhas (some Mahāyāna schools express this by saying that all beings possess the "Buddha-nature" or the seed of enlightenment). By virtue of this common potential for enlightenment it follows that all individuals are worthy of respect. As a corollary of this respect justice demands that the rights of each individual must be protected.

From a Buddhist point of view the Western emphasis on *human* rights may be thought unduly narrow in that it seems to exclude the universe of sentient non-human beings from any entitlement to rights. Buddhists may feel, accordingly, that it is less prejudicial to revert to the older terminology of "natural rights" so as not to exclude animals. Whether or not animals have rights, and whether these are the same rights as human beings, is a matter that requires separate discussion, but the terminology of "natural rights" may be thought less anthropocentric and less prejudicial to the discussion.

See also: **Animals and the environment; Ethics; Ethics, theories of; Moral discipline.**

DAMIEN KEOWN

HWAŎM BUDDHISM

Hwaŏm, Korea's version of Chinese Huayan Buddhism, was one of the dominant forms of scholastic Buddhism in Korea. Its influence on the evolution of Korean Sŏn Buddhism is unmistakable. The first record of Hwaŏm teaching in Korean Buddhism appeared in association with the Silla monk Chajang (590–658) who brought the *Huayan jing* from Tang China. Chajang, however, is better known as a *Vinaya* master. Another Silla monk, Wŏnhyo (617–86) wrote commentaries and essentials on *Huayan jing*, which unfortunately have been lost.

One of Wŏnhyo's contemporary, Ŭisang (625–702), is credited as the founder of the Hwaŏm school. From 661 to 668, Ŭisang studied in Tang China with Zhiyan (602–68), the designated second patriarch of Chinese Huayan Buddhism. During this time, Ŭisang became a colleague of another one of Zhiyan's disciples, Fazang (643–712), who later became the third patriarch of the tradition. Ŭisang's thought on Hwaŏm is well articulated in a small piece entitled *Hwaŏm ilsŭng pŏpkye to* (*The Diagram of Dharmadhātu of the One Vehicle of Hwaŏm Buddhism*), also known as *Pŏpsŏng gye* (*A Verse on Dharma Nature*), which he presented to Zhiyan.

Zhiyan's Huayan thought foregrounds the idea of Nature Origination (Ch. *xingqi*, Kor. *sŏnggi*), the textual source of which is found in the chapter on the "Appearance of the Tathāgata" in the 80-fascicles *Huayan jing* (or *Flower Garland Sūtra*). According to the Buddhist theory of dependent origination, things exist interdependently with other things and, thus, there is no individual self. As things do not have an independent substantial essence of their own, the origination in the theory of dependent origination, in its ultimate sense, is non-origination. This idea of the non-origination of origination is explained in the *Huayan jing* as the reality of the world where things manifest the ultimate truth, or the Tathāgata. This theory is known as Nature Origination and lies at the core of Zhiyan's Huayan thought. Following Zhiyan's dea, Ŭisang in the *Pŏpsŏng gye* explains the Hwaŏm worldview as "Origination of *Dharma* Nature" (Kor. *pŏpkye yŏn' gi*). This *Dharma* nature is the essence of both Tathāgata and all sentient beings. Thus the world as it is manifests the "Origination of *Dharma* Nature." Ŭisang's *Pŏpsŏng gye* generated a series of commentaries, which served as the core of the evolution of Hwaŏm thought in Korea. Commentaries appearing up to the tenth century were collected in a 4-fascicle volume entitled *Pŏpgye to' gi ch' ongsu rok* (*Collected Record of the Cores on the Diagram of the Dharmadhātu*) whose author is not known.

Kyunyŏ (923–73), a monk during the Koryŏ (918–1392) period, left behind voluminous works on Hwaŏm Buddhism. Kyunyŏ's main concern was to clarify the doctrinal ground of Hwaŏm Buddhism through the interpretation of Ŭisang's *Pŏpkye to* and in connection with the Chinese Huayan masters Zhiyan and Fazang. In his *Ilsŭng pŏpkye to wŏn' tong ki* (*Complete and Unified Record on the Diagram of the Dharmadhātu of the One Vehicle*), Kyunyŏ identified Ŭisang's Hwaŏm thought as horizontal *dharmadhātu* (Kor. *hoengjin pŏpkye*) and Fazang's as vertical *dharmadhātu* (Kor. *sujin pŏpkye*). Combining these two ideas, Kyunyŏ described his own Hwaŏm teaching as "round and sided" (or "general and particular") (Kor. *chuch' ŭk*). Kyunyŏ argues that, in Ŭisang's horizontal *dharmadhātu*, part represents whole, whereas in Fazang's vertical *dharmadhātu*, whole is understood by understanding each and every constituent part. In the former, totality is emphasized, whereas in the latter the particulars that construct the whole are emphasized. In comparing these two modes of Hwaŏm thought, both illustrating the interdependence of one and many, Kyunyŏ wanted to bring together, on one hand, the secular and the sacred and, on the other, form and nature.

Kyunyŏ's Hwaŏm Buddhism became a target of criticism with Ŭich'ŏn (1055–1101), who is known as the founder of the Ch' ŏnt' ae (Ch. Tiantai) school in Korea, but who was more a Hwaŏm Buddhist than a Ch' ŏnt' ae patriarch. Ŭich'ŏn was an ambitious scholar, an avid collector of Buddhist texts, and well versed in various different schools of Buddhism. He did not clearly articulate the reason for his criticism of Kyunyŏ, but the context provided in his *Tae'gak kuksa munjip* (*Collected Essays of National Master Great Awakening*) suggests that Ŭich'ŏn believed that Kyunyŏ's philosophical approach to Hwaŏm wrongly served the school and created an imbalance between theory and practice. In various ways Ŭich'ŏn attempted a union between theory and practice, but for him the guiding principle for this harmony was the Hwaŏm doctrine. Unlike Kyunyŏ, who employed Zhiyan and Fazang in his interpretation of Ŭisang, Ŭich'ŏn highly valued Chingguan (738–839) and Zongmi (780–841), and with good reason. Ŭich'ŏn thought that Chingguan emphasized the equal importance of Yogācāra and Madhyaka, and Zongmi harmonized Chan and Huayan. In this context, Ŭich'ŏn came to appreciate the syncretic nature of Wŏnhyo's Buddhism, and placed Wŏnhyo side by side with Ŭisang in the tradition of Korean Hwaŏm Buddhism. Ŭich'ŏn's Buddhism did not produce the results he desired but still prepared a way for Pojo Chinul to incorporate Hwaŏm thought in his Sŏn philosophy.

Hwaŏm Buddhism played a significant role in the formation of Chinul's (1158–1210) Sŏn Buddhism. Chinul shared with

Ŭisang his thought on Nature Origination. In his *Wŏndon sŏngbullon* (*Treatise on Complete and Sudden Attainment of Buddhahood*), Chinul explains that the "Dependent Origination of *Dharma* Nature" discussed by Ŭisang in the *Pŏpgye to* reveals the essence (Kor. *ch' e*; Ch. *ti*) of "Nature Origination," the true nature of sentient beings, which was complete, clear and transparent from the beginning. In this sense, to Chinul, "Nature Origination and Dependent Origination" are not two, but one. This provides the philosophical foundation for the Sŏn Buddhist equation of sentient beings and the Buddha; and at the same time, makes possible sudden enlightenment. Based on this, Chinul developed his idea of the unification of meditational and doctrinal approaches to Buddhism.

During the period between the mid-fifteenth century and the early twentieth century, Korean Buddhism lost its sectarian identity because of the anti-Buddhist policy of the Chosŏn dynasty (1392–1910). However, Ŭisang's *Pŏpgye to* and the 80-fascicles *Huayan jing* continued to serve as major texts of scholastic Buddhism. Among the well-known Chosŏn Hwaŏm scholars were Sŏlcham (1435–93) and Yŏndam (1720–99). They explored the relationship between Hwaŏm's Nature Origination and Sŏn's notion of mind sentient beings; their studies confirm the close relationship between Hwaŏm and Sŏn in Korean Buddhism since Chinul.

See also: **Korea, Buddhism in.**

JIN Y. PARK

HYUJŎNG

Ch'ŏnghŏ Hyujŏng (1520–1604), also known as Sŏsan taesa, was a Sŏn master in Korea who worked to maintain the Buddhist tradition amidst increasing suppression of Buddhism by the Confucian Chosŏn dynasty.

Hyujŏng was trained at Sŏnggyun'gwan, a national academy for Confucian teaching. After an unsuccessful attempt at the national civil examination at the age of fifteen, he took a trip with friends to Mount Chiri in southern Korea, where he encountered Buddhist teachings and later joined a monastery. In 1549, he passed the national examination for monks and took a governmental position, but soon quit the job and devoted his time to personal practice.

In the tradition of Pojo Chinul, a thirteenth-century Korean Sŏn master, Hyujŏng emphasized the importance of Patriarchal Sŏn Buddhism of Kanhwa practice. He made a distinction in *hwadu* (Ch. *huatou*) practice between the investigation of "meaning," which he identified with live words, and the investigation of "word," which he equated to dead words. Hyujŏng considered the quality of earnestness to be of utmost importance in practicing *hwadu*. Together with earnestness, Hyujŏng put forth three essentials of meditation: the great faith, the great intention, and the great doubt.

Like Chinul, Hyujŏng considered *hwadu* practice fit for only practitioners of high capacity, and he felt the time in which he lived lacked practitioners of such capacity. For those not able to directly enter the world of Sŏn through *hwadu* meditation, Hyujŏng proposed what is known as *sa'gyo ipsŏn*, which means to abandon doctrinal teaching and enter into Sŏn. In suggesting *sa'gyo ipsŏn*, Hyujŏng did not completely deny the value of doctrinal teaching. Instead, Hyujŏng thought that doctrinal teaching could facilitate an initial stage in which practitioners of medium or low capacity learned about the Buddhist teachings of causation, sudden awakening, and gradual cultivation and, thus, prepared themselves to practice Sŏn.

In his *Sŏn'ga ku'gam* (*A Paragon of Sŏn Buddhism*), Hyujŏng collected passages from various Sŏn Buddhist texts for practitioners. In this text, Hyujŏng stated that Sŏn is the teaching of seeing one's own mind. To Hyujŏng, reaching the realm of no-language without relying on language is the teaching of Sŏn, whereas to reach there by employing language is that of doctrinal teaching.

Hyujŏng also recorded his thoughts on Confucianism in *Yu'ga ku'gam* (*A Paragon of the Confucian School*), and on Daoism in *To'ga ku'gam* (*A Paragon of the Daoist School*). These texts together with *Sŏn'ga ku'gam* were combined into *Samga ku'gam* (*A Paragon of Three Teachings*), which demonstrates Hujŏng's thought on the oneness of the Three Teachings. During the Chosŏn dynasty, this grouping of the Three Teachings was a major trend amongst Buddhist thinkers in an effort to convince the Confucian literati of the Three Teachings' original oneness.

Hyujŏng and his disciple Yujŏng are well known for being leaders of the monks' militia during the Japanese invasion of Korea (1592–97), for which Hyujŏng has been recognized as a national hero. It remains debatable whether Hyujŏng's involvement with the monks' militia should be celebrated. The close relationship between Buddhism and the state, a major feature of Korean Buddhism, is reconfirmed in the formation of the monks' militia, and its uncritical celebration within the Korean Buddhist tradition.

See also: **Korea, Buddhism in.**

JIN Y. PARK

I

INDIA, BUDDHISM IN

Buddhism began in the republic of Magadha in the Ganges Valley of north-eastern India in, according to traditional accounts, the thirty-fifth year of the life of its founder, Gautama the Buddha, whose dates are now most commonly believed to have been 563–483 BCE. Traditional accounts say that Gautama lived to the age of eighty, by which time he had spent forty-five years teaching and leading a community of monks and nuns, whose number by the time of his death is supposed to have been 1,250. In what Gautama knew were his final days, he was asked who would lead this community after his death, and he responded that the *Dharma* (custom), rather than a human being, should be his disciples' guide. Accordingly, shortly after his death, the *arhants* from his community met with the purpose of arriving at an agreement on what exactly the *Dharma* was.

As the Buddha's cousin Ānanda had been his personal attendant for the last thirty years of his life and had either heard every talk the Buddha had given or had heard a summary of talks he had not personally attended, he was appointed the task of passing final judgment on the authenticity of every account of the Buddha's teachings that was remembered by his disciples. All the accounts that received Ānanda's approval were arranged into collections, and each of these collections was given to several monks to memorize and to pass on to future generations. For several hundred years, these collections of remembered accounts of the Buddha's teachings were passed down from one generation to the next, and one of the principal duties of a newly ordained monk was to commit some portion of the entire collection to memory. The accounts passed down in this way were known as *sūtras*, and these *sūtras* were part of the *Dharma* that was to guide the community.

The other part of the *Dharma* was the set of disciplinary rules known as *Vinaya*. The entire *vinaya* consists of the rules themselves, known as *Prātimokṣa* and an extensive historical record that provides context for how and why each rule was formed and how rules were revised or repealed according to new circumstances. The *Vinaya* provides the only historical record we have of the early Buddhist community in India. The monks who were alive to hear the teachings that were collected into the divisions of the canon known as the *sūtras* and the *Vinaya* were known as the *śrāvakas* (the hearers), and Buddhists who accepted as authentic Buddhism only what the hearers had reportedly heard came to be known as followers of the *Śrāvakayāna* (the way of the hearers).

Self-identification of the early Buddhist community

Aside from attending to the important task of orally transmitting their canon, one of the principal preoccupations of the *Śrāvakayāna* Buddhists was to establish a sense of corporate identity and distinctiveness, in other words to make a case for what made the Buddhist teachings and practices different from (and presumably better than) what other communities were teaching. The only version of the *Śrāvakayāna* canon that is still fully extant is that which is known as the Pāli Canon of the Theravāda community, and it contains numerous traces of the efforts of the Buddhists to distinguish themselves from other communities.

One of the communities against which the early Buddhists defined themselves was that of the Brahmans, the priests whose responsibility was to preserve the teachings and ritual practices associated with the Vedas and their extensive commentaries. Vedic practices were mostly designed to preserve the order of such social institutions as governance, the economy and the family. The Pāli canon contains numerous satirical accounts of Brahmans, who are often portrayed as obsessively concerned with their own power and social status. Indeed, in some *sūtras* (*suttas* in Pāli) the entire Vedic religion is depicted as the work of lazy charlatans who duped the general public into supporting them by hiring them to perform rituals of questionable value. The Buddha is often portrayed as unselfishly offering teachings and practices that genuinely benefit all human beings rather than serving the greed of a privileged few. The Buddhist mendicant (*bhikṣu*, which literally means "beggar") is depicted as a person who actually does what Brahmans ought to do, namely, live an exemplary life of material simplicity, harmlessness and service to others. While the Brahmans are portrayed as fatuous, self-important men interested mostly in maintaining the privileged status of their families, *bhikṣus* are praised as celibates who renounce their biological families so that they can be of service to all people, and not just to their own families. The family tends to be portrayed as a burdensome social unit that makes selfish demands on its members, thereby distracting them from the higher calling of working for the welfare of all living beings. No small part of the *Śrāvakayāna* canons, therefore, is dedicated to celebrating the celibate life of the solitary renunciate as inherently more noble (*ārya*) than family life.

Defining themselves as distinct from follows of the Brahmāṇical religion was only half of what *Śrāvakayāna* Buddhists

Figure 23 Standing Buddha image, Ellorā, India.

had to do to accomplish self-definition. The other half of that task was to distinguish themselves from all the other communities that advocated and practiced renunciation. Collectively, members of these renunciate communities were called *śramaṇas*, a term that is usually interpreted to mean people who undergo the rigors of extraordinary discipline and is often translated as "ascetic." The Buddha and his disciples are often referred to in the *Śrāvakayāna* literature as *śramaṇas*. The Buddhists are distinguished from other ascetics in two ways. First, the Buddha and his disciples are portrayed as less extreme in their renunciation than others, and especially as less extreme than the Jains. So while some ascetics went naked, the Buddhists wore simple robes sewn together from scraps of discarded or donated cloth and dyed with readily available clays or bark. While some ascetics fasted for long periods of time, the Buddhists ate one meal a day of scraps of leftover food donated by householders. While some ascetics remained outdoors all the time and refrained from lying down to sleep, the Buddhists built simple structures and slept on thin woven mats. So while the Buddhist life was one of discipline and simplicity, it was not one of self-denial so severe as to threaten health.

The second way that the Buddhists distinguished themselves from other ascetic movements was by laying emphasis on the reasonableness, practicality and testability of the Buddha's teachings. The Buddha's teachings are repeatedly described to be invitations to try out a particular practice to see whether it produces the expected results; the Buddha's *Dharma* is therefore described in Pāli as *ehipassiko* (a "come and see" thing). It is also described as "timely," which is explained as meaning that it can be known very soon, certainly within this very life, whether the Buddha's teachings produce the promised results; one need not wait until a life after death to see whether following Buddhist practices pays off. Buddhist customs are described as being both good for oneself and good for others; not only will the practitioner benefit, but so will all human beings, and even all living things.

Principal *Śrāvakayāna* teachings

The unambiguously clear focus of the *Śrāvakayāna* teachings is the attainment of *nirvāṇa*, understood as the cessation of afflictions in this life and the cessation of rebirth into any further life after this one. The person who, by following the teachings of a buddha, has attained the cessation of afflictions in this life is known as an *arhant* (feminine, *arhatī*). A person who attains cessation without the benefit of hearing the teachings of a buddha is known as a *pratyekabuddha*, a term that is often translated as "solitary buddha." A person who attains cessation in a time when no buddha's teachings are known in the world and who then teaches others how to attain *nirvāṇa* is known as an unsurpassed perfectly awakened one (*anuttarasamyaksambuddha*). Gautama is regarded the most recent *anuttarasamyaksambuddha*; there will not be another until the *Dharma* of Gautama Buddha has been completely forgotten.

The *Śrāvakayāna* record of the Buddha's teachings on *nirvāṇa* places an emphasis on the endeavor of the individual to follow the path of gradually purifying one's thoughts and actions. While it is easiest to follow this path when one has the support of other individuals who are also dedicated to following it, the resolve to benefit from the support of a community is essentially an individual matter. The purificatory path to *nirvāṇa* is divided into three main phases: the cultivation of good habits (*śīla*), the development of concentration (*samādhi*) and the attainment of wisdom (*prajñā*).

Good habits are to be cultivated in three areas: the way one thinks, the way one speaks and the way one acts. Good habits of thought are those that lead to the elimination of selfish desires, selfish aversions and the principal forms of delusion. Four forms of delusion are especially targeted for elimination, namely, the false views that impermanent things are permanent, that unpleasant things are pleasant, that impersonal things are personal and that impure things are pure. Good habits of speech consist in refraining from deceptive speech, from harsh speech that hurts the feelings of others, from saying what damages the reputations of others and from speaking frivolously or pointlessly. Good habits of action consist in refraining from killing, from taking what is not freely given and from sexual misconduct – most Indian commentators say that misconduct means relations with inappropriate partners, that is, with a person of the same sex, with a minor or with a person married or betrothed to another.

Good habits of conduct are said to enable one to cultivate mental concentration, because they replace those negative habits of body, speech and mind that tend to disturb the mind. Good concentration (*samādhi*) is defined as the single-pointedness of a healthy mind (*kuśalacittasya ekagratā*). It can occur only when the mentality has been cleared of skepticism, drowsiness, anxiety, and worry. More positively, a mentality is said to be healthy when it is characterized by faith, carefulness, self-confidence, equanimity, sense of shame, modesty, absence of greed, absence of hatred, non-violence and courage. There is a wide range of subjects recommended for concentrating the mind on, but all of them can be subsumed under the so-called four foundations of mindful awareness. This exercise consists in observing the general and specific characteristics of the physical body, its various limbs and internal organs, the elements of which it is composed, and its mortality; the pleasant and unpleasant physical and mental feelings that come and go; the six modes of awareness: vision, hearing, smelling, tasting, touching and thinking; and the internal mental factors that arise when different objects are experienced.

The cultivation of *samādhi* is the means by which the mind is prepared to cultivate wisdom (*prajñā*), which is traditionally said to be of three types: the wisdom consisting in listening to teachers and the study of *Dharma* texts; the wisdom consisting in reflecting on what is contained in the teachings one has encountered; and the cultivation of the virtues discussed in those teachings. Wisdom is the natural antidote to delusion, the principal cause of distress (*duḥkha*). The elimination of the cause leads to the elimination of the effect, and the cessation of *duḥkha* is *nirvāṇa*, the final goal of Buddhist practice.

Division of early community into schools

Despite all the efforts to come to an agreement on what the Buddha had actually taught, the early Buddhist community soon realized that there were plenty of issues that were left undecided and that many teachings were subject to more than one interpretation. One of the texts in the Pāli Canon, the *Kathāvatthu*, is a record of some 200 points that were disputed among eighteen early schools of Buddhism. As it is a Theravāda text, this text records the views of other schools and then states the Theravādin position.

Some schools, for example, held the view that there is a permanent self that goes through suffering and then enters *nirvāṇa* when a person becomes enlightened; that becoming an *arhant* is not a permanent achievement; that buddhas pervade all of space; and that buddhas can suspend any of the laws of nature. The Theravādins rejected all those views. Some Buddhists held another view that the Theravādins rejected, namely, that everything the Buddha said, even in discussing the most ordinary matters of everyday life, was *lokottara* or elevated above the plane of ordinary people. Some Buddhists also held that there is a specific quality known as awakening or enlightenment (*bodhi*), and when one acquires that property, then one is a buddha. The Theravāda position is that enlightenment is not a positive quality that one acquires, because if it were a quality that one acquires then one could also lose it again. Rather, enlightenment is a name given to the absence of desire, hatred and delusion; because absence is not a thing, it is not a thing that one can lose. Some Buddhists argued that because the Buddha did not really have any desires and had no real needs, none of the gifts presented to him were really beneficial to him and therefore, there is no real merit in making offerings to the Buddha. The Theravādins responded that giving a gift to a person of great wisdom and virtue brings much benefit, because a wise and virtuous person will use the gift for the benefit of others. As the Buddha was supremely wise and virtuous, giving gifts to him achieved great benefit and therefore generated merit for the donors. A similar matter for discussion was whether the community of monks was a real entity or merely a conventional fiction. If the latter, then giving to it would provide no good. The Theravādins replied that the monastic community uses gifts for the benefit of others. Therefore, the gifts generate merit for the donors. Some Buddhists held that the Buddha did not really live in the world of human beings; rather he sent a manifestation of himself to be among people. The *Dharma* was taught through this manifestation, which was a creation of the cosmic Buddha. The Theravāda position was that the Buddha was a human being who discovered and taught the *Dharma* himself. Some Buddhists held that because the Buddha was perfectly dispassionate, it was impossible for him actually to feel compassion; his apparent displays of compassion were therefore a kind of play-acting done for the benefit of ordinary people. The Theravāda position was that the Buddha did in fact feel true compassion. Finally, a controversy among the early *Śrāvakayānins* concerned the question of whether it is possible for a layperson to be an *arhant*. Some schools argued that a layperson can become an *arhant* and continue living as a layperson. The Theravāda position is that a layperson can become an *arhant*, but an *arhant* cannot continue to live as a layperson; more particularly, an *arhant* cannot have sexual intercourse, own property, wear perfumes and cosmetics, have a wardrobe of fancy clothes, and live in a permanent home. On the question of the relation between an *arhant* and a buddha, some schools argued that buddhas have unlimited knowledge of all things, whereas *arhants* have only a limited knowledge, and therefore, *arhants* must have some fetters that impede them from attaining the full achievements of a buddha. The Theravādin position, however, is that the *arhant* has been completely liberated from all the fetters that keep one bound to the world of rebirth and suffering. To be so liberated was the highest achievement of the Buddha. The achievement of an *arhant* is nothing less. The only difference between a Buddha and an *arhant* is that the Buddha discovered the *Dharma* without being taught by anyone else; and *arhant* learns the *Dharma* by being taught. But, whether it is learned from others or discovered by oneself, the *Dharma* has exactly the same effect on anyone who applies it.

The Mahāyāna expansion of the canon

The canons of the *Śrāvakayāna* were closed in the sense that, theoretically at least, no new texts could be added to them. At approximately the time that these canons were set down in writing, a number of *sūtras* began to emerge that were not previously known. Strict followers of the *Śrāvakayāna* regarded these new texts as forgeries, in the sense that they purported to be records of what the Buddha had said. Critics of these new texts claimed that the texts were written by people motivated by a desire to justify practices that had been forbidden or at least discouraged by the Buddha and to justify doctrinal innovations that were antithetical to what the Buddha had taught. Proponents of the new texts, who came to be called Mahāyāna Buddhists, sometimes claimed that the Buddha had taught the contents of these texts secretly to advanced disciples with the instruction that they not be made public until people were ready to receive them. Perhaps in response to this claim, the *Śrāvakayānins* insisted that the Buddha had never taught anything in secret or held anything back from the general public. Whatever the truth to this matter might be, those who were open to studying the newly available texts usually studied them in addition to, rather than instead of, the canonical texts of the *Śrāvakayāna*. While there may have been some disagreement over the question of whether the new texts were truly the words of the Buddha, this disagreement never resulted in a schism in India; most monasteries reportedly had strictly canonical monks living side by side with those who studied the Mahāyāna texts. Because there was nothing in principle to prevent the addition of new materials, the Mahāyāna corpus of texts was considerably expanded over the centuries. It came to include so many texts that it would be impossible to survey them. What follows is a summary of just a few of those that have been translated into English and that deal with themes that came to characterize the Mahāyāna approach to Buddhist theory and practice.

The *Vimalakīrti Nirdeśa Sūtra* (*Sūtra of Vimalakīrti's Exposition*) is one of the most important of the Mahāyāna texts that expound the doctrine of the *bodhisattva*, proclaim the doctrine of the emptiness of all phenomena, and assert that compassion for all beings is the heart of the Buddhist's career. This text contains a celebration of the ideal Buddhist as being a layperson rather than a monk, and it warns through a number of entertaining satirical stories the dangers of spiritual pride and attachment to purity of life. The text contains a number of inversions of attitudes that were commonplace at the time of its composition. It argues, for example, that females are not intrinsically inferior to males and that in fact gender is purely an illusion and has nothing to do with reality. It also argues, to give another example, that the family of the Tathāgatas (Buddhas) is made up of those who are driven by egoism, ignorance, the thirst for existence, greed, hatred and delusion and who commit the ten unwholesome acts of killing, stealing, sexual promiscuity, lying, harsh speech, gossip, frivolous chatter, covetousness, malice, and false views; for just as lotuses grow in swamps and mud banks, the virtues of a Buddha grow in those living beings who are like swamps and mud banks of passions.

A genre of texts known as *Prajñāpāramitā* (Perfection of Wisdom) deal extensively with the *bodhisattva* ideal. The term "*bodhisattva*" is probably a false Sanskritization of the Pāli term "*bodhisatta*," meaning "one who is dedicated to becoming awakened," but in Mahāyāna, the term comes to mean "one whose essence is awakening." *Bodhisattvas* are described as beings who postpone their own enlightenment until all other creatures have found their way to *nirvāṇa*. That said, these texts also claim that ultimately there is no distinction between *nirvāṇa* and *saṃsāra*, between freedom and bondage or between delusion and wisdom. All the teachings of Buddhism about getting free of *saṃsāra* and achieving *nirvāṇa* are to be understood at the level of conventional truth, not as adequate descriptions of how things really are.

Some of the texts of this genre, such as the *Vajracchedika* (*Diamond-cutter*) *Sūtra*, discuss the concept of the age of decadent *Dharma*, a time when there will be a general collapse of the true *Dharma* of the Buddha; during this time, people should protect themselves by studying and reciting Mahāyāna texts, for these actions will enable people to accumulate vast heaps of merit. Drawing upon a metaphor that first appears in canonical teachings, the *bodhisattva* is described as a teacher who knows better than to pick up a raft and carry it after it has helped one to cross a river. Accordingly, the *bodhisattva* is said not to abide anywhere, not to dwell on any teaching or any practice, not to have any place even the size of an atom that is thought of as home or as a place of refuge. Much of the perfection of wisdom literature is dedicated to expounding the perfections of standard Buddhist virtues, perfection being understood as cultivating the virtues without allowing any idea to arise that they are virtues or that one is a virtuous person for having them.

There were several Mahāyāna *sūtras* that came to be regarded as literary masterpieces in classical Sanskrit literature. One of the most prominent of these was the *Saddharmapuṇḍarīka* (*White Lotus of the True Dharma*). It is important not only as a literary masterpiece, but as one of the most important of a genre of literature that places a strong emphasis on the importance of faith. Unlike many other Mahāyāna texts, it was written in a dramatic style that was accessible to everyone. Its message is conveyed in parables and stories rather than abstractions. Moreover, the main doctrine of the *sūtra* – universal enlightenment – appealed to a wide range of people. One of the most prominent themes in the *Lotus Sūtra* is that there are not two paths, the *Śrāvakayāna* and the Mahāyāna, but just one path, the Buddha path. The *sūtra* first says that the *Śrāvakayāna* is an inferior path or a discarded path (Hīnayāna) and then it denies that this inferior path was ever taught by the Buddha at all; the one path taught by the Buddha, the Buddha path, is in fact just the Mahāyāna. This *sūtra*, like the *Diamond-cutter*, has much to say about the age of degenerate *Dharma*, when all sentient beings become so vitiated through their unwholesome acts that they can barely even form the aspiration to be good; it is in such a time that the only practice that will not lead one to ruin is studying and reciting the *Lotus Sūtra*, a text given by the Buddha to ensure that no sentient being who hears it and has faith in it will fail to attain supreme, prefect awakening. The rigorous practices, purity of life and meditations of the Buddha's first disciples are not necessary, for anyone who hears the *Lotus Sūtra* will by that hearing alone become a buddha. True *Dharma* cannot be acquired through reason or learning, but must be accepted on faith. This is a truth that the *śrāvakas* are incapable of understanding or accepting, and therefore they constitute an actual barrier to those who seek Buddhahood. The teaching of the *Lotus Sūtra*, says the *Lotus Sūtra* itself, was completely unknown to the *śrāvaka*s; the Buddha did not teach this *sūtra* to them, because he knew that the whole world, including the gods, would be terrified by it. The *sūtra* strikes fear into the hearts of those who take pride in their purity of lifestyle, their learning and their ability to reason. Finally the *Lotus Sūtra* warns repeatedly that those who reject the *Lotus Sūtra* will go to hell. Somewhat surprisingly to Chinese pilgrims who had become familiar with this text in Chinese translation and then traveled to India, even this fiery, polemical text did not seem to lead to serious schisms within the Indian Buddhist community.

In all the new literature produced in Indian Mahāyāna Buddhism, some is devotional in nature, some is strictly polemical, while some is more philosophically oriented. The *Āryasaddharmalaṅkāvatāra Mahāyāna Sūtra* (*Noble Mahāyāna Sūtra about the Introduction of the True Dharma to Laṅka*) is among these more philosophical *sūtras*. It is one of the principal scriptural sources for the Yogācāra school of Mahāyāna Buddhism. The *Laṅkāvatāra* is also one of the principal sources for the vegetarian ethic. Among the most important recurrent themes in this *sūtra* are that the entire world is mind only; that there is no dualism, because there is no difference between *nirvāṇa* and *saṃsāra*, or between presence and absence, or between pure and impure, or between subject and object; the notion of different Buddhist paths or vehicles is an illusion; that nothing has a nature of its own (*svabhāva*). The text also claims that the essence of *tathāgatagarbha* is realized only when one casts aside discriminating, dualistic forms of thought. The term *tathāgatagarbha* is said to be synonymous with *dharmakaya*, that is, the totality of phenomena. On a personal level, it is synonymous with *buddhatā* (buddhahood or buddhanature), which in turn is another name for the *ālayavijñāna*, the receptacle of all past experiences and the storehouse of potentials of all future experiences; because it contains the potential for all future experiences, it contains the potential for being a Buddha. The text raises the question: if the notion that there are many paths within Buddhism is an illusion, why do there even appear to be many paths? The answer provided is that the infinite compassion of the Buddha ingeniously contrives methods (*upāya*) of reaching the hearts of all sentient beings and therefore speaks to them in the delusive terms they can comprehend. Eventually, however, he leads them out of delusion and out of discriminating, dualistic thought into a direct experience of the essential nature of the mind, which is pure, calm and nondualistic.

Like many Mahāyāna *sūtras*, the *Laṅkāvatāra* speaks in negative terms of the *Śrāvakayāna*, which is characterized as dualistic and blinded by delusion. In a final section of the *Laṅkāvatāra*, the *śrāvakas* are severely criticized for giving the false teaching that it is sometimes acceptable for a monk to eat meat. The text provides an extensive defense of the view that only those who avoid eating meat, dairy products, honey, leeks and garlic and who avoid wearing wool and leather are living a life of purity in keeping with the Buddha's teachings. This concern with dietary purity is unexpected in a text that places so much emphasis on avoiding false dichotomies such as purity and impurity and may be evidence that the work began as an anthology of several texts that were eventually redacted together without too much concern for logical consistency.

The Sanskritization and Brahmanization of Buddhism

The Buddha reportedly advised his disciples to speak to people in vernacular languages rather than using Sanskrit, a language that even by his time was used only liturgically and among the highly educated. Accordingly, Buddhist texts appeared, once writing became common, in a variety of regional languages. Some Mahāyāna *sūtras*, in discussing the virtues that a *bodhisattva* should cultivate, list a skill in learning many languages as an important qualification. While many Buddhist teachers were undoubtedly polyglots, a tendency grew to use Sanskrit as for communication. The main advantage of using Sanskrit, of course, was that it made communication possible in a larger geographical area, for Sanskrit was used by some people in all of what is now India, Pakistan, Afghanistan, Myanmar (Burma) and Bangladesh. The main disadvantage was that Sanskrit texts were understandable only to those with a

Brahmāṇical education. An irony of history is that because of the relative durability of Sanskrit compared to colloquial languages, it has mostly been the work of the educated Buddhists that has survived, while more popular forms of Buddhism have been much more perishable and difficult for modern historians to recover.

The Sanskritization of Buddhism inevitably led to its Brahmanization. Those who could read and write and speak Sanskrit tended to be people, almost always high-caste males, who had also been trained in Pāṇini's grammatical system and all the metaphysical and methodological structures built into that ingenious system, which many regard as the crowning achievement of Indian culture. Sanskrit users were also routinely educated in Brahmanical systems of religious philosophy, such as Nyāya, Vaiśeṣika, Sāṃkhya, Yoga and Mīmāṃsā. Not surprisingly, then, Sanskrit Buddhism, in contrast to vernacular Buddhism, became increasingly characterized by a preoccupation with showing that the teachings of Buddhism were in every way superior to the teachings of other Indian schools of religious thought and practice, and that the Buddha was unsurpassed as a teacher and in possession of an almost Godlike infallibility. Several Buddhist authors wrote with confidence that *nirvāṇa* was impossible for followers of non-Buddhist systems to attain, and some were convinced (as we saw in the brief outlines of some of the Sanskrit *sūtras* of the Mahāyāna) that only one approach to Buddhism was valid. Along with this doctrinal exclusivism, one also finds a new emphasis on certain kinds of purity, such as dietary purity, and a gradual but undeniable shift to the view that women are seriously handicapped in the quest for *nirvāṇa*, and perhaps even altogether incapable of attaining it.

As Buddhism increasingly became the domain of educated males, its character was no doubt changed. At the same time, it also became a respectable religion among the educated classes. The two Buddhist "universities" (actually large monasteries) at Nālandā and Vikramaśīla attracted some of the best minds of India, both Buddhist and non-Buddhist, and opened their doors to males of all persuasions. For all their exclusivity on some levels, the Buddhist centers of learning were important vehicles for the dissemination of all kinds of philosophy as well as knowledge in medicine, architecture, sculpture and even political science. The high visibility of the great learning centers of Buddhism also made them obvious targets when Arabic, Turkish, and Persian Muslims began to invade India in the eleventh century CE. Invading generals destroyed the Buddhist universities in the north, thus delivering a final blow to a religion that was already becoming somewhat stagnant and lacking in vitality. By the twelfth century there was little evidence of a living Buddhist tradition in the north, and a few centuries later it had all but disappeared in the south of India (See Figure 23).

See also: **Aśoka; Councils; *Dharma*; Kaniṣka; Madhyamaka school; Mahāyāna Buddhism; *Nikāya* Buddhism; Vajrayāna Buddhism; Yogācāra school.**

RICHARD P. HAYES

J

JAPAN, BUDDHISM IN

Buddhism in Japan is part of the wider development of Mahāyāna Buddhism in East Asia. Buddhism was introduced officially from Paekche (Korea) to the ruling court in Japan in the middle of the sixth century, though it is likely that various Buddhist teachings and practices found their way into Japan at an earlier time. The dates 538 and 552 appear in official documents (such as the *Nihon Shoki*, compiled in 720), but the most that can be claimed with any certainty is that the report that Buddhism was transmitted from Paekche, through the presentation of an image of Prince Siddhārtha and other Buddhist objects, during the time of Emperor Kinmei (r. 539–71) was in circulation from about the end of the seventh to the beginning of the eighth century.

The acceptance of Buddhism by the court was not without controversy. The Soga clan supported Buddhism and the importation of continental culture, while the Mononobe clan led the opposition in favor of indigenous deities and customs. Eventually the supporters of Buddhism prevailed, and Buddhism became an important part of Japanese society and culture.

The earliest phase of Buddhism in Japan is referred to as Asuka Buddhism, after the current center of political power, and also the site of the first major Buddhist temple (Asuka-dera). From the beginning one of the major characteristics of Buddhism was providing means for "protecting/guarding the country" (*gokoku*) – such as rituals for rain or a conduit for high culture. The Buddhist art of this period, such as the images of Miroku (Maitreya), are considered by many to be among the most sublime ever produced in Japan.

The earliest record of an ordination was that by the daughter of Soga no Umako, who became a nun and "home-departed-one" in 584 and took the name Zenshin'ni. Women (and nuns) played a major role for Buddhism in Japan, especially in the early days, but their role throughout Japanese history has been generally overlooked.

Prince Shōtoku (Shōtoku Taishi, or Umayado no miko, 574–622) is often presented as the central figure in this period, citing his promulgation of the so-called "Seventeen-Article Constitution," the attribution to him of commentaries on important Buddhist *sūtras*, and his founding of important temples such as Hōryūji, but the historicity of these attributions is uncertain. More important was the establishment of the official clerical hierarchy, with detailed regulations and legal codes, and the building of large temples and monasteries, such as the "national temples" (*kokubunji*) around the country, and the major Nara temples such Kōfukuji and Tōdaiji, with its "big Buddha" (*daibutsu*).

Buddhism in this early period, however, was not limited to the court and capital, and there is evidence that Buddhism spread among the "common" people, of temple construction in local areas by clan families, and of activity by "unofficial" Buddhist figures. Most famous is Gyōki (or Gyōgi, 668–749), who popularized Buddhism and was well known for his social welfare activities. Technically, Gyōki was a monk of the Hossō school at Yakushiji, one of the major temples in the capital of Nara, but he traveled extensively, preaching and performing magical works as well as helping to build roads, dams, and bridges. Emperor Shōmu (701–56), aware of Gyōki's popularity, recruited him to raise funds to construct the *daibutsu* ("big Buddha"), a huge statue of Vairocana at Tōdaiji in Nara. Gyōki also saw no basic opposition between the buddhas and *bodhisattvas* of Buddhism and the local deities (*kami*) of Japan, an idea which was accepted as standard through most of Japanese history.

An important part of the Buddhist tradition with its roots in this period (sixth to eighth century, including the establishment of the capital in Nara) is the standard list of six "Nara schools," not so much independent and self-sufficient sects as academic specialties from the Buddhist tradition that continued to be influential in various degrees throughout Japanese history:

1 Kusha (studies on the *Abhidharma-kośa-śāstra*);
2 Jōjitsu (studies on the *Satyasiddhi-śāstra*);
3 Ritsu (specialists on the *Vinaya* rules);
4 Hossō (studies on the Yogācāra or consciousness-only tradition, based on texts transmitted to China by Xuanzang);
5 Sanron (studies on the "three [Madhyamaka] treatises" of Nāgārjuna [*Mūla-madhyamaka-kārika, Śata-śāstra, Dvādaśa-mukha-śāstra*], as interpreted by Jijang);
6 Kegon (based on the *Avataṃsaka Sūtra*).

Other academic traditions, such as the study of the *Shōdaijō-ron* (*Mahāyāna-saṃgraha*) and the Shutara school (studies on the *Great Perfection of Wisdom Sūtra* [*Mahā Prajñāpāramitā Sūtra*]), were also present, though not included on the official list of six schools.

Outside of the "mainstream" Buddhism of officially ordained monks and nuns were many unofficial, "privately ordained" figures who practiced asceticism and built hermitages in the mountains, preached among the common people in local areas away from the capital, and undertook magical practices (as much Taoist as Buddhist in origin). Many of these figures, such as Gyōki (mentioned above) and Dōkyō (who is said to have cured Empress Kōken's illness through magical practices and later had himself proclaimed "*Dharma* King") straddled both of these worlds. This unofficial "mountain Buddhism" also laid the foundations for the development of Shugendō. Various collections of tales (such as *Nihon Ryōiki* and *Konjaku monogatari*), and "temple and shrine origin stories" (*jisha engi*) indicate the widespread influence of this type of "popular" Buddhism.

The establishment of a new capital in Kyoto (Heian-kyō) in the late eighth century led to the introduction and development of further forms of Buddhism, namely the Tendai tradition introduced by Saichō, and the esoteric Shingon tradition introduced by Kūkai. Saichō and Kūkai traveled to China with the same official embassy in 804 but followed different trajectories. Saichō returned to receive the favor of Emperor Kanmu (r. 781–806) and founded the Tendai school on Mount Hiei, to the immediate northeast of the capital. Kūkai eventually won the favor of Emperor Saga (r. 809–23) and founded the Shingon school with its headquarters at Tōji in Kyoto and on Mount Kōya to the mountains further south of the capital. Tendai Buddhism provided a broad range of teachings and practices from the Mahayana tradition, including Tiantai proper (the "perfect" or "rounded" teachings centered on the *Lotus Sūtra*), Zen meditation, and the *bodhisattva* precepts, which came to be know as "exoteric Buddhism" (in contradistinction to "esoteric Buddhism").

Esoteric Buddhism (especially that transmitted by Kūkai), with its rich array of rituals and artistic objects became increasingly popular and in demand. The esoteric tradition in Tendai was strengthened and developed by prominent figures such as Ennin (794–864), Enchin (814–91), and Annen (841–89?), and other Buddhist groups (such as Kōfukuji) also incorporated esoteric practices. This led to the development of a combination of "exoteric" and "esoteric" (*kenmitsu*) Buddhism that transcended sectarian borders and dominated Japanese society through the early modern period, and is still an important part of Buddhism in Japan today. A central concept in this ethos was the idea of "original enlightenment" (*hongaku shisō*), that all beings are inherently and potentially (or even already are) enlightened.

A prominent part of this "exoteric–esoteric" Buddhism was the amalgamation of Buddhist figures (Buddhas, *bodhisattvas*, and so forth) and the indigenous Japanese deities (*kami*), in which local cults were incorporated into Buddhist teachings and practices, and specific links defined between Buddhist figures and local deities. The Sannō cult, for example, a combination of Tendai Buddhism with the local traditions of Mount Hiei and its environs, was a prominent part of the religious ethos during the Heian period (eighth to thirteenth centuries) and beyond.

Shugendō (a syncretistic Japanese Buddhist tradition of mountain ascetic practices) began to develop into an organized religious movement during the Heian period, with the various mountain ascetic traditions scattered throughout Japan organizing under what eventually became the Honzan branch (with its center at Shōgoin in Kyoto) affiliated with the Tendai school, and the Tozan branch (with its center at Kōfukuji in Nara and Daigoji in Kyoto) affiliated with the Shingon school. The pilgrimage to Kumano was particularly popular during the Heian period, with *yamabushi* (or *shugenja*, Shugendō practitioners) serving as pilgrimage guides and providing religious services.

An important aspect of Buddhism in this period, and a source of much of Buddhist institutional wealth and influence, was the development of the tax-exempt *shōen* ("manor" or "landed estate") system whereby monastic centers came to control large amounts of private land holdings. Many of the elite clergy were from families of the court aristocracy, who often donated land and other wealth to prominent Buddhist centers such as Tōdaiji and Kōfukuji in Nara, and Enryakuji on Mount Hiei. These powerful religious-socio-economic institutions wielded considerable influence until they lost much of their holdings during the armed struggles culminating in the sixteenth century.

In general, the Heian aristocratic culture of this period was strongly influenced by Buddhist ideas of impermanence and karmic retribution and reward, reflected in literary classics such as the *Tale of Genji* and *Tsurezuregusa*, and a large amount of Buddhist art (images, paintings, etc.) was produced. In addition to aristocratic support for artistic Buddhist work, there were popular cults focusing on figures such as Miroku (Maitreya, the future Buddha), Kannon (Avalokiteśvara; the *bodhisattva* of compassion), Fudō (Acalanātha; the *bodhisattva* "unmovable"), and Jizō (Kṣitigarbha; a *bodhisattva* who saves beings in this world or in hell).

These popular movements contributed to the development of Pure Land Buddhism in Japan. The inclusion of Pure Land practices in Tendai (such as the ninety-day practice of walking while chanting the name of Amida, and the habit on Mount Hiei of chanting the *Lotus Sūtra* in the morning and the *nenbutsu* in the evening) are well known, but it is less well known that Pure Land devotion was also a part of the Nara schools and Shingon. Genshin's *Ōjōyōshū* (collection of sayings on rebirth) helped to popularize awareness of the Pure Land and the practice of verbal chanting of the Buddha Amida's name (*shōmyō nenbutsu*). Kūya (903–72) was one of many popular preachers who propagated the *nenbutsu* and offered Buddhist salvation to ordinary people outside the major monastic centers. Ryōnin (1073–1132), also a Tendai monk, promoted the constant repetition on the *nenbutsu* for accumulating merit, based on his idea of *yūzū* ("mutually inclusive") *nenbutsu*, and compiling a book of "pledges" by people who promised to recite the *nenbutsu* in order to be reborn in the Pure Land. Ippen promoted the dancing (*odori*) *nenbutsu*. The chanting of the *nenbutsu* at the time of death became popular, along with paintings of Amida descending from the Pure Land to welcome the dead (*raigōzu*). The most influential Pure Land figures, however, were Hōnen (1133–1212) and Shinran (1173–1262), who founded the first independent Pure Land (Jōdo) schools. Hōnen advocated the "exclusive" practice of *nenbutsu* and started an independent movement of Pure Land devotees, and Shinran's even more radical emphasis on faith (*shinjin*) and "other power" as the essence of the *nenbutsu* rather than the self-power of Buddhist practices (even of chanting the *nenbutsu*) led to the development of what eventually became the largest Buddhist institution in Japan.

An influential Buddhist idea during this period (eighth century and beyond) was that the world had entered into a degenerate age (*mappō*), and it was no longer possible for anyone to successfully practice the Buddha *Dharma*. This idea was a strong impetus for the Pure Land movements, but was also important for other so-called "Kamakura (twelfth to fourteenth century) founders" such as Nichiren (1222–82). Nichiren was a Tendai monk who called for an exclusive faith in the *Lotus Sūtra* as the appropriate teachings and practice for the current degenerate age, and vigorously attacked proponents of other forms of Buddhism. His critical stance against the Kamakura government – such as predicting the occurrence of earthquakes and other disasters (including invasion by a foreign army) if the country did not convert to the *Lotus Sūtra* – and his harsh rejection of other Buddhist traditions, led to his exile but also provided a prophetic Buddhist voice for social criticism and renewal.

Included in the so-called "Kamakura new Buddhism" is the development of exclusively "Zen" schools. The first Chinese Zen master to officially arrive in Japan was Daoxuan though he was also a *Vinaya* master and well versed in the Tendai and Kegon traditions, and the practice of "Zen" meditation was a part of all the Buddhist traditions. Dainichi Nōnin (n.d.) promoted Zen meditation and the "Daruma-shu" tradition in the twelfth century. Eisai (or Yōsai, 1141–1215) was a Tendai monk who went to China (twice) and promoted the Rinzai Zen tradition, though still "mixed" with esoteric and other Buddhist teachings and practices. Eventually Rinzai Zen was supported by the ruling warrior class, leading to the development of the "Five Mountains" (Gozan) system of powerful Buddhist temple complexes. These temples were centers of art and culture, resulting in the construction of magnificent temples, often with famous gardens. Other arts such as calligraphy and painting added much to the wealth of Japanese Buddhist art, and the ethos of the tea ceremony (promoted by figures such as the Rinzai monk Sen no Rikyū [1521–91]) reached a high level of sophistication.

The other prominent "Zen" school in Japan is the Sōtō tradition, transmitted to Japan by Dōgen (1200–53. Dōgen's emphasis on only "sitting" in meditation (*zazen*), and his founding of the monastic center at Eiheiji far from the capital, led to the development of the independent Sōtō school with a vast network of temples throughout Japan.

These "Kamakura founders" were the patriarchs from which grew the schools – Jōdo, Jōdo Shinshū, Nichiren, Rinzai, Sōtō, and so forth – that became the dominant schools in the modern period and are currently known as the schools of "traditional Buddhism" in contemporary Japan. However, they were still a minority – though growing – presence in Japanese society up through the fifteenth and into the sixteenth century. Often they were the targets of suppression, such as the Nichiren groups in Kyoto. The established ethos of exoteric–esoteric Buddhism and its shrine-temple, buddhas-and-*kami* combinatory paradigm – such as the Tendai complex on Mount Hiei, the Shingon tradition centered at Tōji and Mount Kōya (including the cult of Kōbō Daishi Kūkai and itinerant preachers), Shugendō ascetic and pilgrimage centers at mountains throughout Japan, and the networks and shrine-temple complexes of the Nara schools based at temples such as Tōdaiji and Kōfukuji – was still dominant in Japanese society.

Although Buddhist arts flourished with the support of various shoguns, this socio-religious system began to come apart and evolve in the late fifteenth and sixteenth centuries. On the one hand, movements based on the Kamakura founders expanded and gained increasingly large followings, such as the growth in Shin Pure Land groups under the leadership of Rennyo (1415–99), the popularity of Nichiren groups in Kyoto, and the expansion of Sōtō temples of the Eiheiji and Sōjiji lineages. This was a period of social strife and physical conflict, including peasant rebellions among Pure Land followers (*ikko ikki*), and uprisings by Nichiren leagues in Kyoto (*Hokke ikki*), as the society degenerated into warring states. The destruction of powerful Buddhist institutions was seen by the warlord Oda Nobunaga (1534–82) as necessary for the reunification of the country, eventually involving attacks on Pure Land strongholds in Ise, Echizen, and Ishiyama, and killing more than 1,000 monks during an attack on Mount Kōya. His greatest battle against Buddhist forces was the destruction of the Enryakuji complex on Mount Hiei, where it is said that over 3,000 monks were slaughtered and all of the buildings razed. Many of the temples were quickly rebuilt, and Mount Hiei remained the headquarters of Tendai Buddhism, but it never regained the level of its former social and religious influence.

Major changes came with the reunification of the country under the Tokugawa bakufu in Edo (Tokyo) after the decisive battle of Sekigahara in 1600. Buddhism, along with most aspects of society, came under strict control of the central government. Among the earliest actions of the new bakufu was to issue new regulations (*hatto*) establishing strict institutional structures, limiting the freedom of people to convert or change affiliation, and requiring each tradition to study and establish their own doctrinal traditions. Eventually a system of temple affiliation (*danka* or *terauke seido*) was established so that all families were locked into official affiliation with a local temple. "Renegade" Buddhist movements, such as the Nichiren *fuju-fuse* ("neither accepting nor giving" [donations from or to non-Nichiren people]) group and the secret or "hidden" Pure Land (*kakure nenbutsu*) groups, were prohibited, along with Christianity. The powerful Honganji (Jōdo Shinshū) establishment was split in half, into the current Higashi (east) and Nishi (west) Honganji. Tokugawa Ieyasu (1549–1616), the first Tokugawa shogun, also supported the growth of Tendai Buddhism in the Kanto (Tokyo) area, with the Tendai monk Tenkai (?–1642) serving as a close advisor, and constructing the temple Kan'eiji in Tokyo (known as "the eastern Hiei") as headquarters. Eventually Ieyasu was deified as a *bodhisattva* and a temple-shrine complex constructed as his mausoleum in Nikko.

The Tokugawa (Edo), or "premodern" period (1600–1868) is often considered, with regard to Buddhism, as a period of religious degeneration, but this is misleading. It was during this time that Buddhist temples established their current social position of providing a center for social cohesion through family affiliation and providing services such as funeral, memorial, and other rites, as well as serving as a kind of government regulator by keeping track of the populace. The Buddhist temples served also as centers for education, foci of pilgrimage and entertainment, and supporters of Buddhist scholarship.

Such strict regulations did not mean that Buddhist activity was limited to the local Buddhist temple, and the acceptance of combinatory Buddha-and-*kami* practices did not come to an end with the medieval period. Syncretistic deities such as Konpira and Fudō were popular, and had their cultic centers along with those of Jizō, Kannon, and Miroku. Pilgrimage was popular during the Tokugawa period to places such as Mount Fuji, Tateyama, Ise, Zenkōji in Nagano, Sensōji (Asakusadera) in Tokyo, and the Shikoku route focused on Kōbō Daishi, and many confraternities (*kō*) sprung up among people dedicated to certain cultic sites.

Although contemporary Buddhist schools look to the Kamakura period for images of their idealized founders, the temple system and sectarian establishments took their form mostly during this premodern period from the sixteenth to the nineteenth centuries. The period also includes many striking Buddhist figures, such as the following:

- the contrasting Rinzai monks Bankei (1622–93) and Hakuin (1686–1769);
- Jiun (1718–1804), a Shingon monk who strove to revive the practice of the precepts, and a scholar who compiled a massive encyclopedia of Sanskrit studies;
- Manzan Dōhaku (1638–1714), a Sōtō school reformer who advocated a return to emphasizing the centrality of Dōgen;
- Ryōkan (1758–1831), a Sōtō monk and a renowned poet and calligrapher;
- Suzuki Shōsan (1579–1655), a Sōtō monk who applied Buddhist teachings to mundane labor and wrote treatises attacking Christianity;
- Takuan Sōhō (1573–1645), a Rinzai monk and a noted scholar, calligrapher, and painter;
- the Tendai monk Tenkai;
- Tetsugen Dōkō (1630–82), a Jōdo Shishū priest who joined the Ōbaku Zen tradition and helped compile the Buddhist canon known as the Tetsugen-ban Daizōkyō and laid the foundations for modern Buddhist studies in Japan.

Buddhism in Japan – along with Japanese society in general – experienced a "cultural revolution" with the opening of the country to Western forces, the collapse of the Tokugawa regime, and the "Meiji Restoration" in 1868. One of the first actions of the new government was to order the "separation of *kami* and buddhas" (*shinbutsu-bunri*) in an attempt to "restore" an indigenous Shinto tradition independent of the "foreign religion" of Buddhism. Temple-shrine complexes were forced to physically separate, and religious figures had to choose an identity as either a Buddhist or Shinto priest. Movements to "destroy Buddhism" (*haibutsu kishaku*) broke out in various parts of the country, with thousands of Buddhist temples and artworks destroyed, and many Buddhist monks defrocked and returned to lay life. The "secularization" of the Buddhist clergy was advanced when the government, in 1872, rescinded laws banning the "eating of meat and taking of wives" (*nikujiki saitai*) by Buddhist monks, though such practices were not unheard of before then. Some Buddhist leaders responded by re-presenting Buddhism as a modern, scientific religion (unlike, for example, Christianity), a position taken by many at the influential World Parliament of Religions in Chicago in 1893. Figures such as D.T. Suzuki developed an image of "Zen Buddhism" that idealized certain aspects of the Buddhist tradition in Japan in a way that would appeal to Westerners (see essay on Zen).

Another prominent response was to emphasize the historical role of Buddhism as a "protector of the state," and to promote Buddhism as a supporter of the nationalistic cause. Tanaka Chigaku (1861–1939) and his establishment of the Kokuchūkai (Pillar of the State Society) – advocating the unity of Nichiren Buddhism and national polity (*kokutai*) – is only one extreme example, as most Buddhist establishments eagerly supported the nationalist and expansionist policies of the Japanese empire. Thus, for example, when anti-war "socialist" figures were arrested on trumped-up charges in the so-called "Great Treason Incident" (*Taigyaku jiken*) in 1910–11, including the Sōtō activist Uchiyama Gudō and the Jōdo Shinshū priest Takagi Kenmyō, the Sōtō and Shinshū establishments were quick to denounce and defrock their "traitorous" priests and acquiesce in their execution or life imprisonment.

Another aspect of Buddhism in this period was the rapid development of modern Buddhist scholarship. Many young Japanese scholars traveled to Europe to study classical Buddhist languages and philosophy, and returned to Japan to establish a rich and sophisticated tradition of textual and doctrinal studies that is among the best in the world. The Taishō edition of the Buddhist canon, still the most commonly used collection of Chinese texts, was published in 1924. In addition to general Buddhist studies, Buddhist sectarian studies (*shūgaku*), represented by figures such as the Shinshū scholars Kiyozawa Manshi (1863–1903) and Inoue Enryō (1858–1919), also struggled with modern issues, and the major Buddhist schools each established modern universities. The philosophers of the Kyoto school – Nishida Kitarō, Tanabe Hajime, Nishitani Keiji, and so forth – have attempted to apply Buddhist insights to the modern philosophical quest.

New Buddhist lay movements emerged in the twentieth century to fill needs that were not being met by traditional "temple Buddhism." The most successful has been Sōka Gakkai (Value Creating Society), based on the *Lotus Sūtra* and the teachings of Nichiren. It sponsored the formation of a political party, the Kōmeitō (Clean Government Party) in 1964, became independent of the temple-based Nichiren Shōshū in 1991, and has been active both domestically and internationally in various social issues. Risshō

Kōseikai, also based on the *Lotus Sūtra*, is another large-scale new Buddhist lay organization. It plays a pivotal role in the Federation of New Religious Organizations of Japan (Shinshūren) to promote various social causes. Agonshū claims to be based on the Pāli *Āgama sūtras* (*agonkyō*), but its ritual and practices are derived for the most part from esoteric Buddhist traditions. Numerous other Buddhist lay organizations have sprung up to offer Buddhist teachings and practices to lay people who sense a lack in the services of the traditional local family temple.

Regrets over supporting the imperialistic pre-war government policies have helped to propel post-war Japanese Buddhists to emphasize or rediscover Buddhist ideals for peace. There is also a growing awareness of social discrimination, and many of the traditional schools (such as Sōtōshū and Shinshū) have actively promoted movements to rid society of unfair discrimination. Gender-related issues – such as the status and role of nuns in the Sōtō school, or of the status and role of the priest's wife and family (*jizoku*) – are receiving long-overdue attention.

Traditional temple Buddhism is at a crossroads in modern Japan, with a post-war loss in temple land holdings, a steady decline in family affiliations with increased urbanization and the decline of the extended family, and less demand for traditional services such as funerals and ancestor memorial rites. Temples still provide a steady source to meet a popular demand for "practical benefits" (*genze riyaku*) – such as prayers for healing, charms for a variety of benefits, various memorial rites (such as *mizuko kuyō*, rites performed for aborted or stillborn fetuses), and so forth. Some aspects of traditional Buddhism and its institutions, such as its role as depositories of traditional art and culture, sources of tourist visitation (e.g. the temples, gardens, and so forth in Kyoto, Nara, and Kamakura), and as cultic centers and pilgrimage sites, still show signs of strong support. There is also a strong Buddhist academic tradition in Japan that continues to produce a high quality – and quantity (it is said that 90 percent of the books on Buddhism in the world are published in Japan) – of scholarship on Buddhism. It is difficult to predict, however, how Buddhism will evolve in the future, and what role it will play in Japanese society, as Japan struggles (along with the rest of the world) to deal with rapidly changing conditions. (See Figure 24.)

Figure 24 Votive tablets in the Garan precinct of Kōyosan, headquarters of the Japanese Shingon Order.

See also: **Dōgen and Sōtōshū; Hōnen and Jōdoshū; Kūkai and Shingon Buddhism; *Mikkyō* and ritual in Japanese Buddhism; New Buddhist lay movements in Japan; Nichiren and Nichirenshū; Pilgrimage in Japan; Pure Land movements in Japan; Rinzai tradition; Saichō and Tendai; Shugendō; Zen.**

PAUL L. SWANSON

JĀTAKAS AND OTHER NARRATIVE COLLECTIONS

The *Jātaka* (*Birth Stories*), one of nine traditional genres of Buddhist literature, depicts Gautama Buddha's past lives. Each birth story begins by explaining which events prompt the Buddha to tell the story and ends with his identifying himself and his companions with its central characters. Many stories resemble the moral tales in Aesop's *Fables* and in the Sanskrit *Beneficial Instruction* (*Hitopadeśa*). In the Buddhist interpretation of the *Rabbit's Birth Story* (*Śāśa Jātaka*), the rabbit that offers himself as food for an ascetic exemplifies generosity, rather than the ancient Indian theme of hospitality due an honored guest. In the *Vessantara Birth Story* of the Buddha's final past life before his enlightenment, Prince Vessantara gives away everything asked of him. The king of the gods, after praising Vessantara's generous offer of his wife, returns her; Vessantara's father redeems his grandchildren from slavery. Reunited with his family and forgiven for his extraordinary generosity, Vessantara returns from exile to become king. This story, which appears first carved on the second century BCE *stūpa* at Bhārhut, is painted on murals in ancient caves in Ajaṇṭā and Dunhuang and in temples throughout East and Southeast Asia. The recitation of these stories, especially the *Vessantara Birth Story*, often accompanies religious ceremonies, marking the New Year, the commemoration of the Buddha's birth, enlightenment and death (*Visākhā Pūja*), ordinations, family funerals, and house blessings. Following the Buddha's example, Buddhist monks use *Jātakas* in their sermons to teach moral values to a new generation.

The Pāli *Jātaka* collection of 547 stories in verse is arranged numerically, from one verse to the 786 verses of the *Vessantara Birth Story*. The approximately 2,500 canonical verses are embedded in an accompanying prose commentary (*Jātakaṭṭhakathā*) that explains the verses and constructs a story around them. Only the prose of the *Kuṇāla Birth Story* warning ascetics about deceitful women is regarded as canonical. *The Story of the Connections (Nidānakathā)*, the introduction to the Pāli *Birth Story* collection, relies upon stories of the Buddha's past lives in other Pāli canonical texts, the *Lineage of the Buddhas* (*Buddhavaṃsa*) and *the Collection of Deeds* (*Cariyāpiṭaka*) to retell the beginning of the *bodhisattva*'s path when the Buddha Dīpaṃkara predicts that the young Brahmin prostrating to him will become a Buddha. A similar story appears in the Sanskrit *Great Story* (*Mahāvastu*), a text linked to the Lokottaravāda school's *Vinaya*. Other Sanskrit texts, the Mūlasarvāstivāda *Vinaya*, *Divine Stories* (*Divyāvadana*), and *Bodhisattva Collection* (*Bodhisattvapiṭaka*) contain stories about the Buddha's previous lives. The Mahāyāna *Golden Light Scripture* (*Suvarṇaprabhāsottama Sūtra*) tells the story of the *bodhisattva*'s sacrifice of his body to feed a hungry tigress with starving cubs, which inspired artists who illustrated the Dunhuang caves and Nara's Tōdaji temple. Āryaśūrya in his fourth-century *Garland of Birth Stories* (*Jātakamāla*) selects thirty-four stories (many with Pāli parallels) to illustrate the first three virtues – generosity, morality, and patience – that the Mahāyāna *bodhisattva* perfects. Artists painted murals on Ajaṇṭā caves inscribed with Áryaśūrya's verses. Unique to Haribhaṭṭa's fifth-century *Garland of Birth Stories* is the story of the Buddha's past life as woman who gives her severed breasts to an emaciated woman to nourish her hungry baby. These literary and visual narratives of Gautama Buddha's past lives convey his teachings in an accessible way to a wide audience.

The *Jātaka* and *Avadāna* genre of Buddhist literature uses stories of past lives to explain how individuals' past actions influence their present situation and to demonstrate the positive effects of generosity, morality, and devotion. Stories illustrating generosity, some based on Pāli *Jātaka* and others similar to those in the Sanskrit *Avadāna*, are found in the *Fifty Birth Stories* (*Paññasajātaka*, also known as *Zimme Paññāsa* in Burma), a collection of apocryphal birth stories from Chang

Mai in northern Thailand. The *Fifty Birth Stories* provide Buddhist monks in Thailand, Cambodia, and Burma with stories that clarify doctrine on *karma* and rebirth and validate popular devotional practices. The *King Vaṭṭaṅguli Birth Story* about the making of the first Buddha image is retold by the fourteenth-century Sinhala author of the *Kosalabimbavaṇṇā* who emphasizes the merit derived from making Buddha images and from copying texts. Theravāda story collections, both in Pāli and in vernacular languages, extol the results of meritorious actions. The *Brapaṃsukūlānisaṃsa* speaks of the merit acquired through donating robes to the *sangha*. The stories in the thirteenth-century *Jewels of the Doctrine* (*Saddharmaratnāvaliya*), Dharmasena's Sinhala commentary on the *Scripture on Auspicious Things* (*Maṅgala Sutta*), explain how Buddhist values and practices as present create prosperity and happiness in this life and the next.

Mahāyāna beliefs and practices also were incorporated into popular narratives. The *Divine Stories* tells how a seafaring merchant's ship runs aground on a island of female demons, as a consequence of his damaging *stūpa*s and failing to honor the Buddha. Motivated by compassion, the *bodhisattva* Avalokiteśvara intervenes and in the form of a white horse carries Siṃhala to safety. The Nepalese vernacular version of the *Merchant Siṃhala's Story* (*Siṃhalasārthabāhu Avadāna*) identifies prosperity, virtuous conduct and freedom from danger and disease as benefits gained from devotion to Avalokiteśvara. In China, the popularity of the *Hundred Stories* tales, in which gods and ghosts (*preta*) describe the acts that led them to heaven and the underworld, inspired vernacular storytellers to create new stories illustrating the consequences of *karma*. The Chinese genre of miracle tales treats a variety of topics, including *karmic* retribution and desire for the blessings of a healthy and prosperous life. In the *Scripture for Offering Bowls to Repay Kindness* (*Bao'en fengpen jing*) Maudgalyāyana tries to rescue his mother from the underworld but the Buddha explains to him that only donations made to the *sangha* on behalf of the dead can free beings from the sufferings of the lower realms. Other Tang dynasty miracle tales tell how devotion to images of Guanyin (Skt. Avalokiteśvara) and recitation of his name or the *Guanshiyin Sūtra*, free prisoners, spare the condemned from execution, heal the sick, grant children to the barren, and pacify an angry tiger. These tales were told repeatedly to lay and monastic audiences. The Dunhuang caves, sealed early in the eleventh century, also preserve transformation texts (*bien wen*) – illustrated manuscripts in vernacular Chinese – which storytellers used to retell *Jātaka* and *Avadāna* stories and other inspirational Buddhist literature to their audience.

See also: **Buddha; Canons and literature; Chronicles and pilgrimage records; Cosmology and rebirth.**

KAREN C. LANG

K

KABILSINGH, CHATSUMARN

Chatsumarn Kabilsingh is a Thai scholar who recently took full ordination (2003) in the Theravāda school of Buddhism. A Thai national, she holds an M.A. from McMaster University in Canada and a Ph.D. from Magadha University in India. She has written extensively in Thai and English. Her English works are *A Comparative Study of the Bhikkhunī Pāṭimokkha* (1981), *Thai Women in Buddhism* (1991), *A Cry from the Forest* (1987), *Bhikkhunī Pāṭimokkha of the Six Existing Schools* (1991) and *Buddhism and Nature Conservation* (1997–8). She is also the editor of *Yasodhara: Newsletter on International Buddhist Women's Activities*, a co-founder of Sakyadhītā and a past president of the organization, the abbot of Wat Sondhammakalyanī in Nakhonpatham, Thailand, and the director of Baan Santi Pak, a home for unwed mothers.

Chatsumarn Kabilsingh grew up in a religious home and believed that she would be ordained one day. Her mother, Vorami, was ordained when Chatsumarn was ten, the first Thai woman to take ordination in Taiwan. While this ordination was not acknowledged by the Thai monastic establishment, Vorami Kabilsingh, known by her followers as Venerable Luang Ya (grandmother monk), established Wat Sondhammakalyanī and spent her life teaching and in social service. Kabilsingh's father was a politician who spent three sessions in Parliament and was involved in the development of the Democratic Party in the south. He also spent some time in jail because of his politics. With such a background, it is not surprising that Kabilsingh became a professor of Buddhist philosophy and adopted the controversial cause of the establishment of the *bhikkhunī sangha* (female monastic order) in Thailand.

Chatsumarn Kabilsingh taught Buddhist philosophy at Thammasat and Maha Cula universities for over twenty years. At Thammasat she also established the Indian Studies Centre and was its first director. In 1986 she, Ayya Khema and Karma Lekshe Tsomo planned the first conference of nuns (and laywomen) at Bodhgayā, India. The conference took place in 1987 and from it an international association of women, Sakyadhītā, arose. In 1991 while president of the organization she organized a Sakyadhītā conference in Bangkok.

According to an interview with the *Bangkok Post* (17 April 2001), while she felt ordination for her was preordained it was not until the late 1990s that she felt a real "calling" to take the robes. Bored with the world and concerned that if she waited until her retirement she would be too old for ordination, she began the process that led to her transformation into Bhikkhunī Dhammananda in 2003. She divorced her husband, took *bodhisattva* precepts in 2000 and shortly after became vegetarian (although Thai monks are not required to be vegetarian), beginning the mental process from lay to monastic life. As a follower of H.H. the Dalai Lama she was attracted to the Tibetan tradition but as the Theravāda *bhikkhunī sangha* had been revived in Sri Lanka and Thailand's Buddhist lineage was Theravāda, she took novice ordination as a Theravāda nun in 2001.

A survey of articles in the *Bangkok Post* between her taking of novice initiation and full ordination is instructive. Her novitiate stirred considerable controversy. The army-controlled television channel refused to air two interviews with her and senior *bhikkhus* were outraged. The *sangha* hierarchy sent officials to examine the accounts of Wat Sondhammakalyanī. Still, the disapproval was less than in the late 1920s when a previous attempt to establish a *bhikkhunī sangha* in Thailand resulted in the forced disrobing of two women and the passing of a law making it illegal for monks to ordain females. The press in 2001 was generally receptive, some laypeople showed admiration for Dr. Kabilsingh/Bhikkhunī Dhammananda, and a few monks spoke in favor of the possibility of female ordination. This certainly would have not occurred ten years prior, when the Sakyadhītā conference was held in Bangkok. She has noted that, at that time, many Thai laypeople were unaware that there were any *bhikkhunī*. By the time of her full ordination in 2003, a female ordination had occurred in Thailand (2002) and the Senate Committee on Women, Youth and the Elderly had recommended the ordination of women and was holding a series of seminars throughout Thailand to discuss the issue. In March of 2004, Bhikkhunī Dhammananda/Chatsumarn Kabilsingh was given an "Outstanding Women in Buddhism" award by the UN for her work. Commentators generally ascribe this changing tide to lay disenchantment with the Thai male *sangha* which has been riddled by scandals and laxity in the past. One should not, however, discount the decades of work by Dr. Kabilsingh on women's behalf.

Kabilsingh bases her argument for the ordination of women on both scriptural and social grounds and she has a particular idea concerning the role of *bhikkhunī* in society. The fact that the Buddha established an order for women is sufficient scriptural authority to ordain women. The argument that the order was never established in Thailand is, for her, irrelevant. She notes in "Nuns of Thailand" that Thailand did not have discotheques either but they are now common. Further, *bhikkhunī* can play an important role through *Dharma* teaching and social service work. This would provide a measure of security, education and status for women who have few choices in a society that considers female birth to be "lesser" and where women have few choices. This would also, she hopes, provide a viable opportunity for women who are often forced to become prostitutes in Thailand's extensive sex market.

There have been Thai women who adopt the renunciant lifestyle (*mae ji*). Historically, they are poorly educated rural women and elderly women with no options. They sometimes live in temples and serve the monks. While the institute of *mae jis* does organize and assist them, there has not been a widely accepted standard of training and education and the institute has registered only about 4,000 of a probable 100,000 or more. They have not been generally respected or supported, and being a *mae ji* is not seen as a good grounding for the practice and teaching of *Dharma*. The goal of providing a modern *bhikkhunī sangha* is, therefore, tied to improving the education of all mendicant women whether or not they wish to become fully ordained. Kabilsingh's desire is to ensure that Thai women have the opportunity that she has had to develop her own spiritual life and contribute to the betterment of society.

See also: **Women in Buddhism: an historical and textual overview.**

MAVIS L. FENN

KAGYÜ

The Kagyü (bKa' rgyud, "Teaching Lineage") order claims that its teachings originate with the Buddha Vajradhara, who transmitted them to the Indian master Tilopa (988–1069). Tilopa's main student was Nāropa (1016–1100), who passed the teachings to Marpa (1012–97), the first Tibetan master of the Kagyü lineage. Marpa was a translator who traveled to India in search of texts, but after meeting Nāropa pursued the path of a *tantric siddha*. His student Milarepa (1040–1123) is one of the best-known figures of Tibetan Buddhism, and his biography and poems are recited throughout the Tibetan cultural area. All of these masters were lay practitioners, but Milarepa's student Gampopa (1079–1153) developed a monastic structure, which continues today.

Among the distinctive practices of Kagyü are the "six yogas of Nāropa" (*nā ro chos drug*) and the "great seal" (*phyag rgya chen po*, Skt. *mahāmudrā*). The former are an interconnected set of meditation techniques attributed to Nāropa: (1) heat (*gtum mo*); (2) illusory body (*sgyu lus*); (3) dream (*rmi lam*); (4) clear light (*'od gsal*); (5) intermediate state (*bar do*); and (6) transference of consciousness (*'pho ba*). Heat yoga practice is based on tantric physiology, according to which the body contains 72,000 channels through which energies called "winds" and "drops" circulate. Adepts develop the ability to raise their bodily temperature by visualizing fire at various points of the body. This causes winds to move into the central channel, which is roughly contiguous with the spine. The main purpose of this practice is to gain control over the movement of subtle energies.

Illusory body yoga involves visualizing a subtle body, which is endowed with the qualities of a Buddha. This practice is founded on the notion that all phenomena are creations of mind and lack inherent existence, and is the basis for dream yoga, in which meditators learn to take control over the process of dreaming. Dream yoga adepts train in directing the content and events of their dreams, and eventually to develop full awareness of dreaming while asleep.

Clear light yoga is based on the notion that the mind is of the nature of clear light. One visualizes the clear light of mind as radiating throughout the universe, untainted by afflictions or negativity. It is empty of inherent existence, and although the phenomena of existence appear as real things, they are merely manifestations of mind.

Intermediate state yoga focuses on practices connected with the *bardo* period between death and rebirth, during which one's consciousness inhabits a subtle body. One encounters various terrifying sensations, all of which are manifestations of mind. Adepts who realize this and practice successfully can make great progress on the Buddhist path, and may even attain buddhahood. Intermediate state yogas are designed to prepare meditators to take advantage of these opportunities.

Transference of consciousness involves moving one's consciousness from one body to another. It is believed that initiation into this practice can ensure that at the moment of death one's mind will migrate to a Buddhist pure land, where conditions for practice are optimal.

In the Kagyü tradition, the "great seal" system is regarded as the supreme Buddhist practice. Unlike the long periods of training required for traditional Mahāyāna meditation, the yogas of the great seal are said to have the power to fully actualize one's Buddha-nature at any moment. These yogas involve working directly with the clear light nature of mind, which leads to spontaneous self-realization and Buddhahood.

See also: **Tibet, Buddhism in; Vajrayāna Buddhism.**

JOHN POWERS

KĀLACAKRA-TANTRA

The *Kālacakra-tantra* (Tib. *Dus kyi 'khor lo'i rgyud, Wheel of Time Tantra*) is one of the most widely influential Indian tantric texts in Tibet, and every year thousands of Buddhists travel to the Kālacakra initiation given by the Dalai Lama. The text is divided into three parts: inner, outer, and other. The inner teachings are those that discuss the mystical physiology of highest yoga *tantra*, which conceives humans in terms of winds and drops, subtle energies that course through channels and that are manipulated through yogic practices. The outer teachings concern the environments in which sentient beings live. The main interest of the third section is visualization practices that are designed to purify the psycho-physical components of existence, which leads to transformation into a Kālacakra, who is both the central Buddha of this cycle of teachings and the paradigm of meditative training.

The text is divided into five main chapters: (1) a discussion of the external world (Skt. *loka-dhātu*, Tib. *'jig rten gyi khams*); (2) analysis of the individual (Skt. *adhyātma*, Tib. *nang*); (3) initiation (Skt. *abhiṣeka*, Tib. *dbang*); (4) liturgies of visualization (Skt. *sādhana*, Tib. *sgrub thabs*); and (5) wisdom (Skt. *jñāna*, Tib. *ye shes*). Each chapter begins with a request by King Sucandra for instruction on a particular topic, and the text ends with Sucandra's verses in praise of Kālacakra.

Kālacakra is described as having blue skin, three necks, and four faces. The central face is black and has a wrathful appearance and bared fangs. The right face is red and manifests desire. The back face is yellow and is absorbed in meditative equipoise. The left face is white and peaceful in appearance. All the faces have three eyes. Kālacakra's hair is bound on top of his head in the manner of wandering yogins and has a *vajra* ornament woven into it. He has twelve upper arms and twenty-two lower arms. He holds various implements, including a *vajra*, a sword, a trident, and a curved knife.

His consort Viśvamatā is seated in front of him, and the two are in sexual embrace. She has four faces, which are red, yellow, white, and blue. Each face has three eyes, and she has four arms on each side, which hold a curved knife, an iron hook, a *ḍamaru* drum, a string of prayer beads, a skull, a noose, a white lotus, and a jewel.

According to Tibetan tradition, the *Kālacakra* is the most explicit highest yoga tantra. While other texts taught in India employed coded language in order to prevent scholars from mistakenly believing that they had understood the texts and thus neglecting to take the required initiations and following a guru's instructions, the *Kālacakra* was taught for the residents of Shambhala (Skt. Śambhala, Tib. Sham bha la), and because they are advanced practitioners the Buddha gave them his definitive *tantric* teachings. The *Kālacakra* is classed by Tibetan doxographers as a non-dual (Skt. *advaya*, Tib. *gnyis med*) *tantra* because it does not concentrate on the wisdom aspect of practice like mother *tantras* or on the method aspect like father *tantras*, but rather reveals a superior path that combines both in one training program that leads to a state that merges great bliss and realization of emptiness in one consciousness.

In addition to mental training, the yoga of the *Kālacakra* aims at a transformation of the body from gross physical matter into a form composed of subtle energy that transcends both material existence and even winds and drops. This is the state realized by Buddhas, and the *Kālacakra* claims to provide a rapid path to full actualization of both the physical and mental qualities of a Kālacakra. The physical transformation is accompanied by experience of innate great bliss. The text teaches that all beings have the potential to become Buddhas, and the final nature of both sentient beings and their environments is characterized by this innate great bliss. Those who fully realize this fact are Buddhas, while sentient beings fail to perceive reality as it is, and so wander in cyclic existence. But the difference between the two is merely a matter of perspective.

Other highest yoga *tantras* contain explanations for manipulating the winds, but the training of the *Kālacakra* aims at eliminating them. Through this one manifests a body of empty form (Skt. *śūnyatā-bimba*, Tib. *stong pa'i gzugs brnyan*), which arises along with the mind of immutable bliss. Buddhahood is described as a state without winds (Skt. *avāta*, Tib. *rlung med*), and the *nirvāṇa* without support (Skt. *apratiṣṭhita-nirvāṇa*, Tib. *gnas med pa'i nya ngan las 'das pa*) of a Buddha is said to be characterized by an absence of winds. Through eliminating the winds, the mind transcends dualistic thinking, and the subject–object dichotomy is overcome. One's mind and body are both conceived of as empty forms, and the elimination of the winds also entails the eradication of the psycho-physical components of existence; once this occurs, one manifests imperishable bliss.

One of the main practices for experiencing innate great bliss is the practice of sexual yogas, which the *Kālacakra* indicates are performed physically, and not merely as a matter of visualization. The male yogin develops the ability to avoid ejaculation of semen (which is referred to as "*bodhicitta*" and correlated with the mind of awakening that characterizes *bodhisattvas*), which prolongs the experience of orgasm and makes it possible for practitioners to manifest subtle levels of mind, including the most fundamental one, the mind of clear light (Skt. *prabhāsvara-citta*, Tib. *'od gsal sems*). In this state the yogin naturally experiences the empty nature of all phenomena and actualizes the innate potential for Buddhahood.

The text declares that it was spoken on the fifteenth day of the third month after the Buddha's awakening. The Buddha appeared on Vulture Peak wearing monastic robes and taught the *Perfection of Wisdom in 100,000 Lines*, while simultaneously manifesting in south India at the Dhānyakaṭaka *Stūpa*, where he preached the *Kālacakra-tantra* for advanced listeners. The teaching was requested by Sucandra, the king of Shambhala and an emanation of the buddha Vajrapāṇi. Vajrapāṇi compiled the *tantra* in its long form of 12,000 verses (entitled *Paramādhibuddha-tantra*), but this version is held by Tibetan tradition to be no longer extant. The most widely used version of the *Kālacakra* comprises 1,047 verses, and is said to have been edited by Mañjuśrīkīrti. It is referred to as the *Condensed Kālacakra-tantra*.

While other highest yoga *tantras* focus on manipulation of subtle energies, the *Kālacakra* is more concerned with discussions of emptiness, which has two modes: aspected and unaspected. The latter is doctrinally concordant with the Mādhyamaka tradition of Nāgārjuna: it refers to the absence of inherent existence that characterizes all phenomena. The *Kālacakra* contains practices in which the mind of clear light focuses on emptiness as its object of observation. Aspected emptiness refers to the notion that forms are in reality non-material, devoid of any substance and merely creations of mind. The *Kālacakra* is classified as a non-dual *tantra* because it aims at a union of immutable bliss and empty forms, which are conjoined in the meditator's wisdom consciousness directly realizing emptiness. This is the way in which Buddhas perceive reality, and so the *Kālacakra* is said to take the effect stage of practice as its path.

The *tantra* describes a set of fifteen initiations that confer permission for increasingly powerful practices. These are divided into three groups: the first seven are for beginners, the next four are referred to as "high initiations," and the last four are "greatly high initiations." They are said to enable the initiate to alter perceptions and purify their minds in such a way that they transcend ordinariness. Trainees move from the perspective of ordinary beings to that of a Buddha, who perceives phenomena as naturally pure and as the environment of an awakened being. In the generation stage, one visualizes Kālacakra in front of one, endowed with all the physical and mental attributes of a Buddha, and in the completion stage one imagines that one is transformed into Kālacakra and performs a Buddha's activities for the benefit of sentient beings. One develops the divine pride of being a Buddha, untainted by ordinary ego, and through this process gradually comes to approximate the state of Buddhahood.

The core practice of the *Kālacakra* is a six-session yoga, which initiates are expected to perform three times per day: (1) individual withdrawal of winds (Skt. *pratyāhāra*, Tib. *sor 'dus*); (2) concentration (Skt. *dhyāna*, Tib. *bsam gtan*); (3) stopping vitality (Skt. *prāṇāyāma*, Tib. *srog rtsol*); (4) retention (Skt. *dhāraṇā*, Tib. *'dzin pa*); (5) subsequent mindfulness (Skt. *anusmṛti*, Tib. *rjes dran*); and (6) meditative absorption (Skt. *samādhi*, Tib. *ting nge 'dzin*). The early stages involve withdrawing the winds into the central channel (Skt. *avadhūtı*, Tib. *rtsa dbu ma*). The successive stages allow the yogin to develop greater control in the manipulation of winds, which results in actualization of immutable bliss in the sixth stage.

The *Kālacakra* is the basis for the Tibetan astrological calendar and the traditional medical system. The *tantra* is also the seminal source for the notion of the mythical kingdom of Shambhala, which is said to be hidden in a remote valley that is protected from outsiders by magical spells. Various sources provide differing ideas about its location, but most Tibetan Buddhists believe that it exists somewhere north of Tibet. Shambhala is said to be ruled by a succession of Buddhist kings, and the current monarch is the twenty-first to hold the office. He ascended the throne in 1927. The final king (twenty-fifth in the lineage) will be named Rudra; his reign will begin in 2327. He will rule for 100 years (as does every king of Shambhala), but in the 98th year of his reign (i.e. 2425, which according to the *Kālacakra* will be 2,304 years after the death of Śākyamuni Buddha), the enemies of Buddhism will attack the kingdom (which at this point will be the main outpost of the religion), and they will be defeated by its armies. After this Buddhism will flourish for another 1,000 years, but in the 5,140th year after Śākyamuni's passing the period of his dispensation will come to an end.

The *Kālacakra* is generally regarded by contemporary scholars as one of the last *tantras* composed in South Asia, and its late date is indicated by references to Muslim invaders. It was transmitted to Tibet in 1027. The most influential commentary on the *Kālacakra* is the *Stainless Light* (Skt. *Vimālaprabhā*, Tib. *Dri med 'od*), attributed to Puṇḍārīka, who according to tradition was one of the kings of Shambhala. It is the basis for the subsequent *Kālacakra* commentarial tradition in India and Tibet.

See also: **Tibet, Buddhism in; Vajrayāna Buddhism**

JOHN POWERS

KANIṢKA

Kaniṣka was a king of the Kuṣāṇa dynasty from about the first century CE who is remembered as a great patron of Buddhist institutions. Ethnically from a Central Asian community, Kaniṣka consolidated and expanded an empire that stretched across Central Asia, including what is now known as Tajikistan, Uzbekistan, and Turkmenistan, into Afghanistan, Pakistan, and northwest and northern India. Kaniṣka's place in Buddhist history, however, stems not so much from his prominence as a political and military leader, but for his role in transforming Buddhism from a predominantly sectarian religious movement into a civilization. Although Kuṣāṇa rule largely came to an end by the third century, the religious and cultural patterns of Buddhist civilization which began during Kaniṣka's reign, continued for more than a millennium in South Asia and even longer in Tibet and East Asia. Kuṣāṇa rule was a period of civilizational creativity. Increased contacts with the Roman empire allowed for an openness to the conventions of Greek sculpture, with the emergence of some the earliest images of the Buddha in a Greek style the result. Much of what is taken as distinctively Indian in the history of high Indian culture – poetry, drama, art, and the role of religion in all of these – crystallized under Kuṣāṇa reign, ironically a non-Indian dynasty. The extent of Kaniṣka's empire from India to China probably also facilitated some of the first introductions of Buddhism in China. Kaniṣka's place in Buddhist history is so centrally visible that later Chinese sources frequently portray him as another Aśoka.

The specifics of Kaniṣka's life are largely uncertain. He succeeded Vima Kadphises, who was not a relative, to the Kuṣāṇa throne somewhere between 78 CE and maybe seventy years later; his reign is supposed to have lasted about a quarter of a century. Apart from some epigraphic and numismatic evidence, most of what we know about Kaniṣka comes from later Buddhist sources, and it is difficult to disentangle the historical person from the outlines of the idealized image of a Buddhist king. This is particularly the case with accounts of his conversion to Buddhism which seem modeled on accounts of Aśoka's conversion, especially in saying that the immediate cause of Kaniṣka's conversion was remorse over the violence of his various military campaigns.

Whatever the actual motive for his conversion, it is clear that Buddhist practices and institutions began to be associated with the articulation of imperial ambitions and polity, an association which was to continue in South Asia for more than 500 years.

Buddhist sources portray Kaniṣka as convening a council of monks during his reign. The goals of this council are described variously in different sources. Some versions portray Kaniṣka convening the council out of his puzzlement over the variety of doctrines held by different Buddhist schools. Other sources depict the council as being held to standardize the canon of Buddhist scriptures and they say that Kaniṣka had the canon copied and distributed after the council; it is unlikely that this actually took place, but it does indicate that later Buddhists saw Kaniṣka as helping to preserve a complete and fixed canon, although such a canon probably did not exist at his time.

Mahāyāna sources associate the appearance of the Mahāyāna itself with Kaniṣka's council. The Sarvāstivādins depict Kaniṣka's council as under the leadership of Katyāyanīputra and his *Foundations of Knowledge* as a product of this council. It does seem most likely that Kaniṣka's council was only a Sarvāstivādin event.

See also: **Art, Buddhist; Canons and literature; Councils; Katyayanīputra; *Nikāya* Buddhism; Sarvāstivādins.**

CHARLES HALLISEY

Figure 25 Mural of the Buddha's return to Kapilavastu, depicting a story in which Yaśodharā sends her son Rāhula to demand his birthright, Ajaṇṭā, India, cave 17.

KAPILAVASTU

Kapilavastu (Pāli Kapilavatthu), according to traditional Buddhist sources, is Gautama Buddha's childhood home and the capital of the Śākyas over which his father, Śuddhodana, ruled. A number of important events in the Buddha's biography are set there, including the plowing festival when he spontaneously entered a high level of meditative absorption, the archery contest in which he demonstrated his mastery of the skills appropriate to a *kṣatriya* warrior, and his encounter with the four signs that provided the catalyst for his decision to renounce society and seek liberation from the ills of life. Traditional biographical accounts highlight the great luxury and sensuality that surrounded him during his youth, all of which he rejected in his quest for liberating truth.

The present-day location of Kapilavastu remains uncertain, though scholars for more than a century have focused on two possibilities, and each today has its strong proponents. The history of the debate has been influenced by political factors, since the two sites lie in different countries, and considerable prestige and money, in the form of potential income from tourism, are at stake. The two most likely locations of ancient Kapilavastu are Piprāhwā in India and Tilaurakot in Nepal, less than ten miles apart from each other. As in the case of many other sites associated with the life of Gautama Buddha, the records of Chinese pilgrims have played a crucial role in modern efforts to establish their locations. Part of the difficulty stems from the fact that while the site descriptions given by Faxian and Xuanzang are largely in agreement, they disagree on how they orient these sites to other known locations, prompting some scholars to suggest that they may have visited different places. Following the identification of Lumbinī, the Buddha's birthplace, at the end of the nineteenth century, the archeologist A. Führer proposed a region in the Nepalese Tarai (an area near present-day Tilaurakot) as the likely location of Kapilavastu, and he claimed to have found archeological evidence to support his identification. When some of that evidence was found to be forged, Führer's identification was called into question; further excavation in 1899, however, uncovered the remains of a fortified city at Tilaurakot, leading some scholars to favor it as the likely site of Kapilavastu. Meanwhile, W. Peppé's excavation of a ruined *stūpa* at Piprāhwā, just to the south of the India–Nepal border, uncovered a reliquary containing human bones. It bears an inscription that led some scholars to conclude that this was the *stūpa* that, according to textual accounts, the Śākyas built to enshrine their share of the Buddha's relics, though the dating and translation of the inscription was controversial. More recent excavations at both sites have provided additional evidence. A 1972 excavation of the Piprāhwā *stūpa* uncovered additional reliquaries at a deeper level, as well as a large number of terracotta sealings inside the ruins of a monastery that refer to "Kapilavastu." A UNESCO-sponsored excavation at Tilaurakot in 1997 provided further details of the fortified city's plan and, most importantly, indicated that the site's earliest habitation could have been contemporaneous with the dating of the Buddha (though these dates remain controversial, as well). At present, both sites are promoted by their respective countries as the location of Kapilavastu, and both draw Buddhist pilgrims (See Figure 25).

See also: **Aśoka; Bodhgayā; Buddha; Buddha, historical context; Buddha, relics of; Faxiang; Kuśinagara; Lumbinī; Sacred places; Sārnāth.**

KEVIN TRAINOR

KARMA

In popular usage in the West *karma* is thought of simply as the good and bad things that happen to a person, a little like good and bad luck. However, this oversimplifies what for Buddhists is a complex of interrelated ideas which embraces both ethics and belief in rebirth. It did not seem strange to Indian thinkers to conceive of human life following a repeated pattern and passing through an extended series of births and deaths. To this process they gave the name "*saṃsāra*" which literally means "flowing on" but could be translated more poetically as "eternal wandering." Individual existences were thought of like pearls on a necklace – each one separate but strung together in an endless series. The origin of such ideas is pre-Buddhist and they are first mentioned in a body of mystical literature known as the *Upaniṣads* composed over several centuries beginning around the eighth century BCE. Since then belief in reincarnation has been deeply engrained in the Indian worldview and forms a fundamental part of the Buddhist outlook on life. Further details of the various realms of rebirth are given elsewhere in this work, but suffice it to say here that the human world is thought to be the most auspicious for the generation of good *karma*. The gods are so aloof and blissful that they have little opportunity or incentive to do either good or evil, and beings who are reborn as animals, hungry-ghosts (*preta*), or in hell, have little scope for the exercise of moral autonomy.

The doctrine of *karma* is concerned with the ethical implications of *Dharma*, in particular those relating to the consequences of moral behaviour. In the *Abhidharma* (for example, *Atthasālinī* 2.360) it is classified as *karma-niyama*, a law-like aspect of the doctrine of Dependent Origination (*pratītya-samutpāda*) having particular relevance to moral causation. For Buddhism, *karma* is thus neither random – like luck – nor a system of rewards and punishments meted out by God. Nor is it destiny or fate: instead it is best understood as a natural – if complex – sequence of causes and effects.

The literal meaning of the Sanskrit word *karma* is "action," but *karma* as a religious concept is concerned not with just any actions but with actions of a particular kind. Karmic actions are *moral* actions, and the Buddha defined *karma* by reference to moral choices and the acts consequent upon them. He stated, "It is intention (*cetanā*), O monks, that I call *karma*; having willed one acts through body, speech, or mind" (*Aṅguttara Nikāya* 3.415). In this statement the

Buddha reconfigures the traditional understanding of *karma* which tended to see it as a product of ritual acts of a physical kind. In a discussion with a follower of Jainism concerning which the three modes of actions – body, speech or mind – is most reprehensible, the Jain states that bodily action has the greatest power to produce bad *karma*. The Buddha disagrees, stating that mental actions are the most potent of the three, thereby illustrating the innovative ethical perspective adopted by Buddhists.

What, then, makes an action karmically good or bad? From the Buddha's definition above it can be seen to be largely a matter of intention and choice. The psychological springs of motivation are described in Buddhism as "roots," and there are said to be three good roots and three bad roots. Actions motivated by greed (*rāga*), hatred (*dveṣa*) and delusion (*moha*) are bad (*akuśala*) while actions motivated by their opposites – non-attachment, benevolence, and understanding – are good (*kuśala*). Making progress to enlightenment, however, is not simply a matter of having good intentions, and evil is sometimes done by people who act from the highest motives. Good intentions, therefore, must find expression in right actions, and right actions are basically those which are wholesome and do no harm to either oneself or others.

Moral actions are unlike other actions in that they have both transitive and intransitive effects. The transitive effect is seen in the direct impact moral actions have on others; for example, when we kill or steal, someone is deprived of life or property. The intransitive effect is seen in the way moral actions affect the agent, for example by instilling bad or good habits. According to Buddhism, human beings have free will, and in the exercise of free will they engage in self-determination. In a very real sense individuals create themselves through their moral choices. By freely and repeatedly choosing certain sorts of things, an individual shapes his character, and through his character his future. The process of creating *karma* may be likened to the work of a potter who moulds the clay into a finished shape: the soft clay is one's character, and making moral choices is like shaping the clay into a given form.

Another common metaphor is an agricultural one: performing good and bad deeds is like planting seeds that will fruit at a later date, and the remote effects of karmic choices are referred to as the "maturation" (*vipāka*) or "fruit" (*phala*) of the karmic act. Karmic seeds may mature in both the present and future lives. An example given of how *karma* bears fruit in the present life is the way the features of an angry person become progressively distorted and ugly with time (*Majjhima Nikāya* 3.203–6). Certain key aspects of a person's next rebirth are thought of as karmically determined. These include the family into which one is born, one's social status, physical appearance, character and personality. Any *karma* accumulated but not yet experienced is carried forward to the next life, or even many lifetimes ahead. In this sense individuals are said to be "heirs" to their previous deeds (*Majjhima Nikāya* 3.203).

The doctrine of *karma* does not claim that everything that happens to a person is karmically determined, and the Buddha made a distinction between *karma* and deterministic fate (*niyati*). Many of the things that happen in life – like winning the lottery – may be simply the result of luck or chance. In the *Aṅguttara Nikāya* (3.61), the Buddha disagrees with certain of his contemporaries who held the view that "whatever good, bad, or neutral feeling is experienced, all that is due to some previous action." *Karma* does not determine precisely what will happen or how anyone will react to what happens. Individuals are free to resist previous conditioning and establish new patterns of behaviour. The precise manner in which *karma* operates, and the mechanism that links given acts and their consequences, is a matter of dispute among Buddhist schools. The Buddha simply described the process as profound, and as inconceivable (*acinteyya*) to anyone except a Buddha (*Aṅguttara Nikāya* 4.77).

Merit

Buddhists speak of good *karma* as "merit" (Skt. *puṇya*, Pāli *puñña*), and much effort is expended in acquiring it (its opposite, bad *karma*, is known as *pāpa*). Some Buddhists picture merit as a kind of spiritual capital – like money in a bank account – whereby credit is built up as the deposit on a heavenly rebirth. One of the best ways for a layman to earn merit is by supporting the *sangha* or order of monks. This can be done by placing food in the bowls of monks as they pass on their daily alms round, by providing robes for the monks, by listening to sermons and attending religious services, and by donating funds for the upkeep of monasteries and temples. Merit can even be made by congratulating other donors and empathetically rejoicing (*anumodanā*) in their generosity. Based on this commodified understanding of *karma*, some Buddhists make the accumulation of merit an end in itself, and go to the extreme of carrying a notebook to keep a tally of their karmic "balance." This is to lose sight of the fact that merit is earned as a byproduct of doing what is right. To do good deeds simply to obtain good *karma* would be to act from a selfish motive, and would not earn much merit.

In many Buddhist cultures there is a belief in "merit transference," or the idea that good *karma* can be shared with others, just like money. Donating good *karma* has the happy result that instead of one's own karmic balance being depleted, as it would in the case of money, it increases as a result of the generous motivation in sharing. It is doubtful to what extent there is canonical authority for notions of this kind, although the motivation to share one's merit in a spirit of generosity is certainly karmically wholesome, since it would lead to the formation of a generous and benevolent character.

See also: **Cosmology and rebirth; *Dharma*; Ennobling Truths/Realities; Moral discipline; Precepts, lay.**

DAMIEN KEOWN

KARMAPAS, THE GYELWA

One of the most successful innovations of Tibetan Buddhism is the institution of reincarnating *lamas* (*sprul sku*, pronounced *tülku*), which is based on the Mahāyāna ideal of the *bodhisattva*, who pursues Buddhahood for the benefit of other sentient beings. During successive lifetimes, *bodhisattvas* perfect good qualities like wisdom and compassion, which become part of the matrix of attainments of awakened beings. At advanced levels of the path, *bodhisattvas* acquire the ability to consciously choose their rebirth situations, and other advanced practitioners are able to recognize them. These two notions are part of the theoretical background of the *tülku* system.

The first lineage of reincarnating lamas was that of the Gyelwa Karmapas (rGyal dbang kar ma pa), which began in the fourteenth century. This title was first given to the fifth member of the lineage, Teshin Shekpa (De bzhin gshegs pa, 1348–1415), by the Chinese emperor Taiming, and is said to have been based on a dream in which the emperor saw a black hat woven from the hair of 100,000 *ḍākinīs* floating over the head of Teshin Shekpa. A replica of this hat was later fashioned, and it is still worn today by the Karmapas, who are often referred to as the "Black Hat Lamas." Following the bestowal of the title on Teshin Shekpa, it was retrospectively accorded to his previous incarnations, and Tüsüm Khyenpa (Dus gsum khyen pa, 1110–93) was recognized as the first Karmapa.

There is currently a bitter dispute raging between rival claimants to the throne of the Karmapas. Tai Situ Rinpoche (T'ai si tu Rin po che), one of the designated regents of the sixteenth Karmapa, Rangjung Rikpe Dorje (Rang byung rigs pa'i rdo rje, 1924–81), claims that Urgyen Trinle (U rgyan 'phrin las, b. 1985) is the true Karmapa. He was enthroned in Tsurpu (mTshur phu) Monastery in Tibet and certified by the Dalai Lama, but another regent, Shamar Rinpoche (Zhwa dmar Rin po che) asserts that the true Karmapa is Tenzin Khyentse (bsTan 'dzin mkhyen brtse, b. 1982).

Urgyen Trinle managed a dramatic escape from Chinese-controlled Tibet in 2000, and subsequently made his way to Dharamsala, India, where he became closely associated with the fourteenth Dalai Lama, Tenzin Gyatso. At the time of this writing, neither he nor his rival have been allowed to reside at Rumtek (Rum btegs) Monastery in Sikkim, the seat of the Karmapas in exile, founded by Rangjung Rikpe Dorje. There have been several pitched battles at the monastery between the two factions, and the Indian military stationed armed soldiers there in order to prevent further bloodshed. The dispute continues to rage in Indian courts, the Internet, and news media, with both sides accusing their opponents of lying and violent tactics. At issue is control of the Kagyu Order and the charitable trust left by the sixteenth Karmapa, valued at over one billion dollars.

See also: **Tibet, Buddhism in; Vajrayāna Buddhism.**

John Powers

KATYĀYANĪPUTRA

Katyāyanīputra was an Indian scholastic thinker who is credited with compiling *The Foundation of Knowledge* (Skt. *Jñānaprasthāna*), a philosophical text that is often counted among the seven canonical texts of *Abhidharma* in the Sarvāstivāda school and which later served as a root text for the various commentarial compendia (*vibhāṣā*) that came to define the Sarvāstivāda as a distinct, albeit an extended and pluralist doctrinal movement. The significance of Katyāyanīputra for the modern historian, however, lies more in his being representative of the social processes of segmentary lineage inherent in *Nikāya* Buddhism than because of anything that is specifically known about him. Indeed, relatively little is known for certain about Katyāyanīputra.

The dates of Katyāyanīputra are uncertain, with some Chinese sources from the middle of the first millennium dating him 100 years after the death of the Buddha, others saying 300 years, and still others saying 500 years; somewhere between the latter two dates seems most likely, since Katyāyanīputra's *The Foundation of Knowledge* can be dated on independent grounds to approximately the first century BCE. Where Katyāyanīputra lived is equally uncertain, with some sources saying that he lived in northwest India, some specifying Kashmir, and others central India. A fifth-century Chinese text, the *Great Teaching on the Perfection of Wisdom* (Chi. *Da zhi du lun*) which is attributed to Nāgārjuna, says that Katyāyanīputra was a Brahmin by birth – a common feature of the biographies of Buddhist figures at this time – who was possessed of wisdom and sharp cognitive faculties. He was learned in Buddhist texts and compiled *The Foundation of Knowledge* as an aid to understanding the teachings of the Buddha. This same text says that Katyāyanīputra's own disciples were responsible for the various philosophical compendia commenting on *The Foundation of Knowledge*, and in this we see a common feature of the segmentary lineages of *Nikāya* Buddhism where a single foundational figure serves to maintain connections among groups that otherwise would be exclusively differentiated by positions of doctrine or practice.

The Sarvāstivādin school of Buddhism identified different individual authors for all of the seven *Abhidharma* treatises included in their canon. Katyāyanīputra's *The Foundation of Knowledge* was accorded a primacy among these works, however, so much so that, for some, it came to be considered the "body" of the Sarvāstivādin *Abhidharma*, with the other six works described as its "limbs" or "feet" and thus Katyāyanīputra himself came to serve as the key connecting figure of the Sarvāstivādin segmentary lineages labeled as Vaibhāṣikas. *The Foundation of Knowledge* is a definitive systematization of earlier Sarvāstivādin *Abhidharma* works, and not surprisingly it is a long work, comprising about 25,000 verses. Katyāyanīputra is more commonly considered to be the compiler of *The Foundation of Knowledge* rather than its author in a conventional sense. Thus he is thought to have organized in a systematic fashion the teachings of the Buddha himself that had been transmitted in another form; some Chinese texts suggest that Katyāyanīputra came to intuit these teachings of the Buddha directly and atemporally, without the mediation of transmitted texts, through the power of his vows and his religious knowledge, somewhat analogously to what is later seen in the Tibetan tradition of treasure discoverers (*gter-mo*). The organizational structure of *The Foundation of Knowledge* seems to have been widely influential in *Nikāya* Buddhism and beyond with its imprint to be seen in many later *Abhidharma* works, including Vasubandhu's famous *Treasury of Abhidharma* (Skt. *Abhidharmakośa*). In terms of its content, *The Foundation of Knowledge* appears to be an attempt to present a comprehensive and integrated account of major topics in Buddhist teaching and practice.

The social processes of segmentary lineages within the Sarvāstivāda school of *Nikāya* Buddhism are everywhere visible in the evidence connected with Katyāyanīputra and his *The Foundation of Knowledge.* The very existence of *The Foundation of Knowledge* itself suggests this, since the seven *Abhidharma* works of the Sarvāstivādins were composed in different times, seemingly representing different doctrinal positions that came to be attributed to particular individuals, and were only later collected into a composite canon. Indeed, it has been suggested that Katyāyanīputra's own emphasis on the *Abhidharma* led to a schism between the Sarvāstivādins and a more conservative school within the Sthaviravādins, the Haimavata.

The Sanskrit original of *The Foundation of Knowledge* no longer exists, although Sanskrit fragments of it have been discovered in Afghanistan and in Central Asia, an indication in itself of the spread of the textual community focused around Katyāyanīputra. It is extant in two different Chinese translations, one from the fourth century, and the other by Xuanzang in the seventh century. These two translations are significantly different in structure and doctrinal positions, so much so that it seems likely that they came from two different versions of *The Foundation of Knowledge* and reflect the teachings of two different Sarvāstivādin lineages.

The visibility of *The Foundation of Knowledge* in Buddhist intellectual history comes less from anything particular about its content, although it was indeed innovative in its own time, than from its choice as a root text for various commentarial compendia that defined the Sarvāstivāda as a school of Buddhist thought. The significance of these compendia was such that the Sarvāstivādins were alternatively known as the Vaibhāṣikas in contradistinction to the more conservative Sarvāstivādin lineages known as the Mūlasarvāstivādins. These compendia were digests of doctrinal discussions and scriptural proof-texts that often included highly polemical arguments against rival positions as well as doctrinal innovations. There are three extant compendia on *The Foundation of Knowledge*, surviving however only in Chinese translations, but it is likely that there were more. Their legacy can be seen in doctrinal discussions across East Asia in subsequent centuries, defining as they did the structure and categories of reasoned argument in *Abhidharma* thought.

See also: ***Abhidharmakośa*; Dharmaguptakas; *Nikāya* Buddhism; Sarvāstivādins; Sautrāntikas.**

CHARLES HALLISEY

KENMITSU (EXOTERIC–ESOTERIC) BUDDHISM

Kenmitsu (exoteric–esoteric) Buddhism refers to the combination of exoteric and esoteric teachings and practices that was the dominant form of Buddhism, and an integral part of the socio-political structure, of medieval Japan (from around the tenth to the sixteenth century). It is a scholarly term coined by Kuroda Toshio, a historian whose studies of medieval institutions have revolutionized the understanding of the role of Buddhism in Japanese history. Previously it was assumed that the so-called "Kamakura new Buddhism" (*Kamakura shin-Bukkyō*) movements founded by Hōnen, Shinran, Dōgen, Nichiren, and so forth in the Kamakura period (twelfth to fourteenth centuries CE) were the prevailing forms of Buddhism in this period. Kuroda has shown, however, that *kenmitsu* Buddhism was still dominant until the early modern period – when the old socio-political system collapsed – and the Pure Land, Zen, and Nichiren schools (that are prevalent as "traditional Buddhism" today) developed widespread and influential organizations only in the late fourteenth and early sixteenth centuries.

Kenmitsu Buddhism has, at its core, esoteric teachings and practices (*mikkyō*) established firmly for the first time by Kūkai with his transmission of esoteric Buddhism from China and his founding of the Shingon school. Esoteric traditions were soon incorporated into the Tendai school on Mount Hiei, adding to its vast array of "exoteric" (*kengyō*) traditions, starting with Saichō himself and completed by figures such as Ennin, Enchin, and Annen. Other Buddhist institutions, such as the Kōfukuji temple complex and Tōdai-ji in Nara, also incorporated esoteric teachings and practices, especially thaumaturgical rituals, resulting in a variety of combinations under the rubric of exoteric–esoteric Buddhism, which emerged as the orthodox worldview of medieval Japan.

According to Kuroda, the web of large and powerful religious institutions of *kenmitsu* Buddhism was only one part of the dominant socio-political system (*kenmon*; "gates of power") of medieval Japan, along with the imperial court, the aristocracy, and the warriors. The religious authorities provided both spiritual and material benefits – protection from or pacification of spirits (*goryō*), deliverance from passionate delusions and even the realization of Buddhahood within this life (*sokushin jōbutsu*), good fortune, and so forth. The secular powers provided financial and other support as patrons, including the sending of their sons and daughters to join the Buddhist clergy, thus maintaining a balance of power between the Buddhist *Dharma* (*buppō*) and secular/imperial law (*ōbō*). This system recognized only eight official schools of Buddhism: the six schools of Nara–Kusha, Jōjitsu, Ritsu, Hossō, Sanron, and Kegon, plus Tendai and Shingon, and thus from this perspective the new movements of Hōnen and so forth were "heretical" and illegitimate.

Kenmitsu Buddhism included rituals that accessed the powers of not only Buddhist figures but also a variety of spirits, demons, and deities, including local gods (*kami*). It thus incorporated elements that are associated with "Shinto," leading Kuroda to argue that "Buddhism" and "Shinto" were not separate and distinct religions until the modern period, and that "Shinto" is not so much the indigenous religion of Japan but a religion forged through centuries of combinatory associations with Buddhism, and forcibly defined as an independent tradition through the "separation of gods and Buddhas" (*shinbutsu bunri*) by the Meiji government in the late nineteenth century.

Another important aspect of *kenmitsu* Buddhism was the development and prominence of the idea of "original enlightenment" (*hongaku*), especially within the Tendai school on Mount Hiei. This line of thought proclaimed the inherent/original enlightenment of all beings, the absolute non-duality of this world and the world of enlightenment, the total affirmation of this world, and the subjective understanding and interpretation of the Buddhadharma from the perspective of one's contemplative (*kanjin*) practice (see entry on *Hongaku shisō* – original enlightenment). A lineage based on these teachings was developed through secret oral transmissions (*kuden*) from master to disciple, making the *hongaku* tradition a combination of esoteric and (traditional Tendai) exoteric elements.

The characteristics of *kenmitsu* Buddhism as a religious tradition can be summarized as follows:

1 a combination of exoteric and esoteric teachings and practices, often with the assumed superiority of the esoteric;
2 the prominence of the *hongaku* ethos: extreme non-duality, affirmation of this world, and assurance of Buddhahood in this life;
3 the primacy of ritual and practical benefits rather than adherence to a specific set of doctrinal beliefs;
4 oral (secret) transmissions as the basis of legitimacy;
5 the importance of combinatory associations among Buddhas, local deities, other Buddhist and non-Buddhist (such as originally Indian or Chinese) figures, cultural and historical heroes, and so forth (see *honji-suijaku/shinbutsu shūgo*).

The *kenmitsu* system as a socio-political institution broke down in the late medieval period (fifteenth to sixteenth century CE), but *kenmitsu* Buddhism as a religious ethos still lives on; in fact, the list of characteristics given above looks much like the "traditional Buddhism" we see today in contemporary Japan. It can be said that *kenmitsu* Buddhism is not a relic of medieval Japan, but an ongoing legacy.

See also: **Japan, Buddhism in; Mikkyō and ritual in Japanese Buddhism.**

PAUL L. SWANSON

KHEMA, AYYA

Ayya Khema (1923–97) was one of the first Western women to become a Theravāda nun. She took her novice ordination in Sri Lanka in 1979 with the Ven. Nārada Mahā Thera officiating. Full ordination for women was not available in the Theravāda tradition and so she took her full ordination at the Hsi Lai temple in California in 1988. Her desire was to make Theravāda teaching "take root"' in Europe without compromising the teaching. She authored over twenty books on meditation and Buddhist teaching and her books have been translated from German into several languages. One of her books, *Being Nobody, Going Nowhere* (1987), received the Christmas Humphreys award. She was a well-known teacher and advocate for women and worked to establish full ordination for women. She was the first Buddhist nun to address the United Nations and one of the founders of Sakyadhītā. Ayya Khema founded forest monasteries in Australia and Germany, a nuns' training center in Colombo, Sri Lanka, and Nun's Island (Sri Lanka). She traveled extensively in Europe and Asia.

Born Ilse Kussel in Berlin, Ayya Khema's life itself was extraordinary. She grew up in an affluent Jewish family forced to leave Germany in the late 1930s. Separated from her family for a while, in 1940 she joined them in Shanghai, where in 1943 all "European refugees" were confined to a ghetto by the occupying Japanese. After the war she and her husband settled in the United States. It was here, in her thirties and materially comfortable, that she began to feel what she refers to in her autobiography, *I Give You My Life* (1998), as "a vague feeling of incompleteness." She began reading philosophical and spiritual books. Several years later, touring Asia with her second husband, she visited the Sri Aurobindo ashram where she learned meditation. She was immediately comfortable and felt that she had found her path. Although she lived in Australia at the time, she traveled to the United States where she studied Zen at the San Francisco Zen Center. Missing Theravāda teaching, she spent some time at a meditation center in Burma. When her second marriage broke down, she moved to a monastery in Sydney where Phra Khantipalo was teaching. In 1978 she bought land and established a forest monastery, Wat Buddha Dhamma, in New South Wales. She was both the administrator and a teacher while Phra Khantipalo was the abbot. From this time forward she was solely engaged in teaching Buddhism.

Ayya Khema decided to become a nun in 1979. As a means of testing her resolve she spent a rains' retreat in Thailand where she was displeased to discover that female renouncers there (as in Sri Lanka) were not considered to be *bhikkhunīs* but "ladies in white." She was adamant that spiritual development required women to have the option of becoming fully ordained. This motivation led her to organize, with Karma Lekshe Tsomo and Chatsumarn Kabilsingh, the first conference of nuns and laywomen in 1987 at Bodhgayā, India. At the concluding session of the conference Sakyadhītā, a Buddhist women's organization, was created. One of the primary objectives of Sakyadhītā is the restoration of full ordination for women where it is unavailable. Ayya Khema lived long enough to see and participate in the re-establishment of the necessary quorum of *bhikṣuṇī* to conduct full ordinations in the Theravāda tradition, although it is still somewhat controversial.

In *Sakyadhītā: Daughters of the Buddha*, a volume that came out of the 1987 conference proceedings, Ayya Khema writes about the value of a celibate monastic life. The celibate life is particularly important for women, who cross-culturally bear major responsibilities for home and child care, and relationships. Relationships are complex and burdened with the problem of attachment and unfulfilled expectations. A woman gains independence through being single, with time to devote to spiritual development, and her energies can be directed towards aiding all beings rather than her immediate circle. Taking ordination produces a positive mental trace and living by the monastic precepts produces both practical and spiritual benefit. The precepts simplify daily life allowing for mental focus and prevent one from engaging in acts that produce negative *karma*.

In order to provide a more public presence for the ordination movement and organize and train nuns in Sri Lanka, Ayya Khema established the International Buddhist Women's Center. She also established Nuns' Island in 1984 which, according to the website BuddhaNet, is no longer operating. It was at the invitation of the Sri Lankan delegate to the

United Nations that she addressed the Assembly in 1987.

At the request of her students she returned to Germany from Sri Lanka and in 1989 Buddha Haus was established. The building is a converted farmhouse in the Munich area. Ayya Khema's ashes are contained in a *stūpa* in the garden. In 1997 Metta Vihāra, the first forest monastery in Germany was established. The Buddha Haus organization also has a publishing arm and supports aid projects in Ladakh, Bangalore and Assam. Nyanabodhi, who with his brothers was a prime mover in establishing Buddha Haus, was the first abbot of Metta Vihāra and became Ayya Khema's successor at Buddha Haus.

As a Theravāda teacher in the forest tradition Ayya Khema's teaching focuses on meditation. Most of her writings are transcriptions of her talks and meditation instruction. They contain abundant reference to technical Theravāda terms and the style is concise without the use of chatty anecdotes. Chapter titles in *When the Iron Eagle Flies: Buddhism for the West* (2000), a volume in which one might expect elaborate reference to Western culture, reflect her practical and technique-oriented style: "The 'Why' and 'How' of Meditation"; "Dependent Arising: Cause and Effect"; and "Samādhi: The Meditative Absorptions." She moves the instruction systematically through the various types of meditation, explaining them, providing instruction in them, and noting their possible outcomes. Each chapter ends with student questions and her responses.

As a teacher, Ayya Khema appears to have been both revolutionary and traditional. She was revolutionary in that, as a Western woman, she adopted a conservative Buddhist tradition in which female ordination had lapsed rather than a tradition, such as Chinese lineage Mahāyāna, which provided full ordination for women. She was traditional, however, in her focus on meditation and in her presentation of the teaching.

See also: **Sakyadhītā; Tsomo, *Karma* Lekshe; Women in Buddhism: an historical and textual overview.**

MAVIS L. FENN

KŌAN

The *kōan* (Ch. *gongan*) is a short anecdote in which a well-known Zen master of the past has an encounter with a disciple that is understood to be a profound expression of the master's awakened mind. Most *kōans* are contained in two main collections compiled in China, the *Gateless Gate* (Jap. *Mumonkan*) and the *Blue Cliff Records* (Jap. *Hekigan Roku*). Many *kōans* depict the moment at which a disciple has an experience of awakening stimulated by the words or actions of the master. *Kōans* are notoriously difficult to understand, often containing cryptic utterances or startling acts that appear to defy reason or common sense. They are used in Zen meditation as contemplative problems the solution of which yields *satori* or *kenshō*, a glimpse of awakening. Although *kenshō* may seem to be a private realization, it is always verified by the Zen master. The student must bring his or her answer to the *kōan* to the master, who will either verify it as authentic or reject it and ask the student to work more on the problem.

The *kōan* is often presented as a device to propel the mind out of calculating, rational thought, releasing it to the realm of the intuitive and trans-rational. In this sense it poses a verbal, intellectual problem that is impossible to solve rationally, forcing language and reason to their limits and finally breaking through to a trans-linguistic and trans-conceptual insight. This picture, however, is incomplete. Although the emphasis in *kōan* practice is indeed to drive the mind out of fixed patterns and to transcend ordinary dualistic thinking, the *kōan* is not best understood as purely instrumental and without cognitive content, nor as aiming at a blank, non-cognitive state of mind. The existence of a vast commentarial literature on *kōans* and the fact that there is an established curriculum for studying them suggests that the Zen tradition values intellectual comprehension of *kōans*, at least at certain stages in the process. Moreover, many *kōans* have discernable metaphorical and symbolic content. Hakuin's famous *kōan* is one example: "Two hands clap and there is a sound. Now what is the sound of one hand clapping?" Clearly this is a reference to the doctrine of non-duality. The *kōan*, "Show me your original face, the one you had before your father and mother were born," also gestures toward the notion of a primal unity (the "original face") prior to duality (the "father and mother"). Other *kōans* focus the attention on a seemingly ordinary object or phenomenon: a tree, a flower, or the act of washing one's bowl. The point of such *kōans* is to get the practitioner to see non-duality with respect to one thing, then eventually to extend this insight to all things.

While *kōans* have cognitive content and their intellectual study is valued, it is also clear that intellectual comprehension alone is not sufficient for solving the *kōan*. Transcending ordinary words and thought based on binary oppositions is essential. Many *kōans* posit an either/or question that cannot be answered by taking either side, thus forcing the practitioner toward performative demonstrations or performative language. *Kōan* literature is full such demonstrations – putting shoes on the head, slicing a cat in two, burning a house down. Disciples present their masters with answers to *kōans* in a private formal meeting called *dokusan* or *sanzen*. Zen masters will repeatedly reject disciples' answers until they are convinced that the disciples have broken through to a profound insight. Although heavily ritualized, *dokusan* can potentially be an arena for spontaneity, as the disciples attempt to present their understanding of the *kōan* and the masters encourage or excoriate their disciples. After a disciple attains *kenshō* and provides a satisfactory answer, the master assigns another *kōan* to deepen the disciple's awakening. Disciples may eventually work their way through an entire curriculum of *kōans*, after which they themselves can become masters.

See also: **Buddhism in Japan; Chan; Meditation (Chan/Zen); Meditational systems; Zen.**

DAVID L. MCMAHAN

KOREA, BUDDHISM AND COLONIALISM IN

The Korean Buddhist experience during colonialism took a unique form for two reasons. First, Korea was colonized by Japan, a fellow Asian and Buddhist country, unlike the more common pattern of Western non-Buddhist countries colonizing Buddhist Asian countries. Second, colonial history began at a time when Korean Buddhists were desperately trying to revive their tradition after enduring a centuries-long persecution by the neo-Confucian government.

As early as the late 1870s, Japanese Buddhist missionaries arrived on the Korean peninsula for proselytization, and in exchange, progressive-minded Korean monks traveled to Japan to learn its advanced form of Buddhism. One well-known forerunner during this period was Yi Tongin (?–1881), a monk who introduced techniques of modern education to Buddhist lecture halls, and who traveled to Japan to learn about its civilization and progress in order to use them as models for reform in both Korean society and Buddhism. The Korean Buddhist tendency to consider Japan its benefactor increased when the ban on monks and nuns entering the capital city – effective since the mid-fifteenth century – was revoked through an appeal the Japanese monk Sano Zenrei (1859–1912) of the Nichiren sect.

In 1910, when Korea was officially annexed to Japan, Korean Buddhist revival movements were well on their way. In 1899, the Wŏnhŭng monastery in Seoul opened and there, in 1906, Pulgyo yŏn'guhoe (Society for the Study of Buddhism) was founded. In the same year, the first modern-style Buddhist school, the Myŏngjin school, was established to educate young Buddhists. In 1908 a new Buddhist sect under the name Wŏn chong (Consummated school) was created with T'ae'go Pou (1301–82) as its Dharma-origin. Wŏn chong was the first Buddhist sect to appear since 1424, when the sectarian identity of Korean Buddhism was obliterated by the anti-Buddhist policy of the Chosŏn government.

In 1911, the colonial government implemented the Temple Ordinance, which accorded the Governor-General the unique responsibility of appointing abbots and overseeing the properties of the main temples. Many Korean Buddhists considered this measure a means of promoting the status of monks and protecting Buddhist assets.

In 1910, Yi Hoe'gwang, the head of Wŏn chong, attempted a merger with the Japanese Sōtō sect. This infuriated Korean Buddhists, who considered the merger a subordination of Korean Buddhism to the Sōtō sect whose gradualist position was unacceptable to subitist Korean Buddhists. Several Korean Buddhist leaders declared the independence of Korean Buddhism, and in 1911 they made a move to create a new Buddhist sect under the name of Imje (Ch. Linji) chong. By presenting Imje as its sectarian identity, Korean Buddhists tried to distinguish themselves from the Sōtō school.

With the Temple Ordinance in place, the potential conflict between the Wŏn chong and the Imje chong became null. Korean Buddhists continued to defend their independence, and eventually in 1941 a centralized school of the Chogye Order was re-created at the T'ae'go monastery.

As the initial Korean Buddhist response to colonial reality was rather obscure, and as their resistance was religious, not political, in nature, shortly before 1920 critics began to question whether Korean Buddhists could fully grasp the social and political reality of colonialism. After the 1919 March First liberation movement, a group of young Buddhists began to take a critical position towards the colonial government's religious policy, criticizing the naiveté of those who thought well of or disregarded Japanese policies on Buddhism. They criticized the problems of the Temple Ordinance, which prohibited Korean Buddhists from having a centralized organizational body. They also criticized the abuse of power by the abbots of the thirty main temples. They emphasized the practice of *minjung* Buddhism, or Buddhism for the masses, as opposed to Buddhism controlled by the state. By this time, the Korean Buddhists' search for religious identity became intertwined with their attempt to reconfirm their national identity. This combined effort resulted in the creation of the Chogye Order, which did not exist in Japanese Buddhism. Another result was the publication of books on the history of Korean Buddhism. The first comprehensive Korean Buddhist history texts were published in 1917: Yi Nŭnghwa's *Chosŏn pulgyo t'ongsa* (*A Comprehensive History of Korean Buddhism*) and Kwŏn Sangno's *Chosŏn pulgyo yaksa* (*An Abridged History of Korean Buddhism*).

Changes in the interpretation of Korean Buddhist philosophy also followed in a similar manner. Ch'oe Namsŏn (1880–1957) defined Korean Buddhism as ecumenical Buddhism (Kor. *t'ong pulgyo*). He used the Buddhist philosophy of the seventh-century monk Wŏnhyo (617–86) as a way to systematize and unify disparate Buddhist doctrines. Ch'oe's theory of ecumenism as the identity of Korean Buddhism continues to impact Korean Buddhist scholarship today.

During the colonial period, Buddhist journals also began to appear, providing a forum to express and discuss Buddhist philosophy, reform ideas, and literature by Buddhist intellectuals, as well as for the purpose of proselytization and imparting messages from the Governor-General.

One major colonial legacy was the Korean Buddhist adoption of the Japanese Buddhist practices of having a wife and eating meat (Kor. *taech'ŏ sigyuk*). Married monks among Koreans began to appear around the turn of the century before colonization, and the number of married monks rapidly increased during the period between 1910 and 1930. Having maintained the tradition of celibacy and vegetarianism, some Korean Buddhists strongly disapproved of this new form of monkhood.

To group celibacy with religious purity, Korean national identity, and patriotism on the one hand, and to set this against married monks, religious impurity, Japanese invaders, and traitors on the other hand, would oversimplify the situation. Paek Yongsŏng (1863–1940), a leading Buddhist reformer during the colonial period, submitted a petition to the Governor-General requesting a prohibition of monks' marriage, but this did not produce visible results. Meanwhile, Han Yongun (1879–1944), another leading Buddhist during the same period and also a national hero for his anti-Japanese activities, filed a petition in the early 1910s requesting that monks be allowed to marry. In 1926, monks' marriage became officially allowed.

The conflict between married and celibate monks became a long-standing dispute after the liberation, when many Korean Buddhists wanted to restore the purity of their religious and national identity by eliminating the married monks from the Chogye Order. The conflict lasted for more than a decade, from 1954 to 1970, when both sides tentatively reached an agreement by creating T'ae'go chong, an independent order for the married monks.

See also: **Korea, Buddhism in.**

JIN Y. PARK

KOREA, BUDDHISM IN

Korean Buddhism is a part of the East Asian Mahāyāna Buddhist tradition. During its 1,500-year history, which began in the fourth century and continues to today, Korean Buddhism developed closely with Chinese Buddhism, and also influenced the development of Buddhism in Japan. The social and political situation of Korea bears significant impact on the nature of Korean Buddhism. The history began with the founding period during the Three Kingdoms and the Unified Silla periods, when Buddhism settled into Korean society. Korean Buddhism then underwent maturity during the Koryŏ dynasty, suppression during the Chosŏn dynasty, and finally re-emergence in modern time.

Transmission and development: the Three Kingdoms and Unified Silla periods (fourth century CE to 935 CE)

Transmission

When Buddhism was introduced to Korea in the fourth century, the Korean peninsula was divided into three tribal kingdoms. Koguryŏ (37 BCE–618 CE) occupied the northern part of the peninsula; Paekche (18 BCE–660 CE) was located in the southwest; and Silla (57 BCE–925 CE), in the southeast. According to the *Samguk sagi* (*The Historical Records of the Three Kingdoms*), Buddhism was introduced to Koguryŏ around 372 CE by Sundo (Ch. Shundao), who was sent for by King Fujian (r. 357–85) of the

Former Qin (351–85) in China. The same source indicates that the transmission of Buddhism to the kingdom of Paekche occurred around 384 CE, by an Indian monk from the Eastern Jin named Mālānanda. The introduction to Silla took place in the sixth century (528). In all three kingdoms, Buddhism was received by royal families immediately after its arrival. Buddhism was brought to Koguryŏ as part of diplomatic exchanges between Koguryŏ and the Former Qin. Sundo arrived with diplomats and soon became a teacher in the royal family. Within three years, King Sosurim (r. 371–84) of Koguryŏ had two temples constructed. In Paekche, the arrival of the missionary monk was eagerly received by the royal family and within two years a Buddhist temple was already under construction. In the kingdom of Silla, there was a brief period of resistance, but after the martyrdom of Ich'adon (506–27), who was a loyal minister, the ruling class began to embrace Buddhism. Following this initial ordeal, Buddhism was recognized as national religion in 527 by King Pŏphŭng (r. 514–40), who soon prohibited killing (529 CE). Lady Sa (Kor. Sassi), who was the first recorded nun in Korean Buddhism, was the first to be ordained in Silla. After his retirement, King Pŏphŭng and his wife joined the monastery, setting a model for later generations of royal families.

Before Korean Buddhists familiarized themselves with the sophisticated philosophy of Buddhism, Buddhism won the hearts of both the common people and the ruling class with its material culture. Buddhist images provided them with an object for religious devotion in a manner that was not available from the indigenous religious tradition of shamanism. In worshiping the images of the Maitreya Buddha brought by Sundo, people prayed for both their family and nation. As King Sosurim of Koguryŏ advised his people: "Practice Buddhism and thus earn merit (fortune)." For the people of Koguryŏ, family prosperity and national peace were the immediate appeal of Buddhism.

The influence of the material culture of Buddhism on the indigenous culture is not limited to merit-seeking. Acculturation of Buddhism with the indigenous shamanism left an impact still visible in Korean Buddhist temples today. Most Korean Buddhist temples have a small shrine dedicated to the mountain spirit (Kor. *sansin'gak*), with a tiger, which is an old Daoist symbol. The combination reflects the shamanistic element in Korean Buddhism as it was mixed with Daoism.

The major textual sources that chronicle the initial encounter of Buddhism with Korean society include the *Samguk sagi* (*The Historical Records of the Three Kingdoms*), compiled in 1145 CE by the Confucian scholar Kim Pusik (1075–1151); the *Haedong kosŭng chŏn* (*The History of High Monks in Korea*), compiled in 1215 by Kakhun (d.u.) and the *Samguk yusa* (*The Bequeathed History of the Three Kingdoms*), written 1281–9 by the Buddhist monk Iryŏn (1206–89). All three texts were written between the twelfth and thirteenth centuries, far later than the initial arrival of Buddhism in Korea in the fifth century. Records from other East Asian nations provide earlier accounts, if not based on first-hand experience, of early Korean Buddhism. Such texts include: the *Liang gaoseng zhuan* (*The Liang History of High Monks*, 519 CE), the *Liang shu* (*The History of the Liang*, 629 CE), *Tang gaoseng zhuan* (*The Tang History of High Monks*, 645 CE), the *Zu gaoseng zhuang* (*Continuation of the History of Monks*, 664–8 CE), and the Japanese *Nihon shoki* (*Chronicles of Japan*, 720 CE).

The Buddhist schools

During the formative stage, Korean Buddhist schools were most influenced by Chinese Buddhist schools. Soon after the introduction of Buddhism into Korea, Koreans began to travel to China and India to acquire first-hand experience of Buddhist teachings. In the kingdom of Koguryŏ, the teaching of the *Nirvāṇa Sūtra* that all sentient beings have Buddha nature acquired a great appeal. The Samnon school (Ch. Sanlun; Three Treatise school), which is a Chinese form of Indian Madhyamaka, studied in connection with *Prajñā Sūtra*, is believed to have also been popular in Koguryŏ at this time. In the kingdom of Paekche, the study of *Vinaya* was popular, along with the *Abhidharma* literature that was introduced by the Paekche monk Kyŏmik (d.u.) who traveled to India during the mid-sixth century. In the kingdom of Silla, the study of Yusik (the consciousness-only, Yogācāra) was the most popular.

Despite these developments during the first 300 years of Korean Buddhism, the emergence of Korean forms of Buddhism did not take place until the mid-seventh century, when the kingdom of Silla conquered and merged with Koguryŏ and Paekche. The Korean peninsula thus entered into the period called the Unified Silla (668–935). By this time, scriptural studies of Buddhism had developed into the Five Buddhist Schools, which include: Kyeyul chong (*Vinaya* school); Yŏlban chong (*Nirvāṇa* school), Pŏpsŏng chong (*Dharma* Nature school; Mādhyamika); Wŏnyung chong (Huayan school; Kor. Hwaŏm); Pŏpsang chong (*Dharma* Characteristics, Yogācāra). Among the five schools, Hwaŏm became the most influential for its scholastic Buddhism and had a lasting impact on Korean Buddhists.

By the mid-seventh century Korean monks had also become exposed to a new form of Buddhism developed in China called Sŏn (Ch. Chan). The first record of Sŏn in Korea appeared with the Silla monk, Pŏmnang (fl. 632–46), who studied with Daoxin (580–651), the Fourth Patriarch of Chinese Chan Buddhism. After returning to Korea, Pŏmnang transmitted the teaching to his disciples. For the next century and a half, Korean monks traveled to China to study this new form of Buddhism. By the mid-tenth century, their studies developed into what is now known as the Nine Mountains school of Sŏn Buddhism. Most of the founders of the Nine Mountains school studied with Chan masters in the line of Mazu Daoyi (707–86), in the Hongzu sect, the most subitist among the Chinese Chan Buddhist schools.

Major figures

During the founding period of Korean Buddhism, in the kingdom of Paekche, Kyŏmik (d.u.; sixth century) founded the *Vinaya* school. In the kingdom of Silla, Wŏn'gwang (531–630) created the "Five Secular Admonishments" for the training of youth by combining Confucian teaching with Buddhist ethics, demonstrating a mutual reliance between Confucianism and Buddhism even at the early stage of Korean Buddhist development. In the kingdom of Silla, Chajang, a national overseer, established the monks' discipline.

A more scholastic and philosophical aspect of Korean Buddhism at the time is found in the works of Wŏnch'ŭk (613–96), Ŭisang (625–702), and Wŏnhyo (617–86). At the age of fifteen, Wŏnch'ŭk traveled to China where he eventually developed his own interpretation of Yogācāra Buddhism based on Xuanzang's (600–64) New Yogācāra, which later became the basis of Silla Yogācāra studies. The founding patriarch of the Hwaŏm school was Ŭisang, whose interpretation of Hwaŏm Buddhism in *Hwaŏm ilsŭng pŏpkye to* (*The Diagram of Dharmadhātu of the One Vehicle of Hwaŏm Buddhism*) had a significant influence on the evolution of Hwaŏm thought, and spawned a series of commentaries by later generations of Korean Buddhists. Lastly, Wŏnhyo is arguably one of the most important figures in Korean Buddhism.

He left behind voluminous works, of which the most well known are his commentaries on *Dasheng qixin lun* (*Awakening of Mahāyāna Faith*). In his commentaries on *Dasheng qixin lun*, together with *Yijang ŭi* (*Treatises on Two Hindrances*) and *Kŭmgan sammae kyŏngnon* (*Treaties on the Vajrasamādhi Sūtra*), Wŏnhyo discussed the origin of sentient beings' unenlightened nature as well as that of their enlightenment. Wŏnhyo also wrote on *bodhisattva* precepts in three of his works: *Posal yŏngnak ponŏpkyŏng so* (*Commentary on the Sūtra of* Bodhisattva*'s Bead-Ornamented Primary Activities*), *Posalgye bon chibŏm yo'gi* (*Essentials of Observation and Violation of* Bodhisattva *Precepts*) and *Pommanggyŏng posal kyebon sa'gi* (*Personal Records on the Chapter on the* Bodhisattva *Precepts in the Sūtra of Brahma's Net*). In these texts, in line with Mahāyāna teaching of emptiness, Wŏnhyo emphasizes the emptiness of precept, as well as the importance of observing precepts.

Maturity: the Koryŏ period (918–1392)

When the Koryŏ dynasty was established at the beginning of the tenth century, Korean Buddhism had become a major influence and source of power in society. In the "Ten Injunctions" proclaimed by Wang Kŏn (r. 918–43), the Koryŏ dynastic founder, three out of ten injunctions concerned the protection of Buddhism. The three injunctions declared the Buddha as the state protector, planned temples for services, and emphasized the importance of the Buddhist Lantern Festival as a spiritual practice.

Material culture

One memorable achievement of Koryŏ Buddhism was the carving on more than 80,000 wooden blocks of *Tripiṭaka* scriptures, which were based on the Chinese Buddhist *Tripiṭaka* completed during the tenth century. Began in 1010 and completed several decades later, the first production of the wooden blocks was destroyed during the Mongol invasion of Koryŏ. The second series carved between 1236–51 is presently preserved at the Haein Monastery. The Korean *Tripiṭaka* became a major reference for the Japanese Buddhist canon published during the early twentieth century, including the *Taishō shinshū daizō kyō* (1914–22).

Figure 26 1,000 Buddha images, Taeansa Monastery, South Kyongsang, Korea.

The Buddhist schools

During the early period of the Koryŏ dynasty, Korean Buddhist schools were divided into what is now known as the Five Schools of scholastic Buddhism and the Nine Mountains school of Sŏn Buddhism.

As both scholastic Buddhism (Kor. Kyo) and Sŏn (meditational) Buddhism became widespread, the different emphasis in these two forms called for an explanation on their relationship, which became one of main concerns of Koryŏ Buddhists. In response to this task, two incidents should be noted: (1) the Ch'ŏnt'ae school, a Korean version of the Chinese Tiantai, was created by Ŭich'ŏn (1055–1101); and (2) the creation of the Chogye school, a consolidation of the previous Nine Mountains school of Sŏn, was the second incident.

The teaching of Ch'ŏnt'ae and the study of the *Lotus Sūtra* existed in Korea

Figure 27 Temple bell and wooden clapper, on Dobongsan, near Seoul, Korea.

as early as the seventh century. However, the Ch'ŏnt'ae school was not created until Ŭich'ŏn (1055–1101) employed Ch'ŏnt'ae thought with equal emphasis on doctrinal teaching as well as contemplation in his attempt to bring together scholastic and meditational Buddhism. This was his intentional attempt to revive Buddhism, which was only briefly successful.

After the creation of the Ch'ŏnt'ae school, the Nine Mountains school of Sŏn Buddhism was consolidated into the Chogye school. Still maintaining the position of Sŏn master, Chinul claimed the unity between doctrinal and meditational schools through his study of Hwaŏm thought. Hwaŏm later became one of the major philosophical grounds to explain the relationship between doctrinal and meditational schools.

Major figures

Major Buddhist figures of the Koryŏ period can be categorized into three schools: Hwaŏm, Ch'ŏnt'ae, and Sŏn Buddhist schools.

The Hwaŏm school was fully established in Korean Buddhism by Ŭisang and it continued to exert its influence during the Koryŏ dynasty. Clarifications of the doctrinal foundation of Hwaŏm Buddhism can be found in the *Ilsŭng pŏpkye to wŏn'tong ki* (*Complete and Unified Record on the Diagram of the Dharmadhātu of the One Vehicle*), written by Kyunyŏ (923–73), who interpreted Ŭisang's Diagram in connection with the Chinese Huayan masters Zhiyan (602–68) and Fazang (643–712). Chinul was also influenced by Hwaŏm thought in the creation of his own version of Sŏn Buddhism. His strand of Hwaŏm thought and its relation to Sŏn Buddhism is articulated in his posthumous work, *Wŏndon sŏngbul ron* (*Treatise on Sudden and Complete Attainment of Buddhahood*), which emphasized sudden awakening followed by gradual cultivation. Ŭich'ŏn is another notable Hwaŏm scholar, even though he is typically known as the first patriarch of the Ch'ŏnt'ae school. Ŭich'ŏn held high respect for Zongmi, who had put together Huayan and Chan Buddhism, two major influences on Ŭich'ŏn's thought.

In the Ch'ŏnt'ae study, before the Ch'ŏnt'ae school was formally created, Che'gwan (d. 971) elaborated the Tiantai doctrine in his *Ch'ŏnt'ae sa'gyoŭi* (Ch. *Tiantai sijia yi*; *Outline of Fourfold Teaching of Tiantai*), which later became well known in the Chinese Tiantai school. Che'gwan emphasized doctrinal teaching as the entrance into contemplation, whereas Ŭich'ŏn tried to maintain the balance between doctrine and contemplation. A generation after Ŭich'ŏn, Yose Wŏnmyo (1163–1245) attempted a revival of the Ch'ŏnt'ae school by creating the Compact of White Lotus Community (Paengnyŏn kyŏlsa). Yose emphasized repentance practice and the lotus-*samādhi* (*pŏphwa sammae*). The Ch'ŏnt'ae school was revived briefly with Yose but subsided shortly after his death.

Most influential to the later development of Korean Buddhism was Pojo Chinul's Chogye school. His introduction and endorsement of Kanhwa Sŏn became the dominant form of Korean Sŏn Buddhism. In his posthumous work, *Kanhwa kyŏrŭi ron* (*Treatise on Resolving Doubts about Hwadu Meditation*), Chinul introduced *hwadu* (Ch. *huatou*) meditation as the fastest way to attain enlightenment, but reserved it for the high-capacity practitioners. Chinul's successor, Chin'gak Hyesim (1178–1234), solidified and popularized the Kanhwa Sŏn tradition. He compiled 1,125 *kongans* in his *Sŏnmun yŏmsong chip* (*The Collection of Cases and Verses of the Sŏn School*, 1226). T'ae'go Pou (1301–82) practiced *hwadu* meditation and traveled to China to get recognition of his enlightenment. By receiving the transmission from the masters in the Linji school, T'ae'go has been credited as an authentic transmitter of the Linji Chan to Korea.

Persecution: the Chosŏn dynasty (1392–1910)

The privilege that Buddhism enjoyed in Koryŏ society, especially the connections in the political world, eventually caused its own demise as the economic extravagance of the *sangha* was blamed for the financial devastation of Koryŏ society. By the end of the Koryŏ dynasty, the rising neo-Confucian literati launched severe anti-Buddhist polemics, attacking the philosophical foundation of Buddhism as well as its damaging effects on the economy and social ethics. The Chosŏn dynasty replaced Buddhism with neo-Confucianism as the national ideology, and hostility to Buddhism intensified throughout the dynasty. By the late nineteenth century Korean Buddhism was in devastation. Amid governmental suppression, Chosŏn Buddhists were outwardly eager to demonstrate the validity of Buddhism as a religious and philosophical system, and they inwardly took pains to find the identity of Buddhism itself. The Chosŏn neo-Confucian literati also generated a series of edicts prohibiting women from visiting Buddhist temples and being involved with Buddhism-related activities, which produced the dual effect of suppressing women and Buddhism itself.

The Buddhist schools.

The Chosŏn government systematically suppressed Buddhism by abolishing or restructuring most Buddhist schools existing at the time. Within less than forty years after the beginning of the Chosŏn dynasty, six doctrinal schools and five meditational schools were consolidated into the two generic schools of doctrine (Kyo) and meditation (Sŏn) (Kor. *sŏn'gyo yangjong*) (1424), which effectively obliterated sectarian identity in Korean Buddhism. Hence, the Buddhism during the mid- and late-Chosŏn dynasty is known as Mountain Buddhism without sectarian identity.

Major figures.

Hamhŏ Tŭkt'ong (1376–1433), with the epithet Kihwa, was well known during the early period of the Chosŏn dynasty. In his *Hyŏnjŏng ron* (*Exposition of the Correct*), Kihwa challenged the Confucian criticism of Buddhist philosophy and, in conclusion, argued for the original oneness of the traditional Three Schools of Daoism, Confucianism and Buddhism.

Ch'ŏnghŏ Hujŏng (1520–1604) developed his Sŏn thought in his treatise, *Sŏn'ga ku'gam* (*A Paragon of the Sŏn School*, 1590), emphasizing the use of scriptural teaching as an initiating stage to Buddhism, but relinquishing it as practitioners enter into the world of Sŏn. Hujŏng also laid out his thought on the oneness of the Three Teachings in his work, *Samga ku'gam* (*A Paragon of Three Teachings*).

Paekp'a Kŭngsŏn (1767–1852) attempted a systematization of different Sŏn teachings in his *Sŏnmun su'gyŏng* (*A Hand Mirror of the Sŏn School*, 1820). In this work, Paekp'a employed Linji's three phrases, and claimed a hierarchical relationship of Patriarchal Sŏn, Tathāgata Sŏn, and Theoretical Sŏn. Responding to Paekp'a, Ch'oŭi Ŭisŏn (1786–1877) wrote the *Sŏnmun sabyŏn manŏ* (*Talks on the Four Divisions of Sŏn School*) in which he claimed that the existence of different types of Sŏn did not imply a hierarchical relationship among them; the different types meant different methods to be employed according to different characters of practitioners. This debate continued for more than a century and can be understood as a Korean Buddhist effort to recover the identity of Sŏn Buddhism.

Korean Buddhism in East Asian Buddhism

Korean Buddhism developed in close interaction with Korea's neighboring regions. During the fifth century, the Koguryŏ monk Sŭngnang (d.u.) traveled to China, where he became a significant influence on Jizang's (549–623) Sanlun sect (the Three Treatises school). His influence came in the clarification of the differences between the concept of emptiness as stated in the *Chengshi lun* (*The Satyasiddhi Śāstra*) and that as stated in the *Nāgārjuna*. No works by Sŭngnang survived but his thoughts are mentioned by Jizang in several of his texts, and Jizang also credited him as a major figure in the Sanlun teaching.

After the death of Zhiyan (602–68), the designated second patriarch of the school, the Silla monk Ŭisang, who founded the Korean Hwaŏm (Ch. Huayan) school, became one of the leaders of Chinese Huayan Buddhism. Ŭisang and Fazang were colleagues, studying under Zhiyan, and Ŭisang held influence on Fazang's Huayan thought. Fazang was also noticeably influenced by Wŏnhyo's commentaries on *The Awakening of Faith*.

Wŏnch'ŭk had influenced the development of Yogācāra in China and Japan, and as expressed in his *Commentary on the Saṃdhinirmocana Sūtra*, his views on consciousness-only and various other Mahāyāna texts are well known among scholars of Tibetan Buddhism. During the eleventh century, the Kyorŏ monk Che'gwan (d. 971) was brought to China by King Kwangjong, at the request of the Chinese emperor, to re-introduce a copy of the Tiantai manuals lost during the persecution of Buddhism in China. During this visit, Che'gwan composed the *Ch'ŏnt'ae sa'gyo ŭi* (*Tiantai sijiao yi*), which became one of the most important Ch'ŏnt'ae exegetical writings in Tiantai Buddhism.

According to the *Nihon shoki*, Buddhism was spread from the kingdom of Paekche to Japan during the mid-sixth century (552). Around the late sixth century (595), the Paekche monk Haech'ong traveled to Japan where he taught the Japanese Prince Shotoku. Later, Paekche monks Kwallŭk (fl. 602–4) and Tojang (fl. 680–721), who were believed to be well versed in the Sanlun teaching, also traveled to Japan. Tojang composed the *Sŏngsillon so* (*Commentaries on Chengshilun;* Jap. *Jōjitsuron*) which introduced to Japan the Satyasiddhi school, or Jōjitsu shū.

Defining Korean Buddhism

Korean Buddhism has frequently been characterized as syncretic Buddhism (Kor. *t'ongpulbyo*) and state-protecting Buddhism (Kor. *ho'guk pulgyo*). Syncretism in this case goes beyond the simple cultural diffusion that usually takes place between indigenous and imported religions, or when two or more religious traditions come into contact. In the syncretism of

Korean Buddhism, there was an intentional effort to create a unified vision through appropriation of differences within existing thought systems such that conflicting ideas would eventually be reconciled. Syncretism here has been used interchangeably with such expressions as "reconciliation," "harmonization," or sometimes with "interdenomination," and "interpenetration."

During the formative stage of Korean Buddhism (the Three Kingdoms and United Silla periods), syncretism was a result of an effort to create a unified form of teaching out of the sectarian differences within Buddhist schools. The *locus classicus* of the historical and philosophical origin of this syncretic harmony is in a text by Wŏnhyo (617–86), a seventh-century monk-scholar. In his *Simmun hwajaeng ron* (*Ten Approaches to the Harmonization of Doctrinal Controversy*), Wŏnhyo critically warns of the closed attitude of claiming the truth or authenticity of one Buddhist teaching over others. Wŏnhyo considered this attitude to be blind to the reality that the one and the many are reflected in each other. The syncretic effort to resolve doctrinal disputes was further reinforced by the Hwaŏm (Ch. Huayan) Buddhist philosophy of Ŭisang (625–702), which taught the interpenetration of all existing beings.

With the introduction of Sŏn Buddhism around the seventh century, a new pattern of reconciliation began to emerge. Creating a rapport between meditational and doctrinal schools became the major concern of Koryŏ Buddhism, and this resulted in the formation of the Ch'ŏnt'ae school and the Chogye school.

During the Chosŏn dynasty (1392–1910), under the intensified anti-Buddhist polemics, Korean Buddhists developed the idea that the traditional Three Teachings of Buddhism, Confucianism, and Daoism shared one essence: hence they were one in their ultimate teachings. The third pattern of syncretism thus took the form of the harmony of the Three Teachings.

In all three patterns of syncretism, political factors were strongly involved, as is evident from the state-protecting aspect, the second well-known feature of Korean Buddhism. Wŏnhyo's theory of harmonizing doctrinal disputes in his *Simmun hwajaengnon* has been taken to be a contribution to the harmony in the political sphere when the kingdom of Silla, the least developed society among the three kingdoms, overcame to merge the other two. Further, the harmonizing nature of Hwaŏm thought in Wŏnhyo and Ŭisang, as evident in the phrase "one is many and many is one," has also been understood as a major contributor to the unification of Silla. Similarly, there are claims that at the beginning of the Kyorŏ dynasty, the Ch'ŏnt'ae school provided a philosophical grounding which solidified the newly established Kyorŏ society. In an interesting twist, during the Chosŏn period in the late sixteenth century, when Korean Buddhists struggled to prove the essential oneness of Buddhism, Confucianism and Daoism, Buddhist monks created a monk militia (Kor. *sungbyŏng*) to protect the peninsula against the invasion by the Japanese (1592–8).

Claims have also been made that the idea of syncretism as a conspicuous feature of Korean Buddhism was constructed by modern scholarship rather than being a true reflection of history. The Korean intellectual Ch'oe Namsŏn described Korean Buddhism as syncretic (Kor. *hoet'ong pulgyo*) during the 1930s in response to Japanese Buddhist scholarship's disparaging of Korean Buddhism as nothing but an extension of Chinese Buddhism. In the 1960s, the Korean philosopher-scholar Pak Chonghong also identified Wŏnhyo's thought as syncretic. In both cases, the relationship between syncretic Buddhism and its political implications was sustained: for Ch'oe, syncretism as a feature of Korean

Buddhism was employed in the identity formation of Korea in opposition to that of the Japanese colonizer; for Pak, the syncretic nature of Wŏnhyo's thought was promoted, implicit as it may be, in an effort to harmonize the people as Korea transformed herself into a modern nation-state.

Buddhism in modern Korea

Korean Buddhism at the end of the nineteenth and early twentieth century faced dual challenges created by the legacies of its past and the prospects of its future. Most urgent was the recovery of its dignity after centuries-long persecution, which culminated in the banning of monks from entering the metropolitan area beginning in the mid-fifteenth century and remaining effective until 1895. Equally important was the issue proving the function and value of Buddhism within the environment of modern society. The colonization of Korea by Japan (1910–45) only complicated this dual task for Korean Buddhists.

The Buddhist schools

In 1908 Wŏn chong (Complete school) was created, forming the first Buddhist sect since 1424 when all existing Buddhist schools were consolidated into Sŏn and Kyo schools. The school, however, had a short life. Yi Hoe'gwang, the head of the school, made a failed attempt to merge the school with the Japanese Sōtō sect. The attempt to merge faced strong resistance by Korean Buddhists, who responded by creating in 1911 another Buddhist sect under the name Imje (Ch. Linji) chong. As opposed to the gradualism of the Japanese Sōtō sect, Imje chong emphasized the subitist orientation of Korean Buddhism.

Implemented in 1911, the Temple Ordinance (Kor. *sach'allyŏng*) placed Buddhist temples under the control of the Governor-General and acknowledged no sectarian identities of Korean Buddhism, which effectively put an end to both Wŏn chong and Imje chong.

Continued efforts to establish a centralized Buddhist order succeeded in the opening of the Chogye Order in 1941. This order became officially registered in 1962 and has remained the dominant Buddhist school in contemporary Korea.

The identity of Korean Buddhism continues to be an issue of debate within the Korean *sangha*. One major debate was the clash between the celibate and married monks, a division formed during colonialism and lasting for more than a decade (1954–70). The result was the 1969 creation of the T'ae'go chong for married monks.

Revival of Sŏn Buddhism in modern Korea

Korean Buddhism during the late nineteenth century and the first half of the twentieth century can be characterized by two directions: the revival of Sŏn Buddhist tradition and the Buddhist reform movements.

The revival of Sŏn Buddhism began with Sŏn Master Kyŏnghŏ Sŏngu (1849–1912), who has been credited as the founder of modern Korean Sŏn Buddhism. He allegedly obtained enlightenment through *hwadu* meditation, which reconfirms the importance of the Kanhwa Sŏn tradition as introduced and endorsed by Pojo Chinul centuries ago. Kyŏnghŏ's disciples, Song Man'gong (1871–1946), Pang Han'am (1876–1951), Hyewŏl (1861–1937), and Suwŏl (1855–1928), played a major role in modern Korean Sŏn Buddhism, solidifying the position of Kanhwa Sŏn once again as major form of practice in Korean Buddhism.

Buddhist reform movements

The reform movements can be divided into two categories: reform by amending within the traditional Buddhist order, and reform by creating an entirely new Buddhist order. Representatives of the former are Paek Yongsŏng (1864–1940), Kwŏn Sangro (1879–1965), Pak Hanyŏng (1870–1948), Han Yongun (1879–1944) and Yi Yŏngjae (1900–927). As for the latter reform, Won Buddhism, established by Sot'aesan Pak Chungbin (1891–1943) in 1916, is the most prominent example. Both groups share important reform agendas, including the propagation of Buddhist *sūtras* in the Korean language through translation from classical Chinese; the return of Buddhism from its seclusion on the mountain to the life-world of the general public; the blurring of the rigid demarcation between the clergy and lay practitioners; and the modification of Buddhist practice and rituals to fit with modern lifestyles.

Paek Yongsŏng was a pioneer in expanding the audience of Buddhism beyond Buddhist clergy. He emphasized the importance of translating Buddhist scriptures from classical Chinese into the Korean language, and introduced new ways of proselytization. In his *Tae'gak kyo* (*Religion of Great Awakening*) movement, Yongsŏng believed that reaching out to the masses was the path back to the original Buddhism during the time of Śākyamuni Buddha.

Kwŏn Sangno has not been a favorite of Korean Buddhist scholars because of his collaboration with the colonialists. But his essay, *Chosŏn pulgyo kyehyŏk ron* (*Treatise on the Reformation of Korean Buddhism*, 1912–13), was one of the first to appear in a series of articles published by reform-minded Buddhist intellectuals. Kwŏn's reform agenda focused on the importance of education, and on the creation of educational institutions for Buddhists and others.

Among the reform publications of the first half of the twentieth century, the most well known is Han Yongun's *Chosŏn pulgyo yusillon* (*Treatise on the Renovation of Korean Buddhism*, 1913) which contains severe criticism of the situation of Korean Buddhism at the time. The *Treatise* also proposes radical reforms of the *sangha*, including: educating the clerics, unifying the doctrinal orientation of the *sangha*, simplifying practices, centralizing the *sangha* administration, and reforming *sangha* policies and customs. Han's proposals in this essay provided a framework for subsequent *sangha* reformation. Han also showed a strong sympathy for marginalized communities, and emphasized that Buddhism should be for the masses (Kor. *minjung pulgyo*).

These reform-minded Buddhist intellectuals revealed an acute awareness of the distance between Buddhism and the general public. Their reform, however, was limited by their lack of contact and concerns for the laity. Even Han Yongun's *Chosŏn pulgyo yusillon* was focused on the reform of the *sangha*, not of the laity and its practice of Buddhism.

Yi Nŭnghwa was one of the few to direct his reform agenda to the laity. Yi himself never became ordained. Ironically, however, voluminous works on Korean Buddhism in which Yi addressed his contemporary lay practitioners were written in classical Chinese, a language of which the majority of his supposed target audience were ignorant. Even though Yi's lay Buddhist movement failed to produce the expected impact, Yi's *Chosŏn pulgyo t'ongsa* (*History of Korean Buddhism*) was the first comprehensive volume on Korean Buddhist history, and it initiated a new way of studying Buddhism, namely, as a field of objective research.

Present and future of Korean Buddhism

Lay Buddhism became one of main forces in Korean Buddhism after the liberation in 1945 and during the second half of the twentieth century. For lay practitioners, to incorporate Buddhist practice and tradition in the milieu of an increasingly technological and Westernized social setting was a struggle. During the 1970s and 1980s, amid demonstrations against the military regime, Buddhism's concern for the masses materialized into Minjung Buddhism (Buddhism for the masses), criticizing the long history of Korean Buddhism's tie with the powerful in the name of protecting the nation.

Influenced by the Christian Church, many traditional Buddhist monasteries established urban centers where weekly meetings are held. Buddhism began to regain its popularity among the intellectuals as well as the middle and upper classes.

The awareness of the gendered nature of Buddhist discourse and practice, as well as its institutional structure, also began to grow. The population of Buddhist nuns in Korea has reached almost half of the Korean *sangha*; and 80 percent of lay Buddhist practitioners are currently women. Both *bhikṣuṇī sangha* and lay practitioners are making efforts to transform the current patriarchal system of Buddhism into a more equal and open-minded system.

See also: **Korea, the Buddhist–Confucian debate; Hwaŏm Buddhism; Minjung Buddhism; Sŏn Buddhism; Women in Korean Buddhism; Won Buddhism.**

JIN Y. PARK

KOREA: THE BUDDHIST–CONFUCIAN DEBATE

The Buddhist–Confucian debate that took place during the mid-fourteenth to mid-fifteenth centuries reflects the most urgent task Korean Buddhists faced during the early Chosŏn dynasty (1392–1910). The task was to clarify the identity of Buddhism and explicate its relationship with Confucianism, the dominant ideology of society then. In the course of its history, Korean Buddhism's interaction with Confucianism took different forms. Soon after Buddhism's arrival in Korea, Korean monks traveled to China, and upon return, they brought with them Chinese culture, which includes Confucianism. During the formative stage of Buddhism in Korea, the two traditions existed in harmony, each performing relatively separate functions. Confucianism provided a foundation for statecraft and an educational system, while Buddhism formed the spiritual and philosophical foundation of society. The "Five Secular Admonishments" (Kor. *sesok o'gye*) proposed by the Silla monk Wŏn'gwang (531–630) at the beginning of the seventh century illustrates well the combination of Confucian virtues with Buddhist precepts: serve the king with loyalty; tend parents with filial piety; treat friends with sincerity; never retreat from the battlefield; be judicious in the taking of life.

From its early days, Korean Buddhism maintained a close relationship with the state, and at the beginning of the Koryŏ dynasty (918–1392), the relationship was made explicit. In his "Ten Injunctions," promulgated at the establishment of the dynasty, Wang Kŏn (877–?), the Koryŏ dynastic founder, devoted the first two entries to the promotion and protection of Buddhism. Out of the ten entries, three entries specifically addressed Buddhism: the first injunction prohibits activities damaging to the service of the Buddha, deemed the protector of national affairs; the second injunction promises the construction of monasteries and prohibits villainous actions against their property; and the sixth injunction confirms the continuation of the Buddhist Lantern Festival as an important spiritual activity. Wang Kŏn's preference for Buddhism soon faced criticism from Confucian-minded statesmen. As early as the late tenth century, Ch'oe Sŭngno (927–89), a committed Confucian scholar, criticized Buddhism for its extravagance and warned King Sŏngjong (r. 981–97) about the financial waste caused by supporting Buddhist rituals and temple construction. Ch'oe, however, still acknowledged the significance of Buddhism in spiritual cultivation, and limited his criticism of the harmful influence of Buddhism to when it was supported at the state level. He believed that the governing of the state was the job of Confucianism.

The Buddhist–Confucian debate at the beginning of the Chosŏn dynasty (1392–1910) differs in nature from such one-sided criticism as Ch'oe's. With a desire to construct an ideal neo-Confucian society in the newly established Chosŏn dynasty, neo-Confucians challenged the philosophical foundations of Buddhism, making a case for its socially and economically damaging effects on society. Buddhists had to respond to this challenge for survival.

At the time, the most notable critique of Buddhism appeared in the writings of Chŏng Tojŏn (1342–98), a well-known politician and mastermind of statecraft and the creation of institutions in the Chosŏn dynasty. From early on in his life, Chŏng produced a series of anti-Buddhist polemics of which most famous was the essay *Pulssi japbyŏn* (*Array of Critiques against Buddhism*) completed in 1398.

At the beginning of the essay, Chŏng challenges the Buddhist doctrines of transmigration and *karma* by comparing them to the Confucian theories of yin and yang. To Chŏng, the birth and death of humans and changes in the world are all parts of the transformation of yin and yang, as are one's fortunes and misfortunes in life. The Buddhist theory of transmigration claims that after one's death, some elements of an individual remain and return to this world as another being. This Chŏng found untenable. He argues that once the being's energy is dispersed, it could not be recollected to create another being. Chŏng further points out that the Sŏn Buddhist equation of the mind (Kor. *sim*, Ch. *xin*) to nature (Kor. *sŏng*, Ch. *xing*), and its teaching that one can learn about nature by observing the mind, are logically indefensible; for the teaching seems to claim that the mind can see the mind. Chŏng also finds Buddhist compassion for all beings, including animals, ethically problematic. Following the traditional Confucian concept of differentiated benevolence, Chŏng claims that one's sympathy for one's family should naturally come before one's sympathy for others, or for animals. Chŏng compares Buddhists with Yangists and Moists in Chinese history, who were criticized for heterodoxy by classical Confucian Mencius. Buddhist teaching, Chŏng adds, is more sophisticated than that of either Yangists or Moists, and thus has more potential to dangerously delude people. At the end of the essay, Chŏng's philosophical analysis of Buddhism turns into a neo-Confucian political polemic against Buddhism. He concludes: the Emperor Wu of Liang faced a tragic ending because he supported Buddhism; serving the Buddha diligently will shorten the length of one's reign; Buddhism destroys humanity and thus, instead of waiting for sages and worthies to rise against Buddhism, everyone should be on guard against the religion.

A representative Buddhist response to the neo-Confucian challenge is found in the writings of Hamhŏ Tŭkt'ong (1376–1433), posthumously known as Kihwa. Before Kihwa joined a monastery in 1396, immediately after the founding of the Chosŏn dynasty, he received a Confucian education at the Sŏnggyun'gwan, the national institute of Confucian education which was the hotbed of rising anti-Buddhist sentiment. His familiarity with Confucian philosophy enabled him to respond to the major philosophical charges that contemporary neo-Confucians brought against Buddhism. In his *Hyŏnjŏng non* (*Exposition of the Correct*), citing various Confucian texts, Kihwa defends Buddhism on issues including the doctrine of *karma* and rebirth, the Buddhist practice of making offerings, cremation, and the charge of being anti-social in nature. Buddhists, Kihwa argues, cannot be understood as anti-social. Rather, by praying for the ruler and for the state through the purification of body and mind, and by chanting the *sūtras*, they contribute to the well-being of society. Kihwa further claims that the Buddhist teachings of *karma* and transmigration are not illogical as claimed by neo-Confucians, but provide effective social ethics by teaching people to take into account the consequences of their actions, and that the Buddhist practice of cremation is not unfilial or inhuman but allows individuals to cast off defilement caused by the body, and thus selfishness, consequently enabling them to attain purity of spirit. Using Buddhist logic, Kihwa also pointed out inner contradictions of Confucian teachings. In this regard, a most poignant point appeared in his critique of the Confucian encouragement of the sacrificial killing of animals, and of meat-eating, all of which Kihwa finds contradictory to the teaching of benevolence (Ch. *ren*). If benevolence interpenetrates heaven and earth as mentioned in Confucian classical writings, and if a man of benevolence becomes one with all the things in the world, Kihwa argues, then the sacrificial killings and meat-eating encouraged by Confucian teachers amounts to killing one's own children.

After a lengthy defense of Buddhism, Kihwa concludes his essay by noting the similarity in the fundamental philosophy of the Three Teachings of Buddhism, Confucianism, and Daoism. Kihwa defines the Confucian virtue of filial piety as "bright virtue" (Kor. *myŏngdŏk*), which he in turn equates with the Buddhist concept of the "marvelous, clear and bright mind" (Kor. *myojŏng myŏngsim*). Kihwa further points out that the Daoist teaching of "doing and not-doing," the Buddhist teaching of being "quiescent yet eternally luminous," and the Confucian teaching of "extending, yet [being] eternally still" all refer to one and the same truth. There are no two Ways in the world, Kihwa claims, and no two truths. Finally, Kihwah criticizes the narrow attitude of advocating only one of the Three Teachings at the expense of the others, and he then argues for a singular fundamental teaching that exists in all three, which merely bear difference in names.

The idea of unity among the Three Teachings became one of the major tools that Buddhists employed in their efforts to defend their position in the intellectual world of neo-Confucian Chosŏn. The theme of unity appears again in Na'am Po'u's (1509?–65) unfinished work "Iljŏng non" ("Theory of One Correctness"), where he explicates the Confucian unity of heaven and men in connection with the Buddhist concept of Buddha nature. Po'u claims that heaven and men were One in Confucianism, and this corresponded with the Correct in the human mind, and both One and the Correct manifested Buddha nature in the world. A more well-known figure in this theory of unity is Ch'ŏnghŏ Hujŏng (1520–1604). In his *Samga kuigam* (A *Paragon of the Three Teachings*), Hujŏng cited various texts from the three traditions, all of which Hujŏng believed to be teachings of how to learn one's mind, and this singular teaching illustrated unity amongst the three teachings.

The theory of unity reflects the defensive position of Buddhism in its confrontation with neo-Confucianism. Eventually, Buddhists lost the battle, and by the mid-sixteenth century, the status of Buddhism became so low that neo-Confucians no longer considered Buddhists to be worthy opponents. Several of the charges against Buddhism from this debate re-emerged at the beginning of the twentieth century when Korean Buddhism had to deal with colonialism and modernization.

See also: **Korea, Buddhism in.**

JIN Y. PARK

KOREAN BUDDHISM, SUDDEN AND GRADUAL DEBATE IN

Triggered by T'oe'ong Sŏngch'ŏl's (1912–93) publications on the nature of Sŏn enlightenment, the sudden and gradual debate in modern Korean Buddhism opened a space for debates on enlightenment, cultivation and the identity of Korean Sŏn Buddhism.

Sŏngch'ŏl claimed in his *Sŏnmun chŏngno* (*The Correct Path of the Sŏn School*, 1981) that sudden enlightenment followed by gradual cultivation is a heretical teaching in Sŏn Buddhism. He located the origin of this teaching with Pojo Chinul (1158–1210), whose teachings had constituted the dominant form of Sŏn Buddhism in Korea since the thirteenth century. In response to Sŏngch'ŏl's claim, a conference called " Enlightenment and Cultivation in Buddhism" was held in 1990 at the Songgwang monastery, the place where Chinul launched his compact community movement and which has become the head monastery in maintaining the Chinulean tradition. Three years later, the Hae'in monastery, where Sŏngch'ŏl resided as a head-master, hosted a conference in which the sudden–gradual issue was actively debated.

Chinul's idea of the sudden–gradual aspect of awakening and cultivation appeared in his *Susim kyŏl* (*Secrets of Cultivating the Mind*, *c.* 1203–5), and was further elaborated in his *Pŏpchip pŏrhaeng nok chŏryo pyŏngip sagi* (*Excerpts from the Dharma Collection and Special Practice Record with Personal Notes*, 1209), the most comprehensive work of Chinul. In these works, Chinul maintained that one's nature is originally perfect and equipped with undamaged original wisdom. Enlightenment for Chinul means realizing one's own nature; hence it is sudden. Chinul identified this first stage of awakening as understanding-awakening (Kor. *hae'o*). This initial awakening, however, cannot be sustained continuously because of the influence of the habitual energy accumulated within the practitioner throughout many lives. Thus, gradual cultivation after the initial awakening is necessary for the practitioner to reach the ultimate enlightenment (Kor. *ku' gyŏnggak*). To Chinul, sudden awakening followed by sudden practice is also a part of sudden enlightenment followed by gradual practice, because what is meant by sudden practice is none other than the result of gradual practice that practitioners performed in their previous lives, making sudden practice in this life possible.

Sŏngch'ŏl claimed that realizing one's own nature is possible only in the state of ultimate enlightenment; hence, the understanding-awakening that took place in the first of the ten *bodhisattva* stages falls far short of being sudden enlightenment. The sudden awakening in sudden awakening followed by gradual cultivation, Sŏngch'ŏl argued, is mere knowledge, which creates the worst kind of obstacle for Sŏn practitioners. Whoever endorsed sudden awakening followed by gradual cultivation, Sŏngch'ŏl further claimed, was the follower of intellectual knowledge, which is the heretical and wrong way of practicing Sŏn Buddhism.

In the history of Korean Buddhism, Chinul was the first to propose the idea of sudden awakening followed by gradual practice. Ch'ŏnghŏ Hyujŏng (1520–1604) also advocated sudden awakening followed by gradual practice in his *Sŏn'ga ku'gam* (*A Paragon of Sŏn School*), but in his later work, *Sŏn'gyo kyŏl* (*Secrets of Sŏn and Kyo*), Hyujŏng criticized the gradualist position for its reliance on theorization and interpretation, and instructed his disciples to follow the short-cut approach of subitism in which the path of meaning and language was completely cut off.

Sŏngch'ŏl claimed that, in his early days, Chinul mistakenly endorsed a gradualist position, but in his later work, as demonstrated in his *Kanhwa kyŏrŭi ron* (*Treatise on Resolving Doubts about*

Hwadu Meditation), Chinul endorsed the short-cut approach of *hwadu* (Ch. *huatou*) meditation where sudden cultivation followed sudden awakening is emphasized.

The idea of sudden enlightenment is uniquely East Asian Buddhist. Its theoretical origin lies in the Chan Buddhist claim that sentient beings are already Buddha the way they are. In Chinese Chan Buddhism, the subitist and gradualist positions created a division between what is known as Huineng's (638–713) Southern school and Shenxiu's (606?–706) Northern school of Chinese Chan. The sudden in this case designates not so much a temporal dimension of enlightenment as its unmediated nature. Hence, when Sŏngch'ŏl emphasized the subitist nature of enlightenment and practice, he was claiming that awakening should be the state in which all delusions, even in its finest state, are removed. Subitism in this sense represents the original meaning and intention of the Chan school. Such a radical claim by Chan Buddhism, however, invited gradualism as its complement. The gradualist view explains that, in reality, sentient beings need practice in order to realize their own Buddha nature, both before and after awakening. The *bodhisattva* path requires involvement with sentient beings' path to reach enlightenment that inevitably takes a gradualist path with regards to its temporality.

On the one hand, the sudden–gradual debate initiated by Sŏngch'ŏl's Buddhist thought was an extension of the Korean Buddhist attempt to create an authentic identity for Korean Buddhism. This attempt continues from the early nineteenth century when Korean Buddhism was preparing a return to normalcy after centuries of "mountain Buddhism without sectarian identity." As Sŏngch'ŏl considered Chinul's gradualism to be a heretic path in Sŏn school, he also disclaimed Chinul as the founding head of the Chogye Order which was founded after the establishment of Huineng's subitist Southern school. Sŏngch'ŏl claimed T'ae'go Po'u as the authentic founding patriarch of the Chogye Order.

On a practical and social level, the subitist–gradualist debate reflects the status of Korean Buddhism during the late twentieth century. When Chinul acknowledged gradualism in the thirteenth century, it reflected one of the major concerns of Korean Buddhism, which was to create a rapport between Sŏn practice and scholastic teaching. When Sŏngch'ŏl exclusively endorsed subitism as the orthodox path of Sŏn and disparaged gradualism as a heretical teaching, the relationship between the doctrinal and meditational schools was no longer an issue. Instead, amidst of challenges faced by Buddhism in modern society, Sŏngch'ŏl felt it necessary to offer a strictly authentic form of Buddhism.

Subitists and gradualists also differ in their orientation to Buddhism: Sŏngch'ŏl's subitism focused on the nature of enlightenment, whereas Chinul's gradualism emphasized how to attain enlightenment. In the subitist view, enlightenment and practice being one, the issue of how to reach enlightenment is rarely mentioned, and the discussion is geared towards distinguishing true awakening from the immature one. The gradualist view distinguishes cultivation from awakening, and focuses on offering the best practice to reaching enlightenment.

See also: **Korea, Buddhism in.**

JIN Y. PARK

KŪKAI AND SHINGON BUDDHISM

Kūkai (posthumous title: Kōbō Daishi, 774–835) was the transmitter of esoteric Buddhism from China to Japan, and the founder of Shingon Buddhism. Along with Saichō he was one of the two preeminent Buddhist figures of Heian (794–1185) Japan.

Kūkai was born in Sanuki province on the island of Shikoku. He went to the capital to study at fourteen, and eventually entered a national college to study Chinese classics and Confucianism. However, he converted to Buddhism and dropped out of school, and is said to have wandered around the country and practiced severe austerities in the mountains. He visited Tang China (as part of the same mission as Saichō) in 804 in search of training in esoteric Buddhism, making quick progress and received initiation under Huikou (746–805), the disciple of Amoghavajra. Kūkai returned to Japan in 806 as a master of esoteric Buddhism, carrying with him an impressive and important collection of texts and ritual objects. He received the favor of Emperor Saga (r. 809–23), established the headquarters of Shingon Buddhism on Mount Kōya, and was presented the important temple Tōji at the southern entrance of Kyoto. Kūkai traveled extensively, disseminating the teachings and practice of esoteric Buddhism, and also contributed to community projects such as the construction of wells and artificial lakes. Kūkai is said to have "entered *samādhi*" on Mount Kōya, and the faithful believe that he remains in a state of trance awaiting the arrival of Maitreya, the Buddha of the future.

The mystique which has formed around the figure of Kūkai is still strong in Japan. Legends of Kūkai's presence and magical deeds abound in almost every corner of Japan. Mount Kōya and Tōji are strong centers of pilgrimage and faith in Kōbō Daishi, Kūkai's posthumous title. The Shikoku pilgrimage of eighty-eight temples, based on legends of Kūkai's exploits before his trip to China, is one of the major pilgrimage routes in Japan.

Kūkai's reputation as a philosopher and religious thinker is just as formidable. He systematized and perfected the esoteric Buddhist tradition, both in making it distinct from and then showing it to be complementary (though still superior) to exoteric Buddhism. He contributed profound treatises such as the *Jūjūshinron* (*Ten Stages of the Mind*), in which he classified the various Buddhist teachings and argued for the supremacy of esoteric Buddhism; *Benkenmitsu nikyōron* (*The Two Teachings: Esoteric and Exoteric*), in which he compared the esoteric and exoteric teachings; and *Sokushin jōbutsu gi* (*Attaining Buddhahood in This Life*). Through these works he expounded on the basic teachings of Shingon Buddhism as such the permeation of the universe by the *Dharma* Body (Mahāvairocana), the dual aspects of wisdom and compassion as expressed in the Diamond and Womb *maṇḍalas*, and the use of the "three mysteries" (of body, speech, and mind) to attain buddhahood. He also established important rituals at the court, including an enthronement initiation for legitimating the ruler as a Buddhist monarch.

Figure 28 Saitō, West Pagoda, Garan precinct of Kōyosan, headquarters of the Japanese Shingon Order.

Kūkai is also a well-known figure in popular culture, famed as a master calligrapher, engineer, philosopher, savior-figure, and religious genius. He is popularly credited with inventing the Japanese *kana* syllabary, as well as the famous *i-ro-ha* poem, which expresses the Buddhist concept of impermanence through a single use of each of the sounds in the Japanese syllabary.

Unlike the Tendai school after the death of Saichō, the Shingon school in the years after the passing of its founder experienced little in the way of new doctrinal developments or prominent leaders, perhaps through the overwhelming philosophical and ritual legacy, as well as the personal presence, of Kūkai himself. Nevertheless its influence grew quickly through a combination of participation in esoteric rituals for the court, development of ritual lineages, and (again unlike Tendai) institutional cooperation with the traditional Nara schools. (See Figure 28.)

Though the performance of esoteric ritual dominated the activity of the Shingon school, the study of Shingon doctrine and a systematic treatment of Kūkai's works was carried out by Kakuban (1094–1143), founder of the Shingi (New Meaning) school. Kakuban discussed the relationship between Buddhas and Japanese *kami* – such as Dainichi (Mahāvairocana), Amida (Amitābha), and Amaterasu – and brought esoteric teachings to bear on the topic of Pure Land traditions, proposing a "Shingon *nenbutsu*," in works such as *Gorin kuji myō himitsushaku* (*Esoteric Explanation of the Wisdom-Bearing Sounds of the Five Circles*) and *Amida hishaku* (*Esoteric Explanation of Amida*).

An important aspect of Kūkai's legacy is the cult that has developed around his memory as the great Kōbō Daishi (see above). This faith in Kōbō Daishi was spread throughout the country by the itinerant monks known as Kōya *hijiri*, whose origin can be traced to the monks who gathered funds (*kanjin*) to rebuild Mount Kōya after a great fire in the mid-Heian period.

Although the Shingon school itself has been overshadowed in modern times by the growth of the Pure Land, Zen, and Nichiren movements, Shingon (or *mikkyō*) practices continued to play a prominent role in modern and contemporary Japan, and many of the new religious movements (e.g., Agonshū) in Japan derive from or are influenced by the *mikkyō* tradition. Mount Koya is cultural center as well as a museum of artistic treasures, the site of a Buddhist university, and a popular spot for tourists and pilgrims. Its graveyard contains the resting place for many prominent historical figures, as well as the setting for various monuments and memorials (such as the memorial for the spirits of white ants, set up by an association of exterminators).

See also: **Japan, Buddhism in; *Kenmitsu* Buddhism; Mikkyō and ritual in Japanese Buddhism; Pilgrimage in Japan.**

PAUL L. SWANSON

KUMĀRAJĪVA (343–413)

Kumārajīva was a Central Asian Buddhist monk who traveled to China and became one of the "four great translators" of Chinese Buddhist texts. Born into a noble family in Kucha, he entered the monastic order at the age of seven along with his mother, and distinguished himself first in Sarvāstivādin and later in Mahāyāna studies. In 379 his fame had reached even into China, and the Emperor Fu Jian of the Former Qin dynasty sent a delegation to invite him to court. Kumārajīva accepted, but on the way back the general sent to fetch him, Lü Guang, rebelled and held out against the court in northwestern China for seventeen years, during which time he held Kumārajīva captive. While this delay frustrated the court, it gave Kumārajīva a chance to become fluent in Chinese prior to undertaking his translation activities. Seeing Kumārajīva's intelligence and physical capacities, Lü Guang also forced him to have several children with concubines, and while it is clear that Kumārajīva never intended to break his vow of chastity, he himself felt remorse over this episode for the rest of his life.

After Lü Guang's rebellion was suppressed, Kumārajīva arrived in Chang'an in 401 and immediately began producing translations. The combination of his mastery of Indian Buddhist thought and his proficiency in Chinese not only enabled him to produce translations that are still the standard (such as his translations of the *Lotus Sūtra* and the *Diamond Sūtra*), but also to provide instruction that cleared up many misapprehensions of Buddhist doctrine, in particular the teaching of Emptiness (Skt. *śūnyatā*). His main allegiance was to Madhyanaka philosophy, and his work in translating basic texts of this school and its philosophy of the "middle way" led to the formation of the Sanlun ("Three Treatises") school, carried forward by his disciple Sengzhao (374–414). He also corresponded with the great scholar-monk Lushan Huiyuan (334–416) on many points of doctrine, such as the reality of the Buddha Amitābha when seen in dreams.

He worked with over 800 collaborators during his time in the capital, and in his translation activity he stressed clear communication of ideas over exact technical translation. As a result, his translations were so readable that they remained the preferred version for many scriptures, even when later, more precise translations appeared. When he died in 413, it is recorded that his tongue was found unburnt among his cremated ashes.

See also: **China, Buddhism in; China, early schools; *Tripiṭaka*, Chinese.**

CHARLES B. JONES

KUŚINAGARA

Kuśinagara (Pāli Kusinārā) is the name of the town traditionally regarded as the place of Gautama Buddha's final passing away (Skt. *mahā-parinirvāṇa*, Pāli *mahā-parinibbāna*). According to the Pāli *Mahāparinibbāna Sutta*, which provides a detailed account of the events surrounding the Buddha's death, the Buddha and a group of 500 monks stopped in the *śāla*-tree grove in the outskirts of Kuśinagara, the small mud-constructed capital of the Mallā people. As the Buddha lay on his right side between two large *śāla* trees, his head oriented to the north, he conversed with members of his community. When his chief attendant Ānanda complained about the insignificance of the town that the Buddha had chosen for his final passing away, the Buddha responded that in the distant past it had been the location of the magnificent capital of a universal king (*cakravartin*) named Mahāsudassana (Skt. Mahāsudarśaṇa). The account continues with a narration of the Buddha's death, cremation, and the division of his relics.

At the end of the nineteenth century, information preserved in Chinese pilgrim accounts and archeological excavation allowed a preliminary identification of Kuśinagara with a site near the present-day village of Kasia in Uttar Pradesh. Further excavation of the site in the early 1900s revealed a fifth-century copperplate inscription that identified the *stūpa* as the *nirvāṇa-caitya*, thus confirming the site's identity; the remains of eight monasteries were also identified, dating from the Kuṣāṇa period (first to third centuries CE) to the eleventh century. The core of the *stūpa* may date back to the time of Aśoka. The primary religious focus of the site today is the large *stūpa* believed to mark the place of the Buddha's final passing away, which was restored in 1927 and 1972 with support from Myanmar, and the Mahāparinirvāṇa Temple, built by the Indian government in 1956 to commemorate the 2,500th anniversary of the Buddha's death. This temple contains a 20-foot reclining Buddha image carved from red sandstone that dates to the fifth century. The base of the statue depicts three figures responding to the Buddha's death, and bears a fifth-century inscription naming the donor and the sculptor. About a quarter of a mile away, at a place said to be the spot where the Buddha gave his last teaching, stands a temple housing a 10-foot seated Buddha image in the earth-touching posture. The temple was built in 1927 with the support of two Buddhists from Myanmar. Less than a mile to the east of the Mahāparinirvāṇa Temple lie the remains of the Rāmabhār *stūpa*, which measures over 100 feet in diameter. This is believed to mark the site where the Mallās cremated the Buddha's body.

Since its rediscovery at the end of the nineteenth century, Kuśinagara has become an increasingly popular pilgrimage and tourist destination. There are now several Buddhist monasteries in the vicinity providing support for pilgrims, as well as a small archeological museum.

See also: **Aśoka; Buddha; Buddha, relics of; Buddha, historical context; Bodhgayā; Faxiang; Lumbinī; Pāṭaliputra; Sacred places; Sārnāth; *Stūpa*; Vaiśālī.**

KEVIN TRAINOR

KYŎNGHŎ SŎNGU

Kyŏnghŏ Sŏngu (1849–1912) is recognized as the founder of modern Korean Sŏn (Ch. Chan) Buddhism. He joined a monastery at the age of nine (1857), began learning classical Confucian texts from a lay Buddhist when he was fourteen, and later studied Buddhist *sūtras* with Master Manhwa at the Tonghak monastery. Kyŏnghŏ soon became distinguished for his exceptional understanding of Buddhist texts, and at age twenty-three (1871) he was appointed as a *sūtra* lecturer and earned fame as a teacher. Nevertheless, upon experiencing an existential crisis at an epidemic-stricken village on a stormy night in 1879, Kyŏnghŏ gave up his *sūtra* lecture position and devoted himself to *hwadu* (Ch. *huatou*) meditation. After several months of intensive meditation with Master Lingyun's (771–853) *hwadu* "The donkey's affairs are not yet done and the horse has already arrived," Kyŏnghŏ experienced an awakening. From then on, he devoted himself to the practice of meditation, guiding practitioners at various monasteries until 1905 when he suddenly disappeared. His activities from 1905 until his death in 1912 are not clear. Some claim that he wandered around in the northern part of Korea as a beggar, while other sources report that he lived a life of a layperson, letting his hair grow and teaching Confucian classics.

Kyŏnghŏ's life as a Sŏn master shares many similarities with Pojo Chinul (1158–1210) whose teachings of Kanhwa Sŏn (Ch. Kanhua Chan) have been a dominant feature of Korean Buddhism since the thirteenth century. Like Chinul, Kyŏnghŏ emphasized the practice of Sŏn over theoretical debate which dominated Korean Buddhism immediately before Kyŏnghŏ's time. Kyŏnghŏ re-confirmed the efficiency of the *hwadu* meditation, which Chinul introduced and endorsed as a short-cut approach to enlightenment. Like Chinul, who attempted to solidify Sŏn practice through the Compact of Samādhi and the Prajñā Community movement, Kyŏnghŏ created compact communities at the Hae'in monastery in 1899 and at the Pŏmŏ monastery in 1902 in order to revive the Sŏn tradition. Kyŏnghŏ also drafted regulations for Sŏn monasteries (Kor. *ch' ŏnggyu*), which remained as the foundation for regulation in contemporary Korean Sŏn monasteries, together with regulations proposed by Pang Han' am (1876–1951) and Yi Sŏngch' ŏl (1912–93). The importance of Kyŏnghŏ in Korean Buddhism is also demonstrated by the fact that his disciples, including Suwŏl (1855–1928),

Hyewŏl (1861–1937), Man' gong (1871–1946), and Hanam (1876–1951), played a significant role in the *Dharma* transmission of Korean Sŏn Buddhism. By setting a model for Sŏn practitioners at a time when the Sŏn tradition was at its lowest point in the history of Korean Buddhism, Kyŏnghŏ marked a turning point in modern Korean Buddhism. After the awakening experience, Kyŏnghŏ declared himself as being the twelfth generation of Ch' ŏnghŏ Hyujŏng (1520–1604), and thus set up his *Dharma* lineage.

The evaluation of Kyŏnghŏ in Korean Buddhism has been mixed. While Korean Buddhism shows clear influences from Kyŏnghŏ's revival of the *hwadu* Sŏn tradition, his free lifestyle earned him some negative appraisals.

His poems in classical Chinese and short essays written for various occasions in Buddhist monasteries are collected in Kyŏnghŏ chip, first published in 1942.

See also: **Korea, Buddhism in.**

JIN Y. PARK

L

LAITY

Although the primary models for the most effective religious lifestyle in Buddhism are the celibate monastic or the committed *bodhisattva*, members of the laity have always constituted the great majority of Buddhist practitioners. The technical term for male Buddhist lay disciples is *upāsaka*. Becoming a lay disciple in the early Buddhist tradition required a recitation of the *triśaraṇa* or "three refuges" and the formal acceptance of the *pañca-śīla* or "five moral precepts." In so doing, an *upāsaka* sets out on the Buddhist path attempting to perform good *karma*, thus accruing the corresponding merit (*puṇya*) and moving on to a more favorable rebirth, perhaps one in which he might be able to renounce worldly life and join the monastic community. It is also the responsibility of the laity to provide for the welfare of the monastic community through offerings of clothing, food, and the like. Although there are some records in early Buddhism of members of the laity actually attaining *nirvāṇa*, these cases are extremely rare, thus establishing the monastic life as a clearly more desirable path. In Mahāyāna, where the *bodhisattva* ideal is predominant, and with enlightenment clearly more accessible to all disciples, more emphasis is placed upon the laity, thus upgrading the lay disciple's overall status in the community.

The technical term for a female Buddhist lay disciple is *upāsikā*. Although the *upāsikā* recites the same *triśaraṇa* as the male lay disciple, and adheres to the identical *pañca-śīla*, in the earliest tradition her status is theoretically equal to but pragmatically inferior to the male lay disciple. Like her male counterpart, she attempts to perform good *karma*, cultivates merit through acts of giving, and hopes to be reborn as a *male*, in order that she will have a genuinely more accessible opportunity for the attainment of *nirvāṇa*.

It should be no surprise that the interpersonal familial social relationships of the laity are especially important, and were occasionally the focus of Buddha's most pointed and specific instructions. Unquestionably, at the head of the list of important observances for the lay members of the community was adherence to the five moral precepts noted above. These include (1) not harming living beings, (2) abstaining from stealing, (3) abstaining from illicit sexual relations, (4) abstaining from telling lies, and (5) abstaining from taking intoxicants. These five precepts were to be followed comprehensively, and taken together, facilitated the moral purity of lay disciples with respect to matters of body, speech, and mind. Although the precepts appear to have a negative-sounding attitude, they are actually quite positive, fostering important social values.

No doubt because the lay disciples constituted the majority of his followers, Buddha was concerned with offering his *upāsakas* and *upāsikās* serious advice to how to lead a happy lay life. In this regard, Buddha's model for achieving this personal and religious success was based on the ideal family. Indeed, all Buddha's disciples were considered to be part of his spiritual family, and he himself was their foremost spiritual friend (*kalyāṇamitra*). Hammalawa Saddhatissa, in his classic volume *Buddhist Ethics* notes that, "The duties of children to their parents were stressed in India from a very early date." He goes on to point out that the "*Rukkhadhamma Jātaka* expressed the value of the solidarity of a family, using the simile of the trees of a forest; these are able to withstand the force of the wind whereas a solitary tree, however large, is not." Perhaps the most famous and important of Buddha's family-oriented sermons is the *Sigālovāda Sutta* of the *Dīgha Nikāya*, in which Buddha provides explicit instructions to the layman Sigāla, who is trying to honor his father's dying wish that he honor the six directions. Buddha likens worshiping the six directions to proper actions towards six different categories of persons. The six directions: east, south, west, north, nadir, and zenith, respectively correspond to parents, teachers, wife and children, friends and companions, servants and workpeople, and religious teachers and Brahmins. It is not just the *Sigālovāda Sutta* that addresses the issue of social justice and harmony among the laity. Texts such as the *Parābhava Sutta*, *Cakkavatti Sīhanāda Sutta*, *Mahāmaṅgala Sutta*, and *Nakula Sutta* of the Pāli Canon also explicitly address similar issues.

Despite the above, even a cursory reading of the early Buddhist texts reveals that Buddha held the monastic life to be superior to the lay life. In the *Aṅguttara Nikāya* (I.80) Buddha notes, "Monks, there are two kinds of happiness. Which are they? The happiness of the domestic life and that of monastic life. Of the two, the happiness of the monastic life is superior." Again, in the *Pabbajā Sutta* of the *Sutta-nipāta*, he says, "Life in the home is an obstacle, it is the way of passions; life outside is the life of freedom." The life of the two communities – lay and monastic – is, however, inextricably joined in a profoundly symbiotic way. The lay members of the *sangha* provide food, goods, clothing, and the like to the monastics, while the monks and nuns, in the words of the *Sigālovāda Sutta*, show the laity "the way to heaven."

With the rise of the Mahāyāna and Vajrayāna traditions, the role and status of the lay members of the community become redefined in an extremely important new way. With the figure of the *bodhisattva* adopted as the archetypal model for Buddhist practitioners, the monastic vocation, while still important, was no longer deemed essential for spiritual attainment. Stories like that of the layman Vimalakīrti, a highly realized *bodhisattva*, abound in the Mahāyāna literature. As such, the figure of the layman and laywoman was elevated significantly, and the theme of lay spiritual achievement permeates the history of the Mahāyāna and Vajrayāna schools.

The interpenetrating cooperation of the lay and monastic communities continues today as Buddhism continues to aggressively globalize. Moreover Western Buddhism is continuing to develop into an almost exclusively lay tradition, thus expanding the role of the laity in exciting new ways, and with an equal status for both genders. In so doing, it is redefining the definition of the lay *sangha* in modern Buddhism.

See also: **Family life; *Sangha*.**

CHARLES S. PREBISH

LAMOTTE, ÉTIENNE

Born in Dinant, Belgium, in 1903, Étienne Lamotte studied first at the Collège Notre-Dame de Belle-Vue à Dinant (1915–20), eventually joining the Roman Catholic clergy. In addition to his seminary work, he also studied philosophy, theology, and philology at the Catholic University in Louvain. He went on to study Oriental Studies as well as Indian Studies, and received the degree of Licencié in Oriental Languages in 1925. Eventually, he received a doctorate, in 1929, for his thesis on the *Bhagavad-gītā*. Following his studies in Rome 1928–30, he returned to Belgium, where he became the chief disciple of Louis de La Vallée Poussin. For forty-five years (1932–77), Lamotte served as a professor at the Catholic University of Louvain. He was a member of the Académie Royale de Belgique and the Institut de France. He was also an Honorary Fellow of the International Association of Buddhist Studies. Monseigneur Lamotte died in May 1983.

Étienne Lamotte will probably be most remembered for his monumental volume *Histoire du Bouddhisme Indien, des origins à l'ère Śaka*, published in 1958 and translated into English by Sara Boin-Webb in 1988. Additionally, however, Lamotte was able to bring out editions and/or translations of a number of other extremely important Buddhist texts, including the *Saṃdhinirmocana-sūtra* (1936), Vasubandhu's *Karmasiddhiprakaraṇa* (1936), Asaṅga's *Mahāyānasaṃgraha* (1938–9), the *Vimalakīrtinirdeśa-sūtra* (1962), and the Chinese version of the introductory chapter of Nāgārjuna's *Mahāprajñāpāramitā-śāstra* (in five volumes, 1944–80). A prolific writer throughout his long career, Lamotte published a steady stream of articles in leading journals.

Until a trip to Japan at age seventy-three, Lamotte worked exclusively as a textual scholar, drawing all his knowledge of Buddhism from the various literary sources at his disposal and from a small number of Buddhist visitors. He apparently worried, from time to time, about the reaction of the Vatican to his buddhological work. Edward Conze, in Part 2 of *The Memoirs of a Modern Gnostic*, relates a story in which he says:

> When I last saw him, he had risen to the rank of Monseigneur and worried about how his "Histoire" had been received by the Vatican. "*Mon professeur*, do you think they will regard the book as *hérétique*?" They obviously did not. His religious views showed the delightful mixture of absurdity and rationality which is one of the hallmarks of a true believer.

In addition to the honors mentioned above, in 1952 Lamotte became an Honorary Member of the École Française d'Extrême-Orient. In 1960 he became an Honorary Member of the Société Asiatique, and in 1967 an Honorary Fellow of the Royal Asiatic Society of Great Britain. In addition, Pope Paul VI made him Correspondent of the Papal Secretariat for Non-Christians in 1954.

In his obituary note in the 1985 *Journal of the International Association of Buddhist Studies*, Heinz Bechert states,

> Professor Lamotte was acknowledged to be the greatest living authority on Buddhism in the Western world. With his death, we have lost one of the greatest

scholars of our time, and those who had the privilege to know him personally, have lost a most amiable friend and colleague.

See also: **Academic study of Buddhism; Franco-Belgian school of Buddhist Studies.**

CHARLES S. PREBISH

LENINGRAD SCHOOL OF BUDDHIST STUDIES

In the nomenclature utilized by Constantin Régamey in his 1951 volume *Der Buddhismus Indiens*, the Leningrad school of Buddhist Studies developed in the period after around 1915, replacing the older Anglo-German school, which had begun to decline. Its leading scholars were Fedor Stcherbatsky, Otto Rosenberg, and Eric Obermiller. According to Edward Conze, exponents of this school devoted themselves to a very careful study of Buddhist scholastic literature, which they believed was closer to the original doctrines of the Buddha than the notions set forth by other European scholars, predominantly in the Anglo-German school. This school believed that the secret to unraveling the true meaning of Buddhist doctrines might be found in a complete etymological understanding of all the Buddhist technical terms utilized in the various doctrinal formulations. Moreover, this school attempted to draw its information not only from the Indian texts and commentaries, but also from the living Buddhist traditions of Inner, Southeast, and East Asia.

The study of Buddhism had been known in Russia as early as 1825, when the journal *Asiatic Journal* published a biography of the Buddha. Clearly, before Stcherbatsky, Russian Buddhist Studies had benefited from the work of V.P. Vasiliev and I.P. Minayeff. Stcherbatsky was born in 1866 in Poland. He entered St. Petersburg University in 1884 to study Indo-European linguistics under Minayeff and Serge Oldenburg (who in 1897 founded the *Biblioteca Buddhica* series). In 1888 he moved on to study with Georg Bühler in Vienna, but returned to his family's estate between the years of 1893 and 1900. Eventually, he did further studies in Bonn under H. Jacobi. Stcherbatsky is perhaps best known for three publications: his monumental two-volume *Buddhist Logic* (originally published in 1930–2 as part of *Biblioteca Buddhica*), *The Central Conception of Buddhism and the Meaning of the Word "Dharma"* (1923), and *The Conception of Buddhist Nirvāṇa* (1927). He also edited, in 1917, along with Eric Obermiller, the Tibetan text of the *Abhidharmakośa* and its *Bhāṣya*. In 1920 he published *The Soul Theory of the Buddhists*, a translation of Chapter 11 of the *Abhidharmakośa*. Stcherbatsky had a long feud with the great Belgian scholar Louis de La Vallée Poussin, resulting in a blistering review of the Belgian's book *Nirvāṇa*, and the publication of his own book on the subject. According to Guy Welbon, he accuses La Vallée Poussin of "transforming the Buddha into a mere magician and *nirvāṇa* into a simple gross faith object signifying the soul's immortal bliss in paradise."

Otto Rosenberg (1888–1919) had made a significant impact on Stcherbatsky. In 1918, he published a study based on Vasubandhu's *Abhidharmakośa*, advocating the notion that Buddhist philosophy was based on the plurality of *dharmas*. This study was instrumental in Stcherbatsky's understanding of *dharma* theory, and informed his 1923 volume on the topic. Eric Obermiller, also an influence on Stcherbatsky, in 1931 published a translation of Bu-ston's *History of Buddhism*, which was extremely useful in demonstrating to scholars how Buddhists viewed their own histories. Unfortunately, Stcherbatsky and Obermiller died in the 1940s, and with them, the legacy of the Leningrad school.

See also: **Academic study of Buddhism.**

CHARLES S. PREBISH

LOTUS SŪTRA OF THE TRUE DHARMA (SADDHARMAPUṆḌARĪKA SŪTRA)

The *Lotus Sūtra of the True Dharma* (*Saddharmapuṇḍarīka Sūtra*) is one of the best known and most influential of all Mahāyāna scriptures. The original core of the text was very probably composed as early as the first century BCE, which would make it one of the earliest Mahāyāna *sūtras*. In China it was widely studied and frequently translated, the earliest of eight or more Chinese versions dating from the end of the third century CE. Its popularity in Central Asia is attested by the discovery of textual fragments along the Silk Route as well as translations into Uighur and Tibetan. Most significant of all the versions, however, has been Kumārajīva's Chinese translation of 406 CE. It became the core text of the Tiantai (Jap. Tendai) school, which in turn exercised a formative influence on all the indigenous schools of East Asian Buddhism, and particularly on the Nichiren Buddhism of thirteenth-century Japan and its modern offshoots, including the Sōka Gakkai.

The *Lotus Sūtra* is the *locus classicus* for several key Mahāyāna doctrines. Like all Mahāyāna scriptures it sees the path of the *bodhisattva* as the true way of all Buddhists, and it employs several rhetorical strategies to win its readers over to this view. Roughly contemporaneous with the earliest strata of the *Prajñāpāramitā* literature, like them it acknowledges the crucial importance of emptiness (*śūnyatā*) and non-duality (*advaya*), but its primary concern lies elsewhere. The main expository focus of the *Lotus Sūtra* is the working out of a new, more expansive conception of the Buddha and the nature of his soteriological activity in the world. It employs the rhetoric of inspiration and exhortation, relying not on the discourse of non-duality so much as on pragmatic parables illustrating the nature and power of the enlightened mind. Although often associated with the most polemical and sectarian assertions of Mahāyāna triumphalism, the *Lotus Sūtra* in fact offers an irenic and conciliatory stance, especially in the most important opening chapters.

While not having the kind of single sustained narrative story-line found in the later *Vimalakīrti Nirdeśa Sūtra*, the *Lotus Sūtra* nonetheless offers a comprehensive and coherent resolution of the most vexing questions and doubts encountered by the early Mahāyāna Buddhists. Three concerns were especially pressing: (1) how is one to understand the apparent discrepancies or even contradictions between the more conservative canonical scriptures and the more recently circulated Mahāyāna teachings? (2) To what extent, by what means, and to what end do buddhas and *bodhisattvas* intervene actively in the spiritual progress of their devotees? And perhaps most urgently: (3) How is the Buddha's death (*parinirvāṇa*) to be understood and accepted? The first two questions are taken up immediately and directly in the opening chapters of the *sūtra*, providing a basis for taking up the last, which is left hanging until the dramatic climax near the (original) end of the *sūtra*, the point at which the Buddha finally and fully reveals his true nature and infinite life-span.

The first four chapters of the *Lotus Sūtra* address the perplexed or even skeptical reader struggling to understand why the newly circulated Mahāyāna scriptures seem so different and challenging. Through a series of persuasive parables, the *sūtra* illustrates two key doctrines – *upāya* and *adhimukti* – that remain central through the rest of the exposition. *Upāya* ("skillful means"), or alternatively, *upāya-kauśalya* ("skill in means") are terms referring to the ability of buddhas (and advanced *bodhisattvas*) to present the *Dharma* in a manner suited to the capacity and the inclinations of the disciples. Correspondingly, *adhimukti* refers to the disciple's ability and capacity to be inspired by and respond to the *Dharma*, whatever their present level of development. As one progresses up the ladder of teachings, one's *adhimukti* becomes ever more receptive and unshakeable. Translated as "firm resolve" or in Kumārajīva's Chinese as "belief and understanding" (*xinjie*), *adhimukti* combines elements of inspiration, faith, confidence, and resolve with respect to the lofty ideals of the *bodhisattva* ideal and also with regard to the challenges it presents. Confronted with the array of seemingly discrepant teachings stemming from the creativity of the Buddha's *upāya*, the disciple must cultivate *adhimukti* in order to persist and prevail without losing heart and falling into fear and doubt.

In Chapter 2, entitled "*Upāya*," the Buddha explains to Śāriputra that all the buddhas teach the *Dharma* in accordance with what is appropriate to the circumstances, employing countless expedient means (*upāya*) in the form of various doctrines, similes, and parables. But, in fact, these different teachings are all different dispensations of the one and same Single Vehicle (*ekayāna*). Different as the various vehicles and paths may seem, he continues, all beings will ultimately develop to the point where their *adhimukti* will enable them to recognize the ultimate teaching and wholeheartedly follow the one universal path to Buddhahood, i.e., the Mahāyāna. He illustrates his point with the parable of the burning house. A wealthy man dwelling with his family in a large mansion realizes that the building is on fire and that his children are in grave danger. But they are so absorbed in playing, each with his or her own favorite toys, that they do not sense danger, nor do they heed his call to leave the house before it collapses. Realizing that he needs to find another approach, he employs an expedient device (*upāya*): knowing their individual preferences in playthings, he tells them if they leave the burning house, they will find outside the gate even better toys – beautiful goat-carts for some, deer-carts for others, and also ox-carts. The children all run out, each seeking the particular type of cart they prefer, only to find that instead of the various carts promised, their father has in fact provided only a single cart, but one far more magnificent and beautiful than they could ever have imagined. The Buddha then explains that the decrepit, burning mansion is *saṃsāra*, and the carts initially offered are the different paths of Buddhist practice: the Vehicle of the Auditors (*śrāvakayāna*) for those seeking to become *arhats*, the Vehicle of Awakening through Understanding Conditionality for those seeking to become *pratyekabuddhas*, and the *Bodhisattva* Vehicle for those seeking the full and perfect awakening of the buddhas. Just as the children ultimately discover, much to their delight, that there is really only one even more magnificent ox cart waiting outside the gate, so too the three types of disciples will all eventually discover that their three paths, seemingly so different and mutually exclusive, all converge in the Single Universal Path (*ekayāna*). And the stratagem or expedient device of promising what the children think they want, only to deliver something better, is not a deception, the Buddha explains, but an example of the Buddha's highly developed skill in means (*upāyakauśalya*).

Interestingly, and very much in contrast to his role in the *Vimalakīrti Nirdeśa Sūtra*, it is Śāriputra who first fully comprehends the significance of this, the Buddha's ultimate teaching: that all the disciples, whatever path they think they are following – and indeed all the *arhats* and *pratyekabuddhas* thinking they have reached their goal – are destined through the power of their practice eventually to arrive "outside the gate" where they will realize that they have been following the *bodhisattva* path to Buddhahood all along, however unwittingly. The Buddha confirms this point by giving his prediction (*vyākaraṇa*) that Śāriputra will indeed in the (distant) future become the Buddha Padmaprabha (Lotus Radiance). This is the conciliatory note that has sometimes been overlooked or played down: the *ekayāna* or Universal Vehicle of the Lotus Sūtra is big enough for all, and all can eventually find their way aboard – depending on the strength of their *adhimukti*. This latter point is made in Chapter 4, appropriately entitled "*Adhimukti*," in which some of the other *arhats*, on hearing that Śāriputra will become a Buddha, realize the error of their own recalcitrant ways and experience a change of heart which gives rise to *adhimukti* with regard to the Mahāyāna teachings. To illustrate this development, they relate the famous "Parable of the Wayward Son." The immature son of a man forsakes his family and wanders abroad for decades, falling into poverty and despair. One day his father, who has become a wealthy merchant, happens by chance to spot him in the market. He sends servants to bring his son back, but the son, no longer recognizing his father, is intimidated by his wealth and frightened that his life is in danger. Understanding that he must proceed gently, the father has his son employed a laborer on his estate, gradually giving him increasing responsibility to build up his confidence and resolve (*adhimukti*). Finally, when the time is ripe, the father reveals his son's true identity and declares that he is now capable of taking on his inheritance. Father and son are reunited in their common wealth, and prosper together.

In the chapters leading up to the revelation of the Buddha's ultimate *upāya*, he expounds further on the wonders of Buddhahood, predicts that other senior disciples, even Devadatta, will, like Śāriputra, become Buddhas in the future, and then discourses on the merit to be gained by venerating, reciting, copying, and distributing this same *Lotus Sūtra*. That latter theme is taken up again in a number of the concluding chapters, which has led some scholars to see the origins of the Mahāyāna to lie, in part at least, in a "cult of the book." Also to be found are several other now well-known parables, such as the story of the jewel sewn, unbeknownst to him, in the hem of a poor man's coat, and the story of the caravan leader who conjures up the an apparent city where his weary and discouraged companions can seek respite and thus eventually complete their journey to discover a great treasure. Chapter 11 recounts a seemingly unprecedented event: the sudden appearance from the depths of the earth of a giant *stūpa* (or in the Chinese version a multi-tiered pagoda tower). The *stūpa* contains the Buddha Prabhūtaratna, who vowed, Śākyamuni explains, that after his *parinirvāṇa*, his reliquary would manifest in just such a way whenever and wherever any other buddha was preaching the *Lotus Sūtra*. Thereupon the *stūpa* opens to reveal Prabhūtaratna, who invites Śākyamuni to come and share his seat. This sight of two buddhas, teaching side by side, would have been very strange indeed to the first audience of this text, given the prevailing view that there could be no more than one Buddha present in any world-system at the same time. In addition to adding to the drama, this curious manifestation foreshadows the revelations to come, perhaps even anticipating possible objections to the idea that all can become Buddhas and that Buddhas remain active even after their apparent departure from the realm of *saṃsāra*.

This last point is the dramatic revelation which is the climax of the *sūtra*. In Chapter 15 (or 16 in the Kumārajīva's Chinese translation), entitled "The Life Span of the Tathāgata" (*tathāgatāyspramāṇa*) the Buddha returns to the dual theme of *upāya* and *adhimukti*, disclosing his ultimate *upāya*, the one that requires the very highest degree of *adhimukti*. The disciples learn now that it is not just his teachings that are expedient illusions lacking ultimate truth. Even their very notions of him and his career are to be understood as lacking ultimate truth. All the events of his life, including his birth and his apparent death, are just grand expedient means, *upāya*, perpetrated solely for the purpose of bringing beings to enlightenment. His life-span is in fact infinite, his *parinirvāṇa* only a docetic manifestation. He explains this through another parable. A physician who has been away for some time returns home to find that his sons are suffering from an illness so serious that it is distorting their minds as well as their bodies. Fortunately he is able to provide the proper antidote, which some of them promptly take to become quickly cured. Others, however, are so crazed by the illness, that they refuse the medicine. Fearing for their lives, he realizes he must resort to a skillful device. He travels to a distant city, and sends back word that he has died. The recalcitrant sons are shocked back to their senses, realizing in their grief that he has already provided them with just what is needed. They take the medicine and are cured.

Additional chapters follow, some probably later additions, but the key concerns have been resolved. Those with sufficient spiritual resolve (*adhimukti*) can rest assured that the Buddha is still active in the world of human suffering, working for the welfare of all beings. And it is this, his second turning of the Great *Dharma* Wheel, that explains how and why this is so.

See also: **Canons and literature; Mahāyāna Buddhism; Nichiren and Nichirenshū; Tiantai.**

ALAN SPONBERG

LUMBINĪ

Lumbinī is the name of the park traditionally regarded as the place of Gautama Buddha's birth. In the *Sutta Nipāta* of the Pāli Canon, verse 683 refers to his birth "in the Sakyā's village, in the Lumbinī country," and the introduction to the Pāli commentary on the *Jātakas* (*Nidānakathā*) provides a detailed birth narrative, one of several existing versions. According to this account, when the *bodhisattva*'s mother, Queen Mahāmāyā (also called Mayadevī), had carried him in her womb for ten months, she set out on a golden palanquin from Kapilavatthu (Skt. Kapilavastu) to visit her family in Devadaha. Knowing that her time to deliver had come, she stopped in the Lumbinī park which was filled with *śāla* trees, flowers and warbling birds. Approaching a great *śāla* tree, she reached up and the tree bent down a branch for her to grasp. Her attendants drew a curtain around her and she gave birth standing up, as is the custom with the mothers of *bodhisattvas.* Four great Brahmā deities appeared with a golden net in which they received the child and presented him to her, miraculously free from birth fluids and "shining like a precious gem." Two streams of water came down from the heavens and refreshed the *bodhisattva* and his mother; he was then received by four guardian deities and placed on an antelope skin. The *bodhisattva* then stepped down, surveyed the four quarters of the world, took seven steps, and proclaimed, "I am the chief of the world." Other versions of the birth narrative provide additional details and variants, including traditions that Mahāmāyā took purifying baths before and after her delivery, and that the *bodhisattva* was born painlessly from his mother's right side, was received by various gods, and took seven steps in the four cardinal directions.

Near the close of the nineteenth century, the location of Lumbinī was identified at a place called Rummindei in Nepal based on Chinese pilgrim accounts and the discovery of an Aśokan column. The column bears an inscription proclaiming that after the twentieth year of his reign

Aśoka came to venerate this place where the Buddha Śākyamuni was born and he erected a stone column and released the town from taxes. Excavations conducted in 1899 uncovered the remains of the Mayadevi temple, a tank (regarded as the place that the Buddha's mother bathed), *stūpas*, and a partially defaced bas-relief sculpture depicting Mayadevī giving birth to the *bodhisattva*, possibly dating to the Gupta period (fourth–sixth centuries CE). Further excavations of the Mayadevī temple site in the 1990s uncovered several construction levels, the earliest probably dating back to the time of Aśoka. The bas-relief Mayadevi image, which is venerated by Buddhists and Hindus, is now enshrined in a new Mayadevī shrine. The Lumbinī Development Trust, an international organization established in 1970, has created a master plan for Lumbinī that includes the construction of a cultural center, library and research institute, as well as facilities for pilgrims and tourists. A number of Buddhist monasteries have been constructed nearby. Lumbinī was declared a World Heritage Site in 1997.

See also: **Aśoka; Bodhgayā; Buddha; Buddha, relics of; Kuśinagara; Pāṭaliputra; Sacred places; Sārnāth; *Stūpa*; Vaiśālī.**

KEVIN TRAINOR

LUSHAN HUIYUAN (334–416)

Huiyuan was a Buddhist monk of the Eastern Jin dynasty who is known for his contributions to textual and translation theory, his advocacy of clerical freedom from royal authority, and who is also popularly accounted the first patriarch of the Pure Land school.

Early in his life, Huiyuan devoted himself to Confucian and Daoist studies, but turned to Buddhism after reading Buddhist scriptures on the philosophy of the middle way, and became a disciple of the literary genius and bibliographer Daoan (312–85). Huiyuan was the only person Daoan allowed to use the method of *geyi*, or "matching meanings," as a way of coining a much-needed technical vocabulary for Buddhist texts and translations. This technique, which involved looking for terms within pre-existing Chinese religious thought (primarily Daoist), as opposed to using Chinese characters strictly for their sound value as a way of representing Sanskrit words, carried with it the danger that readers unfamiliar with the Sanskrit originals would understand the words in their original, native meaning, thus distorting the Chinese understanding of the texts. Because of this, Daoan had forbidden his own students to use this method in their preaching and teaching. However, he thought Huiyuan's depth of understanding of both the native terms (based on his earlier studies) and their Buddhist meanings would allow him to use them without distortion.

Daoan and Huiyuan were forced to part ways in 378 because of the turmoil of the times. Huiyuan went south, and settled on Mount Lu (Ch. *Lushan*), where local authorities assisted him in constructing the Eastern Grove Temple (Ch. *Donglin si*) in modern Jiangxi Province. He settled there for the remainder of his life, never once leaving its premises. During his time on Mount Lu, Huiyuan carried on his study and writing, composing many treatises on Buddhist doctrine that helped to consolidate the Chinese understanding of Buddhism, an understanding still far from complete. He also encouraged immigrant monks in their translation activities, inviting two prominent translators, Saṃghadeva and Buddhabhadra, to live and work with him in his temple. Later in his life, Huiyuan carried on a correspondence with the great central Asian translator Kumārajīva to further clarify his understanding. In 404 he wrote a treatise defending the proposition that Buddhist monks did not need to prostrate before the king or their parents, a treatise so skillfully argued that it convinced the court. He also wrote works on monastic discipline.

In addition, in the year 402 he gathered a group of 123 disciples, both clerical and lay, to make a statue of the Buddha Amitābha and to vow to take rebirth in the Pure Land. Although the details of their meeting and their understanding of the nature of Pure Land practice show it to be very different from later expositions, it still represents one of the earliest organized efforts at Pure Land practice. Huiyuan also anthologized poems on the Pure Land and inquired into Pure Land practices in his correspondence with Kumārajīva. On these grounds, Huiyuan appears first on the list of Pure Land patriarchs.

See also: **China, Buddhism in; Kumārajīva; Pure Land school, China.**

CHARLES B. JONES

LÜZONG

In China, this was the "*Vinaya* school," or the school of scholar-monks who specialized in studying and commenting upon the monastic regulations and procedures, as well as the study and administration of both lay and clerical precepts. Daoxuan (596–667) is commonly recognized as the founder, and because he lived in the Clear Springs Temple (*Baiquan si*) on South Mountain, it also became known as the "South Mountain school" (Ch. *Nanshan zong*). Daoxuan worked for a time in the capital city of Chang'an assisting Xuanzang with his translation activities, and it was here that he met the monk Daoshi (?–683) of the Ximing monastery. The two of them helped with translation of *Vinaya* texts, and after retiring to their own monasteries continued working on the production of commentaries on these texts. It was under Daoxuan's influence that Chinese Buddhists adopted, from among the four canonical *Vinayas* available in translation, that of the Indian Dharmaguptaka school as the official precepts for the clergy (known in China as the *Vinaya in Four Parts* [Ch. *Si fen lü*]). He felt that this *vinaya* was the most complete, clear, and free of internal contradictions, and thus the most adaptable for actual use. It remains in use today.

The work of the Lüzong focused on three areas: study, commentary, and training. (1) They studied all canonical disciplinary texts intensively, going beyond the *Vinaya in Four Parts* to look at the other *Vinaya* texts, as well as any scripture that contained precepts, whether aimed at laity or clergy, and that prescribed conferral ceremonies. This not only included the monastic precepts, but also the *bodhisattva* precepts, the five lay precepts, and the three refuges. (2) In their commentaries, they dealt with the application of precepts in actual life situations, rendering opinions on what ritual procedures constituted valid conferral and abandonment of precepts, what acts constituted violations, what counted as extenuating circumstances, what penalties ought to apply to infractions, and so on. (3) They also worked directly with those receiving precepts by officiating at conferral rituals, directing training sessions, and giving oral explanations of the precepts and exhortations to observe them faithfully.

The school has always been very small in terms of numbers, but has enjoyed influence and respect for its work in systematizing and providing high-quality guidance for monastic and lay life. Certain monasteries in China were designated "*Vinaya* monasteries" (Ch. *lü si*), or "monasteries of the ten directions" (Ch. *shifang cong lin*), and these provided venues for the specialized study of monastic precepts and the training and ordination of new monks and nuns. The texts of this school were transmitted to Japan, where they became the basis for the Risshū, one of the Six Schools of the Nara period. Its main exponent in China during the modern period was Hongyi (1880–1942), a remarkable monk with great achievements in lay life as an artist and musician, and one of the "four great monks" of the early twentieth century.

See also: **China, Buddhism in; Faxiang; *Vinaya Piṭaka*; *Vinayas*.**

CHARLES B. JONES

M

MACY, JOANNA

Typically counted among the most influential architects of engaged Buddhism in the United States, Joanna Macy espouses an eclectic and activist eco-spirituality with roots in Buddhist philosophy, *vipassanā* meditation, Christian Creation-centered and Native American spiritualities, and Western general systems theory. A charter member of the Buddhist Peace Fellowship's International Advisory Council, as well as an active anti-nuclear activist, religious educator, public speaker, and author of both academic and popular books, Macy is best known for her "Despair and Empowerment Workshops," which offer participants the opportunity to "transform despair and apathy, in the face of overwhelming social and ecological crises, into constructive, collaborative action."

Macy was born Joanna Marie Rogers in Southern California on 2 May 1929, and spent most of her childhood in New York after moving there with her family in 1934. An earnest Presbyterian in her youth, she majored in Biblical History at Wellesley College, where she also experienced a crisis of faith that culminated in her exodus from Christianity before graduation. After graduation, she traveled to France as a Fulbright scholar to study the political tactics of the French Communist Party, and upon her return to the US was recruited by the Central Intelligence Agency to help fight Soviet communism through "cultural activities, journals, broadcasts, and conferences" where, as she puts it, "the only secret was the source of funding." Macy later worked for the American State Department before traveling to India in 1964 with her husband, Peace Corps volunteer Francis Macy, to help a community of 400 Tibetan refugees develop self-sufficiency through cooperative marketing ventures.

It was in India that Macy first encountered Buddhism and began meditation practice. This initial encounter made a deep impression, and, as she reports in her spiritual memoir, *Widening Circles*, it was not long before she was looking for ways to build bridges between Buddhist and Western ways of thinking. The first significant opportunity came in 1972 when she began to study toward her doctorate in religion at Syracuse University, where she concentrated on the Theravādin *suttas* and the "convergence" of the Buddhist teaching of *pratītyasamutpāda* with Western theories of reciprocal causality (see *Mutual Causality in Buddhism and General Systems Theory: The Dharma of Natural Systems*, 1991).

After receiving her Ph.D. in 1978, Macy traveled to Sri Lanka in 1979 with funding from the Ford Foundation to study the grass-roots *Sarvōdaya Śramadāna* community development movement of engaged Buddhist A.T. Ariyaratne. Her findings were published in *Dharma and Development: Religion as aResource in the Sarvōdaya Self Help Movement* in 1983. Upon her return to the US in the early 1980s, she was increasingly taken with what she perceived as a cultural malaise brought on by the prospects of nuclear holocaust and environmental destruction. Her own despair in the face of these threats led her to develop techniques adapted from Buddhist *vipassanā* meditation designed to allow her, and later others, to "work through" their despair and empower them to engage the forces of nuclear and environmental destruction head-on. The Despair and Empowerment Workshops she subsequently developed have been attended by thousands from around the world and her ideas on engaged Buddhism have been even more widely disseminated through her popular books, *Despair and Personal Power in the Nuclear Age* and *World as Lover, World as Self*.

Macy has been sharply criticized by some within the "deep ecology" movement, of which she considers herself a part, for her anti-communist activities and "right-wing" politics which, according to the charge, fail to take seriously the socially and ecologically corrosive effects of Western imperialistic capitalism. At the same time, she is widely respected as an engaged Buddhist social activist who provides not only ideas but also practical tools for overcoming the burn-out so often experienced by those who seek to create a more peaceful and just world.

See also: **Ariyaratne, A.T.; Buddhist economics and ecology; Buddhist peace groups (in Asia and the West); Engaged Buddhism; Global Buddhist networks: selected examples; Maha Ghosananda; Nhat Hanh, Thich; Sulak Sivaraksa.**

JIM DEITRICK

MADHYAMAKA SCHOOL

The Madhyamaka school is the name given to the approach to Buddhism established by Nāgārjuna and the commentators who followed his approach. The name of the school is a Sanskrit term meaning "situated in the middle" and refers to the traditional claim that the teachings of the Buddha are situated between two extreme views, namely, the view that everything exists and the view that nothing exists. The view that everything exists amounts to the belief that everything that we experience is but a transformation or evolute of an underlying ground of being that is eternal, so this view is also known as eternalism (*śāśvatavāda*). At the other extreme is the view that nothing that we experience is real. This view is sometimes associated with the view that everything that we experience exists for a finite time and then is destroyed, a view known in Buddhism as destructionism or cessationism (*ucchedavāda*). At the level of values and style of living, cessationism came to be associated with a hedonistic life, a life dedicated to pursuing fleeting pleasures, while eternalism was associated with an ascetic life, a life of avoiding attachments to any temporary objects of experience that might distract one's attention from the underlying eternal ground of being. According to Buddhist tradition, the Buddha characterized his view, and the set of practices associated with it, as the middle way (*madhyamā pratipad*), because it avoided these two extremes. All of Buddhism, therefore, could be characterized as Madhyamaka. What makes the Madhyamaka school distinctive is its particularly thoroughgoing way of steering a middle course between the extreme views about existence.

The Madhyamaka version of the middle path consists in showing that there are no exceptions to the claim that everything is conditioned and therefore owes its being and its nature to things outside itself, and therefore nothing has a nature it can call its own. The claim that nothing has its own nature (*svabhāva*), or that everything is devoid of its own nature (*svabhāvaśūnya*), entails the claim that nothing is absolute or independent. This claim is given the widest possible scope in the work of Nāgārjuna. He applies it to ontology by showing that nothing comes into existence without dependence on other things and that therefore there is no unconditioned ground of being. He applies it to epistemology by showing that nothing is self-evident nor is any belief ultimately grounded, so that all our beliefs have value only in the context of other beliefs, but none of our beliefs qualify as truths warranted by unquestionable foundations. He applies it to values and goals, contrary to Buddhists before him, by showing that even the ultimate goal of Buddhist practice, *nirvāṇa*, is conditioned and is therefore no different from the conditioned world of rebirth (*saṃsāra*). He applies it to language by showing that no expressions have meanings except in the context of other expressions and that all language is therefore a system of interdefined symbols that lack absolute meaning.

Among the earliest followers of Nāgāruna were Āryadeva and Rāhulabhadra, both of whose works are extant only in Chinese and Tibetan translations and a few surviving Sanskrit fragments quoted in other works. Āryadeva is traditionally said to be a direct disciple of Nāgārjuna, and some sources say that Rāhulabhadra was Āryadeva's successor. Whereas much of Nāgārjuna's work is generically Buddhist and shows no sectarian affiliation, the works of Āryadeva and Rāhulabhadra clearly link the Madhyamaka approach to the *bodhisattva* ideal of Mahāyāna Buddhism and contain explicit criticisms of various *śrāvakayāna* doctrines and attitudes. Moreover, their works contain references to such Mahāyāna works as various *Prajñāpāramitā sūtra*s and to the *Laṅkāvatāra Sūtra*, which works are cited to reinforce Madhyamaka claims. Writings of Āryadeva, translated into Chinese by Xuanzang, joined with works of Nāgārjuna to form the basis of the Chinese Sanlon school.

About 400 years after the first wave of Madhyamaka authors, there was a Madhyamaka renaissance in India. During this second phase of the evolution of the school, two distinctive branches emerged, each of which offered a different approach to arguing and systematizing the Madhyamaka position. The first of this new wave of commentators was Buddhapālita (fl. 500 CE), whose works survive only in Tibetan translation. His commentary on Nāgārjuna's *Mūlamadhyamakakārikā* (MMK) remains close to the original text and to an early commentary known as *Akutobhaya*, which some say was written by Nāgārjuna himself.

About a generation after Buddhapālita came Bhāvaviveka (also known as Bhavya and Bhāviveka), who probably lived in the first half of the sixth century CE. Bhāvaviveka wrote a commentary to the MMK entitled *Prajñāpradīpa*, as well as an independent work entitled *Madhyamakahṛdayakārikā*, which is a verse work accompanied by an extensive prose commentary called *Tarkajvālā*. This latter work contains an extensive discussion and critique of the major schools of Indian philosophy of Bhāvaviveka's time and situates the Madhyamaka philosophy in the context of the cultivation of *bodhicitta*, the desire to become awakened in order to work for the alleviation of the suffering of all sentient beings. Part of the task of cultivating *bodhicitta* according to Bhāvaviveka was to be able to reason clearly and systematically. Accordingly, Bhāvaviveka's presentation of Madhyamaka thought draws heavily on the logical and epistemological methods of Dignāga. It is not sufficient merely to criticize the views of others by showing internal inconsistencies in their positions, said Bhāvaviveka, so one must also produce independent arguments for the position that all things are devoid of their own nature. Because Bhāvaviveka insisted that an independent (*svatantra*) argument need be produced for the doctrine of emptiness, later Tibetan scholastics characterized his approach as *Svātantrika*; and because he drew upon the work of Dignāga, who in turn drew upon Sautrāntika philosophy, Tibetan scholastics also characterized this school as Sautrāntika Madhyamaka. His criticisms of the Vijñānavāda school show that the Madhyamaka and Vijñānavāda schools of Mahāyāna were in sharp disagreement on several issues.

Approximately a century after Bhāvaviveka's time, Candrakīrti came along and defended the approach of Buddhapālita against the criticisms of Bhāvaviveka. Candrakīrti's sharpest critique of other Buddhists was of the school of Dignāga, whose system of logic Candrakīrti characterized as antithetical to the Madhyamaka school. While the school of Dignāga was concerned with striving to establish what is true by relying on empirical observation and the application of reason, Candakīrti defended the insight of Nāgārjuna that all of what we take to be knowledge is, at bottom, unfounded opinion and that therefore the path to liberation must consist of letting go of all views and opinions. The proper use of Madhyamaka analysis, therefore, is just to show of each view that it rests on unwarranted assumptions or that it entails contradictions and other unwanted consequences (*prasaṅga*); the method, used properly, enables one to discard views that impede liberation without taking on any other views to replace them. Candrakīrti's emphasis on pointing out *prasaṅga* led later Tibetan scholastics to give the name Prāsaṅgika to the Buddhapālita-Candrakīrti branch of the Madhyamaka school.

At the beginning of the eighth century, Śāntideva wrote an important text called *Bodhicaryāvatāra* (*Introduction to the Practice of Awakening*) on the cultivation of *bodhicitta* and other virtues connected with the *bodhisattva* path. In connection with the cultivation of wisdom, Śāntideva offers detailed criticisms of other views by using the Madhyamaka style of analysis, and he makes the claim that the mind becomes still when it is freed from attachments to views about existence and non-existence, and these attachments to views cease when one learns no longer to think about things and see things in terms of existence and non-existence. This work was commented upon many times by Indian and, later, by Tibetan authors, and it came to be seen, along with the work of Candrakīrti, as providing a firm foundation to the Prāsaṅgika branch of the Madhyamaka school.

The final phase of the evolution of the Madhyamaka school in India can best be seen as an attempt to reconcile the differences between the Madhyamaka and Vijñānavāda or Yogācāra schools. Associated with this synthesis are the authors Śāntarakṣita and his disciple Kamalaśīla, both of whom flourished in the middle to late eighth century CE. The treatise for which Śāntarakṣita is best known is an extensive verse text known as *Tattvasaṃgraha*, which presents and criticizes all the major schools of Indian philosophy as they were known in his day and defends Buddhist schools against their non-Buddhist critics.

This valuable text is accompanied by an equally valuable prose commentary by Kamalaśīla. The verse text and its commentary together provide historians of Indian philosophy a rich storehouse of information of the state of Indian thought at the end of the eighth century. Because both Śāntarakṣita and Kamalaśīla settled in Tibet and made important contributions to the intellectual aspects of Tibetan Buddhism, their works are still highly valued there. Because these two authors were apparently more interested in defending all of Buddhism against non-Buddhist critics, their work provides an interesting synthesis of all the strands of Indian Buddhism into a single coherent system of theory and practice.

See also: **India, Buddhism in; Mahāyāna Buddhism; Nāgārjuna.**

RICHARD P. HAYES

MAHA GHOSANANDA

Ven. Somdech Preah Maha Ghosananda is often called "the Gandhi of Cambodia" for his efforts to bring peace and reconciliation to his war-ravaged country. Also described as mysterious and even eccentric, Ghosananda is reticent to speak of his past, and little, especially of his early life, is documented. Born in either 1924 or 1929 in Takeo Province, Cambodia (the year and date of his birth are a matter of dispute and Ghosananda has done little to resolve the controversy, reportedly attending celebrations to which he is invited regardless of the date), he was, according to most accounts, ordained as a monk at the age of nineteen at Wat Unallom and studied initially under Cambodia's Supreme Patriarch, Chuon Noth. He later earned a Ph.D. from India's Nālandā University and studied Gandhian social activism with Nichidatsu Fujii, founder of Japan's Nipponzan Myōhōji, before traveling to Thailand in 1965 to study with influential engaged Buddhist monk Buddhadasa and take part in a decade-long forest retreat under meditation master Achaan Dhammadaro.

It was during Ghosananda's sojourn in Thailand that the Khmer Rouge rose to power in Cambodia. Though he escaped the worst of the ensuing turmoil, he nevertheless lost his entire family, including sixteen siblings, to the mass starvation and genocide that followed. His career as a peace activist began in 1979 when he returned to Cambodia subsequent to Vietnam's invasion of the country and the retreat of the Khmer Rouge toward the Thai border. He immediately began visiting refugee camps, where he distributed pamphlets on the *Metta Sutta*, erected simple "shack temples," taught meditation, ordained novice monks, and exhorted reconciliation among Cambodia's war-torn people, insisting that "national peace can only begin with personal peace." As one of the few senior monks to have survived the Khmer Rouge's attempt to eradicate Buddhism, he was greeted enthusiastically by the refugees as a Buddhist authority and has since become renowned for his peaceful and "transformative" character.

During the 1980s, Ghosananda worked with Cambodia's various political factions and the United Nations to negotiate a resolution to Cambodia's civil strife, and, in 1992, led the first annual *Dhammayietra* ("Pilgrimage of Truth") Walk for Peace and Reconciliation, organized by the inter-religious Coalition for Peace and Reconciliation to mark the signing of the Paris Peace Accords in 1991 and begin the process of repatriating hundreds of thousands of refugees to Cambodia. These well-organized events, which provide participants with extensive training in non-violent conflict resolution and draw attention to other important issues facing Cambodia (like the dangers of deforestation and land mines), have been described by one commentator as acting to "sanctify the land" and transform the practice of walking meditation into a form of social commentary.

As with any renowned religious leader, Ghosananda is not without his critics. Some complain, for instance, that his tactics are ineffective, while others, who disparagingly call him the "jet-set monk," charge that his activities as an "international peacemaker" take him too often outside Cambodia and exhibit an unseemly aloofness from the land of his birth. Despite such criticisms, Ghosananda has earned an international reputation for fostering peace and reconciliation through non-violent and non-partisan activism, been promoted to Cambodia's highest ecclesiastical office, and received numerous awards in recognition of his peace efforts, including the Rafto Foundation Prize for Human Rights in 1992, the Niwano Peace Prize in 1998, and several nominations for the Nobel Peace Prize during the 1990s. His reflections on non-violent peace-building are recorded in his book, *Step by Step: Meditations on Wisdom and Compassion*, a collection of *dharma* talks published in the United States in 1992.

See also: **Ariyaratne, A.T.; Dalai Lama (and the Tibetan struggle); Buddhist peace groups (in Asia and the West); Engaged Buddhism; Global Buddhist networks: selected examples; Nhat Hanh, Thich; South and Southeast Asia, Buddhism in; Sivaraksa, Sulak.**

JIM DEITRICK

MAHĀSĀṂGHIKA

The Mahāsāṃghika school was one of the first schools of *Nikāya* Buddhism. It emerged from a schism in the Buddhist monastic order which occurred in about the fourth or third century before the Common Era, about a century or so after the Buddha's death. The name Mahāsāṃghika or "Great Monastic Community" suggests that this school represented the larger group in the previously united monastic order. Its counterpart was known as the Sthaviras or "The Elders." It is with this division of the Buddhist monastic order into the two schools that did not acknowledge each other's ordination lineages or canons that one can properly refer to *Nikāya* Buddhism. Both schools were subject to further subdivisions and are, together, the institutional source for all of the schools and groups of *Nikāya* Buddhism in India. The Mahāsāṃghikas divided into at least six different schools.

There are various explanations in Buddhist sources for the original schism between the Mahāsāṃghikas and the Sthaviras. While the exact reasons are unclear and open to contradictory interpretations, the basic divide seems to have been over issues of conservative and liberal interpretations of thought and practice. One historical account preserved in the Theravāda tradition explains that there was a group of monks in Vaiśālī who had adopted a number of practices that other monks considered to be in violation of monastic precepts. Some of these practices concerned the consumption of food – when one could eat, whether one could keep salt for use as a condiment, and permitting certain foods that ordinarily were avoided – while others involved monastic ritual practice and still others were about the handling of money by monks. In general, it would seem that the new practices assumed and created conditions of practice and interpretation that loosened the requirements of monastic life, although it can also be argued that the Mahāsāṃghikas were resisting an increasingly legalistic approach to monastic practice. Most basically, however, the specific practices were simply at odds with monastic practices found elsewhere. A judgment was made by an appointed set of senior monks (*sthavira*) against the new practices, but many monks refused to abandon them and as a result of this refusal the monastic order came to be divided. Whether or not the details of this Theravādin account are correct, it does make it clear that the formation of separate schools at the beginnings of *Nikāya* Buddhism tended to be over issues of monastic discipline rather than doctrine.

Subsequently, issues of doctrine were more to the fore in the formation of schools in *Nikāya* Buddhism and later Buddhist historians tended to look back on the history of *Nikāya* Buddhism and see doctrinal causes for even the earliest divisions. The division between the Sthaviras and the Mahāsāṃghikas thus came to be seen as resulting from issues of doctrine, particularly over the nature of an *arhat*, a person enlightened through the teachings of the Buddha. A particular monk, commonly called Mahādeva, taught that an *arhat* could have dreams accompanied by nocturnal emissions; that his enlightenment did not mean that he was knowledgeable about everything and indeed could still have ignorance; that he could have doubts, These ideas, along with others, seem to make the *arhat* less exalted than he was portrayed by others; indeed, they may well have been seen as disparaging the state of being an *arhat*. A council was convened in Pāṭaliputra to resolve the doctrinal disagreement, but it failed in its purpose and the Mahāsāṃghika emerged from it as the group which affirmed the doctrinal position of Mahādeva.

It is also plausible that the conditions for the original schism between the Sthaviras and Mahāsāṃghikas represented simply regional differences that inevitably emerged in the Buddhist monastic order as it spread across South Asia. The Mahāsāṃghikas have some associations especially with central and south India, but they were found across India and even beyond; by the seventh century, the Lokottaravādins had made Bāmiyān in present-day Afghanistan into a major Buddhist center. The seventh-century Chinese pilgrim Yijing portrayed the Mahāsāṃghikas as one of the most numerous schools that he observed in India.

Whatever the historical processes by which they emerged, the Mahāsāṃghikas do seem to have been subsequently open to new developments in thought and practice. This seems to have the case even with their canon, although very little of it has survived. They had their own *Vinaya*, as did other some other early schools, and a portion of this survives in a version of Sanskrit. They had their own *Abhidharma*, as did some other schools, but none of it survives. They also had their own collection of *sūtras*, which is also largely lost, but descriptions of it suggest that they considered it as a canonical collection of texts, including *dhāraṇī* or protective texts, that were used but remained uncanonical in other schools of *Nikāya* Buddhism. On the basis of some accounts, it seems that the Mahāsāṃghika canon could have included texts that were considered Mahāyāna texts and it is often thought by modern scholars that there is some connection between Mahāsāṃghika thought and what emerged as distinctive Mahāyāna doctrines.

This is particularly the case with Mahāsāṃghika ideas about the Buddha, especially as these are found in the *Mahāvastu*, a *Vinaya* text of the Lokottaravādins, one of the later subdivisions of the Mahāsāṃghikas. The Mahāsāṃghikas made a sharper distinction between an *arhat* and a Buddha. They held that there are simultaneously many Buddhas in the universe, something that is widely claimed in Mahāyāna texts. The Mahāsāṃghikas also developed a kind of docetic understanding of the career of the Buddha. That is to say, they claimed that the Buddha did not actually act in the world, but only appeared to do so, because he is supra-mundane (*lokottara*).

See also: **Councils; *Nikāya* Buddhism; *Sanghas*, sectarian.**

CHARLES HALLISEY

MAHĀYĀNA BUDDHISM

The Mahāyāna is the single most historically significant development of the Buddhist tradition subsequent to the death of its founder – if we can, in fact, speak of the Mahāyāna as a single historical phenomenon. More likely, it has its origins in a variety of parallel developments, many of them quite early in the history of Buddhism, and some dating back perhaps even to the time of the historical Buddha. The origins of Mahāyāna Buddhism – historical, sociological, and doctrinal – are as obscure as they are complex. Indeed, current research tends increasingly to reduce rather than expand what we can say with certainty about this composite development of Buddhism, which was to be so influential in India, Central Asia and especially East Asia.

What we know today as the Mahāyāna coalesced into a relatively identifiable and self-conscious movement only as late as the fourth century CE, and even then it continued to generate new and diverse devotional cults, beliefs, and doctrines, especially as it evolved into the Central and East Asian forms current today. Rather than seeing the Mahāyāna as a particular sect or school of Buddhism, or even as a broader reformation movement arising in reaction to specific developments within the early schools, we might better begin by imagining it as a certain sensibility or attitude among certain early Buddhists, one as much aesthetic and visionary as doctrinal and dogmatic. It is true that much of the best-known Mahāyāna literature expresses a critical and polemical stance towards the earlier tradition, which the Mahāyānists deemed the Hīnayāna or "Lesser Vehicle," but the emerging scholarly consensus is that this literature presupposes a still earlier phase of development embedded, more directly and less contentiously, well within the mainstream tradition itself.

The earliest sources of Mahāyāna Buddhism, both cultic and scriptural, remain frustratingly obscure even as they have become the focus of much current critical and creative scholarship. What we can say with certainty about the earliest stage of this movement is that it is far less simple, singular, or straightforward than the view that dominated scholarship for much of the twentieth century. Several commonplace assertions, once well entrenched, have been seriously challenged in the last two decades. For example, it was once assumed that the Mahāyāna was a later development stemming from one or another of the traditional "eighteen schools" of early conservative Buddhism – the Mahāsāṃghika school typically put forward as the most likely suspect. But recent scholarship is beginning to reveal that ideas and practices later characterized as "Mahayana" were current, if not universally accepted, in many of the early schools. Again, it was frequently assumed in the past that the Mahāyāna innovations could be localized in one particular geographical region – India's northwest frontier in one view, or south India in another. But now it is clearer that certain aspects of the later Mahāyāna can be traced to several different regional traditions. Similarly, it was once thought that the Mahāyāna was a laicized or even lay-directed dimension of early Buddhism, one that arose as a sort of populist "protestant" rejection of the more conservative and monastic Buddhism of the early schools. But again, more recent scholarship is challenging the bias from Western culture embedded in this view, demonstrating that the authors of the Mahāyāna *sūtras* were, in most if not all cases, monks, and perhaps even monks representing the ascetic forest-dwelling wing of the early monastic community.

Scholarly views on the origins of the Mahāyāna are thus very much in a state of flux. Typically, the history of Buddhism in India has been depicted as a rivalry between major factions, each comprising several schools: first a rivalry among the early conservative and monastic Buddhist schools, and then, later, an even more intense rivalry between the Mahāyānist and all the early conservative schools, which were together deemed to be the inferior "Hīnayāna" ("Lesser Vehicle"). According to this considerably oversimplified account, the Mahāyāna presented itself as superior in every respect – including the authenticity of its expansive literature, which it presented as the final and complete dispensation of Śākyamuni Buddha, taught only at the very end of his life and preserved in a secret transmission until a time when it would be properly understood. Even scholars who rejected these seemingly transparent "origin myth" apologetics still accepted the basic notion of a community of Buddhists divided into two contending camps, with the Mahāyāna camp eventually coming to prevail, except in Southeast Asia where a vestige of the older conservative tradition managed to survive. Recent scholarship leaves very little of this picture intact.

To disentangle the confusion and oversimplification here, one must first distinguish carefully between the various ways in which the early Buddhists identified themselves and their communal affiliations. In particular, there is a distinction to be made between ordination lineages (*nikāyas*), schools of philosophical thought and, at the broadest level, different ways of envisioning and conceptualizing the very nature of the Buddhist path. Within these distinctions, the Mahāyāna is especially associated with a new vision of the path. But at least some of its characteristic attitudes and concerns go back to the earliest days of the Buddhist tradition. The institutional organization of Buddhism has always focused more on orthopraxis ("proper practice") than on orthodoxy ("proper belief"). The different monastic institutions in India were most clearly separated by differences in the ordination lineages, and especially differences having to do with the communal practice of the monastic community – which scriptures and precepts were chanted aloud and how they were to be chanted, and how breaches of the monastic code were to be acknowledged and collectively healed. Differences of belief and individual expression certainly existed in the culture of these early communities, but they were more easily accommodated than differences of collective activity. When monastic communities took on a particular institutional identity, it was that of prevailing ordination lineage. Well into the early centuries of the Common Era, no one thought of "Mahāyāna" or "Hīnayāna" monasteries. The only relevant question at the level of communal practice would have been, "Which *Vinaya* – what kind of ritualized monastic organization and activity – does this community adhere to?" At the level of institutional identity, questions of individual belief and practice were neither definitive nor divisive. This allowed a great diversity of opinion and practice within the same monastic setting.

A given monastery would thus house monks following the same *Vināya* – that of the Sārvastivādin Canon, for instance – but beyond that one common element there would have been room for considerable variation. Some of the monks would have adhered to the Sārvastivāda/Vibhajjavādin school of *Abhidharma* analysis, while others in the same monastery would no doubt have identified themselves as Sautrāntikas (another of the early "schools" of thought). Among the latter there would very likely have been some who would have been drawn to the vision and style of the "newer" Mahāyāna *sūtras*, while others would have been more engaged with treatises exploring the philosophical consistency of the *śūnyavāda* ("emptiness doctrine") as an extension of the Buddha's teaching on conditionality (*pratītya-samutpāda*) and the non-substantiality of the self (*anātman*), and not in the least drawn to the imaginative cosmology characteristic of most Mahāyāna scriptures. Early Buddhism thus comprised a wide and heterogeneous range of options, some of which, over time, eventually coalesced into a broad movement self-consciously identifying itself as the Mahāyāna.

Perhaps the safest way to characterize the Mahāyāna and its relationship to the rest of early Buddhism is to say that the Mahāyāna presented a different vision of both the goal and the course of Buddhist practice, a vision which its adherents would have said was more consistent with the teachings of the Buddha. This difference of vision was expressed in virtually every aspect of the tradition, most noticeably in the Mahāyāna's conception of the Buddha, in its mapping of the path by which one becomes a Buddha, in the methods by which one progresses on that path, and finally in the philosophical and cosmological assumptions underpinning the composite vision. This new vision of the purpose and the method of the Buddhist spiritual life was expressed, moreover, in a distinctive literature, written in a new and more expansive style and serving eventually to pull together the various themes making up the composite whole. Indeed, in the earliest days of the tradition, the only clear way of distinguishing "Mahāyāna" Buddhists from their more conservative colleagues would have been to ask the question, "Which of the *sūtras* do you find the most helpful and inspiring?" All would have accepted the early collections of the Buddha's discourses as authorities. All would have followed the *Vināya* rules of their particular ("Hīnayāna") ordination lineage. And some would also have found inspiration and even spiritual authority in the Mahāyāna *sūtras* that began to be circulated in the first century BCE.

Philosophical innovations

The primary philosophical innovation of the Mahāyāna is its doctrine of *śūnyatā*, the assertion that all phenomena – the "things" of our experience – are empty or void of intrinsic existence, which is to say, in the technical language of the day, that they lack "own-being" (*svabhāva*). In the Mahāyāna view this asserts nothing not already implied in the Buddha's most fundamental teaching, his doctrine of conditionality (*pratītya-samutpāda*), which held that everything exists as part of an ongoing process, dependent on a range of prior causes and conditions. The Buddha had already pointed out that *pratītya-samutpāda* entails *anātman* ("no-self"), the non-substantiality of the self, thereby rejecting the possibility of a permanent, immutable *ātman* as the substrate of personal existence and continuity, a notion that was a key tenet in the *Upaniṣads* of the Brahmāṇical tradition. The Mahāyāna philosophers, especially Nāgārjuna (second century CE), took the teaching of conditionality even further, concluding that non-substantiality must apply to all the phenomena of our experience, to all *dharmas* (*dharmanairātmya*) as well as to the self or *ātman* (*ātmanairātmya*). All existence is an ever-changing, unbifurcated whole, a never-ceasing flow of experience that we break up into experiential moments (*dharmas*) out of which we construct higher-order composite "things." But none of these tactics for comprehending the ongoing flux of existence yield anything more than conceptual constructions, contingent on other conventionally conceptions and thus having no intrinsic existence or ultimate reality themselves.

This basic notion of emptiness is worked out further by the different Mahāyāna schools. The Yogācārins assert that the perceptions of our experience do have a basis in reality; they called this the *paratantra* or dependent aspect of reality.

When we deludedly think that the conceptual constructs by which we reach that *paratantra* experience have some reality themselves, we fail to recognize their ultimately imaginary, constructed nature; this is the *parikalpita* or falsely imagined aspect of reality. For the Yogācārins, the only ultimate truth is reality in its consummate (*pariniṣpanna*) aspect. This is realized only through a long process of moral and meditative practice – a retraining both cognitive and emotional – by which one becomes able to perceive the paratantra aspect of reality directly, free from our normal deluded and imaginary (*parikalpita*) projections.

The Madhyamaka, by contrast, seeks a more rigorously consistent philosophical defense of the emptiness teaching (*śūnyavāda*), one that allows no assertion of any ultimate existence. Recognizing that all of our unenlightened experience is conceptually mediated, and thus at best only conventional truth (*saṃvṛti-satya*), it argues that any attempt to capture reality in a conceptual system, even one of the sort the Yogācārins are willing to adopt pragmatically, is misleading and will ultimately obstruct rather than facilitate the realization of the ultimate truth (*paramārtha-satya*), which is simply acceptance that everything in our experience lacks any intrinsic existence.

Later Mahāyāna philosophers took up epistemological questions such as identifying the means of valid knowledge (*pramāṇa*) and specifying what constitutes a valid sequence of syllogistic reasoning. And finally we must consider also the influential if highly paradoxical and philosophically problematic *tathāgatagarbha* doctrine, which taught that all beings possess congenitally a "Buddha nature" that will eventually be recognized as an already present state of enlightenment. This Buddha-nature is in fact our true nature, which has temporarily and adventitiously been obscured by the cognitive and affective defilements known as greed, hatred and delusion. Once one sees through those defilements, realizing their lack of intrinsic existence, one's ultimate true nature is disclosed, the Buddha nature that has been present all along.

Mahāyana Buddhology and cosmology

The most distinctive feature of the Mahāyāna vision of the Buddhist path and its goal is its conception of the very notion of Buddhahood. The prevailing cosmological assumptions of the more conservative factions of early Buddhists were framed more in terms of time than space. All Buddhists have tended to see the universe as encompassing many parallel world-systems. And all Buddhists have recognized Śākyamuni Buddha as only one of many Buddhas, each deemed a buddha by virtue of having rediscovered or "re-launched" the perennial Truth (*Dharma*) at a time of decline when the teachings of earlier Buddhas had been lost. A Buddha was able to do this by virtue of his practice for countless lifetimes as a *bodhisattva*, "a being (directed towards) awakening (*bodhi*)." A further assumption shared by most early Buddhists was that there would never be – never need to be – two Buddhas active in the same world-system at the same time. From the perspective of conservative or "mainstream" Buddhism this implied that buddhas were, in effect "few and far between." But fortunately there was no need for everyone to become a Buddha, because the buddha's disciples, women and men alike, had access through that Buddha's teaching to the same awakening he had experienced. As *śrāvakas* ("those who listen to the teaching") they could become *arhats* (Buddhist saints) who had conquered greed, hatred and delusion to realize the same liberation from *saṃsāra* and suffering achieved by the buddhas.

The Mahāyāna vision started from many of the same assumptions, but drew different conclusions about the plurality of Buddhas. If both time and space were infinite, then so must be the number of Buddhas. Even though the time required might be immense, there was thus every reason to assume that beings could, and some day would, become Buddhas themselves, thus realizing not only the great wisdom (*mahāprajñā*) of a Buddha, but also his great compassion (*mahākaruṇā*), manifested in his intention to teach what he had realized for the benefit of all beings. This shift to the view that everyone could and should pursue the *bodhisattva* path to Buddhahood was, for the Mahāyānists at least, closer in spirit to the character of the historical Buddha, Śākyamuni. While not neglecting the mental and psychological defilements the *śrāvaka* path sought to overcome, the Mahāyāna vision emphasized the more positively framed virtues or "perfections" (*pāramitās*) which all Buddhists agreed were required of *bodhisattvas* seeking to become Buddhas. Various lists were current, but the standard Mahāyāna enumeration focused on six primary perfections: generosity (*dāna*), morality (*śīla*), forbearance (*kṣanti*), energy (*vīrya*), meditative absorption (*dhyāna*), and wisdom (*prajñā*).

Very likely some early Buddhists found this Mahāyāna emphasis on both wisdom and compassion, coupled with a path of practice stressing the development of positive virtues, more emotionally satisfying and compelling that the less expansive view of the conservative majority. The early Mahāyānists seemed to feel little reason, in the beginning at least, to perceive the two visions of the goal and path as mutually exclusive alternatives. Indeed, early Mahāyāna scriptures often sought to accommodate the more conservative conception, asserting that the seemingly contrary conceptions ultimately converged. In this view, those who think that they are following the path of the *śrāvakas* will eventually come to realize – as many (but not all) do in the *Lotus Sūtra*, for example – that they have, in fact, been pursuing the *bodhisattva* path all along, without realizing it. Thus there is no fundamental conflict, just a temporary difference of how to proceed. Later Mahāyāna scriptures certainly do become more aggressively polemical in their rejection of the "lesser" paths, but even this should be understood more as the rejection of what the Mahāyāna saw as a spiritually limited mind-set – the "Hīnayāna" – than as institutional sectarianism.

In light of the above it becomes easier to understand the special significance the Mahāyāna placed on another key doctrinal innovation, the idea of *bodhicitta* (lit. "awakening mind"). If the paths of the *śrāvaka* and that of the *bodhisattva* were fundamentally the same, the difference being that the *bodhisattvas* were able to see this in a way that the aspiring *śrāvakas* were not, then the most crucial and decisive point on the whole path was the point at which that "re-visioning" came about. It is reaching this point on the path that distinguishes the *bodhisattvas* from the *śrāvakas*, and it is this point that the Mahāyānists sought to specify with their notion of "the arising of awakening-mind" or, as it is sometimes translated, "the arising of the will to enlightenment" (*bodhicittopāda*). This is the crucial turning point on the path, the point at which the aspirant realizes that he or she is seeking enlightenment not simply as a personal goal, but for the sake of all sentient beings. And it is thus the point at which the compassion aspect of the Buddha's enlightenment begins to come to the fore. While the Mahāyāna retained much of the more conservative conception of the stages of the path, this key turning point marked the beginning of *bodhisattva* practice proper, and it led to a richer mapping of the remaining portions of the path, seen now as consisting in the higher cultivation of the *bodhisattva* virtues or "perfections" mentioned above. The Mahāyāna map of the path retained the basic distinction between the insight stage of the path (*darśana-mārga*) and the cultivation stage (*bhāvana-mārga*). But the former was re-envisioned more specifically as the initial transformative insight into *śūnyatā*, i.e. the ultimate non-substantiality of all the "things" (*dharmas*) of our experience, while the latter was now understood in terms of stages in the cultivation of the perfections. Even though this reconceived notion of the path would require the efforts of multiple lifetimes over eons of time, the *bodhisattva* would never despair, as this would simply give all the more opportunity to perfect the compassion that was the natural expression of true wisdom.

The *śūnyatā* doctrine provided the philosophical underpinning for another buddhological innovation central to the Mahāyāna program: to re-envision not just the path but also the ultimate goal it reached. The more conservative view focused on Śākyamuni's *parinirvāṇa* (lit. "final extinguishing") as the ultimate fulfillment of his liberation from the suffering of *saṃsāra*. That entailed, in their view, an end not only to future rebirth, but also to the capacity to work actively in any way for the benefit of *saṃsāric* beings. But this understanding of the nature of Buddhahood went against the Mahāyāna emphasis on the continuing power of a Buddha's great compassion. The solution to this dilemma was reached by reconceiving the very nature of the enlightenment, and this was facilitated by the deconstructive conceptual relativism of the *śūnyavāda* doctrine. Rather than framing the Buddha's enlightenment in terms of his "escape" from *saṃsāra* (and thus from the world of beings) into *(pari)-nirvāṇa*, the early Mahāyāna scriptures shifted the focus onto his awakening (*bodhi*). Using the deconstructive logic of the *śūnya* doctrine, they then rejected the dualism of *saṃsāra* versus *nirvāṇa*, arguing that the Buddha's realization of the ultimate emptiness of all dichotomies – his *bodhi* – not only freed him from suffering, but left him in a state of unbounded or "unfixed" (*apratiṣṭhita*) liberation that took no stand in either *saṃsāra* or *nirvāṇa*. The fully enlightened Buddha was thus able to be completely free of the constraints of rebirth and yet remain an active force of good in the realm of suffering sentient beings. The emotional appeal of this reworking of the mainstream notion of both Buddha and Buddhahood would be difficult to overestimate and must account to a significant degree for the growing popularity the Mahāyāna vision came to enjoy.

Devotional and meditation practice

In the area of practice – both individual meditation and collective worship – we can see further developments arising from the Mahāyāna effort to re-envision the path and the goal of the tradition in terms of the *bodhisattva* ideal. While the Mahāyāna maintained much that was current in more conservative circles – recitation of the Three Refuges, for example – distinctly Mahāyāna forms of practice evolved as well, especially forms that reinforced the centrality of the *bodhisattva* path with its emphasis upon seeking enlightenment for the sake of all sentient beings. This is most obvious perhaps in the liturgical structure of a form of worship popular in Mahāyāna circles, the threefold worship (*triskandhaka*). The focus of the *Triskandhaka* portion of the Mahāyāna *Upālipariprcchā* scripture, which was elaborated further by the Mahāyāna poet-philosopher Śāntideva (seventh century CE), this liturgy began with a ritualized confession of sins, a practice paralleling the collective *Prātimokṣa* recitations common in mainstream Buddhism from its earliest days. That acknowledgment of one's own limitations led next to a rejoicing in the merits of others, a practice again with precedent in the *muditā* portion of the meditation of the four *brahmavihāras*. Finally the practitioner added a petition to all the buddhas that they remain active in the world, working for the benefit of all sentient beings. It is in this third component that we can most clearly see a distinctly Mahāyāna element, a conception of what buddhas could and might do that would make little sense in a non-Mahāyāna context. Conservative mainstream buddhology was based on the assumption that a buddha's death or *parinirvāṇa* represented a complete and irrevocable separation from the world of saṃsāric suffering. But the whole of the *Triskandhaka*, including the first two components, is framed in terms of the pursuit of enlightenment for the sake of all beings.

Innovation in Mahāyāna meditation practice is also significant, and can be best summarized as proceeding in apparently different directions. On the one hand, one can identify a tendency towards "formless" techniques of meditative absorption or concentration, while on the other hand, there was a simultaneous development of increasingly elaborate visualization practices. The first of these trajectories stems from the practical exploration of the *śūnyavāda* insight into the ultimate non-substantiality of phenomenal experience beyond all conceptual construction. Meditation practice within more conservative circles would typically involve training to maintain an object of meditation (*ālambana*) firmly in mind. But in the Mahāyāna context we find more emphasis on cultivating methods of meditation that are object-less (*nirālambana*) and intended to lead to modes of concentration free of all signs (*animitta*) and beyond all conceptualization (*nirvikalpa-samādhi*). The second trajectory begins with modes of devotional cult-practice deriving most likely from earlier "mindfulness of the Buddha" (*buddhānusmṛti*) meditation practices. In their Mahāyāna forms these practices began with a devotional experience of the positive qualities of the chosen cult figure (*iṣṭadevatā*) and then expanded to incorporate not just elaborate eidetic visualizations of a particular archetypal buddha or *bodhisattva* but often their respective Buddha-field (*buddha-kṣetra*) or "pure land" as well. With the later assimilation of Tantric modes of practice into the Mahāyāna, these visualization meditations were taken a step further, with the practitioner not only venerating the enlightened qualities of the object of his meditation but personally identifying with the figure as well.

Mahāyāna literature

In surveying the nature and the role of Mahāyāna literature in shaping the tradition, we should first note that whereas the most conservative, mainstream tradition favored maintaining its teachings in an oral tradition, the Mahāyāna appears to have depended much more on the creation of a written canon of scriptures for its eventual success. Indeed, the fact that the Mahāyāna does not begin to emerge in the historical record until the first century BCE is perhaps because it was impossible for this fledging and minority "revisioning" movement to gain sufficient momentum before the written word was more widely available and accepted in Indian culture. These new scriptures in their written form were so highly valued and venerated that the early Mahāyāna has been characterized, if somewhat misleadingly, as a "cult of the book." And the books generated by this tradition were as expansive in bulk as they were in both imaginative scope and vision.

As with the more conservative versions of the Buddhist canon, the Mahāyāna scriptures fall into the three broad divisions of the *Tripiṭaka* (lit: "three baskets"): *sūtras* or discourses of the Buddha; *Vinaya* or works dealing with the monastic code; and *śāstras* or philosophical treatises.

There is nonetheless a striking difference, in that the Mahāyāna canon was never officially "closed." The texts continued to proliferate, not only with the addition of new works but also with the expansion of the earlier works, including the *sūtras*. The *Vinaya* section of this loosely defined Mahāyāna "canon" was relatively more stable in that most Mahāyāna monastics eventually sought ordination in one of the existing *nikāya* ordination lineages they shared with their more conservative colleagues. But even so, a substantial body of Mahāyāna literature arose, with the addition of works dealing with the vows of the *bodhisattva*, which constituted the contribution of Mahāyāna ethics to the basic monastic code. The Mahāyāna *śāstra* literature shows a much greater degree of proliferation, and this was not just caused by the need to work out the implications of the new Mahāyāna doctrinal innovations. As the Mahāyāna became established in Central and East Asia, new, more localized schools of thought emerged, each developing its own distinctive exegetical traditions and *śāstra* literature.

The *sūtras* of the Mahāyāna movement, vast in both imaginative conception and literary execution, remain its most distinctive literature. Viewed historically, the earliest strata of these scriptures, which probably date from the first century BCE, include the most influential of the tradition, in particular the "Perfection of Wisdom in Eight Thousand Verses" (*Aṣṭasāhasrikāprajñāpāramitā*), the core portions of the *Lotus Sūtra* (*Saddharmapuṇḍarīka*), and the earliest of the "Pure Land" *sūtras*, including the *Akṣobhyavyuhā* and other early works in the *Ratnakuṭa* collection of *sūtras*, along with the earlier of the two *Sukhāvatī Sūtras*. The later Mahāyāna *sūtras* include a number of works presenting expansions of the *Prajñāpāramitā* literature, most notably the 25,000-verse *Prajñāpāramitā* and later still the *Heart Sūtra* (*Prajnāpāramitāhṛdāya Sūtra*) and the *Diamond Sūtra* (*Vajracchedikāprajñāpāramitā Sūtra*). In this period we also find the *Avataṃsaka Sūtra* (including the *Gaṇḍvyuhā Sūtra*) which was very influential in East Asia, as was the *Vimalakīrti Nirdeśa Sūtra*. More directly associated with Yogācāra Buddhism were the *Sandhinirmocana Sūtra* and the *Laṅkāvatāra Sūtra*. Another group of *sūtras* introduced the *tathāgatagarbha* doctrine, including most notably the *Tathāgatagarbha Sūtra*, the *Śrīmālādevī Sūtra* and the later recensions of the Mahāyāna version of the *Mahāparinirvāṇa Sūtra*.

This list includes the most important and historically influential Mahāyāna *sūtras*, all of which are available in modern translations. But there are many, many more. Indeed, it is safe to say that the majority of the Mahāyāna *sūtras* still remain untranslated into any European language. And our understanding of the origins of Mahāyāna Buddhism will certainly continue to evolve as these works receive the scholarly attention they deserve.

See also: **Asaṅga; *Bodhisattva* path; India, Buddhism in; Madhyamaka school; Nāgārjuna; Perfection of Wisdom literature; *Tathāgatagarbha* in Indian Buddhism; Vasubandu; Yogācāra school.**

ALAN SPONBERG

MAJOR PROFESSIONAL SOCIETIES

Introduction

Major professional societies devoted to the study of various aspects of Asia have existed for a very long time. The Royal Asiatic Society, for example, was founded in 1823, and as early as 1834 began publishing its now famous journal. Today it still maintains an impressive membership of over 700. Similarly, the Société Asiatique de Paris began publication of the

Journal Asiatique in 1822. In North America, the American Oriental Society – the oldest discipline-based professional society in the United States – was founded in 1842, and began published the *Journal of the American Oriental Society* the following year. Other professional societies, such as the Association for Asian Studies (founded in 1941), continue to appear to collectively study and explore the various traditions of Asia.

Early Buddhist societies

Yet it was not until the Pāli Text Society was founded in 1881 by Thomas W. Rhys Davids that Buddhism had a professional society devoted exclusively to its textual, historical, and doctrinal study. Its publicity material clearly states that it was founded "to foster and promote the study of Pāli texts," but that study invariably led to a broader consideration of the Theravāda tradition throughout Asia. The society's first tasks involved editing and publishing roman script editions spanning the entire corpus of Pāli literature, including its famous canon. In addition, it published dictionaries, concordances, and an extensive series of ancillary works. Thomas W. Rhys Davids remained president until his death in 1922. By that time, the Pāli Text Society had published sixty-four separate texts in ninety-four volumes. He was succeeded by his wife, Caroline Augusta Foley Rhys Davids, who assumed the presidency in 1922 and remained in the post until her own death in 1942. She was followed by Isaline Blew Horner, the great *Vinaya* scholar, who served as honorary secretary from 1942 to 1959, after which she was president and honorary treasurer until 1981. The current president, Rupert M.L. Gethin, carries on as president from his position at the University of Bristol. On the other side of the globe, the Eastern Buddhist Society was founded in 1921 by D.T. Suzuki. It was primarily interested in various aspects of the Mahāyāna Buddhist tradition, and continues today. In addition to publishing its well-known journal – *The Eastern Buddhist* – it continues to sponsor seminars and occasional lectures.

Current professional societies

The three largest professional venues for the study of Buddhism today are the International Association of Buddhist Studies, the United Kingdom Association for Buddhist Studies, and the "Buddhism Section" of the American Academy of Religion.

The International Association of Buddhist Studies (IABS), created through the singular efforts of A.K. Narain, was launched by a major international conference at the University of Wisconsin in 1976. More than three dozen internationally acclaimed scholars attended the initial meeting, with the conference proceedings eventually being collected and published in two major books, both edited by Narain: *Studies in Pāli and Buddhism* (1979) and *Essays in the History of Buddhism* (1980). An honorary chairperson (Gadjin Nagao) and three honorary vice chairpersons (A.L. Basham, Louis Ligeti, and O.H. de A. Wijesekera) were elected, but the running of the new organization was established in the positions of general secretary, held by Narain; an associate secretary (held by Charles Prebish); and three regional secretaries (Asia: held by Yuichi Kajiyama; Europe: held by Erik Zürcher; and the Americas: held by Bardwell Smith). Throughout its thirty-year history, the organization has held bi-annual meetings at various locations throughout the world. The current location of the headquarters is at the University of Lausanne in Switzerland. The current president is Jukidō Takasaki of Tokyo, and the general secretary is Tom Tillemans. The IABS continues to remain "dedicated to promoting and supporting scholarship in Buddhist Studies in a spirit of non-sectarian tolerance and with scientific research and communication as preeminent objectives."

The United Kingdom Association of Buddhist Studies (UKABS), like the IABS, "aims to act as a focus for Buddhist Studies in the UK, and is open to academics, post-graduates, and unaffiliated Buddhist scholars or interested Buddhist practitioners." Its constitution further states: "The object of the Association shall be the academic study of Buddhism through the national and international collaboration of all scholars whose research has a bearing on the subject." Under the current direction of its current president – Peter Harvey – and secretary – Damien Keown – the UKABS sponsors a yearly conference in London. It has recently assumed direction of the journal *Buddhist Studies Review*, ably edited by Russell Webb until his retirement in 2004. Members of the UKABS span the spectrum of methodological backgrounds and specialties, as well as the scope of philological trainings.

The final professional society to be noted is the "Buddhism Section" of the American Academy of Religion (AAR). For many years, the American Academy of Religion and the Society of Biblical Literature have been the world's two largest societies for the study of religion. As scholars of Buddhism in North America searched for a sympathetic arena in which to meet and share the labors of the research, by the late 1970s it was apparent that the AAR was the logical choice. The Buddhism Section was begun as a "Group" in the infrastructure of the American Academy of Religion in 1981 by George Bond and Charles Prebish, as an outgrowth of its immediate predecessor: the Indian Buddhism Consultation. With Bond and Prebish as its first co-chairs, it concluded its five-year term with an upgrade to status as a "Section," highest category in the AAR. Within a short period, the Buddhism Section – which maintains no formal membership – grew enormously, mirroring the rapid growth of Buddhist Studies on the North American continent. Its five-yearly panels at the AAR annual meeting are profoundly well attended, with much competition for slots on its yearly program. An informal mailing list of "friends of the Buddhism Section" now tallies several hundred members, and its successive list of traditional co-chairs (Leslie Kawamura and Collett Cox, Janice Nattier and John McRae, Jacqueline Stone and John Strong, and Peter Gregory and Anne Blackburn) have included highly influential scholars in North American Buddhist Studies.

See also: **Academic study of Buddhism.**

CHARLES S. PREBISH

MANTRAS, MUDRĀS, AND *MAṆḌALAS*

Mantras

The use of symbolic representations of concepts and meditation practices has a long history in India. In common with the *brahmāṇical* tradition, Buddhists employ *mantras* (Tib. *sngags*, Ch. *zhenyan*, Jap. *shingon*) to encode doctrines, as focal points in meditative training, and as representations of the goals of practice. *Mantras* are important in Vajrayāna Buddhism, but they are found in all Buddhist traditions.

Some Vajrayāna *mantras* are associated with a particular Buddha; chanting a *mantra* creates a *karmic* connection between a practitioner and the buddha evoked by it. Repetition familiarizes the mind with the Buddha's good qualities, enabling one to acquire them for oneself and thus progress along the religious path. Interpretation is often difficult, because *mantras* commonly contain meaningless syllables, and are often written in ungrammatical Sanskrit. Outside of a particular practice and without the instruction of a qualified teacher, some *mantras* have no meaning at all, and derive their effectiveness from the role they play in religious training.

Among Tibetan Buddhists, the *mantra Oṃ maṇi padme hūṃ* (Tib. *Oṃ maṇi padme hūng*) is associated with Avalokiteśvara (Tib. sPyan ras gzigs), who embodies the compassion of all Buddhas. Its translation has been the subject of controversy among scholars, but current research indicates that it should be rendered: "Oṃ in the Jewel Lotus Hūṃ," referring to the notion that one who achieves rebirth in the "pure land" of Sukhāvatī emerges from a jeweled lotus and indicating one's desire to be reborn there. For many Tibetan Buddhists, it is simply an invocation to Avalokiteśvara, and repetition is believed to bring merit for both oneself and others. Meditators who train in practices relating to Avalokiteśvara commonly repeat the *mantra* over and over again as part of their mental training. Repetition leads to familiarization with the exalted attributes of Avalokiteśvara, and through such practice the yogin gradually approximates the state of Buddhahood and acquires these qualities. The *mantra* acquires a range of associations in commentarial literature, and each of the six syllables is correlated to attainment of a particular perfection (*pāramitā*) and removal of a mental affliction. When chanted, each syllable releases sentient beings from a negative rebirth associated with a particular affliction.

The *mantra* is also part of the landscape of Tibetan Buddhism: it is carved on hillsides and rocks, and the entrances to many towns are marked by walls of *maṇi* stones (*maṇi gdong*), each of which has the *mantra* carved onto it. It is also emblazoned on huge prayer wheels, which are filled with millions of repetitions of the *mantra* written on paper; as the wheel is turned, merit is generated both for those who move the wheel and for all sentient beings.

Mantras are also held to possess magical powers, and Vajrayāna texts contain a plethora of spells that are said to be able to alter weather, bring rain, vanquish enemy armies, read the minds of others, gain control over women, subdue demons, etc.

Mudrā

The term *mudrā* (Tib. *phyag rgya*, Ch. *yin*, Jap. *inzō*, "seal") has two primary meanings in Vajrayāna Buddhism: female consorts with whom the yogin unites sexually (either physically or as part of visualization practice) in order to generate spontaneous great bliss in the wisdom consciousness realizing emptiness; and hand gestures that depict aspects of a buddha's qualities or activities. These can also encode doctrines and practices. Tantric practitioners commonly learn a repertoire of *mudrās*, which are enacted at particular points in liturgies of visualization (*sādhana*) and prayers. In *tantric* iconography, the left hand is associated with the male and symbolizes compassion and skill in means, while the right is female and symbolizes wisdom. *Mudrās* often combine the two aspects as symbols of Buddhahood.

Examples of common *mudrās* used in Buddhist iconography include the "fearless gesture" (Skt. *abhaya-mudrā*, Tib. *'jigs med phyag rgya*), in which a Buddha extends the right hand with the palm facing downward in a gesture of protection; the *maṇḍ ala-mudrā* (Tib. *dkyil 'khor phyag rgya*), in which the second and little fingers are held down by the index fingers and thumbs respectively, and which represents Mount Meru and the four surrounding continents; and the "earth-touching *mudrā*" (Skt. *bhūmi-sparśa-mudrā*, Tib. *sa gnon phyag rgya*), which portrays a Buddha extending the fingers toward the ground, thus calling on the

Figure 29 Tibetan monks at Shalu Monastery, Tibet, performing a tantric ritual involving the use of *mantras* and *mudrās*.

earth to bear witness to the veracity of his/her statements.

Maṇḍala

The term *maṇḍala* (Tib. *dkyil 'khor*, Ch. *man to lo*, Jap. *mandara*) can refer both to sacred places – such as the spot beneath the *Bodhi* Tree where Śākyamuni Buddha attained awakening – or to symbolic diagrams that encode aspects of Buddhist doctrine and practice and that commonly serve as templates for the mental transformations meditators aim to achieve through their training.

In Tibetan tantric contexts, a *maṇḍala* often depicts a Buddha realm (Skt. *buddha-kṣetra*, Tib. *sangs rgyas kyi zhing*) or the palace of a particular Buddha, and the various images and symbols in it refer to him/her, to aspects of Buddhist doctrine and practice, and to Buddhist cosmology. *Maṇḍalas* can occur in either two-dimensional or three-dimensional forms; two-dimensional ones are often floor plans of a Buddha's palace (Skt. *kūṭāgāra*, Tib. *khang pa brtsegs pa*), which are intended to provide the template for visualization as a three-dimensional structure. These often reflect the design of palaces in medieval India, and more extensive ones resonate with ideas of kingship and royal power. There is generally a central Buddha, who exercises dominion over the entire region, and each quadrant has another Buddha, surrounded by a retinue and various attendants, who is lord of that area but subordinate to the main Buddha. At the periphery, one sees depictions of marginal areas like cemeteries, cremation grounds, and wildernesses (the borders of civilization in medieval India), as well as fearsome creatures like snakes, wild animals, and demons.

The palace contains various symbols that resonate with the goals and techniques of meditative practice and reflect the good qualities of a Buddha. They represent the body, speech, and mind of a Buddha, along with the performance of awakened activities. Tibetan Buddhist *maṇḍalas* generally have square borders enclosing concentric circles and squares. They are often divided into quadrants of equal size, and are strongly symmetrical and oriented around a central spot in which the main Buddha is depicted, often symbolically.

In *tantric* literature, there are descriptions of various types of *maṇḍalas*, some of which exist in concrete form as painted canvas (*ras bris kyi dkyil 'khor*) or sand *maṇḍalas* (*rdul phran gyi dkyil 'khor*) that are used as aids in meditation or as the focal points of initiation ceremonies. In some texts, the external *maṇḍalas* are said to be representations of natural *maṇḍala*s (Skt. *svabhāva-maṇḍala*, Tib. *rang bzhin dkyil 'khor*), which are non-physical and represent the awakened qualities of Buddhahood. Other *maṇḍala*s are internal: meditational *maṇḍala*s (Skt. *samādhi-maṇḍala*, Tib. *ting nge 'dzin kyi dkyil 'khor*) are visualized by the mind of a practitioner as three-dimensional figures. In *tantric* theory, the body itself is also considered to be a *maṇḍala*, and is the crucible of training designed to transform it into the body of a Buddha.

Once constructed and consecrated, *maṇḍalas* are believed to be imbued with the presence of the relevant Buddha(s), and thus become focal points for devotion and visualized offerings. They are also believed to have magical power, and can prolong life, bring wealth, protect against evil, and are often worn as amulets.

The *maṇḍala* serves as a model for reconstruction of the meditator's mind from that of an ordinary being, afflicted by anxieties and ignorance, into the mind of a Buddha, who has developed wisdom and compassion to their highest level and thus is able to work effectively for the benefit of others. Tantric practice often begins with initiation into a *maṇḍala*, in which a practitioner is brought in front of a specially constructed *maṇḍala* (often made from colored sand elaborately constructed according to traditional models) and given a special empowerment by a guru, who was previously initiated by a qualified teacher who belongs to a lineage of transmission of a particular cycle of practice.

See also: **Tibet, Buddhism in; Tibet: *maṇḍalas*; Vajrayāna Buddhism.**

JOHN POWERS

MARPA

Marpa (Mar pa Chos kyi blo gros, 1012–97) is regarded by the Kagyü Order of Tibetan Buddhism as one of its most influential masters. Born in southern Tibet, he studied with the translator (lo tsā ba) Drokmi ('Brog mi) for fifteen years before deciding to travel to India. There he met the tantric *siddha* Nāropa (Nāḍapāda, 1016–1100). Nāropa accepted him as his student and gave him *tantric* initiations, including the ritual and meditative practices of Cakrasaṃvara (the main tutelary deity of the Kagyü Order), as well as instructions on the "six yogas of Nāropa" (*nā ro chos drug*) and on the "great seal" (*phyag rgya chen po*, Skt. *mahāmudrā*, which is considered by the Kagyüpas to be the quintessence of the Buddha's instructions).

Marpa made two more trips to India, and after returning to Tibet he married Dakmema (bDag med ma) and began attracting students. They had seven sons, but only Darma Dode (Dar ma mdo sde) had the inclination or talent to follow in his father's footsteps. While riding his horse, however, Darma Dode suffered a fatal accident, and as he lay dying Marpa reportedly performed a rite of "transference of consciousness" (*'pho ba*), which caused his son's consciousness to leave his body and enter that of a pigeon. The pigeon flew to India, where Darma Dode's consciousness entered the body of a dying brahman boy.

Marpa became a wealthy landholder and local hegemon, and was renowned as a leading lay *tantric* practitioner (*sngags pa*). According to the Kagyü tradition, he attained a level of awakening equivalent to the Buddha Vajradhara. His most famous disciple was Milarepa (Mi la ras pa, 1040–1123), who sought his teachings after killing a number of people through black magic. Milarepa's biography reports that his family was moderately wealthy, but after his father's death his greedy uncle and aunt deviously took over their land and reduced them to poverty. At his mother's urging, Milarepa took revenge by sending demons to attack a wedding party given by his relatives, but they killed all the guests except the aunt and uncle.

In order to eradicate Milarepa's negative *karma*, Marpa ordered him to engage in a series of painful and arduous tasks, including building several stone towers and then tearing them down. The final tower, however, was left intact, and it gave Marpa control over a trade route through the area and made him the most powerful of the local hegemons.

After completing his study with Marpa, Milarepa went into the wilderness and meditated in a cave for a number of years, during which he also reportedly attained a high level of realization. The religious biographies (*rnam thar*) and ecstatic songs (*dohā*) of Marpa and Milarepa are among the most popular religious works in the

Tibetan Buddhist cultural area, and are regularly recited during Kagyü religious festivals. Marpa and Milarepa are renowned throughout Tibet as paradigms of the lay religious life, which often stands in opposition to the mainstream monastic traditions.

See also: **Tibet, Buddhism in; Vajrayāna Buddhism.**

JOHN POWERS

MEDICAL PRACTICES

Buddhist monks and nuns have been famous throughout Asian history as healers, not only metaphorically, in the sense that they prescribe the cure to ultimate suffering, nor only magically, through their deployment of supernormal forces but also literally, for medicine and monasticism have been interwoven from the very beginning.

Indian medicine did not originate with the Buddhists, but was part of a common stock of *śrāmaṇic* practices that they cautiously appropriated. The Buddha of the *Vinaya*, for example, prohibits monks and nuns from taking on a medical practice but dictates a whole section (Skt. *Bhaiṣajyavastu*, Pāli *Bhesajjakkhandhaka*) devoted to medicines and medical practices. His caution reflects the worldly nature of the profession (including its use of prohibited substances like animal flesh, though even that is sometimes permitted to monks in dire situations) and the classification of medicine among "low sciences" (*tiraścīnavidyā*) whose practitioners should be avoided; the appropriation reflects both the overlap of *śrāmaṇas* (including early Buddhists) with itinerant physicians, some of whom joined the *sangha*, and the variously articulated idea that the members of the *sangha* should be healthy. Thus the Buddha himself is known on occasion to have nursed the sick and to have encouraged his followers to do the same; medicines, defined with an ever-expanding list, were identified as one of the four basic necessities of monks. Both textual and archeological evidence makes certain that from about the third century BCE onwards infirmaries were sometimes attached to large monastic complexes, as was later true in Sri Lanka, China and Tibet. Medicine was a major curricular focus at monastic universities like Nālandā, and on occasion medical texts (such as the *c.* fifth-century CE Bower Manuscript, discovered in eastern Turkestān) were interred in *stūpas* as though they were *dharmadhātu*.

In time Buddhists codified and transmitted collective medical knowledge (including other indigenous practices, such as acupuncture in China) in scholarly treatises that were composed in India (for example, the *c.* fourth-century CE *Suvarṇaprabhāsa Sūtra* and *c.* seventh-century CE *Aṣṭāṅgahṛdayasaṃhitā*) and abroad (e.g. Chinese translations/expansions of numerous *sūtras* no longer extant in Sanskrit, the *c.* 1267 CE Pāli *Casket of Medicines* (*Bhesajjamañjusā*), and the post eighth-century CE Tibetan *Rgyudbźi* attributed to Bhaiṣajyaguru, the Mahāyāna *bodhisattva* of healing).

Although monastic medical practice differed from region to region and coexisted with parallel lay Buddhist and/or non-Buddhist traditions, the *Vinaya* provided it a common holistic basis which treats medicine proper as part of a health regimen that also includes physical type, diet, environment, and extra-medical healing and protective rituals. In general, medicine proper was comprehensively developed in terms of etiology (especially the Ayurvedic theory of three humors), diagnostics (which included special techniques for discerning disease through touch), and treatment (including decoctions, poultices, massage, herbal "pills" and surgery in addition to meditation, change of diet and habit, and healing and protective rites), and addressed a vast range of acute, chronic, infectious, epidemic and psychological ailments, which were sometimes cataloged in expanded legends of Jīvaka, the famous physician contemporary with the Buddha.

See also: **Healing and protective practices; *Sangha*; *Vinaya Piṭaka*.**

JONATHAN S. WALTERS

MEDITATION (CHAN/ZEN)

Chan is a Chinese translation of the Sanskrit *dhyāna* (Pāli *jhāna*), which denotes a state of meditative concentration. The Japanese rendition of the Chinese term is *Zen*, the Korean *Son*, and the Vietnamese *Thiên*. Throughout East Asia, however, Zen refers not just to this technical term for a specific kind of meditative state but to a school of Buddhism that takes meditation as its primary concern. (For convenience I will refer to all forms of this movement as "Zen.") The meditation from which Zen Buddhism takes its name should not be understood in the restricted sense in which it is used in Pāli meditation literature – that is, to the cultivation of specific states of calm concentration – but rather to a broad variety of traditional practices, such as mindfulness, concentration, wisdom, as well as aspects of meditation unique to Zen.

Zen teachings emphasize the value of non-theoretical practice over intellectual understanding – the legendary Bodhidharma said that Zen is "not founded upon words and letters" but "points directly to the mind." Nevertheless it has produced a great deal of literature addressing meditation, only a couple key examples of which we will address here. The *Platform Sūtra of the Sixth Patriarch*, attributed to Huineng (seventh–eighth century), contains many enduring themes regarding meditation and its relationship to enlightenment. It insists that meditation – often thought to entail the cultivation of certain virtues, mental states, and ultimately enlightenment itself – does not actually cultivate anything. The mind, Huineng insists, is already inherently pure, and there is actually nothing to cultivate except the realization of one's own original enlightenment. Formal meditation, scriptures, and ethical conduct don't give rise to wisdom; it is already there, permeating not only the practitioner but everything else as well. It is through maintaining "direct mind" at all times, that is, living in the world with full awareness but clinging to nothing – even Buddhist teachings themselves – that the practitioner realizes complete inner freedom. Seeing directly into any moment is, for Huineng, enlightenment.

With these striking ideas, Huineng articulates some of the dominant themes of Zen meditation. One of the most important is that of radical non-duality, particularly regarding the means and ends of Buddhist practice. Meditation and wisdom (or enlightenment – the ostensible goal of meditation) are not different. The former is not a means to the latter because the primordial nature of all things – variously called original nature, true self, Buddha-nature, or the *dharmakāya* – is already the true reality of everyone and everything. Enlightenment, therefore, is not so much the achieving of a particular state as the unveiling of this primordial reality. This idea also entails another aspect of radical non-dualism: the unity of subject and object or the ultimate oneness of all things. The notion that formal meditation does not bring about enlightenment should not be understood as a repudiation of meditation itself but rather of a particular interpretation of it. Instead of being one activity cut off from all other activities, the notion of meditation here is extended to all elements of daily life: "going, standing, sitting, lying" are all Zen. The enduring influence of this idea can be seen in the fact that Zen monastic practice today construes every aspect of life as meditation and ritualizes even the most everyday activities.

Another crucial work of literature explicating Zen meditation is the *Shōbōgenzō* of the famous Japanese monk and founder of the Japanese Sōtō (Ch. Caotong) school, Dōgen (1200–53). Embracing many of Huineng's principles, Dōgen asserts that *zazen*, seated meditation, is not only sufficient for attaining enlightenment, it is itself enlightenment. When performed correctly, *zazen* is not a method for attaining a different state, but an expression of the true nature of the practitioner, which is, in turn, an expression of the true nature of the cosmos, because the two are one and the same. Dōgen's method of meditation was *shikantaza*, or "just sitting" without expectation of reward, indeed without any ordinary thinking at all. *Shikantaza* is an intensive form of meditation in which the immediate present, whatever its form and content, is the object of meditation. Dōgen refers to it as neither thinking nor blankness, but a process of "un-thinking" (*hi shiryō*) – investigating thought to exhaust the limits of thinking itself, thus allowing for a direct realization of the enlightened mind of the Buddha within the practitioner. Rather than a means to an end, Dōgen insists that it is a process of authenticating this Buddha-mind.

Although *shikantaza* is a form of meditation unique to Zen, the practice of *zazen* draws upon and incorporates forms of meditation common to earlier Buddhist traditions in India, such as tranquility meditation (*śamatha*) – particularly following the movement of the breath – and various techniques for cultivating insight (*vipaśyanā*). Zen meditation also includes walking meditation (*kinhin*) in which meditators take the movement of the feet and legs as an object of meditation. As mentioned above, in the broadest sense virtually all everyday activities of the monastery become forms of meditation; for example, monks eat in a thoroughly ritualized manner and are expected to attend fully to the process of untying their bowls and utensils, consuming food, washing their bowls, and putting them away.

One of the meditation techniques unique to Zen is contemplation of the *kōan* (Ch. *gongan*). *Kōans* are "public cases" or short anecdotes in which a Zen master of the past has an encounter with a disciple that is considered a profound expression of the master's awakened mind. Many *kōans* depict the moment at which a disciple attains an awakening stimulated by the words or actions of the master. *Kōans* are notoriously difficult to understand and often contain cryptic utterances or startling acts that appear to defy reason and common sense. They are used in Zen meditation as contemplative problems, the solution of which yields a glimpse of awakening. The following are a few well-known *kōans*:

> A monk once asked master Jōshu, "Has a dog Buddha-nature?" Jōshu said "*Mu*!" ("no" or "nothing" in Japanese).
>
> Once a monk made a request of Jōshu. "I have just entered the monastery," he said. "Please give me instructions, Master." Jōshu said, "Have you had your breakfast?" "Yes, I have," replied the monk. "Then," said Jōshu, "wash your bowls." The monk had an insight.
>
> A monk once asked Jōshu, "What is the meaning of the Patriarch's [Bodhidharma's] coming from the west?" Jōshu answered, "The oak tree in the front garden."
>
> Hakuin said, "Two hands clap and there is a sound. Now what is the sound of one hand clapping?"
>
> (from the *Mumonkan*)

Hundreds of *kōans*, along with numerous commentaries, make up *kōan* literature. If monastic practitioners take up *kōan* practice, they meditate on a single *kōan*, regularly conferring with the master and presenting him or her with answers in a formal meeting (*dokusan*). Attempts to intellectualize or answer in terms of systematic philosophy are rejected, and students are pushed until they can demonstrate that they have overcome dualistic thinking with regard to the *kōan*. At this point, they have "passed" and may move on to another *kōan*. Discerning the answer to a *kōan* is often accompanied by *kenshō* or *satori*, a glimpse of awakening in which the practitioner overcomes the sense of separation between him or herself and the object of thought, namely the *kōan* or its subject matter. This insight into the non-duality of subject and object is then broadened to include all possible objects, culminating in an experience of a cosmic unity transcending all binary oppositions, yet paradoxically maintaining the distinctiveness of individual things.

Although many contemporary interpreters of the *kōan* emphasize its role in moving the mind toward a trans-rational and non-linguistic state, *kōan* practice involves textual study and intellectual understanding as well. Moreover, most *kōans* do have discernable cognitive content. The *kōans* quoted above, for example, present the doctrine of non-duality in evocative and dramatic ways. The sound of two hands clapping represents familiar dualism, while the one hand suggests the elusive non-dual reality. The monk's famous question to Jōshu about the dog having Buddha-nature is one of many either/or questions (does the dog have it or not?) that make up the first part of some *kōans*, followed by a response that, rather than answering, deflects or "unasks" the question, gesturing beyond the binary opposition – in this case the master yells "*Mu!*" (Ch. "*Wu*") in a way that simulates the sound of a dog barking. Other *kōans* point to ordinary things or activities like an oak tree or washing bowls, implying that full attention to one thing can bring about awakening. While historically both major schools of Zen, Rinzai and Sōtō, have employed *kōan* practice, today it is much more common in the former, while the latter emphasizes *shikantaza*.

Finally, Zen meditation in the modern world, like other forms of Buddhist meditation, has taken an unprecedented twist. Formerly the province of cloistered monks, it has taken on a life of its own among the middle class, both in Asia and the West. Japanese companies sometimes take their employees to monasteries for short retreats, and Zen "centers" that teach *zazen* to people who are not monks and may not even be Buddhists are increasingly common in North America and Europe. Zen meditation has been extrapolated from its monastic context and placed into very different arenas, including therapeutic psychology and even Christian monasticism. Meanwhile more traditional monasteries still train monks in the rigors of meditation for those who want to become temple priests or those few who aspire to live the monastic life indefinitely.

See also: **Chan; Huineng; *Kōan*; Meditation traditions, Vajrayāna; Meditational systems; *Zazen*; Zen.**

David L. McMahan

MEDITATION, MODERN MOVEMENTS

Throughout most of the history of Buddhism, monastics have been the primary practitioners of meditation. While laypeople were not prohibited, most traditions have considered engaging in serious meditation too challenging while maintaining the householder life. In various monastic curricula, serious meditation often involves arduous personal training and takes considerable time. Although many Mahāyāna *sūtras* describe lay Buddhists who are also masters of meditation, most historical evidence suggests serious lay meditation has been the exception. Modern ethnography indicates that even meditation in the monastery is not nearly as common as might be expected, given the prominence of meditation in Buddhist literature. In recent history, monastic specialization in scholarship has been more common, and often only a minority of monastics engage in sustained meditation practice.

Yet, a countervailing trend exists in some modern forms of Buddhism. Revitalization movements throughout Asia and the West have placed a renewed emphasis on meditation. These movements, beginning in the late nineteenth century, stress the rationalistic elements of Buddhism and de-emphasize ritual, devotional elements, and "folk" elements. They draw upon Western philosophy and psychology, which have been persistent influences on the development of Buddhist thought and practice for over a century. These influences have significantly shaped the perception and practice of meditation. Some of the most prominent Buddhists of the twentieth century have suggested that meditation is in some respects detachable from the Buddhist tradition and beneficial outside the context of Buddhism. While not necessarily retreating from the soteriological value of meditation, authors like D.T. Suzuki, Shunryu Suzuki, the Fourteenth Dalai Lama, and Thich Nhat Hanh also present it as a technique conducive to psychological health, peace of mind, and ethical cultivation in no way restricted to monastics or even Buddhists. Thus, while the practice of most lay Buddhists throughout the world still consists of rituals for gaining karmic merit, a growing number of educated middle-class men and women in Asia and the West are taking up Buddhist meditation, not as a part of a renunciate life oriented toward transcending rebirth, but as a means toward greater psychological and spiritual well-being in lay life.

Western Buddhists and Buddhist sympathizers have been perhaps the most forthright in their willingness to extract meditation from the larger doctrinal and praxiological frameworks of Buddhism and use it as a technique for fostering peace of mind in a complex and frenetic world. Yet lay meditation is also an important phenomenon in modernized forms of Asian Buddhism. In Sri Lanka, for example, "meditation centers" have sprung up where people can take classes, go to weekly sessions, and attend occasional retreats. Such centers are neither traditional temples nor monasteries, but incorporate elements of both and add a central focus on meditation for the laity.

A number of new Buddhist movements, or novel variants, with this focus on meditation emerged in the twentieth century. Mahāsī Sayadaw and other Burmese teachers created what would become known as the Vipassana (Pāli *vipassanā*, Skt. *vipaśyanā*), or Insight Meditation movement, which is very now popular in parts of South and Southeast Asia, North America, and Western Europe. The movement takes the *Sūtra on the Foundations of Mindfulness* (*Satipaṭṭhāna Sutta*) as its central text and de-emphasizes ritual, liturgical, and merit-making elements common in Theravāda Buddhism. Americans who have studied with Burmese and other Southeast Asian teachers, especially Joseph Goldstein and Jack Kornfield, have made the Vipassana movement especially popular in North America. They have founded meditation and study centers, most notably Spirit Rock Meditation Center, in California, and the Insight Meditation Center, in Massachusetts, both of which offer meditation classes, retreats, and courses on Buddhist teachings. These organizations focus primarily on meditation practice and philosophical teaching, presenting Buddhism as a meditation-based form of spirituality. Their practices contain few traditional rituals, and while they do not neglect Buddhist ethical concerns, they interpret them liberally and adapt them to liberal Western mores. Many smaller insight meditation centers have emerged across North America and Western

Europe with a similar style, along with small, grass-roots "*sanghas*" practicing *vipassanā* on their own without a teacher – something quite foreign to Asian Buddhism. A number of more traditional Theravāda temples serving immigrants from Sri Lanka, Cambodia, Thailand, and other Southeast Asian countries also offer meditation instruction. While the North American meditation centers cater primarily to middle-class European Americans, some also have monks in residence and offer monastic retreats. Moreover, some more traditional temples serving primarily immigrant populations offer "Western-style" meditation classes.

Zen offers another example of tradition and change in approaches to meditation. While the core of Zen meditation practice in Japan remains the monastery, the tradition makes meditation available to laypeople in a variety of ways. The majority of monks at the monastery are there for training, staying between six months and three years before becoming priests of temples. *Zazen* is an important part of their training, comprising between four and seven hours of their day, and considerably more during *sesshins*, intensive meditation sessions lasting between three and seven days. Meditation also extends beyond formal *zazen*. In monasteries, practitioners are expected to make no distinction between formal meditation and ordinary activities such as bathing, eating, and working. All such activities are heavily ritualized and done with the same reverence and mindfulness as *zazen*. Serious lay practitioners are often allowed to practice at monasteries alongside monks. Some lay practitioners may even stay longer and advance further than the monks. Monasteries make retreats available to employees of corporations, as well, training them in the rigorous discipline that, it is hoped, will transfer to the workplace. A small number of Zen temples, which are distinct from monasteries, offer meditation classes to the public, although the primary service of temple priests is to officiate at calendrical ceremonies and funerals.

In recent decades, Zen meditation has ventured outside the monastery in ways paralleling the emergence of the Vipassana movement. Novel approaches to meditation have been fostered by popular literature on Zen. D.T. Suzuki's highly influential books present Zen as a pure, unmediated encounter with ultimate reality, and the spontaneous living in harmony with that reality. This reality, he claimed, transcends all cultural specificity and, therefore, is not uniquely Buddhist, although he suggested that it achieved its highest expression in Japanese culture. This idea that the goal of meditation was not unique to Buddhism invited the techniques of meditation themselves to be understood as detachable from the complex traditions of ritual, liturgy, priesthood, and hierarchy common in institutional Zen settings. Today, therefore, Zen meditation tends to float more freely across a number of cultures and subcultures, particularly in the West, where Zen meditation centers – again, neither monasteries nor traditional temples – flourish, and grass-roots Zen groups with little or no institutional affiliation meet in homes, colleges, and churches.

Parallels to these laicizing trends in Zen and Theravāda exist in Tibetan Buddhism as well, as Tibetan forms of meditation have rather abruptly gone from being undertaken by a small minority of monks in institutional settings to being offered widely to the public in countries all over the globe. A proliferation of diaspora teachers in India, Europe, and North America now teach meditation to monks and laity alike. Perhaps the most notable change – in presentation if not technique – is that instructions in what were once considered esoteric and advanced practices reserved for monks are now offered liberally to laity through classes and books. Some Tibetan teachers in exile have also been innovators in adapting meditation to modern, secular lifestyles. Chögyam Trungpa's Shambhala training is a popular example, offering methods of mind training stripped of many of the traditional rituals surrounding meditation in institutional contexts.

The separation of meditation from traditional ethical, praxiological, institutional, and doctrinal contexts of Buddhist traditions has been fostered by the proliferation of popular books on Buddhism. The last few decades have seen an explosion of popular Buddhist writings, especially in Western languages. Written both by monks and by lay teachers, many of these works contain detailed meditation instructions that, despite frequent caveats, suggest that meditation can be learned from books and practiced individually. Not surprisingly, this has led to the adaptation of Buddhist meditation techniques in a variety of non-Buddhist settings. Psychotherapists and physicians have begun employing them for stress reduction, lowering of blood-pressure, pain management, and cancer treatment. Today Buddhist and Buddhist-derived meditation is taught in prisons, hospitals, and schools, less for the purpose of achieving enlightenment than for coping with stress and health issues or for living a happier and more fulfilling life.

See also: **Meditation, visualization; Meditation in the Pāli Canon and the Theravāda tradition; Meditation in the *Visuddhimagga*; Meditation traditions, Vajrayāna; Meditational systems; *Śamatha*; South and Southeast Asia, Buddhism in; *Vipaśyanā*.**

DAVID L. MCMAHAN

MEDITATION, VISUALIZATION

A number of meditation practices in Buddhist traditions involve training the visual imagination to produce, control, and manipulate mental imagery. These may be as simple as envisioning a plain clay disk or as complex as visualizing a large and elaborate *maṇḍala* with lavish scenery and many Buddhas and *bodhisattvas*. Although visualization meditation is usually associated with the Mahāyāna and Vajrayāna traditions, it has roots in Theravāda meditation practices that make use of the visual imagination in order to develop the meditator's concentration. Examples include contemplation of external objects or "supports" (*kasiṇas*), devices for training the mind in calm concentration; these include the earth *kasiṇa* (in the form of a clay disc), blue *kasiṇa* (in the form of a basket of blue flowers), light *kasiṇa* (a circle of light on a wall), and others. After contemplating these external objects, the practitioner is instructed to visualize them to develop the ability to manipulate the image, for instance reducing or expanding it in size and maintaining the image with eyes open or closed (*Visuddhimagga* 4).

While rudimentary aspects of visualization are present in Pāli literature, it was the Mahāyāna schools that developed a new genre of meditation practice involving visualization of Buddhas and *bodhisattvas.* Such practices must be seen within the context of the visionary devotionalism (*bhakti*) that infused Buddhism around the time of the development of the Mahāyāna. Another factor is the apparent cleft in early Buddhist communities between emphasis on doctrine (*Dharma*) and emphasis on "seeing" (*darśana*) associated with devotion. Most surviving literature by and for Theravāda monastics stresses the teachings of the Buddha, or the "body of doctrine" (*dharmakāya*), rather than the physical body of the Buddha (*rūpakāya*) and discourages worshipful efforts to evoke the continuing presence of the post-*parinirvāṇa* Buddha. Yet traditions developed that extolled worship of the Buddha as a continuing living presence. Devotional movements, therefore, became a crucial aspect of many Buddhist traditions in India and beyond, and visualization practices were an important feature of these movements.

Most visualization practices are variations on the practice of "recollection of the Buddha" (*buddhānusmṛti*). In Theravāda literature this practice highlights the Buddha's life and teachings, his wisdom and noble characteristics. Mahāyāna literature, while not excluding these, also emphasizes the exquisite physical appearance of the Buddha and his surroundings. Moreover, the subject of these contemplations is not only Gautama Buddha but others in the expanding pantheon of buddhas and *bodhisattvas* – Amitābha, Akṣobhya, Maitreya, Avalokiteśvara, and Manjuśrī.

The *Pratyutpanna Sūtra* is one text illustrative of such practices. It instructs the practitioner to go to a secluded place and concentrate on the Buddha Amitābha constantly for up to seven days and nights until his image is continually before the meditator; then, the *sūtra* asserts, Amitābha will appear to the meditator as clearly as if an ordinary person were standing there. Having obtained such a vision, the practitioner may then worship and receive teachings from him. In the *Sūtra on the Contemplation of Amitāyus* (*Amitāyurdhyāna Sūtra*), those who visualize Amitābha (or Amitāyus) in his pure land and follow the moral precepts increase in faith and merit and, upon death, will see Amitābha standing before them, whereupon he will lead them directly to rebirth in his pure land. The clarity and substantiality of the vision depend on the degree of faith and upon the degree of success with which one has been able to perform the complex visualization. The *Smaller Sukhāvatīvyūha Sūtra*, perhaps recognizing the difficulty for some in performing detailed visualizations, claims that a devotee can obtain rebirth in the pure land simply by invoking the name of Amitābha, a practice that has become widespread among Pure Land Buddhists and continues throughout East Asia today.

Visualization meditation combines a number of meditative and devotional practices: first the concentration and visualization capacities that are encouraged in many Buddhist meditation texts; second, practices intended to influence the place in which one is reborn; and third, devotional practices (*pūjā*) popular across India (and later, across much of Asia) from before the Common Era until today. These consist of approaching a representation of a deity (in this case, a mental image – a kind of internal icon), "seeing and being seen" by the deity (the widespread practice of "taking *darśan*"), and worshiping the deity by making offerings and prayers. These practices and their associated texts became the basis of the very important and influential Pure Land schools of Buddhism which have flourished in many parts of the Buddhist world, especially in East Asia. Visualization meditations were not, however, exclusive to these schools, and practitioners from other Buddhist traditions regularly employed them.

What exactly are devotees of Amitābha and other Buddhas and *bodhisattvas* visualizing when they perform these meditations? The Pure Land *sūtras* give detailed descriptions of Amitābha in his pure land, and many Mahāyāna *sūtras* present accounts of ordinary scenes transformed into purified "Buddha-fields" (*buddhakṣetras*) through the power of the Buddha as he is about to deliver a discourse. At the beginning of the *Gaṇḍavyūha Sūtra*, for example, the park pavilion in which Gautama Buddha is sitting suddenly becomes boundlessly vast, encompassing and making visible the whole universe with its many world systems. The trees are filled with jewels, the pavilion becomes an immense palace, beautiful mountains spring up all around, celestial beings appear in the air, and the Buddhas of other worlds come and array themselves in a circle around Gautama.

Such scenes became fairly standard in Mahāyāna *sūtras*. In the *Amitāyurdhyāna Sūtra*, these resplendent visions become the basis for visualization meditation. This text describes the Pure Land, clearly based on royal palatial imagery, in detail: it has splendid architecture with buildings made of precious stones; its lotus pools are strewn with golden sand and contain immense blooms of many colors; showers of divine blossoms fall throughout the day and night so that devotees can make countless offerings to millions of Buddhas; the land is filled with peacocks and other beautiful birds. It is a lush and lavish paradise with no suffering, no hell-realms, and countless opportunities to hear the *Dharma*. The text also instructs the meditator to visualize Amitābha himself, describing his beautiful physical characteristics in rich detail, along with those of the attending *bodhisattvas* surrounding him. These vivid descriptions are not simply presented as "information" about a far-off place but also as images to be contemplated. Such scenes of Buddhas in their pure lands surrounded by a retinue of other Buddhas and *bodhisattvas* serve as models for the great traditions of *maṇḍalas* art of the Mahāyāna and Vajrayāna, which brings us to the next phase in the development of visualization meditation.

Visualization practice comes to a climax in Vajrayāna, or *Tantric* Buddhism, which carries the practices already mentioned one step further – the identification of the practitioner with the visualized deity. Among the variegated features of the *Tantras* (Vajrayāna scriptures) are visualization practices (*sādhanas* – lit. "means of accomplishment") in which the practitioner evokes a *maṇḍala* and, through the imagination, merges with the primary deity of the image. After preliminary practices such as purification rituals, chanting of syllables, confessions of sins, and dedication of the merit of the practice to all living beings, the practitioner begins the "generation stage" by cultivating an image of the deity in detail. *Sādhana* instructions take care to describe the visual appearance of the figure, often in great detail, including descriptions of clothing, jewelry, facial expressions, and any symbolic implements held in the hands. Some practices instruct the meditator to maintain this complex image for an extended period of time, or to manipulate it in various ways, such as reducing it to the size of a drop or expanding it to envelop the entire cosmos. The culmination of the practice is the "completion stage," the identification of the practitioner with the deity, either through "entering" the *maṇḍala* and merging with the deity or envisioning him or herself at the outset as the deity. This involves cultivating, as well, a sense of "divine pride" (*māna*), the sense that one actually *is* the deity one is envisioning. Finally the *maṇḍala* is dissolved and the practitioner is left with a sense of unity with the deity.

Such practices are clearly attempts not only to construct a world as seen by the Buddhas but also to access that vision and become a Buddha by appropriating a Buddha's vision of things. In this sense Tantric *sādhanas* could be considered ritual re-enactments of the visionary episodes recounted in the visionary Mahāyāna *sūtras*, and attempts to see them from a Buddha's perspective.

See also: **Meditation, modern movements; Meditation in the Pāli Canon and the Theravāda tradition; Meditation in the *Visuddhimagga*; Meditation traditions, Vajrayāna; Meditational systems; *Sādhana*; *Śamatha*; *Vipaśyanā*.**

DAVID L. MCMAHAN

MEDITATION IN THE PĀLI CANON AND THE THERAVĀDA TRADITION

The practice of meditation occupies an important place in the literature of the

Theravāda tradition. The definitive outline of Buddhist life, the Noble Eightfold Path, is divided into three parts: wisdom, ethics, and meditation (*samādhi*), the latter of which includes right effort, right mindfulness, and right concentration. Thus Pāli literature presents meditation as an integral and essential part of Buddhist life and a necessary condition for achieving *nirvāṇa*. The treatments of meditation found in Pāli literature reflect early Buddhist meditation as it was understood by monastics in Buddhist India and Sri Lanka, not only of the Theravāda school but also the other schools (*nikāyas*) of non-Mahāyāna Buddhism.

The Pāli Canon contains some of the definitive formulations of basic meditation techniques that Buddhists in Theravāda traditions continue to practice today. Perhaps one of the most important *sūtras* on meditation is the *Sūtra on the Foundations of Mindfulness* (*Majjhima Nikāya* 1.55). The concept of mindfulness (Pāli *sati*, Skt. *smṛti*) is essential to all Buddhist meditation practice, denoting focused attention to whatever activity in which one is engaged. Meditation literature presents mindfulness both as a prerequisite and an essential aspect of virtually all forms of meditation, and an instrument of penetrating through false concepts to see things as they are. The four foundations of mindfulness are presented as "contemplating the body *as* a body, ardent, fully aware, and mindful," and likewise the feelings (*vedanā*) as feelings, the mind as mind, and the objects of mind as objects of mind. The implication is that in a non-mindful condition one does not see these things as they are. Within each of these four foundations are a number of specific objects of meditation. Mindfulness of the body, for example, includes mindfulness of the breath, in which the practitioner observes the continuous flow of the breath in and out, noting the length of breaths and thereby bringing about the gradual calming of the body. Other meditations on the body include mindfulness of various physical postures (sitting, standing, walking, lying down), movements of the body, the bodily parts (both internal and external), the elements (earth, water, fire, air), and the corpse in various stages of decomposition (for evoking the truth of impermanence, the repugnance of the body, and the inevitability of death). Mindfulness of feelings includes pleasant, painful, or neutral feelings. Mindfulness of the mind itself includes the contemplation of the mind's states when affected or unaffected by desire, hatred, and delusion, and in a state of focused contraction or distraction. Mindfulness of the objects of mind includes contemplation of the "five hindrances" to entering meditative states: sensual desire, aversion, sloth and torpor, restlessness and worry, and doubt. Other objects of mind include the five aggregates, the six sense bases, the seven factors of awakening, and the four noble truths – all important elements of Buddhist doctrine to be considered in the meditative state. The practitioner is supposed to maintain a calm but alert focus on these various objects of mindfulness, noting them but not trying to suppress them. The implication is that seeing all of these "as they are" will lessen clinging to them, allow the mind to transcend its entanglement with destructive states, and facilitate more productive states that naturally to move the practitioner toward greater insight. The fruits of this meditation are said to be nothing less than the possibility of "final knowledge here and now."

Other important elements of meditation in the Pāli corpus are the *jhānas* (Skt. *dhyānas*) – highly refined states of focused awareness in which attention is completely absorbed in its object. The *jhānas* are a succession of states, each more elevated than the last: (1) a state consisting of applied thought, discursive examination, happiness, joy, and one-pointed concentration; (2) the stilling of applied thought, while retaining discursive examination, happiness, joy, and one-pointed concentration; (3) the stilling of discursive examination while retaining happiness and joy, and the arising of equanimity and mindfulness; (4) a state of mindfulness and equanimity transcending pleasure and pain, joy and grief (*Majjhima Nikāya* 3.92). Beyond these are even more refined states of concentration that transcend all physical elements, the four "formless absorptions" (*arūpajhāna*): awareness of endless space, unlimited consciousness, nothingness, and neither perception nor non-perception. Some of the various accounts of stages of meditation include one beyond the *jhānas* – the "cessation of perception and feeling," a condition of deepest calm in which all cognitive processes are temporarily suspended. As elevated as these may appear, the *jhānas* are generally not considered ends in themselves and can even be sources of subtle attachment (*Majjhima Nikāya* 1.294ff., *Visuddhimagga* 18.16ff.).

As elevated as such states appear, the *jhānas* are not themselves sufficient to the attainment of awakening. They are deep states of calm and serenity attained through tranquility meditation (*samatha*, Skt. *śamatha*). Such techniques foster a profoundly restful state and refined concentration (*samādhi*) but are often presented as subordinate or preliminary to insight meditation (Pāli *vipassanā*, Skt. *vipaśyanā*), which comprises a wide variety of practices for seeing the various elements of existence as they truly are. Insight meditation aims at penetrating through the web of false conceptualizations (*maññita, papañca*) that cloud the mind in order to see the true nature of phenomena, particularly their impermanence (Pāli *anicca*, Skt. *anitya*), their lack of permanent and substantial selfhood (Pāli *anattā*, Skt. *anātman*), and the ways in which they cause suffering and dissatisfaction (Pāli *dukkha*, Skt. *duḥkha*). Having seen things in their true nature, the meditator no longer identifies with them or sees them as "me" or "mine," that is, related to a false sense of selfhood. The culmination of such insight is identical to the Buddha's own awakening, in which the practitioner recollects his or her own past lives and those of others, and comprehends the elimination of all *āsavas*, destructive states of being that bind one to *saṃsāra* (*Dīgha Nikāya* 1.74ff.).

By far the most comprehensive source for meditation instruction in the Pāli corpus is Buddhaghosa's fifth century CE *Path of Purification* (*Visuddhimagga*), a voluminous commentary on virtually all aspects of meditation found in the Pāli Canon. This is not only a manual of meditation but a commentary on many facets of the *Dharma*, primarily as it applies to monastic life. It addresses many preliminaries to meditation, such as withdrawal from society and the development of a strong moral basis, which is always a prerequisite for the serious practice of Buddhist meditation. One notable feature of the *Visuddhimagga* as it relates to meditation is its description and analysis of forty meditation subjects. They include thematic meditations such as recollections of the Buddha, his teachings, the community (*sangha*), and contemplations of various aspects of morality, elements of Buddhist doctrine, and the cultivation of beneficent attitudes toward others (*brahmavihāras*) – lovingkindness, compassion, sympathetic joy, and equanimity. Also included are contemplations on the body, for example, the breath, the various components the body, and the bodily functions, as well as contemplations of the human corpse mentioned above. Buddhaghosa says that different people in diverse circumstances are suited to various types of these meditations, though the cultivation of friendliness and awareness of death are beneficial to all. He also analyzes in detail the main elements of Buddhist doctrine, incorporating them finally into a complex map of the various conditions and stages of insight leading to enlightenment.

In modern and contemporary Theravāda communities monastic specialization in scholarship is more common, and in some respects more highly valued, than specialization in meditation. Thus until recently meditation was not especially emphasized in many of the lived traditions of Theravāda Buddhism, even among monastics. Modern reform movements, however, have revitalized meditation not only for monastics but also for the laity. In Theravāda countries, traditional lay "meditation" is quite simple, consisting of reciting Pāli verses – some of which are on meditation topics – at temples on holy days. In the past, the laity were, at most, encouraged to perform meditations on loving-kindness, the recollection of the Buddha, or the repulsiveness and transience of the body. In the twentieth century, however, there has been an increasing interest in meditation among the middle class. In addition to traditional temples, "meditation centers" have emerged, not only in Southeast Asia but increasingly in the West. These cater to individuals who learn meditation at the center then go home and practice on their own, something rather new to the Theravāda tradition. With this comes another novel shift: the idea of meditation as a means for helping lay people in their everyday lives rather than strictly as a means to enlightenment. One important figure in this new orientation is the Burmese monk Mahāsī Sayadaw, who helped popularize the new *Vipassanā* movement, which emphasizes techniques primarily based on the *Satipaṭṭhāna Sutta*. He and a number of Asian and Western teachers have spread this sub-tradition, which highlights meditation while de-emphasizing many traditional elements of Buddhism, throughout the globe. It is through this movement that at least a few of the meditation techniques found in the Theravāda tradition are now practiced throughout the world, not only by monks but by middle-class Thais, Singhalese, Burmese, Indians, Europeans, Australians, and Americans.

See also: **Buddhism in South and Southeast Asia; Meditation, modern movements; Meditation, visualization; Meditation in the *Visuddhimagga*; *Nikāya* Buddhism; *Śamatha*; *Vipaśyanā*.**

DAVID L. MCMAHAN

MEDITATION IN THE *VISUDDHIMAGGA*

Buddhaghosa's *Visuddhimagga*, or *Path of Purification*, is the most extensive and comprehensive work dealing with Buddhist meditation. Written in the fifth century CE, it is a wide-ranging commentary on the *Tripiṭaka* addressing many topics of the canon, but especially techniques of cultivating the mind and body in order to achieve purification and, ultimately, enlightenment.

Buddhaghosa insists in the *Visuddhimagga* that adherence to moral precepts, restraint, and seclusion are prerequisites for formal meditation. As the development of virtue is given special emphasis, the work develops many of the main ethical themes in Buddhism at the outset. The practice of meditation *per se* begins with techniques that foster concentration and calm the mind and body. Buddhaghosa gives forty subjects for contemplation to achieve this calm attentiveness, including contemplation of various mental states, physical functions, Buddhist doctrines, death, the three jewels (Buddha, *Dharma*, and *Sangha*), concentration on various external supports (*kasiṇas*), and cultivation of the *brahmavihāras*: lovingkindness, compassion, sympathetic joy, and equanimity. Buddhaghosa provides specific and detailed instructions for each practice, as well as explanations of their benefits. He also discusses the stages of intensive concentration (Pāli *jhāna*s, Skt. *dhyānas*) explicating their meaning, functions, and limitations. Such practices for developing a calm and concentrated mind are not sufficient for enlightenment, he insists, but are necessary preparation for practices designed to allow the mind to penetrate into the nature of reality.

Before discussing specific practices, Buddhaghosa provides theoretical explications of Buddhist doctrine in which the basic Buddhist categories of experience and existence are described, analyzed, and classified in relation to each other. Particular attention is given to the Four Noble Truths, dependent arising (*pratītya-samutpāda*), and cessation, a state in which all mental functions temporarily cease. This theoretical understanding is also not considered sufficient itself for attaining liberation but is important for gaining right understanding and the capacity to analyze experience in meditative states.

Buddhaghosa asserts that the many methods of concentration and the numerous facets of theoretical knowledge are preliminary to the most important aspect of purification and meditation, the practice of insight (Pāli *vipassanā*, Skt. *vipaśyanā*). For attaining insight, he lays out the "path of knowledge and vision" through which the practitioner sees that all things are impermanent, lacking a self or essence, and conducive to suffering and frustration. As the meditator obtains this insight with regard to all elements of conditioned existence, he or she develops, first, an aversion to all conditioned things, then a sense of equanimity toward them. From the full actualization of this equanimity, even-mindedness, purification of mind, and lack of grasping for permanence and satisfaction in that which cannot give satisfaction, the practitioner finally attains *nirvāṇa*.

See also: **Meditation, modern movements; Meditation, Visualization; Meditation in the Pāli Canon and the Theravāda tradition; Meditational systems; *Nikāya* Buddhism; *Śamatha*; South and Southeast Asia, Buddhism in; *Vipaśyanā*.**

DAVID L. MCMAHAN

MEDITATION TRADITIONS, VAJRAYĀNA

Vajrayāna, or *tantric*, meditation traditions developed in India in perhaps the sixth century and then moved to the Himalayan regions and East Asia, where they evolved particular practices and styles within these unique geographical and cultural areas. Tibetan *tantric* Buddhism and Japanese Shingon constitute the surviving Buddhist *tantric* movements today. Many Vajrayāna schools utilize meditation techniques common to the Theravāda and Mahāyāna, such as tranquility meditation (*śamatha*), insight meditations (*vipaśyanā*), meditations on loving-kindness (*mettā*) and contemplation of death. Vajrayāna, however, has meditation practices specific to it, many of which are contained in the *Tantras* – scriptures unique to this esoteric form of Buddhism. These are elaborate ritual-meditative practices (*sādhanas* – lit. "means of accomplishment") in which the meditators attempt to attain enlightenment by identifying their body, speech, and mind with those of a chosen Buddha or *bodhisattva*. *Tantras* contain, among other things such as magical and ritual practices), *sādhanas* for a great number of deities. In the Tibetan collection of *Tantras*, those classified as Yoga *Tantras* and Highest Yoga *Tantras* (*anuttarayogatantra*) contain the visualization meditations unique to Vajrayāna Buddhism. The Shingon tradition of esoteric Buddhism in Japan relies heavily on the *Mahāvairocana Sūtra*, which depicts the Buddha Mahāvairocana as the cosmic Buddha and the underlying reality encompassing the universe. Some of the contemplation practices of the Vajrayāna contain elements of popular tradition, are highly ritualized, and may contain sophisticated adaptations of pre-Buddhist shamanic practices.

Engaging in *tantric sādhana* invariably requires instruction from a teacher (Skt. *guru*, Tib. *bla ma* [*lama*]) who functions as a guide, initiates the student into progressively higher levels of practice, and even serves in some practices as an object of devotional meditation. Such initiations can be extensive and are meant to ensure the sincerity and purity of the practitioner's motivations and prevent meditators from engaging in practices beyond their capabilities and training. Initiations, or "empowerments" (*abhiṣeka*), are also meant to establish a connection between the practitioner and the chosen Buddha or *bodhisattva*. This deity is often selected by the teacher to suit the practitioner's particular character, and although practitioners have a main tutelary deity, many are initiated into *sādhanas* with other deities as well. The deity has associated *mantras*, ritual verbal formulas, believed to contain and evoke the power of a particular deity, for example, *oṃ maṇi padme huṃ* – "Oṃ, the jewel in the lotus, hail" – the *mantra* of Avalokiteśvara, the *bodhisattva* of compassion. *Mantras* may have some decipherable cognitive content or may be a string of syllables with no particular discursive meaning. Their purpose is not to convey information about a deity, but to embody the deity's power, generate merit for the reciter, and serve as a kind of verbal icon for worship, as well as a device to stabilize and concentrate the mind. *Sādhanas* also utilize hand gestures (*mudrās*) associated with particular deities, believed to attune the body of the practitioner with that of the deity.

Another crucial element of *tantric sādhanas*, particularly in Indian and Tibetan traditions, is visualization of deities. While Pure Land traditions employ visualization techniques, these practices are understood primarily as a means to rebirth in the pure land. *Sādhanas* of the Highest Yoga *Tantras*, however, aim at identifying the practitioner with the Buddha or *bodhisattva* and removing the distinction between them such that the practitioner *becomes* – at least in a symbolic manner – the deity. One of the primary tools for this transformation is the *maṇḍala* (lit. "circle"), a complex image of a Buddha or *bodhisattva*, a retinue of surrounding Buddhas and *bodhisattvas*, and the Buddha-field in which the beings reside. *Maṇḍalas* are not exclusive to Vajrayāna, but it is in *tantric* traditions that they achieved their most intricate development in terms of both iconography and use. Vajrayāna *maṇḍalas* often include the representation of a palace, a central deity, and other enlightened beings arranged directionally around the central figure. While *maṇḍalas* are often physical representations – paintings on walls or parchment, three-dimensional sculptures, or temporary constructions made of sand or chalk – within the context of some *sādhanas* they are also consciously and meticulously created images developed and sustained in the imagination of the meditator. During the *sādhana*, a meditator might gradually put together parts of the complex image, piece by piece, in the imagination while chanting *mantras* and making *mudrās* associated with each part of the image. Utilizing gesture, vocalization, and concentration in this respect, the meditator attempts to identify with the body, speech, and mind of the deity. *Tantric* practitioners believe that this is a faster way to enlightenment than the more conventional meditation practices found in "Hīnayāna" and Mahāyāna *sūtras*.

While *sādhanas* vary in their steps and complexity, most follow a general pattern. After preliminary practices such as purification rituals, chanting of syllables, confession of sins, and dedication of the merit of the practice to all living beings, the practitioner begins the "generation stage" (*utpattikrama*) by cultivating an internal image of the deity, intoning *mantras*, and making *mudrās*. Many *sādhana* instructions take care to describe the visual appearance of the figure in detail, including descriptions of clothing, jewelry, facial expressions, and symbolic implements held in the hands. All of these form a visual vocabulary charged with symbolic significance. Some practices instruct the meditator to maintain this complex image for an extended period of time or to manipulate it in various ways, such as reducing it to the size of a drop or expanding it to envelop the entire cosmos. The culmination of the practice is the "completion stage" (*nispannakrama*), the identification of the practitioner with the deity, either through "entering" the *maṇḍalas* and seeing him or herself as the central deity or envisioning him or herself at the outset as the deity (thus depending on the particular practice, the *sādhana* can be interpreted either as either a means of transformation into the deity or a ritual enactment of the fact that the practitioner is *already* one with the deity). At the conclusion of the practice, the entire *maṇḍala* is dissolved into emptiness. The tantric *sādhana* is, therefore, the imaginative reconstruction of reality as an exalted, symbol-laden world seen from the perspective of an awakened being, and a ritual-meditative re-construction of the self *as* that awakened being.

While such ritual-meditation practices clearly have a strong psychological component, there is also a crucial physiological element. The Highest Yoga *Tantras* contain a complex understanding of "subtle physiology" vital to the advanced practices of deity yoga. Within the body are believed to be three main channels (*nāḍīs*) and thousands of subsidiary veins through which life-energy (Skt. *prāṇa*, Tib. *rlung*) flows. In some *sādhanas* control of this flow of subtle energy is an essential part of the completion stage. The goal of this control is bringing the life-energy into the central channel and raising it up through each energy circle (*cakra*) along the spine until it reaches the crown of the head. This is essentially a way of simulating death, as it is a process through which the energies gradually dissipate and subtler and subtler levels of consciousness emerge, culminating in the emergence of the "mind of clear light," a pure, primordial consciousness that survives death.

The Highest Yoga *Tantras* assert that *sādhana*, at the highest level, involves sexual practices with a partner. Although not widely practiced today, a number of *Tantras* assert the necessity of practicing sexual yoga at least once in order to attain liberation. Although unorthodox, these practices simply extend the logic of the solitary *sādhana*. In sexual yoga, the practitioner and the practitioner's partner are each envisioned as specific deities, and their union produces a state of bliss in which the superficial levels of mind fall away and one is left with the primordial mind of clear light. Such practices are also ways of worshiping and making offerings to deities and contain devotional elements co-mingled with sexual acts. Most *tantric* literature insists that such practices are not performed for the sake of physical pleasure but as means to controlling the subtle energies intimately linked with both sexuality and consciousness. The union is also symbolically significant, representing the union of opposites, the overcoming of duality, and the merging of skillful means (*upāya*, represented by the male) and wisdom (*prajñā*, represented by the female). Overcoming duality is a key feature of the Mahāyāna philosophy of emptiness (*śūnyatā*), which emphasizes the lack of inherent existence in all phenomena and the ultimate non-duality of mind and object, perceiver and perceived. This idea is extrapolated and applied to *tantric sādhanas* such that the practitioner attempts to transcend the binary oppositions of self and deity, skillful means and wisdom, meditator and object of meditation. It also is implicit in some of the antinomian practices of tantric Buddhists who attempt, in a controlled ritual context, to subvert the distinctions between pure and impure with regard not only to sexual practices but also to food, ingesting meat, fish, aphrodisiacs, and other prohibited substances. Sexual yoga and other antinomian practices can also be performed in thc imagination with *maṇḍalas* representing the sexual union of male and female deities. This alternative to the physical performance of such practices is an important reason that *tantra* has flourished in Himalayan areas as a mainstream tradition without posing a threat to traditional morality.

See also: **Meditation, modern movements; Meditation, visualization; Meditational systems; *Sādhana*; *Śamatha*; *Vipaśyanā*.**

DAVID L. MCMAHAN

MEDITATIONAL SYSTEMS

Buddhist meditation comprises a wide variety of techniques designed to produce heightened states of concentration and awareness that lead to knowledge, wisdom, and liberation. While each technique has a particular immediate goal – for example calming the mind, developing deeper insight into Buddhist doctrines, developing compassion, or controlling destructive mental states – the over-arching goal is to achieve wisdom (*prajñā*) and see things "as they are" (*yathābhūta*), which leads to awakening (*bodhi*). Although a great deal of literature on meditation exists, Buddhist traditions have always maintained that such practices must be learned from a teacher. Buddhist literature presents meditation or concentration (*samādhi*) as one of the Three Trainings that make up the path to liberation. While mindfulness and meditation are parts of the Eightfold Path that all Buddhists ostensibly follow, meditation instruction in premodern Buddhist literature was written primarily by and for monastics, and in practice meditation has generally been their province. In most eras, few members of the laity practiced rigorous meditation, although Buddhist modernization movements in both Asia and the West now advocate meditation for laity as well as monastics (see below).

Buddhist meditation techniques have their roots in the wide variety of disciplines and traditions of self-cultivation pre-dating the emergence of the Buddhist tradition. During the time of Gautama Buddha a number of movements arose that rejected the dominant religious culture, often called Brahmāṇism, which revolved around Vedic sacrificial ritual and the Brahmin priests who were empowered to perform them. Members of these movements, who called themselves "strivers" (*śramaṇas*), questioned the efficacy of Vedic ritual, rejected material wealth, and were suspicious of the fleeting pleasures of social status, family, and work. *Śramaṇas* were of many different philosophical positions: from ancient Indian versions of materialism, determinism, and hedonism, to renunciate movements that still maintained elements of Vedic orthodoxy or who were followers of Upaniṣadic doctrine. Many saw life as transient and full of suffering and longed for transcendence. Meditation, along with ascetic lifestyles and sometimes extreme austerities, developed among these groups, which were considered important means toward transcending the suffering of the world and achieving higher states of consciousness. Concern with the altered states of consciousness in order to gain spiritual knowledge, however, did not begin with Buddhism or the even the *śramaṇas*. It can be seen quite early in the use of *soma*, a mind-altering substance used in certain Vedic rituals. Techniques for altering consciousness were an important part of the yoga tradition as well, which developed alongside Buddhism but within the Brahmāṇical orthodoxy and may have had ancient, pre-Buddhist origins. Although the many ascetic movements of the time of the Buddha had divergent views, all shared the notion that developing the powers of concentration and refining consciousness could lead to truer knowledge and liberation from suffering and bondage.

Meditation in *Nikāya* Buddhist literature

No one term in Buddhist source languages translates directly to the English term "meditation." Perhaps the most general term is *bhāvanā*, which means "cultivation" – in this case, cultivation of particular states of consciousness. The most important terms related to meditation that go back to early sources are *smṛti* (Pāli *sati*), *śamatha* (Pāli *samatha*), and *vipaśyanā* (Pāli *vipassanā*). Mindfulness (*smṛti*), the seventh constituent of the Eightfold Path, is the heightened attention necessary to all forms of meditation, and indeed, for a successful life according to Buddhist principles. Virtually all formal meditation practices involve mindfulness, and numerous *sūtras* implore monks to extend it beyond formal meditation to daily activities. Buddhist meditation literature presents mindfulness as the key to seeing things as they are, without delusion, greed, or hatred. The *Sutra on Foundations of Mindfulness* (*Satipaṭṭhāna Sutta*, *Majjhima Nikāya* 1.55) gives detailed instructions on mindfulness meditation. The four foundations of mindfulness are mindfulness of the body, feelings, mind, and objects of mind. Included in the first are exercises devoted to attending to the breath, bodily postures, the various activities of the body, the impurity of the body, and its inevitable decay. The *sūtra* also gives instructions on the contemplation of feelings, mind, and objects of mind, the latter of which entail focused meditations on key elements of Buddhist doctrine.

Śamatha, or tranquility meditation, is meant to foster quietude and one-pointed concentration (*samādhi*) in which discursive thought is brought to a minimum or eliminated. The most common of these meditations is mindfulness of breathing. The simplest form is the silent counting of breaths, from one to ten, then back to one, focusing on the sensation of the air at the tip of the nostrils or the abdomen as it moves in and out. Gradually the meditator is able to keep the mind from wandering, maintaining attention on the breath and nothing else and thereby attaining calm concentration (*Visuddhimagga* 7.190–5). In the *Sūtra on Mindfulness of Breathing* (*Anāpānasati Sutta*, *Majjhima Nikāya* 3.78), the practitioner is instructed to go to a quiet place, sit erect with legs crossed, and concentrate on a variety of sensations, feelings, and thoughts, each connected to the in and out flow of the breath. Buddhaghosa, in his voluminous *Visuddhimagga*, lists other devices to train the mind in calm concentration, such as meditation on various supports (*kasiṇas*) such as earth (in the form of a clay disc), the color blue (in the form of a basket of blue flowers), or light (a circle of light on a wall). The meditator gazes at these devices until he or she achieves a steady, concentrated mind and can maintain the image in the mind's eye. Although this is a calm and tranquil state, it is described as a condition of relaxed alertness, avoiding either strain or dullness.

Tranquility meditation is conducive to achieving the *dhyānas* (Pāli *jhānas*), highly refined states of concentration in which attention is completely absorbed in its object. The *dhyānas* are a succession of states, each more elevated and refined than the last. They include: (1) a state consisting of applied thought, discursive examination, happiness, joy, and one-pointed concentration; (2) the stilling of applied thought, while retaining discursive examination, happiness, joy, and one-pointed concentration; (3) the stilling of discursive examination while retaining happiness and joy, and accompanied by the arising of equanimity and mindfulness; (4) a state of mindfulness and equanimity transcending pleasure and pain, joy and grief (*Majjhima Nikāya* 3.92). Beyond these are even more refined states of concentration that transcend all physical elements, the "formless absorptions" (*arūpadhyāna*): awareness of endless space, unlimited consciousness, nothingness, and neither perception nor non-perception. As elevated as these may appear, the *dhyānas* are not considered ends in themselves and can even be sources of subtle attachment. Accounts of stages of meditation beyond the *dhyānas* include the "cessation of perception and feeling," a condition of deepest calm in which all cognitive processes are temporarily suspended (*Majjhima Nikāya* 1.292ff.; *Visuddhimagga* 28.16ff.)

Pāli literature presents both the *dhyānas* and *śamatha* as preliminary to the cultivation of insight (*vipaśyanā*). Insight meditation includes a number of techniques designed to give the meditator greater understanding of all facets of existence, particularly their impermanence (*anitya*), their lack of selfhood (*anātman*), and the ways in which they cause suffering and dissatisfaction (*duḥkha*). It is, then, both a way of viewing the world in terms of Buddhist doctrine and of attempting to confirm that doctrine through close examination. Buddhaghosa lists forty subjects for meditation designed to develop the power of concentration, many of which, however, are typical of *vipaśyanā* (*Visuddhimagga* 3.105). They include thematic meditations such as recollections of the Buddha, various aspects of morality, elements of Buddhist doctrine, and the cultivation of beneficent attitudes toward others (*brahmavihāras*). Also among these thematic meditations are contemplations of the human corpse in various stages of decomposition, which foster a sense of the body's impermanence, the inevitability of death, and the futility of attachment to corporeality. Buddhaghosa says that different people in different circumstances are suited to different types of these meditations, though the cultivation of lovingkindness and awareness of death is beneficial to all.

Also notable are contemplations designed to decrease destructive emotions directed towards others, such as hatred, jealousy, and ill-will, and to foster compassionate states. These practices underscore the importance of positive regard for others as a part of the meditative path. The four "immeasurables" (*brahmavihāras*) are the proper attitudes towards others that a Buddhist should attempt to nurture – lovingkindness, compassion, sympathetic joy, and equanimity. Buddhaghosa gives detailed commentary on specific meditations to foster unlimited loving kindness (Pāli *mettā*, Skt. *maitrī*). One first contemplates the dangers of hatred and the advantages of patience, then cultivates loving kindness toward oneself, repeating, "May I be happy and free from suffering." The practitioner is then instructed to extend this natural feeling of wanting happiness, life, and lack of suffering for oneself to others, first a friend for whom it is easy to cultivate such positive regard, then a neutral person, then an enemy, then to the entirety of living beings (*Visuddhimagga* 9.1–76). Similar exercises obtain for developing the other immeasurables.

Canonical literature lists five hindrances to the cultivation of any meditation practice. These are deleterious reactions to the disciplined attempt at controlling and training the mind. First is sensual desire, in which the mind seeks something more interesting than the object of meditation. Second is aversion to the practice itself. Third is sloth and torpor, a state of lethargy and sleepiness. Fourth is restlessness and worry, in which the mind becomes overly excited by success and dismayed by failure. Fifth is doubt as to whether or not the practice is worthwhile. The "five factors of *dhyāna*" correspond to and counteract these hindrances: applied thought, examination, joy, happiness, one-pointedness of mind. These are precisely the factors present in the first *dhyāna*; therefore, the overcoming of the five hindrances is tantamount to entering into the first stage of intensive concentration.

Although meditation is clearly a technique for cultivating the mind, it has from its earliest development been connected as well with thaumaturgy. Much traditional Buddhist meditation literature asserts that meditation leads to the development of supernormal powers. While cautioning against attachment to them, cultivating them for their own sake, or using them as a subject of meditation, Buddhaghosa discusses many ways in which a meditator can cultivate them. Some of these abilities relate to contemplation of the *kasiṇas*; contemplation of the earth *kasiṇa*, for instance, allows the meditator to gain control of earth, that is, solidity, such that he or she can walk through walls or manifest the appearance of solid objects. Mastery of contemplation of the water *kasiṇa* allows one to dive into earth as if it were water, cause rainstorms, and manifest bodies of water. Use of the light *kasiṇa* allows one to create luminous appearances (*Visuddhimagga* 4.28ff). The most common supernormal powers discussed in the Pāli literature are the "higher forms of knowledge" (Pāli *abhiññā*, Skt. *abhijñā*), which the meditator can develop in the fourth *dhyāna*. The first consists of various forms of psychokinesis such as the ability to walk on water, fly in the air, and manifest "mind-made bodies" (*manomayakāya*). The second and third forms of higher knowledge are the ability to hear things at a great distance and the capacity to read another's thoughts. The last two recapitulate capacities constitutive of the Buddha's awakening – the abilities to discern all of one's own past lives and those of other beings.

Meditation in Mahāyāna traditions

Developments in South Asia

The Mahāyāna incorporated most of the above meditation techniques but also developed new ones unique to the movement and based in its own literature. Many Mahāyāna *sūtras* contain visionary descriptions of Buddhas and *bodhisattvas* in resplendent surroundings. Some of these *sūtras* begin, for example, with miraculous displays of lavish imagery in which the Buddha transforms an ordinary scene into a display rife with elaborate palaces, jewel trees, beautiful natural scenery, and supernatural beings. While *Nikāya* literature emphasizes understanding the *Dharma* over the presence of the Buddha himself, some Mahāyāna literature also extols the benefits of "seeing the Buddha." Mahāyāna *sūtras* often exalt in such visions, seeing them as recreating the presence of the (or a) Buddha and sometimes even preferring seeing the Buddha over understanding doctrine. Paul Williams has argued that the need for the Buddha to be present – to be seen as well as heard – was a significant factor in the development of the Mahāyāna. Specific visualization meditations arose from this concern, elaborating on the practice of recollection of the Buddha.

Recollection of the Buddha in the Mahāyāna

Both the Mahāyāna and non-Mahāyāna schools developed practices called "recollection of the Buddha" (*buddhānusmṛti*). In the *Nikāyas*, they consist of recalling and contemplating Gautama Buddha's life, teachings, and noble characteristics. Mahāyāna *sūtras*, while not necessarily excluding these elements, stress the exquisite physical appearance of the Buddha and his surroundings, which become purified and transformed by his presence. The subject of these contemplations is not only Gautama Buddha but others in the pantheon of Buddhas and *bodhisattvas* – Amitābha, Akṣobhya, Maitreya, Avalokiteśvara, and Manjuśrī.

The *Pratyutpanna Sūtra* illustrates how the Mahāyāna expanded the recollection of the Buddha into a visualization meditation and devotional practice believed not just to recall a revered figure of the past but to evoke his very presence during meditation. It instructs the practitioner to go to a secluded place and concentrate on the Buddha Amitābha constantly for up to seven days and nights until his image is continually before the meditator; then, the *sūtra* asserts, Amitābha will appear to the meditator as clearly as if an ordinary person were standing there. Having obtained such a vision, the practitioner may then worship and receive teachings from him. The *Sūtra on the Contemplation of Amitāyus* (*Amitāyurdhyāna Sūtra*) contains similar visualization instructions, insuring the reader that those who visualize Amitābha (or Amitāyus) in his Pure Land and follow the moral precepts will obtain a vision of Amitābha at death and be led directly to rebirth in that land. The clarity and substantiality of the vision depend on the degree of faith and on the degree of success with which one has been able to perform the complex visualization. These texts display a combination of meditation and devotionalism characteristic of Mahāyāna *sūtras.* While worship of Buddhas and Buddhist saints was far from absent in early Buddhism, it is played down in canonical Pāli literature. Many Mahāyāna texts, however, are unabashedly devotional. These visionary and devotional elements in the Mahāyāna literature of the early common era reflect a larger of pan-Indic visionary devotionalism (*bhakti*) taking place in Hindu as well as Buddhist traditions during this time.

Tantric visualization

Tantric sādhanas (lit. "means of accomplishment") take visualization meditation a step further. The *Tantras*, a genre of scriptures dating from *c.* the sixth century, contain detailed visualization meditations designed not only to evoke the presence of Buddhas and *bodhisattvas* but to identify the meditator with them. In these *sādhanas*, the practitioner evokes an image of a *maṇḍala* – an often elaborate diagrammatic representation of a Buddha-field with a central deity (a Buddha or *bodhisattva*) surrounded by other deities – and through the imagination identifies with the primary deity (a Buddha or *bodhisattva*) of the image, overcoming the duality between subject and object and evoking the Buddha-nature within the practitioner.

Tantric visualization practices as described in the *Tantras* originating in South Asia vary from text to text, but most follow a general pattern. After preliminary practices that can include purification rituals, chanting of syllables, confessions of sins, and dedication of the merit of the practice to all living beings, the practitioner begins the "generation stage" (*utpannakrama*) by cultivating an image of the deity in detail. *Sādhana* instructions take care to describe the visual appearance of the figure, often in great detail, including descriptions of clothing, jewelry, facial expressions, and symbolic implements held in the hands. Some practices instruct the meditator to maintain this complex image for an extended period of time, or to manipulate it in various ways, such as reducing it to the size of a drop or expanding it to envelop the entire cosmos. The culmination of the practice is the "completion stage" (*sampannakrama*), the identification of the practitioner with the deity, either through entering the *maṇḍala* and merging with the deity or envisioning him or herself at the outset as the deity. This involves cultivating a sense of "divine pride" (*māna*), the sense that one actually *is* the deity one is envisioning. Finally the *maṇḍala* is dissolved and the practitioner is left with a sense of unity with the deity.

Indian and Tibetan adaptations of classical meditation techniques

The Mahāyāna schools also adapted the classical meditation techniques – tranquility and insight meditation – to their own doctrinal and praxiological context. During the flowering of scholasticism in Indic Buddhism, roughly between the seventh and tenth centuries, commentators such as Kamalaśīla developed the themes of tranquility and insight meditation, augmenting them with the *bodhisattva* ideal – the notion that one practices not for personal escape from *saṃsāra* but to remain in the world to help awaken all sentient beings. Mahāyāna commentaries, therefore, see the cultivation of tranquility and insight as a means for developing *bodhicitta*, the aspiration for awakening, not just for oneself but for the sake of others. Mahāyāna accounts of traditional insight meditation also incorporate the Mahāyāna emphasis on seeing all things as *śūnya* – empty, or lacking, any permanent, fixed, inherent existence (*svabhāva*). Insight into things as they are means seeing that they are not independent and permanent but are impermanent and empty of intrinsic nature, being constituted by causes, conditions, and concepts.

Tibetan scholars continued this integration of classical meditation techniques with Mahāyāna themes, incorporating Vajrayāna elements as well. Tsongkhapa (b. 1357) the prolific scholar, reformer, and founder of the Gelukpa school, is the most notable in this regard. His most influential work, *Great Exposition on the Stages of the Path* (*Lamrim Chenmo*) lays out the influential *lamrim* system, which concludes with a discussion of tranquility and insight meditation. According to traditional sources, Tsongkhapa also worked to reconcile Vajrayāna teachings and practices with traditional monastic life. In part, this meant domesticating some of the more antinomian elements of *tantric* practice, such as sexual ritual and ingestion of impure substances, in favor of more symbolic substitutes. It also involved integrating in a comprehensive system virtually all forms of meditation in the classical, Mahāyāna, and Vajrayāna traditions, seeing them as a graduated progression from "Hīnayāna" practices, such as tranquility meditation, to *sādhanas* of the Highest Yoga *Tantras* (*anuttaratantras*), considered to be the most advanced practices.

Tibetans have contributed a great deal of theoretical analysis and practical refinement of Buddhist meditation and developed some approaches unique to Tibetan traditions. One illustrative example is *dzogchen* (*rdzogs chen*, "great perfection"), which comprises a set of teachings on distinctive meditation practices associated with the Nyingma school of Tibetan Buddhism, as well as the non-Buddhist Bön tradition of Tibet. Considered the highest meditation teachings (*atiyoga*) among the *Tantras*, *dzogchen* involves no visualization of deities or the body's subtle energies, but instead works directly with the mind to reveal its own primordially pure nature. This primal nature is not just the personal mind but the ground of all phenomena, identified with emptiness and Buddha-nature and transcending all ideation, linguistic reference, and comparison. It is described as luminous and akin to space – omnipresent, transparent, unobstructed, limitless, and eternal. *Dzogchen* techniques are considered an advanced and rapid path to enlightenment that cuts directly to this primordial level of mind, often in a sudden enlightenment experience.

Developments in East Asia

As in Tibet, Buddhist schools in East Asia continued the traditions of meditation in both *Nikāya* and Mahāyāna literature, adapting them to their unique cultural contexts. Each school of Chinese Buddhism refined meditation, adapting tranquility and insight techniques of the *Nikāyas* while following Mahāyāna interpretations and relegating the "Hīnayāna" teachings to a lower status.

The Chinese monk Zhiyi (538–97), of the Tiantai school, for example, composed a lengthy work *The Great Calming and Contemplation* (*Mohe zhiguan*), which argued for the combination of scholarly learning and meditation practice. Zhiyi studied virtually all of the Buddhist texts extant in China during his time and attempted to integrate the varied and sometimes contradictory doctrines into a comprehensive schema, ranking them from the most elementary – "Hīnayāna" teachings considered to be skilful means (*upāya*) – to the most profound contained in the "Lotus" (*Saddharmapuṇḍarīka Sūtra*) and other Mahāyāna *sūtras*. Zhiyi asserted, however, that even understanding these latter texts that point out the *dharma*-element (*dharmadhātu*), the highest principle underlying the universe, cannot by itself bring about full awakening. Textual learning must be combined with meditation practice. Zhiyi developed a theory of meditation that classified them, as he had classified doctrines, into three categories: *gradual*, which uses skilful means and includes breath awareness, chanting, and contemplation of the *Lotus Sūtra*; *sudden*, which points directly to the ultimate truth, taking the *dharma*-element (*dharmadhātu*) itself as its object; and *variable*, which combines sudden and gradual practices.

Chan/Zen

Zen (Ch. *Chan*, Kor. *Sŏn*, Viet. *Thiên*) is a translation of the Sanskrit *dhyāna* (Pāli *jhāna*), which, as we have seen, means meditative concentration. The Zen schools were founded by monks who specialized in meditation and developed meditative techniques unique to Zen, expanding the meaning of this term beyond that found in the Pāli literature. The theoretical understanding basic to all of Zen practice is that Buddha-nature, sometimes called "self-nature," is immanent in all beings. Meditation, therefore, does not seek to change one's essential condition nor attain anything, as everyone is already a fully awakened Buddha even if he or she does not realize it. One of the seminal texts of the tradition, therefore, the *Platform Sūtra of the Sixth Patriarch*, attributed to Huineng (seventh–eighth century), insists that meditation – often thought to entail the cultivation of certain virtues, mental states, and ultimately enlightenment itself – does not actually cultivate anything. The mind, Huineng insists, is already inherently pure, and there is actually nothing to cultivate except the realization of one's original enlightenment, which has always been there. It is through maintaining "direct mind" at all times – living in the world with full awareness and engagement but clinging to nothing – that the practitioner realizes complete inner freedom.

This idea of enlightenment or Buddhahood as everyone's original nature entails the non-duality of subject and object and of the means and end of Buddhist practice. Huineng insists that meditation and wisdom (or enlightenment – the goal of meditation) are not two different things. The former is not a means to the latter because the true nature of all things already permeates everyone and everything. Enlightenment, therefore, is not so much the achieving of a particular state as the unveiling of this primordial reality.

The fact that this underlying reality is manifest in and as everything implies the unity of subject and object or the ultimate oneness of all things. The notion that formal meditation does not bring about enlightenment should not be understood as repudiation of meditation but rather of a particular interpretation of it. Instead of being one activity cut off from all activities, the meditation is extended to all elements of daily life. Thus Zen monastic practice construes every aspect of life as meditation and ritualizes even the most everyday activities.

The two main schools of Zen, Rinzai (Ch. Linji) and Sōtō (Ch. Caodong), each have different emphases while maintaining these theoretical principles. In both, *zazen*, or seated meditation, is the fundamental meditative practice. *Zazen* is performed seated with back straight and legs crossed in a full- or half-lotus position. It employs methods drawn from early Pāli meditation literature, such as counting breaths and labeling thoughts. Some more advanced techniques, however, are unique to Zen, particularly *shikantaza* and *kōan* practice. *Shikantaza*, espoused by Dōgen Zenji (1200–1253) the founder of the Sōtō school in Japan, is a form of meditation in which the immediate present, whatever its content, is the object of meditation. The meditator calmly but alertly attends to each thought, neither suppressing nor attaching to it. Dōgen refers to it as neither ordinary thinking nor blankness, but a process of "un-thinking" (*hi shiryō*) – investigating thought to exhaust the limits of thinking itself, thus allowing for a direct realization of the enlightened mind of the Buddha within meditator. The practitioner of *shikantaza* must avoid dwelling on thoughts of attaining enlightenment or any other goal and instead simply be aware of everything in the present moment. *Shikantaza* is often presented as an *expression* of enlightenment or one's Buddha-nature rather than a means to attain it.

Both the Rinzai and Sōtō schools practice the contemplation of *kōans* (Ch. *gongan*), but it is far more common in Rinzai, which uses a comprehensive curriculum of *kōans* for training monks. *Kōans* are "public cases" or short legendary anecdotes in which a Zen master has an encounter with a disciple that is considered a profound expression of the master's awakened mind. Many *kōans* depict the moment at which a disciple attains an insight or awakening stimulated by the words or actions of the master. *Kōans* are notoriously difficult to understand, and often contain cryptic utterances or startling acts that appear to defy reason and common sense. They are used in Zen meditation as contemplative problems, the solution of which yields a glimpse of awakening. One well-known *kōan* is about the master Jōshu's dog: A monk once asked master Jōshu, "Has a dog Buddha-nature?" Jōshu said '*Mu!*'" ("no" or "nothing" in Japanese). Another famously asks about the sound of one hand clapping, and yet another asks a monk to show the original face he had before his parents were born. Many present a paradox in which either side of a binary opposition is unsatisfactory: does a dog have Buddha-nature or not? Answering "yes" simply parrots Buddhist doctrine without showing any real insight into its meaning, while answering "no" is simply untrue according to the *Dharma*. Other *kōans* show masters deflecting a monk's desire for an edifying or theoretical discourse in favor of something immediately present: "A monk once asked Jōshu, 'What is the meaning of the Patriarch's [Bodhidharma's] coming from the west?' Jōshu answered, 'The oak tree in the front garden.'"

In *kōan* practice, a monk will sit in *zazen* repeating a condensed phrase or word representing the *kōan* and exhausting all possibilities of dualistic thought until breaking through to an answer. This is not, however, simply a private endeavor.

Monks must regularly consult with their Zen masters in one-on-one meetings, called *dokusan* or *sanzen*, and attempt to express their insight into the *kōan*. The "answers" to *kōans* are a matter of published record, but the master will regularly reject answers he or she deems uninformed by disciples' insights into their own Buddha-nature. Attempts to intellectualize or answer in terms of systematic philosophy are rejected, and students are pushed until they can demonstrate that they have overcome dualistic thinking with regard to the *kōan*. Upon producing a satisfactory answer, they have "passed" and may move on to another *kōan*.

Discerning the answer to a *kōan* is often accompanied by *kenshō* or *satori*, a blissful glimpse of awakening in which the practitioner overcomes the sense of separation between him or herself and the object of thought and realizes his or her true Buddha-nature. This insight into the non-duality of subject and object is then broadened to include all possible objects, culminating in an experience of a cosmic unity transcending all binary oppositions, yet paradoxically maintaining the distinctiveness of individual things.

Buddhist meditation in the modern world

The primary locus of meditation in the history of Buddhist traditions has always been the monastery. While not all Buddhist monastics meditate, many monastic traditions maintain strong meditation traditions, particularly in Tibetan, Zen, and Theravāda Buddhism. The most significant development in meditation in recent history, however, is its movement to the center of lay practice in modern Buddhist revitalization movements in Asia and in novel forms of Buddhism emerging in the West. These movements, which draw on themes from the European Enlightenment and Western psychology as well as ancient Buddhist textual sources, encourage meditation not just for monastics but for laity and even non-Buddhists. While not necessarily retreating from the soteriological value of meditation, prominent modern Buddhists also present it as a technique conducive to psychological health, peace of mind, and ethical cultivation in lay life. Thus, while the practice of most lay Buddhists throughout the world still consists of rituals for gaining karmic merit, a growing number of educated middle-class men and women in Asia and the West are taking up Buddhist meditation.

This revitalization of meditation traditions has fostered new Buddhist movements and has generated a great deal of interest in Buddhist meditation globally. One example is the Vipassana or insight meditation movement, which enjoys popularity in parts of South and Southeast Asia, North America, and Western Europe. This approach sees meditation as central to the Buddhist path and takes the *Sūtra on the Foundations of Mindfulness* (*Satipaṭṭhāna Sutta*) as its main text. Developed by Mahāsī Sayādaw and other Burmese Theravāda teachers, Vipassana was brought to North America by some of his American students, Joseph Goldstein and Jack Kornfield, whose books and meditation centers have made it especially popular in the West. It is primarily a lay movement that dispenses with many ritual, devotional, and merit-making elements of Theravāda, stressing instead seated meditation and bringing meditative awareness to all aspects of life. Zen and Tibetan traditions have also created novel possibilities for non-monastics to practice meditation. Many traditional temples and monasteries now offer meditation classes and retreats for the general public, and meditation "centers" – neither monasteries nor traditional temples – have sprung up, not only the West, but also in Sri Lanka and other parts of Asia.

Especially in the West, Buddhist meditation is increasingly adapted to secular lifestyles and considered detachable from the ethical, praxiological, institutional, and doctrinal contexts of Buddhist traditions. Although tradition insists that practitioners must learn meditation from an experienced teacher, a great deal of popular literature containing meditation instructions has been published in recent decades, leading to a "do-it-yourself" approach. In North America, grass-roots meditation groups with little or no institutional affiliation meet in homes, colleges, and churches. Not surprisingly, this has led to the adaptation of Buddhist meditation techniques in a variety of non-Buddhist settings. Psychotherapists and physicians have begun employing them for stress reduction, lowering of blood-pressure, pain management, and cancer treatment. Today Buddhist-derived meditation is taught in prisons, hospitals, and schools, less for the purpose of achieving enlightenment than for coping with stress and health problems or for living a happier and more fulfilling life.

See also: ***Kōan*; Mahāyāna Buddhism; Meditation (Chan/Zen); Meditation, modern movements; Meditation, visualization; Meditation in the Pāli Canon and the Theravāda tradition; Meditation in the *Visuddhimagga*; Meditation traditions, Vajrayāna; *Nikāya* Buddhism; *Sādhana*; *Śamatha*; South and Southeast Asia, Buddhism in; *Vipaśyanā*; *Zazen*.**

David L. McMahan

MIKKYŌ AND RITUAL IN JAPANESE BUDDHISM

Mikkyō, or esoteric Buddhism, is the Japanese form of tantric Buddhism. Originating in early medieval India, "*tantra*" was originally used as a bibliographic category: that is, as a category of texts distinguished from *sūtra* and *śastra*. In contemporary Buddhist studies discourse, however, it has come to be identified with a particular set of practices, lineages, and ideologies. The terms used by the traditions themselves include terms such as *mantranaya*, *mantrayāna*, and *vajrayāna*. The first character of *mikkyō*, *mitsu*, appears to have been used to translate the Sanskrit term *guhya*, usually translated as "secret."

There exists a fairly standard set of elements that are identified with *tantra* generally, both Buddhist and Hindu forms. These include recitations evoking the presence of a Buddha, *bodhisattva* or guardian deity, and mnemonic formulae (*mantra* and *dhāraṇī*, respectively), hand gestures used in ritual performances (*mudrā*), diagrams portraying a central Buddha surrounded by his retinue (*maṇḍala*), initiation by a teacher into a secret transmission of teachings (*abhiṣeka*), ritualized identification of the practitioner with the deity (*ahaṃkāra*), and worship of the goddess (*śakti*). Indeed, some scholars have attempted to define *tantra* either by reference to a single one of these elements (monothetic definitions) or to various combinations of them (polythetic definitions). There are, however, problems with such approaches. First, many – if not all – of the elements pre-date the medieval rise of identifiably *tantric* traditions. Second, they also exist outside of identifiably tantric traditions. For example, reciting the Heart *sūtra* with its closing *mantra* does not make a Zen practitioner a *tantrika*. What does serve to make the elements into a coherent and meaningful whole is ritual practice.

There are two explicitly *mikkyō* traditions in contemporary Japan, the Tendai (Taimitsu, founded by Saichō, 767–822) and Shingon (Tōmitsu, founded by Kūkai, 774–835). The ritual practices of the two traditions share a great deal, though there are some differences in both ritual details and in certain aspects of the training of priests (Skt. *ācārya*, Jap. *ajari*).

Many of these differences are said to derive from the fact that Ennin (794–864), who traveled in China for ten years (838–47) acquired a copy of a recently translated *tantric* text, the *Sussidhikara Sūtra* (Jap. *Soshitsuji kyō*), which he brought back to Japan. However, not all rituals found in the Tendai and Shingon traditions are specifically *tantric*, but rather are simply part of the broader Mahāyāna ritual tradition. There are also rituals, such as the ritual feeding of hungry ghosts (Skt. *preta*, Jap. *gaki*) performed as part of the annual O Bon festival (*avalambana*, *ullambana*), that include some tantric elements, particularly *mudrā* and *mantra*. While some theorists simply identify *tantric* ritual with ritual identification (see below), the actual situation is more complicated.

There are at least concepts that can help us to understand how *mikkyō* ritual practice is understood to be efficacious. These are the ideas of awakening in this very body (Jap. *sokushin jobutsu*), inherent awakening (Jap. *hongaku*), and ritual identification (Skt. *ahaṃkara*, Jap. *nyūga ganyū*).

Awakening in this very body highlights the potential of esoteric ritual practice to facilitate sudden awakening. It is closely related to the idea of inherent awakening. Inherent awakening has no single Sanskrit source, but rather results from the combination of two concepts from late Indian Buddhism, that is, *tathāgatagarbha* (Jap. *nyoraizō*) and *ālayavijñāna* (Jap. *arayashiki*). The first is the idea that every living being has the potential for full awakening. The second describes a level of mind of which we are usually unaware, but which explains the continuity of personal identity and of *karma*. In China these two concepts were conflated, producing the idea that Buddha-nature is inherent in all living beings. In Japan, inherent awakening was initially formulated in the Tendai tradition. However, the understanding of the efficacy of ritual practice in both traditions shares this understanding of the human potential for awakening in one lifetime, rather than over many eons.

Ritual identification is the ritual action that makes manifest the identity of the practitioner and deity. The practitioner's three actions (Jap. *sangō*) are those of body, speech, and mind. Similarly, the three mysteries of the Buddha (Skt. *triguhya*, Jap. *sanmitsu*) are the deity's body, speech, and mind. Ritual identification allows the practitioner to become aware of the inherently awakened character of human existence. Through ritual identification of the practitioner and the Buddha, the inherently awakened nature of human existence is made increasingly clear. In this way, *mikkyō* thought balances between the two extremes of gradualism and subitism.

The *mikkyō* traditions are esoteric in the sense that initiation is required before one is allowed to engage in the practices of the tradition. This is said to be for the protection of the practitioner and others, just as one would not give a sharp knife or a medicine that is potentially poisonous to a small child. There is therefore a series of initiations marking increasing familiarity with the practices and teachings. The first of these is the initiation that establishes a *karmic* bond (Jap. *kechien kanjō*), usually received by laypersons. The path to priesthood (Skt. *ācārya*, Jap. *ajari*) begins with the novice (Skt. *śrāmaṇera*, Jap. *shami* or *gonsaku*, Skt. *śrāmaṇerī*, Jap. *shamini*) initiation, including the bequeathing of a *Dharma* name. This is then followed by an initiation in which the novice receives the three sets of vows: the *tantric* vows, Mahāyāna vows, and the monastic vows.

Following this initiatory sequence, the practitioner begins the actual training. Three preparatory practices precede the formal ritual training: bowing (*raihai*), full moon *cakra* visualization (*gachirin kan*), and visualization of the syllable "A" (*aji kan*). Upon completion, the practitioner can begin the Fourfold Training (*shidō kegyo*). In the Shingon tradition this begins with a relatively simple ritual, the Eighteen Stages (*jūhachidō*), continues through the Vajradhātu (*kongōkai*) and Garbhakoṣadhātu (*taizōkai*) rituals, and ends with a *homa* (*goma*) of protection. This sequence requires 100 days to complete, at the end of which time the practitioner receives *Dharma*-transmission (*denbo ajari kanjō*).

Rituals are identified as belonging to one of five categories (*goshuhō*), depending on function. These are protection (*sokusai*), merit and prosperity (*sōyaku*), summoning (*kōchō*), love and respect (*keiai*), and subduing enemies (*jōbuku*). *Mikkyō* rituals are still a common part of contemporary Japanese Buddhist practice, especially in the demand for "practical benefits" (see entry on *genze riyaku*).

See also: ***Hongaku shisō* – original enlightenment.**

PAUL L. SWANSON

MINJUNG BUDDHISM (BUDDHISM FOR THE MASSES)

Minjung Buddhism (Buddhism for the masses) is a socially engaged Buddhist movement in Korea whose activities were most visible from the mid-1970s to the late 1980s. The appearance of Minjung Buddhism is closely related to the military dictatorship that existed in Korea from 1961 to 1987. Critical of the collusion between the ecclesiastics and the state in the Korean Buddhist tradition, Minjung Buddhism demanded that the religion change its direction to show concern for the alienated and suffering people.

The idea of Buddhism for the masses first appeared at the beginning of the twentieth century when reform-minded Buddhist intellectuals proposed to change Korean Buddhism to correspond with the life of the general public, especially those marginalized in society. As a movement, however, Minjung Buddhism began together with pro-democratic and anti-government movements in Korean society during the military dictatorship. The expression "Minjung Buddhism" was first used at a college students' meeting held at the Songgwang monastery in 1976 where a paper on the "Theory of Minjung Buddhism" was presented.

A critical event took place in the fall of 1980 when, in the name of purifying Buddhism, the government cracked down on Buddhist headquarters and more than 3,000 monasteries. Known as the 10.27 Persecution, this event brought disillusionment to many Buddhists, which expedited the spread of Minjung Buddhism. Starting in 1981, the concept of Minjung Buddhism was actively disseminated by its adherents, partly in step with the growing democratization movements in Korean society. In 1988 when the Minjung movement went through restructuring, the expression "Minjung Buddhism" was replaced with the phrase "Buddhism for praxis" (Kor. *silch'ŏn pulgyo*) or "engaged Buddhism" (Kor. *ch'amyŏ pulgyo*).

By its founding principles, Minjung Buddhism is Buddhism for the politically suppressed, economically exploited, and socio-culturally alienated. This sets it in clear opposition to traditional Korean Buddhism, which tended to collaborate with the state, isolate itself in mountainside monasteries, and in general be at the service of the upper class.

Philosophically, Minjung Buddhists appeal to the *bodhisattva* ideal and compassion. They are critical of some forms of Mahāyāna Buddhism, including Sŏn, Ch'ŏnt'ae and Hwaŏm, claiming that these forms turned Buddhism into a subjective idealism that overemphasizes the mind and its emptiness, while obscuring the social and political reality of the *minjung*. In contrast, adherents of Minjung emphasize liberation from all forms of suppression, especially that conducted by the state and the ruling class. In this sense, one might consider the rejection of authority in Sŏn Buddhism to be compatible with Minjung, but only if Sŏn can reject also the secluded shelter of subjective idealism.

Minjung Buddhism's literal application of Marxism to Buddhism, and their willingness to employ violence, became a target of criticism. To their credit, however, Minjung Buddhism provided an occasion to awaken Korean Buddhists to the consideration of the often neglected relationship between the ultimate goal of Buddhism, enlightenment, and the reality of the social, political, and historical realm. Minjung Buddhism worked to bring Buddhism back to the life-world of the people, to narrow the gap between Buddhism and socially marginalized groups, and to thus situate Buddhism within the milieu of praxis beyond the Sŏn meditation hall.

See also: **Korea, Buddhism in.**

JIN Y. PARK

MIPHAM

Mipham ('Jam mgon 'Ju Mi pham rnam rgyal, 1846–1912) is considered by the Nyingma Order of Tibetan Buddhism to be one of its greatest scholars, and he was one of the most influential thinkers of the "Non-Sectarian" (*Ris med*) movement in eastern Tibet in the late nineteenth and early twentieth centuries.

Mipham was born in Dingchu (Ding chu) in an area of eastern Tibet under the administrative control of Derge (sDe dge) Monastery. At the age of twelve he became a monk at Mehor Sangngak Chöling (Me hor gsang sngags chos gling) Monastery, and at age fourteen began an eighteen-month period of meditation at Junyung Hermitage ('Ju nyung ri khrod), where he mainly engaged in Mañjuśrī *sādhanas*. According to tradition, he was so successful that Mañjuśrī appeared to him directly, and from that point he was often referred to as "Mañjuśrī Mipham" ('Jam mgon Mi pham).

Beginning in the 1860s, a conflict often called the Nyarong (Nyag rong) War began when the Nyarong leader Gönpo Namgyel fought with Derge. Mipham fled the conflict and went on a pilgrimage to central Tibet, where he spent some time at the Gelukpa monastery of Ganden near Lhasa. During this period he wrote an influential work on the Gesar epic, themes from which became central both to his religious vision and to that of the Non-Sectarian movement, which sought to incorporate indigenous beliefs and cults into mainstream Buddhist practice.

During his travels, Mipham studied with several of the most influential Non-Sectarian teachers, including Kongtrül (Kong sprul bLo gros mtha' yas, 1813–99) and Jamyang Khyentse Wangpo ('Jam dbyangs mkhyen brtse dbang po, 1820–92). His voluminous works include texts on poetics, medicine, divination, and extended commentaries (*mchan 'grel*) on many of the most important Indian Mahāyāna philosophical treatises.

His commentary on the ninth chapter of the *Bodhicaryāvatāra* led to heated debates with Gelukpa scholars, most notably a face-to-face encounter with the noted Geluk scholar Jampa Dongak ('Ja' pa mdo sngags) in the late 1870s. Mipham interpreted the text from a "great perfection" (*rdzogs chen*) perspective, reading it as advocating non-conceptual direct realization of ultimate reality, while his opponent followed the conventional Geluk Mādhyamika reading. The debate was reportedly resolved in Mipham's favor when a light was seen emanating from the heart of an image of Mañjuśrī and entering Mipham's heart, but disputes with other Gelukpa scholars continued for the rest of Mipham's life.

In 1909 he moved to a hermitage called Tashi Belbarling (bKra bshis dPal 'bar gling), where he spent most of the rest of his life. Despite a lingering illness, Mipham continued to be highly productive, and during this period he wrote a number of influential commentaries on Indian philosophical texts, including his extended commentary on the *Mahāyāna-sūtrālaṅkāra*. He was unusual among eminent scholars of his time in that he was not a recognized reincarnation (*sprul sku*), but after his death three reincarnational lineages (body, speech, and mind) were initiated. His literary output was truly phenomenal, both in its scope and in its influence. He remains one of the intellectual giants of twentieth-century Tibetan Buddhism and one of its most original thinkers.

See also: **Tibet, Buddhism in; Vajrayāna Buddhism.**

JOHN POWERS

MONASTIC DWELLINGS

Introduction

In his exhortation to the monks to wander around teaching *Dharma*, Buddha charges his disciples to all go in separate directions, that is, to wander about in as many different places as the existing manpower allowed. This emphasis on solitary wandering finds expression not only in the monastic literature, but also in many of what are considered to be the earliest strata of Buddhist texts, for example the *Sutta Nipāta* and the *Dhammapada*, to cite two sources. In verse 404 of the *Dhammapada*, we read: "He who does not associate with householders or homeless ones, who is homeless and desires nothing, him I call a *Brāhmaṇa*." For his personal requisites, apart from the traditional possessions (three robes, begging bowl, razor, needle, girding for the robes, and water strainer), the monk is advised to depend only on four things: (1) begging food; (2) using rags for robes; (3) dwelling at the foot of a tree; and (4) using urine as medicine. These are traditionally referred to as the four *niśrayas*. The only pause to the mendicant's wandering came during the rainy season or *varṣā*. Of course, travel during the monsoon season was made thoroughly impractical by the severity of the rains, and damage to the crops, which would certainly result from attempts at travel, would prove most harmful. All these factors led to Buddha's injunction to pass the rainy season in settled dwellings. Thus the monks found it most successful to carry out intensified study and meditation in temporary residence. Also blossoming from the foregoing enterprise was an opportunity for the laity to have a brief but sustained interaction with the monkhood, obviously resulting in mutual benefit. During *varṣā*, the monks were also able to engage in scholarly debate, *sūtra* discussion, and similar activities, fully utilizing their close proximity for intellectual as well as spiritual advancement.

Rain retreat settlements

The *bhikṣus* were advised to enter the rainy season dwelling, as recounted in the *Mahāparinibbāna Sutta*, "according to the place where his friends, acquaintances, and intimates may live." As the Buddhist monks begged for their food, rain retreat settlements had to be made in a vicinity where almsfood would be available without extensive travel, so they usually settled near towns or villages. Rain retreat settlements were generally of two types: *āvāsas* and *ārāmas*. The *āvāsas* were monastic dwelling places staked out, constructed, and cared for by the monks themselves. A whole chapter in the Pāli *Mahāvagga* (Chapter III), and in the *Varṣāvastus* of all the various *Vinayas* of the individual Buddhist sects, explains with regard to the *āvāsa*, "its construction, maintenance, regulations for communal living within it, and also manners and points of etiquette to be observed." A necessary part of *āvāsa* construction would, of course, be the demarcation of boundaries (*sīmā*). Often these limits coincided with natural boundaries such as a mountain, rock, tree, or body of water, and great care was taken to ensure that the boundaries of no two *āvāsas* coincided and that no one colony infringed upon another. The house in which each monk resided was called a *vihāra* and amounted to little more than a small hut. Occasionally, however, several monks shared the same *vihāra*, in which case each monk's "cell" was called a *pariveṇa*. Furniture too was kept to a bare minimum, each monk's allotment consisting only of a little wooden bed, a seat, and a spittoon.

The other kind of dwelling place, called an *ārāma*, presents and almost total contrast to the *āvāsa*. Sukumar Dutt, an early researcher on monastic dwellings, remarks that,

> The name, *ārāma*, denotes a pleasure-ground, usually the property within a town or city or in the suburb of a well to do citizen laid out as an orchard or flower garden. When it was given to the monks by the owner, not for temporary use but permanently, it was named a *Saṅghārāma*. The term, meaning originally an *ārāma* owned by the Saṅgha, came later to shed its implication of a donated pleasure-ground and meant simply a campus, and later still a large monastery occupied by a company of monks. The donor of an *ārāma* would not lose interest in it when it had been converted from private property into Saṅgha property. It seems that he would of his own accord continue to look after the property – raise fresh buildings upon it according to the monks' needs and keep it trim and in habitable condition.

Several donations of this sort are mentioned in the legends, one notable example being King Bimbisāra's offer of the Veḷuvana ('bamboo grove') representing the first gift of an *ārāma* to the *sangha*. Some *ārāmas* seem to have persisted for long durations, as with Jetavanārāma, which still existed at the time of Fa-hien's journey to India from China in 399–414 CE.

Within the monastery

With the institutionalization of the rainy season retreat, many communal needs became evident, the most apparent perhaps being a common meeting hall. This common meeting hall is provided for and allowed, at least, in the Pāli sources. Other buildings soon began to appear, strewn over the grounds of the settlement, and usually including a storeroom, kitchen, warehouse, privy, place for walking about, hall in the place for walking about, bathroom, hall in the bathroom, temporary shed for special or festive occasions, well, and hall at the well. All of these structures were the collective property of the *sangha*. From this description, we can also conclude that the management and administration of the monastic settlement was no meager task. At the least, there were a series of permanent officers (1) connected with the commissariat, (2) connected with chambers and wardrobe, and (3) superintendents; and a series of temporary officers and miscellaneous officers.

Further development

Given the physical structure of the monastic dwellings, with their growing numbers of buildings, and the expanding number of monastic officers, one begins to get the feeling that what is being described is not a temporary dwelling for the rainy season only, but rather a permanent residing place (that is, a monastery) for the monks; and most definitely, that is exactly what happened. The three-month rainy season residence generally begins on the full moon of June–July. At that time, the dwellings of "beds and seats" (*śayanāsana*) were assigned to the monks. A second time of assigning dwellings, however, is also mentioned. This second time occurs one month following the full moon of June–July, and accommodated any late-arriving monks. Thus, these two periods should have been more than adequate to meet the monks' needs, because the rainy season dwellings were originally to have been for one year only and were surrendered at the end of the rainy season on the full moon of October–November. However, at the conclusion of the *Pravāraṇā* or "Invitation" ceremony at the conclusion of the rainy season, there was a *third* assignment of dwelling places. The Pāli *Vinaya* describes this third time of assignment as "intervening," with reference to the next rainy season. As assignments for the next rainy season could easily be accommodated at that time, this third assignment is functionally superfluous. The third assignment existed because, in fact, the monks did not wander randomly, settling down with their friends and companions with the onset of the rains, wherever they might be at the time, but rather returned to the dwelling place of the previous year(s). With reservations already made one year in advance, they were assured of satisfactory dwelling for the next year's rains. Once year-to-year assignments were established, it was only a short step for the monks to abolish their eremetical ideal altogether and cease their wanderings even during the dry season. In this fashion, the collective monastic life developed within the Buddhist *sangha*, a life requiring permanent physical structures and administrative officers, as described above. As the permanent individual monastic dwellings arose and proliferated, the texts began to mention these individual *sanghas*, such as the "*Sangha* of Śrāvastī" or the "*Sangha* of Vaiśālī," and the original "*Sangha* of the Four Quarters" seemed to exist no longer. At that point, to call an *āvāsa* or an *ārāma* a place of rain retreat settlement would have been a fiction, and a new term arose to reflect this situation: *vihāra*, reinterpreted to no longer mean a single hut but a complete monastery. It is likely that this process of the emergence of the monastery took perhaps 100 years. Within a relatively short period of time, yet another transition in Buddhist monastic life took place. The *vihāras* gave way to a new kind of collective term for monastic dwellings, referred to in the Pāli legends as a *leṇa*. Five types of *leṇas* were initially identified, but the term later seems to be identified with cave monasteries cut into the hillsides by men rather than reflecting natural structures. It wasn't long before Buddhist universities began to grow up around large monastic centers. Further, as Buddhism rapidly grew beyond India's borders, it was this settled monastic life that became the established Buddhist monastic lifestyle throughout Asia and the West.

Figure 30 Temple bell, Pulguksa Monastery, Korea.

See also: ***Sangha*; *Vihāra*.**

CHARLES S. PREBISH

MONASTIC LIFE

Introduction

While Buddhism identifies four distinct communities of disciples: monks (*bhikṣus*), nuns (*bhikṣuṇīs*), laymen (*upāsakas)* and laywomen (*upāsikās*), in the earliest tradition, the primary emphasis of the Buddhism community or *sangha* was monastic. In the early Theravāda community, for example, the term *sangha* did not include lay followers. Instead, they spoke of a "twofold community" or *ubhatosangha* that included only monks and nuns. The overwhelming majority of Buddha's most significant early disciples were monastics, and young men were encouraged to renounce worldly life in favor of entry into the *sangha* at an early age. The Pāli records suggest that of the first sixty disciples that congregated around Buddha during his first six months of ministry, fifty-five were young laymen who almost immediately renounced lay life in favor of the monastic lifestyle. Indeed, he ordained his own son Rāhula at a very tender age. The emphasis on monastic life that permeated early Buddhism continues throughout Buddhism's history in Asia, despite the development of an important and powerful lay community.

Ordination

One's initial entry to the monastic lifestyle is of paramount importance, so the act of ordination is exceedingly significant. The ritual act of ordination is open to members of both genders in Buddhism, but is an explicit, legal act of the *sangha*, and as such requires certain formal, canonically dictated procedures. The actual ordination process is preceded not only by the stated *voluntary* intention of the ordinand, but also by meeting certain established prerequisites regarding age, status, health, and so forth. In early *Nikāya* Buddhism, two types of ordination are available: (1) initiation as a novice (*śrāmaṇera* for males, *śrāmaṇerī* for females), at which time the ordinand repeats the threefold refuge formula (*triśaraṇa*), agrees to uphold ten specific rules of conduct (*daśa-śīla*) referred to as "precepts" (*śikṣāpada*), is required to follow the monastic code embodied in a text called the *Prātimokṣa*, and is assigned two instructors known as the "teacher" (*ācārya*) and the "preceptor" (*upādhyāya*). At that time, the novice has the head shaved, receives monastic robes, and is given a begging bowl. The first ordination is referred to as *pravrajyā*, literally "going forth." After age twenty, a member of the monastic community can ask for (2) higher ordination as a monk or nun. Higher ordination, carrying with it the full rights and responsibilities of an adult member of the monastic community, is referred to as *upasaṃpadā*. Each of the two ordinations described above *is not considered a lifelong commitment*. At any time, a monk or nun may voluntarily elect to leave the monastic community and return to lay life. In Mahāyāna, a third type of ordination appears, known as the *bodhisattva* ordination, in which case the ordinand takes the formal vow of the *bodhisattva*: to gain complete, perfect enlightenment for the sake of all sentient beings. In each case, the requirements of the monastic member of the *sangha* and his or her teacher and preceptor are carefully spelled out by the *Vinaya*, as are the converse obligations.

Requirements and obligations to monastic law

Each member of the monastic community is required to fulfill the obligations of monastic discipline as detailed in the *Vinaya Piṭaka* and embodied in the text known as the *Prātimokṣa Sūtra*, of which there is a distinct version for monks and another for nuns. The *Prātimokṣa Sūtra* is an inventory of offenses organized into categories classified according to the gravity of the offense. It is recited twice monthly, at the *Poṣadha* observance ceremony on the new-moon and full-moon days, and is employed as a device for insuring proper monastic discipline. As a ritual liturgy, it includes, in addition to the categories of offenses, a set of verses that introduce and conclude the text, an introduction used to call the *sangha* together and instrument the confessional procedure, and an interrogatory formula, recited after each category of offenses, aimed at discovering who was pure and who was not. The monks' version contains eight categories of rules, ranging in number from 218 to 263, depending on which sect one belongs to, while the nuns' version contains seven categories of rules, ranging in number from 279 to 380. The *Poṣadha* ceremony was not considered concluded until all offenses listed in the *Prātimokṣa Sūtra* had been confessed and appropriate punishment meted out, thus guaranteeing on a fortnightly basis that all members of the monastic *sangha* were pure in their behavior and worthy of community respect.

Other monastic business

At first, the only business of the *Poṣadha* ceremony was the *Prātimokṣa* recitation. Later, however, other functions were added to the ceremony, reflecting monastic community decisions carried out according to the *Karmavācanā* method. The *Karmavācanā* is the functional, legalistic device by which the communal life of the *sangha* is regulated. We might say that what the *Prātimokṣa* is to the individual monk or nun, the *Karmavācanā* represented to the *sangha*. At least fourteen items of monastic business are regulated by the *Karmavācanā* procedure: admission into the *sangha*, full ordination, holding the confession ceremony, holding the invitation ceremony, residence obligation during the rainy season, use of leather objects, preparation and use of medicines, robe-giving ceremonies, discipline, daily life of monks, bed and seat apportionment, schisms in the *sangha*, duties of a student and teacher to one another, and rules for nuns. All of these acts are handled under a general procedure called *sanghakarma*, arising either by a general requirement or a specific dispute. To be considered valid, the proper number of competent monks must be assembled, all absentee ballots collected, and a motion set forth. The motion is then read aloud or proclaimed (and *this* is the actual *karmavācanā* or "announcing the action"), and a decision, positive or negative, obtained. On this basis, with a decision democratically obtained, the *sangha* acts as a unified order.

Daily life

From the above, it is quite clear that great attention is paid to the regulation of all aspects of the daily life of monks and nuns. Prior to the establishment of settled monastic life, great attention was placed on the nature of dwelling places during the rainy season retreat known as *varṣā*. After the wandering life was abandoned as the basic normative lifestyle, much care was taken to ensure that dwelling within the monasteries – which came to be known as *vihāras* – was properly maintained. Rules were clear about each and every aspect of monastic life, from the regulation of proper forms of furniture to proper monastic dress (regulated through a formal ceremony known as *kaṭhina*) and the preparation and intake of food. Much attention was given to the distinction between private property and communal *sangha* property, and additionally, with respect to how each was obtained. Occasionally, monks and nuns were obliged to travel outside the monastery, and much concern was taken to ensure that proper decorum and conduct were maintained throughout any travel process.

At the core of monastic life, at least in the early tradition, was the pursuit of training that was consistent with the attainment of salvation, *nirvāṇa*, and with it, the elimination of suffering (*duḥkha*) and continued entrapment in *saṃsāra*. To a large extent, this meant that monastic life was structured so as to provide sufficient, ample time for solitude with which to practice meditation and engage in study of the *Dharma*. Even after the rise of Mahāyāna, and the willful concern of the *bodhisattva* to remain in *saṃsāra* in an attempt to compassionately relieve the suffering of all sentient beings, monastic life still provided time for solitude that was deemed sufficient for proper Buddhist practice.

Because the monastic community in Buddhism exists in a symbiotic relationship with the lay community, monastic members of the *sangha* were also expected to provide *Dharma* instruction and spiritual guidance to the *upāsakas* and *upāsikās* in return for the goods and material support they received. In many cases the monks and nuns were also the best-educated members of the overall Buddhist community and served as treasure troves of learning and information. In so doing, they were considered exemplary in the community. In this respect, the monks and nuns, by their behavior and learning, encouraged the faith of the Buddhist community, and in the process ensured the resulting community from internal schism and discord, which were items highly disparaged by the Buddha.

As Buddhist monastic institutions spread throughout the countries of Asia, some Buddhist monasteries became wealthy institutions, with large and imposing budgets and daily operations. The monasteries became business as much as monastic centers. In cases such as these, various members of the monastic communities maintained institutional jobs consistent with the smooth institutional operation of the entire monastic complex of activities. Additionally, as Buddhist monasteries moved from rural to urban settings, monastic life involved a complicated series of "outreach" activities, adding a new slant to the missionary activities normally associated with spreading the *Dharma* throughout society. Moreover, many modern monasteries have adapted well to the new technologies of the modern world, relying on cyberspace to facilitate the monastery's work and mission. In view of these above innovations, Buddhist monastic life today has become very different from that of its inception in India.

See also: **Monastic rituals; *Sangha*; *Vinaya Piṭaka*.**

CHARLES S. PREBISH

Figure 31 Buddha images on an altar, Daewonsa Monastery, Chunchon, Korea.

MONASTIC RITUALS

Monastic life provides an important exception to the rule that religious life-cycle rituals are underdeveloped in Buddhism. Monasticism not only dictates an all-consuming way of life, but that "life" – conceived according to one's membership in the *sangha* rather than one's biology, paralleling monastic "age" and seniority (which are calculated from higher ordination rather than birth) – is punctuated with rituals to mark its most important transitions: novice ordination (paralleling birth rites), higher ordination (= puberty rites), full moon and rains retreat rituals (= monthly and annual rites of renewal), and funeral and post-funeral rituals.

The *Vinaya*s of the different schools agree in dating the origin of these monastic rituals to the Buddha's original dispensation. Despite admitting an earliest community which, being fully enlightened, needed neither *vinaya* nor rituals – which men joined simply on the utterance of the Buddha's invitation, "Come, Monk" (*ehi bhikkhu*) – the *Vinaya*s explain how burgeoning numbers, expanding geographies and less-enlightened adepts necessitated the creation of both rules and rituals to constitute and maintain the purity of the *sangha* as well as the smooth functioning of the monastery.

Novice ordination (*pravrajyā*)

Novice ordination marks the beginning of one's new life in the *sangha*, whether that change of status is intended to be permanent or temporary (as is particularly common in Thailand and Burma). Because those undergoing ordination are often small boys or youths, parents and other family members may be involved in pre-ordination ceremonies during which the novice typically worships his parents then, after cutting his hair and donning monastic robes, is worshipped by his parents and presented with appropriate gifts. The ordination ceremony proper involves ritual formulas which certify the novice's eligibility and mark his break with his former life through receipt of a new name and sometimes more graphic representations such as the use of a *sambae* or waxed wick in the novice ordination ceremonies of the Korean Chogye Sŏn (Chan) Order, which is burnt down to the skin to represent a new detachment from the body; in some Chinese novice ordinations a whole grid of wicks is placed on the novice's head and lit. The ritual confers on the initiate the status of novice (*śrāmaṇera*) and though formally it requires only the adoption of the ten precepts in practice it is the beginning of the young monk's training in the complete *Vinaya* and related monastic customs and routines. It also marks the beginning of his formal relationship with his monastic preceptor.

Higher ordination (*upasampadā*)

After a stipulated period of time since novice ordination and a stipulated age has been reached, a *śrāmaṇera* may become a *bhikṣ;u* by undergoing higher ordination (*upasampadā*). The *Vinaya* texts contain specific formulas for conducting the *upasampadā* ritual, including set questions to be asked in determining eligibility and competence as well as a period of examination whose content is determined by regional tradition. The *Vinaya* texts also stipulate ritual mechanics such as the requisite quorum's number and nature, special rules for the ordination of nuns (*bhikṣunī*) and rules about when to hold the ceremony.

The formal ritual proceedings are often embedded within elaborate, sometimes days-long festivals in which family members and other supporters accompany a candidate to a central headquarters to witness the *upasaṃpadā*. Depending on regional and sectarian traditions, candidates will be the subject of rituals with fellow monks (including changes of clothing at various points in the ceremony) and lay supporters (famously in the Theravāda world, an elaborate enactment of the renunciation of Prince Siddhārtha, during which the candidate is dressed in royal garb and entertained as a king with music or elephant rides only to renounce these for the saffron robes).

Though formally a matter of monastic regulation, and an occasion for reciting lineages, affirming associations with other monasteries, and expressing commitment to a candidate's future, *upasaṃpadā* rituals sometimes coalesce with state regulation as well, as in Tang and Song China, where ordination occurred through state examination, imperial favor or the purchase of a certificate. Thailand issues ID cards to ordinands (*ngan upasambot*) recording the date and location of *upasaṃpadā*, new religious name, academic achievements, and place(s) of residence. Thai candidates for *upasaṃpadā* submit special applications to supplement their ritual statements about suitability, and monks serving as government officials can revoke ordination on just grounds.

Upasaṃpadā marks one's entry into the formal monastic community, complete with rights and responsibilities, but like puberty rites it is also a beginning, both literally (monastic seniority is calculated from the date of *upasaṃpadā*) and figuratively (one emerges as the least senior of one's cohort, a status symbolically demonstrated by assigning newly ordained monks particularly humbling monastic chores, and during the ceremony itself, which includes forcing candidates to grovel or otherwise demonstrate their submission to senior monks). All the monastic orders offer opportunities for achieving higher ranks as one matures in the *sangha* (see below), and in Tibetan and some Japanese traditions one's further monastic career may be marked with additional esoteric initiations.

Periodic rituals

According to the ancient *Vinayas*, all monks and all nuns living within particular monastic boundaries (*sīmā*) should meet fortnightly to affirm their collective purity by chanting the *Prātimokṣa*. In Sri Lanka, Burma, Thailand, Cambodia and Laos the ceremony still proceeds much as described in the ancient Pāli texts, with monks reciting after a head chanter and either affirming by their silence that in the preceding fortnight they have not violated the code, or confessing such violations as have occurred and receiving appropriate punishment. The full moon day after the rains retreat (see below) marks a different recitation of the code called *Pravāraṇā* ("invitation"), in which fellow monks, having spent the last months in close proximity, are invited to report the transgressions of others.

Rains retreat (*varṣa*)

According to the *Vinayas*, the Buddha instituted the annual rains retreat in response to complaints that the peregrinations of Buddhist monks and nuns harmed microscopic creatures during the monsoons. Restrictions on travel during that period confined monks and nuns to their monasteries and locales, making the rains retreat an ideal time for intensified religious practice, not only for clergy (who use it for more rigorous meditation and study) but also for laypeople (who receive more rituals and sermons because the monks are in residence; in some traditions lay patrons ritually inaugurate the retreat by inviting area monks to spend it under their care). In Thailand temporary ordinations, which function something like coming of age rituals, often occur during this season (Thai *Phansa*), which is calculated according to the "early retreat" of the Sinhala reckoning to fall in July–October. In Sri Lanka, the season (Sinh. *Was*) may also be observed according to the "late calculation" corresponding to August–November, but in neither case does this correspond exactly to the actual Sri Lankan and Southeast Asian monsoons; the ancient north Indian reckoning of time has been preserved as more important than the rains themselves. Japanese Rinzai monks observe an equivalent of the rains retreat twice a year, in May–July and November–January, and in Japan as well as China, and more recently of great popularity among American Buddhists, the retreat – a period of intensive religious

Figure 32 Monk bowing in front of stone Buddha statue, Shilsangsa Monastery, South Kyongsang, Korea.

practice, often made possible by creating or moving to a more secluded environment – has generalized this practice beyond its traditional bounds.

Theravādins consider the end of the rains retreat one of the most important moments in the annual ritual calendar. For monks, it is the time of *Pravāraṇā*, the "invitation" which best certifies the purity of all the members of a given monastic community. For laypeople, and in classical times the king, it is the occasion for a festival (Sinh. *kaṭhina pinkama*) involving almsgiving, sermons and processions and culminating in the presentation of monastic robes to all those who have spent the retreat under the care of a specific group of lay patrons.

The final life-cycle rite for a monk or nun, as for a layperson, is the funeral.

Additional monastic rituals

Vinaya law and regional customs ritualize many additional aspects of monastic life, from the consecration of ritual boundaries (*sīmā*) to the designation of intra-monastic social hierarchies (based on seniority, levels of attainment and as in Nepal and Sri Lanka even caste) and ranks (all the traditions have different levels of rank to which one can aspire, marked with special badges, vocabulary, palladia, titles and/or privileges); ritual time-keeping/bell-ringing, daily *pūjā* at designated shrines, ritual consecration of images, observance of *Vinaya* stipulations about food, dress, and hygiene, and/or meditation may further increase the level of monastic ritual and practice. Moreover, the monastery's importance as a site for Buddhist rituals (such as worship, almsgiving, preaching, chanting, meditation) as well as non-Buddhist rituals (for example, at deity shrines housed within the monastery; monks and nuns are also famous for healing and protective practices) inevitably draws its residents into even more regular ritual activity.

See also: **Holidays and observances; Ritual in Tibetan Buddhism; Ritual texts; Rituals and practices; *Sangha*; *Vinaya Piṭaka*.**

JONATHAN S. WALTERS

MORAL DISCIPLINE

As one of the "three trainings" (*tisso sikkhā*), moral discipline (*śīla*) has been a cardinal virtue of all Buddhists, and practices of restraint, cultivation of good qualities and ritual affirmation of *śīla*, and in some instances ritual confession of breaches, have been important aspects of praxis across the Buddhist world. Of course the paradigmatic moral discipline is the Buddha's own lifestyle as codified in the *Vinaya* traditions of the different schools, which is treated separately, but laypeople also adopt moral codes which the early tradition systematized as the five, eight and ten precepts (*śīla*), and which have been developed into full-blown lay praxis through *Vinaya*-like texts for laypeople, have been expanded into vow-taking liturgies for advanced adepts, and have palpably shaped social etiquette in Buddhist cultures. This article describes the five, eight and ten precepts of the early tradition, some of the ritual contexts which surround them, some of the ways they have been expanded upon in later traditions, and some of their discernible impacts upon Buddhist societies.

Five, eight and ten precepts

All the precepts are phrased according to a set formula, in which one affirms one's commitment to cultivating restraint from specific moral lapses. The five precepts (*pañcasīla*) as set out in the Pāli texts, which constitute the most basic level of participation in the Buddhist community, are thus resolutions to try to refrain from destroying life (*pānātipāta*), taking what is not given (*adinnādāna*), adultery (*kāmesu micchācāra*), false or otherwise bad speech (*musāvāda*) and becoming clouded by drinking alcohol (*surā meraya majja pamādaṭṭhānā*). In the Theravāda Buddhist world recitation of the five precepts, typically preceded by invocations to the Buddha and the three refuges, opens most lay Buddhist rituals, from simple daily worship ceremonies to large-scale festivals. In public settings they are often chanted in unison response to a skilled monastic chanter. Parallel opening invocations and liturgical recitation of vows have been developed in all the Buddhist traditions.

The eight precepts (Skt. *aṣṭāṅgaśīla*, Pāli *aṭṭhasīla*) configuration alters the list of five in two ways. First, the moral lapse against which the third precept enjoins is generalized from adultery to all "non-celibacy" (*abrahmacariya*). Second, it adds three more restraints, against eating at the wrong time – namely after noon – enjoying shows, and wearing ornaments. These alterations mark a transition from an ordinary to a quasi-monastic existence – celibacy and taking only two meals a day being distinctively monastic traits – which is socialized in the use of special titles and forms of address for those who adopt the eight precepts, as well as special dress (in contemporary Theravāda countries a white version of monastic robes) and accoutrements (such as liturgical texts and rosaries). Adoption of the eight precepts may be perpetual, in which case they are recited in daily personal worship, or occasional, as on full moon days, in which case they are "received" from a monk. In this latter case they remain in effect for the ceremony, either twelve or twenty-four hours.

The ten (*daśa*) precepts are stricter still, adding restraint from raised couches and beds and handling silver and gold. They are "given" in formal ceremonies of initiation into the monkhood (the ten precepts being the code of *śrāmaṇeras*) or, in the case of Theravāda women, ceremonies to become "lay nuns" (Sinh. *dasasil mātā*). In both cases the further transition into full monastic life is marked with a change in clothing from white to the typical saffron robes of the monk or nuns, and retirement to a monastic community or solitude. The further transition still is higher ordination (*upasaṃpadā*) which involves adopting the over 200 precepts of the various *vinaya* codes.

Expanded *śīla* practices

While the five, eight or ten precepts may seem to prescribe a specific, somewhat narrow and exclusively negative/repressive moral practice, in actuality maintaining *śīla* involves, at whatever level, a complete commitment of the human being to improving his or her place on the path. Even ordinary five precept holders understand *śīla* to be bigger than avoiding these specific moral lapses. The precepts themselves are open to very wide interpretation such that they can encompass most moral situations, and chanting them daily or at festivals affirms a positive moral discipline that includes cultivation of Buddhist virtues like the four *brahmavihāras* (compassion, pity, sympathetic joy and equanimity). This broader and also positive moral discipline is exemplified for Theravāda Buddhists in the *Jātaka* stories, wherein the *bodhisattva*, far from merely avoiding the five moral lapses, illustrates constantly moral relationships with other beings and the environment; it is spelled out in genres of literature which parallel the Hindu *Dharmaśāstras*. The eight precepts are taken as part of a periodic or perpetual transformation of all aspects of life, the creation of a quasi-monastic identity, while ten precept holders, as monastic novices (*śrāmaṇera*) or lay nuns adopt and grow increasingly socialized into a fully monastic lifestyle.

Echoes of the early Buddhist rituals and practices of moral discipline are evident in the liturgical practices of Mahāyāna and Vajrayāna Buddhists as well, though these have been expanded and altered in several significant ways. First, invocations tend to recognize a plurality of Buddhas and *bodhisattvas* who set the context within which moral discipline proceeds; the *Dharma*-gem is more likely equated with Mahāyāna ideals such as the "perfection of wisdom" (*prajñāpāramitā*) than the early *suttas*/*sūtras*; the *Sangha*-gem is more likely equated with the community of Buddhas and *bodhisattvas* in the entire universe than the specific community of Buddhist monks and nuns in this world. Second, Mahāyāna and Vajrayāna liturgies tend to replace the five, eight or ten precepts of the early tradition and Theravāda with *bodhisattva* vows of varying complexity. Third, Mahāyāna and Vajrayāna liturgies tend to include a formal confession of moral lapses which features in monastic rituals across the Buddhist world but not outside the monastery in the Theravāda context. A particularly elaborate confessional ritual is the "*Dharma* Gathering for Great Compassion Repentance" (*da bei chan fa hui*) popular among Guanyin devotees in China and Taiwan. Tibetan and some Japanese liturgies may also include esoteric invocations and practices. Despite these basic differences, in function these liturgies are quite similar, formally orienting the Buddhist practitioner morally at the beginning of the day or the beginning of a festival or other religious occasion.

Śīla and social mores

While *śīla* is ultimately an individual matter, its anyway obvious social importance is clear in the fact that these varied rituals affirming moral discipline are often public, group events. Buddhist visions of moral society, whether a Theravādin society of precept-observers or a Mahāyāna society of *bodhisattvas*, traditionally centered upon a precept-observing or *bodhisattva* king, presupposed these moral disciplines among the individuals who constituted it. If practiced, the precepts or *bodhisattva* vows, especially in their expanded forms, provide for a social order and interpersonal relationships characterized by non-violence, honesty, propriety, truthfulness, sobriety, compassion, self-sacrifice, equanimity, and other virtues which serve any society well. Recited daily, enforced and modeled by kings, preached by monks, illustrated in Buddhist art and written into laws, *śīla* – especially in the expanded sense described above – proves an important element of social reality writ large. Many observers of Buddhist societies, ancient and modern, have noted the ways in which their specific customs and their overall demeanors exemplify and promote moral discipline.

See also: ***Bodhisattva*; Ethics; Full moon day and other calendrical observances; Monastic rituals; *Vinaya Piṭaka*.**

JONATHAN S. WALTERS

N

NĀGĀRJUNA

Nāgārjuna, who probably lived in the second century CE in south or central India, is credited with writing several influential texts, the most important of which is arguably the *Madhyamikaśāstra* or *Mūlamadhyamakakārikā* (MMK). Authorities differ on the question of which other texts can be attributed to him, but there is general agreement that he also wrote the *Vigrahavyāvartinī* (VV). These two texts are generally regarded as containing the blueprint for what eventually came to be known in India as the Madhyamaka school, a school that had an impact on numerous other schools of Mahāyāna Buddhism in Central and East Asia. Scholars who attribute other texts to Nāgārjuna usually do so on the grounds of that the contents of the other texts agree with the contents of the MMK and VV.

The MMK comprises 450 Sanskrit verses arranged in twenty-seven chapters. As with all Indian treatises written in verse, it is customary to read the MMK with prose commentaries. The Tibetan scholastic tradition had a fondness for classifying the various commentaries of the MMK into competing schools, but it is not obvious that in India such sub-schools could be easily identified. The VV is a much shorter text, also written in verse accompanied by a commentary attributed to Nāgārjuna himself, which anticipates a series of questions that might arise concerning the central issues addressed in the MMK.

The principal argument of the MMK is that everything is empty (*śūnya*) of a fixed, independent nature (*svabhāva*). To say that something is empty, says Nāgārjuna, is to say that it is conditioned, which means that it arises in dependence on other things. A thing's emptiness also means that every word that can be used to express it has its meaning determined by its relationship with other expressions. This means that no thing has absolute, independent existence, and no expression has an absolute, fixed meaning. It is only because a thing is conditioned that it can change. The emptiness of all things means that one's entire being is subject to change. Nāgārjuna's insistence on all this is apparently directed as a criticism of some abhidharmic views whereby all complex things are conditioned, but simple things are not. If a thing were simple as the *Ābhidharmikas* claim, then these simple things could never change; they could neither come into being or pass out of being. This would mean that the allegedly simple building blocks of experience, the *dharmas*, would be eternal and unchanging. If that were the case, then the experience of unhappiness, which is considered to be a *dharma*, would never begin or end. If that were true, says Nāgārjuna, then there would be no point at all in striving to eliminate pain, and hence no point at all to the Buddha's teaching.

A second important theme in the MMK, corroborated in the VV, is that much of our unhappiness stems from rigid beliefs. The doctrine of emptiness is meant to be a cure for that, but, warns Nāgārjuna, there is no cure for anyone who develops a fixation on the doctrine of emptiness itself.

See also: **India, Buddhism in; Madhyamaka school; Mahāyāna Buddhism.**

RICHARD P. HAYES

NĀLANDĀ

In the Buddha's time, Nālandā was a very important town in north central India. The Buddha is said to have visited Nālandā many times and delivered several important discourses there. In the Middle Ages, however, Nālandā became famous as the site of one of the chief centers of Buddhist monastic education, the Nālandā Mahāvihāra, or Nālandā University. From approximately the fifth to the twelfth centuries CE, Nālandā University flourished as a major institution of Buddhist wisdom. The kings of the Gupta and Pāla dynasties patronized Nālandā and established it as a center of learning that was recognized internationally.

The Chinese pilgrim Xuanzang, who studied at Nālandā for several years during the seventh century, provided a good description of the life of the university. In the ninth century, another Chinese traveler, Yizing, also lived at Nālandā for a number of years and wrote an account of his visit. Xuanzang reported that there were 10,000 students and more than 1,500 faculty, but when Yizing stayed there he reported that the students numbered around 3,000. The most famous teacher and the head of the university with whom Xuanzang studied was Śīlabhadra. The curriculum included primarily the works of the Mahāyāna, but also the *Vedas*, Sanskrit grammar, and logic. The university was famous for its libraries filled with manuscripts. The library named Ratnaodadhi (Sea of Jewels) was reported to have been a nine-storey brick building and inscriptions from that time praise the architecture of Nālandā with its rows of monasteries and its lofty turrets. The students were expected to have already studied the major Buddhist texts extensively before entering the university, and the admission exam was administered by gatekeepers who challenged those who sought entry. Those who did gain entry were required to put in long hours studying and debating in Nālandā's "Schools of Discussion" which continued an ancient tradition of monastic education in India. The periods of the day were regulated by a large water clock whose periods were signaled by drumming. The traditional list of famous alumni of Nālandā is said to include such luminaries as: Dharmakīrti, Dignāga, Śāntarakṣita, Kamalaśīla and Padmasambhava. If the tradition concerning these famous scholars being alumni of Nālandā is correct, it would bear out the idea that Nālandā had great significance for the formation of Tibetan Buddhism.

The site of Nālandā University was excavated in the late nineteenth and early twentieth centuries. It is located 90 kilometers southeast of the capital of Bihar, Patna. Many monasteries and temples were arranged in two rows on the campus. The cells of the monastic students opened onto courtyards, and there were many temples and shrines. The seal of Nālandā which was discovered in the excavations shows the wheel of *Dharma* flanked by two gazelles. Today, visitors to this site can see the grandeur and scope of this ancient monastic complex and sense the significance that Buddhist learning had on the culture of India at that time.

Nālandā was destroyed in the twelfth century by Muslim invaders who razed the buildings and burned its texts. However, a modern center for Buddhist studies, the Nava Nālandā Mahāvihāra, was founded nearby in 1951.

See also: **India, Buddhism in; Sacred places.**

George D. Bond

NEW BUDDHIST LAY MOVEMENTS IN JAPAN

The modern and contemporary period, from the end of the nineteenth and into the twenty-first century, has seen the arising of many new Buddhist movements among the so-called New Religions or "new religious movements." Many of them are derived from or inspired by the Nichiren or *Lotus Sūtra* tradition, and are mostly oriented toward lay leaders and followers rather than an ordained clergy. The larger groups are actively involved in social issues, and have an international network. They seek to provide answers for contemporary needs and problems in a way that many people feel is lacking in the traditional Buddhism institutions. Although there are a large number and variety of such movements, both large and small, both relatively old and very new, here we will take a look at some of the major, representative, or influential new Buddhist groups: Sōka Gakkai and Risshō Kōseikai, related to the Nichiren or *Lotus Sūtra* traditions; Shinnyo-en, derived from the Shingon tradition and the *Nirvāṇa Sūtra*; and Aum Shinrikyo, the controversial group that drew on a variety of Buddhist and non-Buddhist traditions to develop a unique mix of teachings and practices, and ended up a deadly cult of the guru.

Sōka Gakkai

Sōka Gakkai (Value Creating Society) is a lay organization originally affiliated with Nichiren Shōshū. It started as a movement (Sōka Kyōiku Gakkai: Value Creating Education Society) founded in 1930 by Makiguchi Tsunesaburō (1871–1944), an educator promoting "value theory" and "the life of great virtue." Toda Jōsei (1900–58) re-established Sōka Gakkai after World War II, emphasizing the idea of "life-force" (the creative power of the universe that emanates from the Buddha) and spreading Nichiren's teachings, and was responsible for its rapid growth in the post-war period. Toda also emphasized the idea of *shakubuku*, a forceful method of proselytization. The Sōka Gakkai grew even larger under its third leader, Ikeda Daisaku (1928–), including expansion abroad with the worldwide organization of Sōka Gakkai International. It currently claims more than twelve million members in over 190 countries.

Sōka Gakkai follows the teachings of Nichiren, stressing faith and the realization of one's inner nature and potential through chanting the title of the *Lotus Sūtra* (the *daimoku*: *namu-myōhō-renge-kyo*), enshrining a copy of a *maṇḍala* created by Nichiren (the *gohonzon*: a combination of the names of various Buddhas in Chinese and Sanskrit that represent the protective functions of the universe) symbolizing the inner Buddhahood of all beings, and reciting portions of the *Lotus Sūtra* (*gongyō*). Sōka Gakkai members are expected to share their faith with others and to be actively involved in changing the world (through "human revolution").

The social engagement of Sōka Gakkai is manifested in their establishment of a political party in Japan, the Kōmeitō (Clean Government Party), which is currently (2005) aligned with the ruling party, and their dedication to a wide variety of social, cultural, and humanitarian activities in the international arena. They manage a major university in Tokyo (Sōka University), with a new campus in Los Angeles. Sōka Gakkai became independent of the Nichiren Shōshū priesthood in 1991, and is currently a fully lay Buddhist organization.

Risshō Kōseikai

Risshō Kōseikai (Society for Establishing Righteousness and Harmony) was founded in 1938 by Niwano Nikkyō (1906–99) and Naganuma Myōkō (1889–1957) for the purpose of promoting Buddhism and the teaching of the *Lotus Sūtra*. Niwano and Naganuma had been members of Reiyūkai, another major new religious movement, but sought a stronger emphasis on the teaching of the *Lotus Sūtra*. Risshō Kōseikai honors the teachings of Tendai and Nichiren, but claims allegiance directly to Śākyamuni and the eternal Buddha as taught in the *Lotus Sūtra*. The current president is Niwano Nichiko, the founder's son, and the society claims over two million member households in Japan, as well as a network of international members.

Risshō Kōseikai at first emphasized overcoming evil *karma* and solving problems by chanting the *Lotus Sūtra*, but now focuses more on the cultivation of personal perfection and the practice of altruistic *bodhisattva*-like activity for world peace and social harmony. It has developed a type of small-group counseling called *hōza* (*Dharma* seat) led by lay teachers. Its practice is focused on chanting, inner reflection, and social activity rather than traditional Buddhist meditation. Its emphasis on *bodhisattva*-like activity in the world is reflected in its promotion of the common good through organizations such as the Brighter Society Movement (an organization for cooperating with local governments, welfare organizations, and volunteer groups), the Donate a Meal Campaign, and the Niwano Peace Foundation, which includes the annual Niwano Peace Prize to honor remarkable religious leaders or groups that contribute to world peace through interreligious dialogue, protection of human rights, and conflict resolution.

Risshō Kōseikai has also been active in promoting inter-religious dialogue and cooperation through leadership and participation in organizations such as the Shinshūren (Federation of New Religious Organizations of Japan) and the World Conference of Religions for Peace (WCRP). They run a seminary for training lay leaders, and publish widely in both Japanese and other languages through Kosei Publishing, including the journal *Dharma World*.

Shinnyo-en

Shinnyo-en was founded by Itō Shinjō (1906–89), an ordinary family man and engineer with a gift for counseling others concerning personal and professional problems. He was ordained in the Shingon esoteric Buddhist tradition at Daigoji (in Kyoto), and started his own lineage in 1948. In 1951 his group took the name Shinnyo-en ("Garden of Thusness") and reincorporated as a legal religious body in 1953. Itō's wife Shojuin also played an important role until her death in 1967. The current leader is Itō Shinso, Itō's daughter and a woman considered the most qualified of his disciples.

Shinnyo-en aims to provide training for people to cultivate their innate Buddha-nature, and a way for lay practitioners to grasp the essence of Buddhist teachings and be liberated from ignorance and craving. Along with traditional Buddhist services, Shinnyo-en provides counseling and meditative training (*sesshin*) based on concepts from the Mahāyāna *Nirvāña Sūtra*. It has established temples and training centers throughout Japan and abroad, in the United States, Latin America, Asia, and Europe, with a membership of almost 900,000 adherents.

Aum Shinrikyō

Aum Shinrikyō began in 1984 as a small yoga training group led by Asahara Shōko (a.k.a. Matsumoto Chizuo). Asahara had studied yoga and esoteric Buddhism as a member of Agonshū, a new religious movement founded by Kiriyama Seiyū. Over the years Asahara taught Buddhist methods of meditation for attaining *satori* (awakening) and *gedatsu* (liberation), as well as non-Buddhist methods such as *kuṇḍalinī* yoga. Asahara claimed to have attained enlightenment, and presented his meetings with the Dalai Lama and other Buddhist leaders as evidence of his attainments. He gathered together a relatively small group of devoted followers (about 10,000 at its height in 1994), many of whom (about 1,000) became world-renouncing ascetics.

Hopes for establishing a utopian Shambhala on earth were replaced around 1990 by an apocalyptic vision of disaster, as Asahara and Aum Shinrikyō faced public criticism for their recruitment activities, and total defeat of their candidates in the national parliamentary elections. Asahara and his followers began a series of crimes – murder of some of their own followers, and of a lawyer (and his family) involved in helping victims of Aum's activities; testing the release of sarin gas in Matsumoto, resulting in numerous deaths; and finally the coordinated release of sarin gas in the Tokyo subway system in March 1995. These activities were justified by Asahara's interpretation of the Buddhist Vajrayāna (said by Asahara to surpass both Hīnayāna and Mahāyāna) teaching of *poa*, saving people by killing them. Asahara and many of his top followers were arrested in 1995, and many have been found guilty of murder and sentenced to death. A small group of followers continue their meditational and yogic practices, having changed the name of their group (in 2000) to Aleph.

See also: **Japan, Buddhism in.**

PAUL L. SWANSON

NEW BUDDHIST ROLES

Buddhism in the West is strongly affected by the increased importance of the laity, the critical evaluation of women's roles, the application of democratic and egalitarian principles, and the championing of social engagement. These emphases, which are strong in most convert groups and catch on in immigrant Buddhist communities, exercise a clear-cut influence on shaping new Buddhist roles. At the same time, these characteristics were reinforced by new roles Western and Asian Buddhists have taken.

To begin with, in the West the Buddhist monk, nun, and priest no longer have the religious monopoly that they have in a number of Asian traditions. Rather, lay teachers also expound the teaching, instruct meditational practices, and may carry out Buddhist rituals. Even more, at times a monk may be criticized and turned back by a lay person. This is hardly imaginable in many Asian contexts, particularly in Theravāda Buddhism. However, in 1957, an uncompromising Australian Buddhist leader named Charles Knight wrote to *bhikkhu* Nārada, at that time one of the world's leading Theravāda authorities, that his expositions and pamphlets were "not in accordance with pure *Dhamma*" and therefore had gone straight to the paper pulp mills. Such an admittedly extreme attitude is nevertheless indicative of the decisively risen self-consciousness of Western lay Buddhists and an evidence of egalitarian principles favored. Monks and nuns themselves have to cope with new demands and roles: in some immigrant communities ordained personnel have to fulfill functions such as social worker, adviser, and political spokesperson for the diaspora group. Hierarchies have been questioned also within the *sangha* and at times a democratic style of leadership instead of the previous autocratic style has been introduced. The feminization of Buddhism in the West has strongly supported the issue of the place and importance of Buddhist nuns (Skt. *bhikṣuṇī*). Western women have sought ordination and reintroduced the Theravāda and Tibetan Buddhist lineages via the Chinese ordination lines. Western women, like the late nuns Jiyu Kennett Rōshi, Ayya Khema, Geshin Prabhasadharma Rōshi, and others have established their own Buddhist organizations and provided prominent and innovative interpretations of Buddhist doctrine and practices. *Bhikṣuṇī* Pema Chödrön, director of Gampo Abbey and well-respected American teacher, introduced modifications to the traditional *Karma* Kagyu three-year retreat in order to meet lifestyle and profession demands of Western practitioners.

On the side of non-monastic people, lay practitioners were instrumental in spreading and establishing Buddhism in Western countries. At times, laypeople have become full-time practitioners and fulfill many roles and obligations traditionally taken by monks and nuns: they teach, practice meditation, study Buddhist texts, instruct in meditation, and spread the *Dharma*. These lay teachers may live in celibacy, in partnership or with a family. Some of them led a monastic life for a few years in Asia but disrobed after their return to the West as they felt it too demanding and difficult to live according to the *Vinaya* rules in a Western setting. Some Buddhist schools invented explicitly new roles, e.g. the Friends of the Western Buddhist Order (FWBO) established the role and function of a *Dharmachari* and *Dharmacharini* (male and female, "*Dharma*-farer"). The committed Buddhists are ordained (in the FBWO) and follow a specific set of precepts. They are not, however, monastics and may follow the lifestyle they prefer. In this respect the role differs from that of an *anagārika* – a "homeless" who has dedicated his life to Buddhism. This role was introduced by Dharmapāla in the late nineteenth century. The laity in immigrant temples and pagodas have also gained importance. Often this is because of their language and organizational skills as well as to the shortage of monastic personnel. Thus laypeople may temporarily take up functions commonly restricted to monks and nuns such as reciting texts and leading through a ceremony.

In many traditions, laypeople have become professionals of Buddhism and are regarded on a par with monastics (especially so in convert groups). Some schools, such as Vipassanā groups, have entirely departed from monastic instructors and rely exclusively on full-time lay teachers. Though some of the "new" roles may have their predecessors in specific Buddhist traditions in Asia, it is the marked emphasis on lay participation, equality of the sexes, and integration of Buddhism into ordinary everyday life that makes some of the roles and functions new.

See also: **Buddhism and Western lifestyle; Buddhism in the Western world; Buddhist adaptations in the West.**

MARTIN BAUMANN

NEW YEAR AND NATIONAL FESTIVALS

In addition to specifically Buddhist calendrical festivals, Buddhists everywhere also participate in numerous indigenous (often pre-Buddhist) annual festivals, most notably New Year celebrations. These are dominated by non-Buddhist (sometimes even un-Buddhist) customs and rites, which during New Year typically include deity-worship, harvest celebrations, gift and greeting exchange, games and competitions, dramas and musical shows, fireworks and decorations, house-cleaning, family reunions, feasting and drinking, and attention to auspicious moments for the first activities of the year, new clothes and/or visits to respected elders.

Yet these New Year celebrations also have come to include Buddhist aspects. This can be recognized generally in the fact that with the exception of Japan (which celebrates New Year on the Gregorian calendar), these celebrations overlap or nearly overlap with a major Buddhist festival, especially celebrations of the Buddha's birth (which in the Theravāda world coincides with his enlightenment and *parinirvāṇa*), such that the two form parts of a single, weeks-long festival season. In their different ways all Buddhists have also added specifically Buddhist rituals and practices to the mix.

Thus in China, Taiwan and the Chinese diaspora, the fifteen-day celebrations of New Year (*Yuan tan*, corresponding to January or February) which culminate in the colorful Lantern Festival on the night of the first full moon of the year, also involve visits to Buddhist temples, monastic blessing rituals at midnight on New Year's Eve, and cycles of monastic worship at various shrines during the first two days of the year. The Tibetan New Year (*Losar*), which corresponds to the Chinese calculation and inaugurates the Great Prayer Festival (*Monlam Chenmo*) in Lhasa, traditionally includes visits to temples for worship and *sūtra* recitation, ritual dances and staged Buddhist debates, *Dharma*-preaching, friendly competitions for the finest butter-carved icons (*torma*), special *pūjās* and other rituals such as burning an effigy (*torjak*) in which has been trapped the evil of the previous year. Though Japanese Buddhists now observe New Year (*Shogatsu*) on 1 January, their celebrations still include Buddhist services of thanksgiving for the past year and renewed dedication to the Buddhist path in the coming one, public *sūtra* recitation by Zen monks for the benefit of all beings, and a ritual known as *Joya-no-kane* in which temple bells chime 108 times, representing the 108 defilements (*kleśa*) which need to be overcome.

Theravāda Buddhists all celebrate the mid-April New Year (Sinh. *Awurudda*, Thai *Songkran*, Burmese *Thingyan*, Khmer *Chaul Chnam*, Lao *Pi Mai*). This date corresponds to the end of the annual rice harvest in much of the region, and Southeast Asian New Year celebrations are especially noted for the practices of dousing others with (sometimes scented or colored) water and building giant sandcastles to represent the past year. But visits to Buddhist temples to hear sermons and *paritta*, offer *pūjās* of festival foodstuffs, conduct processions, receive blessings with oil or water consecrated by a monk or Buddha image, bathe Buddha images, and/or perform rites to transfer merit to the dead likewise give Theravāda New Year celebrations some Buddhist flavor.

Buddhist elements – participation of monks, worship and chanting, Buddhist symbols – are similarly incorporated into numerous additional festivals that are not otherwise particularly Buddhist. Some of these have ancient roots, such as the northeast Thai and Lao rain-making "Rocket Festival" (*Bun Bangfai*) or the celebration of royal birthdays, coronations and weddings; others are clearly more recent, such as "National Day" and May Day festivals.

See also: **Full moon day and other calendrical observances; Holidays and observances; South and Southeast Asia, Buddhism in.**

JONATHAN S. WALTERS

NHAT HANH, THICH

Thich Nhat Hanh is credited with coining the term "engaged Buddhism" in 1963 to describe the socially relevant Buddhism he has sought to construct throughout his career as a Zen Buddhist monk. Through his prolific writing, public speaking, social service, and international peace advocacy, he has become one of the best-known leaders of engaged Buddhism, and indeed of Buddhism itself, throughout the world.

Nhat Hanh was born Nguyen Xuan Bao in 1926 in central Vietnam. He was ordained as a novice monk in Vietnam's *Thien* (Ch. *Chan*, Jap. *Zen*) *Lam Te* (Ch. *Linji*, Jap. *Rinzai*) tradition in 1942 and received full ordination in 1949. The ordination name he took, Nhat Hanh ("One Action"), calls to mind the tenth-century monk Van Hanh ("Ten Thousand Actions"), who was well-versed in Buddhist, Confucian, and Daoist traditions and served as an advisor to Vietnam's kings. Like Van Hanh, Nhat Hanh has also studied widely, both within and without Buddhism, and has consistently involved himself in social and political affairs.

Nhat Hanh's early monastic training incorporated both Mahāyāna and Theravāda traditions, with an emphasis on mindfulness, *gāthā*, and *kōan* practice. After becoming dissatisfied with the narrow curriculum of the Bao Quoc Institute where he began his studies, he enrolled at Saigon University, where he also studied more widely among the disciplines of philosophy, literature, and foreign languages. Upon graduation, Nhat Hanh was invited to return to Bao Quoc Institute to help broaden its curriculum, but soon left again, his ideas reportedly being too "radical" for the institution's elders. His "radical" ideas led him, instead, in 1950 to co-found Ung Quang Temple in Saigon, which later became the An Quang Buddhist Institute, a center of the Buddhist Struggle Movement in the 1960s. During the 1950s, he taught high school and began to disseminate his vision for a socially relevant Buddhism through the writing of books and poems and editing the periodical *Vietnamese Buddhism*, published by the Association of All Buddhists in Vietnam.

In the early 1960s, Nhat Hanh moved to the United States to study comparative religions at Princeton University. He also lectured on contemporary Buddhism at Columbia University, where he was invited to establish a department of Vietnamese Studies. He chose instead to return to Vietnam in 1963, at the request of Vietnam's Buddhist leadership, to help rebuild Buddhism in the wake of recently deposed president Ngo Dinh Diem's persecutions. Toward this end, he was involved in a number of major projects between 1963 and 1966, including the establishment of Van Hanh University in Saigon, the School of Youth for Social Service, the *Tiep Hien* Order or Order of Interbeing (a new "engaged" Buddhist order composed of both lay and monastic practitioners), and a publishing house. He also edited two weekly publications, including the Unified Buddhist Church's *Sound of the Rising Tide*, and wrote prolifically in support of the Struggle Movement. His "neutralist" writings at this time attracted the attention of both the North and South Vietnamese governments, both of which banned his collection of poems, *Prayers for the White Dove of Peace to Appear*.

In 1966, after surviving an assassination attempt, Nhat Hanh began what turned out to be a life of exile when he embarked on an international speaking tour organized by the Fellowship for Reconciliation. The tour promoted his five-point "Proposal for Peace," which called for an immediate and unilateral ceasefire, before members of the United States' Congress, the Canadian and Swedish parliaments, and the United Kingdom's House of Commons. Nhat Hanh also met with Pope Paul VI – who subsequently dispatched a papal mission to Saigon to encourage Vietnamese Catholics to cooperate with Buddhists in the peace effort – and Martin Luther King, Jr. – who publicly repudiated the war for the first time following their meeting and went on to nominate Nhat Hanh for the Nobel Peace Prize.

Toward the end of his speaking tour, colleagues in Vietnam feared for his safety and advised Nhat Hanh not to return. Instead, he took up residence in France and continued to advocate for peace as chair of the Vietnamese Buddhist Peace Delegation to the Paris Peace Talks. Even after the signing of the Accords in 1973, however, he was denied permission to return to Vietnam and retreated for several years from public life. Nhat Hanh has since dedicated himself to advocating reconciliation in Vietnam and teaching his non-violent, engaged Buddhism throughout the world, especially in the West. In 1982, he established Plum Village, a thriving retreat center and his base of operations, near Bordeaux. He has also established centers in California and Vermont.

In 2005, Nhat Hanh and 200 followers were permitted to visit Vietnam for a four-month speaking tour to promote religious freedom; it was Nhat Hanh's first visit home since his exile began in 1966. According to reports, he was greeted "like a rock star." His comments to a reporter during his visit skillfully express his engaged Buddhist teachings in sound-bite form. "I know we will be observed by many people," he said, "even by – especially by – the police. But we don't mind because we believe the police officers also have the Buddha-nature. If you radiate joy, compassion, understanding, peace and calm, they will be able to appreciate it and profit from it."

As his comments to the reporter suggest, Nhat Hanh's engaged Buddhism is grounded in the Mahāyāna doctrine of the universal Buddha-nature and the related teaching of *śūnyatā*, which he renders as "interbeing." Even more basic, perhaps, is the *bodhisattva* vow to root out the suffering of all beings, even the suffering of one's "enemies." Indeed, for Nhat Hanh, the doctrine of interbeing suggests that there is no real separation between oneself and one's enemies, and thus it is not possible to eradicate one's own suffering independently of theirs. Similarly, Nhat Hanh insists that it is not possible even to blame one's enemies for their "evil" actions without also blaming oneself. As he says with reference to his famous poem, "Call Me By My True Names," in which he identifies with a pirate who brutally rapes a twelve-year-old refugee,

> If I had been born in the village of the pirate and raised in the same conditions as he was, I am now the pirate . . . If you or I were born today in those fishing villages, we might become sea pirates in 25 years. If you take a gun and shoot the pirate, you shoot all of us, because all of us are to some extent responsible for this state of affairs.
>
> (*Being Peace*: 62)

For Nhat Hanh, to overcome suffering we must change this state of affairs; indeed, Buddhist liberation is given a mundane interpretation by Nhat Hanh as none other than a new state of affairs, a state in which suffering ceases to arise because its interrelated causes have been mindfully and skillfully eliminated.

Perhaps the most criticized of Nhat Hanh's teachings, especially among engaged Buddhists, is the extreme emphasis he places upon internal change as a means of bringing about social change and the radical non-violence to which this emphasis leads. As he puts it, if we want to "make peace," we have to "be peace"; it is in no circumstances appropriate (that is, expedient) to meet anger with anger or violence with violence. Indeed, he eschews all forms of coercion, even non-violent ones, and encourages followers even to resist fighting against their own anger within; instead, they should be mindful of it and embrace it tenderly as a mother embraces her crying child. For Nhat Hanh, there can be "no battlefields"; only through the gentle embrace of mindfulness can anger and violence truly be assuaged, both within and without.

While engaged Buddhists typically agree that "inner" and "outer" work for peace are interrelated and that such work must progress non-violently, Nhat Hanh represents what might be a minority in the almost exclusive emphasis he places upon "the miracle of mindfulness," that is, the efficaciousness of internal, meditative practices as means for alleviating not only one's own suffering but the suffering of others. While he is confident that one's inner peace will radiate outward through one's relationships and interpersonal interactions, and thereby help create peace in the world, to his critics this approach, which eschews even non-violent attempts to coerce others, is simply naïve. As one American engaged Buddhist put it after participating in a retreat led by Nhat Hanh, "I found myself uncomfortable with what I perceived to be an underlying premise of the retreat: that if enough individuals change, society will change." Despite such misgivings on the part of some engaged Buddhists, however, Nhat Hanh and his followers remain firm in their conviction that mindfulness practice is, indeed, the only realistic way to achieve true peace, not only in oneself but also in society.

Regardless of the effectiveness of the tactics he encourages, as his comments to the reporter above demonstrate, Thich Nhat Hanh is an adept promoter of engaged Buddhism who makes constant use of all available media (interviews, poems, books, articles, speeches, workshops, and the Internet) to promote his ideas. In terms of his writing alone, he has published over eighty books in various genres and languages, which together have sold over 1.5 million copies. Among the more influential of his books in English are *Peace is Every Step*; *The Miracle of Mindfulness*; *Being Peace*; and *Living Buddha, Living Christ*.

See also: **Ariyaratne, A.T.; Buddhist peace groups (in Asia and the West); Dalai Lama (and the Tibetan struggle); Engaged Buddhism; Global Buddhist networks: selected examples; Maha Ghosananda; Vietnam, Buddhism in.**

JIM DEITRICK

NICHIREN AND NICHIRENSHŪ

Nichiren (1222–82) was a Japanese Buddhist monk whose intense faith in the *Lotus Sūtra* brought him into conflict with the existing religious and secular authorities of the day. His disciples and followers formed the Nichiren (or Hokke/Lotus) school.

Nichiren was born in Kominato, a small seaside village in Awa Province (Chiba prefecture). He entered Kiyosumi-dera, a neighboring Tendai temple, at the age of twelve, where he studied Tendai, Pure Land, and esoteric Buddhism, and was ordained at the age of sixteen. After a few years in Kamakura he continued his studies at major centers on Mount Hiei, Mount Kōya, and Nara. In 1253 Nichiren returned home to Kiyosumi-dera where it is said that he proclaimed his faith in the *Lotus Sūtra* and rejected all other forms of Buddhism, proposing instead the chanting of the *daimoku*, *namu myōhō renge kyō* (homage to the *Lotus Sūtra*). His message was not well received and Nichiren went to Kamakura, where he presented his *Risshō ankoku ron* (Treatise on Establishing the Right [*Dharma*] to Bring Peace to the Country) to Hōjō Tokiyori (1227–63), the *de facto* ruler of Japan. Nichiren blamed other Buddhist (especially Pure Land) schools for creating the conditions for various natural disasters (such as famine and epidemics) and predicted further karmic retributions, including foreign invasion, if the government did not accept the "true" Buddhism of the *Lotus Sūtra*. Instead, for his troubles, Nichiren was exiled to Izu.

After being released from exile in 1263, Nichiren traveled widely, and continued his provocative preaching (called *shakubuku*, a method of propagation through confrontation and rebuke). His position was buoyed by the Mongol invasions, which fulfilled his prophesies of foreign attack, but his blistering attacks on other Buddhist schools and their government supporters incurred the wrath of the authorities. Nichiren escaped assassination attempts and a sentence of execution by beheading, and finally faced exile again in 1271, this time to the remote Sado Island in the Japan Sea. Here he wrote *Kaimokusho* (Opening the Eyes), in which he claimed to be a reincarnation of Jōgyō Bosatsu, the figure presented in the *Lotus Sūtra* as one who will appear in latter times to preach and uphold this *sūtra*. He also composed a distinctive verbal/calligraphic *maṇḍala* as a representation of all living beings and buddhas surrounding the letters of the *daimoku* in the center. Another text composed at this time was the *Kanjin honzon sho* (*Contemplating the Object of Worship*), perhaps his most important work. Here Nichiren expands on the Tendai concept of *ichinen sanzen* (all of reality in a single thought) and the ideal of setting up a Buddha land in this world through following the *Lotus Sūtra*.

Nichiren was released from Sado in 1274 and returned briefly to Kamakura, but soon settled at Mount Minobu near Mount Fuji. He gathered many disciples and wrote numerous letters, revealing a sensitivity which belies his reputation as an acerbic fanatic. Nichiren died in 1282 after a long period of illness.

Nichiren is famous for his fierce denunciation of other schools ("*nenbutsu* leads to hell, Zen followers are devils, Shingon ruins the country, and members of the Ritsu school are traitors"). He summed up the true Lotus faith in three parts: (1) *honzon*: Śākyamuni, the personification of truth, as the object of worship, represented calligraphically as a *maṇḍala*; (2) *kaidan*: the ordination platform as a religious center and place of practice to realize the Buddha land in this world; and (3) *daimoku*: the chanting of homage to the *Lotus Sūtra* (with the title embodying the gist of the Buddha Dharma) as an expression of faith.

Just before his death Nichiren named six of his disciples as leaders, and they propagated Nichiren's teachings throughout Japan. Disagreements over various matters – such as how to interpret the *Lotus Sūtra*, and whether or how much to compromise with secular authorities and other Buddhist schools – led to numerous splits and sub-sects. Some, for example, insisted on an uncompromising position known as "neither-receiving-nor-offering" (*fuju-fuse*), such that Nichiren followers should neither accept donations from, nor make offerings to, non-Nichiren followers or groups, while others accepted a more compromising stance. A major incident occurred in the late sixteenth century when Nichiō, abbot of Myōkakuji in Kyoto, refused to participate in memorial services sponsored by the ruler Toyotomi Hideyoshi. All other Nichiren monks followed a policy of *jufuse* (receive but do not give offerings). Nichiō was eventually banished and his *fuju-fuse* movement suppressed, but it was eventually acknowledged by the government as the Fujufuse-ha in the nineteenth century.

Nichiren's rhetoric on the place of Japan in Buddhist history can be easily interpreted in a nationalistic way. One example of this tendency was Tanaka Chigaku (1861–1939), who established the Kokuchūkai (Pillar of the Nation Society) in 1914 to promote nationalism and support the military in its imperialist expansion. On the other hand, Nichiren's uncompromising stance for what is "right" has inspired many to take a principled stand against secular powers, such as numerous Nichiren-tradition leaders in the 1940s who were imprisoned for their defiance of the wartime government.

Nichiren still commands a large following among Buddhists in Japan, and many of the largest new religious movement – such as Sōka Gakkai, Reiyūkai, and Risshō Kōseikai – are derived from or inspired by the Nichiren tradition.

See also: **Japan, Buddhism in; New Buddhist lay movements in Japan.**

PAUL L. SWANSON

NIKĀYA BUDDHISM

The term *Nikāya* Buddhism refers to the pre-Mahāyāna phase of Indian Buddhism during which time the original body of the Buddha's followers subdivided into separate sects (*nikāya*). Later sources, upon which too much reliance should not be placed, speak of there being eighteen such sects in all, but whatever the exact number there were certainly many groups which regarded themselves as distinctive in terms of their doctrines, monastic practices, or both. This article discusses the main factors which lead to fragmentation, and the mechanisms through which it came about, such as the holding of councils. It also characterizes some of the most important schools. More detailed information will be found in the individual entries on the schools mentioned, as well as on other schools which are not dealt with in detail here (references will be found in the "see also" paragraph at the end of the article).

Councils

Councils were the mechanism by which the Buddhist monastic order attempted to limit the social and intellectual fragmentation that was endemic to its organization. The Buddhist monastic order (*sangha*) is organized in a segmentary fashion. Within any segmentary social organization, social identity and location are defined in terms of lineages rather than in terms of identifying characteristics or marked boundaries. In the Buddhist monastic order, one was ordained by someone, one was always the student of someone, and one belonged to his lineage; consequently, one's social location came from one's relations to the monks that one's teacher had also ordained and taught, monks who were fellow members of one's particular lineage. As is easily seen, fragmentation is inherent in segmentary social organizations wherever they occur. In the case of the Buddhist monastic order, students of a teacher go on to have their own students who, in turn, are more related to each other than to the monks who are in lineages of the other students of their teacher's teacher. With this inherent fragmentation of segmentary social organizations, in which an individual is related in varying degrees and in different ways and located within overlapping groups, competition and conflict are not uncommon. It should be no surprise, perhaps, that the earliest divisions in *Nikāya* Buddhism were around issues of monastic practice, and thus consequently about social locations within the larger monastic order.

One way that can be used to settle conflict between segmentary lineages is to claim a deeper genealogical connection between them by saying that the members of groups in competition and conflict are all students of a common teacher – teacher's teacher and so forth – and we can safely assume that such arguments were continually made in the Buddhist monastic order even if these arguments and the monks who made them did not make it into the historical record available to us. We might also speculate that the common tendency found across *Nikāya* Buddhism to identify a particular monk as the founder of a certain school, such as Katyāyanīputra with the Sarvāstivādins, was intended to maintain connections among groups that otherwise would be exclusively differentiated by positions of doctrine or practice.

The Buddhist councils can be seen as similar attempts to maintain relations of harmony among segmentary lineages by claiming the deepest genealogical connection possible: the Buddha and his teachings. When councils failed to establish such a deep connection, however, schism replaced fragmentation, and lineages that had merely been differentiated were subsequently separated by new divisions and perceived as unrelated groups.

Historical sources produced in the different schools of *Nikāya* Buddhism describe five different Buddhist councils. For modern historians, there is considerable doubt about even the broadest accuracy of these accounts, and perhaps they are best taken as descriptions of ideals that could motivate and guide subsequent action in unrecorded councils rather than as accounts of actual events. The different accounts are also frequently sectarian in their historical claims, generally attributing the deep genealogical connection to the Buddha and his teachings to the group or school which produced the account and portraying rival groups as beyond the pale. Such accounts obviously played a centrally visible role in the self-understanding of particular schools of *Nikāya* Buddhism and in defining their place in the history of the Buddha's legacy.

Vinayas

Vinaya denotes the discipline of Buddhist monastics and the associated literature that guides and regulates those who cultivate that discipline. There has always been an important sociological component to *Vinaya* in Buddhist communities. Monastic discipline, the careful observance of regulations in practice, as these regulations are found in *Vinaya* texts, serves to set the Buddhist monastic community off from other religious communities with which it co-existed and interacted within a particular cultural context. It was *Vinaya* that distinguished Buddhist monks and nuns from Jain monastics and from Hindu ascetics in India, for example. With the emergence of *Nikāya* Buddhism, beginning around the third century BCE, this sociological dimension of *Vinaya* was directed to new ends and differences in *Vinaya* observance frequently displayed and maintained divisions that developed with the Buddhist monastic community itself. In this regard, monastic discipline shades into liturgy, and being in communion with other monks in a particular community or *Nikāya* in the performance of rituals prescribed by the *Vinaya* texts became the mark of membership in a particular school.

The multiple functions of *Vinaya* – some individual, some social – can be seen in the ritualized recitation of the *Prātimokṣa*, the summary of monastic precepts, by a community of monks meeting together monthly. This communal recitation served to maintain the discipline of individual monks, even as it promoted the collective cohesion of the group. *Prātimokṣa* texts for eight different schools of *Nikāya* Buddhism survive in some fashion, in addition to the one found from the Theravāda. They are Sarvāstivāda, Mūlasarvāstivāda, Dharmaguptaka, Mahīśāsaka, Mahāsaṃghika, Mahāsaṃghika-lokottaravāda, Kaśyapīya, and Sammatīya. It is clear that the rituals of monastic life were centrally visible in the divisions of monastic life that characterized *Nikāya* Buddhism, even if they were probably not their causes.

Those causes were most likely lay in disagreements over how *Vinaya* was to be practiced and how *Vinaya* was to be applied in new circumstances as Buddhism spread and monastic life changed. With regard to disagreements about how *Vinaya* was to be practiced, the key tension was always between strictness and laxity. Buddhist historiography recounts various instances of disagreements among monks over whether certain practices were permissible or required. As Buddhist institutions spread throughout first India and then across Central Asia, new disagreements emerged with respect to regional differences that began to crystallize in the Buddhist world. The disagreements here moved along a tension between local and trans-local practices. Finally, as Buddhist institutions became more prominent in the public life of the emerging empires of South and Central Asia, new disagreements and competitions for patronage would have emerged over what was permissible according to the *Vinaya* texts and received traditions. These changes were more dramatic even than the earlier transformation in which Buddhist monastic life moved from an ideal of a wandering community to a settled institutional life. Rituals of donations to Buddhist institutions were key elements of the political economy of empires; indeed participation in and sponsoring of Buddhist rituals was one of the most effective ways that a ruler could articulate his identity as an emperor, as opposed to a mere king, in the first 700 years of the Common Era. This meant that Buddhist monasteries received large amounts of patronage and ritual donations. Monasteries came to function as economic and political institutions as well as religious ones. Moreover, through these public rituals, the monasteries of *Nikāya* Buddhism became embedded in the ritual life of mainstream Buddhism, that social grammar that created connections and interactions across the boundaries of monastic schools, regions, and even religious communities. Royal patronage of Buddhist institutions, however, was not an indication of the personal commitments of a ruler, and the social grammar of the rituals and sacred sites of mainstream Buddhism effectively blended into the ritual life of other religious communities, such as the Hindu and the Jain.

When we look at *Vinaya* in mainstream Buddhism, it is obvious that its primary function socially was a ritual one. Individual monks, of course, always pursued their personal religious goals guided by the practice of *Vinaya*, but the prestige that came to communities of disciplined monks only added to their ritual value in mainstream Buddhism. Disciplined monks, monks who strictly observed the *Vinaya* and were indifferent to the allures of public life, were often the most desired "fields of merit" for the donative rituals of mainstream Buddhism.

In this context, *Vinaya* became a way of negotiating the competing claims of different social communities: the received lineage of a particular monastic community; the collective identity of a regional culture: and the trans-local and cosmopolitan visions of imperial cultures.

The performance of the *Prātimokṣa* in a particular school's version would have publicly affirmed the continuity of tradition within a monastic community. Of course, it would have also affirmed to the individual monks who joined in such a performance that the life of discipline entailed by the *Prātimokṣa* itself was key to their religious lives. It would also have affirmed publicly the distinctive identity of the community reciting the *Prātimokṣa* vis-à-vis other monastic communities. Differences in monastic dress, another concern of *Vinaya* literature, would have displayed the school divisions of the monastic order in *Nikāya* Buddhism. But these divisions would have been formally embodied and authorized for monks in the performance of the *Prātimokṣa* rituals. It should come as no surprise that variation in the *Prātimokṣa* and other ritual literature was greater than other kinds of *Vinaya*.

The *Vinaya*, as a canonical collection, survives in the versions of five different schools of *Nikāya* Buddhism, in addition to that found in the Theravāda tradition: Mahāsaṃghika, Sarvāstivāda, Mūlasarvāstivāda, Dharmaguptaka, and Mahīśāsaka. In size and contents, there are significant differences among these *Vinaya* collections, but there is sufficient overlap among them to suggest that they draw on a common backdrop that antedates the formation of different schools in *Nikāya* Buddhism, unlike what is observed with the *Prātimokṣa* texts. Above all, these *Vinaya* collections all seem concerned with the creation of social boundaries that would define who is inside a particular community and who is not, and how to regulate the behavior of those who are within a community, and what to do about those who violate these regulations. *Vinaya* is, somewhat surprisingly, not particularly concerned with many of the practices that are distinctive to Buddhist monastic life, such as meditation. *Vinaya* is concerned with the regulation of sexuality, with the etiquette of monastic hierarchy, with the ownership of property, more than the mental transformation associated with meditation. Monastic literature more generally, of course, included many digests on the practice of meditation but this was not included in *Vinaya* literature proper.

Regional differences were clearly important in the history of *Nikāya* Buddhism, but we do not know just how they were important. Inscriptions do help us to identify the prominence of different schools in different regions of India. The Mahāsaṃghikas, for example, were strong in central India, while the Dharmaguptakas were prominent in the northwest. These regional differences affected *Vinaya* literature as well, with the actual *Vinayas* of different schools sometimes transmitted in the languages of the region with which they were most associated. The Dharmaguptakas, for example, used Ghāndhārī for their *Vinaya*, while the Mahāsaṃghikas seem to have used either a Prākrit or a form of Buddhist hybrid Sanskrit. Later Indian and Tibetan writers tended to idealize the associations of language and school, saying that the Sarvāstivādins used Sanskrit, the Sthaviravādins used Paiśāci, the Mahāsaṃghikas used Prākrit, and the Sammatīyas used Apabhramśa.

The role of *Vinaya* literature in *Nikāya* Buddhism would be misunderstood if it were only perceived as expressing and reinforcing sectarian divisions within the Buddhist monastic order. It did do this, of course, but it also did something else. In the first centuries of the Common Era, *Vinaya* guided monastic participation in the ritual life of mainstream Buddhism. In doing so, *Vinaya* effected an openness in the monastic community to the religious culture that encompassed it and whose support made its existence possible.

The religious culture of mainstream Buddhism focused primarily on worship (*pūjā*), rituals of merit-making (*puṇyakarma*), and donative rituals (*dāna*). There is abundant evidence for monastic participation in these rituals in all versions of the *Vinaya*, and inscriptional evidence gives further confirmation of this. Monks arranged for images of the Buddha to be made, they paid for ceremonies of worship to be performed to these images, and they performed these rituals of worship themselves. We also see ample evidence in the various *Vinayas* for the effects on the monastic communities of this participation in the ritual life of mainstream Buddhism. The control and maintenance of property became a central concern of monastic life, and a reflection of the resources that came to monasteries in regular donative rituals performed by prominent individuals and by rulers themselves, on their own behalf and on the behalf of their states. Buddhist monasteries, far from being places of poverty intentionally chosen within a discipline of world renunciation, were sites for the conspicuous display of wealth, as archeological evidence at monastic sites like Ajaṇṭā in western India make clear. *Vinaya* literature reflects these conditions, with its close attention to the proper ownership of monastic property, whether of institutions or of individuals, and with its rules for the inheritance of property by monks from other deceased monks. Some *Vinaya* collections also included extensive corpuses of narrative literature that provided models for the religious values and practices of mainstream Buddhism.

This openness of the *Vinaya* of the schools of *Nikāya* Buddhism helps us to understand how these collections came to be normative in other communities besides the ones in which they first took shape. A number of *Vinayas* from *Nikāya* Buddhism were used in China by different communities that were otherwise Mahāyāna in their orientation and self-understanding, and the Mūlasarvāstivādin *Vinaya* became normative in the Buddhist communities of Tibet. There are no uniquely Mahāyāna or Vajrayāna *Vinaya* collections. It would seem that when the Mahāyāna or Vajrayāna monastic communities had adopted a particular *Vinaya*, they embraced its catholic openness to mainstream Buddhism rather than its ability to define sectarian boundaries.

Abhidharma

Abhidharma denotes a style of systematic and philosophical interpretation of the Buddha's teachings that was developed by Buddhist scholastics in *Nikāya* Buddhism. The formation of distinct traditions of *Abhidharma* thought and literature was gradual, becoming clearly visible about the third century BCE and reaching an apex around the fourth century CE, but the practice of *Abhidharma* was coincident with the formation of the separate schools that are characteristic of *Nikāya* Buddhism. The philosophical systems subsequently created in these different schools, however, exerted an influence that went beyond the communities of their creation. Their contents were the subject of mutual exchange and debate among different schools and they left an enduring imprint on the philosophical systems that developed in Mahāyāna communities, notably the Yogācāra.

The meaning of the term *Abhidharma* is not easily specified, in large part because the term quickly became overdetermined as a category in the communities that valued *Abhidharma* as an intellectual and religious practice. A straightforward analysis of the word suggests that *Abhidharma* practice is a more advanced or "higher" (*abhi*) study of the Buddha's teachings (*dharma*), and this interpretation was frequently endorsed by Buddhist scholastics. The complexity of meaning that the term quickly acquired in use, however, can be seen in the enumeration of twenty-four different meanings for the word in some texts of the later Sarvāstivāda.

Whatever the complexities of the term might be, it is clear that *Abhidharma* is a method of scholastic analysis and interpretation. As an intellectual practice, *Abhidharma* was philosophical in its concerns for first principles, coherence and consistency, as well as in its rigorous self-consciousness about its methods of interpretation and epistemology. As a religious practice, *Abhidharma* was commonly given three goals. It was meant to be an aid to understanding the world and especially a person through the identification of the metaphysical elements and constitutive processes that make the world and a person what they are. It was also meant to provide assistance in the defense of authentic Buddhist metaphysical positions against the challenges of non-Buddhist rivals and Buddhist heretics. In having this purpose, we can see that *Abhidharma* was a reaction to the conditions of doctrinal difference that characterized *Nikāya* Buddhism as much as it helped to create those differences. Finally, *Abhidharma* was seen as having a soteriological purpose because the discriminatory knowledge that *Abhidharma* contributed to the personal and salvific transformation that was the reason for the existence of Buddhist monastic life. Indeed, the metaphysics discerned through *Abhidharma* analysis came to be identified with the insight gained in the course of higher spiritual attainments.

Three intellectual practices are at the core of *Abhidharma* thinking, each furthering the three religious goals just mentioned. First is standardization. *Abhidharma* standardized the teachings of the Buddha largely through the making of lists of key doctrines which in turn were interpreted as the essential core of Buddhist thought and practice. Second is elaboration. *Abhidharma* literature developed and critically elaborated the basic ideas found in the Buddha's teachings by explaining them in detail and by applying them to new contexts. The third practice of *Abhidharma* thinking is systematization. *Abhidharma* thinkers connected the basic categories of their lists to each other with an eye to removing apparent inconsistencies and also to display their mutual interdependence and coherence.

With respect to their *Vinaya* and *Sūtra* literature, the different schools of *Nikāya* Buddhism showed considerable overlap and commonality, suggesting that these parts of their canons crystallized to a large degree before the process of school formation got well underway. This is not the case with respect to their collections of *Abhidharma* literature. Indeed, the *Abhidharma* collections of the various schools of *Nikāya* Buddhism are so different that we must conclude that *Abhidharma* was integral to the processes by which they became differentiated. This means that *Abhidharma* practices and goals were also put in the service of school formation and the defense of *Abhidharma* positions became as much an apologetic method as a soteriological practice. Inevitably, the apologetic purposes to which *Abhidharma* practice was directed tended to be at the expense of its other intellectual and religious goals, with a defense of mere dogmatism often the result.

Major schools

Mahāsaṃghikas and Sthaviras

The Mahāsāṃghika school was one of the first schools of *Nikāya* Buddhism. It emerged from a schism in the Buddhist monastic order which occurred in about the fourth or third century before the Common Era, about a century or so after the Buddha's death. The name Mahāsāṃghika or "great monastic community" suggests that this school represented the larger group in the previously united monastic order. Its counterpart was known as the Sthaviras or "the elders." It is with this division of the Buddhist monastic order into the two schools that did not acknowledge each other's ordination lineages or canons that one can properly refer to *Nikāya* Buddhism. Both schools were subject to further subdivisions and are, together, the institutional source for all of schools and groups of *Nikāya* Buddhism in India. The Mahāsāṃghikas divided into at least six different schools.

There are various explanations in Buddhist sources for the original schism between the Mahāsāṃghikas and the Sthaviras. While the exact reasons are unclear and open to contradictory interpretations, the basic divide seems to have been over issues of conservative and liberal interpretations of thought and practice. One historical account preserved in the Theravāda tradition explains that there was a group of monks in Vaiśālī who had adopted a number of practices that other monks considered to be in violation of monastic precepts. Some of these practices concerned the consumption of food – when one could eat, whether one could keep salt for use as a condiment, and permitting certain foods that ordinarily were avoided – while others involved monastic ritual practice and still others were about the handling of money by monks. In general, it would seem that the new practices assumed and created conditions of practice and interpretation that loosened the requirements of monastic life, although it can also be argued that the Mahāsāṃghikas were resisting an increasingly legalistic approach to monastic practice. Most basically, however, the specific practices were simply at odds with monastic practices found elsewhere. A judgment was made by an appointed set of senior monks (Sthaviras) against the new practices, but many monks refused to abandon them and as a result of this refusal the monastic order came to be divided. Whether or not the details of this Theravādin account are correct, it does make it clear that the formation of separate schools at the beginnings of *Nikāya* Buddhism tended to be over issues of monastic discipline rather than doctrine.

Subsequently, issues of doctrine were more to the fore in the formation of schools in *Nikāya* Buddhism and later Buddhist historians tended to look back on the history of *Nikāya* Buddhism and see doctrinal causes for even the earliest divisions. The division between the Sthaviras and the Mahāsāṃghikas thus came to be seen as resulting from issues of doctrine, particularly over the nature of an *arhat*, a person enlightened through the teachings of the Buddha. A particular monk, commonly called Mahādeva, taught that an *arhat* could have dreams accompanied by nocturnal emissions; that his enlightenment did not mean that he was knowledgeable about everything and indeed could still have ignorance; that he could have doubts: these ideas, along with others, seem to make the *arhat* less exalted than he was portrayed by others, indeed they may well have been seen as disparaging the state of being an *arhat*. A council was convened in Pāṭaliputra to resolve the doctrinal disagreement, but it failed in its purpose and the Mahāsāṃghika emerged from it as the group which affirmed the doctrinal position of Mahādeva.

It is also plausible that the conditions for the original schism between the Sthaviras and Mahāsāṃghikas represented simply regional differences that inevitably emerged in the Buddhist monastic order as it spread across South Asia. The Mahāsāṃghikas have some associations especially with central and south India, but they were found across India and even beyond; by the seventh century, the Lokottaravādins had made Bāmiyān in present-day Afghanistan into a major Buddhist center. The seventh-century Chinese pilgrim Yijing portrayed the Mahāsāṃghikas as one of the most numerous schools that he observed in India.

Whatever the historical processes by which they emerged, the Mahāsāṃghikas do seem to have been subsequently open to new developments in thought and practice. This seems to have the case even with their canon, although very little of it has survived. They had their own *Vinaya*, as did other some other early schools, and a portion of this survives in a version of Sanskrit. They had their own *Abhidharma*, as did some other schools, but none of it survives. They also had their own collection of *sūtras*, which is also largely lost, but descriptions of it suggest that they considered it as a canonical collection of texts, including *dhāraṇī* or protective texts, that were used but remained uncanonical in other schools of *Nikāya* Buddhism. On the basis of some accounts, it seems that the Mahāsāṃghika canon could have included texts that were considered Mahāyāna texts and it is often thought by modern scholars that there is some connection between Mahāsāṃghika thought and what emerged as distinctive Mahāyāna doctrines.

This is particularly the case with Mahāsāṃghika ideas about the Buddha, especially as these are found in the *Mahāvastu*, a *Vinaya* text of the Lokottaravādins, one of the later subdivisions of the Mahāsāṃghikas. The Mahāsāṃghikas made a sharper distinction between an *arhat* and a Buddha. They held that there are simultaneously many buddhas in the universe, something that is widely claimed in Mahāyāna texts. The Mahāsāṃghikas also developed a kind of docetic understanding of the career of the Buddha. That is to say, they claimed that the Buddha did not actually act in the world, but only appeared to do so, because he is supra-mundane (*lokottara*).

Sarvāstivāda

The Sarvāstivāda was an important school of Indian Buddhism that separated from the main body of the elders (Sthaviras) around three centuries after the death of the Buddha. Its name means "the school that holds that everything exists," or "the school of the reality of all phenomena," this unusual designation deriving from its distinctive and intriguing philosophical views concerning the nature of phenomena or *dharmas*,

Like other early schools such as the Theravāda, the ontology of the Sarvāstivāda was pluralist and realist, and followers of the school believed (not unlike the ancient Greek atomists) that reality could be analyzed into a collection of discrete entities, which were known as *dharmas*. Theories of this kind were developed as a solution to difficulties arising out of the Buddhist denial of enduring substances in the no-Self (*anātman*) doctrine, which gave rise to problems in causation, temporality and personal identity. The conventional scholastic solution was to posit a theory of instantaneous serial continuity according to which phenomena (*dharmas*) constantly replicate themselves in a momentary sequence of change (*dharma-kṣanikatvā*). Thus reality was conceived of as cinematic, like a filmstrip in which one frame constantly gives way to the next: each moment is substantially existent in its own right, and collectively they produce the illusion of stability and continuity. However, this position is not free of problems, not the least of which is what makes an individual or object the same over a span of time. The distinctive Sarvāstivādin solution was to claim that *dharmas* existed in all three times, and enjoyed real existence in the past and future, as well as in the present. Four main theories were proposed to explain this, which we cannot go into here, except to note that according to the first of these, *dharmas* exist from beginningless time and simply undergo a change of mode from latent to manifest in the moment in which they exert causal efficacy (*kāritva*). Time itself was thus seen as a change of mode undergone by *dharmas*, and past, present and future were defined by their relationship to one another rather than as real existents. This made it possible to claim that one and the same phenomenon can exist in all "three times," just as the same woman can be a mother and a daughter simultaneously.

Although the Sarvāstivādins were apparently expelled at the council of Pāṭaliputra, they went on to become extremely influential, particularly in the northwest of India in Kashmir and Gandhāra, where they survived until Buddhism disappeared from the subcontinent. The school possessed its own canon, much of which survives today, and is renowned for its *Abhidharma* texts, especially the *Mahāvibhāṣā* composed under the supervision of Vasumitra at the council of Kaniṣka (second century CE). The school is alternatively known as the Vaibhāṣika, from the name of this text, and gave rise to a dissident tradition known as the Sautrāntika. Later the Sarvāstivāda subdivided into five sub-schools: Dharmagupta, Mūlasarvāstivāda, Kāśyapīya, Mahīśāsaka, Sautrāntika, and the Vātsīputrīya.

Vātsīputrīya

The Vātsīputrīya were one of the earliest schools to emerge in *Nikāya* Buddhism and the first monastic school or *Nikāya* to split off from the Sthaviravādin school. According to some Buddhist sources, this division occurred 200 years after the death of the Buddha, which would place it in the third century BCE. The Vātsīputrīyas took their name from a founding figure, Vātsīputra. He is said to have been a Brahmin by birth and ordained as a monk in a lineage that could be traced to Śāriputra, one of the Buddha's great disciples. While Vātsīputra is described as a master of the *Vinaya*, the texts of monastic law, he is also said to have prepared a new version of the *Abhidharma* from a received tradition that he attributed to Śāriputra and Rāhula; there is no surviving evidence for this collection, although it is said to have existed in nine parts. Vātsīputra is probably best remembered in Buddhist sources, however, for holding a doctrinal position that maintained the reality of a person, *pudgala*, across time. The followers of Vātsīputra were likewise known for holding this position, and thus were frequently reviled as *pudgalavādins*, although they also held a number of other distinctive doctrinal positions.

The Sthaviravādins, from whom the Vātsīputrīyas separated, had constituted themselves about a century earlier in contradistinction to the Mahāsaṃghikas. This first schism of the Buddhist monastic order was also on doctrinal grounds, around disagreements about the nature of an enlightened person (*arhat*). The fact that this first division and the subsequent separation of the Vātsīputrīyas were both on doctrinal grounds suggests that the earliest divisions within the Buddhist monastic order crystallized around doctrinal disputes, but the conditions for these divisions were just as much social as intellectual.

Although relatively little is known about the Vātsīputrīyas as a monastic group in India or elsewhere, what is known includes some details that are sufficient to suggest to us what the first conditions for the emergence of distinct doctrinal "schools" within the Buddhist movement might have been. First, identifying Vātsīputra as a student of Śāriputra identifies him as a member of a particular ordination lineage that would have been simultaneously distinguished and connected to other ordination lineages in a segmentary pattern much like ordinary kinship networks. Awareness of being members of distinct ordination lineages, and sometimes as prestigious as one from Śāriputra, surely must have generated an awareness of difference within the monastic order but would not have ordinarily prompted separations and schisms from it. Second, Vātsīputra's lineage apparently also preserved its own tradition of textual transmission and interpretation which it traced back to Śāriputra and Rāhula as part of its own collective self-understanding and sense of prestige; we are aware of other ordination lineages that included similar collective memories as part of their identities. This received heritage provided the conditions for doctrinal disagreements that, in turn, developed into a desire for division and separation, once reconciliation of difference would have been perceived as an abandonment of a lineage's constitutive authenticity. Separation, once initiated, would have been then reinforced by exclusions in practice between monastic groups and by the codification of distinct *Vinaya* texts, as did happen among some of the Vātsīputrīyas.

As so often happened in the schools of *Nikāya* Buddhism, the Vātsīputrīyas once established as a distinct school were themselves subject to further divisions. Doctrinal disagreements again seem to have structured these divisions, apparently around issues that emerged as the followers of Vātsīputra elaborated and systematized what his *Abhidharma* collection entailed. The Vātsīputrīyas divided into four new schools, the Dhammottarīyas, the Bhadray āṇiyas, the Sammatīyas, and the Ṣaṇṇagarikas. We only have direct knowledge about the Sammatīyas because a few of their texts have survived in Chinese translations. Indeed, it is largely from the Sammatīyas that we have direct knowledge of the Vātsīputrīyas. There is no surviving direct evidence of the Vātsīputrīyas as a group prior to this subdivision in India or elsewhere in the Buddhist world, although they are reported as still surviving in the Pāla empire in eastern India as late as the twelfth century.

See also: ***Abhidharma*; *Abhidharmakośa*; Aśvaghoṣa; Councils; *Dharma*; Dharmaguptakas; Harivarman; Kaniṣka; Katyāyanīputra; Sammatīya / *pudgalavādins*; *Sanghas*, sectarian; Sarvāstivāda; Vasubandhu; Vātsīputrīyas.**

CHARLES HALLISEY AND DAMIEN KEOWN

NIRVĀṆA

Nirvāṇa is the ultimate goal *(paramārtha)* of Buddhist practice, and in most explanations of the act of going for refuge to the three jewels, *nirvāṇa* is regarded as the *dharma*-jewel to which a Buddhist goes for refuge. It is for the sake of helping others attain *nirvāṇa* that all Buddhist teachings are devised. The word "*nirvāṇa*" literally means "blowing out" and is a metaphor that can be understood in two ways. First, it is explained as like the blowing out of a fire, or the extinction of a fire when all its fuel has been consumed. Second, it is explained as the act of cooling something down by blowing, as when a breeze cools people down on a hot day. In either explanation, the prevailing notion is that of relief from something unpleasantly hot.

Buddhism had in common with several other ascetic movements in ancient India a conviction that every consciousness is reborn to another body after the death of the current body. This conviction was accompanied by the belief that every form of conscious existence has the potential for disappointment and frustration, and that this potential is nearly always eventually realized. The pleasantness of the celestial realms, for example, is undermined by worry that eventually one will fall from heaven into less pleasant types of existence, and every form of life on earth or in the hell realms is made unpleasant by disease, injury, the possibility of separation from loved ones and the likelihood of being in contact with what one finds disagreeable. As long as one lives, therefore, there is the inevitability of eventual sorrows. Given these beliefs it follows that the only way to bring an end to the very possibility of enduring sorrows again is to stop being reborn as a conscious being. The name given to the end of rebirth is *nirvāṇa*, a word that is traditionally glossed by commentators as *kleśa-nirodha* and *bhava-nirodha*. In these expressions, the word "*nirodha*" has the twofold meaning of cessation of what has occurred in the past and prevention of that which has previously occurred from occurring again in the future. It is equivalent to eradication, destroying something by destroying its roots.

According to the Buddha's teachings, the root causes of all discontent (*duḥkha*) are greed, hatred, and delusion. Of these, delusion can be seen as the principal root, as both desire and aversion can be explained as arising from the failure to see things as they really are. Seeing clearly (*vipaśyanā*) the way things really are consists in seeing that whatever appears in experience is impermanent. Being impermanent, it is ultimately unsatisfactory.

And being unsatisfactory, it is neither the self nor anything that one can own or control. Realizing that all possible experiences will have these three features of being impermanent, unsatisfactory, and non-self is to be free of delusion.

Another name for the absence of delusion is awakening (*bodhi*). According to the *Abhidharma* tradition, *bodhi* cannot be regarded as an actual thing, for it if were a thing it would be conditioned and therefore impermanent. If it were something that could be gained, it would also be something that could be lost. If it is an absence, however, it is neither conditioned nor anything that can be gained or lost. The same reasoning applies to *nirvāṇa*. In the *Questions of Milinda*, which is considered canonical in some parts of the Theravāda tradition, the monk Nāgasena explains to King Milinda that *nirvāṇa* can be seen either as an absence or as an achievement. He gives the analogy of a man who falls into a pit of burning coals. If he should get out of the pit, he would feel subjectively as if he had achieved something of great value, but objectively he would have gained nothing more than the absence of being burned by the glowing coals.

In Mahāyāna traditions important innovations arose concerning *nirvāṇa*. One innovation occurs in the *Sukhavatī-vyūha Sūtra*, where it is said that the buddha Amitābha has dedicated all his merit to the creation of a happy land (*sukhavatī bhūmi*) in which conditions are ideal for hearing, contemplating, and perfecting all the teachings necessary for attaining *nirvāṇa*. As entry to this happy land is given to all those who sincerely desire entry, even if they cannot earn entry through their own good works, there is an element of grace involved in this doctrine that was not found in earlier phases of Buddhist theory.

A second innovation occurs in several texts of the Mahāyāna tradition that deal with the career of the *bodhisattva*, the being who dedicates every personal resource to helping all sentient beings attain *nirvāṇa* and vows not to attain the final goal until all other beings have attained it. In accordance with this vow, the *bodhisattva* is said to be able to attain a non-enduring *nirvāṇa*, a state that can be entered temporarily and then left behind. Clearly, this doctrine requires a different understanding of what *nirvāṇa* is than the understanding that was found in earlier Buddhism.

One way of seeing *nirvāṇa* that occurs in some forms of Mahāyāna is to see it as the underlying true nature of all phenomena. On this view, while phenomena all appear to be arising, enduring for a while and then decaying and disappearing, their actual nature is peaceful and stable. According to this way of seeing, in reality nothing arises and nothing perishes. The fundamental delusion, according to this view, consists in thinking that there is a difference between the phenomenal world of ordinary experience and the ultimate reality of *nirvāṇa*, whereas really, as Nāgārjuna would put it, "There is not even the most subtle difference between *nirvāṇa* and *saṃsāra*." If the peaceful and stable nature of *nirvāṇa* is seen as the true nature of all experiences, then *nirvāṇa* is not a goal at all but an always-present reality. It is not something to be approached gradually through constant refinement of one's mentality but something to be felt as one's true nature. Between the earlier and the later conceptions of *nirvāṇa*, then, there is almost nothing in common but the name and the sense that the name applies to the greatest possible good.

See also: **India, Buddhism in; Ennobling Truth Reality, the Third: *nirvāṇa*.**

RICHARD P. HAYES

NON-CANONICAL AND APOCRYPHAL LITERATURE

The Buddhist canon's *Collection of Minor Texts* (Skt. *Kṣudrakāgama*, Pāli *Khuddaka*

Nikāya) remained open for some time and disputes occurred among various Buddhist communities over the arrangement and number of texts in this miscellaneous collection. Some refused to accepted commentarial and scholastic texts (*Niddesa*, *Paṭisambhidāmagga*) and others excluded the hagiographical texts (*Apadāna*, *Cariyāpiṭaka*). In Burma, four works were added to the Theravāda canon, a collection of *suttas* including commentary (*Suttasaṅgaha*), two manuals for interpreting texts (*Nettippakaraṇa, Peṭakopadesa*), and the *Questions of King Milinda* (Pāli *Milindapañha*). The *Milindapañha* records the dialog on Buddhism between the monk Nāgasena and Milinda, identified with the Indo-Greek king Menander. The original text composed *c.* 100 BCE and 200 CE, possibly in Gāndhārī, a northwestern Middle Indo-Aryan language, and translated into Chinese before the fourth century CE. The longer Pāli version was completed in Sri Lanka prior to the time of Buddhaghosa (fifth century) who quotes it. The *Words of Dharma* (*Dharmapada*) and other texts included in this miscellaneous collection that may have circulated independently in the monastic centers along the Silk Road are found in Gāndhārī and Chinese translations. Alongside these canonical works, other texts claiming to be the Buddha's word circulated in India and Central Asia and were translated into Chinese and Tibetan. The Chinese and Tibetan canons remained open to the incorporation of new texts. In addition to texts composed in the literary languages of the Buddhist canons, there were numerous non-canonical commentaries, manuals, hagiographies, birth stories (*Jātakas*), story collections (*Avadāna*), ritual and devotional texts composed in local languages.

In China, the composition of texts that claimed to be the word of the Buddha or the word of Indian teachers began not long after the beginning of the Buddhist translation activity in the second century CE. These apocryphal texts, referred to in Chinese as "spurious texts" (*wei jing*) or "texts of doubtful authenticity" (*i jing*), were made to resemble Sanskrit texts because the criterion for authenticity was foreign lineage. Some were forged using false ascriptions to Indian authors or translators to enhance their claims of authenticity. Kumārajīva translated the *Brahmajāla Sūtra (Fanwang Jing)*, an apocryphal text on Mahāyāna precepts, into Chinese in 406 from an alleged Sanskrit original text. This text, which describes the precepts taken by a *bodhisattva* and the stages of *bodhisattva* path, also reflects Chinese concerns with filial piety. These apocryphal texts were often imaginative efforts to make strange foreign teachings more familiar to a Chinese audience incorporating local references and customs. The *Scripture of the Ten Kings (Shiwang jing)* made alien Buddhist teachings on the afterlife seem more acceptable by showing deceased people coming before a succession of magistrates who pass judgment on their past actions. The Dunhuang manuscripts' illustrations of this popular text depict judges and the punishments meted out in a way easily recognizable to a Chinese audience. One of the better-known apocryphal texts, the *Awakening of Faith* (Skt. *Mahāyānaśraddhotpāda*, Ch. *Dasheng Qixin Lun*) was attributed to Aśvaghoṣa and translated by Paramārtha in 550 CE. This influential work synthesizes Mahāyāna teachings on emptiness (*śūnyatā*), suchness (*tathatā*) and embryonic Buddha-nature (*tathāgatagarbha*) to explain how the mind could be inherently enlightened yet also subject to ignorance. Apocryphal texts continued to be written and incorporated into the developing Chinese canonical collections until the first printed edition, the Northern Song edition (971–83), effectively closed the canon. The Dunhuang caves also preserved many Tang dynasty non-canonical Chinese texts, including monks' lectures on *sūtras* and illustrated manuscripts of vernacular stories on the workings of *karma* that reflect an oral storytelling tradition.

The Chinese genre of miracle tales composed by literate monastics or lay people describe popular religious practices. Collections of miracle tales celebrate the miraculous recovery of health, birth of children, and so forth, achieved by pilgrimages to important sites like Mount Wutai or devotion offered to Amita Buddha or the *bodhisattva* Guanyin. Some Tang and early Song miracle tale collections were incorporated into the canon. The popularity of this genre spread to Japan; non-canonical collections attributing miracles to the *bodhisattva* Kannon and the recitation of the *Lotus Sūtra* proliferated. Some Chinese esoteric ritual texts, including one advocating that childless couples recite the incantation (*dhāraṇī*) of the white-robed Guanyin, were preserved outside the canon.

Numerous esoteric ritual texts and manuals were not incorporated into the Tibetan canon. Butön (Bu ston Rin chen grub, 1290–1364) and his "New School" (*gsar ma*) successors doubted the Indian provenance of many "Old *Tantras*" considered authentic by the "Old School" (*rnying ma*). For Butön the important criterion was that the text was an accurate translation of a genuine Indic manuscript. The Nyingma scholar, Ratna Lingpa (Ratna gLing pa, 1403–78), incorporated the *tantras* Butön considered inauthentic into the Nyingma's collection of authoritative texts. *The Collected Tantras of the Ancients (Rnying ma rgyud 'bum)*, contains *tantras* and their commentaries. This compilation of translated materials from Vajrayāna traditions excluded from the mainstream Tibetan canon of Indian Buddhist translations includes numerous alleged translations from Indic sources from the eighth and ninth centuries, rejected by Butön. During the first introduction of Buddhism into Tibet, the ninth-century *yogin* Padmasambhava was said to have buried secret texts (*gter ma*) in Tibet before he returned to India. He transmitted the texts to his disciples and predicted that they will rediscover them in a future incarnation.

The *Buddhist Treasures* claim authenticity by associating themselves with Padmasambhava and the practices of the "Old *Tantras*." Among these texts is the *Tibetan Book of the Dead* (*Bar do thos grol*), a guide for those who seek liberation from the visions of peaceful and wrathful deities that appear during the postmortem intermediate period between death and rebirth. This text lay hidden until the fourteenth-century treasure-discoverer (*gter ston*) Karma Ling (*Karma* gling pa) uncovered it. Treasure-discoverers uncover texts buried in the ground, in a statue, or monastery wall or even a text buried in one's mind. The Nyingma school regards these texts as authentic revelations of the Buddha's teachings, like the *sūtras* and *tantras* of the Buddhist canon. Like the Mahāyāna *sūtras*, these texts are revelations received from Buddhas residing in celestial pure lands. The Buddhist Treasures were not compiled into a collection of their own until the nineteenth century, when Jamgön Kontrul ('Jam mgon Kong sprul bLo gros mtha' yas, 1813–99) edited the *Precious Treasury of Hidden Treasures* (*Rin chen gter mdzod*). Hidden treasures continue to be uncovered to the present day.

See also: **Butön; Hagiographies; Pāli canon; Textual authority: the *Catuḥpratisaraṇa Sūtra*; *Tripiṭaka*, Chinese; *Tripiṭaka*, Sanskrit and Prakrit; *Tripiṭaka*, Tibetan.**

KAREN C. LANG

NORTH AMERICA, BUDDHISM IN

Since the late twentieth century, Buddhism in North America appears to have taken its own shape, self-consciously called by a growing number of United States Buddhists, "American Buddhism." Despite Buddhism's heterogeneity and its many different faces in the United States and Canada, with such characteristics as democratization, feminization, social engagement, and integration, these have emerged as recognizable patterns of an American Buddhism. Buddhism is strongly changing or Americanizing with regard to its organizational forms, interpretations of concepts and methods of practice; nevertheless, the continuity of its dominant social difference – that between immigrants and converts – has been turned into inter- and cross-ethnic activities by a few instances only.

Right from its beginning in the middle of the nineteenth century, Buddhism in North America was formed by both immigrants and converts. Resulting from the discovery of gold in California in 1848, Chinese miners came to the West Coast. Temples were started during the 1850s in San Francisco and other emerging cities. The Chinese were followed by Japanese immigrants in the 1870s. Both East Asian groups, each having grown to over 100,000 people, were faced by social exclusion and racism. The 1882 Chinese Exclusion Act stopped further arrivals of Chinese people, then forty years later this was followed by the Japanese Exclusion Act in 1924. A representation of Japanese Shin Buddhism was founded with the Buddhist Mission to North America in 1914. Developments in Canada were parallel to those in the United States, but with a deferment of time: Chinese miners arrived in British Columbia in 1858. In Canada, a Chinese Immigration (Exclusion) Act was enacted in 1923. Japanese workers, mainly of the Jōdo Shinshū, came in 1889 to British Columbia and Alberta. Both groups were treated as unwelcome immigrants and faced racial stigmatization.

On the East Coast of the United States, Buddhism was perceived much more positively than on the West Coast. The transcendentalists Emerson (1803–82), Thoreau (1817–62), and Whitman (1819–92) gave a glorified image of Buddhist ideas and ethics. In the same vein, the Theosophical Society, founded in 1875, praised Buddhism and Indian religions and was instrumental in spreading knowledge about Buddhist concepts (though interpreted from a Theosophical point of view). It was the written text, not Asian teachers, which served as a means to spread the *Dharma* to the middle and upper-middle strata of society. The 1893 World Parliament of Religions held in Chicago brought the first Buddhist teachers from South and East Asia. Though the presentations by Anagārika Dharmapāla (1864–1933) and Shaku Sōen (1859–1919) were well received and Buddhist societies and Zen groups were founded in the following years, the overall impact remained rather weak. Estimates speak of about 2,000 converts around the turn of the twentieth century.

The years until the late 1940s can be characterized as silent and stagnating. Of major importance for Japanese Shin Buddhism had been the internment of more than 100,000 Japanese during World War II, in both the United States and Canada. Previous processes of adaptation in religious forms, ritual and setting were accelerated, reshaping Shin Buddhism's appearance in line with Christian churches. The turning point for Buddhism reaching out to a wider public came with the lecture tours by D.T. Suzuki (1870–1966) during the 1950s. His reinterpretation of Zen in Western psychological terms was caught up by Alan Watts and others and turned into widely read books. The combination of psychedelic drugs and Zen ideas challenged rational thought and codes of social conduct. Watt's *Beat Zen, Square Zen, and Zen* (1959) caught the spirit of the time, and likewise Jack Kerouac's *The Dharma Bums* (1958). Beat Buddhists such as Kerouac, Allen Ginsberg and Gary

Snyder popularized Buddhist ideas and practices. Their creative employment of poetry and literature paved the way for an Americanizing of Buddhism. Buddhism, as portrayed by these protagonists and the emerging book market, was conceived of as highly individualized, literary based and characterised by the language of humanistic psychology, drugs and experimentation, yet lacking personal discipline or an institutional framework of the kind provided by a monastic order.

The situation started to change as Japanese Zen teachers settled in North America and the United States; and as Americans returned as trained instructors from Japan. Snyder was one of the first to go to Japan (in 1956) to receive training in a Zen monastery, a step followed by many in the years to come. One of those was Philip Kapleau, author of *The Three Pillars of Zen* (1965) and founder of the important Rochester Zen Center in New York (1966). The Americanization of Zen continued, as students of Kapleau retained American dress, received Anglicized Buddhist names, and used English translations of Buddhist texts during training. A few years earlier on the West Coast, the Sōtō Zen master Shunryu Suzuki Rōshi had established the San Francisco Zen Center (SFZC, 1961). In 1966, Tassajara Zen Mountain Center was established as an affiliate center. Richard Baker, a prominent, though later disputed student of Shunryu Suzuki, was ordained as both a monk and a priest in 1966. Kapleau, Shunryu Suzuki, Baker, Robert Aitken and others laid the foundation stones for a disciplined Zen training and lasting Zen institutions in the United States.

Parallel to the explosive interest in Zen in the United States (although less so in Canada), further Buddhist traditions arrived from Asia as a result of changes to the immigration regulations in the early to mid-1960s in both countries. From then on, selection or rather exclusion by race – as clearly stated by the Chinese and Japanese Exclusion Acts – was replaced with selection by education and ability. The 1960s and ensuing decades saw a tremendous influx of skilled workers and professionals from many Asian countries, changing the Buddhist landscape into a multi-cultural and multi-tradition based patchwork. Buddhist teachers and immigrants from Sri Lanka, Thailand, Hong Kong, Taiwan, Korea, Vietnam, Tibet, and Japan came and built their own institutions and Buddhist worlds. Ethnic communities emerged, such as one in Orange County, California, made up of Vietnamese boat people and their offspring, establishing a religious and cultural infrastructure of their own. Notably, one of the most vigorous newly arrived traditions turned out to be the Sōka Gakkai International. It claimed a tremendous growth in membership during the 1970s and 1980s. Also, the ethnic composition of Sōka Gakkai is unique compared to other traditions: it is not mono-ethnically formed, and Hispanics, Blacks, Caucasians and others are to be found among the chanting practitioners.

The two closing decades of the twentieth century saw an explosive growth of Buddhist institutions. Localities ranged from small semi-private groups in a living room (such as meditation groups or Sōka Gakkai groups for joint chanting) to huge and widespread monastic compounds (such as the Taiwanese Hsi Lai complex in the Los Angeles metropolitan area). During the 1990s, Hollywood and the media discovered Tibet. Tibet's spirituality, myth and plight headed the news and cinema films such as *Little Buddha* (1993), *Kundun*, and *Seven Years in Tibet* (both 1997) provided colorful and emotional access to this seemingly endangered world. Celebrities and politicians were portrayed with the fourteenth Dalai Lama, who repeatedly has visited North America. Numbers of ethnic Tibetans in the United States and Canada are comparably low, with about 8,000 and fewer than 1,000 respectively. In contrast to Theravāda and Mahāyāna Buddhism in North America, Tibetan Buddhism is numerically much stronger on the convert side. Well-known *lamas* and teachers such as Chögyam Trungpa, Tarthang Tulku, Lama Surya Das (Jeffrey Miller), Robert Thurman and many ethnic Tibetan and now increasingly Caucasian *lamas* have attracted tens of thousands of Euro-American people. Vajradhatu, renamed Shambhala and associated Nalanda University in Boulder, Colorado, is on the forefront in creating a unique form of American–Tibetan Buddhism. Other Tibetan organizations are less inclined to such experimental innovations and favor a rather close alignment to established forms in Tibet and now India. On the Theravāda side, there is the Insight Meditation Society (founded in 1975) in Barre, Massachusetts, with prominent lay teachers Jack Kornfield, Sharon Salzberg, and Joseph Goldstein. They have been creative with Buddhist forms and ideas in a way that changed Buddhist *vipassanā* meditation approaches into non-religious awareness techniques. Other Theravāda traditions remain rather conservative in transplanting rituals and teachings: this was observable of the South Asian immigrants in particular. Their number in the United States was estimated by Paul Numrich to be about 750,000, with some 200 *wats* or *vihāras* (monasteries). Wat Thai in Los Angeles and Watt Buddhikarana in Washington, D.C., were newly built Thai and Cambodian styled temples, respectively, though the majority of such temples are located in houses, storefronts or old school buildings. Mahāyāna Buddhism differentiates along many national backgrounds and traditions. There are the long-established Chinese and Japanese strands, the former having grown particularly strong with Hong Kong Chinese immigrants in Vancouver and Toronto (some 600,000 in

Figure 33 Sand *maṇḍala* constructed by the monks of Ganden Shardzay College at Grinnell College, Iowa, 1993.

2000). There are Taiwanese, Vietnamese and Korean Buddhists, then the multifaceted spectrum of Zen lineages and centers, and Nichiren Buddhism with the numerically strong Sōka Gakkai. Overall estimates for the United States' Buddhist population range from half a million to six million, but a plausible estimate of three to four million people seems appropriate. With respect to Canada, an estimate of 300,000 Buddhists was made, though the number is most likely higher in view of immigration processes from South and East Asia in recent years.

Buddhism in North America is Americanizing in terms of democratization, feminization, social engagement, and integration. Current issues and controversial debates are directly related to these processes of adaptation and change: questions related to gender equity associated with the role of both women and men; scandals of misuse of authority leading to sexual exploitation; the emergence of a feminist Buddhism; the coming out of a queer community of gays and lesbians; issues linked with authority and hierarchy as well as to renunciation and monasticism. Social engagement and integration are related to issues of the transformation of society in terms of Buddhist social activism, environmentalism, and ecology; to the integration of Buddhist practice and household family life; to the maturing of a generation of Western Buddhist teachers, disciples not of Asian, but of

Western teachers; to intra-Buddhist and inter-religious dialogue; to the rarely raised issue of racism and exclusion of blacks; to the unavoidable shifts and changes of immigrant Buddhist communities with the growing up of the next generation, raising inter-marriage rates and active Christian missionary interference. Critical voices outside and inside the rapidly growing movement have asked to what extent Buddhism is banalized and commercialized as Buddhist practices and ideas have been secularized by certain convert interpretations and are increasingly co-opted by market interests. Buddhism in North America is on its way to becoming a part of the religious mainstream as Americanized forms are in the making, negotiating Asian and American Buddhist forms and contents.

See also: **Buddhism and Western lifestyle; Buddhism in the Western world; Diasporic Buddhism: traditionalist and modernist Buddhism.**

MARTIN BAUMANN

NORTH AMERICAN SCHOOL OF BUDDHIST STUDIES

In the entry on Academic study of Buddhism, the early scholars on Buddhism on the North American continent are highlighted, focusing primarily on such figures as Paul Carus, Henry Clarke Warren, and Charles Rockwell Lanman. They were followed in turn by another series of prolific scholars that included Eugene Burlingame, W.Y. Evans-Wentz, Winston King, E.A. Burtt, Richard Gard, and Kenneth K.S. Ch'en. Until the middle portion of the twentieth century, the vast majority of the work on Buddhism was carried out at Harvard University, Johns Hopkins University, and Yale University, along with the various publication series they fostered.

During the Vietnam War years, and thereafter, Buddhist Studies grew enormously in North American universities. Included among the reasons for this extensive and rapid growth were a significant increase in area studies programs, a general growth in interest in the cultures of Asia, much concern for (and perhaps rejection of) American religion, and an overall sense of social anomie that permeated American culture during this period. In an interesting article in the 1999 issue of the *Journal of the International Association of Buddhist Studies* (*JIABS*), Frank Reynolds says as much, arguing that the first reason for the growth of Buddhist Studies during the 1950s and 1960s was, "a rapidly increasing interest between Buddhism on the one hand, and American religion, culture and society on the other." No doubt the change in US immigration laws in 1965, allowing for a huge influx of Buddhist immigrants from Asia, also impacted on the general awareness of things Buddhist, including its study.

The best known of the newly emergent Buddhist Studies programs was the one initiated at the University of Wisconsin in 1961 by Richard H. Robinson (in conjunction with Robert J. Miller and Murray Fowler), which offered both the M.A. and Ph.D. degrees. In addition to a core faculty that included Robinson and Miller, as well as Minoru Kiyota and Geshe Sopa, the Buddhist Studies program also included a host of language professors spanning all the Buddhist canonical languages. Moreover, the university was fortunate to have frequent visiting faculty that included internationally acclaimed scholars such as Edward Conze, Arthur Link, Yuichi Kajiyama, Alex Wayman, and others. Robinson died a premature death in 1970, following a household accident, which seriously truncated the growth of Wisconsin's program for many years. It has recently begun to revive, under the able direction of Charles Hallisey, with assistance from John Dunne, Gudrun Buhnemann, and others. During its almost five decades of existence, the Wisconsin Buddhist Studies program has turned out more than three dozen doctorates. A number of its students have gone on to distinguished careers elsewhere. Jeffrey Hopkins established a premier Buddhist Studies program at the University of Virginia, and became one of the foremost scholars of Tibetan Buddhism, publishing more than two dozen books. Lewis Lancaster recently retired from the University of California at Berkeley, where he had become a world leader in developing information exchange technology in Buddhism. Charles Prebish co-founded what is now the "Buddhism Section" of the American Academy of Religion (AAR), helped to pioneer the study of Western forms of Buddhism as a sub-discipline within Buddhist Studies, and co-founded the first online peer-reviewed journal in Buddhist Studies: the *Journal of Buddhist Ethics*. José Cabezón has been awarded a named Chair at the University of California at Santa Barbara, and Paul Swanson is a director of the Nanzan Institute in Japan.

Wisconsin, however, was not the only university interested in offering sophisticated training in Buddhist Studies. In 1958 a brilliant young buddhological scholar named Masatoshi Nagatomi joined Harvard's faculty, and within a decade was named its first professor of Buddhist Studies. He not only founded the Harvard Buddhist Studies Forum (in 1985), but was as compassionate a teacher as he was a great scholar, supervising more than thirty dissertations before his retirement. Prior to his death in June 2000, Nagatomi was likely the most beloved academic Buddhist Studies professor on the continent. Through Harvard's Center for the Study of World Religions, dozens of scholars have received sophisticated training in all aspects of Buddhism and gone on to illustrious careers. The best known of Nagatomi's students is undoubtedly Robert A.F. Thurman, who was ordained as a Buddhist monk by the Dalai Lama in the 1960s. Thurman eventually returned to lay life, finished his Ph.D. under his learned master, and currently holds the Jey Tsong Khapa Chair in Buddhist Studies at Columbia University, where he is developing his own generation of buddhologically trained students. Like Hopkins, he is among the discipline's most prolific writers, publishing many scholarly and popular volumes. Perhaps Nagatomi's most brilliant student was Janice Nattier, a multi-talented scholar with a unique language facility and a relentless quest for knowledge in all avenues of Buddhist Studies, from ancient India to modern America. Like Robinson's, the list of Nagatomi's students is far too numerous to cite.

Columbia University, Yale University, the University of Chicago, and the University of California at Berkeley also created Buddhist Studies training programs, either within their Religious Studies departments or through interdisciplinary programs. Following four years at the University of Wisconsin, in the fall of 1966, Alex Wayman joined the Columbia University faculty as a visiting associate professor, and the following year was appointed Professor of Sanskrit. Until his retirement in 1991, Wayman was a fixture on the buddhological scene in North America, gaining a reputation as a relentless scholar and an overwhelming critic, while developing his own impressive list of students. His best-known student is Collett Cox of the University of Washington, who became a co-chair of the Buddhism Section of AAR and has worked diligently with Richard Salomon on the Gāndhārī Buddhist manuscript project. Around the same time Wayman was joining the Columbia faculty, Stanley Weinstein joined the Yale University faculty as Associate Professor of Buddhist Studies. Promoted to professor in 1974, he also turned out an impressive list of

Buddhist Studies students that includes such notable scholars as Luis O. Gómez, who for many years has been the mainstay of Buddhist Studies education at the University of Michigan, William Bodiford, one of the foremost Zen scholars on the continent, David Chappell, and many others. While he was finishing his own Ph.D. in the History of Religions program at the University of Chicago, Frank Reynolds joined its faculty, and until his recent retirement, had a long and illustrious career as a teacher and researcher. He has produced a very long list of scholars, including the above-mentioned Charles Hallisey. Among his other students, John Holt became one of the leading scholars of *Vinaya* studies, and John Strong went on to become a co-chair of the AAR Buddhism Section. As a result of the above, a new generation of young Buddhologists was born, appearing rapidly on the campuses of many American universities and rivaling their overseas peers in both training and insight. For example, in the five years between 1986 and 1991, the attendance of the AAR Buddhism Section's annual business meeting grew from sixty to 140, and its mailing list grew from 106 to 600. About 250 scholars now subscribe to the unit's newsletter.

Despite the above chronology of intense, rapid growth, it remains somewhat unclear precisely how the North American school of Buddhist Studies defines itself. Like all disciplines, Buddhist Studies in North America is rapidly changing, primarily as a result of faculty relocation, altering interests, retirement, and new hires from the continually increasing pool of newly minted scholars entering the field. After surveying many of the issues impacting Buddhist Studies in North America, José Cabezón concluded in 1995,

> All of these factors have contributed to what we might call the diversification of the buddhologist: a movement away from classical Buddhist Studies based on the philological study of written texts, and toward the investigation of more general, comparative and often theoretical issues that have implications (and audiences) outside of Buddhist Studies.

Thus it is no longer clear what constitutes a full-time Buddhologist in North America, and when one factors in the movement in the opposite direction – scholars from other disciplines incorporating Buddhist materials into their work – the entire issue of identifying the number of full-time Buddhologists at any institution becomes quite murky. In 1997, though, Duncan Williams did attempt to at least begin a cursory study of major institutions currently emphasizing Buddhist Studies. In his study, Williams was able to identify six categories of institutions: most comprehensive programs; institutions with strength in East Asian Buddhist Studies; institutions with strength in Indo-Tibetan Buddhist Studies; institutions with strength in Southeast Asian Buddhist Studies; practitioner-friendly institutions; and other noteworthy programs.

In his 1999 *JIABS* article mentioned above, Frank Reynolds aggressively asserts that American Buddhist Studies scholarship has turned away from matters of origin and essence, to increasingly emphasize other matters such as beliefs, practice, modes of communal life, and current Buddhist histories. He also identifies four areas or dimensions of Buddhist Studies scholarship that characterize North American Buddhist Studies. First, is the use of new computer technologies in Buddhist Studies. Second, is the production of what he calls "communally generated research," consisting of edited volumes of multi-author work on issues in Buddhism. Third, he postulates a scholarship related to contemporary issues in Buddhism, including that related to or produced by scholar-practitioners. Finally comes a renewed concern for the importance of theory and method in the study of Buddhism. He concludes: "Given this evidence of growth and progress, it seems reasonable to conclude that Buddhist studies in the United States has, after a long period of marginal existence, finally 'come of age.'"

See also: **Academic study of Buddhism; Robinson, Richard Hugh; Simmer-Brown, Judith.**

CHARLES S. PREBISH

NOT-SELF (*ANĀTMAN*)

In the Buddha's day, the spiritual quest was largely seen as the search for identifying and liberating a person's true Self (Skt. *ātman*, Pāli *attā*). Such an entity was postulated as a person's permanent inner nature, the source of true happiness and the autonomous "inner controller" of action. In Brahmanism, this *ātman* was seen as the ungraspable inner subject, the unseen seer, and as a universal Self, identical with *Brahman*, the divine source and substance of the universe; in Jainism, for example, it was seen as the individual "life principle" (*jīva*).

The five *skandha* analysis

One of the most common analyses of the component processes of a person in Buddhism is in terms of the five *skandhas* (Pāli *khandhas*): "aggregates" or "groups." The first is *rūpa*, "material form" – the material aspect of existence, whether in the outer world or in the body of a living being. It is said to be comprised of four basic elements or forces, and forms of subtle, sensitive matter derived from these. The four basics are solidity (literally "earth"), cohesion ("water"), energy ("fire"), and motion ("wind"). From the interaction of these, the body of flesh, blood, bones, etc., is composed. The remaining four aggregates are all mental in nature; for they lack any physical "form." The second aggregate is *vedanā*, or "feeling." This is the hedonic tone or "taste" of any experience: pleasant, unpleasant, or neutral. It includes both sensations arising from the body and mental feelings of happiness, unhappiness, or indifference. The third aggregate is *saṃjñā* (Pāli *saññā*), which processes sensory and mental objects, so as to classify and label them, for example as "yellow," "a man," or "fear." It is "perception," labeling, recognition, and interpretation – including mis-interpretation – of objects. Without it, a person might be conscious but would be unable to know *what* he or she was conscious of. The fourth aggregate is the *saṃskāras* (Pāli *saṅkhāras*), "constructing activities" or "volitional activities." These comprise a number of states which initiate action or direct, mold and give shape to character (*Visuddhimagga* 462–72). These are mainly active states such as greed, hatred, energy, joy and attention, but also sensory stimulation, an automatically arising state. While some are ethically neutral, many are ethically "skillful" (Skt. *kuśala*, Pāli *kusala*) or "unskillful." The most characteristic "constructing activity" is *cetanā*, "will" or "volition," which is identified with *karma* (*Aṅguttara Nikāya* 3.415). The fifth and final aggregate is *vijñāna* (Pāli *viññāṇa*) "(discriminative) consciousness" or "(perceptual) discernment." This includes both the basic awareness of a sensory or mental object, and the discrimination of its basic aspects or parts, which are actually recognized by *saṃjñā*. It is of six types according to whether it is conditioned by eye, ear, nose, tongue, body or mind-organ (Skt. *manas*, Pāli *mano*). It is also known as *citta*, the central focus of personality which can be seen as "mind," "heart" or "thought." It can also be seen as a "mind set" or "mentality"; some aspects of this alter from moment to moment, but others recur and are equivalent to a person's character. Its form at any moment is set up by the other mental *skandhas*, but in turn it goes on to determine their pattern of arising, in a process of constant interaction.

Much Buddhist practice is concerned with the purification, development, and harmonious integration of these five factors of personality, through the cultivation of moral discipline and meditation. In time, however, the five-fold analysis is used to enable a meditator to gradually transcend the naïve perception – with respect to "himself" or "another" – of a unitary "person" or "self." In place of this, there is set up the contemplation of a person as a cluster of changing physical and mental processes, or *dharmas* (Pāli *dhammas*), thus undermining grasping and attachment, which are key causes of suffering.

The *Anattalakkhaṇa Sutta*

The teaching on not-Self (Skt. *anātman*, Pāli *anattā*) is directly addressed in the *Anattalakkhaṇa Sutta* (*Vinaya* 1.13–14, *Saṃyutta Nikāya* 2.66–8), the "Discourse on the characteristic of *anattā*," seen as the Buddha's second sermon. Here he explains, with respect to each of the five *skandhas*, that if it were truly Self, it would not "tend to sickness," and it would be totally controllable at will, which it is not. This must allude to such facts as that the body gets tired, ill and old, we do not feel pleasure all the time, as we might wish, and our awareness often wanders, being pulled this way and that by external events or inner emotions.

The *sutta* then continues by saying that each *skandha* is impermanent (Skt. *anitya*, Pāli *anicca*), and hence a "pain" (Skt. *duḥkha*, Pāli *dukkha*), and that it is not "fit to consider that which is impermanent, a pain, of a nature to change, as: 'This is mine (*etam mama*), this I am (*eso ham asmi*), this is my Self (*eso me attā*)'." When this is truly recognized as applying to each and every example of each of the five *skandhas*, a person "finds estrangement in/turns away from/feels revulsion for" (*nibbindati*) them, so as to experience dispassion/non-attachment (*virāga*). He or she thus attains liberation and the end of grasping.

Elsewhere the negative aspects of *skandhas* are highlighted by saying that they are to be seen "as impermanent, as a pain (*dukkha*), as a disease, as a boil, as a dart, as a misfortune, as a sickness, as other, as disintegrating, as empty (*suñña-*), as not-Self" (*Saṃyutta Nikāya* 3.167). The tone here is quite clear: what is recognized as being impermanent, a pain and not-Self should be *let go* of. While people long for what is permanent, lasting, reliable, pleasant, controllable, and a reliable possession, this is not how things are. To ignore this and still grasp at things as if they are like this is to continually open oneself to disappointment and frustration.

The meaning of not-Self

The Pāli word *anattā* is a compound made up of *an* +*attā*. *An* is the negative prefix and *attā* is a noun meaning self/Self. In most contexts, it is analyzed grammatically as a *kammadhāraya* compound, like the term *akāla-megha* meaning "an untimely (*akāla*) cloud (*megha*)." On this model, *anattā* technically functions as a noun, and it is generally used as a complement to another noun, just as one says in English "consciousness is *a mystery*" or "John is *a non-smoker*." When it is said "*x* is *anattā*," this means: *x* is a non-Self, is no Self, is not a Self. In the Pāli commentaries it is also sometimes seen as an alternative type of grammatical compound known as a *bahubbīhi*, following the example of *sa-dhañña*, "possessing (*sa*) grain (*dhañña*)," in other words an adjective meaning "grain-bearing." On this model, *anattā* would function as an adjective, meaning that what it is applied to is "without Self." In canonical texts, it behaves as a *kammadhāraya* compound, as the word-ending of *anattā* does not change to agree with the gender of what it is applied to, for example the neuter noun *viññāṇaṃ* (consciousness), as it would if it were being used as *bahubbīhi* adjectival compound. Its use as a *kammadhāraya* compound, however, is still tantamount to an adjectival use: "*x* is *anattā*" is most elegantly rendered "*x* is not-Self," though "*x* is a non-Self" would be most technically correct and "*x* is no Self" is also possible.

When something is said to be *anātman*/*anattā*, not-Self, the kind of "self" it is seen *not* to be is clearly one that would be permanent and free from all pain, however subtle. Such a "Self" is the kind of metaphysical entity that the *Upaniṣads* and Jains postulated, in their different ways. While Pāli and Sanskrit do not have capital letters, in English it is useful to signal such a concept with a capital: thus *S*elf.

The emphasis on non-controllability in the *Anattalakkhaṇa Sutta* relates the Upaniṣadic idea that the Self is the "inner controller" (*antaryamin*). *Bṛhadāraṇyaka Upaniṣad*, 3.7.3 sees the immortal Self as controlling the elements and faculties within a person (and the realms of the world). While the *Upaniṣads* recognized many things as being not-Self, they felt that a real, true Self could be found. When it was found, and known to be identical to *Brahman*, the basis of everything, this would bring liberation. In the Buddhist *suttas*, though, literally *everything* is seen as not-Self.

While *nirvāṇa* is beyond impermanence and *duḥkha*, it is still not-Self. This is made clear in a recurring passage (e.g. *Aṅguttara Nikāya* 1.286–7), which says that all *saṃskāras* (Pāli *saṅkhāras*), or conditioned phenomena, are impermanent and *duḥkha*, but that "all *dharmas* are not-Self." "*Dharma*" (Pāli *dhamma*) is a word with many meanings in Buddhism, but here it refers to any basic component of reality. Most are conditioned, but *nirvāṇa* is the unconditioned (Skt. *asaṃskṛta*, Pāli *asaṅkhata*) *dharma* (*Aṅguttara Nikāya* 2.34–5); both conditioned and unconditioned *dharmas* are not-Self. While *nirvāṇa* is beyond change and suffering, it has nothing in it which could support the feeling of I-ness; for this can only arise with respect to the *skandhas*, and it is not even a truly valid feeling here (*Dīgha Nikāya* 2.66–8).

The non-denial of s/Self

At *Saṃyutta Nikāya* 4.400–1, the wandering ascetic Vacchagotta directly asks the Buddha "Is there a s/Self?" The Buddha remains silent, as he does when he is then asked "Is there not a s/Self?" After Vacchagotta goes away, Ānanda asks the Buddha why he had remained silent. He replies that to say there is a s/Self would be to be associated with "eternalists" – namely those who believe in an eternal *S*elf – and be in contradiction with the knowledge that "all *dharmas* are not-Self" (i.e. "no *dharma* is a Self"). To say that there is not a s/Self would be to be associated with "annihilationists" – namely those who believe only in a "this-life" self which is totally destroyed at death, such that there is no changing empirical *self-process* flowing on to a new rebirth – and would be confusing to Vacchagotta as he would think he had lost a s/Self that he formerly had. It is thus clear that while a Self is not directly *denied*, it is also clear that it is not accepted either (Harvey 1995a: 38–40).

In fact, seeing things as not-Self is a tool to cut off identifying with and clinging to things, including views. It should not itself generate a view "there is no Self." Seeing things as not-Self is a constructed process, and is itself not-Self: it should not be clung to.

The nature and benefit of seeing things as not-Self

While the *suttas* have no place for a metaphysical Self, seeing things as *not*-Self was clearly regarded as playing a vital soteriological role. Given that a Self is not asserted, nor explicitly denied, and that seeing things as not-Self is so important, it becomes apparent that the concept of "Self," and the associated deep-rooted feeling of "I am," are being utilized for a spiritual end. The not-Self teaching can in fact be seen as a brilliant device which uses a deep-seated human aspiration, ultimately *illusory*, to overcome the negative products of such an illusion. Identification, whether conscious or unconscious, with something as "what I truly and permanently am" is a source of attachment; such attachment leads to frustration and a sense of loss when what one identifies with changes and becomes other than one desires. The deep-rooted idea of "Self," though, is not to be directly attacked, but used as a measuring-rod against which all phenomena should be compared: so as to see them as falling short of the perfections implied in the idea of Self. This is to be done through a rigorous experiential examination: as each possible candidate for being "Self" is examined, but is seen to be not-Self, falling short of the ideal. The intended result is that one should let go of any attachment to such a thing. The aim of seeing things as not-Self, then, is to make one see that this, this, this ... *everything* one grasps at, as a result of identifying it as "Self" or "I," is *not* Self and must be *let go* of. This brings *nirvāṇa*. Contemplation of phenomena as impermanent, *duḥkha* and not-Self is a way of undermining craving for and clinging to such phenomena. By seeing things "as they really are," it is believed that attachment and its attendant suffering will be undermined.

One can, perhaps, see the Self idea as fulfilling a role akin to a rocket which boosts a payload into space, against the force of gravity. It provides the force to drive the mind out of the "gravity field" of attachment to the *skandhas*. Having done so, it then falls away and is burnt up as itself an empty concept, part of the unsatisfactory *skandhas*.

The *suttas*, then, use "not-Self" as a reason to let go of things, not to "prove" that there is no Self. There is no need to give some philosophical denial of "Self"; the idea simply withers away, or evaporates in the light of knowledge, when it is seen to be empty of content, or, as the *suttas* put it, when it is seen that all things are "empty" of Self. A philosophical denial is just a view, a theory, which may be agreed with or not. It does not get one to actually examine all the things that one actually *does* identify with, consciously or unconsciously, as Self or I. This examination, in a calm, meditative context, is what the "not-Self" teaching aims at. It is not so much a thing to be thought about as to be *done*, applied to actual experience, so that the meditator actually *sees* that "all *dharmas* are not-Self": no *dharma* can be rightly taken as a Self. A mere philosophical denial does not encourage this, and may actually mean that a person sees no need for it.

That the *anātman* teaching is no bald denial of Self is seen at *Majjhima Nikāya* 1.8, where the ignorant ordinary person unwisely reflects on such matters as: whether "I" existed in the past or not, and in what form and manner; whether or not "I" will exist in the future, and in what form and manner; whether "I" exist now or not, and in what form and manner; and where this being has come from and will go to. This leads on to a variety of views, including "I have a Self" *and* "I do not have a Self." Here, egocentric preoccupation leads to doubts and speculations on "I" and Self, producing a "jungle of views." Buddhist ideas on not-Self are not intended to feed such doubt, but to lead to a different perspective on what it is to exist.

Nevertheless, Buddhism sees no need to postulate a permanent Self, and accounts for the functioning of personality, in life and from life to life, in terms of a stream of changing, conditioned processes. Rebirth is not seen to require a permanent Self or substantial "I," but *belief* in such a thing is one of the things seen to cause rebirth.

Misrepresentations of the not-Self teaching as a denial of "soul" or any kind of "self"

On its own, the word *anātman/anattā* should not be treated as if it were a whole doctrine: "no-self" or "no-soul." While the meaning of "soul" in Christianity varies somewhat, it is primarily that which gives life to the body. As Paul Williams emphasizes, the *anātman* teaching was not "concerned to deny whatever gave life to the body, whatever that is." Moreover, just because the Buddha did not accept anything as an unchanging Self, I or essence does not mean that all talk of "soul" needs to be banished from English language discussion of Buddhism. For example, in the meaning of "soul" as the moral and emotional aspect of a person, the Buddhist term *citta* (heart/mind) seems close in meaning. It is simply that any "soul" must be recognized as not being a fixed, permanent, unitary entity, which at least rules out any idea of an *immortal* soul. Overall, though, Buddhism does not "lack soul"!

The Buddha also accepted many conventional usages of the word "self" (also "*ātman*" or "*attā*"), as in "yourself" and "myself." These he saw as simply a convenient way of referring to a particular interrelated stream of mental and physical states. But within such a conventional, empirical self, he taught that no permanent, substantial, independent, metaphysical Self could be found. This is well explained by an early nun, Vajirā. Just as the word "chariot" is used to denote a collection of items in functional relationship, but not a special part of a chariot, so the conventional term "a being" is properly used to refer to the five *skandhas* relating together (*Saṃyutta Nikāya* 1.135, cf. *Milindapañha* 25–8). None of the *skandhas* is an essential "Being" or "Self," but these are simply conventional terms used to denote the collection of functioning *skandhas.*

Sensitivity to the above variation in self-language should help to avoid such incoherent student statements as: "Buddhism teaches that there is no self . . . The self is the five *skandhas* . . . but these are to be seen as not-self." Again, *anātman/anattā* does not mean "egoless," as it is sometimes rendered. The term "ego" has a range of meanings in English. The Freudian "ego" is not the same as the Indian *ātman/attā* or permanent Self. In more ordinary English, "ego" just means the feeling or sense of being or having an "I" – this feeling is not denied in Buddhism, though it is seen as based on a misperception of reality.

Moreover, the not-Self teaching does not deny that there is continuity of character in life, and to some extent from life to life. But persistent character-traits are merely caused by the repeated occurrence of certain *cittas*, or "mind-sets." The *citta* as a whole is sometimes talked of as an (empirical) "self" (e.g. *Dhammapada* 160 with 35), but while such character traits may be long-lasting, they can and do change, and are thus impermanent, and so "not-Self," insubstantial. A "person" is a collection of rapidly changing and interacting mental and physical processes, with character-patterns recurring over time. Only partial control can be exercised over these processes, so they often change in undesired ways, leading to suffering. Impermanent, they cannot be a permanent Self. Stressful, they cannot be an autonomous true "I," which would contain nothing that was out of harmony with itself.

"Views on the existing group" and the "I am" conceit

The *suttas* often ascribe to those who are spiritually immature – who are not yet stream-enterers – a set of views known as the "views on the existing group" (Skt. *satkāya-dṛṣṭis*, Pāli *sakkāya-diṭṭhis*); the spiritually mature lack such views (e.g. *Saṃyutta Nikāya* 3.114–15). *Satkāya* refers to the five *skandhas* (*Majjhima Nikāya* 1.299), the "group" or "body" (*kāya*) that "exists" or is seen as one's "own." *Satkāya-dṛṣṭi* is sometimes rendered "personality view," which is odd, as the *suttas* do not say that there is no such thing as "personality" – only that "it" is a changing collection of conditioned processes. There are twenty "views on the existing group," which all, in one way or another, relate the *skandhas* to a Self, taking any of the five *skandhas* as: (1) Self; (2) a possession of Self; (3) in Self; or (4) containing Self. One can thus see these as "Self-identity views." The non-acceptance of these views means, for example, that with regard to material form, the body, it is not truly appropriate to say that "I am body," "the body is mine," "body is part of my Self," "I am in the body." Indeed, *Saṃyutta Nikāya* 2.64–5 says that the body does not "belong" to anyone: it simply arises because of past *karma* (albeit interrelated with certain mental states, but these do not "own" it).

At *Saṃyutta Nikāya* 3.127–32, the monk Khemaka first gets rid of any "view on the existing groups," in the form "*this* I am." He still has a lingering feeling of "I am," though, as a vague attitude rather than a specific conceptualized view. Once he overcomes this, he attains *arhat*ship. *Asmi-māna*, the "I-am conceit," is any form of self-importance, self-preoccupation or self-centeredness, expressed in an I-centered self-image which sees oneself as superior, inferior or (competitively or complacently) equal to others (e.g. *Saṃyutta Nikāya* 4.88).

The teaching on phenomena as not-Self, then, is not only intended to undermine the Brahmanical or Jain concepts of Self, but also much more commonly held conceptions and deep-rooted feelings of I-ness. To act as if only *other* people die, and to ignore the inevitability of one's own death is to act as if one had a permanent Self. To relate changing mental phenomena to a substantial self which "owns" them: "*I* am worried ... happy ... angry," is to have such a self-concept. To identify with one's body, ideas, or actions, etc. is to take them as part of an "I."

The interplay of seeing things as not-Self with development of the empirical self

While no permanent Self can be found in the changing, empirical self, one of the constructing activities is the "I-am conceit." As a person develops spiritually, their empirical self becomes stronger as they become more focused, calm, aware and open. The monk should seek to "live with himself as an island, with himself as a refuge, with no other (person) as a refuge, (he lives) with *Dharma* as an island, with *Dharma* as refuge, with no other (Teaching/Path) as refuge"(*Dīgha Nikāya* 3.58). This is done by mindful alertness, so as not to be pulled hither and thither by desirable sense-objects. As a calm centre is better established and grows stronger, one can "expand" as a person. At *Aṅguttara Nikāya* 1.249, the Buddha refers to two kinds of person. The first is "of undeveloped body (of qualities), undeveloped moral discipline, undeveloped *citta* (heart/mind), undeveloped wisdom, he is limited, he has an insignificant self, he dwells insignificant and miserable." The second is "of developed body, developed moral discipline, developed *citta*, developed wisdom, he is not limited, he has a great self (Pāli *mahattā*, Skt. *mahātma*), he dwells immeasurable." Both mindfulness (*Majjhima Nikāya* 1.270) and open-hearted loving kindness (Skt *maitrī*, Pāli *mettā*; *Aṅguttara Nikāya* 5.299) are seen to help to make the *citta* "immeasurable, well-developed." The Path is the way by which "those with great selves travel" (*Itivuttaka* 28–9) and the *arhat* is "one of developed self" (Pāli *bhāvit-atto*; *Itivuttaka* 79–80). As the fully integrated, liberated person, he or she has a very self-controlled, self-contained empirical self. He has an unshakeable "mind like a diamond" (Pāli *vajir-ūpama-citto*; *Aṅguttara Nikāya* 1.124), and, as water runs off a lotus without sticking, sense-objects do not "stick" to him (*Theragāthā* v. 1180). The liberated person has a "boundaryless" *citta* because he/she is "escaped from, unfettered by, released from" the five *skandhas* (*Aṅguttara Nikāya* 5.152) and is one who is "independent," not attracted or repelled by sense-objects (*Majjhima Nikāya* 3.30). That is, being non-attached and self-contained is what, paradoxically, allows the *arhat* to have a boundaryless mind. When a person lets go of everything, such that "his" identity shrinks to zero, then the mind expands to infinity. Each identification with something as "Self" is a limitation, which restricts one and makes one "smaller."

The *arhat* knows that nothing within or beyond his or her empirical self is a substantial Self: so nothing is worth grasping at. This enables his empirical self to be calm, strong and well integrated, and the "boundary" between "self" and "other" is seen as not of ultimate importance. The "I am" conceit is seen as based on an illusion, and leads to both a lack of inner harmony and integration and also a lack of sympathy for others. Once "I am" is seen as an empty mirage, there can be both a profound, imperturbable inner calm and unlimited horizons of awareness and sympathy for others. Insight into all as not-Self leads to a strong and open self that is both Selfless (as everything is Selfless) and without the "I am" attitude: a self which is recognized as a conditioned construct of now only wholesome, still but impermanent states. From the alert openness of such a way-of-being, though, the unconditioned timeless Beyond which is *nirvāṇa* can be experienced.

The Personalists

While the Sarvāstivāda school in time came to include an explicit denial of Self (*Abhidharmakośa* III.18a), a group of schools dubbed the Pudgalavādins, or "Personalists," came to postulate a Self-like *pudgala* or "person" that was neither the same as nor different from the *skandhas*, neither the same nor different over time, and neither conditioned nor unconditioned. They seem to have conceived of it as a kind of organic whole which could not be reduced to its component processes. While they were careful to avoid their "person" being in obvious tension with the agreed teachings of the Buddha, all other schools criticized their ideas.

Mahāyāna extensions of the idea of not-Self

In the *suttas* of the Pāli Canon, the primary sense of something's being "not-Self" is that it is impermanent, a pain, and not controllable at will, because of being conditioned by other factors. In the Mahāyāna it often comes to mean something like "not a separate self," because of the emphasis on the interrelation of everything.

In the Pāli *suttas*, something's being not-Self is often expressed by saying that it is "empty" (*suñña*, Skt. *śūnya*) of Self or what pertains to Self (e.g. *Saṃyutta Nikāya* 4.54). In the *Paṭisambhidāmagga* (2.58), moreover, deep insight into phenomena as not-Self (as compared with their being impermanent or *duḥkha*) leads to an experience of *nirvāṇa* as "emptiness" (Pāli *suññatā*, Skt. *śūnyatā*). In the Mahāyāna, it is emphasized that not only are all components of a person or any other *dharmas* not-Self, but also the *dharmas* themselves are empty of any *svabhāva*, a term meaning own-nature, own-being, inherent nature, or essence. The concept of *svabhāva* had developed in some *Abhidharma* systems, especially that of the Sarvāstivāda, to refer to the individual nature of any *dharma*, such *dharmas* being seen as irreducible real, mental or physical process-events which make up the fabric of reality, onto which ideas of "persons" and commonsense "things" are projected. In the *Prajñāpāramitā Sūtras* and the Madhyamaka school, it was emphasized that as *dharmas* are conditioned in their very nature, they are empty of any separate nature. In their quality of emptiness, moreover, they cannot ultimately be differentiated from nirvanic "emptiness."

See also: ***Abhidharma*; Buddha; Dependent Origination (*pratītya-samutpāda*); Ennobling Truths/Realities; Ennobling Truth/Reality, the First.**

PETER HARVEY

NYINGMA

The Nyingma (rNying ma) Order of Tibetan Buddhism traces itself back to Padmasambhava, who is credited by tradition with playing a decisive role in the first dissemination (*snga dar*) of Buddhism to Tibet. The two main sources of Nyingma doctrines and practices are "treasures" (*gter ma*) and the "teaching" (*bka' ma*) tradition. The former are texts and artifacts believed to have been hidden by Padmasambhava or his disciples during his time in Tibet. They were protected with spells that ensured that only a pre-ordained "treasure discoverer" (*gter ston*) would be able to find a given "treasure." They were then hidden in rocks or hills, and sometimes in the mental continuums of treasure-discoverers, to be revealed at a time appointed by Padmasambhava. The authenticity of these texts has frequently been questioned by the other orders of Tibetan Buddhism, but some are widely disseminated among Tibetan Buddhists.

The texts of the teaching tradition are said to originate with the buddha Samantabhadra, who gives them to "knowledge bearers" (*rigs 'dzin*), who in turn reveal them to human masters. It includes texts, practices, doctrines, and visualizations. The highest meditation practice of the Nyingmapas is the "great perfection" (*rdzogs chen*). It is said to have originated with Samantabhadra, who taught it to Vajrasattva. It was then disseminated to human practitioners and continues today in an unbroken lineage. While it adopts the physiology and major doctrines of *tantra*, it does not rely on visualizations, and instead practitioners focus directly on the nature of mind. According to the system, appearance and emptiness interpenetrate, and the two are inseparable. The nature of the mind is clear light, and great perfection meditative practices allow adepts to directly access the fundamental mind. Training in ethics and traditional *bodhisattva* practices are viewed as superfluous because they rely on merely conceptual dichotomies such as "good" and "bad," "virtue" and "non-virtue." Such limiting constructs are obstacles to liberation.

Great perfection practice aims at cultivating a union of essential purity (*ka dag*) and spontaneity (*lhun grub*). The first term refers to emptiness, which is said to be the final nature of phenomena. Spontaneity refers to the insight that all good qualities are already established in the "basis-of-all" (*kun gzhi*), the psychological continuum of existence. When practitioners realize the essential purity of the basis-of-all, they spontaneously attain buddhahood.

The practice of "cutting through" (*khregs chod*) is central to this path. It involves perceiving the primordially pure mind behind the veil of appearances. According to the system, the mind is of the nature of clear light, and is primordially free from all defilements. Ordinary sentient beings who fail to recognize this wander in cyclic existence, while buddhas directly perceive the nature of mind and so are liberated. Great perfection texts distinguish between ordinary mind (*sems*), which is enmeshed in discursive and dualistic thought, and the "nature of mind" (*sems nyid*), which is the same as the Buddha-nature. This is the fundamental mind, which is never affected by conceptuality or duality, and is the innate capacity for buddhahood that exists in all sentient beings. Unlike traditional gradualist training, advocates of the great perfection claim that practitioners of their system may become liberated at any moment through directly apprehending this truth.

See also: **Tibet, Buddhism in; Vajrayāna Buddhism.**

John Powers

O

ORDINATION (LAY AND MONASTIC)

Admission into the Buddhist monastic community was initially rather simple and straightforward. It required only Buddha's exhortation for the individual to come forth into the monastic life (*ehi bhikṣu* in Sanskrit), with no essential distinction made between the novitiate (*pravrajyā*) and full (*upasaṃpadā*) ordination. Later, when a distinction was made between the novitiate and full ordination, and Buddha allowed monks other than himself to confer these ordinations, additional requirements were added, including the shaving of one's head, taking on yellow robes, and repeating the threefold "refuge formula" (*triśaraṇa*). Moreover, the novice monks called *śrāmaṇeras* were required to observe ten principles of training called *śikṣāpadas*. To normalize the relationship between newly ordained, junior monks and their senior colleagues, and to ensure that proper social decorum was maintained, each prospective junior monk was required to select two individuals to serve as his spiritual mentors: his ordaining monk (known as the *upadhyāya*), and his teacher (called his *ācārya*). The primary function of the *upadhyāya* (or preceptor) involved his ability to teach the novice monk proper discipline and observance of the rules, while the *ācārya*, who was often a *Dharma* master, officiated in the absence of the *upadhyāya*. In this way, the young monk would be properly trained in both the doctrine and the discipline of the Buddhist community. The obligations of the *śrāmaṇera* to his *upadhyāya* and *ācārya* are clearly spelled out in the Pāli *Mahāvagga* (I.25.1–24). More importantly, that same text explicitly states: "Monks, I allow a teacher. The teacher, monks, should arouse in his pupil the attitude of a son; the pupil should arouse in his teacher the attitude of a father." In addition, according to Mohan Wijayaratna, "The preceptor had the right to dismiss his pupil for one of five reasons: if the pupil was not affectionate or polite enough toward him, if the pupil did not trust or respect him, or if he did not make progress under his guidance." These relationships, however, were reciprocal. Pupils were allowed to give advice to their preceptors, to correct doctrinal misinterpretations, and to encourage their teachers if they experienced doubts with regard to the religious life. Although preceptors fulfilled many requirements outlined by the *Mahāvagga*, it was also the case that many preceptors were not *arahants*, and thus, as ordinary people, were still not free from all defilements. As such, the *Vinaya* outlined scandals that occasionally resulted from undeveloped preceptors supervising very bright students.

Alongside the spiritual kinship that developed between preceptors and their disciples, the ongoing preservation of the discipline, in its original form, mandated that some additional relationships needed to be established to sustain the *Vinaya* intact. To accomplish this a tradition of "*Vinaya* masters" (*Vinaya-dharas*) developed. One of the most famous early lineage of "masters" spanned the gap between Śākyamuni's death and the accession of King Aśoka, during which time the *Vinaya* was preserved in turn by Upāli, Dāsaka, Sonaka, Siggava, and Moggaliputta Tissa. Thus, from the very beginning of the tradition, a profoundly strong link between monastic ordination and spiritual lineage in the tradition was established.

Yet it was not just the monastic community that was enjoined to facilitate spiritual kinships through ordination in the early tradition. Following ordination through the formula of "taking refuge" (that is, going for refuge to the Buddha, *Dharma* and *Sangha*) and agreeing to follow the lay precepts embodied in the five vows of the laity known as the *pañca-śīla* (including the injunctions not to kill or injure living creatures; not to take what has not been given; to avoid misconduct in sensual matters; to abstain from false speech; and not to take intoxicants), members of the laity were enjoined to maintain a high level of lay ethics. No text in early Buddhism provides a better, or clearer, statement of lay ethics incumbent on lay ordinands than the famous *Sigālovada-sutta* of the *Dīgha Nikāya*. The text describes a series of familial and social relationships emphasizing the duties and responsibilities of husband and wife, friends, servants and workpeople, duties associated with one's livelihood, and teachers and pupils. According to the text, the pupil should (1) rise from his seat in salutation to the teachers, (2) wait on the teacher, (3) be eager to learn from the teacher, (4) serve the teacher, and (5) be attentive when receiving his teaching. Equally, the teacher should (1) teach the students well, (2) make sure they grasp the teaching, (3) thoroughly instruct them in all the arts, (4) speak well of them among their friends, and (5) provide for their safety. Clearly, the standards of teacher–student interactions are substantially parallel to those of the other familial relationships outlined in the text. And it is not only in the Theravāda or other *nikāya* Buddhist traditions that familial associations are emphasized. Throughout Indian Mahāyāna literature, where both lay and monastic *bodhisattvas* become the ideal type of practitioner, *bodhisattvas* of both genders are referred to as being either a "son of a good family" (*kulaputra*) or "daughter of a good family" (*kuladuhitṛ*), where the "family" is unmistakably Buddha's over-arching spiritual family.

Even after Buddhism extended beyond India, ordination continued to play a significant role. In China, for example, when a member of the laity decided to deepen his commitment to the Buddhist tradition by renouncing lay life and taking his initial, preliminary entry or tonsure into the monastic tradition, he was given the surname Shih, which corresponds to the first syllable of Śākyamuni (or *shih-chia-mou-ni* in Chinese). In so doing, he was considered to be *fo-tzu*, or "a son of the Buddha." Moreover, his tonsure names reflected his tonsure Buddhist family. Unlike the Indian Buddhist tradition, those who underwent the tonsure ceremony and were called *śrāmaṇeras* (*sha-mi* in Chinese) in China did not take the official novice's ordination, which came later. Their official ordination required acceptance of the ten prohibitions (*shou-chieh*), and often a series of higher "*bodhisattva* vows."

Robert Buswell's research on the Korean Zen tradition provides a similar result with regard to ordination. He reports that postulant novices (*śrāmaṇeras*, or *haengjas* in Korean) are assigned a "beneficent master" (*ŭnsa*) who sponsors the postulant for ordination. As in the Chinese tradition, Korean Zen monks' ordinations are significantly more complex than novice ordination. According to Buswell, the *bhikṣu* ordination requires three senior monks: a preceptor (or *ācārya*) who transmits the precepts, a spiritual mentor (often the Sŏn master of the monastery), and a procedural specialist (or *karmācārya*) who effects the proper performance of the entire ceremony.

The same circumstance can be found throughout the Zen tradition in Japan. William Bodiford notes that

> The Zen school places great importance on the master–disciple relationship. According to modern descriptions of this discipleship, the master's goal is to cause his disciple to re-create through his own training the same intuitive cognition of reality that the master himself experiences . . . Traditionally referred to as the "transmission" of the teacher's mind to the disciple, this technique has been termed the crucial "pivot" of the Zen teaching method.

Transmission is the pivot because it affirms the authentic status of the spiritual kinship between the student, his spiritual parent, and Buddha himself. In Sōtō Zen, the acknowledgment of attainment is referred to as *inka shōmei*, while the ritual process of confirmation into the *Dharma* lineage of his master is known as *shihō*, processes we shall soon see are maintained today throughout the modern world of Zen.

In all likelihood, no Buddhist tradition has ever placed more emphasis on lineage and the spiritual kinship inherent in ordination than that of Tibetan Buddhism. The entirety of the Vajrayāna tradition turns on the role and function of ordination and the spiritual kinship it confers. As such, it becomes the exclusive, basic mechanism of the relationship that exists between student and *Dharma* teacher. Moreover, the lineages that develop from these ordination procedures become the cornerstone of each of the four traditional schools of Buddhism in Tibet. John Powers tells us,

> Among adherents of the four main schools of Tibetan Buddhism, Nyingma, Kagyu, Sakya, and Geluk, there is a tendency to emphasize the differences that distinguish them, but much more striking is how much they share in common . . . Each school traces its lineage to particular Indian masters, and there are distinctive differences in their actual tantric practices, but despite these differences there are many points of commonality.

It is the ordination process that contributes significantly to this commonality.

In the aftermath of the Tibetan holocaust, the maintenance of the Tibetan Vajrayāna lineages in the numerous diaspora communities becomes critically important for the ongoing survival of the entire tradition. It is especially interesting to note that within the Gelug tradition, a monk who successfully completes his monastic and academic training, and passes all the appropriate examinations, is referred to as a "*geshe*" (*dge bshes*), the Tibetan equivalent word for the Buddhist Sanskrit term *kalyāṇamitra* or "spiritual friend," identified as the earliest and highest expression of spiritual kinship in Buddhism.

In view of the above, it remains clear that monastic and lay ordination plays a profound role of all Buddhist sectarian traditions throughout the world.

See also: ***Sangha*****; Three Refuges and Going for Refuge.**

CHARLES S. PREBISH

OTHER EMPTINESS AND SELF EMPTINESS IN TIBETAN BUDDHISM

The doctrine of emptiness (Tib. *stong pa nyid*, Skt. *śūnyatā*) figures prominently in Indian Mahāyāna literature, particularly in the *Perfection of Wisdom* (Tib. *Pha rol tu phyin pa*, Skt. *Prajñāpāramitā*) *Sūtras* and the writings of Madhyamaka philosophers. Questions regarding how emptiness should be interpreted have been a major source of debate between the various orders of Tibetan Buddhism, and they continue today.

The two most influential factions advocate respectively the doctrines of "other emptiness" and "self emptiness." The latter position is held by the Gelukpa Order, which follows the interpretation of Madhyamaka developed by its founder Tsong Khapa. He contended that emptiness is a "non-affirming negative" (Tib. *med dgag*, Skt. *prasajya-pratiṣedha*), meaning that it is simply a radical denial of inherent existence (Tib. *rang bzhin*, Skt. *svabhāva*), a quality falsely attributed to phenomena by ordinary beings. From the perspective of an ignorant consciousness, phenomena appear to exist by themselves and are not viewed as composites of smaller parts created by causes and conditions and subject to decay, and persons appear to possess enduring selves (Tib. *bdag*, Skt. *ātman*) that are independent of the vicissitudes of birth, death, and change. The Gelukpas deny that there is any enduring substance and hold that all phenomena are collections of parts that are constantly changing resulting from the influence of causes and conditions.

The advocates of other emptiness are mainly associated with the Kagyü and Nyingma Orders and with the "Non-Sectarian" (*Ris med*) movement. This doctrine was initially propounded by the Jonangpa thinker Dolpopa (Dol po pa Shes rab rgyal mtshan, 1292–1361). According to the other-emptiness interpretation, emptiness is the ultimate truth and is conceived as a self-existent, unchanging reality that pervades all phenomena. It is empty of what is other than itself, that is, the mistaken perceptions attributed to it by deluded beings. But it is not void of itself, as it is the final nature of all phenomena. The emptiness of the Gelukpas is said to be "dead emptiness" (*bem stong*) because it would be a state devoid of any qualities. Proponents of other emptiness claim that it is in fact the repository of all the qualities of buddhahood and is inherent in all beings. It cannot be known by logic or conceptuality, and is only realized by advanced yogins through direct, non-conceptual insight. The Gelukpas denounce this position as an attempt to reify the Absolute and smuggle Indian substantialist notions into Buddhism.

One of the key debates between the Gelukpas and their opponents who advocate the other-emptiness position concerns how the doctrine of the "womb of the *tathāgata*" (Tib. *de bzhin gzhegs pa'i snying po*, Skt. *tathāgata-garbha*) should be understood. This notion, found in some Indian Buddhist texts, holds that all sentient beings have the potential to become buddhas. Advocates of other emptiness conceive of this potential as a positive, self-existent essence that pervades all existence and is made manifest through meditative training, and is not created by it. Buddhahood is the basic nature of mind, and it is said to be subtle, ineffable, and beyond the grasp of conceptual thought.

It cannot be described in words, and can only be understood through direct experience. According to this position, all phenomena are of the nature of mind, which is a union of luminosity and emptiness. They have no substantial existence, and merely exist within the continuum of mind.

The Gelukpas follow the Indian gradualist tradition, which holds that the path to buddhahood consists in progressively perfecting the matrix of good qualities that characterize awakened beings. This is accomplished during many lifetimes of arduous training, during which meditators follow a step-by-step approach and gradually rid themselves of negative propensities while simultaneously acquiring deeper insight and qualities like generosity, ethics, and patience, which they did not have when they began the path. According to this interpretation, *tathāgata-garbha* should be understood as being equivalent to emptiness, conceived as a non-affirming negative. It is another way of expressing the idea that beings lack any enduring essence, and so they have the ability to effect changes in their psycho-physical continuums. If they choose to follow the Buddhist path, they can move toward buddhahood because there is no self, soul, or essence that endures from moment to moment.

See also: **Tibet, Buddhism in.**

JOHN POWERS

P

PAGAN

The city of Pagan (now officially known as Bagan) was the capital of Burma (now officially known as Myanmar) between 1044 and 1287. During this period, more than 2,000 Buddhist monuments were built on the arid plains that surround the city. Together, they make up one of the most impressive monuments in the Buddhist world. Some of the temples house dozens of images and are elaborately decorated with stucco and glazed tiles, depicting scenes from the *Jātakas*, buddhas and *bodhisattvas*, and local deities, or *nats*. Others are *stūpas*, or pagodas, with little adornment.

The temples and *stūpas* at Pagan served a variety of purposes: housing monks, providing places for discourses on the *Dharma*, and opportunities for lay and monastic devotion. Further, Pagan is an awesome physical example of the important link between the king's power and Buddhism, a massive visual display of the royal support of Buddhism. They were begun by the king Anawrahta (1044–77), who is credited with having politically and culturally unified Burma. He is celebrated for having conquered the Mon kingdom of Thaton in the south, and thereby restoring Theravāda Buddhism to the country.

One of the most important of Pagan's *stūpas* is the Shwezigon – there is a very popular replica in the present-day capital, Rangoon (now Yangon) – which was built in the middle of the eleventh century. The Shwezigon seems to be modeled on the classical *stūpa* design found in India, and consists of three square terraces set on a large octagonal base; above the terraces is the gold-covered dome of the *stūpa*, on top of which is a conical spire, topped by an umbrella, a common symbol of royal power in Buddhist architecture. The stairs leading from one terrace to another are decorated with *makaras*, smaller *stūpas*, pots (symbolizing fertility and prosperity), and guardian lions. Around the main *stūpa* are dozens of smaller *stūpas*, enshrining the relics of important monks, and smaller shrines.

Another important structure at Bagan is the Ananda temple. It is a large structure, over 150 feet high. Built in 1090, the temple enshrines four large standing images of Śākyamuni – two are in the teaching position, making the *dharmacakra mudrā*, while one of the others displays the *abhāya* ("no fear") *mudrā*, and the other the *varada* ("wish granting") *mudrā* – in arched recesses on each side of the central terrace. There are six receding terraces; the lower terraces have a complete numbered set of 537 *Jātaka* plaques (with Pāli labels), with a further set of 375 plaques with Mon labels (some of these repeat the upper-level plaques, while some depict local variants of the tales). Along the outer walls of the temple are dozens of small niches housing images of the Buddha and reliefs depicting important scenes from his life. The temple is surrounded by a wall and four integrated arched gateways, containing guardian deities.

Finally, there is a replica of the Mahābodhi temple in Bodhgayā at Pagan, built in the early part of the twelfth century. It is 140 feet high, and is, like its model at Bodhgayā, elaborately decorated on the outside, with well over 400 images set in niches.

See also: **Art, Buddhist; Sacred places.**

JACOB N. KINNARD

PĀLI CANON

Traditional accounts of the life of Gautama Buddha (c. 485–405 BCE) indicate that he taught for forty-five years. The oral teachings he gave to his disciples and that they passed on down to subsequent generations of Buddhists were communicated in local Indian languages, including Māgadhī, the language of the northeastern Magadha region of India where the Buddha spent much of his life. As the Buddha's teachings spread throughout India, some monastics likely made an effort to render these teachings into a common literary language. Several of these languages have left their linguistic traces on Pāli, the literary language in which the Theravāda school of Buddhism has preserved its canonical texts. The Theravāda tradition maintains that after the Buddha's death, 500 of his enlightened disciples met at Rājagṛha, the capital of Magadha, to collect what they remembered of his teachings. The Buddha's death motivated these disciples to gather together and agree on an authoritative corpus of the teachings that he had handed down to them. This recognized corpus of texts would guide the Buddhist community and prevent disputes from dividing it. The oldest of these assembled disciples, Kāśyapa, requested that Ánanda recite the Buddha's discourses (Skt. *sūtra*, Pāli *sutta*) and Upāli recite the rules that govern monastic life (*vinaya*). The communal recitation of these teachings signified agreement on their authenticity.

The Theravāda school, the sole surviving school of at least eighteen schools that flourished in the centuries after the Buddha's death, believes that a third collection of summaries (Skt. *mātṛkā*, Pāli *mātikā*) and scholastic interpretations of Buddhist teachings was added later. Each of these schools had its own collection of authentic texts but the only collection to survive intact is the Theravāda school's canonical collection of Pāli scriptures. This acknowledgement that the three baskets (Skt. *tripiṭaka*; Pāli *tipiṭaka*) of the Buddha's teachings developed over time agrees with modern research that the canon was not closed until centuries after the Buddha's death. The extant Pāli *Tipiṭaka* contains three parts: monastic discipline (*Vinaya*), discourses (*Sutta*) and scholastic texts (*Abhidhamma*). Skilled reciters (*bhāṇakas*) transmitted these authoritative teachings orally for more than 200 years. According to Theravāda tradition, the Buddha's teachings were first brought to Sri Lanka in the third century BCE by the monk Mahinda (*c*. 282–222 BCE), King Aśoka's son. The fourth-century CE chronicles of Sri Lankan history, the *Island Chronicle* (*Dīpavaṃsa*) and the *Great Chronicle* (*Mahāvaṃsa*), recorded that the Theravāda collection of Buddha's teachings and commentaries on them were written down during the reign of King Vaṭṭagāmaṇi (*c.* 29–17 BCE) because of fears that in times of war, famine, and monastic strife, important teachings could be lost. The conflict between monks of the Mahāvihāra, the first monastery built in Sri Lanka by King Devānampiya Tissa (247–207 BCE), and monks of the newer Abhayagiri monastery, built and patronized by King Vaṭṭagāmaṇi, influenced the decision to write the teachings down in manuscript form. The Mahāvihāra monks produced a closed canon of scriptures that legitimated and defined their conservative teachings against newer, controversial teachings favored by Abhayagiri monks. The repeated copying of these manuscripts and careful preservation of these written teachings enabled their canon to survive. It is impossible to know the extent to which this *Tipiṭaka* written down in the first century BCE resembles the present Pāli canon. The selection and order of texts within the extant Pāli canon owes much to the work of the fifth-century Pāli translator and commentator, Buddhaghosa.

Pāli texts, copied and recopied in the various scripts of Theravāda countries (Burma/Myanmar, Cambodia, Sri Lanka and Thailand), have preserved intact the three baskets of the canon. The oldest surviving Pāli manuscript, a fragment of a *Vinaya* text, is earlier than the eighth century CE; most surviving manuscripts are but a few centuries old. The first part of the *Vinaya*, the *Explanation of the [Pāṭimokkha] sutta* (*Suttavibhaṅga*) explains all rules of conduct governing individual monks and nuns. Another set of rules that governs the collective behavior of the monastic community, the *Kammavācā*, is found in the second part, the *Khandaka*. The *Khandaka* is divided into two parts: the *Great Division* (*Mahāvagga*), which begins with the Buddha's enlightenment and ends with the *sangha*'s founding, and the *Small Division* (*Cullavagga*), which describes the monastic assembly at Rājagṛha and 100 years later at Vaiśali to settle disputes over monastic behavior. The third part, the *Appendices* (*Parivāra*), summarizes the first two parts' rules and provides additional information on monastic history. The *Sutta Piṭaka* is divided into five collections (*nikāyas*) with a varying number of discourses, ranging from thirty-four in the *Long Discourses* (*Dīgha Nikāya*) to over 9,000 in the *One-Member-More Discourses* (*Aṅguttara Nikāya*). The *Long Discourses* and the *Middle Length Discourses* (*Majjhima Nikāya*) are arranged by length. The *Connected Discourses* (*Saṃyutta Nikāya*) are arranged topically; the section of discourses on Dependent Origination (*paṭiccasamuppāda*) is followed by a section of discourses on the five aggregates (*khanda*). The *One-Member-More Discourses* arranges its discourses numerically, beginning with discourses in which something, for example, loving kindness (*mettā*), is discussed once, and ending with discourses that discuss a set of eleven members, for example the eleven blessings of loving kindness. The *Collection of Minor Texts* (*Khuddaka Nikāya*) contains fifteen diverse works of varying lengths, ranging from a brief liturgical text, the *Minor Recitations* (*Khuddakapāṭha*) to a lengthy commentary, the *Exposition* (*Niddesa*) on two early texts found in the *Group of Discourses* (*Suttanipāta*) also included in the *Collection of Minor Texts.* The hagiographical material of the *Birth Stories* (*Jātaka*), the *Lineage of the Buddhas* (*Buddhavaṃsa*) and the *Collection of Deeds* (*Cariyapiṭaka*) and the *Stories* (*Apadāna*) about enlightened disciples whose verse collections, *Monks' Verses, Nuns' Verses* (*Theragāthā, Therīgāthā*), along with the *Words of Dhamma*

(*Dhammapada*), are found in the *Collection of Minor Texts*. The *Way of Analysis* (*Paṭisambhidāmagga*), a late *Abhidhamma* text, is also included in this miscellaneous collection. The *Abhidhamma Piṭaka* contains seven texts: the *Compendium of Dhammas* (*Dhammasaṅgaṇī*), the *Explanation* (*Vibhaṅga*), the *Discussion of Elements* (*Dhātukathā*), the *Designation of Persons* (*Puggalapaññatti*), the *Book of Disputed Points* (*Kathāvatthu*), the *Pairs* (*Yamaka*) and the *Conditional Relations* (*Paṭṭhāna*). According to Theravāda tradition, Mogalliputta Tissa (*c.* third century BCE) compiled the *Book of Disputed Points* as a record of the third monastic council held at Pāṭaliputra during the reign of King Aśoka (r. 272–231 BCE).

Some reciters of texts differed over the selection and arrangement of canonical material. The reciters of the *Long Discourses* (*Dīgha bhāṇaka*) excluded the *Stories*, the *Lineage of the Buddhas*, and the *Basket of Conduct* from their *Collection of Minor Texts* and grouped the *Collection of Minor Texts* under their *Abhidhamma Piṭaka*. The Burmese Pāli canon accepted four other texts, including the *Questions of King Milinda* (*Milindapañha*) in their *Collection of Minor Texts*. Decisions about which texts to include in the canon were based upon four guidelines (*mahāpadeśa*) for determining which teachings can be considered the Buddha's word (*buddhavacana*). These guidelines judged a text's authenticity based on its provenance from the Buddha or a learned member of the *sangha* and on its harmony with the received body of his teachings (*sutta*, *vinaya*, *mātikā*). A teaching was considered authoritative if it was heard from the Buddha, a *sangha* of elders, and a group of monastics who were specialists in the *Dharma*, *Vinaya*, or in the *Abhidharma*, or a single monastic who was a specialist in any one of these areas.

Modern scholars distinguish between the formal canon of the Pāli *Tipiṭaka*, the definitive source of interpretative authority, and the ritual or practical canon that contemporary monks draw upon when conducting rituals and preaching sermons. This second type of canon may include selected portions of the *Tipiṭaka* and the ancient commentaries, as well as texts on the *Dhamma* that are consistent with the content of Pāli *Tipiṭaka*. The *Dhamma* for most Theravāda Buddhists includes few Pāli canonical texts, most them popular protective (*paritta*) texts used ritually. Many monasteries have no complete collection of the Pāli *Tipiṭaka*; their manuscript collections consist of popular noncanonical commentaries such as Buddhaghosa's influential *Path of Purification*, collections of paracanonical *Birth Stories* and chronicles of local shrines and Buddhist history.

Modern editions of the Pāli *Tipiṭaka* are based upon manuscript collections from Theravāda countries. The Pāli Text Society, founded in 1881 by Thomas W. Rhys Davids, began publishing romanized editions of Pāli texts in 1882. Their editorial work and translation into English continues to the present day. In 1954 in Yangon, Burma, 2,500 learned monastics and scholars met to review the Pāli *Tipiṭaka* and its commentarial literature and completed their work on the 2,500th anniversary of the birth of Buddha (the full moon day of May 1956). The government of India published Pāli *Tipiṭaka* in the *Devanāgari* script. The Vipassana Research Institute has issued on CD-ROM this 1954–6 edition, along with commentaries and subcommentaries in seven scripts, including *Devanāgari* and romanized script. Another CD-ROM, containing the Thai edition of the Pāli *Tipiṭaka* and commentaries in romanized script, was issued by the Buddhist Scriptures Information Retrieval (BUDSIR) of Mahidol University, Thailand. The Sri Lanka Tripiṭaka Project, in association with the *Journal of Buddhist Ethics*, offers a free public domain edition of the Sri

Lanka Buddha Jayantī Tipiṭaka edition of the *Tipiṭaka* and commentaries in romanized Pāli.

See also: **Canons and literature; South and Southeast Asia, Buddhism in; *Tripiṭaka*, Chinese; *Tripiṭaka*, Sanskrit and Prakrit; *Tripiṭaka*, Tibetan.**

KAREN C. LANG

PANCHEN LAMAS

The Panchen Lamas (*paṇ chen bla ma*) are among the most influential lineages of reincarnating *lamas* (*sprulsku*) in Tibetan Buddhism. Considered by Tibetan tradition to be physical manifestations of the buddha Amitābha, their traditional seat is Tashihlünpo (bKra shis lhun po) Monastery in Shigatse, Tibet. In the seventeenth century, the fifth Dalai Lama gave his teacher, Losang Chögi Gyeltsen (bLo bzang chos kyi rgyal mtshan, 1567–1662), the title "Panchen" ("Great Scholar"), and since that time his recognized reincarnations have inherited it. The title was also retrospectively accorded to his two previous incarnations.

The Panchen Lamas have often been at odds with the Dalai Lamas, and in the past Chinese rulers sometimes played the two off against each other. The ninth Panchen Lama, Losang Tubden Chökyi Nyima (bLo bzang thub bstan chos kyi nyi ma, 1883–1937), spent much of his life in China after fleeing Tibet following a declaration by the thirteenth Dalai Lama that he intended to tax his estates. While in China, he tried to enlist the support of the Chinese Nationalist government, but it lacked the will and resources to help him. He was given an official (but honorary) position and traveled throughout China, but he died in a border area without realizing his dream of returning to Shigatse.

His successor became a controversial figure by actively collaborating with the Chinese authorities after their invasion of Tibet in the 1950s, but he broke with them after writing several letters to Mao Zedong complaining of human rights abuses and declaring that Chinese rule in Tibet had "done more harm than good." He was tortured and imprisoned, and died of a reported heart attack in 1989. In 1994, the Chinese government appointed a group of Tibetan *lamas*, led by Chadrel Rinpoche, the abbot of Tashihlünpo, to search for his reincarnation. The Dalai Lama offered to assist in the process, but was rebuffed. Chadrel Rinpoche, however, reportedly passed information regarding likely candidates to the Dalai Lama, who in 1995 announced that a six-year-old Tibetan boy named Gendün Chökyi Nyima (dGe 'dun chos kyi nyi ma) was the eleventh Panchen Lama. Chinese authorities immediately denounced this move as "illegal and invalid" and added that the Dalai Lama – the highest-ranking reincarnate *lama* in Tibetan Buddhism – had no authority to choose reincarnations. Sole authority in such matters was declared to rest with the Communist Party, which officially holds religion to be the "opiate of the masses" and dismisses the institution of reincarnating lamas as "feudal superstition."

Gendün Chökyi Nyima and his parents were soon arrested by the Chinese military, and have been held under house arrest since. He has been adopted by the European Union as its youngest-ever prisoner of conscience, and despite international pressure the Chinese government refuses to let any outsiders see him or his family. The arrest was followed by an official announcement that the true Panchen Lama was a boy named Gyeltsen Norbu (rGyal mtshan nor bu), who was the son of Tibetan Communist Party cadres. The issue remains unresolved, but the Chinese authorities clearly hope that in time Tibetan Buddhists will come to accept their choice, who can then be used to select the next Dalai Lama.

See also: **Tibet, Buddhism in; Vajrayāna Buddhism.**

JOHN POWERS

PĀṬALIPUTRA

Pāṭaliputra (Pāli Pāṭaliputta) was the capital of several successive north Indian dynasties and an important city in the early history of Buddhism. The *Mahāparinibbāna Sutta* records a tradition that near the end of his life Gautama Buddha visited Pāṭaligāma, then a small town, and predicted its future greatness. The account also states that the gate of the city through which the Buddha departed and the ford where he crossed the Ganges River were named after him. There is also a Theravāda canonical tradition that the Buddha's water pot and belt (important Buddha relics) were deposited there. King Ajātaśatru's son, Udāyin, shifted the capital of the kingdom of Magadha from Rājagṛha to Pāṭaliputra in the fifth century BCE, and the city attained great prominence as the center of Aśoka's kingdom in the third century BCE. Theravāda tradition records that Aśoka convened a great Buddhist council in Pāṭaliputra, the third council by Theravāda reckoning, in order to resolve a major dispute with the Buddha *sangha*. Though the cause of the controversy as well as the council's historicity have been questioned because of conflicting textual evidence, an Aśokan edict condemning schism within the Buddhist *sangha* suggests that some sort of monastic dispute may have taken place there during his reign. Several successive dynasties were centered in Pāṭaliputra until the end of the Gupta dynasty in the sixth century CE. The Chinese pilgrim Xuanzang, who visited the city in the first half of the seventh century, recounts that the city then lay in ruins, marked by the remains of hundreds of temples, *stūpas* and Hindu temples. It was largely deserted until the sixteenth century when it once again became an important regional center; the modern city of Patna, capital of Bihar, now stands over the remains of the ancient city.

Beginning the late nineteenth century, archeologists have conducted several excavations in search of the remains of the ancient city of Pāṭaliputra, with relatively little success, in part, because so much of the area is covered by the densely populated modern city. Among the principal finds are the remains of a large pillared hall at Kumrahar, which early scholarship identified as the likely remains of the great Aśokan stone palace that the Chinese pilgrim Faxian described in his fifth-century CE account, though later excavation indicates that this structure was probably destroyed centuries before Faxian's visit. The remains of a Gupta-era (fourth–sixth century CE) Buddhist monastery have also been uncovered there. The famous Mauryan-period image of a female fly whisk (*caurī*) bearer found at Didarganj, usually identified as a *yakṣī*, presently resides at the Patna Museum.

See also: **Aśoka; Bodhgayā; Councils; Kuśinagara; Lumbinī; Buddha, relics of; Sacred places; Sāñcī; Sārnāth; *Stūpa*; *Vihāra*; Vaiśālī.**

KEVIN TRAINOR

PERFECTION OF WISDOM LITERATURE

The *Prajñāpāramitā Sūtras* represent Buddhism's most consistent effort to fashion what the literary critic Stanley Fish has termed "self-consuming artifact" – which we can understand in this context as a rhetorical creation that systematically deconstructs its own status as an ultimate truth in the very process of asserting the view that it represents is an ultimate truth. Making up a key strand of what eventually became the Mahāyāna tradition, the earliest of this related group of scriptures is generally taken to date from the first century BCE, representing, along with the *Lotus Sūtra*, the *Vimalakīrti Nirdeśa* and the early Pure Land *sūtras*, the foundational scriptures of the Mahāyāna. Two features stand out as especially significant when considering what is most distinctive here. First is the elevation of *prajñā* (wisdom) to the pre-eminent position among the various lists of *pāramitās* in the earliest literature, and second is the assertion that the very nature of this transformative wisdom entails a consummate degree of spontaneous altruistic activity directed towards all sentient beings. Thus the potential tension between the twin goals of cognitive wisdom and effective compassion is resolved with what amounts to the assertion that there can be no truly compassionate activity that is not grounded in the ultimate degree of wisdom, just as the ultimate perfection of wisdom cannot but express itself as compassion in action. While grounding itself firmly and consistently in the doctrine of *śūnyatā* (emptiness or voidness), the *modus operandi* of the Perfection of Wisdom literature is more inspirational than discursive, relying much more on rhetorical induction than on logical argument. Reason has a place in this conception of wisdom (*prajñā*) as a kind of gnostic vision, but its role is to chart the limitations of its own reference. The core Buddhist teaching of the non-substantiality of the self (*anātmavāda*) is relentlessly extended here to every aspect of phenomenal experience in an effort to demonstrate that every "thing" – which is to say every aspect of one's experience – is empty of any independent, self-existing, or intrinsic nature (*svabhāva*). In establishing this ontological position, reason plays a crucial role. But then the *Prajñāpāramitā* continues, making the seemingly paradoxical assertion that as there is ultimately "no act, no recipient of the acting, nor indeed even any acting," it is precisely for that reason that the *bodhisattva* should act compassionately for the benefit of all sentient beings. The resolution of this seeming paradox appears to lie in an assumption that human nature – and indeed the intrinsically empty nature of all existence – is morally good, and that goodness will naturally manifest once the delusional veils sustaining the bifurcation of self and non-self are deconstructed. This conclusion is thus less a matter of logical analysis and much more the culmination of an intuitive or direct perception of the ultimate nature of reality, one that can be cultivated only through a sustained program of meditative training. Even the very reading and recitation of the *Prajñāpāramitā* texts is meant, it would seem, to induce this ethically transformative insight, at least in those who are sufficiently receptive.

This much is common to the whole corpus of *Prajñāpāramitā Sūtras*, even though the successive recensions and augmentation of the core material over at least 1,400 years certainly do reflect development in both style and method. Edward Conze, the modern Western scholar most associated with the *Prajñāpāramitā* studies, has identified some forty different texts existing in Sanskrit, Chinese, Tibetan, and Khotanese, many sharing much material in common, often in the form of extended verbatim stock passages. He further classifies these texts into four periods, the first three of which span roughly two centuries each. The first period is reflected in the earliest surviving texts of the tradition, most notably the *Aṣṭasāhasrikāprajñāpāramitā* or *8,000 Verse Perfection of Wisdom*, the earliest portions of which date from the first century BCE, or perhaps even earlier. The second period shows an expansion of the same core material into increasing longer recensions, yielding successively longer versions of 18,000, 25,000 and eventually 100,000 verses. Reversing that tendency, the third period is characterized by a process of increasing contraction, represented best by the popular *Vajracheddika* or *Diamond-CutterSūtra* and the even more terse *Heart* or *Prajñāpāramitāhṛdāya Sūtra*. The fourth and longest of Conze's phases sees the development of a substantial exegetical literature and the increasing incorporation of Tantric elements into the original material, which ended only with the demise of Buddhism in India. New commentaries have continued to be written in East Asia and Tibet right up to the present, joined more recently by contributions from Western Buddhists as well.

The basic deconstructive or relativistic stance of the *Prajñāpāramitā* tradition has some precedent in the Pāli Canon of the Theravāda school, notably in the two *Suññatā Suttas* of the *Majjhima Nikāya* and even more notably in the "no-views" teaching of the *Aṭṭhakavagga* found in the *Suttanipāta*. Nonetheless, with the *Aṣṭasāhasrikā* we are clearly dealing with a substantial development of the older ideas, expressed in considerably more philosophical depth, though interestingly in a relatively unadorned literary form more reminiscent of the early dialogues of the Buddha than of the fanciful phantasmagoria characteristic of most Mahāyāna *sūtras*. This is especially true of the first two chapters of the *Aṣṭasāhasrikā*, which Conze suggests were the original doctrinal nucleus of the text and thus of the tradition as a whole. Here we find a three-way discussion between Śākyamuṇi, Śāriputra, and Subhūti – Śāriputra representing the more "limited" perspective of the Śrāvakayāna while Subhūti, who is unknown in the earlier canonical scriptures, asserts with the Buddha's sanction the new and more radical Mahāyāna perspective. The general theme is introduced when the Buddha encourages Subhūti to explain how the *bodhisattvas* "go forth into the perfection of wisdom." Their exchange continues, eventually taking up different definitions of a number of key concepts, including *bodhisattva*, *mahāsattva*, and *Mahāyāna*. Subsequent chapters continue the theme of the *bodhisattva*'s training, explaining it as a "no-training" in which all notions of self and other along with all other conceptual formulations are explored as utterly devoid of any substantial or intrinsic reality. *Nirvāṇa* itself is not a "thing," not something to be grasped or attained, a notion that underlies the doctrine of an "unfixed" (*apratiṣthita*) *nirvāṇa*, which is the culmination of the *bodhisattva*'s path, a state of being in the world free of the duality of delusion and awaking, a stance from which the liberated *bodhisattva* is free to employ his or her consummate skillful means (*upāya*) for the welfare of all sentient beings. It is in this sense that the Perfection of Wisdom comes to be seen as the "mother of all buddhas" eventually personified as the goddess Prajñāpāramitā.

See also: **Canons and literature; Mahāyāna Buddhism.**

ALAN SPONBERG

PILGRIMAGE

Indian roots

In the *Mahāparinibbānasutta* (*Dīgha Nikāya* 2.140–1), shortly before passing away the Buddha declares to Ānanda that after his death, those who still wish to wait upon him should visit the sites of his birth, enlightenment, first sermon, and passing away; he predicts that people will do so, reverentially calling to mind the events that occurred at each. That this did in fact become the case at least by the date of our earliest archeological evidence (third century BCE) is clear both in the architectural ruins and in the royal inscriptions discovered at these sites (Lumbinī in modern Nepal and Bodhgayā, Sārnāth, and Kushinagar in India, respectively); Aśoka Maurya, the first and paradigmatic Buddhist emperor, erected stone inscriptions and constructed or enlarged *stūpas* to memorialize his own worshipful pilgrimages to them.

From an early date this four-part Indian pilgrimage circuit was expanded to include eight "Great Wonders" (*aṣṭamahāprātihārya*) through the addition of four more Indian sites connected with the Buddha's taming of the elephant Nālagiri (Rajgir), the "miracle of the pairs" (Śrāvasti/Saheth-Maheth), the gift of honey (Vaiśālī) and the descent from heaven after preaching to his mother (Saṃkāsya/Sankisa). The regular depiction of the four or eight pilgrimage centers in early post-Aśokan Buddhist art is suggestive of their importance, though it is also important to recognize that at the same time, through the spreading out of the Buddha's relics and an ever-expanding repertoire of stories about moments in his life, ultimately thousands of sites in India and later abroad could be treated as "Buddha-fields"(*Buddha-kṣetra*) – or places sanctified by the presence of the Buddha – to which pilgrimage would be valuable.

The archeological record makes clear that each of these sites and associated pilgrimage traditions flourished during the heyday of Indian Buddhism. The travel diaries of Chinese pilgrims Faxian, Xuanzang and Yijing provide vivid pictures of the diversity and complexity of ritual and practice at these sites. Though with much less glory these traditions were preserved (especially by Tibetan, Chinese, Burmese, and Sri Lankan pilgrims) during the period of Indian Buddhism's decline and disappearance, and somewhat selectively pilgrimage to these sites has been revived in the nineteenth and twentieth centuries. Today, pilgrims from all over the world once again come to the Eight Great Wonders and many other restored ancient Indian Buddhist pilgrimage sites; the major sites host pilgrims' rest-houses and temples representing the diversity of the whole Buddhist world, and package tours and modern pilgrimage manuals are available in all Buddhist countries, making pilgrimages easily available to those with the will and the means.

Pilgrimage outside India

Not only have non-Indian Buddhists returned to Indian pilgrimage sites through the centuries, but Buddhist pilgrimage practices were also exported outside India with the religion and the relics. In Sri Lanka, for example, pilgrimage to the Eight or Sixteen Great Sites associated with the Buddha's visits to the island (Sinh. *Aṭamāsthāna*, *Solosmāsthāna*) emerged almost simultaneously with the religion itself, and most of these sites boast an unbroken pilgrimage tradition to this day. In similar fashion, throughout the Buddhist world sites sanctified by the presence of the Buddha, *arahants* and *bodhisattvas*, and/or believed (oftentimes from pre-Buddhist periods) to possess sacred power, have developed into full-blown local or regional pilgrimage traditions of their own. Thus Chinese Buddhists have long made pilgrimages to sacred mountains such as Miaofeng Shan, Tiantai Shan, and the three (sometimes four) "Great Seats of Enlightenment" (*san da dao chang*) associated with specific *bodhisattvas*; similarly, Chinese pilgrims travel to Putuo Island, identified with Mount Polaka (the mythical home of Avalokiteśvara/Guanyin), and many additional local pilgrimages (such as the Pilgrims' Fair of the West Lake (*xi hu xiang shi*), held from mid-February to mid-April in Upper Tianzhu) constitute an important aspect of practice as well as income for Chinese Buddhists. Japan's most famous Buddhist pilgrimage is probably the thousand-mile path encircling the island of Shikoku, during which pilgrims (called *henro*) worship in numerous temples and demonstrate their devotion to Kobo Daishi, founder of Shingon, who supposedly walks with them; but, as in China, numerous local and regional pilgrimage centers and associated traditions, starting with Mount Hiei, exist in Japan. So too do Burmese pilgrims travel to sites such as Kyaikhtiyo Pagoda, where a precarious boulder is said to be held in place by one of the Buddha's hair relics; Cambodians make pilgrimages to the "Grotto of Rebirth" (Phnom Sampau) said to be the womb of the Buddha's mother; for some Thai monks, being on pilgrimage (*doen thudong*) can last a lifetime. Pilgrimage has been especially important in Tibetan tradition and is therefore treated separately.

Types and purposes of pilgrimage

Then as now, a pilgrimage might be as simple as a trip to the local temple (or, more typically, some especially hallowed regional site); but as the various already-mentioned circuits make clear, more elaborate pilgrimages – to multiple sites, and/or covering greater distances – are also commonplace. A pilgrimage may be performed individually or in large groups, may last a day or many years, and may involve a huge variety of specific practices and rituals that have developed in association with the different traditions; each is thus a study in itself. Generalizations about Buddhist pilgrimage are further complicated by the wide variety of motivations and purposes for which pilgrimage is performed. Much of the motivation is doubtless always soteriological, whether conceived as a boon to meditation and moral discipline, a particularly auspicious opportunity for worship and merit-making, or a good way to die. Pilgrims may also be seeking knowledge of Buddhist history, doctrine, customs and praxis, as was clearly the case with the famous Chinese pilgrims. But pilgrimages have also been motivated by more worldly interests including entertainment, escape from routine, social and business networking and prestige, and in some instances they are performed to fulfill vows taken in exchange for some worldly benefit. The *Kaihōgyō* pilgrimage at Mount Hiei is performed by some Tendai monks as an esoteric ritual.

See also: **Aśoka; Bodhgayā; Kuśinagara; Lumbinī; Rituals and practices; Sacred places; Sarnath; *Stūpa*.**

JONATHAN S. WALTERS

PILGRIMAGE IN JAPAN

Pilgrimage is a widely recognized aspect of religious behavior, found in religious cultures across the world, and often holding a central position within many religious traditions, including Buddhism. This is certainly so in Japan, where pilgrimage has been described as "one of the great pillars" of Japanese religion. The act of journeying to and visiting Buddhist centers – whether one single center or, as is often the case in Japan, a number of places that are linked together – has been a dominant religious activity since at least the early Heian period, when the Buddhist monk Ennin (794–864) described his journey to and travels in China in search of the Buddhist *Dharma* as a *junrei* ("pilgrimage"). Whether associated with the travel of ascetics to sacred mountains, the journeys of aristocrats to Buddhist sites renowned for their miraculous efficacy, the wanderings of impoverished or sick peasants on the pilgrimage route of mostly Shingon temples around the island of Shikoku, or the visits of members of new religious movements to the sacred centers of their faiths, the practice of making pilgrimages has been a recurrent strand in Japanese Buddhist and religious history, engaged in by members at every level of Japanese society.

The popularity and variety of pilgrimages can be illustrated by presenting the characteristics of some representative pilgrimages in Japan:

1 The Shikoku *henro* pilgrimage, consisting of a circuit of eighty-eight sacred sites/temples on Shikoku Island (one of the four major islands of Japan), is the most prominent pilgrimage in Japan. The 1,400-kilometer route involves visits to eighty-eight Buddhist (mostly, but not all, Shingon) temples that are the official stages on the route, each of them associated in some way with Kōbō Daishi (Kūkai, the founder of the Shingon school).

Kūkai is said to have wandered around Shikoku and conducted ascetic practices there as a young man in search of his vocation. The veneration of Kōbō Daishi and the pilgrimage practices in Shikoku probably did not begin until the latter part of the tenth century, but have flourished through the centuries. In the early modern (Tokugawa) period, people visited Shikoku from around Japan, and mini- or model 88-circuit Shikoku pilgrimages were created in various parts of Japan. There are also numerous "unofficial" (*bangai*) sites that are visited by many pilgrims.

The Shikoku pilgrimage is still very popular in modern Japan, though many people now visit the circuit by bus or car instead of on foot, collecting calligraphic inscriptions and the temple seal from each site in a special book or scroll. A popular phrase among the pilgrims is *dōgyō ninin* ("two people practicing together"), reflecting the faith that Kōbō Daishi walks the path with, and protects, each pilgrim.

2 The Saikoku Kannon *junrei* pilgrimage is a circuit of thirty-three temples dedicated to the *bodhisattva* Kannon (Avalokiteśvara) in the Saikoku ("western country"; currently Kansai) area of central Japan. The thirty-three temples, of various schools, each house a central sacred object (*honzon*) depicting one of the varieties of Kannon. The number thirty-three reflects the teaching in the *Lotus Sūtra* concerning the number of bodily manifestations of Kannon in his efforts to save beings. The Kannon circuit also involves receiving the temple seal and calligraphical signature in a book containing the poem associated with each temple. The Kannon pilgrimage has been, and still is, popular for its promise of practical this-worldly benefits.

The Bandō and Chichibu Kannon *junrei* (in the Kantō, or Tokyo, area) are modeled on Saikoku but with thirty-three and thirty-four official sites, respectively, and also have a long history. These three sites are often combined to form a nationwide 100-site Kannon pilgrimage.

3 One of the historically most important pilgrimages was the Kumano pilgrimage, with its ninety-nine stations along the way from Kyoto to the Kumano shrines of Hongū, Shingū, and Nachi along the Pacific Ocean on the Kii peninsula. Kumano was a popular goal for many aristocrats and retired emperors in the late Heian period, and four of the retired emperors undertook a total of almost a hundred pilgrimages to Kumano from the late eleventh to the early thirteenth century. Kumano's association with Kannon and other elements of Pure Land faith, esoteric Buddhism, and ascetic practices also made it a popular site for pilgrimage for ordinary people, as well as Buddhist figures such as the poet Saigyō and the Pure Land priest Ippen. Kumano is still a popular, though out-of-the-way, center of retreat, and has recently been designated a World Heritage Site.

In a wide sense the Kumano pilgrimage includes the Yoshino–Kumano route through the Ōmine mountains of the central Kii area used by followers of Shugendō. Mountain centers around Japan – such as Mount Hiko in Kyushu, Mount Ishizuchi in Shikoku, Ontake in central Japan, Mount Fuji, the three mountains of Haguro in northern Japan, and so forth – each with its own mixture of practices and traditions, include aspects of pilgrimage.

4 An example of a single-site pilgrimage is Zenkōji, a temple in Nagano and home to an Amida Triad of mysterious powers that is kept hidden and out of

sight (*hibutsu*). Replicas of the Triad have been distributed throughout Japan, and, in turn, pilgrims from around the country come to Zenkōji. Once every seven years (last held in 2003) there is a special "revealing" of the icon (*gokaichō*), and a string is connected from the Amida Triad to a large pillar in the front yard of the main temple, making the icon and its power more accessible. In the basement there is a dark labyrinth (*kaidan meguri*) where one can enter and, by groping in the dark, touch a large metal key for an assured rebirth in the Pure Land, thus symbolizing a journey of death through the underworld and salvation in paradise. The temple complex is managed, unusually, by both the Tendai and Jōdo schools.

Another example of a popular single-temple pilgrimage site is Sensōji – better known as Asakusa-dera – in Tokyo. The temple is home to Asakusa Kannon, and thrived beginning in the Tokugawa period (1600–1868) when Tokugawa Ieyasu moved the capital to Edo (Tokyo) and chose Sensōji as the temple in charge of prayer for the prosperity of his family. It became a bustling center not only for Buddhist rites and devotion to Kannon (Avalokiteśvara) but also for entertainment – for both "prayer and play" – a role it maintains even today in modern Tokyo.

Another aspect of pilgrimage in Japan is the role of *kō* – confraternities or lay believers' associations. *Kō* can refer to groups with a wide variety of purposes; originally it referred to small groups that gathered to listen to sermons by a Buddhist monk, or to chant *sūtras* or the *nenbutsu*, or share a devotion to a certain figure or sacred place. Pilgrimage-related *kō* include those devoted to sacred mountain sites such as Mount Fuji (Fuji *kō*) or Mount Ontake (Ontake *kō*), temples (Zenkōji *kō*), or other sacred places (Kumano *kō*, Dewa Sanzan *kō*).

See also: **Japan, Buddhism in; Pilgrimage; Pure Land movements in Japan; Shugendō.**

PAUL L. SWANSON

PILGRIMAGE IN TIBETAN BUDDHISM

The Tibetan cultural area has innumerable sacred places, and pilgrimage is perhaps the most widespread activity among Tibetan Buddhists. Prominent features of the landscape, such as mountains, lakes, and caves are often believed to be imbued with religious significance and with the power to confer merit on those who make pilgrimages to them. The two most popular destinations are the holy city of Lhasa and Mount Kailash. Lhasa, which until 1959 was the residence of the Dalai Lamas, is still seen as the sacred center of the Tibetan Buddhist world, and every year thousands of pilgrims travel there to visit the sacred precincts of the Potala and the many monasteries that are found both within and at the periphery of the city. The most important pilgrimage circuit is the Barkhor (Bar 'khor), on which pilgrims circumambulate the Jokhang, a building believed to have been built during Tibet's early dynastic period,

Figure 34 Monks and lay pilgrims circumambulating the most popular pilgrimage spot in Tibet, the Barkhor, Lhasa.

which houses an image of the Buddha as a young prince known as Jowo Rinpoche. (See Figure 34.)

Mount Kailash, the most important of Tibet's holy mountain (*gnas ri*), is sacred to Buddhists, Bönpos, Hindus, and Jains. It draws thousands of pilgrims every year, who circumambulate it in a clockwise fashion (the Bönpos, however, travel in the opposite direction). Many pilgrims make the entire circuit around the mountain in a series of full prostrations.

Although pilgrimage is widely popular among Tibetan Buddhists today, it does not appear to have been practiced during the early period of Tibetan Buddhism. The earliest known pilgrimage account was written by Chak Lotsawa (Chag Lo tsā ba), who traveled to India in the thirteenth century. Since that time, the popularity of pilgrimage has increased, and today there are numerous printed guides for Buddhist pilgrims that provide information on the best time to make certain pilgrimages, the religious significance of Tibet's "power places," and their associations with famous Buddhist masters.

The most common practice in Tibetan Buddhist pilgrimages is circumambulation (*'khor ba*), and most holy places have a designated (and well-worn) path around them. Pilgrims are termed "those who go around a sacred place" (*gnas skor ba*), which can be anything deemed to be imbued with sacred power, such as monasteries, *stūpas*, meditation caves of great masters, or parts of the landscape that have come to be associated with Buddhist deities. Many of these were originally believed to be the abodes of indigenous gods (*yul lha*), but over time these gods have either been supplanted or have become associated with Buddhist deities. Pilgrimage guides often describe the process of ritual subjugation of the indigenous gods and the installation of buddhas and *bodhisattvas* in a sacred *maṇḍala*, which then marks the area as a suitable place for Buddhist pilgrims.

The reasons given for pilgrimage vary, but in general lay Buddhists tend to see the practice as a way to make merit, which will lead to good fortune in the present life and a better rebirth. Monastics and *tantric* adepts often travel to pilgrimage sites because they are believed to be particularly suitable places for religious practice, especially those associated with significant attainments of past masters. Astrological calculations play an important role in determining when to make pilgrimages: certain years are particularly auspicious, and particular times of the year are recommended for visiting certain places. Pilgrimage to Mount Kailash, for example, is believed to be most beneficial during a horse year in the Tibetan calendar and during the fifteenth day of the fourth month.

Pilgrimages were banned by Chinese authorities after their invasion of Tibet in the 1950s, but since the 1980s restrictions have been gradually lifted, and today the practice is enjoying renewed popularity all over Tibet. Much of this is the result of religious fervor – which has remained strong despite the Chinese government's efforts to eradicate it – and pilgrimage has also come to be viewed by Tibetans as a symbol of their cultural and religious identity and as a practice of resistance to Chinese rule.

See also: **Pilgrimage; Tibet, Buddhism in.**

JOHN POWERS

POLITICS

From the very beginning Buddhists have developed a wide range of specifically political paradigms, practices and rituals connected with Buddhist kings or rulers and the actual exercise of political power.

Political paradigms

Buddhist political paradigms, conveyed through religious texts, historical narratives, and lobbying (and in premodern India and China via formal inter-religious debates staged in imperial courts) articulated particularly Buddhist conceptions of the ideal king. They have played an especially important role outside India and China, where non-Buddhist religious traditions have been less firmly entrenched and Buddhism maintains its political importance today.

"The Aśokan paradigm" entails royal-imperial activities associated with Aśoka Maurya, including patronage, assistance to the poor and the environment, pilgrimage and procession, holding of court, regional administration and alliance by marriage, erection of eulogistic stone inscriptions and publicized regret for atrocities. The famous legends of Aśoka created a space for narrating political philosophy and for fighting political battles in post-Aśokan South Asia and later Central, East and Southeast Asia; Aśoka's devotional acts, like abdicating to the *sangha* and "purifying" it of heretics, were imitated by later Buddhist kings and more recently politicians (most recently by former Sri Lankan president Ranasinghe Premadasa [1924–93]).

Varied conceptualizations of the *bodhisattva*-king, an overlapping paradigm, were all based in an understanding of political activity as a domain for the exercise of *bodhisattva* qualities. Especially in the Mahāyāna Buddhist world, wherein multiple (even infinite) Buddhas and *bodhisattvas* are possible, royal identification with *bodhisattvas* was widespread; it persists today in beliefs about the *bodhisattva*hood of the Dalai Lama. From the tenth century CE onwards a comparable *bodhisattva*-king doctrine was developed in the Theravāda context, focused on the single present *bodhisattva* Maitreya (Pāli Metteya), which was invoked most recently by U Nu of Burma (1907–95).

Both these paradigms have lent to political authority a certain sacrality, manifested in ritualized deference to the ruler, taboos surrounding his or her person, inclusion of the ruler's image on altars for worship and transference of merit, and religious festivals celebrating the ruler's birthday or funeral. Once ubiquitous, such practices are still evident in the surviving Buddhist kingships of Thailand and Bhutan, and in exile Tibet; the practice of keeping the British monarch's image on Buddhist altars in Ceylon (Sri Lanka) and Burma (Myanmar) persisted into postcolonial times, and echoes of these practices persist in the treatment of modern Buddhist rulers throughout Asia.

Practices

Emulating these paradigms drew Buddhist rulers into the role of patron and pious leader who employed state and personal funds and energies for Buddhist building projects, supported Buddhist clergy, educational institutions and festivals, and cultivated his/her own religious advancement. These practices continue in sometimes conspicuous shows of piety by modern Buddhist presidents and politicians, where states support Buddhist monuments, educational activities, international exchanges, conferences and publications, etc., often as part of a government bureau of Buddhist affairs.

As patron, the king not only funded but also helped to shape Buddhist practices in his realm. Thus, however often rulers and states have ceremonially placed Buddhism on the throne, in practice they have been powerful regulators and reformers of the *sangha* and related Buddhist institutions as well. In classical times Theravāda rulers enforced periodic "purifications of the religion" (*sāsana-parisodhana*) in which monks were disrobed then re-ordained (often on the basis of an imported *upadampadā*); in modern Thailand the *sangha* is conceived as a branch of the civil service, with head officials selected by the monarch/state (as has been the case in both imperial and modern China); Tokugawa Japanese emperors used the *danka seido* system to track all families through affiliation with local temples; in the Burmese Constitution "religious persons" including monks are denied certain civil rights. Consequently, Buddhists have sometimes also fostered dissent in local, national and international politics, for example Tibetan opposition to Chinese occupation, Burmese pro-democracy activism and Thai anti-logging efforts.

Another important domain in which a ruler's religion and political praxis closely overlap is interregnal (today usually international) diplomacy. In the inscriptions and especially the legends of Aśoka himself diplomacy already proceeds within a Buddhist context, and shared Buddhist paradigms and practices have allowed different rulers to come together for their mutual benefit, in various ways, ever since. Even today, Buddhism plays a key role in the rhetoric and the itineraries of state visits, diplomatic relationships and international projects that occur between Buddhist nations.

Rituals

Specific royal rituals also emerged across Asia as soon as a given kingdom became Buddhist. Their idiosyncrasies were of special concern to Chinese pilgrims like Faxian and Xuanzang, and took a great variety of forms, usually including rituals of coronation (*abhiṣeka*), which persist in Buddhist kingdoms and have been generalized in *tantric* initiations; royal participation in periodic festivals (such as the annual Sri Lankan procession of the Buddha's Tooth Relic, still largely performed as witnessed by Faxian in the fourth century CE); and daily rites in the palace including special liturgies, blessings on the state (such as the Korean *hoguk pulgyo*, which requests *bodhisattvas* to assist the state in return for promotion of *Dharma*), meetings with religious mentors and advisors, and the ruler's own vows and affirmations of moral discipline.

See also: **Aśoka; Buddha and *cakravartins*; Japan, Buddhism in; Rituals and practices; South and Southeast Asia, Buddhism in.**

JONATHAN S. WALTERS

POUSSIN, LOUIS DE LA VALLÉE

Louis de La Vallée Poussin was a Belgian Buddhologist known worldwide for his important translations, articles, and studies, as well as a coterie of brilliant students. He was born in 1869 in Liège, and attended the State University of Liège between 1881 and 1888, focusing his studies on philology and philosophy. Introduced to Sanskrit and Pāli at an early age, once he moved to Paris he was able to study at the Sorbonne with such brilliant Indologists as Sylvain Lévi and Emile Senart while still in his early twenties. Eventually, he moved on to study with Hendrik Kern at Leiden. During his years at Leiden, he also studied Chinese and Tibetan, giving him command of all the primary buddhological languages. In 1895 he became a professor at the University of Ghent, where he remained for over thirty years. He died on 18 February 1938.

He was one of the editors of the journal *Le Muséon*, and in 1921 founded the Société Belge d'Études Orientales. La Vallée Poussin is best known for his multivolume French translation of Vasubandhu's *Abhidharmakośa*, published between 1923 and 1931. He also published a translation of Śāntideva's *Bodhicaryāvatāra* in 1907 and Hsüan-tsang's version of the *Vijñaptimātratāsiddhi* in 1930. Not only an editor and translator, he published important secondary works such as *Bouddhisme, opinions sur l'histoire de la dogmatique*, *Nirvāṇa*, and *The Way to Nirvāṇa*. Additionally, he contributed over two dozen articles to Hastings'

Encyclopedia of Religion and Ethics. Largely through La Vallée Poussin's work, the Franco-Belgian school of Buddhist Studies solidified, giving rise to an entire generation of Buddhist scholarship.

It was La Vallée Poussin's first important publication in 1898, *Études et matériaux*, that signaled his style of buddhological research. The young scholar, who considered himself an intellectual heir to Eugène Burnouf's approach, began by attacking the importance of the Pāli tradition of Buddhism. Without undermining the importance of Pāli Buddhism, he clearly argued that it certainly did not represent *all* of the Buddhist tradition. He felt one needed to study all the sources in all the Buddhist canonical languages. He rejected the assertions of those he referred to as "Pāli-ists," when they maintained that the Buddhist materials of north India, Nepal, and Tibet represented a later, degenerate form of Buddhism. He insisted that the entirety of the Buddhist tradition was far more complex than the Pāli-ists maintained, and that the Theravāda tradition represented only one among many important Buddhist sects. He singled out two of the Pāli tradition's greatest scholars – Thomas W. Rhys Davids and Hermann Oldenberg – for both praise and criticism. The chief locus of his criticism focused on the fact that neither was able to verify the so-called Buddhist origins, or the "Ur-Buddhism," they presumed to be inherent in the Theravāda tradition. The problem of *nirvāṇa* perplexed La Vallée Poussin throughout his life, but he is clear in what he concluded: "As a matter of fact we know what *Nirvāṇa* is as well as the Buddhists themselves, and it is not our fault if we are not able to give an unambiguous statement. The Buddhists were satisfied with descriptions which do not satisfy us."

See also: **Academic study of Buddhism; Franco-Belgian school of Buddhist Studies.**

CHARLES S. PREBISH

PRAMĀṆIKA MOVEMENT

One of the earliest points of contention among Buddhists in India was the question of which texts could be regarded as authentic representations of the teachings of the Buddha. Canonical conservatives, known collectively as Śrāvakayāna Buddhists, had a smaller number of texts that met their strict criteria than did the more liberal movements that eventually came to be known as the Mahāyāna. Members of the various Śrāvakayāna schools, such as the Theravādins, often accused other Buddhists of forging inauthentic texts to justify their non-standard practices. These other Buddhists responded in different ways, offering a variety of strategies to provide legitimacy to the texts that had previously not been widely known. This controversy over the authority of texts had the potential to divide the Buddhist community and to weaken it in the face of non-Buddhist opposition. One way of circumventing this problem of textual authority was provided by a group of thinkers, the best known of them being Dignāga and Dharmakīrti and their many interpreters, who focused on the basic issues of epistemology, the theory of how knowledge (*pramāṇa*) is acquired in general and what the limits of knowledge are. It was in the very nature of this epistemological approach to avoid sectarianism, so it is difficult, and arguably wrong-headed, to try to assign these thinkers to any particular school of Buddhism, or even to see them as primarily Śrāvakayāna or Mahāyāna in orientation.

The principal motivation behind making epistemology the main focus of a Buddhist theory and practice is grounded in an appreciation of the Buddha's claim that all trouble (*duḥkha*) has some form of delusion (*moha*) or misunderstanding (*avidyā*) as its main cause. Delusion is the most fundamental of the three poisons, as the other two, greed and hatred, arise only in the deluded mind. All Buddhist theory and practice, then, can be seen as a collection of methods of eradicating delusion and seeing things as they really are. Once that is done, then greed and hatred will no longer have a basis on which to arise and therefore will disappear by themselves. Delusion itself is often said in Buddhist texts to arise out of careless thinking (*ayoniṣo manaskāra*), so the aim of the Buddhist epistemological movement was to help identify the nature of careful, principled (*yoniṣas*) thinking so that people could cultivate it.

Although not usually thought of as one of the main contributors to the epistemological movement, one of the first Buddhist philosophers to raise the question of how beliefs are grounded was Nāgārjuna (fl. second century CE). In his *Vigrahavyāvartanī* (Averting the Disputes) he made reference to four sources of knowledge: direct sensual experience, inference, analogy and textual tradition. Without going into the details of any of these sources, Nāgārjuna observed that every belief is putatively grounded in one or another of them. One of the beliefs that a person may have is the very belief that beliefs are grounded. One might, for example, have confidence in one's belief that insects exist, because one has experienced them crawling on one's skin. But why should one have confidence in the belief that experience warrants belief? One might reply that it is reasonable to believe that experience warrants belief, but then the question arises: why should one have confidence in reason? What one is left to conclude from this radical questioning of the basis of our beliefs is that none of our beliefs is ultimately warranted. A belief may be nothing more than a form of desire, a desire that some story be true. If desire is one of the root causes of trouble, and if belief is a kind of desire, then it could be that beliefs are one of the root causes of our discontent. The work of the epistemologists Dignāga and Dharmakīrti can be seen as both building upon the insights of Nāgārjuna and offering constraints on their potentially sweeping implications.

Dignāga (fl. fifth and sixth centuries CE) wrote a number of treatises, including a commentary on Vasubandhu's *Abhidharmakośa*, a verse treatise summarizing the insights of the Perfection of Wisdom (*Prajñāpāramitā*) genre, several devotional hymns of praise of the Buddha, and a number of short pieces on logic and epistemology. His reflections on the sources of knowledge were collected in a compiled work called *Pramāṇasamuccaya* (Compilation of Works on the Acquisition of Knowledge). This work presents Dignāga's views, followed by a critique of the views of the main non-Buddhist schools of his time, on such topics as the nature of sense experience, the reliability of inference, the nature of language, and the process of convincing another person through discussion.

In his discussion of sense experience, Dignāga claims that sensation is a direct experience that is not associated with memories of previous experiences or mixed in any way with interpretation or language. When one sees a blue color, for example, one simply sees the color as it is. This direct experience may be, and usually is, followed almost immediately by an attempt to associate this direct experience of the color with previous experiences of colors. Ignoring the subtle differences between what one is currently experiencing and what has been experienced before, one then imagines either that there is a similarity between these experiences or that one is experiencing again what one has experienced on some earlier occasion. It is this imagining that forms the basis of the essentially false beliefs that objects endure through time to be experienced repeatedly and that there is an enduring self that endures through time to experience objects at different times. What Dignāga tries to offer is a means of questioning these imaginings and seeing that much of what one naïvely takes for granted is in fact problematic and that most of our convictions rest on incomplete or faulty reasoning.

Reliable reasoning takes place, said Dignāga in the second chapter of his *Pramāṇasamuccaya*, only when certain conditions are met. Reasoning consists in concluding, on the basis of evidence, that a given subject has a given property. The reasoning is reliable only (1) when the property used as evidence for another property in the same subject is itself actually a property of that subject; (2) the property being used as evidence has been seen in some other subject with the property for which it is evidence; and (3) when the property being used as evidence has never been observed in the absence of the property for which it is evidence. To use Dignāga's canonical example, one can rely on the reasoning that sound is impermanent by observing that sound is produced from conditions. The property of being produced from conditions is a property of sound; it has been observed along with the property of impermanence in many subjects (such as pots) other than sound; finally, being produced from conditions is never observed in the absence of impermanence. We can therefore safely conclude that sound is impermanent. By setting out these strict criteria for deeming an inference safe, Dignāga leaves his readers with the tools to determine which of their beliefs based on inference are warranted by safe reasoning. It turns out that most beliefs fail to pass the test that Dignāga outlines.

In the fifth chapter of his *Pramāṇasamuccaya*, Dignāga presents a theory of language that Indian (and then Tibetan) Buddhist philosophers spent the next thousand years or more refining. The principal insight of this theory is that language is a particular application of inference and therefore operates under the same constraints. A word, or sentence, is a sign for an object in exactly the same way that an observed property, such as the property of being produced from conditions, is a sign for another property. An expression in language is therefore a kind of evidence. Dharmakīrti (fl. seventh century CE), in elaborating on this idea, asks what exactly an expression in language is evidence for, and the answer he gives is that an expression is evidence for nothing but what the user of the expression desires that the hearer of the expression believe. The implications of this observation for the nature of a scriptural tradition are far-reaching, for it suggests that any text used as scriptural evidence that something is true is really evidence only that someone wishes for others to believe that it is true. If a scriptural text says, for example, that God created the world, we cannot reasonably conclude, on that basis alone, that God in fact created the world; all we can know for sure is that someone desires that we believe that we are creatures of God.

Dignāga and Dharmakīrti provide a powerful antidote to delusions arising from a misplaced confidence in scriptural or traditional authority, but a potential problem arises from the fact that this antidote might also undermine a Buddhist's confidence in Buddhist tradition. If one should question the validity of the Veda or some other non-Buddhist text, why should one accept Buddhist texts without questioning them? Dharmakīrti's answer to this question became the standard attitude for many Buddhists of subsequent generations. His answer is that we must question Buddhist texts. It would be irrational to believe a Buddhist doctrine simply because it is traditionally taught. But if one puts the doctrine to Dignāga's test of what qualifies as reliable evidence and it passes, then it is reasonable to hold it. This answer was conducive to a minimalist approach to Buddhist theory and to an experimental approach to Buddhist practice. In general the followers of the Pramāṇika movement helped keep in check the scholastic tendency to multiply dogma.

See also: **Dharmakīrti; India, Buddhism in; Mahāyāna Buddhism.**

RICHARD P. HAYES

PRATYEKA-BUDDHAS

The *pratyeka-buddha* is said to be one of the kinds of people worthy of a *stūpa* (relic mound), along with a perfect Buddha, a (Noble) disciple of a Buddha, and a *cakravartin* emperor (*Dīgha Nikāya* 2.142–3), and in contemporary Theravāda practice, a verse commonly chanted as a blessing, from the *Mahā Jayamaṅgala Gāthā*, is: "By the power obtained by all Buddhas and of *pratyeka-buddhas*, and by the glory of *arhats*, I secure a protection in all ways."

Buddhism postulates three kinds of Buddhas or "awakened ones." The first are *samyak-sambuddhas* (Pāli *sammā-sambuddhas*), perfectly and completely awakened ones: usually referred to simply as Buddhas or perfect Buddhas. These are beings, such as Gautama (Pāli Gotama) Buddha, who are seen to find the path to the end of pain and teach it to others (*Majjhima Nikāya* 3.8). They rediscover the timeless *Dharma* at a time when it has been lost to human society:

> Whether or not there is the arising of *Tathāgatas*, this principle (*dhātu*) stands – this *Dharma*-stability, this *Dharma*-orderliness … The *Tathāgata* directly awakens to that, breaks through to that … he declares it, teaches it, describes it, sets it forth. He reveals it, explains it, and makes it plain.
>
> (*Aṅguttara Nikāya* I.286–7)

The second kind of Buddhas are *śrāvaka-buddhas* (Pāli *sāvaka-buddhas*), "awakened as disciples" or *arhats* (Pāli *arahats*): people who practice the teachings of a perfect Buddha so as to themselves destroy attachment, hatred and delusion and fully realize *nirvāṇa*. They awaken to the same Ennobling Truths/Realities known by a perfect Buddha, and usually teach others, but lack additional knowledges that a perfect Buddha has, such as an unlimited ability to remember past lives (*Visuddhimagga* 411). A perfect Buddha is himself described as an *arhat*, but is more than this alone.

In between these two types of Buddhas are *pratyeka-buddhas* (Pāli *pacceka-buddha*). These came to be seen as people who awaken without the guidance of a perfect Buddha or the tradition established by one, and who do not systematically teach others so as to re-establish Buddhism when it has disappeared (e.g. *Abhidharmakośabhāṣya* III.94c). While they cannot live at a time of a perfect Buddha and his influence, in the Theravāda tradition they are said to arise only in cosmic eons during which a perfect Buddha arises at some time (Sri Lankan commentary on the *Buddhavaṃsa* p. 191). The Lokottaravādin *Mahāvastu* (1.197 and 357) says that when *pratyeka-buddhas* are informed that a *bodhisattva* will soon start the life in which he will become a perfect Buddha, they choose to pass away by rising into the air and burning up. This seems to harden the idea of "is not taught by a perfect Buddha" into a "has to get out of the way in case they are taught by one"!

The *Mahāvastu* (1.47) says that *pratyeka-buddhas* have "won the highest good, but not yet do they turn their thoughts to a knowledge of the whole *Dharma*." Like *arhats*, it is said that they do not know the qualities particular to a perfect Buddha or objects very distant in space or time (*Abhidharmakośabhāśya* I.1); a perfect Buddha can see an unlimited number of world-systems (galaxies), but a *pratyeka-buddha* can see only a million (VII.55a–b). Their qualities are much greater than those of *arhats*, but a world full of *pratyeka-buddhas* would not have the qualities of a perfect Buddha (*Khuddakapāṭha* commentary 178). To become a *pratyeka-buddha* needs much past good *karma*.

The term "*pratyeka-buddha*" is variously translated as "solitary awakened one," "individual Buddha," "one enlightened by himself," "one awakened for himself," and "hermit Buddha." However, K.R. Norman points out that Jainism has a similar concept, which in their Prakrit texts is written *patteya-buddha*, and that the term may well have been borrowed into both Buddhism and Jainism, having previously referred to a kind of enlightened renunciant in some earlier tradition. He sees the term "*pratyeka-buddha*" as probably deriving from the Pāli form *pacceka-buddha*, which may originally have been *pacceya-buddha*, *pacceya* being related to Sanskrit *pratyaya*, "cause," not *pratyeka*, i.e. *prati-eka*, "individually." Indeed, some Sanskrit texts write the term as *pratyaya-buddha* and the Chinese translation means "awakened by conditions". Norman thus holds that the original meaning of the term may have been "one who is awakened by a specific cause, a specific occurrence (not by a Buddha's teaching)". He suggests that the Tibetan explanation of *pratyeka-buddha* as meaning "one who meditates upon conditioned arising (*pratītya-samutpāda*)" is based on a misunderstanding of this.

How a person becomes a *pratyeka-buddha*

In the *Jātaka* commentary, a person becomes a *pratyeka-buddha* by insight into the three marks (impermanence, *duḥkha*, not-Self) on the occasions such as seeing a withered leaf falling, a mango tree ruined by greedy people, bracelets making a noise when placed together on a wrist, birds fighting over a piece of meat, and bulls fighting over a cow (*Jātaka* 3.239, 3.377, 5.248). It is also said that "wise men of old, seeing even a very slight ground (*ārammaṇa*), restrained an arisen defilement and so brought about *pacceka-bodhi* (individual awakening, perhaps originally awakening from a cause)" (*Jātaka* 3.376). One story tells of a man who, having stolen a drink from a workmate's supply, regretted it, and thinking such acts would lead to a bad rebirth, resolved to remove this defilement. "So, having taken as his object (*ārammaṇa*) the state of having drunk the stolen water, he increased his insight (*vipassanā*), and attained the knowledge of *pacceka-bodhi*" (*Jātaka* 4.114). The story continues by referring to four more people in the same locality who likewise become *pratyeka-buddhas* after contemplating some specific regretted deed.

Characterization of *pratyeka-buddhas*

Stories often refer to a person, on becoming a *pratyeka-buddha*, as spontaneously losing their lay appearance, and taking on one which parallels that of a Buddhist monk as to hair length, robe and bowl, and then flying through the air to a cave in the Himalayas (*Jātaka* 4.114–17). *Pratyeka-buddhas* are typically seen as living in such mountain areas. In the *Majjhima Nikāya* (3.68–71), the Buddha refers to 500 *pratyeka-buddhas* as having lived on Mount Isigili, "Gullet of the Seers," at various times in the past, and names eighty-eight of them, including Tagarasikhī. They are described as "without longing, who individually have come to right enlightenment" and as "great seers (*mahesī*) who have attained final *nirvāṇa*." The *Mahāvastu* (3.182), says of a typical *pratyeka-buddha*,

> He was graceful of deportment . . . he had accomplished his task. His faculties and mind were turned inwards. He was steadfast as one who had achieved harmony with *Dharma*. He was mindful, self-possessed, composed and tranquil of heart; his faculties were under control and his gaze firm.

Pratyeka-buddhas often appear in the context of being recipient of either alms or disrespectful behavior, both of which are said to have strong karmic effects for the people concerned. It is said that a man who spat on the *pratyeka-buddha* Tagarasikhī in a past life was born in a hell, and then in his present life as a leper (*Udāna* 50), while someone who gave him alms and then regretted it was reborn in a heaven, and then as a rich man who was a miser (*Saṃyutta Nikāya* 1.92).

Pratyeka-buddhas are often said to live a solitary life. The *Mahāvastu* (1.301, 3.27) says that: "splendid in their silence and of great power, living solitary like a rhinoceros-horn (*khaḍga-visaṇa-kalpa*), they train each his own self." *Khaḍga-visaṇa-kalpa* (Pāli *khagga-visāṇa-kappa*) is part of their stock description (e.g. *Visuddhimagga* 234, *Abhidharmakośa-bhāṣya* III.94c), an Indian rhinoceros having only a single horn. In the *Suttanipāta* (vv. 35–75) is the *Khaggavisāṇa*, or "Rhinoceros-horn" *Sutta*. This is seen by the *Niddesa*, a canonical commentary on very early parts of the *Suttanipāta*, to consist of verses of *pratyeka-buddhas*, a view also found in the *Mahāvastu* (1.357). The first of the verses is: "Laying aside violence in respect of all beings, not harming even one of them, one should not wish for a son, let alone a companion. One should wander solitary as a rhinoceros horn" (v. 35). The last sentence, here, ends all the verses except one: "If one can find a zealous companion, an associate of good disposition, (who is) resolute, overcoming all dangers, one would wander with him, with elated mind, mindful" (v. 45). In fact, there *are* references to groups of *pratyeka-buddhas*: four going for alms together (*Jātaka* 3.407), and 500 living together in a Himalayan cave (*Jātaka* 4.368). The *Abhidharmakośabhāṣya* (III.94c) says that *pratyeka-buddhas* live either alone or in groups.

The latter passage says that the reason *pratyeka-buddha*s do not (systematically) teach is that they have a habit of solitude and wish to avoid the problems that might arise in teaching many people. However, various passages (e.g. *Jātaka* 4.114–17) do have them giving short teachings as the occasion arises. They are sometimes also said to interact with the *bodhisattva* who becomes Gautama Buddha. A *pratyeka-buddha* helps the *bodhisattva* overcome pride in his birth, for he knows he will in future be a perfect Buddha (*Jātaka* 4.328), and the *bodhisattva* teaches someone whose insight was on the point of ripening, who thus becomes a *pratyeka-buddha* (*Jātaka* 4.340).

See also: **Buddha; Buddha, story of.**

PETER HARVEY

PREACHING AND *DHARMA* TRANSMISSION

Whether orally or through the distribution of Buddhist manuscripts and modern publications, transmission of the *Dharma* has always been a central Buddhist concern. The Buddha himself decided to preach at the very beginning of his career (*Majjhima Nikāya* 1.160–75) and his "open-fisted" unqualified willingness to share his whole *Dharma* not only distinguished him from many contemporary teachers but also defined his status as *Samyaksambuddha* and surely constituted one of the primary reasons that the religion spread so quickly and widely. Preaching (*dharmadeśanā*), a privilege granted to the Buddha's monks as one of the first *vinaya* declarations, has remained one of their principal occupations to this day, while listening to sermons has likewise been one of the major means through which Buddhists have cultivated understanding and commitment. Additionally, Buddhists have developed dramatic and theatrical traditions which transmit the *Dharma* through popular stories, and the production and distribution of Buddhist texts have been important practices in all Buddhist cultures.

Sermons

The *sūtras* are almost without exception records of sermons preached by the Buddha (or in some cases famous *arahants* or *bodhisattvas*), *Dharma*-instruction provided in spontaneous response to the queries and circumstances of individuals they encountered. Such one-on-one instruction has certainly remained ubiquitous in Buddhist cultures to this day, but preaching has been formalized in a variety of ways. First, sermons typically take as their topic a passage from one or more of the earlier *sūtras*, which is then explained and expanded upon in the vernacular. Second, these explanations become highly formulaic over time, such that modern preachers have faced a problem engaging their audiences. Third, over time the circumstances in which sermons are delivered have been formalized, dictating the occasions for which they are required (especially full moon days and funerals; the monastic rains retreat is also often a period of intensified preaching), various accoutrements (such as pavilions, special chairs, set styles of speaking and gesturing, processions, formalized invitations and expressions of gratitude) and series of associated rituals and practices which might include chanting, almsgiving or other acts of charity, worship, meditation, and the giving and receipt of protective blessings. While one-on-one transmission is also still practiced (as when preceptors teach novices *sūtras*, village monks counsel congregants, or in esoteric initiations), preaching is primarily a social affair involving large numbers of people and in many instances considerable spectacle.

Modernity has affected preaching across the Buddhist world in two distinct ways. On one hand, it has provided new technologies which make it possible for especially skilled or revered preachers to reach massive national and international audiences, even after they are dead. Loudspeakers, electric lights, advertising, advances in transportation and communications and cassette or DVD markets have similarly left their marks on Buddhist preaching. On the other hand, as preachers have confronted increasing social dislocation, skepticism about tradition and new expectations generated by pop culture, especially among modern Buddhist youth, they have begun to innovate upon the practice of preaching itself, in various circumstances adopting music (and even singing) as accompaniment, taking up current events and popular icons as material, and employing modern language to reach out to wider audiences.

Dharma as drama

Buddhists have also combated the formalism and disinterest that can beleaguer a preaching tradition in any era by expanding the practice beyond the sermon proper to embrace a variety of dramatic and theatrical forms keyed to entertaining as well as instructing. From versified Sinhala *jātakas* and similar folk stories performed at "sermon-festivals" (*baṇa pinkama*) in rural Sri Lankan temples, to elaborate annual performances of the *Vessantara Jātaka* (*Bun Pha Vet, Bun Phrā Wes*) in Laos and Thailand, to ceremonies for the "Recitation of Precious Scrolls" (*xuan juan*) or "Texts of Marvelous Events" (*bianwen*) in China, Buddhists have found ways to vivify the *Dharma* with acting, suspense, dance, props, costumes, humor, and similar widely appealing aspects of theater, sometimes in a carnival atmosphere. Such dramatic festivals increase understanding and motivate practice, thereby resulting in merit for performers and audience alike. They often also play crucial roles in temple fundraising efforts, local prestige, and the livelihood of the performers themselves. As is the case with preaching, modern technologies have expanded audiences for such dramas, which are sometimes televised, and may make use of electric lights, sound effects, and other innovations.

Written *Dharma* transmission

Transmission of the *Dharma* in written form has also played an important role in the history of the spread of the tradition. Prior to the advent of printing, considerable labor was required to produce manuscripts, and their resultant rarity was enhanced, especially in the southern Buddhist world, by an inhospitable climate that required them never to be recopied. Manuscript-production thus came to be regarded as a valuable practice in its own right, evidenced in the long-standing treatment of manuscripts as relics of the Buddha's Dharma-body (*dharma-kāya*) to be worshipped, processed and/or enshrined in *stūpas*, various rituals associated with the presentation and preservation of them, royal patronage and display of *Dharma*-texts (most famously the 729 marble slabs inscribed with the Pāli *Tipiṭaka* at Mandalay) and the claim often found in the colophons of Pāli manuscripts that "writing a single syllable [of the *Dharma*] is the same [merit] as building a *stūpa*" (*akkharaṃ likkhitaṃ ekaṃ thūpaṃ karāpitaṃ samaṃ*).

Printing (which was invented by Chinese Buddhists in the ninth century CE for the reproduction of *Dharma* texts) spread throughout the Buddhist world in its European form during the nineteenth century, largely eliminating the need for manuscript copying (though some Buddhists, notably in Japan, continue the practice for its own sake). But it did make possible mass distribution of printed texts, sermons, pamphlets, magazines and newspapers, which brings merit to publishers, patrons and distributors and is now widespread everywhere, most famously in the placement of the Tokyo-based Bukkyo Dendo Kyokai's *The Teaching of Buddha* in millions of hotel rooms around the world. Many modern Buddhist governments and organizations in the last century have made a project of publishing the entire *Tripiṭaka* and other canons, most recently in electronic form.

See also: **Buddha, style of teaching; Digital research resources; Electronic publications; *Tripiṭaka* and word of the Buddha; *Vinaya Piṭaka*.**

JONATHAN S. WALTERS

PRECEPTS, LAY

The lay precepts in Buddhism are collectively referred to as the five vows of the laity or *pañca-śīla*. The technical term *śīla* refers to a series of moral guidelines that remain internally and only personally enforced, in contrast to the formal rules of the *Vinaya*, which are externally enforced and which carry potentially powerful community and personal sanctions. As such, the lay precepts involve five moral injunctions, traditional to virtually all Buddhist schools throughout the world. Members of the Buddhist laity, in addition to taking refuge in the "three jewels" of Buddha, *Dharma*, and *Sangha*, are required to adhere to these five moral precepts of conduct, which are designed to aid in cultivating the higher life and assist in securing a more favorable rebirth: one that will be consistent with the attainment of salvation as defined by the particular Buddhist tradition in question.

The five precepts include: (1) not to kill or harm living beings; (2) not to take what has not been given; (3) to avoid misconduct in sensual matters; (4) to abstain from false speech; and (5) to avoid intoxicants that cloud the mind. Thus, the *pañca-śīla* are said to constitute the basic ethical framework of the Buddhist laity.

In modern application it appears that they are neither widely followed nor particularly comprehensive. A common practice among Buddhist lay disciples is to observe one precept at a time on the presumption that all five are simply too difficult to be practiced concurrently. A number of Buddhist innovators in the modern world are addressing the problem revealed by the above in order to find new, contemporary applications of the five precepts that make ethical life more genuinely accessible for Buddhists living in a vastly complicated, highly technological world.

One attempt at redefining the lay precepts for the modern world can be found in Thich Nhat Hanh's extension into fourteen precepts created for his "Order of Interbeing." These include:

1 Do not be idolatrous about or bound to any doctrine, theory, or ideology, even a Buddhist one.
2 Do not think the knowledge you currently possess is changeless absolute truth.
3 Do not force others to adopt your views, whether by authority, threat, money, propaganda, or even education.
4 Do not avoid contact with suffering or close your eyes to suffering.
5 Do not accumulate wealth while millions remain hungry.
6 Do not maintain anger or hatred.
7 Do not lose yourself in distraction, inwardly or outwardly.
8 Do not utter words that can create discord or cause your community to split apart.
9 Do not say untruthful things for the sake of personal advantage or to impress people.
10 Do not use the Buddhist community for personal gain or profit, or transform your community into a political party.
11 Do not live with a vocation that is harmful to humans or nature.
12 Do not kill. Do not let others kill.
13 Possess nothing that should belong to others.
14 Do not mistreat your body.

New and creative approaches such as these fourteen precepts are part of a movement of socially engaged Buddhism to try and preserve and extend Buddha's original five vows of the laity.

See also: **Family life, Moral discipline; *Sangha*; *Vinaya Piṭaka*.**

Charles S. Prebish

PROMINENT BUDDHIST STUDIES JOURNALS

Introduction

Throughout its history as an academic discipline, the study of Buddhism has been graced by an energetic group of philologically astute scholars who have been eager to present the results of their research through publication in scholarly journals. Some of the earliest articles devoted to Buddhism found their way into the French publication *Journal Asiatique*, started in 1822, which is the oldest orientalist journal published in France. Initially focusing primarily on philology and history, as the primary publication of the Société Asiatique de Paris, it now spans the entire breadth of the humanities and social sciences. In addition to French language articles, it also publishes work in English, German, Italian and Spanish. Another early journal which included publications on Buddhism was the *Journal of the Royal Asiatic Society*, which began publication in 1834 in London, and included articles and reviews on art, history, anthropology, language, and philosophy, as well as religion. In the United States, the American Oriental Society began publishing its own journal in 1843, and its contents spanned the entire Orient, broadly conceived so as to include the civilizations and literatures of the Near East, North Africa, and the Islamic world as well as Asia.

Buddhist Studies journals

Beginning nearly 125 years ago, the study of Buddhism began developing its own distinct journals. One year after the founding of the Pāli Text Society in London by Thomas W. Rhys Davids, the organization began publishing its own journal: *The Journal of the Pāli Text Society.* The journal had a continuous run of publication from 1882 until 1927, offering articles, texts, and translations relevant to the Pāli Buddhist tradition preserved by the Theravāda school of Buddhism. The journal was revived in 1981, but no longer publishes on a regular calendar, offering issues periodically. This lack of temporal continuity does not mean that the *Journal of the Pāli Text Society* has become minimized, as some of its recent issues have presented some of the most stirring debates in recent scholarly Buddhological history.

Not long before the *Journal of the Pāli Text Society* ceased publication in 1927, a new journal appeared in Japan in 1921 under the energetic editorship of D.T. Suzuki. Devoted to all aspects of the Mahāyāna Buddhist tradition, it was known as *The Eastern Buddhist*, and published not only articles of interest by leading scholars of Buddhism, but also English translations of important Mahāyāna Buddhist texts. It ceased publication during World War II, but began a "New Series" in 1965. Although D.T. Suzuki died in 1966, his editorial work with the journal was continued by Keiji Nishitani. A recent editor, Gadjin Nagao, headed an international editorial board that included such influential scholars as Luis O. Gómez and Lambert Schmithausen.

Some of the prominent Buddhist Studies journals reflect the sectarian affiliation of the founder. *Pacific World*, for example, was initially started in 1925, while its founder – Yehan Numata – was a graduate student at the University of California at Berkeley. After a short run of four years the journal ceased publication, but was revived in 1982 as an annual publication of the Institute of Buddhist Studies in Berkeley. While the Institute of Buddhist Studies is committed to the Jōdo Shinshū tradition, *Pacific World* publishes articles not only on that tradition, but spanning the entirety of the Buddhist tradition, including its Western manifestations. It continues to attract submissions from many of the leading scholars of Buddhism worldwide.

Another significant Buddhist Studies journal is *Buddhist Studies Review*, initially published in London under the editorship of Russell Webb. It is an extension of the now defunct *Pāli Buddhist Review*, and covers the entirety of the Buddhist tradition. Most recently, it has become the official journal of the United Kingdom Association of Buddhist Studies. In 2003, it celebrated its twentieth year of continuous publication. The journal continues to also be sponsored by the Institut de recherche bouddhique Linh-So'n.

Undoubtedly the best-known Buddhist Studies journal is the *Journal of the International Association of Buddhist Studies.* It issued its first volume in 1978, just two years after the founding of the International Association of Buddhist Studies. Its initial editor-in-chief was A.K. Narain, who also served as the General Secretary of the professional association. He was assisted by a team of editors that included several of the best known and respected scholars in the international community of Buddhologists: Leon Hurvitz, Alex Wayman, Lewis Lancaster, Stephen Beyer, A.W. MacDonald, and Heinz Bechert; and by a distinguished editorial board of acclaimed researchers. Published on a twice-yearly basis, it remains the most influential journal in Buddhist Studies. In its short history of barely a quarter of a century, it has grown from a small publication with fewer than 100 pages per issue to a current publication of more than 300 pages per issue, carefully edited under the current direction of Cristina A. Scherrer-Schaub and Tom Tillemans of the University of Lausanne in Switzerland.

Buddhist Studies scholars have also entered into a significant inter-religious dialogue, and that important conversation has produced an interesting journal entitled *Buddhist–Christian Studies*. Begun in 1981 under the editorship of David Chappell at the University of Hawaii, it is an annual publication exploring the intersection of these two significant traditions. It continues today under the editorship of Terry Muck and Rita Gross, and regularly presents, in addition to articles and book reviews, sections on various conferences undertaken by its parent organization, the Society for Buddhist–Christian Studies.

Other prominent Buddhist-related journals

In addition to the journals mentioned above, Buddhist Studies scholars routinely publish in a variety of other international journals which are not confined solely to the study of Buddhism. Results from two surveys conducted in the United States in 1992 and 1995 suggest that the following journals also merit significant attention as venues for Buddhist-related publication: *Journal of Asian Studies*, *Journal of the American Oriental Society*, *Journal of the American Academy of Religion*, *History of Religions*, *Japanese Journal of Religious Studies*, *Philosophy East and West*, *Monumenta Nipponica*, and the *Journal of Chinese Philosophy*.

See also: **Academic study of Buddhism.**

CHARLES S. PREBISH

PURE LAND MOVEMENTS IN JAPAN

Pure Land Buddhist ideas, texts, and practices were transmitted to Japan from an early date. Saichō (767–822), in transmitting the Tiantai/Tendai tradition, included Zhiyi's practice of the "Constantly-walking Samādhi" of chanting the name of Amida (Amitābha) for ninety days, and other commentaries on Pure Land teachings and practices. Ennin (794–864) transmitted Pure Land practices from Mount Wutai in China and established halls on Mount Hiei for the practice of verbal *nenbutsu*. Genshin (942–1017) compiled the *Ōjōyōshū*, a selection of texts on rebirth in the Pure Land, which was influential in the development of pictorial representations of hells and Pure Lands, and the practice of calling on Amida for rebirth in the western Pure Land on one's deathbed. The major founders of new Pure Land schools in the Kamakura period, Hōnen and Shinran, were Tendai monks who developed their own vision of Pure Land Buddhism.

Another major figure in spreading the Pure Land teachings was Ippen (1239–89), founder of the Ji school of Japanese Pure Land Buddhism, and known as an itinerant holy man (*hijiri*) who spread the practice of dancing while chanting the *nenbutsu*. Ippen first studied Tendai Buddhism on Mount Hiei but later went to Kyushu and became a disciple of Shōtatsu of the Seizan branch of Jōdo Pure Land Buddhism. He traveled widely, including pilgrimages to Zenkōji in Nagano, Shikoku, and Shitennōji in Osaka. During a pilgrimage to Kumano in 1274 he had a vision of Amida, who commanded Ippen to distribute talismans (*fuda*) on which were written *namu Amida-butsu* (homage to the Buddha Amitābha). These were to be distributed to all people, whether or not they had any faith or interest. Ippen devoted the rest of his life to traveling and preaching throughout the country. He began and popularized the practice of *odori-nenbutsu* (dancing while chanting the *nenbutsu*) and attracted a large following. The dance served as a celebration of Ippen's belief that all beings are already saved through Amida's enlightenment. Though the Ji sect is now a minor school of Japanese Buddhism, *odori-nenbutsu* is still a part of the popular religious practices of Japan and played a role in the development of Japanese theatre. Ippen's life and teachings are illustrated in the *Ippen Hijiri e*, a masterpiece in the genre of painted scrolls. The most reliable source of Ippen's teaching is the *Ippen Shōnin goroku* (*Record of Ippen*).

Amida's western paradise (*gokuraku*) was not the only Pure Land that caught the attention of the Japanese people. The *bodhisattva* Kannon (Avalokiteśvara) was also a popular figure, and the focus of numerous cults. One example is the practice of *fudaraku tokai* ("crossing the sea to Fudaraku"), physically departing from Nachi beach for the Pure Land of Kannon in the east on a small enclosed boat, nailed shut from the outside in case the person has a change of mind.

A little-known aspect of Pure Land Buddhism in Japan is the secret societies of "hidden *nenbutsu*" (*kakure nenbutsu*). These groups secretly transmit what they believe is the "true" teaching of Shinran, hidden from the official Pure Land institutions. Criticized by the Honganji organization and persecuted by the government, they were forced underground during the Tokugawa (1600–1868) period, but they survive in modern times and continue to orally transmit the "real" secret teachings of Shinran only to those who have undergone proper initiation.

See also: **Hōnen and Jōdoshū; Japan, Buddhism in; Shinran and Jōdo Shinshū.**

PAUL L. SWANSON

PURE LAND SCHOOL, CHINA

This school's core practice is based on a story found in the *Longer Sukhāvatīvyūha Sūtra*. According to this narrative, the Buddha Amitābha, while still a *bodhisattva*, made a series of forty-eight vows, including one which said that he would not accept final Buddhahood unless he brought into being a Buddha-land to which all could come if they but recollected his name ten times. As he indeed achieved Buddhahood, this vow must have been fulfilled and such a land must exist as described. On the basis of this story, devotees believe that, through faith in Amitābha's vow, they can come into his Pure Land without first becoming pure and enlightened themselves, and, once there, they will have a perfect instructor in the person of the Buddha, and ideal conditions for study, practice, and enlightenment.

Amitābha-centered thought and practice first appeared in China in 179 CE, when Lokakṣema produced a translation of the *Pratyutpannasamādhi Sūtra*, a work that extolled a type of meditation which would cause all the Buddhas to appear before the practitioner. In one brief passage, this work states that the practitioner should be aware that Amitābha dwells in the land of Sukhāvatī many millions of Buddha-lands off to the west, and that, by simply calling him to mind, the practitioner can attain a vision of him and all the Buddhas of the cosmos. Although Amitābha practice receives only this brief mention, and although the goal of the practice is a vision of the Buddha in this life rather than rebirth in Sukhāvatī after death, the appearance of this work is regarded as the first instance of Pure Land belief in China, and provided the textual basis for the first example of organized Pure Land practice.

In the year 402 the monk Lushan Huiyuan (334–416) gathered 123 clergy and literati in his Donglin Temple to practice this visualization of Amitābha and affirm their intention to gain rebirth in Sukhāvatī. The group that Huiyuan formed came to be known as the White Lotus Society (Ch. *Bai lian she*), and Huiyuan himself was later placed first on the list of Pure Land patriarchs. Huiyuan also corresponded with the Kuchean translator Kumārajīva (343–413) on a number of points regarding visualization practice, including whether the image of

Amitābha seen in one's dreams was really him or a projection of the mind.

Subsequent developments took place in north central China, around the imperial capitals of Chang'an and Luoyang. New translations of the scriptures that were to become known as the "Three Pure Land *Sūtras*" (The *Longer* and *Shorter Sukhāvatīvyūha Sūtras* and the *Meditation Sūtra*) provided a fuller account of the story of Amitābha Buddha, his vows, and his Pure Land, providing the basis for new developments in Pure Land thought and practice. The master Tanluan (476–542), frightened by a serious illness, left behind the conventional life of the monk-scholar and devoted himself to the oral invocation of Amitābha's name. He enthusiastically taught others this practice, and so became one of the first popularizers of the method of *nianfo* (Buddha-recitation). This shift from visualization to oral invocation was the result of interpreting the Chinese character *nian* to mean "recite" rather than "contemplate."

Another master, Daochuo (562–645), counseled people to recite the Buddha's name as much as possible to purify the mind, using beans as counters. He wrote a commentary on the *Meditation Sūtra* called the *Anle ji* (*Collection of Ease and Bliss*) that included an anthology of scriptural passages supporting and defending the efficacy of the practice. His disciple Shandao (613–81) also wrote in support of the oral recitation of the Buddha's name and composed a number of liturgies and hymns for societies formed for joint practice, and composed a commentary on the *Meditation Sūtra*, a work which teaches a complex set of visualizations as a means of attaining a vision of Amitābha in this life.

While these three masters focused more or less exclusively on Pure Land practice, there were other streams of Pure Land thought as masters identified with other schools sought to incorporate Pure Land practice into wider doctrinal and practical systems. For example, Zhiyi (538–97), the founder of the Tiantai school, included meditative practices aimed at gaining a vision of Amitābha in this life and rebirth in the Pure Land after death within his encyclopedia of meditation, the *Great Calming and Contemplation*. This version of Pure Land practice is very demanding: the practitioner was to repair to a specially consecrated room with an image of Amitābha in the center, and was to circumambulate it for ninety days without stopping or sleeping. Other masters outside of the Pure Land "school" wrote commentaries on the three Pure Land *Sūtras* as part of their overall scholarly program: Zhiyi, the Sanlun master Jizang (549–623), and Jingying Huiyuan (523–92), among others, also composed commentaries on the *Meditation Sūtra* that often differed significantly with commentaries written within the movement on many important points: whether the Pure Land was an expedient illusion devised by Amitābha for the benefit of impure beings or truly reflected his own enlightened nature; whether the Amitābha seen in visualization was a manifestation of his transformation-body (Skt. *nirmāṇakāya*) or his reward-body (Skt. *saṃbhogakāya*); whether the activity of visualization was phenomenal (Ch. *shi*) or noumenal (Ch. *li*); and so on.

Pure Land practice also required defense. The central claim of Pure Land thought – that beings could escape from *saṃsāra* and dwell in a purified Buddha-land without becoming enlightened first – offended many Buddhists. Many critics argued, following the *Platform Sūtra* and the *Vimalakīrti Nirdeśa Sūtra*, that to posit a pure land against the present, impure world, and a Buddha who literally existed outside of the practitioner's own mind, constituted an impermissible dualism from the perspective of emptiness. They argued that the Pure Land is nothing but the present world seen correctly, and Amitābha was only the practitioner's own mind free of all misconceptions. Later literature labeled this position "Mind-Only Pure Land" (Ch. *weixin jingtu*).

To this, many Pure Land apologists, from Daochuo and Huiri (680–748) in the early period to later figures such as Zhuhong (1535–1615), Yuan Hongdao (1568–1610), and Yinguang (1861–1940), replied that to criticize unenlightened beings for not having an enlightened view of non-dualism only castigated them for not being enlightened before being enlightened; such criticism was circular. They explained that Pure Land teachings were compassionately given by the Buddha for those who did not have the time, inclination, or talent for the strenuous and uncertain path to Buddhahood here and now. Once reborn in the Pure Land, they would have perfect conditions for the attainment of enlightenment, at which point they would come to the realization that the Pure Land really was only the present world seen correctly. For the time being, however, they needed expedient teachings that, though admittedly dualistic, would still lead them skillfully to the goal. This position, which left room for a literal understanding of the Pure Land myth, came to be called "Western Direction Pure Land" (Ch. *xi fang jingtu*) or "Other-Direction Pure Land" (Ch. *ta fang jingtu*).

During the Song dynasty (960–1279), one sees the appearance of large-scale Buddha-recitation societies boasting thousands of members, most founded by Tiantai masters working along the southeastern seaboard. Further developments took place in the interaction of Pure Land and other styles of cultivation. The master Yanshou (904–75) attempted to synthesize Pure Land with Chan into a system in which both could be cultivated without contradiction – this came to be known as the "joint practice of Chan and Pure Land" (Ch. *chan-jing shuang xiu*). The main manifestation of this "joint practice" was the so-called "*nianfo gongan*," advocated by Zhongfang Mingben (1262–1323) and Zhuhong. The practitioner, while reciting Amitābha's name, stops periodically to contemplate the *gongan*, "Who is reciting the Buddha's name?" Other masters, however, resisted this synthesis, insisting on the integrity and sufficiency of Pure Land practice alone. Yinguang, for example, decried the "psychological" reading of Mind-Only Pure Land and forcefully defended the literal existence of the Pure Land and the adequacy of traditional Pure Land practice done without mixing in *gongan* or any other extraneous method.

While all defenders of Pure Land practice in China characterized it as an "easy path" in contrast to the "difficult path" of conventional Buddhist practices, one must understand that, as understood in China, the path was far from easy. As Chewu (1741–1810) wrote, the point of Pure Land practice, whether the complex practice of visualization or the simple repetition of the Buddha's name, has purification of the mind and attunement (Ch. *ganying*) with Amitābha as its goal. However, the mind changes constantly: an instant of recitation of the name purifies the mind completely in that instant, but a return to worldly thought in the next instant defiles it once again. The point of using beans and later rosaries as counters was to encourage practitioners to practice repeating the name constantly in order to keep the mind always pure. In addition, visualization and repetition both served to harmonize the practitioner's mind with the Buddha's in order to create karmic links with him and so strengthen the likelihood of rebirth in Sukhāvatī. The ultimate goal was to have the mind focused on Amitābha and the Pure Land at the critical moment of death; distraction at that instant could nullify the results of years of faithful recitation and cause one to veer back into *saṃsāra*. Thus, constant practice was necessary in order to increase the likelihood that one's mind, fortified by habituation, would be unshakeably attuned to the Pure Land at the moment of death.

Since the Song dynasty, Pure Land practice has not been the province of any single "school," despite the recognition of a central line of "patriarchs." With very few exceptions, Chinese Buddhists accept that the chances of attaining enlightenment so complete that it guarantees one an exit from *saṃsāra* through the unaided strength of one's own practice are very slim, and that one must have Pure Land practice as a kind of insurance policy, regardless of what other practices or scholarship one does. Thus, Pure Land thought and practice pervades all of Chinese Buddhism as the guarantor of the path one treads toward Buddhahood. However, in the late twentieth century, a new current of Pure Land thought opened that rejected both the "Mind-only" and "Western-direction" versions of practice as too other-worldly. New masters such as Shengyan (1930–) and Xingyun (1927–) now speak of "building a Pure Land on earth" (*jian renjian jingtu*), meaning that devotees should apply themselves to purifying the present world through social activism and advocacy. Thus, alongside the traditional practices aimed at gaining rebirth in the Pure Land, one may also see action on behalf of the environment, women's issues, and human rights done within a Pure Land framework.

See also: **China, Buddhism in; Pure Land movements in Japan; Pure Land school, China.**

CHARLES B. JONES

R

RATNAKĪRTI

Among the last of the prominent Buddhist thinkers in India, Ratnakīrti flourished in the middle of the eleventh century. He wrote independent treatises on a number of topics that had become mainstays of Indian Buddhist scholasticism. All these treatises are classed by the compilers of the Tibetan canons as works representing the Vijñānavāda point of view.

The central claim of the Vijñānavāda or Yogācāra school is that everything that we are capable of knowing about is mediated by awareness itself. There is no direct experience of objects outside awareness; rather, there is experience only of objects as the contents of acts of awareness. The very idea of external objects, therefore, is a construct of the intellect that is trying to provide a coherent account of the fact of experience, and careful philosophical analysis shows that the idea of external objects is both unwarranted and ultimately untenable. Opponents of the Vijñānavāda position were quick to point out that if there are really no objects external to one's own consciousness, then there cannot be conscious minds other than one's own, because another mind would after all be an object external to one's own mind. For this reason, said the critics, Vijñānavāda entails solipsism, and solipsism is incompatible with the general Buddhist enterprise of teaching and with the Mahāyāna enterprise of cultivating the virtues of a *bodhisattva* for the sake of helping other beings attain liberation. Unlike his predecessors who strove to defend Vijñānavāda from the charge of solipsism, Ratnakīrti wrote a text entitled *Saṃtānāntaradūṣaṇa* (Refutation of Other Continua) in which he tried to show that the idea that there are continua of mental events other than one's own is incoherent. Solipsism, in other words, is true. There really is only one mind, said Ratnakīrti, namely the omniscient mind of the Buddha. All the apparently distinct minds of individual sentient beings are but events within that one mind.

In other treatises, Ratnakīrti argued for standard Buddhist scholastic positions. In

Īśvarasādhanadūṣaṇa he presented criticisms of non-Buddhist arguments for the existence of a single creator god. In *Sthirasiddhidūṣana* he criticizes non-Buddhist arguments for the view that there exist permanent unconditioned beings. And in *Kṣaṇabhaṅgasiddhi* he presents Buddhist arguments for the position of radical momentariness: that is, the doctrine that everything that exists perishes in the same moment that it arises. In addition to these treatises on metaphysical issues, Ratnakīrti wrote several treatises on epistemology, on the theory of inference and on the form of nominalism that was at the heart of the Buddhist philosophy of language. All these were topics that had become important in Indian Buddhism through the writings of Dignāga and Dharmakīrti more than half a millennium before Ratnakīrti's time. He thus comes toward the end of a long debate between Indian Buddhist thinkers and their non-Buddhist critics. By taking into consideration the generations of critics of various Buddhist positions, Ratnakīrti was able to present particularly refined and sophisticated versions of the views advanced by his Buddhist predecessors.

See also: **India, Buddhism in; Mahāyāna Buddhism; Yogācāra school.**

RICHARD P. HAYES

RHYS DAVIDS, CAROLINE AUGUSTA FOLEY

Caroline Augusta Foley Rhys Davids (1857–1942) was the daughter of a vicar and was educated at home. She attended University College in London, and received her MA in 1889. She married Thomas W. Rhys Davids in 1894. While unstated in her online biographies (Faculty of Asian Studies Archives [University of Cambridge], Explore, and World History), it is likely she met Rhys Davids there as he was then Professor of Pāli at the University of London. She was a Lecturer in Indian Philosophy at Manchester University and later in Buddhist History at the School of Oriental and African Studies, London. She was Honorary Secretary of the Pāli Text Society from 1907 to 1922 and President from 1923 to 1942.

C.A.F. Rhys Davids was a productive translator and editor of Pāli texts. She translated the *Saṃyutta Nikāya*, *Theragāthā* and *Therīgāthā* as well as the *Jātaka* and general books on Buddhism. As Teresina Rowell Havens ("Mrs. Rhys Davids' Dialogue with Psychology (1893–1924)") notes, she studied the Buddhist psychology of mind and the dynamic between the notion of a metaphysical self and a psychological one, the emphasis on will, attention and choice without a corresponding acceptance of a soul. Initially, she accepted the notion that self was always "becoming."

Her thoughts on the notion of self and Buddhism and, subsequently, her scholarly reputation changed over the course of the years. This may have been, at least in part, the result of the fact that her only son, Arthur, died in the First World War. Havens states that after this Rhys Davids began to focus on Buddhist texts that dealt with extrasensory perception, audition and other-worldly communication. Indeed, she came to believe that the Buddha had denied the existence of an inauthentic self but affirmed a "true" self. By her description of this self it appears to be the substantial Self or Great Soul of Brāhmaṇical religion, a concept scholars agree was rejected by Buddhism. She also paid attention to the writings of Theosophy which likely influenced her thought in this area as well. As many scholars of the time, she sought to separate the original Buddhist teaching from the various overlays of redactors, but her effort to substantiate a positive teaching of the self led to forced translations.

This change in thinking can be seen in her "Preface" to I.B. Horner's first book,

Women Under Primitive Buddhism (1930). Rhys Davids encouraged Horner to write about women in Buddhism and had herself translated the *Therīgāthā*. In reference to the *bhikkhunī* Soma, she states that Soma would have understood the word "*dhamma*" as the voice of the Deity in "man" (xvi). Interestingly, she states that the story of Mahāpajāpatī is probably not the first entry of women into the *sangha* as tradition asserts. What distinguishes the *Therīgāthā* from the *Theragāthā* for her is its emphasis on liberation and expansion of human nature beyond that "bounded by femininity."

As well as her scholarly work Rhys Davids was involved in social service projects to assist women and children, and the movement for women's suffrage at the turn of the twentieth century.

See also: **Anglo-German school of Buddhist Studies; Women in Buddhism: an historical and textual overview.**

MAVIS L. FENN

RHYS DAVIDS, THOMAS W.

There is little doubt that Thomas W. Rhys Davids was the leading pioneer in the development of Pāli and Theravāda studies in the West. Born in 1843, he studied Sanskrit under Professor Stenzler at the University of Breslau in Germany, eventually earning his Ph.D. He entered the Ceylon Civil Service in 1864, and quickly acquired a working knowledge of both Sinhalese and Tamil. His entry into the study of Pāli and Buddhism was almost accidental, for while serving as a judge in Ceylon he had to adjudicate a case that involved a document in Pāli. That document included a quotation from the *Vinaya Piṭaka*, which fueled an intense interest that led Rhys Davids to study the language under a Buddhist monk named Yatramulle Unnanse.

Rhys Davids left the Civil Service in 1872 and returned to England, studying law and being called to the bar in 1877. Nonetheless, he continued to also study Buddhism, and began contributing regularly to the *Journal of the Royal Asiatic Society*. By that time, the study of Pāli was progressing throughout Europe, involving such scholars as George Turnour, Spence Hardy, Robert Childers, Viggo Fausboll, Hermann Oldenberg, and others, and it was left to Thomas W. Rhys Davids to organize them all. In 1881, he founded the Pāli Text Society, and the following year became Professor of Pāli at University College, London. In 1894 he married Caroline Augusta Foley, and that same year he visited the United States, where he gave a series of lectures at Cornell University (which were eventually published as *Buddhism: Its History and Literature*). He eventually became Professor of Comparative Literature at Victoria University, Manchester, in 1904. Thomas W. Rhys Davids died in 1922.

His work with the Pāli Text Society, which he served as president until his death, cannot be overestimated. He was instrumental in bringing most of the Pāli Canon into publication, in roman characters, and worked aggressively and smoothly in collaboration with a wide range of scholars. He also contributed greatly to the *Sacred Books of the Buddhists* publication series as well as the *Sacred Books of the East* series, and despite his ongoing work with the Pāli Text Society, he continued to play a leading role in the Royal Asiatic Society, serving as its secretary and librarian between 1885 and 1904.

Apart from his many translations, which included both the *Vinaya Piṭaka* and the *Dīgha Nikāya*, one of Rhys Davids' fondest desires was to provide a new and thorough Pāli–English dictionary. With the assistance of one of his longtime collaborators, the philologist William Stede, he was finally able to bring this project to fruition, and it is their *Pāli–English Dictionary* that is still widely used today.

No higher tribute can be paid to him than that of Miss I.B. Horner:

> Rhys Davids bore the stamp of complete integrity of thought and character ... In conversation he was learned, brilliant, and of entrancing interest; but yet people who knew him remember well how the humor that constantly came bubbling out of him, enlivening everything, made his deep wisdom palatable even to the most ordinary or ignorant persons and led them to feel they were making some contribution that was worth-while.

See also: **Academic study of Buddhism; Anglo-German school of Buddhist Studies.**

CHARLES S. PREBISH

RINZAI TRADITION

Rinzai is, along with Sōtō, one of the two major schools of Zen Buddhism in Japan. It carries on the Linji Chan tradition in emphasizing the use of *kōans* (Ch. *gongan*) – stories or "precedents" involving a riddle to be solved – as a central practice to attain enlightenment.

The Rinzai tradition was first transmitted to Japan by Eisai (Yōsai, 1141–1215), who studied at the Tendai headquarters on Mount Hiei and then in 1168 traveled to China. He made a second trip to China in 1187, but his plans to make a pilgrimage to India were thwarted by Chinese officials. Instead, Eisai studied the Chan/Zen tradition of Linji.

After his return to Japan in 1191, Eisai began to propagate Rinzai teachings, along with the Tendai and esoteric Buddhist teachings and practice, also emphasizing the importance of observing the Buddhist precepts. Faced with opposition from the Tendai establishment, Eisai wrote *Shukke taikō* (*Essentials of the Monastic Life*) and *Kōzen-gokoku-ron* (*Dissemination of Zen for the Defense of the Nation*) in which he claimed that Zen teachings should reform and not threaten Tendai Buddhism, and would strengthen rather than weaken society. In 1199 Eisai went to Kamakura to seek the support of the new shogunate. Eventually he was put in charge of Kennin-ji, a new monastery, where he served the shogunate by performing religious services and became involved in the restoration of various temples, such as Tōdai-ji in Nara.

Eisai is recognized as the founder of the Rinzai school of Zen Buddhism in Japan, but Eisai himself taught an eclectic "mixed" form of Buddhism that included many elements from the esoteric tradition. He also saw himself as a reformer of Tendai rather than the founder of a new movement. He is most famous for introducing tea to Japan, which he recommended to monks for their health and as an aid to meditation.

The Rinzai Zen tradition after Eisai, reinforced by cultured Chinese monks escaping to Japan to avoid the Mongols, was patronized by the warrior elite and aristocratic families, eventually forming the cultural centers of the Five Mountains (*gozan*) temples. Temples such as Nanzanji and Daitokuji became great centers of the arts.

A representative figure from this period is Musō Soseki (or Musō Kokushi; 1275–1351). Musō first studied esoteric Tendai and Shingon Buddhism before studying Zen under the Chinese master Yishan Yining (1247–1317), and then under Kōhō Kennichi (1241–1316) in Kamakura. He spent many years wandering and meditating in the mountains. Eventually he was invited to be abbot of Nanzenji, and played a central role in the establishment of the Gozan system. He headed a number of major Zen temples (including Nanzanji and Enkakuji), trained numerous disciples, founded many more temples (including Tenryūji), and was an influential figure in the political world of his day, ushering the Gozan temple system into a leading role in the culture and life of medieval Japan.

Musō taught a traditional Rinzai combination of seated meditation and *kōan* study, as well as incorporating elements of esoteric Buddhism. His many works include *Muchū mondō* (Dialogue in a Dream) in which he explains Zen Buddhism in response to questions raised by the Shogun Ashikaga Tadayoshi. He also compiled strict rules for the community of Zen monks. Musō was also a designer of gardens, the most famous being the "moss garden" at Saihō-ji in Kyoto.

The wars of the sixteenth century put an end to the Gozan system as a dominant cultural establishment, and the lineages of Daitokuji and Myōshinji became most important for the Rinzai tradition. Two contrasting representatives of Daitokuji and the Rinzai Zen of this period are Ikkyū and Takuan Sōhō.

Ikkyū Sōjun (1394–1481) was an eccentric Japanese Zen master and noted poet and calligrapher who disdained worldly conventions and the Gozan Zen establishment. He was the son of Emperor Go-Komatsu (r. 1382–1412) and was schooled from childhood at the Zen temple Ankoku-ji in Kyoto. He came to detest the sophisticated Zen establishment and left Ankoku-ji to practice with Ken'ō Sōi (d. 1415) and then Kasō Sōdon (1352–1428), under whose strict tutelage he experienced enlightenment. Ikkyū spent many years in Sakai (currently Osaka), where he frequented the local taverns and brothels and exhibited a mad eccentricity, such as marching down the street waving a human skull. Ikkyū accepted an appointment as abbot of Daitoku-ji in 1474, and succeeded somewhat in its restoration from the ravages of the Ōnin war, but he soon left the position. His love affair late in life with the blind singer Mori is well known, and the subject of many of his poignant poems. Ikkyū is also famed for his many striking poems in the classic Chinese style, and his dynamic calligraphy. His finest collection of poetry is the *Kyōunshō* (Crazy Cloud Anthology), containing over 1,000 poems. Ikkyū is well known in the modern popular mind, because of his role as the hero of a Japanese cartoon, as an adolescent novice monk who betters his superiors through wit and clever antics. He also lives on in legend as an exemplar of the unconventional Zen monk whose eccentric behavior exposes the vanity of worldly pretensions.

Takuan Sōhō (1573–1645), in contrast, was also a noted scholar, calligrapher, and painter. Appointed abbot of Daitokuji at the young age of thirty-five, he made important contributions to the Zen art of tea, swordsmanship, calligraphy, poetry, and painting. He was spiritual advisor to the Shogun Tokugawa Iemitsu, and Takuan's relationship with Iemitsu's sword master Yagyū Munenori is especially well known. Takuan also wrote extensively on Zen theory and was well acquainted with Confucian studies. His *Ri-ki sabetsu ron* (The Difference between *Ri* and *Ki*) is a study of Confucianism from the perspective of Zen Buddhism.

The Myōshinji branch was influenced by the arrival of the Ōbaku lineage, a third (though smaller) school of Japanese Zen. A famous, though not necessarily representative, monk of the Myōshinji branch is Bankei Yōtaku (1622–93). Bankei was born into a Confucian family in Hamada, a small village on the Inland Sea, but studied Rinzai Zen under Umpo Zenjō (1568–1653) at Zuiōji in Akō, and with the Ming Chinese monk Dezhe. During a time of extreme physical illness he experienced the insight that "all things are resolved in the Unborn (*fushō*)." He was affiliated with the Zen temple Myōshinji but spent most of his time traveling, training disciples and preaching to the people. He tirelessly proclaimed the principle of *fushō*, the Unborn, which for him expressed the essence of Buddhism and the universality of the unborn Buddha mind. He rejected the traditional Rinzai use of the *kōan*, and was famed as a preacher who spoke to the people in simple, ordinary language.

The most important figure for modern Rinzai, however, was Hakuin Ekaku (1686–1769). Hakuin showed an inclination for the religious life from the time he was a child and entered the Zen temple Shōin-ji at the age of fifteen. When he was twenty-four Hakuin experienced a "Great Doubt," which was in turn shattered like the smashing of a sheet of ice or a jade tower. Driven by this enlightening experience, he visited the master Shōju Rōjin (1643–1721) at his hermitage of Shōju-an in Nagano. Further intense practice and struggling with *kōans* resulted in a deeper understanding of the Zen way. Further travels provided many more intense experiences of enlightenment, each revealing a new level of awareness. Hakuin also suffered from repeated bouts of psychosomatic disturbances, called "Zen sickness;" these were slowly cured after a visit to the hermit Hakuyū, who pointed out that these symptoms were based on Hakuin's extreme ascetic and meditational practices. This experience aided Hakuin in providing methods which he in turn used to help his disciples with regard to health problems. Hakuin finally returned to Shōin-ji in 1716, where he guided a growing number of disciples and his fame spread throughout Japan.

Hakuin's many writings include *Yasen kanna* (*Talks on a Boat in the Evening*). Even more famous is *Orategama* (*The Embossed Tea Kettle*) in which Hakuin outlines his theories on health and long life. Hakuin is also famous for his bold and original calligraphy. Hakuin emphasized a strict regimen of meditation accompanied by active participation in daily chores in order to "perceive one's (true) nature" (*kenshō*). He revitalized the Rinzai process of meditating on *kōans*, and his teachings became the central Rinzai tradition in Japan. All modern Rinzai masters in Japan trace their lineage to Hakuin.

See also: **Japan, Buddhism in; Meditation (Chan/Zen); Zen.**

PAUL L. SWANSON

RIS MED (NON-SECTARIAN) MOVEMENT IN TIBETAN BUDDHISM

Sectarian controversy has been a recurring feature of Tibetan Buddhism since earliest times. Every order has produced vast quantities of polemical literature, and the history of Tibetan Buddhism is marked by oral debates between rival traditions as well as persecutions and factional wars. In the late nineteenth century, several prominent *lamas* in eastern Tibet began a counter-movement, commonly referred to as "Non-Sectarian" (*Ris med*). It was a direct challenge to the scholastic approach of the Gelukpa Order, whose educational system mainly relies on textbooks (*yig cha*) that summarize key philosophical and doctrinal points. The definitions (*mtshan nyid*) they contain are derived from Indian "root texts"; these are memorized by students and form the basis of their curriculum and examinations.

The Non-Sectarian *lamas*, by contrast, required their students to study Indian *sūtras* and philosophical texts, and much of the Non-Sectarian literature consists of original commentaries on them. The philosophical basis of most Non-Sectarian lamas is the "other emptiness" (*gzhan stong*) view, which posits a self-existent ultimate reality that can only be understood by direct meditative perception. Another important aspect of the movement is the vision of the "great perfection" (*rdzogs chen*) developed by the "treasure discoverer" (*gter ston*) Jikme Lingpa ('Jigs med gling pa, 1730–98). His revelation of the *Heart Essence of Longchenpa* (*kLong chen snying thig*) cycle of practice is one of the foundational sources of the movement.

His reincarnation Jamyang Khyentse Wangpo ('Jam dbyangs mkhyen rtse dbang po, 1820–92) became one of the leading figures in the Non-Sectarian movement. He was a *lama* in the Sakya Order, but was also a practitioner of Nyingma great perfection teachings. Like other Non-Sectarian lamas, he advocated a universalist approach to Buddhist teachings, according to which all were said to have value for particular practitioners. Students were encouraged to study extensively in various traditions, and as Gene Smith has pointed out, one of the key features of the movement was an encyclopedic orientation. Non-Sectarian lamas produced a number of compendiums of Buddhist learning, most notably Kongtrül's ('Jam mgon Kong sprul blo gros mtha' yas, 1813–99) *Compendium of All Knowledge* (*Shes bya kun khyab*). Unlike some scholars of his time, who focused on certain texts as normative and rejected others, Kongtrül and his students traveled throughout Tibet searching for texts, initiations, and oral lineages, both those that were widely popular and others that were obscure and local, and brought them together in huge collections. Contrary to those who claimed that one approach is superior to all others, they sought to make available as many teachings and practices as possible so that students could choose those that were most effective.

In keeping with its non-dogmatic approach, the Non-Sectarian movement was not a distinct school with fixed doctrines. Instead, its proponents maintained allegiance to their own lineages, but adopted elements from the various Buddhist traditions available to them. A number of Non-Sectarian *lamas* were lay *tantric* practitioners (*sngags pa*), but others were monastics. No one approach to Buddhist doctrine and practice is dogmatically asserted, and the essence of the movement is an openness to different approaches.

See also: **Tibet, Buddhism in.**

JOHN POWERS

RITUAL IN TIBETAN BUDDHISM

For Tibetan Buddhists, all religiously significant aspects of life are marked by rituals. Some of these are private, while others involve large numbers of people and may last for days. Community rituals are performed on all religious holidays, and monks and nuns generally devote part of every day to the performance of rituals for lay sponsors. Rituals pervade the daily routines of Tibetan monastics, and even academic study follows prescribed ritual patterns.

Tibetan rituals are sometimes divided into two types: those performed for one's own benefit, and those performed for others. The former include, for example, solitary tantric meditation, and the latter encompass such activities as consecration of *stūpas.* While this division has some utility, there is also considerable overlap between the two categories. Private meditation, for example, generally includes an aspect of dedicating the merit of the practice for the benefit of others, and those who perform rituals for others are said to acquire merit for themselves.

The general term for ritual is *cho ga* (Skt. *vidhi*), which encompasses a vast range of practices, including meditation techniques, fire rituals (Tib. *sbyin sreg*, Skt. *homa*), consecrations, and ceremonies to mark religiously significant events like the taking of monastic vows, tantric initiations, and death. Even such activities as oral debate are highly ritualized, and the majority of works by Tibet's most influential *lamas* are devoted to the performance of rituals.

One of the most common activities for Tibetan Buddhist practitioners is the performance of *tantric* ritual cycles (Tib. *grub thabs*, Skt. *sādhana*). *Sādhana* practice requires that one be initiated by a qualified *lama*, and the ceremony provides a *karmic* connection between initiates and the tutelary deity (Tib. *yi dam*, Skt. *iṣṭa-devatā*) that authorizes them to practice.

In addition, initiation generally entails daily commitments. These often include performance of the requisite *sādhana*, which involves visualizations of the main Buddha (as well as an accompanying retinue, various *tantric* symbols, etc.). Ideally, the visualized images are generated out of the wisdom consciousness realizing emptiness, and are dissolved into emptiness at the end of the ritual. The *sādhana* also involves recitation of certain *mantras* and accompanying hand gestures (Tib. *phyag rgya*, Skt. *mudrā*).

Consecration rituals are important communal activities. These are performed for most religious objects and buildings, and it is generally thought that devotion to an unconsecrated image or building brings no merit. During the consecration ritual of an image, the *tantric* master (Tib. *rdo rje slob dpon*, Skt. *vajrācārya*) visualizes a "wisdom being" (Tib. *ye shes sems dpa'*, Skt. *jñāna-sattva*) and causes it to enter the image, which then becomes imbued with its sacred presence. The wisdom being is asked to remain for as long as cyclic existence lasts for the benefit of sentient beings. As a result of the ritual, the image becomes a suitable object for worship, which confers merit on those who perform religiously sanctioned devotions.

In Tibetan *tantra*, meditative practice, communal worship, and even philosophical debate are highly ritualized. The goal of most rituals is to transform the consciousness of practitioners, so that the world they perceive comes to more closely approximate that of the Buddhas and *bodhisattvas*. *Tantric* rituals create an imagined space in which practitioners learn to view themselves as awakened beings, and over time the identification moves from the merely imaginary to the actual.

See also: **Rituals and practices; Ritual texts; Tibet, Buddhism in; Vajrayāna Buddhism.**

JOHN POWERS

RITUAL TEXTS

Monastic libraries contain large numbers of ritual texts and ritual manuals. The performance of rituals is an important part of life of a Buddhist temple. The rituals of ordination, prescribed by the *Statement of Action* (*Karmavācanā)*, permit entrance into the Buddhist order (*sangha*). The members of the Buddhist order gather together on full moon and new moon days for the ritual recitation of another *Vinaya* text, the *Prātimokṣa*, a list of the more than 200 rules that control their lives. Ritual manuals guide monks in the performance of consecration rituals, which bring together the lay and monastic communities for consecration of a temple, *stūpa*, or an image. Thai monks recite the *Consecrating the Buddha [Image] (Buddha Abhiṣekha)*, a text that both instructs and empowers the image as the Buddha's life is recited. The recitation of the Buddha's virtues functions as a conduit for their entrance into the empowered image. Tibetan Vajrayāna consecration manuals guide the monks or *lamas* performing the ritual through the process of transforming themselves into Buddhas and summoning from the Buddha-land the particular Buddha that is asked to enter and empower the image. These Tibetan ritual specialists also rely on Tantric practice manuals (*sadhāna*), which describe the ritual invocations of divine power and meditation techniques that transform their bodies, speech and minds into those of Buddhas. After the ritual of consecration, the Thai or Tibetan image becomes the focus of devotional actions that create merit for all in attendance.

The primary ritual texts that Theravāda Buddhists memorize and recite are found in *The Book of Protection*, a collection of protective texts (*paritta*), found in the *Sutta Piṭaka* of the Pāli canon. Both lay and monastics recite daily the popular *paritta* text, the *Loving Kindness Scripture* (*Metta Sutta*). In this text, the Buddha encourages the Buddhist community to develop lovingkindness toward all beings, in the same way as a mother's lovingkindness nourishes her only child. The Buddha and his disciples first recited these *paritta* texts to protect people from suffering and danger. The recitation of one text (the *Khandha paritta*) extends lovingkindness to poisonous snakes so that no harm will ensue. The recitation of the *Jewel Scripture* (*Ratana Sutta*) protects people from the malevolent spirits that cause sickness, drought, and famine. The Buddha's disciple, Aṅgulimāla, first recited the text that bears his name, *Aṅgulimāla Paritta*, to ease the pain of childbirth. Lay people invite monks to chant *paritta* for protection against illness and misfortune, but also as blessings for new houses, new businesses, and new marriages.

Mahāyāna Buddhists recite incantations (*dhāraṇī), which,* like *paritta*, offer protection from disease and danger. *Dhāraṇī* first occur in chapters of the *Lotus Sūtra* (*Saddharmapuṇḍarīka*) and the *Golden Light Sūtra* (*Suvarṇaprabhāsottama*) as concise embodiments of the *sūtra*'s teachings that aid retention of its meaning. Independent *dhāraṇī* texts are incorporated into the Chinese and Tibetan canons. Certain *dhāraṇī* texts become like *mantras*, endowed with supernatural power that protects those who recite them from demons and diseases. These esoteric *dhāraṇī* texts, extensively used in East Asian and Tibetan cultural areas, invoke the power of Buddhas and *bodhisattvas* for material and spiritual purposes. The recitation of *dhāraṇī* destroys the obstacles to success and ensures health, wealth, and birth of children. *Dhāraṇī* recitation may destroy ignorance and the obstacles that impede enlightenment. The *Mahāmāyūri dhāraṇī*, which invokes the goddess *Mahāmāyūri*'s protection from snakebite, became part of a popular collection, the *Five Protective Scriptures* (*Pañcarakṣa*), that survives in Tibetan translation and in abundant Sanskrit and Newari manuscripts in Nepal. The recitation of the *Five Protective Scriptures* creates merit and a wide range of blessings that include honor, fame, easy childbirth, and protection against snakebites, serious illness, natural disasters, and the miseries of hell. Protection from harm is sought also for the state. One of the *Five Protective Scriptures*, the *Mahāpratisarā*, protects cities from enemy invasions. Theravāda rulers request monks to recite *paritta* to avert dangers of natural disasters and of invading armies. The Chinese apocryphal text, the *Scripture on Perfect Wisdom for Humane Kings who Wish to Protect their States* (*Renwang hu guo banrou boluomiduo jing*) was used by the Tang emperor Daizong to deter a Tibetan invasion of China. Twentieth-century Japanese rulers used this text in an attempt to prevent the American invasion of Japan in World War II.

The most important ritual activities that Buddhist monastics perform for the laity concern the dead and the dying. Theravāda monks recite *paritta* to create merit for the dead and protect the living from the malevolence of death. Chinese rites for the dead developed in the esoteric (*mijao*) tradition of feeding hungry ghosts (*preta*). The ritual feeding of hungry ghosts is based on Buddha's discourse on the eighth-century *Scripture of the Spell for Saving the Burning-Mouth Hungry Ghost* (*Fo shuo quiba yankou tuoluoni jing*). In this text, the Buddha advises Ānanda that recitation of *dhāraṇī* will enable him to feed thousands of hungry ghosts and bring about their rebirth as gods. Chinese monastics recite this ritual text and others based on it during the annual ghost festival. This rite, introduced into Japan, became the foundation for the Obon midsummer festival to honor ancestors. Buddhist priests perform the *Abbreviated Ritual for Feeding the Hungry Ghosts* (*Segaki ryaku sahō*) for the benefit of all the dead. The Japanese esoteric tradition, Shingon, advocates that Buddhist priests recite the *Ritual of the Clear*

Light Mantra (*Kōmyō shingon bō*) at the time of death. The Tibetan esoteric tradition similarly advises reading texts to the dying person, such as the *Tibetan Book of the Dead* (Tib. *Bar do thos grol*), that explain how to transform the three stages of death, the intermediate state, and rebirth into the three bodies of a Buddha. If the mind of clear light is recognized at the moment of death and used to contemplate *Dharma*, it is said that death can be transformed into liberation.

See also: **Canons and literature; Monastic rituals; Ritual in Tibetan Buddhism; Rituals and practices.**

KAREN C. LANG

RITUALS AND PRACTICES

Praxis – including specific rituals and spiritual techniques as well as generalized life-ways – constitutes a central dimension of all religions, and is especially pronounced in the Buddhist case. From the time of the Buddha himself, Buddhists have devoted enormous energy to inventing, developing, categorizing and above all participating in a vast array of rituals and practices while simultaneously attacking and/or adapting and appropriating the praxis of competing religious adepts. The importance of this industry is clear in the fact that disputes over ortho*praxy* rather than ortho*doxy* have dominated Buddhist sectarian history and inter-religious relations. In Buddhist languages the religion is not primarily something which one "believes," "has faith in," "converts to" or "is"; the religion is something which one "does," so much so that many modern Western and Buddhist commentators have argued that Buddhism should be conceived not as a religion at all, but rather as a technology, medical system, secular philosophy or science. Yet it is ironically the ritualistic aspects of praxis, especially worship, which serve as the best rebuttal to such a portrayal. Even philosophical and doctrinal thought and discussion have been conceived by Buddhists, in various ways, as aspects of praxis, as have been ethics, artistic expression, and literary production; Buddhist hagiographies, histories, and soteriologies consistently track the path to enlightenment in terms of deeds (*karma*) and generalized life-ways. In fact, the enacted or embodied dimension of religiosity, praxis, is so central to Buddhists that it is difficult to identify anything in "Buddhism" which is not ultimately encompassed by "Buddhist praxis," broadly conceived.

Scope and definitions

Given its centrality and ubiquity, elements of praxis figure heavily in all the sections of this encyclopedia. Meditation is a practice of such great importance to all Buddhists that it is treated as a section unto itself, while praxis also figures especially prominently in the sections on *sangha*, ethics, engaged Buddhism, sacred places, Buddhist art, Buddhism and technology, and sections on the various regional Buddhist traditions. The present section of this encyclopedia is designed to provide a general orientation to religious praxis across the Buddhist traditions, making praxis a topic in its own right rather than merely an aspect of something else, and to supplement coverage of it by detailing additional Buddhist practices and rituals which, like meditation, have been especially significant and widespread. While covering Buddhist praxis comprehensively lies beyond the scope of any single-volume work, it is hoped that this general orientation and supplemental detail will allow readers to organize and situate references to aspects of praxis found throughout the other sections, and thereby to develop a solidly substantive and theoretically nuanced sense of the topic as a whole.

The present article introduces both scholarly and Buddhist conceptualizations of Buddhist praxis in general, and methodological approaches to the topic as a whole. Separate entries on worship, moral discipline, charity and monastic rituals chart out four major components of praxis as such, while additional entries on deity cults, healing rituals, pilgrimage, preaching, chanting, full moon day festivals, life-cycle rites, medical practices, New Year and other national festivals and political practices broadly sketch the range of practical and ritual forms that have emerged in Buddhism's long and complex history.

Scholars of Buddhism, historians of religions, anthropologists, sociologists and psychologists, among many others, have generated a large and still open discourse on the role and meaning of religious praxis in general as well as specific religious rituals and practices. Needless to say it is not within the present scope to attempt to adjudicate such long-standing debates as that about the relative primacy of myth (and other forms of religious thought) or ritual (and other forms of religious praxis) in how religion functions, nor to advance a comprehensive theory of religious praxis. But it is useful to specify the meanings of these terms as employed here, and to introduce some general insights into the nature of religious praxis which the scholarship has generated, toward the pragmatic end of providing readers a holistic take on Buddhist praxis.

"Praxis" or "practice," in the singular, is used here to signify the whole of what a person does, as (at least partially) distinct from what he or she intends, believes, and/or thinks, allowing of course that what one does is always complexly related to what one thinks or believes. This distinction is also made in Buddhist sources, such as the Theravāda distinction between *pariyatti* (that which is textual, thought) and *paṭipatti* (that which is part of practice, performed). The adjectives "religious" or "Buddhist" specify those aspects of praxis which are primarily connected to religious soteriology, that employ religious symbols and authority, and/or that are performed in the name of religion, here as conceived within the different Buddhist traditions.

Praxis can be subdivided into the specific "practices," in the plural, and "rituals" that make it up. "Ritual" is used here in its ordinary sense, to designate a formalized occasion of religious activity, whether periodic (daily, monthly, annual) or occasional (for example, performed as specific needs arise), which whether performed individually or collectively enacts (with whatever degree of innovation and idiosyncrasy) patterned procedures perceived to be authentic or original to the purpose. I employ "practices" as the more general term; a Buddhist's "practices" will likely include "rituals" in the specified sense, such as worshiping Buddha images or conducting ordination ceremonies, but will also include other, less formalized aspects of his or her overall religious praxis whether perpetual (such as practicing moral restraint or compassion for others, or following the daily monastic routine) or periodic or occasional practices (such as participating in gifts of labor to build a Buddhist monument or political rallies for a Buddhist cause, practicing meditation, or attending a festival). These practices may have ritual components, and the categories obviously overlap, but whereas all rituals are practices, not all practices are rituals.

Interpreting rituals and practices

The scholarly discourse mentioned above has provided many useful though not always mutually consistent perspectives for understanding the roles played by praxis – in general, and by specific practices and rituals – in Buddhism. Though scholars have often argued for the primacy of one perspective over all others, this section of the encyclopedia takes as axiomatic that most rituals and practices can best be understood from a variety of different perspectives, each of them contributing to the holistic picture which, though never fully achieved, must remain our goal in pursuing interpretation of Buddhist praxis.

Soteriological perspectives

One important such insight is that despite popular misperceptions of rituals and other religious practices as inherently mindless or mechanical, in fact they can involve the whole person in a creative and spiritually enriching process directly linked to the religion's loftiest, ultimate goals. This link is especially explicit in the case of meditation, which most Buddhists portray as both prerequisite to and the fullest embodiment of enlightenment, but Buddhists have also stressed this link between praxis and soteriology in schematizations that are holistic enough to include the entire range of additional Buddhist rituals, practices and corresponding virtues within which an ideal, meditative life is located.

For example, the early Pāli texts (e.g. *Saṃyutta Nikāya* III.83) classify the religious life as "three trainings" (*tisso sikkhā*), namely the cultivation of moral discipline (*sīla*), wisdom (*paññā*) and mental clarity (*samādhi*) to perfect a practitioner in each of his or her three aspects (body, speech and mind respectively), a state of being which encompasses all the varieties of praxis and which equates to *arahant*ship. A similar schematization, shared across the Buddhist world, is that of the *bodhisattva* path as a cultivation of praxis-encompassing perfections (*pāramitā*) which, fully realized, characterize full Buddhahood. Mahāyāna texts sometimes enumerate these as five perfections (namely, charity [*dāna*], moral discipline [*śīla*], patience [*kṣānti*], vigor [*vīrya*] and meditation [*dhyāna*]), though more often wisdom (*prajñā*) is added to make a list of six perfections, and in some lists skill in means (*upāya-kauśālya*) is also added to make a total of seven. Theravāda texts alter and expand the list to ten perfections (namely charity [*dāna*], moral discipline [*sīla*], aversion [*nekkhamma*], wisdom [*paññā*], vigor [*viriya*], patience [*khanti*], truthfulness [*sacca*], resolution [*adhiṭṭhāna*], lovingkindness [*mettā*], and equanimity [*upekkhā*]), but the principle remains the same: fully participating in and perfecting these various aspects of Buddhist praxis are one and the same as full achievement of Buddhist soteriological goals. Theravādins, among others, have made the same claim for fully living the monastic discipline (*vinaya*): if one lives the *vinaya*, one will achieve *arahant*ship; if one has achieved *arahant*ship, one will live the *vinaya*.

Achievement of perfected praxis – full cultivation of the three trainings, or the five, six, seven or ten perfections, or the *Vinaya* – is understood in Theravāda texts to require hundreds of lifetimes and millions of years. This "gradual path" to human perfection begins with the simplest ritual (such as placing a flower before a Buddha image) or practice (such as giving food to a beggar or hungry animal) which becomes a "seed" for accomplishments later in life and in future lives, during which one becomes increasingly accustomed to all aspects of Buddhist praxis until in one's final existence that praxis is fully lived as a perfected being. Some Mahāyāna schools, notably some schools of Chan/Zen, place greater emphasis on achieving this full, embodied perfection "suddenly" in the present moment, though the gradual path is admitted for those who are slower and *bodhisattva* praxis is often conceived of as all but perpetual, reaching an end only when every sentient being has been enlightened.

Indeed, in all the traditions constant praxis – a life fully occupied with Buddhist practices and rituals, exclusively devoted to achieving or fully embodying soteriological goals – is clearly the ideal.

But it is not enough to view praxis solely in soteriological terms, for praxis, embedded in the daily lives of those who engage it, also entails overlapping but more worldly concerns. Just as Buddhist schematizations substantiate the scholarly recognition that praxis can be integral to soteriology, so Buddhists have in various ways articulated for themselves the scholarly recognition that praxis can also be central to and fruitfully analyzed according to the perspectives of psychology, sociology, politics, and aesthetics. We will briefly examine each of these intersections in turn.

Psychological perspectives

Psychologists of religion have noted that in addition to cultivating specifically religious consciousness, rituals and practices can also affect and reflect more ordinary (as well as pathological) psychological states. While Buddhists traditionally did not employ modern psychological terminology – such as wish fulfillment, projection, individuation, placebo effect, repression or past lives therapy – in making sense of the connections between praxis and psychology, aspects of Buddhist praxis and anthropology overlap sufficiently with psychological thought that they can fruitfully be interpreted according to psychological theories, producing perspectives, interpretations and practices which are new for psychologists and Buddhists alike.

Buddhist rituals and practices have proven especially interesting to psychologists and psychiatrists because they are based in anthropologies and epistemologies quite foreign to those which produced the modern disciplines. The construction of *karma*-based or mutually interpenetrating theories of human action which are not predicated on any sort of soul or psyche, as in the early Buddhist/Theravāda and Huayan cases, respectively, as well as phenomenologies of various supramundane mental states and associated special mental and physical powers which are detailed in all Buddhist traditions, and the religion's general emphasis on praxis/action over self or psyche/reflection, for examples, can challenge as well as enrich psychology in both theory and practice. As detailed in the articles on Healing and protective practices and Medical practices, Buddhists have long served as functional equivalents of modern psychiatrists and psychologists, and in fact Buddhist meditational practices (especially *vipassanā* and *zazen*) and even exorcistic rites (such as the Sinhala *yak tovil*) have been successfully adapted for use in some contemporary psychotherapeutic contexts. Buddhists have described and explored the connections among the different states of mind which are said to accompany effective rituals and practices, including mental pleasure (such as the *citta-pasāda* that figures prominently in the Pāli *Apadāna* hagiographies), faith (*śraddhā*) and devotion (*bhakti*), and Buddhist rituals and even the most mundane daily practices have been variously conceived as foci, devices or containers for meditative pursuits (such as the Pāli *kasiṇa* or object of meditation, or the Japanese *dō* or activity which embodies enlightenment).

Sociological perspectives

Sociologists of religion have noted many additional aspects of praxis which have less to do with the individual psyche than with the individual's position in society, and with society as a whole. Participation in rituals particular to a given community affirms one's identity within it, whether as a general member of the social group it constitutes or, more directly, as an explicit form of initiation into that group and its various ranks (see Monastic rituals for the most telling case, but we could also include initiations in Tibetan and esoteric Japanese/Shingon traditions, or Buddhist royal coronation ceremonies, as additional examples). Participation in rituals and practices may also reflect and enhance the participant's prestige within society – generous donors, for example, have been eulogized in texts and inscriptions across the Buddhist world – and the colossalism which characterized Buddhist artistic and architectural monuments in ancient and medieval times, each monastery outdoing the others in size, amount of ornamentation, and audacity (carving Buddhas out of mountains or making mountains into *stūpas)*, reflects the degree to which patrons employed elements of praxis to raise the prestige not only of themselves but also of the social institutions which they supported. Especially large-scale rituals such as regional festivals have long served as meeting points for conducting trade, making marriage alliances and exchanging technologies and texts, while they – and many of the specific rituals and practices they involved, such as chanted statements of "refuge" and disciplinary vows (see Chanting practices, Moral discipline) and listening to sermons – reinforced a certain social and moral vision which often formed the foundation for law and social order.

The importance of rituals and practices in the creation of individual and institutional social identities and roles extends beyond whatever particular Buddhist group produces and practices them. Since the time of the Buddha himself, Buddhists have always existed in societies which included significant non-Buddhist populations, and at least since the time of Aśoka Maurya (third century BCE) they have always existed in societies wherein Buddhism itself is diverse and contested. Rituals and practices have been vital sites for establishing and negotiating social relationships with those perceived by any particular group of Buddhists as "other." The records of the Chinese pilgrims are rich sources for ancient and medieval world Buddhist praxis, because praxis – especially unusual customs and special rituals and festivals – was precisely what they sought to know and felt compelled to describe about the "others" they encountered in their travels; the pilgrims sought out what others *did* more than what they *thought*, as is epitomized by the overriding importance they gave to *vinaya* texts in their quests for authentic *Dharma*.

A clear illustration of the importance of praxis in such inter-communal sociology is the famous division of the Buddhist world into separate "vehicles" (*yāna*) predicated (as the metaphor implies) on the sort of praxis each promotes: Hīnayāna or Śrāvakayāna (represented today by the Theravāda) promoting practice of moral restraint (especially the monastic discipline or *vinaya*) and the gradual path to enlightenment; Mahāyāna or Bodhisattvayāna, promoting the cultivation of bodhisattvic virtues like compassion and universal Buddhahood; Tantrayāna or Vajrayāna, promoting tantric rites and initiations aimed at enlightenment as well as worldly powers. This tripartite vision can be both unifying (the three vehicles taken as different aspects of a single Buddhist religion as opposed, say, to Hinduism or Taoism) and divisive (especially because in different enunciations of this and similar holistic schematizations of the Buddhist world there are always explicit or implicit hierarchies of truth and appropriateness, and concomitant attacks on other Buddhists as somehow lesser).

Likewise the monastic disciplinary code (*vinaya*) unites all Buddhist monks and nuns in a theoretically single *sangha* distinct from non-Buddhists as well as from Buddhist laypeople, and variations among the different *vinaya* recensions and local monastic cultures have been small enough that the shared code has often allowed monks and nuns from China and Kashmir or from Andhra and Angkor to meet each other as members of a single community, staying in each other's monasteries, exchanging texts and images, or spending the rains retreat together. Yet in different circumstances, and sometimes much closer to home, Buddhists have found it impossible to overlook divergence on minor points of *vinaya* practice, which is often made out to be the primary reason for "splitting" within sectarian histories of the *sangha* (for example, *Dīpavaṃsa* 22.66–74).

Political perspectives

Because the patrons of Buddhist rituals such as large-scale festivals, as well as the monasteries and temples that made them perpetually possible, were often kings (or in modern times presidents) and other elites, and because Buddhist praxis and ideology figured heavily in Buddhist political philosophies, both the unifying and the divisive dimensions of rituals and practices have specifically political connotations as well; the politics of praxis also constitutes an important interpretive domain.

The importance of politics to praxis, and vice versa, should already be clear from what has been said above about the relationships of praxis to social order, law, and intra- and inter-communal relationships and identities, which of course always have political edges. Sectarian disputes and contention often overlapped with specifically political factionalism, festivals and monuments patronized by particular kings often actively broadcast their accomplishments and programs, and Buddhists whether monastic or lay often invoked Buddhist ideas and themes in mobilizing political forces, whether conservative or revolutionary.

Although the assertion that Prince Siddhārtha was born as heir-apparent to an important Indian (Śākyan) throne is probably a later tradition, the close connection of Buddhism and politics which that assertion conveys dates back to the earliest *suttas* and *vinaya* texts, in which kings play various roles in the Buddha's life including interlocutor, patron, and negative or positive example. By about the third-century BCE reign of Aśoka Maurya, the association of kingship with the Buddha's biography had been projected back into numerous previous lives when as *bodhisattva* he himself was a king or, more often, a world-conquering "universal monarch" (*cakravartin*), as related in several late *sutta*s and elaborated in the various *jātaka* traditions. These stories provided foundations for a specifically Buddhist royal praxis which, especially with the advent of Aśoka Maurya, became *sine qua non* for subsequent Buddhist political formations in India and abroad. Not so much a single regimen as a very long-lived diversity of specifically Buddhist political practices – though certain themes and structures do remain consistent throughout Buddhist history – the superstructure built upon these foundations provided Buddhists significant places in royal/national and interregnal/international political relationships and spheres from the time of Aśoka to the present; at points during the last two millennia Buddhists controlled or at least participated in all the major kingdoms of Asia, and Buddhism continues to be an important political force in much of the continent and, increasingly, on the contemporary global stage. A rich history of particularly Buddhist political practices and rituals has emerged, developed, and changed into the present as a result. This is explored further in the article on Politics.

In addition to specifically political practices and rituals, we can note in this context that Buddhist conceptualizations of power include not only worldly power (the force, persuasion, contract and/or established order that constitutes the stuff of politics) but also the supernormal powers of beings like demons and deities who can both protect and threaten Buddhists and their culture depending on ritual relationships with them, as well as extra-human powers which certain advanced practitioners are believed capable of achieving and exercising. Whatever modern interpreters may make of these claims about supernormal power, it is important to recognize that for Buddhists these were (and in some instances still are) very real, potent forces in the world.

Aesthetic perspectives

It is finally important that any holistic analysis also recognize the aesthetic and performative dimensions of rituals and practices. As has been true in religious cultures around the world, religion and aesthetics have been deeply intertwined for most of Buddhist history: much of the great Buddhist art was produced as a Buddhist practice for use in Buddhist rituals; much of the great Buddhist literature was produced to illustrate and motivate Buddhist praxis, evaluating religious action and its consequences through story-telling and poetry; moral standards, themes and subjects, styles and performative contexts likewise closely overlapped with Buddhist praxis in the realms of painting, music, architecture, drama, hagiography and history, all of which figure, in different ways, as religious practices in their own right which are in turn created for and employed in religious rituals, festivals, and other practices. As a result of this close overlap between religion and aesthetics, any particular Buddhist ritual or practice can be understood as both reflecting and helping to constitute aesthetic canons of the society in which it occurs. Aesthetic appreciation and outright enjoyableness may take us very far in understanding its popularity and efficacy, as well as the considerable expenditure of time and resources which has often been made in the service of beautifying particular practices and rituals besides more permanent sites for them such as temples, parks, monuments and monasteries. The connection between aesthetics and religious praxis has been especially well theorized, and cultivated, by Chan/Zen Buddhists.

Generalization and specificity

We can then affirm that a holistic understanding of Buddhist praxis must take into consideration at least its spiritual importance to practitioners, its psychological relevance, its sociological effects, its political implications and its aesthetic appeal; likewise, any understanding of Buddhist spirituality, psychology, sociology, politics, and aesthetics would be incomplete without consideration of various dimensions of Buddhist praxis. But the wider the lens, the more blurry the picture: a holistic perspective on the whole of Buddhist praxis is a never-achieved ideal because any generalization can always be challenged by the details of specific rituals and practices, while the whole of Buddhist praxis is so vast – ranging as it does across time (for 2,500 years) and space (for long all of Asia, and now the entire world), embracing various scales of complexity (from individual worship or meditation and family- or village-only rituals to those performed on regional, national or international stages, such as large-scale festivals and pan-Buddhist political activities), periodicity (annually, monthly, daily, occasionally, often, constantly), publicity (some rituals and practices are private, or by initiation only, or open to only certain "publics") and so forth – as to render generalization inherently suspect.

Thus while discussion of Buddhist praxis in general serves the valuable purpose of providing an orientation to the specifics, that value is realized only by moving away from the general orientation to look in greater detail at those specific forms of praxis, which is the goal of the separate articles which make up this section of the encyclopedia. But the value of those more specific articles is realized when they in turn serve as an orientation to specific rituals and practices within the sub-categories they address, a process which likewise renders them obsolete. Put differently, general discussion of praxis is best viewed as a guide to the dimensions worth investigating when looking at any particular ritual or practice in some particular time and place, rather than as an achievable end in itself; the present article has sketched broadly the sorts of spiritual, psychological, sociological, political, and aesthetic aspects one might look for in any particular Buddhist practice or ritual, while the more specific articles within this section of the encyclopedia will help readers place any particular ritual or practice within broader, pan-Buddhist contexts and trends; but in both events the payoff comes in better understanding the ever-inexhaustible depth of that particular ritual or practice itself.

One important way to unlock the unique significance of whatever ritual or practice one confronts is to remember that it is necessarily situated in and therefore evidence of particular histories that coalesced to provide the context of its possibility or existence. In tracing its roots we discover not only what is traditional, common and most deeply meaningful about it, but also how and why its performers have innovated in different historical circumstances. Even when a ritual or practice is literally repeated from the past, changing external histories give it different meanings in each iteration, such that the study of any particular ritual practice really is bottomless. Indeed, it is possible – even likely – that any single practice or ritual will have vastly different meanings for different people in a single audience, or even for a single individual at two different times.

See also: **Art and ritual; Art as ritual; Aśoka; Mahāyāna Buddhism; Meditational systems; Monastic rituals; Politics; Ritual in Tibetan Buddhism; Ritual texts; *Sangha*; South and Southeast Asia, Buddhism in; *Vinaya Piṭaka*.**

JONATHAN S. WALTERS

ROBINSON, RICHARD HUGH

Richard H. Robinson was a famous Buddhologist and Madhyamika specialist who was the founder of the Buddhist Studies program at the University of Wisconsin. He was born in Alberta on 21 June 1926. He received his B.A. degree, focusing on economics and modern languages, from the University of Alberta in 1947. He had been interested in Buddhism since his youth, and in 1948–9 continued his friendship with the Japanese Canadian Buddhists by assisting Reverend Takashi Tsuji of the Toronto Buddhist Church. In 1950 he enrolled in the School of Oriental and African Studies at the University of London, earning a second B.A. in classical Chinese. While in London, he studied with well-known buddhological scholars such as Edward Conze and David Snellgrove. During his studies in London, he met his future wife, Hannah; they had two children (Sita, born in 1955, and Neil, born in 1957). In 1954, he joined the faculty of the University of Toronto, before moving on to Wisconsin. His doctorate from the University of London was awarded in 1959. In 1960 Robinson joined the University of Wisconsin–Madison faculty, teaching Indian philosophy and Indian civilization in addition to Buddhism. In 1961, he collaborated with Professors Robert J. Miller and Murray Fowler to establish the Ph.D. program in Buddhist Studies. During his tenure at Wisconsin, he became chairman on the then-named Department of Indian Studies, and director of the South Asian Area Center. He also served as secretary of the American Institute of Indian Studies.

Following a horrifying explosion in a home accident in 1970, Richard Robinson died a premature death at age forty-four.

Fluent in all the Buddhist canonical languages, Robinson was primarily interested in the work of Nāgārjuna and the other Madhyamika writers, especially in China, but he also possessed an extensive background and intense curiosity that produced fruitful results across the whole of Buddhist Studies. Like Louis de La Vallée Poussin and other major scholarly figures of the twentieth century, Robinson trained a large number of scholars before his untimely death, and many of these have gone on to further develop his lineage in North American Buddhist Studies. Some of these include Lewis Lancaster, Francis Cook, Nancy Lethcoe, Stephen Beyer, Stefan Anacker, Douglas Daye, Roger Corless, Mark Ehman, Jeffrey Hopkins, Harvey Aronson, and Charles Prebish.

Robinson's major publications include *Chinese Buddhist Verse* (1954), *Early Mādhyamika in India and China* (1967), and his textbook *The Buddhist Religion*, published in 1970. This latter volume, now updated primarily by Willard Johnson, is in its fifth edition, and continues to be perhaps the most popular of all introductory textbooks on Buddhism. A number of his former students are still at work editing his last projects in hopeful anticipation that they might one day appear, albeit posthumously. These include an English translation of the *Vimalakīrti Nirdeśa-sūtra*, the *Awakening of Mahāyāna Faith*, a Sanskrit primer, and an additional textbook tentatively titled *The Eastern Buddha Lands*. He has been honored with two memorial volumes. First, a textbook titled *Buddhism: A Modern Perspective*, was published in 1975, consisting of forty-five chapters composed by eight of his former students. Second, Minoru Kiyota edited *Mahāyāna Buddhist Meditation: Theory and Practice* in 1978.

See also: **Academic study of Buddhism; North American school of Buddhist Studies.**

CHARLES S. PREBISH

S

SACRED MOUNTAINS

Introduction

People from many diverse cultures have long regarded mountains as objects of majesty and power. The importance of mountains for Buddhists over roughly two millennia might seem natural, given the way mountains impose their presence upon those who live around them even without the intrusion of human artifice. The importance of particular mountains in the history of Buddhism, however, also reflects the dynamic interaction of several factors, including distinctive Buddhist ideas and practices, indigenous religious cults that preceded the advent of Buddhist traditions, the influence of local cultures and histories, and the features of particular regional landscapes. This article first explores some of the factors that have contributed to the importance of mountains in the history of Buddhism and then examines briefly some specific examples.

Buddhist cosmology and indigenous religion

Indian Buddhism drew upon a rich Indian mythological and cosmological tradition that was grounded in Vedic and Brahmanic scriptures. However unequivocally early Buddhism rejected a number of fundamental Vedic religious ideas, including notions of divine creation and the infallibility of Vedic revelation, its scriptures preserve many passages in which gods, spirits, and other superhuman agents play prominent roles. Each of these various non-human beings has its place in an extended hierarchy of rebirth statuses that extends from the lowest hells to the most ethereal and sublime celestial realms. This cosmic hierarchy can be plotted along a great vertical axis organized according to the effects of *karma*, with the denizens of each realm of rebirth finding their place along an ascending scale of perfection according to their relative degree of moral, mental, and physical purity. Indian Buddhist tradition also assimilated the currently accepted map of the physical world, including the idea that the various landmasses and oceans radiate outward from the base of a great mountain, Mount Sumeru, also called Mount Meru, which projects upwards into the heavens and upon which various deities have their dwellings.

Another important element in the Indian Buddhist worldview that contributed to a reverence for mountains was the tendency to correlate a hierarchy of interior mental states, ascending in their purity and immateriality, with the hierarchy of cosmic realms outlined above. Indian Buddhist literature includes many accounts detailing the travels of the Buddha and his religiously advanced followers into celestial realms empowered by their mastery of advanced meditative states. Moreover, textual schematizations of these internal states, including *dhyānas* (Pāli *jhānas*) and other mental absorptions, identify them with the higher levels of the celestial hierarchy that ascend upwards from Mount Sumeru.

This hierarchical cosmology, homologizing internal mental states and external rebirth statuses, provided a potent ideological system for assimilating and organizing a wide range of elite and popular beliefs and practices in ancient India, one that was flexible enough to move and take root in different cultural communities as Buddhist traditions moved outside the Indian sub-continent. In many of these cultures, diverse practices aimed at propitiating and gaining the favor of localized superhuman powers who were commonly identified with mountains and other natural features of the landscape had wide currency among elites and non-elites. As was the case in South Asia, many of these local and regional spirits were "converted" and incorporated into the Buddhist pantheon as supporters and protectors of the tradition. It is not surprising, then, that mountains came to be regarded as important sites for the establishment of Buddhist relic monuments and temples.

Another contributing factor was the association of mountains with the early Buddhist ideal of forest-dwelling renunciation; retreat to mountainous regions was linked with the attainment of higher-level meditational states, visionary experiences, and the development of extraordinary powers such as the capacity to pacify wild animals and subdue supernatural agents. The reverence for nature expressed in many Daoist and Shinto ideas and practices also contributed to the development of a tradition of sacred mountains among Chinese and Japanese Buddhists. Shugendō, for example, is a Japanese mountain-centered tradition aimed at the attainment of special powers through rigorous ascetic practices and the invocation of both Shinto and Buddhist deities. As in South Asia, the incorporation of East and Southeast Asian gods and spirits into the Buddhist pantheon helped ground a tradition that privileged elite social renunciants and that, at least in theory, disparaged the pursuit of sensual pleasure and worldly prosperity. The presence of shrines dedicated to mountain gods and local spirits within Buddhist temple complexes drew people to visit and propitiate these supernatural beings whose power could be brought to bear on mundane concerns, and their offerings provided an important source of economic support for the *sangha*.

Examples

A map of Buddhist sacred places in Asia shows a number of mountains that have played important roles in the history of Buddhism. Some of the more prominent are: Kailaś in Tibet; Sri Pada in Sri Lanka; Wutai, Emei, Putuo, and Jiuhua in China; Kumgangsan and Kayasan in Korea; Fuji, Hiei, and Koya in Japan; Doi Suthep, Doi Kham, and Doi Ang Salung in Thailand; and Popa in Myanmar. Even when mountains have not been a part of the natural landscape, Buddhist kings in Southeast Asia appropriated Mount Meru symbolism and an ideology linking divine power and kingship (*devarāja*) in their construction of awe-inspiring royal capitals with extensive monastic and temple complexes built on the plan of *maṇḍalas*, including Angkor Thom in Cambodia, Pagan in Myanmar, and Sukhothai and Ayutthaya in Thailand. Such complexes gave material form to a number of religious and political ideals that served the consolidation of royal authority. Mount Meru symbolism has also informed the construction of Buddhist *stūpas* in Sri Lanka, and mountain–*stūpa* (Tib. *mchod rten*) connections have likewise been important in Tibetan Buddhist tradition, as at Dakpa Sheri.

The Sri Lankan mountain known as Sri Pada ("resplendent footprint"), also commonly called Adam's Peak, is consistently among the sites included on a traditional list of the sixteen most important Buddhist pilgrimage sites in Sri Lanka, and it also serves as a popular pilgrimage site for non-Buddhists, including Hindus who attribute the footprint to the god Śiva as well as Muslims who trace it to Adam. The story of the Buddha's visit to Sri Pada is recounted in the Pāli *vaṃsa* literature, and it reflects the widespread conversion dynamic in which a pre-Buddhist mountain deity, in this case the *deva* Saman or Mahāsumana, submits to the authority of the Buddha and becomes a protector of Buddhism. According to the *vaṃsa* tradition, Saman encountered the Buddha at Mahiyaṅgana after the Buddha had first purified the island of the impure and malevolent *yakkhas* (Skt. *yakṣas*). Upon hearing the Buddha's teaching, Saman gained the fruit of stream entry and requested that the Buddha leave him something to venerate; the Buddha responded by giving him hairs from his head which Saman enshrined in a golden *stūpa* and venerated. It was during the Buddha's third visit to the island that he left his footprint on the top of Saman's mountain, and also made use of a cave at the bottom of the mountain (Dīghavāpi) as a resting place, thus converting the mountaintop and cave into *pāribhogika* relics ("relics of use"). There is textual and inscriptional evidence of pilgrimage to the mountain by the twelfth century, and the *vaṃsa* literature records the visits of many Sri Lankan kings to the site. The modern pilgrimage season extends from December until the festival of Wesak in May or June, and it has been estimated that each week during the height of the season tens of thousands of pilgrims make the arduous ascent to the top of the mountain to venerate the footprint. Buddhist pilgrims traditionally observe a variety of practices, including a purifying bath in a local stream, special clothing for first-time pilgrims, chanting of traditional songs, the observance of special linguistic conventions during the climb, and the ringing of the bell at the summit of the peak, once for each time that the pilgrim has made the ascent.

Mount Putuo, which is dedicated to the *bodhisattva* Guanyin (Avalokiteśvara), is one of a set of four Chinese mountains frequently grouped together as holding particular importance for Chinese Buddhists; the others are Wutai, Emei, and Jiuhua, which are dedicated to the *bodhisattvas* Mañjuśrī, Samantabhadra, and Kṣitigarbha respectively; each was also identified with one of the four cardinal directions as well as with one of four great elements. While other sites in China had earlier Guanyin associations, beginning in the ninth century Putuo began gradually to gain pre-eminence as Guanyin's *Potalaka* or island dwelling place as described in two influential Buddhist *sūtras*. This *bodhisattva*, who began as a male figure in India, was gradually transformed by Chinese Buddhists into a female, in keeping her reputation for boundless compassion, and Putuo came to be regarded the place where she revealed herself in miraculous visions.

Putuo is a small mountainous island off the eastern coast of China (the name refers to the island as a whole) that in the tenth century benefited from the emergence of a major trade network linking northern and southern China as well as China with Japan and Korea. Not surprisingly, merchants, diplomats, and sailors in particular were drawn to the island in hope of the *bodhisattva*'s protection during their travels. A wide range of pilgrims contributed to Putuo's fame, including monastic and lay elites who wrote literary accounts of their visits, as well as great numbers of ordinary pilgrims who visited the island's numerous sacred places and brought home tales of miraculous occurrences that they either witnessed or heard about through word of mouth. The most important site on the island was initially the Cave of Tidal Sound where Guanyin was believed to be most likely to bestow a miraculous vision, though over the course of several centuries the island went through cycles of decline and reconstruction, and other places on the island rose to prominence.

As these examples suggest, Buddhist sacred mountains have played an important role in the establishment of Buddhist traditions outside India, providing one very effective means for its integration into a variety of physical, cultural, and historical landscapes.

See also: **Angkor; Borobudur; Cosmology and rebirth; *Dhyānas*; *Mantras*, *mudrās*, and *maṇḍalas*; Pāṭaliputra; Sacred places; Shugendō; *Stūpa*.**

KEVIN TRAINOR

SACRED PLACES

Introduction

Buddhism, as presented in the West, has been closely linked with time and place. Despite considerable uncertainty about its historical origins as late as the beginning of the 1800s, the story of Buddhism was by the middle of the nineteenth century a story that began with a particular man who lived in north India centuries before the birth of Christ. And one could make the case that this concern to root Buddhism in time and place is paralleled in the opening formula characteristic of many Buddhist canonical texts: "Thus have I heard: At a certain time the Buddha was dwelling at ... " This formula simultaneously evokes the tradition that the Buddha's teachings were authoritatively fixed at a communal recitation convened following his death, and locates each particular teaching in the life of the Buddha, specifying where the teaching was given and to whom. This concern to specify the connection between a given teaching and the particular audience to whom it was communicated parallels the tradition that the Buddha had an extraordinary capacity to communicate the *Dharma* in a form appropriate to his hearers, each of whom had a particular capacity to grasp his teaching in keeping with their respective degree of progress along the path to enlightenment.

At the same time, one can easily find Buddhist texts that emphasize the timelessness and universality of the Buddha's *Dharma*, and that represent each particular verbal or written expression of it as fragmentary and inadequate. Seen from this perspective, finite expressions of the *Dharma*, as put forth in particular times and places, appear secondary to the unchanging truth about the nature of reality that persists whether or not there are any beings capable of grasping it and communicating it to others. There are, moreover, Buddhist traditions that portray the key elements in Gautama Buddha's life story as but the most recent instantiations of a timeless pattern. There have been countless Buddhas in the past, and there will be countless more in the future. From this perspective, the unique events, spatially and temporally delimited, that constitute the biography of Gautama Buddha recede before an unchanging archetype of Buddhahood, of which they are merely the most recent examples.

This tension between the timeless and limitless truth about reality and the physical embodiment of that truth through individual Buddhas lies behind Buddhist formulations about multiple Buddha-bodies. Buddhist schools such as the Theravāda, while recognizing a succession of previous and future perfectly enlightened Buddhas, have placed primary emphasis on the most recent Buddha, Siddhārtha Gautama (Pāli Siddhattha Gotama), envisioning the end of his teaching and of his physical continuity in the form of relics as the necessary prerequisite for the arrival of the next Buddha, Maitreya (Pāli Metteyya). Thus Theravāda reflections on the Buddha's two bodies, his *rūpa-kāya* ("form-body") and *dhamma-kāya* ("truth-body), have principally addressed the issue of the Buddha's continued presence and agency in the world following his final passing away, a period that came to be defined as extending for 5,000 years. Other Buddhist communities asserted that the temporally and spatially limited physical bodies of Gautama and other Buddhas were a kind of strategic illusion by means of which the perfect and eternal *Dharma* manifested itself in a provisional form that could be grasped by beings mired in ignorance and sensual craving. From this perspective, there could be countless Buddhas simultaneously dwelling in their respective Buddha-lands to help ignorant beings in accordance with their varying needs and religious aspirations. Other related teachings emphasized that Buddha-nature was itself imminent in all beings and even in all dimensions of the material world. Seen from the perspective of ultimate truth, every place could be seen as sacred.

These diverse traditions about the relationship between perfect enlightenment and its embodiment in the material world, including divergent interpretations of the significance of the person commonly known in the West as "the Buddha," open up a wide range of possibilities for defining and relating to sacred place. In fact, activities for defining and interacting with particular places set apart by virtue of their religious significance and power have played a formative role throughout the history of Buddhism. Precisely because there are so many prominent sacred places in the long history of Buddhism, an essay of this sort cannot describe them all, and will necessarily emphasize broader themes and dynamics that have characterized a number of important sites. These broader dynamics, however, must always be considered in relationship to the concrete and non-generalizable particulars of individual places and the specific historical communities who defined and interacted with them. In what follows I identify two basic strategies through which religiously significant places have been defined in the history of Buddhism, discuss several functions that sacred places have performed, and briefly sketch some distinctive characteristics of Buddhist sacred places in the context of modernity.

Ways of constructing sacred place

Historical connections

Scholars have long recognized the close connection between the development of a continuous and detailed Buddha biography and the identification of important cultic sites associated with events in his life. The early Buddhist canonical collections do not provide a continuous narrative of the Gautama Buddha's life, though they do present accounts of his enlightenment and the founding of the Buddhist *sangha*, and an extended narrative of the final weeks of his life. The story of the Buddha's death as recounted in the *Mahāparinibbāna Sutta* (*Dīgha Nikāya*

2.140–1) of the Theravāda canon recounts that not long before his final passing away, Gautama Buddha identified four places associated with formative events in his life as places "that ought to be seen" and that are "productive of strong religious feeling." These are the places of his birth, Lumbinī, his enlightenment, Bodhgayā, his first teaching, Sārnāth, and his final passing away, Kuśinagara. He predicts that Buddhist monks, nuns, and male and female lay disciples alike will visit these places, reflecting on their connection with the important events that occurred there, and concludes by noting that whoever dies while traveling to visit such a shrine (*cetiya*) with a serenely confident mind will, at death, gain a fortunate heavenly rebirth.

The immediate setting of this passage in the *Mahāparinibbāna Sutta* is noteworthy, for it follows two sections that highlight the religious importance of beholding the Buddha's body and the bodies of *sangha* members who have made progress along the path to *nirvāṇa*. In the first, the text recounts that the Buddha requests a monk named Upavāṇa, who has been standing at his side fanning him, to step aside. When asked why, the Buddha explains that many celestial beings have gathered for a final viewing before he passes away, and the monk is blocking their line of sight. It turns out, according to the fifth-century Pāli commentary, that the deities, who normally can look right through ordinary people, could not see through the monk, an *arhant*, because of his extraordinary virtue; the commentary further explains that his great virtue was the result of offerings he made in past lives at the *stūpas* of two previous Buddhas. In the second passage, the Buddha's chief attendant Ānanda, worries that after the Buddha passes away, the community will lose the opportunity to see the mentally cultivated monks who used to visit the Buddha at the end of the rains retreat. Responding to this concern, the Buddha details the four sites that will draw pilgrims after his death.

Taken together, these passages bring into focus one common strategy through which sacred place has been defined in Buddhist tradition. The narrative highlights the vital importance that being in the presence of the Buddha's physical body held for those who encountered him during his lifetime and, in particular, the importance of beholding that body. At the same time, it communicates the transient and historically limited nature of the Buddha's body. And by constructing a religiously significant landscape linked to pivotal moments in the Buddha's life, it establishes a temporal distance between the past Buddha and present Buddhist devotees while simultaneously providing the means to bridge that distance: devotees are encouraged to journey from wherever they find themselves to specific places marked by a special connection to the Buddha's physical presence, places that retain the power to transform in various ways those who come in physical contact with them. While the particular forms of power associated with these sites are not detailed, it is clear that they have the capacity to alter the mental states of those who visit them, and that those who undertake journeys to such places are engaging in highly meritorious activities that can dramatically improve their future rebirths. This text can be regarded as one in a long succession of texts that, through the use of historical narrative, forge a relationship with Buddhas of the past and important places in the present that mediate their religious power. In these texts, sacred biography and sacred geography are inseparably linked.

The earliest reliably datable records we have of Buddhist pilgrimage survive in the form of Aśokan inscriptions from the third century BCE that recount the emperor Aśoka's visits to the sites of the Buddha's birth and enlightenment, as well as two visits to a *stūpa* dedicated to an earlier Buddha (Koṇāgamana) at Nigālī Sāgar in present-day Nepal. These texts indicate a direct connection between Aśoka, who became a paradigm of Buddhist kingship and lay devotion, and two of the four sacred sites referred to in the *Mahāparinibbāna Sutta*, though it is impossible to know whether Aśoka's pilgrimage activity reflects an ongoing Buddhist pilgrimage tradition or was an innovation.

Beginning in the fourth century CE, lengthier narrative texts survive that provide a more detailed picture of Buddhist sacred places and the activities with which they were associated. Two genres of narrative sources have been particularly important: Pāli *vaṃsa* texts from Sri Lanka and Chinese pilgrim accounts. The Pāli *vaṃsa* ("chronicle" or "history") literature, beginning with the fourth- or fifth-century CE *Dīpavaṃsa* (*History of the Island*), recounts Gautama Buddha's legendary visits to the island, where he is said to have marked several sacred places through physical contact. This literature provides a chronologically organized history of Buddhism in Sri Lanka that highlights the role of kings as builders of *stūpas* and monasteries; many of the most prominent of these are located at sites defined through the narrative of the Buddha's three visits to Sri Lanka. This tradition of Gautama Buddha's travels outside of India is a significant theme echoed in many Buddhist texts, including Pāli *vaṃsa* texts composed in Southeast Asia. Often, sites sanctified by the physical presence of Gautama Buddha during his lifetime are associated with sites marked by previous Buddhas, and by the later enshrinement of important relics and Buddha images; in many cases the future enshrinement of these powerful objects is the subject of prophecies pronounced by the Buddha before his final passing away.

Again, we see a close connection between strategies for constructing a religiously significant landscape and for defining the passage of time. These texts highlight the forward progress of time, marked by a succession of important events in the life of the Buddha and by the activities of specific Buddhists through history whose relationship to him are defined by an understanding of what he did for them in the past, a understanding that evokes feelings of gratitude toward him expressed through ritualized offerings at sites associated with his physical presence. They also sound the overarching theme of *anitya*, transience, highlighting the finitude of the Buddha's body and of his *śāsana* (Pāli *sāsana*, "instruction" or "religion"). But this is not the only message: these narratives communicate a complementary theme, highlighting a series of repeating patterns that reinforce a sense of stability and support. Thus the unique events of Gautama Buddha's life can be seen as reflections of an unchanging pattern that marks the lives of all Buddhas, past, present, and future. A striking example of this is the tradition that Bodhgayā is not only the site of Gautama Buddha's enlightenment, but the place of enlightenment of all past and future Buddhas.

Among the most important early sources for the study of Indian Buddhist pilgrimage sites are the travel records of Chinese monks. The most influential of these in the West are the accounts of Faxian (*c*. 337–418), Xuanzang (*c*. 600–64), and Yijing (635–713). All three monks made lengthy and arduous journeys from China to India to collect Buddhist texts that could further the establishment of an authentic Chinese Buddhist tradition. Their accounts provide vivid depictions of important Buddhist sacred places, of the ritual practices centered around them, and of the Buddhist communities they encountered. They also testify to the dramatic expansion of the Buddhist sacred geography which was linked the developing narrative of Gautama Buddha's life, especially stories connected with miraculous occurrences.

The tradition of the "eight great marvels" (Skt. *aṣṭamahāprātihārya*) represents one influential example of this elaboration of Buddhist sacred geography in connection with the Buddha biography. This formulation includes, in addition to the four sites found in the *Mahāparinibbāna Sutta*, the cities of Sāṇkāsya, Śrāvasti, Rājagṛha, and Vaiśālī, each of which was the scene of a major display of the Buddha's extraordinary powers. At Sāṇkāsya Gautama Buddha was said to have descended along a jeweled ladder, flanked on either side by Brahmā and Indra, after spending three months in the Trāyatriṃśa heaven preaching to his mother, who had been reborn there as a male deity. Śrāvasti is the place where he displayed his supremacy over a group of rival teachers by producing multiple forms of his body and rising up into the sky, emitting fire and water from the opposite sides of his body. At Rājagṛha he displayed his power of lovingkindness to subdue an enraged elephant sent by his cousin Devadatta to kill him. And at Vaiśālī a band of monkeys dug a water tank for him and made an offering of honey, a display of the extraordinary *karmic* benefits that gifts offered to him bear.

All eight of these sites were described in Chinese pilgrims' accounts, though they were not given special attention as a group. They begin to appear together iconographically by the eighth century, and are a frequent subject of Pāla-era sculptures from eastern India. The typical form of the Pāla images displays the Buddha seated in the earth-touching posture at Bodhgayā, a depiction of his victory over Māra just prior to his enlightenment, with smaller depictions of the seven other scenes encircling the central figure. Taken together, the eight episodes encapsulate the life and career of the Buddha, highlighting the moment of his perfect enlightenment at Bodhgayā. Some of these images are sculpted in stone, but many more survive in clay, pressed from molds, and variations of this iconographic theme have been found in India, China, Tibet, and Burma. It appears likely that at least some of these images served as a kind of pilgrim's memento, though it is also possible that the images could themselves have been regarded as embodiments of the power associated with the eight pilgrimage sites that they depict, thus effectively making those sites ritually present wherever the images were taken and rendering a physical journey to the actual sites in India unnecessary.

Ritual consecration

The sacred places treated above owe their special status to traditions, framed as narratives about the past, that link them with events in the life of Gautama Buddha. These places, by virtue of their immediate physical connection with his body and with actions he is said to have performed while located at those places, are attributed special religious significance. As we have seen, these traditions included accounts of the Buddha's travels far beyond north India, in keeping with the belief that his supreme enlightenment and meditational attainments empowered him to fly through the air and to manifest his physical body in a variety of forms. There are, however, many places throughout the Buddhist world that are regarded as possessing special religious significance entirely apart from claims that they were visited by the Buddha during his lifetime, and these owe their status to various techniques of ritualized consecration.

The most widespread of these ritual techniques for defining sacred place is relic enshrinement. The use of relics to distinguish places of special religious importance can be seen as a bridge between sites set apart by virtue of some past connection with the Buddha and sites that owe their special status to the activities of later communities of Buddhists.

Relics, as objects that have some tangible connection to the Buddha (post-cremation remains or objects rendered powerful through the Buddha's use of them), are like sacred places set apart through their historical connection with the Buddha in that they owe their specialness to some sort of physical continuity with the Buddha's body, and there are many narratives that recount the peregrinations of the Buddha's relics from the time and place of his cremation in north India to their ultimate places of enshrinement across Asia. They represent a different strategy for defining sacred place, however, in that their place of enshrinement is not limited to the sphere of the Buddha's travels during his lifetime. Virtually any place, through a ritual of enshrinement, can be rendered religiously powerful, and in that respect relic enshrinement provides a wider set of possibilities for defining sacred places than those dependent stories about the life of the Buddha. In this second strategy for making places sacred, the actions of the individuals responsible for constructing relic monuments (*stūpas*) and enshrining the relics they contain play a primary role. And not all *stūpas* enshrine corporeal relics; some Mahāyāna Buddhist communities commonly enshrined Buddhist texts, including the widely disseminated *pratītyasamutpāda* verse, or so-called "Buddhist creed" ("*ye dharmā hetu* . . . ": "Those *dharmas* which arise from a cause/The Tathāgata has declared their cause/And that which is the cessation of them./Thus the great renunciant has taught").

A passage in the *Mahāparinibbāna Sutta* relates that the Buddha enjoined his followers to cremate his body and enshrine his remains in a *stūpa* erected at a crossroads, and another section of that text describes his funeral rites in some detail, including an account of how his post-cremation remains were divided into eight portions that were distributed among eight different groups in the region for enshrinement in *stūpas*, thus averting a battle over possession of his remains. The vessel in which the relics had been placed after the cremation, as well as the embers from the funeral pyre, formed the basis for two additional enshrinements. The text concludes (*Dīgha Nikāya* 2.166–8) with two lists of places where relics were enshrined, the first list detailing the ten sites just discussed, and the second, attributed in Buddhaghosa's commentary to Sri Lankan monks, providing an updated and expanded account of relic enshrinements. This second list details the locations of the eight portions of corporeal relics originally enshrined in north India, noting that one portion had moved into the possession of a group of serpent-deities (*nāgas*), and specifies, as well, the location of the Buddha's four eye-teeth, which are not mentioned in the first list.

This account of the eightfold division of relics (which should not be confused with the sites of the *aṣṭamahāprātihārya* or "eight great marvels" discussed above) and their subsequent enshrinements provides the classical formulation for later accounts. Another influential narrative tradition recounts how the emperor Aśoka collected the relics from the original eight sites and redistributed them in 84,000 *stūpas* constructed across this realm. The accounts of Chinese pilgrims make frequent reference to these Aśokan *stūpas* in their descriptions of the sites that they visited. A third narrative, which has been very important in Sri Lankan relic histories, draws upon the two accounts just mentioned, and explains that Aśoka was prevented from removing the relics that were enshrined by the *nāgas* when he redistributed the Buddha's relics throughout India; these relics, according to a prophecy pronounced by the Buddha just before his final passing away, were destined for enshrinement in the Great *Stūpa* built by the Sri Lankan king Duṭṭhagāmaṇi in the second century BCE, and accounts of this enshrinement play a prominent role in several relic histories composed in Sri Lanka and Southeast Asia.

While Buddha relics have been highlighted in enshrinement accounts, there is considerable evidence that the relics of Buddhist *arhant*s and other revered Buddhist monastics have also played an important role in establishing sacred places. By the time of Buddhaghosa's fifth century Pāli commentaries, Theravāda Buddhist monasteries were clearly expected to have *stūpas* within their monastery grounds. At the famous monastic complex at Sāñcī in central India, which has no claim to a connection with the living Buddha, the site is dominated by a large Aśoka-era *stūpa* that probably enshrined Buddha relics. Many other relic monuments were also constructed at the site, including a *stūpa* enshrining relics of two of Gautama Buddha's most prominent followers, the *arhants* Śāriputra and Mahāmaudgalyāna, and another enshrining the remains of ten monks, including a second-century BCE Haimavata monk named Gotiputra. Reliquary inscriptions from *stūpas* at Andher and Sonāri, two other monastic sites in the area, also mention Gotiputra, and it is likely that he was responsible for initiating major renovations at Sāñcī as well as new monastic complexes at Andher and Sonāri. A variation on this basic dynamic appears in the tradition of self-mummified Chan Buddhist masters in medieval China. In place of relics, the mummified bodies of Chan masters were carefully preserved and enshrined in their *Dharma* halls as objects of special authority and power, functioning in some cases as the basis for pilgrimage.

The physical orientation and relative elevations of the three *stūpas* at Sāñcī reflect a clear hierarchy of status, illustrating how relic enshrinements can serve to differentiate positions of relative status within the confines of monastic complexes, which are themselves generally set apart as places of greater purity and religious significance in relation the dwellings of the laity. The importance of ritual techniques for differentiating sacred places in the context of monastic complexes can be seen in accounts of the construction of the Sri Lankan Mahāvihāra in Anurādhapura. These include ritual practices related to the establishment of the monastic boundary (*sīmā*), as well as those connected with the construction of the Thūpārāma *stūpa* and the ceremony of enshrining the relics. Monastic boundaries play an important role in marking Theravāda disciplinary lineages, as well as in the performance of important monastic ceremonies such as ordination.

The complementarity of historical and ritual strategies for defining Buddhist sacred places is apparent in the tradition of the sixteen pilgrimage sites in Sri Lanka. As mentioned above, several of these sites are named in *vaṃsa* accounts that narrate the tradition that Gautama Buddha made three visits to Sri Lanka. These sites are spread across the island, and they are linked with a tradition that the Buddha prophesied that the island of Sri Lanka was a special preserve where his true *Dharma* would shine forth. All of these places, with the exception of Sri Pada which is sanctified by an imprint of the Buddha's foot, are also the sites of later relic enshrinements, including several locations in Anurādhapura. The basic formulation of sixteen sacred places on the island goes back at least to the eighteenth century, but the actual sites included have been subject to some variation. It is a striking anomaly that the location of one of the sixteen sites on the list, Dīvāguhā, a cave where the Buddha is said to have rested at the foot of the mountain of Sri Pada, is unknown and thus cannot be visited.

The importance of Sri Pada as a Buddhist sacred place points to a characteristic of many important Buddhist religious sites across Asia. They are located at places noteworthy for their natural features – for example, mountains and caves, features that have been further distinguished by means of historical narratives (accounts of visits by Buddhas, *bodhisattvas* other important Buddhist figures) and/or through the ritualized activities of later communities of Buddhists (including enshrinement and the construction of special religious structures). The natural prominence of mountains makes them well suited for use in religious contexts where height is associated with higher levels of purity and status. The local deities identified with a number of mountains throughout Asia have been transformed into supporters and protectors of Buddhas and other important Buddhist figures with the introduction of a universalizing Buddhist tradition. For example, the Tibetan pilgrimage site of Pure Crystal Mountain (Dakpa Sheri) in southeastern Tibet was transformed from a site associated with local deities to a great Tibetan Buddhist *gnas ri* ("mountain abode") through a process of "mandalization" based on Indian *Tantric* traditions. Central to this process of subjugation and incorporation was the activity of heroic *Tantric lamas* who, by means of meditative and visionary powers gained through a process of interior perfection, exerted mastery over a series of external forces, including local superhuman beings, as well as competing religious and political groups. The subjugation of these various external forces was accomplished in part through the *Tantric lamas'* visions of the mountain as a great *maṇḍala* palace with an extensive hierarchy of positions and statuses into which local powers were assimilated. These visions employ complex sets of homologies between the bodies of deities, various features of mountain topography, and the bodies of *Tantric* adepts. The homologizing of sacred mountains, *maṇḍala* palaces, and *stūpas* (Tib. *mchod rten*) has also been noted. The activities of these great *Tantric* heroes and the sublime reality they revealed, as handed down through oral and written narratives, have provided the model for the ritual activities of later pilgrims who circumambulate the mountain in hopes of purification. Pure Crystal Mountain took its place within a network of Tibetan mountain abodes that eventually shifted the scene of the cosmic dramas preserved in the Indian narrative traditions from a network of Indian sacred sites to the Tibetan landscape. Similar *maṇḍala*-based schema took root and developed considerable influence in East and Southeast Asia.

Functions

As these examples of mandalization suggest, many Buddhist sacred sites incorporate hierarchies of supernatural beings who are oriented vertically and horizontally in a manner that locates them in complex systems of purity and power. These hierarchies have functioned effectively as a means of assimilating Buddhist systems of thought and practice into a wide variety of local circumstances. Such systems have, in addition, enabled Buddhist sacred sites to serve a variety of purposes, from the attainment of lofty soteriological goals to more mundane benefits such as averting misfortune and gaining material prosperity. Buddhist sacred sites have also served the interests of kings and other political figures eager to consolidate their power and authority by marshaling material and human resources for Buddhist construction projects such as *stūpas* and temples, often with explicit reference to the Aśokan ideal. Finally, the economic power of Buddhist sacred sites should not be ignored. The movement of large numbers of pilgrims to Buddhist sacred places, whether small local shrines or great pilgrimage centers, brought economic benefits to surrounding communities and, in particular, to the nearby Buddhist monastic communities with which they were associated. The power of Buddhist sacred places to attract material support from both Buddhist monastics and laypeople is apparent, for example, from the hundreds of donative inscriptions found at the *stūpa* sites at Sāñcī and Bhārhut in central India.

Buddhist sacred space and modernity

As I suggested at the beginning of this essay, the picture of Buddhism that emerged in the West in the latter half of the nineteenth century was closely connected with the efforts of historians, philologists, and archeologists to uncover the origins of the religion in India. In their search for the material remains of the places where the historical Buddha lived and taught, they were often guided by the surviving records of Buddhist pilgrims from past ages, relying particularly heavily on the accounts of Chinese pilgrims. In many cases these accounts functioned as the equivalent of treasure maps by means of which excavators, digging into the ruins of *stūpas* and monastic complexes, sought to confirm the location of the principal sites of the Buddha's life. As recent scholarship has emphasized, a marked tendency to equate authenticity with the earliest origins of the tradition has in many cases diverted scholarly attention away from the study of later Buddhist communities and their material artifacts, or, when they have been studied, has resulted in their being characterized as evidence of Buddhism's decline.

One of the characteristic dynamics affecting Buddhist sacred places in the age of modernity is the complicated interdependence of scholars trained in historical and archeological methods that originated in the West and diverse communities of Asian Buddhists. At times their respective aims and activities have converged, and at other times they have been in conflict. For example, the identification and renovation of ancient sites in India and Sri Lanka during the nineteenth and early twentieth centuries contributed to a revival of Buddhism in those countries. And the recognition of several Buddhist sacred places as World Heritage Sites has brought international funding for their renovation and upkeep, as well as a heightened international profile and crowds of free-spending tourists possessed of varying degrees of attunement to the religious sensibilities of local Buddhist communities. The interests of scholars committed to preserving particular historical features of an archeological site have sometimes conflicted with the goals of modern Buddhist patrons seeking to restore it to a past ideal, or expand and enhance it as did exemplary royal patrons of the past.

Buddhist sacred places have also played a key role in the confluence of Western historical discourses with efforts by Asian Buddhists to consolidate ethnic and religious identities in the context of modern anti-colonialist and nationalist movements. Both the international movement to free Tibet from Chinese political and cultural hegemony and the ongoing ethnic conflict in Sri Lanka bear witness to the sometimes tragic role that Buddhist sacred places have played in bringing together historical narratives, ethnic and religious identities, and nationalist struggles.

Finally, the consequences of modern technology for the future of Buddhist sacred places remain uncertain. Technological advances in transportation and global communication have greatly facilitated the movement of people to Buddhist sites around the world, though perhaps in a manner that vitiates the transformative effects of more traditional modes of access which often entailed considerable physical difficulty. The influence of the Internet is particularly interesting in this regard, given its capacity to facilitate immediate virtual access to visual and aural representations of Buddhist sites around the world without regard to their actual locations in the physical world. It remains to be seen whether future Buddhists will find in these disembodied representations an enticement to follow in the footsteps of earlier Buddhist pilgrims or will regard them as effective substitutes for the places they represent.

See also: **Ajanta; Angkor; Anurādhapura; *Arahant*; Aśoka; Ayutthaya; Bodhgayā; Borobudur; Buddha, bodies of; Buddha, relics of; Cave temples; Councils; Faxiang; Kuśinagara; Lumbinī; *Mantras*, *mudrās*, and *maṇḍalas*; Pagan; Pāṭaliputra; Sacred mountains; Sāñcī; Sārnāth; Shugendō; *Stūpa*; *Stūpas* of Sāñcī, Bhārhut, and Amarāvatī; Vaiśālī; *Vihāra*.**

KEVIN TRAINOR

SĀDHANA

Sādhana is a Sanskrit term denoting a "means of accomplishment." Although the word has various applications, in Vajrayāna (*tantric*) Buddhism it refers to a type of ritual-meditative practice in which practitioners attempt to attain enlightenment by identifying their body, speech, and mind with those of a chosen Buddha or *bodhisattva*. The main literary source for *sādhanas* in the Tibetan tradition are the Yoga *Tantras* and the Highest Yoga *Tantras* (*anuttarayogatantra*), the most important of which are the *Kālacakra Tantra* and the *Guhyasamāja Tantra*. In Shingon Buddhism, the tantric sect of Japan, the most important sources of *sādhanas* are the *Mahāvairocana Sūtra* and its commentaries.

Sādhanas are practices intended symbolically to transform the practitioner into a Buddha or *bodhisattva* (often called "deities" [*devas, devīs*] in the context of *sādhanas*). They entail often elaborate practices requiring the total involvement of the practitioner, who must balance verbal formulations (*mantras*) associated with the deity, physical gestures (*mudrās*), and visualization of the deity's *maṇḍala*, a complex image of the deity in his or her purified realm, often surrounded by other deities. Prior to engagement in *sādhanas*, practitioners must go through initiations or empowerments (*abhiṣeka*) to purify the intentions and prepare the mind and body for the practice. Initiations also establish a relationship between the practitioner and his or her deity, and new initiations must take place for each deity with which the practitioner is empowered to practice.

Although *tantric sādhanas* vary in content, using many different deities as objects of contemplation, most show basic structural similarities. The following summary of a *sādhana* from the eleventh-century collection, *Sādhanamāla*, features a *sādhana* of Tārā, a benevolent female deity, and is fairly typical of the main features of *sādhanas*.

Preliminary practices:

1 Ritual purification of both the practitioner and the site of meditation prior to engaging in the practice. This often involves ritual bathing and adorning the site – a private place outdoors – with flowers and incense.
2 Preliminary visualization of the letters corresponding to a number of "seed syllables" associated with the particular deity.
3 Paying homage to the Buddhas and *bodhisattvas*; making offerings of flowers, incense, etc.
4 Confession of any sins one has committed against any beings.
5 Rejoicing in the merit of all beings; taking refuge in the Buddha, *Dharma*, and *Sangha*; expression of reliance on the path of the Buddha; and appeal for the Buddhas to remain in the world and continue to teach the *Dharma*.
6 Dedication of merit gained through this practice to the attainment of full awakening of all beings.

7 Cultivation of the four holy states (*brahmavihāras*): friendliness, compassion, joy, and equanimity.
8 Meditation on the inherent purity and emptiness of all things and of oneself. It is out of this emptiness, visually represented as an empty space, that one creates the *maṇḍala*.

The core of the *sādhana* consists of two stages, the generation (*utpattikrama*) and completion stages (*niṣpannakrama*). In the generation stage the meditator imagines an image of the deity in detail. From a Tārā *sādhana*:

> Then one should visualize the blessed, holy Tārā proceeding from the yellow seed syllable *tāṃ* situated on the spotless sphere of the moon, which is inside the filaments of a lotus in full flower, in the middle of the moon already visualized in one's heart. One should conceive her as deep green in color, with two arms, a smiling face, endowed with every virtue, and free of all defects, adorned with jewelry of heavenly gold, rubies, pearls, and jewels. Her two breasts are decorated with beautiful garlands, her arms wrapped in bracelets and bangles ... She is a radiant and seductive figure in the prime of youth, with eyes like a blue autumn lotus, her body dressed in heavenly garments, seated in a half-lotus posture in a circle of light rays as large as a cart-wheel. With her right hand, she makes the sign of granting wishes; in her left she holds a blue lotus flower in full bloom ...
>
> Then, the [image of] the blessed one [Tārā] is led away on numerous bundles of light-rays illuminating the triple world. [The rays] issue from the yellow seed syllable *tāṃ*, which is in the filaments of the lotus in the circle of the moon situated in one's heart ... When she has been brought forth and established on the firmament, one should receive her by offering oblation at her feet with scented water and fragrant flowers in a jeweled vase. One should worship her ... with flowers, incense, lamps, food, scents, garlands, perfumes, garments, umbrellas, flags, bells, banners, and so on.
>
> (*Sādhanamāla*, pp. 208–9)

During or after visualizing the deity, the practitioner forms the hand gestures (*mudrā*) and pronounces *mantras* appropriate to the deity.

The culmination of the practice is the completion stage, the identification of the practitioner with the deity, in some cases through envisioning him or herself merging with the deity or initially imagining the deity as him or herself. Some *sādhanas* contain a physiological component in the completion stage. The Highest Yoga *Tantras* contain a complex understanding of "subtle physiology" which maintains that there are within the body three main channels (*nāḍīs*) and thousands of subsidiary veins through which life-energy (Skt. *prāṇa*, Tib. *rlung*) flows. In some *sādhanas* controlling the flow of this energy is an essential part of the completion stage. The goal of this control is bringing the life-energy into the central channel and raising it up through each energy circle (*cakra*) along the spine until it reaches the crown of the head. Through this process the coarser energies gradually dissipate and subtler levels of consciousness emerge, culminating in the emergence of the "mind of clear light." After all of these visualizations are concluded, the *maṇḍala* is dissolved back into emptiness through a series of stages.

See also: **Meditation, modern movements; Meditation, visualization; Meditation traditions, Vajrayāna; Meditational systems; *Śamatha*; *Vipaśyanā*.**

DAVID L. MCMAHAN

SAICHŌ AND TENDAI

Saichō (posthumous title: Dengyō Daishi; 767–822) was the founder and transmitter of the Tendai (Ch. Tiantai) school and (with Kūkai) one of the two pre-eminent Buddhist figures of Heian (794–1185) Japan.

Saichō was born in Ōmi near Lake Biwa and entered a nearby temple at the age of twelve, where he studied under Gyōhyō (1222–1797). Shortly after he was ordained, Saichō forsook the established Buddhist temples for a simple retreat on the nearby Mount Hiei. His *Ganmon* (vows) written at this time (such as the vow to share any of his merit with all sentient beings so that they can attain enlightenment) reveals his idealism and dedication.

Saichō traveled to China in 804 to study Tiantai Buddhism. While in China he also received initiations in Ox-head Chan, the *Fanwang* Mahāyāna *bodhisattva* precepts, and esoteric Buddhism. After returning to Japan Saichō founded the Tendai school on Mount Hiei on the basis of these four pillars: esoteric Buddhism, Zen, the Mahāyāna *bodhisattva* precepts, and the "perfect" or "complete" teachings of Tiantai proper. The new Tendai school was recognized by the court in 806 through the approval of two annual ordinands, one to focus on Tendai proper and one to focus on esoteric Buddhism.

For the rest of his life Saichō was busy defending and building up his new school. He sought to establish an independent official ordination platform, based on the Mahāyāna *bodhisattva* precepts, to prevent his disciples from defecting to the established Nara schools. His petitions submitted to the court concerning annual ordinands (*Rokujōshiki* and so forth) were written at this time. Saichō also carried on a long debate with Tokuitsu (780?–842?) of the Hossō school over the respective worth of their schools' teachings, with Saichō supporting the idea of the universal attainment of Buddhahood in works such as *Shugo kokkaishō* (*Essays on Protecting the Nation*) and *Hokke shūku* (*Elegant Words on the Lotus Sūtra*). Saichō also sought to incorporate esoteric Buddhism under the rubric of Tendai, but in this area he was overshadowed by Kūkai, and the completion of Tendai esoteric Buddhism (*taimitsu*) was accomplished by Saichō's successors Ennin, Enchin, and Annen.

Although Saichō was outshone by Kūkai during his lifetime, the Tendai school he founded grew to be the largest and most influential school of Buddhism during much of Japanese history. Saichō's belief in universal Buddhahood became the accepted norm of Japanese Buddhism, and his Mahāyāna ideals have had incalculable influence throughout Japanese history.

The Tendai school received full independence when, one week after Saichō's death in 822, the court approved his petition for autonomous ordination with the *bodhisattva* precepts on Mount Hiei. The Tendai institution continued to grow in influence and popularity until it was a dominant force in Japanese society. Ennin (794–864) and Enchin (814–91) visited China to study and strengthen Tendai's position with regard to esoteric (*mikkyō*) Buddhist teachings and practice. The dominance of esoteric Buddhism (*taimitsu*, in contrast to the *tōmitsu* of Kūkai's Shingon) climaxed doctrinally with the work of Annen (841–89?).

Throughout the Heian period (eighth to twelfth centuries) and beyond, the Tendai establishment was heavily involved in social and political affairs, catering to demands for esoteric rituals and ceremonies, and accumulating power and wealth. Ryōgen (942–85), the eighteenth Tendai abbot (*zasu*), introduced his "26-Article Regulations" to encourage scholarship and a stricter religious life. Nonetheless, Tendai involvement in worldly affairs continued at a high level, including the maintenance of "warrior monks" (*sōhei*) to promote its interests.

Ryōgen's disciple Genshin (942–1017) was a wide-ranging Tendai scholar most famous for his compilation of Pure Land texts in the *Ōjōyōshū*. Another example of the high level of Tendai scholarship is Hōchibō Shōshin (twelfth century), whose detailed commentaries on the central works of Tiantai represent a major contribution to classical textual studies. Again, Jien (1155–1225), a Tendai abbot, lamenting the decadence of his age, composed the *Gukanshō*, a history of Japan and an analysis of contemporary secular struggles, reflecting the prevalent view that the current age was the degenerate Age of the Latter *Dharma* (*mappō*).

As for Tendai Buddhist practice, in addition to the plethora of meditative and ritual activities practiced in various parts of the Mount Hiei/Enryakuji complex, Sōō (831–918) established the *kaihōgyō* (circling the peaks) ascetic practice of walking and performing other practices in the mountains of Hiei, centered at Mudōji. These practices, such as the 100-day or 1,000-day *kaihōgyō*, continue to be practiced on Mount Hiei.

Another aspect of Tendai is its amalgamation with local beliefs and deities, in particular the merging with local deities and ritual known as the Sannō cult.

Tendai Buddhism, with its headquarters at Enryakuji on Mount Hiei, was the womb from which sprang many of the new movements of Kamakura Buddhism, and nurtured such major figures as Eisai/Yōsai, Dōgen, Hōnen, Shinran, Ippen, and Nichiren.

Another important aspect of Japanese Tendai is *Hongaku hōmon*, the tradition and lineage based on the idea that all beings are endowed with enlightenment.

Tendai reached a nadir in 1571 when the warlord Oda Nobunaga burned down its headquarters on Mount Hiei, destroying hundreds of temples and killing thousands of residents. Mount Hiei recovered with the support of Oda's successor, Toyotomi Hidoyoshi, and the Tokugawa family. Tendai flourished in the Kanto area with the Tokugawa shogunate. The Tendai monk Tenkai (?–1642) was supported by Tokugawa Ieyasu and oversaw the printing of the entire Buddhist canon (the Tenkai edition). Tenkai also was in charge of the Tendai temple at Nikkō, which became the final resting place for Ieyasu.

A movement worthy of note during the Tokugawa period is the Anraku school of Myōryū (1637–90) and Reikū (1652–1739), which urged a revival of the precepts in response to what they perceived as a decadence encouraged by the philosophy of "original enlightenment," and propagated the philosophy of the Tiantai interpretations of Zhili. It was from around this time that the Tendai "Five Periods and Eight Teachings" classification system as presented by Chegwan in his *Tendai shikyōgi* (*An Outline of the Fourfold Teachings*) began to be used as an introduction to Tendai Buddhism.

Tendai Buddhism remains alive in the modern world, though its temples and adherents are not as numerous as other schools. Its teachings are studied at universities throughout Japan and across the world, and Tendai missions have been established abroad (e.g. in Hawaii). Recent activities include sponsoring interreligious prayer and dialogue with leaders of religions around the world. On a more popular level, *ichigu oterasu* ("lighting a corner") – a famous saying by Saichō – has been used as a catch phrase in a modern campaign to proclaim the message of contemporary Tendai.

See also: **Dōgen and Sōtōshū; Hōnen and Jōdoshū; *Hongaku Shisō* – original enlightenment; *Honji-suijaku/shinbutsu shūgo* – Buddhist syncretism in Japan; *Kenmitsu* (exoteric–esoteric) Buddhism; Nichiren and Nichirenshū; Shinran and Jōdo Shinshū; Shugendō.**

PAUL L. SWANSON

SAKYA

The Sakya tradition traces itself back to the Indian siddha Virūpa, who was a scholar-monk at Somapurı Monastery but found the constraints of monasticism to be incompatible with his *tantric* practice. After leaving the monastery, he developed the "path and result" (*lam 'bras*) system that is the core of Sakya meditative training.

The hierarchs of Sakya come from the aristocratic Khön family. The main figure in the lineage is the "Throne Holder of Sakya" (Sa skya Khri 'dzin), who is a male member of the Khön family. The Khön were originally affiliated with the Nyingma Order, but a split occurred when Sherap Tsültrim saw Nyingma monks publicly performing *tantric* rituals. Believing that this practice violated *tantric* rules of secrecy, he and his followers severed ties with the Nyingma and founded a new order that was to be devoted to scholarship and *tantric* practice.

In the thirteenth century, the Sakyapas became the most powerful order in Tibet as a result of Sakya Pandita's (1182–1251) trip to Mongolia at the invitation of Godan Khan. He and his nephew Pakpa established an arrangement called "priest–patron" (*mchod yon*), in which they became the court chaplains of the Mongol khans and the khans in turn made them viceroys of Tibet. When Mongol power waned in the following century, so did the influence of the Sakyapas, and today they are the smallest order of Tibetan Buddhism in terms of numbers, though highly influential as scholars and teachers.

The "path and fruit" system is a comprehensive program of Buddhist practice based on the *Hevajra-tantra*. This text teaches that *saṃsāra* and *nirvāṇa* are indivisible, and that there is no real difference between them. Rather, beings who live in *saṃsāra* do so because of adventitious afflictions based on mistaken ideas, while awakened beings have eliminated these. They are merely false perceptions, and so the key to making the transition from affliction to awakening lies in a shift in understanding and perspective. From the point of view of the awakened state, all dichotomies vanish, and the result of practice is seen as being inseparable from the path itself. The role of the teacher is stressed, and one begins with the essential instructions (*gdams ngag*) of a master who has successfully followed the path, and who also provides *tantric* empowerments (*dbang skur*), which provide an essential authorization to practice.

Other important Sakya doctrines include the "triple appearance" (*snang gsum*) and the "triple continuum" (*rgyud gsum*). The former consists of: (1) the appearance of phenomena as impure error; (2) the appearance of experience in meditation; and (3) pure appearance. This represents a progressive advance in understanding, beginning with the mistaken perspective of ordinary beings, then the partial awakening of advanced meditators, and culminating in the wisdom of fully awakened masters. The triple continuum refers to: (1) basis; (2) path; and (3) result. As with the triple appearance, these are fundamentally non-different, and distinctions are only made from the point of view of ordinary conceptuality. The basis refers to the two truths (conventional and ultimate). The path involves cultivating method and wisdom, and the result is the pure vision.

See also: **Tibet, Buddhism in; Vajrayāna Buddhism.**

John Powers

SAKYADHĪTĀ

Sakyadhītā is a Buddhist women's organization founded in 1987. It was created from the first international conference of Buddhist nuns held in Bodhgayā in 1987. The conference was organized by Karma Lekshe Tsomo, an American Tibetan nun; Ayya Khema, a German-born Theravādin nun; and Chatsumarn Kabilsingh, a Thai professor at Thammasat University in Bangkok, Thailand. The focus of the conference was to bring together, for the first time, nuns from a variety of traditions to foster mutual understanding, discuss their common concerns and encourage others in the practice of *Dharma*. There were representatives from twenty-six countries and all Buddhist traditions. At the final evaluation session the decision was made to make Sakyadhītā a women's organization of both lay and monastic women. The founding goals of the organization are:

1 The creation of a network of communication for Buddhist women throughout the world.
2. Education and improvement of facilities for women to study, practice, and teach Buddhism.
3 Support for the full ordination of women in every Buddhist tradition where it does not now exist.
4 Facilitation of understanding among the various Buddhist traditions.
5 The promotion of world peace through Buddhist teachings.

Since its inception, it has held a series of eight international conferences in Asia as well as conferences in North America and Germany that focused primarily on Western practitioners: Bodhgayā, India, 1987; Bangkok, Thailand, 1992; Sri Lanka, 1993; Ladakh, India, 1995; Phnom Penh, Cambodia, 1998; Lumbini, Nepal, 2000; Taipei, Taiwan, 2002; Seoul, Korea, 2004. The North American conference on Buddhist women was held at Pitzer College, California in 1998 and the European conference on Buddhist women was held in Cologne, Germany, 2000. It has produced a series of books based upon these conferences (all edited by Karma Lekshe Tsomo): *Sakyadhita: Daughters of the Buddha* (1988); *Buddhism Through American Women's Eyes* (1995); *Innovative Women: Swimming Against the Stream* (2000); and *Buddhist Women Across Cultures: Realizations* (1999). It has also produced a newsletter and website (which contains past volumes of the newsletter): http://www.sakyadhita.org. It has further engaged in a wide variety of projects for the improvement of women, and worked towards the re-establishment of the full ordination of women in the Theravāda and Tibetan (Vajrayāna) traditions.

The conferences are generally held in Asia for a variety of reasons, cost being one. By having the conferences in Asia it becomes possible to invite many Asian nuns who would not otherwise have the financial resources to attend. Their presence provides a multitude of benefits for both them and other conference participants. For many, it is their first trip away from their local area. Their horizons are expanded by seeing the large numbers of *bhikkhunīs* who exist worldwide and by meeting nuns from other Buddhist traditions. As e-mail is available to all but the remotest areas, there is the opportunity to make contacts worldwide and develop outreach programs. The workshops are a practical benefit and some have developed into ongoing programs, for example in women's health care. The respect these nuns receive from the laity empowers them and serves to notify laity in countries which do not have a tradition of an order of fully ordained *bhikkhunīs*, such as Thailand, that such orders are possible and a benefit. The presence of Westerners should also not be underestimated as it tends to bring the attention of local officials.

The conferences tend to blend scholarly presentations with updates on the situation of nuns in various countries and practical workshops on health care, family relationships, and peace building. The volumes that have issued from these conferences have, of necessity, been in English and written by scholars or practitioners who are well educated. Each volume, however, contains articles that address the problems and achievements of Buddhist women from a wide variety of economic and social backgrounds, including the stories of non-literate women from remote areas.

Any organization that is international, multi-cultural, multi-ethnic, that cuts across class and economic lines and is run by volunteer labor is bound to have some tensions. The issues that confront Asian and Western women often differ. The conference in the United States was convened specifically to deal with the situation of Western Buddhist women. There has been some tension regarding the format of some of the conferences. Some feel they have been too Western and academically orientated rather than oriented towards Buddhist practice and teaching. Asian and Western women may also differ on protocol or on ways the issue of ordination should be approached. Translation can also be a problem when volunteers are unable to show up. And, of course, money is always a problem.

Regardless, Sakyadhītā has had a good deal of success. The conferences appear to have been a catalyst for change with nunneries and educational programs for both secular and monastic education being launched. Jamyang Choling, for example, was established by Sakyadhītā organizer Karma Lekshe Tsomo and has six educational programs for girls. There has also been progress on the ordination front. When Sakyadhītā held a conference in Colombo, Sri Lanka, they were told by government officials not to mention the ordination issue as it would raise "false hopes." Now, however, ordinations are being done in Sri Lanka (which has a nuns' training center) and the opposition to them is considerably less. So too in Thailand, where in 2003 the full ordination of one of Sakyadhītā's founders, Chatsumarn Kabilsingh (now Bhikkhunī Dhammanada), was greeted with far less hostility than her novice ordination in 2001. While the conferences are giving women's issues more prominence in Asia, the volumes produced are bringing knowledge of Buddhist women's issues to the West. The organization and its efforts have stimulated scholarly research and raised awareness and interest.

As Sakyadhītā has grown, the organization has tended to localize, with branches in England, Germany and Australia, for example. This allows for the consideration of local needs while the website and newsletter keep all informed of upcoming events and conferences. Sakyadhītā is an example of how much can be done with a small but dedicated group.

See also: **Tsomo, *Karma* Lekshe; Women in Buddhism: an historical and textual overview.**

MAVIS L. FENN

ŚAMATHA

Śamatha (Pāli *samatha*), or tranquility meditation, is meant to foster calm, serenity, and one-pointed concentration (*samādhi*) in which discursive thought is brought to a minimum or eliminated. Buddhist discussions of meditation often assert that the untrained mind is a jumble of fleeting thoughts, deluded ideas, and destructive emotions. Tranquility meditation is the first line of attack against this "monkey mind" and is generally considered a prerequisite for more advanced forms of meditation involving the cultivation of insight (*vipaśyanā*) into the nature of reality. The idea is that one must have a certain degree of calm and concentration of mind before consciousness can penetrate the true nature of things.

In tranquility meditation, attention is focused on one object to the exclusion of all others. The most common is the continual in-and-out flow of the breath. One form of this practice entails the silent counting of breaths, from one to ten, then back to one, focusing on the sensation of the air at the tip of the nostrils as it moves in and out. Gradually the meditator is able to keep the mind from wandering and maintain attention simply on the breath and nothing else, thereby attaining calm concentration (*Visuddhimagga* 7.190–5). In the *Sutta on Mindfulness of Breathing* (*Majjhima Nikāya* 1.55), the meditator is instructed to go to a quiet place, sit erect with legs crossed, and concentrate on the breath. He or she then concentrates on a variety of sensations, feelings, and thoughts, each connected to inhalation and exhalation. For example: "I breathe in contemplating impermanence; I breathe out contemplating impermanence"; "I breathe in experiencing the whole body; I breathe out experiencing the whole body"; "I breathe in concentrating the mind; I breathe out concentrating the mind" (*Majjhima Nikāya* 1.56ff.).

In the *Visuddhimagga* Buddhaghosa lists other devices to train the mind in calm concentration, such as meditation on various kinds of supports (*kasiṇas*) such as earth (in the form of a clay disc), blue (in the form of a basket of blue flowers), or light (a circle of light on a wall). The meditator gazes at these devices until he or she achieves a steady, concentrated mind and can maintain its image in the mind's eye. Although this is a calm and tranquil condition, it is also described as a condition of relaxed alertness, avoiding either strain or drowsiness. In the Pāli *suttas*, tranquility meditation leads directly to the states of profound concentration (Palī *jhānas*, Skt. *dhyānas*) in which the mind is completely absorbed in its object (and even, at the highest levels, absorbed in the absence of all objects). This concentrated state, in turn, leads to insight into the nature of things, particularly their impermanence (*anitya*), lack of permanent and substantial selfhood (*anātman*), and their tendency to cause suffering and dissatisfaction (*duḥkha*). Although the basic elements of tranquility meditation are laid out in the Pāli *suttas* and the *Visuddhimagga*, a number of Mahāyāna texts also explicate this practice. It is considered essential in Tibetan forms of meditation as well as in the Chan/Zen schools.

See also: **Meditation (Chan/Zen); Meditation, modern movements; Meditation, visualization; Meditation in the Pāli Canon and the Theravāda Tradition; Meditation in the *Visuddhimagga*; Meditational systems; *Nikāya* Buddhism; South and Southeast Asia, Buddhism in; *Vipaśyanā*.**

DAVID L. MCMAHAN

SAMMATĪYAS/ *PUDGALAVĀDINS*

The Sammatīya was one of the schools within the Vātsīputrīya division of the Sthaviravādins. A basic difficulty faces the student of Buddhism in taking the measure of the significance of the Sammatīyas historically. On the one hand, as a Vātsīputrīya school, the Sammatīyas held a doctrinal position that affirmed the existence of a person (Skt. *pudgala*) who endured across time, and thus they were reviled by other Buddhist communities as heretics and *pudgalavādins*. This encourages the historian to ignore the Sammatīyas on the grounds that they are unrepresentative of mainstream Buddhist thought. On the other hand, it seems likely that until the seventh century at least the Sammatīyas were numerically one of the most dominant Buddhist communities in India. They were also widespread geographically, stretching across northern India.

The Sammatīyas were especially dominant in the west of India and they were particularly associated with the great Buddhist university at Valabhī, which significantly was also associated with the Vijñānavāda school of the Mahāyāna. The Chinese pilgrim Yijing also reports that Sammatīya monks were found in Southeast Asia. This encourages the historian to examine the Sammatīyas as not only representative, but centrally visible in mainstream Buddhism in many geographical areas.

The meaning of the name of the Sammatīyas is unclear. Among the possible interpretations suggested are meanings that refer to "the group that lives harmoniously" or "the group that is to be respected." Some Buddhist sources, expecting another instance of the common pattern in *Nikāya* Buddhism where a group takes a name that is derivative from that of a founding monk, trace the Sammatīyas back to a monk named Sammata; nothing is known otherwise about him. The time of the Sammatīyas' emergence as a distinct group among the schools of the Vātsīputrīyas is equally unclear. Buddhist sources sometimes say they emerged about a century after the separation within the monastic order that defined the Vātsīputrīyas; this would make them appear in the second century BCE. Inscriptional evidence, however, only attests to their existence from the second century CE.

Some monastic practices of the Sammatīyas clearly set them apart from other Buddhist monastic communities. They are said to have cut their monastic robes in a distinctive way and they wore them in an equally distinctive style. They had their own *Vinaya* literature, a small portion of which survives in Chinese translation. For some Buddhist historians, what was especially important about the Sammatīya *Vinaya* was the language in which it was transmitted. This is sometimes said to be Paiśacī and sometimes Apabhramśa, two of the trans-local literary languages which developed in middle-period India as counterparts to Sanskrit as a language of cosmopolitan aspirations; if the Sammatīyas did use either Paiśacī or Apabhamśa as their authoritative language, then in this their choice of language to distinguish themselves as a distinct sect (*nikāya*) would have been like the choice of Pāli as a trans-local language of religious authority by the Theravādins in Sri Lanka and south India and the choice of Gandharī by the Dharmaguptakas in northwest India.

As already noted, however, it is neither their monastic practices nor their *Vinaya* literature that set the Sammatīyas apart from other Buddhist schools. It was their association with a particularly controversial understanding of the metaphysics of a person that seems to have been their defining feature for Buddhists of the past and for modern historians. This position was designated "The Doctrine of a Person" (Skt. *pudgalavādin*) and it was a mainstay of doctrinal discussions in the *Abhidharma* literatures of the various schools of *Nikāya* Buddhism. Typically these discussions, in texts like the *Kathāvatthu* of the Theravādins and the *Vijñānakāya* of the Sarvāstivādins, create standardized questions addressed to a *pudgalavādin* who is often identified as belonging to the Vātsīputrīyas or one of their subschools about whether a person exists, how such a person is known, whether a person is the same across lifetimes. Stock answers are then provided for the *pudgalavādin* and these are immediately refuted on the basis of their purported inconsistency with what is stated in Buddhist canonical texts and on the basis of logical inadequacies. It is important to keep in mind that the appearance of the Vātsīputrīyas and the Sammatīyas in scholastic digests of schools in *Nikāya* Buddhism was always as a representative of an essentialized and generalized position that inevitably was to be rejected. As the discussions in these digests are obviously tendentious, even while they appear relatively accurate to the modern historian, there should be a remaining uneasiness about the adequacy of their representations of the particular doctrinal positions of a school like the Sammatīyas.

The scholastic sources of the Sammatīyas and other Vātsīputrīya schools, unfortunately, are limited. Only one text of the Sammatīyas survives, the *Treatise of the Sammatīyas* (Skt. *Sammatīyaśāstra*), in a Chinese translation and it is the only surviving example of Vātsīputrīya literature. Not surprisingly, this text is concerned with the defense of the Sammatīya understanding of the metaphysics of a person as neither the same as nor different from the constituent elements (Skt. *skandha*) that make up a person.

This understanding of the metaphysics of a person does indeed seem to have been the key position of the Sammatīyas and of other Vātsīputrīya groups as well. The Sammatīya position seems to have been a middle position between Hindu concepts of an eternal self (Skt. *ātman*) and other Buddhist positions that allowed for nothing other than the five constituent elements of body, mental co-efficients, emotions, perceptions, and consciousness, in the metaphysics of the person. Other Buddhist schools interpreted statements of the Buddha in which reference to a "person" (*pudgala*) occurs as just using a figure of speech, but the Vātsīputrīyas understood these statements to refer to a real entity that did transmigrate uniquely from one life to the next. Just as what transmigrated was "neither the same nor different" across lifetimes, so the existence of a real person in the present, as defended by the Vātsīputrīyas and the Sammatīyas, was "neither the same nor different" with respect to the five metaphysical constituents of a person. They also held that this "person" could be known by consciousness, although it could not be described independently of the five metaphysical elements of a person.

See also: **Katyāyanīputra; *Nikāya* Buddhism; Sarvāstivāda; Sautrāntika; Vātsīputrīyas.**

CHARLES HALLISEY

SĀÑCĪ

The Buddhist monuments at Sāñcī in present-day Madhya Pradesh, India, which date from the third century BCE to the twelfth century CE, provide a unique overview of the history of Indian Buddhism. The hilltop complex, which includes the remains of *stūpas*, monasteries, and temples, is located about four miles from the ancient city of Vidiśā (Pāli Vedisa), a prosperous trade and mercantile center that dominated the region during the Śuṅga dynasty (second–first centuries BCE). Sāñcī's location, neither too far from a community of prosperous laity capable of supporting the *sangha*, nor too close to the sort of urban distractions that might disrupt the religious pursuits of the resident monks and nuns, exemplifies the ideal of separation with ready access that facilitated the interdependence of Indian Buddhist monastics and their lay supporters.

After many centuries of obscurity following the disappearance of Buddhism from the region in the thirteenth century, the site was first rediscovered in 1818 by a British officer who stumbled across it while camping nearby during a military operation. Once identified, the ruins were damaged greatly by treasure hunters and amateur excavators, until Alexander Cunningham and F.C. Maisey undertook somewhat more rigorous excavations in 1851. The present condition of most of the monuments, as well as much of our current knowledge of their history, dates back to John Marshall's extensive 1912–19 excavations.

The early core of the Śuṅga-era *stūpa* no. 1 (the "great *stūpa*") at Sāñcī is generally dated to the Aśokan era (270–230 BCE), and it thus represents one of the earliest surviving Buddhist relic monuments. An aerial view of the Sāñcī hilltop clearly reveals the dominant architectural presence of *stūpa* 1 in relation to the remains of the other structures. The *stūpa* structure visible to a viewer today dates mostly to the second-century BCE. During Marshall's excavation and repair of this *stūpa*, he noted that the third-century BCE Mauryan remains showed evidence of considerable destruction and thus could not be accurately measured; however, he estimated that its diameter was similar to that of the Mauryan *stūpa* at Sarnath, about 60 feet at the base. He conjectured that the Mauryan *stūpa*, in addition to the hemispherical dome, included a circular wooden balustrade marking a processional path around the base, a raised terrace probably also surrounded by a wooden balustrade, a structure of some sort surmounting the dome with one or more umbrellas raised above it, probably encircled by a wooden railing. Though an earlier excavation failed to discover any relics within the *stūpa*, Marshall was confident, based on the size and centrality of the structure in relation to the other *stūpas* at the site, that it originally contained relics of the Buddha.

The Śuṅga-era reconstruction of the great *stūpa*, probably undertaken toward the end of the second century BCE, brought the structure to its present dimensions, more than 120 feet in diameter and 54 feet high (not including the railings and umbrella). In this period, the elevated terrace with its surrounding stone balustrade and the two stone staircases which offered access to it for procession, the stone processional path at the base of the *stūpa*, and a stone *harmikā* enclosing a stone relic box were all added, with the whole structure surmounted by a third stone balustrade and stone umbrellas. The four stone gateways (*toraṇas*) marking the entrances to the processional pathway at the four cardinal directions date to the first centuries BCE–CE.

Stūpa no. 1 is only one of many *stūpas* that were constructed at the site. The remains of numerous smaller *stūpas* at Sāñcī were documented in the nineteenth century, though most of these were demolished during work conducted in the 1880s. A comparison of the great *stūpa* to the other extant relic monuments suggests how variations in physical size, proximity, and relative elevation were used to articulate degrees of status. *Stūpa* no. 3, which is located to the northeast of *stūpa* no. 1 and which also dates largely to the Śuṅga period, contained two relic chambers, each preserving a steatite reliquary engraved with the name of one of the Buddha's most venerable followers (Śāriputra and Mahāmaudgalyāna). The third large *stūpa* at the site, *stūpa* no. 2, is located on a terrace constructed upon the hillside more than 100 yards below the hilltop terrace where *stūpas* 1 and 3 are situated; it too dates to the Śuṅga period, and it was found to preserve four steatite reliquaries containing relics identified by inscriptions as those of ten enlightened elder monks from the Aśokan era. The gradations in size and elevation, from *stūpas* no. 1 to 3 to 2, manifest a hierarchy of relative worthiness. Their inscriptions also cast considerable light on the history of Sāñcī and other *stūpa* sites in the vicinity of Vidiśa, as they link the *stūpas* to a particular second-century BCE Buddhist monk of the Haimavata fraternity, Gotiputa, whose name appears on reliquary inscriptions at Sāñcī, Andher and Sonāri.

Sāñcī is known most commonly in the modern era for its spectacular bas-relief sculptures, in particular those found on the four gateways that surround *stūpa* 1. The so-called "aniconic" depictions of the Buddha found here and at other Buddhist sites have given rise to considerable controversy. The appeal of this imagery to a broad popular audience has also been noted, with its celebration of sensuous form, its depictions of legions of celestial beings, and its evocations of fertility and material abundance. Once again one can see the importance of hierarchy in the formal organization of the site and in the ritual behavior centered upon it. The art of Sāñcī portrays a world inhabited by diverse orders of beings, all of whom share a common condition of dependence upon the Buddha, the highest embodiment of Buddhist virtue. Those who approach the monuments see depicted a panorama of possible birth statuses, each individually articulated according to the principle of karmic effects, and at the same time joined together in the shared activity of venerating the Buddha, the one most deserving of their offerings, whose example and teaching offer them the means to end the cycle of rebirth altogether.

See also: **Ajaṇṭā and Ellora; Aśoka; Buddha, relics of; Disciples of the Buddha; Sacred places; *Stūpa*; *Stūpas* of Sāñcī, Bhārhut, and Amarāvatī; *Vihāra*.**

KEVIN TRAINOR

SANGHA

The *sangha* defined

Tradition generally acknowledges that Buddha spent forty-nine days in the vicinity of the *Bodhi* Tree following his experience of enlightenment. Eventually, he was persuaded to propagate the *Dharma* by a deity known as Brahmā Sahampati, and upon so doing, his first followers were two merchants who became lay disciples. Buddha moved on to Benares, where he preached his first sermon to five old ascetic friends who had previously wandered around with him for six years practicing austerities. As noted above, this initial sermon was followed by a second, and in short order the five ascetics attained *nirvāṇa*. The five ascetics requested both preliminary ordination into monkhood (called *pravrajyā*) and full ordination as well (called *upasaṃpadā*). Buddha accomplished this with a simple exhortation of "Come, O Monk!" (*ehi bhikṣu*). Thus the monastic order, or *sangha*, was born, and within a short period this monastic community expanded rapidly and enormously.

Despite the fact that the term *sangha* is used today in a more extended and comprehensive fashion than originally, referring to almost any community or group loosely associated with Buddhism, in the time of the Buddha the term was used in a radically different fashion. The Sanskrit word *sangha* simply connotes a society or company or a number of people living together for a certain purpose. In the midst of many religious *sanghas* in the general wanderers' (*parivrājaka*) community, the Buddha's followers appropriated the term in a rather distinct fashion, one that gave their fledgling community a clear and unique identity. While outsiders may have referred to the Buddha's first disciples as *Śākyaputrīya-śrāmaṇas* or "mendicants who follow the Buddha," the original community referred to itself as the *bhikṣu-sangha*, or "community of monks." Later, when the order of nuns was founded, they became known as the *bhikṣuṇī-sangha*, and the two units were collectively known as the *ubhayato-sangha*, the "twofold community." In Theravāda countries, this quite narrow usage of the term *sangha* has remained the predominant meaning of the word, as is pointed out by most modern scholars writing on the Buddhist community. Occasionally, in the early literature, the Buddha uses the term *cāturdisa-sangha* or the "*sangha* of the four quarters," but it seems clear from his usage that he still means the monastic *sangha* exclusively.

Monastic life

Initially, Buddha conferred all ordination himself. However, the dramatic growth of the *sangha* required certain adjustments to be made in the formal ordination procedure for monastics, and over time this became rather formalized. Monks were allowed to confer ordinations, and the entire process was preceded by a threefold recitation of the following formula:

I go to the Buddha for refuge,
I go to the *Dharma* for refuge,
I go to the *Sangha* for refuge.

The actual ordination procedure itself was also altered, not only dividing the initial and full ordination into separate activities, but also adding more extensive requisites to the process, such as shaving one's head, taking on yellow robes, and agreeing to follow special rules of training. Moreover, novice monks were assigned two teachers: an ordaining monk (*upadhyāya*) and a teacher (*ācārya*).

Both the monks' and nuns' communities were charged to wander continually teaching *Dharma*, settling down only during the rainy season when traveling about was simply not practical in India. Requisites for the monastic were kept to a minimum, generally including only their three robes, a begging bowl, razor, needle, girding for the robes, and a water strainer. Additionally, the monks and nuns were allowed to depend on four requisites known as the four *niśrayas*, consisting of begging for their food, using robes made from rag materials, dwelling at the foot of trees, and relying only on cow's urine for medicine.

Initially, the Buddha's plan for community life worked admirably. Monks and nuns settled down only during the rainy season or *varṣā* in one of two types of dwelling: (1) a self-constructed hut known as an *āvāsa*, or (2) a donated hut known as an *ārāma*. In each case, furniture and requisites were kept to a bare minimum, and the monastic dweller engaged in serious study and meditation for the roughly three-month period of rain retreat confinement. As might be anticipated, within a short time after Buddha's death, the rain retreat became institutionalized, expanding communal needs considerably, and the wandering ideal became largely a fiction in early Buddhism. Large monastic units developed, usually identified as *vihāras*, and often catalogued by their location as "the *Sangha* of Vaiśālī" or "the *Sangha* of Śrāvastī," and so forth. Obviously, the growth of these large monasteries necessitated changes within the physical structure of the monastic units themselves, and rather quickly additional buildings arose to meet the more detailed needs of the monastic dwellers. Moreover, officers from within each monastic unit needed to be appointed to handle the now extensive management and administrative needs of the institution. Although the movement toward settled, lasting monasteries contradicted Buddha's injunction regarding settled permanent dwelling, it did provide the opportunity for the development of Buddhism as a religious tradition. And it was this social institution that was exported by various rulers in the Buddhist missionary enterprise. In time, the monasteries that developed in diverse Buddhist cultures became formidable units, serving as festival and pilgrimage sites and commanding economic and political, as well as religious, respect.

Within the monasteries, life was defined by the twice-monthly *Poṣadha* ceremony. At first, the only business transacted by this ceremony was the recitation of the code for monastic conduct known as the *Prātimokṣa Sūtra* (see below). As the monastic units became more increasingly complex, however, the *Poṣadha* ceremony became the institutional methodology for transacting monastic business. Decisions were transacted that regulated all aspects of monastic life, from ordination to the duties of students and teachers to one another.

Much attention was also given to the routine of daily life within the monasteries. Clearly, the core activity of monastic life was the potential attainment of *nirvāṇa*. As such, the monks and nuns planned their daily routine so as to provide sufficient time for study of the *Dharma* and to engage in rigorous meditation. Despite their obligation to offer *Dharma* instruction and counsel to the members of the laity, much time for solitude was scheduled into their everyday activities.

Although the monastic vocation was by no means ascetic, in keeping with Buddha's insistence on a "middle path" between asceticism and luxury, it was certainly a serious step that *most* individuals were not capable of making. As such, Buddhist history records that the Buddha also admitted lay members – male disciples or *upāsakas* and female disciples known as *upāsikās* – into his community, and they eventually became a vital, symbiotic part of that community (see below). Nevertheless, the lay community was initially considered autonomous, and even distinct from, the monastic community.

The *Vinaya Piṭaka*

Buddhist scholar Michael Carrithers is quoted to have said, "No Buddhism without the *Sangha* and no *Sangha* without the Discipline." In other words, in order to effect the highest level of ethical conduct from the monastic and lay communities, disciplinary codes for each unit were enacted. For the monastic community, this took the form of a portion of the canon known as the *Vinaya Piṭaka*.

The *Vinaya Piṭaka* is the first portion of the Buddhist canon, generally rendered as the "Basket of Discipline." It consists of three parts. First, there is a compendium of rules (called the *Sūtravibhaṅga*) for the individual behavior of the monks and nuns. The formal canonical text is an extension of the brief monastic liturgy known as the *Prātimokṣā Sūtra*, a category-by-category inventory of offenses arranged in decreasing order of severity. It extends the text by offering a story or stories surrounding the promulgation of each specific rule, presents the rule itself, continues with a word-for-word commentary on the rule, and concludes with further stories identifying mitigating circumstances in which exceptions to the rule or deviations in punishment might be made. There are separate versions of this first portion for the monks and for the nuns. The second portion of the canonical text, known as the *Skandhaka*, deals with the collective rules for the smooth and proper running of the *sangha* as a religious institution. This section is divided into approximately twenty chapters, considering such topics as ordination, schisms, rainy season retreats, and the like. The formal canonical text is an extension of an earlier text known as the *Karmavācanā*, which deals with these matters in a democratic and liturgical, less inclusive manner. The third general section of the text includes appendices that consider matters best termed "miscellaneous." Virtually every major *Nikāya* Buddhist school preserved its own version of the *Vinaya Piṭaka*, manifesting a high general agreement regarding the basic content of the rules, but differing significantly in several areas, thus affording a glimpse as to how individual Buddhist schools changed in response to differing times and locations. We have the complete *Vinaya Piṭaka* for only one school in its original language: the Pāli Canon of the Theravāda school. A number of other schools present Sanskrit fragments and mostly complete translations into Chinese and/or Tibetan. A significant amount of "paracanonical" literature, or texts that preceded the actual, finalized canonical versions, has also been preserved in a variety of languages, as well as copious amounts of commentarial material. Much of the commentarial literature is enormously important for understanding the way in which the *Vinaya* tradition was applied in the various sectarian groups and the manner in which the rules of the tradition were shaped and altered by changing times, locations, and circumstances.

There are also a number of texts which outline moral practices for those pursuing the *bodhisattva* path of the Mahāyāna tradition. Just as the *Vinaya Piṭakas* of the various *Nikāya* Buddhist schools describe, in great detail, the regulations governing the proper and expected moral conduct of monks and nuns, as well as their method of application, so also practitioners of the Mahāyāna path are expected to maintain high ethical conduct. However, because Mahāyāna does not dictate an absolutely monastic way of life, a series of texts emerged that addressed ethical conduct more generally, without specific distinctions between the religious professional and lay disciple. These texts can collectively be referred to as the Mahāyāna *Vinaya*. The most well known of these texts include the *Bodhicaryāvatāra* and *Śikṣāsamuccaya* of Śāntideva, the *Brahmajāla* Bodhisattva *Śīla Sūtra*, and the Bodhisattva *Prātimokṣa Sūtra*. Additionally, portions of a variety of other texts address issues applicable to Mahāyāna practice. Taken together, they describe an ethical life that is the embodiment of wisdom (*prajñā*) compassion (*karuṇā*), and skill in means (*upāya*).

The laity

Although the basic model for the ideal Buddhist lifestyle was that of the monk or nun, or the committed *bodhisattva*, the majority of Buddhist membership has always been constituted by the faithful community of lay disciples, known as *upāsaka* (male) and *upāsikā* (female) respectively. Many Buddhist scholars have pointed out that the basis of Buddhist spiritual life is merit (*puṇya*). For the male and female lay disciples, this merit could be cultivated in two primary ways. First, they could practice wholesome acts which created the attainment of merit or "good *karma*." But additionally, they could establish the monastic *sangha* as a special "field of merit" (or *puṇya-kṣetra*). By providing acts of giving (*dāna*) and generosity to the entire monastic community, they enhanced their own spiritual growth while supporting the religious professionals of their faith. This "giving" usually consisted of providing offerings of food, clothing, goods, and the like to the monastic community and its members. In return for their support, the laity received the wise counsel and *Dharma* instruction from the monastic community. It is no surprise, then, that the rigor of disciplinary rules for the monastic community is easily explained in the context of understanding this symbiotic nature of the monastic–lay relationship. As the monastic vocation required a retreat from worldly life and an eremitic ideal, the individual monk or nun had to remain worthy of the highest respect in order to retain the support of the laity.

For the lay community, ethical conduct was governed by adherence to five vows, generally known as the *pañca-śīla*: (1) to abstain from taking life, (2) to abstain from taking that which is not given, (3) to abstain from sexual misconduct, (4) to abstain from false speech, and (5) to abstain from intoxicating substances. In some variants, this formula was expanded to eight and to ten precepts. The word *śīla* is often translated as "conduct or "virtue." Unlike the formal and externally enforced code embodied in the *Vinaya Piṭaka*, *śīla* appears to be a non-formal, internally enforced ethical guideline designed to assist in the development of proper human conduct. The majority of the guidelines that can be identified as *śīla* appear to come from outside the *Vinaya*, in a number of famous discourses, like the Pāli *Sigālovāda Sutta*, *Metta Sutta*, and *Maṅgala Sutta* which regulate ethical conduct within the various relationships that occur in normal social intercourse. While the major focus of the earliest Buddhist communities, in various Asian Buddhist cultures, was clearly monastic, we will see later in this book that Buddhism's globalization, and spread to Western cultures, yields a profound shift in emphasis from the monastic lifestyle as the normative, ideal pattern for Buddhists to a new and profound accent on the lay lifestyle as the more usual choice for modern Buddhists. As an outgrowth of this new modern emphasis on the lay lifestyle, creative ethical guidelines also began to appear, such as Thich Nhat Hanh's fourteen precepts formulated as part of his "Order of Interbeing," and reflecting an extensive expansion on the traditional *pañca-śīla*. Additionally, as noted above, with the rise of Mahāyāna, new texts appeared which defined *śīla* for *bodhisattvas*, emphasizing wisdom, compassion, and skill in means in application to everyday life.

Because the laity represents the majority of Buddhist practitioners, much attention is given in the literature to this aspect of *sangha* life. In many respects, Buddha's *sangha* was modeled upon the ideal and efficiently functioning family. In this regard, entry into the *sangha* is often marked by the phrases "son of a good family" (*kulaputra*) or "daughter of a good family" (*kuladuhitṛ*), in which case the "family" is none other than Buddha's spiritual family or *sangha*. Consequently, the various relationships within the family structure are very carefully defined within Buddhist scripture to reflect the profound respect required for proper social and familial relating. These concerns became especially important as Buddhism spread from India to other Asian countries. Additionally, in the modern world, this concern for proper family life among the laity has given rise to a spate of popular books and articles devoted to such issues as marriage, intimacy, death, raising children, divorce, and so forth. Especially important has been the concern for emphasizing the role of Buddhist festivals and holidays in the life of the lay *sanghas*.

The most important Buddhist holidays and festivals focus on the start of the Buddhist New Year in mid-April, offering an occasion for personal reflection; the holiday one month later known as *Vesākha Pūja*, celebrating Buddha's birthday, enlightenment, and death; the *Āsālha Pūja*, commemorating Buddha's renunciation and the preaching of the first sermon; the beginning of the rainy season retreat; and the *Pavāraṇā* ceremony marking the end of the rain retreat. Other ceremonies have been added by individual Buddhist sectarian traditions in the various Asian countries, often reflecting holidays that are distinct to Mahāyāna or Vajrayāna Buddhism, such as the Hungry Ghost Festival in China.

Important disciples in the early *Sangha*

During the time period immediately following Buddha's attainment of enlightenment, many disciples became an integral part of the early history of the Buddhist community. What follows is a brief mention of some of the most important disciples, classified under the headings of "Monks," "Lay disciples," and "Royal patrons."

Monks

Ānanda

Ānanda was Buddha's cousin and was converted to Buddhism during Buddha's visit to Kapilavastu. During the twentieth year of Buddha's ministry, he became Buddha's personal attendant, and remained so for the rest of Buddha's life. Most notable among his accomplishments were his recitation of all the *sūtras* at the first council after Buddha's death, and his role in helping to establish the order of nuns (*bhikṣuṇīs*) by coming to the aid of Mahāprajāpatī, who became the first nun.

Upāli

Belonging to a barber's family, Upāli also became a monk at Kapilavastu, eventually becoming a master of the *Vinaya*, which he recited in total at the first council.

Rāhula

Following his enlightenment, Buddha eventually returned to Kapilavastu to visit his family. At that time Buddha's former wife Yaśodharā sent their son Rāhula to receive his birthright. Instead, however, Buddha ordained the young boy (who was only seven years old at the time) as a novice (*śrāmaṇera*). Rāhula is known as the chief of the novices.

Śāriputra and Maudgalyāyana

Śāriputra was originally a follower of a wanderer named Sañjaya. One day he met a novice Buddhist monk named Aśvajit, who expounded to *Dharma* to him. Śāriputra immediately perceived the true meaning of the teaching and became an *arahant*. Śāriputra then recited the *Dharma* to his close friend Maudgalyāyana, who also immediately became enlightened. The two young men became monks, and established themselves as two of Buddha's closest and wisest disciples. Śāriputra is often associated with the *Abhidharma*, while Maudgalyāyana was known for his miraculous powers.

Mahākāśyapa

A very senior and highly disciplined monk, Mahākāśyapa was selected to head the first council, held at Rājagṛha in the first rainy season following Buddha's death. He is reputed to have selected the 500 monks who attended, and to have personally questioned Ānanda on the *Sūtras* and Upāli on the *Vinaya*.

Devadatta

Also related to the Buddha, Devadatta became a monk but, unlike Buddha's other followers, was a threat to the *sangha* by constantly, toward the end of Buddha's ministry, trying to usurp leadership of the community. After several unsuccessful attempts to murder Buddha, Devadatta founded his own order based on more austere religious practices. When his followers eventually left him to return to Buddha's *sangha*, he coughed up blood and died.

Lay disciples

Anāthapiṇḍika

He was a wealthy banker in Śrāvastī. After becoming a lay disciple, he built a monastery known as Jetavana, where Buddha spent the final twenty-five rainy seasons of his ministry.

Viśākhā

She was a banker's daughter. Born into a Buddhist family, she was eventually married into a family who followed a rival religious system. Although instructed by her father-in-law to support this new system and its followers, she rebelled, eventually bringing her father-in-law to Buddhism. She is known for having performed social services for the *sangha*, engaging in activities such as offering daily food for the monks, offering medicine to the sick, and providing robes for the monks.

Royal patrons

King Bimbisāra

Bimbisāra ruled Magadha from his chief city of Rājagṛha. Having become a disciple of Buddha after hearing a *Dharma* discourse, he built the very first monastery offered to the *sangha*: Veṇuvana Ārāma (literally "Bamboo Grove Park"). He was responsible for Buddha's adoption of the twice-monthly confessional meeting known as *poṣadha*. He was eventually caught in a court intrigue involving his son, Prince Ajātaśatru and the murderous Devadatta, and briefly imprisoned before regaining his freedom.

King Prasenajit

Unlike King Bimbisāra, Prasenajit, King of Kośala, did not give his unqualified support to the Buddha, although he did offer gifts to the *sangha*. Eventually, though, he became a Buddhist lay disciple and ardent patron of the religion.

Monastic life

During the early history of Buddhism, the *sangha* existed as simply another sect of the community of wanderers known as *parivrājakas*. One custom which seems to have been observed by all these sects was that of suspending the wandering life during the rainy season. The Buddhists used this temporary settling down as a means to cultivate living together in concord, establishing careful rules for the observance of the rainy season (*varṣā*), and thus differentiated themselves from the rest of the wanderers' community by establishing the rudiments of Buddhist monastic life.

Buddhist rainy season settlements were generally of two types: *āvāsas* or dwelling places which were determined, constructed, and kept up by the monks themselves, and *ārāmas* or parks which were donated and maintained by some wealthy patron. With the *āvāsas* and *ārāmas*, huts called *vihāras* were constructed for monks' residences. Later, when monastic dwellings became more fully developed, the term *vihāra* came to designate the whole monastery. In these residences, monks' accommodations were of the simplest kind. Most monasteries were built on the outskirts of towns and villages, so their close proximity to the town made alms procurement easy but provided enough isolation for the monks to pursue their meditative vocation undisturbed by the hustle and bustle of city life.

Figure 35 Senior monks of the Chogye Order at Chogyesa, Seoul, Korea.

The three months of enforced communal living quickly made a profound impact on the Buddhist *sangha*. Various institutions within the *sangha* began to emerge to mold the *sangha* into a cohesive body. The recitation of the code of monastic law (*Prātimokṣa*) was adopted on a twice-monthly basis. The preparation and distribution of robes (*kaṭhina*) took on collective features, eventually becoming a distinct ceremony, as did the "Invitation" or *Pravāraṇā* held at the end of the rainy season residence and dealing with purity during the rainy season. Initial and full ordination procedures (*pravrajyā* and *upasaṃpadā*, respectively) were administered by the *sangha* rather than by individual monks.

The monastery as a unit, however, was by definition a self-limiting institution at the outset. At the end of each rainy season the monks were to abandon the settlement and begin wandering once again. Nevertheless, monks did tend to return to the same monastic residence year after year. Eventually, blending motivations of self-preservation and usefulness to their lay communities, monks ceased to wander at all. Thus individual *sanghas* grew up, such as the *sangha* of Śrāvastī. Gradually, as the wandering life became a fiction, the Buddhists established themselves as a distinct group, bound by the teaching and discipline of the Buddha and committed to their own attainment of *nirvāṇa*, as well as the spiritual uplift of the laity; but with the rise of distinct *sanghas*, the maintenance of commonality became acute. As each *sangha* became increasingly more individualized and removed geographically from other *sanghas*, the first seed of sectarianism was sown (See Figure 35).

Geographic dispersal of the *sangha*

During Buddha's lifetime, his religion and *sangha* did not spread far. Most of his preaching was conducted in and around the great regions of Magadha and Kośala. Within Magadha three places seem to be most noteworthy. First was the capital city of the region: Rājagṛha. Here Bimbisāra's patronage resulted in the first gift of an *ārāma* to the *sangha*. Also in Magadha, Pāṭaliputra was later to become the stronghold capital of perhaps the greatest king of Indian history, Aśoka. Besides these two cities, on the outskirts of Rājagṛha was Nālandā, later to become the seat of one of the most important early Buddhist universities. Magadha also marks the birthplace of the religion, as it was in Bodhgayā that Buddha's enlightenment was attained. In Buddha's early wanderings, he gained his largest group of followers in Magadha. Kośala, ruled by Prasenajit, was most important for its capital of Śrāvastī, where Buddha received his two early patrons Anāthapiṇḍika and Viśākhā, and where he spent the last twenty-five rainy seasons of his ministry. Within the kingdom of Kośala was Kapilavastu, Buddha's home.

To the east of Kośala and north of Magadha were several other kingdoms which, although being strongholds of the Brāhmaṇical tradition, felt Buddha's impact: the Licchavis, the Videhas, and the Koliyas, to name a few. Also to the east was the region of Aṅga, mentioned occasionally in the early texts, as is the city of Kauśāmbī. The west and north seem to have been much less frequented by the early Buddhists. Consequently, we can see from the above that during its earliest history, the Buddhist *sangha* spread within some rather closely defined limits.

The wide dispersal of Buddhism, both within India and outside its borders, belongs to a period at least several hundred years after Buddha's death.

Other issues

In addition to the items mentioned above, a number of other factors impacted on the growth and development of *sangha* life. The first, and most obvious, of these is sectarianism. Current research suggests that the beginning of Buddhist sectarianism in India developed within a very short time after the second Buddhist council held at Vaiśālī, reputed to have taken place 100 years after Buddha's death. The initial schism in Buddhism separated the previously unified "*sangha* of the four quarters" into two groups: the Mahāsāṃghikas and Sthaviras. Within a short time, and certainly less than a generation, these two trunk groups began to subdivide internally, resulting in the growth of several dozen distinct Buddhist sectarian *sanghas* within two centuries. Each of these *sanghas* created their own version of the *Vinaya Piṭaka* and developed their own distinct lay and monastic lifestyle. The problem of sectarianism was further exacerbated by the development of Mahāyāna, and then Vajrayāna Buddhism, each of which subsequently subdivided internally. Thus, as Buddhism moved throughout South, Southeast, Central, and East Asia, an enormous variety of quite distinct Buddhist sectarian *sanghas* developed, radically altering the Buddhist landscape, and turning the study of the overall Buddhist *sangha* into a profoundly multifaceted, highly variegated pursuit. In some case, the widely divergent Buddhist *sanghas* have experienced significant difficulty in communicating with one another across sectarian boundaries. Some attempts have been made to create Buddhist ecumenical organizations, such as the European Buddhist Union, but to some degree these have been neither efficient nor effective in addressing issues of interests to all Buddhist communities worldwide.

Not the least of the issues impacting the development of the Buddhist *sangha* was the role of women, both as nuns and lay members, as Buddhism spread throughout Asia and the world. Stories surrounding the creation of the order of nuns abound in the early Buddhist tradition, and although the *bhikṣuṇī-sangha* survived for many centuries in Theravāda countries, it eventually died out, and has only been reinstituted in recent times. The order, however, did not die out in China, and there remains a significant order of nuns and a proper nuns' ordination platform in China today. Additionally, in the midst of changing gender roles in modern culture, many Western women have become Buddhist nuns in the various traditions, but especially so in Vajrayāna. In the Zen tradition, too, an increasing number of women have begun to ordain as priests, and become lineage holders in the various Zen sects. Some writers have suggested that Buddhism is becoming "post-patriarchal" as it develops in global Buddhism.

In addition to the increased role of women in Buddhist *sanghas* throughout the world, Buddhism's increasing globalization has highlighted two other important features which are impacting the development of the Buddhist *sangha*. First, there is an increasing development of urban Buddhist *sanghas*. Unlike the ancient world, in which most Buddhist *sanghas* were essentially rural communities, the modern world is witnessing the rapid growth of urban Buddhist *sanghas*, appealing to a more highly educated, increasingly professional community of city dwellers. This development has brought some degree of conflict within Buddhist sectarian communities as rural members and urban members strive to communicate with, and understand, each other's needs and requirements. This problem is further compounded by the second development with Buddhist *sangha* life: the astronomical growth of Western Buddhist communities. During the past two centuries, Buddhism has spread aggressively throughout North America, Europe, and Australia/New Zealand. It has also spread, but to a lesser degree, in South America and Africa. North America, for example, boasts approximately 2,000 Buddhist communities, with a total population of roughly six million members. Many of these members – likely 20 percent – are "convert" Buddhists, and the majority of them have very different goals than had been previously understood in traditional ethnic communities.

The above issues underscore the general concern for "modernization" within all Buddhist communities. Buddhists worldwide are becoming increasingly concerned with the well-being of their individual *sanghas* and the overall health of the entire Buddhist community worldwide. At the core of such a concern is a consideration of such topics as *Vinaya* modernization, reinterpretation of the various general Buddhist ethical emphases in light of dynamic new issues in bioethics, matters of human rights and "just war" philosophies in the face of worldwide terrorism, the utilization of expanding modes of technology, and so forth. These issues span the entire landscape of the Buddhist tradition, involving monastic, textual, ritual, social, and pragmatic concerns. Buddhist *sanghas* across the face of the globe, and from within each of the various sectarian traditions, have attempted to seriously address these issues, keenly aware of the truth of the law of impermanence: that just as Buddhist *sanghas* have grown and prospered in various cultures, they may also wither and die without intra-Buddhist and inter-Buddhist communication and cooperation.

See also: **Monastic dwellings; Precepts, lay; Rituals and practices; Three Refuges and Going for Refuge; *Vihāra*; *Vinaya Piṭaka*.**

CHARLES S. PREBISH

SANGHA GENDER ISSUES

Stories about Buddha's reluctance to begin an order of nuns are legion in the scholarly Buddhist literature devoted to the development of the early *sangha*. Articles and books about the contribution of Buddhist nuns, or *bhikṣuṇīs*, to the growth of the Buddhist tradition are not. Until the publication of I.B. Horner's *Women under Primitive Buddhism: Laywomen and Almswomen* in 1930, not much had been written about women in Buddhism. More recently, there has been a small but continually growing corpus of scholarly literature on women in Buddhism.

In a paper entitled "The Future of American Buddhism," Rick Fields noted that two specific tendencies have emerged from a feminist critique of traditionally male forms of Buddhism: first, a tendency to "critique forms of practice from the vantage point of a 'woman's spirituality'"; second, a strong movement to recover the full *bhikṣuṇī* lineage, and correspondingly to have Western nuns play a leading role in teaching Westerners. This is especially significant because, in the Tibetan tradition, the nuns' ordination was never introduced from India, and in the Theravādin tradition, the nuns' lineage died out no later than the thirteenth century. While there is currently an increase in the number of Theravādin nuns in Asia, the chief locations from which to receive the full nun's ordination remain Taiwan and Korea, which have preserved the ordination lineages intact, and a first nuns' ordination in the United States was held in 1988. Although the monastic tradition represents only a tiny portion of Buddhist communities, many Buddhist women see the role of nuns as instrumental in cultivating gender equality in Buddhism.

The degree to which male Buddhist practitioners and teachers welcome women into the Buddhist community remains the challenge of changing gender roles in Buddhism. It is an important challenge because the changing of gender roles in Buddhism and the elevation of females to positions of prominence in their respective communities seem to be coincident with the emergence of a number of outstanding and influential female teachers in the various traditions, some of whom are lineage holders or *rōshis*. Moreover, almost all of these female teachers are now, or have been, monastics.

The growing community of female teachers is significant in that it bridges the gap between the small *sanghas* of monastic members and the overwhelmingly larger number of female lay practitioners in Buddhism. Few would contest the necessity of spiritual authority in Buddhism; nor would most Buddhists challenge the necessity of a top-down rather than bottom-up orientation for the successful recognition of leadership figures. The changing of gender roles in Buddhism, however, requires that women achieve spiritual authority and discharge the proper duties associated with its attainment. As Rita Gross indicates, "Thus, there is no question that Buddhism cannot become post-patriarchal until women wield authority in Buddhism – however that comes to be defined and structured eventually." In so doing, a Buddhism that is more open to women's needs, more receptive to women's spiritual leadership, and less dependent on formerly hierarchical, male-dominated Buddhist social institutions may well develop in this century.

See also: ***Sangha.***

CHARLES S. PREBISH

SANGHA MODERNIZATION

Introduction

In the "Introduction" to *Buddhism in the Modern World* (edited by Steven Heine and Charles Prebish), the editors note, "As with other major world religions, the history of Buddhism has been long characterized by an ongoing tension between attempts to preserve traditional ideals and modes of practice and the need to adapt to changing social and cultural conditions." They go on to remark that, "At the same time, these monastic, textual, ritual, or social conditions have been inalterably affected by continuing encounters with modernization." And finally: "The cultural forces include the inseparability and intertwining of industrialization with Westernization, that is, the identity on many levels of becoming modernized with the importing of values and modes of behavior from the West." In the light of the above, a number of critical issues in *sangha* modernization are considered below.

Modernizing the *Vinaya*

If the defining element of the Buddhist tradition's establishment in any country is, as maintained by scripture, the foundation of a monastic community in that country, then the modernization of the monastic *sangha* and the *Vinaya Piṭaka* that governs it is critical for the ongoing history and development of the Buddhism as a religion. As the *Vinaya* itself notes and Mohan Wijayaratna cites in his book *Buddhist Monastic Life*, the rules of discipline for the monastic community have ten intentions:

1. Protecting the community
2. Insuring the community's comfort
3. Warding off ill-meaning people
4. Helping well-behaved monks and nuns
5. Destroying present defilements
6. Preventing future defilements
7. Benefiting non-followers
8. Increasing the number of followers
9. Establishing the discipline
10. Observing the rules of restraint.

How these intentions, and the specific rules of the *Vinaya*, are applied to modern Buddhist communities in Asia and the West is no simple matter, as times and circumstances have changed enormously since the *Vinaya Piṭaka* was codified in the first centuries following Buddha's demise.

Tradition surrounding the first Buddhist council records that, despite reproving Ānanda for not ascertaining *which* rules the Buddha considered lesser and minor, and therefore subject to exclusion from the codified *Vinaya*, the council's participants were nevertheless faced with an obviously difficult decision on this matter, prompting Mahākāśyapa, as president of the council, to put forth a motion – unanimously accepted by the *sangha* – that rules would be neither added to nor deleted from those recited by Upāli, the master of the *Vinaya*. It did not take long for the *sangha* to face the grim reality that the decision made at the first council was profoundly impractical. Eventually, and necessarily, monks discovered ways to overcome this difficulty by reinterpreting the law in a non-compromising fashion. These decisions were eventually collected in a book titled *Pālimuttaka-vinayavinicchaya*, written by the thirteenth-century Sri Lankan monk Sāriputta Thera. Despite the fact that *pālimuttaka-vinicchaya* resolutions, or "decisions standing outside the canonical texts," could only be arrived at by a consensual agreement of the monks (called *katikāvata*), Paul Numrich describes the process as a "paradoxical hermeneutic." Unfortunately, Numrich also notes that the *katikāvata* hermeneutical principle has not been utilized in Theravāda countries since the thirteenth or fourteenth century, and is only now being discussed in Western Theravāda communities. Truly effective *sangha* modernization would seem to require utilization of this device to produce a new *Vinaya* for modern conditions.

Changing patterns of authority

Studies of the Buddhist monastic tradition in various Asian countries reveal the importance of the monastic community for the surrounding community and the degree to which its monks and nuns were venerated for their effort and, often, their education. In other words, the ideal lifestyle for Buddhist practitioners was that of the monastic. In the modern world that is becoming less and less the norm. As such, *sangha* modernization apparently needs to recognize more effectively a genuine interpenetration of the lay and monastic lifestyles. Included in that realization is a more effective recognition of the importance of changing gender roles throughout Buddhism, resulting in the development of a truly post-patriarchal Buddhism. Along with developing changing gender roles, modernizing Buddhist *sanghas* will necessarily need to confront a growing membership who practice various alternative lifestyles, including the acknowledgement of a large homosexual membership.

Social issues

Although many people perceive Buddhism and Buddhists to be world-rejecting and passive, choosing isolation in preference to social action, there is little support for such a position, and especially so in the modern world. Thus, *sangha* modernization involves a genuine concern for what has been identified as "socially engaged Buddhism." Largely owing to the work of Thich Nhat Hanh and his development of the Tiep Hien Order, new concerns for activism in Buddhist *sanghas* are readily apparent. These concerns involve such activities as supporting the peace movement, developing prison reforms and prison *sanghas*, hospice work, voter mobilization, and a host of other society-oriented activities.

Because the modern Buddhist tradition has become so diverse, *sangha* modernization also requires an important role for Buddhist ecumenicism. This does not suggest that Buddhists should eschew their traditional sectarian affiliations, but rather that Buddhists learn to speak to each other across these sectarian affiliations, and for the promotion of the *entire* tradition. Some organizations, such as the European Buddhist Union and the American Buddhist Congress, have begun to make inroads in this direction.

The role of technology

Because so much progress has been made in information exchange technology, *sangha* modernization will profit from a careful utilization of its fruits. Apart from simply facilitating better communication via e-mail, Buddhist *sanghas* are posting Buddhist scriptures on the World Wide Web, and creating informational sources for Buddhists of all sects to digest. Additionally, *sanghas* are better able to advise community members of *sangha* activities and to facilitate institutional identity more effectively than before these advances appeared.

Looking forward

Buddhist leaders throughout the various traditions have begun to write about ways of constructing a truly global Buddhism – one that respects the individual traditions of each Buddhist culture, but recognizes the necessity for implementing the realizations that spill forth from the Buddhist notion of *anitya*, impermanence, and the need to continually and dynamically keep the tradition meaningful in the modern world.

See also: **Sangha.**

CHARLES S. PREBISH

SANGHAS, SECTARIAN

The Indian Buddhist tradition reveals that within two centuries of Buddha's death, there were literally dozens of sectarian *sanghas*, each reflecting differing monastic and doctrinal inclinations of the group in question. Until quite recently, though, there was little agreement on when the sectarian movement began in Indian Buddhism, or what precipitated the initial schism in the so-called "*sangha* of the four quarters." The initial theory suggested that disciplinary laxity on the part of the future Mahāsāṃghikas, coupled with the notorious five theses about the nature of the *arhant* propounded by the monk Mahādeva, brought about the schism. More recently, a newer theory has rather conclusively established quite the opposite position: that the future Mahāsāṃghikas were actually disciplinary conservatives who reacted negatively to proposed *Vinaya* expansion on the part of the future Sthaviras, and that the notion of *Vinaya* expansion was the *sole* basis of the schism (that is, doctrinal concerns played no role in the split). In either, once begun, many *Nikāya* Buddhist schools developed in the next centuries, and while only one of these early schools remains today – the Theravāda – all of the schools contributed significantly to the Buddhist schools that populate the scene today. It was the Theravāda tradition, however, which was exported to South and Southeast Asia, and which almost exclusively represents the Buddhist tradition there today in Sri Lanka, Laos, Cambodia, Thailand, Burma, and portions of Vietnam.

Beginning around 200 BCE, the Mahāyāna movement began, presumably as a reaction against the highly ecclesiastic, somewhat pedantic, and self-motivated Buddhism of the time, and this new movement attempted to re-emphasize Buddhism as a liberating vehicle for the masses of Buddhist practitioners. Apart from its profound and important development in India, Mahāyāna was exported to East Asia, forming *sanghas* in China, Korea, Japan, and Vietnam. Like earlier Buddhism, Mahāyāna also became highly sectarian, establishing Ch'an/Zen/Sŏn and Pure Land *sanghas*, as well as new varieties of Buddhism, such as the Nichiren school of Buddhism in Japan, and a continuation of Indian esoteric Buddhism.

With the development of Vajrayāna Buddhism in the early centuries of the Common Era, still further Buddhist *sanghas* were created as this aspect of the Buddhist tradition spread in India, and throughout Central Asia and Tibet. As such, within a few centuries, *sanghas* with affiliations to the Nyingma, Kagyu, Sakya, and Gelug traditions of Vajrayāna Buddhism were established.

With the onset of Buddhism's globalization over the past two centuries, many of these sectarian *sanghas* from the Buddhist cultures of Asia have begun to appear in Western countries. In some cases, the *sanghas* and traditions, such as the various Zen sectarian lineages and the schools of Tibetan Buddhism, have been "imported" by Western countries. In other cases, *sanghas* and traditions, such as that of Sōka Gakkai from Japan or the Fo Kuang Shan of Taiwan, have been ostensibly "exported" to other cultures. And in yet other instances, sectarian *sanghas* emerged around immigrant communities who brought their tradition with them to the new land. Now it is quite ordinary to find Buddhist *sanghas* from all Buddhist traditions in the same city, and sometimes even in the same neighborhood, making a revolutionary shift in the nature of sectarian *sanghas* from ancient to modern times.

See also: **Sangha.**

CHARLES S. PREBISH

SANGHAS, URBAN AND RURAL

In ancient India, as the wandering eremitical life of the Buddhist monks and nuns gradually transformed itself into a life largely maintained in permanent, settled *vihāras*, it nevertheless remained the case that these permanent monasteries were almost exclusively found in rural areas. The primary reason for this almost self-imposed seclusion was pragmatic. The initial rainy season dwellings known as *āvāsas* and *ārāmas* that housed the monastic wanderers, and which were eventually transformed into *vihāras*, were built just close enough to villages to make alms-gathering both possible and accessible, while affording the monastic community with sufficient solitude to engage their yearly three-month period of meditation and study without being confronted by the hustle and bustle of city life.

As the temporary monastic dwellings became permanent, it was almost inevitable that Buddhist communities or *sanghas*, both monastic and lay, would develop in urban as well as rural settings. This growing urbanization encouraged a wider population base for Buddhist communities, and created a more substantial economic foundation from which to support the general Buddhist activities of each individual *sangha*. While rural Buddhist communities remain the normative model for most Asian countries in which Buddhism thrives, it is nonetheless clear that in major cities, there is an increasing growth of Buddhist *sanghas*, and this urban expansion creates an entirely new and challenging set of problems associated with Buddhist outreach activities. As Buddhism has moved into Western countries, *sangha* creation and growth has manifested the converse circumstance. Rather than finding the majority of Buddhist communities in rural settings, Western Buddhism has become an almost exclusively urban phenomenon.

In Western countries, until quite recently, Buddhists who lived in rural areas had virtually no nearby *sanghas* to join. Instead, they joined city-based communities, and visited their home center when they could. One Western Buddhist noted, "'There's nothing lonelier than a Buddhist in Alabama' is the kind of comment I hear from many Buddhists who live in the outlying regions of North America where their *sangha* is small or nonexistent and information about Buddhist practice and philosophy is scarce." Fortunately, the advance of computer technology has closed the information gap for these *sangha* members by providing online access to the parent community in the city. There are even Buddhist "cyber*sanghas*," which have no real existence in real, geographic space.

City *sanghas*, which have become the norm in Western countries, provide more obvious access to Buddhist resources, and additionally, more lines of communication with city-dwelling practitioners of other traditions. Noted theologian Harvey Cox has argued that city dwellers of one tradition often communicate more effectively with city-dwelling practitioners of other religions than with members of their own faith who live, physically and spiritually, in the countryside. Problems such as how to creatively manage the *Vinaya* regulations for monastic *sangha* members, and how to follow the precepts inherent in the *pañcā-śīla* amidst the obvious temptations of city life, complicate the issue for city *sanghas*, but they remain a vital complement to rural *sanghas*. In any case, modern Buddhist *sanghas* have now become an exciting, vital mix of rural and urban communities.

See also: ***Sangha.***

Charles S. Prebish

SANGHAS, WESTERN

The original Buddhist community referred to itself as the *bhikṣu-sangha*, or community of mendicants who followed the Buddha. Later, when the order of nuns was founded, they became known as the *bhikṣuṇī-sangha*, and the two units were collectively known as the *ubhayato-sangha* or "twofold community." Eventually, as laymen and laywomen joined these two groups, the *sangha* became fourfold, and was sometimes referred to as the "*sangha* of the four quarters." At that time, it was also simple to determine who belonged to this collective *sangha*. Lay Buddhists "took refuge" in the Buddha, *Dharma*, and *sangha*, and agreed to follow the five vows of the laity (*pañca-śīla*), while monastic members added five additional vows and agreed to follow the precepts included in the *Vinaya*.

At the heart of identifying and characterizing Western *sanghas* and their membership is the issue of determining just who is a Buddhist today, and what determines the requisites for membership in individual *sanghas*. Is taking refuge and following the five vows of the laity sufficient for establishing Buddhist identity? Is attendance at religious observances and ritual functions necessary? Must one be a financial contributor? Is personal meditational practice required? Are the requirements different for Asian immigrant Buddhists than for American convert Buddhists? It's a truly murky issue. The problem is further exacerbated by the fact that Westerners tend to be, in Jan Nattier's terms, "notorious non-joiners." Indeed, one researcher even considers such colorful and creative terms as "nightstand Buddhists" and "sympathizer." The current consensus is that the safest, and most reasonable approach to defining membership in Western Buddhist *sanghas* is to accept the method known as "self-identification," or to acknowledge that a person who says he or she is a Buddhist is a Buddhist.

In this environment, Western *sanghas* tend to be of three kinds: monastic communities, lay communities, and "in between" communities in which the members live the full Buddhist life of a monastic while maintaining families and outside employment. Lay communities frequently house one or more monastic members, and monastic communities often have accommodations for lay members.

Some Western *sanghas* are established as very formal – irrespective of whether they are primarily monastic or lay communities – while others are very informal. Formal communities may even build communities on land acquired by the *sangha*, such as Hsi-Lai Temple in California, while less formal communities may establish impromptu *zendōs* in people's homes. Any of these communities may be located in cities, suburbs, or even rural areas.

The specific nature of each Western *sangha* is generally determined by the sectarian affiliation of the group and the nature of its membership. Asian immigrant *sanghas* tend to establish temples in ethnic neighborhoods, and the temple itself becomes the place of personal, and community identification. While the temple is the location of formal religious practices, it also establishes the social as well as religious identity of the group. American convert communities tend to be less a locale for social and community affairs than as an explicitly religious center for various practices, but mostly focused on meditation. As such, Western *sanghas* are multifaceted, multifunction, dynamic institutions that reflect the changing face of modern globalized Buddhism.

See also: **Buddhist adaptations in the West; *Sangha*.**

CHARLES S. PREBISH

ŚĀNTIDEVA

Among the most important treatises written in India on the practices developed to help a person cultivate the virtues of the *bodhisattva* was *Bodhicaryāvatāra* by Śāntideva, who is traditionally said to have been born a prince of Surāṣṭra in the early eighth century CE and to have renounced his kingdom in favor of the religious life.

The *Bodhicaryāvatāra* begins with a discussion of all the advantages of cultivating the desire to become awakened so that one can dedicate oneself to liberating other sentient beings from their turmoil. The arising of this desire, known as *bodhicitta*, is the beginning of a *bodhisattva*'s career. Śāntideva describes it as occurring in two stages. First, *bodhicitta* occurs as a resolve, and after considerable work it manifests as an accomplished fact. Cultivating it is facilitated by acts of worship and veneration of the buddhas and *bodhisattvas*, and by acknowledgment of one's shortcomings and the resolve not to repeat unskillful ways of thinking and acting that have led to one's own suffering and the suffering of others in the past. After reinforcing one's resolve through these acts of worship and contrition, the follower of the *bodhisattva* path should work on focusing the mind so as to avoid distractions from the task of becoming awakened and on cultivating mindfulness: that is, a constant recollection of one's purpose. Various obstacles may arise in this process, so Śāntideva devotes chapters to discussing the damaging consequences of anger and to offering strategies for overcoming anger through the cultivation of patience. Chapters on the perfection of zeal (*vīrya*) and concentration (*dhyāna*) lead up to a long chapter on the perfection of wisdom (*prajñāpāramitā*), in which Śāntideva provides a textbook on the sort of Madhyamaka analysis that results in the elimination of all attachments to views and dogmas, such detachment being necessary to enable the *bodhisattva* to deal convincingly with all beings, regardless of their persuasions. The final chapter of this work is a discussion of how the *bodhisattva* then dedicates all the merits of his or her work to the well-being of all sentient beings everywhere, regardless of their situations or their level of merit. So long as any being anywhere in the incalculable reaches of infinite space is in need, says Śāntideva, then he will remain in this world to serve them as selflessly as the elements sustain the material world. This remarkable text serves as an inspirational poem, a guide to worship and meditation and a sophisticated philosophical treatise, all rolled into a single work that has the added attraction of being written in uncommonly beautiful poetic form. Few works in the history of Indian Buddhism come close to its versatility in theoretical and practical matters and to its aesthetic beauty. It is accompanied by a second work called *Śikṣāsamuccaya*, which contains copious quotations from Mahāyāna *sūtras* meant to inspire the practitioner in all the aspects of Buddhist practice, all arranged and commented upon by Śāntideva.

See also: **India, Buddhism in; Mahāyāna Buddhism.**

RICHARD P. HAYES

ŚĀNTIRAKṢITA

One of the most influential thinkers of the last phase of Indian Buddhism, Śāntirakṣita flourished in the middle to late eighth century CE. Traditional accounts of his life report that he was born in what is now Bengal into a royal family. He had a long and distinguished career as a scholar and teacher in various monasteries in northern India before going to Nepal and then to Tibet. He seems to have reached Tibet in 766 CE and to have died there in or around 788. While in Tibet he served as abbot of Bsam-yas monastery, which was the main monastery in Tibet in his day. His disciple Kamalaśīla continued his work in Tibet and helped to establish the Indian approach to Buddhism in Tibet and to mute the influence of Chinese Buddhism, and especially Chan, there.

One of Śāntirakṣita's most important works is a collection of verses called *Tattvasaṃgraha*, which is still extant in the original Sanskrit along with its prose commentary by Kamalaśīla. This important treatise begins with critiques of non-Buddhist schools that posited that the entire world of multiplicity ultimately derives from a single source. In this connection, he presents and refutes the Sāṃkhya claim that the world of multiplicity is an evolution out of a primordial matter known as *pradhāna* or *prakṛti*. He then presents and criticizes the view advanced by the Nyāya school that the world is a creation of God. Having dismissed the claims that the world comes out of some single source, he then criticizes the view that the world is somehow independent and self-arising. His treatise then turns to a discussion of various views of the self (*ātman*) advanced by the Sāṃkhya, Nyāya and Vedānta schools; he also presents a criticism of the Vātsiputrīya Buddhists who smuggled an *ātman* into Buddhist theory by positing an ineffable person (*pudgala*) that is said to be neither identical to nor different from the phenomena of personal experience. The treatise then deals extensively with epistemology, logic, and theory of language.

In his work called *Madhyamakālaṃkāra* Śāntirakṣita argues that the mind only (*cittamātra*) doctrine of the Yogācāra school serves as a useful bridge between naïve realism and the Madhyamaka view that all beings are empty of their own nature. The Yogācāra view helps one to see that all apparent objects are but appearances in the mind. Then the application of logic (*yukti*) enables one to see that mind, like all other things, has no nature of its own. He argues that mind has neither a simple nature nor a complex nature. As there is no kind of nature other than simple or complex, mind must therefore have no nature at all. He applies this same strategy to everything he analyses and thus shows that all supposed beings, whether conditioned like *dharmas* or unconditioned like *nirvāṇa*, have neither simple nor complex natures and thus are entirely empty of their own natures (*svabhāvaśūnya*). This synthesis of Madhyamaka and Yogācāra philosophies became the foundation of much of later Tibetan Buddhism.

See also: **India, Buddhism in; Madhyamaka school; Mahāyāna Buddhism; Yogācāra school.**

RICHARD P. HAYES

SĀRNĀTH

Sārnāth is the modern name of the place where Gautama Buddha is traditionally believed to have first taught the *Dharma*, an event often described as "setting in motion the wheel of the *Dharma*" (*dharma-cakra-pravartana*). Early Buddhist texts refer to this place as Mṛgadāva, the "Deer Park," and Ṛṣipatana, "Sages' Alighting Place." It is located a few miles north of Vārāṇasī (Benares) in Uttar Pradesh. According to Pāli commentarial tradition, this, like the place of the Buddha's awakening, is one of the "unchanging spots"; all Buddhas begin their teaching at this location. Traditional accounts describe how the Buddha initially hesitated to teach because of the futility of communicating what he had realized to beings mired in ignorance and craving, but the god Brahmā Sahampati interceded and convinced him that there were beings who could profit from his instruction. He set off to meet the group of five ascetics with whom he had earlier practiced austerities before abandoning the path of extreme asceticism and found them in the Ṛṣipatana deer park. As they saw him coming, they agreed among themselves that they would not stand to honor him because they believed he had abandoned the religious life, but his presence was so powerful that they rose and paid him the appropriate civilities. He then taught them the *Dharmacakra pravartana Sūtra*, which includes the Four Ennobling Truths. When the five, one by one, gained profound insight into the *Dharma* and were admitted into *sangha*,

Gautama Buddha's religion *śāsana* (Pāli *sāsana*) was established.

The Deer Park at Sārnāth had an illustrious place in Buddhist history into the twelfth century, but with the disappearance of the Buddhist community from north India, its location was lost for many centuries. Sārnāth came to the attention of British scholars when Jonathan Duncan, a colonial official, published an article in 1807 about the 1794 discovery of a reliquary containing human bones inside some ruins at Sārnāth that a local ruler had been excavating for bricks. A series of archeological excavations, beginning in the 1830s, revealed an Aśokan column, *stūpas*, the remains of monasteries and a major Buddhist temple, and a rich collection of Buddhist sculpture. The history of Buddhist architecture at the site extends from the third century BCE to the twelfth century. Among the most important monuments are the Dharmarājikā *stūpa*, where the reliquary was discovered in 1794, the 100-foot tall Dharmekh *stūpa*, the core of which probably dates to the time of Aśoka (third century BCE), possibly the traditional site of the Buddha's first teaching, and the remains of the Buddha's original residence at Sārnāth, the "perfumed chamber" (the *Mūlagandhakuṭī*). The broken column bears an Aśoka's edict warning against schism within the *sangha*; it was originally surmounted by the well-known capital carved with four lions seated back to back that was adopted as the emblem of the Republic of India. The capital is now preserved in the local archeological museum, which also houses a substantial collection of Buddhist sculptures, including a famous Gupta-era seated Buddha image in the "turning the *Dharma* wheel" posture.

See also: **Bodhgayā; Buddha; Ennobling Truths/Realities; Kuśinagara; Lumbinī; Pāṭaliputra; Sacred places; *Vihāra*.**

KEVIN TRAINOR

SARVA-TATHĀGATA-TATTVA-SAṂGRAHA AND *MAHĀVAIROCANA-ABHISAMBODHI SŪTRA*

The *Sūtra of the Awakening of Mahāvairocana* (*Mahāvairocana-Abhisambodhi Sūtra*) and the *Compendium of the Truth of All Buddhas* (*Sarva-tathāgata-tattva-saṃgraha*) are the two most important scriptural sources for Japanese *tantric* (*mikkyō*) Buddhism. *The Compendium of Truth* is found in three versions in the Chinese canon: (1) a translation by Vajrabodhi in four sections (*juan*) (T 866); (2) one by Amoghavajra in three sections (T 865); and (3) one by Dānapāla (*c.* late tenth century) in thirty (T 882). Unlike the *Awakening of Mahāvairocana*, the *Compendium of Truth* has little concern with doctrinal exposition, and instead focuses on description of the *vajra* realm *maṇḍala*, which is one of the two main *maṇḍalas* for Shingon, along with the womb realm *maṇḍala*.

The first is divided into nine "assemblies" with the five Buddhas (*jina*) in the central section, known as the "*Karma* Assembly." There are total of 1,461 deities in the *maṇḍala*, 1,061 of which are in the *Karma* Assembly, which depicts the buddhas' activity of bringing sentient beings to awakening. The *vajra* symbolizes the indestructible truth of all reality, and the *maṇḍala* as a whole represents the wisdom of Buddhas who apprehend it. It is a microcosm of the universe, which is composed of phenomena (*dharma*). They are pervaded by and inextricably mixed with primordial principle (Ch. *li*, Jap. *ri*). Principle is equated with suchness (Skt. *tathatā*, Jap. *shinnyo*) and is said to transcend causation and time and to be immutable and eternal. The universe is "contained, sustained, nurtured, and protected" by principle. All *dharmas* are equal and undifferentiated, and there are no real distinctions between them. The *maṇḍala* is associated with the compassion aspect of buddhahood and the Buddha-body. According to the *Compendium of Truth*, "your own body is a *vajra*, firm and indestructible," and is the basis for actualization of buddhahood in this lifetime.

In this *maṇḍala*, the five celestial Buddhas are associated with the five primary wisdoms of awakened beings: Mahāvairocana represents the essential wisdom of the *Dharma* realm (*dharmadhātu-svabhāva-jñāna*), which perceives the fundamental nature of all phenomena; Akṣobhya and Ratnasambhava are connected with mirror-like wisdom *(ādarśa-jñāna*, which reflects the world as it is) and the wisdom of equality (*samatā-jñāna*, which understands the fundamental sameness of all *dharmas*) respectively (these contribute to one's own awakening); and Amitābha and Amoghasiddhi are associated with investigative wisdom (*pratyavekṣaṇā-jñāna*, which understands the workings of phenomena) and wisdom of accomplishment (*kṛtyā-nuṣṭhāna-jñāna*, which enables Buddhas to skillfully work for the benefit of sentient beings) respectively, both of which bring others to Buddhahood.

The *Compendium of Truth* indicates that its practices are particularly effective for beings who have committed evil deeds and who have strong passion:

> With regard to entering the great *maṇḍala* [of the *Compendium of Truth*,] one should make no distinctions between those who are worthy recipients and those who are not. Why? All living beings who have committed great evil who see the great *maṇḍala* of the vajra realm and enter into it will be rescued from bad rebirths. Those beings who are greedy for all manner of things – food, drink, and sexual pleasures – who break their pledges and who are not skilled in the preliminaries and so forth ... will have all their aspirations fulfilled.

It goes on to describe how inferior trainees also benefit from the teachings of the *Compendium of Truth*, and adds that advanced practitioners who are diligent will make great progress through entering into its *maṇḍala* and will quickly attain buddhahood for the benefit of all others without difficulty, along with supreme accomplishments (*siddhi*).

The *Sūtra of the Awakening of Mahāvairocana* describes how the Buddha Mahāvairocana's awakening is manifested in the world through a variety of *maṇḍalas*, *mantras*, and *mudrās*, which allow trainees to follow his example and use ritual practices to attain awakening themselves. It was originally composed in Sanskrit, but now only exists in Chinese and Tibetan translations. The most widely used version was translated by Śubhākarasiṃha and Yi Xing from two Sanskrit manuscripts.

The first thirty-one chapters are concerned with an exposition of Buddhist doctrine from the tantric perspective, and the later sections focus on ritual performance. The opening chapter is the most influential, and it provides an outline of the path to awakening, which is summed up in the phrase: "the mind of awakening (*bodhicitta*) is the cause, compassion is its roots, and skill in means is its result." *Bodhicitta* is said to be inherent in the minds of all sentient beings, and so it is not something that one must create. Rather, according to the *tantra*, "*bodhicitta* is knowing one's true self," and it becomes fully manifest through practice, particularly familiarization with *tantric* symbolism. According to Yixing's *Commentary on the Mahāvairocana-Abhisambodhi Sūtra* (*Dari jing su*), actualization of the mind of awakening is related to realization of emptiness, and he indicates that *mantra* recitation awakens one's innate potential for Buddhahood. The "true self" is equated with realization of emptiness, and *mantra* is the means to awaken *bodhicitta*. Although it is innate, it must be cultivated, because the potential for *bodhicitta* is obscured by mental afflictions in ordinary beings. Training in compassion is the primary means by which this is achieved, and according to the *Awakening of Mahāvairocana* this involves working within the six destinies into which sentient beings may be reborn in order to help them overcome suffering.

Among its important doctrines is the notion of three *kalpas* (Jap. *sangō*), which here does not refer to world ages but to the three basic aspects of the mind that grasp illusions (*mithyā-grāha*): (1) coarse (*sthūla*); (2) subtle (*sūkṣma*); and (3) very subtle (*parasūkṣma*). The first refers to the perspective of ordinary beings, who are afflicted by ignorance and thus cling to the notion of a truly existent self. The second involves perceiving *dharmas* as having real existence. The text asserts the standard Mahāyāna doctrine that all persons and *dharmas* are empty of inherent existence. The third *kalpa* is the delusion of categorizing *dharmas* as either conditioned (*saṃskṛta*) or unconditioned (*asaṃskṛta*), which is mistaken because in reality all of reality is a universal network of interconnected causality and change.

The *Awakening of Mahāvairocana* is the main source for the theory and practice of the womb realm *maṇḍala*, which is an iconographic illustration of the generation and practice of the mind of awakening. The *maṇḍala* has twelve halls, and each hall represents the seat of a central Buddha, surrounded by attendant *bodhisattvas*. The configuration of the halls illustrates the dynamic relationship between the mind of awakening, compassion, and skill in means, which is compared to the relationship between the truth body (*dharma-kāya*), enjoyment body (*saṃbhoga-kāya*), and emanation bodies (*nirmāṇa-kāya*). In this *maṇḍala*, Mahāvairocana is situated in the center seated on an eight-petaled lotus, surrounded by the four other celestial Buddhas, and beyond the perimeter of the central hall are numerous buddhas, *bodhisattvas*, and other figures.

In the text, Mahāvairocana states that the *maṇḍala* resides in the minds of Buddhas and *tantric* practitioners: "it does not differ from consciousness, and consciousness does not differ from the *maṇḍala*. Why? Because consciousness and the *maṇḍala* are identical." The *maṇḍala* is also said to be "that which gives rise to all buddhas, which has an incomparable and most excellent flavor. That is the meaning of the world '*maṇḍala*'."

The date of composition of the text has been the subject of dispute among scholars. It is not mentioned by Xuanzang (596–664), who traveled to India from 629 to 645, or by other early Chinese pilgrims to India, but is noted in the account of Yijing (635–713), who entered India in 671 and who refers to the text in his *Biography of Eminent Monks Who Sought the Dharma in the Western Region* (*Shiyu qiu fa gao*). Wuxing, who arrived in India around the same time as Yijing, reportedly sent a copy of the text to China, but he died in Central Asia. It was brought to China by Śubhākarasiṃha. He and Yixing translated it into Chinese in 725. Saichō, the founder of the Japanese Tendai tradition, traveled to China and studied under Shanxia, whose teacher had been a student of Śubhākarasiṃha. Kūkai, the founder of the Japanese Shingon Order, also traveled to China and studied *tantric* Buddhism under Huiguo, who was a student of Śubhākarasiṃha's disciple Xuanchao. He received instructions in the *Compendium of Truth* from Amoghavajra. After its transmission to China, esoteric Buddhism enjoyed a brief period of popularity, but was later amalgamated into other schools of Chinese Buddhism. In Japan, however, it became a central part of the teaching and practice of both Shingon and Tendai, and is still influential today in those traditions.

See also: **Tibet, Buddhism in; Vajrayāna Buddhism.**

JOHN POWERS

SARVĀSTIVĀDA

The Sarvāstivāda was an important school of Indian Buddhism that separated from the main body of the Elders (Sthaviras) around three centuries after the death of the Buddha. Its name means "the school that holds that everything exists," or "the school of the reality of all phenomena." This unusual designation derives from its distinctive and intriguing philosophical views concerning the nature of phenomena or *dharmas*,

Like other early schools such as the Theravāda, the ontology of the Sarvāstivāda was pluralist and realist, and followers of the school believed (not unlike the ancient Greek atomists) that reality could be analysed into a collection of discrete entities, which were known as *dharmas*. Theories of this kind were developed as a solution to difficulties arising out of the Buddhist denial of enduring substances in the no-self (*anātman*) doctrine, which gave rise to problems in causation, temporality, and personal identity. The conventional scholastic solution was to posit a theory of instantaneous serial continuity according to which phenomena (*dharmas*) constantly replicate themselves in a momentary sequence of change (*dharma-kṣanikatvā*). Thus reality was conceived of as cinematic, like a filmstrip in which one frame constantly gives way to the next: each moment is substantially existent in its own right, and collectively they produce the illusion of stability and continuity. However, this position is not free of problems, not the least of which is what makes an individual or object the same over a span of time. The distinctive Sarvāstivādin solution was to claim that *dharmas* existed in all three times, and enjoyed real existence in the past and future, as well as in the present. Four main theories were proposed to explain this, which we cannot go into here, except to note that according to the first of these, *dharmas* exist from beginningless time and simply undergo a change of mode from latent to manifest in the moment in which they exert causal efficacy (*kāritva*). Time itself was thus seen as a change of mode undergone by *dharmas*, and past, present and future were defined by their relationship to one another rather than as real existents. This made it possible to claim that one and the same phenomenon can exist in all "three times," just as the same woman can be a mother and a daughter simultaneously.

The Sarvāstivādin classification of *dharmas*

Sarvāstivādin sources distinguish seventy-five *dharmas* in total, of which seventy-two are "conditioned" (*saṃskṛta*) and three are "unconditioned" (*asaṃskṛta*). The three unconditioned *dharmas* are (1) space (*ākāśa*); and two states of emancipation: (2) through discerning knowledge (*pratisankhyānirodha*) and (3) through non-discerning knowledge (*apratisankhyānirodha*). These three are unconditioned in the sense that they are not subject to the law of causality and so do not pass through the phases of production (*jāti*), duration (*sthiti*), decay (*jarā*) and destruction (*anityatā*) which affects all conditioned phenomena. The remaining seventy-two *dharmas* were grouped into four main categories: matter (*rūpa*), mind (*citta*), mental concomitants (*caitta*), and formations not connected to thought (*cittaviprayukta*).

Matter (*rūpa*)

Matter or form consists of the first five of the six sense faculties (*indriya*) and their respective objects (*viṣaya*). Thus the senses of seeing (*cakṣur-indriya*), hearing (*śrotra-indriya*), smell (*ghrāṇa-indriya*), taste (*jihvā-indriya*) and touch (*kāya-indriya*) have material form (*rūpa*), sound (*śabda*), smell (*gandha*), taste (*rasa*), and touch (*spraṣṭavya*) as their objects. The eleventh *dharma* in the group was "unmanifest action" (*avijñapti*), a problematic concept not accepted by all branches of the Sarvāstivāda which relates to inward dispositions as yet not manifest in physical action. The intention, choice or resolution to do something was thought of as a kind of internal shadow of the outward act which left a subtle material trace in the body of the agent at some level.

Mind (*citta*)

The second category contains only one element, that of pure thought or consciousness.

Mental concomitants (*caittas*)

The third category contains forty-six elements or factors associated with mental activity. The first ten of these are general factors thought to be of broad scope (*mahābhūmika*) that accompany all mental activity. These are:

1 Feeling (*vedanā*)
2 Conception (*saṃjñā*)
3 Volition (*cetanā*)
4 Contact (*sparśa*)
5 Attention (*manaskāra*)
6 Motivation (*chanda*)
7 Inclination (*adhimokṣa*)
8 Mindfulness (*smṛti*)
9 Meditation (*samādhi*)
10 Understanding (*prajñā*).

Ten further basic factors accompany every good (*kuśala*) moment of consciousness. These are:

1 Faith or confidence (*śraddhā*)
2 Energy (*vīrya*)
3 Equanimity (*upekśā*)
4 Modesty (*hrī*)
5 Embarrassment at wrongdoing by others (*apatrāpya*)
6 Non-craving (*alobha*)
7 Non-hatred (*adveṣa*)
8 Non-injury (*ahiṃsā*)
9 Serenity (*praśrabdhi*)
10 Non-heedlessness (*apramāda*).

Six "general defiled factors" (*kleśa-mahābhūmika-dharmas*) accompany negative thoughts:

1 Delusion (*moha*)
2 Heedlessness (*pramāda*)
3 Torpor (*kausīdya*)
4 Lack of faith (*aśraddhā*)
5 Sloth (*styāna*)
6 Restlessness (*auddhatya*).

Ten minor defiled factors (*upakleśa*) which may be present at specific times are:

1 Anger (*krodha*)
2 Hypocrisy (*mrakṣsa*)
3 Stinginess (*mātsarya*)
4 Jealousy (*īrṣyā*)
5 Envious rivalry (*pradāsa*)
6 Causing harm (*vihiṃsā*)
7 Enmity (*upanāha*)
8 Deceit (*māyā*)
9 Trickery (*śāṭhya*)
10 Conceit (*mada*).

Two factors are present alongside all negative states of mind. These are known as "universally unwholesome elements" (*akuśala-mahābhūmika-dharma*) and are:

1 Shamelessness (*āhrīkya*)
2 Immodesty (*anapatrāpya*).

Eight indeterminate (*aniyata*) factors can be associated with good, bad or indeterminate states of mind. These are:

1 Attention (*vitarka*)
2 Discursive thought (*vicāra*)
3 Drowsiness (*middhā*)
4 Remorse (*kaukṛtya*)
5 Greed (*rāga*)
6 Hatred (*pratigha*)
7 Pride (*māna*)
8 Doubt (*vicikitsā*).

Factors disassociated from thought (*cittaviprayukta*)

The following fourteen factors do not fall into the category of either mind or matter and for the most part are natural forces which control the way *dharmas* interact.

1 Acquisition (*prāpti*): a force which binds *dharmas* together into groups.
2 Rejection (*aprāpti*): a force which disengages *dharmas* from one another.
3 Homogeneity (*sabhāgatā*): a force which unites similar *dharmas*.
4 Non-perception (*āsaṃjñnika*): a force which brings out the attainment of the meditative state of non-perception.
5 Attainment of non-perception (*asaṃjñisamāpatti*) produced by the effort to attain a trance state.
6 The "attainment of cessation" (*nirodhasamāpatti*), a trance in which all thought and feeling are suspended.
7 The life force (*jīvitendriya*), the faculty which determines lifespan.
8 Origination (*jāti*).
9 Duration (*sthiti*).
10 Decay (*jarā*).
11 Impermanence (*anityatā*).
12 Force imparting meaning to letters (*vyañjana-kāya*).
13 Force imparting meaning to sentences (*nāmakāya*).
14 Force imparting meaning to phrases (*pādakāya*).

Later history

Although the Sarvāstivādins were apparently expelled at the council of Pāṭaliputra, they went on to become extremely influential, particularly in the northwest of India in Kashmir and Gandhāra, where they survived until Buddhism disappeared from the sub-continent. The school possessed its own canon, much of which survives today, and is renowned for its *Abhidharma* texts, especially the *Mahāvibhāṣā* composed under the supervision of Vasumitra at the Council of Kaniṣka (second century CE). The school is alternatively known as the Vaibhāṣika, from the name of this text, and gave rise to a dissident tradition known as the Sautrāntika. Later the Sarvāstivāda subdivided into five sub-schools: Dharmagupta, Mūlasarvāstivāda, Kāśyapīyah, Mahīśāsaka, Sautrāntika and the Vātsīputrīya.

See also: ***Abhidharma***; ***Abhidharmakośa***; ***Dharma***; **Dharmaguptakas; Kaniṣka; Sautrāntrika; Vasubandhu; Vātsīputrīyas.**

DAMIEN KEOWN

SAUTRĀNTIKA

The Sautrāntika is an interpretative position found among scholars in the Sarvāstivādin sect of *Nikāya* Buddhism. Sautrāntika scholars practiced *Abhidharma* thinking but they were distinguished from their Sarvāstivādin peers by their rejection of *Abhidharma* texts as the Word of the Buddha; this rejection explains the name of the interpretative position as those who accepted only the *sūtras* as authoritative (Sautrāntika). The name can be misleading, however, as the Sautrāntikas were, in fact, *Abhidharma* thinkers, as the titles of Vasubandhu's *Treasury of Abhidharma* (*Abhidharmakośa*) and Skandhila's *The Instanciation of Abhidharma* (*Abhidharmāvatāra*) make clear. The Sautrāntikas were *Abhidharma* thinkers who rejected the idea that doctrinal positions could be anchored by solely by the authority of the Sarvāstivādin *Abhidharma* literature.

The Sautrāntikas were not a community defined by a common sociological and institutional basis, as the *Vinaya* sects of *Nikāya* Buddhism were, such as the Mahāsāṃghikas, Dharmaguptakas, and Sarvāstivādins; in fact they belonged to the Sarvāstivādin *Vinaya* sect. Nor were the Sautrāntikas a textual community, unified in thought if not in sociology by a shared and distinctive focus on a foundational text, as their doctrinal opponents in the Sarvāstivāda, the Vaibhāṣikas, were. And they were not a doctrinal "school," thinkers that could be grouped together across *nikāyas* by a common affirmation of a particular doctrinal position, as the Pudgalavādins were held to be, although the Sautrāntikas do seem to have commonly rejected some of the most basic positions of Sarvāstivādin thought. At most, the Sautrāntikas were held to be a "school," it seems, on the basis of what they rejected, not what they affirmed.

This suggests that the Sautrāntikas are best understood as thinkers who held a variety of doctrinal positions. They were grouped together by opponents more for their common rejection of orthodox Sarvāstivādin thought and texts than for any consistent doctrinal position or shared textual basis of their own. In this regard, the term "Sautrāntika" seems to function in Indian Buddhist literature much like the term "Mahāyāna": the term creates an image of commonality among thinkers and doctrinal positions on the basis of what they are not and what they reject rather than on the basis of any consistently shared characteristics among these thinkers and doctrinal positions. In both cases, the name also creates the image of a community where there probably was none. It is thus important to keep in mind that it is misleading to think of, say, the Dharmaguptakas, who had their own *Vinaya*, and the Sautrāntikas as somehow being similar insofar as both are "schools" within *Nikāya* Buddhism. The Dharmaguptakas had far more of a concrete social presence than the Sautrāntikas. Sociologically, they existed as a community. Groups of monks met together for ritual purposes on the basis of a shared monastic lineage identified as Dharmaguptaka, something that never occurred among Sautrāntikas, and Dharmaguptakas were concretely visible enough to be designated as the recipients of gifts by patrons.

The great Buddhist scholastic Vasubandhu presented himself as a Sautrāntika and the positions that he takes and calls Sautrāntika in his *Treasury of Abhidharma* (*Abhidharmakośabhāṣya*) are frequently taken by modern historians as their benchmark for Sautrāntika thought; indeed, it is only with Vasubandhu that we first have the term "Sautrāntika" used in a clearly visible fashion, although the manner in which he writes suggests that he understood himself as inheriting a received position. Modern historians use Vasubandhu's doctrinal positions to identify other texts and the doctrinal positions found in them as possibly belonging to the Sautrāntika fold. Vasubandhu apparently converted to Yogācāra Buddhism, but it has been noted that many of the positions which he describes as Sautrāntika in his work can be found in central Yogācāra texts. Yogācāra is, of course, considered to be one of the main doctrinal schools of the Mahāyāna. Vasubandhu apparently converted to the Yogācāra later in his life, but whether or not he already held Yogācāra positions when he wrote the *Treasury of Abhidharma* and merely called them Sautrāntika, or these viewpoints only subsequently became accepted among Yogācāra thinkers, is unclear.

This doctrinal commonality between the Sautrāntikas and the Yogācārins is important, whatever the actual history of who came first may be. It reminds us that even on doctrinal grounds, there was sometimes less of a gap between *Nikāya* Buddhism and Mahāyāna Buddhism than might be expected if these two affiliations are approached on the basis of the polemical contrast between Hīnayāna Buddhism and Mahāyāna Buddhism and this in turn is a reminder of just how vigilant the modern historian must be against allowing the shadows of Buddhist polemics, always inherent in any use of the term "*Nikaya* Buddhism," to guide our reconstructions of the history of

Buddhist thought and practice. The overlap of the Sautrāntikas and the Yogācārins in doctrine echoes what is seen in the case of *Vinaya*, where there are no separate *Vinaya* collections or schools found in the Mahāyāna. It also echoes the public practices of mainstream Buddhism that were shared among all of the internal divisions of early medieval Indian Buddhism.

The history of the Sautrāntika orientation within the Sarvāstivādin school is obscure. In some instances, the Sautrāntikas are identified as the same as another interpretative affiliation within the Sarvāstivādins, the Dārṣṭāntikas, "those who illustrate their arguments with concrete examples." There is some possibility that this term is pejorative, and thus the terms "Sautrāntika" and "Dārṣṭāntikas" may have referred to the same interpretative position, albeit with a different valuation. It is also possible that the Sautrāntikas were a development out of the Dārṣṭāntikas.

The Sautrāntikas, like so many other affiliations within *Nikāya* Buddhism, seem to have had a regional connection. They were particularly associated with the area of north India near Mathurā whereas the Vaibhāṣika orthodoxy of the Sarvāstivādin school was associated with Kashmir.

With the passing of the prominence of the Kashmiri Vaibhāṣika orthodoxy in Indian Buddhism, and the emergence of the Mūlasarvāstivādin school of Sarvāstivāda, the interpretative position within the Sarvāstivāda that the Sautrāntikas represented seems to have lost its reason for preservation and the visibility of the Sautrāntika position disappeared. This is made clear, perhaps, in the Tibetan reception of Buddhism, where the Mūlasarvāstivādin *Vinaya* and Vasubandhu's *Treasury of Abhidharma* are translated, but the *Vinaya* of the Sarvāstivādins and the literature produced by the Vaibhāṣikas are not. Sautrāntika positions continued to be discussed among Chinese Buddhist thinkers, such as Kuiji, long after their disappearance in India, and positions associated with the Sautrāntikas continued to be defended independently by Yogācārin thinkers.

See also: ***Abhidharmakośa*; Councils; *Nikāya* Buddhism; Sarvāstivāda; Vasubandhu.**

CHARLES HALLISEY

SAYADAW, MAHĀSĪ (1904–82)

Burma's acclaimed meditation teacher, the Mahāsī Sayadaw U Sobhana Mahāthera, was also a prolific scholar of Pāli texts. He wrote an introduction to Buddhaghosa's Path of Purification (*Visuddhimagga Aṭṭhakathā*) in Pāli and prepared *nissaya* translations of the *Visuddhimagga* and of Dhammapāla's *Visudhimagga Mahāṭīkā*. Much of his work focused on the theory and practice of *vipassanā* mediation. His biography follows the trajectory of a traditional career monk of rural origins whose intellectual acumen led to prominence at the monastic centers of the Burmese Buddhist revival since the 1950s. In addition to developing popular insight meditation techniques taught through the Mahāsī network of meditations centers in Burma and abroad, he also undertook numerous missions to India, Sri Lanka, Thailand, Cambodia and Japan, and the West.

Growing up in a village near Shwebo, Upper Burma, he became a novice at age six, and was fully ordained in 1923. Among his monastic teachers was the famous Mingun Jetavan Sayadaw who introduced him to *vipassanā* meditation in 1938. He pursued advanced monastic examinations in Mandalay and became especially interested in the *Mahāsatipaṭṭhāna sutta* for which he completed a *nissaya* translation in 1949. He achieved the *dhammacariya* (monastic teacher) degree in 1941 and was awarded the distinguished monastic title of *Aggamahāpaṇḍita* by the U Nu government in 1952.

The Mahāsī Sayadaw assumed prominent roles in the popularization of lay meditation during U Nu's Buddhist revival. Sir U Thwin, president of the *Buddha Sāsana Nuggaha Ahpwe* (BSNA), the lay steering committee overseeing the Buddhist revival and monastic reforms initiated by U Nu and the *Buddha Sāsana Council* (BSC), requested the Mahāsī Sayadaw to set up the first mediation center at the Thathana Yeiktha compound in Rangoon in 1949. The Mahāsī meditation center was also the headquarters for the BSC and still functions today as the main Mahāsī Meditation Center. By certifying meditation teachers, institutions, methods and the individual achievements of lay meditators in techniques of satipatthana *vipassanā* (mindful insight meditation), the center created a loosely organized, vast network of several hundred meditation centers throughout Burma. The center estimates that several hundred thousand meditators have attended retreats since its inception and credits this success to Mahāsī's simplification of Buddhaghosha's structure of the path to perfection.

The Mahāsī Sayadaw had significant roles in the *Sanghayāna*, the Sixth Buddhist Synod (1954–6). As final editor of the council's textual work on the Theravāda canonical *tipiṭaka*, the Sayadaw incorporated the editing of commentaries (*aṭṭhakathā*) and subcommentaries (*ṭīkās*). At the opening of the *sanghayāna*, he served as questioner in the *tipiṭakadhāra* examination of the Ven. U Vicittasarabhivamsa. This type of examination requires memorization of the entire Pāli Canon and signifies complete knowledge of the *dhamma* and, hence, enlightenment.

Of the more than sixty-five books he authored, *The Satipaṭṭhāna Vipassanā Meditation*, *Practical Insight Meditation*, and *Progress of Insight* were published abroad. His legacy rests in monastic scholarship on the theory and practice of insight meditation and its popularization, institutionalization, and missionization. He went on more than twenty missions to establish meditation centers abroad in Asia and in the West. His teaching lineage continues through respected meditation teachers who carry on his work and mission at the Thathana Yeiktha Center in Yangon.

See also: **Famous Buddhists and ideal types.**

JULIANE SCHOBER

SCHOLAR-PRACTITIONERS IN BUDDHIST STUDIES

Although there have been only a few scholarly studies chronicling the academic investigation of Buddhism by Western researchers, and fewer still of the academic discipline known as Buddhist Studies, until quite recently the issue of the religious affiliation of the researcher has not been part of the mix. Almost exclusively, the founding mothers and founding fathers of Buddhist Studies in the West have had personal religious commitments entirely separate from Buddhism. Now, however, it is quite ordinary for individuals teaching Buddhist Studies in universities throughout the world to be "scholar-practitioners," involved in the practices of various Buddhist traditions and sects. Georges Dreyfus' new book *The Sound of Two Hands Clapping: The Education of a Tibetan Buddhist Monk*, for example, traces his monastic career through many years of study in Tibetan Buddhist monasteries in India. Nevertheless, it is not always easy for academics to reveal their religious orientation in an environment that is not uniformly supportive of such choices.

Stories reflecting the study/practice dichotomy in Buddhism are abundant in both the primary and secondary literature on the subject. Walpola Rahula's *History of Buddhism in Ceylon* provides a good summary of the issue. During the first century BCE, in response to a concern over the possible loss of the *Tripiṭaka* during a severe famine, a question arose. What is the basis of the "Teaching" (that is, *Sāsana*) – learning or practice? A clear difference of opinion resulted in the development of two groups: the Dhammakathikas, who claimed that learning was the basis of the *Sāsana*, and the Paṃsukūlikas, who argued for practice as the basis. The Dhammakathikas apparently won out.

The two vocations described above came to be known as *gantha-dhura*, or the "vocation of books," and *vipassanā-dhura*, or the "vocation of meditation," with the former being regarded as the superior training (because surely meditation would not be possible if the teachings were lost). Moreover, not the least characteristic of these two divisions was that the *vipassanā-dhura* monks began to live in the forest, where they could best pursue their vocation undisturbed, while the *gantha-dhura* monks began to dwell in villages and towns. As such, the *gantha-dhura* monks began to play a significant role in Buddhist education. It would probably not be going too far to refer to the *gantha-dhura* monks as "scholar-monks." Why is this distinction so important? It is significant for at least two reasons. First, and most obviously, it reveals why the tradition of study in Buddhism, so long minimized in popular and scholarly investigations of the Buddhist tradition, has such an impact on that same tradition, and resulted in the rapid development of Buddhist schools and institutes of higher learning in the latter quarter of the twentieth century. Second, it explains why the Buddhist movement has encouraged a high level of "Buddhist literacy" among its practitioners. However, it also highlights the fact that the global Buddhist movement has been almost exclusively a lay movement. While many leaders of various Buddhist groups may have had formal monastic training (irrespective of whether they continue to lead monastic lifestyles), the vast majority of their disciples have not. Thus the educational model on which modern global Buddhists pattern their behavior is contrary to the traditional Asian Buddhist archetype. It is, in fact, the converse of the traditional model. As such, at least with regard to Buddhist study and education, there is a leadership gap in this global Buddhist community, one largely not filled by a *sangha* of "scholar-monks."

Above, it was noted that in Asia the monastic renunciants were almost exclusively responsible for the religious education of the lay *sangha*. In the absence of the traditional "scholar-monks" so prevalent in Asia, it may well be that the "scholar-practitioners" of today's Western community of Buddhism will fulfill the role of "quasi-monastics," or at least of treasure-troves of Buddhist literacy and information, functioning as guides through whom one's understanding of the *Dharma* may be sharpened. In this way, individual practice might once again be balanced with individual study so that Buddhist study deepens one's practice, while Buddhist practice informs one's study. Obviously, such a suggestion spawns two further questions: (1) Are there sufficient scholar-practitioners currently active in Buddhism to make such an impact? (2) Are they actually making that impact?

With regard to the former question, much of the information reported above is necessarily anecdotal. By simply making mental notes at the various conferences attended by Western Buddhologists, one can develop a roster of scholar-practitioners who are openly Buddhist; and while such a roster is not publishable in a volume such as this, the number is quite clearly at least 25 percent. A better estimate might be that at least another 25 percent of Western scholars of Buddhism are almost certainly Buddhists, but careful not to make public expressions of their religiosity for fear of professional reprisal, keenly felt or perceived.

The second question is perhaps not so difficult to assess as the first. As one surveys the vast corpus of literature that surrounds the academic programs sponsored by numerous Western Buddhist groups, the names of academic scholars of Buddhism have begun to dominate the roster of invited presenters, and these individuals are almost exclusively Buddhists. In other words, many Western Buddhist masters have come to acknowledge and incorporate the professional contributions of these American Buddhist scholar-practitioners into the religious life of their communities, recognizing the unique and vital role they fulfill. This is a new and emerging phenomenon as well. In 1977, a conference at Syracuse University devoted to the theme of "The Flowering of Buddhism in America" offered academic-sounding titles in many of the presentations, but nearly all of the papers were prepared by non-academic practitioners. Seventeen years later, when the Institute of Buddhist Studies in Berkeley, California, sponsored a semester-long symposium called "Buddhisms in America: An Expanding Frontier," every single participant had impressive academic credentials, and more than two-thirds of the nearly twenty presenters were Buddhist practitioners.

See also: **Academic study of Buddhism; North America, Buddhism in.**

CHARLES S. PREBISH

SERVICE AND RELIEF ORGANIZATIONS

Buddhism is, perhaps, most basically a remedy for suffering, and Buddhists have worked compassionately throughout the centuries to relieve not only their own suffering, but the suffering of others as well. In the contemporary world, this concern to relieve others' suffering is expressed commonly through the formation of service and relief organizations which seek to alleviate suffering in all of its forms – religious, physical, psychological, social, environmental, and so on. Many of these groups and their members actively identify themselves as "engaged Buddhists," regarding all forms of suffering as interrelated aspects of a single suffering which is best treated, not only through traditional Buddhist religious practices, but also through overt activity directed at removing suffering's immediate and remote causes in the world. The liberation which engaged Buddhists seek is often construed, therefore, as a "mundane awakening," although engaged Buddhists are reluctant to draw distinctions between mundane and supra-mundane dimensions of reality and so also eschew distinctions between ordinary and spiritual forms of suffering. As already noted, for them all suffering is ultimately one, and can, therefore – indeed must – be combated through the skillful combination of personal religious practices and social action engineered to relieve suffering in all its forms, relative to its myriad (material, social, and spiritual) causes.

The Taiwan-based Tzu Chi Foundation, for instance, which today boasts over four million members in twenty-eight countries, was founded in 1966 with the fourfold mission of charity, medical care, education, and culture, a mission which it creatively derives from and equates with the traditional four *brahmavihāra* (compassion, lovingkindness, equanimity, and sympathetic joy). Its most significant contributions to date have come in the areas of health care and disaster relief, working, for instance, to make health care free in Taiwan, establishing the world's third-largest bone marrow data bank, and providing relief to the victims of natural disasters throughout the world. In addition to the *brahmavihāra*, Tzu Chi's charismatic founder, Taiwanese nun Cheng Yen, bases her social work on her own "*bodhisattva*-like" vows to "purify minds; harmonize society; and free the world from disasters." Implied by these vows' recognition of the interrelatedness of personal, social, and natural suffering is the idea that work directed toward the relief of others' suffering is not a distraction from the pursuit of one's own liberation, but contributes to that liberation by working to lead all beings interdependently toward the goal of freedom and joy for all.

The *Sarvōdaya Śramadāna* Movement in Sri Lanka also works to provide relief to the victims of poverty, social oppression, violence, and natural disasters as an expression of Buddhist compassion directed toward the interdependent goal of liberation from suffering for others and self. Like the Tzu Chi Foundation, *Sarvōdaya* creatively grounds its service activities in traditional Buddhist teachings, in this case relating the charitable activity of its "*śramadāna*" ("giving one's energy") work camps to the traditional Buddhist virtue of *dāna* (giving or generosity). While *dāna* has traditionally been understood in Theravāda Buddhism as the giving of alms to Buddhist monastics, a form of merit-making directed primarily at gaining a better rebirth for the giver, *Sarvōdaya* broadens the scope of giving to include giving to one's entire community, and lays emphasis on the possibility of giving not just material goods, but also one's efforts to benefit others. Such giving is taken, in turn, as a means of advancing toward the interrelated "dual awakening" of self and society. While the movement's founder, A.T. Ariyaratne, is sometimes criticized by traditionalists for the "mundane" character of the "awakening" he promotes, he nevertheless conceives of the *Sarvōdaya* Movement as empowering people, not only to improve their present existence, but to work toward ultimate, spiritual liberation as interrelated aspects of a thoroughly integrated *nirvāṇa*.

Influenced by the *Sarvōdaya* Movement, the Buddhist Peace Fellowship's (BPF) Buddhist Alliance for Social Engagement (BASE) also brings Buddhist practitioners together for the purpose of serving others as a means of achieving the interrelated liberation of self and others from suffering in its various forms. This program, which was begun in the San Francisco Bay area in 1995, organizes six-month-long training programs in which participants work within established social service organizations while simultaneously engaging in more traditional Buddhist practices under the guidance of experienced "mentors" and meeting regularly with other practitioners for study, support, discussion, training, and meditation. The overall goal of the program is to allow participants "the opportunity to deepen their understanding of the interface of Buddhist practice with 'social change practice.'"

In like manner, Bernard Glassman Rōshi's Greyston Mandala Foundation provides service to victims of poverty, disease, and social injustice as a means for deepening awareness of the interconnectedness of all phenomena and leading all beings toward liberation from suffering. The Foundation connects a multi-million-dollar network of enterprises – including Greyston Bakery, Greyston Family Inn, and Maitri House – which provides housing and job development, social services, child care, and HIV-related health care for "the economically disenfranchised" of New York and, through its international affiliates, other locations throughout the world. As with the other organizations discussed here, participation in these enterprises is regarded not merely as helping to relieve the suffering of others, but also as a kind of "work-practice," wherein activist practitioners enact the enlightenment they seek for themselves and others.

As seen in these and countless other cases around the world, engaged Buddhists rely on the fundamental notion of interrelatedness, in this case the interrelatedness of one's own and others' suffering, to construct modes of social service that simultaneously conduce to the liberation of others and self from worldly and spiritual forms of suffering. Ultimately unwilling to draw distinctions between self and other, mundane and supra-mundane, these engaged Buddhists view "inner" practices, such as meditation, and "outer" practices, such as giving, as interrelated aspects of a single practice which ultimately leads all to the experience of freedom from suffering in all its forms. While Buddhist traditionalists sometimes criticize their activities as distorting basic Buddhist teachings, engaged Buddhist service providers nevertheless see their activities as not only consonant with, but even as more true to, Buddhism's essence than practices that concentrate unduly on the "spiritual" liberation of individuals alone. Regardless of how they are viewed by Buddhists, these service and relief organizations represent important ways in which the tradition is seeking to come to terms with the widespread suffering made possible by current technologies and emergent social forms and contribute greatly to the lessening of suffering around the world.

See also: **Ariyaratne, A.T.; Buddhist peace groups (in Asia and the West); Engaged Buddhism; Glassman, Bernard Rōshi; Global Buddhist networks: selected examples; Maha Ghosananda; Nhat Hanh, Thich.**

JIM DEITRICK

SEXUAL ETHICS

Buddhism in general adopts a wary attitude towards sex. As an ascetic tradition it teaches that control of the appetites and desires is a prerequisite for spiritual development. In this respect the Buddha provides the perfect role model: at the age of twenty-nine he turned his back on family life and remained celibate for the rest of his days. The Buddha said that he knew of nothing that overpowers a man's mind so much as "the form of a woman" (*Aṅguttara Nikāya* 3.68f). Such advice is, perhaps, best seen not as evidence of a misogynist streak in Buddhism (although this is often alleged) but as a realization of the danger posed by sexual desire to members of a celibate community. He makes similar points about female sexual desire too, warning of the dangers of the desires women feel for men. Although women are said to be "a snare of Māra" (the Buddhist devil), it is not basically women who are the problem, nor men, but the sexual desire which the physical proximity of the genders can create and which binds both to *saṃsāra*.

Marriage

For those who are unable to cope with the rigours of the celibate monastic life the status of married householder is recommended. While monogamy is the preferred and predominant model, there is much local variation in marriage patterns across the Buddhist world. Early texts mention a variety of temporary and permanent arrangements entered into for both emotional and economic reasons, and in different parts of Buddhist Asia both polygamy and polyandry have been (and still are) practised. The various forms of marriage arrangements found among Buddhists are determined more by local custom than Buddhist teachings, and such matters are seen as essentially the responsibility of the secular authorities. As it does not regard marriage as a religious matter, Buddhism has no objection to divorce, but because of social pressures in traditional societies this is much less common than in the West.

The third precept

Various precepts were laid down in the *Vinaya* to regulate sexual behavior for monks and nuns, while the sexual morality of the laity is governed primarily by the third precept. This precept prohibits "misconduct (*mithyācāra*) in things sexual (*kāmeṣu*)." The wording of the precept is imprecise, and it does not define what forms of behavior constitute "misconduct." Although it makes no explicit reference to "coveting another man's wife" as does the Third Commandment, the third precept is almost universally interpreted in Buddhist societies to prohibit first and foremost adultery. Little is said about pre-marital sex but the impression is given that marriage is the only appropriate forum for sexual intimacy. Some early sources specify certain classes of women that are precluded as sexual partners, such as close relatives and vulnerable young girls.

Other more general moral teachings also have a bearing on sexual behaviour. For example, the principle of *ahiṃsā* would require that one should not intentionally harm another person physically or emotionally, thus precluding rape, paedophilia, sexual harassment, and perhaps incest. Further, all relationships, including sexual ones, should be informed by the virtues of lovingkindness (*mettā*) and compassion (*karuṇā*). The "Golden Rule" would counsel that you should do nothing to others you would not like done to yourself. This is specifically applied to adultery at *Saṃyutta Nikāya* 5.354, where it is said that just as you would not like another to commit adultery with your wife, you should not do it yourself with another man's wife. Furthermore, the *śīla* component of the Eightfold Path relating to Right Speech, Right Action and Right Livelihood would impose certain general restraints upon conduct, such as a requirement to speak the truth and be straightforward and honest in relationships, thereby avoiding the lies and deceit common in extra-marital affairs. Adultery also involves breaking the solemn vow of fidelity typically made in a wedding service, and so would be prohibited by these more general standards of moral conduct as well as by the third precept.

Homosexuality

The Buddha himself never passes judgment on the moral status of homosexual acts and in early sources homosexuality is not discussed as a moral issue. There are, however, numerous references to homosexual practices in the context of monastic law. For monks and nuns, any kind of sexual activity, whether of a heterosexual or homosexual nature, is prohibited by the *Vinaya*, and there are severe penalties for those who break the rules. Any monk or nun found guilty of sexual intercourse (*maithuna-dharma*) faces the penalty of lifelong expulsion from the community. More minor offences, such as masturbation or lewd conduct, are punished less severely.

The question of homosexuality arises specifically in connection with admission to the Order. Certain types of people were not allowed to be ordained as monks, among them hermaphrodites and a class of individuals known in the Pāli texts as *paṇḍakas*. Apparently transvestites or male prostitutes, these individuals were excluded from ordination by the Buddha following an incident of lewd conduct by one of their number (*Vinaya* 1.85f). However, there seems to have been no bar on the admission of non-practicing homosexuals who did nothing to draw attention to their sexual orientation. Buddhism believes that gender can change from one life to another, and some Buddhists explain homosexuality as the result of a past gender reasserting itself in the present life. There are even stories in the early sources of gender changing within the same lifetime, such that because of *karmic* factors men become women and vice versa (*Vinaya* 3.35), but such changes were not seen as a hindrance to spiritual progress. Sexual orientation and even gender were seen as somewhat fluid, therefore, and not in themselves morally problematic.

In modern times homosexuality has become a source of controversy. In July 2003 Phra Pisarn Thammapatee, one of Thailand's most famed monks, called for homosexual monks to be expelled and for stricter screening of candidates for ordination. In discussions with gay Buddhist representatives the Dalai Lama has affirmed the dignity and rights of gays and lesbians but stated that masturbation and oral or anal intercourse are improper activities and are proscribed for Buddhist practitioners. The conflict between traditional Buddhist ethics and Western liberal values on the issue of homosexuality mirrors the division over this issue in other religions and may prove as divisive for Buddhists as it has been for Christians.

See also: **Abortion; Ethics; Moral discipline; Precepts, lay; *Vinaya Piṭaka*.**

DAMIEN KEOWN

SHINRAN AND JŌDO SHINSHŪ

Shinran (1173–1262) was a Tendai monk who found refuge in faith in Amida's grace expressed through invoking his name (*nenbutsu*), and became the founder of the Jōdo Shinshū (True Pure Land Sect) of Japanese Buddhism.

Shinran entered Enryakuji as a novice at the age of eight (in 1181), and lived as a Tendai *dōsō* (menial monk) on Mount Hiei for twenty years. His attempt (and failure) to maintain various Buddhist practices brought him to the conviction that he could not reach liberation by his own efforts. In 1201 he left Mount Hiei to join the community of Hōnen in Kyoto and "abandoned the difficult practices and took refuge in the Primal Vow" of Amida. In 1207 he was sent into exile to Echigo province (present Niigata prefecture), where he married and started a family of seven or eight children, declaring himself to be "neither monk nor lay." Life among the common people of the provinces put a deep mark on his spirituality. Pardoned, he migrated to the Kantō region in 1214 to propagate his Pure Land Way. Around 1235 Shinran returned to Kyoto and lived there quietly until his death, forever amending his *magnum opus*, the *Kyōgyōshinshō* (*True Teaching, Practice and Realization of the Pure Land Way*), a reasoned anthology of passages on the Pure Land Way found in the *sūtras* and the writings of the patriarchs of Pure Land Buddhism. He also wrote many short treatises and hymns in the vernacular (*wasan*) for the instruction of the common people. After his death one of his disciples, Yuienbō, collected some of his sayings into the *Tannishō* (*Treatise Lamenting Dissensions*), possibly the most popular religious booklet in Japan, and known for its advocacy of salvation for the evil person.

Like Hōnen, of whom he considered himself a loyal disciple, Shinran carried on the Indo-Chinese Pure Land tradition. At the same time, however, he radicalized it by way of a very personal reinterpretation of the transmitted texts, so that his doctrine came to show a marked originality over against that of his master. While Hōnen felt the need to stress the independence of the Pure Land Way (other-power) over against the "Path of the Sages" (self-power) by rejecting many of its notions (such as original enlightenment (*hongaku*), the aspiration for enlightenment (*bodhicitta*), and, in general, the wisdom tradition), Shinran tends to reinterpret these same notions so as to reconcile them with the basic tenets of the Pure Land Way. While Hōnen found his inspiration mainly in the *Meditation Sūtra* and Shandao (631–81), Shinran sees the *Larger Pure Land Sūtra* as the true doctrine and relied much on the other Chinese patriarch, Tanluan (476–542).

Shinran rids the Pure Land Way of all lingering traces of self-reliance. All activity of salvation is exclusively Amida's doing and the role of sentient beings is one of pure receptivity. Thus, transference of merits (*ekō*) does not occur among sentient beings but only from Amida to us; the *nenbutsu* is no longer seen as a work we perform as a condition for salvation, but as a spontaneous echo in us of the mutual *nenbutsu* of the Buddhas (17th Vow); and faith itself is the working of Amida without any contribution on our part. Shinran also redirects the future-oriented (toward the moment of death and the Pure Land after death) Pure Land religiosity towards the present by centering everything on the "one moment of faith" in this life.

After Shinran's death, his tomb was built at Ōtani in Kyoto, and managed by his daughter Kakushin. This tomb became the focus of Shinran's followers, and grew into the Honganji establishment, eventually the largest Buddhist institution in Japan.

Rennyo (1415–99) is often called the second founder of Shinshū, because, by his organizational talent and missionary activity, he made Honganji the center of Shinshū and one of the strongest religious organizations in Japan. He succeeded his father Zonnyo as *hossu* in 1457, and his success soon attracted the enmity of the warrior-monks of Mount Hiei, who burnt down his head temple in 1465. From then on he moved his headquarters to several places, especially Yoshizaki in Hokuriku (1471–5) and Yamashina near Kyoto (from 1483). Historians tend to see in him not so much a religious man as a clever politician, organizer, and propagandist. In Shinshū itself, however, his pastoral letters (*gobunsho* or *ofumi*), wherein he teaches the Pure Land doctrine in a popular way, have long been the most quoted sources of their doctrine. Some have argued that he compromised the purity of Shinran's religiosity by bringing it in line with the requirements of the "Japanese spirit" by enjoining the faithful to respect all Buddhas and all *kami*, and to be obedient to civil authorities in the same way as to the Buddha. This justification of cooperation with the authorities contributed to the Honganji's role as a strong supporter and advocate of the government and its militaristic expansion in pre-war (early twentieth-century) Japan.

After the time of Rennyo, the Honganji organization grew so large and powerful that at the beginning of the seventeenth century the shogun Tokugawa Ieyasu arranged for the group to be split into two, the Eastern (Higashi Honganji) and Western (Nishi Honganji).

Modern Shinshū continues to be the largest traditional Buddhist school in Japan, and also has many centers abroad, especially among Japanese immigrants in North and South America. It sponsors a number of modern universities (Ōtani University, Ryūkoku University) and is active in translating Shinran's and Shinshū works into Western languages. As with other schools of traditional Buddhism in post-war Japan, Shinshū is actively involved in peace movements and the attempt to rid society of discrimination. One recent controversy has been a debate over whether Shinshū should acknowledge and in some way accept the "folk" or "magical" practices that are common among their parishioners at the local level (called "Shinshū C" for "Catholicism"), or should adhere strictly to the orthodox rejection of all practices outside of faith in Amida ("Shinshū P" for "Puritanism").

See also: **Japan, Buddhism in; Pure Land movements in Japan.**

PAUL L. SWANSON

SHŌTOKU TAISHI AND BUDDHISM IN ANCIENT JAPAN

Shōtoku Taishi (574–622) was prince regent during the reign of Empress Suiko

(r. 593–628), famed as an early supporter and interpreter of Buddhism in Japan.

The historical facts concerning Prince Shōtoku are in doubt, but it has long been believed that he was a distinguished statesman and devout follower of Buddhism who contributed greatly both to the political development of Japan and to the early progress of Buddhism in Japan. Many of the stories connected with him (miraculous birth in a stable, and his ability to predict the future, or listen to ten people at once and reply correctly to all) have long been regarded as legendary, but recent scholarship has argued that most of the activities attributed to him were established on the occasion of the compilation of the *Nihon shoki*, an imperial "history" compiled around the middle of the eighth century, and expanded as part of a cult of Prince Shōtoku.

The accomplishments attributed to Prince Shōtoku made him a model statesman and religious figure. It is said that he sent embassies to China which opened the way for Chinese Buddhism and culture to enter and flourish in Japan, and that in 604 he promulgated the so-called "Seventeen-Article Constitution," more a set of moral injunctions than a set of laws, which included the admonition to "revere the three treasures (Buddha, *Dharma, Sangha*)." He is also credited with support for the building of major Buddhist temples such as Asukadera, Shittenōji, and Hōryūji.

Shōtoku is also credited with composing commentaries on three major Mahāyāna texts, the *Lotus Sūtra*, *Vimalakīrti Sūtra*, and *Śrīmālādevī Sūtra*, all of which have proven to be important texts for Japanese Buddhism. The famous inscription on an embroidery at Hōryūji, said to have been written as a testament to his wife, that "the world is an illusion, only the Buddha is real," is also thought to be a later attribution, but is well known as an insightful observation based on Buddhist teachings.

Shōtoku has been revered by many Buddhists throughout Japanese history, including major leaders such as Saichō and Shinran, and he remains a figure idealized for his reputed political accomplishments, religious devotion, and commitment to harmony (*wa*). Prince Shōtoku has thus served as a focus and symbol for the introduction and early propagation of Buddhism in Japan, though care should be taken not to understand this period solely in terms of his purported historical accomplishments (for details see the entry on Japan, Buddhism in).

See also: **Japan, Buddhism in.**

PAUL L. SWANSON

SHUGENDŌ

Shugendō is a syncretistic Japanese Buddhist tradition of mountain ascetic practices, influential for much of Japanese history, which combines elements from esoteric Buddhism, shamanism, indigenous beliefs concerning mountains and spirits of the dead, Yin-Yang traditions, and Taoist magic. Shugendō literally means "the way of cultivating supernatural power." Its followers are known as *yamabushi* (those who lie down in the mountains) or *shugenja* (ascetics, or "those who cultivate power"). Although their role has evolved and changed over the years, these figures were expected to accumulate religious power by undergoing severe ascetic practices in the mountains – such as fasting, meditating, reciting spells or Buddhist texts, sitting under waterfalls, gathering firewood, abstaining from water, hanging over cliffs to "weigh" one's sins, retiring in solitary confinement to caves, and performing rituals such as fire ceremonies. The *shugenja* then drew on this power to provide services such as a guide for pilgrimage, the demonstration of superhuman feats like walking on fire, and the performance of various religious rites like divination, exorcism, and prayers.

In pre-Buddhist Japan, religious activities included festivals and rites celebrating the descent of the agricultural deities from the mountains in the spring and their return to the mountains after the autumn harvest. There was also a belief in mountains as the residence of the dead, or as a borderland between this world and the other world. As Buddhism was being introduced and assimilated into Japanese society in the sixth century (if not earlier), ascetics were entering mountainous areas to undergo religious austerities. These persons were not necessarily Buddhist monks, but included an assortment of solitary hermits, diviners, exorcists, "unordained" Buddhist specialists (*ubasoku*), and wandering religious figures (*hijiri*). The most famous of these was En-no-Gyōja (En the Ascetic, or En-no-Ozunu), a prototypical ascetic with shamanic powers and the semi-legendary founder of Shugendō. En-no-gyōja is said to have practiced asceticism on Mount Katsuragi, a mountain west of the Yamato plain, and attained supernatural powers. Many stories tell of his ability to command spirits and demons, or bind disobedient ones with a spell. One story relates that he ordered spirits to build a bridge of rock between Mount Katsuragi and Kinpusen in Yoshino. According to the *Nihon shoki*, a man named En-no-Ozunu was banished in 699 to the island of Ōshima in Izu on trumped-up charges of using his supernatural powers to control and mislead the people. Legend has it that En-no-gyōja would fly to Mount Fuji every night to continue his practices. En-no-gyōja is important mainly as a model of the mountain ascetic. He is a common figure in Japanese lore and literature, and his name and image are found throughout Japan on mountains and sites used for ascetic practice.

By the early ninth century many Buddhist ascetics, especially those associated with the esoteric traditions of Tendai and Shingon, were entering not only Mount Hiei and Mount Kōya but also other mountains, such as Mount Kinbu in the Yoshino region. Various mountainous areas throughout Japan developed their own traditions, among them Hakusan and Mount Fuji in central Japan, the Haguro peaks in the north, Ishizuchi in Shikoku, and Hikosan in Kyushu. Each had its own religious history, its own set of deities, its own web of associations with other sacred sites, and its own community of Shugendō practitioners. *Shugenja* from these areas performed religious services and guided pilgrims to popular sacred sites like Mitake and Kumano. By the middle of the tenth century, these *shugenja* gradually became organized, usually in connection with the pilgrimages of retired emperors and aristocrats. In time the institutional structure formed two major pillars: the Honzan-ha headquartered at Shōgo-in and affiliated with Tendai Buddhism, and the Tōzan-ha headquartered at Kōfukuji and Daigoji and affiliated with Shingon Buddhism. In this way the older shamanistic and mountain ascetic practices were incorporated within the categories, teachings and practices of esoteric Buddhism, and Shugendō came to represent a large part of the dominant syncretistic worldview of medieval Japan. In the early modern period (seventeenth to nineteenth century) the most common role of the *shugenja* shifted from that of ascetic wanderer to that of someone settled in a local society, in the role of *oshi* ("teacher") or *kitōshi* (a diviner who offers "prayers").

Buddhist aspects of Shugendō are reflected in its doctrinal and ethical teachings, rituals, cosmology, and ascetic practices, based mainly on esoteric Buddhism as it evolved in the Tendai and Shingon traditions. Examples include the reinterpretation of traditional Buddhist categories – such as the ten realms of existence (from hell to Buddha) and the six perfections (*pāramitā*) – in terms of the physical and spiritual progress made by ascetics as they advance through the mountain trails and trials. *Goma* fire ceremonies and other Buddhist rituals also underwent transformation. Cosmological and symbolic significance were assigned to Shugendō geographical sites based on the configuration of the womb realm (*taizōkai*) and diamond realm (*kongōkai*) *maṇḍalas*. The mountains came to be identified with the body of the cosmic Buddha Mahāvairocana (Jap. Dainichi), and entering them took on the added significance of becoming integrated with the Buddha and attaining enlightenment. The belief that Buddhahood can be attained within this life is a central tenet of Shugendō faith and a major goal of its practice. Traditional Buddhist figures (buddhas, *bodhisattvas*, guardian deities) were incorporated into Shugendō worship, along with completely new figures. Especially important is Fudō-myō-ō (the "unmovable"), a fiery and angry-looking representation of the role of the cosmic Buddha in destroying the passionate afflictions of this world. Buddhist practices such as meditation (seated, walking, or otherwise on the move) and the recitation of scriptures are a central part of Shugendō activities. Thus, while it is misleading to speak of Shugendō only in terms of Buddhism, its adherents consider themselves Buddhists and it is not inaccurate to consider it part of the Buddhist tradition.

Today Shugendō is only a shadow of its former glory. Shugendō-related activities (such as the *kaihōgyō* Tendai practices of "circling the peaks" on Mount Hiei, and Shugendō-influenced rituals and activities in some of the new religious movements of Japan) are still practiced. A syncretistic mix of various traditions, Shugendō was outlawed in the late nineteenth century as part of the attempt by the Japanese government to "purify" Shinto of its "foreign" elements. Shugendō specialists were forced to identify themselves either as Buddhist monks or Shinto priests. With the post-war declaration of religious freedom in the second half of the 1940s, Shugendō organizations recovered their independence and many activities (such as the Yoshino-Kumano pilgrimage along the Ōmine range, and the seasonal retreats at Haguro) have been revived by their former institutional centers.

See also: ***Honji-suijaku/shinbutsu shūgo* – Buddhist syncretism in Japan; Japan, Buddhism in.**

PAUL L. SWANSON

SIDDHĀRTHA GAUTAMA, LIFE OF

This essay considers the life of Siddhārtha Gautama as a religious modality that finds expression in various contexts, including Buddhist culture, ritual, and art. Some Buddhists consciously emulate his hagiography in the ways in which they conduct their own lives. Familiar fragments of the Buddha's biographical narrative also inform powerfully evocative representations in visual and performative art, including temple murals, theatrical performances and so forth. For discussions of historical and textual biographies of the Buddha, readers should consult entries on Buddha, story of; Hagiographies; and *Jātakas* and other narrative collections.

For about 100 million Buddhists who comprise the Theravāda world today, the life of Siddhārtha Gautama, the Buddha, is a foundational narrative that describes for the community his model for mastering enlightenment. As such it is a master narrative shaping the imagination of all Buddhist communities, while continually undergoing local reinterpretations in Sri Lanka, Myanmar, Thailand, Laos, and Cambodia. Its numerous versions are commonly known and its paradigmatic significance is refracted in just about every aspect of popular Buddhist belief and practice. Prominent themes of the

Buddha's final life include his miraculous birth, the predictions Brahmin sages offered about his future, the privileged life he led as a prince, his renunciation of attachment, the ascetic trials, his temptation by Māra, the King of Hells, his ultimate enlightenment, his sermon to set the Wheel of Law into motion, his ministry to his community, and his Final Departure from the world, *pārinirvāṇa*. The life of the Buddha, and the tradition of his sacred biography more generally, constitute an encompassing cultural idiom or a root metaphor, in Victor Turner's terms, that continues to engage the imagination of Buddhist communities and creates meaning in practice, doctrine, and belief.

Myth and cultural realities

In 1977, Frank Reynolds noted that the narrative structures of the Buddha's sacred biography informed emergent doctrinal and institutional formations in the early Buddhist tradition. The mythic qualities of the Buddha's sacred biography helped shape the process by which the early community moved from a focus on the Buddha's charisma to the cultural institutions that emerged after his death. In the story of the life of Gautama, court Brahmins predict upon his birth that he will become either a world-conquering universal monarch (*cakkavatti*) or renounce worldly matter to attain Buddhahood. These complementary biographical themes are expressed in terms of the dual Buddhist roles of a world conqueror and a world renouncer. This division of social roles lies at the core of traditional Theravāda cultural practices. The religious practice of a Buddhist king (*dhammarāja*) and of his subjects was focused on making merit by providing material support for the monastic community of world renouncers, the *sangha*. Those who join the *sangha* are ordained into a community of world renouncers. In an analogy to the Buddha's son, Rāhula, who became ordained, the *sangha* is sometimes also referred to as the Sons of the Buddha. Some Theravāda Buddhist kings and monks have also been inspired to emulate the life of the Buddha in the conduct of their own lives. The hagiographies of Buddhist saints frequently evoke analogies with salient events or themes in the life of the Buddha. By implication, such analogies imply that the saintly person's spiritual achievements are in some ways comparable to those of the Buddha and legitimated by the paradigm and significance of his story.

Teaching about the Buddha through narratives and art

The story about Siddhārtha Gautama Śākyamuni is not just about the founder of the tradition, it also frequently conveys the foundation of knowledge about the Buddhist tradition. There is no single or original version of the story of the life of the Buddha and the Buddhist traditions encompass numerous authoritative versions of the narrative. The life of the Buddha is commonly the subject of storytelling, sermons, mural paintings, and even popular entertainment like movies and children's literature. The narrative teaches listeners about mastering the path to enlightenment and invites interpretations and illustrations of his message. Many Buddhists are taught, at an early age, the narrative episodes and moral values conveyed in this story and Buddhist audiences are generally familiar with its salient episodes. A modern version by the Burmese monk Ashin Janakabhivamsa (1951) including captivatingly didactic illustrations is accessible online at http://nibbana.com (http://web.ukonline.co.uk/buddhism/).

The text that accompanies these illustrations is easily accessible to young audiences and others unfamiliar with this story. Its narrative structure follows a familiar pattern, while rendering this particular version in a cultural style that is specifically Burmese. The illustrations are depicted in a modern artistic style characteristic of the 1930s and retain many of the story's mythic and miraculous elements.

Narrative episodes of this story are commonly represented in Buddhist iconography and through visual and performative media. Such frames are themselves reminders of the broader biographical paradigm of the Buddha's life. They illustrate specific teachings of the Buddha. A catalog of standardized representations provides a symbolic index to central events in this story. Buddhist iconographic art such as the Buddha's footprint or Buddha images may bring to mind specific episodes in the biographical narrative. Such representations index his particular achievement as well as the possibility of enlightenment in general (See Figure 36).

Murals carved in stone or painted on plaques often depict scenes from the Buddha's life on the walls of temples or surrounding the base of a *stūpa*. The earliest illustrations of narrative frames taken from the life of the Buddha appear in the Buddhist art found at Bhārhut and dating to the second century BCE. Artistic representations of the life of the Buddha are also commonly found in later Buddhist temples, like those at Borobudur and Pagan.

Figure 36 Wall mural in Hwagaesa Monastery, Seoul, Korea, depicting the Buddha defeating Māra during the night of his awakening, and turning arrows shot at him into flowers.

Buddha images depicting the moment of his enlightenment typically show him in a cross-legged posture, seated on a lotus throne, and with his right hand extended toward the earth (*mudrā*). Icons of Gautama's *parinirvāṇa*, the moment of his departure from the world of impermanence, show him reclining on his side and resting his head in his right hand. Some icons, like the Emerald Buddha in Bangkok or the Mahāmuni Image in Mandalay, are believed to embody Gautama's extraordinary powers. Burmese myths recount that, while on a visit to southern Burma, Gautama enlivened and conversed with the Mahāmuni Image that is now enshrined in Mandalay. The image is said to have advised many kings, but has fallen silent because of the moral decline of the world.

Ritual participation in the life of the Buddha

The cultic celebration of the life of the Buddha allows Buddhist communities to incorporate into their own lives mythic times, places, and events associated with the Buddha. Such rituals allow Buddhists to create karmic links between the life of the Buddha and their own lives. In the same way, they also bring the universal message of the Buddha into the local contexts of Buddhist communities. Rituals that focus on the Buddha and his biography give him a presence among Buddhist communities in religiously meaningful ways, despite his absence from the world of rebirth.

Theravādins participate in the life of Gautama through various kinds of ritual performances. These may include pilgrimages to places associated with his relics, famous *stūpas*, or images. Pilgrimage destinations may also include traveling to places associated with biographical events, such as the place of the Buddha's birth at Lumbinī, the place of his Enlightenment at Bodhgayā, the Deer

Park in Vārānasi (Benares) where he preached his first sermon, and the village of Kusinārā where the Buddha passed into *pārinirvāṇa*. Calendrical rituals also commemorate his enlightenment, his first sermon and his *pārinirvāṇa*.

Ritual veneration of the Buddha's presence may also consist of meditating on and emulating Ānanda's service to the Buddha. Communal rituals celebrating the Buddha's ritual presence generally involve the veneration of his physical remains (*sārīra*), *stūpas*, and icons. Novice initiation in Burma similarly emulates biographical themes from the last life as the young boys begin their ritual initiation dressed in the garments of princes who ride on horses in procession. During the *Shinbyu* (White Lord) initiation to novicehood, the boys attend the rituals dressed in the royal garments and honors that the tradition ascribes to the life of Prince Siddhartha. They then have their heads shaven and change into the orange robes of the *sangha*.

In contrast to other religions of the world, the Buddhist biographical genre extends beyond the life of its founder to encompass his countless rebirths that lead up to his culminating and final rebirth, as well as the lives of many of his disciplines and companions who traverse with him the cycle of rebirth (*saṃsāra*). In that sense, the final life of Siddhārtha Gautama is merely the culminating episode within an encompassing narrative of many lives. The foundational life of Siddhārtha Gautama thus engenders a biographical genre within the Theravādin tradition that spans not merely the life of the founder but, more significantly, the many rebirths that link moments in his unfolding dispensation to the dispensation and lineages of Buddhas of the past and the future.

See also: **Famous Buddhists and ideal types; India, Buddhism in.**

JULIANE SCHOBER

SIMMER-BROWN, JUDITH

Until relatively recently, combining academic study and being openly Buddhist was considered to compromise one's academic credibility. Judith Simmer-Brown was one of the first academics to combat the prejudice that one could not be a good academic *and* a Buddhist. With a B.A. from Cornell, an M.A. from Florida State University and a Ph.D. from Walden University (with studies at Columbia and the University of British Columbia as well) her academic credentials are solid. She has been a Buddhist practitioner for over thirty years, and is a respected teacher. Her books include *Ḍākinī's Warm Breath* (2001) and *Benedict's Buddhists Comment on the Rule of St. Benedict* (2001) with Br. David Steindl-Rast, Joseph Goldstein *et al.* She is on the board of the Society for Buddhist–Christian Studies, is a member of the Lilly Buddhist–Christian Theological Encounter, and has been a professor at Naropa University for almost thirty years.

Simmer-Brown initially studied Zen with Suzuki Rōshi. After his death she became a student of Chögyan Trungpa Rinpoche. She has clearly absorbed many of his teachings, including that regarding "spiritual materialism" and his ideas, constructing a Buddhism that is suited to Western needs. Although he has been dead for many years, his name came up frequently in a recent interview (2005, for *Eastern Horizon*) with Simmer-Brown (http://dannyfisher.blogspot.com/2005/03/interview-acarya-judith-simmer-brown.html).

Her interviews and articles, recently "The Roar of the Lioness", indicate that she has spent considerable time contemplating the development of Buddhism in the West, especially the United States. She notes that development of Buddhism in the West will be driven by the lay tradition. Certainly monasticism functions as a spiritual archetype but it has not been a predominant tradition in the West and appears to be in decline within the

Christian tradition and, she notes sadly, within Tibetan monasteries in India. Her approach to the development of Buddhism in America is one that, in effect, monasticizes the laity. That is, it provides laypeople with the opportunity to do retreats and learn practices formerly done only by monastics in Asia. She applauds the move by Thrangu Rinpoche of Gampo Abbey to institute the practice of taking "temporary" vows for a period of time.

Simmer-Brown is also one of the few to struggle seriously with the question of hierarchy and patriarchy in Buddhism. She raises the thorny question regarding whether or not patriarchy and hierarchy are inevitably entwined. She raises concerns that some women may be moving away from male Asian masters too quickly, out of cultural concerns, before they have absorbed their wisdom. Further, she discusses the cultural inclination of American society to challenge hierarchy, tradition, authority, and privilege. She notes that this tendency must also be examined along with the cultural trappings of Buddhism. She seeks a balance between innovation and tradition.

While Simmer-Brown notes that women's participation in the construction of American Buddhism has been quite remarkable, with half of all lay teachers being women, she adds a warning. American Buddhism is still new, still marginal to mainstream society. Sociological studies show that as marginal groups become more mainstream, they adopt the organizational patterns of the broader society. In this case, those patterns are patriarchal and androcentric.

Simmer-Brown's combination of scholarship and practitioner experience provides one of the most thoughtful approaches to women in Western Buddhism.

See also: **Women in Buddhism: an historical and textual overview.**

MAVIS L. FENN

SIVARAKSA, SULAK

Sulak Sivaraksa is one of Thailand's (or Siam's, as he prefers) best-known and most controversial engaged Buddhist reformers and social activists. A lay Theravādin with a fiery tongue, Sulak has done more than most through his prolific writing, publishing, ecumenical networking, and founding of non-governmental organizations (NGOs) to influence engaged Buddhism's development, not only in Thailand, but around the world.

Sulak was born on 27 March 1933, within months of the signing of Thailand's first constitution by King Prajadhipok (Rama VII) in December 1932. He was educated in temple schools in Bangkok before earning university and law degrees in Great Britain. Seemingly boundless in energy, he has lectured extensively throughout the world's colleges and universities; is responsible for the publication and editing of numerous periodicals (including Thailand's respected and influential *Social Science Review*); has authored countless articles and books (including *Seeds of Peace: A Buddhist Vision for Renewing Society*; *Conflict, Culture, Change: Engaged Buddhism in a Globalizing World*; and *Loyalty Demands Dissent: Autobiography of an Engaged Buddhist*); all the while founding an ongoing series of NGOs and foundations in Thailand and abroad (including the Komol Keemthong Foundation and the International Network of Engaged Buddhists). In all of these activities, Sulak has demonstrated his dedication, on the one hand, to addressing vital social needs – especially the needs of the poor, women, and children – and, on the other, to creating ecumenical networks of educators, social workers, and peace activists throughout the world. An acerbic critic of Thailand's military government and the corrosive effects of Western consumer culture, Sulak has twice been forced into exile, and twice arraigned and once arrested on charges of *lèse majesté*, spending four months in prison in 1984 before charges were eventually dropped (reportedly through the intervention of Thailand's King Bhumibol). In 1994 he was nominated by the American Friends Service Committee for the Nobel Peace Prize and in 1995 was given the so-called "Alternative Nobel Prize" or Right Livelihood Award "for his vision and commitment to a future rooted in democracy, justice and cultural integrity."

Sulak's cosmopolitan vision for the transformation of Siamese society and the world aptly takes inspiration from a variety of sources. An advocate of what he calls "small 'b' Buddhism," he is especially indebted to Bhikkhu Buddhadasa's notion of "dhammic socialism" and Thich Nhat Hanh's teachings on "interbeing" and "being peace"; at the same time, traces of the Christian social gospel, Gandhi's and Martin Luther King, Jr.'s non-violent social activism, and the quietist spiritualities of Thomas Merton and the Society of Friends are also noticeably present in his work. At the base of Sulak's vision is an unremitting criticism of the structural causes of suffering which he sees at work in Western-style capitalism and militaristic societies throughout the world, and an unflinching commitment to building "a spiritual, green and just society" founded upon Buddhist-inspired principles of social and economic development. In typical engaged Buddhist fashion, he insists that "the transformation of society must first begin with the self" through the cultivation of wisdom, compassion, and lovingkindness.

See also: **Ariyaratne, A.T.; Buddhist economics and ecology; Buddhist peace groups (in Asia and the West); Dalai Lama (and the Tibetan struggle); Engaged Buddhism; Global Buddhist networks: selected examples; Maha Ghosananda; Nhat Hanh, Thich; South and Southeast Asia, Buddhism in; Thailand, Buddhism in.**

JIM DEITRICK

SKILLFUL MEANS (*UPĀYA-KAUŚALYA*)

The notion of Skillful Means has its roots in the Buddha's skill in teaching the *Dharma*, particularly as demonstrated in his ability to adapt his message to the context in which it was delivered. For example, when talking to Brahmins, the Buddha would often explain his teachings by reference to their rituals and traditions, leading his audience step by step to see the truth of a Buddhist tenet. Parables, metaphors, and similes formed an important part of his teaching repertoire, skillfully tailored to suit the level of his audience. This is the primary sense in which the term *upāya-kosalla* is found in Pāli sources.

Mahāyāna developments

The Mahāyāna developed this idea in a radical way by intimating, in texts such as the *Lotus Sūtra* (*c.* first century CE), that the early teachings were not just skillfully delivered, but were a means to an end in their entirety. In chapter two of the *Lotus Sūtra* the Buddha introduces the doctrine of Skillful Means and demonstrates through the use of parables throughout the text why it is necessary for him to make use of stratagems and devices. The text depicts him as a wise man or kindly father whose words his foolish children refuse to heed. To encourage them to follow his advice he has recourse to "Skillful Means," realizing that this is the only way to bring the ignorant and deluded into the path to liberation. Although this involves a certain degree of duplicity, such as telling lies, the Buddha is exonerated from all blame because his only motivation is compassionate concern for all beings.

This development has certain implications for ethics. If the early teachings were provisional rather than ultimate, then perhaps the precepts they contain could also be of a provisional rather than an ultimate nature. Thus the clear and strict rules encountered in the early sources which prohibit certain sorts of acts could be interpreted more in the way of guidelines rather than as ultimately binding. In particular, *bodhisattvas*, the new moral heroes of the Mahāyāna, could claim increased latitude and flexibility based on their recognition of the importance of compassion. A *bodhisattva* takes a vow to save all beings, and there is evidence in many texts of impatience with rules and regulations which seem to get in the way of a *bodhisattva* going about his salvific mission. The new imperative was to act in accordance with the spirit and not the letter of the precepts, and some sources go so far as to allow *karuṇā* to override other considerations and even sanction immoral acts if the *bodhisattva* sees that it would reduce suffering.

The pressure to bend or suspend the rules in the interests of compassion results in certain texts establishing new codes of conduct for *bodhisattvas* which sometimes allow the precepts to be broken. In some of these, such as the *Upāyakauśalya Sūtra* (*c.* first century BCE), even killing is said to be justified to prevent someone committing a heinous crime and suffering *karmic* retribution in hell. Telling lies, abandoning celibacy, and other breaches of the precepts are also said to be permissible in exceptional circumstances. It is not always clear, however, whether such behavior is held up by the texts as normative and a model for imitation by others, or to make a point about the great compassion of *bodhisattvas*, who willingly accept the *karmic* consequences of breaking the precepts as the price of helping others.

See also: **Buddha, style of teaching; *Dharma*; Ethics; Mahāyāna Buddhism.**

DAMIEN KEOWN

SŌKA GAKKAI INTERNATIONAL

One of Japan's most successful and controversial new religions, Sōka Gakkai International (SGI) traces its origins to the publication of *Sōka Kyōikugaku Taikei* (*The Theory of Value-Creating Pedagogy*) in 1930 by reformist educator and lay Nichiren Shōshū practitioner Tsunesaburō Makiguchi, and later to the founding of the Sōka Kyōiku Gakkai (Value Creation Educational Society) in 1937 by Makiguchi and his protégé Josei Toda. Critical of Japan's militaristic educational system and refusing to require Society members to enshrine imperial talismans, Makiguchi and Toda, along with eighteen other Society leaders, were imprisoned and the Society disbanded by the Japanese wartime government in 1943. Tragically, Makiguchi died in prison of malnutrition in 1944, while Toda, who revived the Society and became its second president in the years following World War II, was released in 1945.

Toda claimed while in prison to have recited the *daimoku* (*namu myōhō renge kyō*) two million times, culminating in a religious experience that cemented his commitment to the *Lotus Sūtra* and propagation of Nichiren Shōshū Buddhism. In 1951, he re-established the Society as a lay organization of the Nichiren Shōshū and renamed it simply Sōka Gakkai (Value Creation Society) to stress its now decidedly religious character. Owing to Toda's fanatical efforts and the aggressive proselytizing tactics in which he encouraged members to engage (notoriously called *shakubuku*, lit. "break and subdue"), Sōka Gakkai grew at a fervent pace, claiming a membership of over one million families by Toda's death in 1958.

Toda was succeeded by Daisaku Ikeda as the Society's third president in 1960. A controversial figure, Ikeda has overseen the group's continued dramatic growth, not only in Japan but around the world – especially in the United States and Brazil. SGI, which presently claims a membership of over twelve million people in 190 countries and territories, was founded in 1975 under Ikeda's leadership to unify the

Society's growing international constituency. Ikeda is responsible for reviving the Society's commitment to education with the establishment of its own schools and universities in Japan and abroad, broadening its interests to include support for culture and the arts, and cultivating cooperative relations with other religions and Buddhist sects. It is also under Ikeda's leadership that ties between SGI and Nichiren Shōshū were dramatically severed in 2001 with the excommunication of Ikeda and the entire SGI membership. In response, SGI leaders have since assumed responsibility for many activities once reserved for Shōshū priests and there is little indication of SGI suffering significant harm as a result of the excommunications.

According to its charter, the fundamental aim of SGI is that of "contributing to peace, culture, and education based on the philosophy and ideals of the Buddhism of Nichiren Daishōnin." For SGI, Nichiren's is fundamentally a humanistic philosophy which "enables individuals to cultivate and bring forth their inherent wisdom ... and realize a society of peaceful and prosperous coexistence." Although some engaged Buddhists are reluctant to include this controversial organization among their ranks (see Queen and King 1996: 3–4), SGI's reformist commitment to the cultivation of peace in society through the practice of Buddhism and active social engagement no doubt justifies its inclusion.

See also: **Buddhist peace groups (in Asia and the West); Engaged Buddhism; Global Buddhist networks: selected examples; Japan, Buddhism in.**

JIM DEITRICK

SŎN BUDDHISM

The import of Chan Buddhism and the Nine Mountains school of Sŏn

The first record of Chinese Chan Buddhism in Korea, where it is pronounced Sŏn, appears in connection with the Silla monk Pŏmnang (fl. 632–46) who studied with Daoxin (580–651), the Fourth Patriarch of Chinese Chan Buddhism. Pŏmnang returned to Korea during the mid-seventh century and passed down his teachings to Sinhaeng (?–779), who in turn traveled to China and studied with Puji (651–739), a successor of Shenxiu (?–706) the head of the Northern school of Chan. For the next two centuries Korean monks continued to travel to China to learn this new form of Buddhism, eventually developing what has been known as the Nine Mountains school of Sŏn Buddhism.

The Nine Mountains school of Sŏn does not denote nine different schools of Sŏn Buddhism, but rather the nine sites of Sŏn Buddhism located in the nine different mountains, and created by the nine pioneers of Korean Sŏn Buddhism, all of whom studied in China. Although Sinhaeng brought with him the Northern school of Chan, all but one of the founders of the Nine Mountains school studied with disciples of Mazu Daoyi (707–86), who was the founder of the most subitist Chinese Chan sect, the Hongzu sect of the Southern school.

The Nine Mountains school of Sŏn developed over a period of a century. Toŭi (fl. 821), who returned from China in the early ninth century and founded the Kaji Mountain school of Sŏn, is credited as the first patriarch of Korean Sŏn Buddhism. The first record of the Nine Mountains school, however, is dated the late eleventh century (1084), suggesting that the formation of the Nine Mountains school might be later than the end of the Unified Silla period (668–935) as scholars have speculated.

Kanhwa Sŏn tradition

By the eleventh century when Sŏn Buddhism established itself in Korea, Korean Buddhists were already well versed in the scholastic teachings of Buddhism and had established what has been known as the Five Schools, which include: Kyeyul chong (*Vinaya* school), Yŏlban chong (*Nirvāṇa* school), Pŏpsŏng chong (*Dharma* Nature school), Hwaŏm chong (Huayan school), and Pŏpsang chong (Yogācāra school). Given the radically different emphasis with which Sŏn Buddhism distinguishes itself from existing scriptural Buddhism, its appearance in Korea called for efforts towards mutual understanding and rapprochement between Sŏn and the scholastic teachings of Buddhism (Kor. Kyo). Indeed, this became one of the main concerns for Korean Buddhists during the Koryŏ period (918–1392). In this context, two figures are noteworthy: Ŭich'ŏn (1055–1101), who created the Ch'ŏnt'ae school (Ch. Tiantai), and Pojo Chinul (1158–1210), who created the Chogye school. The relationship between Sŏn and scriptural teaching in Ŭich'ŏn stands in opposition to that in Chinul. Ŭich'ŏn thought that Sŏn meditational practice could be incorporated into doctrinal Buddhism, whereas Chinul tried to incorporate doctrinal teachings into Sŏn by confirming the sameness between the two. When Ŭich'ŏn opened the Ch'ŏnt'ae school, those who joined the school were mostly Sŏn monks, and within Koryŏ Buddhism Ch'ŏnt'ae was categorized as a sect of Sŏn Buddhism, which obscured the identity of both Ch'ŏnt'ae and Sŏn in Ŭich'ŏn's Buddhism. Ŭich'ŏn's limited vision of Sŏn Buddhism and his early death undermined Ŭich'ŏn's project to bring together meditational and doctrinal teachings.

Chinul discovered in the Huayan theory of Nature Origination, which asserts that all existing beings in the world are manifestation of the Tathāgata nature, a doctrine equivalent to the Sŏn adage that the mind is Buddha. Chinul's Buddhism is characterized by an equal emphasis on doctrinal teaching and Sŏn practice, with a special focus on Kanhwa Sŏn (Ch. Kanhua Chan) practice as the ultimate way to reach enlightenment, as is well articulated in his posthumous work, *Kanhwa kyŏrŭi ron* (*Treatise on Resolving Doubts about Hwadu Meditation*). Understood as a sudden awakening followed by gradual practice, Chinul's Sŏn teaching is identified as Pojo Sŏn, to be distinguished from Imje (Ch. Linji, d. 866–67) Sŏn which was officially introduced to Korea at the end of the Koryŏ dynasty.

Chinul's successor, Chin'gak Hyesim (1178–1234), solidified the Kanhwa Sŏn tradition endorsed by Chinul. Without much concern for the philosophical relationship between doctrinal issues and Sŏn practice, Hyesim exclusively emphasized *hwadu* (Ch. *huatou*; critical phrase) meditation, and compiled a comprehensive collection of 1,125 *kongans* in his *Sŏnmun yŏmsongjip* (*The Collection of Verses and Cases of Sŏn School*, 1226) which has served as a textbook for Korean Sŏn practitioners. Hyesim also encouraged female practitioners to practice *hwadu* at a time when women's Buddhist practice was limited to chanting and *sūtra*-readings.

Kanhwa Sŏn, as introduced by Chinul and popularized by Hyesim, was the version taught by Chinese Chan Master Dahui Zonggao (1089–1163), the seventeenth-generation successor of the Yanggi branch of the Linji school. By the end of the Koryŏ dynasty, three Sŏn masters had begun introducing Sŏn teachings to the Linji school: T'ae'go Pou (1301–82), Na'ong Hye'gŭn (1320–76), and Paegun Kyŏnghan (1299–1375). All three experienced enlightenment by practicing *hwadu*, and traveled to China where they received recognition of their experience and *dharma* transmission from the masters in the Linji school. T'ae'go Pou has been credited as the authentic transmitter of the teachings of the Linji school. This raised a debate as to whether the founding patriarch of the Chogye Order should be Pojo Chinul, who was the first to introduce Linji's Buddhism in his teaching of Kanhua Sŏn, or T'aego Pou, who received recognition in person from a master in the Chinese Linji school.

Mountain Buddhism and the debate of the three types of Sŏn

During the Chosŏn dynasty (1392–1910) Sŏn Buddhism suffered from neo-Confucian, anti-Buddhist policy. Sŏn masters emphasized the validity of Sŏn teaching by proposing the oneness of the traditional Three Teachings of Buddhism, Confucianism, and Daoism. As Buddhist schools were variously merged and abolished according to government policy, there had been no Buddhist sectarian identity in Korea since 1424, a period called Mountain Buddhism which centuries later resulted in an identity crisis for Sŏn Buddhists.

Hamhŏ Dŭkt'ong (1376–1433) was a leading Sŏn master at the beginning of the Chosŏn period. Hamhŏ challenged Confucians in the midst of the Buddhist–Confucian debate. Unlike Sŏn masters before him, Hamhŏ Dŭkt'ong left behind commentaries on Buddhist *sūtras* including *Wŏn'gakkyŏng so* (*Commentaries on the Complete Enlightenment Sūtra*) and *Kŭmganggyŏng o'gahae sŏrŭi* (*Commentaries on the Five Master Interpretations of the Diamond Sūtra*).

Ch'ŏnghŏ Hyujŏng (1520–1604) reserved the patriarchal Sŏn of Kanhwa for the practitioners of superior capacity and proposed to incorporate doctrinal teaching at the initial stage that guides medium- to low-capacity practitioners to Sŏn Buddhism.

Around the beginning of the nineteenth century, an attempt was made to overcome the decline of Buddhism by critically exploring the identity of Sŏn Buddhism. Paekp'a Kŭngsŏn (1767–1852) proposed a systematization of Sŏn Buddhist teachings in his work *Sŏnmun su'gyŏng* (*Hand Mirror of Sŏn School*, 1820), and Ch'oŭi Ŭisŏn (1786–1866) critically responded to Paekp'a's theory in his *Sŏnmun sabyŏn manŏ* (*Talks on the Four Divisions of Sŏn School*). The debate lasted for over a century. Paekp'a identified the three phrases of Linji with the three types of Sŏn – Patriarchal Sŏn, Tathāgata Sŏn, and Theoretical Sŏn – and he understood their relationship as hierarchical. Paekp'a also identified the first phrase in the Linji's three phrases with live words (Kor. *hwalgu*) and with Patriarchal Sŏn, whereas the third phrase was identified with that of dead words (Kor. *sagu*) and with Theoretical Sŏn.

Ch'oŭi warned that Paekp'a's theory of the three types of Sŏn could distort Sŏn teaching. Ch'oŭi argued that the Linji's three phrases did not stand in a hierarchical order, nor did the four classifications of Patriarchal Sŏn, Tathāgata Sŏn, Outside-formal Sŏn (Kor. *kyŏgoesŏn*) and Theoretical Sŏn. Ch'oŭi considered all four types of Sŏn to be skillful means of Buddhist teachings in which different methods could and should be used according to different levels and characters of practitioners. Ch'oŭi's non-hierarchical view on the different types of Sŏn reveals a new approach to Sŏn teachings.

Son Buddhism in modern Korea

While the debate on the identity of Sŏn Buddhism revived the scholastic zeal in Sŏn Buddhism, Kyŏnghŏ Sŏngu (1849–1912) set the foundation of Sŏn Buddhism in modern Korea by reviving the Kanhwa Sŏn tradition. After spending some time as a renowned *sūtra* lecturer, Kyŏnghŏ condemned the doctrinal approach to Buddhism, practiced *hwadu* meditation, and went through an awakening experience. He created a compact community to revive Sŏn Buddhism, drafted rules for the Sŏn monastery, and trained disciples, including Man'gong (1871–1946) and Hanam (1876–1951), both of whom played a pivotal role in defending an independent identity for Korean Buddhism during the colonial period (1910–45) and in establishing modern Korean Buddhism after the liberation.

T'oe'ong Sŏngch'ŏl (1912–93) influenced Korean Sŏn Buddhism with his rigorous Sŏn practice. Sŏngch'ŏl made efforts to renovate Sŏn monastic life, emphasized the sudden awakening followed by sudden cultivation as the orthodox form of Sŏn practice, and challenged Pojo Chinul's position as the founding patriarch of the Chogye Order.

Sŏn Buddhism is still one of the most dominant forms of Buddhism in modern Korea. The Chogye (Ch. Caoqi) school, with its origin in the Nine Mountains schools of Sŏn, closed in 1424, but was re-established in 1962 and has since become a main Buddhist school in contemporary Korea.

See also: **Chan; Korea, Buddhism in; Meditation (Chan/Zen); Zen.**

JIN Y. PARK

SŎNGCH'ŎL

Yi Sŏngch'ŏl (1912–93), with the epithet T'oe'ong, was one of the most influential figures in Korean Buddhism during the second half of the twentieth century. Sŏngch'ŏl joined a monastery in 1936 after practicing *hwadu* (Ch. *huatou*) as a lay practitioner. He was appointed as the first *pangjang* (Sŏn master) of the Hae'in *ch'ongnim* (a cluster of monasteries) in 1969 and served as the supreme patriarch of the Chogye Order from 1981 to 1993. Sŏngch'ŏl's Buddhism is characterized by his teaching of the middle path and his emphasis on subitism and rigorous Sŏn practice.

Sŏngch'ŏl understood the history of Buddhism as an evolution of the teaching of the middle path. In his *Paegil pŏpmun* (*One Hundred Days Dharma Talks*, 1992), Sŏngch'ŏl interpreted the Buddha's first turning of the wheel of *Dharma* as a declaration of the middle path, which he considered to be the core of both early Buddhism and Mahāyāna Buddhism. This, to Sŏngch'ŏl, demonstrated that Mahāyāna Buddhism is an authentic successor of early Buddhism.

Sŏngch'ŏl was an advocate of strict subitism in Sŏn practice. In his *Sŏnmun chŏngno* (*The Right Path of the Sŏn School*, 1981), Sŏngch'ŏl stressed that the goal of Sŏn practice is to be awakened to the true suchness of one's self-nature. The best way to see one's nature, Sŏngch'ŏl argued, is to investigate *kongan* (Ch. *gong'an*), which to Sŏngch'ŏl inevitably takes the path of sudden awakening and sudden cultivation. The theory of sudden enlightenment followed by gradual cultivation, Sŏngch'ŏl contended, is the heretic way of "the followers of speculation and interpretation." Sŏngch'ŏl's claim that Pojo Chinul (1158–1210) was the originator of this inauthentic practice kindled a polemic among Korean Buddhists: the polemic is known as the sudden–gradual debate. Sŏngch'ŏl's challenge to Chinul also appeared in *Han'guk pulgyo ŭi pŏpmaek* (*The Dharma Lineage of Korean Buddhism*, 1976), in which Sŏngch'ŏl contested Chinul's position as the founding patriarch of the Chogye Order, the dominant Buddhist order in contemporary Korea, and claimed that T'aego Pou (1301–82) should be the original head of the school.

For lay practitioners, Sŏngch'ŏl emphasized the importance of making offerings to the Buddha, offerings through which one practices compassion for others. This teaching constitutes one core of his *Dharma* talks collected in *Yŏngwŏnhan chayu* (*Eternal Freedom*, 1988) and *Cha'gi rŭl paro popsida* (*Take a Good Look at Yourself*, 2003).

A relentlessly strict Sŏn practitioner, Sŏngch'ŏl undertook for eight years the practice of never lying down (Kor. *changjwa purwa*), and for ten years isolated himself from the outside world (Kor. *tonggu pulch'ul*, 1955–5). He was also obstinate in his belief that practitioners should remain isolated on the mountain without getting involved in worldly affairs. In order to renovate monastic life, he created a compact community at the Pongam monastery in 1947. The "*Kongju kyuyak*" (Community regulations) he drafted for the occasion is now one of three major regulations for Sŏn monasteries in Korea.

The gap he kept between the secular world and his mountain Buddhism was a target of criticism. He remained uninvolved during the decade-long conflicts between married and celibate monks; he also kept silence about what is known as the 10.27 Persecution when the martial law government persecuted the Buddhist *sangha* in the name of purification.

See also: **Korea, Buddhism in.**

Jin Y. Park

SŌSHIKI BUKKYŌ (FUNERAL BUDDHISM)

Sōshiki Bukkyō (funeral or "funerary" Buddhism) is a modern term that refers to the current state of, and major role played by, Buddhism in contemporary Japan, in which funeral services and memorial rites are the primary activities of, and provide the major economic support for, Buddhist temples.

Funeral services and memorial rites, of course, have been performed by Buddhist clergy from the earliest times and through the medieval period, but it was in the early modern (Tokugawa) period (1600–1868) that the role was institutionalized through government action. In the early seventeenth century, the Tokugawa bakufu passed a series of laws to consolidate its control over the country. Known as the "temple registration system" (*terauke seido*), this required all people to register their family at a Buddhist temple, which would then provide the government with certification on the activities (births, marriages, deaths, travel, etc.) of its parishioners (*danka*). The system was established, in part, to prevent people from belonging to proscribed religious movements such as Christianity and the Nichiren *fuju-fuse* movement. Once registered, neither individuals nor families were allowed to "convert" to a different religion or change affiliation to a different school. Religious affiliation thus became a social, family affair that was passed down from generation to generation (*danka seido*, "parishioner system").

As a result of this Tokugawa government policy, funerary rites and memorial services became almost exclusively the province of Buddhism. At the same time, and as a result, mortuary rites and memorial services became the major source of income for Buddhist temples. Even after the registration system was officially abandoned in the late nineteenth century, temple affiliation by family tradition (*danka seido*), the maintenance of a family grave at a Buddhist temple, and the conducting of funeral services and memorial rites by Buddhist clergy, continues to be a major part of Buddhism in contemporary Japan

One of the controversial aspects of this Buddhist funeral practice is the conferral of a posthumous Buddhist name (*kaimyō*, "precept name," or *hōmyō*, "*Dharma* name"). Originally the religious name one received upon ordination or "taking the precepts" during one's life, the *kaimyō* currently serves as a posthumous name to put on the grave-stone and to refer to the deceased. It is commonly believed that everyone "becomes a Buddha" (*jōbutsu*) after death and after passing through various stages during set periods of time (such as seven weeks or one year), requiring memorial rites at certain death anniversaries. The *kaimyō* is chosen by the Buddhist priest who presides over the funeral ceremonies, and is supposed to reflect the personality and status of the deceased, but often is determined by price. Various prefixes, suffixes, and terms that suggest or confer various levels of status originally were given to reflect the actual social status of the deceased during his or her life, but now can often be conferred according to the wishes of the deceased's family and according to the level of donation. The Jōdo Shinshū, however, is exceptional in limiting the use of *kaimyō* to two Chinese characters (the Buddhist name) preceded by the character *shaku* (for [disciple of] Śākyamuni).

Modern urbanization, the movement of people away from traditional rural areas to urban areas, and the accompanying breakdown of the extended family, have caused a weakening of traditional ties to the family Buddhist temple. There is less and less reliance on the family temple for funeral services, leading some temples to establish "open" graveyards or grave sites for people not traditional parishioners but seeking long-term memorial rites (*eitai kuyō*). Others seek solutions apart from the Buddhist temples. Recently some have sought to establish the practice of "natural funerals" (*shizensō*), such as scattering the ashes of the dead in the mountains or in the ocean, thus precluding the need for a grave and its accompanying memorial rites. This movement threatens the financial security of Buddhist temples, and (according to some Buddhist priests) breaks the links that people have with traditional Buddhist values, undermines the solidarity of the extended family, and thus weakens the basis of Japanese society.

See also: **Japan, Buddhism in; Rituals and practices.**

PAUL L. SWANSON

SOUTH AND SOUTHEAST ASIA, BUDDHISM IN

Although many people in the West associate Buddhism primarily with East Asia, in both its early history and its thought, Buddhism was a product of South Asia. The Buddha was born in what is today Nepal and spent his life as a peripatetic monastic teacher in the basin of the Ganges river in what is today India. The Chinese, by contrast, always understood this association, as is shown by the numerous occasions in Chinese history when Buddhism was criticized and opposed as a foreign religion. Buddhism was shaped in many ways by the distinctive culture and civilization of South Asia in the sixth and fifth centuries BCE and it was preserved and developed further in the surrounding cultures of Southeast Asia in the following centuries.

The traditional dates for the Buddha's life are 563–483 BCE, but recent scholarship has questioned this dating and argued for later dates: *c.* 480–400 BCE. In either case the Buddha lived and worked during what Jaspers has termed the Axial Age when many of the great philosophies and religions of the world were being formulated. Jaspers argued that the hallmark of the Axial Age was that human beings became self-reflective and sought to understand the nature of their existence and consciousness. This was certainly true in South Asia where a social and cultural revolution was taking place in the time of the Buddha. A new urban civilization arose in the Ganges valley around the sixth century BCE. Based on the use of iron, this culture developed new farming techniques that led to the expansion of agriculture and new weapons that led to military superiority. Because of the increased prosperity from agriculture, many important cities emerged and came to dominate the society, including Rājagṛha, Śrāvastī, Kauśāmbī, Kāśī and Vaiśālī. These cities came to be the centers of new kingdoms such as Kośala and Magadha. The Buddhist texts relate that the Buddha lived and taught in all of these cities and kingdoms during his long career. Both the teachings and the religion that the Buddha founded reflect the influences of this rising new culture, and the religion and teachings of the Buddha were spread along the trade routes that led from the emerging cities of north central India to other parts of Asia.

The *samaṇas*

One of the distinctive features of this period of Indian history was the emergence of the *samaṇas* (Skt. *śramaṇas*) or *paribbājakas* (Skt. *parivrājakas*), the spiritual seekers who had "gone forth from home to homelessness." In the Buddha's time, there were many of these *samaṇas* professing a variety of views but generally opposing the orthodox Brahmins and rejecting the religion of the *Vedas* with its emphasis on the sacrifice. The hallmark of their teaching was that renunciation was necessary for liberation and fulfillment. Accordingly, the *samaṇas* renounced their ties to family and their attachments to material possessions. The goal of most of the *samaṇas* was liberation from material existence by means of asceticism and meditation. This emphasis on renunciation may have represented, in part, their response to the new prosperity, complexity and materialism of that emerging South Asian civilization, but it also represented an important theme in South Asian culture that may have pre-dated the rise of the new culture.

According to tradition, the Buddha began his own quest for liberation by following two of the leading *samaṇa* masters of his day. Apprenticing himself first to Āḷāra Kālāma and then to Uddaka Rāmaputta, Gotama trained as a *samaṇa*. The legend says that although these two teachers both declared that Gotama had mastered their paths, he was dissatisfied and left to seek wisdom elsewhere. He next tried the path of asceticism, which was also central to many of the *samaṇas*. The Buddha accepted the reasoning of the ascetics who said that just as wood had to be dried out before it would burn, so the body had to be dried out through asceticism before wisdom could blaze forth. The legends state that with regard to asceticism too, Gotama attained great success and was recognized as a master ascetic. But eventually, feeling disillusioned and unenlightened, Gotama abandoned this path also and went out on his own in search of wisdom. These legends of the Buddha's teachers signified for the early Buddhists a critique of the other *samaṇa* traditions and an assertion of the superiority of the Buddha's version of the path. Having rejected the leading *samaṇa* teachers and paths of the time, the Buddha, meditating on his own at Bodhgayā, had discovered a path to the highest wisdom and *nirvāṇa*.

The Pāli Buddhist *suttas* refer frequently to the Buddha's encounters with some of the most important *samaṇa* sects and leaders. The *Sāmaññaphāla Sutta* (*Dīgha Nikāya* 1.47ff.) compares the views of some of the major *samaṇas* with the Buddhist views. It is instructive to study the ideas of these schools because their distinctive teachings represent, in varying degrees, both complements to and contrasts with the Buddhist teachings. One of the most important sects was the Jains, whose teacher, *Mahāvīra*, was a contemporary of the Buddha. Jain teachings parallel Buddhist teachings in many ways, for example in their ethical ideals. One major difference, however, was the Jain teaching that all beings are essentially defined by their spirit or *jīva*. *Mahāvīra* taught that the *jīva*, an individual's eternal spirit or soul, is trapped in material existence but can be liberated by following the Jain path, which included asceticism as a key element. Another sect prominent in the Buddha's time was the group called the Materialists who denied the existence of any form of self or *jīva*, and taught that beings were annihilated at the end of this existence.

Dharma and *Vinaya*

When the Buddha began to teach after attaining enlightenment at Bodhgayā, he described his *Dharma* as a "middle way."

In the history of Buddhism this designation has been given numerous interpretations, but in terms of the South Asian context of the Buddha's day, it seems probable that the Buddhists understood their *Dharma* to represent a "middle way" between the eternalism of groups such as the Jains and the annihilationism of groups such as the Materialists. The central Buddhist idea of *anattā*, for example, seems to critique both the Jain view of a permanent soul-essence and the Materialist view that there is no essence to human existence. The Buddhists adopted a middle view that human existence represents a process of changing mental and physical states. These changing and evolving states both constitute an individual and make it possible for that individual to seek liberation. Among the central teachings of the Buddha, the corollaries to the teaching of *anattā* (Skt. *anātman*) or no-self, were those about *anicca* (Skt. *anitya*) or impermanence, and *dukkha* (Skt. *duḥkha*) or suffering. These ideas, central to the Buddha's first sermon in which he set out the Four Noble Truths, constituted his distinctive analysis of existence.

The Buddha – along with the other *samaṇa* teachers – probably had no intention of establishing a separate religion, such as Buddhism. Rather, he and the other teachers intended to set out paths to wisdom and liberation. The Buddha described his path as *Dharma* and *Vinaya*, the doctrine and discipline, and he addressed it to his followers. As the Buddha taught for approximately fifty years after attaining enlightenment, he had time to put his own stamp on the *Dharma* and *Vinaya* that was handed down to later Buddhists. Not that everything that has been handed down is authentically from the Buddha, but during his long career he set the course for his followers and established the general direction that the path should go. The Buddhists themselves acknowledged this when they declared that in order to decide whether a teaching could be considered "the word of the Buddha" or *Buddhavacana*, it should be compared with the core of *Dharma* and *Vinaya* that the tradition had already accepted.

The *sangha*

Although some scholars, following Weber, have argued that the Buddha's *Dharma* and *Vinaya* were intended primarily for monastics, the Buddha described his followers as a "fourfold *sangha*" consisting of male and female monastics, laymen and laywomen. Although all four groups could follow the path, they were believed to be at different levels of spiritual development and were assigned different guidelines for the path. The inclusion of women in the *sangha* and the recognition that women could go forth as monastics indicates the progressive nature of both the early Buddhist community and the *samaṇa* movement generally. The Buddhist texts say, however, that the Buddha was originally reluctant to allow women to become *bhikkhunīs*. Although his own stepmother, Mahāpajāpatī, requested that he establish ordination for women and an order of *bhikkhunīs*, the Buddha is reported to have refused at first, until Ānanda, his disciple, interceded on her behalf. The reasons for the Buddha's reluctance in this matter are not clear and have long been a matter of debate. Assuming that this legend had a historical basis, some argue that it might reflect the Buddha's wish to protect women or his view that the time was not yet right to allow women to join the male monastics. But the legend may not have had a historical basis and could simply represent the views of the paternalistic *bhikkhus* of a later period. In any case, it is clear that the *bhikkhunī* order was established and that female monastics went on to play important roles in the *sangha*, with the *suttas* recounting their becoming *arahants* and serving as advisers to kings.

What primarily set the male and female monastics apart from the laymen and laywomen was the act of renunciation. The *bhikkhus* and *bhikkhunīs* followed the *samaṇa* ideal of going "forth from home to homelessness," and the early monastics, both male and female, seem to have lived a wandering, homeless lifestyle in quest of liberation and *nirvāṇa*. As the Buddhist tradition developed, however, the *bhikkhus* and *bhikkhunīs* eventually came to live more or less permanently in one place and served pastoral roles for the laity. The Theravāda and other schools of Buddhism came to see the goal of *nirvāṇa* as very remote and difficult to attain in one lifetime for either monastics or laypersons. Thus, Theravādins, at least, came to view the path to liberation as a long, gradual path that extended over many lifetimes. Rather than understanding the path as a single course which led directly to the ultimate goal, the Theravāda saw it as a series of soteriological strategies adapted to the needs of people, monastics and laity, with differing levels of wisdom and spiritual perfection. The dimensions of this gradual path were worked out in texts such as the *Nettipakaraṇa* and the *Paṭisambhidāmagga*, but it was Buddhaghosa who gave the gradual path its definitive expression for Theravāda in the *Visuddhimagga*. The path was gradual and extended but it led through its various stages to one goal, *nirvāṇa*. Dividing the path into two levels, mundane, *lokiya*, and supramundane, *lokuttara*, enabled the tradition to subsume mundane means and goals under the supramundane in order to relate the *Dharma* to all persons. The existence of these two levels also provided a means of grounding devotional practices and a *cultus* that addressed the needs of the laity.

Early councils

Buddhist sources have traditionally recounted the evolution of Buddhism after the death and *parinirvāṇa* of the Buddha in terms of a series of great councils or *saṅgīti*. According to almost all sources, the First Council was held in Rājagṛha (Pāli Rājagaha) immediately after the passing of the Buddha. The purpose of this council was to recite and commit to memory the teachings of the Buddha in order to prevent any dissent about the teachings. The account in the *Cullavaga* of the Pāli *Vinaya Piṭaka* states that at the First Council 500 disciples of the Buddha who had all become *arahants* met and recited the *Sutta Piṭaka* and the *Vinaya Piṭaka*.

A Second Council is reported to have been held in *Vaiśālī* about 100 years after the First Council, although some scholars today suggest that the time between these two councils may actually have been only about sixty or seventy years. All sources agree that this council was called to resolve a dispute that had arisen in the monastic *sangha*; however, the sources disagree about the exact nature of the dispute. The Theravāda texts say that the council was called to deal with disagreements about ten points of monastic discipline, including questions of whether monks could accept money and eat after noon. The Mahāyāna sources, however, tend to say that the cause for the council was a largely doctrinal disagreement about the *arahants*. Whatever the nature of the dispute, most Buddhist sources say that the significance of this council was that either at the council or shortly afterward the community experienced its first major schism. According to the Theravāda accounts of this event, the *Mahāsāṃghikas* split off from the Sthaviras. This schism was to become the basis for further divisions which led eventually to the two major branches of Buddhism, Mahāyāna which descended from the Mahāsāṃghikas, and Hīnayāna which descended from the Sthaviras.

Aśoka and the Third Council

According to Theravāda sources, a Third Council was held during the reign of

Aśoka (*c*. 268–*c*. 239 BCE) and although Mahāyāna sources do not mention this council, the traditions concerning both this council and the reign of Aśoka had great significance for the evolution of Buddhism in South and Southeast Asia. Aśoka extended the Mauryan Empire and established a kingdom that united most of the Indian sub-continent under one rule. We know about his reign because he inscribed edicts on rocks and pillars throughout his kingdom describing his accomplishments and extolling the *Dharma*. From one of these edicts we learn that although Aśoka had been a powerful warrior, conquering and ruling by force of arms, after the conquest of Kalinga where his army killed thousands of his opponents the king seems to have adopted Buddhism and become a model Buddhist ruler. From that point on, Aśoka became the moral exemplar of Buddhist kingship, embodying the Buddhist ideals of the linkage of *Dharma* and political power. Aśoka seems to have attempted to rule according to the Buddhist ten royal virtues, *dasa rāja dhammā*, which included such qualities as generosity, morality, piety, patience, non-anger, and non-violence. Non-violence, *ahiṃsā*, figures prominently in Aśoka's edicts and proclamations to his subjects. Aśoka is said to have banned the sacrifices of animals and to have adopted a largely vegetarian diet so that animals would not be killed unnecessarily. He is remembered as a monarch who worked for the welfare of his subjects, building rest houses, roads and wells and planting thousands of trees to provide fruit and shade. He also established medical clinics for people and animals throughout his kingdom.

Aśoka's support for Buddhism also included addressing edicts to his people explaining the *Dharma* and sending missions to foreign lands to promote the *Dharma*. He encouraged his subjects to live by the *Dharma*: following *sīla*, being generous to monks and nuns, respecting their parents, loving their children, honoring their friends, and treating their servants with kindness. To promote Buddhism and to assist the laity in their practice of the *Dharma*, Aśoka established thousands of *cetiyas* to enshrine the relics of the Buddha and the *arahants*. Later Buddhists came to revere Aśoka as a *Cakkavattin* (Skt. *Cakravartin*), a "wheel-turning" ruler whose mundane role in promoting and establishing the *Dharma* complements that of the supramundane Buddha.

According to the Theravāda textual sources, Aśoka convened the Third Council to purify the *sangha*. In addition to expelling heterodox monastics, the council also chanted and confirmed the *Tipiṭaka*. Following this council, Moggaliputta Tissa Thera, the council's leader, is said to have dispatched *Dharma* missions to various regions as part of Aśoka's campaign of conquest by *Dharma*. Aśoka's edicts confirm some of the *Dharma* emissaries mentioned in the Theravāda accounts of this council and they enumerate many other missions to foreign lands such as Egypt and Macedonia, as well as the Himalayan regions, Sri Lanka, and Southeast Asia.

Developments after Aśoka

Following the reign of Aśoka, Buddhism expanded and evolved in India in many ways. The *Sthaviravāda* schools continued to flourish and grow in importance. This included the *Sarvastivāda* and the *Puggalavāda* schools. From the first century BCE to the first century CE, Mahāyāna began to emerge as a significant new force. Mahāyāna seems to have begun as a loose movement in various parts of India, whose evolution was shaped by several factors, including new social forces, foreign influences on Indian culture, and new doctrinal and ritual emphases in Buddhism. The proponents of the new movement were diverse, but united in their desire to provide a path for all beings and in their emphasis on the *bodhisattva* ideal as a key element in that path. The Mahāyāna schools grew slowly but by about the seventh century they seem to have achieved parity with the *Sthaviravāda* or Hīnayāna schools. All of these Mahāyāna and *Sthaviravāda* schools continued to develop and many spread beyond the sub-continent of India by the beginning of the Common Era. This expansion and development of Buddhism, begun during the time of Aśoka and continued in the following centuries, ensured the survival of the religion after it declined in India in the eleventh and twelfth centuries CE because of both external and internal factors.

In Southeast Asia and Sri Lanka, the Aśokan heritage and the tradition of the Third Council were influential in shaping the forms of Theravāda Buddhism that evolved and came to be dominant in these regions. Theravāda Buddhists of Sri Lanka, Myanmar, and Thailand all trace the beginnings of Buddhism in their countries to the missions sent out following the Third Council. The account of the Third Council in the *Mahāvaṃsa* lists nine destinations to which missions were sent following that council, and the *Sāsanavaṃsa* of Myanmar places five of these in Southeast Asia. Although the Thai Buddhists have traditionally believed that the missions to the places identified in the chronicles as Mahāraṭṭha and the Yona region indicated Thailand, the historical and inscriptional evidence for this appears weak. Similarly, the Buddhists of Myanmar have traditionally believed that the missions to the locations identified as Vanāvasa, Aparantaka, and Suvaṇṇabhūmi indicated different places in Myanmar. The chronicles' accounts of the emissaries say that two of the missionaries, the *arahants* Soṇa and Uttara, came to Suvaṇṇabhūmi or Thaton. This claim is somewhat stronger than that of the Thais because these missions are also mentioned in the Kalyani inscriptions of Pegu (*c.* 1476), but other historical evidence points to a later date for the introduction of Buddhism to Myanmar. The Buddhists of Sri Lanka, however, have somewhat more basis for their belief that the mission of Mahinda Thera following the Third Council came to Sri Lanka. The Sinhala chronicles relate the legend of Mahinda, a monastic and a son of King Aśoka, who traveled to Lanka with a delegation of other *bhikkhus* to establish the *Dharma*. After meeting and converting the king of Lanka, Devānampiya Tissa, Mahinda proclaimed the *Dharma* and sanctified the sites of future Buddhist shrines in Anurādhapura. Mahinda's sister, the *bhikkhunī* Sanghamittā, came to Lanka after him to establish ordination for women. She also is said to have brought a branch from the sacred *Bodhi* Tree which was then planted in Lanka and became an important Buddhist shrine.

The legends of the Buddha's visits and of the missions sent out following the Third Council have been read as sacred history by Theravāda Buddhists in Sri Lanka and Southeast Asia. These accounts have provided charters for Theravāda Buddhism and legitimated the connections between the religion, the ruler and the state. The legend of Mahinda's mission to Sri Lanka, for example, relates the Buddhism of Sri Lanka to the golden age of Buddhism in India and the archetypal Buddhist ruler, Aśoka. Mahinda's mission effectively transfers to Sri Lanka all of the essential elements of Aśokan Buddhism: Mahinda proclaims the *Dharma*, establishes the *sangha*, and finally brings even the Buddha in the form of the relics that are enshrined at Anurādhapura. The king of Sri Lanka, Devānampiya Tissa, acquires the mantle of Aśoka and adopts the role of the defender of the faith. The parallel legends of Aśokan missions to other countries have had the same significance for other

Theravāda Buddhists. Regarded as the *Cakkavattin*, Aśoka became both an exemplar and a charter for rulers in the region. Kings in Sri Lanka, Thailand, and Burma have historically sought to emulate Aśoka and by doing so have legitimated their reigns. Following the Aśokan example, kings such as Tilokarāja of Thailand, Aniruddha of Burma, and Duṭṭhagāmaṇi of Sri Lanka supported the *sangha*, convened Buddhist councils, built temples and erected massive *stūpas*. In addition these kings sought to follow and were judged by their performance of the ten royal virtues, *dasa rāja dhammā*. The history of this region is replete with rulers who sought to embody the archetype for Buddhist kingship established in the Aśokan legends and this pattern of mimesis and legitimation by the ruler and the state has continued only slightly changed in the modern period.

The forms of Theravāda Buddhism in Sri Lanka and the various countries of Southeast Asia have many similarities because of this Aśokan heritage and because of the historic interconnections that have existed. These forms of Theravāda, however, also have distinctive differences because of the ways that they have combined with the popular religion and culture of each region. The Mahāvihāra became the center of Theravāda orthodoxy in Sri Lanka during the Anurādhapura Period (*c*. 250 BCE–tenth century CE) because of a combination of political strength and the monastic scholarship of commentators such as Buddhaghosa. The influence of the Mahāvihāra's form of Sinhala Theravāda radiated out into Southeast Asia during the classical period. There were also frequent exchanges of monks between these countries with monks traveling to the other Theravāda centers to study the scriptures, to reform the *sangha*, and to restore the ordination lineages whenever they lapsed. In the eleventh century CE, for example, King Vijayabāhu I of Sri Lanka and King Aniruddha of Burma arranged exchanges of monks and scriptures to strengthen the religion in their countries. Other exchanges took place between Burma and Sri Lanka during the sixteenth and seventeenth centuries, with Burmese monks coming to Sri Lanka to restore the ordination lineage.

Whereas these monastic exchanges led to more uniformity between the Buddhism of various Theravāda countries, the need to accommodate Buddhism to the local religion made the forms of Theravāda distinct. The Buddhism of Sri Lanka incorporated a popular religion of gods and spirits that derived both from Brahmanical sources and from local tradition. Almost all Buddhist temples in Sri Lanka include shrines to these *devas* in addition to the shrines to the Buddha, and many Buddhist festivals feature the *devas* in prominent roles. Similarly, the Theravādins of Myanmar, Thailand and other countries found ways to incorporate into their religious practice a range of indigenous gods and spirits.

The modern period

In the modern period in Sri Lanka and Southeast Asia, Theravāda Buddhism experienced a decline during the colonial reigns in many of the countries but then underwent a great resurgence and revival across the region. Several themes have marked the resurgence of Buddhism, including the emergence of new roles for the laity, the reform and revitalization of the *sangha*, and the re-establishment of powerful links between Buddhism and polity. During the colonial period, the colonial governments in Sri Lanka, Burma and other countries introduced policies that displaced Buddhism and discriminated against the Buddhists. The *sangha*, in particular, suffered from the colonial policies, losing their traditional roles as advisers to the government and their status as leaders and teachers in society. The modern resurgence of Buddhism is often dated from 1864 when some *bhikkhus* in Sri Lanka responded to the challenge of the Christian missionaries by agreeing to a series of public debates. For years the missionaries had attacked Buddhism and criticized the religion as an inferior, negative faith, but the debates, which were open-air events attended by thousands of Buddhists, gave new confidence and pride to the Buddhists. In addition, news of the debates spread widely and came to the attention of the leaders of the Theosophical Society in New York and London, Madame Helena Blavatsky and Colonel Henry Olcott, who then traveled to Sri Lanka to assist the Buddhists. In their work with the Buddhists, the Theosophists met a young man named David Hewavitarne whom they trained to be a leader in the Buddhist revival. This young man eventually took the name Anagarika Dharmapala and became the leading figure in the movement to revitalize Buddhism and overcome the colonial oppression. Living a homeless life but without becoming a monk, Dharmapala became the voice of the Buddhists and protested the treatment of the Buddhists in Sri Lanka and India. In his prolific writings and speeches, Dharmapala spoke out against the British and the Western influences that were destroying Asian culture. A keen student of the texts, Dharmapala used the Pāli *suttas* and the *Mahāvaṃsa* to assert the superiority of Buddhism and to raise the Buddhists' pride in their noble heritage and their identity. With a sharp wit, he compared the Sinhala Buddhists to their British colonial rulers, observing that when the ancestors of the British were living in the forests with their bodies painted, the ancestors of the Buddhists were already following the lofty *Dharma* of the Buddha.

The work of Dharmapala and the Theosophists strengthened the revitalization of the *sangha* in Sri Lanka and other Theravāda countries. This revitalization had already begun as early as 1753 when the reformist *bhikkhu* Saranaṃkara persuaded Kīrti Śrī Rājasinha, the ruler of the Kandyan kingdom, to bring monks from Thailand to re-establish the ordination lineage in Sri Lanka, continuing the long tradition of monastic exchanges between Sri Lanka and Southeast Asia. The monks that came founded the Siyam Nikaya, which became a reforming branch of the *sangha* and the dominant branch in Sri Lanka. About a century later, monks from Thailand went to Sri Lanka to study and learn from the *sangha* there and then returned to Thailand and founded the Thammayut sect to reform Buddhism. The reforms of the *sangha* influenced the reforms of the Buddhist laity in many ways, including the rise of the *vipassanā* meditation movement in Myanmar in the mid-twentieth century. U Narada and his pupil Mahāsī Sayadaw originated what has been called the "New Burmese Method" of meditation and taught at the government-sponsored meditation center, Thathana Yeiktha, in Rangoon. When Myanmar Buddhists hosted the Sixth Buddhist Council in 1955, lay Buddhists from Sri Lanka went to Burma to learn these new methods of meditation and upon their return they formed a meditation society. Inviting the leading Burmese monastic teachers, including Mahāsī Sayadaw, to come to Sri Lanka, they conducted *vipassanā* meditation classes and retreats that attracted large numbers of laity. The laity eventually came to control the *vipassanā* movement and found in it new roles and new freedom. The new forms of meditation appealed to the laity because they did not require a lengthy period of study and training as the traditional teachings about meditation and the *sangha* had held. The meditation movement had the effect of opening both the Buddhist path and the ultimate goal, *nibbāna* (Skt. *nirvāṇa*), to the laity in a way that was virtually unprecedented in Theravāda history.

A key outcome of the resurgence of Buddhism in the modern period in Sri Lanka and Southeast Asia was that the laity and the *sangha* came together to advocate political independence and the restoration of traditional ties between Buddhism and nationalism. The Buddhist leaders appealed once again to the Aśokan paradigm of the close relation between the *Dharma* and the ruler. In Sri Lanka, the Buddhist Committee of Inquiry, which was commissioned by the laity-controlled All Ceylon Buddhist Council to investigate the status of Buddhism under the colonial powers, issued a report advocating that Buddhism should be restored to its "rightful place." This came to mean that Buddhist values should become the foundation for the national government and should be given priority in decision-making about issues such as education, economics, and social policy. Elements of the *sangha* in Sri Lanka had advocated this since the 1930s when Walpola Rahula wrote his revolutionary book *The Heritage of the Bhikkhu*, in which he argued for the relevance of Buddhism, and particularly the *sangha*, to the state. Building on the earlier work and writings of Dharmapala, Rahula and other Buddhist nationalists agitated against colonial rule and advocated Buddhist patriotism. The work of the Buddhist nationalists came to fruition when the colonial states of South and Southeast Asia received their independence after World War II. The pivotal event for this movement was the Buddha Jayanti, the 2,500th anniversary of the Buddha's entry into *nirvāṇa*, which was celebrated in 1956. Buddhists regarded the Jayanti as the dawn of a new age when the *Dharma* would once again flourish and spread all over the world, and the event inspired many new initiatives to restore the religion. In Sri Lanka, Myanmar, and Thailand, the governments that came to power around this time advocated Buddhist nationalism and emphasized the necessity for the ruler to follow the *Dharma*.

Figure 37 Entrance to Siong Lim Temple, Singapore.

Myanmar elected U Nu prime minister in 1948 on a platform of Buddhist socialism. His government advocated that people should limit their material desires for the good of the state and other beings. In Sri Lanka, S.W.R.D. Bandaranaike came to power in 1956 on a platform of Buddhist socialism. Many elements of the *sangha* were instrumental in campaigning for his election and expected him to restore the fortunes of the religion. Appealing to the Buddhist middle class that felt it had suffered the most from the colonial and Christian policies, Bandaranaike made two campaign pledges: he promised to restore Buddhism as the national religion and to restore Sinhala as the national language. That he was ultimately unable to fulfill either promise led, in part, to his assassination in 1959 by some of the same elements that had supported his election. Subsequent governments in Sri Lanka have continued to pursue versions of this ideal of Buddhist nationalism, with some leaders invoking more explicitly the Aśokan ideals. Buddhist nationalism and its programs have definitely benefited the Buddhist majorities in Sri Lanka and Southeast Asia, but they have also proved to be divisive forces because they have alienated the non-Buddhist minorities and generated protracted civil conflicts in Sri Lanka and Myanmar.

See also: **Anagarika Dharmapala; Aśoka; Buddha, historical context; Buddha and *cakravartins*; Buddhism in the Western world; Burma (Myanmar), Buddhism in; Cambodia and Laos, Buddhism in; Sri Lanka, Buddhism in; Thailand, Buddhism in; Vietnam, Buddhism in.**

George D. Bond

SOUTHERN HEMISPHERE, BUDDHISM IN THE

Recent studies have documented and analyzed the history and presence of Buddhism in South America and Africa. Commonly, these continents are not connected with Buddhism because of biased perspectives and expectations. Also, some will question whether these continents are part of what is commonly subsumed under the category "the West." However, "the West" is an historically produced category and, from this perspective, a society and nation is considered Western not when it is located in a discrete, geographically specified region, but when it is developed, industrialized, urbanized, capitalist, secular, and modern. Undoubtedly, certain parts of the society in Brazil and South Africa, the two countries focused on here, are Western, modern, and metropolitan – and specific parts of the social middle and upper strata are strongly connected to Buddhism. For some of these, Buddhism is a signifier of modernity and avant-garde status, and therefore an incentive to turn to. However, as in all other "Western worlds" (i.e. beyond Asia), Buddhism is heterogeneous and not restricted to specific sections of society.

South America

Buddhism may have entered South America as early as 1810 when Chinese workers disembarked in Rio de Janeiro on short-term labor contracts. As no records of religious, and specifically Buddhist, activities exist, the story of Buddhism and South and Latin America starts a century later. Again, immigrants from East Asia play a vital role. A work force was needed for the plantations as sugar and coffee production boomed in the second half of the nineteenth century. Japanese migrants were recruited and they arrived in Mexico in 1897, in Peru in 1899, and in São Paulo, Brazil, in 1908. Brazil received 33,200 Japanese immigrants from 1908 to 1923, the number quadrupling to 142,000 during the next decade. The laborers' hopes were to prosper quickly and then return to Japan. Most often, however, their stay turned into a long-term residence. During the 1920s and 1930s, the Japanese workers built provisional installations that functioned as temples and Buddhist monks from Jōdo Shinshū, Shingon, Tenrikyō and other traditions stayed to serve their religious and cultural needs. The only lasting temple was the Kōmyōji temple (Jōdo Shinshū) in Cafelândia in São Paulo, founded in 1932. Generally, however, Japanese State Shinto proliferated among the workers and Buddhism had only a low profile. Importantly, Japanese workers were expected to assimilate to Brazilian culture, including the abandonment of their Japanese religious practices and a conversion to Roman Catholicism. Quite a number of Japanese saw conversion as necessary to the process of Brazilianization and became Christian. Quite a number, however, preserved their Japanese culture and religious identity. World War II and Japan's defeat brought an end to the migrants' hopes of return. With the expectation of staying permanently, Buddhist Japanese and their descendants established more temples. The early 1950s saw the arrival of Buddhist missionaries from Japan and the institutionalization of Jōdoshū, Sōtō and Nichiren activities. The Mission of Sōtō Zenshū in Brazil founded the important Busshinji temple as the official seat of this mission for South America in 1956. Also, new Japanese immigrants brought the Sōka Gakkai, and its president, Daisaku Ikeda, visited Brazil in 1966. Chinese immigrants established the Mo Ti temple in São Paulo in 1962.

A different line of Buddhism in Brazil was constituted by scholars, called universalistic philosophical or intellectualized Buddhism. The academics Murillo Azevedo and Ricardo Mário Goncalves propagated Buddhist ideas and revived the previously Theosophical-oriented Buddhist Society of Brazil in 1955. This convert interest in Buddhism marks the prelude to the increasing interest in Buddhism within the better-off urban circles in Brazil. As in other countries beyond Asia, traveling Zen teachers and Tibetan *lamas* also started to visit South America. The Sōtō monk Ryotan Tokuda, sent by the Sōtōshū headquarters to cater for the Japanese Brazilians in 1968, developed a wide impact among Japanese and non-Japanese in Brazil. He propagated sitting meditation and founded three Zen monasteries, a Sōtō temple and affiliated Zen groups. Conspicuously, members of Brazilia's cultural elite adopted the practice of Zen as a symbol of cosmopolitanism, modernity, class distinction, and being a part of "the West." Other Zen teachers, Tibetan *lamas*, Pure Land and Shingon priests, and teachers of various other traditions came and founded groups, centers, societies and temples during the 1980s and the 1990s in particular. According to the census for 2000, 246,000 Brazilians declared themselves as Buddhists (0.14 percent of 170 million). The clear center of Buddhist institutionalization and activities is the southeastern and urbanized state of São Paulo, where half of the 309 groups, centers, and temples were located in 2003. There and in Rio de Janeiro, Buddhism has evolved into a trendy religion among the intellectual elite.

Compared to Brazil, fewer Buddhist activities are so far documented for the other South and Latin American countries. However, developments and processes of institutionalization have increased from the 1990s. In 2005, Peru was home to five Tibetan Buddhist centers and two more Buddhist groups, according to BuddhaNet. In Columbia, likewise, Tibetan Buddhist and Zen groups sprang up. In 2005 eight of the eighteen groups were part of the Diamond Way directed by Ole Nydahl. In Venezuela, with its twenty-two groups and centers, Zen and Tibetan Buddhism were also strong. Chile was home to fifteen different groups and centers, again mainly of Zen and Tibetan orientation. Zen groups came into being in Argentina and Uruguay through the visits of Moriyama Rōshi, formerly priest at the Brazilian Busshinji temple. Argentina's capital Buenos Aires maintains four temples serving the Chinese and Korean immigrant minorities. Zen practitioners founded Sōtō and Rinzai groups. Tibetan *lamas* and Japanese *rōshis* also visited the country. Within a short time, a Buddhist plurality had come into existence. BuddhaNet documented twenty-four groups and centers for Argentina in 2005.

Activities are also reported for Latin America. For example, a Mexican novice was ordained as a Theravāda monk in the Dhamma Vihara monastery, Xalapa (Veracruz) in autumn 2004. Some forty-five Buddhist groups and centers of various Buddhist schools and traditions were established in Mexico in 2005. Groups and centers were also listed for Costa Rica (four), El Salvador (five), Guatemala (six), and a few other countries. Except for Brazil, thus far South and Latin America have hardly been researched and future studies will unearth fascinating stories of immigrant and convert Buddhists, of the foundation of groups and centers and the localization of Buddhist concepts and practices.

Africa

South African scholars documented that Buddhism's history in Africa started as early as the late seventeenth century, when three Thai *bhikkhus* were shipwrecked off the west coast of the Cape Colony. The monks were sent as emissaries of the Siamese king, heading for Portugal. This early encounter between Southern Asia and Western Europe, between Buddhism and Roman Catholicism, failed and it was more than a century until Buddhists again came to Southern Africa. During the eighteenth century large numbers of Chinese stayed as workers in South Africa, but no records are available as to their religious practices. Reliable information is on record with regard to a Buddhist conversion movement among low-caste Hindus in Kwazulu-Natal province. Rajaram Dass had formed the Overport Buddhist Sakya Society in 1917 and approached low-caste Hindus to adopt Buddhism. The Society had some success during the 1920s and 1930s though the small Indian Buddhist community steadily declined.

From the 1970s onward, sections of the urbanized middle class became interested in Buddhist teachings and practices. This interest was restricted to white South Africans and took its input from developments in Europe, North America, and South Asia. Though different groups came into existence along Theravāda, Tibetan Buddhism, Zen, and Nichiren lines, during the 1970s and early 1980s emphasis was less on tradition-wise divisions. One of South Africa's main Buddhist reference points became the Buddhist Retreat Center near Ixopo (Southern Natal), formally inaugurated in 1980. In contrast to a prevalent ecumenical spirit, since the mid-1980s the various groups have begun sharpening their doctrinal identity and lineage adherence. In many cases hitherto loose bonds with the Asian parent tradition or headquarters have been strengthened. During the 1990s, Tibetan Buddhism gained a strong following as teachers started to stay for longer in South Africa. Likewise, Zen teachers and Theravāda *bhikkhus* settled in the politically new, democratic country which strove to leave apartheid behind. These teachers, a few of them South Africans returned from longer education abroad, firmly established their traditions with groups and centers in the urban environment. In 1992, the Fo Kuang Shan Order started to build a huge temple and cultural complex in Bronkhorstspruit, near Pretoria. The order actively recruits novices in Tanzania, Congo, and other sub-Saharan countries. The educational programs of the Nan Hua Temple are uncompromisingly Chinese, which so far has slowed down wider success. On the other hand the order is able to attract black people and novices, and thus successfully trespasses on the almost exclusively white milieu and clientele. Only the Sōkka Gakkai has also attracted significant numbers of black members. Informed estimates put the number of Buddhists in South Africa at from 6,000 to 30,000 people, organized in about forty groups, centers, and temples in the early years of the twenty-first century.

Apart from in South Africa, small pockets of Buddhists and the establishment of groups and centers have occurred in various African states. Sōka Gakkai gained a growing membership in Western Africa and some sub-Saharan countries. The Association Zen International was able to establish centers in Cameroon, Bukina Faso, Ivory Coast, and the Mali Republic. The Ixopo Buddhist Retreat Center attracted people from neighboring countries for retreats; on their return, small groups have established themselves in the course of time, among others in Mozambique, Botswana, and Zimbabwe. The spreading of Buddhist concepts, ethics, and practices in Africa overall is in process, though so far mainly restricted to educated, white, Western-oriented people. Buddhist organizations with a global distribution and orientation play a vital role.

See also: **Buddhism in the Western world.**

MARTIN BAUMANN

SRI LANKA, BUDDHISM IN

The arrival of Buddhism

Tradition holds that Buddhism arrived in Sri Lanka very early. According to the chronicles *Mahāvaṃsa* and *Dīpavaṃsa*, the Buddha himself visited the island on three occasions to prepare the way for the *Dharma*'s flourishing there. By describing the Buddha's visits to various places in Sri Lanka, these accounts provide both an explanation and an authorization for many of the most important later Buddhist sacred spaces. On his first trip, said to have been made some nine months after his enlightenment, the Buddha visited an assembly of *yakkhas* (Skt. *yakṣas*) or demons, and persuaded them to leave Sri Lanka, thus preparing a place for the *Dharma*. On this visit he sanctified the future site of the Mahiyaṅgaṇa *stūpa*. In the fifth year after attaining enlightenment, the Buddha again visited Sri Lanka in order to establish peace between two *nāga* (serpent) kings who were preparing to go to war. On that trip, the Buddha preached the *Dharma* to a large delegation of *nāgas* and sanctified places in the Nāgadīpa region of the island. Finally, eight years after his enlightenment, returning to Sri Lanka at the invitation of one of the *nāga* kings, the Buddha is said to have visited and sanctified a number of important Buddhist shrines. He sat on a throne on the site of the future *Kalyāṇī cetiya*, left his footprint on the top of the mountain, Sumanakūṭa, and then went to Anurādhapura and meditated at the place where the branch of the *Bodhi* tree would later be planted and at several other future sacred spaces. The chronicles report that the Buddha himself predicted that Lanka would be the place where the *Dharma* would "shine in glory" even after it faded in India.

Following the accounts of the visits of the Buddha, the chronicles detail the introduction of Buddhism to the island by Mahinda Thera. This cycle of stories serves to further legitimate Buddhism in Sri Lanka by linking it to the golden age of its flowering in India under King Aśoka, who is regarded as the ideal ruler and defender of the faith. The effect of this account is to transfer the Aśokan Buddhist heritage, with its implications for both the monarchy and the *sangha*, to Sri Lanka. The chronicles set the stage by explaining that there were strong ties between Aśoka and Devānaṃpiya Tissa even though they had never met. The two kings exchanged gifts when Tissa was crowned, with Aśoka bestowing the gift of the *Dharma* and recommending that Tissa seek the Three Refuges. This admonition provides the warrant for the transfer of the Aśokan Buddhist orthodoxy in the form of Buddha, *Dharma*, and *Sangha*. Mahinda Thera, who is described as Aśoka's son, serves as the agent for this transfer. After the Third Council, which Theravāda sources say was held by Aśoka (*c*. 250 BCE), nine missions were sent to various countries, and Mahinda was chosen to lead the one to Sri Lanka. Coming to Sri Lanka, he preached the *Dharma* to King Devānaṃpiya Tissa and his subjects in Anurādhapura. Tissa and large numbers of the citizens converted to Buddhism in response to Mahinda's presentation of the *Dharma*.

Revering the *Dharma*, the king worked with Mahinda to establish the *sangha* in Sri Lanka. The king presented Mahinda and his accompanying *bhikkhus* (monks) with the park that was to become the Mahāvihāra. As the king and Mahinda toured Anurādhapura dedicating the sites of future sacred shrines, such as the Great

Stūpa, the earth quaked in response. The sages declared that the *bhikkhus* would become the "masters on the island." Then, to conclude this founding of the *sangha*, Mahinda and the Tissa established the first *sīmā*, or monastic boundary, setting apart the Mahāvihāra [xv.192].

At the request of the women followers, Mahinda invited his sister, Sanghamittā, to bring *bhikkhunīs* from India to establish ordination for women. Sanghamittā brought with her a branch from the *Bodhi* tree which was transplanted in Anurādhapura at a site sanctified by the *Bodhi* trees of three previous Buddhas.

Having established two of the three refuges, Mahinda told the king that they had not seen their master, the Buddha, for a long time. Surprised, the king replied that he understood that the Buddha had passed into *nirvāṇa*. But Mahinda explained that they longed to behold the relics of the Buddha. Thus, numerous relics, including the collar-bone of the Buddha, arrived from India and were enshrined in the *stūpas*. The establishment of Buddhism in Sri Lanka and the transfer of the Aśokan heritage was complete when the son of King Devānaṃpiya Tissa was ordained a *bhikkhu* and recited the *Vinaya Piṭaka*.

The Anurādhapura period

King Devānaṃpiya Tissa began the Anurādhapura period which lasted from *c*. 250 BCE until the end of the tenth century CE. This pivotal period of Sri Lanka's history, marked by a close connection between the monarchy and Buddhism, witnessed the rise of many notable kings who saw their duty to be the protectors of Buddhism. These kings unified the island and built Anurādhapura into both an important center for government and a magnificent sacred city for Buddhism. From Anurādhapura, the elders of the Mahāvihāra spread their version of Theravāda Buddhism to other countries in the region.

One of the most notable kings of this period was one of the earliest, Duṭṭhagāmaṇi (r. 101–77 BCE). He came to power by defeating a warrior from south India who had usurped the throne. That king, Eḷāra, is depicted by the *Mahāvaṃsa* as an enemy of Buddhism, while Duṭṭhagāmaṇi is depicted as the defender of the *Dharma*. During his reign, Duṭṭhagāmaṇi oversaw the establishment of Anurādhapura as a sacred city. He built some of the most important *stūpas* including the Mahāthūpa or Ruvanavālisāya. Succeeding monarchs built numerous other Buddhist shrines including the enclosure for the *Mahā Bodhi* tree and a temple for the Tooth Relic which arrived in the fourth century CE.

Although the Mahāvihāra seems to have been the center of Theravāda orthodoxy, it was challenged by several other monasteries, most notably the Abhayagiri and the Jetavana, that vied for favor with the king and the people. In addition to religious shrines, the kings of Anurādhapura also built a network of irrigation tanks and canals that strengthened agriculture and stabilized the economy. These impressive works of hydraulic engineering protected the people against drought and enabled the farmers to be more productive. Although these measures led to long periods of stability and peace, the Anurādhapura period was also marked by numerous invasions from south India.

The Polonnaruwa period

Partially because of the continuing threats from south India, the capital was moved to Polonnaruwa and remained there from *c*. 993 to 1250 CE. King Vijayabāhu I (1055–1110) defeated the Cola invaders and built up the new capital. To restore Buddhism, Vijayabāhu I requested King Aniruddha of Burma to send monks to re-establish the ordination lineage. In return, Vijayabāhu I sent Aniruddha a copy of the *Tipiṭaka* and relics, thus beginning a long period of Buddhist relations between Burma and Sri Lanka.

Parākramabāhu I (1153–86) unified the island and constructed many of the great buildings and temples at Polonnaruwa. He continued the tradition of hydro-engineering works that aided the people. Following the Aśokan ideal of a *cakkavattin* (Skt. *cakravartin*), Parākramabāhu I held a purification of the *sangha* which brought unity by expelling hundreds of heterodox monks and strengthening Theravāda orthodoxy. The renewed vigor of the Sri Lankan *sangha* during this period attracted monks from Burma who came to Polonnaruwa to receive ordination. These exchanges contributed to the dominance of the Mahāvihāra's form of Theravāda Buddhism in Burma and Southeast Asia.

The Kandyan and later periods

When the Polonnaruwa kingdom fell *c.* 1250 CE, the capital of Sri Lanka, after moving to several locations, was finally established in Kandy by the sixteenth century to ward off invasions from south India and also from the Europeans. The kings of the Kandyan period balanced political power to keep the Portuguese and the Dutch at bay. To legitimate their rule, the Kandyan kings again invoked the Aśokan model of the king as the *cakkavatti* and as the *dhammarāja* or "*Dharma* king." King Kīrti Śri Rājasiṃha (1751–82 CE) dedicated his reign to the support and reform of Buddhism. He appointed a monastic reformer, Saranaṃkara, to be *sangharāja* and he enlisted the aid of the Dutch to bring monks from Thailand in 1753 to re-establish higher ordination in the island. The newly ordained *bhikkhus* formed the Siyam *Nikāya* which became the dominant branch of the *sangha*. Later missions to Burma/Myanmar in the early nineteenth century led to the establishment of two other reforming branches of the *sangha*, the Amarapura and the Rāmañña *Nikāyas*.

The British period and modern period

The Kandyan kingdom ended in 1815, when the British gained control of Kandy and signed a treaty called the Kandyan Convention, which promised that Buddhism would be "maintained and protected." Despite what may have been the sincere intentions of the British officials who negotiated this treaty, the *sangha* and Buddhism declined significantly during the British period because of pressures from Christian missionaries, colonial policies, and a general Westernization. In the late nineteenth century, however, a movement to revive and reform Buddhism began to stir. In 1873, senior Buddhist *bhikkhus* engaged the Christian missionaries in a series of debates at Panadurā. Hearing of these debates, the Theosophists Madame Helena Blavatsky and Colonel Henry Olcott traveled to Sri Lanka to lend their support to the Buddhists. The Theosophists selected Anagarika Dharmapala, who became the inspirational leader of the movement to revive Buddhism. The momentum of the Buddhist resurgence helped bring independence from Britain in 1948 and generated a series of political leaders who aspired once again to be seen as successors to Aśoka and defenders of the *Dharma*. Although the emerging Buddhist nationalism sought to "restore Buddhism to its proper place," it eventually drove a wedge between the Sinhala majority and the Tamil minority and led to a lengthy ethnic conflict in the island that has yet to be resolved.

See also: **Anagarika Dharmapala; Aśoka; Buddhism in the Western world; Burma (Myanmar), Buddhism in; South and Southeast Asia, Buddhism in.**

GEORGE D. BOND

STEM CELL RESEARCH

Many researchers believe that human stem cells have an important role to play in the development of genetic therapies. Stem cells have the ability to divide for indefinite periods in culture and to give rise to other more specialized cells. Because of the power they have to grow into any kind of somatic cell – such as a brain cell, a liver cell, a heart or blood cell – they are described as "pluripotent." This means they function a bit like the joker in a pack of playing cards, which can take on any value as the context requires. Researchers working with stem cells believe they can learn much about the process through which an organism develops from a single cell and how healthy cells replace damaged ones. It is felt that this knowledge will contribute much to the developing field of regenerative or reparative medicine. Diseases such as Parkinson's Disease, a neurodegenerative disorder affecting around 2 per cent of the population, may be the first disease amenable to treatment by stem cell transplantation.

The stem cells used for research are obtained from two main sources, the first being excess embryos left over after infertility treatment. Here, the inner cell mass of the embryo which consists of the pluripotent cells is cultured to produce a pluripotent stem cell line. The second method is to isolate pluripotent stem cells from fetal tissue obtained from terminated pregnancies, and here we encounter dilemmas familiar from the abortion debate. As in these cases an abortion will already have been carried out and the cells to be used would otherwise simply be destroyed along with the fetal remains, some observers feel that there is nothing immoral in the use of this tissue for scientific research. Others consider that the research itself is tainted by its association with the abortion, even when this was carried out in accordance with legal requirements, the consent of the mother was obtained, and the research holds the promise of alleviating suffering. Stem cells are also found in adults (for example, stem cells reside in the bone marrow and perform the critical role of replenishing our supply of blood cells), and recent experiments have shown that these may retain a greater capacity to diversify than had hitherto been thought. If adult cells can be utilized an important objection to stem cell research could be removed, but as yet the flexibility of adult stem cells has only been observed in animals and in limited tissue types. The view one comes to regarding stem cell research will be influenced by the view one takes on abortion, and although as we have seen traditional Buddhist teachings oppose abortion, in practice Buddhists are as likely to be as divided on this question as any other group.

See also: **Abortion; Cloning; Ethics; Precepts, lay.**

DAMIEN KEOWN

STŪPA

Introduction

The Sanskrit term *stūpa* refers to a structure that enshrines relics for the purposes of veneration. *Stūpas* are among the most characteristic and widespread of Buddhist architectural forms. The Pāli *Mahāparinibbāna Sutta* (Skt. *Mahāparinirvāṇa Sūtra*), a Buddhist canonical text that survives in several parallel versions, recounts that Gautama Buddha gave detailed instructions for cremating his body and placing his remains in a *stūpa* erected at a prominent crossroads, concluding: "Those who there offer a garland, or scent, or fragrant powder, or make a salutation, or feel serene joy in their heart, that will be to their benefit and happiness for a long time" (*Dīgha Nikāya* 2.142). The same text further specifies whose remains are worthy of enshrinement in a *stūpa*: Tathāgatas (Buddhas

Figure 38 Maṇi wall (*maṇi gdong*) and *stūpas* at entrance to a village in Nepal.

such as Gautama), Paccekabuddhas (Skt. *Pratyekabuddha*, Buddhas who do not teach), *sāvakas* (Skt. *śrāvakas*; disciples of a Tathāgata) and *cakravartin* kings (a "wheel-turning" king who governs with universal sovereignty in accordance with the *Dharma*). These passages set forth the basic elements of Buddhist *stūpa* veneration: a distinctive structure enshrining relics (either cremated remains or objects rendered venerable through physical use or contact) of Buddhas or other significant religious figures, erected in a prominent location, that serves as the focus for devotional offerings understood to be beneficial for future rebirths and, ultimately, for the realization of *nirvāṇa*. (See Figure 38.)

Historical background

The Pāli terms *thūpa* (Skt. *stūpa*) and *cetiya* (Skt. *caitya*) came to be used interchangeably to refer to relic monuments in Pāli Buddhist literature by the fifth century CE, though in earlier Buddhist usage the term *cetiya* and its cognates had a broader meaning that included places or objects worthy of special reverence for reasons other than their association with relics, such as sacred groves or trees. The etymologies of both *stūpa* and *caitya* are uncertain. The word *stūpa* first occurs in Vedic literature, though with a meaning apparently unrelated to its later Buddhist usage, which is first attested in a third-century BCE inscription referring to Aśoka's expansion of a *stūpa* for the former Buddha Konākamuni. Most commentators trace *caitya* back to a word meaning "funeral pile," based on the Sanskrit root *ci*, "to pile up." *Caitya* appears in Sanskrit literature with a range of associations, designating sites for Vedic fire sacrifices, places of cremation and burial, and sacred groves and trees associated with powerful spirits.

Buddhist *stūpas* and the religious practices centered around them probably did not suddenly appear on the Indian horizon without historical and cultural precedent, and one line of analysis locates the antecedents of the Buddhist *stūpa* in megalithic burial mounds. As Gregory Schopen has noted, there is considerable evidence of Buddhist *stūpa* construction on sites in India where earlier traces of megalithic burials have been excavated, and in some cases it appears that there was a period of overlap between the communities responsible for the megalithic burials and Buddhist monastic communities. A similar pattern has been noted in Sri Lanka and Burma. One possible explanation for the connection was a general tendency to concentrate burial sites on land unsuitable for habitation or cultivation, though it is an intriguing possibility that as Buddhism spread into new regions, Buddhist monastics intentionally appropriated sites with longstanding cultic associations for their own religious complexes.

Another line of historical analysis centers on connections between Buddhist *stūpa* practices and pre-Buddhist traditions related to *cakravartin* kings. It has been argued that the funeral rites described in the *Mahāparinirvāṇa Sūtra*, perhaps reflecting local non-Aryan practices, may represent later efforts on the part of the Buddha's followers to exalt his status by according him the rites of a universal king, though there is as yet no archeological evidence of pre-Buddhist *cakravartin* burial mounds. *Stūpa* veneration was also a part of early Jain tradition, though again the connections with Buddhist practice remain unclear, since the earliest archeological evidence of Jain *stūpas* post-dates the oldest remains of Buddhist *stūpas*. Some scholars have also looked to Vedic burial mounds (*śmaśānas*), known only through textual references, for the origins of Buddhist *stūpas*.

Whatever the historical connections between pre-Buddhist burial practices and the emergence of Buddhist *stūpa* veneration, the significance of Buddhist *stūpa* practices clearly came to extend well beyond a basic concern with burial. Given consistent anxieties about corpse pollution in Brahmanic religion, the central role of relic veneration in the religious practice and institutional development of early Buddhism marks a significantly new development in Indian religion. The narrative of the Buddha's death and funeral rites highlights the purity and auspiciousness of his cremated remains, emphasizing the respective roles of *sangha* members and lay Buddhists, as well as the involvement of celestial beings, in honoring his relics. As Schopen emphasizes, Buddhist *stūpas* were also constructed for the local monastic dead, and not only for those of high religious attainment. At the same time, there is textual and material evidence (at Sāñcī, for example) pointing to a clear hierarchy of enshrinement, with the *stūpa* enshrining Buddha relics occupying a centralized position, and the smaller *stūpas* containing the remains of other monastics arrayed around it at varying distances in keeping with their relative status. There is considerable evidence that *stūpas* enshrining Buddha relics were believed to embody the living presence of the Buddha, and the construction of additional *stūpas* to enshrine the remains of *sangha* members may thus reflect a desire to maintain some sort of continued proximity to that powerful presence. A similar motivation may be reflected in the large numbers of donative inscriptions placed around and in *stūpas*, often containing little more than the name of the donor, in keeping with a belief that a person's written name continues to manifest their physical presence.

While the earliest remains of a few currently known Buddhist *stūpas* may date to a period earlier than the third century BCE, during the reign of the emperor Aśoka (270–230 BCE) Buddhist *stūpa* construction gained a major impetus, and the earliest securely dated *stūpa* remains belong to this period. Both textual sources and material remains testify to Aśoka's patronage of Buddhism, including *stūpa* construction. Widespread and highly influential textual traditions, including the Sanskrit *Aśokāvadāna* and the Pāli *vaṃsa* texts, maintain that Aśoka constructed 84,000 *stūpa*s throughout his kingdom and undertook a comprehensive redistribution of the Buddha's relics. Though the Aśokan inscriptions do not refer to this major program of *stūpa* construction and the remains of only a few *stūpas* have been securely dated to his reign, the ideal of Aśoka as a righteous Buddhist ruler and *stūpa* builder established a paradigm for Buddhist kingship that proved very attractive to later rulers throughout Asia.

Structure and symbolism

Given the wide geographic and temporal spread of Buddhist *stūpa* construction and the diversity of cultures in which it was adopted, it is not surprising that the architectural forms of Buddhist *stūpas* vary considerably. Nevertheless, there are a number of characteristic features. The earliest Indian *stūpas* were probably hemispherical mounds of earth or clay erected upon the ground or upon a simple base, possibly surrounded by a circular fence that defined a walkway for circumambulation (*pradakṣiṇā*) and surmounted by one or more umbrellas atop a central pole (a symbol of royal stature). Bricks and stone were first used in Mauryan (third century BCE) *stūpa* construction. During the second century BCE through the first century CE, the basic form of Indian *stūpas* received increasing elaboration, including more formally articulated berms or terraces (*medhis*), in some cases forming elevated circumambulatory walkways, decorated ground-level balustrades (*vedikās*) and elaborately illustrated entrance gateways (*toraṇas*), enlarged, reshaped, and resurfaced domes (*aṇḍas*), and more complex superstructures, sometimes comprised of multiple stone umbrellas (*chatrāvalis*) raised upon a central shaft (*yaṣṭi*) set into a square stone base (*harmikā*) surrounded by a railing (*vedikā*).

The basic structure detailed above is largely reflected in Sri Lankan *stūpas*. Sri Lankan *vaṃsa* accounts as well as excavated Sri Lankan relic chambers provide evidence of a detailed cosmological symbolism depicting the Buddha, represented by relics and images, enthroned at the top of a cosmic pantheon. Multichambered stone receptacles (*yantragalas* or *garbhapātras*) were commonly placed beneath the central relic chamber in the dome of the *stūpa*, oriented toward the four cardinal directions, with the chambers typically containing small figures that represented guardian deities, each with their respective realms of authority according to their location. The central relic chambers in some *stūpas* included a central four-sided stone carved to represent Mount Meru, the cosmic mountain at the center of the universe, which provided the reliquary base, and in some cases a central shaft extended from the lid of the relic chamber upward through the dome and superstructure. It is also clear from Indian and Sri Lankan *stūpa* excavations that relic chambers were often located in multiple sites within *stūpas* and a wide diversity of objects were enshrined, including images, jewelry, coins, and Buddhist texts. The form of the *stūpa* and the materials used to construct it underwent considerable modification in Central, East, and Southeast Asia, though the primary function of enshrining relics remained largely consistent. (See Figure 39.)

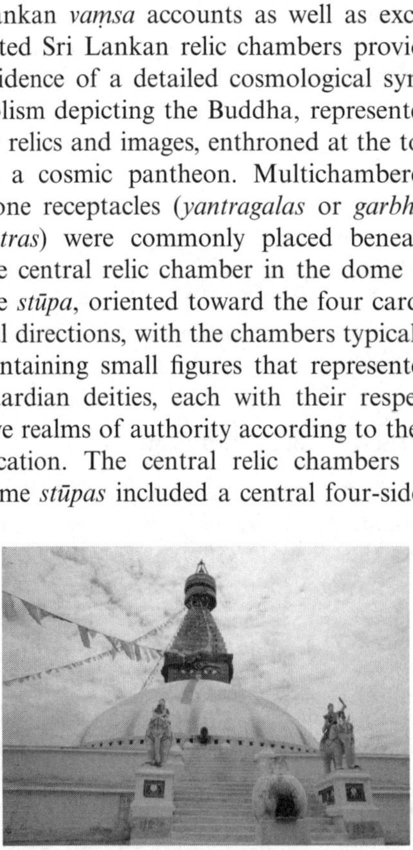

Figure 39 The Great *Stūpa* at Swayambunath, in Kathmandu, Nepal.

Associated texts and rituals

Textual accounts of *stūpa* construction and relic enshrinements provide ample evidence that *stūpas* have functioned as vital cultic centers for coordinating the respective statuses and activities of Buddhist monastics and lay supporters, often in conformity with the Aśokan ideal. *Stūpa* construction and reconstruction are a primary means through which many Asian rulers have manifested and enhanced their political and religious authority. Kings were also frequently the organizers and patrons of annual *stūpa*-centered festivals. From the laying of the foundation to the final raising of the pinnacle, *stūpa* building is a highly ritualized activity well suited to reinforcing social roles and collective identity. *Stūpas* also provide a central focus for individual devotional activity, in the form of material offerings (*pūjā*) and ritualized gestures, including circumambulation and prostration. *Stūpas* are, moreover, key elements in the spatial and ritual organization of monastic complexes and in the construction of a sacred landscape defined by pilgrimage routes. All this *stūpa*-centered activity reflects and reinforces the over-arching Buddhist principle of intentional actions and their karmic consequences, in accordance with which a "skillful" (*kuśala*) action can appear both as the fruition of previous meritorious actions and as a primary means through which future benefits, both mundane and supramundane, will be realized. *Stūpas*, through their tangible and enduring representation of Buddhas and other powerful religious figures, have been and continue to be formative elements in the organization, maintenance, and enhancement of Buddhist religious life.

See also: **Angkor; Aśoka; Borobudur; Buddha, relics of; Buddha and *cakravartins*; *Mantras*, *mudrās*, and *maṇḍalas*; Pāṭaliputra; Sacred places; Sāñcī; *Stūpas* of Sāñcī, Bhārhut, and Amarāvatī; Worship.**

KEVIN TRAINOR

STŪPAS OF SĀÑCĪ, BHĀRHUT, AND AMARĀVATĪ

The Mauryans' dynastic rule ended in the early part of the second century BCE; they were followed by a lineage of kings known as the Śuṅgas. Under the Śuṅgas – and the other regional rulers of this period – Buddhism continued to flourish, and it is in this period that we see particularly significant developments in Buddhist art: the development of large-scale free-standing architectural monuments and the introduction of human figures and narrative motifs. Perhaps the most significant of these early monuments are Sāñcī and Bhārhut, two sprawling monastic complexes located in modern Madhya Pradesh which date to about 100 BCE (although artistic work at the sites probably was ongoing, continuing for several hundred years), and Amarāvatī in modern Andhra Pradesh.

The Great *Stūpa* at Sāñcī (also referred to as *Stūpa* I) is one of the best-known monuments in the history of Indian art. Located atop a hill on a major trade route outside of the ancient city of Vidiśā, Sāñcī developed into a sprawling monastic complex (See Figure 40). At the center of this complex was a huge *stūpa* enshrining relics of the Buddha. It is the four gateways (*toraṇas*) that provide entrance to the *stūpa*, though, that are most significant in the context of Buddhist art: funded by the donations of hundreds of Buddhist laypersons (including, significantly, women) and monks, they were elaborately carved with Buddhist symbols and scenes, scenes that were intended to be seen by Buddhist monks and laypersons as they ritually circumambulated the *stūpa* itself. These scenes range from *Jātaka* stories of the Buddha's previous lives to depictions of key moments in his life – his birth, the first sermon, his death, and so on. Significantly, Buddhist artisans began to include human figures in these relief carvings; the Buddha himself, however, is absent from these early scenes.

The *Vessantara Jātaka*, for instance, is presented in a complex series of images across one of the monument's gates, forming a kind of collage effect that seems to be intended to visually narrate the story – although it is important to point out that the viewers of such an image were also no doubt already familiar with at least the basic outlines of the story – and also to create the opportunity for a monk or educated layperson to emphasize particular aspects of it. Indeed,

Figure 40 Stūpa and *toraṇa*, Sāñcī, India.

it is difficult to imagine that such a complex visual image would have only been seen; it would also, necessarily, have been discussed. In this sense, then, images around the Great *Stūpa* at Sāñcī may have functioned as opportunities for monks – and well-educated laypersons – to offer instructions and meditations on particular aspects of the *Dharma*.

The *stūpa* at Bhārhut, like that at Sāñcī, was marked by very elaborately carved gateways, decorated with *makaras* (mythical beasts associated with fertility), *yakṣas* and *yakṣīs* (spirits of varying character), *cakras*, *triratnas* (the "triple gem," symbolizing the Buddha, *Dharma*, and *Sangha*), and various animals. On the railings that surrounded the *stūpa*, as at Sāñcī, are scenes from the *Jātakas* and from Śākyamuni's life. There are also a great many scenes depicting various forms of ritual veneration, with men and women worshiping the *Bodhi* tree, the Buddha's footprints, the *dharmacakra*, and small *stūpas*. In one such scene, from a piece of the monument now in the Indian Museum, four figures, two standing and two kneeling, worship what appears to be a reliquary topped a small *stūpa* and two *dharmacakras*. Likewise, at Sāñcī depictions of ritual veneration are quite common; on the north *toraṇa* of the Great *Stūpa*, for instance, is a scene that depicts an assembly of men and women – along with a group of musicians and a collection of heavenly beings (*devas*) – worshipping a *stūpa* that looks very much like the Great *Stūpa* itself.

At Amarāvatī another huge *stūpa* was built at about the same time as those at Sāñcī and Bhārhut. Again, surrounding the *stūpa* with railings, gateways, and pillars were elaborately carved scenes from the *Jātakas* and the Buddha's life story. Although there are significant stylistic differences between the various images at these different sites, there is also a basic thematic similarity which allows them to be discussed in the same general terms. Indeed, it seems clear that Buddhist artisans and monks traveled between these various sites, exchanging doctrinal ideas as well as artistic one. Although much has been written on the images, and a great deal of care has been paid to linking a particular image or motif to a particular textual episode, such links are frequently quite tenuous. Indeed, although many of these images clearly "illustrated" a particular textual episode, it is equally clear that some images had a quite different contextual function.

On one of the pillars from Amarāvatī, for instance (Knox 1992: 51, or Barrett, *Sculptures from Amaravati in the British Museum* [London: Trustees of the British Museum, 1954], pl. 21) there are several scenes that are clearly related to the Buddha's enlightenment, scenes that are illustrative of the nature and function of the art from these early monuments. At the center of the pillar, the main image presents a small *Bodhi* tree, a pedestal with two footprints, and a group of worshipers, all of whom appear to be women, some bearing offerings. At the bottom of the pillar is a similar scene, with two men offering what appears to be a length of cloth to the footprints. At the top of the pillar a river is depicted, along with several footprints (in what is perhaps sand or mud), as well as a tree with a hand emerging from it: the river here is no doubt the Phalgu, along the banks of which Śākyamuni began his meditations (the hand is rather puzzling, but may be that of a *vānadevata*, a forest spirit, who in some versions of the story offers it to assist the Buddha in crossing the river). The other two scenes are more difficult to interpret.

Several scholars have suggested that the central scene is the well-known episode, from the Buddha's life story, of the laywoman Sujatā offering food to the Śākyamuni prior to his enlightenment. This is an extremely important scene in Buddhism: the Buddha-to-be has nearly starved himself to death through the practice of severe austerities, and Sujatā, who does not know who this starving man is but is simply overcome with compassion for him, offers the humble gift of rice-water that allows him to gain the necessary physical strength to apply himself to his mediation and thus, ultimately, to attain enlightenment. The scene serves as a ritual template, a kind of visual guide, for proper, humble giving (*dāna*) on the part of the layperson. Although seeing this image as a depiction of the Sujatā is certainly a plausible interpretation, in the textual narrative Sujatā is alone, whereas in the carved image she is in the company of several other women. This image could just as plausibly be a depiction of generic worship of the Buddha by a group of his followers. Perhaps more puzzling, though, is that in this image the offerings are not made to the Buddha, but to the footprints. Indeed, as in the case of virtually all of the early images from Sāñcī, Bharhūt, and Amarāvatī, the Buddha is not actually depicted at all.

It is possible that the footprints here were intended to represent the living Buddha, symbolically, and that is how it has been typically interpreted, in keeping with the basic gist of the oft-repeated aniconic thesis. It seems just as likely, though, that this scene from Amarāvatī represents precisely what it seems, on its face, to represent: the veneration of images of the Buddha's footprints, a most physical index of his absence, a common visual theme in the Buddhist art of India and a ritual practice that continues to the present day, especially in and around Bodhgayā. In this sense, then, this image – as well as many similar ones found at Sāñcī and Bhārhut – is perhaps best seen not so much as a "visual text," but rather as a depiction of the sort of worship that was appropriate after the *parinirvāṇa* of the Buddha. As such, then, these images may have served, collectively, as a kind of ritual guide for Buddhist devotees. In this regard, an important challenge to the dominance of the aniconic thesis has been put forth in recent years, one that sees scenes such as this one from Amarāvatī, in which the Buddha is not actually depicted – as well as similar ones from Bārhut, Sāñcī, and elsewhere in the early Buddhist world – not as "texts" at all, but rather as records of actual practice, as well as visual guides to such practice.

Thus it may be that Buddhists did not prohibit the physical depiction of the Buddha at all – certainly there is no textual evidence to support such an idea – but rather that, after his death, Buddhists worshipped images of his absence, such as the empty throne, the footprints, and the *Bodhi* tree. Such ritual activity is in keeping with one of the core philosophical tenets of Buddhism, *anitya*, the impermanence of all things, including the physical person of the Buddha. It is likely, certainly, that Buddhist monks and artisans did not make artistic images with only one intent, but rather that such images served different functions – narrative, ritual, philosophical – depending on the particular context in which they were situated, contexts which, moreover, were probably never static, but changed as the religious tradition itself changed. Likewise, the function of any single image was also determined by the viewer him- or herself. In this sense, then, it is essential to understand that visual images in the Buddhist context are inherently multivalent, able to convey different messages – and to serve different ritual functions – depending on the context, and one must always be very wary of any sort of overgeneral or essentialized interpretations.

See also: **Art, Buddhist; Sacred places; *Stūpa*.**

JACOB N. KINNARD

SUICIDE

Many striking examples of suicide can be found throughout the Buddhist world. In modern times the suicide of the seventy-three-year-old Vietnamese monk Thich Quang Duc made headlines throughout the world in 1963 when he burned himself alive on 11 June on a main street in Saigon. Sitting quietly in the lotus posture, the elderly monk ordered two of his followers to douse him with petrol and then calmly set himself alight. Thich Qang Duc's suicide was a protest against the religious policies of the dictator Ngo Dinh Diem, who had persistently favored the country's Catholic minority. Thich Quang Duc's final testimony read: "Before closing my eyes to go to Buddha, I have the honor to present my words to President Diem, asking him to be kind and tolerant towards his people and enforce a policy of religious equality."

Thich Qang Duc was not the originator of the dramatic act he performed in Saigon, and stands within a long tradition of self-immolation in East Asian Buddhism. In China there are historical precedents for individuals burning either themselves or parts of their bodies for religious reasons. Burning of the body in a token way has formed part of the monastic ordination ritual in China and Korea down to modern times. In the course of the ordination ceremony a small cone of incense is placed on the monk's shaven head and ignited. When it burns away it leaves a permanent mark on the scalp. Other, more dramatic, examples feature in the historical records, including burning off fingers or entire limbs (usually the arms), and in extreme cases burning the whole body. A tenth-century treatise by the Chinese monk Yongming Yanshou (904–75) commends these practices to ordinary monks and nuns. Such deeds were seen by those who approved of them as sacrifices to the Buddha, recalling the master's own cremation, and demonstrating great piety and devotion. Other authorities disagreed, arguing that such extreme acts were only appropriate for great *bodhisattvas.*

Suicide has also been common in neighboring Japan in the ritualized form which goes by the name of *seppuku* (also known as "hara kiri," a more vulgar term meaning "to slice the abdomen"). This act involves making two small crosswise slices across the gut while in a kneeling position, after which a second would behead the samurai with a sword (in practice the first step was rarely carried out). Beginning in the Tokugawa period, samurai warriors came to see this sacrifice as the penalty for a failure in their duty and as something enjoined by their professional code of honor. In modern times large numbers of suicides occurred among the Japanese military in the wake of the country's defeat in the Second World War. As many *samurai* turned to Buddhism, some commentators have come to see suicide as legitimized by Buddhist teachings, and have gone so far as to claim that the practice of suicide was approved of by the Buddha.

An alternative view is that the practices described previously owe more to the indigenous cultures to which Buddhism spread and have little basis in the early Indian teachings. In China, the two texts which seem to validate the practice of auto-cremation (the *Brahmajāla Sūtra* and the *Śūraṃgamasamādhi Sūtra*) are both apocryphal Chinese compositions with no Indian ancestor. Further, auto-cremation has ancient roots in pre-Buddhist China in the practice of moxibustion and in ceremonies designed to produce rain. The practice of ritual suicide in Japan, likewise, may be thought to owe more to Japanese military honor codes than to Buddhist teachings.

Reaching a moral evaluation of the examples discussed above is complicated by the fact that it is not always easy to define what counts as "suicide." If we take as our definition of suicide something like "cases where a person knowingly embarks on a course of action that will lead to his or her death," we may find that the category is too broad. For instance, is the soldier who throws himself on a grenade to save his comrades "committing suicide"? And what of the martyr who refuses to recant knowing that the stake awaits him, or the pilot who remains at the controls of his plane to avoid crashing into a school? Depending on how we classify these examples our moral assessment can be very different. Rather than being associated with the stigma of suicide, the individuals in these examples may in fact be praised and even regarded as heroes. The fact remains, however, that they all freely and knowingly chose a course of action that they knew would lead to their deaths. Given the nuances which distinguish the different kinds of self-inflicted death, some commentators prefer to avoid pejorative terms like "suicide" and speak instead of "voluntary death." Perhaps a separate category of "altruistic suicide" is needed within this to encompass the examples cited, and also one of "religious suicide" for cases like that of Thich Qang Duc.

Turning to the earliest sources, there is a possible precedent for condoning suicide in Indian Buddhism in the form of a small number of well-known cases in the Pāli Canon where monks who were sick and in pain took their own lives and apparently received a posthumous endorsement from the Buddha. Three cases are particularly important: those of the monks Channa, Vakkali and Godhika. A special feature of these cases is that the monks in question attained *arhant*ship as they died and were not reborn. Because of this something of a consensus has emerged among scholars that while Buddhism is generally opposed to suicide it is prepared to make an exception in the case of the enlightened, because they in some sense or other have transcended conventional moral norms. Further, one early school (the Sarvāstivāda) seems to have supported the view that suicide may be permitted to avoid loss of *arhant* status, and we are also told that the Buddha renounced his "life principle" (*āyusaṃskāra*) three months before he died (*Dīgha Nikāya* 2.106) (whether this constitutes "suicide" would seem to involve definitional problems of the kind described earlier).

An alternative interpretation of the early sources, however, suggests that although the Buddha felt great sympathy for those involved, there is little evidence that he ever condoned suicide. His position rather was to see suicide as wrong, but not to judge too harshly those who took their own lives in circumstances of great pain or distress. Leaving to one side the problematic cases relating to the special category of suicide by the enlightened, there is little support for suicide elsewhere in the early sources. In general it is strongly discouraged as the futile waste of a precious human rebirth, because the person who commits suicide will simply be reborn with the additional bad *karma* of the suicide to contend with.

See also: ***Ahiṃsā*; Ethics; Euthanasia; Moral discipline; Precepts, lay; *Vinaya Piṭaka*.**

DAMIEN KEOWN

T

TATHĀGATAGARBHA IN INDIAN BUDDHISM

The doctrine of *tathāgatagarbha* occurs in several *sūtras* of the Mahāyāna tradition and in a small number of Indian Buddhist scholastic texts. Although the doctrine evidently began in India and did have adherents there, it seems never to have been as influential in India as it eventually was in East Asia and Tibet. The expression literally means the womb or embryo (*garbha*) of the Tathāgata or Buddha, and it refers, in some interpretations, to the potential that every sentient being has to become fully awakened. In other interpretations it refers to the beginningless fact of being awakened that is inherent, though obscured, in every sentient being. As not all the texts that use this term use it in exactly the same way, one must consider each text separately.

A short Mahāyāna sūtra called the *Tathāgatagarbha Sūtra* says simply that in the midst of all the unwholesome and afflicted mental events in every sentient being there is an always pure and wholesome core that is the potential of awakening. This core is said to be the nature of all things and is present even when no buddhas are to be found in the world. The *Laṅkāvatāra Sūtra*, the full title of which means "Introduction of the True *Dharma* of the Mahāyāna into Laṅka," is a complex compilation of teachings, many of which were eventually systematized in the Yogācāra or Vijñānavāda school. In section 82 of this *sūtra* it is suggested that the *tathāgatagarbha* is the same as the *ālayavijñāna* (underlying awareness or storehouse consciousness), which is the repository of all traces left from previous experiences in the current life and all past lives and the source therefore of all future experiences. Equating the *tathāgatagarbha* with the storehouse consciousness is a way of emphasizing that the roots of awakening lie within one's own thought processes and modes of awareness; the potential of being a buddha is already present in one's experiences and one's personality. In introducing these ideas, *Laṅkāvatāra Sūtra* is careful to make the point that the storehouse consciousness (and therefore the *tathāgatagarbha*) must not be seen as the self (*ātman*); in fact, says the text, the Buddha refrained from teaching about these doctrines at first, lest fools fall into the mistaken view that there is an *ātman*.

Another Mahāyāna *sūtra*, the *Mahāparinirvāṇa Sūtra*, claims that all sentient beings, even the very wicked who cannot even form the wish to be good, are destined for buddhahood. Moreover, this text, unlike the *Laṅkāvatāra*, clearly identifies the *tathāgatagarbha* with the self (*ātman*). The true self of all sentient beings is nothing other than the *tathāgatagarbha*. The Buddhist teaching of non-self (*anātman*) is to be understood as saying only that the afflictions (*kleśas*) and unwholesome mental events are not really the self at all and that it is therefore a delusion to identify with them. It is not, however, a delusion to realize that one's true nature is that of a buddha and that this buddha nature is permanent, blissful and pure.

Yet another Mahāyāna *sūtra*, the *Śrīmālādevīsiṃhanāda Sūtra* (*The Lion's Roar of Queen Śrīmālā*), gives an even more elaborate and detailed account of the *tathāgatagarbha*, saying of it that it is beginningless, unconditioned, unborn, undying, eternal, calm, pure, and impossible to contaminate. There are as many *tathāgatagarbhas* or Buddha-natures as there are sands on the shores of the Ganges. Moreover, says this *sūtra*, *tathāgatagarbha* is just another name for the *dharmakāya*, the essential body of the buddha, when the *dharmakāya* is in the presence of defilements. When this Buddha-nature is accompanied by defilements, by which its actual nature is not at all affected but by which its presence is temporarily concealed, it becomes the basis for rebirth, or at least for the illusion of rebirth. Once the defilements are removed, however, the Buddha-nature shines fully, and it becomes apparent that it is undivided and one. It is one and the same *dharmakāya* that is mistakenly seen as a multitude of *tathāgatagarbhas*.

The earliest of the still-extant scholastic treatises to deal with the *tathāgatagarbha* doctrine is the *Ratnagotravibhāga*, also known as *Mahāyānottaratantra Śāstra*, the exact authorship of which is unknown, although a commentary to it is attributed to Asaṅga. This text consists mostly of quotations from Mahāyāna *sūtras*, especially the *Śrīmālādevīsiṃhanāda Sūtra*. This treatise, like the *Śrīmaladevī*, argues that when the Buddha outlined his list of delusional views, he said that it is delusion to regard as permanent what is in fact impermanent, and to regard as pleasant what is in fact unsatisfactory, and to regard as self what is in fact not self. The Buddha did not say, however, that it is delusion to regard as permanent, pleasant and self what in fact is permanent, pleasant and self. Indeed, it would be delusion to regard as impermanent what is in fact permanent. What is permanent, pleasant and self, says this treatise, is nothing other than *tathāgatagarbha*. The teaching of *tathāgatagarbha* is then said to be more inspiring than the teaching of emptiness (*śūnyatā*) that is found in much Mahāyāna literature. The teaching of emptiness has a specific purpose, and it should be taken as the antidote to a particular malady. This antidote, however, is a medicine that carries with it certain risks. The doctrine of emptiness carries the risk of generating despondency, even despair. It should therefore be taken only to clear away the self-centered mental states that obscure the reality of an unconditioned, pure, blissful, wholesome unity that is in fact the true self of all beings.

The ideas set forward in the *Ratnagotravibhāga* and Asaṅga's commentary did not meet with wide acceptance in India until similar arguments were made by Ratnakīrti in the eleventh century. The doctrine of *tathāgatagarbha* was met with suspicion in most quarters of Indian Buddhism because of its being seen as a form of eternalism, one of the two extreme views that the Middle Path of Buddhism was supposed to avoid. Followers of *tathāgatagarbha*, in contrast, would argue that rejecting the doctrine would entail cessationism (*ucchedavāda*), the other extreme view avoided by the Middle Path.

See also: **Buddha nature and *tathāgatagarbha*; India, Buddhism in; Mahāyāna Buddhism; Yogācāra school.**

RICHARD P. HAYES

TECHNOLOGY AND BUDDHISM

The Buddhist tradition has been profoundly affected by information technology throughout much of its history. The first major use of such technology in Buddhism came with the advent of writing as a method of storing and disseminating the teaching. The earliest examples of written material in the Indian sub-continent appear on stone and pillar inscriptions from the time of King Aśoka (*c.* 272–232 BCE). Relying on the alphabet of neighboring kingdoms to his west, Aśoka was able to convey messages about his rule throughout the realm. The literacy rate among his subjects must have been very limited when these edicts were cut into stone, but the number and range of locations of the inscriptions indicate that Aśoka was fully supportive of writing as a medium of communication. The use of stone, whether natural or polished, insured the survival of his written edicts. While there are no extant examples of other written material from this era, a few references in texts indicate the possibility of an earlier use of the medium. The oldest extant reference to the use of writing in Buddhism appears in the Chinese translation of the *Aṣṭasāhasrikāprajñāpāramitā Sūtra* in 179 CE.

Writing requires other adjunct technologies before it becomes a useful or widespread activity. The first necessity is a surface on which to place the letters and scripts. While the earliest Indian examples are on stone, we know that progress was being made on developing other "surface technologies." Eventually this search resulted in the treatment of palm leaves (*olla* or *ola*) as a renewable and readily available source for the needed surface material. The Talipot (Skt. *tālapāt*) palm, *Corypha umbraculifera*, had large leaves that could be cut into strips for writing. The Palmyra palm, *Borassus flabelliformis*, was also used. The undried *olla* contained within its own structure a sticky sap that could be exploited for "inking" the surface. Soot, applied to the incised outlines of written characters, dissolved into the sticky substance to create a written text. Once this process was in place, it was feasible to construct volumes of multiple loose folios that were tied together with string passed through a prepared hole in the *olla*. With this new technology, the Buddhists could begin to transmit their teachings apart from the original oral tradition. Recitation required that a group of monks gather together to assess the accuracy of chanted memorized words. Written texts, by contrast, constituted their own authority. Having the teaching in a form that could be disseminated without a reciter created an entirely different climate for the spread of Buddhism. Some scholars have suggested that the technology of writing may have facilitated the rapid development of Mahāyāna. Certainly it is the early Mahāyāna texts that first claim that writing, or causing someone to copy, a written document brings enormous merit. The use of the technology of writing, with its attendant palm leaves or other surfaces, was declared to be equal, or even superior, to other religious activities, such as constructing *stūpas*. Thus, writing is the first example of the Buddhist tradition adopting a new information technology and making it an integral part of religious life.

As Buddhism spread into Central Asia, it was no longer practical to rely on tropical palm-leaf surfaces. A new surface material was needed, one that could grow in higher and colder altitudes. This led to the use of bark from the Himalayan birch (*Betula utilis*). Indians referred to this material as *bhoja-patra*, retaining in the word *patra* the metaphor of a "leaf." Like palm leaves, the natural surface of the birch bark was used with some preparation; it was not manufactured into a fabric. The size of the birch bark could have allowed for changes in the formatting of texts. However, the older method of using long, narrow *olla* strips determined the way the bark was shaped for use. The new material was made to look as much like the palm leaf as possible. Volumes were long and narrow so as to imitate the technology of the Indian sub-continent.

When Buddhism reached the capital of the Han dynasty shortly after the beginning of the Common Era, China had a long-established culture of writing. Because of this history, Chinese scribes had found a great variety of surfaces for the creation of volumes. Some of these were like the palm leaves and birch bark used in India and Central Asia – that is, natural surfaces requiring only some degree of processing before use. One of the most widely used was the bamboo slip. Because of the way bamboo grows, it is easy to slice lengthwise into long narrow slips. These narrow panels, or columns, of bamboo were dried by fire until completely free of sap. They were then laid in order and secured with fiber to make rolls for storage. Bamboo-slip technology probably was a determining factor in the writing of Chinese text in vertical lines. One of the drawbacks to the use of bamboo was its weight; several men or a cart might be needed to lift and transport it. In some cases, the Chinese used other natural writing surfaces, such as bone, shell, horn, wooden panels, stone, and soft metal.

The technology available to the Buddhists in China had ramifications for the dissemination of written material that still pertain today. Instead of relying on the natural surfaces of rocks or organic matter, China introduced the idea of manufactured surfaces. The construction of a fabric on which writing could be placed was a major innovation. It allowed the creation of large amounts of usable surface material. The first of these constructed fabrics came from a "biotechnology" based on extracting long fibers from the cocoons of moths, most notably those of the silkworm, *Bombyx mori*. In ancient times the Han people had invented the process of heating silkworm cocoons to dissolve the sericin gum holding the strands in a mass that protected the moth worm. The cloth produced from the woven strings of silkworm cocoons was easily adapted to scrolls that could be rolled and stored in an efficient manner. The drawback to widespread use of silk cloth for writing was the high cost of production and its popularity in other uses, such as clothing and decorations. Another issue for the Buddhists was the fact that sericulture involved killing the caterpillar encased in the fiber.

A cheap and easily manufactured surface was needed to handle the increasing demand for writing surfaces among the Han people. The solution to the problem was the invention of paper. First made by pulping used cloth made from hemp (*Cannabis sativa*), paper came to dominate all other surfaces and remains today the most common material for writing and printing. Hemp cloth was in wide use in China when the technology of pulping it for paper was introduced. It was also used in Europe, where it was made into canvas (a word derived from *cannabis*) for ship sails. As in China, the finest European paper was composed of plant fiber reclaimed from hemp cloth. This technology allowed the production of a constant supply of long-lasting and easy-to-handle surfaces for written texts. And, unlike papyrus, sometimes called the "paper" of the Egyptians, hemp produces true paper. While papyrus stalks were flattened and laminated to form a page, hemp fibers were completely separated by being soaked and then poured onto a sieve to produce China's paper.

New technologies usually require other, supporting, technological developments in order to be optimally usable. In the case of paper and silk, as well as the other natural surfaces, an instrument was needed to deliver liquid ink to the writing surface. One instrument used was the sharpened or frayed point of a bamboo or wooden stylus that could be dipped into ink or supplied by a tube of ink that seeped onto the point. But these did not always deliver enough ink for the rapid absorption rate of paper, and the hard-edged stylus sometimes damaged the silk or paper writing surface. So scribes looked for a softer instrument that would allow saturation of the surface and produce a more flowing form to the glyphs. By the time Buddhism arrived in China, brushes made of animal hair were already in use. Early examples of these brushes indicate that hair, such as that of the deer, was used to produce a very stiff, but elastic, pointed nib that could be used and replaced. The technology of making ink for use with these brushes was also being pursued. Scribes wanted an ink that was easy to control, thick enough to be transferred to the writing surface, and contained pigmentation that would last for a long period without fading. Early inks were made from pinewood soot mixed with gelatin from the hooves of animals such as donkeys.

Just as the technology of text preparation had been incorporated into the religious life of India's Buddhists, so too the technology of paper, brush, and ink in China became an important element of China's Buddhist traditions. Starting in the middle of the second century, translations of texts from Indic languages into Chinese became a major enterprise. Hundreds of thousands of pages of paper were required to keep up with the demand for these new "publications." The process by which so many documents could be disseminated and preserved went hand in hand with the use of the technology that created the manuscripts. The demand for copies of texts resulted in the creation of copy centers and monastic establishments that catered to this enterprise.

As large collections of silk and paper scrolls developed, library science was needed to index and shelve them. When the first Buddhist translation bureau was set up in the capital in the second century CE, the Buddhists were allowed to call their texts *jing*. This designation was important, for it implied that the Buddhist texts were similar to the classic texts that preserved the words of China's ancient sages. As the number of *jing* increased, monasteries developed a need for a place to house them. Following the pattern of the royal court, library buildings appeared and indexed collections of manuscripts marked the adaptation of paper technology to Chinese Buddhism. As a result, the Chinese Buddhist canon was arranged by cataloguers from the shelf lists of monastic libraries.

By the time of the Northern Song, manuscript technology was challenged by the new and developing technology of printing. Following the Tang dynasty's production of single-sheet almanacs, calendars, and individual texts on carved wooden blocks, the court of the Northern Song started to make standard copies of the classics and the Buddhist canon. Tenth-century print technology was to have a great impact on the way the teachings were preserved and understood, and expanded the technology far beyond any previous use. We know, for example, that the Northern Song court in Kaifeng made more than 130,000 separate printing blocks to hold the entire library of Buddhist translations and compilations that were housed in a monastery in Chengdu.

At first, the technology's potential for making large numbers of identical prints was not fully exploited. The set of thousands of blocks containing the Buddhist canon was used to make only a few highly prized, complete prints of the xylographs. This small number of rubbings meant that every set was a rare and valuable item. Because of the value placed on them, records of how they were distributed are preserved in historical documents. The Chengdu rubbings were sent from the Kaifeng court to the leaders of the Liao, Jin, Koryŏ, and Japanese empires. The transmission of the new technology was not one of slow diffusion, but a hierarchical spread from one ruling elite to another. The courts received not only the set of prints, but also information about how to reproduce the sophisticated technology that created them. Within a few years, the Liao, Jin, and Koryŏ courts made their own sets of printing blocks. The Jin and the Koryŏ traced the outline of the characters from the Northern Song edition, making blocks that were exactly the same in content, format, and even in character spacing and glyph construction. Only the Liao court turned to their own manuscripts as the basis for their block prints, and did not rely on the edition sent to them from Kaifeng. As so few sets of rubbings were made from the Northern Song blocks, it was necessary to continue the former method of manuscript copying, using the block prints as the standard. This changed in the Southern Song when local monasteries started to produce their own sets of xylographs and to make multiple copies from them. And, because a well-preserved printing block is thought to be capable of making as many as 100,000 copies, printing eventually replaced most of the manuscript procedures of the past. Copying Buddhist texts became a ritual act carried out for the sake of merit, and a single text was sufficient for the purpose. Just as with writing, print technology became a part of the structure of Buddhist life and practice and was associated with merit-making.

The information technology associated with writing, palm leaves, birch bark, silk, paper, ink, brushes, and printing blocks has remained in place for more than 1,000 years. While refinements of the printing process arrived with the advent of movable and, finally, metal type, these were not completely new technologies.

In addition to textual technology, Buddhism also made use of a wide range of graphic arts to depict and spread the doctrine. The creation of metal statues, frescoes, murals, bas-reliefs, stone sculpture, and paintings was a very important part of Buddhist history. Each of these art forms required technologies and training that were crucial elements in the spread of Buddhism from South Asia along the mercantile routes to East and Southeast Asia. Much of our information from the early centuries of the religion comes from these artistic and architectural productions. The most important examples of these materials are found in the caves that were excavated and decorated along the trade routes, and the tombs of royal and elite families. These were decorated with images on surfaces and in dimensional forms whose artistic achievement would remain uncontested for centuries.

Archeology used to explore and interpret these ancient sites is an application of modern technology and expertise to Buddhist studies. Cave and tomb information is most helpful when it can be dated, and some Buddhist material has undergone carbon dating to identify the era in which it was produced. In Japan, tombs can now be explored using digital cameras on fiber-optic cables. These small cameras can be inserted into the tombs, allowing information to be gathered without destructive excavations. This is an example of technology used to explore technology.

In the nineteenth century, many technological inventions paved the way for the modern era of scientific research and applications (Marvin 1988). The most important of these for information dissemination came from research on light. In 1827 Nicéphore Niépce produced the first photograph, though the term "photograph" (from the Greek, "light writing") was not used until 1839. The first microphotograph was made in the same year, proving that images could be magnified or reduced in size. This "photo technology" used chemicals and light to create an exact image on paper, glass, and gelatin film. The ability to record images of places and events changed the way religious life was depicted and studied. In the nineteenth century, the Archaeological Survey of India, using chemically treated paper negatives and sunlight exposure, created some of the first images of ancient Buddhist sites. These beautiful photographs are now housed in the British Library. The technology of light heralded a new era in the way information was recorded. For more than a century scholars and officials have exposed thousands of films, adding a visual component to the study of religion. Of special note are films that preserve rituals and ceremonies as well as art and architecture. One of the best examples of this type of archiving of Buddhist imagery is the John C. and Susan L. Huntington Photographic Archive at the Ohio State University.

A further refinement in the technology of light came with the advent of motion pictures and inventions that allowed the rapid streaming of still images to appear as real-time action. While cinematography has been used mainly for entertainment, a sizable and growing body of cinematographic work records the details of events at Buddhist sites. Motion pictures were further enhanced by the addition of sound synchronized with the images, permitting individuals to appear and to be heard speaking. Interviews and recordings of Buddhist teachers became possible, and many groups undertook to capture and preserve on film speeches delivered by their esteemed leaders. In the 1930s Buddhist activities in the remote area of Tibet were even captured on film.

Photography and cinematography had been integrated into Buddhist scholarship by the middle of the twentieth century, when a further application of the technology began to greatly impact the field. While the first microphotograph had been made in 1839 and the potential value of this technology for storing and preserving documents was recognized by 1853, it was almost a century before the technique was in widespread use. A little-known scientist, Emanuel Goldberg, developed the first high-resolution microfilm in the 1920s, and laid the groundwork for microdot technology. Photographic miniaturization and the storage of large amounts of data on small surfaces were developed in response to the needs of military intelligence in World War II. The military use of miniaturization technology allowed for the rapid development of microfilm. Libraries and government offices recognized the value of being able to photograph and archive large numbers of images in a small space. Records could be kept in a fraction of the space required for filing the original documents. This technology was soon applied to textual studies in many fields of scholarship, including Buddhism. Microfilming of manuscripts allowed scholars to record and preserve thousands of pages on small spools of 35mm film. Projects such as Nepal and Germany's joint efforts to film and archive Sanskrit and Tibetan documents created a whole new resource for study. The Institute for Advanced Studies of World Religions, originally housed at the campus of the State University of New York, Stony Brook, also used these methods to disseminate Buddhist manuscript materials in the miniaturized format of microfiche.

Photographic technology created and preserved textual data in a new way. Rather than applying pigment to surfaces or incising glyphs in stone or metal, photography embeds a chemical image within the structure or coating of the surface. Like printing, photography creates a facsimile of the original, rather than a new construct. But film has significant advantages for the preservation of texts. It is thought that microfilm, stored under optimal conditions, can last for 500 years. The storage space needed is small relative to that required by the original volumes. However, one of the great drawbacks to microfilm has been the difficulty of searching and retrieving. While it was possible to provide an index using the "address" of the frame holding the desired data, this proved to be cumbersome. Researchers sought ways to attach the index in the frame itself and design a reader using light to identify the indexed item. None of this research managed to reach Buddhist studies. While microfilm became a necessary part of textual archiving for the field, the early index strategies were overtaken by technological advances. Computer Aided Retrieval (CAR) replaced the need for embedded indexing and the search and retrieval technology shifted to the digital realm.

In the 1940s an entirely different approach to recording, storing, and retrieving data came into existence. In January 1944, at Bletchley Park in England, a machine called "Colossus" was completed in time to help decipher military codes of the German navy. This was probably the first full application of computer technology. Based in part of the work of Alan Turing, "Colossus" executed complicated tasks in a few hours. At the end of the war ten of these machines were still in use. All were dismantled and their diagrams burned to prevent the discoveries being used by other governments. This decision held back the development of computer technology. By 1952 vacuum tubes were being used as the inner core of machines that processed data, banks being among the first institutions to rely on this new methodology. The initial attempt to create a digital computer resulted in a 30-ton machine with 18,000 vacuum tubes. It did not seem promising for Buddhist Studies to be tied to such a costly venture. Fortunately, the invention of the transistor in 1947 removed the dependence on vacuum tubes, and a decade later the first integrated circuit was constructed. As a result of these developments, primitive computers based on binary input were built, and by 1960 the full potential of this advance was being demonstrated. In the early 1970s, the silicon "chip" and the technology of photolithography opened the door for compact machines at relatively reasonable costs. The use of integrated circuit technology allowed enormous amounts of data to be stored on a single silicon computer chip. There was nothing comparable in previous centuries. The digital era represented a truly new technology that would provide an alternative to both writing and print. As computers became smaller, cheaper, and easier to use, Buddhist scholars, like those in other disciplines, began to use them for research.

In its early use by Buddhist scholars, the computer was viewed as a "standalone" tool. The strategic use of the technology required major shifts in the way data was recorded and retrieved. Individual scholars had their own data located only in their local machine or on personal disks. These systems often required that users write special programs designed for their specific needs, and these were not easily shared with other scholars. Thus, individual scholars' data remained locked in their own computer. The distribution of the data required having it printed on paper and published. The multilingual nature of Buddhist studies exacerbated these problems. For example, scholars who wanted to display national scripts or Romanized texts with diacritical marks were faced with the daunting task of writing idiosyncratic code for their own computers. Under these circumstances, the new machines hampered rather than enhanced the sharing of data among scholars. Governments and computer experts alike recognized that international standards were essential for effective use of computers. This resulted in the adoption of standard markup language for the communication of data. SGML (Standard General Markup Language) provided a set of common codes for the recognition of commands to control the printing of lines, paragraphs, word spacing, and other elements of page layout. The earliest standards were written to mimic the older technology of printing.

Scholars within Buddhism were attracted by the idea that computers could be used to archive textual materials. Creating such archives was still quite difficult, and the work was often hampered by the state of hardware and software development. In the late 1980s, however, the complete Pāli Canon was digitized, and the dreamed-of potential became a reality. Since that time a steady stream of canonic collections has been digitized. As with all new technology, the early applications mirrored the older practices: until the 1990s most Buddhist scholars viewed computers as nothing more than better typewriters. By the turn of the twenty-first century, however, with many new developments in software, multilingual input, standard coding, and faster machines, scholars were using the digital canons for research and reading. The early impact of these data sets of the canonic texts was evident in the ease with which every example of a word or a string of words could be searched and retrieved. Paper publications of concordances and indexes, such as the multiple volumes of the Taishō Canon indexing, waned. Research tools were changing rapidly as digital data expanded. The input cost of the basic data was underwritten mainly by Buddhist groups, who viewed their contributions as the equivalent of their previous underwriting of manuscript and print productions. The computer was brought into the Buddhist system of merit-making.

The question that remained unanswered in the use of the computer was how to share data. Subsequent developments have already begun to address this question. The ability to link computers around the world has changed the way information about Buddhism is used. In 1962 Dr. J.C.R. Licklider took over the Advanced Research Projects Agency (ARPA) that had been set up in response to the launch of the first satellite by the USSR. Dr. Licklider's vision was that computers should be more interactive, and he used his office and resources toward achieving that goal. The promise of that type of research began to be demonstrated in 1969 when the Interface Message Processor (IMP) allowed a four-node network to connect UCLA, UC Santa Barbara, Stanford Research Institute, and the University of Utah in Salt Lake City. In 1981 CERNET was set up to connect Switzerland, Italy, and the United Kingdom with ARPA. Then, in 1990, CERN built the first Web server and client machines using NeXT's object-oriented technology. The key figure in developing the World Wide Web (WWW) was Tim Berners-Lee. It was he who helped launch the Uniform Resource Locator (URL), Hypertext Transfer Protocol (HTTP), and Hypertext Transfer Markup Language (HTML) standards for servers and browsers. The World Wide Web was developed to provide a set of standards for accessing information and hypermedia distributed on desktop computers around the world. The next great advance came from Marc Andreessen's development of the first user-friendly browser, NCSA Mosaic, at the University of Illinois. With Tim Berners-Lee's protocols and Marc Andreessen's browser capability, the World Wide Web in two years became one of the most widely used technologies ever. The capability of worldwide information dissemination far surpassed anything available for Buddhist studies in the past. Computer technology and its Internet applications are without precedent. Future advances in the Internet environment promise both great challenges and benefits for scholarship. Grid computing, for example, is an emerging technique for solving large computational problems by combining the processing power of many disparate computers. When this becomes a working reality, Buddhist Studies may benefit from thousands of sites available for collection and analysis of digitized material.

Buddhist websites were among the first to be available on the Internet. While scholars were slow to enter into the communication linkage system, individuals and religious centers recognized early on the power of reaching a worldwide audience for the spread of ideas and religious teachings. The term "cyber-Buddhist" was coined to express the idea of a single virtual community of individuals linking themselves to one another through the computer. It was thought that the community could exist and disseminate information without reference to any sectarian structure. Technology might create a new kind of Buddhism. Within a ten-year period browsers were able to locate millions of sites containing Buddhist information and ideas. Rather than a centralized single portal for cyber-Buddhists, the Internet proved to be a distributed system where sectarian as well as personal data could appear. The Internet was characterized by multiplicity, and competing voices represented a wider range of opinions about Buddhism than ever appeared in the print medium. Electronic journals, full text articles, books, images, and research tools allowed students and researchers to have access to large amounts of data in the new medium.

While the earliest scholarly use of the Internet tended to be dominated by individuals, institutions and governments are becoming increasingly involved. In 1995, for example, the National Science Foundation released a report recommending the establishment of a national digital library (NDL) for science, technology, engineering, and mathematics (STEM). The recommendations included a plan to digitize one million books. One decade later, Google Corporation announced a plan to digitize more than eight million books from four universities (Oxford, Stanford, Harvard, and Michigan) and the New York Public Library. In the UK, the Arts and Humanities Data Service has constructed a large and important collection of information from a variety of nationally funded projects. Academia Sinica in Taiwan launched an eight-year project to digitize images and texts for the entire corpus of Chinese materials held in the country. China has digitized all volumes of more than 7,000 academic journals published since 1994. Spread throughout these massive national ventures are primary and secondary Buddhist resources at a level not available in any one center or national library. An example of how Buddhist material is adapted to this type of archive can be seen in the Tibetan and Himalayan Digital Library at the University of Virginia.

In 2005 the need for digital tools in the humanities came to be recognized as critical. Advanced computers, standardized programs, and massive data sources raised questions about how to pursue research in Buddhist studies. The scholar's role shifted from information collection to management and analysis. With this development, digital technology became the third technology, joining the ancient ones of writing and printing, to which Buddhism and its scholars have had access.

LEWIS R. LANCASTER

TEXTUAL AUTHORITY: THE *CATUḤPRATISARAṆA SŪTRA*

Before the Buddha passed into *parinirvāṇa*, he advised his grieving disciples that they must look to his words, the *Dharma*, for inspiration and guidance after he had gone. He did not choose to appoint any one of his numerous disciples to succeed him but instead gave each of them the responsibility for guiding their lives according to the precepts he had set down for them during his lifetime. His parting advice encouraged his disciples to gather together and come to an agreement on the teachings that he had handed down to them. Traditional accounts of early Buddhist history recorded that 500 enlightened disciples met during the first rainy season retreat after the Buddha's death to collect what they had remembered of the talks he had given during the forty-five years of his teaching career. Successive generations of disciples passed down these teachings orally and transmitted the Buddha's word into different regions of India, each with its own language or dialect. The fallibility of human memory, the problems of translation, contested interpretations of scripture, and the composition of new scriptures, prompted questions over which teachings could be relied upon as the Buddha's word.

The *Scripture on the Great Guidelines* (*Mahāpradeśa Sūtra*) judges a text's authenticity based on its provenance from the Buddha or a learned member of the *sangha* and on its harmony with the received body of his teachings (*sūtra*, *vinaya*, *abhidharma*). A teaching is considered authoritative if it is heard from the Buddha, a *sangha* of elders, a group of monastics who were specialists in the *Dharma*, *Vinaya*, or in the *Abhidharma* (*mātṛkā*), or a single monastic who is a specialist in any one of these. Other criteria occur in the Pāli paracanonical text, the *Guide* (*Nettipakaraṇa*), and in the *Mūlasarvāstivāda Vinaya*: a teaching is authoritative if it agrees with recognized *sūtras*, is reflected in the *vinaya*, and does not contradict reality (*dharmatā*).

The *Scripture on the Four Reliances* (*Catuḥpratisaraṇa Sūtra*) sets forth additional criteria for determining which texts should be recognized as the Buddha's word. This text does not survive in extant canonical collections of *sūtras* but quotations from it occur in several canonical works associated with the Vaibhāṣika, Mādhyamika, and Yogācāra schools, including the *Treasury of Abhidharma* (*Abhidharmakośa*), the *Commentary on the Middle Way* (*Madhyamakavṛtti*), and the Bodhisattva *Stages* (*Bodhisattvabhūmi*). The *Scripture on the Four Reliances* describes four reliances or refuges (*pratisaraṇa*). One should rely on (1) the teaching (*Dharma*) rather than the person (*pudgala*); (2) the meaning (*artha*) rather than the letter (*vyañjana*); (3) the definitive meaning (*nītārtha*) rather than the interpretable meaning (*neyārtha*); and (4) direct intuitive knowledge (*jñāna*) rather than conceptual, discursive knowledge (*vijñāna*). The *Scripture on the Four Reliances* advises the practitioner to reject personality cults centered on a charismatic teacher, blind adherence to the letter of the law, and teachings whose meanings require explanation or are apprehended through discursive modes of thought. The *Scripture on the Four Reliances*' criteria for determining which texts are authentic indicate that the proof of a text's authenticity resides in its ability to produce the intuitive and transformative insight that is characteristic of Buddhas.

See also: ***Abhidharma*; Canons and literature; Pāli canon; Tibet, Buddhism in; *Tripiṭaka*, Chinese; *Tripiṭaka*, Sanskrit and Prakrit; *Tripiṭaka*, Tibetan; *Tripiṭaka* and word of the Buddha; *Vinayas*.**

KAREN C. LANG

THAILAND, BUDDHISM IN

Buddhism as a Theravāda religious culture came to Thailand in the thirteenth century CE. The first Buddhist state, Sukkothai, was established in north central Thailand after the fall of the Khmer Empire and the expulsion of the Khmer and Mon. Mahāyāna Buddhism, Brahmanism, and animistic practices were already in existence. They lingered on within the larger Theravāda tradition.

The early Buddhist kingdoms of Sukkothai (*c.* 1253–1350), Ayuthya (1350–1767), and Thonburi (1767–82) manifested themes that continued into modern times. The symbiosis between the church and state, the king as the Dharmarāja, the protector of the *Dharma* and the *sāsana* (Buddhist tradition), the preservation of the canonical texts, the maintenance of the integrity of the *sangha*, orthodoxy, doctrinal purity and the hierarchical order within the monkhood, were paramount. Great importance was attached to the maintaining of fraternal links with Sri Lanka in a commonly shared Theravāda tradition. Thai rulers made Buddhism adaptive, responsive to change, ensuring the survival of the paradigm.

Rāma Khamhaeng (1283–1317), referred to as father by his subjects, was typical in his support of monks and emphasis of the *Tripiṭaka*. His grandson, Li Thai, enthusiastically supported the monks and the *sāsana*. He followed the *Dasa rāja dharmā*, the ten norms guiding the policies of a ruler. According to tradition he was involved in the compilation of the *Tribhūmikathā*, a treatise on the three planes of mundane and cosmic existence. The Sukkothai period was considered the golden age of Thai Buddhism, and set the tone for dynastic policies that followed.

In the Ayudhya period Buddhism suffered serious setbacks, because of Brahamanical influences. The king became as much a Hindu god king, assuming the title of *Devarāja*, as he was a Buddhist *Dharmarāja*. The Ayudhya was accessible by sea to commercial and cosmopolitan cultural influences, notably from India. The tide turned with King Paramatrailokanath (1441–81), a particularly able ruler sympathetic to Buddhism. He followed traditional practices to foster Buddhism and like many Thai rulers became a monk. During his reign a deputation from Chiangmai left for Sri Lanka, studying Buddhism and being ordained as monks. They retuned accompanied by Sri Lankan monks, which led to the formation of a new Buddhist sect, named Warnaratvongsa, in northern Thailand.

The early kings of the Chakri dynasty, Rāma II and Rāma III, focused their attention on the monkhood, which had declined in the periods of political turmoil. Reform involved the purification of the *sangha* and the restoration of monastic learning. Contact with Buddhist Sri Lanka was restored. In the last days of Ayudhya, Thai monks were sent to Sri Lanka to restore *upasampadā*, or higher ordination, disrupted by colonial rule and the weakening of Buddhist secular power.

The reigns of Mongkut, Rāma IV (1851–68) and his son Chulalongkorn, Rāma V (1868–1910), saw existing policies toward Buddhism carried out under altered circumstances brought about by the presence of European colonial powers in Southeast Asia. The Portuguese and the Dutch were superseded by the French and the British, who brought pressure on the rulers of Thailand for economic and political concessions with far-reaching consequences, not least a critical abbreviation of the *de facto* sovereignty of the states. The French incorporated Laos, a part of Thailand, to create French Indochina. Meanwhile, the British made Burma a colony. There was a real fear of collusion between the two powers to extend their influence into Thailand. Thai rulers, particularly Chulalongkorn, successfully cultivated relationships with Russia and Germany to neutralize the threat, helped by British distractions with incipient nationalism in India.

Traditional policies took on new meaning. The symbiosis of a Buddhist king enlightened by the *Dharma*, providing guidance to state policies, and a reformed dynamic *sangha* was the best antidote to foreign political and cultural inroads. Both Mongkut and Chulalongkorn, while they accepted the benefits of education and technology, were not enamored with Western ideologies of democracy. Chakri rulers beginning with Chulalongkorn closely studied the fate of Buddhism in Sri Lanka capitulating over time to colonial rule politically and culturally. They also observed, closer to home, the fall of Burma in spite of its traditions of Buddhist rule. The ruling elite in Thailand felt that Siam was the last line of defense for Buddhism. The classic Thai paradigm of a dharmically unified and integrated society acquired a deeper messianic dimension.

The full impact of aggressive European colonialism had not unfolded when Mongkut as Rāma IV ascended the throne in 1851. Mongkut, who had himself been a monk ordained in the stricter Mon tradition before he became the ruler of Siam, was a Pāli scholar familiar with the *Tripiṭaka*. He favored a literalist interpretation of the Pāli texts, which laid out monastic conduct in its ideal normative form. He inaugurated a new monastic order called the *Dhammayuttika* sect, reflecting high standards vis-à-vis the traditional order of the *Mahānikāya* sect. Mongkut moreover downplayed the emphasis on the Tribhūmi, and favored the Pāli *Tripiṭaka*, with its teleological vision of attaining *nirvāṇa* as the culmination of self-transcendence. Mongkut also saw in the *Tripiṭaka* potential modern social contexts. In contrast to his predecessors he was "modern," and often spoke of affinities between Buddhism and modern science.

Buddhism in the reign of Chulalongkorn (Rāma V) is best seen against the larger canvas of modernization, a policy the king followed with commitment. In 1872, on an official visit to India, Chulalongkorn was critical of some elites in Indian society who glorified India's past. In Siam the king presided over the modernization of the administrative apparatus, the judicial system, the fiscal and financial instruments of government, and in building the critical infrastructure of transport and communications.

Policies towards the *sangha* and Buddhism in general were directed at making traditional institutions stronger, so that Buddhism would serve as an effective countervailing cultural force. The reforms virtually reduced Buddhism to another government department controlled directly by royal authority. An imperial act in 1902 made Buddhism subordinate to the state. Only two Buddhist sects were officially recognized, the older traditional *Mahanikāya* sect and the *Dhammayuttika* sect that his father had founded. The Chinese and Vietnamese sects were officially downgraded. The king founded two modern universities functioning under the aegis of the main sects. A notable feature was the revision of the *Tripiṭaka* and its translation to the Thai language, making Buddhism more widely accessible and in a sense less dependent on monastic ideological influence.

Chulalongkorn downplayed the Brahamanical ideal of a divinely ordained *Devarāja*, projecting instead the Buddhist image of the *Dharmarāja* guided by the ten norms of an ideal ruler. However, Brahmanical influences in their ritualistic forms did not altogether disappear, but added to the overall legitimation of a traditional Siamese ruler.

Chulalongkorn believed, in apocalyptic vein, that he was the last Buddhist king. The apocalypse, however, took the form of a peaceful revolution in 1932 when the centuries-old absolute monarchy ended, its place taken by a democratic constitutional form of government. Although some members of the military establishment wanted the monarchy abolished outright, the king became the titular head of state, constitutionally a Buddhist king in a Buddhist country. The king was more than ever a unifying element given the factionalism inherent in a political democracy. The post-1932 period is clearly characterized by the active role played by the *sangha* in Thailand to address social, economic and political issues brought about by cataleptic forces unleashed by modernization. The post-revolutionary period stands in contrast to an old repertoire of state policies marked by monastic discipline, purification of the *sangha* and an emphasis on textualism.

Although Thailand did not become a European colony, as did other Buddhist countries, it was not immune to colonialism marked by newer ideologies, individualism, materialism, and consumerism, bringing in its train an imperceptible alienation from traditional modalities of thinking

Economic pressures from structural imbalances as well as chronic regional instability in Vietnam, Cambodia, and Laos following the Second World War and exacerbated by the American presence in Thailand brought massive capital investments and inflationary pressures. These changes devastated the vulnerable rural segment of Thai society, while benefiting a plutocratic elite that traditionally wielded political influence. Politics in the post-1932 period and well into the 1980s was characterized by an alliance between the military and the ruling elite.

The state was alarmed at the very real possibility of a communist-inspired *coup d'état* or the infiltration of communist cadres into rural Thailand. The strategy was to rejuvenate the rural sector, with Buddhist monks reinforcing traditional values, in a well-organized massive development program, worked on a modest outlay with monks going on foot or bus to remote villages to distribute medicines, school books, and provisions. The monks were naturally empathic to the work of spreading the *Dharma*, and were often volunteer recruits from the major universities.

The issue is best viewed within the larger ideological paradigm. In early Buddhist literature, there is a narration of factors harmful to the *sāsana* such as wars, disorder, social unrest, and famines, and of how Buddhism could suffer as a result of schisms, laxity in discipline, worldliness of the monks, and too-intimate connections with the laity. The state alone could secure the integrity of the *sangha*. Successive dynasties made it their particular business to preserve the *sangha* from the self-inflicted pathologies within its ranks. The symbiosis was clearly to their mutual advantage. Mindful of the symbiosis, the monks became part of political and social processes. The Buddha, however, had cautioned the monks to be circumspect in their relations with lay authorities, giving advice when asked, but at the same time keeping their distance.

The crisis atmosphere of the post-1960 period, however, did not inhibit the vigorous growth of Buddhism. Some monks became leaders in the movement to build

Figure 41 Statue of the Buddha, Ko Samui, Thailand.

up infrastructure in impoverished areas. Other Buddhist monks made the preservation of the forests their primary concern. These monks gained national and international attention by "ordaining" trees and persuading the authorities to declare extended areas as reserves. The controversial monk Buddhadāsa began to popularize the idea that seminal Buddhist ideas oriented to transmundane goals like *paṭicca-samuppāda* (Dependent Origination) and the notion of *anicca* (impermanence) could be used to understand social phenomena. The tradition of forest monks, revived in its modern form by virtuosos like Ajan Mun, Ajan Cha, and Ajan Lee, remained a shining city on the hill but achieved a new dimension of depth and relevance with the notion that *nirvāṇa* was achievable in this lifetime here on earth and the forest monks were its living exemplifications. Buddhism in this phase of empowerment in modern Thailand by creative adaptations became a *dharma* of immediate practical relevance and applicability.

ooking to future trends, it is possible that in keeping with their increasing importance in the secular sphere, women in Thailand will achieve a greater degree of parity, despite built-in structural prejudices. The ordination of *bhikkunīs* (nuns), however, seems more distant. Meanwhile, Buddhism in Thailand will be increasingly challenged by secularism and the pervasive influence of globalization, the latter in its previous incarnations no stranger to Thailand.

See also: **Buddhadasa; Buddhism in the Western world; *Sangha*; South and Southeast Asia, Buddhism in; Sri Lanka, Buddhism in.**

ANANDA WICKREMERATNE

THREE REFUGES AND GOING FOR REFUGE

The "three refuges" in Buddhism refer to the three major features of the Buddhist tradition. The first identifies Buddha as the enlightened one, an individual who put an end to entrapment in the cycle of perpetual rebirth in *saṃsāra*. Consistent with the meaning of the title "Buddha," derived from the Sanskrit verb root *budh*, the first refuge identifies the one who has become awakened. The second refuge identifies *Dharma* as the basic teaching of the Buddha. Generically, it includes the various doctrines maintained by all the Buddhist schools. The *Sangha* or community is the third refuge. Although most Buddhist think of this refuge as inclusive of all those groups in the lay and monastic community, in the strictest sense this refuge includes only those individuals who are included in the *Ārya-sangha*, that is, persons who have attained status as "noble persons" (or *ārya-pudgalas*). These three refuges are also referred to as the "three jewels" of Buddhism.

The Sanskrit technical term *triśaraṇa* refers to a ritual formulary utilized as part of one's formal entrance into the Buddhist faith, irrespective of whether one is initially joining the lay or monastic *sangha*, and it may be considered to be a profession of faith in the Buddhist religion. It involves a threefold repetition of the formula:

> I go to the Buddha for refuge (*buddhaṃ śaraṇam gacchāmi*).
>
> I go to the *Dharma* for refuge (*dharmaṃ śaraṇam gacchāmi*).
>
> I go to the *Sangha* for refuge (*sanghaṃ śaraṇam gacchāmi*).

The repetition of the formula means that each individual who recites it puts his or her faith in Buddha as a man who accomplished what is ascribed to him in the tradition: that he put an end to suffering by uprooting its cause, becoming fully awakened in the process. It means that each individual puts his or her faith in the *Dharma* as reflective of those doctrines deemed by Buddha to be essential for practice leading to the eradication of suffering and the end of rebirth. It means that each individual puts his or her faith in the *Sangha*, the community of noble persons who have attained as least the first stage on the path, that of "streamwinner" (*śrotāpanna*). The completion of this formula, in conjunction with acceptance of the five vows of the laity (called the *pañca-śīla*), constitutes acceptance into the traditional Buddhist lay community. The completion of this formula, in conjunction with acceptance of the five vows of the laity, five additional higher vows, and a number of other, more rigorous and difficult requirements, constitutes acceptance into the traditional monastic community. In Tibetan Buddhism, a fourth refuge – the guru – is added to the formula because the guru serves as the living embodiment of the Buddha, and it is through his kindness and compassion that access to the other three refuges is made possible.

The ritual of "taking refuge" or "going for refuge" is routinely included in the various liturgies and holiday proceedings of Buddhist schools of all denominations, and it is equally important to Theravādins, Mahāyānists, and Vajrayānists.

See also: ***Sangha.***

CHARLES S. PREBISH

TIANTAI

Tiantai is a school of Chinese Buddhism that is named after the site of its head temple, Mount Tiantai in Zhejiang Province on China's eastern seaboard. The *de facto* founder is Zhiyi (538–97), but tradition regards him as the third patriarch of the school after Huiwen (fl. *c.* 550), and Zhiyi's teacher, Huisi (515–77). Tiantai is known for a number of innovations: its doctrinal classification system (Ch. *panjiao*), its highly articulated system of meditation, and its doctrine of the Three Truths.

Doctrinal classification

One of the problems with which Zhiyi dealt was that of making sense of the mass of Buddhist texts that had been translated into Chinese by the end of the sixth century. Buddhism had entered China at a time when Indian Mahāyāna teachings were just forming, and texts reflecting doctrinal controversies, as well as older Hīnayāna texts, circulated throughout China. It was difficult to understand how these heterogeneous and often contradictory scriptures, all purporting to be the word of the Buddha, formed any sort of coherent teaching. In response, Zhiyi created a set of criteria that placed scriptures in three contexts: the period of the Buddha's life in which they were preached, the audience to whom they were directed, and the teaching method the Buddha employed. The first criterion yielded the scheme of "Five Periods":

1 *Avataṃsaka* period (three weeks): This period immediately followed the Buddha's enlightenment, and was preached to convey the entire content of his vision. However, his audience could not grasp the totality of the message, so the Buddha quickly changed his approach.
2 *Āgama* period (twelve years): During this time, the Buddha preached the Hīnayāna scriptures as an easy introduction into the teachings.
3 *Vaipulya* period (eight years): In this period, the Buddha began to introduce Mahāyāna themes and undercut the teachings of the previous period so as to clear the way for a fuller understanding.
4 *Prajñāpāramitā* period (twenty-two years): During this period, the Buddha taught the full Mahāyāna doctrine of universal emptiness.

5 *Lotus* and *Nirvāṇa Sūtra* period (eight years): During this period, the Buddha switched from the negative language of the *Prajñāpāramitā* scriptures to the positive language of the *Lotus Sūtra*, affirming the Buddha-nature of all beings and the identity and common goal of the so-called "three vehicles" of Buddhism. Because the Buddha at this time returned to teaching the full content of his enlightenment, the Tiantai school considers the *Lotus Sūtra* the highest of all scriptures, expressing most directly the Buddha's enlightenment.

The criterion of intended audience produced four divisions: (1) the "*Piṭaka* teachings" were given for the two vehicles of the *śrāvakas* and *pratyekabuddhas*; (2) the "Common teachings" were intended for the above two groups, and also for *bodhisattvas* just starting on the Mahāyāna path; (3) the "Distinct teachings" were only for *bodhisattvas* on the Mahāyāna path; and (4) the "Perfect teachings" gave a complete account of the teachings for the highest *bodhisattvas*.

Finally, the criterion of teaching method produced another four categories: (1) the "Abrupt teaching," intended to jolt practitioners into a sudden realization of the complete truth; (2) the "Gradual teaching," which took a step-by-step approach to teaching and led practitioners systematically to the truth; (3) "Secret teaching," where the Buddha spoke to a large crowd, but veiled his message so that only a specific person or persons would understand his meaning (this also indicates a situation in which not all members of the audience are aware of each other, as when in several Mahāyāna scriptures it is revealed that gods and *bodhisattvas* have been attending a teaching undetected by the less spiritually advanced hearers); (4) the "Indeterminate teachings," where the members of the audience are aware of each other's presence, but the Buddha speaks to each one individually while appearing to address the crowd at once.

Meditation

Zhiyi and his teacher Huisi were both masters of meditation, and two of Zhiyi's works, the *Mohe zhiguan* (*Great Calming and Contemplation*) and *Xiao zhiguan* (*Small Calming and Contemplation*), systematize a great number of methods. These comprehensive classifications of techniques fed into other traditions that would arise with or after Tiantai. For example, they included methods of exercising mindfulness in everyday activities and of perceiving the ultimate truth through the contemplation of ordinary reality; these would influence the development of Chan. They also included methods of invoking the name of and visualizing the Buddha Amitābha, which would give new impetus to the already existing Pure Land tradition.

The Three Truths

Zhiyi felt some dissatisfaction with the essentially negative metaphysical analysis of the Madhyamika teachings. The problem, as he saw it, was that the Two Truths of Madhyamika presented "emptiness" as simple negation: it said what things were *not*, without making any affirmation of what they *were*. Thus, Zhiyi proposed the Three Truths of emptiness, provisionality, and the middle. The first broke down illusions about things, denying their permanence or the possession of any essence. The second affirmed their existence as impermanent objects that arose, abided, decayed, and ceased according to cause and effect. The third truth, that of the middle, synthesized these into a positive statement about the nature of reality. The impermanence and interdependence of all phenomena was the ultimate truth about them. In this way, Zhiyi denied that emptiness and provisionality were two different and unrelated aspects of things, or that emptiness negated provisionality, but that the contingency of things was in itself the ultimate truth about them.

Zhiyi also turned this middle truth from a statement about ontology to one that affirmed agency operating within the universe. Whereas Madhyamaka teachings of emptiness asserted how things existed in a dry and static way, saying merely that they lacked any self-nature, Zhiyi characterized the final nature of things as consciousness, which he called Middle-Way Buddha-Nature (Ch. *zhongdao foxing*). The omniscient mind of the Buddha took in all reality, and so everything in the world was within his consciousness. His mind thus operated through all things to work compassionately for the liberation of all beings. The fact that this Mind took in defiled phenomena as well as pure phenomena led to a unique teaching: that the Absolute Mind had defiled as well as pure aspects; in other words, that even immoral and impure things in the world served as the vehicle for the saving activity of the Buddha mind alongside things that were pure. Tiantai is the only school of Chinese Buddhism that attributes impure aspects to the Buddha-mind. Tiantai doctrine thus does not look for a pure, undefiled realm that is above and beyond the present, defiled world. Rather, it affirms that the absolute abides in and through the contingent, not outside or beyond it. This found expression in one of the characteristic doctrines of the school: that of the non-obstruction of phenomena with the absolute (Ch. *li shi wu ai*).

History after Zhiyi

Tiantai is the only school of Chinese Buddhism that derives its name from its geographical center (Mount Tiantai) rather than from a central text (as the Huayan school does) or its method of practice (as Chan or Pure Land). This gave it a measure of stability and continuity, as those who resided on Mount Tiantai felt the need to keep the vision and practices of the school alive. This allowed it to survive even the great persecution of Buddhism in 845 that destroyed all the other schools save the highly decentralized Chan and Pure Land.

Zhiyi was succeeded by his disciple of twenty years, Guanding (561–632), who composed commentaries on the *Nirvāṇa Sūtra* in Zhiyi's style. The sixth patriarch, Zhanran (711–82) was instrumental in revitalizing Tiantai after it lost ground to the newly arisen Huayan, Chan, and Esoteric schools. He composed commentaries on scriptures and the works of Zhiyi, and is also credited with an interesting doctrinal development. Building on Zhiyi's doctrine of the pervasion of Absolute Mind through all phenomena, Zhanran asserted that all things, both animate and inanimate, possess Buddha-nature, and can thus attain enlightenment; even "grass and trees" could be enlightened. The school flourished greatly under his leadership.

Two generations later, the persecution of 845 broke out, and the temple complex on Mount Tiantai was destroyed, along with its library, and its clergy scattered. The school went into a steep decline after this, but did not die out. Korean disciples responded to invitations to bring the texts and teachings of the school back to the mountain, and it began to rebuild. During the Song dynasty, two eminent Tiantai monks, Zhili (960–1028) and Zongshi (964–1032) were very active, not only in propagating Tiantai teachings, but in establishing large-scale Pure Land societies among clergy and laypeople.

In 1000, Zhili also initiated a controversy that split the Tiantai school into two factions for the next several centuries. This became known as the Shanjia ("mountain house") versus Shanwai ("outside the mountain") controversy, and it touched on four separate issues: (1) authenticity of a particular version of one of Zhiyi's works; (2) where to place a particular doctrine of conditioned origination within the school's classification scheme; (3) the relationship between the evil inherent in the absolute principle and the evil within particular beings; and (4) the nature of the Pure Land. The Shanjia/Shanwai controversy provided fodder for a steady stream of treatises and letters well into the Ming dynasty.

After this time, the school settled into a quiet existence, and by the end of the Ming dynasty was less a self-standing school than a set of texts and doctrines in which some might choose to specialize (although certain clergy still claimed to be part of the Tiantai school). Also, starting in the ninth century with the visit of Saichō to China in search of Mount Tiantai, the school came to Japan, where it became known as the Tendai school.

See also: **China, Buddhism in; Japan, Buddhism in; Sacred mountains; Zhiyi.**

CHARLES B. JONES

TIBET: AN EXPANDED PANTHEON

Buddhism first appeared in Tibet in the seventh and eighth centuries CE, and gradually became established over the course of the next three centuries. It was brought there by monks who were based in the large northeastern Indian monastic complexes (Nalāndā, Vikramaśīla, Bodhgayā, Uddaṇḍandapura). These monks gradually moved into Tibet to missionize, certainly, but some of them were also no doubt seeking a degree of freedom to follow doctrinal and meditational pursuits that were not received favorably in the highly scholastic context of the Indian monasteries. In particular, they brought with them the nascent *tantric* (or Vajrayāna) doctrines and practices that were, in some of these monasteries, viewed with a degree of disfavor. Further, these monks brought with them not only a complex doctrinal structure, but also a wide range of iconographic forms.

By this time the mainstream Mahāyāna pantheon included Śākyamuni, various prior Buddhas, *bodhisattvas* such as Avalokiteśvara, Mañjuśrī, and Maitreya, and also a variety of female figures, such as Tārā, Bhṛkutī, and Prajṇāpāramitā, as well as numerous minor figures and gods from the Brahmanical pantheon (often in subservient positions, reflecting a desire on the part of the artisans to demonstrate the superior status of the Buddhist figures). The Vajrayāna (or *tantric*) schools that had begun to establish themselves in the northeastern part of India, as well as in various southern locales such as Ellorā, developed a range of sculpturally and pictorially represented figures specific to the tantric tradition. Further, as Buddhism established itself in Tibet it also adopted a great many indigenous beings into its iconographic repertoire. In short, the artistically represented Buddhist pantheon increased tremendously when the religion moved into Tibet, and expanded to a seemingly limitless degree, with a vast range of Buddha families, *bodhisattvas*, goddesses, *yoginīs*, and all manner of fierce divinities.

Benign figures

Although the most striking development in Buddhist art when it reaches Tibet is no doubt the many fierce deities that populate the pantheon, there are also all manner of benevolent beings as well. Perhaps because the concept of lineage is so important in Tibetan Buddhism, and because of the exalted position of the *lama* (guru), significant teachers and saints are common in Tibetan painting and sculpture. Most significant of these figures is Padmasambhava.

According to Tibetan mytho-history, when Buddhism was first introduced into Tibet the region was inhabited by all manner of demons and deities who were opposed to the new religion. The *tantric mahāsiddha* Padmasambhava (later called by his Tibetan name, Rinpoche) was summoned from south India to tame and convert the local deities. The great saint journeys through the Tibetan landscape and subdues and binds a succession of named deities at specific places; these exploits are celebrated in a great range of myths and hymns, and are also the subject of paintings and sculptures. He is often depicted as mustached yogin or teacher, dressed as a monk. Typically he holds a *vajra* in his right hand and a begging bowl made of a human skull in his left (which contains *amṛta*, the elixir of immortality). Against his shoulder leans a magician's staff, projecting his status as a highly accomplished one (*siddhi*) with magical powers.

One of the most popular figures in all of Tibet is Mi-la-ras-pa or Milarepa, the eleventh-century saint whose life story is extremely well known and who stands as an example and model for all Tibetan Buddhists, whether monk, hermit, or layperson, and regardless of social origin or condition of life. The model that Milaraspa's life provides, with its humanity and universality, can be summarized by his emergence from low beginnings, his search for a teacher and the relationship between them, the importance of solitary meditation to his spiritual growth, and his success as a *tantric* master. He is most commonly depicted as a meditating yogin or monk, sometimes with an alms bowl in one hand, holding up the other to his ear, listening to the *dharma*. The medieval saint Tsongkhapa (1357–1419), commonly known as Je Rinpoche ("Precious Lord"), the great reformer and founder of the Gelug school, is also a popular figure in Tibetan Buddhist art. He is often depicted flanked by his main two disciples, Gyaltsab Je and Khedrub Je, with Maitreya above his head.

A wide variety of *bodhisattvas* are also depicted in Tibetan Buddhist art, from the more mainstream Mahāyāna figures of Avalokiteśvara, Maitreya, and Mañjuśrī, who are depicted essentially as they are in India, to specifically Tibetan manifestations of the *bodhisattvas* and various Buddha qualities. They include Samantabadra, who is textually prominent in the *Lotus* and *Avataṃsaka Sūtras*, and who personifies the transcendental practices and vows of the Buddhas and is usually depicted seated on an elephant with six tusks (symbolic of the six perfections, or *pāramitās*). He is also frequently depicted in an explicitly *tantric* form (see below). Bhaiṣayaguru (Sangye Menlha), the "medicine Buddha" sometimes associated with Avalokiteśvara, is also a commonly depicted being in Tibet. He is typically bright blue, seated, forming the gift-giving gesture (*varada mudrā*) with his right hand offering a branch of myrobolan (a universal remedy), and a bowl of *amṛta* in his left; he is sometimes also surrounded by a group of seven other healing Buddhas.

The five celestial Buddhas (sometimes *dhyāni* Buddhas, or *jinas*) who first appear in medieval Indian Buddhist are also commonly depicted in Tibet, especially in *maṇḍala* paintings. Vairocana is usually located in the center of *maṇḍalas* of the *Dhyāni* Buddhas; his color is white (or blue), which symbolizes pure consciousness. Akṣobhya is usually positioned in the east (at the bottom of the *maṇḍala*) – although sometimes he occupies the center position – and is typically blue; he generally forms the *bhūmisparśa mudrā*, conveying his unshakeable wisdom. Ratnasambhava, who transforms pride into *prajñā*, is the Buddha of the south. His color is yellow, and he sometimes holds the *ratna* (gem) or *cintamaṇi* (the wish-fulfilling jewel that grants all desires). Amitābha, who is typically red in Tibetan images, is positioned to the west, and embodies insight and wisdom. Finally, Amoghasiddhi represents the practical realization of the wisdoms; he is usually green, and his special symbol is the *viśva-vajra*, or double *vajra*.

Another benevolent figure who warrants specific mention is Vajradhara – literally the "holder of the thunderbolt," and thus the bearer of the unchanging *Dharma* which this ubiquitous Tibetan symbol denotes. He holds sometimes one, sometimes two *vajras*, often also holding a bell in the other hand, which conveys the resounding, penetrating quality of the teachings. His hands are typically crossed at the wrists, a gesture symbolizing highest energy and the union of compassion and wisdom necessary to reach enlightenment. In paintings he is deep blue, denoting the profound and boundless nature of his omniscient mind.

Fierce figures

There are numerous categories of wrathful (*krodha*) beings in the Vajrayāna pantheon, including *vajradhāras*, *herukas*, *lokapālas*, and *dharmapālas*. These beings, fundamentally, are projections of the base aspects of human nature: lust, anger, delusion, greed, and so on. Properly propitiated, however, these figures are transformed into saviors and destroy the passions of the mind and protect the faithful. Their faces are depicted with strikingly wrathful expressions, their mouths contorted into angry smiles, from which protrude long fangs, sometimes dripping with blood. Perhaps the most commonly represented figures are the eight *dharmapāla*s, the fierce protectors of the Buddha's teachings. They are: Yāma, Mahakala, Yamantaka, Kubera, Hayagriva, Palden Lhamo, Tshangs pa, and Begtse. Although space does not permit a discussion of each of these figures, a discussion of a few of them sheds considerable light on the nature of artistic images in Tibetan Buddhism.

Avalokiteśvara is the patron *bodhisattva* of Tibet; according to Tibetan mytho-history, he made Tibet his special abode, a kind of earthly Pure Land, and chose the people of Tibet as his special charges. As a *bodhisattva*, he is devoted to assuring the salvation of all Tibetans. Typically in Indian Buddhism, Avalokiteśvara is a savior *bodhisattva*, that being who comes to the aid of his devotees. He is the embodiment of compassion and also the supreme practitioner of *upāya*, skillful means. In artistic representations produced in Tibet, Avalokiteśvara wields his *upāya*, particularly, as the fierce defender of Buddhism and as the defeater of Tibet's many indigenous demons. In his fierce form, as Hayagriva, the *bodhisattva* is most simply depicted as a horse-headed being with one face, two arms and two legs. He has an aggressive, scowling face, with three bulging eyes; he has an open, roaring mouth with long protruding fangs; he poses as a frightening warrior, his stomach bulging, with a sword raised in his right hand and his left hand poised to strike.

According to popular mythology, the god of death, Yāma, came to be when thieves attempted to rob a hermit on the verge of enlightenment, and then threatened to kill him. He asked them to wait, as if he were killed all of his effort would be for naught; they ignored him and cut off his head. The hermit then transformed into the ferocious Yāma, placed a bull's head in place of his own severed head, and then killed the thieves and drank their blood from cups made from their skulls. Iconographically, he is often depicted with his consort, Chamundi, a horrific feminine deity, and is naked, wearing a garland of severed human heads. Tibetan Buddhists frequently appeal to Mañjuśrī to tame Yāma, with Mañjuśrī appearing in the form of Yamantaka, a superior version of Yāma himself with eight faces and multiple arms, each holding a different weapon. In paintings and sculpture, Yamantaka is often accompanied by a whole collection of fierce beings.

Each of these fierce figures – and there are many, many more in the Tibetan pantheon – is to be venerated and, in the process, the devotee mentally transforms the superficially threatening and horrendous into that which protects. This is analogous to the fundamental transformation that is at the core of tantric Buddhism, the transformation of selfishness and lust into selflessness and compassion. Likewise, Tibetan Buddhist art is also marked by a high degree of apparent eroticism, but this, too, is to be transformed from the superficial visual realm to the deeper mental one.

Eroticism in Tibetan Buddhist art

If these ferocious figures pose a challenge to the uninitiated viewer, other motifs and images in Tibetan Buddhist art are substantially more shocking and open to misunderstanding. Tantric paintings and sculpture often present a male and a female in sexual embrace, a form known as *yab–yum* (father–mother). On one level, this iconographic motif conveys the joining of the female wisdom (*prajñā*) with the male skillful means (*upāya*). There is a further symbolic valence with such images, however. One of the fundamental tenets of *tantric* Buddhism (and Buddhism in general) is that the reality/illusion dualism is false. This is perhaps most famously articulated by Nāgārjuna, who posited that there was not distinction between *saṃsāra* and *nirvāṇa*. It is *prajñā* that allows one to cut through this false dualism, but in Tibetan Buddhism this cutting wisdom is conjoined with *upāya*, in a kind of "any means necessary" understanding of the path to enlightenment. The *yab–yum* image, then, rather than being erotic, is symbolic of this union.

See also: **Art, Buddhist; Tibet, Buddhism in.**

JACOB N. KINNARD

TIBET, BUDDHISM IN

The "first dissemination" of Buddhism

According to traditional Tibetan histories, the importation of Buddhism was initiated in the distant past when a monkey (who was an incarnation of the buddha Avalokiteśvara) mated with an ogress. Their children were the first Tibetans; from their father they inherited their propensity for religious practice and good qualities such as compassion, while their mother imparted their negative aspects. During the following centuries, Avalokiteśvara and other Buddhas worked to educate the sometimes unruly Tibetans in order that they would eventually embrace the *Dharma*. Tibetan histories (most of which were written by Buddhist clerics whose primary concern was the progress and glorification of the religion) report that the violent and warlike tendencies of the Tibetans made this difficult, and so several buddhas decided to incarnate as Tibetan kings.

The first recorded royal dynasty had its capital in the Yarlung Valley of central Tibet. The early Yarlung kings reportedly descended to earth via a rope, and at the end of their reigns climbed back up it to heaven. Beginning in the sixth century, they began to consolidate their power and brought other local rulers under their control, and following this started a program of expansion. In the seventh to ninth centuries, Tibet was a growing military power that was engaged in frequent battles with its neighbors, particularly China. These military encounters made Tibet's kings aware of their country's cultural backwardness, and beginning with Songtsen Gampo (Srong btsan sGam po, *c.* 618–50) there was a growing interest in importing culture and technology to Tibet in order to rectify this situation.

As part of the king's efforts to modernize his country, he sent the scholar

Tönmi Sambhota (Thon mi Sam bho ṭa) to India to develop a written script for the Tibetan language, and he married princesses from neighboring China and Nepal in order to forge political ties. His marriage to the Chinese princess Wencheng is used by the government of the People's Republic of China as part of its claim to overlordship of Tibet. China asserts that she was not a war bride, as contemporary histories indicate, but rather a cultural ambassador whose mission was to sinicize the Tibetans and bring them up to the level of the Han. Songtsen Gambo is portrayed by contemporary Chinese historians (and in popular culture) as a barbarian ruler overwhelmed by the cultural superiority of the Chinese enemies he had defeated in battle who worked to destroy his own culture and replace it with that of China. Contemporaneous records, however, provide a picture of a pragmatic military commander who took only those elements of foreign cultures that he thought would benefit him and his country.

Later Tibetan tradition conceives of Songtsen Gampo as a "religious king" (*chos rgyal*) and as a physical emanation of Avalokiteśvara who worked to propagate Buddhism in Tibet, but dynastic records indicate that he had little interest in Buddhism, and when he died he was buried according to the rites of the royal cult.

Some of his successors, however, were devout Buddhists, and the second "religious king," Trisong Detsen (Khri srong lDe btsan, ca. 740–98), actively worked to promote the *Dharma*. Later tradition presents him as an incarnation of Mañjuśrī and reports that he invited the Indian scholar-monk Śāntarakṣita to Tibet to spread Buddhism. When he arrived, however, he met with opposition from Tibet's indigenous demons, who were supporters of the pre-Buddhist religion of Bön. He was forced to leave the country, but before he departed Śāntarakṣita advised Trisong Detsen to invite the tantric master Padmasambhava to travel to Tibet in order to overcome demonic resistance to his mission.

The king followed his advice, but when Padmasambhava neared the border, Tibet's demons sent a huge snowstorm to prevent him from entering the country. Padmasambhava retreated to a cave and meditated, and the power of his practice stopped the storm. As he proceeded into Tibet he challenged its demons to personal combat. None of them were able to stop him. One by one, each demon "offered up its life force," and Padmasambhava spared their lives in exchange for vows that henceforth they would become guardians of the *Dharma*. This began a process of incorporating Tibet's indigenous spirits into Buddhism. Some were reconceived as *Dharma* protectors, and others came to be associated with various buddhas and *bodhisattvas*. The land itself was said to be a huge demoness, and in order to subdue her temples were built on top of her four limbs and another over her heart, which rendered her powerless to hinder the spread of the *Dharma*.

The Tibetans who witnessed Padmasambhava's display were so impressed by one man's ability to fight their feared demons and apparently emerge victorious that from this point Padmasambhava made rapid progress in introducing Buddhism. This account is found in most traditional Tibetan histories, but there is scant reference to Padmasambhava in early sources, in which he is either not mentioned or briefly referred to as an Indian water diviner. Later Tibetan histories are unanimous regarding his influence and the success of his mission, however, and they report that following his victory over the demons, Padmasambhava, Trisong Detsen, and Santirakṣita consecrated Tibet's first monastery, which was named Samye (bSam yas). Shortly thereafter, the first seven Tibetan probationers (*sad mi bdun*) received monastic vows.

As Buddhism increased in influence, the government sponsored Tibetans to travel to the great monastic universities of north India to study, and also brought eminent Indian masters to Tibet. At the same time, Chinese Buddhist missionaries began to appear in Tibet, and some of them attracted significant numbers of disciples. Many of the Chinese masters propounded teachings and practices that differed from mainstream Indian Mahāyāna Buddhism, and conflicts developed between rival schools. According to Pudön (Bu ston rin chen grub, 1290–1364), Trisong Detsen decided to settle the matter by sponsoring a public debate between the Chinese master Hashang Mahāyāna (Hva shang Ma hā yā na; Chinese: Heshang Moheyan) and the Indian scholar-monk Kamalaśīla, a student of Śāntarakṣita. Pudön reports that Śāntarakṣita had foreseen the conflict and counseled the king to invite Kamalaśīla to defend Buddhist orthodoxy.

According to Pudön, the Hashang advocated a form of antinomian Chan Buddhism which taught that the practice of morality is unnecessary in pursuit of Buddhahood and that all one needs to do is empty the mind of thoughts. Awakening is instantaneous, and the traditional Mahāyāna gradualist path is only suitable for practitioners of limited capacities. Advanced trainees leap into Buddhahood all at once by eliminating thoughts. Kamalaśīla is reported to have replied that nothing happens all at once, no one climbs a mountain in an instant, and he demanded that the Hashang provide an example of a truly instantaneous phenomenon. He responded that a sword cuts through a rope instantaneously, and a baby is born all at once, but his Indian opponents pointed out that these things actually happen in stages. They further contended that the thoughtless state advocated by the Hashang is like deep sleep and has nothing in common with scriptural descriptions of Buddhahood. Pudön reports that the Chinese master was finally reduced to silence and unable to answer his critics, and so Trisong Detsen declared the Indian side victorious and ordered that Chinese Buddhist teachings henceforth be regarded as heterodox and proscribed.

There is considerable debate among contemporary scholars regarding the veracity of traditional accounts of the "debate." Luis Gómez and others have argued that it is likely that it never actually took place (Gómez thinks that it is more probable that a series of haphazard encounters were later recast in the story of a winner-take-all contest), but traditional Tibetan histories are unanimous regarding its details and outcome, and regardless of its historicity Tibetan Buddhists believe that it happened and that from that point Chinese Buddhism was regarded as heterodox. Tibetan histories report that one outcome of the debate was that India became the sole source for the importation of the *Dharma*. Traditions like the "great perfection" (*rdzogs chen*) and the "great seal" (Tib. *phyag rgya chen po*, Skt. *mahāmudrā*), which were influenced by Chinese subitist practices, often feel compelled to defend themselves against the charge that they propound doctrines similar to those of Hashang Mahāyāna. The Hashang is a comical figure in many Tibetan ritual dances (*'cham*), in which he is portrayed as a bumbling monk wearing Chinese brocade and with exaggerated Chinese facial features. He has a retinue of disciples who try to keep him from hurting himself, and his antics are immensely entertaining for Tibetan refugee audiences, who see him as a symbol of their Chinese enemies.

Trisong Detsen's successors continued to support Buddhism, and the apogee of royal patronage was the reign of King Relpachen (Ral pa can, r. 815–36), who is said to have been an incarnation of Vajrapāṇi. He reportedly spent large amounts of money on Buddhist projects, and as a result severely depleted the kingdom's coffers. Because of this and his neglect of royal duties, he was assassinated by his ministers, and he was succeeded by Lang Darma (gLang dar ma, r. 838–42), who according to Tibetan histories instituted a massive persecution of Buddhism. Contemporaneous accounts suggest that while he was opposed to Buddhism, his persecutions were fairly minor, and mainly involved withdrawing royal sponsorship from Buddhist institutions and forcing some monastics to return to lay life. He was assassinated by a Buddhist monk, and after this the Yarlung dynasty collapsed.

Relpachen's death marks the demise of the "first dissemination" (*snga dar*) of Buddhism to Tibet, and with the end of royal patronage Buddhism survived mainly in local cults and with individual practitioners. In the following centuries Tibet was ruled by local hegemons. No one was able to exercise power over the whole country, and there was little support for large monastic institutions.

The "second dissemination"

In the eleventh century, the kings of western Tibet invited the Indian scholar-monk Atiśa (one of the four directors of the monastic university of Nālandā) to travel to the country to propagate the *Dharma*. His arrival in 1042 marks the beginning of the "second dissemination" (*phyi dar*) of Buddhism. Atiśa advocated the traditional Mahāyāna gradualist paradigm of the *bodhisattva* path, in which a person progresses in stages toward Buddhahood, motivated by compassion for suffering sentient beings. His teachings mingled both sūtric and tantric techniques and philosophies, and they became the dominant version of Buddhism in the order he founded, the Kadampa (bKa' gdams pa). This was later revived by Tsong Khapa, who referred to his Gelukpa Order as the "New Kadampa" and saw himself as following the model taught by Atiśa.

The western Tibetan king Yeshe Ö (Ye shes 'od) also sent the scholar Rinchen Sangpo (Rin chen bzang po, 958–1055) to India to learn Sanskrit. When he returned, he began translating Buddhist scriptures into Tibetan and writing commentaries on many of them. His literary activity was a key aspect of the regeneration of Buddhism in Tibet. He also played an important role in re-establishing the monastic code (*Vinaya*) in Tibet. The translators of the second dissemination instituted a program of systematic rendering of Sanskrit Buddhist texts into Tibetan. Translation bureaus were formed which generally combined Tibetan and Indian scholars, who developed standard Sanskrit–Tibetan lexicons. In a remarkably short time, huge numbers of Indian Buddhist texts were translated into Tibetan, and in the fourteenth century Pudön redacted them into a canon that is still normative today. He divided the Buddhist scriptures into two groupings, "Translations of Teachings" (*bKa' 'gyur*) and "Translations of Treatises" (*bsTan 'gyur*). The former mainly includes Indian *sūtras* and *tantras*, and the latter comprises Indian philosophical texts, commentaries, and a few Chinese works.

At the same time, *tantric* lineages entered Tibet from India (mainly Bengal and Bihar) that challenged – and often rejected outright – the monastic and scholastic streams that came to Tibet from the north Indian monastic universities. These lineages were propagated by sometimes iconoclastic *siddhas* like Tilopa and Virūpa, whose biographies report antisocial and paradoxical behavior that showed their disdain for worldly conventions and the norms of cenobitic monasticism. These two streams (scholastic monasticism and charismatic *tantra*) continue to dominate Tibetan Buddhism, and in modern times most orders mingle elements of both. The Kagyüpa Order in particular sees itself as descending from the Indian *siddhas* Tilopa and Nāropa, and the Sakyapas consider Virūpa to be one of their main progenitors. However, the Gelukpa Order traces itself back to Atiśa and emphasizes the institutional monastic paradigm. These three traditions are collectively called the "New Orders" (*gsar ma*), because they rely on translations of *tantras* prepared during the second dissemination, while the Nyingma ("Old Translation") Order prefers the translations of the first dissemination, which they contend were written by realized masters who grasped the essential meaning of the Indian texts.

Mongol power and Sakya hegemony

In the thirteenth century, Tibet was threatened by the expansion of the Mongol empire. The Mongol ruler Godan Khan demanded that Tibet surrender to him and become part of his domain, and the Sakya hierarch Sakya Pandita (Sa skya Paṇḍita Kun dga' rgyal mtshan, 1182–1251) was ordered to travel to the Mongol capital to acknowledge Godan's overlordship. Tibetan sources report that when the *lama* arrived in 1244 Godan was deeply impressed by him and offered to establish a special "priest–patron" (*mchod yon*) relationship, in which the Sakya *lamas* would become chaplains of the Mongol rulers, and the khans in turn would serve as protectors of the Sakyapas. Tibetan sources present this as a conversion of Godan Khan by Sakya Pandita, but Mongol records (and a letter Sakya Pandita wrote to his compatriots in Tibet) are more ambiguous. They suggest that it was an arrangement of convenience and indicate that Sakya Pandita's nephew Pakpa ('Phags pa blo gros, 1235–89) was kept as a virtual hostage in order to ensure Tibetan compliance.

Godan Khan's successor Kubilai Khan (r. 1260–94), however, seems to have forged a close personal and religious bond with Pakpa, and with his sponsorship the Sakyapas became the dominant power in Tibet. Until Mongol power waned in the fourteenth century, the Sakyapa hierarchs were the effective rulers of the country, and by all accounts the Mongols avoided interfering with internal Tibetan affairs.

The government of the People's Republic of China asserts that Sakya Pandita's submission to Godan marked the official incorporation of Tibet into China, but Tibetan historians point out that when he traveled to Mongolia China had not yet been conquered by the Mongols. When they annexed China, it was added to an already substantial empire that included much of Asia and large areas of eastern Europe. Tibet ceded overlordship to the Mongols, and not to China, and when Mongol power waned both Tibet and China regained their independence, but at different times and by different means. Tibetans did not help China regain its independence, nor were the Chinese involved when Tibet freed itself from Mongol rule. Contemporary Chinese historians, however, claim that the Mongols are one of the many ethnic groups of China and that their political ascendancy was achieved within this multi-ethnic framework. They were a Chinese dynasty, and from this point forward, according to the Chinese, Tibet became a inalienable part of China.

Tibetan Buddhism among the Mongols

Sakya Pandita and Pakpa were successful in missionizing members of the royal court, but Buddhism failed to spread widely among the populace. Contacts between Tibetan Buddhism and the Mongols were revived in the sixteenth century, when Altan Khan's (1507–83) armies made military conquests in eastern Tibet. The third Dalai Lama, Sönam Gyatso (bSod nams rgya mtsho, 1543–88), visited the khan's palace in 1578, and this initiated a new phase of Buddhist missionary activity among the Mongols. A number of Tibetan Buddhist teachers traveled to Mongolia, including Neyichi Toyin (1557–1653), who converted the eastern Mongols, and Zaya Pandita (fl. seventeenth century), who converted the western and northern Mongols. Abadai Khan, the leader of the Khalkha tribe, became a supporter of Buddhism, and is reported to have commissioned the construction of Erdini Juu Monastery to house images that Sönam Gyatso gave him. Newly converted Mongol rulers also banned live animal sacrifices and hunting, and every yurt was required to have an image of the Buddha Mahākāla (Mon. Yeke gara). At this time Mongol scholars also began the process of translating the Tibetan Buddhist canon into Mongolian. From this point until the present, Tibetan Buddhism has been the dominant religion among most Mongols, despite efforts to eradicate it during the Soviet era and the Chinese Cultural Revolution of the 1960s and 1970s.

The rule of the Dalai Lamas

Despite their diminished empire and power, Mongol armies continued to be influential in Asian politics and were courted by both Tibet and China. An important link between the Gelukpas and the Mongols was forged in the sixteenth century, when the fourth Dalai Lama was discovered in the Mongol royal house. From this point onward, the fortunes of the Gelukpas were closely tied to Mongol patrons, culminating in the installation of the fifth Dalai Lama, Ngawang Losang Gyatso (Ngag dbang blo bzang rgya mtsho, 1617–82), as the ruler of Tibet by the armies of the Mongol chieftain Gushri Khan. From then until 1959, the Dalai Lamas were (at least nominally) the rulers of Tibet, although several of them died before they reached maturity. For most of the period following the fifth Dalai Lama's death, Tibet was ruled by regents, and only the thirteenth and fourteenth Dalai Lamas were able to exert significant political authority.

Under the rule of the Dalai Lamas, Tibet was politically stable, but it became increasingly militarily weak. The thirteenth Dalai Lama, Tupden Gyatso (Thub bstan rgya mtsho, 1876–1933), recognized the threat that China posed for his country and attempted to modernize Tibet's medieval military and education systems, but his reforms were scuttled after his death by the conservative monasteries and aristocracy, which feared that the proposed changes would undermine their power. Because of its geographical position and the government's decision to close Tibet's borders to most foreigners, the country was able to remain largely isolated for centuries, but its archaic and inefficient government and military were utterly unable to adapt to the changing circumstances they faced in the mid-twentieth century, when troops of the Chinese People's Liberation Army launched an invasion into eastern Tibet. China claimed that Tibet was under the control of foreign "imperialists" and that it intended to "liberate" the country from them and would leave when this goal was achieved.

The Chinese invasion and Tibetan resistance

On the eve of the Chinese invasion, the central government headquartered in Lhasa was led by the regent Taktra Rinpoche (sTag sgra Rin po che), a reincarnate *lama* who had come to power following the abdication of his corrupt predecessor, Reting Rinpoche (Rva sgreng Rin po che 'Jam dpal ye shes). Although it claimed sovereignty over most of the Tibetan plateau, in fact the government only exercised authority over the central provinces and adjoining areas. Much of the country was under the control of monasteries, which while nominally subject to the central government were in fact autonomous. In addition, large areas of eastern Tibet had been conquered by Chinese warlords who moved into the power vacuum following the demise of China's last imperial dynasty, the Qing.

The Nationalist government that succeeded the Qing emperors claimed sovereignty over Tibet, but lacked the resources to exert any real control over the central provinces. The Tibetan government was invited to voluntarily rejoin the Chinese "motherland," but this request was rebuffed. Despite an official declaration of independence by the thirteenth Dalai Lama in 1911, China continued to proclaim that Tibet was a part of its territory. The Nationalists were overthrown by the Communists, led by Mao Zedong, in 1937, and after consolidating their power they set their sights on Tibet. Mao conceded that there were no Chinese in Tibet, but like other Han of his day he believed that it was a part of Chinese territory and that without Tibet China would fall prey to the intrigues of foreigners. In 1949, soldiers of the People's Liberation Army began exploratory strikes into Tibetan territory in order to assess the mettle of Tibetan militias.

The invaders' first skirmishes demonstrated that they would encounter no significant resistance. Tibet's military commanders were traditional aristocrats who generally had no military training, and the leader of Tibet's defenses in the east surrendered without a fight and later became a leading collaborator.

Belatedly realizing the threat China posed, the monastic and lay authorities in Lhasa, the capital of Tibet, decided that the fourteenth Dalai Lama, Tenzin Gyatso (bsTan 'dzin rgya mtsho, b. 1935, who was sixteen at the time), should be invested with full secular authority. This decision was prompted by the Nechung Oracle (the state oracle, who goes into trance and is possessed by a disembodied being named Pehar), who reportedly pointed to the young Dalai Lama and said, "Make him king." He was still studying for his final examinations, but after he successfully completed them he was put in charge of the government.

With no opposing force to stop them, Chinese troops proceeded to Lhasa and announced that Tibet had for centuries been an integral part of the Chinese "motherland" and that their Chinese brothers had arrived to reintegrate the region and bring the Tibetans the benefits of their superior culture. The Tibetan government protested that Tibet was a sovereign country and had never been ruled by China, and further pointed out that there were no foreign imperialists in the country, and so there was no need for China to "liberate" Tibet. Despite Tibetan objections, the Chinese soon formed an administration to rule the country, but initially left the Dalai Lama's government intact. The Dalai Lama tried to cooperate with the Chinese and worked to establish cordial relations with them, but friction increased as Chinese control deepened.

At first the Chinese avoided openly antagonizing residents of central Tibet, but in eastern parts of the country they began forcing the population into communal work units, and in an attempt to weaken the influence of religion began destroying monasteries and killing monks and nuns. A resistance movement soon formed in eastern Tibet, and the Chinese responded with a show of force, which prompted large numbers of refugees to flee into the central provinces. As the new arrivals told of religious persecution and killings in the east, people in the capital became increasingly radicalized. At the same time, the presence of thousands of Chinese troops put a strain on Tibet's small economy, and the price of food and other necessities skyrocketed. Tibetans began to take to the streets to call for an end to Chinese rule, and the invaders – who had been told by their leaders that they would be welcomed as brothers and as liberators – were increasingly confronted by angry mobs yelling "Han go home!"

Exile and repression

As tensions mounted, the Chinese responded with increasingly harsh measures. Matters came to a head in March 1959, when a rumor that the Dalai Lama had been invited to a theatrical performance by the Chinese military commander swept through Lhasa. Fearing that the Chinese intended to capture him, a large crowd gathered outside the Norbulingka (his summer residence) to prevent his abduction. On 10 March, Chinese troops began shelling the compound with mortars, which prompted the Dalai Lama's advisors to suggest that he flee the country. Disguised as a soldier, he slipped out of the Norbulingka with a small retinue. They were met by resistance fighters from eastern Tibet, who escorted them to the Indian border, narrowly beating Chinese troops that had been sent to intercept them. Mao Zedong later claimed that he knew of the escape and allowed it to happen, but this seems highly unlikely.

Once in India, the Dalai Lama declared that Tibet was an independent country and denounced China's invasion. The Indian prime minister, Jawaharlal Nehru, offered to let the Tibetans establish a headquarters in the former British hill station of Dharamsala, Himachal Pradesh. The Dalai Lama soon formed a government-in-exile, which remains the central authority for Tibetan refugees.

Soon after word reached Tibet of the Dalai Lama's flight, tens of thousands of Tibetans joined him in exile. As the numbers grew, it became clear that there were too many for Dharamsala to accommodate, and so Nehru decided to give the Tibetans uncleared land in south India where they could establish new settlements. During this period conditions worsened in Tibet, and the Chinese authorities increasingly resorted to force to subdue the restive population. Both Chinese leaders and soldiers had apparently believed that Tibetans would welcome them as liberators and eagerly throw off the shackles of their traditional culture and religion when presented with the superior culture of the Han Chinese. Tibetan intransigence was incomprehensible to the invaders, to whom their own superiority was obvious and who viewed the Tibetans as backward and uncivilized.

In the immediate aftermath of the Dalai Lama's flight, Chinese troops killed scores of Tibetans, and repression increased in the following years. During the Cultural Revolution, communist cadres flocked to Tibet, seeking to destroy its traditional "feudal" culture and make way for the full introduction of socialism. Religious practitioners and institutions were a particular target of attack, and by the end of this period only a handful of approximately 7,000 monasteries and other religious structures remained. Most religious leaders who stayed in Tibet were killed or imprisoned, and the Tibetan government-in-exile estimates that over 1.2 million Tibetans perished. While these figures are probably inflated, they still fail to convey the enormous suffering inflicted on the Tibetan people and the extent of the devastation of their traditional culture because they focus only on those who

Figure 42 Tibetan Buddhists turning prayer wheels along the Barkhor, Lhasa, Tibet.

died; many who suffered greatly under Chinese rule survived, and only a handful of their stories have been told.

Beginning in the 1980s, there was a slight relaxation of religious repression, but this led to Tibetan protests against Chinese rule and prompted another brutal crackdown and the declaration of martial law. During the 1990s and the early part of the twenty-first century, repression has waxed and waned, but at the time of this writing (2004) it is on the increase, and over 3,000 Tibetans escape into exile every year. An untold number are arrested in the attempt, many die while crossing some of the world's highest passes, and others are turned back by Nepali border patrols. The majority of new refugees are monks and nuns, who claim that religious practice is impossible in Tibet and that Chinese authorities allow no freedom of religion.

Independent human rights groups concur with this assessment, and the future of Tibetan Buddhism in the country of its origin is bleak. The refugees in India and elsewhere have made preservation of Tibetan religion and culture a priority, and most of the monasteries and other religious institutions destroyed by the Chinese have been rebuilt in exile. Large numbers of monks and nuns study traditional curricula, practice meditation, and perform Buddhist rituals, and a school system has been created that teaches children a combination of modern subjects and Tibetan language, religion, and culture. Recognizing the importance of unity for this small refugee community, the Dalai Lama has labored to counteract sectarianism, which was a divisive force in old Tibet and continues to threaten the cohesion of Tibetan exiles. He has publicly sought to forge ties between all four orders of Tibetan Buddhism, and has even reached out to the non-Buddhist Bönpos, declaring at one point that they are the "original Tibetan Buddhists." His ecumenical stance has angered many traditionalists, but has been highly effective in helping the exile community to maintain cohesion and to present a unified face to the world.

Tibetan Buddhism in the West

Ironically, during the past few decades, as Tibetan Buddhism comes under increasing threat in the land of its origin, it is thriving in exile, and has attracted foreign adherents in unprecedented numbers. There are now thousands of Tibetan Buddhist centers in the West, and Tibetan *lamas* often draw large crowds when they tour. Increasing numbers of Westerners consider themselves to be Tibetan Buddhists, and books by the Dalai Lama and other Tibetan teachers have reached the top of the best-seller lists. As Tibetan Buddhism slowly dies in Tibet, it is enjoying new popularity in other countries, and it seems clear now that early pronouncements of the tradition's demise were overly pessimistic. Tibetan Buddhism is flourishing as never before outside of Tibet, and many Tibetan *lamas* view the West as the next great missionizing field for their religion. A number of recent studies of this phenomenon have shown that Tibetan Buddhism is already adapting to its new environment and that Buddhist centers in the West are generally very different from Tibetan institutions. Western centers tend to be democratic and non-hierarchical, and even when a Tibetan *lama* is the spiritual head of a center, he is often officially a chaplain who is an employee of its members. Centers are commonly run by boards of directors, who are mostly lay disciples, and they are non-profit organizations governed by constitutions. Many traditional *lamas* have expressed shock and dismay at the notion that they are under the control of their students (which they claim undermines the role of the *lama* and makes the traditional devotion of tantric guru yoga practices problematic), but such arrangements are generally necessary in order for a religious organization to gain tax-exempt status. It is likely that as Tibetan Buddhism continues to gain adherents in the West it will make further cultural adjustments and that it will shed many of the accoutrements of Tibet's traditional culture and adopt elements of the societies of Western adherents.

See also: **Buddhism in Tibet today; Dalai Lamas; Geluk; Kagyü; Nyingma; *Ris med* (Non-Sectarian) movement in Tibetan Buddhism; Ritual in Tibetan Buddhism; Sakya; Tibetan Buddhism in exile; Tsong Khapa; Vajrayāna Buddhism; Women in Tibetan Buddhism.**

JOHN POWERS

TIBET: *MAṆḌALAS*

The Sanskrit word *maṇḍala* literally means "circle," although its valence is considerably more complex than this. In its most rudimentary form, then, the *maṇḍala* is a circular diagram intended, in meditational and ritual contexts, to focus the mind. In a broader sense, a *maṇḍala* can be seen as a distinctly sacred realm, the abode of a deity, a map of the entire cosmos. In Tibetan Buddhist art and practice, there is a vast array of *maṇḍalas* with very different functions and meanings. Some *maṇḍalas* are presented as basic diagrams, geometrical line drawings; others are extremely complex, presenting in great detail a complexly rendered Buddhist cosmos populated by dozens of Buddhas, *bodhisattvas*, benign and wrathful deities, saints, *lamas*, and lay practitioners. *Maṇḍalas* are an integral part of a variety of ritual practices in Tibetan Buddhism, particularly the complex visualization rituals that are at the core of the tradition. Although there is a tremendous range of *maṇḍala* types, the structure of the *maṇḍala* generally allows the ritual actor (or meditator) to move mentally from the external world depicted on the outer rim of the *maṇḍala* – the material, human realm – into the realms of the various *bodhisattvas* and deities, through the pure realms of existence, and then finally to the pure heart of the *maṇḍala*, where resides the central deity of the *maṇḍala*.

The basic *maṇḍala*

The history of Tibetan Buddhism, and therefore Tibetan Buddhist art, is extremely complex, and it is difficult to locate, with precision, the introduction of the *maṇḍala* into the region. That said, the first *maṇḍalas* to appear in Tibet seem to have been produced in the eighth century, following Indian models. A *maṇḍala* can be constructed in a number of ways out of a variety of materials – stone images, metal engraving, temples, sand – but in Tibet they are perhaps most typically painted on cloth, as a *thangka*, and are often hung on the walls of monasteries. The central *bodhisattva* or deity of the *maṇḍala* typically is represented at the very center of the image, surrounded by concentrically placed *bodhisattvas* and deities, as well as various symbols such as lotuses, *vajras*, flames. Specific colors are used to represent specific figures, as dictated by a wide range of iconographic manuals.

Although a painted *maṇḍala* is a two-dimensional object, it is intended to convey a three-dimensional world. Indeed, the *maṇḍala* is in many ways intended to create an image of a *stūpa* or temple; presenting an image of the classical Indian temple, they thus typically depict a central square with four gates at the cardinal points, in which are circles, intended to create the image of a rising structure. This central structure is then often encircled by another circle, a band sometimes embellished with variously colored lotuses, sometimes with flames, sometimes simply with geometrical patterns. This band encircles the pure center of the *maṇḍala*, in much the same way that the pure zone of the temple is, in the material world, encircled by a wall. Outside of this band is the material, profane world.

The particular *bodhisattva* or deity who resides in the inner sanctum of the *maṇḍala* temple varies widely, as do the various details presented by the *maṇḍala* image. Sometime there is only a single deity, while in some *maṇḍalas* there are several deities at the center of the image, surrounded by their various attendants, relative deities, sacred symbols.

For instance, *maṇḍalas* that focus on Śākyamuni present an image of the Buddha at the center – very often, in Tibet, the Buddha in the *bhūmisparśamudrā*, the earth-touching gesture that signifies the defeat of Māra – surrounded by various scenes from his life, such as his birth, departure from the palace, various miracles, death, etc. The prototype for this *maṇḍala* form is no doubt the *aṣṭamāhapratiharya* that began to be produced in Indian Buddhist sculpture sometime around the eighth century. Such an image presents a kind of image of the whole of the Buddha's life, and, by extension, the whole of his teachings.

A more distinctly Tibetan *maṇḍala* might be one devoted to Vairocana, one of the *pañcatathāgatas*, the five so-called celestial Buddhas (or *dhyāni* Buddhas) that become particularly prominent in the Vajrayāna Buddhism of Tibet. Typically, Vairocana sits in mediation at the center of the *maṇḍala* in his two-armed, one-faced form (other *maṇḍalas* might depict him in one of his other guises). Around him, in concentric circles, are three palace (or temple) levels occupied by hundreds of attendants. Sometimes these attendants are specific Buddhas, *bodhisattvas*, and deities, while in other images each figure is specifically identified with a particular monk – sometimes specifically identified on the back of the image – in the Vairocana teaching lineage. In this sense, then, the *maṇḍala* presents not only an image of Vaircocana's Pure Land, an image to aid in meditation, but also a historical record of a particular monastic lineage.

Hevajra is one the most commonly represented fierce, or *krodha*, deities in the Tibetan pantheon. He is classified as a *yidam*, or protector deity, or sometimes as a *dharmapāla* (literally a "protector of the *Dharma*"). He is sometimes represented as Hevajra Kapaladhāra, "holder of the skull cup," because he carries a cup made out of a human skull, out of which he drinks the blood of his victims (who represent the negative psychological forces that he defeats). He often has eight faces, four legs (with which he tramples the evil Māras), and sixteen arms in which he carries a variety of items – weapons, garlands of skulls and severed heads, rosaries and *vajras*. He is surrounded in his *maṇḍala* by various *yoginīs* who dance on lotus petals and a whole host of fierce and benign deities and monks. In each of the four corners of the *maṇḍala* are cremation grounds with other forms of Hevajra. Sometimes he is depicted in sexual union with his consort, while in others he appears menacingly alone.

Maṇḍalas, then, can depict both benign figures such as Vairocana, fierce deities such as Hevajra, or figures in explicitly sexual positions. One of the most important and popular *maṇḍala* deities is Cakrasṃvara, who is depicted in a wide variety of forms, some of which present the deity in sexual union with his consort, Vajravārahī. At the center of the *maṇḍala* are the central figures, locked in embrace, trampling Bhairava and Kālārātrī. They are accompanied, in concentric rings, by the four major *yoginīs* in their fierce guises in the innermost ring, and then various *ḍākinīs*, buddhas, deities in charnel grounds, and, in the outermost ring, important *lamas*, priests, patrons, etc.

The concentric bands of the *maṇḍala* thus present various members of the central figure's entourage, or family, along with important historical figures and contemporary monks and priests. All of these figures, however, also symbolically represent the various realms of the mind that are progressively traveled through as one makes progress on the Buddhist path. As the mind becomes progressively trained, or focused, it moves from the tainted outer world, the world of lust and greed and material, toward the purity of the center, the still point where resides the deity.

Visualizations

An integral aspect of the *maṇḍala* is ritual visualization of the particular *bodhisattva* or deity to which the *maṇḍala* is dedicated, often referred to simply as "deity yoga." Such visualization rituals can be extremely complex, involving prayers, prostrations, hand gestures, and *mantras*, and although they do not always or necessarily involve *maṇḍalas* – sometimes they use only texts – the two-dimensional visual world presented in the *maṇḍala* can act as an aid in the meditational entry into the realm of the deity. Ritual practitioners frequently use *sādhanas*, which are verbal descriptions of the particular deity's *maṇḍala*, along with two-dimensional images, in order to create a vivid mentally constructed *maṇḍala* in meditation. The meditator is to envision him or herself as not merely encountering the deity, but as entering into the deity's world, as represented by the *maṇḍala*; in advanced visualization practices, the meditator attains union with the deity at the *maṇḍala*'s center – either through symbolic sexual union, as in the case of the consort, or through actual embodiment of the deity.

A common ritual practice in this regard is referred to as *maṇḍala* offering. Here, the practitioner uses the *maṇḍala* to conjure a vision of the deity, and then physically offers that being various substances, such as rice, jewels, gold, etc. In some instances, the ritual agents actually construct a kind of *maṇḍala* in the physical world: on a pure plate – ideally made of gold, symbolizing the innate purity of every individual – grains are offered in a series of ritual gestures. A pile of grain is made at the center of the plate, symbolizing Mount Meru, the center of the Buddhist cosmos, and other smaller piles are formed to symbolize the four continents (as traditionally described in Buddhism), the sun and moon, and so on. Essentially, the worshipper creates a three-dimensional *maṇḍala* while at the same time mentally constructing a more elaborate version that corresponds with the detailed two-dimensional painted *maṇḍalas*, populating it with precisely the deities that are artistically represented.

See also: **Art, Buddhist; Tibet, Buddhism in.**

JACOB N. KINNARD

TIBETAN BUDDHISM IN EXILE

Beginning in the late 1950s, the People's Republic of China began sending its military into eastern Tibet. After meeting no real resistance, Chinese troops proceeded to Lhasa and announced that Tibet was a part of Chinese territory and that their incursion was the beginning of a "peaceful liberation" of the Tibetan people.

In eastern Tibet, the Chinese destroyed a number of monasteries and forced the population into collective farms, which led to the formation of a resistance movement. As conflict intensified, large numbers of refugees fled to central Tibet with tales of persecution and violence. In 1959 a series of anti-Chinese riots erupted in Lhasa, and after a Chinese mortar attack on his residence the fourteenth Dalai Lama, Tenzin Gyatso (bsTan 'dzin rgya mtsho, 1935–), decided to flee to India. His party was guided by resistance fighters from eastern Tibet, and narrowly managed to reach the border ahead of Chinese patrols sent to intercept them.

Once they were in India, Prime Minister Jawaharlal Nehru permitted the Dalai

Lama and his followers to set up headquarters in the former British hill station of Dharamsala. They formed a government-in-exile, which remains the central administration for Tibetan refugees. Following the Dalai Lama's flight, tens of thousands of Tibetans left their homeland to join him in exile. To accommodate the new arrivals, the Indian government gave them large tracts of land (mostly uncleared jungle) in south India. The two largest settlements were at Mundgod and Bylakuppe, where the Tibetans cleared the jungle and established farming communities.

Donations by international aid organizations and private sympathizers were an important part of the process of building Tibetan communities in exile. Though many of the refugees are poor by Western standards, the money the community has received from foreign donors has allowed the government-in-exile to establish what amounts to a cradle-to-grave welfare system. Many Tibetans have personal sponsors from overseas, and most of the monastic institutions have ongoing networks of sponsorship. The Tibetan refugee communities today are significantly better off than their Indian neighbors, which has been a source of friction between the two groups.

From the beginning, the exile government decided that preserving religious traditions would be its core mission, and all of Tibet's major monasteries (most of which were destroyed by the Chinese) have been rebuilt in exile. These are supported by the exiles themselves, but their main source of income is foreign money. Their numbers are greatly reduced from pre-invasion times, but many of the best teachers managed to escape into exile, and after an initial period of dislocation, the process of rebuilding monastic institutions began in earnest. Today thousands of monks and nuns study in these new center, most of which bear the names of their Tibetan counterparts. In addition, the exile government has established school systems for refugee children, which combine religious and secular education.

One of the strains on refugee institutions is the constant influx of new arrivals; during the 1990s an average of 3,000 Tibetans managed to escape into exile every year. The majority were monks and nuns, who cited ongoing human rights abuses and denial of religious freedom as their reasons for leaving. There are often conflicts between newcomers and established refugees, who are suspicious of fellow Tibetans who have lived under Chinese rule. Tibetan Buddhist religious practice and study is flourishing in exile, but is gradually dying in the land of its origin as the Chinese authorities continue to torture and imprison the people they claim to have "liberated."

See also: **Buddhism in the Western world; Tibet, Buddhism in.**

JOHN POWERS

TRIPIṬAKA, CHINESE

Buddhism spread across the Silk Road through Central Asia to China with monks and pious laity bringing hand-copied Buddhist manuscripts. The *Scripture in Forty-two Sections* (*Sishi'er zhang jing*), a short collection of passages from Buddhist scriptures (*Āgamas*), is traditionally regarded as the first text translated into Chinese at the request of Emperor Ming (r. 58 – 75 CE). Central Asians, who had a copy of Sanskrit or Prakrit manuscript in hand or had memorized the text, worked with Chinese scholars to translate these Buddhist scriptures into classical Chinese. An Shigao (fl. 148–70 CE), the Chinese name of a Parthian Buddhist monk, translated more than twenty works, mostly mainstream (*Śrāvakayāna*) *Sūtra* and *Abhidharma* texts in the capital city of Luoyang. Daoist interest may have influenced the translation of meditation texts that teach techniques based on counting the breath. The Indo-scythian monk Lokakṣema (fl. 170–90), also working in Luoyang, is credited with the introduction of Mahāyāna Buddhism. He translated many Mahāyāna *sūtras*, including a partial translation of *the Perfection of Insight Sūtra in Eight Thousand Lines* (*Aṣṭasāhasrikāprajñāpāramitā*), the *Sūtra of Concentration of Direct Encounter with the Buddhas of the Present* (*Pratyutpannabuddhasammukhāvasthitasamādhi Sūtra*) and the *Land of Bliss Sūtra* (*Sukhāvatīvyūha*) which introduced the meditative practice of visualizing Amitābha Buddha and his western Buddha Land. Dharmarakṣa (233–310 CE), a bilingual monk from Dunhuang, worked at Chang An with a team of lay and monastic assistants and translated over 150 mainstream and Mahāyāna texts. Several important Mahāyāna *sūtras*, the *Lotus Sūtra* (*Saddharmapuṇḍarīka*), the *Teaching of Vimalakīrti Sūtra* (*Vimalakīrti Nirdeśa*) and the *Ten Stages* (*Daśabhūmika*) *Sūtra* were among them. These early translation teams of foreigners and Chinese often used a translation method that matched foreign Buddhist terms and concepts with local equivalents (*ge yi*). The word *Dao* translated the way to *nirvāṇa* and Buddhist *arhats* were identified with Daoist sages.

The Chinese monk Dao'an (312–85) blamed the earlier translations' inaccuracy and awkwardness on the difficulties that arose from the collaboration of foreign monks and Chinese assistants who were not fluent in each other's languages, and rejected the earlier method of matching terms. The standard for elegant and accurate translations was set by Kumārajīva (343–413), a Central Asian from Kucha who was fluent in Chinese and Sanskrit. Kumārajīva and his team of assistants at Chang An translated nearly 100 texts into Chinese, including translations of the *Lotus Sūtra* and the *Teaching of Vimalakīrti Sūtra* that improved on earlier efforts. He also translated Sarvāstivāda *Vinaya* works, the three treatises (*san lun*) on which the Chinese branch of the Madhyamaka school was based and the *Great Perfection of Insight Treatise* (*Dazhidulun*), which incorporates some of his oral commentary on these Madhyamaka treatises. Chinese readers preferred Kumārajīva's stylish translations to those of Xuanzang (596–664), whose meticulous translations retain traces of Sanskrit syntax and grammar that he had studied during his years in India.

Chinese catalogs of translated scriptures in monastic libraries provided information on the dating and translation of Buddhist scriptures. The earliest extant catalog, *A Compilation of Notices on the Translation of the Tripiṭaka* (*Chu sanzang jiji*) by Sengyou (445–518) preserved portions of an earlier catalog by Dao'an. Sengyou's catalog distinguishes between new or old translations, authentic Indian texts and spurious scriptures, complete and abridged translations, mainstream and Mahāyāna works, and those scriptures with know and unknown translators. The Tang dynasty (618–907) catalogs were compiled after the translation of most scriptures into Chinese was completed. Zhisheng's *Catalog of the Kaiyuan era on Buddhism* (*Kaiyuan shijao*) completed in 730 was the most thorough in its chronological arrangement of translations and descriptions of different translators and translations. This catalog influenced the organization of all subsequent East Asian editions of the canon, including the modern Taishō. The compilers of these early catalogs made an effort to determine which of the plethora of scriptures in monastic libraries were genuine Chinese translations of Indic originals and which were spurious texts (*wei jing*) or texts of doubtful authenticity (*i jing*). Not all of their efforts succeeded; some apocryphal texts credited to well-known foreign translators were accepted as genuine, such as Kumārajīva's translation of the *Brahma's Net Sūtra* (*Fanwang Jing*) and the *Awakening of Faith* (*Dasheng Qixin Lun*), attributed to Aśvaghoṣa (first to second century CE) and translated by Paramārtha (499–569).

For centuries Buddhist scriptures were hand-copied on silk and paper scrolls. Some of these Tang manuscripts were preserved in the Dunhuang caves, sealed shut early in the eleventh century. Other Tang manuscripts were engraved on stone slabs found in caves in Fang shan. A complete canon of scriptures was not produced until the Song dynasty when block-printing technology facilitated the massive undertaking. In 927 the Song court authorized the carving of the canon onto wooden printing blocks. The massive work of carving 13,000 with the contents of over 1,000 works was completed in 984 and the resultant Shu edition was widely disseminated. In northern China, the Mongol rulers of the Liao dynasty printed another set of blocks in 1055 based on the Shu edition. These two editions formed the basis for the Korean Koryŏ dynasty editions, made during the reigns of Hyeonjong (r. 1009–31) and Munjong (r. 1046–82). In 1232 a new set of blocks was ordered and the 81,000 carved blocks were completed in 1251. The monk Sugi and his staff compared manuscripts and old blocks to check readings and make editorial changes. The blocks of the Sugi edition, housed in Haein-sa monasteries, are the oldest version of the Chinese canon. The Research Institute of the Tripiṭaka Koreana of the Haein Monastery in South Korea has published a CD-ROM version of the 1236–51 edition of the Korean Buddhist canon.

Sponsored by courts and large temples, other editions of the Chinese canon, based on the Shu edition, were produced during the Chin (1115–1234) and Yuan (1280–1368) dynasties. The abbots of Dong chan temple in the Fukien province sponsored a new and enlarged edition, begun in 1080 and completed in 1176. This edition's enlarged content and its reader-friendly format, with paper folded accordion-style rather than rolled in scrolls, influenced the production of later editions. During the Mongol Yuan dynasty, other editions were printed at Pu ning Temple in Hangzhou during the years 1278–94, at the Hung fa temple in Beijing from 1277 to 1294, and a court-sponsored edition in the Tangut script printed at the Da wan shou temple in Hangzhou. Two editions were printed during the Ming dynasty; one, sponsored by Emperor Hung wu (r. 1368–98) and printed in Nanjing, was based on the southern Dong Chan edition; the other, based on the northern Shu edition, was printed in Beijing.

The first complete edition of the Chinese canon in Japan was begun by the monk Tenkai in 1633 and completed in 1645; a second edition was completed by Tetsugen in 1681. The nineteenth and early twentieth centuries saw the completion of three Japanese editions. The Dainippon Kōtei Daizōkyō, known as the Tokyo edition, was printed in 1880–5 by the Kōkyō Shoin of Tokyo. This edition was based on the Korean Koryŏ edition and compared earlier Chinese and Japanese editions. During the years 1902–5, the Zōkyō Shoin of Kyoto put out another edition, the Dainippon Kōtei Zōkyō, known as the Kyoto edition. The 1924–34 Taishō Shinshū Daizōkyō edition, in eighty-five volumes containing 2,920 texts, has become the standard reference for the Chinese canon; citations from this edition are indicated by the abbreviation T. followed by the document number. The editors, under direction of Takakusu Junjiro, used the Koryŏ edition as their primary source. They compared its readings with previous Chinese and Korean editions, and consulted the Pāli and Tibetan canons for Pāli and Tibetan translations of parallel texts. The Taishō edition of the canon contains more the traditional *tripiṭaka* of *Sūtra*, *Vinaya*, and *Abhidharma* texts. Historical works, biographies of eminent monks and nuns, meditation and ritual manuals, and even reproduction of iconographies are included. The first fifty-five volumes of the Taishō edition contain the scriptures of the Chinese canon; Japanese texts are included in Volumes 56 to 84. Volume 85 contains Dunhuang texts and apocryphal texts composed in China; Volumes 86 to 97 reproduce iconographies, and Volumes 98 to 100 provide bibliographical information. An international team of Buddhist scholars, assembled by Dr. Yehan Numata, began translating the Taishō collection of Chinese texts into English in 1982. The Chinese Buddhist Electronic Text Association (CBETA) has made the Indian and Chinese sections of the Taishō available online.

See also: **Digital research resources; Electronic publications; Pāli canon; Textual authority: the *Catuḥpratisaraṇa Sūtra*; *Tripiṭaka*, Sanskrit and Prakrit; *Tripiṭaka*, Tibetan; *Tripiṭaka* and word of the Buddha.**

KAREN C. LANG

TRIPIṬAKA, SANSKRIT AND PRAKṚIT

In a well-known and much-discussed passage in the Pāli *Vinaya* (2. 139) two brahmin converts complain to the Buddha that monastics from different backgrounds spoil the discourses by reciting them in accord with their own manner of speaking (*sakāya niruttiyā*). They request permission to recite the discourses in the same manner as the *Vedas*. The Buddha responds by prohibiting these monastics from reciting the discourses (Skt. *sūtra*, Pāli *sutta*) in such a manner and enjoins all monastics to transmit the texts in their own manner of speech. The *Vinayas* of other schools contain similar versions of this story. All these versions indicate the Buddhist preference for retaining regional speech over the Sanskrit of the educated brahmin class, thus ensuring the widespread dissemination of the Buddha's teachings.

As Buddhism spread into different regions of India, the Buddhist teaching, passed down orally from one generation of disciples to another, must have been transmitted and preserved in number of different languages or dialects. At some point, the schools that developed in these regions may have chosen to render their *sūtra* holdings which had been collected and preserved up to that point in the multitude of different regional dialects into a *lingua franca*, capable of being understood by monastics from different regions. Sanskrit became a "church" language used for translating scriptures by monastics who were most likely more fluent in local languages or dialects. The anomalous forms that occur in "church" languages such as Pāli and Buddhist Sanskrit may represent the remnants of recensions in other languages. Buddhist scriptures found in Afghanistan, northern India and Pakistan, the oases of Central Asia and Xinjiang, show varying degrees of adaptation from earlier Prakrit or Middle Indo-Aryan languages to classical Sanskrit.

Manuscripts continue to be found, but much of the Buddhist canonical literature composed in Sanskrit is now lost and known only through Tibetan and Chinese translations. The *Vinayas* of several schools have survived, along with some *Sūtra* and *Abhidharma* texts. Early twentieth-century expeditions led by Aurel Stein, Paul Pelliot, Albert Grünwedel, and Kozui Otani excavated Central Asian ruins along the Silk Road and brought back to Europe and Japan numerous manuscripts in Buddhist Sanskrit. The excavation of a *stūpa* in the Gilgit region of Kashmir in 1931 also yielded a large cache of Sanskrit texts – 3,000 folios written on birch bark and some paper manuscripts – dating from sixth and seventh centuries CE. Other recently discovered Buddhist Sanskrit manuscripts, the Schøyen collection, may have come from a monastic library in Bāmiyān. The Bāmiyān manuscripts, written on palm leaf, birch bark, vellum, and leather, date from second to eighth century CE. The manuscripts from Bāmiyān and Gilgit include several Mahāyāna texts, unlike the Gandhārī Buddhist manuscript collections that date from first to the third centuries CE.

Buddhist settlements flourished in Gandhāra (northern Pakistan and eastern Afghanistan) under the first century CE patronage of the Kuṣāṇa dynasty king, Kaniṣka. The fifty-five Gandhārī manuscripts in the "Senior Collection" and the twenty-nine Gandhārī scrolls of the British Library collection suggest that there was a canon or proto-canon in Gandhārī, a middle Indo-Aryan vernacular language. Many of the fifty-five *sūtras* in the "Senior Collection" correspond to Pāli canonical texts that comprise the "Connected Collection," the "Middle Length Collection" and the "Long Collection" (*Saṁyutta Nikāya*, *Majjhima Nikāya*, and *Dīgha Nikāya*). The British Library collection of fragmentary birch-bark manuscripts reflects the contents of a Gandhāran Buddhist monastery's library of the first centuries CE. This cache of manuscripts, found in Afghanistan buried in clay pots, include *Abhidharma* texts, *sūtra* and many hagiographical *Avadāna* texts. Parallels to known canonical literature include the *Words of Dharma* (*Dharmapada*) and the *Rhinoceros Horn Sūtra* (*Khaḍgaviṣāṇasūtra*) of the "Collection of Minor Texts" (Skt. *Kṣudraka*, Pāli *Khuddaka Nikāya*). Some of the *Avadāna* texts have no known parallels and may be locally composed materials unique to the Gandhāran region.

A Mahāyāna canon

Around the first century CE, debate over the interpretation of the Buddha's word (*Buddhavacana*) contributed to the writing and rewriting of new *sūtras* with new analyses of the Buddha's teachings. Although the origins of the Mahāyāna movement remain obscure, most scholars agree that it developed in monastic circles. Chinese pilgrims report that the minority of monks who supported its vision lived in the same monastic institutions as the other monks whom they criticized for following an inferior path (*Hīnayāna*). The new *sūtras* they created, though often longer in length, were modeled on older paradigms. These *sūtras* were presented in the form of dialogs between Śākyamuni Buddha and his disciples that took place in various regions in central India, often on Vulture Peak. The anonymous creators of these Mahāyāna *sūtras* and the *Dharma*-preachers (*dharmabhāṇakas*) who memorized and recited them in public regarded these works as the Buddha's word: "Whatever is well spoken is the word of the Buddha." The Buddha to these anonymous authors and *Dharma*-preachers revealed some of these *sūtras* in meditations, visions, and dreams. Other *sūtras*, the "Perfection of Insight" texts (*Prajñāpāramitā Sūtra*), claimed to be teachings entrusted by the Buddha to semi-divine beings, the serpent-like *nāgas*, until the time came when there were people receptive to their profound, deep teachings. The *Dharma*-preachers also encouraged others to copy and preserve these texts.

The earliest extant manuscript copy of a Mahāyāna *sūtra* was produced around the second century CE, although these scriptures may have been circulating orally and in manuscripts centuries earlier. This incomplete manuscript of *The Perfection of Insight Sūtra in Eight Thousand Lines* (*Aṣṭasāhasrikāprajñāpāramitā*) was recovered among the fragmentary palm-leaf manuscripts from Bāmiyān. The language in the text is a kind of Buddhist Sanskrit, a mixture of Sanskrit and Prakrit. Later compositions varied in length from the short versions, the *Diamond* (*Vajracchedika*) *Sūtra* and the *Heart (Hṛdaya) Sūtra*, to the lengthy *The Perfection of Insight in 100,000 Lines* (*Śatasasrikāprajñāpāramitā*). Manuscript copies of the *Diamond Sūtra* have been found in Bāmiyān and Gilgit, but the *Heart Sūtra* may have been an original composition in Chinese, translated back into Sanskrit, possibly by Xuanzang (596–664). The *Perfection of Insight Sūtras* criticize the path of the *arhat* for its self-centered concern with the attainment of *nirvāṇa*. As an alternative, these *sūtras* advocate the *bodhisattva*'s path because this practice balances the pursuit of insight with compassion for others. This path is greater, they argued, because it begins with the intention (*bodhicitta*) to work for the awakening of all sentient beings. *Bodhisattvas* in the course of their careers must perfect six virtuous qualities (*pāramitā*), beginning with generosity, moral conduct, patience, energy, meditation, and culminating with insight.

Some early Mahāyāna *sūtra*s, such as the *Immovable One's Pure Land* (*Akṣobhyavyūha*), the *Pure Land of Bliss(Sukhāvatīvyūha)*, and the *Bhaiṣajya Guru Sūtra*, found at in Bāmiyān and Gilgit depict the pure lands of Mahāyāna Buddhas, Akṣobhya (the Immovable) Buddha, Amitābha (Infinite Light) Buddha, and the Bhaiṣajya (Medicine) Buddha, and the vows they took as *bodhisattvas* that resulted in the creation of their pure lands. The stages of *bodhisattva* path and the *bodhisattva*'s journey are also the focus of two influential scriptures included within the vast *Avataṁsaka* collection, the *Ten Stages* (*Daśabhūmika*) and the *Array of Flowers* (*Gaṇḍavyūha*). Because of this focus on the acts of *bodhisattvas*, collections of Mahāyāna *sūtras* are described as a *bodhisattva* canon (*bodhisattvapiṭaka*).

Manuscript copies of several of these Mahāyāna *sūtras* survive in large numbers of medieval and modern Sanskrit manuscripts because Buddhists in Nepal use nine of these scriptures – the *Perfection of Insight Sūtra in Eight Thousand Lines*, the *Lotus Sūtra*, the *Descent to Laṅka* (*Laṅkāvatāra*), the *Ten Stages Sūtra*, the *Array of Flowers Sūtra*, the *King of Concentrations* (*Samādhirāja*) *Sūtra*, the *Golden Light* (*Suvarṇaprabhāsa*) *Sūtra*, the *Graceful Description* (*Lalitavistara*, a hagiography of the Buddha), and the *Secret Assembly* (*Guhyasamāja*) *Tantra* – in the ritual practice of devotion to the *Dharma*.

The *Secret Assembly Tantra* is one of a new genre of Buddhist scriptures, attributed to Śākyamuni Buddha. These *tantras*, like some early Mahāyāna *sūtras*, claimed to be revelations acquired from Buddhas through meditation, visions, and dreams. Some of these scriptures may date back as early as the fifth century CE but most were composed between the eighth and eleventh centuries, when the Vajrayāna path was followed in both lay and monastic circles. The *tantras* were written in a non-standard Sanskrit, which often used coded language (*sandhya bhāṣā*) that required that a teacher (*guru*) initiate and instruct disciples about these scriptures' hidden meanings. Teachers' explanations also aided students in the practice of specific rituals and visualization techniques incorporated in the *tantras*. The scriptures from the highest class of *tantras* (*anuttarayoga*), such as the *Secret Assembly Tantra*, the *O Thunderbolt* (*Hevajra*) *Tantra*, and the *Wheel of Time* (*Kālacakra*) *Tantra*, employed sexual imagery to depict the stages of the Vajrayāna path. These *tantras* also generated an extensive commentarial literature, composed by monastic exegetes, to explain the esoteric context of these sexual images. The eleventh-century *Wheel of Time Tantra*, the last *tantra* composed in India, refers to the Muslim invaders' conquest of India; the commentaries explain that the real war is between the forces of ignorance and enlightenment within the Vajrayāna practitioner's own mind.

The libraries of the great Indian monastic universities, Nālandā, Odantapurī, and Vikramalaśīla, contain manuscript copies of *sūtras* and *tantras* and an extensive commentarial literature on both genres. The manuscript collections of these monastic libraries may have constituted a

Sanskrit canon but there are no extant catalogs that might have determined whether there was a separate Mahāyāna *bodhisattva* canon or, even less probable, a Vajrayāna canon.

See also: **Canons and literature; Mahāyāna Buddhism; Pāli canon; *Tripiṭaka*, Chinese; *Tripiṭaka*, Tibetan.**

KAREN C. LANG

TRIPIṬAKA, TIBETAN

The Tibetan edition of the Buddhist *Tripiṭaka* is divided into two parts: translations (*'gyur*) of the word (*bka'*) of the Buddha, known as the Kanjur (*bka 'gyur*), and translations of the treatises (*bstan*) attributed to Indian masters, known as the Tenjur (*bstan 'gyur*). The Kanjur and Tenjur refer to various edited collections of Buddhist scriptures translated into Tibetan from Indic languages and Chinese. The Kanjur collections contain over 1,000 discourses (*sūtras*, *tantras*) and the Tenjur collections contain over 3,000 commentaries and independent treatises (*bstan bcos*). Early in the fourteenth century, at Narthang (*Snar thang*) monastery, Tibetan scholars compiled translations made over a 500-year period and determined which of these to include in an authoritative collection of Buddhist scripture.

The transmission of Buddhism into Tibet

According to Tibetan historical works, the first transmission of Buddhism began with the reign of Songtsen Gampo (Srong bstan sgam po, *c*. 622–50), whose minister, Thonmi Sambhoṭa, devised a Tibetan script based on Indian models and completed the first translations of Buddhist *sūtras* into Tibetan. Trisong Detsen (Khri srong lde brtsan, r. 755–97) sent Tibetans to collect Buddhist texts from India, Nepal, China, and Central Asia, and invited scholars from these regions to assist in translating these texts into Tibetan. These early Tibetan translations from texts composed in Sanskrit, Chinese, and various Indic and Central Asian languages were difficult to comprehend and unsystematic. Trisong Detsen's son and grandson, Tride Songsen (Khri lde srong brtsan, r. 800–15) and Relpa Chen (Ral pa can, r. 815–38), commissioned Indian and Tibetan scholars to develop grammars, dictionaries, and guidelines that would simplify and standardize the translation of Buddhist texts. These scholars revised old translations with the aid of the *Great Dictionary* (*Mahāvyutpatti*) and made them more accurate and readable.

At Samye (Bsam yas) monastery and other smaller monasteries, teams of Tibetan translators working with Indian and Chinese collaborators, had produced a large body of translated texts, kept in monastery and palace libraries. The ninth-century catalog of translations held in the Denkar (Ldan/Lhan dkar) palace listed *sūtras*, followed by *tantras* and *dhāraṇīs*, hymns of praise, texts on monastic disciple (*vinaya*), and *sūtra* commentaries and other treatises. Nearly 500 of its 736 titles are *sūtras*, beginning with the *Perfection of Insight (Prajñāpāramitā) Sūtras*, *Flower Garland (Avataṃsaka) Sūtras*, *Jewel Peak* (*Ratnakūṭa*) *Sūtras*, miscellaneous Mahāyāna *sūtras*, and ending with Hīnayāna *sūtras*. A small number of *sūtras* and *sūtra* commentaries were listed as translations from Chinese. Outside central Tibet, many Tibetan translations made from Chinese texts were found in the Silk Road oasis of Dunhuang. This collection of Tibetan manuscripts included both translations with archaic orthography and terminology, dating back to the Tibetan occupation of Dunhuang in the eighth century, and newer, revised translations, all sealed in a cave early in the eleventh century.

With the assassination of Relpa Chen, the first transmission of Buddhism came to a close. The second transmission began with the efforts of kings in western Tibet to re-establish close relations with Indian Buddhists. Yeshe Ö (Ye she 'od) sent twenty-one young Tibetans to Kashmir to study Buddhism and collect Buddhist texts. Rinchen Zangpo (Rin chen bzang po, 958–1056), one of two survivors to return to Tibet, brought back several Indian scholars to assist him in translating. After Yeshe Ö's death, his grandson, Ö de ('Od lde) persuaded Atiśa (982–1054) to leave the Indian monastic university of Vikramaśīla for western Tibet, where he trained disciples and assisted in translation work. Rinchen Zangpo and Atīśa revised many older, inaccurate translations and also translated many previously unknown texts, including *tantras* that had surfaced in India after the ninth century. Indian scholars and their textual tradition shaped the direction of the Tibetan Buddhist canon.

The formation of the Tibetan canon

Early in the fourteenth century, Narthang monastery became a central repository for thousands of original manuscripts and copies brought together from monastic libraries all over central and western Tibet. Monks learned in the canon (Skt. *piṭakadhara*, Tib. *sde snod 'dzin pa*) began work in 1311 on the first Kanjur and Tenjur collections, each totaling over 100 volumes. The colophons to the *sūtra* section of this "Old Narthang" canon state that the Kanjur was compiled from more than 3,000 translations, from the *sūtra* collections of a dozen monasteries. Butön Rinchendrup (Bu ston Rin chen 'grub, 1290–1364) played a major role in selecting, editing, and classifying these texts. He compared the massive collection of manuscripts at Narthang with those listed in the Denkar catalog and in the catalogs of several monastic libraries. His arrangement of texts was based on the catalogs' lists, but he went beyond their simple inventories of manuscripts to establish criteria for limiting the number and type of texts included in the Kanjur and Tenjur. The most important criterion was that the text was an accurate translation of a genuine Indic manuscript. Among the texts he included in the Kanjur were thirteen texts recently translated from Pāli by the Sinhalese monk Ānandasri and his Tibetan collaborator, Nyima Gyaltsen (Nyi ma rgyal mtshan). The fifteenth-century Tibetan historical work, the *Blue Annals* (*Deb ther sngon po*), stated that Butön brought the Tenjur from Narthang to his home monastery in Zwalu, removed the duplicate texts, and added over 1,000 new texts. Many monasteries in the fourteenth and fifteenth centuries commissioned copies of the Narthang Kanjur and Tenjur for their own libraries. These canonical collections conveyed prestige upon the monasteries holding them and the manuscripts were themselves the focus of Buddhist devotion.

The Kanjur has three main sections: *Vinaya*, *Sūtra*, and *Tantra*. The *Vinaya* section's texts on monastic discipline are from the Mūlasarvāstivādin schools. The *Sūtra* section includes *Perfection of Insight Sūtras*, *Flower Garland Sūtras*, *Jewel Peak Sūtras*, and miscellaneous *sūtras*, primarily Mahāyāna. The *Tantra* section's more than 300 texts follow Butön's arrangement into four main classes: *Action Tantra* (*Kriyā Tantra*), *Performance Tantra*(*Caryā Tantra*), *Yoga Tantra* and *Highest Yoga* (*anuttarayoga*) *Tantra*. The arrangement of the Tenjur's collection of more than 3,000 texts begins with *Hymns of Praise to the Buddhas*, followed by *Commentaries on the Tantras* and *Commentaries on the Perfection of Insight Sūtras*, Mādhyamika treatises, Yogācāra treatises, *Abhidharma* treatises, *Vinaya* commentaries, *Avadāna* and *Jātaka* stories, letters, and technical treatises on logic and epistemology (*pramāṇa*), linguistics (*śabdavidyā*), medicine, iconography, poetic meters, political treatises (*nītiśāstra*), and Atiśa's minor treatises.

The sections and the number and order of the individual texts within sections are not the same in all Tibetan *Tripiṭakas.* Differences occur in classifying the sequence of the Buddha's teachings and reflect sectarian preferences in the inclusion and order of specific *tantras.* Some Kanjur collections include the Nyingma (Rnying ma) *tantras* that Butön excluded because he doubted their Indian provenance. *The Wheel of Time* (*Kālacakra*) *Tantra* commentaries come first in the Peking Tenjur, which follows Butön's preference for the Kālacakra cycle, while in Derge Tenjur the commentaries on the *O Vajra* (*Hevajra*) *Tantra* favored by the Sakya school (Sa skya) come first. Transmissions of texts occurred outside of the Kanjur and Tenjur collections. The Nyingma scholar, Ratna Lingpa (Ratna gLing pa, 1403–78), incorporated the Tantras Butön considered inauthentic into the Nyingma's canon of authoritative texts, the *Collected Tantras of the Ancients* (*Rnying ma rgyud 'bum*).

There is no standard edition of the Tibetan canon. Kanjurs and Tenjurs come from different regions of Tibet and have a complex history of transmission. Most editions of the Kanjur come from manuscript collections of Tshal and Zhwalu monasteries. The Tshal manuscripts were used for the first woodblock print of the Kanjur, completed in Beijing in 1411. The texts were carved on long narrow blocks of wood shaped like palmleaf manuscripts, the blocks were inked and paper placed to them to make copies. This Chinese printing technology simplified and encouraged the production of Kanjurs and Tenjurs, although elegant hand-written copies, especially of *Perfection of Insight Sūtras*, continued to be made. In the eighteenth century numerous editions of the *Tripiṭaka* were produced based on "Old Narthang" manuscripts: the Ganden (dGa' ldan) monastery's *Golden Manuscript of the Tenjur*; the New Narthang blockprint edition of the Kanjur in 1731 and the Tenjur in 1742; the Peking edition of the Kanjur and Tenjur prepared in 1737; and the Derge (sDe dge) and Chone (Co ne) editions completed by 1772. The variant readings of these editions are attributable to errors in carving the blocks or differences in orthography, which confirm the close connection between the Peking and Narthang editions and the Derge and Chone editions. Modern published editions of the Tibetan canon include the Chone, published in microfiche by the Institute for the Advanced Studies of World Religions, Stonybrook, New York; 1974; the Derge, published by the Faculty of Letters, Tokyo University, 1981; and the Peking, published by the Tibetan Tripitaka Research Institute, Tokyo and Kyoto, 1955–61.

See also: **Canons and literature; Pāli canon; Tibet, Buddhism in; *Tripiṭaka*, Chinese; *Tripiṭaka*, Sanskrit and Pāli; *Tripiṭaka* and word of the Buddha.**

KAREN C. LANG

TRIPIṬAKA AND WORD OF THE BUDDHA

The *Tripiṭaka* ("three baskets") represents the collection of scriptures of Buddhism. Although almost all schools of Buddhism agree on the use of the term *Tripiṭaka* (Pāli *Tipiṭaka*) to refer to their scriptures, the schools do not agree on the contents of the *Tripiṭaka*. The Theravāda school's *Tipiṭaka* comprises some forty volumes (including multivolume works) while the various Mahāyāna schools include many more texts in their respective *Tripiṭakas.* The Theravāda understanding of the *Tripiṭaka* (which will constitute the focus of this brief article) divides the scriptures into three collections: the *Sutta Piṭaka*, the *Vinaya Piṭaka* and the *Abhidhamma Piṭaka*. As their names imply, the three sections of the *Tripiṭaka* contain different kinds of texts. The *Sutta Piṭaka* contains narratives and philosophical teachings, the stories of the Buddha's discourses and those of his disciples to various audiences in various places in India. The *Vinaya Piṭaka* contains primarily the rules governing the monastic life and other related material such as monastic legal opinions concerning the rules and historical accounts of the First and Second Councils. The *Abhidhamma Piṭaka* contains seven texts that analyze the *Dharma* in various philosophical, psychological, contemplative and scholastic ways. These three collections of texts are all held to represent "the word of the Buddha" or *buddhavacana*.

According to Buddhist tradition, a council was held at Rājagṛha soon after the death or final *nirvāṇa* of the Buddha. At this First Council, the *arhats* who had accompanied the Buddha met and recited his teachings in order to commit them to memory. Ānanda, the chief disciple of the Buddha, recited the *Dharma* in the form of the *Sutta Piṭaka* and Upāli recited the *Vinaya Piṭaka* or rules for the order. The earliest Theravāda accounts of the First Council do not mention the *Abhidhamma Piṭaka* being recited at that council, but it is mentioned by other and later sources. The Theravāda *Tipiṭaka* was transmitted orally until the end of the first century BCE, when it was written down at Alu Vihāra in Sri Lanka because the elders of the Mahāvihāra wanted to protect and preserve the *Dharma* at a difficult and dangerous time.

By designating the *Tripiṭaka* "the word of the Buddha," or *buddhavacana*, Buddhists identified these texts with the authoritative *Dharma* taught by the founder. Within the Theravāda school two interpretations of this designation arose. Some Theravādins held that the phrase "the word of the Buddha" meant that all of the material in the scriptures had been literally spoken by the Buddha. The Pāli Commentaries to the *Tripiṭaka*, for example, defined "the word of the Buddha" as all the words said by the Buddha from his first words after attaining enlightenment to his final words before entering *parinirvāṇa*.

Buddhists who have accepted this view have believed that the councils served as the medium for preserving and transmitting these truths. Another interpretation of "the word of the Buddha" seems to have arisen quite early, however, to deal with problems inherent in this literalist view. Buddhists recognized that the *Tripiṭaka* contained a great variety of material and that some of that material could not literally be considered "the word of the Buddha." A number of *sūtras*, for example, are explicitly said to be teachings given by disciples, and some *sūtras* mention kings and other persons who lived after the time of the Buddha. In addition there is the problem of the *Abhidhamma Piṭaka*, which was not mentioned in the accounts of the First Council and contains material that seems clearly secondary and analytical in nature.

The second interpretation of "the word of the Buddha" suggests a more liberal approach that is consonant with the diverse nature of the material in the *Tripiṭakas* of the various schools of Buddhism. This explanation allows the view that the contents of the *Tripiṭaka* developed over a long period of time rather than being fixed soon after the death of the Buddha. The roots for this interpretation can be found in the *Tripiṭaka* itself in the *Mahāpadesa Sutta* (*Dīgha Nikāya* 2.123) which sets out the criteria and a procedure for deciding which teachings can be accepted as "the word of the Buddha." The key criteria here are called the "four great authorities" or *Mahāpadesa*, and the *sutta* explains how to weigh the validity of teachings heard from these authorities. The "four great authorities" are (1) the Buddha, (2) a complete *sangha* with wise *theras* (elders), (3) a group of *theras* who are learned in at least one of the three *piṭakas*, and (4) a single *thera* who is learned in at least one of the three *piṭakas*. On receiving a teaching from one of these four authorities, the hearer should neither accept nor reject the status of the teaching as "the word of the Buddha." Rather, while suspending judgment, the hearer should compare the teaching in question with an established core of teachings called "*sutta* and *vinaya*." If it compares favorably, that is, if it is consistent with the accepted core of teachings, it can be regarded as "the word of the Buddha." Clearly, this procedure and these guidelines seem to point both to the way in which the *Tripiṭaka* evolved during the early history of Buddhism and to the explanation for how some apparently late texts came to be included. According to this procedure, "the word of the Buddha" becomes a formal category that does not necessarily mean that the Buddha actually spoke these words, but only that they conform in some way to what were taken to be the basic lines of his teachings. The reasoning here is similar to the idea expressed in one of Aśoka's edicts which says, "All the words of the Buddha are well said." In this case, however, the idea is interpreted to mean also that anything that is well said represents a "word of the Buddha." This explanation of the "word of the Buddha" emphasizes the wisdom of the Buddha rather than his historical career as the primary source of these "words." Although a wise teaching may not have actually been spoken by the Buddha, it could be considered the "word of the Buddha" because of the Buddha's omniscience, his boundless "granary" of wisdom.

See also: **Canons and literature; Textual authority, the *Catuḥpratisaraṇa Sūtra*; *Tripiṭaka*, Chinese; *Tripiṭaka*, Sanskrit and Prakrit; *Tripiṭaka*, Tibetan.**

GEORGE D. BOND

TSOME, KARMA LEKSHE

Karma Lekshe Tsomo is an American-born nun ordained in the Tibetan tradition (Vajrayāna). She is an Assistant Professor in the Department of Theology and Religious Studies at the University of San Diego. She graduated from the University of Hawaii with a doctorate in comparative philosophy. She also holds M.A. degrees in Asian Studies and in Religion (both from the University of Hawaii), and a B.A. from the University of California, Berkeley, in Japanese. She is one of the founders of Sakyadhītā, along with Chatsumarn Kabilsingh and Ayya Khema. She has organized nine Sakyadhītā conferences on women in Buddhism and edited the volumes that have issued from them: *Sakyadhītā: Daughters of the Buddha* (1989); *Buddhism Through American Women's Eyes* (1995); *Buddhist Women Across Cultures: Realizations* (1999); and *Innovative Buddhist Women: Swimming Against the Stream* (2000). She has also edited *Buddhist Women and Social Justice: Ideals, Challenges, and Achievements* (2004), and co-edited (with David W. Chappell) *Living and Dying in Buddhist Cultures* (1997). She has written on Buddhist monastic discipline for women, *Sisters in Solitude: Two Traditions of Buddhist Monastic Ethics for Women* (1996) and translated *Jorcho: Preparatory Practices* (n.d.). She has written numerous articles, participated in countless forums, given a plethora of talks, produced the *Sakhyadhītā* newsletter and coordinated the website, and in 1994 she was awarded a United Nations' Outstanding Women in Buddhism Award for her work.

Born Patricia Jean Zenn, she grew up around the Malibu Beach area of California. In the foreword to *Sisters in Solitude*, she notes that teasing about her surname, which sounded to schoolmates like "Zen," caused her to read about Buddhism and at age eleven she announced to her Southern Baptist mother that she was a Buddhist. She later dropped out of Occidental College, spent a few years in Japan and traveling in Asia, then returned to the United States to study at Berkeley. In 1972 she traveled to Dharamsala, India, to study Tibetan and there met Geshe Ngawang Dhargyey. Her interaction with him convinced her that she was meant for the monastic life. She took her novice vows in France in 1977, unaware that full *bhikṣuṇī* ordination was not available in the Tibetan Vajrayāna tradition. She took full ordination in 1982 in Korea and then in Taiwan.

Karma Lekshe Tsomo has dedicated her life to improving the situation of women within Buddhism, particularly those women who wish to become fully ordained *bhikṣuṇī*. It is her belief that a strong *bhikṣuṇī sangha* would not only benefit Buddhism but could act as a link between women cross-culturally. The challenges are many and the issues facing women vary culturally: Western women and Asian women frequently face different obstacles to religious life. In two recent articles, "Family, Monastery, and Gender Justice" and "Buddhist Nuns: Changes and Challenges," she reflects on the issues with which she has grappled for thirty years. Two issues that affect women's ability to develop spiritually are, ironically, the same for women from both Asia and the West. The first has to do with education. In Asia it is a question of both secular and religious education. Without education, women have neither the confidence nor the tools to work towards equal opportunity in lay or monastic life. Without education, women in religious life are not respected by lay people and as a consequence they receive fewer donations, compounding their inability to sustain themselves. Nunneries that do exist are often in quite remote areas, making access to teachers difficult. As well, many people believe that birth as a woman is evidence of a lesser birth and thus women do not possess the ability to learn the *Dharma*. Finally, there is plain sexism. Tsomo talks of the difficulty she had in getting male teachers to teach nuns in the Himalayan region. Twice male teachers were harassed by members of their home monastery for teaching women. She founded Jamyang monastery in Ladakh in 1987 and it now has six different educational programs for women.

Religious education can be a problem for women in the West as well. There are few teachers. Asian male teachers often travel extensively, making teaching and guidance difficult. Asian teachers may not have experience with female students and may be reluctant to teach them. Some do not have good English language skills. As more Western women become teachers this problem is lessening.

A second major issue is one with which Karma Lekshe Tsomo herself has grappled. That is, the question of maintaining oneself. In both Asia and the West the problem is the provision of the necessaries of life. While nuns in Asia are generally poorly supported and monasteries for them must struggle, there is a tradition of lay donations for support. The West, particularly North America, is not a culture that embraces monasticism and donations are not readily forthcoming. There are few monasteries to provide a supportive environment for learning and practicing. Some, like Tsomo herself, are highly educated and can support themselves, but they also may be isolated from a community of common interest.

In her writings, Tsomo constantly points to the model provided by Taiwan and Korea for examples of what a *bhikṣuṇī sangha* can provide for Buddhism, monastic women and society in general. Nuns from these countries are well educated and quite active in social service. They hold positions of authority and have achieved some equality with monks. They provide a model of well-disciplined and hard-working nuns for countries without a *bhikṣuṇī sangha*.

Tsomo continues to work for improvement in the lives of female nuns in Buddhism and for full ordination where it does not exist. While she notes in "Buddhist Nuns: Changes and Challenges" that full ordination has been more of a concern to Western women, she, with Chatsumarn Kabilsingh, Ayya Khema, Ranjanī de Silva and others, has created an international network of Buddhist women. This is a first for Buddhism.

As well as her work with Sakyadhītā, Karma Lekshe Tsomo has worked on the scholarly aspects of the ordination issue. Her own work has included a translation of the *Mūlasarvātivāda Bhikṣuṇī Prātimokṣa Sūtra* and a comparison of it with the Chinese Dharmagupta version (translated by Shu-lien Miao). One of the arguments given by some Tibetan and Theravāda scholars for rejecting the ordinations of *bhikṣuṇī* by Chinese or Korean nuns and monks is that these traditions are Mahāyāna and so not acceptable for Vajrayāna or Theravāda *bhikṣuṇī*. Translations of the various *Vinayas* and comparison between them serves to indicate whether they are sufficiently similar in nature to be acceptable, and whether the rules that are additional to one may be considered "minor" and ignored according to the Buddha's instructions that the minor rules might be suspended after his death.

Tsomo notes that although every *Vinaya* extant contains more rules for *bhikṣuṇīs* than it does for *bhikṣus*, and many of these rules seem to either subordinate or denigrate women, this does not support the conclusion that Buddhism is irredeemably sexist, nor does it support some male commentators who would argue that they show the unsuitability of women for religious life. It is necessary to look at these additional rules and try to determine their intent given the social circumstances of the time. In "Is the Bhikṣuṇī *Vinaya* Sexist?" Tsomo examines some of the additional rules and the eight special rules (*gurudharma*) for women instituted at the time of the creation of the *bhikṣuṇī sangha*. Her conclusion is that many of the rules for women were instituted as a means of protecting them from men, including monks. The *gurudharma* she sees as having an administrative function and, although discriminatory to women, it was based on the only model available at that time in Indian society. The Buddhist record is mixed. From its origins in a patriarchal culture it integrated some of that milieu; it did, however, make some important divergences from the status quo. These can form the basis for actualizing the ideal of women's equal participation in Buddhist practice.

See also: **Sakyadhītā; Women in Buddhism: an historical and textual overview.**

MAVIS L. FENN

TSONG KHAPA

Tsong Khapa Losang Drakpa (Tsong kha pa bLo bzang grags pa, 1357–1419) was one of Tibet's most influential scholars and reformers. Born in the Tsongkha Valley of Amdo, he was ordained as a monk by the fourth Gyelwa Karmapa, Rolbe Dorje (rGyal dbang Kar ma pa Rol pa'i rdo rje, 1340–83), at the age of three. He received his novice vows at the age of seven and was given the name Losang Drakpa. At an early age, he began traveling throughout the Tibetan cultural area and studying with teachers from a range of traditions, and is said to have excelled in comprehension of Indian Buddhist philosophical literature and *tantra*. He was also renowned as a debater, and oral philosophical debate continues to be an important component of the educational system of the order he founded, the Gelukpa (dGe lugs pa).

His writings indicate a deep concern with what he perceived as a tendency toward laxness with regard to monastic discipline (Tib. *'dul ba*, Skt. *Vinaya*) among his contemporaries. The sexual techniques of highest yoga *tantra* (Tib. *bla na med pa'i rnal 'byor*, Skt. *anuttara-yoga-tantra*) were regarded by most Tibetans of his time as the supreme of all Buddhist meditative practices, but they are incompatible with cenobitic monasticism, which Tsong Khapa believed to be the best path for the majority of Buddhists. While acknowledging the supremacy of highest yoga *tantra*, he contended that it is only appropriate for a few elite practitioners and that it should be restricted to people with unusually strong compassion who have directly realized emptiness (Tib. *stong pa nyid*, Skt. *śūnyatā*). According to tradition, he set an example for his followers by abstaining from the practice of sexual yogas until he was in the intermediate (Tib. *bar do*, Skt. *antarābhava*) state after his death.

The order he founded was first called Gandenpa (dGa' ldan pa) after its first monastery, and later came to be known as Gelukpa ("System of Virtue"). He believed himself to be re-establishing the Kadampa (bKa' gdams pa) Order that had been founded by Atīsa (982–1054) and his disciple Dromdön ('Brom ston). Like Atīśa, Tsong Khapa emphasized the importance of intensive study and of practice that combined elements of both exoteric subjects like epistemology and logic and the esoteric texts and techniques of *tantra*.

His most influential works are: the *Great Exposition of the Stages of the Path* (*Lam rim chen mo*, which focuses on the traditional Mahāyāna gradualist path of the *bodhisattva*); the *Great Exposition of Secret Mantra* (*sNgags rim chen mo*, which discusses the tantric path to buddhahood); and the *Essence of Good Explanations* (*Legs bshad snying po*, which is concerned with Buddhist hermeneutics).

According to the Gelukpa tradition, Tsong Khapa was an incarnation of the buddha Mañjuśrī and had frequent meetings with him. He is credited with four main achievements: (1) establishing the "Great Prayer Festival" (sMon lam chen mo), which was held every Tibetan New Year until it was banned by Chinese authorities in the 1960s; (2) restoring an important statue of Maitreya; (3) establishing the importance of strict adherence to the rules of monastic discipline; and (4) the construction of several major monasteries.

See also: **Tibet, Buddhism in; Vajrayāna Buddhism.**

JOHN POWERS

U

U NU (1907–95)

A deeply religious person, consummate politician and published author, U Nu served as Burma's first parliamentary prime minister between 1948 and 1956, 1957 and 1958, and 1960 and 1962. During his lifetime, Burma underwent rapid social and political transformations, from British colonial rule to independence and military rule. His influence shaped these changes profoundly in political and religious ways.

A leader of the nationalist Thakin (Master) student group, U Nu was suspended from Rangoon University in 1936. Between 1945 and 1947, he served as president and vice-president of the AFPFL before becoming Burma's prime minister in the aftermath of Aung San's massacre. He was imprisoned from 1962 until 1966 by his military successor, Ne Win, and formed a government in exile in Thailand from 1969 until 1973. Returning to Burma in 1980 as part of a general amnesty, he agreed to oversee a new edition of the Burmese *Tipiṭaka* published by the Ministry of Religious Affairs in conjunction with the Ne Win monastic reforms. The State Law and Order Restoration Council (SLORC) put U Nu under house arrest in 1988 when he proclaimed a parallel government following the popular uprising and subsequent collapse of the government. He remained under house arrest until 1992 and passed away in 1995.

Burma's Buddhist culture was central to U Nu's plan for nation building. Partially to discourage communist sympathies and also to construct a religious legitimation for his post-independence government, U Nu actively promoted a national Buddhist revival upon assuming the premiership in November of 1947. Together with Sir U Thwin, a private businessman, and several cabinet ministers, including U Ba Khin, Accountant General, he set up the Buddha Sāsana Nuggaha Ahpwe (BSNA) to consolidate under lay control functions of religious reform traditionally located in the court. Its mission was to promote the expansion and stability of Buddhism and the progress of monastic education (*pariyatti*) and practice (*paṭipatti*), and to establish a library to serve as a repository for Buddhist texts. U Thwin's land donation in Yangon became the site of a monastic compound that headquartered the Buddha Sāsana Council (BSC) charged with organizing the Sanghayāna, the Sixth Buddhist Synod (1954–5), and the religious construction and convocations it entailed, as well as the Thathana Yeiktha Center, the initial Mahāsī Sayadaw's meditation center that soon popularized *satipathana vipassanā* (mindfulness insight) meditation across Burma and abroad.

Hallmarks of the Sixth Buddhist Synod include the construction of Kaba Aye, also called the World Peace Pagoda; the purification of the Theravāda *Tipiṭaka*; the reorganization of the *sangha* into lineages approved by the government; and the celebrated pilgrimage of the Sri Lankan Tooth Relic to Burma. Its occurrence was timed to coincide with millennial expectations in the Theravāda world celebrating the midpoint of the Buddha's dispensation (*sāsana*). U Nu's frequent meditation retreats furthered his popular charismatic appeal as Burma's *cakkavatti*. Promoting meditation practice among civil servants and urbanites generally lent religious support to U Nu's utopian vision of the Burmese Way to Socialism that advocated national development within the framework of the Eightfold Noble Path, linking national prosperity and welfare to the eventual spiritual enlightenment of the Burmese people. His declaration of Buddhism as Burma's state religion, ethnic insurgencies, and tensions within Buddhist monastic factions ultimately invited a military coup led by Ne Win in 1962 that eclipsed U Nu's political career. In the course of his life, U Nu authored countless speeches, sermons, translations and several books, including an autobiography entitled *Saturday's Son* and a novel.

See also: **Famous Buddhists and ideal types.**

JULIANE SCHOBER

V

VAIŚĀLĪ

Vaiśālī (Pāli Vesālī) was the capital of the Licchavī people, who are characterized in early Buddhist texts as an important north Indian political power with a republican form of government. It was at Vaiśālī that Gautama Buddha agreed to grant ordination to a group of women led by his aunt Mahāprajāpatī, thus establishing the women's monastic lineage. The second Buddhist council is also said to have been convened there a century following the Buddha's final passing away. Vaiśālī is also connected with one of the "eight great marvels" (Skt. *aṣṭamahāprātihārya*), a biographical motif widely represented in Buddhist art. According to this tradition, a group of monkeys dug a pool for his use and offered him a bowl of honey, acts of generosity that resulted in their heavenly rebirth. Vaiśālī figures prominently in the *Mahāparinibbāna Sutta*'s account of the end of the Buddha's life. It was there that he accepted a meal from the wealthy courtesan Ambapālī and received her gift of a grove of mango trees. He also gave a final admonition to his followers there, announcing that he would pass away at the end of three months, and exhorting them to strive diligently along the path. This text also records that as he was setting out on the last leg of his journey to Kuśīnagara, the place of his final passing away, he turned completely around to gaze upon Vaiśālī one last time. According to this text, after his death and cremation, the Licchavīs received one-eighth share of his bodily relics and they built a *stūpa* in Vaiśālī to enshrine them.

Vaiśālī has been identified with present-day Basarh in Bihar. Chinese pilgrims' accounts detail several important monuments there, though by the seventh century, when Xuanzang wrote, the site was already in decline. Buddhist images found at Vaiśālī indicate that it continued as a Buddhist site into the twelfth century. It was first identified in the modern period by Cunningham in 1861 who relied upon the Chinese pilgrims' accounts as well as the presence of a ruined *stūpa* and an uninscribed Mauryan-era column. An excavation in the first decade of the twentieth century uncovered seals that referred to Vaiśālī, thus confirming Cunningham's identification. A pond at the site is presently associated with the tradition of the pond dug by the monkeys for the Buddha's use. The most notable Buddhist structure there is a low *stūpa* that was excavated in 1958–62. The earliest core of the *stūpa* was constructed of mud, with several successive enlargements. On the basis of pottery finds and stratigraphic analysis, the archeologists responsible for the excavation have proposed an early fifth-century BCE date for the earliest *stūpa*, leading some to conclude that this may be the original *stūpa* built by the Licchavīs over the Buddha's remains. While their dating has been questioned, this *stūpa* remains one of the few Buddhist monuments excavated to date that may have been constructed before the time of Aśoka.

See also: **Aśoka; Bodhgayā; Councils; Kuśinagara; Lumbinī; Pāṭaliputra; Sacred places; Sāñcī; Sārnāth; *Stūpa*; *Vihāra*; Women in Buddhism: an historical and textual overview.**

KEVIN TRAINOR

VAJRAYĀNA BUDDHISM

Vajrayāna and Indian Buddhism

The core texts of Vajrayāna Buddhism are the *tantras* produced in India, which constitute a third wave of Buddhist scripture. The oldest stratum of scriptural works is the Pāli Canon and the texts of other early schools that only exist today in Chinese translations. According to Indian tradition, shortly after the passing of Śākyamuni Buddha, a council of *arhats* was convened to recite his teachings, and at its conclusion the canon was declared closed. The canon contained discourses (*sūtra*) attributed to him (or in some cases his disciples) along with rules for monastic conduct (*vinaya*), and later scholastic treatises (*abhidharma*) were added. According to one tradition, the *Abhidharma* had been taught by the Buddha to his mother while he visited her in the Heaven of the Thirty-Three (Trāyastriṃśa), and it was recited at the first council by Mahākāśyapa. Despite the claim that the canon was closed, several centuries after his death a new group of texts, also claiming to have been spoken by the Buddha, began to appear in India, and over the next few centuries many more were added to what later became the canon of the Mahāyāna.

Another several centuries later, a new wave of discourses, generally called *tantra* (and sometimes *sūtra*), began to circulate in India, and their adherents claimed that they had also been taught by the Buddha during his lifetime (some were attributed to other buddhas). This new dispensation followed the main outlines of Mahāyāna thought and practice, and assumed the *bodhisattva* ideal of a practitioner who is motivated by compassion (*karuṇā*) to strive for buddhahood in order to benefit others. According to one popular myth, the *tantras* were taught during Śākyamuni's lifetime, but because there was no one who could properly comprehend and apply them, they were hidden in the Heaven of the Thirty-Three or Tuṣita, and later the buddha Vajrapāṇi gave them to King Indrabhūti of Zahor. He was unable to make sense of them, but the sage Kukura was given a special direct transmission by the buddha Vajrasattva, following which he understood them in all aspects and was able to explain them to Indrabhūti.

Vajrayāna and other Mahāyāna traditions

Like earlier Mahāyāna scriptures, the *tantras* emphasized the doctrine of emptiness (*śūnyatā*), which holds that all persons and phenomena lack inherent existence (*svabhāva*), that they are composed of parts and produced by causes and conditions. Like other forms of Mahāyāna, tantric Buddhism also placed great emphasis on "skill in means" (*upāya-kauśalya*), the ability to adapt teachings and practices to the proclivities and capacities of trainees. Although Vajrayāna claims the status of a separate and superior vehicle, it also incorporates key aspects of the two other vehicles. Thus Tibetan monks who practice Vajrayāna take the vows of the Mūlasarvāstivāda *Vinaya*, as well as the Mahāyāna *bodhisattva* vows. Tantric vows are generally regarded as additional commitments, but most Tibetans agree that they do not abrogate other ones.

The main difference between the *tantras* and earlier Mahāyāna texts lay in the new practices they proclaimed – which adherents believe are vastly more effective than the mainstream Mahāyāna path and have the ability to greatly shorten the time required to become a Buddha. These included extensive use of spells (*mantra*), hand gestures (*mudrā*), symbolic diagrams (*maṇḍala*), and often elaborate systems of visualization and ritual. One of the most important practices of Indian and Tibetan Vajrayāna is deity yoga (Skt. *devatā-yoga*, Tib. *lha'i rnal 'byor*), in which one first creates a vivid mental image of a buddha in front of oneself, and then imagines that the deity merges with one's body, and that one's body, speech, and mind are transformed into those of a Buddha. The first part is called the "generation stage" (Skt. *utpatti-krama*, Tib. *bskyed rim*), and the second is the "completion stage" (Skt. *niṣpanna-krama*, Tib. *rdzogs rim*). According to the Tibetan scholar Tsong Khapa (Tsong Kha Pa, 1357–1419), deity yoga is the main differentiating factor that separates mainstream Mahāyāna from Vajrayāna, but other Tibetan scholars dispute this idea. Ngorchen Günga Sangpo (Ngor Chen Kun Dga' Bzang Po, 1389–1456), for example, pointed out that some *tantras* make no mention of deity yoga.

From India, *tantric* Buddhism spread throughout Southeast Asia, and there are tantric images and motifs in ancient sites in Thailand, Pagan in Burma, and Angkor in Cambodia, although Vajrayāna was later supplanted by Theravāda in these areas. Vajrayāna was also influential in Tang dynasty China (618–907) and entered Japan during the Heian period (794–1185), but it had its greatest influence in Tibet and surrounding areas, including Nepal and Mongolia.

Vajrayāna is referred to by its current adherents by a variety of names, including "*mantra* vehicle" (*mantra-yāna*, because of the prominence of *mantras*) and "method vehicle" (*upāya-yāna*, because of its superior methods), in contrast to mainstream Mahāyāna, which is termed "*sūtra* vehicle" (*sūtra-yāna*, because it follows the early Mahāyāna *sūtras*) or "perfection vehicle" (*pāramitā-yāna*), because it emphasizes the path of the *bodhisattva* who trains in the Six Perfections (*Pāramitā*) in limitless ways over a vast expanse of time, unlike Vajrayāna practitioners, who train more effectively and so are able to attain buddhahood far more quickly. Its central symbol is the *vajra* (Tib. *rdo rje*, Ch. *jingang*, Jap. *kongō*) which can represent a thunderbolt used by the Indian god Viśṇu to slay enemies or an indestructible substance like a diamond. The *vajra* is also a sort of scepter that exists in various configurations and that represents the method aspect of practice, while the bell (*ghanta*) represents wisdom. According to the *Vajra Crown Tantra* (*Vajraśekhara-tantra*), a *vajra* is "adamantine, hard, nonempty, with a nature that is imperturbable and indivisible; because it cannot be burned and is indestructible and empty, it is called 'vajra'." In some *tantric* texts, the *vajra* is also associated with the male penis.

Origins of Vajrayāna

The origins of Vajrayāna Buddhism are obscure and have been the subject of considerable debate among scholars. There is little surviving archeological evidence from India to indicate how this form of Buddhism developed or who its earliest practitioners were. Some scholars have speculated that early *tantric* or proto-*tantric* texts and practices began to appear in India around the middle of the first millennium CE, but when the Chinese pilgrim Xuanzang (596–664) traveled to the Indian sub-continent from 629 to 645, his extensive chronicles of Buddhist sites and practitioners contain no mention of anything recognizably *tantric*. It may be that he encountered *tantrists* but did not recognize them as Buddhists, or he may have been scandalized by some of their doctrines and practices, but in any event it appears that during his visit if Vajrayāna existed it was not part of the Buddhist mainstream.

By the late seventh century, however, Vajrayāna had been incorporated into the curriculum of the great north Indian monastic universities that later became the main source for the importation of Buddhism into Tibet. The Chinese pilgrim Wu Xing, writing some time around 680, reported that Vajrayāna had entered the monastic mainstream in the north Indian monastic centers, and he indicated that this was a recent phenomenon. The earliest Tibetan translations of *tantric* texts were done in the eighth century, and around the same time Chinese translators also began to import and translate *tantras* and commentaries from India.

Tantric tradition claims a number of Indian masters as part of its lineage, including Nāgārjuna (*c*. 150–250 CE) and Asaṅga (*c*. fourth century CE), and it is not impossible that elements associated with the developed *tantric* systems began to emerge around this time. The *vajra* predates Buddhism, as does the use of *mantras*, symbolic diagrams, and fire rituals (Skt. *homa*, Jap. *goma*), all of which are central to Vajrayāna, but it is not until the seventh century that we see evidence of comprehensive systems of doctrine and practice codified in texts called *tantras* and the self-conscious formation of a separate "vehicle." *Mantras*, *maṇḍalas*, and visualizations are aspects of other Buddhist traditions, but in Vajrayāna they are parts of a unified system with a distinctive iconography, structure of practice, and doctrine.

Moreover, the emergence of Vajrayāna also coincides with the development of a sense of community on the part of its practitioners, who perceive themselves as belonging to a vehicle that is both different from and superior to other Buddhist traditions. An important aspect of the development of community is the requirement that in order to enter the *Vajra* Vehicle one must receive initiation from a qualified guru (Tib. *bla ma*; pronounced "*lama*"), and those who receive it are sworn to secrecy. The initiations commonly emulated aspects of royal consecrations, and initiates were instructed in practices involving visualization of themselves as buddhas surrounded by retinues of subordinate Buddhas, a feature that is not found in other forms of Buddhism, and which is not attested until the late seventh–early eighth century. In light of Wu Xing's comments that Vajrayāna's entry into the monastic establishment was a recent event and the lack of previous evidence of *tantric* practices, practitioners, texts, or images, it appears that its emergence was probably quite rapid, and that it developed as a distinctive system in the course of a few decades, following which it continued to expand and produce new paradigms and texts. After the composition of the first recognizably *tantric* texts, new practices were developed, and new texts were composed to accommodate them. The process continued into the twelfth century, and possibly later. During this time, Nālandā became one of the main centers of *tantric* study, along with Vikramaśilā. The destruction of Vikramaśīla by Muslim invaders in 1203 was one of the climactic events in the demise of Vajrayāna in India.

The socio-political environment for the emergence of Vajrayāna

Following the demise of the Gupta dynasty and the Vākāṭas (*c.* 320–550), India moved from a time of relatively stable centralized government to a period of smaller states. Larger and more powerful kingdoms commonly had allies and vassals, and war between these states was frequent. Records of the time speak of devastation wrought by war and large population shifts as a result of conflict, along with a corresponding breakdown in trade and the sort of royal sponsorship that had been essential to the maintenance of large monastic institutions. In this new environment, Buddhism borrowed doctrines, practices, and social models from rival groups like the Pāśupatas and Kāpālikas, and the emerging *tantric* movement can be viewed as an attempt to adapt to changing social conditions and develop new paradigms to suit the times.

Not surprisingly, much of the symbolism and organization of the new movement reflects the shifting social realities of this period. An example is the *tantric maṇḍala*, which often depicts a medieval Indian royal residence or a central deity with a surrounding retinue of subordinates. In visualization practices, one generates the *maṇḍala* and populates it with various deities, each with its own subsidiary entourages, and at the conclusion of the rite dissolves them into one's own mind. This is said to be accompanied with a feeling of divine pride – the pride of a lordly Buddha who exerts legitimate dominion – which is not afflicted by negative mental states such as envy, anger, or desire.

Tantric consecration rituals have a number of elements that parallel those of medieval Indian kings, and even the stated goal of *tantra* – becoming a supreme lord with dominion over a particular area – reflects the attitudes and social realities of the time. The notion that *bodhisattvas* accumulate vast stores of merit that allow them to create buddha realms (*buddha-kṣetra*) for the benefit of particular types of beings was already present in Mahāyāna Buddhism, and a number of such lands (for instance Sukhāvatī, the Pure Land of Amitābha) are well known in Indian Buddhism and became the focus of popular cults. The buddha who creates a Buddha-realm also rules over it. The imperial metaphor is extended in *tantric* Buddhism, in which adepts are said to become "supreme overlords" (*rājādirāja*), to possess great magical power, and to be able to conquer both sorcerers and gods.

Consecration rituals still in use today employ the accoutrements of royal ceremonies from the Indian feudal period that followed the demise of the Guptas, and initiates commonly wear crowns and carry *vajras* which in some texts are explicitly correlated with the staff of office (*daṇḍa*), the symbol of kingly power in medieval India. The language and imagery of these ceremonies also contain elements of the regal paraphernalia of the time. In these rites, initiates are instructed to conceive of themselves as kings who acquire power through the performance of rituals and meditation, which enables them to exercise dominion in the manner of a universal monarch (*cakravartin*). Initiates also learn *mantras* that purportedly enable adepts to defeat rival armies, ensure good crops, control the weather, etc., all of which are elements of kingship in medieval India.

Despite the incorporation of core symbols of Indian kingship and social structures, Indian *tantra* also had antinomian aspects, and some of its most influential practitioners situated themselves outside the mainstream and engaged in practices that were regarded as polluting by brahmanical orthodoxy.

Early recognizably *tantric* texts speak of communities of wandering adepts (*siddha*), who frequented such marginal areas as cemeteries and cremation grounds and who gathered for special "feasts" (*gaṅacakra*) in which prohibited substances such as alcohol and dishes made from human flesh were consumed. Some of them focused their practices on Hindu gods, although they rejected traditional brahmanical norms. Others had a Buddhist orientation, and there is evidence of mutual borrowing between the two groups, particularly in terms of techniques of practice.

Doctrine and practice

One of the core doctrines of Vajrayāna is the non-difference of cyclic existence (*saṃsāra*) and *nirvāṇa* (Skt. *saṃsāra-nirvāṇa-abheda*, Tib. *'khor 'das dbyer med*). According to the *Hevajra-tantra*: "Then the essence is declared, pure and consisting in knowledge, where there is not the slightest difference between *saṃsāra* and *nirvāṇa*." In putting this idea into practice, *tantric* adepts created practices involving prohibited actions and substances as means to break attachment to orthodoxy and directly understand that nothing is inherently good or bad, but thinking makes it so. The *Hevajra-tantra* thus proclaims: "That by which the world is bound, by the same things it is released from bondage."

Compassion is central to Vajrayāna thought and practice. The standard *bodhisattva* path takes a minimum of three countless eons (*asaṃkhyeya-kalpa*) to complete, but the special techniques of *tantra* are said by adherents to be able to greatly shorten the time required to attain buddhahood. Texts of the highest yoga *tantra* (Skt. *anuttara-yoga-tantra*, Tib. *rnal 'byor bla na med kyi rgyud*) class, for example, assert that practitioners can become Buddhas in one human lifetime. But *tantric* texts warn that only trainees with especially keen compassion who want to attain Buddhahood quickly in order to benefit suffering sentient beings should undertake these practices. If one is attracted by the possibility of acquiring extraordinary powers (Skt. *siddhi*, Tib. *dngos grub*) or wants to practice *tantra* simply because it is reputed to be the fastest and best path, one is not a "suitable vessel" for the teachings and should instead enter another system concordant with one's capacities. Development of compassion is an important aspect of preliminary training in Vajrayāna Buddhism, and there are a number of popular techniques designed to foster and strengthen one's concern for others, as this is essential for successful practice.

Vajrayāna in the Tibetan cultural area

In the Tibetan cultural area, where Vajrayāna is viewed as the supreme Buddhist system, practitioners are initiated into particular *tantric* cycles, which are generally based on a root *tantra* (e.g. the *Kālacakra*, *Guhyasamāja*, *Hevajra*, *Cakrasaṃvara*, etc.), which is often associated with a number of supplementary texts in the canon, along with ritual manuals that describe visualization liturgies (Skt. *sādhana*, Tib. *grub thabs*), and later textual commentaries. This is further augmented, transmitted, and explained by traditions of oral instructions by *lamas*, who are the main repositories of the lore of each tantric cycle. Most Tibetan lineages maintain a history of transmission going back to early Indian masters and sometimes to Buddhas who are believed to have originally imparted the teachings.

Lineage plays a crucial role in all tantric traditions, and only texts and practices that are able to establish a connection to recognized authorities are accepted. In the early period of the transmission of Buddhism to Tibet, the primary criterion for determining the authority of a particular *tantra* was the existence of a Sanskrit original. There are number of cases of particular texts being regarded as spurious until a Sanskrit manuscript was discovered.

In addition to the extensive *tantric* literature in the Tibetan Buddhist canon and the scriptural collections of the four orders of Tibetan Buddhism (Nyingma, Sakya, Kagyu, and Geluk), new revelations and practices are introduced from time to time through the mechanism of "hidden treasures" (*gter ma*), which their adherents believe were delivered by Padmasambhava or his disciples during the early period of transmission of Buddhism to Tibet (*snga dar*) and protected with spells that ensure that they will only be discovered at a pre-ordained time by a particular "treasure-discoverer" (*gter ston*), who is a reincarnation of one of Padmasambhava's students. These are particularly associated with the Nyingma (rNying ma) tradition, but all orders of Tibetan Buddhism have particular "hidden treasures" that they regard as normative and that are part of their doctrine and practice.

Each order emphasizes particular *tantras* and bases its Vajrayāna practices on them. The Nyingma (Old Order) prefers the translations of *tantras* that were made during the first dissemination, which began in the seventh century. They assert that while the later translations may be more technically accurate in some cases, the early translators (*lo tsā ba*) were highly realized practitioners, whose translations captured the essence of the Sanskrit texts. The Sakya (Sa skya) Order bases its "path and result" (*lam 'bras*) tradition on the *Hevajra-tantra*, and the Kagyu (bKa' rgyud) and Geluk (dGe lugs) orders emphasize the *Guhyasamāja-tantra*, the *Cakrasaṃvara-tantra*, and the *Kālacakra-tantra*.

Types and divisions

Tibetan Buddhism has two main collections of tantric texts: the "old translations" that were prepared during the first period of transmission to Tibet, and the "new translations" that are followed by the three "New Orders" (*gsar ma*): the Kagyu, Sakya, and Geluk. The first group is particularly important for the Nyingmapas, but some of these texts are also used by the New Orders. Another important textual distinction is the division of early teachings (*bka' ma*) – *tantras* found in the canons of Tibetan Buddhist orders – and the "hidden treasures."

Tibetan exegetes also divide the new *tantras* into four sets: (1) action *tantras* (*kriyā-tantra*, Tib. *bya rgyud*); (2) performance *tantras* (*caryā-tantra*, Tib. *spyod rgyud*); (3) yoga *tantras* (*yoga-tantra*, Tib. *rnal 'byor rgyud*); and (4) highest yoga *tantras*. This division probably roughly reflects the chronology of the production of various types of *tantras* and the practices they contained in India: the texts of the first two sets probably were produced first, followed by the yoga *tantras*, and the highest yoga *tantras* were the last wave of tantric texts. Tibetan exegetes, however, presume the traditional notion that they were spoken by the historical Buddha and regard each set as a teaching specific to a particular type of practitioner. The schema is hierarchical, and each successive class is considered to be superior to the preceding one. It was developed in the thirteenth and fourteenth centuries by Pudön (Bu ston rin chen grub, 1290–1364), who is credited with editing the Tibetan canon. The lines of division are somewhat hazy, and different exegetes posit various reasons for separating them. Theoretically, the basis of division is the sort of practices described in a particular *tantra*, but there is considerable overlap within tantric texts classified in different sets.

In action *tantra*, one relates to the deity as a servant to a master and gives offerings, engages in rituals of worship, and intones prayers. The focus is on external activities, and the main trainees are people who are unable to engage in meditation on emptiness but who have strong faith and are inclined toward worship.

In action *tantra*, one uses symbolism in acting out religious practice. This form of yoga emphasizes images or other representations of deities, and one makes offerings to them, while imagining that the deities are actually present and accept one's worship. Other activities include purificatory practices like bathing, in which one imagines that the external activity eliminates mental afflictions. The main trainees of such *tantras* are not suited to internal visualization but can benefit from using external symbols as supports for practice.

Performance *tantras* use both external activities and internal yogas. One relates to the deity as friend or brother/sister and strives to attain the status of a Buddha through a combination of practices relating to external purity and internal meditation. Meditation involves generating a mental image of oneself as a deity and also creating an image of the deity as a model for one's practice. One views the buddha as a friend and strives to become like him/her.

Practitioners of yoga *tantra* are able to visualize themselves as actual deities, and not merely as aspirants. The emphasis is on internal yoga, and the rituals of purification and worship found in the lower *tantras* are now merely aids that contribute to one's practice. Practitioners of yoga *tantra* strive to view all phenomena as naturally pure and free from the signs of mental projection. They are understood as manifestations of luminosity and emptiness, and initially trainees regard phenomena as aspects of the *maṇḍalas* of deities. This is a "pure vision" (Tib. *dag snang*), unlike one's ordinary perceptions. The *maṇḍala* is an idealized cosmos, but one that is regarded as more true and pure than ordinary reality, a template for training that through repetition can lead to real transformation of one's environment into the realm of a buddha. There are often elaborate homologies between aspects of the *maṇḍala* and the cosmos, and ideally the meditator should learn to perceive phenomena of the environment as aspects of the *maṇḍala*.

In the next stage of practice, the "yoga without signs" (Skt. *animitta-yoga*, Tib. *mtshan ma med pa'i rnal 'byor*), one no longer requires external symbols and meditates directly on suchness (Skt. *tathatā*, Tib. *de kho na nyid*). One understands that it is non-dual and views it as inseparable from the appearances of deities, and the deities are regarded as manifestations of perfect awakening.

Highest yoga *tantra* texts include the *Hevajra-tantra*, *Kālacakra-tantra*, *Cakrasaṃvara-tantra*, and *Guhyasamāja-tantra*, all of which assume the developed mystical physiology of the subtle body (Skt. *māya-deha*, Tib. *sgyu lus*) and which contain instructions for generation stage and completion stage yogas. Symbolism of deities in sexual embrace is occasionally found in the lower *tantras*, but it is much more widespread and developed in highest yoga *tantras*, which present elaborate homologies between aspects of human physiology and the universe. In these texts, the male figure represents compassion and method, while the female represents wisdom. Their joining symbolizes the union of the two that characterizes full actualization of buddhahood.

Tibetan commentators generally regard the lower *tantras* as preparatory and as sources for attainment of worldly ends (such as long life, wealth, good health, destroying enemies or evil forces) and supernatural abilities, as well as purificatory practices that lay a foundation for more advanced training. The highest yoga *tantras* are regarded as the most effective and rapid means for attaining buddhahood, and according to some exegetes like Tsong Khapa, in the final analysis it can only be attained through these practices.

This idea is found in the *Compendium of the Truth of All Buddhas* (Skt. *Sarvathatāgata-tattva-saṃgraha*, Tib. *De bzhin gshegs pa thams cad kyi de kho na nyid bsdus pa'i mdo*, Ch. *Jinggang ding yiqie rulai zhenshi shedashen xianzheng dajiaowang jing, Jinggang ding jing* (T 866), Jap. *Kongōchō-gyō*), which considers the problem that the standard biographies of Śākyamuni Buddha make no mention of him engaging in *tantric* ritual activities or in the sexual yogas that are supposedly required for the attainment of full awakening. In this text, the story is rewritten at a crucial point: Siddhārtha Gautama is sitting under the *Bodhi* Tree in meditation in the final stages of preparation for buddhahood, but he is interrupted by the buddhas of the ten directions, who inform him that he can only complete the path through the special practices of *tantra*. He subsequently leaves behind his physical body, and he sends a mentally created body to a transcendent *tantric* realm, where he is given the highest consecrations, following which he is able to attain final awakening.

The second dissemination and socialization of *tantra*

During the period of the first dissemination, Indian Buddhist teachers traveled to Tibet and Tibetans went to India, where they studied at north Indian monastic institutions or privately with *tantric* masters. Many Indian texts were translated, and government sponsorship of Buddhism ensured that it would spread widely, but with the assassination of the last king of the Yarlung dynasty, Lang Darma (gLang dar ma, r. 838–42), the Tibetan empire began to collapse, and there was an interregnum period during which no central government existed.

In the eleventh century, the kings of the western Tibetan kingdom of Guge decided to revive Buddhism, and the Indian scholar Atiśa (982–1054) was invited to spread the *Dharma* in Tibet. Following his arrival in 1042, he propounded a vision of the path that incorporated *tantric* practices with the mainstream Mahāyāna path of the *bodhisattva* and which emphasized celibate monasticism as the most effective route to Buddhahood for the majority of practitioners. His arrival is viewed by traditional historians as the inception of the "second dissemination" (Tib. *phyi dar*) of Buddhism in Tibet.

Atiśa regarded the sexual yogas of highest yoga *tantra* as uniquely effective, but taught that they are only appropriate for the most elite practitioners, who had directly realized emptiness and who had unusually strong compassion. The majority of Buddhists should recognize their limitations and not attempt to employ techniques that would be too difficult and powerful for them. Tsong Khapa and the Gelukpa Order – who viewed themselves as Atīśa's successors – continued this model and emphasized the centrality of deity yoga (using visualizations rather than an actual consort), while also asserting that at the highest levels of the path one must physically engage in sexual yogas in order to attain final Buddhahood. The other orders of Tibetan Buddhism have differing interpretations, and the Nyingmapas, for example, hold that visualization can be sufficient for Buddhahood.

The Nyingmapas also have a non-tantric practice, the "great perfection" (*rdzogs chen*) – which assumes the physiology of highest yoga *tantra* but does not rely on visualizations – that they claim is superior to highest yoga *tantra* and can lead to buddhahood in an instant of realization. The Kagyupas make the same claim for their own non-*tantric* path, the "great seal" (Skt. *mahāmudrā*, Tib. *phyag rgya chen po*), which has many similarities with the great perfection in both theory and practice.

Today *tantric* practice is regarded as the supreme Buddhist path throughout the Tibetan cultural area, and most

Tibetan Buddhists receive some form of tantric empowerment. Most serious practitioners are monks or nuns, most of whom consider adherence to the *vinaya* rules (including those that enjoin celibacy) to be an essential aspect of Buddhist practice. There are also lay *tantric* practitioners (Tib. *sngags pa*), who may engage in sexual yogas (though many do not), and who often deride the monastics as plodding and conventional. These lay *tantrics* generally trace themselves back through a lineage that began with one of the early Indian *mahāsiddhas*, such as Tilopa or Virūpa.

Vajrayāna in China

Beginning in the seventh and eighth centuries, *tantric* texts began to arrive in China. The origins of Vajrayāna (Ch. *Mizong*, Jap. *Mikkyō*, "esoteric") Buddhism in East Asia are traditionally traced to the efforts of three missionary monks: Śubhākarasiṃha (Ch. Shan Wuwei, Jap. Zenmui, 637–735), Vajrabodhi (Ch. Jin Gangzhi, Jap. Kongōchi, 671–741), and Amoghavajra (Ch. Bukong, Jap. Fukū, 705–75). According to the Japanese Shingon tradition, Vajrabodhi was a student of the Indian *tantric* master Nāgabodhi, whose teacher was Nāgārjuna (although this connection would have required lifespans of several centuries for both men). Shingon regards Nāgabodhi as its fourth patriarch. Vajrabodhi is the fifth patriarch, and he was succeeded by Amoghavajra. Śubhākarasiṃa and his student Yi Xing (Jap. Ichigyō, 683–727) translated the *Sūtra of the Awakening of Mahāvairocana* (*Mahāvairocana-Abhisambodhi Sūtra*, Ch. *Da pilushena chengfo shenbian jianchi jing*, *Dari jing*; T 848). Vajrabodhi translated the *Compendium of the Truth of All Buddhas* into Chinese, and Amoghavajra later published another translation.

These texts were central to the Chinese Vajrayāna (Zhenyan, literally "True Words," the Chinese translation of *mantra*) tradition, and later in the Japanese Shingon school. Both portray Mahāvairocana (Ch. Dari, Jap. Dainichi) as the fundamental Buddha, who manifests in the forms of manifold other buddhas. Their *maṇḍalas* depict him in the center, surrounded by large retinues, and they describe rituals and visualizations that help practitioners to identify their "three mysteries" (Skt. *triguhya*, Jap. *sanmitsu*) – of body, speech, and mind – with those of Mahāvairocana. Through repeated familiarization, one comes gradually to approximate the state of Mahāvairocana, and finally fully actualizes the innate potential for Buddhahood. These texts represent early periods in the development of Indian *tantric* literature. The *Sūtra of the Awakening of Mahāvairocana* is classed as a performance *tantra* in Tibet, while the *Compendium of the Truth of All Buddhas* is considered to be a yoga *tantra*. The later texts of highest yoga *tantra* (Jap. *mujōyuga*) only arrived in East Asia after the formative period of esoteric Buddhism, and never had a significant impact in either China or Japan.

Some important events in the history of Chinese esoteric Buddhism

Śubhākarasiṃha traveled from Nālandā in India to China and arrived in 716. He was joined by Vajrabodhi and Amoghavajra in 720. Śubhākarasiṃha was a well-known teacher, and when he arrived in China the emperor Xuan Zong (r. 712–56) welcomed him and installed him in a temple in the capital of Changan. He later moved to Luoyang, where he began translating texts. Following the revolt of An Lushan in 755, Xuan Zong fled the capital, and later his successor, Su Zong, requested that Amoghavajra perform esoteric rituals to defeat the rebels. When Emperor Dai Zong (762–80) finally quelled the rebellion, esoteric Buddhism received some credit and became associated with protection of the state.

Amoghavajra later built a temple on Mount Wutai, which became a major center for Vajrayāna, and he was successful in spreading the teachings widely. His disciple Hui Guo (Jap. Keika, 746–805) is regarded by Shingon as its seventh patriarch, and he transmitted the esoteric teachings to Kūkai (774–835), who became the founder of Shingon in Japan. Hui Guo performed esoteric rituals for the court, but later rulers preferred Daoism to Buddhism, and Vajrayāna's fortunes declined. The government-sponsored persecution of Buddhism in 845 was a major blow to the tradition, particularly because the authorities prohibited the practice of Buddhist ritual magic.

In the mid-eleventh century, there was a brief revival of interest in esoteric Buddhism in the Northern Liao dynasty in northern China. The main focus was the performance of rituals for magical purposes, but the interest appears to have been short-lived. Later under the Mongol Yuan dynasty (1279–1368), Vajrayāna again became popular in the court, but it was the Tibetan variety. The Manchu Qing dynasty (1644–1911) also supported Tibetan Buddhism, and rulers received tantric initiations and sponsored rituals, but there was no revival of East Asian forms of Vajrayāna during these periods.

Vajrayāna in Japan

In Japan, esoteric traditions are retained today in the Tendai and Shingon orders. Tendai includes esoteric practices within an eclectic mix of Buddhist traditions, but Shingon conceives of itself as solely tantric in its doctrines and practices. An important event in the transmission of Vajrayāna to Japan was a mission to China in 804, in which Kūkai and Saichō (767–822) traveled by separate boats to study Buddhism. Saichō was only able to remain a short time and studied Vajrayāna for about two months, while Kūkai remained for three years and immersed himself in esoteric study. During his stay, he became a student of Hui Guo, who according to tradition appointed Kūkai as his *dharma*-successor.

Shingon hagiographies claim that Kūkai mastered all aspects of Vajrayāna during the six months he studied with Hui Guo, but given the complexity of Vajrayāna texts and practices, this is unlikely. He may have engaged in some prior study of Vajrayāna in Japan, and probably also continued to learn after his return, but according to Shingon hagiographies he was immediately recognized by Hui Guo as his successor, and Shingon further claims that Hui Guo was the first teacher in history to receive the transmissions of both the *Compendium of Truth* and the *Awakening of Mahāvairocana*. He imparted these initiations to Kūkai, who brought them to Japan, following which the complete tradition died out in China. Records from before and after this time indicate, however, that a number of other masters received both transmissions, and that Hui Guo also passed them on to some of his Chinese students.

After returning to Japan, Kūkai sent a message to the emperor outlining his activities and the texts, images, and ritual implements that he had brought back with him. Saichō had also brought *tantric* texts and images to Japan and had performed a number of esoteric rituals for the royal court, which had earned him imperial favor and patronage; consequently, when Kūkai announced that he was the *dharma*-successor to Hui Guo, this presented a problem for the court, because Saichō had already established a reputation as a master of esoteric Buddhism. Probably for this reason, for several years Kūkai was not allowed to travel to the capital. When Emperor Saga (r. 809–23) ascended the throne, however, his fortunes improved, and around the age of thirty-nine he was allowed to establish Shingon as a separate Buddhist sect. Following a rebellion in 810, Kūkai was asked to perform tantric rituals for the protection of the country, and he subsequently enjoyed royal patronage.

During this time, he had generally cordial relations with Saichō, who wanted to further his knowledge of esoteric Buddhism. He began to borrow texts from Kūkai, and in 812 was given initiation into the two main *maṇḍalas* of Shingon, the womb realm *maṇḍala* (Skt. *garbha-dhātu-maṇḍala*, Jap. *taizōkai mandara*) and the vajra realm *maṇḍala* (Skt. *vajra-dhātu-maṇḍala*, Jap. *kongōkai mandara*). When Saichō requested a highly esoteric initiation, however, Kūkai refused and indicated that he would need to become his disciple and undergo a period of study. When Saichō's student Taihan refused to return to him after studying with Kūkai, the two had a falling out. They remained rivals, both claiming to be masters of Vajrayāna, although it only constituted a part of the Tendai tradition, which also emphasized the centrality of the *Lotus Sūtra* and incorporated Chan practices.

In 816 Kūkai received permission to establish a monastery on Mount Kōya, which was named Kongōbuji; it remains the main seat of Shingon today. He also continued to perform *tantric* rituals for the royal court and initiated several emperors into esoteric practice. Toward the end of his life, an esoteric temple was built on the palace grounds, indicating how popular it was with the court.

Kūkai on the difference between exoteric and esoteric Buddhism

Kūkai drew a distinction between exoteric and esoteric teachings and practices. The former are taught by emanation bodies (Skt. *nirmāṇa-kāya*, Jap. *ōjin*) like Śākyamuni and are adapted to the needs and proclivities of sentient beings, but esoteric traditions are revealed directly by the ultimate truth body (Skt. *dharma-kāya*, Jap. *hosshin*), manifested as Mahāvairocana, and express the ultimate truth. Mahāvairocana's teachings are eternal and absolute, while the exoteric teachings are conditioned and relative. In his *Treatise on Exoteric and Esoteric Teachings* (*Benkenmitsu Nikyō-ron*), Kūkai proclaims: "The teaching of the truth body is deep and profound, while the teachings adapted to circumstances are shallow and limited. Thus the name 'esoteric' is used."

Exoteric Buddhism assumes that beings are not awakened and that they need to develop new qualities in order to become buddhas, but esoteric Buddhism teaches the original awakening (*hongaku*) of all things just as they are. Because all beings are inherently Buddhas, awakening is a matter of making this fully manifest, rather than creating something new.

According to Kūkai, Mahāvairocana is the primordial Buddha, and as the truth body pervades all of reality. Buddhahood is a potential in sentient beings, and is manifested in all the phenomena of existence. Esoteric practices enable trainees to attain awakening immediately by providing techniques that actualize the potential of their three mysteries and bring them into harmony with those of Mahāvairocana. When one successfully attunes the three mysteries with Mahāvairocana's, one becomes a Buddha.

This is accomplished by special techniques. *Mudrās* (Jap. *ingei*) serve to harmonize one's body with Mahāvairocana's, and other physical aspects of practice – such as the smoke of fire rituals, the manipulation of ritual implements, the taste of certain herbs, and examination of statues and paintings containing esoteric symbolism – involve the senses and attune the body to the pervasive reality of the truth body. The mystery of speech is linked to Mahāvairocana through chanting of *mantras* (Jap. *shingon*), which have innate power that conveys understandings beyond words and concepts. *Mantras* are the very speech of the truth body, and are used to convey truths that cannot be expressed in words.

Maṇḍalas, images of *tantric* Buddhas, visualizations, etc., all are used to bring one's mind into harmony with that of the primordial Buddha. The sounds of the *mantras*, images of *maṇḍalas*, and physical gestures of *mudrās* all encode the mysteries of the truth body and contain its primordial energy. They are a direct communication by Mahāvairocana to the individual practitioner that is not different from one's true self, and so they are more powerful than exoteric methods. When one uses these techniques in the way prescribed in tantric texts and under the instruction of a master, one's three mysteries generate a response from those of Mahāvairocana, which are also manifest in each element of existence. Both Buddha and practitioner are affected by this process, resulting in mutual empowerment (*kaji*) through which the three mysteries of the practitioner unite with those of Mahāvairocana, thus actualizing their highest potential.

Kūkai claims that traditional Mahāyāna conceives of the truth body as static and inactive, but in reality it is dynamic and interacts with the world. It continually evolves and manifests itself in phenomena, and is conceived as all-illuminating and all-pervasive life energy. It transcends duality and is beyond the reach of conceptual thought, but it can be realized through symbols and visualizations. One who successfully engages in Vajrayāna practice is able to attain Buddhahood in this very body (*sokushin jōbutsu*). One accomplishes this by fully comprehending the three minds (*sanshin*) – of self, other, and Buddha – which are conceived as an inseparable unity because all participate in the universal reality of innate Buddhahood. Buddhahood is the realization of the equality of the three minds.

Shingon after Kūkai

After Kūkai's death, several disciples carried on his teachings. Two of the most important were Jichie (786–847), who became abbot of Tōji Monastery, and Shinzei (800–860), who succeeded him. After Kūkai, Shingon came to be increasingly perceived as a sect devoted mainly to rituals and magic, and this was certainly an important aspect of its appeal. Most of its rituals were designed to produce worldly benefits or protect the state, but there was less interest within the tradition with development of doctrine or practice.

During the tenth and eleventh centuries, a number of sub-schools developed, mainly based on lineages of transmission from particular masters. Two early orders, the Ono and Hirosawa, further subdivided into twelve more sects, and by the thirteenth century these had become thirty-six, most of which were separated by fairly minor differences in style or emphasis, but which were sometimes in open conflict.

Today there are eighteen major temples (*honzan*) that serve as headquarters for a particular Shingon sect. Historically there have been conflicts between the sects over doctrine and practice, but they all share the same basic doctrinal framework, derived primarily from Kūkai's teachings. Shingon has an estimated ten million followers, but actual religious affiliation in Japan is often difficult to gauge. There are about 3,000 Shingon priests and about 11,000 temples throughout Japan.

See also: **Japan, Buddhism in; Ritual in Tibetan Buddhism; Tibet, Buddhism in.**

JOHN POWERS

VAJRAYĀNA PANTHEON

From earliest times, Buddhist texts indicated that the state of Buddhahood is not confined to Śākyamuni Buddha and that he had been preceded by other buddhas. There will also be Buddhas in the future, the most important of whom is Maitreya, who currently resides in Tuṣita Heaven waiting for the ideal time to take his final rebirth as a Buddha. In Mahāyāna literature, the pantheon of Buddhas and *bodhisattvas* expanded dramatically, and the Mahāyāna universe is populated by a vast number of beings who are either on their way to Buddhahood or who have already become buddhas and continue to work for the benefit of sentient beings. Vajrayāna Buddhism increased this pantheon still further and added not only prominent individual Buddhas associated with various aspects of *tantric* practice and theory, but also whole classes of Buddhas, such as the *ḍākinīs*, female Buddhas who are custodians of *tantric* lore and who are strongly associated with the *siddha* traditions. Many Buddhas function both as focal points of devotion and as archetypes that represent aspects of Buddhist thought and practice. Avalokiteśvara, for example, is said to embody the compassion of all Buddhas, while Mañjuśrī represents their wisdom.

Vajrapāṇi, Vajradhara, Heruka

In Tibetan Buddhism, one of the most important knowledge-holder (Skt. *vidyādhara*, Tib. *rig 'dzin*) Buddhas is Vajrapāṇi (Tib. Phyag na rdo rje, "Vajra Hand"), who is commonly depicted with blue skin, wearing a tiger skin around his waist and with long hair in the manner of yogins. He appears in two-armed and four-armed versions: in the four-armed depiction, two of his hands make a threatening gesture that overcomes obstacles, while the other two hold a *vajra* and a lasso. In early Indian texts, he is said to be a mere demon (*yakṣa*) or a lord of demons, but the *Lotus Sūtra* describes him as an emanation of Avalokiteśvara. In some *tantras*, he is referred to as Vajrasattva and Vajradhara, but in later *tantric* traditions the three are distinct figures.

In Indian *tantric* texts, he is described as "Lord of the Mysterious" (*Guhyakādhipati*), which appears to have originally indicated that he was the ruler of a class of mysterious *yakṣas*, but later marks him as the guardian of *tantric* mysteries and those who practice them. In East Asia, he is a guardian figure at the entrances to temples, and is considered to be a *bodhisattva*. In Tibetan Buddhism, he becomes a major figure in his own right, and is said to represent the power of all the Buddhas and their ability to overcome obstacles. He is commonly depicted together with Avalokiteśvara and Mañjuśrī.

In traditional Tibetan histories he plays a crucial role in the early dissemination of Buddhism: when Padmasambhava's mission to bring the *Dharma* to Tibet was thwarted by its indigenous demons, he withdrew into a cave and meditated on Vajrapāṇi, who used his power to frighten the demons, allowing Padmasambhava to conquer them and convert them to Buddhism. In some Tibetan traditions, he will be the final Buddha of the present era.

He is also referred to as "the greatest of those who subdue [beings] that are difficult to tame" (*durdāntadamakaḥ paraḥ*), and perhaps his best-known exploit is his subjugation of the Hindu god Śiva (Maheśvara) as reported in the *Compendium of the Truth of All Buddhas.* Here he is said to be a manifestation of the *bodhisattva* Samantabhadra, whose purpose is to protect the *Dharma* and defeat heretics. The story recounts that Śiva is deceiving beings with his false doctrines, leading to various forms of wrong-doing by those who follow him. At Vairocana's request, Vajrapāṇi agrees to put an end to his malicious activities.

He first recites a *mantra* that causes the Indian gods to appear before him in his palace at the top of Mount Sumeru. Despite this show of power, Śiva is unimpressed, and declares that Vajrapāṇi is a lowly tree spirit (*yakṣa*) and that he is the most powerful god, following which the two engage in a magic contest. Vajrapāṇi triumphs, and he then places his feet on Śiva and his wife Umā, a grave insult in

India, where the feet are regarded as the most polluting part of the body. Śiva's retinue submit to Vajrapāṇi and become subordinate deities in Vairocana's *maṇḍala*, promising to use their power on behalf of Buddhism, but Śiva himself still refuses to acknowledge Vajrapāṇi's overlordship. Vajrapāṇi then slays him and transfers his life force into another realm, where it is transmuted into a Buddha named "Soundless Lord of Ashes" (Bhasmeśvara-nirghoṣa), a reflection of the standard iconography of Śiva, in which he is depicted smearing the ashes from cremation grounds on his skin. This story is clearly a sectarian attempt to place Buddhism ahead of Hinduism by creating a narrative in which the chief *tantric* Buddha defeats, slays, and finally converts one of the most powerful Hindu gods.

Vajradhara (Tib. rDo rje 'chang, "Vajra Holder") is often said to be the primordial Buddha (Skt. *ādi-buddha*, Tib. *dang po'i sangs rgyas*), particularly in the "New Translation" orders of Tibetan Buddhism (Kagyu, Sakya, Geluk). According to the Kagyupas, their teachings derive from him, and they claim that Vajradhara was the *mahāsiddha* Tilopa's teacher.

Iconographically, he is depicted with dark blue skin, with arms crossed on his chest, holding a *vajra* and bell in his hands as a representation of the combination of wisdom and compassion that characterizes Buddhas. His consort is Prajñāpāramitā, who embodies wisdom, and the two are often in sexual embrace (*yab yum*). In Tibetan *sādhana* practice, Vajradhara is closely associated with the guru, who is often visualized as Vajradhara. Vajradhara is said to manifest in the form of human gurus, and reincarnate *lamas* (*sprul sku*) often have the title "*rdo rje chang*" as an indication of the close association of this Buddha with teachers. Many tantric texts speak of the goal of practice as "becoming a Vajradhara."

Heruka (Tib. Khrag 'thung dpa' bo, "Blood Drinker") is a term for wrathful meditational deities (Skt. *iṣṭa-devatā*, Tib. *yi dam*) in Tibetan Buddhism, and is often particularly applied to the wrathful manifestation of Cakrasaṃvara. In the Nyingma Order, there is a well-known set of eight Herukas that are represented in various *maṇḍalas*. Heruka also stands alone as an important *tantric* deity, often associated with cremation grounds and cemeteries (which may be the source of the Tibetan translation of his name as "Blood Drinker," because these places soak up the blood of corpses). In the *Connection of All Buddhas* (*Sarvabuddha-samāyoga*), he defeats Māra and Śiva and incorporates them into his *maṇḍala* as subordinate figures.

The five Celestial Buddhas and Samantabhadra

The five Jinas (Victors, often referred to as "Celestial Buddhas") are a group of buddhas depicted together iconographically throughout East Asia and the Tibetan cultural area. Each has a specific iconography and is associated with a particular direction, and they also appear as separate figures in Mahāyāna *sūtras* and *tantras*. The five are: (Mahā)Vairocana, Akṣobhya, Ratnasambhava, Amitābha, and Amoghasiddhi.

Vairocana (Tib. rNam par snang mdzad, Ch. Palushena, Jap. Birushana, Dainichi Nyorai) is commonly depicted with white skin with his hands making the "turning the wheel of Dharma gesture" (*dharma-cakra-mudrā*). He is associated with Samantabhadra, and in East Asia is regarded in some traditions as the primordial Buddha. In the *Heroic Concentration Sūtra* (*Śūraṅgama-samādhi Sūtra*), Śākyamuni declares that Vairocana is another aspect of himself. When the five transcendent buddhas are depicted together, Vairocana is generally in the center, and according to the Shingon tradition the others are manifestations of him. His name means "Resplendent," and he is associated with the sun, and in Japan with the sun *kami* Amaterasu. Vairocana plays a central role in Shingon, where he is the central Buddha of its two main *maṇḍalas*, the *vajra* realm *maṇḍala* and the womb realm *maṇḍala*.

Akṣobhya (Tib. Mi 'khrugs pa, Ch. Achu, Jap. Ashuka Nyorai, "Imperturbable") is the lord of the eastern paradise of Abhirati. Iconographically, he has dark blue (sometimes gold) skin and rides an elephant. In his right hand is a *vajra*, and his left makes the "earth-touching" *mudrā*. When depicted with the other four Jina buddhas, he appears in the eastern quadrant. His name is said to derive from a vow never to become angry at another being.

Ratnasaṃbhava (Tib. Rin chen 'byung ldan, Ch. Baosheng Fo, Jap. Hōshō Nyorai, "Jewel Born") is the central Buddha of the southern pure land, and is depicted with golden skin and sitting in the lotus position (*padmāsana*), holding a wish-granting gem (*cintā-maṇi*) and making the wish-granting gesture (*varada-mudrā*). His consort is Māmakī, and in Tibetan depictions the two are often shown embracing.

Amitābha (Tib. 'Od dpag med, Ch. Omituofo, Jap. Amida, "Limitless Light") is one of the most popular Buddhas in East Asia and the central figure of the "Pure Land" (Ch. Qingtu, Jap. Jōdo) traditions. He presides over the western paradise of Sukhāvatī, which was created by the power of his meritorious deeds. In this land, the conditions for attainment of Buddhahood are optimal, and those fortunate enough to be reborn there will definitely attain it. His past practice and present activities are described in the short and long versions of the *Sukhāvatī-vyūha Sūtra*. The latter is the main source for the well-known series of past vows, particularly the eighteenth, which states that anyone who invokes his name ten times will be reborn in Sukhāvatī. He is depicted in a wide variety of ways throughout the Mahāyāna Buddhist world, and in esoteric representations he generally has red skin and wears red monk's robes. His hands often make the meditation gesture (*dhyāna-mūdrā*) or the explanation gesture (*vitarka-mūdrā*), and in Japanese Buddhist art he is commonly shown residing in Sukhāvatī or descending to earth to bring devotees there.

Amoghasiddhi (Tib. Don yod grub pa, Jap. Fukūjōju, "Unfailing Accomplishment") is situated in the northern direction, and has green skin; his left hand is in his lap, palm up, and his right hand makes the "fearless gesture" (*abhaya-mudrā*). He is seated in the lotus position, generally accompanied by a retinue of four great *bodhisattvas*.

In *tantric* Buddhism, these five Buddhas are associated with purification of the five aggregates, as well as the five elements that comprise material things, the five directions, the five colors, five Buddha families, and transmutation of the five primary mental afflictions into their opposites. Akṣobhya is the paradigm for transforming the energy of hatred and anger into the perfection of wisdom. Vairocana transmutes delusion into mirror-like wisdom. Ratnasambhava is associated with changing pride and envy into the wisdom of equanimity. Amitābha transforms desire and lust into discriminating wisdom. Samantabhadra (Tib. Kun tu bzang po, Ch. Puxian, Jap. Fugen, "All-Good") is described as a *bodhisattva* who protects those who propagate *sūtras* in early Mahāyāna texts, but later becomes one of the most important figures in the Mahāyāna pantheon. He is often depicted riding on a white elephant with six tusks, and he holds a lotus, a wish-fulfilling jewel, or a scroll. In both Tibet and East Asia, he is often said to be the primordial Buddha and the embodiment of the truth body of all buddhas, and is regarded as such by the Nyingma Order of Tibetan Buddhism. In tantric representations, he is commonly shown with dark blue skin (symbolic of emptiness) and is often in sexual embrace with his consort Samantabhadrī.

See also: **Tibet: an expanded pantheon; Tibet, Buddhism in; Vajrayāna Buddhism.**

JOHN POWERS

VAJRAYĀNA PRACTICE

Vajrayāna and other Mahāyāna traditions

Adherents of Vajrayāna claim that the special practices of their traditions provide a more rapid path to Buddhahood than those of the standard Mahāyāna, which is commonly referred to as the "*Sūtra* Vehicle" – because it follows the Mahāyāna corpus of *sūtras* that are attributed to Śākyamuni Buddha but which only began to appear centuries after his death – or "Perfection Vehicle," based on the notion that *bodhisattvas* on this path gradually cultivate the six perfections over a period of three countless eons (*asaṃkyeya-kalpa*) in pursuit of Buddhahood.

The practices of the Perfection Vehicle are concordant with awakening (*bodhi*), but Vajrayāna claims to be faster because it takes the effect of path – Buddhahood – as the practice itself, and so tantrists familiarize themselves with the various aspects of being a Buddha and performance of activities for the benefit of sentient beings.

Initiation and instruction

Each *tantric* cycle is essentially a lineage of practice. The primary aim is to attain Buddhahood in order to benefit other beings, and intermediate goals include acquisition of magical powers (*siddhi*) and advanced states of consciousness. Vajrayāna practice normatively begins with initiation (Skt. *abhiṣeka*, Tib. *dbang*), which in order to be authentic must be conferred by a qualified spiritual teacher. The master in turn received the same instructions from his or her teacher, and each lineage traces itself back through a succession of human gurus, and generally to a particular Buddha who is said to have given the teachings to their first human recipient. In Tibetan Buddhism, most orders first require that aspirants complete the "preliminary practices" (*sngon 'gro*), which include: (1) 100,000 repetitions of the refuge prayer, through which one commits oneself to reliance on the Buddha, the *Dharma*, and the monastic community (*tantric* practitioners generally add refuge in the guru, and sometimes in the *ḍākinīs*); (2) 100,000 prostrations (Tib. *phyag 'tshal*), generally in front of an image or painting of the main Buddha of a particular *tantric* cycle, which serves to develop one's faith and reduce egotism; (3) 100,000 recitations of the *mantra* of the Buddha Vajrasattva, which is believed to purify the mind; (4) 100,000 *maṇḍala* offerings, in which one generally uses small plates which one fills with gems or grains, which are visualized as offerings of all the precious things of the universe to the Buddhas and *bodhisattvas*; and (5) 100,000 sessions of guru yoga, in which one learns to visualize the guru as the embodiment of the Buddha.

In order to practice Vajrayāna, a student should first receive empowerment (Tib. *dbang skur*), which creates a *karmic* connection with the main buddha of a particular *tantric* cycle and opens up the potential for Buddhahood in one's mind. This is generally combined with an oral transmission (Tib. *rlung*) of relevant texts, during which the guru often reads them quickly – not expecting that the students will comprehend the teachings or practices – which is believed to enhance the newly awakened potential for practice. The guru also provides formal teachings (Tib. *khrid*) and additional advice (Tib. *man ngag*), often as an ongoing activity. The actual initiations employ terminology, symbolism, and practices from royal consecrations that were performed in India during the period the *tantras* were composed (seventh to eleventh centuries).

The *tantras* commonly employ coded language, and many parts of the texts are deliberately incomprehensible at the literal level. Thus instructions by a master of the oral lineage are essential. The connections that develop between master and disciple are particularly close in Vajrayāna Buddhism, and the tradition abounds with stories of recurring relationships over the course of many lifetimes. In some texts it is even asserted that unless a particular student has past *karmic* connections with a guru, it will not be possible for them to establish a *tantric* master–student relationship.

Sādhana

In Tibetan traditions, recipients of initiations generally pledge to maintain ongoing commitments. These include the fourteen root vows (Skt. *samaya*, Tib. *dam tshig*), which include promises not to contradict the guru, not to engage in sectarian controversy with fellow *tantrists*, not to denigrate women, and not to develop doubts regarding *tantric* teachings or practices. Students also commonly promise to perform *sādhanas*, which range from simple rituals that can be done in a relatively short time to elaborate combinations of prayers, offerings, and visualizations of vast numbers of deities in various patterns. *Sādhanas* generally begin with recitation of the refuge prayer and an indication of one's intention to manifest the mind of awakening. This is followed by visualization of the central deity, generally accompanied by other buddhas and various attendants.

The next phase involves paying homage to the deity and recitation of his/her *mantra*, and one may imagine that all sentient beings are also participating in the practice and deriving merit from it. The deity is viewed as responding positively to one's prayers and bestowing blessings. In the next phase one visualizes the deity being dissolved into emptiness, and one abides in non-conceptual contemplation of suchness. The concluding part of the ritual involves dedication of the merit generated by it to all sentient beings and hoping that they benefit from one's practice.

More elaborate *sādhanas* may involve initial purificatory practices for oneself and the surrounding environment, elaborate visualizations, extended verses of homage and dedication of merit, and detailed sequences of imagery that are built up progressively and then comprehensively dissolved into emptiness. The dissolution is crucial because ideally the visualization itself is generated from the wisdom consciousness realizing emptiness, which enables one to understand that there is no real difference between oneself and the deity. This fundamental non-difference makes possible the transformation of an ordinary being into a fully actualized buddha, and comprehending that both oneself, the deity, and the environment are empty serves as a counteragent to false pride and afflicted perceptions.

Deity yoga

One of the central practices of Tibetan tantra is deity yoga, which involves generating a vivid mental image of a Buddha, often accompanied by other Buddhas and various attendants. In highest yoga *tantra*, this is divided into two main phases: the generation stage; and the completion stage. In the first, one generates a vivid mental image of a Buddha in front of oneself, complete with all the exalted qualities of the body, speech, and mind of a fully awakened being. When one is able to maintain the image for extended periods of time without wavering, one has accomplished the generation stage. In the completion stage, one invites the Buddha to merge with oneself, and one imagines that one is transformed into a Buddha and that one performs activities for the benefit of sentient beings. This is said to be a rapid path to Buddhahood because instead of engaging in practices that are merely concordant with Buddhahood, like the six perfections (as is done in the Perfection Vehicle), one trains in the effect of the path, Buddhahood itself. The more one familiarizes oneself with these meditations, the more one comes to approximate the state of Buddhahood in reality. For this reason, Vajrayāna is sometimes referred to as the "Effect Vehicle" (Skt. Phala-yāna, Tib. 'Bras bu'i theg pa) because trainees take the effect of the path as the basis for their practice.

Subtle body

Generation-stage yogas assume the physiology of the "subtle body" (Skt. *mayādeha*, Tib. *sgyu lus*), consisting of winds and drops and the channels through which they circulate. There are said to be 82,000 channels, the most important of which are the right, left, and central channels. Generation-stage yogas are also closely connected with practices relating to the intermediate state between lifetimes (Skt. *antarābhava*, Tib. *bar do*), which commences when the winds coalesce into the heart *cakra* (a place where the left and right channels wrap around the central channel in the region of the heart). At this point, the last of the coarser levels of mind disappears, and all that remains is the most subtle level, the mind of clear light. Following the manifestation of the mind of clear light, one acquires an intermediate state body and enters the *bardo*, during which one encounters various frightening sounds and visions. Advanced meditators who have previously trained in generation and completion-stage yogas are able to recognize them as manifestations of their own minds and can take control over the intermediate-state process, which represents a significant opportunity for spiritual progress for those who are prepared, but which also contains numerous pitfalls for the untrained and for beginning practitioners.

In the completion stage, one simulates the process of dying by moving through the subtle physical processes that occur in the moments before death. During the completion stage, one draws the winds into the central channel (which occurs naturally at the time of death). After this one causes them to move upward through the *cakras*. In this practice, there is no clear differentiation of mind and body, as the subtle energies are said to be the "mounts" (Skt. *aśva*, Tib. *rta*) of minds, and they are also mentally manipulated by the meditator. In addition, when they are brought into the central channel and moved through the *cakras*, this process is accompanied by the manifestation of various mental states.

Sexual yogas

Some completion-stage practices involve sexual yogas with a partner who is either real or imagined. According to *tantric* theory, at the moment of orgasm coarser levels of mind drop away and a subtle mind manifests. Sexual yogas make use of this natural occurrence by manipulating winds and employing visualizations of oneself and one's partner as male and female Buddhas whose sexual embrace symbolizes the actualization of compassion and wisdom in the completion of Buddhahood. The bliss of orgasm is associated with the innate great bliss that is fully known by Buddhas.

Some lineages of Tibetan Buddhism contend that one may attain Buddhahood by merely visualizing a consort in the act of sexual union, but others – including Tsong Khapa and the Gelukpa tradition generally – maintain that one must employ an actual partner (referred to as an "action seal": Skt. *karma-mudrā*, Tib. *las kyi phyag rgya*) in the final stages of practice. The bliss of union – which is combined with the wisdom consciousness realizing emptiness – approximates the mental state of Buddhas, who perceive all appearances as manifestations of luminosity and emptiness and who are untroubled by the vicissitudes of phenomenal reality. Sexual yogas often involve retention of semen by male practitioners. In such contexts, the semen is referred to as "mind of awakening" (*bodhicitta*), and the movement of subtle energies through the central channel is equated with generation of the aspiration to become a Buddha.

According to *tantric* theory, sexual yogas are only appropriate and effective for advanced practitioners who have ideally directly realized emptiness – or those at least who have acquired significant control over energies within the subtle body. Among contemporary Tibetan Buddhists, actual practice of these techniques appears to be quite rare, despite the assertion by some masters that they are necessary for final attainment of Buddhahood. Many *tantric* practitioners are monks or nuns who have taken vows of monastic celibacy, and so sexual congress would be a violation of those vows. In the Gelukpa Order, Tsong Khapa is said to have waited until the intermediate state to engage in sexual yogas, which were performed in a subtle *bardo* body, and his example is often cited by his contemporary followers.

Guru yoga

Prior to undertaking *tantric* practice, one must receive initiation from a qualified master, and during the initiation the guru plays the role of the central Buddha. Students are required to imagine the guru as undifferentiable from the Buddha, and visualizations often involve mentally projecting the Buddha in front of one with the guru's face. The guru's blessing (Skt. *adhiṣṭhāna*, Tib. *byin rlabs*) provides direct access to the power of the Buddha, and each stage of practice requires a new empowerment by the guru. These are accompanied by oral explanations, reading of texts, and instructions in the performance of *sādhanas*.

Tibetan *tantric* theory emphasizes the necessity of learning to visualize one's guru as the Buddha in his *tantric* form of Vajradhara (rDo rje 'chang), the transmitter of *tantric* lore. *Tantric* texts commonly claim that unless one is able to do so, attainment of Buddhahood is impossible. One first conceives of the guru as possessing all the exalted qualities of a buddha, and through this one is able to acquire them oneself. Even if the guru does not have these qualities, one's imagination can still actualize them for oneself. Similarly, any faults one attributes to the guru – even faults that s/he actually has – are transferred to oneself if one fails to develop the devotion necessary for successful guru yoga.

Tantric texts sometimes contain admonitions to examine gurus thoroughly before committing to a master–disciple relationship because it is easier to develop sincere devotion if the guru is a good exemplar of the tradition and its values. But once the relationship has been formalized, the student is expected to maintain unfailing reverence for the guru. This will lead to rapid progress on the Buddhist path, and students who fulfill their obligations can expect to meet the guru again and again in future lives. The importance of guru yoga is indicated by the fact that *sādhana* visualizations often place the guru in the form of the central Buddha at the center of the *maṇḍala*, and many *tantric* lineages have elaborate pantheons stretching back through generations of luminaries to the Buddha who revealed the teachings, with one's own guru at the center.

Further, all of the figures of the pantheon are said to be manifestations of the guru, who is identical with Vajradhara. At the same time, however, the doctrine of emptiness permeates the theory and practice of guru yoga; one realizes that both oneself and the guru are empty of inherent existence, and so finally the guru is an external model for the goals of one's own training. Ultimately one aims to become the guru, and thus the duality of student and teacher is transcended at the higher levels of practice. One can become a Buddha because the potential for Buddhahood is inherent in all beings. The guru symbolically represents the actualization of this potential, but one engages in guru yoga not simply in order to acknowledge a master's attainments but to enable one to acquire them oneself. One initially projects Buddhahood onto an external figure (the guru or a Buddha) as a means for making the transition to Buddhahood.

See also: **Vajrayāna Buddhism.**

JOHN POWERS

VASUBANDHU

One of the most prolific of all Indian Buddhist writers, Vasubandhu reportedly lived in the fourth century CE, probably dying around 396 at the age of eighty. His writings contributed to the scholasticism of the Vaibhāṣika and Sautrāntika schools of canonical Buddhism as well as to the Yogācāra school of Mahāyāna Buddhism. His most enduring philosophical contribution to the Vaibhāṣika school was the *Abhidharmakośa* (for more on which see *Abhidharma* schools). His principal writings from the Yogācāra perspective were the *Viṃśatikā kārikā* (*Twenty-verse Treatise*), the *Triṃśikā kārikā* (*Thirty-verse Treatise*), the *Trisvabhāvanirdeśa* (*Description of the Three Natures*) and a commentary on Asaṅga's *Madhyāntavibhāga* (*Distinguishing the Middle from the Extremes*). For more on these works see Yogācāra school. In addition, Vasubandhu made contributions to logic and debate theory in his *Vādavidhi* (Method of Debate).

According to traditional biographies, most of which are based on a biography written by Paramārtha (499–569), Vasubandhu was born in the kingdom of Gāndhāra, now part of Pakistan, into a Brahman family. His father was a learned priest in the royal court, and this circumstance probably enabled the young Vasubandhu to study the Nyāya and Vaiśeṣika schools of the Brāhmaṇical tradition; it is clear from his writings that he knew those systems well and was influenced by them. His older brother eventually took the religious name Asaṅga and became one of the most important figures in the early Yogācāra school. Vasubandhu eventually followed Asaṅga into Buddhist monastic life but retained his given name rather than taking on a religious name.

In Gandhāra during Vasubandhu's time, the Vaibhāṣika school was influential among Buddhists, and it is likely that Vasubandhu heard debates among the great *abhidharma* specialists of his time. His largest work by far, the *Abhidharmakośa*, presents an extensive summary of the principal doctrines of that school arranged in eight chapters. The title of the work is explained by the author to mean a scabbard (*kośam*) in which the sword of wisdom is kept, wisdom being the highest virtue (*abhidharma*) which leads to the highest reality (*abhidharma*), namely, *nirvāṇa*. In this work he dedicates chapters to the constituents of experience, the various faculties of sentient beings, the various world systems in the universe, the working of *karma*, the latent impurities that bring about suffering, the four stages of progress toward *nirvāṇa*, the nature of liberative knowledge, and the theory and practice of meditation. A short work refuting the doctrines of the Buddhist personalists (*pudgalavādins*) often circulates now as a ninth chapter to this work. The verses of *Abhidharmakośa* are said to present the views of Vaibhāṣika orthodoxy, but the author's own prose commentary shows that he was willing to question the orthodox position and to consider the views of the Sautrāntika school. Eventually Vasubandhu's uneasiness with Vasibhāṣika and even Sautrāntika views led to his becoming more interested in Mahāyāna principles, and especially the Yogācāra system. In this connection he wrote his commentary to his brother's work and composed several influential treatises of his own.

See also: **Asaṅga; India, Buddhism in; Mahāyāna Buddhism; Yogācāra school.**

RICHARD P. HAYES

VĀTSĪPUTRĪYAS

The Vātsīputrīyas were one of the earliest schools to emerge in *Nikāya* Buddhism and the first monastic school or *nikāya* to split off from the Sthaviravādin school. According to some Buddhist sources, this division occurred 200 years after the death of the Buddha, which would place it in the third century BCE. The Vātsīputrīyas took their name from a founding figure, Vātsīputra. He is said to have been a Brahmin by birth and ordained as a monk in a lineage that could be traced to Śāriputra, one of the Buddha's great disciples. While Vātsīputra is described as a master of the *Vinaya*, the texts of monastic law, he is also said to have prepared a new version of the *Abhidharma* from a received tradition that he attributed to Śāriputra and Rāhula; there is no surviving evidence for this collection, although it is said to have existed in nine parts. Vātsīputra is probably best remembered in Buddhist sources, however, for holding a doctrinal position that maintained the reality of a person, *pudgala*, across time. The followers of Vātsīputra were likewise known for holding this position, and thus were frequently reviled as *Pudgalavādins*, although they also held a number of other distinctive doctrinal positions.

The Sthaviravādins, from whom the Vātsīputrīyas separated, had constituted themselves about a century earlier in contradistinction to the Mahāsaṃghikas. This first schism of the Buddhist monastic order was also on doctrinal grounds, around disagreements about the nature of an enlightened person (*arhat*). The fact that this first division and the subsequent separation of the Vātsīputrīyas were both on doctrinal grounds suggests that the earliest divisions within the Buddhist monastic order had crystallized around doctrinal disputes, but the conditions for these divisions were just as much social as intellectual.

Although relatively little is known about the Vātsīputrīyas as a monastic group in India or elsewhere, what is known includes some details that are sufficient to suggest to us what the first conditions for the emergence of distinct doctrinal "schools" within the Buddhist movement might have been. First, identifying Vātsīputra as a student of Śāriputra identifies him as a member of a particular ordination lineage that would have been simultaneously distinguished and connected to other ordination lineages in a segmentary pattern, much like ordinary kinship networks. Awareness of being members of distinct ordination lineages, sometimes as prestigious as one from Śāriputra, surely must have generated an awareness of difference within the monastic order but would not have ordinarily prompted separations and schisms from it. Second, Vātsīputra's lineage apparently also preserved its own tradition of textual transmission and interpretation which it traced back to Śāriputra and Rāhula as part of its own collective self-understanding and sense of prestige; we are aware of other ordination lineages that included similar collective memories as part of their identities. This received heritage provided the conditions for doctrinal disagreements that, in turn, developed into a desire for division and separation, once reconciliation of difference would have been perceived as an abandonment of a lineage's constitutive authenticity. Separation, once initiated, would have been then reinforced by exclusions in practice between monastic groups and by the codification of distinct *Vinaya* texts, as did happen among some of the Vātsīputrīyas.

As so often happened in the schools of *Nikāya* Buddhism, the Vātsīputrīyas once established as a distinct school were themselves subject to further divisions. Doctrinal disagreements again seem to have structured these divisions, apparently around issues that emerged as the followers of Vātsīputra elaborated and systematized what his *Abhidharma* collection entailed. The Vātsīputrīyas divided into four new schools: the Dhammottarīyas, the Bhadrayāṇiyas, the Sammatīyas, and the Ṣaṇṇagarikas. We only have direct knowledge about the Sammatīyas because a few of their texts have survived in Chinese translations. Indeed, it is largely from the Sammatīyas that we have direct knowledge of the Vātsīputrīyas. There is no surviving direct evidence of the Vātsīputrīyas as a group prior to this subdivision in India or elsewhere in the Buddhist world, although they are reported as still surviving in the Pāla Empire in eastern India as late as the twelfth century.

See also: ***Nikāya* Buddhism; Sammatīya/*pudgalavādins*; Sarvāstivāda; Sautrāntika.**

CHARLES HALLISEY

VEGETARIANISM

The instructions the Buddha laid down concerning diet in the earliest sources were intended mainly for monks and nuns as recipients of alms food rather than for the laity. An important practice in Buddhist monasticism is that monks go out daily into the local community to beg for food. As regards the type of food that may be consumed, the general principle is that monks should accept with gratitude whatever they are given and not be selective in preferring or rejecting particular dishes. To selectively refuse an offering from a householder would be seen as very bad form, and possibly bring the *sangha* into disrepute. Accordingly, in Theravāda Buddhism there is no prohibition on eating meat providing that the monk has not, in the words of the *Jīvaka Sutta* of the *Majjhima Nikāya*, "seen, heard or suspected" that the animal was slaughtered specifically on his behalf. By observing these requirements it was felt that the monk avoided complicity in the animal's demise and was innocent of breaking of the First Precept against taking life.

The Buddha did not categorically prohibit his followers from eating meat, even when it was suggested to him as a way of intensifying the religious practice of the community. Further, according to the *Mahāparinibbāna Sutta*, towards the end of his life the Buddha himself became gravely ill after consuming pork, although the precise nature of this dish (called *sūkara maddava* or "soft pig's flesh" in Pāli) has been disputed. Ten specific kinds of flesh, however, were thought to be inappropriate for human consumption, for instance the flesh of elephants, tigers, and serpents. Monks and laypeople in Theravāda countries still consume meat, although they may refrain from it on certain days, and they also regard the occupation of butchery as being a form of wrong livelihood. This is also the case in Tibet and Mongolia, where the harsh climate makes the mass adoption of a vegetarian lifestyle impractical. Meat-eating was accepted in Tibetan Buddhist circles on account of the lack of vegetable produce in Tibet, and today even the Dalai Lama does not follow a wholly vegetarian diet.

In sharp contrast to Theravāda attitudes, the rise of Mahāyāna Buddhism saw a movement towards the total abstention from meat-eating on the grounds that it opposed the development of compassion (*karuṇā*) by a *bodhisattva*. A number of Mahāyāna texts such as the *Nirvāṇa Sūtra* and the *Laṅkāvatāra Sūtra* condemn meat-eating, as do sources associated with *tathāgata-garbha* teachings, holding as they do that all living beings are embryonic Buddhas. The popularity of these texts in East Asia has resulted in almost universal vegetarianism among members of the *sangha*. Japan and Korea, while sharing this concern for vegetarianism early in their history, have in recent centuries been more tolerant of meat-eating among the clergy, while still admiring vegetarianism as an additional discipline that some may choose.

The difference between Theravāda and Mahāyāna Buddhism seems to turn on the question of whether a distinction can be made between the act of eating meat and the act of taking life. For the Theravāda, eating meat does not necessarily involve complicity in causing the death of the animal consumed, whereas for the Mahāyāna the two are morally inseparable.

See also: **Animals and the environment; Cosmology and rebirth; *Karma*; Mahāyāna Buddhism; Moral discipline; Precepts, lay.**

DAMIEN KEOWN

VIETNAM, BUDDHISM IN

Buddhism in Vietnam is traced to both India and China. Buddhist monks joined caravans returning eastward to China along the Silk Road. The caravans touched India as they passed through the Hindu Kush mountains. More frequently, monks accompanied Indian merchants in a direct route across the China seas. The merchants broke journey in Tonkin, in north Vietnam, before sailing further east. Tonkin, with its Buddhist *stūpas*, monasteries, itinerant Buddhist scholars, and missionaries, was a flourishing center of Buddhism.

Certain pioneer figures from India were associated with this phase, which also marked the beginnings of the translation of Indian Buddhist texts from Sanskrit to Chinese. However, considering the proximity of Vietnam to China and the gradual decline of Buddhism in India, China became the paramount source of Buddhist influence in Vietnam.

With the older traditions of Confucianism and Taoism, Buddhism was one of three religions imported to Vietnam from China. The stigmatization of being foreign, a sensitive cultural issue in the ancient world, was officially associated with Buddhism during the long period of Chinese colonial rule over Vietnam, which lasted well into the eleventh century of the Christian era. Chinese policies oscillated between spasmodic spurts of support, to apathy and open hostility, inspired by a perception that Buddhism had little pragmatic use as an appendage to secular state policies. The ruling Chinese Mandarin power elite feared Buddhism in a political sense, although the politicization of Buddhism came much later in the second half of the nineteenth century.

Characterized as an exotic import, Buddhism harmonized with the indigenous cultures of animism and ancestor worship. Buddhism was seen in this light among Vietnam's peasant communities who made up the bulk of the population. *Dukkha* (Skt. *duḥkha*) (suffering) taken in its literal, rudimentary and universal form, harmonized with grim realities of quotidian living, its burdens alleviated by concerned ancestors who watched over the living. The deeper metaphysical dimensions of Buddhist theories of suffering made little sense.

It augured well for Buddhism that it came to Vietnam in Mahāyāna rather than the Theravāda form. The Mahāyāna *bodhisattva* moved by compassion for suffering humankind postpones his entry into *nirvāṇa* until all other beings are able to achieve the status of an enlightened *bodhisattva*. The robust optimistic vision that every human being has the potential of achieving *bodhisattva* status projected a warm encompassing inclusive vision of things, linking ancestors to the living.

Over and above interfacing with older traditions and religious cultures, Buddhism developed an identity of its own. Its strengths were resilience and visibility. In the absence of the classic symbiosis between Buddhism and the state, individual Vietnamese rulers reacted idiosyncratically to Buddhism. Some rulers marked their tenures by erecting new *stūpas* (*pagodas*), renovating old ones, building new monasteries, making generous grants of state land for the support of the monasteries, and exempting monks from the payment of taxes and from compulsory service in the military. Other rulers, however, reversed these very policies, bringing monks under the strict security and regimentation of the state. Attempts were also made to run monasteries bureaucratically as a secular government department. Underlying these policies was the ancient fear that the monks politically were potentially an *Imperium in Imperio* threatening the state. Instances of charismatic monks, one of whom claimed to be a reincarnation of the Buddha, raising the standard of rebellion, gave certain credence to this fear.

A different order of things was ushered in with the coming of the colonial powers, the Portuguese, the Dutch, the French and the British, to Southeast Asia, and their successful establishment of enclaves of economic, political, and cultural power. In Vietnam, as elsewhere, the foreign presence engendered an atmosphere of unease, uncertainty, and spasmodic movement toward ontological self-definition. European commercial activity in the entrepot and inland created a comprador bourgeois class in Vietnam. In Vietnam, the comprador elements did not become irreversibly anglicized as they did to a great extent in Sri Lanka. Instead, they were useful as a medium to make sense of the foreign presence in both its institutional and its cultural forms. The comprador elements became relatively affluent, making their wealth available for the Vietnamese countercultural Buddhist response.

The European presence helped the Buddhist revitalization in Vietnam through technology. Print technology, telegraphic communication overseas, possibilities of overseas travel, all contributed to revivalist impulses. Reformist-minded Buddhist organizations made contact with foreign Buddhist countries, notably with Sri Lanka, which had seen a successful revivalist movement and provided a modular paradigm for countries struggling with colonialism. In time overseas trans-regional communications made Vietnam privy to revivalist organizations such as the Young Men's Buddhist Association, the Mahā *Bodhi* Society, the World Fellowship of Buddhists, and the World Buddhist Congress. These influences led to new Buddhist practices like the adoption of the tradition of celebrating Vesak as a day of international significance to all Buddhists. Within Vietnam, as Buddhist consciousness rose, print technology played a part in interweaving a bewildering plethora of Buddhist associations, creating thereby a common Buddhist – at times a crypto-militant Buddhist – solidarity transcending the old sectarian divisions. Print technology saw the prolific reproduction of traditional Buddhist scriptural texts.

It seemed that the reformist societies, typically styled innocuously as associations, had the potential to spearhead a combined movement to achieve the decolonization of Vietnam. They were, however, oriented to making Vietnamese Buddhist society stronger. This took the form of programs of welfare and social amelioration, as well as a retooling of attitudes under the concept of self-cultivation, which gave Buddhists the capacity to adapt to new social environments, and presumably the political status quo without being confrontational. Moreover, Buddhist reformist organizations during the first three decades of the twentieth century took care to emphasize their non-political orientation, possibly as a tactical ploy to allay the fears of an alien European power ruling Vietnam. Mahāyāna-inspired apocalyptic and millenarian visions may have given the reformist movements their inspiration leading to an earthly Utopia, or at least a better order of things. The Amitābha-inspired Pure Land perfectibility served to encourage earthly endeavors when all seemed hopeless.

Women were very much part of Buddhism in Vietnam. They formed their own associations and launched a Buddhist weekly magazine as part of the immense ephemeral literature that the era of reform generated. In the process, women drew attention to gender discrimination and the tendency of colonial authorities in general to take institutionalized discrimination for granted. The rather unique feminist manifestation of the *bodhisattva* Avalokiteśvara and the immense popularity of female goddesses, notably Quam Am, the Goddess of Mercy, and Ba Chua Xu, the Lady of the Realm, clearly stressed the strong feminine presence in the Vietnamese culture. However, the phenomenon was not seen in a narrow sectarian feminist light because the goddesses' appeal was translocal and transcending gender.

As in other Asian countries, Buddhism in effect meant invariably a focus on the *sangha*, its only institutional form and the most conspicuous feature. In Vietnam, the recurring stereotypes were that monks were distracted by rituals, magic, sorcery, and had not immersed themselves sufficiently in the *Dharma* to reach the people at large. In both China and Vietnam, official policies of the state tended to be stern and often draconian, and constantly questioned the utilitarian value of the Buddhist monkhood. The authorities encouraged the monks to become well versed in the *Dharma* and in canonical Buddhist texts, and to preach to Buddhist laymen. The rationale was plain: the Buddhist emphasis on pacifism, non-violence, and of non-involvement in worldly activism and the placing of a strong emphasis on transcendence, helped overall in the perpetuation of the existing political and social status quo. The official calculation that a Buddhist monk could not in good conscience espouse violence held true and may account for the comparative political passivity of monks in Vietnam till the end of World War II.

It was easy to underestimate the power of a seemingly quiescent *sangha*. At the end of the Second World War, a critical catalyst in the colonial history of Asia, increasing numbers of Buddhist monks and nuns joined the Vietminh, whose sights were set on the elimination of French power and the ultimate unification of an independent Vietnam. The dramatic fall of Dienbienphu paved the way for the successful creation of the new state of North Vietnam. What weighed as a critical factor were the intemperate policies followed by the French puppet Bao Dai and his enactment of the notorious Decree No. 10, which reduced all religions other than Catholicism and Protestantism to the level of associations requiring the formal permission of the state to legally function. The crisis took on ominous proportions when the new state of South Vietnam, established under the aegis of American power, imprudently retained this decree and banned the traditional Vesak celebrations in 1957. Events took a dramatic turn when a young monk, Thich Quang Duc, assuming the sitting position of a monk in meditation, set himself on fire in Saigon, drawing worldwide attention to his martyrdom. Six other monks at various points followed his example. The event was the symbolic prelude to the fall of Diem and after a long searing war, the incorporation of South Vietnam within the framework of a unified country under the banner of communism. The monks withdrew to their monasteries.

Given the traditional conservatism of the laity, the monks stepped in to restore the state of things conducive to the practice of the *Dharma*, a recurring pattern in the decades that followed in other Asian countries confronted with similar dilemmas.

After the Vietminh succeeded in achieving the total unification of Vietnam as one political entity, not previously accomplished in a country which, like its neighbors in Southeast Asia, was really a congeries of micro-polities at the best of times, Ho Chi Minh was deified and achieved apotheosis. He in one sense is part of a pantheon of those leaders who in the course of time will be remembered entirely as religious figures when the present historical contexts have lost their relevance. The heroic figure of a successful communist revolution in a secular state will be subsumed by the greater religious tradition of religious apotheosis – all ironically within a communist state constantly made nervous these days by revival of religion, especially after the state adopted policies of economic liberalization and the inroads of globalization.

See also: **Buddha and *cakravartins*; Buddhism and Western lifestyle; Buddhism in the Western world; China, Buddhism in; Politics; South and Southeast Asia, Buddhism in.**

Ananda Wickremeratne

VIHĀRA

This article discusses the history of Buddhist monastic dwellings with a focus on their significance as sacred places and centers of ritual practice. The entry on Monastic dwellings provides an overview of the development of early Buddhist monastic residences. The term *vihāra*, "abode" or "dwelling," is one of a number of terms applied to the dwelling places of Buddhist monks and nuns in early Indian Buddhist literature. While the term was sometimes used to refer to the individual structures in which members of the *sangha* resided, the word came to be applied to whole monastic complexes, which eventually comprised a wide range of structures such as residential cells, relic monuments (*stūpas*), *Bodhi* tree shrines, image halls, teaching halls, structures dedicated to the important *sangha* rituals of higher ordination and bi-monthly *Pratimokṣa* recitation, libraries, and a number of buildings devoted to various practical purposes such as food preparation and sanitation (See Figure 43).

Figure 43 Interior of monastery on Dobongsan, near Seoul, Korea.

Scholars generally agree that the earliest members of the *sangha* moved from place to place, begging for their food. This is consistent with the ideal of solitude and detachment from all material possessions found as a continuing theme throughout early Buddhist literature. This ideal was just that: a highly valued standard that has been central to the community's distinctive ethos but that is probably not indicative of how most Buddhist monks and nuns have actually lived. The disciplinary provisions set forth in the surviving *Vinaya* texts point to a form of monastic life far more enmeshed in reciprocal relationships of interdependence with lay supporters than this ideal of solitude, detachment, and homelessness would suggest. This ideal nevertheless continued to be ritually and symbolically enacted through ordination rituals (including head shaving and the donning of distinctive monastic clothing), comprehensive rules prescribing the external deportment of monks and nuns, and through the material organization of monastic spaces which have served both symbolic and practical purposes. And it has remained an ideal more actively pursued by the minority of Buddhist renunciants who have chosen to live in remote caves and forest hermitages.

The earliest surviving evidence of Buddhist monastic structures dates to the third century BCE and includes rock-cut caves in western India, *stūpa* remains in northern India, and Sri Lankan donative inscriptions associated with cave residences for Buddhist renunciants. The rock-cut cave complexes in western India are particularly important sources of evidence, because most early monastic residences were constructed of perishable materials that have not survived to the present day. The rock-cut *vihāras* were typically built on a simple rectangular plan with monastic cells arrayed around three sides of a walled central hall; these residential structures were situated near rock-cut *caitya* halls containing *stūpas* at one end that served as devotional centers for rituals of circumambulation and offering; the halls likely also served as places where monks and laity could receive *Dharma* instruction. This basic pattern is repeated at early free-standing Indian monastic complexes such as Sāñcī, where the monastic residences were organized according to a similar rectangular plan with cells on three sides of an open-air courtyard located in close proximity to *stūpas*. Early monastic complexes tended to be constructed along trade routes and on the outskirts of towns and urban centers, affording lay patrons ready access to *Dharma* instruction and opportunities for merit-making, while providing the resident *sangha* members with some degree of solitude for their religious practices.

The rectangular plan of *vihāra* construction continued to dominate throughout South Asia, with a general tendency toward expanding the scale of temple complexes and adding more stories. One of the most significant shifts in the spatial and ritual organization of monastic complexes occurred with the emergence of Buddhist image veneration. *Stūpas*, and the ritual activity oriented around them, were central to the organization of Buddhist monastic communities from very early in the history of *sangha*. The earliest sculptural depictions of scenes from the Buddha's life such as those found on the railings and gateways surrounding the *stūpas* at Bhārhut, Sāñcī, and Amarāvatī do not depict his physical body, representing him instead symbolically; the earliest surviving images that portray the Buddha in bodily form date from the first centuries BCE and CE. As image veneration became an important element in Buddhist religious practice, centrally located image shrines began to appear in Indian *vihāras*, often at first located immediately across from the main entrance to the interior courtyard; Buddhist images were also placed in niches on *stūpas*. Even with the advent of image veneration, *stūpas* continued to be central to South Asian Buddhist ritual; their primacy is reflected in the Theravāda commentarial ranking of bodily relics, which are typically enshrined in *stūpas*, at the top of a threefold classification and images at the bottom, a hierarchy commonly reflected in an ideal ritual sequence in accordance with which the *stūpa* is first venerated, then the *Bodhi* tree shrine (considered a "relic of use"), and finally the Buddha image. When Buddhism became established in China, the prominence of *stūpa* veneration in South Asian traditions was reflected in the spatial centrality given pagodas (*stūpas*) in early Chinese monasteries. The earliest Chinese monasteries were built along a north–south axis with the main gateway oriented to the south; as one entered the main courtyard, the pagoda was the first structure encountered, followed by the image hall and teaching hall, with the residential spaces located outside the main courtyard. A similar pattern was used in the construction of early Korean and Japanese monasteries. The early importance of the pagoda was supplanted by the image hall, however, and later Chinese and Japanese monasteries either omitted the pagoda altogether or located it outside the central courtyard. As a variety of Buddhist schools took root in East Asia reflecting varying emphases in religious practices, monastery plans came to reflect these differences. Chan and Zen monasteries, for example, gave special prominence to meditation halls and special quarters for the abbot.

Given the central roles that monastic ordination and adherence to monastic discipline have played in defining a fundamental separation between members of the *sangha* and the community of lay Buddhists, it is not surprising that special ordination halls and rituals for establishing monastery boundaries (*sīmā*) developed. Apart from the special shrines within the monastery precincts that represent the Buddha's continued presence within the community (e.g. *stūpas*, image halls), the ordination hall holds the greatest ritual significance for *sangha* members. This prominence is often reflected in its physical construction, by elevating it or physically separating it from the surrounding space. The *sangha* members gather regularly within this ritually and physically defined space to reaffirm their disciplinary purity through the *Prātimokṣa* ceremony, and to recall the transition that each of them has made from the householder's life to membership in the *sangha* as they introduce new members to the community. And as Buddhist monks and nuns ritually mark their more enduring symbolic and spatial separation from the life of the laity, a separation physically embodied in the *vihāra*'s distinctive structures, so too lay Buddhists commonly prepare for their temporary ascent to the higher religious status of the *vihāra* through purifying gestures such as removing their footwear and washing their hands.

The precincts of Buddhist temples also frequently include shrines devoted to various gods and spirits who occupy different levels in the Buddhist hierarchy of rebirth statuses. These shrines often reflect both the historical process through which Buddhist institutions have been integrated into a multiplicity of local cultures and functional accommodation to the diverse mundane and supramundane needs of Buddhists. Typically, the spatial orientation of these shrines reflects the subordination of these lower-level supernatural agents to the Buddhas and *bodhisattvas* represented in the central image halls.

See also: **Ajaṇṭā; *Bodhi* tree; Cave temples; Monastic rituals; Sacred places; *Stūpa*; *Stūpas* of Sāñcī, Bhārhut, and Amarāvatī; *Vinaya Piṭaka*.**

KEVIN TRAINOR

VIMALAKĪRTI NIRDEŚA SŪTRA

The Teaching of Vimalakīrti (*Vimalakīrti-Nirdeśa Sūtra*) is one of the most popular Mahāyāna scriptures in East Asian Buddhism, and its historical significance is surpassed perhaps only by that of the *Lotus Sūtra*. Relatively brief by later Mahāyāna literary conventions, it is a work of expansive vision and imagination tightly structured within a strikingly dramatic and carefully sustained narrative. This degree of structural coherence is especially remarkable in a text dating from no later than the second century, and perhaps earlier. This work would surely claim a much higher position among the classics of Indian and indeed all of world literature, had the original Sanskrit text not been lost. Fortunately it has survived in both Chinese and Tibetan translations with its literary quality largely intact, especially in the elegant Classical

Chinese of Kumārajīva's translation, which was completed in 406 CE.

Taking as its core teaching the doctrine of non-duality, *The Teaching of Vimalakīrti* stands in close relationship to other *śūnyavāda*-class scriptures, and in particular to the philosophical vision of the Perfection of Wisdom literature on the one hand and the mythopoetic extravagance of the *Avataṃsaka* and the *Ratnakūṭa Sūtras* on the other. As an early, proto-Madhyamaka work, it is an exposition of the ultimately inexpressible and even inconceivable nature of Buddhist liberation understood as insight into the absence of any intrinsic nature in the world of phenomenal existence. While enacted on a stage that spans the vast cosmology of multiple parallel world systems so characteristic of the *Mahāyāna* imagination, the narrative opens in the familiar geography of the Gangetic plane. Set amongst the opulent precincts of Vaiśālī at the time of Śākyāmuṇi's ministry, the story focuses on the multifaceted figure of a certain Vimalakīrti, who is portrayed as a highly developed *bodhisattva*-adept, equally skilled in fantastic magical displays and profound *Dharma* discourse. Like the householder *bodhisattva* Dharmodgata in the *Aṣṭasāhasrikā Prajñāparamitā Sūtra*, Vimalakīrti lives the life of a respected and exemplary layman of "immaculate reputation" (*vimalakīrti*). Indeed he moves freely and skillfully through all aspects of worldly existence, from guild hall to brothel, board-room to bar-room. Fully within the world, he is, through the power of his skillful means (*upāyakauśalya*), utterly untainted by it, living always within "the flavor of meditative absorption" (*dhyānarasa*). He is said to have served numerous buddhas in previous lifetimes, and to have acquired with ease all the great superknowledges and magical incantations (*dharāṇī*). He has penetrated the most profound principle of the *Dharma* and achieved the perfection of wisdom.

The narrative begins conventionally enough, with the Buddha dwelling at Āmrapālī's grove, just outside Vaiśālī, the capital city of the Licchavis. Very quickly, however, the reader is transported from the familiarity of historical specificity to the exuberance of mythic imagination. After the conventional "thus-have-I-heard" opening (*evaṃ mayā śrutaṃ*) we are quickly informed that the Buddha is, on this occasion, attended by 8,000 enlightened *arhats*, 32,000 *bodhisattvas*, 10,000 Brahmās, and 12,000 Śakras – along with sundry other beings, including Lokapālas, Devas, Nāgas, Yakṣas, Gandharavs, Asuras, Garuḍas, Kiṃnaras, Mahoragas – and, finally, also the fourfold community of ordinary human aspirants: monks, nuns, laymen, and laywomen. Five hundred Licchavi youths soon arrive on the scene to pay their respects, led by the *bodhisattva* Ratnākara. On receiving their gifts the Buddha manifests an impressive display of the manifold range of natural phenomena throughout the great trichiliocosm, all within the span of a single parasol. Following that preamble, Ratnākara proceeds to ask the Buddha to explain how a *bodhisattva* should go about the key practice of purifying his (or her) future Buddha-field (*buddha-kṣetra*). The Buddha instructs him in the various virtues and practices of the *bodhisattva*, concluding that the *bodhisattva* who wishes to purify his Buddha-field must first of all adorn and purify his own mind.

This opening exchange might seem unconnected to the *sūtra*'s broader theme, the inconceivable non-dual nature of all existence, but in fact it serves as an appropriate introduction, grounding the abstract (and abstruse) philosophical discussion to follow in a very practical and immediate concern. It also locates the crux of the *bodhisattva*'s practice directly in the cognitive transformation that is the necessary basis for any successful cultivation of the ethical qualities making up the path. And finally it also serves to introduce one of the text's most effective tropes – the sly and playful depiction of the venerable Śāriputra as a well-intended but rather fussy and doltish schlemiel. Throughout the narrative, just at the point when the rarefied discourse threatens to leave the reader behind, this Mahāyāna "puppet-Śāriputra" steps in with some narrow and literalistic concern, only to be put in his place by those with greater *Dharma* insight. First it is the Buddha who sets him straight, then Mañjuśrī, and then the layman Vimalakīrti – several times. Finally, and most humiliatingly of all, it is a woman, a goddess. Seeing the full measure of ironic humor in these dramatic interludes is crucial to a full appreciation of the skillful rhetorical structure of the text, by means of which the potentially top-heavy discourse of non-duality is lightened.

With the introduction completed, the text moves on to the central drama of the story: Vimalakīrti has decided, as a skillful means (*upāya*), to feign illness in order to create the opportunity for *Dharma* discourse with all those who may visit to wish him well. Knowing this, the Buddha asks who among his attendants will go to convey his regards to Vimalakīrti. One by one, beginning with Śāriputra, they all beg off, each recounting some prior occasion when the inadequacy of their own understanding was revealed by the layman's far superior insight. Finally only Mañjuśrī is left, and though even he is reluctant, he agrees to be the Buddha's envoy, much to the delight of all present, who follow along, keen to experience an encounter between two such accomplished *bodhisattvas*.

On arriving, the guests are astounded to find that Vimalakīrti's house magically expands to accommodate not only themselves but myriads of other beings. When Śāriputra worries whether the monks will have a proper place to sit, the layman *bodhisattva* brings in magnificent thrones from a parallel world-system, so grand and tall that Śāriputra and his cohorts are unable to sit in them. Then, noticing amongst the assembled venerables a goddess (*devī*) in the guise of a princess, Śāriputra seeks to test her understanding. After several exchanges that do not go well for the monk, he asks her why, if she has such understanding, she is not capable taking on the (more desirable) form of a man. Replying with a gentle discourse on the emptiness of all such distinctions, the goddess proceeds to transform the monk Śāriputra into a woman! Later in the story, Śāriputra worries whether there will be sufficient food in time for the monks and others to eat. Sensing his concern, Vimalakīrti magically enables all present to see into a universe far away where the Buddha Sugandhakūṭa presides over his Buddha-field, called Sarvagandhasugandha ("most excellent of all fragrances"), teaching the *Dharma* not in terms of words and concepts, but by means of subtle and alluring fragrances. He, on learning of the hunger of Vimalakīrti's guest, dispatches wondrous food flavored with all the fragrances.

Each of these wry episodes provides occasion for Vimalakīrti (and the goddess) to discourse ever more deeply on the inconceivable nature of full and perfect awakening. But the climax of the story comes when the layman *bodhisattva* challenges all the Buddha's retinue, *arhats* and *bodhisattvas*, to take a turn at explaining the entry-way into the profound doctrine of non-duality. Each makes an attempt, their responses becoming ever more subtle, with the final effort of Mañjuśrī seemingly not to be surpassed. But then Vimalakīrti responds with his famous "thunderous silence" – surely one of the most poignant and powerful moments in all of Buddhist literature.

See also: ***Bodhisattva* path; Canons and literature; Mahāyāna Buddhism; Skillful Means.**

ALAN SPONBERG

VINAYA PIṬAKA

Introduction

Buddhist scholar Michael Carrithers is quoted to have said, "No Buddhism without the *Sangha* and no *Sangha* without the Discipline." In other words, in order to effect the highest level of ethical conduct from the monastic and lay communities, disciplinary codes for each unit were enacted. For the monastic community, this took the form of a portion of the canon known as the *Vinaya Piṭaka*. In the case of the monks and nuns, this was especially important because the monastic community depended on the lay community to provide institutional support consisting of food, clothing, and the like in return for the monastic community's offering of the *Dharma*. If, as a result of their individual and collective moral conduct, the monastics did not maintain the highest level of the laity's respect, the lay members of the *sangha* could easily withhold their support, thus disrupting – or even destroying altogether – the symbiotic relationship between the two communities.

The *Vinaya Piṭaka* is that portion of the Buddhist canon regulating the monastic life of the monks and nuns. Properly speaking, though, a consideration of the monastic aspect of Buddhist life must be taken in broad spectrum, focusing not just on that portion of the monastic law which was canonized, but on *Vinaya* literature in general, thus affording us an opportunity to view the developmental process going on within the early Buddhist community in the first few centuries after Buddha's death. For convenience, then, we arrive at the following schema:

- Paracanonical *Vinaya* literature
  - *Prātimokṣa Sūtra*
  - *Karmavācanā*
- Canonical *Vinaya* literature
  - *Sūtravibhaṅga*
  - *Skandhaka*
- Appendices
- Non-canonical *Vinaya* literature
  - Commentaries
  - Miscellaneous texts

Paracanonical *Vinaya* literature

Prātimokṣa

The *Prātimokṣa* is an inventory of offenses organized into several categories classified according to the gravity of the offense. Many scholars now agree that the *Prātimokṣa*, as a technical term in the Buddhist lexicon, seems to have undergone at least three stages of development: as a simple confession of faith recited by Buddhist monks and nuns at periodic intervals, as a bare monastic code employed as a device insuring proper monastic discipline, and as a monastic liturgy, representing a period of relatively high organization and structure within the *sangha*. We find the following classes of offenses within the monks' text:

1 *Pārājika dharmas*: offenses requiring expulsion from the *sangha*.
2 *Sanghāvaśeṣa dharmas*: offenses involving temporary exclusion from the *sangha* while undergoing a probationary period.
3 *Aniyata dharmas*: undetermined cases (involving sexuality) in which the offender, when observed by a trustworthy female lay follower, may be charged under one of several categories of offenses.
4 *Naiḥsargika-Pāyantika dharmas*: offenses requiring forfeiture and expiation.
5 *Pāyantika dharmas*: offenses requiring simple expiation.
6 *Pratideśanīya dharmas*: offenses which should be confessed.
7 *Śaikṣa dharmas*: rules concerning etiquette.
8 *Adhikaraṇa-Śamatha dharmas*: legalistic procedures to be used in settling disputes.

The nuns' text contains only seven categories, the third being excluded. The number of rules cited varies in the texts of the diverse Buddhist schools, ranging from 218 to 263 for the monks and from 279 to 380 for the nuns. When formalized into the *Prātimokṣa Sūtra* recited as a confessional at the twice-monthly *Poṣadha* or fast-day ceremony, concurrent with the new and full moon days, three new features were added to the text: a series of verses preceding and following the text, praising the virtuous, disciplined life; an introduction used to call the *sangha* together and instrument the confessional procedure; and an interrogatory formula, recited after each class of offense, aimed at discovery of who was pure and who was not. Thus within a short time after the founder's death, the monks had provided themselves with an organizational tool for implementing purity in the monastic order.

Karmavācanā

The *Karmavācanā* is the functional, legalistic device by which the communal life of the *sangha* is regulated. We might say that what the *Prātimokṣa* represented to the individual monk or nun, the *Karmavācanā* represented to the *sangha*. At least fourteen *Karmavācanas* can be listed:

1 Admission into the order (*pravrajyā*).
2 Full ordination of monks (*upasaṃpadā*).
3 Holding the confession ceremony (*poṣadha*).
4 Holding the invitation ceremony (*pravāraṇā*).
5 Residence obligation during the rainy season (*varṣopagamana*).
6 Use of leather objects (*carman*).
7 Preparation and use of medicines (*bhaiṣajya*).
8 Robe-giving ceremony (*kaṭhina*).
9 Discipline.
10 Daily life of monks.
11 Beds and seats in dwellings (*śayanāsana*).
12 Schisms in the order (*sanghabheda*).
13 Duties of a student and teacher to one another.
14 Rules for nuns.

All of these are handled under a general procedure called *sanghakarma* (literally, "an act of the *sangha*") arising either by a general requisition or a dispute. To be considered valid, the proper number of competent monks must be assembled, all absentee ballots gathered, and a motion (or *jñapti*) set forth. The motion is then read aloud or proclaimed (this is the *Karmavācanā* or "announcing the action") and a decision, positive or negative, obtained. On the basis of the decision, democratically elicited, the *sangha* acts as a unified order.

Canonical *Vinaya* literature

Sūtravibhaṅga

The term *Sūtravibhaṅga* is literally translated as "analysis of a *sūtra*." Thus the *Sūtravibhaṅga* is a detailed analysis of the offenses recorded in the *Prātimokṣa Sūtra*. As we should expect, the *Sūtravibhaṅga* has the same general categories of offenses as the *Prātimokṣa Sūtra*. Regarding each of the *Prātimokṣa* rules, the *Sūtravibhaṅga* has a fourfold structure: (1) a story (or stories) explaining the circumstances under which the rule was pronounced; (2) the *Prātimokṣa* rule; (3) a word-for-word commentary on the rule; and (4) stories indicating mitigating circumstances in which exceptions to the rule or deviations in punishment might be made. In addition to the *Prātimokṣa* offenses, several new terms are found in the *Sūtravibhaṅga*: *sthūlātyaya* or grave offense, *duṣkṛta* or light offense, and *durbhāsita* or offense of improper speech. These new terms were added because by the time the *Sūtravibhaṅga* was compiled, the *Prātimokṣa* had become fixed (that is, closed) with new rules considered inadmissible. To provide the flexibility of a situational ethics, the *Sūtravibhaṅga* expanded necessarily in this direction. Like the *Prātimokṣa*, there is both a monks' and nuns' *Sūtravibhaṅga*.

Skandhaka

The *Skandhaka* contains the regulations pertaining to the organization of the *sangha*. It functions on the basis of the acts and ceremonies dictated by the *Karmavācanās*. We might say that the *Karmavācanās* are to the *Skandhaka* what the *Prātimokṣa* is to the *Sūtravhibhaṅga*. There are twenty sections in the *Skandhaka*, each referred to as a *vastu*:

1 *Pravrajyāvastu*: admission to the *sangha*.
2 *Poṣadhavastu*: the monthly confession ceremony.
3 *Varṣāvastu*: residence during the rainy season.
4 *Pravāraṇāvastu*: the invitation ceremony at the end of the rainy season.
5 *Carmavastu*: use of shoes and leather objects.
6 *Bhaṣajyavastu*: food and medicine for the monks.
7 *Cīvaravastu*: rules concerning clothing.
8 *Kaṭhinavastu*: rules concerning the production and distribution of robes.
9 *Kośambakavastu*: dispute between two groups of monks in Kauśāmbī.
10 *Karmavastu*: lawful monastic procedure.
11 *Pāṇḍulohitakavastu*: measures taken by the *sangha* to correct disciplinary problems.
12 *Pudgalavastu*: ordinary procedures for simple offenses.
13 *Pārivāsikavastu*: behavior during the *parivāsa* and *mānatvā* probationary periods.
14 *Poṣadhasthāpanavastu*: prohibiting a monk from participating in the *poṣadha* ceremony.
15 *Śamathavastu*: procedures to settle disputes.
16 *Sanghabhedavastu*: schisms in the *sangha*.
17 *Śayanāsanavastu*: monastic residences.
18 *Ācāravastu*: behavior of the monks (not discussed elsewhere).
19 *Kṣudrakavastu*: miscellaneous, minor matters.
20 *Bhikṣuṇīvastu*: rules specifically for nuns.

In addition to the twenty *vastus*, there is an introductory section discussing Buddha's genealogy, birth, and life history up to the conversion of Śāriputra and Maudgalyāyana, and also a concluding section covering Buddha's death, the council of Rājagṛha, the history of the patriarchs, and the council of Vaiṣālī.

Appendices

Appendices are attached to several of the *Vinayas* as a supplement. They serve two basic functions: providing summaries of the rules found in the *Sūtravibhaṅga* and *Skandhaka*, and providing interesting bits of monastic history.

Non-canonical *Vinaya* literature

Fortunately, a wide variety of *Vinaya* commentaries have come down to us, and their importance for the student of *Vinaya* literature cannot be stressed enough. They provide interesting bits of monastic and sectarian history that have helped to define and understand the significant differences between the early Indian Buddhist sects. It is clear that the most complete commentarial traditions have been preserved in the Theravādin (in Pāli) and Mūlasarvāstivādin (preserved in Tibetan) schools. We also possess Chinese translations for *Vinaya* commentaries in virtually all of the major *Nikāya* Buddhist schools but unfortunately we are almost totally lacking in Sanskrit *Vinaya* commentaries.

Virtually every major early *Nikāya* Buddhist school preserved its own version of the *Vinaya Piṭaka*, manifesting a high general agreement regarding the basic content of the rules, but differing significantly in several areas, thus affording an important glimpse as to how these individual Buddhist schools changed in response to differing times and locations. The issue of the regulation of monastic behavior continues to be important in the modern world as Buddhism rapidly continues its process of globalization, and especially so in the West, where significant changes in technology, community, and membership are redefining the *sangha* in bold new ways.

See also: **Buddhist canons and literature; *Sangha*; *Vinayas*.**

CHARLES S. PREBISH

VINAYAS

Vinaya denotes the discipline of Buddhist monastics and the associated literature that guides and regulates those who cultivate that discipline. The single word "vinaya" thus refers both to an ideal within Buddhist monastic life and to a specific corpus of Buddhist literature. The latter names one of the three divisions of Buddhist scriptures accepted in the schools of *Nikāya* Buddhism, but *Vinaya* literature extends beyond the canonical collections.

There has always been an important sociological component to *Vinaya* in Buddhist communities. Monastic discipline, the careful observance of regulations in practice, as these regulations are found in *Vinaya* texts, serves to set the Buddhist monastic community off from other religious communities with which it co-existed and interacted within a particular cultural context. It was *Vinaya* that distinguished Buddhist monks and nuns from Jain monastics and from Hindu ascetics in India, for example. With the emergence of *Nikāya* Buddhism, beginning around the third century BCE, this sociological dimension of *Vinaya* was directed to new ends, and differences in *Vinaya* observance frequently displayed and maintained divisions that developed with the Buddhist monastic community itself. In this regard, monastic discipline shades into liturgy and being in communion with other monks in a particular community or *nikāya* in the performance of rituals prescribed by the *Vinaya* texts became the mark of membership in a particular school.

The multiple functions of *Vinaya* – some individual, some social – can be seen in the ritualized recitation of the *Prātimokṣa*, the summary of monastic precepts, by a community of monks meeting together monthly. This communal recitation served to maintain the discipline of individual monks, even as it promoted the collective cohesion of the group. The ritual required that individual monks confess their faults and violations of the *Vinaya* in the company of their monastic peers, and once this was done and penalties assigned, the assembled community would recite the *Prātimokṣa* that was the mark of its received heritage as a school.

Some features of this ritual seem to emphasize its collective functions at the expense of its effectiveness in guiding the lives of individuals. It is striking that confession of faults and violations would take place at the outset of the ceremony, although in this practice the *Prātimokṣa* seems to be consonant with what is commonly observed more generally in the legal cultures of Buddhist communities. Legal proceedings were less about ascertaining wrong-doing and assigning responsibility than about restoring the social fabric of a community that had been breached. Equally striking is the received heritage itself. It enjoined the performance of the *Prātimokṣa* as a key component of Buddhist monastic life. As foundational as the *Prātimokṣa* is to Buddhist monasticism, the texts that are recited, albeit extremely authoritative, are not actually canonical. Indeed, the *Prātimokṣa* texts as well as other texts concerned with ordination and other monastic rituals (*Karmavācana*) seem to have been given shape after the initial formation of the *Vinaya* portions of the canon, and also after the beginning of school formation within *Nikāya* Buddhism. *Prātimokṣa* texts for eight different schools of *Nikāya* Buddhism survive in some fashion, in addition to the one found from the Theravāda. They are Sarvāstivāda, Mūlasarvāstivāda, Mahīśāsaka, Mahāsaṃghika, Mahāsaṃghika-Lokottaravāda, Kaśyapīya, and Sammatīya. It is clear that the rituals of monastic life were centrally visible in the divisions of monastic life that characterized *Nikāya* Buddhism, even if they were probably not their causes.

Those causes most likely lay in disagreements over how *Vinaya* was to be practiced and how *Vinaya* was to be applied in new circumstances as Buddhism spread and monastic life changed. With regard to disagreements about how *Vinaya* was to be practiced, the key tension was always between strictness and laxity. Buddhist historiography recounts various instances of disagreements among monks over whether certain practices were permissible or required. As Buddhist institutions spread throughout first India and then across Central Asia, new disagreements emerged with respect to regional differences that began to crystallize in the Buddhist world. The disagreements here moved along a tension between local and trans-local practices. Finally, as Buddhist institutions became more prominent in the public life of the emerging empires of South and Central Asia, new disagreements and competitions for patronage would have emerged over what was permissible according to the *Vinaya* texts and received traditions. These changes were more dramatic even than the earlier transformation in which Buddhist monastic life moved from an ideal of a wandering community to a settled institutional life. Rituals of donations to Buddhist institutions were key elements of the political economy of empires; indeed, participation in and sponsoring of Buddhist rituals was one of the most effective ways that a ruler could articulate his identity as an emperor, as opposed to a mere king, in the first 700 years of the Common Era. This meant that Buddhist monasteries received large amounts of patronage and ritual donations. Monasteries came to function as economic and political institutions as well as religious ones. Moreover, through these public rituals, the monasteries of *Nikāya* Buddhism became embedded in the ritual life of mainstream Buddhism, that social grammar that created connections and interactions across the boundaries of monastic schools, regions, and even religious communities. Royal patronage of Buddhist institutions, however, was not an indication of the personal commitments of a ruler, and the social grammar of the rituals and sacred sites of mainstream Buddhism effectively blended into the ritual life of other religious communities, such as the Hindu and the Jain.

When we look at *Vinaya* in mainstream Buddhism, it is obvious that its primary function socially was a ritual one. Individual monks, of course, always pursued their personal religious goals guided by the practice of *Vinaya*, but the prestige that came to communities of disciplined monks only added to their ritual value in mainstream Buddhism. Disciplined monks, monks who strictly observed the *Vinaya* and were indifferent to the allures of public life, were often the most desired "fields of merit" for the donative rituals of mainstream Buddhism.

In this context, *Vinaya* became a way of negotiating the competing claims of different social communities: the received lineage of a particular monastic community; the collective identity of a regional culture:

and the trans-local and cosmopolitan visions of imperial cultures.

The performance of the *Prātimokṣa* in a particular school's version would have publicly affirmed the continuity of tradition within a monastic community. Of course, it would have also affirmed to the individual monks who joined in such a performance that the life of discipline entailed by the *Prātimokṣa* itself was key to their religious lives. It would also have affirmed publicly the distinctive identity of the community reciting the *Prātimokṣa* vis-à-vis other monastic communities. Differences in monastic dress, another concern of *Vinaya* literature, would have displayed the school divisions of the monastic order in *Nikāya* Buddhism. But these divisions would have been formally embodied and authorized for monks in the performance of the *Prātimokṣa* rituals. It should come as no surprise that variation in the *Prātimokṣa* and other ritual literature was greater than other kinds of *Vinaya*.

The *Vinaya*, as a canonical collection, survives in the versions of five different schools of *Nikāya* Buddhism, in addition to that found in the Theravāda tradition: Mahāsaṃghika, Sarvāstivāda, Mūlasarvāstivāda, Dharmaguptaka, and Mahīśāsaka. In size and contents, there are significant differences among these *Vinaya* collections, but there is sufficient overlap among them to suggest that they draw on a common backdrop that antedates the formation of different schools in *Nikāya* Buddhism, unlike what is observed with the *Prātimokṣa* texts. Above all, these *Vinaya* collections all seem concerned with the creation of social boundaries that would define who is inside a particular community and who is not, how to regulate the behavior of those who are within a community, and what to do about those who violate these regulations. *Vinaya* is, somewhat surprisingly not particularly concerned with many of the practices that are distinctive to Buddhist monastic life, such as meditation. *Vinaya* is concerned with the regulation of sexuality, with the etiquette of monastic hierarchy, with the ownership of property more than the mental transformation associated with meditation. Monastic literature more generally, of course, included many digests on the practice of meditation but this was not included in *Vinaya* literature proper.

Regional differences were clearly important in the history of *Nikāya* Buddhism, but we do not know just how they were important. Inscriptions do help us to identify the prominence of different schools in different regions of India. The Mahāsaṃghikas, for example, were strong in central India, while the Dharmaguptakas were prominent in the northwest. These regional differences affected *Vinaya* literature as well, with the actual *Vinayas* of different schools sometimes transmitted in the languages of the region with which they were most associated. The Dharmaguptakas, for example, used Ghāndhārī for their *Vinaya*, while the Mahāsaṃghikas seem to have used either a Prākrit or a form of Buddhist Hybrid Sanskrit. Later Indian and Tibetan writers tended to idealize the associations of language and school, saying that the Sarvāstivādins used Sanskrit, the Sthaviravādins used Paiśāci, the Mahāsaṃghikas used Prākrit, and the Sammatīyas used Apabhramśa.

The role of *Vinaya* literature in *Nikāya* Buddhism would be misunderstood if it were only perceived as expressing and reinforcing sectarian divisions within the Buddhist monastic order. It did do this, of course, but it also did something else.

In the first centuries of the Common Era, *Vinaya* guided monastic participation in the ritual life of mainstream Buddhism. In doing so, *Vinaya* effected an openness in the monastic community to the religious culture that encompassed it and whose support made its existence possible.

The religious culture of mainstream Buddhism focused primarily on worship (*pūjā*), rituals of merit-making (*puṇya-karma*), and donative rituals (*dāna*). There is abundant evidence for monastic participation in these rituals in all versions of the *Vinaya*, and inscriptional evidence gives further confirmation of this. Monks arranged for images of the Buddha to be made, they paid for ceremonies of worship to be performed to these images, and they performed these rituals of worship themselves. We also see ample evidence in the various *Vinayas* for the effects on the monastic communities of this participation in the ritual life of mainstream Buddhism. The control and maintenance of property became a central concern of monastic life, and a reflection of the resources that came to monasteries in regular donative rituals performed by prominent individuals and by rulers themselves, on their own behalf and on the behalf of their states. Buddhist monasteries, far from being places of poverty intentionally chosen within a discipline of world renunciation, were sites for the conspicuous display of wealth, as archeological evidence at monastic sites like Ajaṇṭā in western India make clear. *Vinaya* literature reflects these conditions, with its close attention to the proper ownership of monastic property, whether of institutions or of individuals, and with its rules for the inheritance of property by monks from other deceased monks. Some *Vinaya* collections also included extensive corpuses of narrative literature that provided models for the religious values and practices of mainstream Buddhism.

This openness of the *Vinaya* of the schools of *Nikāya* Buddhism helps us to understand how these collections came to be normative in other communities besides the ones in which they first took shape. A number of *Vinayas* from *Nikāya* Buddhism were used in China by different communities that were otherwise Mahāyāna in their orientation and self-understanding, and the Mūlasarvāstivādin *Vinaya* became normative in the Buddhist communities of Tibet. There are no uniquely Mahāyāna or Vajrayāna *Vinaya* collections. It would seem that when the Mahāyāna or Vajrayāna monastic communities had adopted a particular *Vinaya*, they embraced its catholic openness to mainstream Buddhism rather than its ability to define sectarian boundaries.

See also: **Monastic life; *Nikāya* Buddhism; Ordination (lay and monastic); *Sangha*; *Sanghas, sectarian*; *Vinaya Piṭaka*.**

CHARLES HALLISEY

VIPAŚYANĀ

Insight meditation (Skt. *vipaśyanā*, Pāli *vipassanā*) is comprised of a number of techniques designed to give the meditator greater understanding of all facets of existence, particularly their impermanence (*anitya*), their lack of selfhood (*anātman*), and the ways in which they cause suffering and dissatisfaction (*duḥkha*). Mahāyāna traditions emphasize developing the insight into things as being empty (*śūnya*) of inherent, independent existence (*svabhāva*). While tranquility meditation (*śamatha*) emphasizes serenity and stability aiming concentration (*samādhi*), insight meditation aims at wisdom (*prajñā*). Attaining wisdom requires observing the various shifting and changing phenomena of *saṃsāra* to see their true nature. Buddhist thought asserts that what keeps the mind from insight into things as they are is a host of cravings, attachments, and repulsions rooted in a network of false conceptions (*vikalpa*) and discursive elaborations upon those conceptions (*prapañca*). Insight meditation is a set of techniques for penetrating through these false conceptions to a cognition of the actual nature of phenomena.

One of the most important literary sources for insight meditation is the *Sutra on the Foundations of Mindfulness* (*Satipaṭṭhāna Sutta*, *Majjhima Nikāya* 1.55), which presents the basic technique of developing insight through the "four foundations of mindfulness." These include "contemplating the body *as* a body," the feelings (*vedanā*) as feelings, the mind as mind, and the objects of mind as objects of mind. The implication is that in a non-mindful condition one does not see these things as they are or in their true nature. Within each of these four foundations are a number of specific objects of meditation. Mindfulness of the body, for example, includes mindfulness of the breath, in which the practitioner observes the continuous flow of inhalation and exhalation, noting the length of breaths and thereby bringing about the gradual calming of the body and insight into its nature. Other meditations on the body include mindfulness of various physical postures (sitting, standing, walking, lying down), movements of the body, the bodily parts (both internal and external), the elements (earth, water, fire, air), and the corpse in various stages of decomposition (for vividly evoking the truth of impermanence, the potential repugnance of the body, and the inevitability of death). Mindfulness of feelings includes pleasant, painful, or neutral feelings. Mindfulness of the mind itself includes the contemplation of the mind's states when affected or unaffected by desire, hatred, and delusion, and in a state of focused contraction or distraction. Mindfulness of the objects of mind includes contemplation of the "five hindrances" to entering meditative states: sensual desire, aversion, sloth and torpor, restlessness and worry, and doubt. Other objects of mind include the five aggregates, the six sense bases, the seven factors of awakening, and the four noble truths – all important elements of Buddhist doctrine to be considered in the meditative state and experienced personally. The practitioner should maintain a calm but alert focus on these various objects of mindfulness, noting them but not trying to suppress them. The implication is that seeing all of these "as they are" (*yathābhūta*) will lessen clinging to them, allow the mind to transcend its entanglement with destructive states, and facilitate states that move the practitioner toward greater insight.

See also: **Meditation, modern movements; Meditation, visualization; Meditation in the Pāli canon and the Theravāda tradition; Meditation in the *Visuddhimagga*; Meditation traditions, Vajrayāna; Meditational systems; *Śamatha*; South and Southeast Asia, Buddhism in**.

David L. McMahan

W

WAR AND PEACE

Buddhist teachings strongly oppose the use of violence, analyzing it in psychological terms as the product of greed (*rāga*), hatred (*dveṣa*) and delusion (*moha*). The false belief in a self (*ātman*) and a desire to protect that self against "others" who are thought to threaten it is seen as the underlying cause of aggression. Buddhism holds that drawing a sharp boundary between self and others leads to the construction of a self-image which sees all that is not of "me and mine" (such as those of another country, race or creed) as alien and threatening. When this strong sense of self is reduced by practicing Buddhist teachings, such egocentric preoccupations are thought to subside and be replaced by a greater appreciation of the kinship among beings. This dissipates the fear and hostility which engender conflict and so removes one of the main causes of violent disputes. When threatened, Buddhists are encouraged to practice patience (*kṣānti*), and there are many stories of exemplary patience as well as practices designed to cultivate toleration and forbearance. Anger is seen as a negative emotion which only serves to inflame situations and inevitably rebounds causing negative karmic consequences.

Early Buddhist literature contains numerous references to war. The view expressed almost unanimously in the texts is that because war involves killing, and killing is a breach of the first precept, it is morally wrong to fight in either offensive or defensive wars. In marked contrast to the teachings of the Qu'ran, the Buddha states (*Sutta Nipāta* 4.308–11) that warriors who die in battle go not to heaven but to a special hell, because at the moment of death their minds are intent on killing living beings. According to Vasubandhu in the *Abhidharmakośabhāṣya*, a soldier "even if conscripted, is guilty of killing unless he makes the firm resolve that he will definitely not kill anybody, even for the sake of saving his own life." The same text affirms that killing is bad *karma* even in the case of self-defence or when done for the sake of defending friends. A legend in the commentary to the *Dhammapada* narrates how the Buddha's kinsmen, the *śākyas*, offered only token resistance when attacked by King Viḍūḍabha, and allowed themselves to be slaughtered rather than break the precept against taking life. The *Jātakas* contain stories concerning princes and kings who were so horrified by violence that they renounced their kingdoms to become ascetics or refused to defend themselves in the face of attack.

The example of the Emperor Aśoka in the third century BCE is often given as the model for a Buddhist ruler. After a bloody campaign in the thirteenth year of his reign, Aśoka renounced violence and vowed henceforth to rule by *Dharma*. The edicts promulgated throughout his extensive empire speak of tolerance and compassion and state that conquest by *Dharma* is preferable to conquest by force or coercion. Aśoka modeled himself on the classical concept of the *Cakravartin*, the righteous Buddhist king. It is notable, however, that although the *Cakravartin* is portrayed as conquering peacefully through the power of *Dharma*, he nonetheless retains his army and is accompanied by it on his travels to neighbouring kingdoms.

The pacifist ideal of the classical sources has not prevented Buddhists from fighting battles and conducting military campaigns from a mixture of political and religious motives. The historical background to the Buddhist involvement in war in different countries is complex. The early history of Sri Lanka was convulsed by war between Sinhalese and Tamils, and King Duṭṭhagāmaṇi (first century BCE) is regarded as a national hero for defeating the Tamil general Elāra who had invaded the island from south India. Duṭṭhagāmaṇi's victory was glorified in a famous chronicle known as the *Mahāvaṃsa* (fifth–sixth century CE) which relates that his army was accompanied by Buddhist monks and that Buddhist relics adorned the spears of the soldiers. Monks disrobed and joined the army to fight in what the chronicle depicts as a "holy war," although no such concept exists in orthodox Buddhism. Despite this apparent endorsement by the *sangha*, after his victory Duṭṭhagāmaṇi felt remorse at the loss of life whereupon, according to the chronicle, he was reassured by enlightened monks (*arhants*) that he was responsible for the deaths of just "one and a half people." The meaning of this cryptic remark seems to be that in contrast to Buddhists, Tamils count only as half persons, because they are "evil men of wrong views" little better than "beasts."

East Asia has also seen the involvement of monks in insurrections and military campaigns. This was most noticeable in Japan, where monasteries became wealthy landowning institutions employing bands of warrior monks (*sōhei*) to provide protection and intimidate opponents. The teachings and practices of Zen Buddhism were found helpful by the military caste (*bushi*) as techniques to discipline the mind in battle and dispel the fear of death. Martial arts such as swordsmanship and archery were influenced by Zen teachings, and the doctrine of emptiness (*śūnyatā*) helped provide justification for both taking life and contemplating the loss of one's own life with equanimity. In the final analysis, so the reasoning of teachers such as Takuan Sōhō Zenji (1573–1645) went, there is only emptiness or the void: life is like a dream and the one who strikes and the one who is struck are merely phantoms.

In the modern period, Buddhist religious groups have had a close involvement with Japanese nationalism and militarism. The Zen and Pure Land denominations provided financial support for the 1937–45 war with China, and in the Second World War most Buddhist schools (with the notable exception of Sōka Gakkai) supported the Japanese war effort against the Allies.

From the foregoing it seems that with respect to war there is a tension in Buddhism between precept and practice. On the one hand the classical sources teach strict pacifism, while on the other Buddhist states have never shunned the use of force, and have sometimes invoked religion as a justification for military campaigns. It should be noted, however, that in contrast to the Western crusades, war has rarely been used by Buddhists for purposes of religious coercion.

See also: ***Ahiṃsā*; Ethics; Moral discipline; Precepts, lay.**

DAMIEN KEOWN

WESTERN BUDDHISM: DIAMOND SANGHA

Founded in 1959 by the American Robert Aitken (1917–), the Diamond Sangha has grown to an international Zen Buddhist organization. The Diamond Sangha has created a Western form of Zen with an inculcation of the equality of the sexes, decision-making by consensus, and radical social engagement. Since the late 1980s, Aitken has given *Dharma* transmission to seven of his students, thus starting a Western Zen lineage with Western *Dharma* heirs.

Aitken came into contact with Zen while in a World War II internment camp in Japan with R.H. Blyth, an English disciple of D.T. Suzuki. After his return to California he met Nyōgen Senzaki (1876–1958) in 1947 and began Zen and *kōan* practice. He continued Zen training in Japan and Hawaii and became a student of Rinzai master Nakagawa Sōen Rōshi (1907–84). In 1959, Sōen gave Aitken permission to establish a sitting meditation group at his home in Hawaii. This small group, led by Aitken and his wife Anne Aitken (1911–94), was named the Diamond Sangha. It became an important link between Zen tradition in Japan and the widespread interest in Zen within California's counterculture. Aitken and the Diamond Sangha had a significant impact on the early stages of Zen in North America and its transition from a mystical fascination to the more practice-oriented approach.

During the 1960s, Aitken continued his Zen training with Hakuun Yasutani Rōshi (1885–1973), founder of the Zen-ecumenical Sanbō Kyōdan lineage. Both Yasutani and his *Dharma* heir Koun Yamada Rōshi (1907–89) taught Aitken and students in the Diamond Sangha. Aitken received *Dharma* transmission from Yamada Rōshi in 1974. Aitken's influence on Zen in North America continued with his widely used translations of Buddhist texts and being a respected Zen master and social activist. Ever since the end of World War II, Aitken had been a radical pacifist; together with Gary Snyder and Joanna Macy he founded the Buddhist Peace Fellowship in 1978.

In 1985, Yamada gave Aitken the additional qualification of Shōshike ("correctly qualified teacher"). This gave Aitken the authority to teach independently of the Sanbō Kyōdan lineage, and he and the Diamond Sangha separated, with it becoming a lineage in its own right. Nevertheless, the Diamond Sangha has similar practices to those of the Sanbō Kyōdan and the students train in meditation and most in *kōan* practice. Depending on the group, residential training programs in meditation are on offer which last two to four weeks. Teachers encourage students to take their practice outside the Zen center and to apply the practice to their everyday life. Texts are chanted in Sino-Japanese and also in English. Conspicuously, the organization has lay teachers – no monastic personnel – and is directed towards lay practitioners. Also, students are not necessarily Buddhist, though the teachers must be Buddhists. This does not, however, exclude that other religious beliefs can be held concurrently. As a number of teachers in the Diamond Sangha are also qualified psychologists or psychotherapists, psychological ideas and approaches have been incorporated in the Zen practice. As a grass-root social activist, Aitken is critical of hierarchies and power relations. Consequently and in sharp contrast to the hierarchical levels of etiquette and organizations so characteristic of Zen in Japan, the Diamond Sangha emphasizes consensual decision-making and equality of the sexes. Also, the organization has become an international network of affiliated Zen Buddhist centers with no central headquarters (though the *zendō* at Maui, Hawaii, is of much importance).

Aitken, aged eighty-eight in 2005, lives as a retired master in Hawaii and continues to write and study, working with a few long-term students. Nelson Foster and John Tarrant, authorized as first independent masters by Aitken, head the *Dharma* transmission ceremonies, having given permission to a further three students in the Diamond Sangha. The total membership was approximately 2,500 students in 2000. In 2005, there were eighteen officially affiliated Diamond Sangha centers worldwide. Apart from the United States with eleven centers, Australia – thanks to Aitken's teaching during the 1980s – was the second strongest with five centers; New Zealand and Germany each had one affiliate.

See also: **Buddhism in the Western world; North America, Buddhism in.**

MARTIN BAUMANN

WESTERN BUDDHISM: FRIENDS OF THE WESTERN BUDDHIST ORDER

The organization of the Friends of the Western Buddhist Order (FWBO) was founded by the English monastic Sangharakshita (Dennis Lingwood, b. 1925) in London in 1967. A year later, the Western Buddhist Order came into being, composed of both women and men. The FWBO seeks to give Buddhism a modern, up-to-date shape, fitting Western conditions, as it claims. The FWBO is not aligned to a specific Buddhist tradition in Asia, but rather strives to create a Western form of Buddhist interpretation, practice, and organizational form.

The FWBO uses texts and teachings of various Buddhist developments and traditions. Basic to the FWBO is its reference to the spirit of the original teaching, as Sangharakshita calls it. In order to reawaken this "spirit," Western art and literature from individuals such as William Blake, Goethe, and Nietzsche, are introduced as so-called bridges to an understanding of the *Dharma*. This eclectic intra-Buddhist and inter-philosophical approach also applies to the practices favored by the FWBO. Common are Buddhist meditation exercises from the Theravāda tradition, as are techniques from Zen and Tibetan traditions. Members regularly take part in *pūjās* ("worship"), which comprise of chanting, bowing and prostration.

The authoritative and organizational focal point of the movement is the Western Buddhist Order. Order members are ordained in a ceremony, taking specific precepts, the title *Dharmachari* and *Dharmacharini* (male or female, "*Dharma*-farer") and a religious name in Sanskrit or Pāli. Sangharakshita strongly emphasized the importance of "going for refuge" to the Buddha, *Dharma*, and *Sangha*. According to him, this is the central act of the Buddhist life, commitment and spiritual development. Order members may be single or married, living in celibacy, or in full-time employment. Many, although not all, order members live together in residential communities. Such communities, most often single-sex, are usually found near a center of the FWBO. The centers are visited by interested people and "friends," that is, those who have become members of the FWBO. At the centers, order members offer regular programs including meditation classes, public talks, study on Buddhist themes and texts and "bodywork" such as t'ai chi, yoga, and massage. In addition to the communities and the Buddhist centers, the FWBO has founded "Right Livelihood" cooperatives, such as vegetarian restaurants, wholefood shops, and the successful wholesale and retail gift business Windhorse Trading in Cambridge (UK). The movement's three pillars of community, centre, and cooperative aim to change local as well as general Western society and to bring about a "New Society."

Founded in Britain in the late 1960s, the FWBO began to gain a foothold in other European countries and overseas within a decade. An especially strong branch exists in western India, where Sangharakshita had supported Dr. Ambedkar's conversion movement during the mid-1950s. Apart from in Europe and India, FWBO institutions exist in Australia, New Zealand, Venezuela, Mexico, Canada, and the United States. In spring 2005, some fifty centers and local groups, six retreat centers and twenty-nine Buddhist businesses existed in Britain. As such, the FWBO is one of Britain's principal Buddhist organizations. Outside of Britain, there were about fifty city centers and groups, nine retreat centers and eleven cooperatives (spring 2005). The order's size was about 1,250 members; the number of supporters and friends is estimated to be about 100,000, the vast majority of them being Buddhists in India. The FWBO has launched several journals, among them the *Dharma Life Magazine*, and is a prolific book publisher (Windhorse Publications).

From the 1990s, Sangharakshita started passing on responsibilities to senior order members. He authorized these members to conduct ordinations, previously performed only by him. As the first chairman of a committee called the College of Public Preceptors, Sangharakshita appointed senior member Dharmachari Subhuti in 2000. In the ensuing years Subhuti and others started to convert the centralized organizational structures into decentralized and more flexible forms. Inevitably, a tension has become apparent between the overall coherence and unity of the FWBO and local developments and emphases, transforming the experimental movement of the 1960s, and the consolidated organization of the 1980s and 1990s into a globally spread spiritual network.

See also: **Buddhism in the Western world; Buddhist adaptations in the West; Europe, Buddhism in; North America, Buddhism in.**

MARTIN BAUMANN

WESTERN BUDDHISM: INSIGHT MEDITATION SOCIETY

The Insight Meditation Society (IMS) was founded in 1975 by four American lay teachers, disciples of prominent Asian modernist meditation masters. The approach favored by Joseph Goldstein (b. 1944), Jack Kornfield (b. 1945), Sharon Salzberg (b. 1952), and Jacqueline Schwartz/Mandell proved attractive to a growing number of people interested in practicing *vipassanā* meditation in an American-adapted style and interpretation. As such, the IMS, together with the Spirit Rock Meditation Center and their many affiliated centers and local sitting groups, is the most widely known and recognized organization among the multifaceted *vipassanā* movement in North America.

The adoption of meditation practice in this South Asian form by lay Westerners would not have been possible without previous changes in South Asia itself. Reformist monks in Burma and Thailand laid emphasis on meditation, enabled lay participation, and underscored the possibility of reaching final liberation or awakening, *nibbāna*, in this life. This contrasted with traditionalist Buddhism, with its centrality on *Dhamma* teachings by monks and devotional practices such as rituals, chanting, and reciting formulaic lists, intended as means for accumulating merit (*puñña*) for a better next life. The instruction in meditational practices by eminent monks such as Ledi Sayādaw (1846–1923), U Nàrada (1868–1955), and his most influential disciple, Mahāsī Sayādaw (1904–82), to both ordained and laity was new and decisive, first because the practice of meditation had not traditionally constituted an option for lay Buddhists and, second because the tradition of meditation had been lost for centuries among the Buddhist order, at least among the village- and town-dwelling monks.

IMS founders Salzberg, Kornfield, and Goldstein had been disciples of Mahāsi Sayādaw during the 1960s, spending years in Burma and India. Mahāsī Sayādaw instructed them and others using his approach of teaching *vipassanā* meditation exclusively during intensive periods of silent retreats on a strict daily schedule. The term *vipassanā* drives from the Pāli verb *vipassati*, "to see clearly"; *vipassanā* is understood to be a way of seeing or gaining an insight into the reality of things as they are. Closely related to *vipassanā* is *sati*, mindfulness or awareness. *Vipassanā*, insight meditation, is developed through the practice of *sati*, starting with focused practices of the mindfulness of breathing.

Having returned to the United States, Kornfield and Goldstein met for the first time in 1974 at Chögyam Trungpa's Naropa Institute when giving courses in *vipassanā*. A year later they founded the IMS as a non-profit organization for the practice of *vipassanā* or insight meditation in Barre, Massachusetts. The basic practice taught was the Mahāsī approach, structured in ten- and thirty-day retreats modeled according to the courses taught by S.N. Goenka, grand-disciple of Ledi Sayādaw and teacher to Salzberg. The courses consisted of daily periods of meditation, instruction and *Dhamma* talks in the evening, a day ranging from 5.00 a.m. to 10.00 p.m. In 1981 Kornfield moved to California, where a few years later he co-founded Spirit Rock Meditation Center in Marin County (near San Francisco) as a West Coast sister center to IMS. During the 1980s and 1990s interest in *vipassanā* meditation grew steadily. The number of IMS-affiliated meditation centers and sitting groups rose from nine in 1984 to 120 fully staffed retreat centers, such as those in Barre (the IMS headquarters), Cambridge, New York, Washington, Woodacre (West Marin), Seattle, Maui, and Honolulu, in 2000. However, the number of centers and sitting groups is an indication of the growth alone. Overall, the grade of institutionalization of the *vipassanā* movement is low, as participation in a retreat offered by the main centers proves to be the main form of adherence.

In order to meet the growing interest in *vipassanā* meditation, in the mid-1980s Kornfield set up a four-year program to systematically train teachers. The aim of the program, which is now run by both IMS and Spirit Rock, was and still is to certify teachers. A teacher's code of ethics is part of the training, the code having been issued in response to ethical breaches, abuse of power, and sexual abuse by a number of American Buddhist teachers during the 1980s. The ethos of Buddhism offered through IMS carries a number of Americanized characteristics: apart from being overwhelmingly lay-oriented and focusing exclusively on the practice of meditation, teachers of IMS eschew using Pāli vocabulary and keep to South Asian etiquette. The practice of *vipassanā* meditation is designed to be integrated into the practitioner's daily life and to form a practical part of American life. Features of democratization rank high, observable in the number of lay teachers; the retreats conducted are often team-based and gender-equal. The IMS supports ideals of individualism in emphasizing personal and inward experience. Organizational forms display soft institutional structures, with practitioners coming together for retreats at main centers, thus rarely aiming to establish local centers as in other Buddhist traditions and organizations. Importantly, the religious orientation of a practitioner is of no importance. *Vipassanā* or insight meditation is not presented as a religion but rather as an awareness technique which supports psychological healing and pursuits of happiness. Strikingly, instructions make much use of psychotherapeutic vocabulary, praising the ideals of personal transformation and freedom. So far, IMS and its well-trained teachers have succeeded in combining American adaptations of insight meditation with the basic Buddhist perspective towards individuals, reality and the goal of awakening.

See also: **Buddhism in the Western world; Buddhist adaptations in the West; Meditational systems; *Vipaśyanā*.**

MARTIN BAUMANN

WESTERN BUDDHISM: SHAMBHALA INTERNATIONAL

Shambhala International is the successor organization of Vajradhatu, the latter founded by the eminent Chögyam Trungpa Rinpoche in 1973 in Barnet, Vermont. Chögyam Trungpa Rinpoche (1939–87), born in Geje (eastern Tibet), was recognized as the eleventh Trungpa Tulku at less than two years of age, became a novice monk at age nine, and received full ordination in at age nineteen (1958). He received teachings and initiations from the Kagyu, Nyingma and Rismed traditions, though generally Chögyam Trungpa is categorized within the Kagyu lineage of Tibetan Buddhism. Forced to flee Tibet, Trungpa stayed in India before coming to Oxford on the basis of a Spalding Fellowship. He studied comparative religion, philosophy, and art. In 1968, Trungpa and Akong Rinpoche (b. 1943) founded Samye-Ling in Scotland, the first Tibetan meditation center in the West. As a result of a debilitating car accident, Trungpa gave up his monastic vows in 1969. A year later, he married Diana Pybus and moved to the United States the same year.

During the 1970s Trungpa generated a great interest among artists and the counterculture movement in the United States. His capacity to combine Tibetan Buddhist teachings and practices with United States/American pragmatism, and his outrageousness, became legendary. Trungpa's *Cutting Through Spiritual Materialism* (1973) became a bestseller and an American Buddhist classic. Trungpa and the many Vajradhatu centers founded in the US and Canada during that decade had a huge impact on Buddhism in North America. Apart from founding Vajradhatu as the umbrella organization for the growing international network of religious centers, Trungpa established the Naropa Institute as part of the educational Nalanda Foundation as well as a secular path of spiritual training, named Shambhala Training.

The death of Trungpa in 1987 was followed by a time of turbulence. Although Trungpa had empowered Ösel Tendzin (Thomas Rich, 1944–90), an American pupil of Trungpa, as his successor, his early death in 1990 resulting from AIDS and the scandal of having infected a Vajradhatu member caused confusion and strife. Trungpa's eldest son, Mipham Rinpoche, born 1962, became his successor and the new head of the movement. He consolidated the various religious and educational programs his father had established and renamed the entire institution Shambhala International in 1992. In 1995, Mipham Rinpoche was installed as Sakyong, or leader, of the various wings, which were all united under the organization of Shambhala International.

Shambhala International, like its predecessor Vajradhatu, constitutes a unique blend of Tibetan Buddhism, Japanese art, and an American way of life. Buddhist teachers and instructors can be ordained or lay persons, male or female. Converts are engaged in monastic training such as studying texts and practicing meditation, at times for many hours a day. The vision of Shambhala is to bring about an "enlightened society." To this end three "gates" are distinguished: Vajradhatu Gate assembles the various Buddhist centers, called Dharmadhatus, to practice meditation and pursue Buddhist studies; Shambhala Training is the secular path of spiritual training designed for everyone, regardless of whether the person is Buddhist, Christian, Jew or religiously non-affiliated; and Nalanda Gate offers training in a variety of disciplines such as the arts, health, education, and business, accompanied by instructions in poetics, archery, flower arranging and others. Naropa Institute, now an accredited university, founded in 1974 in Boulder, Colorado, and the Nalanda Translation Committee are two of the more prominent enterprises. All the various programs of Shambhala International aim for the cultivation of a contemplative life to be pursued in everyday life as well as in Buddhist environments. The creation of the envisaged enlightened society has become real in educational and economical endeavors: a pre-school, an elementary school, an accredited college, a credit union, bookstores and various profit-run businesses. However, this area is much less prominent than the Buddhist Dharmadhatu centers and the Shambhala meditation programs.

Trungpa had moved the headquarters in 1983 to Halifax, Nova Scotia (Canada), now the central administration for Shambhala International. In 1984 Gampo Abbey was established nearby as the main monastic center. The monastery, with its abbot, the American-born nun Pema Chödrön, has devised a special variation of the traditional three-year retreat to become a *lama* ("advanced teacher"). Participants alternate periods of six or more months with equal periods leaving the monastery in order to work and earn a living. In spring 2005 Ṣhambhala International had about 190 centers with ninety-two in the USA, thirty in Canada, fifty-seven in Europe and a few more in Japan and Australia. The organization is still growing, especially so in North America and Europe. The head of Shambhala International, the Sakyong, is increasingly recognized as an important voice and person within Buddhism in the West and Tibetan Buddhism in India.

See also: **Buddhism in the Western world; Buddhist adaptations in the West; Europe, Buddhism in; North America, Buddhism in.**

MARTIN BAUMANN

WETZEL, SYLVIA

Sylvia Wetzel is, as she notes in "Neither Monk nor Nun", a representative example of a Western *Dharma* teacher, a non-robed, non-titled laywoman. She has been involved with Buddhism for almost thirty years and is considered to be a European Buddhist pioneer (www.sylvia-wetzel.de/english/biographie.htm). In 1977 she met and studied with Lama Thubten Yeshe in Dharamsala and Zopa Rinpoche, founders of the Federation for the Preservation of the Mahāyāna Tradition (FPMT).

Her Buddhist background is also typical of teachers in the West in that she has received training in a variety of traditions: Zen, Theravāda, and Tibetan. She experienced the monastic side of Buddhism, spending two years as a Korean Buddhist nun.

Her early interest in political science and the women's movement led her seamlessly into issues concerning women and Buddhism and the adaptation of an ancient religion to a modern Western context. She was a founding member of Sakyadhītā in 1987 and also of Women Awake (1999). During the first Conference on Western Buddhism in 1993 in Dharamsala she spoke frankly to senior Tibetan monks, including the Dalai Lama, regarding the barriers faced by women in Buddhism. She was a founding member of the Network of Western Buddhist Teachers that grew out of that conference. Her teaching is known to be innovative and she encourages the integration of other fields such as psychotherapy to create a practice suited to Western needs. Among the meditation practices she regularly teaches is the Green Tara meditation.

Wetzel was a board member of the German Buddhist Union for fifteen years, and editor of the quarterly *Lotusblätter* ("Lotus Leaves") for twelve years. Since 2001 she has been the president of the Buddhist Academy Berlin Brandenburg.

The Buddhist Academy functions as a network for European Buddhists. A non-profit organization, it is composed of various interest groups which produce papers and organize conferences. These interest groups are reflective of the wide variety of interests of Western Buddhists: psychotherapy, economy and politics, women artists. There are classes in Sanskrit and Tibetan and members have produced a database of Buddhist terms in five languages. In addition, there are public talks and inter-religious dialogue with the Catholic Academy (http://buddhistischeo-akademie-bb.de/english/academy.htm). Wetzel's background and experience make her a perfect president for the organization.

Sylvia Wetzel has also translated numerous talks and books into German and is most well known for her *Das Herz des Lotos* (1999). The English print version appeared in 2002 and there is a translation by Jane Anhold into "American" English (also produced in 2002) available on the Relaxation Meditation Buddhism website (www.sylvia-wetzel.de/english/WomenAndBuddhism.htm). Her teachings take a critical eye to sexism in the Buddhist tradition and she dispels any attempt to "ignore" or provide apologetics for the issue. Yet, she shows how women can both call the tradition to account and make their place in it. Drawing on philosopher Luce Irigaray she envisions a tradition that does not deny women identity under the rubric of emptiness but offers equality with the recognition of difference.

See also: **Women in Buddhism: an historical and textual overview.**

MAVIS L. FENN

WILLIS, JAN

Jan Willis is a professor of religion at Wesleyan University and the Walter A. Crowell Professor of Social Sciences. She was the Acting Director of the Center for African Studies (1985–6) and Chair of the Department of Religious Studies at Wesleyan and Commonwealth Professor of Religious Studies at the University of Virginia (1984–5). She did her B.A, and her M.A. at Cornell and her Ph.D. at Columbia University. She has studied Buddhism for over thirty years and taught for over twenty-five. She has published extensively: *The Diamond Light* (1972), *On Knowing Reality* (1979), *Enlightened Beings* (1995). She has also edited *Feminine Ground: Essays on Women and Tibet* (1989) and published numerous articles and book reviews as well as a memoir, *Dreaming Me: An African American Baptist–Buddhist Journey* (2001). In December 2000, *Time* noted that she was a "spiritual innovator of the new millennium" and a "philosopher with a bold agenda" (http://time.com/innovators/spirituality/profile_willis.html).

As well as being one of the first scholar-practitioners in the West, Willis has had to deal with the difficulties of being black in America. Prior to heading off to Nepal to study meditation she was politically very active and even contemplated becoming a Black Panther during the 1960s. Trained in both Western and Tibetan philosophy, Willis has deeply considered questions of prejudice, their origination and their dissipation. She has developed a series of meditations on race and has tried to broaden Buddhism's base in America where only Sōka Gakkai Buddhism has managed to attract a number of black practitioners. In "Diversity and Race: New Koans for American Buddhism" she presented interviews and discussion with several black American Buddhists about Buddhism and race. This was a rare opportunity to hear these voices. In "Buddhism and Race" she presents her experience with Buddhism as a black woman. In her memoir she also deals with her cultural background (Southern, American, Baptist) and the way in which Buddhism helped her to deal with her "blackness." The memoir validates the *Time* profile of her: it is thoughtful, passionate and deeply moving.

In an interview with *Southern Scribe* Willis described a series of workshops she has developed with Marles Bosch for women at the York Correctional Institute for Women in Connecticut. These workshops teach practical techniques including meditation and visualization designed to enhance self-esteem and counter prejudice (http://southernscribe.com/zine/authors/willis_jan.htm). She and Bosch intend to eventually publish a book based upon the workshops, to be entitled *Transforming Prejudice: Practical Exercises and Meditations.*

Willis studied with both Thubten Yeshe and his teacher, Geshe Rabten. Her range of scholarship is quite broad. She combines the traditional scholarly skills of language training and translation (Sanskrit and Tibetan) with an interest in modern issues regarding race and gender. Her interest in history has been applied to the role of women in early Buddhism through a comparison of scriptural texts on women and secular histories regarding their impact on the tradition.

A pioneer scholar-practitioner in the West, Willis has demonstrated that it is possible to do both well.

See also: **Women in Buddhism: an historical and textual overview.**

MAVIS L. FENN

WOMEN IN BUDDHISM: AN HISTORICAL AND TEXTUAL OVERVIEW

Buddhism originated and developed in the northeastern part of India during a chaotic time of social, political and religious change. It rejected, adapted, and adopted ideas of the time, including views about women. The Brahmanical religious system, rapidly becoming the dominant religious force in India, asserted that the hierarchical structure of society was also religious in nature. One's place in society – priest, noble, peasant, slave – was a product of one's acts (initially ritual acts, later moral acts as well). This held for gender too. Birth as male or female was determined by *karma*. Buddhism did not reject this system as a means of organizing labor and the social order. It did, however, reject the notion that the social order reflected religious merit. A good man or woman was such because of their moral deeds regardless of their gender or place in the social order. A corollary of this is that both men and women are capable of attaining the ultimate religious goal, *nirvāṇa*. Following this logic, both the Jains and Buddhists provided monastic ordination for women. This was controversial. Women were to be mothers (especially of sons) and wives, positions in which they received social praise. This kept women subordinate to men, a position considered necessary because of a general notion that birth as a female was a lesser birth – lesser physically, morally and spiritually. The religious life itself was frowned upon because it was an individual, independent life that removed people (especially young people) from the divinely created social order. This was doubly so for women because the religious life not only cut off their reproduction, necessary for the survival of society, but removed women from male control. While there might be an occasional female renunciant, the idea of an entire order of nuns was socially threatening.

The Jains were the first to ordain women, although Buddhism is frequently given credit as the first ascetic group to establish an organized religious community for women (*sangha*). Establishment of the *bhikṣuṇī sangha* (monastic order for women) occurred about five years after the foundation of the monastic order for men (*bhikṣu sangha*). The Buddha was approached by Mahāprajāpatī, who was his aunt and foster-mother. Mahāprajāpatī wished him to establish a *sangha* for women. Initially she was refused but after the intervention of Ānanda, his attendant and cousin, the Buddha agreed. The turning point was the Buddha's admission that women were equally as capable as men of attaining *nirvāṇa*. The Buddha, however, required the acceptance of eight additional rules (*gurudharma*) as a condition of their ordination. The narrative ends on a sour note with a prediction that the introduction of women into the *sangha* will shorten its existence by half, likening their introduction into the *sangha* to mildew infesting a rice field. This story of the origination of the *bhikṣuṇī sangha*, told in *Cullavagga X* of the Pāli *Vinaya*, has raised a number of issues, and its interpretation has been varied and sometimes controversial. Why, if the Buddha believed that women and men were spiritually equal, did he initially refuse to ordain women? Why did he impose the *gurudharma*? And, what is the significance of the appalling prophecy at the end? While these issues will be discussed below, generally scholars have held that the Buddha's apparent reluctance to ordain women is a reflection of the cultural prejudices of the time and was added at a later date.

Women appeared to embrace Buddhism from the beginning, both as lay supporters and as nuns. Donations by laywomen are lauded in the texts and we know from inscriptions that nuns made donations as well. Women joined the *bhikṣuṇī sangha* for a wide variety of reasons: death of a husband or loved one, desire to follow a husband or son into the religious life, a wish to avoid marriage and, of course, the desire to pursue a religious life and attain *nirvāṇa*. The nuns' stories are told in a collection of verses, the *Therīgāthā*, and the texts of the Pāli *Nikāyas* speak of both monastic and lay women who excelled in a variety of skills and who attained *nirvāṇa*.

A now classic article by Nancy Auer Falk notes that after the third century CE records of nuns' donations – indeed, any mention of nuns at all – begins to drop off quite radically. By the time of the Chinese pilgrim Yijing's visit in the eighth century CE nuns were extremely poor. While Buddhism was in decline in India generally, the *bhikṣuṇī sangha* declined at a far greater rate. The most likely reason for this is the social perception of women and its relationship to the notion of religious merit. When the laity makes donations to the *sangha* they accrue religious merit. The amount of merit is proportional to the status of the receiver. That is, the higher the status of the monk or nun, the more merit is made. The most meritorious gifts are those given to scholar-monks. But women were not allowed to be educated at the great monasteries such as Nālandā and Valabhī that produced such monks. Further, as males were considered to be "higher" than females, the *bhikṣu sangha* was a better "field of merit" than the *bhikṣuṇī* and received larger and more frequent donations. This lack of education, resources and status prevented the development of a strong, educated and productive *bhikṣuṇī sangha*. This is a situation that still occurs in some places where nuns spend most of their time chanting for the benefit of patrons who support them. These nuns lack time to devote to education, self-improvement and meditation. The situation is further complicated in countries like Tibet, where nuns may live in remote areas, and in many countries where the nuns are seen, and may see themselves, as domestics for monks.

Buddhism became extinct in India by the end of the twelfth century CE. Prior to this it was exported to the rest of Asia. By then, it had developed into three broad strands: Theravāda, Mahāyāna and Vajrayāna or Tantric Buddhism. Theravāda Buddhism has as its scriptural corpus the Pāli *Nikāyas*, the oldest known surviving Buddhist texts and the only complete set of texts extant. *Bhikṣuṇīs* as well as *bhikṣus* engaged in these missionary outreaches, although the *bhikṣuṇī sangha* was never established in Tibet or Thailand. The form of Buddhism exported to Sri Lanka was Theravāda and while there were elements of Mahāyāna introduced they never developed into a strong presence.

It was the monk Mahinda (son of King Aśoka) who brought Theravāda Buddhism to Sri Lanka from India. The accounts of this are found in the *Dīpavaṃsa*, *Mahāvaṃsa*, *Cūlavaṃsa* (known collectively as the Chronicles) and in Chinese sources. The Chinese sources are important, not only historically regarding the establishment of the *bhikṣuṇī sangha* in China in the fifth century CE but also to modern efforts to re-establish the *bhikṣuṇī sangha* in Sri Lanka and Burma and to establish it for the first time in Thailand and Tibet. The late Tessa Bartholemeusz studied the Sri Lankan texts in great detail in *Women Under the Bo Tree* (1994).

The nun Saṅghamittā (Mahinda's sister/Ashoka's daughter) and the correct number of nuns required in order to ordain *bhikṣuṇīs* traveled to Sri Lanka bringing with them a cutting from the Bō tree. There Saṅghamittā found a group of 500 women (a traditional number in Buddhist texts), headed by Queen Anulā, waiting to be ordained. Unable to be properly ordained by Mahinda, they had taken the ten precepts, donned robes and cloistered themselves in separate quarters built for them by the king. After the foundation of the order, Anulā and all 500 of her companions attained *nirvāṇa*. The history of the nuns in Sri Lanka seems to parallel that of nuns in India. In the *Dipavaṃsa* nuns play a major role in the establishment of Buddhism. It extols nuns for their teaching, scholarship, and attainment of *nirvāṇa*, and states that even the kings honored them. Bartholomeusz notes, however, that the *Mahāvaṃsa* rarely mentions nuns and when it does it is always in conjunction with monks. The implication is that they are less worthy and receive less. The last recorded evidence of the order occurs in the tenth century in the *Cūlavaṃsa* where it is recorded that the king built a large residence for nuns. From then on, the record is silent. While both the monks' and nuns' orders became extinct in the eleventh century, there are only records of the re-establishment of the *bhikṣu sangha* from Burma in the late eleventh century. Were attempts never made to rejuvenate the *bhikṣuṇī sangha*? Were the Burmese unable to marshal the needed quorum? Did women not agitate for a new community? The texts are silent.

While the *bhikṣuṇī sangha* was transmitted to Burma in the eleventh century CE and appears to have been active in the late thirteenth century, it did not last much longer than that. The order of nuns did not reach Thailand. Vietnam received a wide variety of Buddhist teachings throughout its history: Theravāda,

Mahāyāna, Pure Land, and Chan. The Vietnamese tended to blend these traditions, as Chan meditation and Pure Land devotional practices. Religious women, and men, face additional problems in countries such as Vietnam, Laos, and Cambodia. There Buddhism itself struggles to remain vital after years of political and social strife, and modernization.

Tibetan Buddhism also faces this challenge. Since the Chinese occupation of Tibet (1959) Buddhist monasteries have been destroyed. Monks and nuns have been killed and many have fled into exile. The Chinese policy of flooding the area with Han Chinese settlers threatens traditional Tibetan culture which is inherently Buddhist. While the *bhikṣuṇī sangha* did not reach Tibet, monks have traditionally bestowed the novice ordination and historically there have been a large number of nuns in Tibet. As in Vietnam, they have frequently been in the forefront of political struggle. In addition, Tibet has a category of non-celibate female tantric practitioners called *yoginī*. *Yoginī* are not ordained nor do they take a vow of celibacy. Like their male counterparts, they sometimes live around monastic compounds or in isolated areas.

The practice of monks giving novice initiation to women where there is no quorum of full ordained nuns (twelve) is common in South and Southeastern Asia as well as in Tibet. Karma Lekshe Tsomo, an American-born Vajyayāna nun who is at the forefront of the movement to provide full *bhikṣuṇī* ordination where it does not exist, has commented on the problematic nature of this in "Family, Monastery, and Gender Justice,". While commending the monks' honoring of women's desire to fully participate in Buddhist monastic life, Tsomo believes that if ordination is not complemented with education and training, it can cause difficulties both for the women and for any communities they may join. Further, it erodes the monastic authority of the women's community to relinquish ordination to monks.

Only China, Korea and Vietnam have been able to maintain a lineage of full *bhikṣuṇī* ordination. The *Vinaya* lineage is Dharmagupta, brought to China from Sri Lanka in the first third of the fifth century (429–34 CE). This is significant in that the core of Buddhism has been monasticism and the core of monasticism has been the *vinaya*. Indeed, texts of the Pāli *Vinaya* assert that Buddhism will last only as long as the *Vinaya* lasts. It is this fact, that the Dharmagupta was one of the early Buddhist schools related in lineage to the Theravāda (the only early school to survive), that proponents of the re-establishment of full *bhikṣuṇī* ordination in Southeast Asia and Tibet argue for its legitimacy. Those who oppose full ordination argue that it is not legitimate because Chinese Buddhism is Mahāyāna. More on this debate will be said below in the discussion of non-ordained, or semi-ordained religious women, numerous throughout Asia.

Buddhism had some difficulty establishing itself in China. One of the main reasons was the strong Confucian ethic with focus on family and ancestors. Women, in particular, were charged with the care of their husband's parents and ancestors. Once established, however, the *bhikṣuṇī sangha* was well supported and respected and provided a good deal of autonomy for women. Having said that, however, sources are minimal, confined to the upper classes, and no works written by females remain. Nancy Barnes notes in "Buddhist Women and the Nuns' Order in Asia" that even before the communist revolution this support and respect had begun to drop off and Buddhism was on the decline. The move to Taiwan by large numbers of Buddhist monastics when the communists won the civil war in 1949 stimulated a rejuvenation of Buddhism in which Buddhist nuns have played a significant role. Ciji, a Buddhist welfare society, was founded by the Ven. Zhengyan. Foguangshan, which promotes a humanistic Buddhism focused on people's religious and practical needs in daily life, attracts a large number of young, educated women who play central roles as organizers, teachers, outreach workers and administrators. The majority of those who seek ordination in Taiwan are female. The *gurudharma* have not been stressed by Taiwanese masters and several of the most prominent, including Yinshun (1906–2005), have promoted equality between monks and nuns.

Buddhism reached Korea from China in the fourth century. The *bhikṣuṇī sangha* was established some time after the monks' order. Korean *bhikṣuṇī* live a disciplined life. Nunneries are self-sufficient and meditation is emphasized, as is pilgrimage to other temples throughout Korea. Education is greatly valued and there are two major monastic training centers for nuns. As a result of the influence of Japanese Buddhism during the occupation of Korea by Japan (1909–45), monks in some sects were allowed to marry. While the dual platform ordination (monks and nuns) died out in Korea for some time, it was reinstituted in the early 1980s. Bhikṣuṇī Karma Lekshe Tsomo recounts her experience of this dual platform ordination in "Nuns of the Buddhist Tradition".

Buddhism came to Japan in the middle of the sixth century CE. According to Paula Arai in her important work on nuns in the Sōtō Buddhist tradition, the first ordained person in Japan was a female, Zenshin-ni, who was ordained in 584 CE. While there are many sects in Japan, the two traditions best known in the West are Zen and Pure Land Buddhism. Karma Lekshe Tsomo notes that three Japanese women were ordained as nuns in Korea in 590 CE but there were insufficient nuns in number to establish a *bhikṣuṇī sangha* upon their return to Japan. Thus, while Japanese nuns take *bodhisattva* vows, there is not a full order of nuns according to *Vinaya*. The early periods of Buddhism in Japan saw nuns as well respected. Arai notes that during the Asuka period (550–710 CE) and the Nara period (710–84 CE) eight empresses were ordained. This period in which nuns were considered to be influential leaders gradually faded as Confucian values permeated and became entrenched in Japanese society. Diana Wright, who has noted the dearth of material on pre-modern nuns, has written about Mantokuji, a Tokugawa-period (1603–1868) Jishū temple-shrine complex known as a "divorce temple". This temple may have been an exception to this trend, perhaps because it was also the ancestral temple of the Tokugawa shogunal line. Their public performances of rituals for the shogunate attest to their importance. They also had important religious and political connections to a wide variety of temple complexes of other sects. During the Meiji Restoration period (1865–1911 CE) there was a liberalization of monastic rules. Monks and nuns were allowed to marry. While monks tended to take advantage of this, nuns chose to remain celibate. This can be particularly problematic where the primary source of revenue is from temple income. Temples are generally passed on to children whose training in a monastery is a preparation to take over the family temple. Nuns who have no children are disadvantaged in this system. (They can pass the temple headship on to a disciple.) Arai details the means by which Sōtō nuns moved from a position of extremely low status at the beginning to the twentieth century to a position of complete acceptance by the sect. One key factor in this transformation was education. Further, they agitated for changes to regulations that gave preference to monks, and became guardians of traditional monastic life and Japanese arts. There have been changes in the demographics of women who chose the monastic life. As was the case for men,

Figure 44 Nun sweeping in early morning, Daewonsa Monastery, North Kyongsang, Korea.

before 1960 women who became nuns usually came from large families with some temple association. Currently, the majority are mature women who have had a previous career and family and likely no prior temple association.

While not all Buddhist countries received the full *bhikṣuṇī* lineage and while it may have died out in some countries which did receive it, all Buddhist countries have had groups of religious women. These are women who have adopted the celibate life, have taken eight or ten or more precepts, donned robes and practice a religious life. In Sri Lanka they are known as *dasa sīla mātāvo* (ten precept nuns), as *maeji* in Thailand, and as *thila shin* in Burma. Religiously, they are neither fully ordained nor are they simply laywomen. Their ambiguous nature is revealed in the fact that, in Thailand, they cannot vote as they are considered "religious." Their status has been low and they receive little economic support. Laity has not considered them to be a "field of merit." Frequently, they have been poor rural women and widows, poorly educated in both secular and religious terms. When they are young, they are often considered to be women who could not find husbands or who are defective in some way. Because they are women, few expect them to be capable of spiritual discipline or attainment. When attached to a temple or monastery, they may spend their days cleaning the temple or doing domestic service for the monks (See Figure 44). Their religious practice tends to focus on devotional practice for themselves and their benefactors (if they have any). The novice nuns of Tibet share this situation, one which is aggravated by the remoteness of the nunneries which do exist. There have been attempts to improve the conditions of these women in education and health care, and to organize them for training purposes. These efforts have been greeted with mixed responses by those whom they are intended to benefit.

Tied to the condition of these religious women is the concern for the re-institution of the *bhikṣuṇī sangha* where it does not exist. In order for this to be accepted by the laity there needs to be a demonstration that women are fully capable of a disciplined religious life and are a good "field of merit." Training programs have been established for those who wish to become nuns and full ordination is now reestablished in Sri Lanka. Although this is still somewhat controversial, great progress has been made since Sakyadhītā held its 1993 conference there. Chatsumarn Kabilsingh (now Bikkhunī Dhammananda) commented that until the Sakyadhītā conference in Bangkok, Thailand, in 1991, Thai laity did not even realize that there were nuns. Indeed, this is one of the reasons why Sakyadhītā holds the majority of its conferences in Asia, to show the laity what a benefit fully trained, ordained nuns can be for society. This also holds for many of the nuns themselves. Karma Lekshe Tsomo has commented that it gives nuns who may come from remote areas an opportunity to meet nuns from other areas and Buddhist traditions.

This is not to say that there has not been some resistance to this, including from the religious women as well. Reasons given for not wishing ordination vary. Not wanting to accept the *gurudharma* (eight special rules) which brings them under the monks' control is one reason given. They prefer their independence to the possibility of more stable economic support. They also point out that they don't need to be ordained to attain enlightenment. The modern vision of the *bhikṣuṇī sangha* is one that sees the nuns doing social service work, counseling and so on, as is the case with the majority of the Taiwanese nuns. Some religious women prefer to devote their time to their private devotions, turning in rather than turning out. Finally, there is some tension surrounding the high visibility of Western and upper-class Asian women in the movement. Some Asian women see Western participation as evidence of a lack of humility and an aggressive individualism, combined with a colonial attitude that assumes they need help in order to improve their situation. Some Western women feel that Asian religious women have been trained to be too shy, humble, and deferential, and need to acknowledge their own talents. Regardless of this tension, there has been a great deal of East–West dialogue between nuns and other religious women in the past fifteen or so years and progress has been made in improving both the living and the educational opportunities of religious women throughout Asia. Whether or not women choose to be ordained, it is clear that education is crucial to raising the status of women in general. In countries where education is encouraged and full ordination is available, respected teachers are produced and nuns have a much higher status.

Buddhism came to the attention of the West through processes of colonization and immigration. The British wished their administrators to be familiar with the language and customs of those they ruled. This produced the translations of T.W. Rhys Davids (civil servant in Sri Lanka), and the founding of the Pāli Text Society in England late in the nineteenth century. His wife, Caroline Augusta Foley Rhys Davids, was a scholar in her own right. She encouraged Isaline Blew Horner, who wrote the first scholarly work on women in the early Buddhist tradition. The Theosophical Society, established in 1875 in New York, played an important role in bringing Eastern concepts to the West. They also had branches in India, England, and Sri Lanka. One of the founders, Madame Blavatsky, took Buddhist precepts in Sri Lanka in 1880 (with Col. Henry Olcott, the other founder of the society). She also claimed to have received, telepathically, the secret wisdom of Tibetan masters. Alexandra David-Neel traveled in Tibet and claimed to have learned the esoteric practices of Tibetan mystics. The Parliament of Religions at the Chicago World's Fair in 1893 was an important impetus for bringing Buddhism, especially Zen Buddhism, to the West.

While Buddhism in Asia is centered on the monastic community, practice in Europe and North America is more lay centered. Few men become monks and even fewer women become nuns. Western women studied with male Asian masters and it was the late 1970s to early 1980s before women teachers appeared. This situation changed rapidly. Lenore Friedman, who did a study of female Buddhist teachers in America states that when she began her research in 1983 she knew of only three female teachers. Four years later, she could name a dozen.

Karma Lekshe Tsomo has surveyed the history and situation of Western Buddhist nuns and female teachers in "Buddhist Nuns: Changes and Challenges". Several of these women, herself included, studied extensively in Asia before beginning their teaching careers. Two of the earliest were Kechong Palmö (1911–77), a British woman ordained in the Tibetan tradition in 1966, and Ayya Khema (1923–97), ordained in 1977 in the Theravāda tradition.

Several have gone on to be well-known teachers and administrators: Pema Chödrön of Gampo Abbey on Cape Breton Island (Canada); Lobsang Chodron, senior nun for the Foundation for the Preservation of the Mahāyāna Tradition; and Tenzin Palmo of Dongyu Gatsal Ling Nunnery (India), who is well known in the West for her twelve-year cave retreat.

Monasteries in the West also tend to differ from those in Asia in that they may house monks and nuns, as well as dedicated laypeople in the same space. This is true of Kagyu Samye Ling in Scotland which is also noted for being the first Tibetan monastery outside of India. Other European monastery complexes with resident nuns include Amaravati (Theravāda) in England and Plum Village (Order of Interbeing) in France. In North America, as well as Gampo Abbey there is Maple Forest Monastery (Order of Interbeing) in Vermont, Shasta Abbey in California and the City of Ten Thousand Buddhas, Talmage (California). City of Ten Thousand Buddhas is the largest, established by Hsüan Hua (1908–96) in 1976 with numerous branches throughout the world. Tsomo lists several others, including Tassajara Zen Mountain Center, the first monastic community in the United States which provides summer vacation retreats for families. Also notable is the fact that, while individuals at Tassajara may shave their head and wear robes, their vows do not include celibacy. This highlights one of the challenges of developing Buddhism for a modern, Western venue. In Asian Buddhism there has been a strict division between lay life and monastic life. While the West has had some tradition of monasticism with the Catholic Church, North America in particular has been resistant to a stark division between lay and specialist practice. Western Buddhists tend to accept Buddhism primarily through meditative practice, a specialist practice in Asian Buddhism. Thus, Western Buddhists have adapted various aspects of the tradition. The most conscious of these re-workings has been by the Friends of the Western Buddhist Order.

Women in Buddhist texts: Theravāda, Mahāyāna, and Vajrayāna

The narrative concerning the establishment of the *bhikṣuṇī sangha* (*Cullavagga X*) is contained in the tenth chapter of the *Vinaya* (rules of monastic discipline). As noted above, monasticism has been the core of Buddhism. Thus, the narrative is not only canonical but central to the self-identity of the monastic tradition. Seen in this light, the text takes on more importance than it would if found anywhere else in the Pāli *Nikāyas*. While the text deals only with those women who wish to become *bhikṣuṇī* it necessarily reflects views about women in general. These views are mixed: they affirm women's equality in spiritual matters; they teach female subordination and they express misogyny. The Buddha is recorded as refusing the request for ordination three times without explanation. According to protocol at that time, this should have ended the matter. Mahāprajāpatī and her relatives were not to be deterred, however. They returned home, cut their hair, donned robes and walked to Vesāli where the Buddha and his entourage had gone. Scholars have argued about the symbolism of this. According to Jonathan Walters and Kate Blackstone this is a case of symbolic parallelism, Mahāprajāpatī as a female Buddha figure. Liz Wilson and Bernard Faure disagree. According to Wilson the parallels are superficial and, in fact, Mahāprajāpatī's path is shown to be dependent upon her male relatives in the time of her renunciation, her choice of teacher, even in her time of death. In short, while she may be a Buddha figure and her path a model for Buddhist women, it is clearly a subordinate path and position.

There is also the question of their ordination. Ānanda must wrest foundation of the order from the Buddha through argument. Are women as capable as men are of attaining *nirvāṇa* if given the opportunity? Yes, certainly they are, the Buddha responds. Ānanda repeats this and adds that as Mahāprajāpatī was his aunt, foster-mother and wet-nurse after his mother's death (the mothers of all Buddhas die seven days after their son's birth) he should establish a monastic order for women. The Buddha agrees.

What is notable here is that the Buddha responds not simply to the logic of Ānanda's argument but to the appeal to Mahāprajāpatī's family connection. The fact that women are capable of *nirvāṇa* is insufficient on its own to justify an order for women. Further, there is the implication of a debt owed to Mahāprajāpatī. This notion that a child (particularly a male child) owes a debt to their mother becomes important in Chinese Buddhism (see below).

As a condition of ordination he requires Mahāprajāpatī to accept eight additional rules (*gurudharma*) specific to the female monastic order:

> Even a senior nun must bow to a monk, even if he is newly ordained.
> The rains retreat must be spent near the monks.
> Nuns must ask the monks for the date of the recitation of the monastic rules (twice monthly) and when the monks are coming to recite it.
> After the three-month rains retreat a nun must "invite" both orders to note her offences.
> A nun who breaks any of the rules for which discipline is required must serve her punishment before both orders.
> After two years' probation, she must ask for ordination from both orders.
> A nun must never criticize a monk.
> A nun must never correct a monk.

Each of these rules serves to subordinate the female order to the male order. Some may be only administrative and others may be rationalized by reference to concerns for women's safety (residing near the monks).The rule that requires senior nuns to bow to junior monks and the rules that state that nuns cannot correct or admonish monks are more problematic. Karma Lekshe Tsomo has argued that in the social context of the time it would have been rude for women to contradict their protectors and unacceptable for men to bow to women. That this explanation is likely is reflected in the Buddha's rejection of Mahāprajāpatī's request to waive the bowing rule. He states that not even poorly organized groups allowed this. The *sangha* was dependent upon the goodwill of the laity for its existence and to move too far beyond social norms could have been costly. One can then argue that, as times have changed, there is no need and it is undesirable to bind nuns to these rules. Simply saying that they were added later or are inconsistent is insufficient in that they have been accepted as authoritative "words of the Buddha" since the beginning.

Given the variety of voices one finds in this text, one is hard pressed to discover "the" view about women in this narrative. The same is true for the Pāli *Nikāyas* as a whole and, indeed, Buddhist literature generally. Alan Sponberg has identified four views about women found in the early texts of the Theravāda, Mahāyāna, and the Vajrayāna: soteriological inclusiveness, institutional androcentrism, ascetic misogyny, and soteriological androgyny. Despite the prophecy of *Cullavagga X*, really nasty verses on women are rare in the Pāli texts and cautions for monks to "watch out" for women are often followed by verses cautioning women against men. Diana Paul in her classic *Women in Buddhism* also finds a variety of views regarding women's spiritual abilities in Mahāyāna texts, including texts that later became popular in China and Japan such as *The Sutra of Queen Śrīmālā Who Had the Lion's Roar*. Some texts state that a woman cannot become a Buddha or advanced *bodhisattva* in the female form, others have women transforming into men at the point of enlightenment, and still others state that sex is irrelevant to becoming a *bodhisattva*. There are also texts that foretell a woman's rebirth in the future in the Pure Land.

Alan Cole argues that in rooting itself in Chinese culture Buddhism had to put its own mark on the notion of filial piety, a primary element of which is the child's (especially male child's) duty to care for their parents. While Buddhism's integration into Chinese society is a multifaceted matter, Cole's work does shed some light on at least one attitude towards women in Chinese Buddhism. A series of Buddhist texts reworked the mother–son relationship. The mother, either through her own sin or simply because she is a woman, has been reborn in a hell. The son can redeem his mother through a series of donations or rituals involving donations to the monastic community. He should do this because he is indebted to his mother for her care of him, particularly her breastfeeding of him. The notion that a woman is inherently impure or prone to sinful deeds appears to be universal and is sometimes cited as a reason why women should not be ordained or cannot be truly religious. In Japan, for example, for a period of time women were refused access to sacred sites as they might pollute them and male pilgrims.

The literature that appears to be the most positive with regard to women is the literature of the Vajrayāna. The goal of the texts and rituals is, as Sponberg has said, "soteriological androgyny" – that is, an integration of all human potential in "emptiness." Thus all aspects of a person are symbolically represented in the Buddhas, *bodhisattvas*, and varieties of male and female deities. This is vividly symbolized in iconography which presents a male Buddha in sexual union with a female deity. However, because of the symbolic nature of the texts scholars do not always agree that the symbolism transfers to actual women. We know that traditions which have a strong tradition of goddess worship, like Hinduism, have not translated that worship into respect for actual women. Are the women who are not to be denigrated by a male disciple real women or are they female aspects of the men for whom the texts are written? Are the women co-participants or conceived of as ritual implements? Scholars have tended to be skeptical regarding the historical role of real women in *tantra*. Working with forty texts written by female *tantric* teachers and after two years with *tantric* practitioners in Nepal, Miranda Shaw has challenged this view. She states that women were important teachers, respected and independent, who not only practiced but contributed to the development of *tantra*. Even the skeptical recognize the potential of these texts for female empowerment if placed within a supportive cultural context.

The multiplicity of voices found in Buddhist texts do not pose problems for scholars who accept that these texts grew up over time, redacted by the hands of many in different cultural contexts. For those, however, who accept them equally as the "words of the Buddha" things are more complicated. Writings that support the full ordination of women and their potential for enlightenment as women can be found, as can texts that warn of the moral depravity of women. Like people of all religions, Buddhists must struggle with such inconsistencies, attempting to maintain their tradition through times of rapid and sometimes tumultuous change.

See also: **Feminist approaches in Buddhism; Horner, Isaline Blew; Sakyadhītā.**

Mavis L. Fenn

WOMEN IN KOREAN BUDDHISM

Women have made a significant contribution to the development and maintenance of Korean Buddhism. The first known nun in the tradition was Lady Sa (Kor. Sassi), who lived in the sixth century. She was a sister of the person named Morok who helped Master Ado spread Buddhism in the kingdom of Silla (57 BCE–925 CE). Lady Sa was, in fact, the first person to be ordained in Silla, where later the *sangha* of nuns developed to an extent that required a separate position to oversee the organization.

As early as the late sixth century, Korean nuns also traveled to Japan to spread Buddhism. Even from the limited historical records, we can still ascertain that the nuns' *sangha* began with the spread of Buddhism in Korea, and that among the ordained were women from royal families and the upper class, as well as courtesans and commoners.

During the Koryŏ period (918–1392), activities of nuns increased along with increased national support of Buddhism. By the thirteenth century, the names of nuns began to appear on the epitaphs of renowned monks, suggesting that nuns as a class had gained higher status in society. Nuns' practice at this time consisted mainly in chanting and *sūtra* reading, but records show that, encouraged by Sŏn masters like Hyesim (1178–1234) and Naong Hye'gŭn (1320–76), nuns also practiced *hwadu* (Ch. *huatou*) meditation. Memorial inscriptions discovered on the tombs of upper-class women indicate that the practices of chanting, *sūtra* reading, and performing other Buddhist rituals to mark various occasions in life were popular among lay practitioners as well.

Beginning in the fifteenth century, along with other Buddhists, Buddhist nuns suffered from persecution as a result of the anti-Buddhist policy of the Chosŏn dynasty (1392–1910). The neo-Confucian government prohibited women from visiting monasteries in 1404, citing as reason the protection of women's chastity. In 1413, all nuns from good families who had become nuns as virgins were ordered to be laicized and married. In 1428, women were forbidden to attend the Lantern Festival. Finally, in 1451, nuns and monks were prohibited from entering the capital city. The Chosŏn government's anti-Buddhist policies, combined with neo-Confucianism's strict gender hierarchy, amounted to the dual discrimination, based on religion and gender, against lay and ordained Buddhist women alike.

As the neo-Confucian patriarchal system became more oppressive, and as their tactics to isolate nuns from social and political milieu intensified, the Chosŏn Buddhist women became ever more devoted to Buddhism. The support of Buddhism by female members of the royal family during the Chosŏn dynasty was crucial to the survival of the tradition. Supporting Buddhism meant violating governmental policy. Yet the women of the royal family, through the privilege of their social position, supported Buddhism with generous donations that funded the reconstruction of monasteries. Among royal Buddhist supporters were Queen Mother Insu (1437–1504), Queen Mother Inhae (?–1498), and Queen Mother Munjŏng, who revived the government examination of monks (Kor. *sŭnggwa*). Royal and upper-class women were also avid supporters of the Buddhist arts during this time. By supporting Buddhism, women challenged patriarchal power; in practicing Buddhism, they prayed for the safety and prosperity of their family and nation, which are major Confucian values. This illustrates the complex relationship between religion and gender in Choson society.

Buddhism in contemporary Korea is still patriarchal. However, the Korean nuns' *sangha* is the only existing tradition in which nuns receive full ordination from senior nuns, instead of from monks. As of 2003, the number of nuns in Korea reached 7,000, slightly outnumbering monks. An almost equal number of monks and nuns received full ordination in 2003, and about 80 percent of lay practitioners are women.

Korean nuns receive training in two ways: basic education received in the seminary (Kor. *kangwŏn*), and self-cultivation practiced in the meditation hall (Kor. *sŏnwŏn*). The first meditation hall for nuns, the Kyŏnsŏng hermitage at the Sudŏk monastery, opened in 1928, and in 1935 the first modern seminary for nuns opened at the Po'mun monastery in Seoul. Immediately after its opening, the Kyŏnsŏng hermitage became a force in revitalizing the Sŏn tradition among Korean nuns, and today it continues to generate leading female Sŏn teachers. Myori Pŏphŭi (1887–1975) is credited as a pioneer of the Sŏn lineage of nuns in modern Korea. At the age of four, she joined the monastery and later became a disciple of Man'gong Wŏlmyŏn (1871–1946), a leading Sŏn master in the early twentieth century. Among Man'gong's disciples was Master Iryŏp (1896–1971), who was a writer and leading female intellectual before joining the monastery. After a failed search for identity and freedom in a patriarchal society, Iryŏp resorted to Buddhism, where she finally found personal fulfillment in the idea that the great "I" (Kor. *tae'a*) liberates the small "I" (Kor. *so'a*). For her, this idea delivered the freedom and true identity she was seeking. Another prominent nun in contemporary Korea is Master Daehaeng (1927–) who opened the Hanmaum Seon Center in 1972; it currently has 30,000 families registered as members. Daehaeng's teaching is succinctly summarized in the expression "doing without doing." This is a spiritual practice through which one lets go of the selfish concept of "I" and realizes the fundamental nature of reality, thus also helping others to experience the inherent oneness of all life. From the perspective of reformed Buddhism, achieving gender equality is a major part of the agenda. As demonstrated in the case of Won Buddhism, the founder of the school, Pak Chungbin, made it clear that men and women are to be educated equally and given equal opportunities to participate in social activities.

Nevertheless, Buddhist nuns today still face challenges. These include the practice of the Eight Chief Rules, the unequal division of administrative workload in the *sangha*, and the lack of resources on women's involvement in Korean Buddhism. In response to these challenges, changes are also taking place: efforts have been made to eliminate the Eight Chief Rules, and projects have been underway to compile material on women and Buddhism.

See also: **Korea, Buddhism in.**

JIN Y. PARK

WOMEN IN MODERN BUDDHISM

Charles S. Prebish outlines five criteria that will influence the development of Buddhism in America. One of these is democratization, the involvement of women (and laity) in ways that have not been common in Asian Buddhism. Another criterion is adaptation, adapting a tradition rooted in Asian soil to the Western context. Those tendencies, while perhaps more pronounced in the West, are visible throughout Buddhism. There have been numerous ordinations in the conservative Theravāda tradition of Sri Lanka and the full ordination of Chatsumarn Kabilsingh in Thailand produced far less negative press than her novice ordination a few years earlier. Even if one argues that the press is more progressive than the populace, there are more indicators of the growing move towards the full ordination of women. Some members of the laity have embraced full ordination as they find it easier to talk with nuns or find them generally more disciplined than the monks. Some have also expressed their feeling that nuns can provide good role models for young women in countries where marriage and prostitution have been the only options. Further, while some religious women may not wish to become fully ordained because they do not wish to come under the control of monks or do not share the proposed vision of a nun's life as one including social service work, the wish of some will inevitably raise the opportunities for others. It will, hopefully, also raise the overall economic and social situation of religious women in general. The Dalai Lama has given his support to the movement and many senior Asian monks realize that Buddhism will not expand in the West without women's participation.

Buddhism has been in the West long enough for it to have passed beyond the "honeymoon" period. Studies of Buddhist women in Asia and scandals in American Buddhism in the 1980s brought American Buddhism to a new maturity as women struggled with teacher–student abuses of power and the traditional patriarchal structure of Buddhism. The production of women teachers has gone some way to restoring confidence, as has the establishment of "women only" *sanghas*. Women who have begun to raise children demand assistance so that they can have equal time for meditation. Indeed, the family influence in the West has caused well-known teacher Thich Nhat Hanh to redefine the *sangha* in broader terms to include a community at large, and feminist scholar Rita Gross has long argued for the need to provide support for women with families.

Scholarship on and by women has multiplied and the study by Western women of Asian nuns has added to the maturation process of Buddhism in the West. In terms of Buddhist Studies, topics regarding women are considered to be legitimate and studies on women are no longer ghettoized, that is, confined to women scholars. Course offerings on both Buddhism and Buddhist women continue to grow and organizations such as Sakyadhītā provide Buddhist women worldwide the opportunity to meet, network and work for change.

See also: **Women in Buddhism: an historical and textual overview.**

MAVIS L. FENN

WOMEN IN TIBETAN BUDDHISM

Western enthusiasts of Tibetan Buddhism commonly claim that women in Tibetan society enjoy virtual equality with men, and this has become an important theme in materials presented for foreign consumption by the Tibetan government-in-exile. There are a number of reports by travelers to Tibet prior to the Chinese invasion of the 1950s that remark on the power of women in domestic affairs and commerce relative to their counterparts in other Asian societies, but it is clear from all accounts that the position of women was still decidedly inferior to that of men, and this situation continues today in Tibet itself and among the exile community.

One indication of women's status in Tibet is the most common term used for woman, *skyes dman*, literally "inferior birth." This etymology is well known among Tibetans, and it appears even in the religious biography (*rnam thar*) of one of Tibet's great female saints, Yeshe Tsogyel (Ye shes mtsho rgyal, ca. eighth century). The inferior position of women is nowhere more evident than in the religious sphere, which is overwhelmingly dominated by men. All the major monastic establishments are controlled by men, and all of the most powerful reincarnate lamas (*sprul sku*) are men. While there have been a few outstanding female religious practitioners, the overwhelming majority of religious biographies – which are written about people who are considered to have lived the most religiously significant lives – are about men.

The actual situation of women stands in stark contrast to Tibetan Buddhist theory, which conceives of women as the embodiment of wisdom. One of the vows taken by *tantric* practitioners enjoins them from "denigrating women, who are the bearers of wisdom." Some important tantric practices and lineages have been instituted by women, and there is some evidence that women played an important formative role in Indian *tantra*. "Cutting off" (*chod*), one of the most popular tantric practices in Tibet, was instituted by the great yoginī Machik Lapdrön (Ma gcig lab sgron, 1055–1143). It involves visualizing one's body being cut up and devoured by demons, and is designed to overcome attachment to physical things.

Yeshe Tsogyel is probably the most widely revered female figure in Tibetan Buddhism. According to her religious biography, she was a student and consort of Padmasambhava and played a key role in encoding and transmitting his "secret treasure" (*gter ma*) teachings and artifacts. She is credited with having manifested the "rainbow body" (*'ja lus*), an apotheosis that is a sign of the attainment of full awakening in *tantric* Buddhism.

The inferior status of women in Tibetan Buddhism generally is manifest in the lives of Tibetan nuns (*a ni*). The full monastic ordination for nuns died out centuries ago in Tibet, and today most women can take only the novice ordination. Comparing the few nunneries (*a ni dgon pa*) to nearby monasteries, it is clear that the latter have far greater resources and status, and monks vastly outnumber nuns, both in Tibet and in exile. A few Tibetan nuns have traveled to other Buddhist countries to take the full ordination, but many men in the monastic establishment have denounced this move and hold that women can only take novice vows. In addition, Tibetan nuns are mainly involved in devotional activities and rituals, which are not valued as highly as scholarship within the largest Tibetan order, the Gelukpa. There have been notable attempts to allow nuns to engage in academic study and debate in the exile community, but only a small number of nuns have been permitted to do so.

In theory, Tibetan Buddhism holds that gender distinctions are merely part of conventional reality and have no ultimate validity. Moreover, a number of prominent teachers have declared that women have religious capacities equal to men, and some Nyingma texts state that women have a superior aptitude for tantric practice, but despite these egalitarian sentiments the actual status of women remains below that of men.

See also: **Tibet, Buddhism in; Vajrayāna Buddhism; Women in Buddhism: an historical and textual overview.**

JOHN POWERS

WON BUDDHISM

Founded in 1916 by Sot'aesan Pak Chungbin (1891–1943) upon his enlightenment experience, Won Buddhism is a representative form of the new Buddhism in modern Korea. The initial organization for the school was established in 1918 under the name "Society for the Study of Buddha-dharma" (*Pulpŏp yŏn'guhoe*). The school was known by that name until 1947 when the second Dharma-Master Chŏngsan (1900–62) renamed the order Won Buddhism (*Wŏn pulgyo*).

Sot'aesan claimed that his enlightenment experience had not been initiated by Buddhist teaching. After the enlightenment, Sot'aesan reviewed scriptures from major world religious traditions and realized that the teachings of the śākyamuni Buddha were the closest to what he realized through his enlightenment experience. Sot'aesan retroactively declared the śākyamuni Buddha as the origin of his teaching.

In the *Chosŏn pulgyo hyŏksillon* (*Treatise on the Renovation of Korean Buddhism*, 1935), which constituted the first chapter of the *Won Buddhist Canon* before it was redacted in 1962, Sot'aesan identified the agenda of his Buddhist reform as the change of Korean Buddhism: "from the Buddhism of abroad to Buddhism for Koreans; from the Buddhism of the past to the Buddhism of the present and future; from the Buddhism of a few monks residing on the mountain to the Buddhism of the general public."

Social aspects of Pak's reform focus on expanding Buddhism beyond the monastic community by popularizing and simplifying its teaching and practice. The doctrinal ground of Pak's reform is anchored in the Mahāyāna idea of the existence of Buddha nature in all beings. Combining this doctrine and his vision for popular Buddhism, Pak replaced in his order the Buddha statue with the One Circle Symbol of Buddha nature (*Pulsŏng Irwŏnsang*). This symbol marks one of the most visible distinctions between Won Buddhism and traditional Buddhism.

Pak interpreted the doctrine of dependent origination through the idea of Fourfold Beneficence (Kor. *saŭn*), which includes: Beneficence of Heaven and Earth, Beneficence of Parents, Beneficence of Brethren, and Beneficence of Law. They illuminate the Buddhist non-substantialist view of being by defining environmental, biological, communal, and social aspects as the net in which one exists. Pak also reformulated the traditional concepts of the precept (*śīla*), wisdom (*prajñā*), and concentration (*samādhi*), into the Threefold Practice (Kol. *samhak*), rendering them as training in the investigation of things, training in the cultivation of mind, and training in the mindful choice. Pak's vision of new Buddhism reflected well the reform spirit of his time, a spirit shared by Buddhist intellectuals including Han Yongun, Paek Yongsŏng, and Pak Hanyŏng, to name a few. Whereas these reform-minded Buddhists launched their reform within the traditional Korean Buddhist order, Pak made his way independent of it. Pak's reform also included his emphasis on gender equality. He stressed that women must be educated like men and participate in social activities together with men.

Won Buddhism has been one of the fastest growing schools of religion in modern Korea, actively proselytizing both in Korea and abroad. One challenge it faces now is whether the current system of Won Buddhism can maintain the revolutionary spirit with which its founder created the school.

See also: **Korea, Buddhism in.**

JIN Y. PARK

WŎNCH'ŬK

Wŏnch'ŭk (Ch. Yuance, Tib. Wen tshegs, 613–96) was a monk from the kingdom of Silla (57 BCE–925 CE) in ancient Korea, known for his contribution to the development of Yogācāra Buddhism in China, Tibet, and Japan as well as Korea. The son of a royal family, Wŏnch'ŭk joined the monastery at the age of three and traveled to Tang China when he was fifteen (627). He attended lectures on Yogācāra given by Fachiang (567–645) and Sengbian (568–642), and participated in a translation project with Xuanzang (600–64) and Xuanzang's protégé, Kuiji (632–82), who was posthumously appointed first patriarch of the Faxiang school of Chinese Yogācāra Buddhism. The Tang emperor issued Wŏnch'ŭk an identification which allowed him to stay at Yuanfa si in Changan, where he studied various Buddhist *sūtras* and commentaries. In recognition of Wŏnch'ŭk's scholarship, the emperor appointed him Great Virtue at Ximing temple. In his later years, Wŏnch'ŭk moved to Loyang, where he devoted his time to translating the *Huayan Sūtra* in eighty fascicles, which was interrupted by his death at the age of eighty-four (696).

When the renowned Xuanzang returned from India, he gave lectures on Yogācāra in line with Dhamapāla's (Ch. Hufa, sixth century) interpretation, which recognized up to the eighth consciousness without accepting Paramārtha's (Ch. Zhendi, 499–569) proposal on the ninth consciousness. The former is known as New Yogācāra whereas the latter is called Old Yogācāra. Wŏnch'ŭk followed Xuanzang's interpretation but not without his own modification. Unlike Xuanzang, Wŏnch'ŭk understood the eighth consciousness as having both contamination and the element of purity (Original Enlightenment), which in Paramārtha's version were assigned to the ninth consciousness. Wŏnch'ŭk considered that this original enlightenment made possible the later transformation of consciousness into the level of enlightenment. Wŏnch'ŭk's interpretation was criticized by the disciples of Kuiji (632–82), especially in Huizhao's (650–714) *Cheng weishi lun liaoyi deng* (*Commentary on Cheng weishi lun*) where Huizhao criticized the interpretation of Wŏnch'ŭk and another Korean Yogācāra monk Tojŭng (*c.* 640–71).

Silla Buddhist monks Tojŭng and T'aehyŏn (fl. 753) followed Wŏnch'ŭk's interpretation and developed it into Korean Yogācāra, which is called the Ximing school after the name of the temple (Ximing) where Wŏnch'ŭk developed his theory. Similarly, Kuiji's Yogācāra was named the Cien school followed the name of the temple (Cien temple) where he stayed. Japanese Yogācāra scholars who considered Kuiji's school as the orthodox version considered Wŏnch'ŭk's interpretation a "heterodox" version of Yogācāra. The tension between Wŏnch'ŭk's and Kuiji's schools caused a negative portrayal of Wŏnch'ŭk in *Song gaoseng zhuan* (*Biographies of Eminent Monks Written During the Song Dynasty*).

Wŏnch'ŭk located Yogācāra teaching in the third stage of the development of Buddhism, following the second stage of Madhyamaka. Madhyamaka negates both being and non-being, Wŏnch'ŭk claimed, whereas Yogācāra accepts both being and non-being. In this manner Wŏnch'ŭk attempted to include Madhyamaka within Yogācāra and thus to create the Buddhist teaching of "one taste."

Extant works by Wŏnch'ŭk include: *Pulsŏl panya paramilda simgyŏng ch'an* (*Eulogy to the Heart Sutra*), *Inwanggyŏng so* (*Commentary on the Humane Kings Sūtra*), and *Haesimmilgyŏng so* (*Commentary on the Saṃdhinirmocana Sūtra*). His *Sŏng yusingnon so* (*Commentary on the Cheng weishi lun*) was lost, but collections of quoted passages from this work in various sources were recently collected into a volume by Korean scholars.

See also: **Korea, Buddhism in.**

JIN Y. PARK

WŎNHYO

Arguably one of most important figures in Korean Buddhism, Wŏnhyo (617–86) set the foundation of Korean Buddhist philosophy and also influenced East Asian Buddhism with his commentaries on major Mahāyāna texts.

Wŏnhyo's life

Wŏnhyo joined the monastery in his teens. Without specific teachers, he read widely and wrote commentaries on almost all the major Mahāyāna texts. He twice attempted traveling to China, but never made it. An awakening experience during his second unsuccessful journey to China is frequently cited as the moment of his awakening to the truth that the three worlds are dependent on one's mind. The story of the experience tells that one night in a dark cave Wŏnhyo blindly drank water out of a container which he later realized was a human skull. When the darkness hid the reality of the container, Wŏnhyo had enjoyed the fresh taste of water; when he saw the next morning that the container was actually a human skull, he vomited. It is one's consciousness, Wŏnhyo realized, that made the same water either fresh or nauseous; outside the mind there is no *Dharma*.

Wŏnhyo later had a relationship with the princess Yosŏk with whom he fathered a son. This son grew up to be the well-known scholar Sŏlch'ong. In his later days, Wŏnhyo is said to have traveled villages in tattered clothes, sometimes even wearing masks, singing and dancing to teach the Buddha's words in music, and urging people to practice Buddhism.

The hagiography of Wŏnhyo's life has been an inspiration for scholars, who interpreted it as a symbolic rendering of Wŏnhyo's Buddhist thought, as well as for fiction writers, who modeled their novels after his life. The realization that one's mind is the primary cause of one's understanding of the external world reflects Wŏnhyo's Yogācāra (or consciousness-only) philosophy; his attempt to spread Buddhism among the commoners in his later years has been understood as acting out the *bodhisattva* path of Mahāyāna Buddhism.

Works

Wŏnhyo was a great reader and writer who is believed to have authored more than 200 works, of which only twenty-two are extant. Most well known among his works are his commentaries on the *Awakening of Mahāyāna Faith*. In the commentaries, Wŏnhyo employs the idea of opening (or analysis) and closing (or synthesis), construction and destruction, and giving and taking as a middle path between Madhyamaka and Yogācāra. To Wŏnhyo, the Madhyamaka school explored in Nāgārjuna's *Mādhyamaka-kārikā* (Ch. *Zhonglun*; *Verses on the Middle Way*) and *Dvādaśdvāra śāstra* (Ch. *Shier men lun*; *Treatise of the Twelve Gates*) attempts to destroy all attachments without constructing after destruction, whereas Yogācāra teachings, as in Maitreiyanātha's (Ch. Milu) *Yogācārabhūmi Śāstra* (Ch. *Yuqie lun*) and Asaṅga's *Mahāyāna-saṃgraha Śāstra* (Ch. *She dasheng lun;Summary of the Great Vehicle*), explain Buddhist teaching by constructing ideas but without letting go of what they constructed. Wŏnhyo understood the *Awakening of Mahāyāna Faith* as reconciling the two modes of Madhyamaka and Yogācāra, and he applied this idea in explaining how the mind of sentient beings, originally clear, came to create delusions. The One Mind, equated with the mind of sentient beings, is a gate with two aspects: the mind as true suchness, and the mind of arising and ceasing. The gate of the mind as true suchness is empty and thus does not make distinctions between the Buddha and sentient beings. However, because the true mind does not change and is filled with truth *dharma*, it is not empty. The mind of arising and ceasing is *tathāgata-garbha* (the womb of Tathāgata) as it is mixed with afflictions (*kleśa*). The self-nature of true suchness and the mind of arising and ceasing are not the same, nor are they different. Hence, *ālayavijñāna* (storehouse consciousness) has both enlightened and unenlightened aspects. Wŏnhyo explains the paradox that equates the sentient being to the Buddha by employing the distinction between initial enlightenment and original enlightenment. Original enlightenment emphasizes the idea that the mind of the sentient beings is originally enlightened, whereas initial enlightenment focuses on the process of awakening to that reality. The *Awakening of Mahāyāna Faith* thus emphasizes the sentient beings' faith in the fact that there is *dharma*. Unlike the Yogācāra of Xuanzang, which considered *ālayavijñāna* to be contaminated, Wŏnhyo thought *ālaya-vijñāna* combined consciousness of both purity and impurity, from which the elimination of impurity generates pure *dharma* for practitioners to proceed toward *nirvāṇa*.

In his *Yijang ŭi* (*Treatises on Two Hindrances*), Wŏnhyo discusses in detail the reasons for the failure to attain enlightenment. Wŏnhyo's thought on how sentient beings remove defilements and recover their original nature is further reiterated in his *Kŭmgan sammae kyŏngnon* (*Treaties on the Vajrasamādhi Sūtra*). In this *Treatise*, which is actually Wŏnhyo's commentary on the *Vajrasamādhi Sūtra*, Wŏnhyo uses original enlightenment and initial enlightenment as the basis of his discussion on enlightenment.

Wŏnhyo wrote seventeen *jongyos* (doctrinal essentials), including *Pŏphwa jongyo* (*Doctrinal Essentials of the Lotus Sūtra*) and *Yŏlban jongyo* (*Doctrinal Essentials of the Nirvāṇa Sūtra*).

His works constitute the major texts for *Vinaya* studies and *Vinaya* in Korean monasteries. His discussions on *bodhisattva* precepts can be found in three of his works: *Posal yŏngnak ponŏpkyŏng so* (*Commentary on the Sūtra of* Bodhisattva*'s Bead-Ornamented Primary Activities*), *Posalgye bon chibŏm yo'gi* (*Essentials of Observation and Violation of* Bodhisattva *Precepts*) and *Pommanggyŏng posal kyebon sa'gi* (*Personal Records on the Chapter on the* Bodhisattva *Precepts in the Sūtra of Brahma's Net*). All three provide seminal points on Mahāyāna Buddhist ethics. In these texts, Wŏnhyo emphasizes the emptiness of precepts; hence, from Wŏnhyo's perspective, neither the observing nor the violation of *bodhisattva* precepts can be the path to observing precepts in its ultimate sense. However, in Wŏnhyo's understanding of Mahāyāna ethics, non-existence of set paths or precepts is not meant to encourage the anything-can-happen mode of thinking. Rather, Wŏnhyo argues that because there is no set path to awakening and maintaining precepts, there is no limit in finding situations and things that can function as *bodhisattva* precepts.

To Wŏnhyo, a genuine understanding of a precept violation is not limited to the realization of the mistake made by the act of violation. More important is the realization of the emptiness of the violation itself. Like Zen Buddhists who try to learn that there is nothing to practice while practicing, Wŏnhyo's Mahāyāna ethics demands that the observation of precepts in its ultimate sense amounts to the awareness that there is nothing to abide by. Wŏnhyo's thought on this topic can be broadly outlined according to three levels. On the first level, Wŏnhyo foregrounds emptiness as the basis of Mahāyāna ethics; precepts themselves should be considered empty. On the second level, Wŏnhyo discusses actual precepts but emphasizes the importance of observing them while simultaneously and constantly keeping in mind the emptiness of the precepts. On the third level, Wŏnhyo discusses how ethical modes take place within a practitioner, and proposes faith as a foundation or initiator of Mahāyāna ethics in the practitioner. This view is consistent with his interpretation of Mahāyāna Buddhism, as it appears in his commentaries on the *Awakening of Mahayana Faith*, where he emphasizes the importance of faith in the existence of *dharma*.

Wŏnhyo's views on *bodhisattva* precepts, particularly his *Palsim suhaeg jang* (*Raise Your Mind and Practice*), have been used as a text for *śramaṇa* division in the lecture halls of Korean Buddhist monasteries.

Wŏnhyo and Korean Buddhist schools

Wŏnhyo's Buddhism set the foundation of several important Buddhist schools in Korea. The official launch of the Ch'ŏnt'ae school (Ch. Tiantai) in Korea did not take place until the eleventh century. However, the expression *Ch'ŏnt'ae* first appeared in Wŏnhyo's *Yolban jongyo* (*Doctrinal Essentials of the Nirvāṇa Sutra*). In his *Pŏphwa jongyo* (*Doctrinal Essentials of the Lotus Sūtra*), Wŏnhyo also explicated the teachings of the *Lotus Sūtra*. He also wrote commentaries and essentials about *Huayan jing*, which unfortunately have been lost. Wŏnhyo's Hwaŏm thought is best illustrated in his interpretation of the *Awakening of Mahāyāna Faith*. The commentary had a great influence on Fazang (643–712), the designated third patriarch of Chinese Huayan Buddhism, as well as Ŭisang (625–702), the founder of Korean Hwaŏm school. In the eleventh century, Ŭich'ŏn (1055–1101) acknowledged Wŏnhyo's influence on Hwaŏm thought by attributing to Wŏnhyo the creation of Korean Hwaŏm thought. Wŏnhyo's thought on Yogācāra also served as the grounding for Pŏpsang chong (*Dharma* Characteristics school).

Wŏnhyo's Buddhism has been frequently identified with "reconciliation," as reflected in his posthumous title National Master of Reconciliation of Conflicts. His commentaries on the *Awakening of Mahāyāna Faith* reconcile the seemingly binary positions of Madhyamaka and Yogācāra. This reconciliation between the two great schools in the history of Buddhism was further understood as his effort to emphasize the oneness of the secular and the sacred. Finally, his treatise, *Simnun hwajaeng non* (*Treatise on Reconciling Doctrinal Conflicts*) shows his attempt to create a unified teaching of Buddhism out of the doctrinal diversities that existed in his time.

Wŏnhyo's contribution to Korean Buddhism was first acknowledged by Ŭich'ŏn (1055–1101). The modern writer and intellectual Ch'oe Namsŏn (1890–1957) used the ecumenical vision of Wŏnhyo's Buddhism when Ch'oe tried to define the identity of Korean Buddhism to oppose the Japanese disparagement of Korean Buddhism as a mere extension of Chinese Buddhism. During the 1960s, the Korean philosopher–scholar Pak Chonghong (1903–76) rediscovered Wŏnhyo and credited him as a major figure in Korean Buddhist philosophy.

See also: **Korea, Buddhism in.**

JIN Y. PARK

WORSHIP

Buddhist worship traditions originated in the respect and hospitality customarily provided to an honored guest in Vedic India, which his followers and well-wishers provided to the Buddha himself. Almost without fail, throughout his long career the Buddha is depicted being welcomed with invocations and greetings, water for washing, food and drink, appropriate seating and/or lodging as required, and an etiquette of deference including keeping him to the right (*pradakṣinā*), using polite forms of address and gesture, speaking words of praise, and avoiding objectionable behavior in his presence.

Buddhist worship traditions vary considerably in size and level of patronage (from an individual's genuflection before a home altar to massive public festivals sponsored by powerful elites), duration (from an instant to many months or years; perpetual worship traditions have emerged in various schools), longevity (*stūpa*-worship has been occurring for millennia, whereas Buddhist pop devotional music in Sri Lanka, Thailand, and Japan is strictly modern) and form and function, but in general can be understood as an elaboration of those original hospitality practices in the special circumstances created by the Buddha's *parinirvāṇa*. That is, given the caveat that in his absence the Buddha must be represented by surrogates such as images or paintings, Buddhist worship continues to treat the Buddha (and other Buddhist saints) as he is believed to have been treated during his lifetime.

One can get a handle on this diversity by recognizing that it occurs within a relatively small and widely shared set of basic forms, which can be grouped as concerning (1) objects of worship, (2) specific worship practices, and (3) ideas about the efficacy and purpose of worship, each of which is explored in turn.

Objects of worship

The *Mahāparinibbāna Sutta* (*Dīgha Nikāya* 2.141–3) makes clear that Buddhists believed the Buddha himself to have recommended the continuance of such honoring (*vandana*) and offering (*pūjā*) after his death. In that text he instructs Ānanda that his bodily remains should be enshrined in *stūpas*, where lay followers can develop happy thoughts that lead to heavenly rebirth. While scholars have certainly over-determined this passage as a prohibition on monastic participation in *stūpa* worship – historically, monks and nuns were consistent and sometimes dominant participants therein – *stūpas* were clearly the first surrogates for the Buddha-in-*nirvāṇa* which subsequent Buddhists revered as though the Buddha himself.

Scholars are agreed that by the third-century BCE reign of Aśoka Maurya numerous *stūpas* had been constructed and embellished throughout South Asia. The relics within *stūpas* which stood in for the Buddha included identified pieces of his corpse (for example, the collar-bone or forehead bone or, especially popularly across the Buddhist world, teeth, hair and nail parings) or (more often) unidentified pieces, and also objects he had used (such as robe, bowl, staff) and, by about the first century CE, manuscripts of Buddhist texts. We have important evidence that, at least from the third or second century BCE onwards, the relics worshipped in *stūpas* were not only the Buddha's own, but sometimes also or rather those of respected saints such as Śāriputra, Mahāmaudgalyayāna and Moggaliputtatissa.

In time Buddhists began to worship additional Buddha-surrogates, often originally within *stūpa* courtyards but later altogether independent of them. These included Buddha-footprints (in carved slabs or identified rock-indentations), carved *Dharma*-wheels (*dharmacakras*) and royal umbrellas, empty seats, *Bodhi* trees, places associated with the Buddha's life or carved or painted pictures of scenes from it, and finally two-dimensional and three-dimensional Buddha images. As was true of relics, so images or paintings were sometimes – and in the Mahāyāna world increasingly – not of the Buddha himself but rather of particularly famous *arahants* who in some cases (as in the cults of the Sixteen or Eighteen *Arahants*) would intercede on behalf of petitioners, or of *bodhisattvas* who similarly could respond to the needs and wishes of worshippers; in addition to corporeal relics and visual images of them, objects which they used or blessed and/or places associated with them likewise have often become objects of worship.

Finally, it is important to notice that living monks and nuns, especially those considered spiritually advanced, *arahants*, *bodhisattvas* or Buddhas, may also become objects of worship for their followers, truly standing in for the living Buddha.

Forms of worship

The ancient tripartite understanding of human action as involving body, speech, and mind serves well to categorize the great variety of forms which Buddhist worship has taken. With their bodies Buddhists have given respectful "salutes" (*añjalī*) to the Buddha and to surrogate objects of worship, with the hands folded in front of the face or over the head, and have also developed forms of prostration from simple bowing to the Tibetan grand prostration (*kyang chak*) which involves lying down at full length, sometimes moving one body length at a time in circumambulation of the object of worship; ordinary circumambulation is also a common form of bodily worship of *stūpas*, Buddha images and similar objects of worship, and may include the use of prayer wheels in Tibet. In some schools, notably in Tibet and Japanese Shingon, bells and *vajras* as well as *mudrās* or hand gestures (Jap. *shuin*) indicative of particular mental states, deities, and/or aspects of Buddhahood, may also accompany acts of worship.

Making an offering is itself a bodily act, and one which exhibits great diversity across the Buddhist world. While flowers, rice and other foodstuffs, water and tea, incense and candles, and oil lamps or other forms of light are ubiquitous offerings, regional customs vary considerably: Sri Lankans regularly offer betel leaves and nuts; Burmese altars might contain cigars; Thai altars, cigarettes or alcohol; Tibetan altars, figures constructed of colored butter and dough (*torma*), colorful diagrams (*maṇḍala*) made of sand or other perishable material (Shingon practitioners also developed a large-scale public festival for "giving diagrams," Jap. *mandara-ku*), and even skull bowls filled with water to represent blood and semen. Tibetan and Japanese *homa* or burnt-offering ceremonies (Jap. *goma*) involve

Figure 45 Worshipers burning joss sticks and praying, Sing Lim Temple, Singapore.

specific pleasant or distasteful objects offered in return for positive and negative effects, respectively (See Figure 45).

Acts of worship include not only bodily gestures and material offerings but also verbal or otherwise sounded speech-acts and visualizational and meditative acts of the mind. They invariably begin with invocations, and regularly include additional speech-acts such as hymns of praise (*stotra*), affirmation of moral precepts (*śīla*), confession of wrongs, recitation of *bodhisattva* vows, recitations of *mantras* and seed syllables (in *Tantric sādhanas*) and/or petitions, aspirations or other prayers offered to the object of worship. Many Buddhist cultures have also developed musical and drumming traditions as accoutrements to their worship routines.

Worship involves the mind in a number of ways. Certain religious states of mind – including devotion and faith, insight, determination, joy and enlightenment – are understood in various schools to be affected by, exercised in and/or prerequisite to the efficacy of worship, which often includes meditative reflections. More explicitly, the object of worship, the act of offering and/or its results may be entirely mental constructions, as in *sādhanas* and other visualization meditations.

Reasons for worship

By the reign of Aśoka Maurya in the third century BCE, Buddhists had begun to systematize the benefits of worshiping *stūpas* (and later other Buddha-surrogates), which were conceived in terms of short-term benefits like a happy heart, a good reputation, a death without fear and rebirth in better circumstances, as well as long-term benefits which would be realized during a succession of future rebirths in which one grows increasingly accustomed to performing such acts of merit (*puṇyakarma*), culminating in *arahant*ship during the time of a future Buddha. In worship one literally practiced or trained for such a future time, providing for the Buddha as one would were he still alive/when a future one is alive.

Thus despite a superficial appearance of similarity to Buddhist and non-Buddhist deity cults, in which the object of worship is ontologically present in an image or at a sacred space, much Buddhist worship has been instead what scholars term "commemorative," that is, focused on remembering the Buddha and cultivating his virtues rather than in directly petitioning him. However, in various ways some worshippers seem to treat the Buddha as somehow "present" in images or *stūpas*, and many more believe that even in the absence of his personal presence a sort of mysterious power (*ānubhāva*) facilitates the granting of wished-for results during worship. This somewhat ambiguous presence of the Buddha in *stūpas* and images is apparent in the fact that the Buddha qua *stūpa* was treated as a resident member of the *sangha* and given various rights in ancient Indian monasteries, or in the special eye-painting ceremonies accorded Theravāda images (Sinh. *netra pinkama*).

The very different ontology of Mahāyāna and Vajrayāna traditions renders unproblematic the assumption that Śākyamuni is somehow "in" an image or *stūpa*, and thereby capable of being petitioned in worship. This is especially the case, however, in terms of other objects of worship such as images of *bodhisattvas* and "living *arahants*," whose very nature and religious path is to be available to help others. As examples, Chinese and Japanese Buddhists will often petition *bodhisattvas* such as Bhaiṣajyaguru for health or Avalokiteśvara/Guanyin/Kannon for assistance, while Burmese and Thai Theravādins will call on Upagupta at the beginning of ceremonies to protect them and ensure their success. But even in these traditions worship is not always nor even primarily conceived of as an exchange with a living deity, such as one finds in, say, Hindu worship.

See also: **Chanting practices; Charity (*dāna*); *Mantras*, *mudrās*, and *maṇḍalas*; Ritual in Tibetan Buddhism; South and Southeast Asia, Buddhism in.**

JONATHAN S. WALTERS

Y

YOGĀCĀRA SCHOOL

Indian Mahāyāna Buddhists traditionally recognized two major philosophical schools within the Mahāyāna, namely Madhyamaka and Yogācāra. The name of the latter school suggests an affinity with the meditative practices of yoga. Other names for this school are *Cittamātra* (thought only) and *Vijñaptimātra* (representation only). Like the Mahāyāna itself, the two schools evolved slowly and their early adherents probably did not see themselves as belonging to a distinct school of thought; it was the work of such Indian Buddhist scholastics as Jitāri (tenth century CE) to put earlier scholastics into neat categories and schools. According to the latter scholastics, the Yogācāra movement began with the works of Asaṅga and Vasubandhu in around the fourth century CE. Many of the doctrines that they defended had already been found in early versions of such Mahāyāna *sūtras* as the *Saṃdhinirmocana*, the *Laṅkāvatāra*, and the *Samādhirāja*, but extant versions of these texts apparently incorporate later material influenced by Asaṅga, so it is difficult to sort out the historical evolution of this school in any but general terms. The names of the texts written by Asaṅga and Vasubandhu can be found in the entries on them. The present entry will present an outline of four key doctrines associated with the Yogācāra school, namely *cittamātra*, eightfold awareness, "receptacle" awareness and three natures.

Cittamātra

Already in undisputedly early Buddhist texts there occur passages emphasizing the primacy of thought. The *Dhammapada*, for example, opens with the famous line "Thought precedes all mental states. Thought is their leader; they all consist of thought. If with an impure thought a person speaks or acts, trouble follows him like the wheel that follows the foot of the ox." Later texts from the Mahāyāna tradition claim that all the Buddhas and *bodhisattvas* originate in thought and are made of (or by) thinking and indeed are nothing but thought (*cittamātra*). In his

Abhidharmakośa, a non-Mahāyāna scholastic work, Vasubandhu states that the entire physical world in which sentient beings dwell is the collective effect of the *karma* of all its innumerable dwellers and that all *karma* begins with thought. The idea, therefore, that the physical world is born of thoughts is not radically new. If Yogācāra has any novelty, it is an emphasis on the recognition that there is no means of knowing how anything that one experiences is in itself, independent of one's personal experience of it. Moreover, it is recognized that one's overall mentality has such a powerful influence on how something is experienced that there is no means of knowing how something is in itself, independent of one's feeling about it and attitude towards it. Much harm can come from the naïve assumption that one's awareness simply reflects the external world just as it is. A preventive to that potential harm takes the form of realizing that one's mentality actively constructs what one experiences rather than passively receiving it, with no value added, from the external world. In effect, then, what one experiences is inseparable from the process of experience itself; that of which one is conscious is really just an aspect of consciousness itself.

All schools of Buddhism proclaim some version of the notion that all uneasiness (*duḥkha*) stems from delusion, and what distinguishes one school from another is what each understands the fundamental delusion to be. For the Yogācāra school, the fundamental delusion is the belief that the subject of awareness and the object of awareness are radically different from each other rather than two inseparable aspects of the same thing, like the two sides of a coin. The realization that the apparent duality of subject and object is in fact erroneous consists in realizing that there is no real distinction between self and other. This means that one of the benefits of realizing that the apparent other is not really an other is that one also realizes that the apparent self is not really a self. Therefore, the Yogācāra emphasis on both subject and object being nothing but thought (*cittamātra*) turns out to be just another way of stating the traditional Buddhist doctrine that no factor of experience is a self.

Eightfold awareness and "receptacle" awareness

Canonical Buddhism teaches that the notion of a self is unnecessarily superimposed upon five collections or aggregates (*skandha*) of phenomena: *rūpa*, the aggregate of sensible properties, namely colors, sounds, tastes, smells and tactile sensations; *vedanā*, the aggregate of reacting to those sensible properties by feeling them as pleasures, pains or neutral feelings; *saṃjñā*, the aggregate of associating present sensations with past experiences and thereby naming them and categorizing them; *saṃskāra*, the aggregate of all *karma*-producing affects and volitions; and *vijñāna*, the aggregate of six types of awareness, namely seeing, hearing, smelling, tasting, touching and introspecting. The Yogācāra analysis expands upon this teaching by adding two more dimensions of awareness to the six traditional types.

The first addition is usually called *ālayavijñāna*. The term "*ālaya*" means an abode or dwelling or receptacle. It is often translated into English as "storehouse" on the basis of a common way of describing this type of awareness as a storage facility into which all past actions are stored as seeds until they are ready to ripen into new experiences. The *ālayavijñāna*, then, is a sort of experiential warehouse in which are kept all the potentials for future experiences. What makes different people (and other sentient beings) individuals is that each has a slightly different store of potentials from which to draw; therefore, no two people have exactly the same experience, even though if they were to compare notes on their experiences, they might come to believe that they had both experienced the same thing, albeit from slightly different perspectives. The receptacle awareness is constantly changing, because new experiences occur at every moment, thereby bringing an old "seed" to fruition and giving rise to a new *karmic* seed to store for future use. Because it is always changing, the *ālayavijñāna* is not a self, for a self is that which remains the same as other things change. It is, however, the basis of the delusion that there is a self.

The mechanism by which that delusion occurs is the second Yogācāra addition to the classical six types of awareness. This second addition is called afflicted mind (*kliṣṭamanas*), and its principal function is to superimpose a subject–object dualism upon the experiences that arise out of the receptacle awareness. Because all dissatisfaction and affliction arises out of this perception of a subject, or self, receiving information about objects, or others, from the outside, this dualistic mentality is said to be afflicted (*kliṣṭa*). The process of becoming liberated from those afflictions consists in bringing about an "overturning of the receptacle" (*ālaya-parāvṛtti*), a figurative dumping of the receptacle awareness and turning it over so that it no longer functions as a receptacle and store of future experiences. The process by which this is done involves, among other things, coming to a clearer understanding of the nature of experience.

The three natures (*trisvabhāva*)

If someone besides a Buddha relates how experience feels to the experiencer, the usual account would be that there seems to be a more or less steady flow of information coming into awareness from the outside world and that this outside world consists of a great multiplicity of different objects: birds, shrubs, trees, blossoms, insects, cats, clouds, and mountains. One bird spies the cat and flies away, and another unsuspecting bird takes its place. All these players in the drama seem to be independent of one another. They also seem to be independent of the experiencing subject, for it seems obvious that they would continue to go about their business if one were to go and take a nap instead of watching them. This apparently independent nature of the manifold things is, however, imagined (*parikalpita*). It is a superficial reading of a text that if read more deeply would prove to be a complex net of interdependent things, none of which could be just what it is in the absence of all the others. So the real nature of things is dependence (*paratantra*) on causes and conditions, and the real nature of everything that can be construed as a cause is that it is dependent on everything else to be what it is; it even depends on something being perceived as its effect in order for it to be perceived as a cause, and it depends on a perceiver to be perceived at all, and the perceiver depends on the perceived to be a perceiver, and so on *ad infinitum*. The imagined independent nature (*parikalpitasvabhāva*) of things is a superimposition upon the true nature of things, which is dependence (*paratantrasvabhāva*), another name for which is emptiness (*śūnyatā*). When this dependence-nature of things is realized without any false imaginings, then it is said to be a perfected nature (*parinispannasvabhāva*). In reality, there is but one nature, and it can either be seen as it is or it can be imagined to be other than it is.

The process of becoming liberated, according to Yogācāra, begins with the cultivation of the desire to become awakened (*bodhicitta*) so that one can help all sentient beings become awakened. This resolve is followed by an intense effort to cultivate good character through study and contemplative practices. Proficiency in study and contemplation leads to seeing all things as interdependent, or empty. This leads in turn to all imaginings of independence fading away, which can also be seen as overturning the receptacle discussed above. Finally, one abides in a purified awareness of the constantly changing flow of interdependent events on which there is no superimposition of subject and object, self and other. This is the mentality of a Buddha.

See also: **Asaṅga; India, Buddhism in; Mahāyāna Buddhism; Vasubandhu.**

RICHARD P. HAYES

Z

ZAZEN

In Japanese *zazen* means "sitting meditation," the primary form of meditation in the Chan/Zen schools of Buddhism. Adapted from seated meditation practices imported to East Asia from South Asia, *zazen* involves sitting with the back straight and legs crossed in full or partial lotus position. An alternative position is sitting on a small bench. Exactly what the practitioner does while sitting depends on the specific tradition, teacher, and goals of the practitioner. *Zazen* often employs methods drawn from early Pāli meditation literature, such as counting breaths in order to develop concentration and attentiveness, labeling thoughts, or attempting to cut off all discursive thought. A more advanced method of *zazen* is "just sitting" (*shikantaza*), allowing each moment of awareness to be the object of meditation while minimizing discursive thinking and intellectual activity. Another method employed in *zazen* is the contemplation of a *kōan*, a short, often abstruse, anecdote of an encounter between a master and disciple, the understanding of which is believed to constitute a profound insight.

Different schools of Zen understand the significance and purpose of *zazen* in different ways. Both Sōtō and Rinzai schools assert that all individuals have intrinsic Buddha nature, but they understand the relationship of *zazen* to this true nature differently. The Rinzai school emphasizes strenuous exertion in order to achieve the sudden seeing into one's nature (*kenshō* or *satori*) and emphasizes *kōan* practice as a means to this end. Use of *kōans* is designed to restructure awareness in such a way that there is no ultimate separation perceived between oneself and others; everything is a part of a non-dual harmony, and *kenshō* is a sudden breakthrough to an understanding of that nonduality. When *zazen* is combined with *kōan* practice, regular private meetings (*dokusan* or *sanzen*) with the Zen master (*rōshi*) in which monks attempt to express their insight into the *kōan* are essential. The master will question the monks individually and either reject their answers, in which case they must continue to sit in *zazen* working on the *kōan*, or accept them, in which case they will be assigned another *kōan* in order to deepen and integrate their realization.

Zazen in the Sōtō school is considered an *expression* of one's original Buddha-nature rather than a means by which to realize it. This approach tends to de-emphasize the pursuit of *kenshō* in favor of cultivating an awareness of one's original nature in meditation and ordinary activities. *Kōans* are not absent in Sōtō *zazen* but play a limited role, as they are sometimes seen as harsh and goal-oriented. Instead, the Sōtō school views *shikantaza* as the most important form of *zazen*.

See also: ***Dhyānas*; Meditation (Chan/Zen); Meditational systems; *Śamatha*; *Vipaśyanā*; Zen.**

David L. McMahan

ZEN

The word "Zen" is the romanized form of the Japanese pronunciation of the first of the two-character Chinese compound (Ch. *chan-na*) that transliterates the Sanskrit term *dhyāna*, which in the Buddhist context refers to the state, or experience, of various stages of meditative concentration. In current Western parlance, "Zen" means much more (and much less) than this.

The various uses of "Zen" can be categorized in at least the following ways:

1a the transliteration/translation of the Sanskrit term *dhyāna* (the technical, etymological sense);
1b an altered state of consciousness brought about through specific practices of concentration and calming the mind and heart, resulting in well-delineated stages of altered consciousness and meditative concentration, such as the four stages of *dhyāna*, leading to enlightenment (the Buddhological sense);
2a the teachings and practices of the tradition that is believed to have been transmitted to China by Bodhidharma and passed on through various lineages in East Asia, such as a form of practice centered on sitting in meditation (*zazen*) (the historical sense);
2b the institutional traditions of various schools, such as the "Zen" schools of Rinzai, Sōtō, and Ōbaku in Japan (the sectarian sense);
3 Zen as a mystical or intuitional experience that transcends history or verbal, doctrinal explanations (including the Buddhist scriptures), an "immediate experience" or awareness of the world as-it-is that is beyond words and expression (the experiential sense).

In addition to, or as extension of, these meanings one could speak of the promiscuous uses of the term in "pop Zen" – inspired by the works of modern commentators such as D.T. Suzuki, Alan Watts, and Eugen Herrigel – as a mysterious way to master a subject, or the "joyful/awesome" experience felt through a high level of concentration and full mastery of an activity (in martial arts or other sports), such as "the Zen of snowboarding" or "Zen and the art of motorcycle maintenance." However, should we not include funeral ceremonies and memorial rites as important "Zen" activities, because that is the dominant activity of most modern Zen temples in Japan today? If not, what is the relationship between Zen and such funerary rituals?

Let us take a step back and look at the historical background to this situation. The popularity of Zen in the West can be attributed in large part to the influence of D.T. (Daisetz Teitarō) Suzuki (1870–1966), a Japanese Zen Buddhist scholar and layman. Born in Kanazawa (where his lifelong friendship with Nishida Kitarō [1870–1945], Japan's pre-eminent modern philosopher, began), he underwent Zen training under Shaku Sōen Rōshi in Kamakura while studying in Tokyo. He lived in the United States for two long periods: from 1897 to 1908 as a collaborator of the Orientalist Paul Carus, and again from 1949 lecturing in various universities. In Japan he held the chair of Buddhist philosophy at Ōtani University (from 1921). His American wife, Beatrice Lane, whom he married in 1921, was his faithful collaborator until her death in 1939. Among his voluminous literary output (thirty-two volumes in Japanese and almost thirty in English) his introductions to Zen are best known in the West: *Essays in Zen Buddhism* (3 vols); *An Introduction to Zen Buddhism* (1934); *Zen and Japanese Culture* (1938; revised edn 1959); and so forth. Through such writings Suzuki popularized Zen as an "immediate experience" that transcends history and religion, and does not rely on words or concepts. However, Suzuki also contributed to the present flowering of Buddhist studies in Japan as well as in the West by his many translations of and introductions to Buddhist *sūtras* and treatises.

Another important influence on the understanding and practice of Zen in the West is the Sanbō Kyōdan (Three Treasures Association), a movement founded by Yasutani Hakuun (1885–1973) to integrate the best of the Sōtō and Rinzai traditions, though he officially became independent of the Sōtō school. Yasutani emphasized training laypeople through the use of *sesshin* (intensive Zen retreats) to attain *kenshō* (seeing one's true nature). Many of the prominent Zen figures in the West (including Philip Kapleau, Robert Aitken, and Fr. Enomiya-Lassalle) have links to Sanbō Kyōdan, and it has been pointed out that it shares some of the characteristics of the "new religious movements," such as institutional independence, a prominent and charismatic "founder," and emphasis on lay practitioners.

These are only two examples of the influences on "Zen" in the modern world. Zen, often cut off from its historical roots and used in a promiscuous and ambiguous sense, continues to hold a fascination for many in the West and has developed its own social and cultural aura. There are also signs that Zen Buddhism has begun to develop its own Buddhist tradition in the West, with the success of numerous Zen centers (such as the San Francisco Zen Center), and popular publications such as the quarterly magazine *Tricycle.*

To return to the list of various ways the word "Zen" is used today, which of these meanings are "really" Buddhist? What is the relationship between "Zen" and "Buddhism"? Does it matter? To give a "Zen" reply: "The answer is blowing in the wind."

See also: **Japan, Buddhism in; New Buddhist lay movements in Japan; Meditation (Chan/Zen); *Sōshiki Bukkyō* (funeral Buddhism).**

PAUL L. SWANSON

ZHENGYAN, VENERABLE

Ven. Zhengyan is the founder and head of the Taiwanese Buddhist social welfare organization known as the Tzu Chi Compassion Relief Foundation (Ciji). André Laliberté notes that about two million of Taiwan's Buddhist population are members of Ciji, and it has many members overseas. The largest group within the organization is composed of laywomen who come from a variety of ethnic backgrounds. Ciji provides hospitals, clinics, universities, publishing houses, and a television channel. The entire organization is centered on Zhengyan, although there is a board of directors to assist her.

As Zhengyan self-tonsured, the Buddhist Association of the Republic of China (BAROC) refused her ordination initially. Yinshun, whom she recognizes as her teacher, agreed to sponsor her. Given the BAROC's initial reluctance, it is not surprising that Ciji is registered as a charity and thus does not come under its supervision. Yinshun is one of the founders of "humanistic Buddhism" and Zengyan and Ciji fit into the humanistic pattern with some variation. Humanistic Buddhism is centered on this world. It takes *bodhisattvas* as ideals for human behavior rather than deities for devotion. Through selfless, compassionate care of others, one makes the *bodhisattva* path concrete for oneself and participates in the creation of an earthly pureland. Given the illness in her family background and belief that poverty is the result of illness, it is no wonder that the initial focus of the organization was on health-related service. They have since expanded into international relief efforts (1991) and since 1994 have included relief to mainland China. For her humanitarian efforts Zengyan has been called the "Mother Theresa of Asia" and has received numerous awards, among them the Eisenhower International Peace Prize and Asia's Most Outstanding Woman Award.

The most important *bodhisattva* for Zhengyan is Guanyin, the *bodhisattva* of compassion. Within the framework of humanistic Buddhism and its humanization of iconic figures, she sees Ciji as the arms of Guanyin, accomplishing her compassionate goals in the earthly realm. Ng Zhiru notes that a triad of icons (Sahā triad) has become associated with Ciji: Sakyamuni in the middle, flanked by Guanyin and Dizang. While these figures are the central devotion icons in many public and private Ciji settings, they are understood to be venerated for their qualities: pursuit of enlightenment, compassion, and strength of dedication, rather than as objects of worship.

Julia Huang has done an interesting study in which she applied the "three body" doctrine of Buddhism to Ciji. Zhengyan's personal charisma as leader represents the body of the *dharma* with which the individual wishes to absorb. The *sangha* is represented by the personal provision of aid combined with communal symbols such as uniforms. The third body is that of the follower whose expression of devotion is often expressed through weeping and "silent melody" (sign language for hymns).

Zhengyan's following, primarily women, makes Ciji a powerful presence in Taiwan. Its overseas outreach is largely Chinese but may expand over time.

See also: **Women in Buddhism: an historical and textual overview.**

MAVIS L. FENN

ZHENYAN ZONG

Zhenyan ("True Word" or *mantra*) is a school of Chinese Buddhism sometimes referred to as the Esoteric school, representing an importation of Tantric Buddhism from India into China. Once in China, however, it changed to fit the temperament and mores of Chinese religious culture. Evidence of this importation can be detected as far back as the third century, but the real transmission of the school into China may be said to begin with the arrival of the India monks Śubākarasiṃha (Ch. Shanwuwei, 637–735), Vajrabodhi (Ch. Jingangzhi, 671?–741), and Amoghavajra (Ch. Bukong, 705–74) at the capital in the eighth century. These three men were also responsible for the translation of most of its foundational scriptures and formularies, and for training the first generation of Chinese practitioners.

Zhenyan shares the following features in common with its Indian sources:

1 It is based primarily on practice and action rather than learning and knowledge. The object of the practice is to master the "three *karmas*" of body, speech, and mind through the practices of *mudrā* (ritual hand gestures associated with specific deities,

bodhisattvas, and Buddhas); *mantra* or *dhāraṇī* (spoken formulae transliterated directly from Sanskrit ritual utterances which have no semantic meaning but contain power in the sounds); and visualizations of specific deities, *bodhisattvas*, or Buddhas.

2 It organizes the cosmos ritually into a series of energies that emanate from the center and radiate outward, each energy symbolized by a particular deity, *bodhisattva*, or Buddha. The central Buddha is Vairocana, the Sun Buddha, who emanates all other Buddhas and divine beings. This scheme is represented visually in the *maṇḍala* that depicts all divine beings in their proper locations relative to one another.
3 Its transmission depends upon *abhiṣeka*, or initiation into a line of masters and disciples. No one can practice authentically and successfully without having been initiated into the practice by a guru who stands in a valid succession of masters.
4 The practice also depends upon the protection and support of a specific Buddha, *bodhisattva*, or guardian deity. This divine guardian is chosen in the course of the initiation ceremony, when the neophyte drops a flower upon the *maṇḍala*, and takes as his patron the being upon whose image it falls.
5 Zhenyan sees its practice as a short-cut that dispenses with the usual gradual cultivation of wisdom on one's own in favor of powerful practices, empowered by beings more advanced in the path who lead the practitioner directly to the goal of enlightenment and liberation in one lifetime, or even instantaneously.
6 The power of its practices could also be used for purposes other than religious advancement, such as healing, rainmaking, acquiring wealth, national protection, and so on.

Having noted these similarities, one must also be aware that the Chinese school differed from its Indian counterpart in at least two respects. First, the sexual element in iconography and practice is not as strong as it was in India and was to become in Tibet. This element appears to have offended Chinese sensibilities. Second, it did not base itself on a body of literature called *tantras*, but used the *sūtra* literature, giving it esoteric interpretations.

Esoteric practices have existed continuously, though at a low level, in Chinese Buddhism since its first transmission. At first, it was confined to the court and the nobility because of the expense of building the elaborate ritual facilities and acquiring the vestments, texts, and implements necessary. Some groups exist today who devote themselves to esoteric rituals. In addition, esoteric elements pervade almost all corners of the Chinese Buddhist world. For example, every monastery's devotional liturgies contain *mantras* and make occasional use of *mudrās*, and many monasteries, whether esoterically based or not, make use of esoteric rituals such as the "Release of the Flaming Mouths" or the "Mengshan Ceremony for Feeding the Hungry Ghosts."

See also: **China, Buddhism in.**

CHARLES B. JONES

ZHIYI

The Tiantai school officially recognizes Zhiyi (538–97) as its third patriarch, but in fact he founded the school and proposed its most distinctive teachings.

He was born in south China into a family with aristocratic connections, but realized the transitoriness of life at a young age after witnessing troops destroying a library. He became a monk, and studied with the northern meditation master Huisi (515–77), later recognized as the second patriarch of Tiantai. After a stay in Jinling (modern Nanjing), he went to Mount Tiantai on the eastern seaboard in Zhejiang province, and remained there for the rest of his life; it is from his residence there that his school derived its name. An early visionary experience aroused his faith in the supremacy of the *Lotus Sūtra*, and later he wrote two commentaries on it, one a general survey of its meaning, the other a line-by-line exegesis. When China was reunited by the Sui dynasty in 581, his family's connections brought him to the attention of the court, where he was invited to preach and received honors. Imperial patronage allowed him to buy up the fishing rights along the coastline adjacent to Mount Tiantai and to obtain a ban on fishing in the area.

Zhiyi achieved distinction as both a meditator and a scholar. He studied and mastered many forms of meditation, which he set forth systematically in his textbook *The Great Calming and Contemplation* (*Mohe zhiguan*). In doctrinal study, he put forth many distinctive new ideas, including:

1. the Tiantai method of classifying scriptures and teachings (Ch. *panjiao*), which honored the *Lotus Sūtra* as the supreme scripture and explained other Buddhist schools and teachings, even apparently contradictory ones, as steps in a graded curriculum aimed at practitioners at different points in their paths and having different pedagogical needs;
2. the Three Truths (emptiness, the provisions, and the middle) that overcame the disconnection between the traditional Two Truths of Mādhyamika teaching by positing a third truth that integrated them;
3. the idea that transcendent principle (Ch. *li*) and phenomenal reality (Ch. *shi*) mutually interpenetrate without obstruction, which clarified the point that transcendent truth is not to be found outside of phenomenal realities close at hand, but within them; and
4. the idea of One Mind or Absolute Mind that underlay all of reality, in both its pure and defiled aspects, which made truth a living, compassionate reality rather than an abstract idea.

This last doctrine proved controversial later in Tiantai history, as it made impurity an integral part of reality as realized by an enlightened mind. Many later followers preferred the view that impurities in the world reflected impurities in the mind itself, and that once one was enlightened and could see the world correctly, all impurities would be seen as delusions. Zhiyi defended this doctrine of the pure and defiled aspects of Absolute Mind by comparing the practitioner to a great general who needs real enemies in order to achieve great victory. In the same way, the world must present the practitioner with real suffering and defilement if she or he is to have genuine accomplishments.

See also: **China, Buddhism in; China, early schools.**

CHARLES B. JONES

Guide to the Buddhist scriptures

The Pāli Canon

The Pāli Canon is the complete scripture collection of the Theravāda school. As such, it is the only complete set of scriptures for any Hīnayāna sect, preserved in the language of its composition. It is often called the *Tipiṭaka* or "Three Baskets" because it includes the *Vinaya Piṭaka* or "Basket of Discipline," the *Sutta Piṭaka* or "Basket of Discourses," and the *Abhidhamma Piṭaka* or "Basket of Higher Teachings." There is an especially good summary of the Pāli Canon on pp. 265–76 of *The History of Buddhist Thought* (2nd edition; New York: Barnes and Noble, 1963) by Edward J. Thomas.

1 *Vinaya Piṭaka* ("Basket of Discipline")
  - (a) *Suttavibhaṅga* ("Analysis of Rules"): Rules of the *Pātimokkha* code with commentarial explanations.
    - (i) *Mahāvibhaṅga* ("Great Section"): 227 rules for monks.
    - (ii) *Bhikkhunī vibhaṅga* ("Division for Nuns"): 311 rules for nuns.
  - (b) *Khandhaka* ("Sections"): chapters relative to the organization of the sangha.
    - (i) *Mahāvagga* ("Great Group"): regulations for ordination, *Uposatha* (Observance) Day, rainy-season retreat, clothing, food, medicine, and procedures relative to the *Sangha*'s operation.
    - (ii) *Cullavagga* ("Small Group"): regulations for judicial matters, requisites, schisms, travel, ordination and instruction of nuns, history of the first and second councils.
  - (c) *Parivāra* ("Supplement"): summaries and classifications of the *Vinaya* rules.

2 *Sutta Piṭaka* ("Basket of Discourses")
  - (a) *Dīgha Nikāya* ("Collection of Long Discourses"): thirty-four suttas.
  - (b) *Majjhima Nikāya* ("Collection of Middle Length Discourses"): 152 suttas.
  - (c) *Saṃyutta Nikāya* ("Collection of Connected Discourses"): fifty-six groups of suttas, grouped according to subject matter.
  - (d) *Aṅguttara Nikāya* ("Collection of Item-More Discourses"): discourses grouped according to the number of items in an ascending list.
  - (e) *Khuddaka Nikāya* ("Collection of Little Texts")
    - (i) *Khuddaka-pāṭha* ("Collection of Little Readings"): short *suttas* for recitation.
    - (ii) *Dhammapada* ("Verses on Dhamma"): collection of 423 verses, in many cases concerned with ethical maxims.

(iii) *Udāna* ("Verses of Uplift"): eighty solemn utterances spoken by Buddha.
(iv) *Itivuttaka* ("Thus it is Said"): 112 short *suttas*.
(v) *Sutta-nipāta* ("Group of *Suttas*"): seventy verse *suttas* containing legendary material.
(vi) *Vimāna-vatthu* ("Stories of Heavenly Mansions"): *suttas* concerning heavenly rebirths.
(vii) *Peta-vatthu* ("Stories of the Departed"): fifty-one poems on unfortunate rebirths.
(viii) *Thera-gāthā* ("Verses of the Male Elders"): verses attributed to 264 male disciples of Buddha.
(ix) *Therī-gāthā* ("Verses of the Female Elders"): verses attributed to about 100 female disciples of Buddha.
(x) *Jātaka* ("Birth Stories"): 547 stories of the previous lives of the Buddha.
(xi) *Niddesa* ("Exposition"): commentary on portions of the *Sutta-nipāta*.
(xii) *Paṭisambhidā-magga* ("Way of Analysis"): an *Abdhidhamma*-style discussion of doctrinal points.
(xiii) *Apadāna* ("Stories"): verse stories of lives and former lives of various monks and nuns.
(xiv) *Buddhavaṃsa* ("Lineage of the Buddhas"): history of twenty-four previous Buddhas.
(xv) *Cariyā-piṭaka* ("Basket of Conduct"): *Jātaka* strories emphasizing a bodhisatta's practice of the perfections.

3 *Abhidhamma Piṭaka* ("Basket of Higher Teachings")
(a) *Dhammasaṅgaṇi* ("Enumeration of Dhammas"): discussion of mental and bodily factors, with reference to ethical issues.
(b) *Vibhaṅga* ("Analysis"): continued analysis of various doctrinal categories.
(c) *Dhātu-kathā* ("Discussion of Elements"): ordering of various factors under a variety of major categories.
(d) *Puggala-paññatti* ("Designation of Human Types"): classification of individuals according to a variety of traits.
(e) *Kathā-vatthu* ("Subjects of Discussion"): polemical treatise concerning doctrines disputed by rival schools.
(f) *Yamaka* ("Book of Pairs"): pairs of questions addressing basic categories.
(g) *Paṭṭhāna* ("Book of Relations"): analysis of causality in twenty-four groups.

The Chinese Canon

The Chinese Buddhist Canon is called the Decang Jing or "Great Scripture Store." The first complete printing of the "Three Baskets" or *Tripiṭaka* was completed in 983 CE, and known as the Shupen or Szechuan edition. It included 1,076 texts in 480 cases. A number of other editions of the Chinese Canon were made thereafter. The now standard modern edition of this work is known as the *Taishō Shinshū Daizōkyō*, published in Tokyo between 1924 and 1929. It contains fifty-five volumes containing 2,184 texts, along with a supplement of forty-five additional volumes. A fine chapter titled "The Chinese Tripitaka" can be found on pp. 365–86 of *Buddhism in China* (Princeton: Princeton University Press, 1964) by Kenneth K.S. Ch'en.

1 *Āgama* Section: Volumes 1–2, 151 texts. Contains the equivalent of

the first four Pāli *Nikāyas* and a portion of the fifth *Nikāya*.

2 Story Section: Volumes 3–4, sixty-eight texts. Contains the *Jātaka* stories.
3 *Prajñāpāramitā* Section: Volumes 5–8, forty-two texts. Contains the Perfection of Wisdom literature.
4 *Saddharmapuṇḍarīka* Section: Volume 9, sixteen texts. Contains three versions of the *Lotus Sūtra* and some additional material.
5 *Avataṃsaka* Section: Volumes 9–10, thirty-one texts. Contains material on the *Flower Garland Sūtra.*
6 *Ratnakūṭa* Section: Volumes 11–12, sixty-four texts. Contains material on a group of forty-nine texts, some of which are extremely early Mahāyāna treatises.
7 *Mahāparinirvāṇa* Section: Volume 12, twenty-three texts. Contains the Mahāyāna version of the conclusion of Buddha's life.
8 Great Assembly Section: Volume 13, twenty-eight texts. Collection of Mahāyāna *sūtras*, beginning with the "*Great Assembly Sūtra*."
9 *Sūtra*-Collection Section: Volumes 14–17, 423 texts. Collection of miscellaneous (primarily Mahāyāna) *sūtras*.
10 *Tantra* Section: Volumes 18–21, 572 texts. Contains Vajrayāna *Sūtras* and *Tantric* materials.
11 *Vinaya* Section: Volumes 22–4, eighty-six texts. Contains the disciplinary texts of a variety of Hīnayāna schools as well as texts on *bodhisattva* discipline.
12 Commentaries on *Sūtras*: Volumes 24–6, thirty-one texts. Commentaries by Indian authors on the *Āgamas* and Mahāyāna *Sūtras.*
13 *Abhidharma* Section: Volumes 26–9, twenty-eight texts. Translations of Sarvāstivādin, Dharmaguptaka, and Sautrāntika *Abhidharma* texts.
14 Madhyamaka Section: Volume 30, fifteen texts. Contains texts of this important school of Mahāyāna Buddhist thought.
15 Yogācāra Section: Volumes 30–1, forty-nine texts. Contains texts of this important school of Mahāyāna Buddhist thought.
16 Collection of Treatises: Volume 32, sixty-five texts. Miscellaneous works on logic and other matters.
17 Commentaries on the *Sūtras*: Volumes 33–9. Commentaries by Chinese authors.
18 Commentaries on the *Vinaya*: Volume 40. Commentaries by Chinese authors.
19 Commentaries on the *Śāstras*: Volumes 40–4. Commentaries by Chinese authors.
20 Chinese sectarian writings: Volumes 44–8.
21 History and biography: Volumes 49–52, ninety-five texts.
22 Encyclopedias and dictionaries: Volumes 53–4, sixteen texts.
23 Non-Buddhist doctrines: Volume 54, eight texts. Contains materials on Hinduism, Manichean, and Nestorian Christian writing.
24 Catalogs: Volume 55, forty texts. Catalogs of the Chinese Canon, starting with that of Seng-yu (published 515 CE).

The Tibetan Canon

The Tibetan Canon consists of two parts: (1) the *bKa'-gyur* ("Translation of the Word of the Buddha"), pronounced Kanjur, and (2) the *bStan-'gyur* ("Translation of Teachings"), pronounced Tenjur. Because this latter collection contains works attributed to individuals other than the Buddha, it is considered only semi-canonical. The first printing of the Kanjur occurred not in Tibet, but in China (Peking), being completed in 1411. The first Tibetan edition of the canon was at sNar-thang (pronounced Narthang) with the Kanjur appearing in 1731, followed by the Tenjur in 1742. Other famous editions of the canon were printed at Derge and Co-ne. Almost fifty years ago, Kenneth K.S. Ch'en provided a short article on the Tibetan Canon titled "The Tibetan Tripitaka," published in the *Harvard Journal of Asiatic Studies*, 9, 2 (June, 1946), pp. 53–62, that is still quite useful today.

1 *bKa'-gyur* (Kanjur): translation of the Word of the Buddha; ninety-eight volumes according to the sNar-thang (Narthang) edition.
   (a) *Vinaya*: thirteen volumes.
   (b) *Prajñāpāramitā*: twenty-one volumes.
   (c) *Avataṃsaka*: six volumes.
   (d) *Ratnakūṭa*: six volumes.
   (e) *Sūtra*: thirty volumes. 270 texts, 75 percent of which are Mahāyāna, 25 percent Hīnayāna.
   (f) *Tantra*: twenty-two volumes. Contains more than 300 texts.
2 *bStan-'gyur* (Tenjur): Translation of Teachings; 224 volumes (3,626 texts) according to the Peking edition.
   (a) *Stotras* ("Hymns of Praise"): one volume; sixty-four texts.
   (b) Commentaries on the *Tantras*: eighty-six volumes; 3,055 texts.
   (c) Commentaries on the *Sūtras*: 137 volumes; 567 texts.
      (i) *Prajñāpāramitā* Commentaries, sixteen volumes.
      (ii) Madhyamaka treatises, seventeen volumes.
      (iii) Yogācāra treatises, twenty-nine volumes.
      (iv) *Abhidharma*, eight volumes.
      (v) Miscellaneous texts, four volumes.
      (vi) *Vinaya* commentaries, sixteen volumes.
      (vii) Tales and dramas, four volumes.
      (viii) Technical treatises: forty-three volumes.
         A Logic: twenty-one volumes.
         B Grammar: one volume.
         C Lexicography and poetics: one volume.
         D Medicine: five volumes.
         E Chemistry and miscellaneous: one volume.
         F Supplements: fourteen volumes.

Contributors' biographical notes

Martin Baumann is Professor of the Study of Religions at the University of Lucerne, Switzerland. He obtained his Ph.D. with a thesis on the history and processes of adaptation of Buddhism in Germany (1993). His post-doctorial thesis (habilitation) on Hindu tradition in the Caribbean analyzed patterns of diaspora identities and changes (1999). He has been research fellow at the University of Hanover and visiting professor at the university of Bremen (both Germany), writing a study on Vietnamese Buddhists and Tamil Hindus in Germany (2000). His fields of interests are the spread and adaptation of Buddhist and Hindu traditions outside of Asia, diaspora and migrant studies, and theory and method in the study of religions. He is the general editor of the online *Journal of Global Buddhism* and author of numerous articles in both German and English. He has co-edited *Westward Dharma: Buddhism Beyond Asia* (2002) with Charles S. Prebish, *Religions of the World: A Comprehensive Encyclopaedia of Beliefs and Practices* (2002) with J. Gordon Melton, and *Tempel und Tamilen in zweiter Heimat* (2003) with Brigitte Luchesi and Annette Wilke. He is member of the board of the Swiss Association for the Study of Religions, research affiliate of the Pluralism Project, Harvard University, member of the editorial boards of the *Journal of Contemporary Religion*, King's College London, and the RoutledgeCurzon Critical Studies in Buddhism Series, and member of the editorial advisory board of the series Contemporary Religions in Global Perspective, Ashgate Publishing, Aldershot UK.

George D. Bond is Professor of Religion in the Religion Department of Northwestern University. Specializing in Buddhist studies and the history of religion, he works primarily on Theravāda Buddhism studying the texts and the practices of Buddhism in Sri Lanka and Southeast Asia. He received his Ph.D. from Northwestern University and also studied at the University of Sri Lanka. One of his doctoral mentors was the Venerable Dr. Walpola Rahula. His teaching focuses on Buddhism, Hinduism, and the history of religion. He has been a recipient of the Charles Deering McCormick Professorship of Teaching Excellence, the Northwestern Alumni Association's Award for Excellence in Teaching and the Weinberg College of Arts and Sciences Teaching Award. His publications include: *The Buddhist Revival in Sri Lanka* (1988), *The Word of the Buddha* (1980), *Sainthood: Its Manifestations in World Religions* (1988), which he co-authored and edited with Richard Kieckhefer; and *Buddhism at Work: Community Development, Social Empowerment and the Sarvodaya Movement* (2004). He has also written numerous articles on Buddhist texts and Buddhist practice, including a recent article, entitled "The Contemporary Lay Meditation Movement and Lay Gurus in Sri Lanka," which appeared in *Religion* (2004). Currently he is working on a book about socially engaged Buddhist movements. He has served as president of the Midwest region of the American Academy of Religion and as co-chair, with Charles Prebish, of the Buddhism Section of the national American Academy of Religion. He has been an officer and a board member of the American Institute for Sri Lanka Studies and has served as the Overseas Director for the Center of the American Institute for Sri Lanka Studies in Colombo, Sri Lanka.

Jim Deitrick holds a Ph.D. in Religion and Social Ethics from the School of Religion at the University of Southern California. He is Assistant Professor of Comparative Philosophy and Religion and Director of the Interdisciplinary Programs in Religious Studies and Asian Studies at the University of Central Arkansas. His teaching and research focus on Western engagements with Asian philosophical and religious traditions and the consequences of such engagements for contemporary social ethical theory and practice. He was awarded the Yvonne Leonard Dissertation Fellowship for his doctoral dissertation, "Mistaking the Boat for the Shore? A Critical Analysis of Socially Engaged Buddhist Social Ethics in the United States."

Mavis L. Fenn received her Ph.D. from McMaster University, Hamilton, Ontario, Canada. She is at St. Paul's College (University of Waterloo), Ontario, Canada. She teaches Asian Religion for the Department of Religious Studies. Her research interests include women in Buddhism and the adaptation of Buddhism to the West. Her most recent articles are "Buddhist Diversity in Ontario" co-authored with Kay Koppedrayer at Wilfrid Laurier University, Ontario, Canada, and "The Kutadanta Sutta: Tradition in Tension." She is currently working on two projects: "Buddhism on a Canadian Campus" and "Buddhist Women in Canada" with Janet McClellan at Wilfrid Laurier University.

Charles Hallisey is Associate Professor of Languages and Cultures of Asia at the University of Wisconsin-Madison. He completed his doctoral research on Devotion in the Buddhist Literature of Medieval Sri Lanka at the Divinity School, the University of Chicago, and subsequently taught at Loyola University of Chicago and Harvard University. He has published widely in the fields of South Asian Buddhism and Buddhist ethics.

Peter Harvey is Professor of Buddhist Studies at the University of Sunderland, UK, from where he teaches a web-based MA Buddhist Studies (http://www.sunderland.ac.uk/buddhist). Co-founder of the UK Association for Buddhist Studies (http://www.sunderland.ac.uk/~os0dwe/bsa.shtml), we he was President 2002–6. He is the author of *An Introduction to Buddhism: Teachings, History and Practices* (Cambridge University Press, 1990, with a second edition to be published by 2007), *The Selfless Mind: Personality, Consciousness and Nirvāṇa in Early Buddhism* (Richmond, UK: Curzon Press, 1995), *An Introduction to Buddhist Ethics: Foundations, Values and Issues* (Cambridge University Press, 2000), *Buddhism* (edited volume, London and New York: Continuum, 2001). He is a meditation teacher in the Theravādin Samatha Trust tradition (http://www.samatha.org).

Richard P. Hayes got his doctorate in Indian philosophy in the South Asian Studies program at University of Toronto in 1982. After completing his studies he taught in the Department of Philosophy and the Religious Studies Program at University of Toronto. He taught Buddhist Studies in the Faculty of Religious Studies at McGill University from 1988 until 2003. He is currently in the Department of Philosophy at the University of New Mexico. His principal research focus has been on Indian Buddhist scholastics who wrote in Sanskrit, especially on the school of Dignāga and Dharmakīrti.

Charles B. Jones is an Associate Professor in the School of Theology and Religious Studies in the Catholic University of America. Aside from publishing in the area of East Asian Buddhism, he is also the executive director of the Institute for Interreligious Study and Dialogue, in which capacity he has published articles on Buddhist–Christian dialogue and Christian theological responses to other religions. He was the recipient of a Fulbright research fellowship in 2004–5, during which time he was a visiting scholar at the Institute of History and Philology, Academia Sinica, Taipei, where he pursued research on Pure Land Buddhist belief among the literati of late Ming dynasty China. His latest book is *The View from Mars Hill: Christianity in the Landscape of World Religions* (Cowley, 2005).

Damien Keown is Professor of Buddhist Ethics at Goldsmiths College, University of London, where he has taught Buddhism since 1981. After taking a first degree in Religious Studies at Lancaster University he specialized in Buddhism and completed a doctorate at the Oriental Institute, University of Oxford, on Buddhist ethics. Since then he has helped pioneer the development of this field and has published widely on the subject, authoring and editing numerous books and many articles and chapters and speaking at international conferences. In 1994 he and Charles Prebish co-founded the award winning *Journal of Buddhist Ethics*, and subsequently the Routledge-Curzon Critical Studies in Buddhism Series and the Journal of Buddhist Ethics Online Books series of electronic textbooks on religion. Damien Keown was elected a Fellow of the Royal Asiatic Society in 1985, and was Spalding Trust Visiting Fellow in Comparative Religion, Clare Hall, Cambridge, in 1996–97 and a visiting professor at the Katholieke Universiteit Leuven, Belgium, in 2002. He is a member of numerous professional bodies in religion and was Secretary of the UK Association of Buddhist Studies 2002–5.

Jacob N. Kinnard is Assistant Professor of Comparative Religious Thought at Iliff School of Theology, where he teaches graduate courses on the religions of India and methodological and theoretical issues in the history of religions. He holds a B.A. from Bowdoin College, and an M.A. and Ph.D. from the University of Chicago. He is the author of *Imaging Wisdom: Seeing and Knowing in the Art of Indian Buddhism* (Routledge Curzon, 1999) and *The Emergence of Buddhism* (Greenwood, 2006), and co-editor of *Constituting Communities: Theravāda Traditions in South and Southeast Asia* (SUNY, 2003). He has written numerous articles on a variety of issues in Buddhist studies, and is currently working on a book on the relationship between Hinduism and Buddhism as it is played out at several shared pilgrimage places in India. Professor Kinnard is editor of the Cultural Criticism series for Oxford University Press/AAR, and a member of the Publication Committee of the American Academy of Religion.

Lewis R. Lancaster is President of University of the West, Rosemead, California, and Professor Emeritus of East

Asian languages and Buddhist Studies at the University of California, Berkeley. For many years Professor Lancaster was in charge of University of California at Berkeley's Ph.D. program in the Group in Buddhist Studies. His recent publications include "The Koryŏ Edition of the Buddhist Canon: New Sources for Research" (in Sang-oak Lee and Duksoo Park, eds., *Perspective on Korea*, Honolulu: University of Hawai'i Press, dist, 1998); "The Dunhuang Manuscripts: The Current State of Research" and "Fragments and Forgeries: Strategies for Judging Authenticity," (in Susan Whitfield, ed., *Dunhuang Manuscript Forgeries*, London: British Library Studies in Conservation Science, Vol. 3, 2002); and "Virtual Reality Within the Humanities," (in Maurizio Forte, ed., *The Reconstruction of Archaeological Landscapes through Digital Technologies*, BAR International Series 1379: London, 2005). His print publication, *The Korean Buddhist Canon: A Descriptive Catalogue* (in collaboration with Sung-bae Park, Berkeley: University of California Press, 1970), has been digitized by Charles Muller and posted at his website (http://www.hm.tyg.jp/~acmuller/descriptive-catalogue/). Professor Lancaster has been active in the world of computers, organizing the Electronic Buddhist Text Initiative, a consortium of more than forty groups around the world dealing with Buddhism and the new technology, and the Electronic Cultural Atlas Initiative (ECAI) which makes use of GIS software. As one of the organizers of the Summit Conference on Digital Tools for the Humanities at the University of Virginia in 2005, he continues to work toward a more effective use of technology in scholarship.

Karen C. Lang is Professor of Buddhist Studies in the Department of Religious Studies at the University of Virginia. She teaches undergraduate and graduate courses on Buddhism and reading courses in Sanskrit, Pāli and Tibetan languages. Her research interests focus on the intellectual history of Indian Buddhism. Her publications include *Āryadeva's Catuḥśataka: On the Bodhisattva's Cultivation of Merit and Knowledge* (Akademisk Vorlag, 1986) and *Four Illusions: Candrakīrti's Advice on the Bodhisattva's Practice of Yoga* (Oxford University Press, 2003), and numerous articles on Indian Buddhist philosophy and literature.

David L. McMahan is Associate Professor of Religious Studies at Franklin and Marshall College in Pennsylvania and received his Ph.D. from the University of California at Santa Barbara. He is the author of *Empty Vision: Metaphor and Visionary Imagery in Mahayana Buddhism* (RoutledgeCurzon, 2002) and is writing on a book on the development of modern Buddhism to be published by Oxford University Press.

Jin Y. Park is Assistant Professor of Philosophy and Religion at American University. She is editor of the forthcoming *Buddhisms and Deconstructions* (Rowman and Littlefield), translator of *Getting Familiar with Death* (Won Publications, 1999) and author of journal articles and book chapters including: "Zen and Zen Philosophy of Language," "Zen Language in Our Time: The Case of Pojo Chinul's Huatou Meditation," and "Gendered Response to Modernity: Kim Iryeop and Buddhism."

Richard K. Payne is Dean of the Institute of Buddhist Studies, an affiliate of both the Graduate Theological Union, Berkeley, and Ryukoku University, Kyoto. He is also a Shingon Buddhist priest (*acari*), ordained on Koyasan in 1982. While specializing in the study of Shingon ritual, he has published on the Pure Land tradition as well. His recent publications include *Discourse and Ideology in Medieval Japanese Buddhism* (co-edited with Taigen Dan Leighton, RoutledgeCurzon, 2005), *Tantric Buddhism in East Asia* (Wisdom Publications, 2005), and *Approaching the Land of Bliss* (co-edited with Kenneth K. Tanaka, University of Hawai'i Press, 2004). He is Chair of the Editorial Committee for *Pacific World: Journal of the Institute of Buddhist Studies*, and Editor in Chief of the Pure Land Buddhist Studies Series, jointly published by Brill Academic and University of Hawai'i Press.

John Powers received his Ph.D. in Buddhist Studies from University of Virginia in 1991. He is the author of nine books, including *Introduction to Tibetan Buddhism* (Ithaca: Snow Lion Publications, 1995) and *History as Propaganda: Tibetan Exiles Versus the People's Republic of China* (New York: Oxford University Press, 2004). He has also published over seventy articles on a variety of subjects, including Buddhist philosophy, human rights issues, and contemporary Buddhist movements.

Charles S. Prebish has been Professor of Religious Studies at the Pennsylvania State University for more than thirty-five years. He holds a Ph.D. from the University of Wisconsin, where he served as Research Assistant to Richard H. Robinson. He is the author of seventeen books, and nearly 100 articles and chapters. He is a former officer in the International Association of Buddhist Studies and a founding Co-Chair of the Buddhism Section of the American Academy of Religion. He is also a past president of the Association of Peer Reviewed Electronic Journals in Religion. In 1994, along with Damien Keown, he co-founded the award-winning *Journal of Buddhist Ethics*, and in 2000 co-founded the *Journal of Global Buddhism* with Martin Baumann. With Damien Keown, he is co-editor of the RoutledgeCurzon Critical Studies in Buddhism series. Also with Damien Keown, he created the Journal of Buddhist Ethics Online Books series, which was the first scholarly eBook textbook series. In 1993 he held the Numata Chair in Buddhist Studies as "Distinguished Visiting Professor" at the University of Calgary, and in 1997–8 won a Rockefeller Foundation National Humanities Fellowship to conduct research on North American Buddhism at the Centre for the Study of Religion at the University of Toronto. His major research work has focused on the Indian Buddhist monastic and sectarian traditions, on the academic study of Buddhism, and on the development of Western Buddhism, an area in which he is considered the leading pioneer whose efforts led to the emergence of this topic as a legitimate sub-discipline in the larger field of Buddhist Studies. His long contribution to Buddhist Studies has recently been honored by the publication of a festschrift volume entitled *Buddhist Studies from India to America: Essays in Honor of Charles Prebish.*

Juliane Schober (Ph.D., Anthropology) is Associate Professor of Religious Studies and a former director of the Program for Southeast Asian Studies at Arizona State University. Her research focuses on Theravāda Buddhism in Burma, particularly on ritual, sacred geography, and veneration of images. Her publications include an edited volume on *Sacred Biography in the Buddhist Traditions of South and Southeast Asia* (University of Hawai'i Press, 1997). She has contributed to a number of encyclopedia projects. Her recent essay on "Buddhist Visions of Moral Authority and Civil Society: The Search for the Post-Colonial State in Burma" appeared in *Burma at the Turn of the Twenty-First Century* (M. Skidmore, ed., Honolulu: University of Hawai'i Press, 2005: 113–33). Her present project traces the genealogies on modern Buddhism in Burma during the country's precolonial, colonial and independent eras. "Buddhism and Modernity in Myanmar" appears in *Buddhism in World Cultures: Contemporary Perspectives* (ABC-Clio, S. Berkwitz, ed., forthcoming 2006).

Alan Sponberg has taught Buddhist Studies for twenty-five years at Princeton University, Stanford University, and currently at the University of Montana, where he is Professor of Asian Philosophy and Religion and Director of the Asian Studies Program. He also teaches courses periodically at the Buddhist Library of Singapore and the Nagarjuna Institute in Nagpur, India. His publications focus on the transmission of early Mahāyāna Buddhism from India to China and reflect additional ongoing interests in Buddhist ethics and contemporary Buddhism in Asia and the West. He has lived in Nepal, India and Japan, and is currently helping to organize Dharmapala College, an internationally based two-year Buddhist seminary program under the auspices of the Western Buddhist Order.

Paul L. Swanson is a permanent Research Fellow and Director of the Nanzan Institute for Religion and Culture, and Professor in the Faculty of Humanities at Nanzan University in Nagoya, Japan. His major focuses of research are on Tiantai/Tendai Buddhism and Shugendo. In addition to editing the *Japanese Journal of Religious Studies*, he has published widely in the field of Buddhist Studies and Japanese religions, including *Foundations of Tien-t'ai Philosophy* (Asian Humanities Press, 1989), *Religion and Society in Modern Japan* (Asian Humanities Press, 1993), *Pruning the Bodhi Tree* (University of Hawai'i Press, 1997), and the *Nanzan Guide to Japanese Religions* (University of Hawai'i Press, 2006). His annotated translation of the Chinese Buddhist classic *Mo-ho chih-kuan* has been released in provisional digital form on CD-ROM as *The Great Cessation and Contemplation* (2004).

Kevin Trainor is Associate Professor of Religion at the University of Vermont. He received his Ph.D. from Columbia University in 1990. His areas of research include Indian Buddhism and Theravāda Buddhism in Sri Lanka, with a particular focus on the history of Buddhist relic veneration. His book publications include *Relics, Ritual, and Representation in Buddhism: Rematerializing the Sri Lankan Theravāda Tradition* (Cambridge University Press, 1997), *Buddhism: The Illustrated Guide* (Oxford University Press, 2004; general editor), and *Embodying the Dharma: Buddhist Relic Veneration in Asia* (SUNY Press, 2004; co-editor with David Germano). His articles, including work on the *Therīgāthā* (Verses of the Elder Nuns), on relic theft in Sri Lankan Buddhism, and on Sāñcī, have been published in *Journal of the American Academy of Religion*, *Numen*, and *Mārg*. He was co-organizer and co-chair, with David Germano, of a four-year seminar on Buddhist relic veneration at the annual meeting of the American Academy of Religion, 1994–7. He has been a Fulbright senior scholar at the University of Kelaniya in Sri Lanka and a visiting scholar at Cornell University. He is currently completing a book exploring the modern history of the *Dhammapada* as an object of cultural exchange and appropriation.

Jonathan S. Walters (B.A., Bowdoin; A.M., Ph.D., University of Chicago) is currently Associate Professor of Religion and Asian Studies, and Paul Garrett Fellow in the Humanities at Whitman College, Walla Walla, Washington. He previously taught at the University of Chicago, Northwestern University and the University of Peradeniya, Sri Lanka, and his research and long-term fieldwork in rural Sri Lanka have been supported by the Fulbright Foundation, the National Endowment for the Humanities and the Arthur and Lois Graves Foundation. He is author or editor of *The History of Kelaniya*, *Finding Buddhists in Global History*, *Querying the Medieval: Texts and the History of Practices in South Asia* (with Ronald B. Inden and Daud Ali) and *Constituting Communities: Theravada Buddhism and the Religious Cultures of South and Southeast Asia* (edited with John C. Holt and Jacob Kinnard), in addition to numerous shorter publications in the general area of South Asian (and especially Sri Lankan) Buddhist history, culture and politics, ancient to contemporary. He currently serves on the Board of Directors of the American Institute of Sri Lankan Studies and as International Representative of the Committee for the Protection of the Eppawala Phosphate Deposit, a grassroots Buddhist environmentalist movement in Sri Lanka's ancient North Central Province.

Ananda Wickremeratne graduated with honors in History from the University of Ceylon in 1961, and soon became a member of its faculty. The award of a Commonwealth Scholarship from the UK in 1963 enabled him to pursue his doctoral research in Oxford, which he successfully completed in 1966. Following the grant of a Commonwealth Academic Staff Fellowship, also by the British government, he spent 1974–5 as a visiting fellow to the University of London. He left Sri Lanka in 1979 to assume to two fellowships in Harvard in the Department of Anthropology and the Center for the Study of World Religions. At the time he left Sri Lanka he had obtained a merit promotion to an Associate Professorship. He relocated to Chicago and continues to be an Associate Member of the University of Chicago. Currently, he is a Senior Lecturer in the Theology Department of Loyola University Chicago and teaches courses in Buddhism at the Northwestern University, and religion in the School of Continuing Studies, also at Northwestern University. Wickremeratne is the author of *The Genesis of an Orientalist: Thomas William Rhys Davids in Sri Lanka* (Missouri: South Asia Books, 1994), *Buddhism and Ethnicity in Sri Lanka: A Historical Analysis* (New Delhi: Vikas, 1995), and *The Roots of Nationalism in Sri Lanka* (Colombo: Marga Institute, 1995). Wickremeratne has in addition published numerous articles in academic journals in Sri Lanka, England, and the USA.

References and further reading
Arranged by major topic

Academic study of Buddhism

Cabezón, José. "Buddhist Studies as a Discipline and the Role of Theory." *Journal of the International Association of Buddhist Studies* 18, no. 2 (Winter 1995), 231–68.

Conze, Edward. "Recent Progress in Buddhist Studies." In Edward Conze, *Thirty Years of Buddhist Studies*. Columbia, SC: University of South Carolina Press, 1968, 1–32.

de Jong, Jan W. *A Brief History of Buddhist Studies in Europe and America*. Second, revised and enlarged edition. Delhi: Sri Satguru Publications, 1987.

Eckel, Malcom David. "The Ghost at the Table: On the Study of Buddhism and the Study of Religion." *Journal of the American Academy of Religion* 62, no. 4 (Winter 1994), 1085–110.

Gómez, Luis. "Unspoken Paradigms: Meanderings through the Metaphors of a Field." *Journal of the International Association of Buddhist Studies* 18, no. 2 (Winter 1995), 183–230.

Peiris, William. *The Western Contribution to Buddhism*. Delhi: Motilal Banarsidass, 1973.

Prebish, Charles. "The Silent Sangha: Buddhism in the Academy, 173–202." In Charles Prebish, *Luminous Passage: The Practice and Study of Buddhism in America*. Berkeley, CA: University of California Press, 1999.

Webb, Russell. "Contemporary European Scholarship on Buddhism." In *The Buddhist Heritage*, edited by Tadeusz Skorupski, Buddhica Britannica Vol. 1, 237–76. Tring: Institute for Buddhist Studies, 1989.

Welbon, Guy Richard. *The Buddhist Nirvāṇa and Its Western Interpreters*. Chicago, IL: University of Chicago Press, 1968.

Art

Bentor, Yael. *Consecration of Images and Stupas in Indo-Tibetan Tantric Buddhism*. Leiden: E.J. Brill, 1997.

Bhattacharya, Benoytosh. *The Indian Buddhist Iconography, Mainly Based on the Sadhanamala and Other Cognate Tantric Texts of Rituals*. London: Humphrey Milford/Oxford University Press, 1924.

Bunce, Frederick W. *An Encyclopedia of Buddhist Deities, Demigods, Godlings, Saints, and Demons with Special Focus on Iconographic Attributes*, 2 vols. New Delhi: D.K. Printworld, 1994.

Chandra, Lokesh. *Dictionary of Buddhist Iconography*, 2 vols. Revised edition. New Delhi: Aditya Prakashan, 1999.

Coomaraswamy, Ananda K. *The Origin of the Buddha Image*. New Delhi: Munshiram Manoharlal, 1980.

Davidson, J. Leroy. *The Lotus Sutra in Chinese Art: A Study in Buddhist Art to the Year 1000*. New Haven, CT: Yale University Press, 1954.

Dehejia, Vidya. *Early Buddhist Rock Temples*. Ithaca, NY: Cornell University Press, 1972.

Fisher, Robert E. *Buddhist Art and Architecture*. London: Thames and Hudson, 1993.

Gómez, Luis O., ed. *Barabudur: History and Significance of a Buddhist Monument*. Berkeley, CA: Asian Humanities Press, 1981.

Hallade, Madeleine. *Gandharan Art of North India and the Graeco-Buddhist Tradition in India, Persia, and Central Asia*. New York: Harry N. Abrams, 1968.

Huntington, Susan L. and John C. Huntington. *Leaves from the Bodhi Tree: The Art of Pala India (8th–12th centuries) and Its*

International Legacy. Seattle, WA: The Dayton Art Institute, 1990.
Karetsky, Patricia Eichenbaum. *Chinese Buddhist Art*. Oxford, UK: Oxford University Press, 2004.
Kinnard, Jacob N. *Imagining Wisdom: Seeing and Knowing in the Art of Indian Buddhism*. London: RoutledgeCurzon, 1999.
Klimburg-Slater, Deborah E., ed. *The Silk Route and the Diamond Path: Buddhist Esoteric Art on the Trans-Himalayan Trade Routes*. Los Angeles, CA: UCLA Arts Council, 1982.
Knox, Robert. *Amaravati: Buddhist Sculpture from the Great Stupa*. London: The British Museum Press, 1992.
Lauf, Detlef Ingo. *Tibetan Sacred Art: The Heritage of Tantra*. Berkeley, CA: Shambhala, 1976.
Leoshko, Janice, ed. *Bodhgaya: The Site of Enlightenment*. Bombay: Marg Publishing, 1987.
Malandra, Geri H. *Unfolding the Mandala: The Buddhist Caves at Ellora*. Albany, NY: SUNY Press, 1993.
Nehru, Lolita. *Origins of the Gandharan Style*. Delhi: Oxford University Press, 1989.
Pal, Pratapaditya. *The Arts of Nepal, Part 1: Sculpture*. Leiden: E.J. Brill, 1974.
—— *The Arts of Nepal, Part 2: Painting*. Leiden: E.J. Brill, 1978.
Sanford, James H., William R. LaFleur and Masatoshi Nagatomi, eds. *Flowing Traces: Buddhism in the Literary and Visual Arts of Japan*. Princeton, NJ: Princeton University Press, 1992.
Seneviratna, Anuradha and Benjamin Polk. *Buddhist Monastic Architecture in Sri Lanka*. New Delhi: Abhinav, 1997.
Sharf, Robert H. and Elizabeth Horton Sharf, eds. *Living Images: Japanese Buddhist Icons in Context*. Stanford, CA: Stanford University Press, 2002.
Snodgrass, Adrian. *The Symbolism of the Stupa*. Ithaca, NY: Southeast Asia Program, Cornell University, 1985.
Tucci, Giuseppe (Uma Marina Vesci, trans. and Lokesh Chandra, ed.). *Stupa: Art, Architectonics, and Symbolism*. New Delhi: Aditya Prakashan, 1988.
Weidner, Marsha Smith, Richard K. Kent, Patricia Ann Berger and Julia K. Murray, eds. *Latter Days of the Law: Images of Chinese Buddhism, 850–1850*. Honolulu, HI: University of Hawaii Press, 1994.
Weiner, Sheila L. *Ajanta: Its Place in Buddhist Art*. Berkeley, CA: University of California Press, 1977.
Woodward, Hiram W. Jr. *The Sacred Sculpture of Thailand: The Alexander B. Griswold Collection*. Seattle, WA: University of Washington Press, 1997.

Buddha

Basham, A.L. *History and Doctrines of the Ājīvikas: A Vanished Indian Religion*. Delhi: Motilal Banarsidass, 1981.
Bechert, Heinz, ed. *Dating of the Historical Buddha/Die Datierung des historischen Buddha, Parts 1–2*. Göttingen: Vandenhoeck und Ruprecht, 1991–2.
Bodhi, Bhikkhu. "A Look at the Kalama Sutta" (1988). Available http://www.accesstoinsight.org/lib/bps/news/essay09.html
Collins, Steven. *Nirvana and Other Buddhist Felicities*. Cambridge: Cambridge University Press, 1998.
Conze, Edward. *Buddhist Scriptures*. Harmondsworth: Penguin Books, 1959.
Conze, Edward, I.B. Horner, D. Snellgrove, and A. Waley, eds. *Buddhist Texts Through the Ages*. Oxford: Cassirer, 1954; London: Luzac, and New York: Harper Torchbooks, 1964; London: One World, 1995.
Coomaraswamy, Ananda. *Elements of Buddhist Iconograpy*. Cambridge, MA, 1935; reprinted New Delhi: Munshiram Manoharlal, 1972; Philadelphia, PA: Coronet Books, 1998.
Cousins, L.S. "The Dating of the Historical Buddha: A Review Article." *Journal of the Royal Asiatic Society* 6 (1996), 57–63 (review of Bechert 1991–2).
Gethin, Rupert. *The Foundations of Buddhism*. Oxford and New York: University Press, 1998.
Gombrich, Richard. *Precept and Practice: Traditional Buddhism in the Rural Highlands of Ceylon*. Oxford: Clarendon Press, 1971.
—— *Theravāda Buddhism: A Social History from Ancient Benares to Modern Colombo*. London and New York: Routledge and Kegan Paul, 1988.
—— "Dating the Buddha: A Red Herring Revealed." In Heinz Bechert, ed. *Dating of the Historical Buddha/Die Datierung des historischen Buddha, Parts 1–2*. Göttingen: Vandenhoeck und Ruprecht, 1991–2, II.237–57.
—— *How Buddhism Began: The Conditioned Genesis of the Early Teachings*. London

and Atlantic Highlands, NJ: Athlone, 1996.
—— "Discovery of the Buddha's Date." In Lakshman S. Perera, ed. *Buddhism for the New Millennium: Sri Saddhatissa International Buddhist Centre 10th Anniversary Celebrarory Volume*, 9–25. London: World Buddhist Foundation, 2000.
Härtel, Herbert. "Archaeological research on Ancient Buddhist Sites." In Heinz Bechert, ed. *Dating of the Historical Buddha/Die Datierung des historischen Buddha, Parts 1–2*. Göttingen: Vandenhoeck und Ruprecht, 1991–2, I.68–9.
Harvey, Peter. *An Introduction to Buddhism: Teachings, History and Practices*. Cambridge: Cambridge University Press, 1990.
—— *The Selfless Mind: Personality, Consciousness and Nirvana in Early Buddhism.* Richmond: Curzon Press, 1995.
—— "Contemporary Characterisations of the 'Philosophy' of Nikāyan Buddhism." *Buddhist Studies Review* 12, no. 2 (1995b), 109–33.
—— *An Introduction to Buddhist Ethics: Foundations, Values and Issues.* Cambridge: Cambridge University Press, 2000.
Holt, John C. *Buddha in the Crown: Avalokiteśvara in the Buddhist Traditions of Sri Lanka*. Oxford and New York: Oxford University Press, 1991.
Nagapriya, Dharmachari. "Knowledge and Truth in Early Buddhism." *Western Buddhist Review* 3 (no date). Available http://www.westernbuddhistreview.com/vol3/Knowledge.htm
Norman, K.R. "The *Pratyeka-buddha* in Buddhism and Jainism." In Philip Denwood and Alexander Piatigorsky, eds. *Buddhist Studies: Ancient and Modern*, 92–106. London: Curzon, 1983.
—— "Observations on the Dates of the Jina and the Buddha." In Heinz Bechert, ed. *Dating of the Historical Buddha/Die Datierung des historischen Buddha, Parts 1–2*. Göttingen: Vandenhoeck und Ruprecht, 1991–2, I.300–12.
—— *A Philological Approach to Buddhism.* London: School of Oriental and African Studies, 1997.
Obeyesekere, Gananath. "Myth, history and numerology in the Buddhist chronicles." In Heinz Bechert, ed. *Dating of the Historical Buddha/Die Datierung des historischen Buddha, Parts 1–2*. Göttingen: Vandenhoeck und Ruprecht, 1991–2, I.152–82.
Olivelle, Patrick. *Upaniṣads: A New Translation.* Oxford: Oxford University Press, 1996.
Ratnayaka, Shanta. "The Bodhisattva Ideal of the Theravāda." *Journal of the International Association of Buddhist Studies*, 8, no. 2 (1985), 85–110.
Reynolds, Frank E. and Mari B. Reynolds, *A Buddhist Cosmology*. Berkeley, CA: Asian Humanities Press, 1982.
Sponberg, Alan and Helen Hardacre, eds. *Maitreya, the Future Buddha*. Cambridge and New York: Cambridge University Press, 1988.
Strong, John S. *The Buddha: A Short Biography*. Oxford: One Word, 2001.
—— *The Experience of Buddhism: Sources and Interpretations*. Second edition. Belmont, CA: Wadsworth, 2002.
—— *Relics of the Buddha*. Princeton, NJ: Princeton University Press, 2004.
Swearer, Donald K. The *Buddhist World of Southeast Asia*. Albany, NY: SUNY Press, 1995.
Ṭhānissaro Bhikkhu. *The Mind Like Fire Unbound*. Barre, MA: Dhamma Dana Publications, 1993. Also available on Access to Insight website: http://www.accesstoinsight.org/lib/modern/thanissaro/likefire/2–2.html
Walters, Jonathan S. "Gotamī's Story." In Donald S. Lopez Jr., ed. *Buddhism in Practice*. Princeton, NJ: Princeton University Press, 1995, 113–38.
Williams, Paul. *Mahāyāna Buddhism: The Doctrinal Foundations*. London and New York: Routledge, 1989.
—— *Buddhist Thought: A Complete Introduction to the Indian Tradition*. London and New York: Routledge, 2000.

Buddhism and technology

Abercrombie, John R. *Computer Programs for Literary Analysis*. Philadelphia, PA: University of Pennsylvania Press, 1984.
App, Urs, ed. *The Electronic Bodhidharma*. Kyoto: IRIZ, 1991.
Boulnois, L. *The Silk Road*. London: George Allen and Unwin, 1966.
Buckland, Michael. "Emanuel Goldberg, Electronic Document Retrieval, and Vannevar Bush's Memex." *Journal of the American Society for Information Science* 43, no. 4 (1992), 284–94.
Cowan, Ruth Schwartz. *A Social History of American Technology*. New York: Oxford University Press, 1997.
Das, Sarat Chandra (revised by G. Sandberg and A.W. Heyde). *A Tibetan–English*

Dictionary with Sanscrit Synonyms. Calcutta, 1902 (reprint China, 1951).

Davis, Erik. *TechGnosis: Myth, Magic, and Mysticism in the Age of Information*. New York: Three Rivers Press, 1998.

Hockney, Susan. *A Guide to Computer Applications in the Humanities*. Baltimore, MD: Johns Hopkins University Press, 1980.

Hori, Victor Sogen, Richard P. Hayes, and James Mark Shields, eds. *Teaching Buddhism in the West: From the Wheel to the Web* (Curzon Critical Studies in Buddhism, 20). Richmond: Curzon Press, 2002.

Hsing, Yun, ed. *Fo Guang Buddhist Dictionary*. Taiwan: Fo Guang Publishing, 1988–99.

Jaeschke, H.A. *A Tibetan–English Dictionary*. London, 1881 (reprint 1934, 1949, 1959).

Lancaster, Lewis and Sung-bae Park. *The Korean Buddhist Canon: A Descriptive Catalogue*. Berkeley, CA: University of California Press, 1979.

Li, Hui-Lin. "An Archeological and Historical Account of Cannabis in China." *Economic Botany* 28, no. 4 (1974), 437–48.

Māhathera, Nyānatiloka (revised and ed. Nyānaponika Mahāthera). *Buddhist Dictionary: Manual of Buddhist Terms and Doctrines*. Kandy, Sri Lanka: Buddhist Publication Society, 1980.

Marvin, Carolyn. *When Old Technologies Were New: Thinking About Electric Communication in the Late Nineteenth Century*. New York: Oxford University Press, 1988.

Mial, David S., ed. *Humanities and the Computer: New Directions*. Oxford: Oxford University Press, 1990.

Muller, Charles. *CJKV–English Dictionary*. Available at http:// http://www.acmuller.-net/dealt/

—— *Digital Dictionary of Buddhism*. Available at http:// http://www.acmuller.net/ddb/

Nichiren Shoshu International. *A Dictionary of Buddhist Terms and Concepts*. Tokyo: Nichiren Shoshu International Center, 1983.

Obeyesekere, Gananath. "A Review of *The White Buddhist: The Asian Odyssey of Henry Steel Olcott*." *Journal of Buddhist Ethics* 4 (1997).

Perry, Edmund. "Buddhism Transformed: Religious Change in Sri Lanka." *The Journal of the American Oriental Society* 117, no. 2 (1997), 339–42.

Prebish, Charles. *Luminous Passage:The Practice and Study of Buddhism in America*. Los Angeles, CA: University of California Press, 1999.

Prothero, Stephen. *The White Buddhist: The Asian Odyssey of Henry Steel Olcott*. Bloomington, IN: Indiana University Press, 1996. (For review see Obeyesekere 1997.)

Ray, Paul. *The Integral Survey: A Study of the Emergence of Transformational Values in America*. Sausalito, CA: Institute of Noetic Sciences, 1996.

Rhys Davids, T.W. and William Stede, eds. *The Pali Text Society's Pali–English Dictionary*. Chipstead: Pali Text Society, 1921–5 (reprints include London: Luzac, 1966).

Rojas, Raúl and Ulf Hashagen, eds. *The First Computers: History and Architectures*. Cambridge, MA: MIT Press, 2000.

Soka Gakkai *The Dictionary of Buddhism*. Tokyo: Soka Gakkai, 2002.

Taylor, Isaac. *The Alphabet: An Account of the Origin and Development of Letters*. New Delhi: Asian Educational Services, 1991 (reprint of London, 1883). See also: http://www.visopsys.org/andy/essays/darius-bisitun.html

Taylor, Jim. "Cyber-Buddhism and Changing Urban Space in Thailand." *Space and Culture* 6, no. 3 (2003), 292–308.

Buddhism and the Western world

Batchelor, Stephen. *The Awakening of the West: The Encounter of Buddhism and Western Culture*. Berkeley, CA: Parallax Press, 1994.

Baumann, Martin. *Deutsche Buddhisten: Geschichte und Gemeinschaften*, Second edition. Marburg: Diagonal, 1995.

—— "Global Buddhism. Developmental Periods, Regional Histories and a New Analytical Perspective." *Journal of Global Buddhism* 2 (2001), 1–43.

Cadge, Wendy. *Heartwood: The First Generation Practices Theravada Buddhism in America*. Chicago, IL: University of Chicago Press, 2004.

Chandler, Stuart. *Establishing a Pure Land on Earth: The Foguang Buddhist Perspective on Modernization and Globalization*. Honolulu, HI: University of Hawai'i Press, 2004.

Clasquin, Michel and Kobus Krüger. *Buddhism and Africa*. Pretoria: University of South Africa Press, 1999.

Croucher, Paul. *Buddhism in Australia, 1848–1988*. Kensington: New South Wales University Press, 1989.

Fields, Rick. *How the Swans Came to the Lake. A Narrative History of Buddhism in America*, third edition, revised and updated. Boulder, CO: Shambhala, 1992.

Halbfass, Wilhelm. *India and Europe: An Essay in Understanding*. Albany, NY: SUNY Press, 1988.

Hammond, Phillip and David Machacek. *Soka Gakkai in America: Accomodation and Conversion*. New York: Oxford University Press, 1999.

Journal of Buddhist Ethics, online at: http:// jbe.gold.ac.uk/

Journal of Global Buddhism, online at: http:// www.globalbuddhism.org

Kay, David N. *Tibetan and Zen Buddhism in Britain: Transplantation, Development and Adaptation*. London: RoutledgeCurzon, 2004.

Learman, Linda, ed. *Buddhist Missionaries in the Era Of Globalization*. Honolulu, HI: University of Hawai'i Press, 2005.

Machacek, David and Bryan Wilson, eds. *Global Citizens: The Soka Gakkai Buddhist Movement in the World*. Oxford: Oxford University Press, 2000.

McLellan, Janet. *Many Petals of the Lotus: Five Asian Buddhist Communities in Toronto*. Toronto: University of Toronto Press, 1999.

Molino, Anthony, ed. *The Couch and the Tree: Dialogues between Psychoanalysis and Buddhism*. San Francisco, CA: North Point 1998.

Morreale, Don. *The Complete Guide to Buddhist America*. Boston, MA: Shambhala, 1998.

Numrich, Paul David. *Old Wisdom in the New World: Americanization in Two Immigrant Theravada Buddhist Temples*. Knoxville, TN: University of Tennessee Press, 1996.

Obadia, Lionel. *Bouddhisme et Occident: La Diffusion du bouddhisme tibétan en France*. Paris: L'Harmattan, 1999.

Prebish, Charles S. *American Buddhism*. North Scituate, MA: Duxbury Press, 1979.

—— "Two Buddhisms Reconsidered." *Buddhist Studies Review* 10 (1993), 187–206.

—— *Luminous Passage. The Practice and Study of Buddhism in America*. Berkeley, CA: University of California Press, 1999.

Prebish. Charles S. and Martin Baumann, eds. *Westward Dharma: Buddhism beyond Asia*. Berkeley, CA: University of California Press, 2002.

Prebish, Charles S. and Kenneth K. Tanaka, eds. *The Faces of Buddhism in America*. Berkeley, CA: University of California Press, 1998.

Queen, Christopher S., ed. *Engaged Buddhism in the West*. Boston, MA: Wisdom, 2000.

Rawlinson, Andrew. *The Book of Enlightened Master: Western Teachers in Eastern Traditions*. Chicago, IL: Open Court, 1997.

Rocha, Cristina. *Zen in Brazil: The Quest for Cosmopolitan Modernity*, Honolulu, HI: University of Hawai'i Press, 2006.

Schwab, Raymond. *The Oriental Renaissance: Europe's Discovery of India and the East, 1680–1880*. New York: Columbia University Press, 1984.

Seager, Richard Hugh. *Buddhism in America. Columbia Series on Contemporary American Religions*. New York: Columbia University Press, 1999.

Sharf, Robert H. "Buddhist Modernism and the Rhetoric of Meditative Experience." *Numen* 42 (1995), 228–83.

Spuler, Michelle. *Facets of the Diamond: Developments in Australian Buddhism*. Richmond: Curzon, 2002.

Tweed, Thomas A. *The American Encounter with Buddhism 1844–1912: Victorian Culture and the Limits of Dissent*. Bloomington, IN: Indiana University Press, 1992.

Tweed, Thomas A. and Stephen Prothero. *Asian Religions in America: A Documentary History*. New York: Oxford University Press, 1992.

Tworkov, Helen. *Zen in America: Profiles of Five Teachers*. San Francisco, CA: North Point Press, 1989.

Waterhouse, Helen. *Authority and Adaptation: A Case Study in British Buddhism*. Leeds: Religions Community Project, 1997.

Williams, Duncan Ryūken and Christopher S. Queen, eds. *American Buddhism: Methods and Findings in Recent Scholarship*. Richmond: Curzon Press, 1999.

Wilson, Bryan and Karel Dobbelaere. *A Time to Chant: The Soka Gakkai Buddhists in Britain*. Oxford: Oxford University Press, 1994.

Buddhism in China

Ch'en, Kenneth. *Buddhism in China: A Historical Survey*. Princeton, NJ: Princeton University Press, 1964.

Cook, Francis H. *Hua-yen Buddhism: The Jewel Net of Indra*. University Park, PA: Pennsylvania State University Press, 1977.

Dumoulin, Heinrich (trans. James W. Heisig and Paul Knitter). *Zen Buddhism: A History*, 2 vols. London: Macmillan, 1988–90.

Gregory, Peter N., ed. *Traditions of Meditation in Chinese Buddhism*. Studies in East Asian Buddhism, 4. Honolulu, HI: Kuroda Institute, University of Hawai'i Press, 1986.
—— ed. *Sudden and Gradual Approaches to Enlightenment in Chinese Thought*. Honolulu, HI: University of Hawai'i Press, 1987.
Kieschnick, John. *The Impact of Buddhism on Chinese Material Culture*. Princeton, NJ: Princeton University Press, 2003.
Kraft, Kenneth, ed. *Zen: Tradition and Transition: A Sourcebook by Contemporary Zen Masters and Scholars*. New York: Grove Press, 1988.
McRae, John R. *The Northern School and the Formation of Early Ch'an Buddhism*. Honolulu, HI: University of Hawai'i Press, 1986.
—— *Seeing Through Zen – Encounter, Transformation, and Genealogy in Chinese Chan Buddhism*. Berkeley, CA: University of California Press, 2004.
Ng, Yu-kwan. *T'ien-t'ai Buddhism and Early Mādhyamaka*. Honolulu, HI: University of Hawaii Press, 1993.
Swanson, Paul L. *Foundations of T'ien-t'ai Philosophy: The Flowering of the Two Truths Theory in Chinese Buddhism*. Berkeley, CA: Asian Humanities Press, 1989.
Watson, Burton, trans. *Cold Mountain; 100 Poems by the T'Ang Poet Han-Shan*. New York: Columbia University Press, 1970.
—— trans. *The Lotus Sutra*. New York: Columbia University Press, 1993.
—— trans. *The Vimalakirti Sutra*. New York: Columbia University Press, 1997.
Welch, Holmes. *The Practice of Chinese Buddhism, 1900–1950*. Harvard East Asian Studies, no. 26. Cambridge, MA: Harvard University Press, 1967.
—— *The Buddhist Revival in China*. Harvard East Asian Studies, no. 33. Cambridge, MA, Harvard University Press, 1968.
Yu, Chun-fang. *Kuan-yin: The Chinese Transformation of Avalokiteśvara*. New York: Columbia University Press, 2001.
Zürcher, Erik. *The Buddhist Conquest of China; The Spread and Adaptation of Buddhism in Early Medieval China*, 2 vols. Leiden: E.J. Brill, 1959.

Buddhism in India

Anacker, Stefan. *Seven Works of Vasubandhu: The Buddhist Psychological Doctor*. Delhi: Motilal Banarsidass, 1984.
Boisvert, Mathieu. *The Five Aggregates: Understanding Theravāda Psychology and Soteriology*. Waterloo, Ontario: Canadian Corporation for Studies in Religion, 1995.
Brassard, Francis. *The Concept of Bodhicitta in Śāntideva's Bodhicaryāvatāra*. Albany, NY: SUNY Press, 2000.
Carrithers, Michael. *The Buddha*. Oxford: Oxford University Press, 1983.
Collins, Steven. *Selfless Persons: Imagery and Thought in Thevavāda Buddhism*. Cambridge: Cambridge University Press, 1982.
—— *Nirvana and Other Buddhist Felicities*. Cambridge: Cambridge University Press, 1998.
Conze, Edward. *Buddhist Thought in India: Three Phases of Buddhist Philosophy*. Ann Arbor, MI: University of Michigan Press, 1967.
Dreyfus, Georges B.J. *Recognizing Reality: Dharmakīrti's Philosophy and Its Tibetan Interpreters*. Albany, NY: SUNY Press, 1997.
Dunne, John D. *Foundations of Dharmakīrti's Philosophy*. Boston, MA: Wisdom Publications, 2004.
Garfield, Jay L. *The Fundamental Wisdom of the Middle Way: Nāgārjuna's Mūlamadhyamakakārikā*. Oxford: Oxford University Press, 1995.
Gethin, Rupert. *The Foundations of Buddhism*. Oxford: Oxford University Press, 1998.
Griffiths, Paul J. *On Being Buddha: The Classical Doctrine of Buddhahood*. Albany, NY: SUNY Press, 1994.
Gunaratana, Henepola. *The Path of Serenity and Insight: An Explanation of the Buddhist Jhānas*. Delhi: Motilal Banarsidass, 1985.
Harvey, Peter. *An Introduction to Buddhism*. Cambridge: Cambridge University Press, 1990.
—— *The Selfless Mind: Personality, Consciousness and Nirvana in Early Buddhism*. Surrey: Curzon Press, 1995.
Hayes, Richard P. *Dignāga on the Interpretation of Signs*. Dordrecht: Kluwer Academic Publishers, 1988.
Hirakawa, Akira. *A History of Indian Buddhism: From Śākyamuni to Early Mahāyāna*. Honolulu, HI: University of Hawai'i Press, 1990.
Hoffman, Frank J. *Rationality and Mind in Early Buddhism*. Delhi: Motilal Banarsidass, 1987.
Jayatilleke, Kulatissa Nanda. *Early Buddhist Theory of Knowledge*. London: Allen and Unwin, 1963.
Kochumuttom, Thomas A. *A Buddhist Doctrine of Experience: A New Translation and*

Interpretation of the Works of Vasubandhu the Yogācārin. Delhi: Motilal Banarsidass, 1982.
Lindtner, Christian. *Nāgārjuniana: Studies in the Writings and Philosophy of Nāgārjuna.* Delhi: Motilal Banarsidass, 1987.
Schmithausen, Lambert. *Ālayavijñāna: On the Origin and the Early Development of a Central Concept of Yogācāra Philosophy.* Tokyo: International Institute for Buddhist Studies,1987.
Stcherbatsky, Th. *Buddhist Logic.* New York: Dover Publications. 1962 [reprint].
—— *The Conception of Buddhist Nirvana.* The Hague: Mouton, 1965.
Vasubandhu. *Abhidharmakośabhāṣyam.* Translated by Leo M. Pruden from La Vallée Poussin's 1923 French translation. Berkeley, CA: Asian Humanities Press, 1988.
Verdu, Alfonso. *Early Buddhist Philosophy in the Light of the Four Noble Truths.* Delhi: Motilal Banarsidass, 1985.
Vetter, Tilmann. *The Ideas and Meditative Practices of Early Buddhism.* Leiden; New York: E.J. Brill, 1988.
Warder, A.K. *Indian Buddhism.* Dehli: Motilal Banarsidass, 1980.
Williams, Paul. *Mahāyāna Buddhism: The Doctrinal Foundations.* London; New York: Routledge, 1989.
Willis, Janice Dean. *On Knowing Reality: The Tattvārtha Chapter of Asaṅga's Bodhisattvabhūmi.* New York: Columbia University Press, 1979.

Buddhism in Japan

Abé Ryūichi. *The Weaving of Mantra: Kūkai and the Construction of Esoteric Buddhist Discourse.* New York: Columbia University Press, 1999.
Adolphson, Mikael S. *The Gates of Power: Monks, Courtiers, and Warriors in Premodern Japan.* Honolulu, HI: University of Hawai'i Press, 2000.
Bielefeldt, Carl. *Dōgen's Manuals of Zen Buddhism.* Berkeley, CA: University of California Press, 1988.
Bodiford, William M. *Sōtō Zen in Medieval Japan.* Kuroda Institute Studies in East Asian Buddhism 8. Honolulu, HI: University of Hawai'i Press, 1993.
Colcutt, Martin. *Five Mountains: The Rinzai Zen Monastic Institution in Medieval Japan.* Harvard East Asian Monographs 85. Cambridge, MA: Harvard University Press, 1981.
Dobbins, James C. *Jōdo Shinshū: Shin Buddhism in Medieval Japan.* Bloomington, IN: Indiana University Press, 1989.
—— ed. *The Legacy of Kuroda Toshio.* Special issue of *Japanese Journal of Religious Studies* 23 no. 3–4 (Fall), 1996.
Dumoulin, Heinrich. *Zen Buddhism: A History.* Vol. 1: India and China; Vol. 2: Japan. New York: Macmillan, 1990. (Reprinted, with new introductory essays by John McRae and Victor Hori, Bloomington, IN: World Wisdom, 2005.)
Faure, Bernard. *The Rhetoric of Immediacy: A Cultural Critique of Chan/Zen Buddhism.* Princeton, NJ: Princeton University Press, 1991.
—— *Visions of Power: Imagining Medieval Japanese Buddhism.* Princeton, NJ: Princeton University Press, 1996.
Groner, Paul. *Saichō: The Establishment of the Japanese Tendai School.* Berkeley Buddhist Studies Series 7, 1984. (Reprint Honolulu, HI: University of Hawai'i Press, 2000.)
Hubbard, Jamie, and Paul L. Swanson. *Pruning the Bodhi Tree: The Storm Over Critical Buddhism.* Nanzan Library of Asian Religion and Culture 2. Honolulu, HI: University of Hawai'i Press, 1997.
Hur, Nam-lin. *Prayer and Play in Late Tokugawa Japan: Asakusa Sensōji and Edo Society.* Cambridge and London: Harvard University Press, 2000.
Jaffe, Richard M. *Neither Monk nor Layman: Clerical Marriage in Modern Japanese Buddhism.* Princeton, NJ: Princeton University Press, 2001.
Kasahara Kazuo, ed. *A History of Japanese Religion.* Tokyo: Kosei Publishing, 2001.
Kashiwahara, Yusen, and Koyu Sonoda, eds. *Shapers of Japanese Buddhism.* Tokyo: Kōsei Publishing, 1994.
Ketelaar, James Edward. *Of Heretics and Martyrs in Meiji Japan: Buddhism and Its Persecution.* Princeton, NJ: Princeton University Press, 1990.
LaFleur, William R. *The Karma of Words: Buddhism and the Literary Arts in Medieval Japan.* Berkeley, CA: University of California Press, 1983.
McCallum, Donald F. *Zenkōji and Its Icon: A Study in Medieval Japanese Religious Art.* Princeton, NJ: Princeton University Press, 1994.
McMullin, Neil. *Buddhism and the State in Sixteenth-Century Japan.* Princeton, NJ: Princeton University Press, 1984.
Matsunaga, Daigan and Alicia Matsunaga. *Foundation of Japanese Buddhism*, 2 vols.

Tokyo: Buddhist Books International, 1974.
Payne, Richard K., ed. *Re-Visioning "Kamakura" Buddhism*. Kuroda Institute Studies in East Asian Buddhism 11. Honolulu, HI: University of Hawai'i Press, 1998.
Reader, Ian, *Making Pilgrimages: Meaning and Practice in Shikoku*. Honolulu, HI: University of Hawai'i Press, 2005.
Reader, Ian and George J. Tanabe, Jr. *Practically Religious: Worldly Benefits and the Common Religion of Japan*. Honolulu, HI: University of Hawai'i Press, 1998.
Ruppert, Brian D. *Jewel in the Ashes: Buddha Relics and Power in Early Medieval Japan*. Cambridge, MA: Harvard University Press, 2000.
Sanford, James H., William R. LaFleur, and Masatoshi Nagatomi, eds. *Flowing Traces: Buddhism in the Literary and Visual Arts of Japan*. Princeton, NJ: Princeton University Press, 1992.
Stone, Jacqueline I., *Original Enlightenment and the Transformation of Medieval Japanese Buddhism*. Kuroda Institute Studies in East Asian Buddhism 12. Honolulu, HI: University of Hawai'i Press, 1999.
Tamura Yoshiro, *Japanese Buddhism: A Cultural History*. Tokyo: Kosei Publishing, 2001.
Tanabe, George J., Jr., ed. *Religions of Japan in Practice*. Princeton, NJ: Princeton University Press, 1999.
Teeuwen, Mark and Fabio Rambelli, eds. *Buddhas and Kami in Japan: Honji suijaku as a Combinatory Paradigm*. London and New York: RoutledgeCurzon, 2003.
Thelle, Notto R. *Buddhism and Christianity in Japan: From Conflict to Dialogue, 1854–1899*. Honolulu, HI: University of Hawai'i Press, 1987.
Williams, Duncan Ryūken. *The Other Side of Zen: A Social History of Sōtō Buddhism in Tokugawa Japan*. Princeton and Oxford: Princeton University Press, 2005.

Buddhism in Korea

Buswell, Robert E., Jr. *Tracing Back the Radiance: Chinul's Korean Way of Zen*. Honolulu, HI: University of Hawai'i Press, 1991.
—— *The Zen Monastic Experience: Buddhist Practice in Contemporary Korea*. Princeton, NJ: Princeton University Press, 1992.
—— "The Koryo Period." In Takeuchi Yoshinori, ed. *Buddhist Spirituality II: Later China, Korea, Japan, and the Modern World*. New York: Crossroad Publishing Company, 1999, 134–59.
—— ed. *Currents and Countercurrents: Korean Influences on the East Asian Buddhist Traditions*. Honolulu, HI: University of Hawai'i Press, 2005.
Keel, Hee-Sung. *Chinul: The Founder of the Korean Son Tradition*. Berkeley, CA: Center for South and South East Asian Studies, University of California, Berkeley, Institute of Buddhist Studies, 1984.
Lancaster, Lewis R. and C.S. Yu, eds. *Introduction of Buddhism to Korea: New Cultural Patterns*. Berkeley, CA: Asian Humanities Press, 1989.
—— eds. *Assimilation of Buddhism in Korea: Religious Maturity and Innovation in the Silla Dynasty*. Berkeley, CA: Asian Humanities Press, 1991.
—— eds. *Buddhism in the Early Chosŏn: Suppression and Transformation*. Berkeley, CA: Center for Korean Studies, University of California at Berkeley, Institute of East Asian Studies, 1996.
Lancaster, Lewis R., Kikun Suh and Chaishin Yu, eds. *Buddhism in Koryŏ: A Royal Religion*. Berkeley, CA: University of California, Berkeley, Institute of East Asian Studies, 1996.
Mu Seong Sunim. *Thousand Peaks: Korean Zen-Tradition and Teachers*. Cumberland, RI: Primary Point Press, 1991.
Muller, A. Charles. *The Sutra of Perfect Enlightenment: Korean Buddhism's Guide to Meditation* (with the commentary by the Sŏn monk Kihwa). Albany, NY: SUNY Press, 1999.
Park, Sung Bae. *Buddhist Faith and Sudden Enlightenment*. Albany, NY: SUNY Press, 1983.
—— "Silla Buddhist Spirituality." In Takeuchi Yoshinori, ed. *Buddhist Spirituality II: Later China, Korea, Japan, and the Modern World*. New York: Crossroad Publishing Company, 1999, 57–78.
Shim, Jae-Ryong. *Korean Buddhism: Tradition and Transformation*. Seoul: Jimoondang, 1999.
Sørensen, Henrik H. "Buddhist Spirituality in Premodern and Modern Korea." In Takeuchi Yoshinori, ed. *Buddhist Spirituality II: Later China, Korea, Japan, and the Modern World*. New York: Crossroad Publishing Company, 1999, 109–33.

Buddhism in South and Southeast Asia

Basham, A.L. *The Wonder that was India*. New York: Macmillan, 1954.

Bond, George D. *The Word of the Buddha: The* Tipiṭaka *and its Interpretation in Theravāda Buddhism.* Colombo: M.D. Gunasena, 1982.
—— *The Buddhist Revival in Sri Lanka.* Columbia, SC: University of South Carolina Press, 1988.
—— *Buddhism at Work: Community Development, Social Empowerment and the Sarvodaya Movement.* Bloomfield, CT: Kumarian Press, 2004.
De Silva, C.R. *Sri Lanka: A History.* New Delhi: Vikas Publishing House, 1987.
Gombrich, Richard. *Precept and Practice: Traditional Buddhism in the Rural Highlands of Sri Lanka.* Oxford: Clarendon Press, 1971.
Gombrich, Richard and Obeyesekere, Gananath. *Buddhism Transformed: Religious Change in Sri Lanka.* Princeton, NJ: Princeton University Press, 1988.
Harris, Ian, ed. *Buddhism and Politics in Twentieth Century Asia.* London: Continuum, 1999.
Holt, John C. *The Religious World of Kīrti Śrī: Buddhism, Art and Politics in Late Medieval Sri Lanka.* New York: Oxford University Press, 1996.
Horner, I.B. *The Early Buddhist Theory of Man Perfected.* London: Williams and Norgate, 1936.
Kabilsingh, Chatsumarn. *Thai Women in Buddhism.* Berkeley, CA: Parallax Press, 1991.
Lester, Robert. *Theravada Buddhism in Southeast Asia.* Ann Arbor, MI: University of Michigan Press, 1973.
Malalasekera, G.P. *The Pali Literature of Ceylon.* Colombo: M.D. Gunasena, 1928.
Oliver, Victor L. *Caodai Spiritism: A Study of Religion in Vietnamese Society.* Leiden: E.J. Brill, 1976.
Prebish, Charles S. "A Review of Scholarship on the Buddhist Councils." *Journal of Asian Studies* 33 (February 1974), 239–54.
Prebish, Charles S. and Janice J. Nattier, "Mahāsāṃghika Origins: The Beginning of Buddhist Sectarianism." *History of Religion* 16 (1977), 237–72.
Rahula, Walpola. *History of Buddhism in Ceylon: The Anuradhapura Period.* Colombo: M.D. Gunasena, 1956.
Ray, Niharranjan. *An Introduction to the Study of Theravada Buddhism in Burma.* Bangkok: Orchid Press, 2002.
Ray, Reginald A. *Buddhist Saints in India: A Study in Buddhist Values and Orientations.* New York: Oxford University Press, 1994.
Reynolds, Holly and Bardwell Smith, eds. *The City as a Sacred Center: Essays on Six Asian Contexts.* Leiden: E.J. Brill, 1987.
Sivaraksa, Sulak. *Trans Thai Buddhism and Envisioning Resistance: The Engaged Buddhism of Sulak Sivaraksa.* Bangkok: Suksit Siam, 2004.
Smith, Bardwell, ed. *Religion and the Legitimation of Power in Thailand, Laos, and Burma.* Chambersburg, PA: Anima Books, 1978.
Suksamran, Somboom. *Political Buddhism in Southeast Asia: The Role of the Sangha in the Modernization of Thailand.* New York: St. Martin's Press, 1976.
—— *Buddhism and Politics in Thailand.* Singapore: Institute of Southeast Asian Studies, 1982.
—— *Buddhism and Political Legitimacy.* Bangkok: Chulalongkorn University Printing House, 1993.
Swearer, Donald K. "Buddhism in Southeast Asia." In Joseph Kitagawa and Mark Cummings, eds. *Buddhism and Asian History.* New York: Macmillan, 1987, 107–29.
—— *The Buddhist World of Southeast Asia.* Albany, NY: SUNY Press, 1995.
Tambiah, S.J. *Buddhism and Spirit Cults in Northeast Thailand.* Cambridge: Cambridge University Press, 1970.
—— *Buddhism Betrayed? Religion, Politics and Violence in Sri Lanka.* Chicago, IL: University of Chicago Press, 1992.
Taylor, Philip. *Goddess on the Rise: Pilgrimage and Popular Religion in Vietnam.* Honolulu, HI: University of Hawai'i Press, 2004.
Unger, Ann Helen and Walter Unger, eds. *Pagodas, Gods, and Spirits of Vietnam.* New York: Thames and Hudson, 1997.
Vander Cruysse, Dirk. *Siam and the West 1500–1700.* Chiang Mai: Silkworm Press, 1991.
Von Der Mehden, Fred. *Religion and Modernization in Southeast Asia.* Syracuse, NY: Syracuse University Press, 1986.
Wyatt, David K. *Siam in Mind.* Chiang Mai: Silkworm Books, 2002.

Buddhism in Tibet

Blondeau, A.M. and Ernst Steinkellner, eds. *Reflections of the Mountain: Essays on the History and Social Meaning of the Mountain Cult in Tibet and the Himalaya.* Vienna: Österreichische Akademie der Wissenschaften, 1996.

Dreyfus, Georges B.J. *Recognizing Reality: Dharmakīrti's Philosophy and Its Tibetan Interpreters*. Ithaca, NY: SUNY Press, 1997.

Dudjom Rinpoche and Jikdrel Yeshe Dorje (trans. Matthew Kapstein). *The Nyingma School of Tibetan Buddhism: Its Fundamentals and History*, 2 vols. Boston, MA: Wisdom Publications, 1991.

Goldstein, Melvyn C. and Matthew T. Kapstein, eds. *Buddhism in Contemporary Tibet: Religious Revival and Cultural Identity*. Berkeley, CA: University of California Press, 1998.

Gyatso, Janet. *Apparitions of the Self: The Secret Autobiographies of a Tibetan Visionary*. Princeton, NJ: Princeton University Press, 1998.

Gyatso, Janet and Hanna Havnevik. *Women in Tibet: Past and Present*. New York: Columbia University Press, 2004.

Kapstein, Matthew T. *The Tibetan Assimilation of Buddhism: Conversion, Contestation, and Memory*. Oxford: Oxford University Press, 2000.

Klein, Anne C. *Meeting the Great Bliss Queen: Buddhists, Feminists, and the Art of the Self*. Boston, MA: Beacon Press, 1995.

Klieger, P. Christiaan, ed. *Tibet, Self, and the Tibetan Diaspora*. Leiden: E.J. Brill, 2002.

McKay, Alex, ed. *Pilgrimage in Tibet*. Richmond: Curzon, 1998.

Powers, John. *Introduction to Tibetan Buddhism*. Ithaca, NY: Snow Lion Publications, 1995.

—— *History as Propaganda: Tibetan Exiles Versus the People's Republic of China*. New York: Oxford University Press, 2004.

Ray, Reginald. *Secret of the Vajra World: The Tantric Buddhism of Tibet*. Boston, MA: Shambhala Publications, 2001.

Richardson, Hugh. *High Peaks, Pure Earth: Collected Writings on Tibetan History and Culture*. London: Serindia Publications, 1998.

Ruegg, David S. *Buddha-Nature, Mind, and the Problem of Gradualism in a Comparative Perspective*. London: School of Oriental and African Studies, 1989.

Samuel, Geoffrey. *Civilized Shamans: Buddhism in Tibetan Societies*. Washington, DC: Smithsonian Institution Press, 1993.

Smith, E. Gene. *Among Tibetan Texts: History and Literature of the Himalayan Plateau*. Boston, MA: Wisdom Publications, 2001.

Sobisch, Jan-Ulrich. *Three-Vow Theories in Tibetan Buddhism: A Comparative Study of Major Traditions from the Twelfth through Nineteenth Centuries*. Wiesbaden: Dr. Ludwig Reichert Verlag, 2002.

Sogyal Rinpoche. *The Tibetan Book of Living and Dying*. San Francisco, CA: Harper, 1992.

Tenzin Gyatso, Dalai Lama XIV. *Path to Bliss: A Practical Guide to Stages of Meditation*. Ithaca, NY: Snow Lion Publications, 1991.

Canons and literature

Bechert, Heinz, ed. *The Language of the Earliest Buddhist Tradition*. Göttingen: Vandenhoeck und Ruprecht, 1980.

Blackburn, Anne M. "Looking for the Vinaya: Monastic Discipline in the Practical Canons of the Theravada." *Journal of the International Association of Buddhist Studies* 2, no. 2 (1999), 281–309.

Bond, George. *The Word of the Buddha: Tipiṭaka and Its Interpretation in Theravāda Buddhism*. Colombo: Gunasena, 1982.

Braarvig, Jens, Paul Harrison, Jens-Uwe Hartman, Kazuno Matsuda and Lore Sander, eds. *Buddhist Manuscripts of the Schøyen Collection*, 2 vols. Oslo: Hermes, 2002.

Buswell, Robert, Jr., ed. *Chinese Buddhist Apocrypha*. Honolulu, HI: University of Hawai'i Press, 1990.

Cabezon, Jose Ignacio and Roger R. Jackson, eds. *Tibetan Literature*. Ithaca, NY: Snow Lion Press, 1996.

Collins, Stephen. "On the Very Idea of the Pāli Canon." *Journal of the Pāli Text Society* 15 (1990), 89–126.

Davidson, Ronald M. "An Introduction to the Standards of Scriptural Authority in Indian Buddhism." In Robert Buswell, Jr., ed. *Chinese Buddhist Apocrypha*, 291–325. Honolulu, HI: University of Hawai'i Press, 1990.

Eimer, Helmut, ed. *Transmission of the Tibetan Canon*. Vienna: Verlag der Osterreichischen Akademie der Wissenschaften, 1997.

Eimer, Helmut and David Germano, eds. *The Many Canons of Tibetan Buddhism*. Leiden: E.J. Brill, 2002.

Gyatso, Janet. "Drawn from the Tibetan Treasury, the gTerma Literature." In Jose Ignacio Cabezon and Roger R. Jackson, eds. *Tibetan Literature*. Ithaca, NY: Snow Lion, 1996, 147–69.

Harrison, Paul. "A Brief History of the Tibetan bKa' gyur." In Jose Ignacio Cabezon and Roger R. Jackson, eds. *Tibetan Literature*. Ithaca, NY: Snow Lion, 1996, 70–94.

Kieschnick, John. *The Eminent Monk: Buddhist Ideals in Medieval Chinese Hagiography*. Honolulu, HI: University of Hawai'i Press, 1997.

Lamotte, Etienne, "Assessment of Textual Interpretation in Buddhism." In Donald Lopez, Jr., ed. *Buddhist Hermeneutics*. Honolulu, HI: University of Hawai'i Press, 1988, 11–27.

—— trans. Sara Boin. *History of Indian Buddhism from the Origins to the Śaka Era*. Louvain: Peeters Press, 1988.

Lewis, Todd E. *Popular Buddhist Texts from Nepal*. New York: SUNY Press, 2000.

Link, Arthur. "The Earliest Chinese Account of the Compilation of the Chinese Tripiṭaka." *Journal of the American Oriental Society* 81 (1961), 87–103, 281–92.

Lopez, Donald S., Jr., ed. *Buddhism in Practice*. Princeton, NJ: Princeton University Press, 1995.

—— ed. *Religions of China in Practice*. Princeton, NJ: Princeton University Press, 1996.

McDaniel, Justin, "The Curricular Canon in Northern Thailand and Laos." *Manusya* 4 (2002), 20–59.

Mair, Victor, ed. *The Columbia History of Chinese Literature*. New York: Columbia University Press, 2001.

Nattier, Jan. "Church Language and Vernacular Language in Central Asian Buddhism." *Numen* 37 (1990), 195–219.

Newman, John. "Itineraries to Shambhala." In Jose Ignacio Cabezon and Roger R. Jackson, eds. *Tibetan Literature*. Ithaca, NY: Snow Lion, 1996, 485–99.

Norman, K.R. *Pali Literature*. Wiesbaden: Otto Harrassowitz, 1983.

Obermiller, E., trans. *The History of Buddhism in India and Tibet*. Delhi, India: Sri Satguru Publications, 1986.

Ruegg, D.S., trans. *The Life of Bu Ston Rin Po Che*. Roma: Instituto Italiano per il Medio ed Estremo Oriente, 1966.

Salomon, Richard, *Ancient Scrolls from Gandhara*. Seattle, WA: University of Washington Press, 1999.

Schoening, Jeffrey D. "Sūtra Commentaries in Tibetan Translation." In Jose Ignacio Cabezon and Roger R. Jackson, eds. *Tibetan Literature*. Ithaca, NY: Snow Lion. 1996, 111–37.

Skilling, Peter. "Theravādin Literature in Tibetan Translation." *Journal of the Pāli Text Society* (1993), 69–201.

—— " From bKa' bstan bcos to bKa' 'gyur and bsTan 'gyur." In Helmut Eimer, ed. *Transmission of the Tibetan Canon*, 87–111. Vienna: Verlag der Osterreichischen Akademie der Wissenschaften 1997.

Skorupksi, Tadeusz. "The Canonical Tantras of the New Schools." In Jose Ignacio Cabezon and Roger R. Jackson, eds. *Tibetan Literature*. Ithaca, NY: Snow Lion, 1996, 95–110.

Smith, E. Gene. *Among Tibetan Texts*. Boston, MA: Wisdom Publications, 2001.

Tokuno, Kyoko. "The Evaluation of Indigenous Scriptures in the Chinese Buddhist Bibliographical Catalogues." In Robert E. Buswell, Jr., ed. *Chinese Buddhist Apocrypha*. Honolulu, HI: University of Hawai'i Press, 1990, 31–74.

von Hinuber, Oskar. *A Handbook of Pāli Literature*. Berlin and New York: De Gruyter, 1996.

Wilson, Joe Bransford. "Tibetan Commentaries on Indian Śāstras." In Jose Ignacio Cabezon and Roger R. Jackson, eds. *Tibetan Literature*. Ithaca, NY: Snow Lion, 1996, 125–37.

Zurcher, Erik. *Buddhist Conquest of China: The Spread and Adaptation of Buddhism in Early Medieval China*, 2 vols. Leiden: E.J. Brill, 1959.

Dharma

Carter, John Ross *Dhamma: Western Academic and Sinhalese Buddhist Interpretations, a Study of a Religious Concept*. San Francisco, CA: Hokuseido Press, 1978.

Frauwallner, Ernst (trans. Sophie S. Kidd). *Studies in Abhidharma Literature and the Origins of Buddhist Philosophical Systems*. Albany, NY: SUNY Press, 1995.

Gethin, Rupert. *The Foundations of Buddhism*. Oxford: Oxford University Press, 1998.

Nyānatiloka, Mahāthera *Guide through the Abhidhamma Piṭaka*. Kandy: Buddhist Publication Society, 1971.

Potter, Karl H., ed. *Encyclopedia of Indian Philosophies, Vol. 8: Buddhist Philosophy from 100 to 350 A.D.* Delhi: Motilal Banarsidass, 1998.

Rhys Davids, Caroline A.F. *A Buddhist Manual of Psychological Ethics: Dhammasangaṇi*, third edition. Oxford: Pali Text Society, 1997.

Stcherbatsky, Theodore. *The Central Conception of Buddhism and the Meaning of the Word "Dharma"*, 4th edition. Delhi: Indological Book House, 1970.

Vasubandhu and Louis de La Vallée Poussin (trans. Leo M. Pruden). *Abhidharmakośabhāṣyam*. Berkeley, CA: Asian Humanities Press, 1988.
Williams, Paul. *Mahāyāna Buddhism: The Doctrinal Foundations*. London; New York: Routledge, 1989.

Engaged Buddhism

Aitken, Robert. *The Mind of Clover: Essays in Zen Buddhist Ethics*. San Francisco, CA: North Point Press, 1984.
Badiner, Allan Hunt, ed. *Dharma Gaia: A Harvest of Essays in Buddhism and Ecology*. Berkeley, CA: Parallax Press, 1990.
Chappell, David W., ed. *Buddhist Peacework: Creating Cultures of Peace*. Boston, MA: Wisdom Publications, 1999.
Coleman, James William. *The New Buddhism: The Western Transformation of an Ancient Tradition*. New York: Oxford University Press, 2000.
De Silva, Padmisiri. *The Search for Buddhist Economics*. Kandy: Buddhist Publication Society, 1975.
Dresser, Marianne. *Buddhist Women on the Edge: Contemporary Perspectives from the Western Frontier*. Berkeley, CA: North Atlantic Books, 1996.
Eppsteiner, Fred, ed. *The Path of Compassion: Writings on Socially Engaged Buddhism*. Berkeley, CA: Parallax Press, 1988.
Glassman, Bernie. *Bearing Witness: A Zen Master's Lessons in Making Peace*. New York: Bell Tower, 1998.
Gross, Rita M. *Buddhism after Patriarchy: A Feminist History, Analysis, and Reconstruction of Buddhism*. Albany, NY: SUNY Press, 1993.
Jones, Ken. *The Social Face of Buddhism*. London: Wisdom Publications, 1989.
Kaza, Stephanie and Kenneth Kraft, eds. *Dharma Rain: Sources of Buddhism Environmentalism*. Boston, MA: Shambhala, 2000.
King, Sallie B. *Being Benevolence: The Social Ethics of Engaged Buddhism*. Honolulu, HI: University of Hawai'i Press, 2005.
Kotler, Arnold, ed. *Engaged Buddhist Reader: Ten Years of Engaged Buddhist Publishing*. Berkeley, CA: Parallax Press, 1996.
Kraft, Kenneth, ed. *Inner Peace, World Peace: Essays on Buddhism and Nonviolence*. Albany, NY: SUNY Press, 1992.
Macy, Joanna. *Dharma and Development: Religion as Resource in the Sarvodaya Self-help Movement*. West Hartford, CN: Kumarian, 1983.
—— *Mutual Causality in Buddhism and General Systems Theory: The Dharma of Natural Systems*, New York: SUNY Press, 1991.
—— *World as Lover, World as Self*. Berkeley, CA: Parallax Press, 1991.
Nhat Hanh, Thich. *Being Peace*. Berkeley, CA: Parallax Press, 1987.
Payutto, P.A. *Buddhist Economics: A Middle Way for the Market Place*. Bangkok: Buddhadhamma Foundation, 1994.
Prebish, Charles S. and Martin Baumann, eds. *Westward Dharma: Buddhism Beyond Asia*. Berkeley, CA: University of California Press, 2002.
Prebish, Charles S. and Kenneth K. Tanaka, eds. *The Faces of Buddhism in America*. Berkeley, CA: University of California Press, 1998.
Prothero, Stephen. *The White Buddhist: The Asian Odyssey of Henry Steel Olcott*. Bloomington, IN: Indiana University Press, 1996.
Queen, Christopher S., ed. *Engaged Buddhism in the West*. Boston, MA: Wisdom Publications, 2000.
Queen, Christopher, Charles Prebish, and Damien Keown, eds. *Action Dharma: New Studies in Engaged Buddhism*. New York: RoutledgeCurzon, 2003.
Queen, Christopher S. and Sallie B. King, eds. *Engaged Buddhism: Buddhist Liberation Movements in Asia*. Albany, NY: SUNY Press, 1996.
Rahula, Walpola. *What the Buddha Taught*, second edition. New York: Grove Press, 1974.
Schumacher, E.F. *Small is Beautiful: Economics as if People Mattered*. London: Blond and Briggs, 1973.
Sivaraksa, Sulak. *Seeds of Peace: A Buddhist Vision for Renewing Society*. Berkeley, CA: Parallax Press, 1992.
Tucker, Mary Evelyn and Duncan Ryuken Williams, eds. *Buddhism and Ecology: The Interconnectedness of Dharma and Deeds*. Cambridge, MA: Harvard University Press, 1997.

Ethics

Harvey, Peter. *An Introduction to Buddhist Ethics*. Cambridge: Cambridge University Press, 2000.
Keown, Damien. *Contemporary Buddhist Ethics*. London: Curzon Press, 2000.

—— *Buddhism and Bioethics*. London: Palgrave, 2001.
—— *The Nature of Buddhist Ethics*. Basingstoke: Palgrave, 2001.
King, Winston L. *In the Hope of Nibbana: The Ethics of Theravada Buddhism*. La Salle, PA: Open Court, 1964.
Kraft, Kennet. *Inner Peace, World Peace. Essays on Buddhism and Nonviolence*. Albany, NY: SUNY Press, 1992.
Queen, Christopher, Charles Prebish and Damien Keown, eds. *Action Dharma. New Studies in Engaged Buddhism*. London: Routledge, 2003.
Saddhatissa, Hammalava. *Buddhist Ethics*. Boston, MA: Wisdom, 1997.

Famous Buddhists and ideal types

Ashin Janakabhivamsa. *The Illustrated History of Buddhism* (U Ba Kyi, artisti) 1951. Accessed online at nibbana.com (http://web.ukonline.co.uk/buddhism/) on 4 August 2005.
Aung San Suu Kyi. *Freedom from Fear and Other Writings*. New York: Penguin Books, 1991.
—— *Empowerment for a Culture of Peace and Development*. Address to World Commission on Culture and Development, Manila, 21 November 1994.
—— *Letters from Burma*. New York: Penguin Books, 1997.
Buddhagosha (trans. Bhikkhu Nanamoli). *The Path of Purification*. Colombo: R. Semage, 1960.
Butwell, R. *U Nu of Burma*. Stanford, CA: Stanford University Press, 1963 (reprinted 1969).
Carrithers, Michael. *The Forest Monks of Sri Lanka: An Anthropological and Historical Study*. Delhi: Oxford University Press, 1983.
Clement, Alan and Aung San Suu Kyi. *The Voice of Hope*. New York: Seven Story Press, 1997.
Holt, John Clifford. *Discipline: The Canonical Buddhism of the Vinayapiṭaka*. Columbia, MO: South Asia Books, 1983.
Holt, John, Jacob Kinnard and Jonathan Walters, eds. *Constituting Communities: Theravāda Buddhism and the Religious Cultures of South and Southeast Asia*. Albany, NY: SUNY Press, 2003.
Kamala Tiyavanich. *Forest Recollections*. Honolulu, HI: University of Hawai'i Press, 1997.
Kloppenborg, Ria. *The Paccekabuddha, A Buddhist Ascetic*. Leiden: E.J. Brill, 1974.
Lopez, Donald S., Jr. *The Heart Sūtra Explained: Indian and Tibetan Commentaries*. Albany, NY: State University of New York, 1988.
—— *The Story of Buddhism: A Concise Guide to its History and Teachings*. San Francisco: HarperSanFrancisco, 2001.
Mendelson, Michael E. (ed. J.P. Ferguson). *Sangha and State in Burma, A Study of Monastic Sectarianism and Leadership*, Ithaca, NY: Cornell University Press, 1975.
Nu, U. *Burma Looks Ahead*. Rangoon: Ministry of Information, Government of the Union of Burma, 1953.
—— (trans. U Law Yone). *Saturday's Son*. New Haven, CT: Yale University Press, 1975.
—— *Buddhism: Theory and Practice*. Bangkok: Mahachulalongkorn Buddhist University, n.d.
—— "Nats." *Crossroads: Journal of Southeast Asian Studies* 4, no. 1 (1988).
Nyanaponika Thera and Hellmut Hecker (ed. Bhikkhu Bodhi). *Great Disciples of the Buddha, Their Lives, Their Work and Their Legacy*. Boston, MA: Wisdom Publications, 2003.
Ray, Reginald. *Buddhist Saints in India*. New York: Oxford University Press, 1994.
Reynolds, Frank E. "The Several Bodies of the Buddha." *History of Religions* 16, no. 4 (1977), 374–89.
Santikaro, Bhikkhu. "Buddhadāsa Bhikkhu: Life and Society through the Natural Eyes of Voidness." In Christopher Queen and Sally King, eds. *Engaged Buddhism: Buddhist Liberation Movements in Asia*. Albany, NY: SUNY Press, 1996.
Sarkisyanz, Emanuel. *Buddhist Backgrounds of the Burmese Revolution*. The Hague: Martinus Nijhoff, 1965.
Sayadawb, Mahāsī. *Practical Insight Meditation*. San Francisco, CA: The Unity Press, 1971.
—— *The Satipatthana Vipassana Meditation*. San Francisco, CA: The Unity Press, 1977.
—— (trans. Nyanaponika Thera). *The Progress of Insight (Visuddhiñana-katha)*. Kandy: Buddhist Publication Society, 1994.
Schober, Juliane. "Religious Merit and Social Status among Burmese Lay Buddhist Organizations." In N. Tannenbaum and C. Kammerer, eds. *Blessing and Merit in Mainland Southeast Asia*. New Haven, CT: Yale University Southeast Asia Monograph Series, 1996, 197–211.

—— ed. *Sacred Biography in the Buddhist Traditions of South and Southeast Asia*. Honolulu, HI: University of Hawai'i Press, 1997.
—— "Buddhist Visions of Moral Authority and Civil Society: The Search for the Post-Colonial State in Burma." In Monique Skidmore, ed. *Burma at the Turn of the Twenty-First Century*. Honolulu, HI: University of Hawai'i Press, 2005, 113–33.
—— "Venerating the Buddha's Remains in Burma: From Solitary Practice to the Cultural Hegemony of Communities." *The Journal of Burma Studies* 6 (2001), 111–39.
Smith, Donald E. *Religion and Politics in Burma*, Princeton, NJ: Princeton University Press. 1965.
Strong, John. *The Legend and Cult of Upagupta: Sanskrit Buddhism in North India and Southeast Asia*. Princeton, NJ: Princeton University Press, 1992.
—— *Relics of the Buddha*. Princeton, NJ: Princeton University Press, 2004.
Swearer, Donald. *The Buddhist World of Southeast Asia*. Albany, NY: SUNY, 1996.
—— *Becoming the Buddha: The Ritual of Image Consecration in Thailand*. Princeton, NJ: Princeton University Press, 2004.
Tambiah, Stanley J. *World Conqueror and World Renouncer*. Cambridge: Cambridge University Press, 1977.
—— *The Buddhist Saints of the Forest and the Cult of Amulets*. Cambridge: Cambridge University Press, 1984.

Mahāyāna Buddhism

Chang, Garma C.C., ed. *A Treasury of Mahāyāna Sūtras: Selections from the Mahāratnakūṭa Sūtra*. University Park, PA: Pennsylvania State University Press, 1983.
Cleary, Thomas, trans. *The Flower Ornament Scripture: Avatamsaka-sutra*. Boston, MA: Shambhala, 1983.
Conze, Edward. *The Prajñāpāramitā Literature*. 's-Gravenhage: Mouton, 1960.
—— *The Perfection of Wisdom in Eight Thousand Lines and its Verse Summary*. Bolinas, CA: Four Seasons Foundation, 1973.
Dutt, Nalinaksha. *Aspects of Mahāyāna Buddhism and its Relation to Hīnayāna*. London: Luzac, 1930.
Gomez, L.O. "Buddhism: Buddhism in India." In Mircea Eliade, ed. *The Encyclopedia of Religion*. New York: Macmillan, 1987.
—— *The Land of Bliss: The Paradise of the Buddha of Measureless Light*. Honolulu, HI: University of Hawai'i Press, 1996.
Griffiths, P.J. *On Being Buddha: The Classical Doctrine of Buddhahood*. Albany, NY: SUNY Press, 1994.
Griffiths, P.J. and J.P. Keenan, eds. *Buddha Nature: A Festschrift in Honor of Minoru Kiyota*. Reno, NV: Buddhist Books International, 1990.
Hakeda, Y., trans. *The Awakening of Faith*. New York: Columbia University Press, 1967.
Harrison, Paul. "Who Gets to Ride in the Great Vehicle? Self-image and Identity among the Followers of the Early Mahāyāna." *The Journal of the International Association of Buddhist Studies* 10, no. 1 (1987), 33–89.
Hirakawa, Akira (trans. Paul Groner). *History of Early Buddhism: From Śākyamuni to Early Mahāyāna*. Reprint, Delhi: Motilal Banarsidass, 1998.
Howard, A.F. *The Imagery of the Cosmological Buddha*. Leiden: E.J. Brill, 1986.
Hurvitz, Leon, trans. *Scripture of the Lotus Blossom of the Fine Dharma (The Lotus Sūtra). Translated from the Chinese of Kumārajīva*. New York: Columbia University Press, 1976.
Kiyota, Minoru, ed. *Mahayana Buddhist Meditation: Theory and Practice*. Honolulu, HI: University of Hawai'i Press, 1978.
Kloetzli, Randy. *Buddhist Cosmology: From Single World System to Pure Land-Science and Theology in the Images of Motion and Light*. Delhi: Motilal Banarsidass, 1983.
Lamotte, Étienne (trans. Sara Boin Webb). *The Teaching of Vimalakīrti (Vimalakīrtinirdeśa)*. London: Pali Text Society, 1976.
Liu, Ming-wood. "The Doctrine of the Buddha-Nature in the Mahāyāna Mahāparinirvāṇ Sūtra." *Journal of the International Association of Buddhist Studies* 5, no. 2 (1982), 63–94.
Ñāṇamoli, Bhikkhu, trans. [Buddhaghosa's] *Path of Purification* (*Visuddhimagga*). Kandy: Buddhist Publication Society, 1975.
Pagel, Ulrich. *The Bodhisattvapiṭaka: Its Doctrines, Practices and their Position in Mahāyāna Literature*. Tring: Institute of Buddhist Studies, 1995
Pye, Michael. *Skilful Means: A Concept in Mahāyāna Buddhism*. London: Duckworth, 1978.
Ruegg, David. S. and Lambert Schmithausen, eds. *Earliest Buddhism and Madhyamaka*, Leiden: E.J. Brill, 1990.

Schopen, Gregory. *Bones, Stones, and Buddhist Monks: Collected Papers on the Archaeology, Epigraphy, and Texts of Monastic Buddhism in India.* Honolulu, HI: University of Hawai'i Press, 1997.

—— *Buddhist Monks and Business Matters: Still More Papers on Monastic Buddhism in India.* Honolulu, HI: University of Hawai'i Press, 2004.

—— *Figments and Fragments of Mahāyāna Buddhism in India: More Collected Papers.* Honolulu, HI: University of Hawai'i, 2005.

Schroeder, John W. and Thomas P. Kasulis. *Skillful Means: The Heart of Buddhist Compassion.* Honolulu, HI: University of Hawai'i Press, 2001.

Snellgrove, David L. *Indo-Tibetan Buddhism.* London: Serindia, 1987.

Sponberg, Alan and Helen Hardacre, eds. *Maitreya, the Future Buddha.* Cambridge: Cambridge University Press, 1988.

Suzuki, D. T. "The Development of the Pure Land Doctrine in Buddhism." *The Eastern Buddhist* 3 (1925), 285–326.

—— *On Indian Mahāyāna Buddhism.* New York: Harper Torchbook, 1968.

Takasaki, J. "The Tathāgatotpattisaṃbhava-nirdeśa of the Avataṃsaka and the Ratnagotravibhāga," *Journal of Indian and Buddhist Studies* (Tokyo) 7, no. 1 (1958), 48–53.

Thurman, Robert A.F. *The Holy Teaching of Vimalakīrti: A Mahāyāna Scripture.* University Park and London: Pennsylvania State University Press, 1976.

Tucci, Giuseppe. *The Theory and Practice of the Maṇḍ ala*, London: Rider, 1969.

Vessantara. *Meeting the Buddhas: A Guide to Buddhas, Bodhisattvas and Tantric Deities.* Glasgow: Windhorse Publications, 1993.

Vetter, Tillman. *The Ideas and Meditative Practices of Early Buddhism.* Leiden: E.J. Brill, 1988.

Watson, Burton, trans. *The Lotus Sutra.* New York: Columbia University Press, 1993.

Williams, Paul. *Mahāyāna Buddhism: The Doctrinal Foundations.* London: Routledge, 1989.

Meditational systems

Bielefeldt, Carl. *Dōgen's Manuals of Zen Meditation.* Berkeley, CA: University of California Press, 1988.

Benoytosh Bhattacharya, ed. *Sādhanamāla.* Baroda: Oriental Institute, 1968.

Buddhaghosa (trans. Bhikkhu Ñyāṇamoli). *Path of Purification (Visuddhimagga).* Colombo: A. Semage, 1964.

Conze, Edward. *Buddhist Meditation.* New York: George Allen and Unwin, 1956.

Cozort, Daniel. *Highest Yoga Tantra.* Ithaca, NY: Snow Lion, 1986.

Dalai Lama. *Dzogchen: The Heart Essence of the Great Perfection.* Ithaca, NY: Snow Lion, 2000.

Dalai Lama, Tsong-ka-pa and Jeffrey Hopkins. *Deity Yoga: In Action and Performance Tantra.* Ithaca, NY: Snow Lion, 1981.

English, Elizabeth. *Vajrayoginī: Her Visualizations, Rituals, and Forms.* Boston, MA: Wisdom Publications, 2002.

Gómez, Luis O. "Two Tantric Meditations: Visualizing the Deity." In Donald S. Lopez, Jr., ed. *Buddhism in Practice.* Princeton, NJ: Princeton University Press, 1995, 318–27.

Gregory, Peter N., ed. *Traditions of Meditation in Chinese Buddhism.* Honolulu, HI: University of Hawai'i Press, 1986.

Griffiths, Paul J. *On Being Mindless: Buddhist Meditation and the Mind–Body Problem.* La Salle, PA: Open Court, 1986.

Harrison, P.M. "Buddhānusmrti in the *Pratyutpanna-buddha-saṃmukhāvasthita-samādhi-sūtra*" *Journal of Indian Philosophy* 9 (1978): 35–57.

Heine, Steven and Dale S. Wright. *The Kōan: Texts and Contexts in Zen Buddhism.* New York: Oxford University Press, 2000.

Hopkins, Jeffrey. *Meditation on Emptiness.* Boston, MA: Wisdom Publications, 1996.

Hori, Victor. *Zen Sand: The Book of Capping Phrases for Zen Practice.* Honolulu, HI: University of Hawai'i Press, 2003.

King, Winston L. *Theravāda Meditation: The Buddhist Transformation of Yoga.* College Park, PA: University of Pennsylvania Press, 1980.

Kiyota, Minoru. *Mahāyāna Buddhist Meditation: Theory and Practice.* Honolulu, HI: University of Hawai'i Press, 1978.

McMahan, David L. *Empty Vision: Metaphor and Visionary Imagery in Mahāyāna Buddhism.* New York and London: Routledge Curzon, 2002 (Ch. 5).

Swearer, Donald K. *Secrets of the Lotus.* New York: Macmillan, 1970.

Yampolsky, Philip B., trans. *The Platform Sutra of the Sixth Patriarch.* New York: Columbia, 1967.

Nikāya Buddhism

Bareau, André. *Les Premiers Conciles bouddhiques*. Paris: Presses Universitaires, 1955.
—— *Les Sectes bouddhiques du petit véhicule*. Saigon: École Française d'Extrême-Orient, 1955.
Blackburn, Anne M. "Looking for the Vinaya: Monastic Discipline in the Practical Canons of the Theravada." *Journal of the International Association of Buddhist Studies* 2, no. 2 (1999), 281–309.
Bond, George. *The Word of the Buddha: Tipiṭaka and Its Interpretation in Theravāda Buddhism*. Colombo, Sri Lanka: Gunasena, 1982.
Frauwallner, Ernst (trans. Sophie S. Kidd). *Studies in Abhidharma Literature and the Origins of Buddhist Philosophical Systems*. Albany, NY: SUNY, 1995.
Hallisey, Charles. "Councils as Ideas and Events in the Theravada." *The Buddhist Forum* II (1991), 133–48.
Holt, John C. *Discipline: The Canonical Buddhism of the Vinayapiṭaka*. Delhi: Motilal Banarsidass, 1981.
Holt, John C., Jonathan S. Walters and Jacob N. Kinnard, eds. *Constituting Communities: Theravāda Buddhism and the Religious Cultures of South and Southeast Asia*. Albany, NY: SUNY Press, 2003.
Lamotte, Etienne (trans. Sara Boin). *History of Indian Buddhism from the Origins to the Śaka Era*. Louvain: Peeters Press, 1988.
Nakamura, Hajime. *Indian Buddhism. A Survey with Bibliographical Notes*. Delhi: Motilal Banarsidass, 1989 reprint.
Prebish, Charles. "A Review of Scholarship on the Buddhist Councils." *Journal of Asian Studies* 33, no. 2 (February 1974), 239–54.
Prebish, Charles and Janice Nattier. "Mahāsāṃghika Origins: The Beginnings of Buddhist Sectarianism." *History of Religions* 35, no. 3 (February 1977), 237–72.
Schopen, Gregory. *Bones, Stones and Buddhist Monks: Collected Papers on Archaeology, Epigraphy and Texts of Monastic Buddhism in India*. Honolulu, HI: University of Hawai'i Press, 1997.
—— *Buddhist monks and Business Matters: Still More Papers on Monastic Buddhism*. Honolulu, HI: University of Hawai'i Press, 2004.
Strong, John S. *The Experience of Buddhism: Sources and Interpretations*. Belmont, CA: Wadsworth, 1995.

Rituals and practices

Beal, Samuel, trans. *Si-yu-ki: Buddhist Records of the Western World: Translated from the Chinese of Hiuen Tsiang (AD 629)*. London: Kegan Paul, Trench and Trübner, 1884. Reprint London: Routledge, 2000.
Beyer, Stephan. *The Cult of Tārā: Magic and Ritual in Tibet*. Berkeley, CA: University of California Press, 1973.
Birnbaum, Raoul. *The Healing Buddha*. Boulder, CO: Shambhala, 1979.
Bunnag, Jane. *Buddhist Monk, Buddhist Layman: A Study of Urban Monastic Organization in Central Thailand*. Cambridge: Cambridge University Press, 1973.
Ch'en, Kenneth. *Buddhism in China*. Princeton, NJ: Princeton University Press, 1964.
Deegalle, Mahinda. "Buddhist Preaching and Sinhala Religious Rhetoric: Medieval Buddhist Methods to Popularize Theravāda." *Numen* 44, no. 2 (1997), 180–210.
De Silva, Lily. *Paritta: A Historical and Religious Study of the Buddhist Ceremony for Peace and Prosperity in Sri Lanka*. Colombo: National Museums, 1981.
Deegalle, Mahinda. "Marathon Preachers: The Two-Pulpit Tradition in Sri Lanka." *Asiatische Studien* 52, no. 1 (1998), 15–56.
Dummer, Tom. *Tibetan Medicine*. London: Routledge, 1988.
Faure, Bernard, ed. *Grafting the Bodhi Tree: The Chan and Zen Traditions in Ritual and Cultural Contexts*. London and New York: RoutledgeCurzon, 2003.
Gombrich, Richard. *Precept and Practice: Traditional Buddhism in the Rural Highlands of Ceylon*. Oxford: Clarendon Press, 1971.
Holt, John C. *Discipline: The Canonical Buddhism of the Vinayapiṭaka*. Delhi: Motilal Banarsidass, 1981.
—— *Buddha in the Crown: Avalokiteśvara in the Buddhist Traditions of Sri Lanka*. New York and Oxford: Oxford University Press, 1991.
—— *The Religious World of Kīrti Śrī: Buddhism, Art and Politics in Late Medieval Sri Lanka*. New York and Oxford: Oxford University Press, 1996.
—— *The Buddhist Visnu: Religious Transformation, Politics and Culture*. New York: Columbia University Press, 2004.
Holt, John C., Jonathan S. Walters and Jacob N. Kinnard, eds. *Constituting Communities: Theravāda Buddhism and the*

Religious Cultures of South and Southeast Asia. Albany, NY: SUNY Press, 2003.

Kasulis, Thomas P. *Zen Action/Zen Person.* Honolulu, HI: University of Hawai'i Press, 1981.

Kitagawa, Joseph M. and Mark D. Cummings, eds. *Buddhism and Asian History.* New York: Macmillan, 1989.

Legge, James, trans. *A Record of Buddhistic Kingdoms; Being an Account by the Chinese Monk Fâ-hien of his Travels in India and Ceylon (AD 399–414) in Search of the Buddhist Books of Discipline.* Oxford: Clarendon Press, 1886. Reprint New York: Paragon, 1965.

Lewis, Todd T. *Popular Buddhist Texts from Nepal: Narratives and Rituals of Newar Buddhism.* Albany, NY: SUNY Press, 2000.

Lopez, Donald S., ed. *Buddhism in Practice.* Princeton, NJ: Princeton University Press, 1995.

Mus, Paul. *Barabadur: esquisse d'une histoire du bouddhisme, fondée sur la critique archéologique des texts*, 2 vols. Hanoi: Impr. d'Extrême-Orient, 1935.

Numrich, Paul David. *Old Wisdom in the New World: Americanization in Two Immigrant Theravada Buddhist Temples.* Knoxville, TN: University of Tennessee Press, 1996.

Oldenberg, Hermann, trans. *The Dīpavaṃsa: An Ancient Buddhist Historical Record.* London: Williams and Norgate, 1879.

Ortner, Sherry B. *Sherpas through their Rituals.* Cambridge: Cambridge University Press, 1978.

Perera, G. Ariyapala. *Buddhist Paritta Chanting Ritual: A Comparative Study of the Buddhist Benedictory Ritual.* Dehiwala: Buddhist Cultural Centre, 2000.

Plutschow, Herbert E. *Matsuri: The Festivals of Japan.* Surrey: Japan Library, 1996.

Reynolds, Frank E. and Jason A. Carbine, eds. *The Life of Buddhism.* Berkeley, CA: University of California Press, 2000.

Richardson, Hugh and Michael Aris, eds. *Ceremonies of the Lhasa Year.* London: Serindia, 1994.

Samuels, Jeffrey. "Toward an Action-Oriented Pedagogy: Buddhist Texts and Monastic Education in Contemporary Sri Lanka." *Journal of the American Academy of Religion* 72, no. 4 (2004), 955–71.

Sarkisyanz, Emanual. *Buddhist Backgrounds of the Burmese Revolution.* The Hague: M. Nijhoff, 1965.

Schober, Juliane, ed. *Sacred Biography in the Buddhist Traditions of South and Southeast Asia.* Honolulu, HI: University of Hawai'i Press, 1997.

Schopen, Gregory. *Bones, Stones and Buddhist Monks: Collected Papers on Archaeology, Epigraphy and Texts of Monastic Buddhism in India.* Honolulu, HI: University of Hawai'i Press, 1997.

—— *Buddhist Monks and Business Matters: Still More Papers on Monastic Buddhism.* Honolulu, HI: University of Hawai'i Press, 2004.

Seneviratne, H.L. *Rituals of the Kandyan State.* Cambridge: Cambridge University Press, 1978.

Smith, Bardwell L., ed. *Religion and Legitimation of Power in Sri Lanka.* Chambersburg, PA: Anima Books, 1978.

—— ed. *Religion and Legitimation of Power in Thailand, Laos and Burma.* Chambersburg, PA: Anima Books, 1978.

Snellgrove, David. *Indo-Tibetan Buddhism*, 2 vols. Boston, MA: Shambhala Press, 1987.

Strong, John S. *The Legend and Cult of Upagupta: Sanskrit Buddhism in North India and Southeast Asia.* Princeton, NJ: Princeton University Press, 1992.

—— *The Experience of Buddhism: Sources and Interpretations.* Belmont, CA: Wadsworth, 1995.

Swearer, Donald. *Becoming the Buddha: The Ritual of Image Consecration in Thailand.* Princeton, NJ: Princeton University Press, 2004.

Takakusa, J., trans. *A Record of the Buddhist Religion as Practiced in India and the Malay Archipelago (AD 671–695) by I-Tsing.* Oxford: Clarendon Press, 1896.

Tambiah, Stanley J. *Buddhism and the Spirit Cults in North-east Thailand.* Cambridge: Cambridge University Press, 1970.

—— *World Conqueror and World Renouncer: A Study of Buddhism and Polity in Thailand against its Historical Background.* Cambridge: Cambridge University Press, 1976.

—— *The Buddhist Saints of the Forest and the Cult of Amulets.* Cambridge: Cambridge University Press, 1984.

Teiser, Stephen F. *The Ghost Festival in Medieval China.* Princeton, NJ: Princeton University Press, 1988.

Tiyavanich, Kamala. *Forest Recollections: Wandering Monks in Twentieth Century Thailand.* Honolulu, HI: University of Hawai'i Press, 1997.

Walters, Jonathan S. *The History of Kelaniya.* Colombo: Social Scientists Association, 1996.

—— *Finding Buddhists in Global History*. Washington, DC: American Historical Association, 1998.
Welch, Holmes. *The Practice of Chinese Buddhism*. Cambridge, MA: Harvard University Press, 1967.
Yamasaki, Taikō. *Shingon: Japanese Esoteric Buddhism*. Boston, MA: Shambhala Press, 1988.
Yü, Chün-fang. *Kuan-yin: The Chinese Transformation of Avalokiteśvara*. New York: Columbia University Press, 2001.
Zysk, Kenneth G. *Asceticism and Healing in Ancient India: Medicine in the Buddhist Monastery*. Delhi: Motilal Banarsidass, 1991.

Sacred places in Buddhism

Ayutthaya

Ayutthaya Historical Study Centre. *Ayutthaya Historical Study Centre*. Phra Nakhon Si Ayutthaya: The Centre, 1990.
Swearer, Donald K. *The Buddhist World of Southeast Asia*. Albany, NY: SUNY Press, 1995.
Van Beek, Steve and Luca Invernizzi. *An Introduction to the Arts of Thailand*. Hong Kong: Travel Pub. Asia, 1986.

Bodhgayā

Cunningham, Alexander. *Mahâbodhi, or the Great Buddhist Temple under the Bodhi Tree at Buddha-Gaya*. London: W.H. Allen, 1892.
Kinnard, Jacob N. "When Is the Buddha Not the Buddha? The Hindu/Buddhist Battle over Bodhgayā and Its Buddha Image." *Journal of the American Academy of Religion* 66, no. 4 (1998), 817–39.
Lahiri, Nayanjot. "Bodh-Gaya: An Ancient Buddhist Shrine and Its Modern History (1891–1904)." In Timothy Insoll, ed. *Case Studies in Archaeology and World Religion: The Proceedings of the Cambridge Conference*. Oxford: Archaeopress, 1999, 33–43.
Leoshko, Janice. *Bodhgaya, the Site of Enlightenment*. Bombay: Marg Publications, 1988.
—— *Sacred Traces: British Explorations of Buddhism in South Asia*. Burlington, VT: Ashgate, 2003.
Nugteren, Albertina. "Rituals around the Bodhi-Tree in Bodhgayā, India." In Jan Platvoet and Karel van der Toorn, eds. *Pluralism and Identity: Studies in Ritual Behaviour*. Leiden: E.J. Brill, 1995, 145–65.

Bodhi tree

Gombrich, Richard. "A New Theravadin Liturgy." In Frank E. Reynolds and Jason A. Carbine, eds. *The Life of Buddhism*. Berkeley, CA: University of California Press, 2000, 180–93.
Gombrich, Richard, and Gananath Obeyesekere. *Buddhism Transformed: Religious Change in Sri Lanka*. Princeton, NJ: Princeton University Press, 1988.
Nissanka, H.S.S. *Maha Bodhi Tree in Anuradhapura, Sri Lanka: The Oldest Historical Tree in the World*. New Delhi: Vikas Pub. House, 1994.

Cave temples

Cohen, Richard S. "Nāga, Yakṣiṇī, Buddha: Local Deities and Local Buddhism at Ajanta." *History of Religions* 37 (1998), 360–400.
Dehejia, Vidya. *Early Buddhist Rock Temples: A Chronology*. Ithaca, NY: Cornell University Press, 1972.
Katz, Nathan. "The Modernization of Sinhalese Buddhism as Reflected in the Dambulla Cave Temples." In Steven Heine and Charles S. Prebish, eds. *Buddhism in the Modern World: Adaptations of an Ancient Tradition*. New York: Oxford University Press, 2003, 27–44.
Mitra, Debala. *Buddhist Monuments*. Calcutta: Sahitya Samsad, 1971.
Spink, Walter M. "Ajanta's Chronology: Politics and Patronage." In Joanna Gottfried Williams, ed. *Kalādarśana: American Studies in the Art of India*. New Delhi: Oxford University Press and IBH, 1981, 109–26.
Wang, Eugene Yuejin. *Shaping the Lotus Sutra: Buddhist Visual Culture in Medieval China*. Seattle, WA: University of Washington Press, 2005.
Whitfield, Roderick, Susan Whitfield and Neville Agnew. *Cave Temples of Mogao: Art and History on the Silk Road*. Los Angeles, CA: Getty Conservation Institute and the J. Paul Getty Museum, 2000.

Kapilavastu

Coningham, Robin. "The Archaeology of Buddhism." In Timothy Insoll, ed.

Archaeology and World Religion. London: Routledge, 2001, 61–95.
Mitra, Debala. *Buddhist Monuments*. Calcutta: Sahitya Samsad, 1971.
Rijal, Babu Krishna, and P.C. Mukherji. *100 Years of Archaeological Research in Lumbini, Kapilavastu and Devadaha*, first edition. Kathmandu: S.K. International Pub. House, 1996.

Kuśīnagara

Mitra, Debala. *Buddhist Monuments*. Calcutta: Sahitya Samsad, 1971.
Ghosh, A. *An Encyclopaedia of Indian Archaeology*. Leiden; New York: E.J. Brill, 1990.

Lumbinī

Coningham, Robin. "The Archaeology of Buddhism." In Timothy Insoll, ed. *Archaeology and World Religion*. London: Routledge, 2001, 61–95.
Mitra, Debala. *Buddhist Monuments*. Calcutta: Sahitya Samsad, 1971.
Rijal, Babu Krishna, and P.C. Mukherji. *100 Years of Archaeological Research in Lumbini, Kapilavastu and Devadaha*, first edition. Kathmandu: S.K. International Pub. House, 1996.

Pāṭaliputra

Ghosh, A. *An Encyclopaedia of Indian Archaeology*. Leiden and New York: E.J. Brill, 1990.
Kumar, Brajmohan. *Archaeology of Pataliputra and Nalanda*. Delhi: Ramanand Vidya Bhawan, 1987.

Sacred mountains

Living Heritage Trust of Sri Lanka. "Sri Pada: Myth, Legend and Geography" http://sripada.org/ (accessed 8 June 2004).
Mason, David A. *Spirit of the Mountains: Korea's San-Shin and Traditions of Mountain-Worship*. Elizabeth, NJ: Holly, 1999.
Naquin, Susan and Chün-fang Yü, eds. *Pilgrims and Sacred Sites in China*. Berkeley, CA: University of California Press, 1992.
Swearer, Donald K. *The Buddhist World of Southeast Asia*. Albany, NY: SUNY Press, 1995.
Tyler, Royall and Paul L. Swanson, eds. "Shugendo and Mountain Religion in Japan." *Japanese Journal of Religion* 16, no. 2–3 (June–September 1989), 53–253.

Sacred places

Boucher, Daniel. "The *Pratītyasamutpādagāthā* and Its Role in the Medieval Cult of the Relics." *Journal of the International Association of Buddhist Studies* 14 (1991), 1–27.
Byrne, Denis. "Buddhist Stupa and Thai Social Practice." *World Archaeology* 27, no. 2 (1995), 266–81.
Coningham, Robin. "The Archaeology of Buddhism." In Timothy Insoll, ed. *Archaeology and World Religion*. London: Routledge, 2001, 61–95.
Huber, Toni. *The Cult of Pure Crystal Mountain: Popular Pilgrimage and Visionary Landscape in Southeast Tibet*. New York: Oxford University Press, 1999.
Huntington, John C. "Pilgrimage as Image: The Cult of the *Aṣṭamahāprātihārya*." *Orientations* 18, no. 4, 8 (1987), 55–63; 56–68.
Leoshko, Janice. *Sacred Traces: British Explorations of Buddhism in South Asia*. Burlington, VT: Ashgate, 2003.
McKay, Alex, ed. *Pilgrimage in Tibet*. Richmond, Surrey: Curzon, 1998.
Naquin, Susan and Chün-fang Yü, eds. *Pilgrims and Sacred Sites in China*. Berkeley, CA: University of California Press, 1992.
Reader, Ian, and Paul L. Swanson. "Pilgrimage in the Japanese Religious Tradition." *Japanese Journal of Religious Studies* 24 (1997), 225–70.
Schopen, Gregory. "The Phrase '*sa pịtivīprade?śaś caityabhūto bhavet*' in the *Vajracchedikā*: Notes on the Cult of the Book in Mahāyāna." *Indo-Iranian Journal* 17 (1975), 147–81.
Trainor, Kevin. *Relics, Ritual, and Representation in Buddhism: Rematerializing the Sri Lankan Theravāda Tradition*. Cambridge: Cambridge University Press, 1997.
Willis, Michael D. *Buddhist Reliquaries from Ancient India*. London: British Museum Press, 2000.

Sāñcī

Dehejia, Vidya, ed. *Unseen Presence: The Buddha and Sanchi*. Mumbai: Marg Publications, 1996.

Marshall, John, Alfred Foucher and N.G. Majumdar. *The Monuments of Sāñchī*, 3 vols. Reprint of 1940 edition, Delhi: Swati Publishers, 1982.
Willis, Michael D. *Buddhist Reliquaries from Ancient India*. London: British Museum Press, 2000.

Sārnāth

Ghosh, A. *An Encyclopaedia of Indian Archaeology*. Leiden; New York: E.J. Brill, 1990.
Leoshko, Janice. *Sacred Traces: British Explorations of Buddhism in South Asia*. Burlington, VT: Ashgate, 2003.
Mitra, Debala. *Buddhist Monuments*. Calcutta: Sahitya Samsad, 1971.

Stūpa

Brown, Robert. "Recent Stupa Literature: A Review Article." *Journal of Asian History* 20 (1986), 215–32.
Dallapiccola, Anna Libera, ed. *The Stūpa: Its Religious, Historical and Architectual Significance*. Wiesbaden: Franz Steiner Verlag, 1980.
Dehejia, Vidya, ed. *Unseen Presence: The Buddha and Sanchi*. Mumbai: Marg Publications, 1996.
Mitra, Debala. *Buddhist Monuments*. Calcutta: Sahitya Samsad, 1971.
Schopen, Gregory. *Bones, Stones, and Buddhist Monks*. Honolulu, HI: University of Hawai'i Press, 1997.
—— *Buddhist Monks and Business Matters*. Honolulu, HI: University of Hawai'i Press, 2004.
Willis, Michael. *Buddhist Reliquaries from Ancient India*. London: British Museum Press, 2000.

Vaiśālī

Ghosh, A. *An Encyclopaedia of Indian Archaeology*. Leiden; New York: E.J. Brill, 1990.
Sinha, B.P. and Sita Ram Roy. *Vaiśālī Excavations, 1958–1962*. Patna: Directorate of Archaeology and Museums, 1969.

Vihāra

Bandaranayake, Senake. *Sinhalese Monastic Architecture: The Vihāras of Anurādhapura*. Leiden: E.J. Brill, 1974.
Coningham, Robin. "The Archaeology of Buddhism." In Timothy Insoll, ed. *Archaeology and World Religion*. London: Routledge, 200, 61–95.
Dehejia, Vidya. *Early Buddhist Rock Temples: A Chronology*. Ithaca, NY: Cornell University Press, 1972.
Mitra, Debala. *Buddhist Monuments*. Calcutta: Sahitya Samsad, 1971.
Prip-Møller, Johannes. *Chinese Buddhist Monasteries: Their Plan and Its Function as a Setting for Buddhist Monastic Life*, second edition. Hong Kong: Hong Kong University Press, 1967.

Sangha

Bareau, André. *Les Premiers Conciles bouddhiques*. Paris: Presses Universitaires, 1955.
Baumann, Martin and Charles Prebish, eds. *Westward Dharma: Buddhism Beyond Asia*. Berkeley, CA: University of California Press, 2002.
Dutt, Sukumar. *Buddhist Monks and Monasteries of India*. London: George Allen and Unwin, 1962.
Frauwallner, Erich. *The Earliest Vinaya and the Beginnings of Buddhist Literature*. Volume VIII of Serie Orientale. Roma: Instituto per il Medio ed Estremo Oriente, 1956.
Holt, John. *The Canonical Buddhism on the Vinayapiṭaka*. Delhi: Motilal Banarsidass, 1981.
Keown, Damien. *The Nature of Buddhist Ethics*. New York: St. Martin's Press, 1992.
Misra, G.S.P. *The Age of Vinaya*. New Delhi: Munshiram Manoharlal, 1972.
Prebish, Charles S. *Buddhist Monastic Discipline: The Sanbskrit Prātimokṣa Sūtras of the Mahāsāṃghikas and Mūlsarvāstivadins*. University Park, PA: Pennsylvania State University Press, 1975.
—— *A Survey of Vinaya Literature*. London: RoutledgeCurzon, 1994.
Wijayaratna, Mohan (trans. Claude Grangier and Steven Collins). *Buddhist Monastic Life*. Cambridge: Cambridge University Press, 1990.

Vajrayāna Buddhism

Beer, Robert. *The Encyclopedia of Tibetan Symbols and Motifs*. Boston, MA: Shambhala, 1999.

Bentor, Yael. *Consecration of Images and Stūpas in Indo-Tibetan Tantric Buddhism*. Leiden: E.J. Brill, 1996.

Berzin, Alexander. *Kalachakra and Other Six-Session Yoga Texts*. Ithaca, NY: Snow Lion, 2004.

Brauen, Martin. *The Mandala: Sacred Circle in Tibetan Buddhism*. London: Serindia Publications, 1997.

Cozort, Daniel. *Highest Yoga Tantra: An Introduction to the Esoteric Buddhism of Tibet*. Ithaca, NY: Snow Lion, 1986.

Dalton, Jacob. "The Development of Perfection: The Interiorization of Buddhist Ritual in the Eighth and Ninth Centuries." *Journal of Indian Philosophy* 32, no. 1 (2004), 1–30.

Davidson, Ronald M. *Indian Esoteric Buddhism: A Social History of the Tantric Movement*. New York: Columbia University Press, 2002.

Dorje, Gyurme. *The Guhyagarbhatantra and Its XIVth Century Commentary Phyogs-bcu mun-sel*. Ph.D. dissertation, School of Oriental and African Studies, University of London, 1987.

Farrow, G.W. and I. Menon. *The Concealed Essence of the Hevajra Tantra: With the Commentary Yogaratnmālā*. Delhi: Motilal Banarsidass, 1992.

Fremantle, Francesca. *A Critical Study of the Guhyasamāja Tantra*. Ph.D. dissertation, University of London, 1971.

—— "Chapter Seven of the *Guhyasamāja Tantra*." In Tadeusz Skorupski, ed. *Indo-Tibetan Studies. Papers in Honour and Appreciation of Professor David L. Snellgrove's Contribution to Indo-Tibetan Studies*. Tring: Institute of Buddhist Studies, 1990, 101–14.

Guenther, Herbert V. *Matrix of Mystery: Scientific and Humanistic Aspects of rDzogs-chen Thought*. Boulder, CO: Shambhala, 1984.

Gyatso, Tenzin (Dalai Lama XIV) (trans. Jeffrey Hopkins). *The Kalachakra Tantra: Rite of Initiation*. London: Wisdom Publications, 1985.

Karmay, Samten. *The Great Perfection (Rdzogs Chen): A Philosophical and Meditative Teaching in Tibetan Buddhism*. Leiden: E.J. Brill, 1988.

Martin, Dan. "Illusion Web: Locating the *Guhyagarbha Tantra* in Buddhist Intellectual History." In Christopher Beckwith, ed. *Silver on Lapis: Tibetan Literary Culture and History*. Bloomington, IN: The Tibet Society, 1987, 175–220.

Matsunaga, Yukei. *The Guhyasamāja Tantra: A New Critical Edition*. Osaka: Toho Shuppan Showa, 1978.

Powers, John. *Introduction to Tibetan Buddhism*. Ithaca, NY: Snow Lion, 1995.

Rambelli, Fabio. "Re-inscribing Maṇḍ ala: Semiotic Operations on a Word and Its Object." *Studies in Central and East Asian Religions* 4 (1991), 1–8.

Ray, Reginald A. *Indestructible Truth: The Living Spirituality of Tibetan Buddhism*. Boston, MA: Shambhala, 2000.

—— *Secret of the Vajra World: The Tantric Buddhism of Tibet*. Boston, MA: Shambhala, 2001.

Samuel, Geoffrey. *Civilized Shamans: Buddhism in Tibetan Societies*. Washington, DC: Smithsonian Institution Press, 1993.

Snellgrove, David L. *The Hevajra Tantra: A Critical Study*, 2 vols. London: Oxford University Press, 1959.

Snodgrass, Adrian. *The Matrix and Diamond World Mandalas in Shingon Buddhism*. Delhi: Motilal Banarsidass, 1988.

Sopa, Geshe Lhundub, Roger Jackson and John Newman. *The Wheel of Time: The Kalachakra in Context*. Ithaca, NY: Snow Lion, 1991.

Studholme, Alexander. *The Origins of Oṃ Maṇipadme Hūṃ: A Study of the Kāraṇḍ avyūha Sūtra*. Albany, NY: SUNY Press, 2002.

Wallace, Vesna A. *The Inner Kālacakra: A Buddhist Tantric View of the Individual*. Oxford: Oxford University Press, 2001.

—— *Kālacakratantra: The Chapter on the Individual together with the Vimālaprabhā*. New York: Columbia University Press, 2005.

Wayman, Alex. *Yoga of the Guhyasamāja*. Delhi: Motilal Banarsidass, 1991.

Willson, Martin and Martin Brauen. *Deities of Tibetan Buddhism*. Boston, MA: Wisdom Publications, 2000.

Yamasaki, Taikō. *Shingon: Japanese Esoteric Buddhism*. Boston, MA: Shambhala, 1988.

Yuthok, Lama Choedak. *Lamdre: Dawn of Enlightenment*. Canberra: Gorum Publications, 1997.

Women in Buddhism

Adiele, Faith. *Meeting Faith: The Forest Journals of a Black Buddhist Nun*. New York: W.W. Norton, 2004.

Allione, Tsultrim. *Women of Wisdom*. New York: Arkana, 1986.

Arai, Paula Kane Robinson. *Women Living Zen: Japanese Soto Buddhist Nuns*. Oxford: Oxford University Press, 1999.

Barnes, Nancy J. "Buddhist Women and the Nuns' Order in Asia." In Christopher S. Queen and Sallie B. King, eds. *Engaged Buddhism: Buddhist Liberation Movements In Asia*. New York: SUNY Press, 1996, 259–94.

Bartholomeusz, Tessa. *Women Under the Bo Tree*. Cambridge: Cambridge University Press, 1994.

Batchelor, Martine. *Walking on Lotus Flowers*. New York: Thorsons, 1996. Republished as *Women on the Buddhist Path*. New York: Thorsons, 2002.

Blackstone, Kate. "Damming the Dhamma: Problems with Bhikkhunīs in the Pāli Vinaya." *Journal of Buddhist Ethics* 6 (1999), 292–312.

Boucher, Sandy. *Turning The Wheel: American Women Creating the New Buddhism*. New York: Harper and Row, 1988.

Chodron, Pema. *When Things Fall Apart: Heart Advice for Difficult Times*. Boston and London: Shambhala, 1997.

Cole, Alan. *Mothers and Sons in Chinese Buddhism*. Stanford, CA: Stanford University Press, 1998.

Falk, Nancy Auer. "The Case of the Vanishing Nuns: The Fruits of Ambivalence in ancient Indian Buddhism." In Nancy Auer Falk and Rita M. Gross, eds. *Unspoken Worlds: Women's Religious Lives In Non-Western Cultures*, 155–65. Belmont, CA: Wadsworth, 1989.

Faure, Bernard. *The Power of Denial: Buddhism, Purity and Gender*. Princeton, NJ: University Press, 2003.

Friedman, Lenore. *Meetings with Remarkable Women: Buddhist Teachers in America*. Boston, MA: Shambhala, 1987.

Grimshaw, Anna. *Servants of the Buddha: Winter in a Himalayan Convent*. Cleveland, OH: Pilgrim Press, 1994.

Gross, Rita. *Buddhism after Patriarchy: A Feminist History, Analysis, and Reconstruction of Buddhism*. New York: SUNY Press, 1993.

Gutschow, Kim. *Being a Buddhist Nun: The Struggle for Enlightenment in the Himalayas*. Cambridge and London: Harvard University Press, 2004.

Halifax, Joan. *Shamanic Voices: A Survey of Visionary Narratives*. New York and London: Penguin, 1991.

—— "A Buddhist Life in America: Simplicity in the Complex." Wit Lecture, 1998. available online: http://upaya.org/htmls/Buddhist_life.pdf

Horner, I.B., trans. "Cullavagga X" In *The Book of Discipline V*. Sacred Books of the Buddhists Vol. XX, edited by Max Müller, 352–92. Great Britain: Pali Text Society, 1988 (1952).

—— *Women Under Primitive Buddhism: Laywomen and Almswomen*. London: Routledge and Kegan Paul, 1930 (reprint, New Delhi: Motilal Banarsidass, 1989).

Kabilsingh, Chatsumarn. *Thai Women in Buddhism*. Berkeley, CA: Parallax Press, 1991.

Khema, Ayya (trans. Sherab Chodzin Kohn). *I Give You My Life: The Autobiography of a Western Buddhist Nun*. Boston and London: Shambhala, 1998.

King, Sallie B. "Egalitarian Philosophies in Sexist Institutions: The Life of Satomi-san, Shinto Miko and Zen Buddhist Nun." *Journal of Feminist Studies in Religion* 4, no. 1 (1988), 7–26.

Klein, Anne Carolyn. *Meeting the Great Bliss Queen: Buddhists, Feminists and the Art of the Self*. Boston, MA: Beacon, 1995.

Koppedrayer, Kay. "Reading Pema Chodron." *Contemporary Buddhism* 3, no. 1 (2002), 51–79.

Laliberté, André. "Buddhist Organizations and Democracy in Taiwan." *American Asian Review* 29, no. 4 (2002), 97–129.

Lang, Karen. "Lord Death's Snare: Gender-Related Imagery in the Therāgāthā and the Therīgāthā." *Journal of Feminist Studies in Religion* 2, no. 1 (1986), 63–79.

Paul, Diana Y. *Women in Buddhism: Images of Women in the Mahāyāna Tradition*. Berkeley, Los Angeles, London: University of California Press, 1979.

Rhys Davids, C.A.F., and K.R. Norman, trans. *Poems of the Early Buddhist Nuns: Therīgāthā*. London: Pali Text Society, 1989.

Schuster, Nancy. "Striking a Balance." In Yvonne Y. Haddad and Ellison B. Findly, eds. *Women, Resistance, and Social Change*. New York: SUNY Press, 1985.

Shaw, Miranda. *Passionate Enlightenment: Women in Tantric Buddhism*. Princeton, NJ: Princeton University Press, 1994.

Simmer-Brown, Judith. *Dakini's Warm Breath: The Feminine Principle in Tibetan Buddhism*. Boston and London: Shambhala, 2001.

Sponberg, Alan. "Attitudes Toward Women and the Feminine in Early Buddhism." In Jose Ignacio Cabezon, ed. *Buddhism, Sexuality, and Gender*. New York: SUNY Press, 1992, 3–36.

Tsai, Kathryn A., trans. *Lives of the Nuns: Biographies of Chinese Buddhist Nuns from the Fourth to the Sixth Century*. Honolulu, HI: University of Hawai'i Press, 1994.

Tsomo, Karma Lekshe. *Sakyadhita: Daughters of the Buddha*. Ithaca, NY: Snow Lion; 1988.

—— ed. *Buddhist Women and Social Justice: Ideals, Challenges, and Achievements*. Albany, NY: SUNY Press, 2004.

Walters, Jonathan. "A Voice from the Silence: The Buddha's Mother's Story." *History of Religions* 4 (May 1994), 358–79.

Willis, Janice Dean, ed. *Feminine Ground: Essays on Women and Tibet*. New York: Snow Lion, 1989.

—— *Dreaming Me: An African American Baptist–Buddhist Journey*. New York: Riverhead Books, 2001.

Wilson, Liz. *Charming Cadavers: Horrific Figurations of the Feminine in Indian Buddhist Hagiographic Literature.* Chicago and London: University of Chicago Press, 1996.

Young, Serinity. *Courtesans and Tantric Consorts. Sexualities in Buddhist Narrative, Iconography and Ritual.* London: Routledge, 2004.

Zhiyu, Ng. "The Emergence of the Sahā Triad in Contemporary Taiwan: Iconic Representation and Humanistic Buddhism." *Asia Major* 13, no. 2 (2000).

Index

Dharmakīrti **283–4**
Pramāṇika movement, epistemology 597, 599
Dharmapala 707
dharmas, Sarvāstivāda classification of 277–9, 673
Dhyānas **284**
Diamond *Sangha* 379, 814–15
Diamond Way Buddhism 379
Diasporic Buddhism: traditionalist and modernist Buddhism **285–8**
parallel worlds 287
religious concepts perspective 286
strands of Buddhism 285–6, 287
traditionalist and modernist Buddhism 286–7
"two Buddhisms" 285
Western Buddhists 286
digital input of Buddhist texts **288–96**
Buddhist response to digital canonic developments 295–6
Central Asian languages 292
Chinese Buddhist canon 292, 293–4
Chinese Buddhist Electronic Text Association 293–4
Chinese Buddhist manuscripts 295
Fragile Palm Leaves manuscript preservation project 290
Hong Kong 295
Koryŏ edition, Chinese Buddhist canon 293
overview 288
Pāli 288–9
Pāli Text Society and Dhammkaya Foundation 289–90
persistence of digital data 295
Sanskrit editions 291–2
SAT (*Samganikikritam Taishō Tripitakam*), digital input of texts 294
Tibetan canon editions and commentaries 290–1
Zen texts project of Hanazono University 292–3
digital research resources **296–9**
Cologne Digital Sanskrit Lexicon (CDSL) 298
dictionary of multilingual equivalents 297
digital tools production, early developments 296–7
Pāli Text Society's Pāli–English Dictionary and other dictionaries 297–8
Tibetan online dictionaries 298–9
Dignāga and *Pramāṇika* movement, epistemology 597, 598–9
Dilun school 226
disciples of the Buddha **299–302**
Ānanda 301
Buddha preaching the first sermon, Sārnāth, India *300*
disciples during the Buddha's ministry 300–1
disciples, meaning and concept of 299–301
Mahākassapa 302
Moggallāna 302
Sāriputta 301
types of 300
"Discourse on Setting in Motion the Wheel of the *Dhamma*, The" 272–3
devas and celestial pantheon 37–9
"Doctrine of a Person, The" (Sammatīyas/ *pudgalavādins*) 649, 650–1
Dōgen 302–3, 501
Dōgen and *Sōtōshū* **302–4**
founder of *Sōtō* school 303
life of *Dōgen* 303–4
duḥkha see Ennobling Truths/Realities, the first
Dunhuang complex (China) 62
Dzogchen (*rdzogs chen* or "great perfections") **304–5**

Eastern Buddhist Society 494
Eastern Buddhist, The, journal 606
ecology *see* Economics and ecology
Economics and ecology
Buddhist, attempts towards 181–2
suffering, objective of abolishing 182–3
Western economies, criticism of 182
ecumenicism and intra-Buddhist activities **306–7**
"eight great marvels" pilgrimage sites 637
eightfold awareness and "receptacle" awareness 844–5
Eightfold Path and its three divisions, Buddhist ethics 338
see also Ennobling Truths/Realities, the fourth, the Ennobling Eightfold Path
Eisai (Yōsai), Rinzai tradition 615
Electronic Cultural Atlas Initiative 242–3
electronic publications **307–10**
digital libraries 309–10
early approaches 307–8
Electronic Buddhist Archive, Australian National University 17
electronic and print proliferations in 1990s 308
internet 308–9
online course websites 309
see also digital research resources
Ellorā cave temple complex *see* Ajaṇṭā and Ellorā
"engaged Buddhism" **310–18**
active and systematic work, need for 316
Ambedkar, B. R. 24–6
Ariyaratne, A. T., and the *Sarvōdaya Śramadāna* movement 43–5, 681
Buddhist economics and 182

founding goals 647
later conferences 647–8
samaṇas see śramaṇas
Ṣamantabhadra 787–9
Śamatha **648–9**
meditation on various supports 649
tranquility meditation 648–9
Sammatīyas/*pudgalavādins* **649–51**
"Doctrine of a Person, The" 649, 650–1
historic background 649
meaning of name 649–50
monastic practices 650
samyak-sambuddhas (*sammāsambuddhas*) 600
Sāñcī **651–3,** 719
bas-relief sculptures at 652–3
"great *stūpa*", the 651–2, 719
historic background 651
sacred place as 639
site 114
smaller *stūpas* 652
Stūpa and *toraṇa 719*
toraṇa, Jātaka carvings 719
toraṇa, Vessantara Jātaka 719–20
wheel design *110*
Sangha **653–61**
Buddha and 702–3
community life, initial 654
community of wanderers, originally a 659
defined 653, 659, *659*
Diamond *Sangha* 814–15
disciples in the early *Sangha* 657–9
geographic dispersal of 660
globalisation, increasing, issue of 661
ideal community (ordained monastic community) 359
issue, other 660–1
Karmavācanā 804, 805
lay disciples 658
lay members 655, 656–7
life within 654
modernisation, issue of 661–2
monastic life 653–5, 659
monks 657–8
ordination 653–4
rainy season settlements 659
royal patrons 658–9
sectarianism 660
Skandhaka 806
three refuges, *Sangha* as one of the 738, 739
Vietnam, role in 798
Vinaya Piṭaka 655–6
women, role of 661
see also bhikṣuṇī sangha
Sangha gender issues **661–2**
Sangha modernization **662–4**
changing patterns of authority 663–4
looking forward 664
preservation of ideals and need to adapt tension 662–3
social issues 664
technology, role of 664
Vinaya, modernising the 663
Sangharakshita 815, 816
Sanghas, sectarian **664–5**
globalization effect 665
Māhāyana and Vajrayāna movements 665
origins of 664–5
Sanghas, urban and rural **665–6**
Sanghas, Western **666–7**
Buddhist, determining what is a 667
Diamond *Sangha* 814–15
original Buddhist community, the 666–7
types of Western *sanghas* 666, 667
urban 666
Sanghayāna (Sixth Buddhist Synod 1954–6) 678
Sanlun school, China 224
Ṣanskrit editions, digital input of texts 291–2
Śāntideva **667–8**
Bodhicaryāvatāra 667–8
Śāntideva *Madhyamaka* school 482
Śāntirakṣita **668–9**
Madhyamakālaṃkāra 669
Sāriputra 658
Sāriputta, disciple of the Buddha 301
Sārnāth **669–70**
place where Gautama Buddha first taught the *Dharma* 669–70
rediscovery of 670
Sarvāstivāda **673–5**
Abhidharma, *dharma* and 275–6
dharmas, classification of 277–9, 673
matter (*rūpa*) 277–8
mental concomitants (*caittas*) 278–9
mind (*citta*) 278; overview 277
factors disassociated from thought (*cittaviprayukta*) 675
Foundation of Knowledge (*Jñānaprasthāna*) 440–2
later history 675–7
matter (*rūpa*) 277–8, 673–4
mental concomitants (*caittas*) 278–9, 674
mind (*citta*) 278, 674
ontology of 673
School 3–6, 556–7
sarvāstivāda school 4–6, 277, 556–7
Dharmas, classification of 277–9
Dharmas, classification of by three major schools, Table 4 280
Sarva-tathāgata-tattvasaṃgraha (*Compendium of the Truth of All Buddhas*)
content 670–1
effectiveness of practices for evil-doers and those with strong passions 671
yoga, highest *tantras* 780, 781

Zhengyan, Venerable **849–50**
humanitarian efforts 850
life and works 849–50
Tzu Chi Foundation, founder 849
Zhenyan Zong **850–1**
differences with Indian sources 851
features shared with Indian sources 850–1
origin 850
Zhiyi **851–2**
doctrinal studies of 852
life of 851–2
Three Truths 852
Tianti 739, 740–1, 851
Tianti method of classifying scriptures and teachings 852